# Western Civilization

## THE CONTINUING EXPERIMENT

# Western Civilization

## THE CONTINUING EXPERIMENT

FOURTH EDITION

VOLUME I
TO 1715

**Thomas F. X. Noble**
University of Notre Dame

**Barry Strauss**
Cornell University

**Duane J. Osheim**
University of Virginia

**Kristen B. Neuschel**
Duke University

**William B. Cohen**
Late of Indiana University

**David D. Roberts**
University of Georgia

**Rachel G. Fuchs**
Arizona State University

Houghton Mifflin Company    Boston  New York

Publisher: Charles Hartford
Editor-in-Chief: Jean L. Woy
Senior Sponsoring Editor: Nancy Blaine
Senior Development Editor: Julie Dunn
Editorial Associate: Annette Fantasia
Senior Project Editor: Christina M. Horn
Editorial Assistant: Teresa Huang
Senior Art and Design Coordinator: Jill Haber
Senior Photo Editor: Jennifer Meyer Dare
Senior Composition Buyer: Sarah Ambrose
Senior Designer: Henry Rachlin
Senior Manufacturing Coordinator: Marie Barnes
Senior Marketing Manager: Sandra McGuire
Marketing Assistant: Ilana Gordon

**Volume I cover image:** Franceso del Cossa (1435–1478), *Women Embroidering,* detail from the *Month of March: Triumph of Minerva,* fresco, Palazzo Schifanoia, Ferrara, Italy. Photograph: Scala/Art Resource, NY.

**Illustration credits:** Global Encounters: © Corbis Images; The Continuing Experiment: © Getty Images; Weighing the Evidence: Library of Congress.

**Text credits: Page 82:** Quote by Sappho from *Ancient Greek Literature and Society,* Second Edition, by Charles Rowan Beye. Copyright © 1987 by Cornell University Press. Reprinted by permission. **Page 137:** Poem from *The Aeneid of Virgil,* trans. Allen Mandelbaum. Copyright © 1971 by Allen Mandelbaum. Reprinted by permission of Bantam Books, a division of Bantam, Doubleday, Dell Publishing Group, Inc. **Page 344:** "Down there, around Ventadorn" from *The Lyrics of the Troubador, Trouveres,* translated by Frederick Goldin. Copyright © 1973 by Frederick Goldin. Used by permission of Doubleday, a division of Random House, Inc. "Friend, if you had shown consideration" from lyrics by Castellozza, in *The Women Troubadours* by Meg Bodin (W. W. Norton, 1976). Copyright © 1976 by Magda Bogin. Reprinted by permission of Magda Bogin. **Page 407:** Poem by Michelangelo from *The Italian Renaissance Reader,* edited and translated by Julia Conaway Bondanella and Mark Musa. Copyright © 1987 by Julia Conaway Bondanella and Mark Musa. Used by permission of Dutton Signet, a division of Penguin Group (USA) Inc.

Printed in the U.S.A.

Library of Congress Control Number: 2003110158

ISBN: 0-618-43277-9

123456789-VH-08 07 06 05 04

# In Memoriam
# William Benjamin Cohen
## 1941–2002

**B**ILL COHEN was born in Jakobstad, Finland, amid the horrors of World War II. His parents were German Jews who had fled Hitler's regime. Bill's father was a doctor, and his connection with an influential patient saved the family when Nazi sympathizers among the Finns began rounding up German Jews. When Bill was 2, his family moved to Sweden. Three years later they moved to Ethiopia, and then eight years later back to Sweden. One enduring result of Bill's peregrinations was that he learned six languages: Swedish, German, Amharic, Italian, French, and English. He always joked that he spoke six languages with an accent. Remarkably, Bill's maternal great-grandfather had served in the U.S. Civil War in Texas, and his grandfather was permitted to immigrate to the United States during World War II. Bill's father died when Bill was 16, and his mother moved the family to southern California. Bill acclimated himself quickly enough to earn substantial winnings on a game show and to complete high school early. He won a scholarship to Pomona College and then undertook graduate study in history at Stanford. Bill taught briefly at Northwestern and then moved to Indiana University, which was to be his professional home and where he chaired the history department on two occasions. Through a long series of distinguished publications, Bill became one of the world's pre-eminent historians of modern France and French colonialism. Almost never without one of his prodigious collection of hats, Bill was a connoisseur of fine foods, a formidable critic of music, a voracious reader, a world traveler, a cunning wit, and a deeply sympathetic person. A friend said of him, "He was a multinational, multicultural, multilingual being, who crossed borders of all kinds effortlessly as a natural dimension of life." Bill's untimely death in November 2002, at the height of his intellectual powers and in the happiest moments of his life, was an inconsolable loss to all who knew him.

# Brief Contents

# Contents

**CHAPTER 17**

# A Revolution in World-View   573

# Maps

# Documents

# Weighing the Evidence

# Information Technology

# Preface

Chance discoveries reveal that fifteen centuries ago, boys in Ireland and in what is now Afghanistan were copying the biblical psalms with a view to memorizing them. Young Christians were learning these Latin and Greek translations of ancient Hebrew poems. This arresting development points to three big themes that inform this book and that contribute to an understanding of why we should study Western Civilization in the early twenty-first century.

First, what or where is the "West"? The West is sometimes understood geographically and sometimes culturally. For most people, the West means western Europe. And yet western Europe itself is the heir of the peoples and cultures of antiquity, including the Sumerians, Egyptians, Persians, Greeks, Romans, Jews, Christians, and Muslims. In fact, Europe is the heir of even earlier civilizations in Asia and Africa.

Let us turn back to the psalm-learning boys of Ireland and Afghanistan. Although Ireland is now considered European, it was not part of the classical world. In fact, the Romans placed the island "at the end of the world." Christian missionaries prepared Ireland's entry into Western Civilization, and it has been at the heart of the West for more than a millennium. Consider Saint Patrick, the exuberant beauty of Celtic art, the English entanglement with Ireland, the poetry of William Butler Yeats or Seamus Heaney, and the novels of James Joyce—all of these are part of our Western heritage. The question of Afghanistan is trickier. Persians touched this land, as did the soldiers of Alexander the Great. The Silk Road—that great artery of objects and ideas—passed through it. A few years ago, to the horror of the world, the Taliban, radical Muslims, destroyed two monumental Buddha statues at Bamiyan. The psalm-learning boys, their psalms, and their heirs had religious competitors. But those statues had unmistakably Greek features, and today Western troops police much of Afghanistan. It would be a fascinating thought exercise to ask whether Afghanistan is "East" or "West."

As a cultural phenomenon, "Western" implies many things: freedom and free, participatory political institutions; economic initiative and opportunity; monotheistic religious faiths (Judaism, Christianity, and Islam); rationalism and ordered thought in the social, political, and philosophical realms; an aesthetic sensibility that aspires to a universal sense of beauty. But the West has felt free to evoke tradition as its guiding light and also to innovate brilliantly; to accommodate slavery and freedom simultaneously; to esteem original thought and to persecute people who deviate from the norm. "Western" indeed has meant many things in various places at different times. This book constantly and explicitly attempts to situate its readers in place, time, and tradition.

Second, what exactly is civilization? No definition can win universal acceptance, but certain elements of a definition are widely accepted. Cities are crucial; with cities emerge complex social organizations that involve at least a minimal division of labor. Some people work in the fields, some in the home. Soldiers defend the city, and artisans provide its daily goods. Governing institutions have a wide measure of acceptance and have the ability to enforce their will. Complex cultures also develop religious ideas and authorities; a literature and law that may be oral or written; monumental architecture, especially fortifications, palaces, and temples; and arts such as music, painting, and sculpture.

Western Civilization has had an influence on almost every person alive today. The West deserves to be studied because its tale is compelling, but it demands to be studied because its story has been so central to the development of the world in which we live. Many of the world's dominant institutions are Western in their origin and in their contemporary manifestations—most notably parliamentary democracy. Commercial capitalism, a Western construct, is the world's dominant form of economic organization, and even its greatest rival, communism, is fundamentally Western: its theoreticians were Europeans who drew on utopian ideals, classical economics, Enlightenment doctrines, and the ideologies of the French Revolution. Western styles in architecture dominate the skyline of every major city in the world. Western popular culture, from movies and music to fast food, may be found everywhere. Communications technologies, from cell phones to e-mail, are as global in spread as they are Western in origin.

It must be said that some people, inside and outside the West, have grave reservations about the extent of Western influence in the modern world. Were those boys of fifteen centuries ago heirs and beneficiaries of a great tradition? Or were they dupes and victims of Western cultural aggression? Some critics challenge Western religious, philosophical, political, and economic ideas at their core. Others have no quarrel with Western ideas as such but regret that local cultures around the globe are vanishing before a relentless Western onslaught. Still others wonder why Western achievements in political stability and economic prosperity cannot be more widely shared. In other words, to say that the West is dominant is only to state the obvious, not to insist that such domination is inevitable or desirable. But the sheer, unassailable fact of that domination makes the careful study of the West essential for informed, responsible participation in the modern world. And such study can help us understand and appreciate an impressive cultural heritage.

Third, the subtitle of this book, "The Continuing Experiment," was chosen to signal our third theme, contingency or unpredictability. This subtitle conveys our resolve to avoid a deterministic approach. For students and teachers, an appreciation of continuity and change, or unity and diversity, can foster sympathetic participation in this often-bewildering world. We try to give individual actors, moments, and movements the sense of drama, possibility, and contingency that they actually possessed. We, with faultless hindsight, always know how things came out. Contemporaries often did not have a clue. We respect them. Much of the fascination, and the reward, of studying Western Civilization lies precisely in its richness, diversity, changeability, and unpredictability. No one in Israel in 500 B.C. or in Rome a millennium later could have predicted that Irish and Afghan boys would simultaneously cultivate a new and similar religious sensibility by reading Jewish poems in the Christianized versions of the classical languages. Who, a generation ago, could have predicted the collapse of the Soviet Union or the rise of Osama bin Laden? The experiment continues.

## BASIC APPROACH

More than a decade ago the six authors of *Western Civilization: The Continuing Experiment* set out to create a textbook that would play a role in a course that will, as a total effort, inform students about essential developments within a tradition that has powerfully, though not always positively, affected everyone in the contemporary world. Although each of us found something to admire in all of the existing textbooks, none of us was fully happy with any of them. We were disappointed with

books that claimed "balance," but actually stressed a single kind of history. We regretted that so many texts were uneven in their command of recent scholarship. Although we were convinced of both the inherent interest of Western Civilization and the importance of teaching the subject, we were disconcerted by the celebratory tone of some books, which portrayed the West as resting on its laurels instead of creatively facing its future.

We decided to produce a book that is balanced and coherent; that addresses the full range of subjects that a Western Civilization book needs to address; that provides the student reader with interesting, timely material; that is up-to-date in terms of scholarship and approach; and that is handsome to look at—in short, a book that helps the instructor to teach and the student to learn. We have kept our common vision fresh through frequent meetings, correspondence, critical mutual readings, and expert editorial guidance. We have come together as one, and because each of us has focused on his or her own area of specialization, we believe that we have attained a rare blend of competence, confidence, and enthusiasm. Moreover, in moving from plans for a first edition to the preparation of a fourth, we have been able to profit from the experience of using the book, the advice and criticism of dozens of colleagues, and the reactions of thousands of students.

Western Civilization is a story. Therefore, we aimed at a strong chronological narrative line. Our experience as teachers tells us that students appreciate this clear but gentle orientation. Our experience tells us, too, that an approach that is broadly chronological will leave instructors plenty of room to adapt our narrative to their preferred organization, or to supplement our narrative with one of their own.

Although we maintain the familiar, large-scale divisions of a Western Civilization book, we also present some innovative adjustments in arrangement. For instance, Chapter 2 treats early Greece together with the whole eastern Mediterranean region in the period from about 1500 to 750 B.C. This approach both links kindred cultures and respects chronological flow better than customary treatments, which take western Asia to a certain point and then backtrack to deal with early Greece. We incorporate a single chapter on Late Antiquity, the tumultuous and fascinating period from about A.D. 300 to 600 that witnessed the transformation of the Roman Empire into three successors: Byzantine, Islamic, and European. One chapter studies those three successors, thereby permitting careful comparisons. But we also assign chapters to some of the greatest issues in Western Civilization, such as the Renaissance, the age of European exploration and conquest, the Scientific Revolution, and the industrial transformation. Our twentieth-century chapters reflect an understanding of the last century formed in its closing years rather than in its middle decades. What is new in our organization represents adjustments grounded in the best scholarship, and what is old represents time-tested approaches.

In fashioning our picture of the West, we took two unusual steps. First, our West is itself bigger than the one found in most textbooks. We treat the Celtic world, Scandinavia, and the Slavic world as integral parts of the story. We look often at the lands that border the West—Anatolia/Turkey, western Asia, North Africa, the Eurasian steppes—in order to show the to-and-fro of peoples, ideas, technologies, and products. Second, we continually situate the West in its global context. We must be clear: this is not a world history book. But just as we recognize that the West has influenced the rest of the world, we also carefully acknowledge how the rest of the world has influenced the West. We begin this story of mutual interaction with the Greeks and Romans, carry it through the European Middle Ages, focus on it in the age of European exploration and conquest, and analyze it closely in the modern world of industry, diplomacy, empire, immigration, and questions of citizenship and identity.

Another approach that runs like a ribbon throughout this textbook involves balance and integration. Teachers and students, just like the authors of this book, have their particular interests and emphases. In the large and diverse American academy, that is as it should be. But a textbook, if it is to be helpful and useful, should incorporate as many interests and emphases as possible. For a long time, some said, Western Civilization books devoted excessive coverage to high politics—"the public deeds of great men," as an ancient Greek writer defined the historian's subject. Others felt that high culture—all the Aristotles and Mozarts—were included to the exclusion of supposedly lesser figures and ordinary men and women. In the 1970s books began to emphasize social history. Some applauded this new emphasis even as they debated fiercely over what to include under this heading.

In this book, we attempt to capture the Western tradition in its full contours, to hear the voices of all those who have made durable contributions. But because we cannot say everything about everybody at every moment, we have had to make choices about how and where to array key topics within our narrative. Above all, we have tried to be integrative. For example, when we talk about government and politics, we present the institutional structures through which power was exercised, the people who possessed power as well as the people who did not, the ideological foundations for the use of power, and the material conditions that fostered or hindered the real or the would-be powerful. In other words, instead of treating old-fashioned "high politics" in abstract and descriptive ways, we take an approach that is organic and analytical: How did things work? Our approach to the history of women is another example. A glance at this book's table of contents and then at its index is revealing. The former reveals very few sections devoted explicitly and exclusively to women. The latter shows that women appear constantly in every section of this book. Is there a contradiction here? Not at all. Women and men have not been historical actors in isolation from one another. Yet gender is an important variable that has shaped individual and collective experience. Hence we seek to explain why certain political, economic, or social circumstances had differing impacts on men and women, and how such conditions led them to make different choices.

Similarly, when we talk of great ideas, we describe the antecedent ideas from which seemingly new ones were built up, and we ask about the consequences of those ideas. We explore the social positions of the authors of those ideas to see if this helps us to explain the ideas themselves or to gauge their influence. We try to understand how ideas in one field of human endeavor proved to be influential in other fields. For instance, gender is viewed as connected to and part of the larger fabric of ideas including power, culture, and piety.

We invite the reader to look at our narrative as if it were a mosaic. Taken as a whole, our narrative contains a coherent picture. Viewed more closely, it is made up of countless tiny bits that may have their individual interest but do not even hint at the larger picture of which they are parts. Finally, just as the viewer of a mosaic may find his or her eye drawn especially to one area, feature, color, or style, so too the reader of this book will find some parts more engaging or compelling than others. But it is only because there is, in this book as in a mosaic, a complete picture that the individual sections make sense, command our attention, excite our interest.

One word sums up our approach in this book: "balance." We tell a good story, but we pause often to reflect on that story, to analyze it. We devote substantial coverage to the typical areas of Greece, Rome, Italy, France, Great Britain, and so forth, but we say more about western Europe's frontiers than any other book. We do not try to disguise our Western Civilization book as a world history book, but we take great pains to locate the West within its global context. And we always assume that context means mutuality and reciprocity. We have high politics and big ideas alongside household management and popular culture. We think that part of the fascination of the past lies in its capacity to suggest understandings of the present and possibilities for the future.

## DISTINCTIVE FEATURES

To make this book as accessible as possible to students, we have constantly been aware of its place in a program of teaching and learning. Each chapter begins with a vignette that is directly tied to an accompanying picture. These vignettes introduce the reader to one or more of the key aspects of the chapter. Then the reader encounters a thematic introduction that evokes interest while pointing clearly and in some detail to what follows.

To make our chapter introductions more effective, which means to give students greater confidence as they proceed through the book, we have taken five steps. First, for this as for past editions, we reviewed and revised our opening vignettes to connect text and picture more closely and to use both to invite the reader into the chapter.

Second, we place on the first page of each chapter a succinct outline that immediately and dramatically tells the reader what he or she is going to encounter in the following pages.

Third, we put at the end of each chapter's introduction a list of Questions to Consider that are designed to work with the introduction and outline to give the student a clear orientation to what will follow.

Fourth, we include a list of Terms to Know that also alert the student to people or issues that demand special attention. As a complement to text coverage, a ready reference, and a potential study guide, all of the Terms to Know are gathered into a Glossary at the back of the book.

Fifth, as the student begins to read the chapter proper, he or she will see a Chronology, which serves as yet another orientation to the material contained in the chapter. Subject-specific chronologies still appear in various parts of the book, but we felt that readers would benefit from a chronological orientation to each chapter.

In addition to this fundamental attention to the chapter opening, we also sought to improve the book's teachability by adding a pronunciation guide. Whenever we use an unfamiliar name or term, we show the reader how to pronounce it. Instead of using the intricate rules of phonetics, we provide commonsense guides to pronunciation at the foot of the page.

Careful chapter summaries draw together major topics and themes and link the present chapter to the one that follows. To encourage students to strike out on their own historical discoveries, each chapter offers a few carefully selected suggestions for further reading.

We have been conscious of how the book *looks* to the reader from the very beginning. Attractively laid-out pages, a handsome full-color design, engaging maps, and beautifully reproduced pictures enhance the book's appearance. In keeping with our desire to integrate the components of the book into a coherent whole, we carefully anchor the maps and pictures into the volume. The authors chose the maps in this book, labeled them to complement its text, and captioned them to advance its teaching role. The same is true of the pictures: the authors selected them, worked with the book's designers to place them advantageously (and not just decoratively), and wrote all the captions. All the maps are cross-referenced in the text, some of them several times, and the text often refers directly to the pictures. Our diverse boxed documents—usually five per chapter—are referred to and tightly anchored in the text and support the surrounding discussion. As with the maps, familiar documents are blended with pleasing newcomers.

Another important component of this book is the two-page feature Weighing the Evidence, presented at the end of each chapter. This feature introduces students to the fascinating array of sources that historians use and invites them to think critically about the nature of historical information and inquiry. Each opens with a description of the evidence presented in the feature—topics ranging from images of Cleopatra, the Ravenna mosaics, and Renaissance marriage chests to eighteenth-century political symbols, the layout of the British Museum, and postmodern architecture—and then discusses how the professional historian examines this evidence to reconstruct the past. When Samuel Butler said that God cannot change history but that historians can and often do, he meant that history itself arises from new or different acts of interpretation. With Weighing the Evidence, students look over the shoulder of the historian to become active participants in this interpretive process. The sources examined are interesting and instructive in their own right, but the Weighing the Evidence also contributes to the teaching program of the book. As always, these boxes are carefully integrated into the text. There are references to them at appropriate points in the narrative, they contain cross-references to other sections or illustrations, and they support ongoing discussions.

Many textbooks have boxed documents. In four different respects, we have taken special care with our documents for this edition. First, we have included more than fifty new documents as this book has proceeded through its four editions. Second, we have included in most chapters at least one document that permits a gendered analysis of a key historical person or problem. Third, we have included in each chapter one Global Encounters box. The documents under this heading depict either a Western person commenting on the non-Western world, or a non-Western person commenting on the Western world. They further our intention to situate our story in its global context. Fourth, because some documents cry out for more discussion or context than we can provide on the page, we have supplied web activities in the *Student Study Companion,* a website that grows continually but that, right away, expands on some of the documents included in our text—at least one per chapter. (See the Supplements section later in this Preface for more information about the *Student Study Companion.*)

This book is flexible in format as well as substantive organization. Because schools use different academic calendars, organize Western Civilization courses according to different chronologies, and require or recommend different parts of the course, we issue this book in three formats:

- **One-volume hardcover edition** (Chapters 1–30)
- **Two-volume paperback edition:** Volume I, To 1715 (Chapters 1–17); Volume II, Since 1560 (Chapters 15–30)
- **Three-volume paperback edition:** Volume A, To 1500 (Chapters 1–12); Volume B, 1300–1815 (Chapters 11–19); Volume C, Since 1789 (Chapters 19–30)

Volume II begins with a comprehensive Introduction that situates the student reader in the late sixteenth century and surveys the course of Western Civilization from ancient times to the early centuries of the modern era. This Introduction is designed particularly for students who did not take the first semester of the course or who are new to this book.

# CHANGES IN THE NEW EDITION

In preparing our fourth edition, we thought hard about our own experiences in using the book and paid strict attention to the advice given to us by many instructors, including both those who use the book and those who do not. Two main lines of revision guided our changes.

## The Continuing Experiment

Helpful advice suggested to us that our "Continuing Experiment" theme was welcome but less fully developed than it might have been. Accordingly, each chapter now has a boxed document called The Continuing Experiment. The authors have chosen a document that shows contingency, possibility, or uncertainty. The document is carefully introduced and then followed by a series of focus questions that are designed to invite the reader to imagine how things might have been different. Readers will encounter topics such as Egypt's startling religious experimentation, Archimedes' anticipation of the scientific method, Charlemagne's attempts to reform education, the stupendous achievement of Brunelleschi's dome for Florence's cathedral, France's premature efforts at religious toleration, the ambiguous appeal of Marxism, the complexities of Keynesian economics, and the varying outcomes of "women's liberation." Again and again, readers are encouraged to think imaginatively and creatively.

## Organization and Content Changes

As always, we have paid close attention to how our chapters "work." Accordingly, Chapter 5 includes revised material on Roman politics and the conflict of the orders, as well as material on the Roman household and the connection between family and government. Chapter 7 has reorganized material on the Catholic Church, and Chapter 9 has expanded coverage of the Crusades. The material on the Thirty Years' War in Chapter 15 has been fully reworked and now includes a section on the developments in eastern and central Europe. New material on the slave trade has been added to Chapter 18. In Chapter 23, a new discussion of women and charity has been added, focusing on Josephine Grey Butler, Annie Wood Besant, and others. Chapter 28 incorporates new scholarship on the role of Pope Pius XII during the Holocaust, as well as an expanded account of the Warsaw uprising. Finally, in light of the drastic changes in the world since this book was last revised, Chapter 30 has been thoroughly reworked to include coverage of the Iraq War, recent environmental issues, the expanding European Union, the changing demographics of Europe, and the issues of unilateralism and Western responsibility in an increasingly global community.

## SUPPLEMENTS

We have assembled with care an array of supplements to aid students in learning and instructors in teaching. These supplements include the new *History Companion,* the *Instructor's Resource Manual, Test Items,* WebCT and Blackboard course cartridges, and a collection of map transparencies for Western Civilization courses.

The new *Houghton Mifflin History Companion* is a collection of resources designed to complement the use of this edition. It is organized according to the chapters in the text and has three parts—the *Instructor Companion,* the *Student Research Companion,* and the *Student Study Companion.* The *Instructor Companion* is a free, searchable CD-ROM featuring hundreds of historical images and maps in PowerPoint format. Each image is accompanied by notes that place it in its proper historical context. The maps and images are correlated to the text's table of contents and are also searchable by other criteria. They are formatted for easy presentation in the classroom. The CD-ROM also includes the *HM Testing* program, a computerized version of the *Test Items* to enable instructors to alter, replace, or add questions, as well as resources from the *Instructor's Resource Manual.*

The *Student Research Companion* is a free web-based tool with one hundred interactive maps and hundreds of primary sources. The primary sources include headnotes that provide pertinent background information and questions that students can answer and e-mail to their instructors. This website also provides students and teachers with additional information for the documents that are featured in the text. It has lengthy, searchable bibliographies that permit students to launch research assignments or pursue personal interests while giving teachers an outstanding opportunity to get directed guidance to the best historical literature in fields outside their own areas of expertise.

The *Student Study Companion* is a free, online study guide to accompany our text. It contains a variety of tutorial resources, including self-tests (ACE questions) with feedback, chronological exercises, flash cards to test vocabulary, and web activities that correspond to the chapter features. In addition, the site features an electronic *Study Guide* containing chapter outlines, chapter summaries, review questions, and more. This versatile, interactive study tool satisfies different learning styles and can improve students' chances of success.

The print *Instructor's Resource Manual,* written by Matthew Lenoe, includes learning objectives, annotated outlines, suggested lecture topics, discussion questions, classroom activities, and paper topics for each chapter of the text. It also features suggestions for integrating the web exercises into your teaching. Each chapter of the print *Test Items,* by Diane Moczar, offers key terms, short-answer and essay questions, map questions, and multiple-choice questions. An answer key for the multiple-choice questions is located at the end of the *Test Items.*

## ACKNOWLEDGMENTS

The authors have benefited throughout the process of revision from the acute and helpful criticisms of numerous colleagues. We thank in particular: **James Burns,** Clemson University; **Eleanor A. Congdon,** Youngstown State University; **Eugene Cruz-Uribe,** Northern Arizona University; **Janusz Duzinkiewicz,** Purdue University North Central; **Ann R. Higginbotham,** Eastern Connecticut State University; **Vejas Gabriel Liulevicius,** University of Tennessee; **David A. Reid,** University of North Florida; and **Alice N. Walters,** University of Massachusetts, Lowell.

Each of us has also benefited from the close readings and careful criticisms of our coauthors, although we all assume responsibility for our own chapters. Barry Strauss has written Chapters 1–6; Thomas Noble, 7–10; Duane Osheim, 11–14; Kristen Neuschel, 15–19; William Cohen, 20–24; and David Roberts, 25–30.

Many colleagues, friends, and family members have helped us develop this work as well. Thomas Noble wishes to thank Linda Noble for her patience and good humor. He is also grateful to John Contreni, Wendy Davies, Thomas Head, Elizabeth Meyer, Julia Smith, Richard Sullivan, John Van Engen, Robert Wilken, and Ian Wood.

Barry Strauss is grateful to colleagues at Cornell and at other universities who offered advice and encouragement and responded to scholarly questions. He would also like to thank the people at Cornell who provided technical assistance and support. Most important have been the support and forbearance of his family. His daughter, Sylvie; his son, Michael; and, above all, his wife, Marcia, have truly been sources of inspiration.

Duane Osheim wishes to thank his family for support during the writing and revising of this book. He is also grateful to colleagues at the University of Virginia, who helped to clarify the many connections between Western Civilization and the wider world. He would specifically like to thank Erik Midelfort, Arthur Field, Janis Gibbs, and Beth Plummer for comments and advice.

Kristen Neuschel thanks her colleagues at Duke University for sharing their expertise. She is especially grateful to Sy Mauskopf, Bill Reddy, John Richards, Tom Robisheaux, and Alex Roland. She also thanks her husband and fellow historian, Alan Williams, for his wisdom about Western Civilization and his support throughout the project, and her children, Jesse and Rachel, for their patience, joy, and curiosity.

Rachel Fuchs wishes to thank two of her graduate students, Ute E. Chamberlin and Richard S. Hopkins, for their enthusiasm for this project and their very able assistance.

David Roberts wishes to thank Bonnie Cary, Linda Green, and Nancy Heaton for their able assistance and Timothy Cleaveland, Joshua Cole, Karl Friday, Thomas Ganschow, John Haag, Michael Kwass, John Morrow, Douglas Northrup, Miranda Pollard, Eve Trout Powell, Judith Rohrer, William Stueck, and Kirk Willis for sharing their expertise in response to questions. He also thanks Beth Roberts for her constant support and interest and her exceedingly critical eye.

The first plans for this book were laid in 1988, and over the course of fifteen years, there has been remarkable stability in the core group of people who have been responsible for its growth and development. The author team suffered the loss of a member, but Rachel Fuchs, a student of Bill Cohen's, joined us to revise the chapters dealing with the nineteenth century. Our gratitude to Rachel is as immense as our pleasure at the quality of her work. Our original sponsoring editor, Jean Woy, has become Editor-in-Chief for History and Political Science but has never missed a meeting with us or weakened in her interest in and commitment to this book. Christina Horn, our Senior Project Editor, has been the wizard behind the curtain for all four editions. She understood from the beginning our desire to have maps, pictures, and boxes closely integrated with their pertinent text, and she has never let us down. Our picture researcher, Carole Frohlich, also has been with us from the start, and she has always understood the spirit of this book and the wishes of its authors. Our sponsoring editor, Nancy Blaine, has imparted wisdom and encouragement, sympathy and understanding. We have been fortunate in our editors: Elizabeth Welch, Jennifer Sutherland, and Julie Dunn. They have been by turns friends, confidantes, critics, advisers, and cheerleaders. We are a team, a veteran team, a team with what sports enthusiasts call "good chemistry." We authors are grateful to all the people who have taught us so much and who have prodded us to do better than we could possibly have done on our own or under the guidance of anyone else.

Thomas F. X. Noble

# About the Authors

**Thomas F. X. Noble**  After receiving his Ph.D. from Michigan State University, Thomas Noble taught at Albion College, Michigan State University, Texas Tech University, and the University of Virginia. In 1999 he received the University of Virginia's highest award for teaching excellence. In 2001 he became Robert M. Conway Director of the Medieval Institute at the University of Notre Dame. He is the author of *The Republic of St. Peter: The Birth of the Papal State, 680–825; Religion, Culture and Society in the Early Middle Ages; Soldiers of Christ: Saints and Saints' Lives from Late Antiquity and the Early Middle Ages;* and *Images and the Carolingians: Tradition, Order, and Worship.* Noble's articles and reviews have appeared in many leading journals, including the *American Historical Review, Byzantinische Zeitschrift, Catholic Historical Review, Revue d'histoire ecclésiastique, Speculum,* and *Studi medievali.* He has also contributed chapters to several books and articles to three encyclopedias. He was a member of the Institute for Advanced Study in 1994 and the Netherlands Institute for Advanced Study in 1999–2000. He has been awarded fellowships by the National Endowment for the Humanities (twice) and the American Philosophical Society.

**Barry S. Strauss**  Professor of history and Classics at Cornell University, Barry Strauss holds a Ph.D. from Yale. He has been awarded fellowships by the National Endowment for the Humanities, the American School of Classical Studies at Athens, the MacDowell Colony for the Arts, the Korea Foundation, and the Killam Foundation of Canada. He is the recipient of the Clark Award for excellence in teaching from Cornell. He served as Director of Cornell's Peace Studies Program. His many publications include *Athens After the Peloponnesian War: Class, Faction, and Policy, 403–386 B.C.; Fathers and Sons in Athens: Ideology and Society in the Era of the Peloponnesian War; The Anatomy of Error: Ancient Military Disasters and Their Lessons for Modern Strategists* (with Josiah Ober); *Hegemonic Rivalry from Thucydides to the Nuclear Age* (co-edited with R. Ned Lebow); *War and Democracy: A Comparative Study of the Korean War and the Peloponnesian War* (co-edited with David R. McCann); *Rowing Against the Current: On Learning to Scull at Forty;* and *The Battle of Salamis, the Naval Encounter That Saved Greece—and Western Civilization.*

**Duane J. Osheim**  A Fellow of the American Academy in Rome with a Ph.D. in history from the University of California, Davis, Duane Osheim is a professor of history at the University of Virginia. A specialist in late medieval and Renaissance social and institutional history, he is the author and editor of *A Tuscan Monastery and Its Social World, An Italian Lordship: The Bishopric of Lucca in the Late Middle Ages,* and *Beyond Florence: The Contours of Medieval and Early Modern Italy.*

**Kristen B. Neuschel**  After receiving her Ph.D. from Brown University, Kristen Neuschel taught at Denison University and Duke University, where she is currently associate professor of history. She is a specialist in early modern French history and is the author of *Word of Honor: Interpreting Noble Culture in Sixteenth-Century France* and articles on French social history and European women's history. She has received grants from the National Endowment for the Humanities and the American Council of Learned Societies. She has also received the Alumni Distinguished Undergraduate Teaching Award, which is awarded annually on the basis of student nominations for excellence in teaching at Duke. She is currently Director of Undergraduate Studies for the History Department.

**William B. Cohen**  After receiving his Ph.D. at Stanford University, William Cohen taught at Northwestern University and Indiana University, where he was professor of history. At Indiana, he served as chairman of the West European Studies and History Departments and was Director of Graduate Studies for the History Department. A previous president of the Society of French Historical Studies, Cohen received several academic fellowships, including a National Endowment for the Humanities and a Fulbright fellowship. He was the author of many works on French history and his research focused on the Algerian war and French memory.

**David D. Roberts**  After taking his Ph.D. in modern European history at the University of California, Berkeley, David Roberts taught at the Universities of Virginia and Rochester before becoming professor of history at the University of Georgia in 1988. At Rochester he chaired the Humanities Department of the Eastman School of Music, and he chaired the History Department at Georgia from 1993 to 1998. A recipient of Woodrow Wilson and Rockefeller Foundation fellowships, he is the author of *The Syndicalist Tradition and Italian Fascism; Benedetto Croce and the Uses of Historicism;* and *Nothing but History: Reconstruction and Extremity After Metaphysics,* as well as two books in Italian and numerous articles and reviews. He is currently the Albert Berry Saye Professor of History at Georgia.

# Western Civilization

## The Continuing Experiment

# CHAPTER 1

# The Ancestors of the West

**T**HEY look at us with an up-to-date intensity, this nearly 5,000-year-old couple from early Egypt. Dressed in simple clothes, they each have movie star good looks, heightened by well-made wigs and expensive jewelry. Their bodies are shown in the regular way of Egyptian art: The man's body is largely bare, while the woman's is mostly covered; his skin is dark brown, hers is light yellow. They are depicted as partners but not as equals.

The writing identifies them as Rahotep and Nofret, husband and wife. We see them here in sculptures from their tomb of about 2600 B.C. The painted limestone statues, with inlaid eyes of quartz and rock crystal, show a powerful pair. Both were part of the royal court, and Rahotep was a general and high priest. The sculptures show us that early civilization was literate, technologically sophisticated, structured by rank and status, religious, and fascinated by the relationship between men and women.

The rich and complex world of Rahotep and Nofret rested on the most momentous inventions in human history. They began approximately 100,000 years ago, when the first modern humans evolved from humanlike ancestors. Human beings wrestled with an often-hostile environment, engaging in a continuing series of experiments, until beginning about 10,000 B.C. they learned how to plant crops and tame animals. The shift from a food-collecting to a food-producing economy dramatically increased the amount of human life that the earth could support. Between 3500 and 3000 B.C., human society became well organized in urban centers, supported by farmers in the surrounding territories, and able to keep written records: it had, in short, achieved civilization.

What we call Western civilization, however, was still more than two thousand years away. As a term, *Western civilization* is imprecise, inviting disagreement about its definition and about the lands, peoples,

Statues of Rahotep (*left*) and Nofret (*right*), Old Kingdom, Egypt. (Egyptian Museum, Cairo)

Origins, to ca. 3000 B.C.

Mesopotamia, to ca. 1600 B.C.

Egypt, to ca. 1100 B.C.

Widening Horizons: The Levant and Anatolia, 2500–1150 B.C.

and cultures that it embraces at any given time. In this book we give Western civilization an evolving definition that permits comparison and reflection over time and space. In the strictest sense, Western civilization means the "West," and that, in turn, has traditionally meant the lands and peoples of western Europe.

Initially, however, the West embraced the Greek and Roman peoples, plus the foundational monotheistic religions of Judaism and Christianity. These first Westerners in turn borrowed many ideas and institutions from the earlier civilizations of western Asia and Egypt. (These civilizations are sometimes referred to as the Ancient Near East.) Indeed, civilization began in those lands and came only relatively late to Europe.

Western Asia and Egypt contributed greatly to the cultures of Greece and Rome and to the religious visions of the Jews and Christians. Yet those earlier civilizations are sufficiently different from the West and its society, politics, and religion that they are better considered as ancestors or forerunners of the West rather than as its founders. (For a longer discussion of the definition of Western civilization, see the Preface.)

So, after briefly surveying the origins of the human species, the historian of the West must begin with the emergence of civilizations after 3500 B.C. in two great river valleys: the valley of the Tigris° and Euphrates° in Mesopotamia (today, Iraq and Syria), and the valley of the Nile in Egypt. Impressive in

their own right, Mesopotamia and Egypt influenced a wide range of other early civilizations in western Asia and northern Africa. Among them were the Hittites and the Syro-Palestinian city-states, whose own cultural contributions make them ancestors of the West as well. They are studied in this chapter. The Hebrews and the Greeks were also influenced by Mesopotamia and Egypt, but with the Hebrews and the Greeks, Western civilization begins, and so they are covered in Chapter 2.

## QUESTIONS TO CONSIDER

- When, where, and how did modern humans evolve?

- How did people shift from a food-collecting to a food-producing economy?

- What is civilization? When, where, and why did it begin? What is Western civilization, or the West?

- What did the civilizations of Egypt and western Asia contribute to the West between about 3500 and 1200 B.C.?

## TERMS TO KNOW

| | |
|---|---|
| hominids | Sumerians |
| hunter-gatherers | city-state |
| Neolithic Revolution | pharaoh |
| cuneiform | Amarna reform |
| papyrus | Ugarit |

## ORIGINS, TO CA. 3000 B.C.

THE earth is old; modern human beings are young; and civilization is a very recent innovation. Physical anthropologists, archaeologists, geneticists, and biochemists have made great strides in explaining human origins. Great disagreement still

reigns nonetheless. Each decade seems to bring an exciting new discovery that calls for the reassessment of previous theories.

We can be more certain about the series of processes, beginning around 10,000 B.C., that led to the emergence of civilization by 3500 to 3000 B.C. The period studied in this chapter includes both prehistory—the term often used for time before the invention of writing—and recorded history. Writing appeared last among the complex of characteristics that marks the emergence of civilization. Over a period of several thousand years, many humans aban-

---

**Tigris** (TY-gris)   **Euphrates** (yoo-FRAY-tees)

doned a mobile existence for a sedentary one. They learned to domesticate animals and to cultivate plants. They shifted from a food-collecting economy to a predominantly food-producing economy. They developed the first towns, from which, over several millennia, the first urban societies slowly evolved. The result—the first civilizations, found in western Asia and Egypt—laid the groundwork on which later would be built the founding civilizations of the West: Greece, Rome, and ancient Israel.

## The First Human Beings

Anatomically modern human beings, *Homo sapiens sapiens*—genus *Homo*, species *sapiens*, subspecies *sapiens*—first appeared about 100,000 years ago. The human family, or hominids, are much older, however. The hominids include many ancient and extinct species.

Both the first hominids and, much later, the first *Homo sapiens sapiens* were found in Africa, the continent that is the cradle of humanity. The first hominids appeared in Africa's tropics and subtropics over 4 million years ago. By 2.5 million years ago they had evolved into creatures who invented the first technology, simple stone tools. Prehistory is traditionally referred to as the Stone Age because stone was the primary medium from which hominids made tools. The hominids were migratory: not less than 1.6 million years ago and perhaps much earlier, they appeared in East Asia and the eastern edge of Europe. The next important stage in human evolution is *Homo erectus* ("upright person"), a hominid with a large brain who used more complex stone tools and may have acquired language. The appearance of *Homo erectus* is usually dated to 1.8 million years ago, but a recent discovery in China may date *Homo erectus* as early as 2.25 million years ago. Slowly, separate *Homo erectus* populations in different places gave way to the gradual emergence of various archaic forms of *Homo sapiens*.

But the most recent research suggests that all anatomically modern humans are descended from a single African ancestor. This conclusion is supported both by DNA evidence and by three recently discovered skulls in Ethiopia. These skulls are about 160,000 years old and represent the probable immediate ancestors of anatomically modern humans. About 89,000 years ago, the *Homo sapiens sapiens* from whom we are all descended was born in Africa. About 70,000 years ago, descendants of that man left Africa for the other continents. All humans today may be descended from only about two thousand individuals in Africa.

For many millennia humans struggled with the ebb and flow of glaciers. They lived during the Ice Age, as

| CHRONOLOGY | |
| --- | --- |
| ca. 4.4 million years ago | Earliest hominids |
| 800,000 years ago | First humans in Europe |
| ca. 100,000 years ago | *Homo sapiens sapiens* |
| 40,000–10,000 B.C. | Upper Paleolithic era |
| 10,000–2500 B.C. | Neolithic era |
| 3500–3000 B.C. | First civilizations |
| 3500–3100 B.C. | First writing in Mesopotamia |
| 3300–3200 B.C. | First writing in Egypt |
| ca. 3200 B.C. | Unification of Nile Valley |
| 2800–2350 B.C. | Early Dynastic Period |
| 2695–2160 B.C. | Egyptian Old Kingdom |
| 2500–2350 B.C. | Cuneiform texts from Ebla |
| 2025–1786 B.C. | Egyptian Middle Kingdom |
| 1650–1180 B.C. | Hittite Old, Middle, and New Kingdoms |
| 1550–1075 B.C. | Egyptian New Kingdom |
| 1450–1300 B.C. | First international system |
| 1400–1200 B.C. | Height of prosperity at Ugarit |
| 1250–1150 B.C. | Sea Peoples invade |

(All dates in this chapter are approximate.)

scholars refer to the period of fluctuating cycles of warm and cold, beginning about 730,000 years ago and ending only about 10,000 years ago. Early humans existed amid great contrasts in temperature, seasons, and landscapes, requiring considerable adaptation—but adapt they did.

Archaic humans first appeared in Europe about 800,000 years ago. Beginning about 400,000 years ago, Europe was home to the ancestors of the best-known archaic people, the Neandertals. Fully evolved by 130,000 years ago, Neandertal people lived in Europe and western Asia for the following 100,000 years, to about 30,000 years ago. Their strong and stocky physiques were perhaps an adaptation to the rugged climate of the Ice Age. The Neandertals were far from being the brutes they are usually imagined to be. They were, for example, among the first people to bury their dead, often with grave offerings—for example, flint, animal bones, or flowers—a practice that suggests they were sensitive enough to mourn their losses. Recent research shows both that Neandertals were clever enough to use tools to attack one another and caring enough to nurse their wounded back to health.

Neandertals, however, were not modern humans. Modern humans entered Europe about 40,000 years ago, having originated in Africa. Within 10,000 years Neandertals had disappeared—whether through war, disease, or an inability to compete with modern humans, we do not know. The first modern humans tended to be taller and less muscular than Neandertals and other archaic people. They also used their hands more precisely and walked more efficiently, and they lived longer. The modern human skull, with its high forehead and tucked-in face, is distinctive, but differences between the modern and archaic human brain are a matter of scholarly debate. What no one debates, however, is that, with the disappearance of Neandertals, modern humans put into effect a revolution in culture.

## The Revolution in Human Culture, ca. 70,000–10,000 B.C.

Before the emergence of modern humans and perhaps before Neandertals, people had relatively little ability to change the natural environment. Modern humans changed that. They exploited natural resources largely by means of technology and organization. Thus they began the process of human manipulation of the environment that—sometimes brilliantly, sometimes disastrously—has remained a leading theme of the human experience ever since. The key to this change was a dramatic increase in the amount and complexity of information being communicated—what might be called the first information revolution. The twin symbols of the revolution are cave paintings and notations made on bone, signs that humans were thinking about their environment and their experiences.

It was long thought that these dramatic changes began in Europe about 40,000 B.C.* Recently, however, they

have been traced to southern Africa, probably more than 70,000 years ago. The discovery there of carefully worked bone tools and stone spearheads pinpoints the dawn of modern human technology. Still, it is not in Africa but elsewhere that we can best trace the early evolution of the modern human mind. Europe from about 40,000 to about 10,000 B.C. provides reliable evidence of the way of life and the culture of early human hunter-gatherer societies, complex organizations that survived by a food-collecting economy of hunting, fishing, and gathering fruits and nuts. This period is sometimes called the Upper Paleolithic (Greek for "Old Stone") era. Then, around 10,000 B.C., western Asia offers evidence of a second revolution: the invention of a food-producing economy, consisting of the domestication of animals and the cultivation of crops. The period from about 10,000 to 3000 B.C. is sometimes called the Neolithic (Greek for "New Stone") era.

Archaeology tells us something about early people's way of life. So do analogies from contemporary anthropology, for even today a tiny number of people still exist in hunter-gatherer societies in isolated corners of the globe—for example, in the Kalahari Desert of Africa and in the Arctic. It is reasonable to speculate that early humans lived in small groups, numbering perhaps twenty-five to fifty persons, related by kinship or marriage. Early hunter-gatherers moved from place to place, following the seasonal migration of game, but by the eve of the invention of agriculture, some hunter-gatherers had settled down in villages. Hunting was largely a male preserve, while gathering nuts and berries fell into the female domain. Perhaps women brought their children with them as they worked or relied on kin or friends for child-care.

It was probably common for men and women to pair off, have children, and establish a family, much as marriage is a near-universal practice among humans today. Compared with other animals, humans produce extremely dependent infants requiring years of attention. In order to ensure the survival of the young to adulthood, men as well as women need to play a role in child rearing.

Early people found shelter by building huts or, frequently, by living in caves or rock shelters—hence our notion of the "caveman." Caves offered shelter, could be heated, and made a naturally good vantage point for observing prey and hostile humans. In the Upper Paleolithic era, about 30,000 years ago, caves were the site of the earliest representational art. The most spectacular Upper Paleolithic paintings discovered so far have been found in caves in southern France (for example, at Lascaux° and at Chauvet° Cave) and in Spain (at Altamira). European

---

*We follow the traditional practice in the West of expressing historical dates in relation to the birth of Jesus Christ (actually, to a now discredited calculation of his birth date, because in fact Jesus was not born in A.D. 1; see page 193). Dates before his birth are labeled B.C. (which stands for "before Christ"), and dates after his birth are labeled A.D. (*anno Domini*, Latin for "in the year of the Lord"). A widely used alternative refers to these dates as B.C.E. ("before the common era") and C.E. ("of the common era").

Lascaux (lass-CO)   Chauvet (show-VAY)

**Chauvet Cave Art**    This black-painted panel shows horses, rhinoceroses, and wild oxen. This painting and others in the cave, discovered in 1994 in southern France, are over 30,000 years old, making them perhaps the oldest known paintings in the world.    *(Jean Cottes/Ministère de la Culture/Corbis Sygma)*

cave paintings of animals such as the bison, horse, reindeer, and woolly mammoth (a huge, extinct member of the elephant family with hairy skin and long, upward-curving tusks) attest to early human artistic skill. The presence of abstract shapes attests to an interest in symbols. The purpose of cave paintings is unknown, but perhaps they served as illustrations of myths or as attempts to control the environment through magic.

Other early representational art includes engravings on stone of animals, birds, and stylized human females, as well as female figurines carved from ivory or bone. Usually represented with exaggerated breasts or buttocks, the carvings are called Venus figurines, after Venus, the Roman goddess of love. They may represent an attempt to control fertility through magic.

Upper Paleolithic craftsmanship is as impressive as the art. The early human tool kit included the first utensils in such easily worked materials as antler and ivory. Stone tools became longer and the first polished bone

tools appeared, as did the first stone and bone spear points and the first bows and arrows. The presence of bone needles and awls (pointed tools for punching holes) implies sewing, probably of animal skins.

The existence of Upper Paleolithic artists and skilled craftspeople demonstrates at least a limited specialization of skills and division of labor: society required organization, albeit on a limited scale. Hunting was a communal enterprise. Related families are likely to have joined together in clans, which in turn may have formed tribes. It is often thought that each of these groups was patriarchal (literally, "ruled by the father"); that is, the family was governed by the father, the tribe by a male headman or chief. To be sure, some later myths (for example, among the ancient Greeks) argue that women were the rulers of prehistoric society. Today some historians see the possibility of matriarchy (literally, "rule by the mother") in the Venus figurines. There is, however, no firm evidence of matriarchy. Male chiefs probably did exist, as in later periods, but some tribes may have had no chief at all, following the decision of the community rather than an individual leader.

## The Coming of Agriculture, ca. 10,000–5000 B.C.

The human discovery of agriculture was dramatic, meriting the name "Neolithic Revolution" that scholars sometimes give it. Yet if dramatic, the discovery spread slowly and unevenly. In most areas, hunting and fishing continued to be a major source of food, even though agriculture fed more people. Agriculture was first discovered sometime after 10,000 B.C. in western Asia, then discovered again independently in other parts of the world. By 5000 B.C. information about the new practices had spread so widely that farming could be found in many places around the world.

The story begins about 13,000 B.C., when humans began to specialize in the wild plants they collected and the animals they hunted. They had good reason to do so because hunter-gatherer society had become increasingly complex, and in some places permanent settlements had appeared. A settled existence probably produced more mouths to feed, stimulating the need for more food. The next step is not surprising: learning how to domesticate plants and animals.

People seem to have begun by domesticating dogs, which were useful in hunting. Then they learned to keep sheep, goats, and cattle. Next came farming. Humans learned first how to grow wheat and barley, then legumes (beans). With males occupied in hunting, it may well have been females who first unraveled the secrets of agriculture.

The earliest area of domestication is a zone of land stretching in a crescent shape west to east from what is

**Map 1.1　Western Asia**　The Neolithic Revolution began after 10,000 B.C. in the Fertile Crescent, an arc-shaped region of dependable annual rainfall. In this area between the Tigris and Euphrates Rivers known as Mesopotamia, the world's first urban civilization took root about 3500 to 3000 B.C.

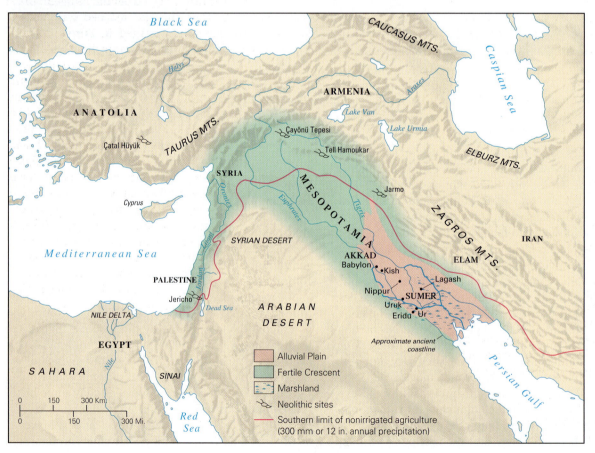

today southern Jordan to southern Iran. Scholars call this region of dependable annual rainfall the Fertile Crescent (see Map 1.1). With domestication came small agricultural settlements, which were increasingly common after 7000 B.C. Thus was born the farming village, probably the place that most people have called home since the spread of agriculture around the world.

Scholars once thought of Neolithic villages as simple places devoted to subsistence agriculture, with no craft specialization, and as egalitarian societies lacking social hierarchies. In recent years, new evidence and a rethinking of older information have altered this picture considerably. The Neolithic village site of Çayönü Tepesi° in eastern Anatolia, for example, provides evidence of metalworking (of copper) and specialization of labor (in beadmaking) from approximately 7000 to 6000 B.C. The site also contains the world's earliest known example of cloth, probably linen, woven around 7000 B.C. Other contemporaneous village sites reveal experiments in ironworking and craft specialization. Evidence points to long-distance trade between villages in pottery and in obsidian (a sharp volcanic glass used in tools). Artwork shows men wearing loincloths and headdresses, women wearing pants and halter tops, and both sexes wearing jewelry.

Consider the case of Jericho°, in Palestine near the Dead Sea (see Map 1.1), perhaps the oldest settled community on earth. A small village around 9000 B.C., Jericho had by about 7000 B.C. become a town surrounded by massive walls 10 feet thick and 13 or more feet high. The walls, about 765 yards long, probably enclosed an area of about 10 acres. The most prominent feature of the walls was a great tower 33 feet in diameter and 28 feet high with an interior stairway. Inside the walls lived a densely packed population of about two thousand people.

An even larger Neolithic town was Çatal Hüyük° in south-central Anatolia (see Map 1.1). Its population of six thousand people in 6000 B.C. made it by far the largest settlement of the era. It was probably a trading center and perhaps a religious shrine. Carbonization from fire has preserved a wealth of artifacts attesting to Çatal Hüyük's sophistication, including woven fabrics, obsidian mirrors, wooden vessels, and makeup applicators.

Agriculture made human populations richer and more numerous, but the resulting concentrations of population bred disease and probably increased the scale of war. More men than ever before were available to fight because agriculture proved to be so efficient a source of food that it freed people for specialized labor. Some became craftsmen, some artists, some priests, and some warriors.

This is not to say that war in Neolithic times was sophisticated. Indeed, the phenomenon perhaps consisted of group skirmishes and sporadic raids rather than systematic warfare. People added new weapons to the spear and the bow: the sling, the dagger, and the mace (a heavy war club). Spanish rock art shows a confrontation between two groups of archers, one following what seems to be a leader. The scene may be a ritual rather than a violent conflict, but we have physical cases of actual bloodshed. The earliest known evidence of organized warfare comes from a cemetery along the Nile River in the Sudan dating from 12,000 to 4500 B.C. The cemetery contains fifty-nine human skeletons, nearly half of whom died violently. Some were speared, some clubbed, and some killed by arrowheads. Some suffered multiple wounds. The victims include women and children.

## Neolithic and Copper Age Europe, 7000–2500 B.C.

Europe was one day to become the center of Western civilization, but the region lagged behind its neighbors at first. Innovations from the east reached Europe after 7000 B.C. and slowly transformed it. Europe was no empty vessel to be filled by eastern technologies, however: Europeans developed their own unique culture.

The term *Europe* refers to a vast peninsula of the Eurasian continent with several very distinct regions. Southern Europe is made up of a rugged and hilly Mediterranean coastal strip, linked to northern Africa and western Asia by the sea and by similarities in climate and landscape. High mountains are found in the Alps of south-central Europe, from which chains of lower mountains radiate toward the southwest and southeast. Northern Europe, by contrast, consists in large part of a forested plain, indented here and there by great rivers. In the southeast the plain, or steppe, becomes open and mostly treeless. The eastern boundaries of Europe are, in the north, the Ural Mountains and, in the south, the Caucasus Mountains. Georgia, Armenia, and Azerbaijan are all considered parts of Europe.

Before 7000 B.C. Europeans lived a traditional hunter-gatherer existence. Farming began in southeastern Europe around 7000 B.C., when migrants from western Asia introduced the settled way of life of the Neolithic village. That food-producing economy spread across Europe between about 6000 and 4500 B.C., borne alternately by colonization and by native adaptation of new technologies.

---

**Çayönü Tepesi** (CHAH-yer-ner TEH-peh-see)
**Jericho** (JEH-rih-co)    **Çatal Hüyük** (CHAH-tal Her-yerk)

The farmers of Early Neolithic Europe (ca. 7000–ca. 4500 B.C.) were pioneers, living in hamlets or villages surrounded by larger hunter-gatherer populations. Not until 2500 B.C. did the majority of Europeans adopt a food-producing way of life. Between 4500 and 2500 B.C., a give-and-take between pioneers and natives led to the development of regional cultures. This era of European prehistory is known as the Late Neolithic Age, or the Copper Age, because copper came into use on the Continent during this time, as did gold. Both metals were used primarily as status symbols: the most dramatic example is a Bulgarian burial site dating from about 4000 B.C. in which a 45-year-old man is buried with 990 gold objects as well as copper and flint weapons.

Between about 4500 and about 3500 B.C., Copper Age Europeans developed their own cultures in relative isolation from the more advanced East. For example, European metallurgy probably developed independently. On Europe's northern and western edges people began to set up megaliths—stone tombs and monuments—often of huge blocks. Such monuments may illustrate an awareness of time created by the spread of agriculture, with its seasonal rhythms.

Between about 3500 and 2500 B.C., Copper Age Europe grew in sophistication. The urbanization of Mesopotamia (in modern-day Iraq; see Map 1.1) had an impact on southeastern Europe, which supplied raw materials for western Asia. Greece underwent the greatest transformation, to the extent that it developed its own urban civilization by about 2000 B.C. (see Chapter 2). Elsewhere, especially in the Balkans, technological innovations came into use, from the wheel, to complex metal-casting, to wine cups (evidence of a new taste). The recent discovery of a Copper Age corpse preserved in the ice of the Italian Alps opens a window into northern Italian society of about 3200 B.C. (See the feature "Weighing the Evidence: The Iceman and His World" on pages 36–37.)

In western Europe stone monuments are the most dramatic cultural achievements. On the Mediterranean island of Malta, for example, people built elaborate temple complexes constructed of massive limestone blocks. In Britain megalithic architecture reached its peak with Stonehenge, built in stages from about 2800 to 1500 B.C. This famous monument consists of a circle of stones oriented precisely on the rising sun of midsummer—a sign

**The Maltese Female**    The "Sleeping Lady," a terra-cotta statuette of the late fourth millennium B.C. from Malta, shows a reclining woman, perhaps a goddess or priestess. Her double-egg–shaped buttocks are thought to symbolize fertility or regeneration.    *(Erich Lessing/Art Resource, NY)*

both of early Europeans' interest in the calendar and of their skill in technology.

Neolithic and Copper Age sculpture consists of many representations of females but few of males. Consider, for example, the ample, sculpted female figures found in Malta's temples. The enlarged buttocks and thighs of these statues might be symbols of fertility. Some scholars speculate that early Europeans worshiped goddesses, until warlike invaders after 2000 B.C., who brought male deities with them. The theory is, however, controversial.

## The Emergence of Civilization, 3500–3000 B.C.

Civilization is derived from the Latin word *civitas*, meaning "commonwealth" or "city." The first civilizations, beginning in Mesopotamia and Egypt between 3500 and 3000 B.C., probably contained the first cities. What differentiated them from their predecessors, however, was not so much size (a city versus a town) as complexity. Civilization allowed human beings to think big. A large and specialized labor force, organized by a sufficiently strong government, made it possible to expand control over nature, pursue advances in technology, and trade and compete over ever widening areas. An elite class emerged that was able to pursue ever more ambitious projects in art and thought and to invent systems of writing. In short, the advent of civilization in the fourth millennium B.C. marked a major turning point. Thereafter, the human horizon expanded forever.

Civilization arose in Iraq, in the valley between the Tigris and Euphrates Rivers (see Map 1.1), a region that the Greeks named Mesopotamia (literally, "between the rivers"). At around the same time or shortly afterward, civilization also began in the valley of the Nile River in Egypt. Although these civilizations each developed largely independently, some borrowing between the two nonetheless took place.

Both Mesopotamia and Egypt are home to valleys containing alluvial land—that is, a relatively flat tract where fertile soil is deposited by a river. Otherwise, the two regions are quite different. Although the Nile Valley was easy to farm, much of the Tigris-Euphrates plain had to be tamed by would-be farmers. Every summer the Nile flooded in a relatively regular and predictable manner, bringing north to Egypt the waters of the monsoon rains of the Ethiopian highlands, where one of the river's sources—the Blue Nile—rises. The spring deluges of the Tigris and Euphrates were more sudden and less predictable. Moreover, the Nile's waters spread so broadly that it took less human effort than in Mesopotamia to ir-

**Eye Idol**   This tiny figurine, made from bone and named for its prominent eyes, may represent a person rather than a god. It comes from Tell Hamoukar in northeastern Syria (ca. 3500 B.C.), which is one of history's earliest cities. *(Oriental Institute Hamoukar Expedition)*

rigate most of the available farmland. In southern Mesopotamia, by contrast, most of the soil was alternately so dry or so marshy that agriculture would not have been possible without considerable irrigation and drainage—that is, the use of channels, dikes, or dams to control floodwaters and improve the fertility of the land. One Mesopotamian text describes a farmer as "the man of dike, ditch, and plow." Making matters worse, Mesopotamia was given to extreme heat and scorching winds. Some scholars argue that the very hostility of Mesopotamia's environment generated the cooperation and control that civilization requires.

It has long been thought that the first cities developed in southern Mesopotamia. A recent discovery, however, suggests that cities were found in northern Mesopotamia around the same time—that is, during the Uruk° Period (3800–3200 B.C.). An excavation at Tell Hamoukar° in northeastern Syria, near the Iraqi border,

---

**Uruk** (OO-rook)   **Tell Hamoukar** (tell ha-moo-CAR)

| Uruk IV ca. 3100 B.C. | Sumerian ca. 2500 B.C. | Old Babylonian ca. 1800 B.C. | Neo-Babylonian ca. 600 B.C. | SUMERIAN Babylonian |
|---|---|---|---|---|
| | | | | **APIN** epinnu plow |
| | | | | **ŠE** še'u grain |
| | | | | **ŠAR** kirû orchard |
| | | | | **KUR** šadû mountain |
| | | | | **GUD** alpu ox |
| | | | | **KU(A)** nunu fish |
| | | | | **DUG** karpatu jar |

**Figure 1.1   Early Mesopotamian Writing**   The pictographs of early writing evolved into a system of phonetic syllables and abstract symbols. Simplified and standardized, this writing was *cuneiform,* or "wedge-shaped." Over time, it was adapted from Sumerian to Babylonian and other languages throughout western Asia.   *(Source: From Babylon, by Joan Oates. Published by Thames and Hudson Ltd., 1978. Reprinted by permission of the publisher.)*

uncovered what appears to be a city from around 3500 B.C. The excavators found ovens and pottery, apparently used for large-scale food production, and they unearthed stamp seals and clay seal impressions, which may indicate a bureaucracy. A mud-brick fortification wall has tentatively been identified. In short, several signs point to a city.

If cities developed simultaneously in northern and southern Mesopotamia in the mid-fourth millennium B.C. they may share a common, earlier source: the Ubaid° culture of mid-fifth-millennium B.C. Mesopotamia. Many questions arise, among them whether Ubaid cities existed as early as 4500 B.C., a thousand years earlier than cities

were thought to have first appeared. We will have to wait for future excavation and study to answer such questions.

The first cities emerged through a slow, incremental process of action and reaction. Labor became more specialized, and agricultural production was maximized. When part of the population moves to a city, those who remain on the land must work harder or use better farming techniques or increase the amount of land under cultivation. In fourth- and third-millennium B.C. Mesopotamia, farmers did all three. Meanwhile, both the number and variety of settlements increased. Urban populations required the support of people in smaller units—towns, villages, and hamlets—clustered around a city.

Along with the growth of cities came the development of writing, about 3500 to 3100 B.C. in Mesopotamia. The development of writing from simple recordkeeping

**Ubaid** (oo-BA-id)

can be traced step by step. Before writing, Mesopotamian people used tiny clay or stone tokens to represent objects being counted or traded. By 3500 B.C., with 250 different types of tokens in play, the system had grown unwieldy enough for people to start using signs to indicate tokens. It was a short step to dispensing with the tokens and placing the signs on a clay tablet by making indentations in the clay with a reed stylus: writing. New words were soon added through pictographs (pictures that stand for particular objects). In time the pictographs evolved into ideograms—that is, abstract symbols that are no longer recognizable as specific objects and thus can be used to denote ideas as well as things.

In the centuries following its introduction, Mesopotamian writing became standardized. Scholars call the signs *cuneiform,* from the Latin for "wedge-shaped," a good description of what early writing looks like (see Figure 1.1). In its first centuries, cuneiform was used almost entirely for economic records or commercial transactions. Then it was adapted to make brief records of offerings to the gods. By 2350 B.C. cuneiform had evolved into a mixed system of about six hundred signs, most of them phonetic (syllabic), with relatively few ideograms.

Experts used to think that writing began in Mesopotamia and spread to Egypt. Recent excavations, however, have found examples of early Egyptian writing securely dated to 3300 to 3200 B.C. In other words, Egyptian writing was independent: it was not derived from or related to cuneiform. Whether writing began in Egypt or Mesopotamia, therefore, is now an open question. What is clear, however, is that writing was invented to meet economic rather than creative needs. In Egypt the earliest writing includes records of the delivery of linen and oil as taxes to King Scorpion I. The writing consists of early *hieroglyphs* (literally, "sacred carvings"), a system of pictures and abstract signs that represent sounds or ideas, later to become more formal and standardized.

As we shall see, incising cuneiform on clay was much clumsier than writing with pen and ink on papyrus, as became possible in Egypt. (See the feature "Information Technology: Papyrus.") Nonetheless, cuneiform was flexible enough to record the spoken language and to be used for poetry as well as for bookkeeping. Moreover, cuneiform became the standard script of various languages of western Asia for several thousand years. Clumsy it may have been, but cuneiform was writing, and writing is both a catalyst for change and the historian's best friend. Mesopotamia after 3000 B.C. was dynamic, sophisticated, and, best of all, intelligible to us.

# MESOPOTAMIA, TO CA. 1600 B.C.

A FTER 3000 B.C. the people of Mesopotamia flourished. They experimented in government, in cooperation and conflict among different ethnic groups, in law, and in the working out of class and gender relations. Keenly aware of human limitations and vanity, they sought divine justice, as their literary and religious texts show. Their engineering skill, mathematics, and astronomy set ancient science on an upward path. In later centuries, Western civilization would build on these foundations, and then take off in new directions.

Archaeologists sometimes refer to the third and second millennia in the eastern Mediterranean and western Asia as the Bronze Age. In this period people mastered the technology of making bronze, an alloy of copper and tin, and bronze frequently replaced stone as a primary material for everyday use.

## The City-States of Sumer

Though their culture is long dead, the Sumerians live on. Whenever someone today counts the minutes, debates politics, or quotes the law, the Sumerians live, for these are all legacies of that ingenious society.

The dominant inhabitants of Mesopotamian civilization in its first flowering are named Sumerians. Present in southern Mesopotamia by 3200 B.C. and probably earlier, the Sumerians entered their great age in the third millennium B.C., when their city-states enjoyed a proud independence (see Map 1.1).

The formative era of Mesopotamian civilization is known as the Uruk Period (ca. 3800–3200 B.C.), after one of its major archaeological sites. During the Uruk Period the Sumerians invented the wheel and the plow, planted the first orchards—of dates, figs, or olives—and developed the first sophisticated metal-casting processes. They built some of the first cities, for example, Uruk. They expanded the size of territories and populations, the scale of war, the complexity of society, and the power of government. Finally, as if to cap a period of remarkable change, at the end of the Uruk Period the Sumerians invented cuneiform writing.

Mesopotamian cities flourished in this era. By the period that scholars have named the Early Dynastic Period (2800–2350 B.C.), named for the first royal dynasties (ruling families), a large Mesopotamian city had grown to the point where it might cover 1,000 acres surrounded by more than 5 miles of walls, within which lived about

## Papyrus

It grew in the marshes of the Nile River valley, a tall and graceful plant. Once it was picked, it might be eaten, woven into baskets or rope, used as construction material for lightweight boats or shelters, or burned for fuel or as incense. But, most important, this versatile vegetation generated a paperlike writing material that had a huge impact on ancient civilization. Today most paper comes from wood, following a technology developed in China. In the ancient West, however, people wrote on rolled sheets produced from an Egyptian plant. In fact, we derive our word *paper* from the name of the plant, *papyrus.* The Greeks called it *byblos,* from which came the Greek word for book and, eventually, our word *bible.*

Harvested papyrus was transformed into writing material by cutting the stalks into thin strips and laying them in a crosshatched fashion to form sheets, which were then glued together into rolls, in which form it was sold. The roll was the standard form of both writing paper and books in ancient times. Although sizes varied, a typical roll was about 8 or 9 inches high by about 15 feet long (when unrolled). A sheet of paper was white, shiny, and smooth.

Rolls manufactured from papyrus became the primary writing material of the ancient world, outstripping all competing media. Papyrus was durable and easy to write on, which facilitated all written communication, from paying taxes to reading Plato. Even if they had had only stone or bone or animal skin to write on, humans would have made progress, but papyrus-making technology made things simpler. Progress requires a process of trial and error, which is easier to carry out on paper than in any other nonelectronic medium.

Unlike people in western Asia, where clay tablets were the standard writing medium, Egyptians wrote on papyrus, beginning around 3000 B.C. Carving cuneiform in clay with a reed stylus was cumbersome, but writing on paper with brush and ink was easy, flexible, and even elegant (see the photograph of the Egyptian *Book of the Dead* on page 25). Not only did papyrus allow Egyptians to develop several different written scripts, but it may also have helped stimulate the development of the alphabet. The first alphabet appeared in Egypt in the second millennium B.C., in a Semitic script with Egyptian influences. Although written on stone, that alphabet was probably developed through experimentation more easily done on papyrus.

People wrote everything on papyrus, from contracts to curses, from public documents to poetry, from trivial jottings to holy books. Highly prized because it was durable and flexible, papyrus grew more common than other writing materials available in antiquity, such as parchment (manufactured from animal skins), potsherds, stone, bone, or tablets of wood, wax, or clay. Although expensive for ordinary people, papyrus was cheap for the elites, who had a near monopoly on literacy.

The papyrus plant has a tall triangular stem and a fluffy crown. It was often the subject of pharaonic art. Look, for example, at this painting from an Egyptian tomb of the fifteenth century B.C. The man on the right has poled the boat into a grove of papyrus plants. The man on the left is pulling a plant out by the stalk, while his coworker in the center is tying stalks into a sheaf.

Papyrus grew in several places around the Mediterranean, but in ancient times its main habitat was Egypt.

fifty thousand people. Such a city was part of a network of thirty such city-states with a common culture, commerce, and propensity to make war on one another. Hence the city-states of Mesopotamia may be called the first civilization.

It was a land of cooperation and conflict. The Sumerian cities had much in common: language, literature, arts and sciences, and religion. Yet the cities often quarreled. In some cases conflict erupted over the boundaries of adjacent farmlands. The scarcity of fresh water also led to disputes among cities over water rights.

Each city had its own small urbanized area and a larger agricultural hinterland irrigated by canals. Cities traded with one another and with the outside world. The primary political units of southern Mesopotamia for most of the third millennium B.C., Sumerian city-states were an incubator of civilization.

How were the Sumerian city-states governed? A Sumerian might have responded that they were governed by the gods, for the Sumerians believed that the gods had created, and thus owned, everything on earth. Historians study human government, but the lack of evidence makes it difficult to say much with assurance about Sumerian government before the Early Dynastic Period.

The Nile Valley, particularly the delta, became the center of a vast international trade in papyrus in Greek and Roman times, from around 600 B.C. on. Yet the trade began much earlier, at least by around 1100 B.C., when it is known that paper was brought from Egypt to Phoenicia. In pharaonic times the manufacture of papyrus in Egypt may have been under royal supervision. The word *papyrus* itself may mean "that of the pharaoh."

The Classical Greeks got their papyrus from Egypt, at first possibly via the Phoenician port city of Byblos. The Romans considered papyrus to be "an indispensable necessity of public and private business," as one Roman writer put it. From Britain to Iraq, papyrus was in almost universal use during Greek and Roman times for more than a thousand years after 600 B.C.

**Harvesting Papyrus**  This Egyptian wall-painting, from a tomb dating to about 1450 B.C., shows boatmen gathering papyrus plants.  *(The Metropolitan Museum of Art [30.4.11])*

Certainly in early times Sumerian temples were wealthy and powerful. A simple structure around 5000 B.C., the temple had become by 4000 B.C. an elaborate, monumental work of architecture built on a raised platform. Each city had at least one temple, the house of its patron god and the common symbol of the community. There is no evidence, though, for the once-prominent theory that the early Sumerian cities were temple-states governed by priests.

By the beginning of the Early Dynastic Period, around 2800 B.C., political power in a Sumerian city rested largely in the hands of its Council of Elders, whose members were probably wealthy landowners. Some scholars argue that the council shared power with a popular assembly, creating, in effect, a bicameral legislature and perhaps even a primitive democracy. The evidence is ambiguous, however, leaving it highly debatable whether ordinary people took part in Sumerian government.

In Sumer, as elsewhere in western Asia and Egypt throughout ancient times, ordinary people often faced limits on their freedom. True, there seem to have been many free peasants. Yet these small "free" farmers often had to provide forced labor for the state as a kind of taxation—maintaining the vast Mesopotamian irrigation system, for example. There also seems to have been a large group of people who were only semi-free because they owned no land of their own but worked others' land. Finally, there were slaves—that is, people who could be bought and sold. Slaves were never very numerous in these societies because no large policing system existed yet to keep them from running away. Still, wealthy people usually had a few slaves to help in the household. Slaves were usually brought from abroad as war booty or merchandise, although some slaves were local people who had been sold into slavery to pay off a debt; often they were children (especially daughters) sold by their parents.

By about 2700 B.C. political power shifted. It was a time of chronic intercity warfare, and the times demanded a strong hand. The new ruler was not a Council of Elders but rather a "big man" (*lugal*) or, less often, a "governor" (*ensi*)—that is, a king or, occasionally, a queen. The monarch was first and foremost a warrior. He claimed to be the earthly representative of the gods, a position that gave him general responsibility for his subjects' welfare. Accordingly, kings sponsored irrigation works, raised fortification walls, restored temples, and built palaces.

The earliest Sumerian kings, dating from the period 2700 to 2600 B.C., are Enmebaragesi of the city of Kish; his son and successor, Agga; and Gilgamesh° of Uruk, a hero of epic poetry whom many scholars consider a genuine historical personage. In the cities of Ur and Lagash, the king's wife was often a power in her own right. Kish was ruled by Ku-baba (r. ca. 2450 B.C.), the first reigning queen of recorded history.

Though warriors, Sumerian monarchs also recognized a responsibility for promoting justice. History's earliest known reformer of law and society was Uru-inim-gina, king of Lagash around 2400 B.C. Surviving documents describe Lagash as a society in which wealthy landowners encroached on the temples and oppressed the poor, and royal administrators mistreated ordinary people. The king's aims seem to have been both to correct abuses and to weaken independent sources of power threatening royal authority. Uru-inim-gina attempted to manage the bureaucracy, protect the property of humble people, and guard the temples. He also put into effect the first known wage and price controls. Uru-inim-gina's proclaimed intention was to promote impartial justice, a goal that he expressed in the formula "[the king] will protect the mother that is in distress, the mighty man shall not oppress the naked and the widow."

If at the same time he also managed to increase his own power, then so much the better. As it turned out, Lagash was conquered only a few years after Uru-inim-gina's reign. His reforms nonetheless survived as the precedent for a long Mesopotamian tradition of royal lawgiving.

## Conquest and Assimilation, ca. 2350–1900 B.C.

Mesopotamian cities faced competition from the surrounding peoples of the desert and the mountains. Poor and tough, these people coveted Mesopotamia's wealth. Some conquerors came directly from the hinterland to the walls of the city they were attacking; others climbed to power from within the Sumerian city-states. Both groups were sufficiently impressed by Sumerian culture to adopt a great many Sumerian customs and ideas. The most successful warrior-king was Sargon (r. 2371–2316 B.C.), an unusual figure who rose from obscurity to a high position under the king of Kish before founding his own capital city, Agade°. Even more important, Sargon was a native speaker not of Sumerian but of Akkadian.

The Akkadians were originally a seminomadic people who lived on the edge of the desert. Shepherds, they moved their flocks with the seasons. Their language, Akkadian, belongs to the Semitic group of languages, which also includes Arabic and Hebrew. Scholars formerly believed that the Akkadians came directly from the desert to conquer Sumer, but it is now known that they had begun settling in the northern cities of southern Mesopotamia by the end of the Uruk Period. This northern part of southern Mesopotamia was known as Akkad.

As commander of one of history's first professional armies, Sargon conquered all of Mesopotamia, and his power extended westward along the Euphrates and eastward into the Iranian Plateau. Rather than rule conquered peoples directly, the Akkadians generally were satisfied with loose control, as long as they could monopolize trade. They adopted Sumerian religion and wrote Akkadian in cuneiform.

Sargon's son inherited his throne. His dynasty boasted that it reigned over "the peoples of all lands" or "the four quarters of the earth." The Akkadian empire reached its greatest height in the reign of Sargon's grandson, Naram-sin (r. ca. 2250–2220 B.C.), but it did not survive the next reign. Sargon nonetheless proved to be one of western Asia's most influential figures. His dynasty's ideal of universal empire was one to which future conquerors would lay claim.

---

**Gilgamesh** (GIL-ga-mesh)

**Agade** (ah-GAH-day)

**Statuette of a Goddess**   This copper figurine (ca. 1800–1600 B.C.) from the city of Ur represents a *lamma*, that is, a kindly goddess. She wears a headdress and a pleated dress, while the counterweight to her necklace hangs down her back. She stands about 4 inches tall and 1 inch wide.   *(Courtesy of the Trustees of the British Museum)*

**Akkadian Bronze**   This stern-faced, life-size cast-bronze head, with its stylized ringleted beard and carefully arranged hair, shows Mesopotamian craftsmanship at its finest. Thought by some to be Sargon (r. 2371–2316 B.C.) or Naram-sin (r. ca. 2250–2220 B.C.), it was deliberately mutilated in ancient times.   *(Claus Hansmann, München)*

Sargon proved adept at using religion to legitimize his rule. A self-made monarch, he was sensitive to the charge of having stolen power. Indeed, he chose the throne name Sargon (Sharrum-ken in Akkadian) because it means "the king is legitimate." By claiming the status of the gods' representative on earth, Sargon strengthened his authority. He once paraded a defeated enemy in a halter before the temple and priests of Enlil, the chief Sumerian god, confidently proclaiming that Enlil was on his side.

Assimilation was another lasting Akkadian legacy. Although Sargon made Akkadian the official language of administration, he made politic concessions to Sumerian sensibilities. For instance, his daughter Enkheduanna°, whom he appointed high priestess at Ur and Uruk, wrote poetry in Sumerian, poetry powerful enough to be quoted often in later Sumerian texts. The first known woman poet, Enkheduanna described the union of Sumerians and Akkadians.

Around 2200 B.C. the Akkadian empire broke up into a series of smaller successor states. Then, after a century of rule by invaders from the Zagros Mountains on the eastern border of Mesopotamia, the Sumerians returned to power under the Third Dynasty of Ur (2112–2004 B.C.). Far from stripping away all Akkadian influence, the revived Sumerian rulers spoke of themselves as "kings of

---

**Enkheduanna** (en-khe-du-AN-na)

Sumer and Akkad." It was a title that would have a long and potent history: for the next fifteen hundred years, many of the great kings of western Asia would label themselves, among other honorifics, "king of Sumer and Akkad." By using this title, the Sumerian kings of Ur showed that they recognized the existence of a composite, common Mesopotamian society.

This society survived renewed political turmoil around 2000 B.C. A new kingdom under the rule of the Amorites, one of several raiding peoples, emerged around 1900 B.C. in southern Mesopotamia. The kingdom of the Amorites, Semitic-speakers, shared Mesopotamian culture and traditions. Babylon, northwest of Ur in the central part of Mesopotamia, became the Amorite capital. From Babylon, Amorite kings issued cuneiform decrees that, although written in a Semitic language, drew heavily on Sumerian material.

## Hammurabi's Code

The most famous Amorite king, Hammurabi (r. 1792–1750 B.C.) ruled in Babylon about six hundred years after Sargon. Much of his forty-two-year reign was devoted to creating a Mesopotamian empire. A careful administrator who ushered in an era of prosperity and cultural flowering, Hammurabi is most famous for the text known as Hammurabi's Code. Although the work was less a "code" than a collection listing various crimes and their punishments—a kind of treatise on justice glorifying Hammurabi's qualities as a judge—we shall use the familiar name. Hammurabi's Code became both a legal and a literary classic, much copied in later times.

Hammurabi's Code offers a remarkable portrait of Mesopotamian society. The document contains nearly three hundred rulings in cases ranging from family to commercial law, from wage rates to murder. The administration of justice in Mesopotamia was entirely practical: we find no notion of abstract absolutes or universal principles, not even a word for "law."

Though occasionally less harsh than earlier law codes, which date as far back as around 2100 B.C., Hammurabi's Code was by no means lenient. Whereas earlier codes were satisfied with payment in silver as recompense for crime, Hammurabi's Code was the first to stipulate such ruthless penalties as mutilation, drowning, and impaling. It also introduced the law of retaliation for wounds: "If a man has destroyed the eye of a member of the aristocracy: they shall destroy his eye. If he has broken his limb: they shall break the (same) limb." Moreover, children could be punished for the crimes of their fathers. (See the box "Reading Sources: King Hammurabi Dispenses Justice.")

Inscribed in forty-nine vertical columns on a stone stele about 7½ feet high and displayed in a prominent public place, Hammurabi's Code symbolized the notion that the law belonged to everyone. Although ordinary people could not read, it was possible for them to find a patron who could. Yet the societies of western Asia and Egypt were anything but egalitarian, and Hammurabi's society was no exception. Punishments there, as elsewhere, were class-based: crimes against a free person, for example, received harsher punishment than crimes against a slave or a semi-free person. Debt seems to have been a serious and widespread problem, frequently leading to debt slavery. Women could own and inherit property and testify in court. The overall direction of the code, however, was patriarchal: it enshrined the power of the male head of the family. For example, a son who struck his father had his hand cut off, while a woman who brought about the death of her husband "because of another man" was impaled on stakes.

## Divine Masters

The Sumerians were polytheists—that is, they had many gods—and their gods (like the later gods of Greece) were anthropomorphic, or human in form. Indeed, Sumerian (and Greek) gods were thought to be much like human beings, by turns wise and foolish, except that they were immortal and superpowerful. Many Sumerian gods arose out of the forces of nature: An, the sky-god; Enki, the earth-god and freshwater-god; Enlil, the air-god; Nanna, the moon-god; and Utu (Semitic, Shamash), the sun-god. Other Sumerian gods embodied human passions or notions about the afterlife: Inanna (Semitic, Ishtar), goddess of love and war; and Ereshkigal, goddess of the underworld.

The Sumerians sometimes envisioned their gods holding an assembly, much like a boisterous Sumerian prototype. The Sumerians and Akkadians considered Enlil, city-god of Nippur, to be the chief god. The Babylonians replaced him with Marduk, city-god of Babylon.

Every Mesopotamian city had its main temple complex, the most striking feature of which was a *ziggurat*, or stepped tower. Constructed originally as simple raised terraces, ziggurats eventually became seven-stage structures. Unlike the pyramids of Egypt, ziggurats were not tombs but "stairways" connecting humans and the gods.

The keynote of Mesopotamian religion was a certain pessimism about the human condition. It is not surprising that the Mesopotamians, living in a difficult natural environment, regarded the gods with fear and awe. Although the gods communicated with humans, their lan-

**READING SOURCES**

## KING HAMMURABI DISPENSES JUSTICE

*The Code of Hammurabi, king of Babylon (r. 1792–1750 B.C.), is one of the best-known documents of antiquity. Less a code than a treatise on justice, the text illustrates both the image of himself that the king wished to promote and the class and gender hierarchies of Mesopotamia in the second millennium B.C. The following excerpts are from the preface and body of the text.*

The gods] named me to promote the welfare of the people, me, Hammurabi, the devout, god-fearing prince, to cause justice to prevail in the land, to destroy the wicked and the evil, that the strong might not oppress the weak, to rise like the sun over the black-headed (people), and to light up the land. . . . I established law and justice in the language of the land, thereby promoting the welfare of the people. At that time (I decreed):

128: If a free man acquired a wife but did not draw up the contracts for her, that woman is no wife.

129: If the wife of a free man has been caught while lying with another man, they shall bind them and throw them into the water [that is, submit to the water ordeal, with the river as divine judge]. If the husband of the woman wishes to spare his wife, then the king in turn may spare his subject. . . .

170: When a free man's first wife bore him children and his female slave also bore him children, if the father during this lifetime has ever said "My children!" to the children whom the slave bore him, thus having counted them with the children of his first wife, after the father has gone to (his) fate, the children of the first wife and the children of the slave shall share equally in the goods of the paternal estate, with the first-born, the son of the first wife, receiving a preferential share. . . .

196: If a free man has destroyed the eye of a member of the aristocracy, they shall destroy his eye. . . .

198: If he has destroyed the eye of a commoner or broken the bone of a commoner, he shall pay one mina [approximately one pound] of silver. . . .

202: If a free man has struck the cheek of an aristocrat who is superior to him, he shall be beaten sixty (times) with an oxtail whip in the assembly. . . .

237: When a free man hired a boatman and a boat and loaded it with grain, wool, oil, dates, or any kind of freight, if that boatman was so careless that he has sunk the boat and lost what was in it as well, the boatman shall make good the boat which he sank and whatever he lost that was in it.

Source: Adapted from James B. Pritchard, ed., *Ancient Near Eastern Texts Relating to the Old Testament,* 3d ed., with Supplement, pp. 164, 171, 173, 175–176. Copyright © 1969 by Princeton University Press. Reprinted by permission of Princeton University Press.

guage was mysterious. To understand the divine will, the Mesopotamians engaged in various kinds of divination: the interpretation of dreams, the examination of the entrails of slaughtered animals, and the study of the stars (which stimulated great advances in astronomy, as we will see). By building temples, offering prayers and animal sacrifices, and participating in public rituals and processions, Mesopotamians hoped to appease their gods and discern their wishes.

Most people expected nothing glorious in the afterlife, merely a shadowy existence. It was thought that with a person's last breath, his or her spirit embarked on a long journey to the Netherworld, a place under the earth. More than one Mesopotamian text describes the Netherworld as the "Land-of-no-return" and "the house wherein the dwellers are bereft of light, / Where dust is their fare and clay their food, / Where they see no light, residing in darkness."[1] The dead resided there permanently, though in some texts their spirits return to earth, often with hostile intent toward the living.

Archaeological evidence indicates a possible shift in such attitudes toward death, at least on the part of the Mesopotamian upper classes, by the late third millennium B.C. The kings and nobles of the Third Dynasty of Ur were buried with rich grave goods and with their servants, who were apparently the victims of human sacrifice following the master's death. Perhaps the rulers now expected to have the opportunity to use their wealth

## READING SOURCES

# HEROISM AND DEATH IN MESOPOTAMIA

*The* Epic of Gilgamesh *sheds light on categories of gender and power in Mesopotamia. Men such as King Gilgamesh and his friend Enkidu have heroic adventures and risk death. Women lead quieter lives but are wiser and more realistic, as the following excerpts show. Here Gilgamesh, who wanders in his grief over the death of Enkidu, comes to the cottage of the barmaid Siduri.*

Then she took pity on him / And let him enter and lie down and rest. / She gave him her bed to fall into and sleep / And rubbed his back and neck and legs and arms / When he was coming out of sleep, still muttering / About the one "who went with me through everything." / Like those old people who forget their listeners / Have not lived through their past with them, / Mentioning names that no one knows. / Enkidu, whom I loved so much, / Who went through everything with me / He died—like any ordinary man. / I have cried both day and night. / I did not want to put him in a grave. / He will rise, I know, one day. / But then I saw that he *was* dead. / His face collapsed within / After several days, / Like cobwebs I have touched / With my finger.

She wiped his face with a moist cloth / Saying: Yes yes yes yes, / As she made him cooler / Trying to help him forget / By the steady softness of her flesh. / She moved her lips across his chest / And caressed the length of his tired body / And lay over him at night until he slept.

You will never find an end to grief by going on, / She said to the one half sleeping at her side, / Leaning forward to wipe the perspiration from his face. / His eyes were open though his whole self felt asleep / Far off alone in some deep forest / Planted in his flesh / Through which he felt his way in pain / Without the help / Of friends. / She spoke as to a child who could not understand / All the futility that lay ahead / Yet who she knew would go on to repeat / Repeat repeat the things men had to learn. The gods gave death to man and kept life for / Themselves. That is the only way it is. / Cherish your rests; the children you might have; / You are a thing that carries so much tiredness.

Source: Herbert Mason, *Gilgamesh: A Verse Narrative* (Boston: Houghton Mifflin, 2003), pp. 63–65. Copyright © 1970 by Herbert Mason. Reprinted by permission of Houghton Mifflin Company. All rights reserved.

**For additional information on this topic, go to college.hmco.com/students.**

again in a comfortable immortality, possibly influenced by Egyptian ideas (see pages 25–26).

## Arts and Sciences

The people of Mesopotamia were deeply inquisitive. They focused on the beginning and the end of things. "How did the world come into being?" and "What happens to us when we die?" are perhaps the two fundamental questions of their rich literature. Consider, for example, the Babylonian creation epic known from its first line as *Enuma Elish*° ("When on high"). An epic poem is the story of heroic deeds, in this case the deeds

---

**Enuma Elish** (eh-noo-MAH EH-lish)

of the gods of order, who triumphed over the forces of chaos. This poem also commemorates the political ascendancy of Babylon. The poem was recited annually during the New Year's festival by Babylonian priests. Another important Babylonian literary genre, known as wisdom literature, responded to life's vicissitudes with precepts that are sometimes simple, sometimes sophisticated. It proved eventually to influence the wisdom literature of the Hebrew Bible.

The best-known example of Mesopotamian literature is the *Epic of Gilgamesh*. Frequently translated and adapted by various western Asian peoples, *Gilgamesh* may be a Sumerian work dating to about 2500 B.C. Gilgamesh, king of Uruk, was probably a real historical personage, but the poem primarily concerns his fictionalized personal life, in particular his painful pilgrimage from arrogant youth to wise maturity. The main themes are friendship, loss, and the inevitability of death. Much of the poem discusses Gilgamesh's close relationship with Enkidu, who is first his rival, then his friend, and finally his educator. Enkidu's untimely death makes Gilgamesh aware of his own mortality. Distraught by his friend's passing, Gilgamesh goes on a vain quest for immortality. The *Epic of Gilgamesh* contains stories that presage the later biblical Eden and Flood narratives; there is little doubt but that those narratives found their way from Mesopotamia to the Hebrew Bible. (See the box "Reading Sources: Heroism and Death in Mesopotamia.")

The Mesopotamians made advances in mathematics, astronomy, medicine, and engineering. The Sumerians had two systems of numbers: a decimal system (powers of ten) for administration and business and a sexagesimal system (powers of sixty) for weights and mathematical or astronomical calculations. Like the Babylonians, we still divide hours by sixty today. Furthermore, our modern system of numerical place-value notation—for example, the difference between 42 and 24—is derived, through Hindu-Arabic intermediaries, from the Babylonian system. The Babylonians were adept at arithmetic and could solve problems for which we would use algebra. A millennium before the Greek mathematician Pythagoras (who claimed to have studied the Mesopotamian tradition) proved the validity of the theorem that bears his name, they were familiar with the proposition that in a right triangle the square of the longest side is equal to the sum of the squares of the other two sides. In the first millennium B.C. the Babylonians developed a sophisticated mathematical astronomy (see page 44). As early as the seventeenth century B.C., they made systematic, if not always accurate, recordings of the movements of the planet Venus.

In medical matters they demonstrated considerable critical ability. Physicians made advances in the use of plant products for medicines and in very rudimentary surgery. The Babylonians had a simple pregnancy test of moderate accuracy, for example, and their surgeons were experienced at setting broken bones. When they became ill, however, most people in Mesopotamia set more store by magic and incantations than by surgery or herbal medicine.

Mesopotamian sculptors, particularly the Sumerians, were adept and sophisticated. They did not produce realistic representations of reality—that was not their purpose. Rather, they aimed at creating symbols of religious piety or political or military power. Sumerian statues tend to be stiff and solemn. The head and face are carved in detail, and the body is neglected, sometimes little more than a geometric form.

The most common type of Mesopotamian sculpture is relief sculpture, in which figures or forms are projected from a flat surface. Steles (upright stone slabs or pillars), plaques, and cylinder seals (small, carved stone or metal cylinders rolled over wet clay to make a stamp, indicating ownership) are all found.

# EGYPT, TO CA. 1100 B.C.

FROM Babylon to the valley of the Nile River was about 750 miles by way of the caravan routes through Syria and Palestine—close enough to exchange goods and customs but far enough for a distinct Egyptian civilization to emerge. As in Sumer, civilization in Egypt arose in a river valley, but Egypt was much earlier than Mesopotamia in becoming a unified kingdom under one ruler. Moreover, ancient Egypt survived as a united and independent kingdom for over two thousand years (to be sure, with some periods of civil war and foreign rule). Egypt made great strides in a variety of areas of human achievement, from the arts to warfare. Western civilization borrowed much from Egypt, especially in technology and religion.

## Geography as Destiny

Ancient Egypt is a product of the unique characteristics of the Nile River (see Map 1.2). Egypt was "the gift of the Nile," to use the well-known phrase of Herodotus, a Greek historian who visited Egypt in the fifth century B.C.

Yet most of present-day Egypt is desert. Only about 5 percent is habitable by humans, including a few oases, the Nile Delta, and the Nile Valley itself, which extends about 760 miles from Cairo to Egypt's modern southern border: Upper Egypt, a long and narrow valley never more than about 14 miles wide. North of Cairo, in Lower Egypt, the Nile branches out into the wide, low-lying delta before flowing into the Mediterranean Sea.

The fertility of the Nile River gave ancient Egypt a prosperous economy and optimistic culture. The river's annual floods, which took place during late summer and autumn, were generally benign. With less human effort than was required in Mesopotamia, the floodwaters could be used to irrigate most of the farmland in the Nile Valley. As a result, Egyptian agriculture was one of the wealthiest in the ancient world. Bread and beer were the national staples.

**Map 1.2    Ancient Egypt and the Levant**    The unique geography of the Nile Valley and its fertile soil left a stamp on ancient Egypt. Egypt enjoyed trade and cultural contact—and sometimes went to war—with nearby lands such as Nubia and the Levant.

Egyptian culture celebrated the Nile's bounty. "Hail to Thee, O Nile, that gushest forth from the earth and comest to nourish Egypt!" So proclaims an ancient hymn that indicates the Egyptians' confidence in their natural environment. With its plentiful water and fertile land, Egypt suffered far less of the warfare that damaging floods and relative economic scarcity provoked in Mesopotamia.

Egyptian art and literature betray little of the despair over the unpredictability of the universe that developed in the harsher climatic conditions of Mesopotamia. The behavior of the Nile, furthermore, encouraged a static quality in Egyptian ideology. Change seemed undesirable. Even death appeared to be a minor event compared with the eternal regularity of the Nile, which may help explain the prominence in Egyptian religion of belief in the afterlife. In addition, the static outlook helped promote the idea of an absolute, all-powerful, and all-providing king—namely, pharaoh.

Early Egypt developed a distinctive civilization, with no major invasion for nearly 1,500 years after the beginning of the historical period around 3100 B.C. Just how isolated was early Egypt, however, and just how distinctive was its civilization? Debate has arisen in recent years about the relationship of Egypt with western Asia, Europe, and the rest of Africa. Before World War II, most Egyptologists tended to think of Egypt more as part of the Near East (that is, of the culture of western Asia) than as part of Africa. Many imagined that ancient Egyptians looked much like modern Europeans: part of "the Great White Race."[2] More recently, with the liberation after World War II of Europe's former African colonies and with the awakening of a growing interest in Africa by African Americans, some people have argued that Egypt was primarily African in character and that the ancient Egyptians were black.

The truth lies in between these two positions. Much of Egypt's earliest culture is African, as evidenced by both artifacts, such as Neolithic artwork and pottery, and ideas, such as the notion that the ruler represents the ancestors and guarantees the fertility of the soil. Yet in its late Neolithic era (ca. 3400–3050 B.C.), Egypt imported new styles and techniques in art, architecture, ceramics, and metallurgy from western Asia. As for the population, it seems from the fourth millennium B.C., if not earlier, to have consisted of Africans mixed with immigrants from western Asia. The Egyptians considered themselves a distinct ethnic and racial group, unlike their neighbors in Africa or elsewhere. Egyptians were generally darker skinned than the ancient peoples of Europe or western Asia but often lighter skinned than the peoples of Africa south of the Sahara. They included a considerable variety of skin colors and body types. The Egyptians of the southerly Upper Nile were more likely to have the dark skin and facial features characteristic of sub-Saharan Africans.

Egypt was in continual contact with other regions of Africa, particularly the neighboring areas of ancient Libya and Nubia (roughly, modern Sudan). The people of Nubia, who were black Africans, borrowed from Egypt and were perhaps borrowed from in turn. Some scholars believe, for example, that the early Egyptian notion of monarchy originated in Nubia. In West Africa certain important institutions—including sacred royalty, the cult of the ram, and belief in the afterlife existence of a double of one's physical person—may be of Egyptian origin.

## Divine Kingship

Agriculture and settled village life emerged in Egypt around 5000 B.C. By 4000 B.C. villages had grown into towns, each controlling a strip of territory. About a thousand years later, around 3100 B.C., the Nile Valley had become one unified kingdom of Egypt, with a capital city perhaps at Memphis. We do not know precisely how this process unfolded. Egyptians writing after 3000 B.C. assumed that the Nile Valley had originally been home to two kingdoms roughly corresponding to Upper and Lower Egypt. Then, around 3100 B.C., Menes, king of Upper Egypt, is said to have conquered Lower Egypt and united the two into a single realm.

We do not know how much (if any) of this tradition is true. We *do* know that between about 5000 and 3100 B.C., Egyptian communities up and down the Nile Valley succeeded in clearing marshes and expanding the amount of land under cultivation, which in turn could support a larger population. By 3200 B.C., monumental architecture, writing, and kingship appeared. For several centuries Egyptians consolidated their institutions. Although few specifics are known about this Archaic Period (3200–2695 B.C.), it clearly laid the groundwork for the next era. Around 2700 B.C., a remarkable, distinctive, and relatively well-documented period of creativity began, the Third (2695–2600 B.C.) and Fourth (2600–2500 B.C.) Dynasties (that is, ruling families) of the Old Kingdom.

The history of third- and second-millennium B.C. Egypt is usually divided into three distinct eras of great prosperity: the Old Kingdom (2695–2160 B.C.), the Middle Kingdom (2025–1786 B.C.), and the New Kingdom (1550–1075 B.C.). Between the kingdoms, central authority broke down in the Intermediate Periods. Broadly speaking, the Old Kingdom was an era of spectacular creativity and originality, symbolized by the building of the Great Pyramids; the Middle Kingdom, an era of introspection and literary production; and the New Kingdom, an era in which Egypt's traditional isolation gave way to international diplomacy and expansion.

The early Egyptian government was the first government in recorded history to govern a large territory. Indeed, a chart of Egypt's power structure would be strictly hierarchical, resembling a pyramid, with a broad base of laborers and artisans supporting a small commanding elite. The occupant of the highest point of power was considered so important that for centuries Egyptians referred to the office rather than to the person, calling it "the Great House"—in Egyptian, *per-aa,* or "pharaoh," as the ruler himself (or occasionally herself) was eventually called.

Egyptian kingship was sacred monarchy. In Mesopotamia, the king generally claimed to have been appointed by the gods. In Egypt pharaoh was deemed to *be* a god. He was referred to as the "good god" in his lifetime and the "great god" after death. Considered the physical child of the sun-god, Re, he was also equated with the sky-god Horus, and after dying he became Osiris, god of the underworld. Just as Egyptian myth recounted how the world was created when a god, sitting on a hill, made the waters recede, so pharaoh was thought to make the Nile rise and fall each year.

A wall of language and ceremony separated kings from ordinary human beings. Egyptians did not speak "to" the king but rather "in his presence." He was outfitted with a variety of crowns, headdresses, and scepters. Pharaoh's exalted status was apparent on the occasion of a "glorious appearance" before his subjects, especially at the Sed festival or jubilee, a ceremony designed to rejuvenate the king's divine powers.

The most dramatic symbol of the king's divinity, however, was not a festival but a building—or, rather, a series of buildings—the pyramids. The ancients built thirty-five major and many smaller pyramids, of which the best known are the Great Pyramids of Giza—three gigantic, perfectly symmetrical limestone tombs constructed during the Fourth Dynasty. Nearly five thousand years after its construction, the pyramid of King Khufu (r. 2589–2566 B.C., better known by his Greek name, Cheops) is still the largest all-stone building in human history. Near the Great Pyramids stands the Great Sphinx, a human-headed lion carved out of a huge rock outcropping, perhaps representing Khufu's son, King Khafre (r. 2558–2532 B.C.; Greek name, Chephren), for whom the second pyramid at Giza was built.

The pyramids were not just monuments to an ego but also temples where the king would continue to be worshiped and served in the afterlife. The structures served a political purpose as well. When the Great Pyramids were constructed, the kingdom of Egypt was still young and fragile. By carrying out an astonishingly large

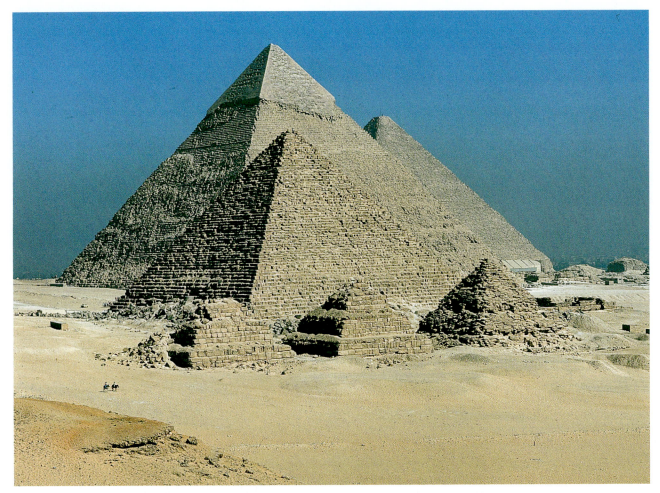

**Great Pyramids of Giza**    Royal funerary monuments of three Egyptian kings of the twenty-sixth century B.C., the pyramids symbolize the power and ambition of the Old Kingdom. The pyramid of King Khufu (or Cheops, rearmost in the photo) is still the largest all-stone building in human history.    *(Michael Holford)*

project focused on his person, the king made a statement of his power—an eloquent, simple, and irrefutable statement. The sheer size of the Great Pyramids demonstrated the king's ability to organize a vast labor force. Indeed, it has plausibly been suggested that the encampment of workers at Giza represented the largest gathering of human beings to that date. Moreover, the pyramids and the rows of tombs surrounding them reinforced the hierarchical structure of Egyptian society, of which the king was the capstone. Only princes and select officials were given the privilege of erecting a tomb beside the royal pyramids, a privilege that Fourth Dynasty Egyptians viewed as a prerequisite to gaining access to

eternal life. The principal royal wives were permitted to be buried in small pyramids of their own.

In theory, the king owned all the land, but in practice Egypt's economy was a mixture of private enterprise and centralized control. The king was thought to watch over Egypt carefully. In the Middle Kingdom, for example, he was represented as a good shepherd, appointed by the sun-god, Re, as one text says, "to keep alive the people and the folk, not sleeping by night as well as by day in seeking out every beneficial act, in looking for possibilities of usefulness." Even sleepless pharaohs needed help, however, and they delegated authority to a large group of officials. Indeed, Old Kingdom Egypt was one of the earliest great bureaucracies. The country was supervised by governors, mayors, military commanders, judges, treasurers, engineers, agricultural overseers, scribes, and others. The highest official was the vizier, a sort of prime minister who had more day-to-day power than pharaoh himself.

The essence of good government was what the Egyptians called *ma'at,* whose basic meaning is "order"—in government, society, or the universe. *Ma'at* can also mean "truth" or "justice." The god-king embodied what we would call law, but the administration of justice rested mainly on others' shoulders. Egypt had a well-functioning system of judges who heard lawsuits, and it probably also had a detailed law code, although few written laws survive.

## Life and Afterlife

Later peoples, beginning with the Greeks, have assumed that the ordinary Egyptian chafed under royal power. It is true that Egyptians were burdened with a variety of taxes (paid in agricultural produce) and that free people, both men and women, had an obligation of forced labor service on public works, from irrigation projects to the pyramids. Sometimes this service caused resentment. We hear of worker discipline maintained by beatings, of desperate fugitives, of the pious hope that there would be no forced labor in the afterlife, and even, in one unusual case, of a workers' strike.

Both piety and practicality, however, dictated that most people make peace with their public burdens. Far from resenting the king's claim to divinity, ordinary people may have been reassured to be ruled by a god. Nor were the pyramid-builders slaves laboring under a tyrant, as Greek writers assumed. In fact, they might have given their labor gladly to raising the man-god's tomb, as an act of faith, just as people centuries later donated time and money to build medieval cathedrals. The workers reaped material compensations, too: ration supplements for ordinary laborers, steady employment for specialized craftsmen.

Egyptian life was suffused with religious practices, from daily rituals and seasonal festivals to ethical teachings and magic. Egyptian religion tended toward *syncretism*—that is, the blending of mutually opposed beliefs, principles, or practices. For example, Egyptian mythology taught variously that the sky was a cow, was held up by a god or by a post, or was a goddess stretched over the earth. No one was troubled by such inconsistencies, as a modern worshiper might be, because Egyptians believed that a fundamental unity underlay the varieties of nature. Another example of syncretism is the most important Egyptian god, Re, the sun, often called "universal lord." From time to time, Re was syncretized with other gods to create a powerful new god—for example, Re-Atum, a combination of Re and a creator-god.

But Egypt's religion had an abundance of greater and lesser deities, including human, animal, and composite

**Egyptian Book of the Dead**    This scene from a lavishly illustrated papyrus shows a dead person's appearance before a divine court of judgment. His heart is being weighed in the balance to determine his fate in the afterlife.    *(Courtesy of the Trustees of the British Museum)*

gods. Various animals, from cats and dogs to crocodiles and serpents, were thought to represent the divine. Innumerable local deities and demons, as well as gods and goddesses of all of Egypt, peopled the spirit world. Important deities included Thoth, the moon-god and god of wisdom; Nut, goddess of the sky; Ptah, a creator-god; Osiris, who invented agriculture and became lord of the dead; Horus, son of Osiris, a sky-god imagined as a giant falcon; and Isis, wife of Osiris and mother of Horus, a mother-goddess. Temples were numerous and lavish.

Probably the most striking feature of Egyptian religion was its focus on the afterlife. Unlike the Mesopotamians, the Egyptians believed that death could be an extremely pleasant continuation of life on earth. Hence, they actively sought immortality. The wealthy placed great emphasis on building tombs, decorating them with paintings and inscriptions, and stocking them with cherished possessions for use in the world beyond. The most cherished possession of all, of course, was the body itself, and the Egyptians provided for its preservation through their mastery of the science of embalming—thus the Egyptian mummies. The Egyptians believed that a person's spirit could live on after death, but unlike later civilizations, they were not prepared to jettison the body altogether, believing instead that from time to time a person desired to return to the body after death. That belief made mummification necessary.

Reserved for the king and his officials in the Old Kingdom, the afterlife became, as it were, democratized by the Middle Kingdom. The Middle Kingdom and the First and Second Intermediate Periods were in many ways an inward-looking and reflective era, one in which materialism was de-emphasized and a sense of common humanity appears.

By the Middle Kingdom, even ordinary Egyptians believed they could enjoy immortality after death, as gods, as long as they could purchase for their graves funerary texts containing the relevant litanies. The texts emphasize ritual—incantations, magic spells, prayers—as the key to eternal life. Yet from time to time we find other texts, especially from the Middle Kingdom, that say that ritual is not enough; ethical behavior also is required. New Kingdom texts describe the details of a dead person's appearance before a divine court for judgment. Before forty-two judges of the underworld, the dead person declares his or her innocence of a variety of sins. A god then weighs the dead person's heart in the balance against a feather, the symbol of *ma'at*, or truth. The sinless are admitted into eternal life in the kingdom of the blessed. The guilty, their heavy hearts devoured by a beast, suffer a second, final death.

Such absolute judgments were not found in daily life. Consider relations between the sexes. Egyptian women did not enjoy equal status with men, but they had a considerably greater measure of equality than women in other ancient societies, particularly in legal matters. As in Mesopotamia, so in Egypt a woman could buy or sell, bequeath or inherit, sue or testify in court, but a married Egyptian woman, unlike her eastern sisters, could do so without a male guardian's approval. A married woman in Egypt retained the status of complete legal independence. She could even own property without her husband's involvement. But how often did women exercise such privileges? Relatively little evidence of female property owners survives from Egypt. Although Egyptian women could work outside the home in a variety of enterprises, they were rarely managers. Women worked in agriculture and trade, in the textile and perfume industries, in dining halls, and in entertainment, and women served as priestesses of various kinds. Yet in Egypt, as elsewhere, women were expected to make the home the focus of their activities. So although Egyptian women had more freedom outside the home than most ancient women, they exercised nothing like the freedom enjoyed by women in North America today.

## Expansion, Reform, and Power Shifts, 1786–1075 B.C.

The humane attitudes of the Middle Kingdom were swept away after about 1700 B.C., when Semitic-speaking immigrants from Palestine—the Hyksos°, to employ the commonly used Greek term—conquered much of Egypt. In many ways gentle conquerors, the Hyksos worshiped Egyptian gods, built and restored Egyptian temples, and intermarried with natives. As foreigners, however, the Hyksos were unpopular. Eventually a war launched from Upper Egypt, which had retained a loose independence, drove the Hyksos out.

The first restored Egyptian ruler of the New Kingdom was Ahmose° I (r. 1550–1525 B.C.). His proved to be a new Egypt indeed. The Hyksos had brought advanced military technology to Egypt, including the horse-drawn war chariot, new kinds of daggers and swords, and the composite bow. Made of laminated materials including wood, leather, and horn, the composite bow could hit a target at 600 yards. Having tasted foreign occupation, Egypt's new rulers determined to use such weapons in aggressive military campaigns abroad.

Warlike, expansionist, and marked by a daring at-

**Hyksos** (HICK-sos)    **Ahmose** (AKH-mose)

**Egyptian Queen**    This elegant, red granite statue of the pharaoh Hatshepsut (r. 1479–1457 B.C.) is one of the few to depict her as a woman. She is usually shown as a man, complete with beard, to symbolize her royal power. Centuries later the proportions and carving techniques of Egyptian stone sculpture would influence the Greeks, although Greek artists chose less to copy the Egyptians than to try to outdo them (see the photo on page 82).    *(Brian Brake/Photo Researchers, Inc.)*

tempt at religious reform, the New Kingdom's Eighteenth Dynasty (1540–1293 B.C.) has long held a special fascination for historians. One of the dynasty's memorable names is that of Queen Hatshepsut°. Widow of

Thutmose° II (r. 1491–1479 B.C.), Hatshepsut first served as regent for her young stepson and then assumed the kingship herself (r. 1479–1457 B.C.). Other Egyptian queens had exercised royal power before, but Hatshepsut was the first to call herself king. Some statues show her wearing a false beard, and some of her inscriptions refer to Hatshepsut as "he," not "she." Although Hatshepsut dispatched Egyptian armies to fight, her reign is best known for peaceful activities: at home, public works and temple rebuilding; abroad, a commercial expedition over the Red Sea to the "Land of Punt" (perhaps modern Somalia, in eastern Africa).

After her death Hatshepsut was succeeded by her stepson, Thutmose III (r. 1479–1425 B.C.). Late in his reign, he tried to erase his stepmother's memory by having Hatshepsut's statues destroyed and her name expunged from records—an attempt, perhaps, to cut off a claim to the throne by her supporters. A warrior-pharaoh, Thutmose III led his dynasty's armed expansion in western Asia and northern Africa. Thutmose won his greatest victory during his first campaign, at the Battle of Megiddo in Palestine in 1457 B.C. (see Map 1.2), where Egypt's triumph prevented the kingdom of Mitanni from expanding southward. Egypt now ruled an empire with territory in Nubia, Palestine, and Syria.

Empire brings power, and power often causes conflict. In imperial Egypt during the fourteenth century B.C., kings and priests struggled over authority. Consider the Amarna° reform, named for a major archaeological site at the modern town of Tell el-Amarna.

The Amarna reform was carried out by Thutmose III's great-great-grandson, King Amenhotep IV (r. 1352–1336 B.C.). Earlier, the god Amun-Re had become the chief deity of the New Kingdom. As supporters of the ideology of imperialism, his temple priests had been so richly rewarded with land and wealth that their power now rivaled pharaoh's own. Amenhotep IV's dramatic response was to forbid the worship of Amun-Re and replace him with the god Aten, the solar disk. Changing his own name to Akhenaten ("pleasing to Aten"), the king ordered the erasure of Amun-Re's name from monuments throughout Egypt. As a further step, Akhenaten created a new capital city in central Egypt at an uninhabited site at the desert's edge: Akhetaten (modern Amarna). The new town had a distinctive culture. Akhenaten's wife, Nefertiti, figures prominently in Amarna art, and she too may have played an important role in the reform. (See the box "The Continuing Experiment: The Amarna Reform.")

---

**Hatshepsut** (HAT-shep-soot)

**Thutmose** (THUT-mose)    **Amarna** (a-MAR-na)

# The Amarna Reform

The Amarna reform under King Amenhotep IV, or Akhenaten (r. 1352–1336 B.C.), changed Egypt's religion from polytheism to the worship of the god Aten, or disk of the sun. While generally considered the first experiment in monotheism, the reform permitted only the king and his family to worship the god directly. This selection, "The Great Hymn to Aten," is from a text found in a tomb at Akhetaten, the new capital city of Egypt. After Akhenaten's death, the Aten cult was abolished and the Egyptians' polytheistic beliefs were restored. Later, however, Hebrew monotheism would prove a lasting part of the West.

Splendid you rise in heaven's lightland, / O living Aten, creator of life! / When you have dawned in eastern lightland, / You fill every land with your beauty. / You are beauteous, great, radiant, / High over every land; / Your rays embrace the lands, / To the limits of all that you made. / Being Re, you reach their limits, / You bend them [for] the son whom you love; / Though you are far, your rays are on earth, / Though one sees you, your strides are unseen.

How many are your deeds, / Though hidden from sight, / O Sole God beside whom there is none! / You made the earth as you wished, you alone, / All peoples, herds, and flocks; / All upon the earth that walk on legs, / All on high that fly on wings, / The lands of Khor and Kush. / The land of Egypt. You set every man in his place, / You supply their needs; / Everyone has his food, / His lifetime is counted. / Their tongues differ in speech, / Their characters likewise; / Their skins are distinct, / For you distinguished the peoples. . . .

You are in my heart, / There is no other who knows you, / Only your son, *Neferkheprure, Sole-one-of-Re,* / Whom you have taught your ways and your might. / [Those on] earth come from your hand as you made them, / When you have dawned they live, / When you set they die; / You yourself are lifetime, one lives by you. / All eyes are on [your] beauty until you set, / All labor ceases when you rest in the west; / When you rise you stir [everyone] for the King, / Every leg is on the move since you founded the earth. / You rouse them for your son who came from your body, / The King who lives by Maat [ma'at], the Lord of the Two Lands, / *Neferkheprure, Sole-one-of-Re,* / The Son of Re who lives by Maat, the Lord of crowns, / *Akhenaten,* great in his lifetime; / (And) the great Queen whom he loves, the Lady of the Two Lands, / *Nefer-nefru-Aten Nefertiti,* living forever.

## QUESTIONS

1. What is the power of Aten, and what are his deeds? How is the god of Egypt linked with the rest of the world?

2. What is the relationship between Aten and the king of Egypt?

3. In what ways does this text show radical changes in Egyptian religion? In what ways does it show continuity with the old religion?

SOURCE: Miriam Lichtheim, *Ancient Egyptian Literature,* vol. 2, *The New Kingdom* (Berkeley: University of California Press, 1976), pp. 96–99. Copyright © 1976 by the Regents of the University of California. Reprinted by permission of The University of California Press.

The reform shifted power away from the priests and toward the king, but we need not doubt the reformers' sincerity. Contemporary literature suggests intense religious conviction in Aten as a benevolent god and one who nurtured not only Egypt but all countries. Although the Aten cult focuses on one god, only Akhenaten and his family were permitted to worship Aten directly; the rest of the Egyptian population was expected to worship the god through pharaoh.

Bold as the reform was, sustaining so dramatic a break with tradition proved impossible. After Akhenaten's death his son-in-law and successor, Tutankhaten (r. 1336– 1327 B.C.) restored good relations with the priests of Amun-Re, which he signaled by changing his name to Tutankhamun. The Amun-Re cult was revived, the Aten cult was abolished, and the city of Akhetaten was abandoned. After Tutankhamun's death the military exercised great influence over the remaining pharaohs of the Eighteenth Dynasty. Then, in 1291 B.C., a military officer founded a new dynasty as Ramesses° I (r. 1291–1289 B.C.).

---

**Ramesses** (RAM-zeez)

The Nineteenth (ca. 1291–1185 B.C.) and Twentieth (ca. 1185–1075 B.C.) Dynasties are known as the Ramesside Era, from the most common name of the pharaohs. Although the era witnessed great warrior-pharaohs and builder-pharaohs, over time the kings lost power to the priests of Amun. Abroad, Egypt remained a formidable power, but it faced armed invasions, some of which required major efforts to repel (see page 34). In any case, many foreigners settled peacefully in the rich farmland of the Nile Delta, giving Egypt a more cosmopolitan character. Both their presence and the building of a great new city in the delta by the Ramesside kings led to a power shift within Egypt. When the Twentieth Dynasty ended in 1075 B.C., the New Kingdom ended with it, and regional conflict between the Nile Delta and Upper Egypt broke out.

## Arts and Sciences in the New Kingdom

The Egyptians were superb builders, architects, and engineers. In addition to pyramids and irrigation works, they constructed monumental royal tombs, palaces, forts, and temples, and they erected looming obelisks. At their best, Egyptian architects designed buildings in harmony with the unique landscape—one of the reasons for the structures' lasting appeal. Their most original and enduring work was done in stone. Stone temples, for example, culminated in the imposing pillared structures of the New Kingdom. That period also saw the construction of rock-cut temples, the most famous of which is Ramesses II's (r. 1279–1213 B.C.) project at Abu Simbel (see Map 1.2). In front of the temples sit four colossal statues of Ramesses, also carved out of rock. Obelisks were slender, tapering pillars carved of a single piece of stone. Inscribed with figures and hieroglyphs, and usually erected in pairs in front of a temple, obelisks were meant to glorify the sun-god.

Throughout history royal courts have excelled as patrons of the arts; the Egyptian court was one of the first and greatest. Egyptian craftsmen were master goldsmiths, glassmakers, and woodworkers. The major arts are well represented in tombs, which were decorated with rich, multicolored wall paintings, the first narrative depictions. Scenes of the gods, court ceremony, ordinary life, war, and recreation amid the crocodiles and hippopotamuses of the Nile Valley adorn subterranean walls. Like so much else in Egypt, painting had a religious purpose. Representations of living people were meant to perpetuate them in the afterlife.

Sculpture was another art form in which Egyptians excelled. Carved in stone, wood, or metal, Egyptian sculpture is a study in contrasts. The body posture is usually rigid and stiff, the musculature only sketchy; the face, in contrast, is often individualistic, the expression full of character and drawn from life. Statues represent kings and queens, gods and goddesses, husbands and wives, adults and children, officials, priests, scribes, animals. Mirroring broader cultural trends, statues of pharaohs underwent stylistic changes through the centuries. In the Old Kingdom, the royal expression was usually one of majesty and power, but in the Middle Kingdom, the king's face often appeared more human and weak. Statues of New Kingdom pharaohs often suggested imperial power, whereas Amarna sculptors emphasized introspective gazes and experimented with the grotesque. Eighteenth Dynasty sculpture often shows a striking interest in feminine beauty and grace.

Ancient Egyptian literature is notable for its variety. Religious subjects, historical and commemorative records, technical treatises in mathematics and medicine, and secular stories survive alongside business contracts and royal proclamations. A good example of Egyptian writing is the *Story of Sinuhe,* a Middle Kingdom prose tale. Sinuhe reveals both the charm of ancient Egyptian literature and its cultural chauvinism. (See the box "Global Encounters: Egyptian Attitudes Toward Foreigners.")

The vastness and variety of ancient Egyptian literature were made possible by the invention of a far more convenient medium for writing than the clunky clay tablets of Mesopotamia—papyrus. (See the feature "Information Technology: Papyrus" on pages 14–15.) Egyptian writing is best known for hieroglyphs. Elaborate and formal, hieroglyphs were generally used after the Archaic Period only for monuments and ornamentation. Two simplified scripts served for everyday use.

The people who built the pyramids had to be skilled at arithmetic and geometry. Egyptians were able to approximate pi (the ratio of the circumference of a circle to its diameter) and to solve equations containing one or two unknowns. Mathematical astronomy never reached the heights in Egypt that it reached in Babylon (see page 44), but the Egyptian calendar was a remarkable achievement. Based on observation of the star Sirius, the Egyptian calendar, with its 365-day year, approximates the solar calendar. Corrected to 365¼ days, it survives to this day as the calendar of Europe, the Americas, and much of the rest of the world.

Egyptian medical doctors were admired in antiquity and in demand abroad. They knew how to set a dislocated shoulder and used a full battery of splints, sutures, adhesive plasters, elementary disinfectants (from tree

# Egyptian Attitudes Toward Foreigners

The story of Sinuhe is a well-known piece of Middle Kingdom prose literature. A court official, Sinuhe fled Egypt for Syria-Palestine after the assassination of the king. There he married the daughter of a tribal chief and became a successful chief himself. In his old age he received permission to return home. The tale demonstrates Egyptian curiosity about Palestine and Syria, at the same time revealing Egyptian cultural snobbery toward what another Egyptian text calls "the miserable Asiatic."

This decree of the King: . . . Come back to Egypt! See the residence in which you lived! Kiss the ground at the great portals, mingle with the courtiers! For today you have begun to age. You have lost a man's strength. Think of the day of burial, the passing into reveredness.

A night is made for you with ointments and wrappings from the hand of Tait [goddess of weaving]. A funeral procession is made for you on the day of burial; the mummy case is of gold, its head of lapis lazuli. . . . You shall not die abroad! Nor shall Asiatics inter you. You shall not be wrapped in the skin of a ram to serve as your coffin. Too long a roaming of the earth! Think of your corpse, come back! . . .

Copy of the reply to this decree:

The servant of the Palace, Sinuhe, says: In very good peace! . . . May the fear of you resound in lowlands and highlands, for you have subdued all that the sun encircles! . . .

Re [the sun-god] has set the fear of you throughout the land, the dread of you in every foreign country. Whether I am at the residence, whether I am in this place, it is you who cover this horizon. The sun rises at your pleasure. The water in the river is drunk when you wish. The air of heaven is breathed at your bidding. . . . This servant has been sent for! Your Majesty will do as he wishes! One lives by the breath which you give.

[Sinuhe returns to Egypt and is brought into the king's presence.]

Then the royal daughters were brought in, and his majesty said to the queen: "Here is Sinuhe, come as an Asiatic, a product of nomads!" She uttered a very great cry, and the royal daughters shrieked all together. They said to his majesty: "Is it really he, O kings, our lord?" Said his majesty: "It is really he!" . . .

His majesty said: "He shall not fear, he shall not dread! He shall be a Companion among the nobles. He shall be among the courtiers. Proceed to the robing-room to wait on him!"

I left the audience-hall, the royal daughters giving me their hands. We went through the great portals, and I was put in the house of a prince. In it were luxuries: a bathroom and mirrors. . . . Every servant was at his task. Years were removed from my body. I was shaved; my hair was combed. Thus was my squalor returned to the foreign land, my dress to the Sand-farers. I was clothed in fine linen; I was anointed with fine oil. I slept on a bed. I had returned the sand to those who dwell in it, the tree-oil to those who grease themselves with it.

## QUESTIONS

1. What evidence does the text give that Egyptians had a low opinion of "Asiatics"?

2. According to the king's decree, why should Sinuhe want to return to Egypt?

3. How do the king's servants make Sinuhe feel Egyptian again? What does this tell us about the ways Egyptians judged a person?

SOURCE: Miriam Lichtheim, *Ancient Egyptian Literature, vol. 1, The Old and Middle Kingdoms* (Berkeley: University of California Press, 1973), pp. 229–233. Copyright © 1973. Reprinted by permission of the University of California Press.

leaves), and burn treatments (fatty substances). A brilliant treatise, the Edwin Smith Papyrus, demonstrates their sophistication and rationalism. Dating from around 1750 B.C., the document claims to be a copy of an original from 2700 B.C. (the veracity of that claim is uncertain). Possibly a manual for the treatment of battlefield wounds, it is an ancient prototype of modern triage, dividing diseases into three categories: treatable, possibly treatable, and untreatable. In addition to signs of careful observation is tantalizing evidence that Egyptian doctors undertook postmortem dissection in order to understand the human body better.

# WIDENING HORIZONS: THE LEVANT AND ANATOLIA, 2500–1150 B.C.

EGYPT and Mesopotamia tend to capture our attention, but other early, nearby civilizations are, if less important, also significant contributors to the West. Not only were they the cradle of Western languages and writing systems, but they took part in the first international system of states, a forerunner of later international relations between the West and its neighbors. Let us look in particular at the city-states of the Levant°—the geographic region known today as Syria and Palestine or Israel—and at a kingdom in Anatolia, today's Turkey.

## The City-States of Syria-Palestine, ca. 2500–1200 B.C.

The discovery in 1974 of a huge cuneiform archive at Ebla° (modern Tell Mardikh) in northern Syria revolutionized our knowledge of one such city-state in the mid-third millennium B.C. Another Levantine city-state, Ugarit° (modern Ras Shamra), a cosmopolitan port, flourished in the second millennium B.C.

A prosperous city, Ebla was known for commerce and artisanry as well as scholarship. Its extensive cuneiform archives include the world's earliest known dictionaries. Sometime between 2500 and 2300 B.C., Ebla ruled a large kingdom, extending over much of Syria and possibly containing as many as 250,000 people, of whom perhaps 30,000 lived in the city (see Map 1.3). Ebla's government fostered trade by negotiating commercial treaties and arranging dynastic marriages. The treaty between Ebla and Ashur, a city about 435 miles to the east, is the earliest known agreement between two states. When diplomacy failed, Ebla resorted to war, with great success. Ebla's most notable conquest was Mari, a commercial competitor 300 miles downstream on the Euphrates.

Ebla was ruled by an oligarchy (a small, elite group) headed by fourteen regional governors who were probably also clan elders. The king, a sort of first among equals, was chosen by election rather than inheritance; his power was limited by the oligarchic council. Eblaites seem to have conceived of the state as a large family, the "children of Ebla." The queen and queen mother had significant government authority. The queen had her own properties, administered by officials who answered to her. If she was still alive, the queen mother, officially addressed as "the honored mother of the king," had considerable say in the succession.

Ebla fell to the Amorites around 2000 B.C. It remained a wealthy city, though much diminished in power. To find a much more vibrant city in Syria after 2000 B.C., we need only look at the coast and the city of Ugarit (see Map 1.3). Ugarit was a thriving Mediterranean port, especially around 1400 to 1200 B.C. Its cosmopolitanism made Ugarit distinctive among western Asian city-states. As a trading center, it linked ships coming from the eastern Mediterranean island of Cyprus or the Anatolian ports with land caravans heading to Babylonia. The native inhabitants of Ugarit spoke a Semitic language. Their culture and that of large numbers of people in southern Syria and Palestine is called Canaanite (from the Hebrew Bible, which calls Palestine "the land of Canaan"). The merchants of Ugarit, however, were often foreigners, and the bazaars echoed with a multitude of languages.

Ugarit played an important role in the spread of one of history's most important writing systems: the alphabet. Unlike the pictographic or syllabic systems of Mesopotamia, Egypt, and China, in an alphabet each sign stands for one and only one sound. In the 1300s B.C. scribes in Ugarit developed an alphabet. It was not the first alphabet, however. In Egypt, in the desert west of the Nile, limestone inscriptions have recently been found in a Semitic script with Egyptian influences. Dated to about 1900 to 1800 B.C., during the Middle Kingdom, the writing is now recognized as the earliest known example of an alphabet.

We do not know whether that alphabet was invented by Egyptians or by speakers of a Semitic language who were visiting Egypt. Nor do we know if that alphabet influenced Ugarit. What is clear is that Ugaritic scribes invented thirty cuneiform signs as an alphabet to write their Semitic language. Later adapted by the Phoenicians and, through them, the Greeks, the Ugaritic alphabet is the source of the Roman alphabet, used today by English and many other languages around the world.

## The Hittites, 1650–1180 B.C.

Almost all the peoples of western Asia and Egypt whom we have discussed so far spoke a language belonging to the large Afro-Asiatic language family. But none of these languages survived antiquity in Europe. Instead, virtually every modern European language—as well as the dominant languages of Iran and India—are descendants of the long-lost proto–Indo-European language. These languages,

---

**Levant** (le-VANT)    **Ebla** (EH-bla)    **Ugarit** (OO-ga-rit)

**Map 1.3    The International System, ca. 1500–1250 B.C.**   This era of competing kingdoms and city-states witnessed considerable war, especially between Egypt and the Hittites for control of Syria and Palestine. Yet it was also a period of international trade, diplomacy, and, from 1450 to 1300 B.C., peace.

from English and Russian to Iranian and Hindi, are said to belong to the Indo-European language family.

Indo-European–speakers probably originated between 4500 and 2500 B.C. in southern Russia, in the region of the Dnieper and Volga Rivers. A warlike, mobile people, they emigrated east and west. The first speakers of an Indo-European language to establish a civilization in western Asia were the Hittites, who came to Anatolia sometime before 1800 B.C. The Hittites were masters of the horse, which they harnessed to chariots and used in battle. They ruled Anatolia from their city of Hattusas (modern Boghazköy). Rich in minerals and farmland, Anatolia provided a solid foundation for power.

Hittite history is divided into several periods. After conquest and consolidation in the Old Kingdom (ca. 1650–1450 B.C.) came a period of retrenchment and loss of territory known as the Middle Kingdom (ca. 1450–1380 B.C.). During the New Kingdom (ca. 1380–1180 B.C.), the Hittites' power extended into Syria and northern Mesopotamia (see Map 1.3). Afterward came the Neo-Hittite era (ca. 1180–700 B.C.), when the Hittite kingdom had disintegrated into small successor states.

The Hittite Old Kingdom was a warrior society with a strong nobility and weak kings. Nobles supplied the king with troops and horses in return for land. The monarch was neither a god nor god's representative but only first among equals. The power of the nobility spelled trouble for central authority in the sixteenth century B.C., when conspiracy, feud, and assassination came close to destroying the Hittite kingdom. The powerful King Telepinu finally established himself and his family securely on the throne around 1500 B.C. In the Hittite New Kingdom the balance of power swung further in favor of the king, who was now addressed as "my Sun" during his lifetime and was deified after death.

Hittite queens and queen mothers had strong and independent positions, as at Ebla. Puduhepa°, wife of King Hattusilis° III (r. 1278–1250 B.C.), played a memorable role in state affairs. Puduhepa seems to have been the prime mover in making the Hurrian sun-goddess of Arinna (a shrine near Hattusas) the chief deity of the Hittite state.

---

**Puduhepa** (pu-du-HE-pa)    **Hattusilis** (hat-tu-SIL-is)

# PRAYERS OF A HITTITE QUEEN

*Puduhepa, wife of the Hittite king Hattusilis III (r. 1278–1250 B.C.), played an important role in state religious ritual and propaganda. The following selections from her recorded prayers show Puduhepa's official devotion to her royal husband as well as a belief, common in ancient religion, that women had a special closeness to the gods.*

### Prayer to the Sun-Goddess Herself

To the Sun-goddess of Arinna, my lady, the mistress of the Hatti lands, the queen of heaven and earth. . . . I, Puduhepa, am a servant of thine from of old, a heifer from thy stable, a foundation stone upon which thou canst rest. Thou, my lady, rearedst me and Hattusilis, thy servant, to whom thou espousedst me, was closely associated with the Storm-god of Nerik, thy beloved son. The place in which thou, Sun-goddess of Arinna, my lady, didst establish us was the residence of the Storm-god of Nerik, thy beloved son. How the earlier kings had neglected it, that thou knowest, Sun-goddess of Arinna, my lady. The earlier kings let fall into ruins even those countries which thou, Sun-goddess of Arinna, my lady, hadst given them. . . .

Sun-goddess of Arinna, my lady, yield to me, hearken to me! Among men there is a saying: "To a woman in travail the god yields her wish." Since I, Puduhepa, am a woman in travail and since I have devoted myself to thy son, yield to me, Sun-goddess of Arinna, my lady! Grant to me what I ask. Grant life to Hattusilis, thy servant [who was ill]! Through the Good-women and the Mother-goddess long and enduring years and days shall be given to him. Since thou, an exalted deity, holdest a place set apart from the gods, all the gods are subservient to thee, and no one appeals to thee in vain. In the assembly of the gods request thou the life of Hattusilis! May thy request be received with favor! Because thou, Sun-goddess of Arinna, my lady, hast shown favor to me and because the good of the land of its realm is close to thy heart, thou shalt enjoy the reverent worship of my family.

### Prayer to Lelwanis [probably Ishtar]

. . . Hattusilis, that servant of thine, who is ill. In the presence of Sum . . . , the physician, they spoke charms over him. . . . If Hattusilis is accursed, and if Hattusilis, my husband, has become hateful in the eyes of you, the gods; or if anyone of the gods above or below has taken offence at him; or if anyone has made an offering to the gods to bring evil upon Hattusilis— accept not those evil words, O goddess, my lady! Let evil not touch Hattusilis, thy servant! O gods, prefer not our adversaries, our enviers, . . . to us!

### Prayer to the Storm-God of Zippalanda

. . . This word, which I, Puduhepa, thy handmaid, have spoken in prayer, announce and relay thou to thy parents, Storm-god of Zippalanda, my lord! O god, my lord, yield to this word of mine! Because as a woman in travail I have in my own person made reparation to the god, my lord, intercede for me, god, my lord, with the Storm-god, thy father, and the Sun-goddess of Arinna, thy mother! Hattusilis, thy servant, wore himself out in the god's service; he gave himself body and soul to the restoration of Nerik, the beloved city of the god, my lord. So be thou, O god, my lord, favorably inclined toward Hattusilis, thy servant!

Source: Adapted from James B. Pritchard, ed., *Ancient Near Eastern Texts Relating to the Old Testament,* 3d ed., with Supplement, pp. 393–394. Copyright © 1969 by Princeton University Press. Reprinted by permission of Princeton University Press.

---

(See the box "Reading Sources: Prayers of a Hittite Queen.") Hattusilis publicly declared that he would not have rebelled against the previous king had Puduhepa not first dreamed of divine support for the coup.

Hittite political thought stands out as sophisticated and original. Earlier peoples had kept lists and chronicles; Hittite annals are livelier and better argued. The royal annals of King Hattusilis III, for example, read in parts like a lawsuit, carefully pleading a justification of the king's actions. Hattusilis excused his usurpation of the throne by stating that the former king had unjustly stripped him of territory; furthermore, Hattusilis rebelled openly. Hittite treaties with lesser states similarly argue their cases: each begins with an introduction providing historical background and justifying the relationship sworn to in the body of the text.

**Hittite God** This figurine in gold, standing only 1.5 inches high, represents Hittite art of the Old Kingdom (ca. 1650–1450 B.C.). The clothes, shoes, and conical hat are typical of Hittite depictions of gods. *(Louvre/R.M.N./Art Resource, NY)*

## The First International System and Its Collapse, ca. 1500–1150 B.C.

The Hittites and New Kingdom Egyptians exercised great military power, yet what is even more remarkable about these states and others is their ability to make and maintain peace. The years from about 1450 to about 1300 B.C. marked a period of peace among the great powers from Egypt to Anatolia and Mesopotamia—what historians call the first international system. The arts of peace are illustrated in surviving treaties and letters between monarchs, the most important of which comes from Amarna.

The Amarna Archives (mid-fourteenth century), written in Akkadian cuneiform, illustrate formal communication among states. Rulers of great powers addressed each other as "brother," while Canaanite princes called pharaoh "my lord and my Sun-god" and assured him that they were "thy servant and the dirt on which thou dost tread." The texts reveal a system of gift exchange and commerce, politeness and formality, alliance and dynastic marriage, subjects and governors, rebels and garrisons. Two factors seem to have supported peace. First, shared values among kings created mutual respect and a willingness to compromise. Second, although no such concept as our balance of power existed then, a rough equality of power did prevail. Since no great power was likely to defeat the others, the parties avoided all-out war, preferring instead to compete by jockeying for allies among the small border states of Syria and Palestine.

But peace was not to last. By the late fourteenth century B.C., Egypt and the Hittites were back at war. At the Battle of Qadesh in northern Syria in 1274 B.C., twenty thousand Egyptian troops faced seventeen thousand Hittites. Predictably, neither of the two evenly matched powers managed to conquer the other. Instead, they used resources that would soon be dearly needed for defense.

Between about 1250 and 1150 B.C., the international system came to a crashing end. From Mesopotamia to Greece, from Anatolia to Egypt, one state after another collapsed during this time. Surviving evidence is fragmentary, but it suggests that both foreign and domestic problems led to the collapse. Raiders and invaders beset the eastern Mediterranean in this period. Called "Sea Peoples" by the Egyptians, they attacked both on land and at sea. We do not know precisely who they were. In addition, some evidence of regional famine and climatic change indicates that natural causes may have led to disruption and rebellion.

Whatever the cause, what followed would prove to be a different world. Yet the end of the international system did not result in the disappearance of ancient cultures. Although new peoples appeared and old peoples changed, both continued to borrow from the cultures that had flowered before 1250 B.C.

## SUMMARY

**T**HIS chapter covers not just the history of the ancestors of Western civilization but the very origins of civilization itself. Yet that milestone is only a small part of the vast era that ranges from the first hominids to the heirs of the great kingdoms of Egypt and western Asia after the collapse of the thirteenth century B.C. The achievements of this period may make it the most creative epoch in human history. First, probably beginning before 70,000 B.C., came the invention of human culture—that is, the development of communications to the degree that humans could cooperate to exploit their natural environment by means of technology and social organization. Next came the move from a food-collecting to a food-producing economy. After a series of independent discoveries beginning in the Fertile Crescent region of western Asia shortly after 10,000 B.C., food production spread to many places around the globe by 5000 B.C.

Over the thousands of years following the emergence of agriculture, we can trace the development of ever more complex organizations of human beings and ever increasing control of the natural environment, culminating in the emergence of civilization in Egypt and Mesopotamia after 3500 B.C. Elaborate though such large Neolithic towns as Çatal Hüyük and Jericho were, civilization marked a major step forward in sophistication. Civilization brought cities commanding the manpower, technology, and degree of labor specialization needed to build a monumental urban architecture and reshape the agricultural hinterland; civilization brought governments and armies controlling wide areas; civilization brought, finally, writing. By 3000 B.C. civilization was present in the Levant as well. Through trade networks, civilization affected a vast hinterland, including Europe. European societies, especially in southeastern Europe, were reshaped by trade with more advanced neighbors. European civilization emerged in the Aegean around 2000 B.C.

Mesopotamia and Egypt are the first and best remembered of the early civilizations. Their extraordinary achievements, later built on by the Greeks and Hebrews, laid the foundation for important Western concepts in government, religion, technology, art, and literature. It is hard to avoid the appearance of exaggeration when listing the inventions of Mesopotamia and Egypt, among them the first cities, kingdoms, and multi-ethnic empires; the first monumental architecture; the first advances in agriculture sweeping enough to support a large urban population; the first writing, and with it the first written attempts to explore the most profound subjects of life and death.

The years from 2000 to 1000 B.C. were a period of competition, exchange, and warfare among the various civilizations of the eastern Mediterranean region. They were also an era of further advance in literature and science. Then, around 1250 to 1150 B.C., the great kingdoms of the period collapsed, one after another.

It was not long before new states arose in Egypt and western Asia to replace those destroyed in the era of the Sea Peoples. In the first half of the first millennium B.C., new regions joined southern Mesopotamia, Egypt, the Levant, and Anatolia in making lasting contributions to the West: among them, Assyria (northern Mesopotamia), Persia, ancient Israel, and Greece. We turn to those regions in the next chapter.

## ■ Notes

1. James B. Pritchard, ed., *Ancient Near Eastern Texts Relating to the Old Testament,* 3d ed., with Supplement (Princeton, N.J.: Princeton University Press, 1969), p. 107.
2. James H. Breasted, *The Conquest of Civilization* (New York: Harper & Bros., 1926), p. 112. Quoted in Brian Tierney, Donald Kagan, and L. Pearce Williams, eds., *Great Issues in Western Civilization from Ancient Egypt Through Louis XIV* (New York: McGraw-Hill, 1992), pp. 68–69.

## ■ Suggested Reading

Bertman, Stephen. *Handbook to Life in Ancient Mesopotamia.* 2003. A useful and informative introduction, offering thumbnail sketches, in encyclopedia form, of a wide variety of subjects from archaeology to ziggurats.

Bottéro, Jean, et al. *Everyday Life in Ancient Mesopotamia.* 2001. One of the most readable introductions to the subject.

Bryce, Trevor. *The Kingdom of the Hittites.* 1999. The best and most up-to-date introduction.

Cunliffe, Barry, ed. *The Oxford Illustrated Prehistory of Europe.* 1994. An introduction to European material culture from the Paleolithic era to the early medieval period, with chapters written by a dozen archaeologists. Especially valuable for its treatment of the early period and for its integration of Greco-Roman civilization and the wider continental context.

Johanson, D. C., and Edgar B. Johanson. *From Lucy to Language.* 1996. Excellent and relatively up-to-date introduction to human evolution, with outstanding photographs.

Murnane, William J. *The Penguin Guide to Ancient Egypt.* 1983. Both a well-illustrated travel guide and a scholarly, basic introduction.

Oates, Joan. *Babylon.* Rev. ed. 1986. A well-illustrated historical and archaeological introduction, from Sargon of Agade to the Greeks.

**www.** **For a searchable list of additional readings for this chapter, go to college.hmco.com/students.**

# The Iceman and His World

On September 19, 1991, a German couple went hiking in the Italian Alps. At 10,530 feet above sea level, in a mountain pass, they thought they had left civilization and its problems behind until they stumbled on an unexpected sight: the body of a dead man lying in the melting ice. Nor was that their only surprise. At first they thought the corpse was the victim of a recent accident. When the authorities arrived, however, the body was discovered to be very old. A helicopter was ordered, and the body was brought to a research institute in Innsbruck, Austria. When the investigators were through, it was clear that the hikers had chanced upon one of the most remarkable archaeological discoveries of the century.*

He was 5,300 years old. The Iceman—as the corpse has become known—is a natural mummy, preserved under the snow: the oldest known remains of human flesh. If that weren't striking enough, consider the clothes and extensive gear that survived with him—they are a window into the European world of about 3200 B.C. The most difficult and most fascinating question is this: Who was the Iceman?

His body offers an introduction. The Iceman stood 5 feet 2 inches tall. He was in his mid-40s and probably had a beard. Genetic testing shows that he was a European, a close relative of modern northern and alpine Europeans. Other tests indicate a difficult life. His growth was arrested by periods of illness, grave hunger, or metal poisoning. His teeth are badly worn, the result perhaps of chewing dried meat or, alternatively, of working leather. He may have undergone a kind of acupuncture; at any rate, he is tattooed, which in some cultures is a medical treatment rather than a form of decoration. He has several broken ribs, which indicates either damage under the ice, mishandling when the body was discovered, or an ancient accident or fight.

And it was a fight—a hand-to-hand combat—that killed him. Blood tests indicate a long fight involving four people besides the Iceman. The Iceman was shot through the chest with an arrow and cut severely by a rough blade on his right hand. The arrow caused a very painful death. After the fight, he might have managed to escape up the mountain until he fell down and died in the snow.

Not long before he died, the Iceman was in the valley to the south. There he ate his last meal, which consisted of goat meat and bread cooked in a charcoal oven. We might guess that the Iceman's fatal struggle took place in a farming village in the valley.

But his enemies did not find him on the mountain; otherwise they would have stripped the gear found with him. Today that gear provides tantalizing clues to his social status. Look at the artist's drawing. A woven grass or

**Mummy of Iceman**   *(Copyright Photo Archives, South Tyrol Museum of Archaeology)*

reed cape lies over the Iceman's deerskin coat, which in turn covers a leather loincloth and garter, held in place by a leather belt. A bearskin hat, skin leggings, and calfskin shoes, stuffed with grass for insulation, complete his wardrobe. The Iceman and his contemporaries knew how to dress for the cold weather of the mountains.

The Iceman carries a rich tool kit. Notice his copper ax and 6-foot-long bow, made of yew, the best wood then available for making bows. A quiver (arrow case), two birch-bark containers, a waist pouch, and a frame—probably part of a backpack—hang from his body. Among his items of equipment are flint tools (including a dagger, a retouching tool, and a scraper); a piece of net; two birch-fungus-like "polypores" threaded on a leather thong, probably used as a natural antibiotic; and fourteen arrows, all, oddly, broken. In short, it appears that the Iceman was equipped with a state-of-the-art mountain survival kit of his day. It is not clear why he carried broken arrows, but he would not have had time to change his gear before he fled.

Scholars differ about the Iceman's occupation. Guesses range from a hunter to a trader to a warrior to an outlaw to a shaman (a priest who uses magic). The Iceman's complex weapons and well-made clothing point to a sophisticated culture. The copper ax is the key to that culture and its relationship with the wider world. Similar axes have been found in northern Italian tombs in Remedello, about 240 miles south of the Alps. Before the discovery of the Iceman, archaeologists believed that Italians learned the metalwork technology needed for such an ax from Anatolia, where similar pieces of metalwork are dated to approximately 2700 to 2400 B.C. Hence the Remedello culture was usually also dated to that period. The discovery of the Iceman means that Remedello must be backdated by about five hundred years. It is clear, then, that by about 3200 B.C. northern Italians not only borrowed from the more advanced eastern Mediterranean areas but also created their own original technology and culture. Thus a small object (a copper ax), placed within a larger body of evidence (Italian and Anatolian metalwork), permits broad generalization about the interaction and independence of ancient cultures.

---

*For an introduction to the Iceman, see Brenda Fowler, *Iceman: Uncovering the Life and Times of a Prehistoric Man Found in an Alpine Glacier* (Chicago: University of Chicago Press, 2001), and James H. Dickson, Klaus Oeggl, and Linda L. Handley, "The Iceman Reconsidered," *Scientific American* (May 2003).

**Artist's Rendition of the Ice Man**   *(New York Times Photo Sales)*

 **For additional information on this topic, go to college.hmco.com/students.**

# CHAPTER 2

# The Sword, the Book, and the Myths: Western Asia and Early Greece

THE bull in brick relief shown on the left symbolizes power even today, twenty-six hundred years after it was molded and glazed. About 4 feet high, this bull was one of several dozen figures of bulls and dragons that decorated the massive Ishtar Gate, which led through the inner town wall of Babylon° into the palace. The gate represents only a small part of a magnificent reconstruction of the city by the Neo-Babylonian° kings who ruled western Asia around 600 to 539 B.C.

Imagine the king's surprise had he known that under his nose an obscure prophet—we know him only as "Second Isaiah°"—was preaching a bold message to his compatriots, a conquered people living in exile in Babylon. Isaiah reminded them that Yahweh°, their god, was a god of justice and mercy—the one and only true god of the entire world—and that Yahweh had chosen the king of mountainous, backward Persia to conquer western Asia and redeem Yahweh's people. The Neo-Babylonian king might have laughed at the idea. Yet the Persians under Cyrus the Great conquered Babylon in 539 B.C. and proclaimed the freedom of Yahweh's people—the Jews—to return to Palestine and re-establish the Temple to their god in the city of Jerusalem°. They did so, and around this time they wrote down their religious and historical traditions in large sections of what would become the Hebrew Bible, or Old Testament.

Also in the sixth century B.C., Pisistratus°, the ambitious ruler of Athens, a tiny city-state a thousand miles northwest of Babylon, sponsored a literary project to preserve the religious and historical traditions of his people. The literary works whose texts were standardized under his patronage are the *Iliad* and *Odyssey*, the epic

---

**Babylon** (BAB-eh-lon)   **Neo-Babylonian** (NEE-oh bab-eh-LONE-ee-an)
**Isaiah** (eye-ZAY-ah)   **Yahweh** (YAH-way)   **Jerusalem** (juh-ROO-suh-lem)
**Pisistratus** (pie-SIS-trah-tus)

Bull from Ishtar Gate, Babylon.   (Staatliche Museen zu Berlin, Museum für Vor- und Frühgeschite/Bildarchiv Preussischer Kulturbesitz. Photo: Reinhard Saczewski)

Assyrians, Neo-Babylonians, and Persians, ca. 1200–330 B.C.

Israel, ca. 1500–400 B.C.

Early Greece, to ca. 725 B.C.

poems of Homer, who had composed them about two centuries before.

Both the Hebrew Bible and the Homeric poems are deeply religious in outlook, but there the similarities end. The Hebrew Bible is monotheistic and focuses on the individual's subordination to God. Homer is polytheistic and glorifies the hero, who, though doomed to fail, aspires to godlike achievement. For most scholars the Bible and Homer represent two poles of Western civilization: the sacred and the worldly, the reverent and the heroic, holy writ and poetic craftsmanship.

Israel and Greece are, along with Rome, the founders of the West. Israel's holy book, the Hebrew Bible, founded the Western religious tradition. Greece, which founded the Western tradition of philosophy and politics, had its first great literary flowering in the works of Homer, whose epic poems are based on Greek myths.

The Neo-Babylonians, along with the other great empires of the era, the Assyrians and Persians, are ancestors of the West. Conquerors, they came to power by the sword, but once in power they spread civilization, serving as conduits through which the achievements of Mesopotamia were transmitted. They built great empires whose institutions were eventually transformed into notions of mass citizenship under law and justice in a universal empire by the third founder of the West, Rome.

The first half of the first millennium B.C., therefore, left a divergent legacy to the West. On the one hand, new empires arose that were more systemat-

ically organized, farther-flung, and more diverse ethnically than those created before. On the other hand, prophets, philosophers, and poets looked in new and deeper ways into the human soul.

In this chapter we look at the deeply influential developments in empire, religion, and thought forged in the first half of the first millennium B.C. At the same time, we consider the peaceful expansion in this era, through trade and colonization, particularly under the Phoenicians. Finally, we examine the material innovation that has earned the period the title "Iron Age."

> ### QUESTIONS TO CONSIDER
>
> - What made the first-millennium B.C. empires of the Assyrians, Neo-Babylonians, and Persians so much more effective than earlier empires?
> - How did monotheism develop in ancient Israel, and what is its legacy today?
> - What are the Homeric poems, and what light do they shed on the culture of early Greece?

> ### TERMS TO KNOW
>
> | | |
> |---|---|
> | Assyrians | Neo-Babylonians |
> | Phoenicians | Persian Empire |
> | Zoroastrianism | Torah |
> | covenant | Israel |
> | monotheism | Minoans |
> | Mycenaeans | Homer |

## ASSYRIANS, NEO-BABYLONIANS, AND PERSIANS, CA. 1200–330 B.C.

ANCESTORS of the West, three great multiethnic empires emerged between the 800s and 500s B.C. Ruthless soldiers, brutal conquerors, and innovative administrators, the Assyrians established an empire in western Asia and Egypt during the ninth

through seventh centuries B.C. They were followed in turn by a Neo-Babylonian empire in the late seventh and sixth centuries. However, neither of these was as successful or as durable as the empire of the Persians (ca. 550–330 B.C.). At its height the Persian Empire stretched from central Asia and northwest India in the east to Macedonia and Libya in the west (see Map 2.1). Persia's vast empire was loosely governed by a Persian ruling elite and its native helpers. Unlike the ironfisted Assyrians, the Persians were relatively tolerant and respectful of their subjects' customs. Many of Persia's kings were followers of Zoroastrianism, an ethical and forceful religion. A period of relative peace in most of Persia's domains from the 530s to the 330s B.C. fostered widespread economic prosperity.

Borrowing the administrative methods of the Assyrians and Medes° and the long-established officialdom of Babylon, the Persians built a new and durable imperial government. Their official art stressed the unity of the peoples of the empire under Persian leadership. Persian rule represented the greatest success yet in implementing the notions of universal kingship that dated back to Sargon of Agade (r. 2371–2316 B.C.; see page 16). In turn, Persia transmitted the trappings of absolute kingship to later ambitious rulers, from Alexander the Great to the caesars of Rome and from the Byzantine emperors to the Muslim caliphs.

## Assyrians and Neo-Babylonians

The Assyrians, whose homeland was in what is today northern Iraq, spoke a Semitic language. For most of the second millennium B.C., they were a military and commercial power. Around 1200 B.C. the Assyrians' state collapsed during that era of international crisis (see page 34), but they held on to a small homeland of about 5,000 square miles, roughly the size of Connecticut. The toughened survivors emerged with an aggressive, expansionist ideology.

Assyria's greatest successes came in the eighth and seventh centuries. One by one, states large and small fell—Babylonia, Syria, the kingdom of Israel, Cilicia in southern Anatolia, even Egypt (though Assyrian rule there lasted only a generation). Assyria became the first state to rule the two great river valleys of the ancient Near East, the Nile and the Tigris-Euphrates (see Map 2.1).

The Assyrians were warriors. Ashur, their main deity, was a war-god. Theirs was an ideology of power, conquest, and control. (See the box "Reading Sources: The Banquet of Ashurnasirpal II.") The key to Assyria's success was its army—100,000 to 200,000 men strong—which made an unforgettable impression on observers and foes. The Israelite prophet Isaiah of Jerusalem ("First Isaiah") said of Assyrian soldiers: "[Their] arrows are sharpened, and all their bows bent, their horses' hoofs are like flint, their chariot wheels like the whirlwind. Their growling is like that of a lion" (Isaiah 5:28–29). He might have added that Assyrian spearmen, archers, and cavalrymen were equipped with weapons and armor of iron.

Medes (meedz)

| | CHRONOLOGY | |
|---|---|
| 2000 B.C. | First Minoan palaces on Crete |
| 1800–1550 B.C. | Height of Minoan civilization |
| 1626 B.C. | Eruption of Thera volcano |
| 1550 B.C. | Mycenaeans conquer Crete |
| 1375 B.C. | Palace at Knossos destroyed |
| 1400–1200 B.C. | Height of Mycenaean civilization |
| 1250–1150 B.C. | Sea Peoples invade Palestine |
| 1200 B.C. | Mycenaean palaces destroyed |
| ca. 1200–1000 B.C. | Israelites settle Palestinian hill country |
| ca. 1050–750 B.C. | Height of Phoenician city-states |
| 1004–928 B.C. | Reigns of David and Solomon |
| ca. 725 B.C. | Homer |
| 722 B.C. | Assyrians conquer kingdom of Israel |
| 612 B.C. | Conquest of Nineveh ends Assyrian power |
| 598 B.C. | Neo-Babylonians conquer kingdom of Judah |
| 559–530 B.C. | Reign of Cyrus the Great |
| 550–331 B.C. | Achaemenid Persian Empire |
| 539 B.C. | Cyrus conquers Babylon; permits Jews to return to Palestine |
| ca. 425 B.C. | Judean assembly accepts the Torah |

Thanks to new heating and cooling techniques, metal smiths in the ancient world produced an alloy of carbon and iron that was harder and more durable than bronze. It was also easier to obtain since iron ore is widespread—unlike tin, an essential element of bronze. Iron tools and weapons were often stronger and cheaper than their bronze predecessors, which opened up new technical and military possibilities.

Adding to its might, Assyria was the first major state to employ regular cavalry units (rather than charioteers) as the main strike force. The Assyrians were also excellent engineers, adept at taking walled cities by siege.

**Map 2.1   The Assyrian and Persian Empires**   In the 660s B.C. the Assyrians ruled the largest empire the ancient world had seen, extending from the Tigris to the Nile. The Persian Empire was even greater. Around 500 B.C. it reached from its heartland in southwestern Iran westward to Macedonia and eastward to India.

In addition, the Assyrians displayed superb organizational skills. The central standing army was supplemented with draftees conscripted from around the empire. Provinces were kept small to prevent the emergence of separate power bases, and independent-minded nobles were regularly checked by the kings.

To control the restive subjects of their far-flung empire, the Assyrians met rebellion with ferocious reprisals. Disloyal cities were attacked and, if need be, destroyed. Sculptured reliefs and inscriptions were set up to show, often in gruesome detail, the fate awaiting Assyria's enemies. We see or read of cities burned to the ground; of men flayed alive, even though they had surrendered, and walls covered with their skin; and of piles of human skulls. (See the feature "Weighing the Evidence: The Siege of Lachish" on pages 66–67.)

The Assyrians also engaged in mass deportations. They uprooted the people of a conquered country, resettled them far away—often in Assyria itself—and colonized their land with Assyrian loyalists. The so-called Ten Lost Tribes of Israel—the people of the northern Israelite

kingdom (see pages 53–54)—were conquered by Assyria in 722 B.C., and many of them were transported to Mesopotamia, where they disappeared from history. (Those who remained in Israel mixed with colonists, and the new group became known, and scorned, as Samaritans.)

Assyrian policy was the result of careful calculation. The political goal was to punish rebellion, the economic goal to create a varied labor force. For example, although it is estimated that the Assyrians deported several million people, they deported not whole populations but a carefully chosen cross section of professions. They also deported entire families together, to weaken deportees' emotional ties to their former homes.

Assyria's success also was due in part to the relative weakness of other powers. Egypt had been at the mercy of factions and invaders for much of the Third Intermediate Period (1075–656 B.C.). Around 950, for example, the kingship came into the hands of Libyan mercenaries. From the eighth century on, their rule was challenged in turn by invaders from the south, rulers of a new Nubian kingdom called Kush (see Map 1.2 on page 22). Kushite

# THE BANQUET OF ASHURNASIRPAL II

*This inscription comes from the palace of the Assyrian king Ashurnasirpal II (r. 883–859 B.C.) at his new capital city of Calah (Nimrud). The first two paragraphs illustrate the expansive claims to power of the Assyrian kings. The third shows the effort made to bring in subjects from far and wide to the inaugural festival of the palace in order to awe them.*

This is the palace of Ashurnasirpal, the high priest of Ashur, chosen by Enlil and Ninurta, the favorite of Anu and of Dagan who is destruction personified among the great gods—the legitimate king, the king of the world, the king of Assyria, son of Tukulti-Ninurta, great king, legitimate king, king of the world and king of Assyria—the heroic warrior who always acts upon trust-inspiring signs given by his lord Ashur and therefore has no rival among the rulers of the four quarters of the world; the shepherd of all mortals, not afraid of battle but an onrushing flood which brooks no resistance; the king who subdues the unsubmissive and rules over all mankind; the king who always acts upon the trust-inspiring signs given by his lords, the great gods, and therefore has personally conquered all countries; who has acquired dominion over the mountain regions and received their tribute; he takes hostages, triumphs over all countries from beyond the Tigris to the Lebanon and the Great Sea, he has brought into submission the entire country of Laqe and the region of Suhu as far as the town of Rapiqu; personally he conquered the region from the source of the Subnat River to Urartu. . . .

Ashur, the Great Lord, has chosen me and made a pronouncement concerning my world rule with his own holy mouth (as follows): Ashurnasirpal is the king whose fame is power! . . .

When I inaugurated the palace at Calah I treated for ten days with food and drink 47,074 persons, men and women, who were bid to come from across my entire country, also 5,000 important persons, delegates from the country Suhu, from Hindana, Hattina, Hatti, Tyre, and Musasir, also 16,000 inhabitants of Calah from all ways of life, 1,500 officials of all my palaces, altogether 69,574 invited guests from all the mentioned countries including the people of Calah; I furthermore provided them with the means to clean and anoint themselves. I did them due honors and sent them back, healthy and happy, to their own countries.

pharaohs governed Egypt from around 719 until 656, when they withdrew back south. It was they who faced the Assyrian attacks in 671 and 667.

The conquest of Egypt marked imperial Assyria's greatest extent—and its overextension (see Map 2.1). A coalition army consisting of soldiers from a revived Babylonian kingdom and of Medes (who had formed a powerful state in Iran; see page 45) conquered Nineveh°, the Assyrian capital, in 612 B.C. and defeated the remnants of the Assyrian army in battles in 609 and 605. Few of its subjects mourned the empire's passing.

The destruction of Assyria led to revival for Babylon, whose rulers attempted to recapture the glories of Hammurabi's day (see page 47). For a short period, until the Persian conquest in 539 B.C., the Neo-Babylonian dynasty (founded in 626 B.C.) and the Medes of Iran were the dominant military forces in western Asia. The Neo-Babylonian king Nebuchadrezzar° II (Nebuchadnezzar in the Hebrew Bible; r. 605–562 B.C.) conquered the kingdom of Judah (in southern Palestine) in 598 and destroyed Jerusalem, its capital, in 586. He deported many thousands of Judeans° to Babylon, an event remembered by Christians and Jews as the Babylonian Captivity. Most of the rest of western Asia also fell to Nebuchadrezzar's troops. His most enduring achievement

---

**Nineveh** (NIN-eh-veh)

**Nebuchadrezzar** (neh-boo-khad-REZ-zar)
**Judeans** (joo-DEE-unz)

**Assyrian Winged Genie** This alabaster relief comes from a temple of Ashurnasirpal II (r. 883–859 B.C.) at his capital of Calah (Nimrud). The figure holds an incense pouch in one hand and a pine cone in the other, perhaps symbols of the tree of life. *(The Metropolitan Museum of Art, Gift of John D. Rockefeller, Jr., 1931 [31.72.1])*

was rebuilding Babylon on a grand scale. In addition to the city's numerous temples, shrines, and altars, he created the so-called Hanging Gardens celebrated by later Greek writers. They describe the structure as a large terraced complex that Nebuchadrezzar built for his queen, although it may have been a plant-covered ziggurat.

The Neo-Babylonians and Assyrians both made great strides in astronomy. Their primary motive was not scientific but religious—that is, a belief in astrology (the study of the movements of heavenly bodies in the belief that they influence human affairs). Astrology led to advances in the scientific observation of the heavens. Assyrian priests had produced relatively accurate circular diagrams (astrolabes) that showed the positions of the major constellations, stars, and planets over the course of the year. By 600 B.C. Assyrian and Neo-Babylonian astronomers could predict solstices, equinoxes, and lunar eclipses.

Astronomy in Mesopotamia reached its heights in the centuries after 500 B.C. The zodiac, a diagram showing the movement of the sun and planets relative to the constellations, was invented in Persian-ruled Babylon in the fourth century B.C. In the third and second centuries B.C., when Babylonia was under Hellenistic Greek rule, native scientists made impressive advances in mathematical astronomy, composing tables that could be used to calculate movements of the moon and planets. More sophisticated mathematical astronomy would not be produced in the West until the Scientific Revolution of the sixteenth century A.D.

Another western Asian society during this period was created by trade, not war. In both the Hebrew Bible and Homer, the Phoenicians° loom large as merchants and seamen, as "traders the world honored" (Isaiah 23:8). Phoenicians were Canaanites°, speakers of a Semitic language and heirs to the civilization that had prospered in Ugarit around 1400 B.C. (see page 31). After the invasions of the Sea Peoples and others around 1200 B.C., the Canaanites' once-large territory was reduced to a narrow strip along the Mediterranean in the area of modern Lebanon and northern Israel (see Map 2.2 on page 54). Between 1050 and 750 B.C., the inhabitants of the area flourished; historians call them, as did the ancient Greeks, "Phoenicians." Their purple-dyed textiles gave the Greeks their word for the color purple: *Phoenician.*

The Phoenicians were master shipbuilders and sailors. Around 600 B.C. their ships accomplished the first known circumnavigation of Africa. Around 450 B.C. they made the first known commercial sailing trip to the British Isles. Some scholars think they even reached Brazil. The most lasting Phoenician achievement at sea, however, was the planting of colonies in the Mediterranean, probably beginning in the ninth century B.C. Many of their colonies eventually became independent states. The greatest Phoenician colony was Carthage°, founded by the city of Tyre around 750 B.C. It was the major port city of the western Mediterranean for much of the next thousand years.

Phoenician culture was open to outside influences. Phoenician religious art is full of Egyptian sphinxes, coffins that look like mummy cases, and women wearing wigs in the style of Egypt's New Kingdom. But Phoeni-

---

**Phoenicians** (fuh-NEESH-anz)    **Canaanites** (CAY-nan-ites)
**Carthage** (CAR-thidge)

cian art also contains Near Eastern seals and figures out of Greek myths.

Phoenician traders introduced advanced material goods, slaves, and possibly law codes to the Greeks. It was probably from the Phoenicians, whose alphabet derived from Ugarit, that the Greeks adapted their alphabet.

Around 750 B.C. the Phoenician city-states lost their independence to the Assyrians, and in later years Neo-Babylonians, Persians, and other foreign conquerors followed. But Phoenician culture survived—at home, in the colonies, and among the many Mediterranean peoples influenced by it. The result, though unintended, was that Phoenician colonists exported the civilization of western Asia to the western Mediterranean.

## Building the Persian Empire

A thousand miles east of Phoenicia, a great empire took root. Indo-European–speaking peoples, the Medes and Persians arrived in western Iran probably around 1500 B.C. but perhaps not until 900 B.C. The two peoples were closely related in language and customs. The Medes lived in the central Zagros Mountains. The Persians made their homeland farther south in Anshan (modern Fars). At first the Medes ruled the Persians, but in 550 B.C. the tables were turned when the Medes were suddenly conquered by the young Persian king Cyrus the Great (r. 559–530 B.C.).

It took Cyrus only twenty years to conquer most of western Asia and much of central Asia. Within five years of his death in 530 B.C., his son and successor, Cambyses° (r. 530–525 B.C.), added Egypt and Libya. Cambyses' successor, Darius° (r. 521–486 B.C.), corralled northwestern India and Thrace. The frontier regions, especially Egypt, were often in revolt, and the attempt of Darius and his successor, Xerxes° (r. 486–465 B.C.), to extend Persian rule to Greece ended in failure (see pages 88–91). The Achaemenid° Persian Empire (named after a legendary founder, Achaemenes) survived for two hundred years, until a Greco-Macedonian army under Alexander the Great, king of Macedon (r. 336–323 B.C.), destroyed it.

Let us consider several reasons for the success of Achaemenid Persia. The first was military prowess. Persia was ruled by a warrior aristocracy whose traditional values, according to the Greek historian Herodotus, were "riding, hunting, and telling the truth." The state was able to field a huge army of about 300,000 men, conscripted from the various subject peoples. Although the

**Phoenician Ivory**    This delicately carved plaque of a cow and calf, just 3 inches high, illustrates the wealth of artistic talent at the disposal of the Phoenicians, whose civilization reached its peak between 1050 and 750 B.C.    *(Iraq Antiquities Department)*

resultant hodgepodge of soldiers from across the empire did not always fight as a unit, a crack infantry group, the 10,000 Immortals, provided a solid core. The Persians excelled as bowmen and cavalrymen. Following the Assyrians, they made cavalry into the decisive strike force of the battlefield, assigning a more minor role to chariotry. Persia was even more innovative at sea, where it had its subjects build the first great navy. Although Persians served as marines and sometimes as commanders, the rowers and seamen were usually Phoenicians or Greeks.

The second reason for Persia's success was political. Unlike the Assyrians, the Persians considered generosity and tolerance to be more effective than terrorism and brutality. As Cyrus prepared to attack Babylon, he portrayed himself as the champion of the traditional Babylonian religion, and Babylon surrendered to him without a fight. Cyrus also emphasized his continuity with earlier Mesopotamian history by adopting the traditional title of "King of Sumer and Akkad." Nor did he hesitate to break with Assyrian and Neo-Babylonian population transfers, as witnessed in his edict permitting the Jewish exiles in Babylon to return to Judea. (See the box "Reading Sources: Cyrus and His Subjects' Gods.")

**Cambyses** (kam-BYE-seez)    **Darius** (dah-RYE-us)
**Xerxes** (ZURK-seez)    **Achaemenid** (ah-KEE-men-id)

## CYRUS AND HIS SUBJECTS' GODS

*Although the Persians sometimes used brutal tactics, they preferred to gain their subjects' loyalty by gestures of goodwill, such as winning the favor of the religious leaders. Excerpt (a), a Babylonian inscription, demonstrates the political skill by which Cyrus the Great secured the surrender of Babylon in 539 B.C. without a battle. Excerpt (b), from the Hebrew Bible, records the favor that Cyrus showed to the Jewish exiles in Babylon.*

**(a)**

He [Marduk] scanned and looked (through) all the countries, searching for a righteous ruler willing to lead him [i.e., Marduk] (in the annual procession). (Then) he pronounced the name of Cyrus, king of Anshan, declared him to be(come) the ruler of all the world. . . . And he [Cyrus] did always endeavor to treat according to justice the black-headed whom he [Marduk] has made him conquer. Marduk, the great lord, a protector of his people/worshipers, beheld with pleasure his [i.e., Cyrus's] good deeds and his upright mind (and therefore) ordered him to march against his city Babylon. . . .

I am Cyrus, king of the world, great king, legitimate king, king of Babylon, king of Sumer and Akkad, king of the four rims (of the earth), son of Cambyses. . . .

When I entered Babylon as a friend and (when) I established the seat of the government in the palace of the ruler under jubilation and rejoicing, Marduk, the great lord, [induced] the magnanimous inhabi-

tants of Babylon [to love me], and I was daily endeavoring to worship him. My numerous troops walked around in Babylon in peace, I did not allow anybody to terrorize (any place) of the [country of Sumer] and Akkad. I strove for peace in Babylon and in all his other sacred cities.

**(b)**

In the first year of King Cyrus of Persia [539 B.C.] the Lord, to fulfill his word spoken through Jeremiah, inspired the king to issue throughout his kingdom the following proclamation, which he also put in writing: The decree of King Cyrus of Persia. The Lord the God of the heavens has given me all the kingdoms of the earth, and he himself has charged me to build him a house at Jerusalem in Judah. Whoever among you belongs to his people, may his God be with him; and let him go up to Jerusalem in Judah, and build the house of the Lord the God of Israel, the God who is in Jerusalem. Let every Jew left among us, wherever he is settled throughout the country, be helped by his neighbours with silver and gold, goods and livestock, in addition to the voluntary offerings for the house of God in Jerusalem.

Sources: Excerpt (a): Adapted from James B. Pritchard, ed., *Ancient Near Eastern Texts Relating to the Old Testament,* 3d ed., with Supplement, pp. 315–316. Copyright © 1969 by Princeton University Press. Reprinted by permission of Princeton University Press. Excerpt (b): Ezra 1:1–3, in *The Oxford Study Bible: Revised English Bible with the Apocrypha.* © Oxford University Press and Cambridge University Press, 1989.

The third reason for Persia's success was its skill at administration and organization. Darius played a crucial role in reorganizing the imperial administration and finances. Like the Assyrian Empire, the Persian domain was divided into provinces, called *satrapies*°. Each of the twenty satrapies was a unit of administration and tax collection. For the first time, taxes could be paid with a stable, official coinage: the gold daric (named after Darius) and the silver shekel. Coins had been invented in the kingdom of Lydia in western Asia Minor in the seventh

century B.C. Croesus (r. 560–547 B.C.), Lydia's king, was known for his wealth—hence the expression "rich as Croesus"—before Cyrus conquered him in 547 B.C.

The provincial governors, or *satraps,* were powerful, often quasi-independent figures. But the king tried to keep a firm hand on them. Each province had a royal secretary and was visited regularly by traveling inspectors called "the king's eyes." A network of good roads radiated from the capital cities of Susa and Persepolis. The most famous road, the so-called Royal Road, stretched 1,600 miles from western Iran to western Anatolia (see Map 2.1). Covering the whole distance took most travelers three months, but the king's relay messenger corps

**satrapies** (SAY-truh-peez)

**Achaemenid Persian Silver**    This silver rhyton (drinking vessel) is in the shape of a griffin, a mythological animal that is part lion and part eagle. Persian rulers commanded the talents of western Asia's best artists and craftsmen, silversmiths among them.    *(Courtesy of the Trustees of the British Museum)*

could make the trip in a week, thanks to a series of staging posts furnished with fresh horses.

Another unifying element was a society that was law-abiding and prosperous. Darius proclaimed in an inscription that he had fostered the rule of law: "These countries [of the empire] showed respect toward my law; as was said to them by me, thus it was done." Darius and other Persian kings helped create the conditions for compliance and security by taking an interest in the economy. For example, they opened to commercial traffic Persian roads and a canal connecting the Red Sea and the Nile.

Language, too, built unity. Not Persian, which relatively few people spoke, but Aramaic, the most widespread language of western Asia, became the empire's basic language of commerce and administration. A Semitic language related to Hebrew, Aramaic was first used by the Aramaeans°, a nomadic people who settled in northern Syria about 1100 B.C. and ruled an area extending into Mesopotamia before succumbing to Assyrian conquest about 725 B.C. The Aramaeans dominated the overland trade routes, which, combined with the simple and easily learned Aramaic alphabet, contributed to the spread of their language. Aramaic facilitated the development of literacy and recordkeeping. Aramaic would become the common language of western Asia for over a thousand years, until Arabic replaced it; Jesus Christ was to be its most famous native speaker.

## The King of Kings

Despite its success, Persia's empire was fraught with several weaknesses. First, Cyrus had bequeathed a legacy as a charismatic war leader. Feeling the need to live up to his example, his successors sometimes undertook ambitious and expensive expeditions that failed, such as wars with the Scythians (a tough nomadic people in Ukraine) and the Greeks. Second, however mild Persian rule, however peaceful and prosperous, it was still rule by foreigners and it still involved taxation. Persian officials, military garrisons, and colonists were found—and were resented—in every corner of the empire. Native resentment, particularly in Egypt, and the independence of certain satraps led to intermittent provincial revolts.

The exaltation of the Persian king served as a counterweight to rebellious tendencies. From Darius on, the Persian monarch tried to overawe his officials with his majesty and might. The "King of Kings," as the monarch called himself, sat on a high, gold and blue throne, dressed in purple, decked out in gold jewelry, wearing fragrant oils and cosmetics, and attended by corps of slaves and eunuchs (castrated men employed in high positions). Although he was not considered a god, he had to be treated with reverence. Persians spoke of the king's *khvarna*, his "kingly glory," a mysterious aura of power. Anyone who came into the royal presence had to approach him with a bow to the ground, face-down.

Impressive as the court ceremonial was, Persian kings were not all-powerful. They were bound by the rule of law and by the considerable power of Persia's proud nobility, on whom they relied to fill the top administrative positions. Competing factions of ministers, wives, concubines, eunuchs, and sons often brought intrigue and discord to court, especially in the fourth century B.C., a time of frequent rebellion.

---

**Aramaeans** (air-uh-MAY-unz)

# The Subject Peoples of a Multicultural Empire

The Persian Empire ruled more people than ever before, and the kings were proud of that. This inscription from the capital city of Susa, dated probably about 520 B.C., emphasizes the participation of a variety of peoples, from India to Egypt and the Aegean Sea, in the construction of King Darius's palace.

§2. I am Darius, the Great King, the king of kings, king of the lands, king of this earth, son of Hystaspes, an Achaemenid. And Darius the king says: "Ahura Mazda, who is the greatest of the gods, has created me, has made me king, has given me this kingdom, which is great, and which has good horses and good men. By the favor of Ahura Mazda, my father Hystaspes and Arsames, my grandfather, were both alive when Ahura Mazda made me king on this earth. Thus it was the desire of Ahura Mazda to choose me as his man on this entire earth, he made me king on this earth. I worshipped Ahura Mazda. Ahura Mazda brought me aid. What I ordered (to be done), this he accomplished for me. I achieved all of what I did by the grace of Ahura Mazda.

§3. "This palace which I built at Susa: its materials were brought from afar. The earth was dug down deep, until the rock was reached in the earth. When the excavation had been made, then rubble was packed down, some 40 cubits (ca. 65 feet) deep, another (part) 20 cubits deep. On that rubble the palace was constructed. And that earth, which was dug deep, and that rubble, which was packed down, and the sun-dried bricks, which were molded, the Babylonian people—they performed (these tasks).

§4. "The cedar timber was brought from a mountain called Lebanon. The Assyrian people brought it to Babylon. From Babylon the Carians and Ionians brought it to Susa. The sissoo-timber was brought from Gandara and from Carmania. The gold which was worked here was brought from Sardis and from Bactria. The precious stone lapis lazuli and carnelian which was worked here was brought from Sogdi-ana. The precious stone turquoise, which was worked here, this was brought from Chorasmia. The silver and the ebony were brought from Egypt. The ornamentation with which the wall was adorned was brought from Ionia. The ivory which was worked here was brought from Ethiopia, and from India and from Arachosia. The stone columns which were worked here were brought from a village called Abiradu, in Elam. The stonecutters who worked the stone were Ionians and Sardians. The goldsmiths who worked the gold were Medes and Egyptians. The men who worked the wood were Sardians and Egyptians. The men who worked the baked brick were Babylonians. The men who adorned the wall were Medes and Egyptians."

§5. Darius the king says: "At Susa a very excellent work was ordered, a very excellent work was brought to completion. May Ahura Mazda protect me, and Hystaspes my father and my country."

## QUESTIONS

1. What does Darius consider to be special signs that heaven favored him? Why does he choose these signs?

2. List all the different materials in the palace and all the different ethnic groups that brought them to Susa. What do you think was the most valuable material? Least valuable?

3. How does the variety of peoples and materials demonstrate Darius's power?

SOURCE: LACTORs 16, *The Persian Empire from Cyrus II to Artaxerxes I,* translated and edited by Maria Brosius. Copyright 2000. Reprinted by permission of L.A.C.T. For more information, contact http://www.kcl.ac.uk/humanities/cch/lactor.

 **For additional information on this topic, go to college.hmco.com/students.**

Royal authority was symbolized in the decoration of the great palaces at Susa and Persepolis, a project begun by Darius I and completed by his son and successor, Xerxes. The Susa palace, the larger of the two, reflected the universality of the empire in the variety of hands that built it Craftsmen from east and west took part in the construction. (See the box "Global Encounters: The Subject Peoples of a Multicultural Empire.") The Persepolis palace, too, displayed the heterogeneity of the empire in its architecture. The palace was placed on a terrace, as in Mesopotamia, but contained columned halls as in Egypt, with Assyrian-style column capitals or tops. In Persepolis, a frieze of sculpted relief panels lining a monumental stairway leading to the palace emphasized the king's vast power. The panels depict an endless procession of the peoples of the world paying homage to the

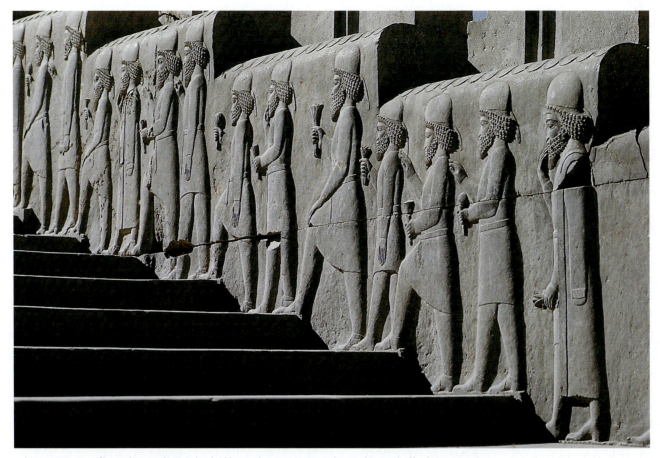

**Frieze at Persepolis**    This sculptured relief lines the stairway to the audience hall of King Darius (r. 521–486 B.C.). It depicts Persian nobles, well groomed and formally dressed, carrying flowers for the New Year's feast.    *(Rony Jaques/Photo Researchers)*

King of Kings: from the nobility to the Immortals, to Median and Persian soldiers, to tribute-bearing subjects from the ends of the earth. The overall feeling of the scene is static, as if the Persian Empire would last forever.

## Zoroastrianism

Like ancient Israel, Persia developed a highly ethical religion in the first millennium B.C. From obscure beginnings, Zoroastrianism° became the religion of Persia that persisted until the Muslim conquest in the seventh century A.D. Although largely extinct in today's Iran, an Islamic country, Zoroastrianism still survives in small communities elsewhere, primarily in India. Some scholars argue that Zoroastrian beliefs eventually influenced Judaism and Christianity, as well as Roman paganism and Indian Buddhism.

It is easier to describe ancient Zoroastrianism in broad strokes than in detail, partly because the religion changed radically over the course of its ancient history, and partly because relatively little information survives before A.D. 300. This much is clear: The religion was founded by a great reformer and prophet named Zarathustra° (Zoroaster in Greek). Zarathustra lived in eastern Iran. His teachings survive in the *Gathas* ("Songs"), a portion of the Zoroastrian holy book called the *Avesta*. Some scholars date Zarathustra as late as 550 B.C.; others prefer an earlier date, 750 or even 1000 B.C.

Zarathustra's society was dominated by warriors whose religion consisted of blood cults, violent gods,

---

**Zoroastrianism** (zoh-roh-AS-tree-un-izm)

**Zarathustra** (zah-ruh-THOOS-truh)

animal sacrifice, and ecstatic rituals in which hallucinogens were eaten. Zarathustra rejected such violent practices in favor of an inward-looking, intellectual, and ethical religion. He favored ceremonies involving fire, considered a symbol of purity. Zarathustra was not a strict monotheist like the Jews, but he did emphasize the power of one god over all people, the supremely good and wise creator of the universe, whom he called Ahura Mazda ("Wise Lord"). Unlike the Jews, Zarathustra considered the problem of evil to be the central question of religion. If god was one, good, and omnipotent, how could evil exist?

Zarathustra's answer might be called *ethical dualism* (dualism is the notion of a grand conflict between good and evil). Ahura Mazda had twin children: the Beneficent Spirit and the Hostile Spirit. Each spirit had made a free choice: one for the "truth" and the other for the "lie"—that is, one for good and the other for evil. Every human being faces a similar choice between good and evil. "Reflect with a clear mind—man by man for himself—upon the two choices of decision, being aware to declare yourselves to Him before the great retribution," says Zarathustra.[1] Indeed, humanity is caught in a great cosmic struggle in which individuals are free to make a momentous choice. Zarathustra distinguished between two states of being: the spiritual and the material. The more a person pursued spiritual purity, the greater was the person's ability to choose good rather than evil.

Zarathustra held a linear conception of history, similar to that in the Hebrew Bible. His religion is marked by a strong *eschatology* (interest in the end of the world) as well as *soteriology* (belief in a savior). He believed that one day, through an ordeal by fire, Ahura Mazda would judge all the people who had ever lived. Those who had chosen good would be rewarded, and those who had chosen evil would be punished. Then would follow a Last Judgment in which the dead would be transfigured and restored to a glorious bodily existence. There would be, Zarathustra promised, "long destruction for the deceitful but salvation for the truthful." The notion of a savior who would initiate the Last Judgment is an early Zoroastrian belief, if perhaps not a doctrine of Zarathustra himself.

In later centuries, Zarathustra's followers eased his uncompromising rejection of Iranian paganism. Under the leadership of priests, known as *magi*° in western Iran, the religion changed considerably. Lesser deities beneath Ahura Mazda were added to the Zoroastrian pantheon, in part to suit the religion to the needs of the huge, multicultural Persian Empire.

**magi** (MAY-jye)

It is tempting to attribute Cyrus's policy of toleration to the ethical teachings of Zarathustra, but it is uncertain whether Cyrus was Zoroastrian. We are on firmer ground with later Persian kings, particularly Darius I, who had an image of himself alongside Ahura Mazda carved on the face of an Iranian cliff. In an accompanying inscription Darius announces: "For this reason Ahura Mazda bore aid, and the other gods who . . . [exist], because I was not hostile, I was not a Lie-follower, I was not a doer of wrong—neither I nor my family. According to righteousness I conducted myself."[2]

# ISRAEL, CA. 1500–400 B.C.

In the first millennium B.C. a small, often-conquered people turned imperialism on its head. Human achievement is meaningless, they argued; only the power of divinity matters. There is only one god, they said; all other gods are false. The one true god had revealed himself not to the awesome, imperialistic Assyrians but to the less powerful Hebrews—ancient Jews. They founded the Western tradition of religion. The God of ancient Israel eventually gave rise to the God of Christianity and of Islam as well as of modern Judaism.

The Hebrews, also known as Israelites, had existed as a people since about 1200 B.C. and perhaps for centuries earlier. They spoke a Semitic language.

## The Hebrew Bible

As literature and as religious teaching, the Bible is one of the most important books in Western civilization. As a source of history, however, it presents difficulties. Much of the Hebrew Bible (called the Old Testament by Christians) is based on written sources that probably date back at least as far as the early Israelite monarchy of about 1000 B.C. Other parts of the Hebrew Bible are probably the product of an oral tradition, and the nature, antiquity, and reliability of that tradition are the subject of much scholarly debate.

Archaeological evidence from the area of ancient Israel, a small number of inscriptions (almost all after 800 B.C.), and some information in Greek and Roman writings provide an alternative source of information. Yet little of that alternative evidence sheds light on the period before about 1200 B.C., and it offers only partial insight into the later period. The historian needs both to pay attention to the Bible and to consider its nature.

The Hebrew Bible reached something close to its current form a century or two before the birth of Christ.

It consists of three main sections: (1) the Torah° (literally, "teaching"), also known as the Pentateuch, or five books of Moses (that is, the first five books of the Bible); (2) the Prophets, that is, the "historical" books of the early prophets (Joshua, Judges, Kings, and Chronicles) and the books of the later prophets (Isaiah, Jeremiah, Ezekiel, and the twelve "minor prophets"); and (3) the Writings, various books of poetry, proverbs, and wisdom literature.

The books of the Hebrew (and Christian) Bible are canonical: one by one, each was accepted by established authority as sacred. Two key dates stand out in the canonization of the Hebrew Bible: 622 B.C. and about 425 B.C. On the first date, Josiah, king of Judah (see page 54), assembled "the entire population, high and low" to swear to obey "the scroll of the covenant which had been discovered in the house of the Lord" (the scroll probably was Deuteronomy, now the fifth book of the Torah). On the second date, a similar assembly of the people, called by the religious leader Ezra, swore to accept the five books of the Torah that had by then been assembled. The introduction of the Torah made its worshipers into what they have been ever since: "a people of the Book," as the Muslims would put it many years later. The written tradition and literacy became central to the Hebrews.

The Hebrews are the first people we know of to have a single national history book. That book was written not as secular history but as sacred history. It is the story of the working out of God's pact, or covenant, with the Hebrews, his chosen people. All ancient peoples told stories of their semidivine foundation. Only the Hebrews imagined the nation created by an actual treaty between the people and their God.

The central fact of human existence in the Hebrew Bible is God's covenant with the Hebrews. Because of the covenant, history has meaning. History is the story of the success or failure of the Hebrew people in carrying out God's commandments. The emphatic focus is on the individual: on individual people taking actions that have not just moral but military and political consequences that unfold over time.

Many of the themes, narrative details, and styles of writing in the Hebrew Bible derive from earlier cultures. The biblical Flood story, for example, seems to have been modeled on a similar flood in the *Epic of Gilgamesh* (see page 20). Biblical poems in praise of God are often similar to Egyptian poems in praise of pagan gods, and biblical wisdom literature (that is, works containing proverbs and rules of conduct) often recalls Egyptian or Babylonian parallels. In spite of such borrowings, the

**Statuette of Bull**    This bronze statuette of a Canaanite deity (ca. 1200–1100 B.C.) comes from a sanctuary in the hills of Samaria. At this time, most Israelites still worshiped pagan gods.    *(The Israel Museum, Jerusalem)*

Hebrew Bible is dramatically different from its predecessors because it subordinates everything to one central theme: God's plan for humanity and, in particular, for his chosen people—the Hebrews.

## The Emergence of Hebrew Monotheism, ca. 1500–600 B.C.

The earliest nonbiblical evidence of the Hebrews is an inscribed monument of the New Kingdom Egyptian pharaoh Merneptah (r. 1224–1214 B.C.). After a military expedition into Canaan° (that is, roughly, Palestine), pharaoh declared triumphantly that "Israel is laid waste." Most scholars accept this as evidence of an Israelite presence in Canaan, but the question is, how did they get there? The Bible says that the Israelites settled Palestine by conquering its earlier inhabitants. Most scholars now reject that account. Archaeological evidence suggests, rather, a more complex process. Perhaps the Israelites were a combination of three groups: armed conquerors, shepherds who gradually entered the country and later settled down to farming, and dispossessed and oppressed Canaanites who rebelled against their masters.

---

**Torah** (TOE-rah)

**Canaan** (KAY-nan)

From such sources the Israelites may have emerged. The Bible, however, tells a different story of Israelite origins. Although much of it is credible, none of it is confirmed by nonbiblical sources. Still, the biblical story of Israelite origins has been so influential in later Western culture that we must examine it. If one follows the Bible, Hebrew history began sometime during the period 2000 to 1500 B.C. with the patriarchs, or founding fathers. Abraham, the first patriarch, migrated to Canaan from the city of Haran in northern Mesopotamia. A seminomadic chieftain, Abraham settled on territory north and west of the Dead Sea, where he grazed his herds. Seminomadic clans in the region frequently made long migrations in antiquity, so the biblical account of Abraham and his descendants, Isaac and Jacob, is plausible.

The Bible, however, emphasizes the implausible: Abraham's extraordinary decision to give up Mesopotamian polytheism for belief in one god. This god commanded Abraham to leave Haran; indeed, he made a treaty, or covenant, with Abraham. In return for Abraham's faith, said the god, "As a possession for all time I shall give you and your descendants after you the land in which you are now aliens, the whole of Canaan, and I shall be their God" (Genesis 17:8). Abraham was not a strict monotheist: although he worshiped only one god, he did not deny the existence of other gods. (See, for a comparison, the discussion of Akhenaten on page 27.) Nevertheless, he took a giant step on the road to pure monotheism by coming to believe that only one god rules *all* peoples.

According to the Bible, the next important step took place several hundred years later. In a time of famine in Canaan, many of Abraham's descendants left for prosperous Egypt. At first they thrived there, but in time they were enslaved and forced to build cities in the Nile Delta. Eventually, Moses, a divinely appointed leader, released the Hebrews from bondage in Egypt and led them back toward Canaan and freedom.

The Exodus ("journey out," in Greek), as this movement has been called, is a rare example of a successful national liberation movement in antiquity. Among those who accept its historicity, a date in the thirteenth century B.C. is frequently assigned to the Exodus. According to the Bible, the Exodus marked the key moment of another covenant, this time between the god of Abraham and the entire Israelite people. At Mount Sinai°, traditionally located on the rugged Sinai Peninsula between Egypt and Palestine, the Israelites are said to have first accepted as their one god a deity whose name is represented in Hebrew by the letters corresponding to YHWH. YHWH is traditionally rendered in English as "Jehovah," but "Yahweh" is more likely to be accurate. The Israelites accepted Yahweh's laws, summarized by the Ten Commandments. In return for obedience to Yahweh's commandments, they would be God's chosen people, his "special possession; . . . a kingdom of priests, . . . [his] holy nation." (See the box "The Continuing Experiment: The Covenant.")

The Ten Commandments are both more general and more personal than the laws of Hammurabi's Code. They are addressed to the individual, whom they commit to a universal standard. They emphasize prohibitions, saying more about what one should *not* do than about what one should do. The first three commandments establish Yahweh as the sole god of Israel, prohibit any sculpture or image of God, and forbid misuse of the divine name. The next two commandments are injunctions to observe the seventh day of the week (the Sabbath) as a day free of work and to honor one's parents. The sixth and seventh prohibit destructive or violent acts against neighbors, in particular adultery and killing. The final three commandments regulate community life by prohibiting stealing, testifying falsely, and coveting another man's wife or goods. In contrast to the starkness of the Ten Commandments, an enormous amount of detailed legal material is also found in the Hebrew Bible.

Many scholars doubt whether Hebrew monotheism emerged as early as the thirteenth century. In any case, the Bible makes clear that many ordinary Hebrews remained unconvinced. For centuries afterward, many Israelite worshipers deemed Yahweh their greatest god but not their only god. Unready for the radical innovation that monotheism represented, they carried out the rituals of various Canaanite deities, whom they worshiped on hilltop altars. Forging a national consensus for monotheism took centuries.

From the thirteenth to the late eleventh century B.C., the Hebrews were governed by a series of tribal leaders, referred to as "judges" in the Bible, but eventually the military threat posed by the Philistines° persuaded the tribes to accept a centralized monarchy. The Philistines, one of the Sea Peoples, had captured the Palestinian coast in the twelfth and eleventh centuries and seriously endangered Israel. The first Israelite king, Saul (r. ca. 1020–1004 B.C.), had some success against them but eventually fell in battle along with his son, Jonathan. The next king,

---

**Sinai** (SYE-nye)

**Philistines** (FILL-uh-steenz)

## The Covenant

The central event in the history of ancient Israel was the establishment, during the Exodus, of the covenant, or treaty, at Sinai (see Map 2.2) between God and his chosen people. Before this time, ancient peoples had worshiped gods and tried to gain their favor, but with only a loose relationship. The covenant uniquely uses a treaty—something typically reserved for legal or political obligations—to bring God and man closer together and to make the relationship permanent. As this text of Moses demonstrates, the covenant required the Israelites to follow certain obligations in order to receive the protection and blessings of God.

Moses summoned all Israel and said to them: Israel, listen to the statutes and the laws which I proclaim to you this day. Learn them, and be careful to observe them. The Lord our God made a covenant with us at Horeb [Sinai]. . . .

It was not because you were more numerous than any other nation that the Lord cared for you and chose you, for you were the smallest of all nations; it was because the Lord loved you and stood by his oath to your forefathers, that he brought you out with his strong hand and redeemed you from the land of slavery, from the power of Pharaoh king of Egypt. Know then that the Lord your God is God, the faithful God; with those who love him and keep his commandments he keeps covenant and faith for a thousand generations, but those who defy him and show their hatred for him he repays with destruction: he will not be slow to requite any who so hate him.

You are to observe these commandments, statutes, and laws which I give to you this day, and keep them.

What then, Israel, does the Lord your God ask of you? Only this: to fear the Lord your God, to conform to all his ways, to love him, and to serve him with all your heart and soul. This you will do by observing the commandments of the Lord and his statutes which I give you this day for your good. To the Lord your God belong heaven itself, the highest heaven, the earth and everything in it; yet the Lord was attached to your forefathers by his love for them, and he chose their descendants after them. Out of all nations you were his chosen people, as you are this day. So now you must circumcise your hearts and not be stubborn any more, for the Lord your God is God of gods and Lord of lords, the great, mighty, and terrible God. He is no respecter of persons; he is not to be bribed; he secures justice for the fatherless and the widow, and he shows love towards the alien who lives among you, giving him food and clothing. You too must show love towards the alien, for you once lived as aliens in Egypt.

### QUESTIONS

1. What is the covenant between God and the Israelites? Why did God choose the Israelites?

2. What are the basic obligations of the Israelites? What does God promise the Israelites in return?

3. What does it mean to "show love towards the alien"? Why is that important?

SOURCE: Exodus 19:1, 3–6; 20:1-9, 12–17, in *The New English Bible with the Apocrypha.* © Oxford University Press and Cambridge University Press, 1989.

---

David (r. 1004–965 B.C.), a former mercenary captain for the Philistines, defeated them decisively.

David was Israel's greatest king. He extended the kingdom into parts of modern Jordan, Lebanon, and Syria and conquered the Canaanite city of Jerusalem, which he made Israel's capital. David's son and successor, Solomon (r. 965–928 B.C.), was also a great king, a centralizer who moved from a loose kingship toward a tightly organized monarchy. His most famous accomplishment was the construction of the magnificent Temple in Jerusalem. The Temple priesthood and sacrifices became the focus of the national cult of Yahweh. Previously, that focus had been a humble, movable wooden chest known as the Ark of the Covenant.

Solomon's reign represented the high-water mark of the power of the Israelite monarchy. Under his successors the monarchy was split into a large northern kingdom of Israel with a capital at Samaria and a smaller southern kingdom of Judah° centered on Jerusalem (see Map 2.2). In 722 B.C., the Assyrians conquered the

**Judah** (JOO-duh)

kingdom of Israel and deported its inhabitants. Judah survived, first as a state controlled by Assyria and then as an independent power.

The religious history of the period of the two kingdoms (928–722 B.C.) and the Judean survivor-state (722–587 B.C.) is marked by an intense drive toward monotheism. The kings of Judah in the seventh century B.C., especially Hezekiah (r. 715–686 B.C.) and Josiah (r. 640–609 B.C.), aggressively attacked the worship of all gods other than Yahweh and all centers of Yahweh worship other than the Temple in Jerusalem. The kings also began the process of canonizing the Hebrew Bible. Ambitious and independent, Hezekiah joined in a revolt against Assyria that was brutally suppressed in 701 B.C. and almost cost him his kingdom.

The Judean kings could not have succeeded without the help of the prophets, who were prominent from approximately 900 to 500 B.C. Seers uttering divinely inspired predictions were universal figures in ancient religion. No other culture of antiquity, however, has anything like the Hebrew prophets: charismatic, uncompromising, terrible figures who announced God's anger and ultimate forgiveness. The prophets remind us of the most radical spiritual teachings of Israel: absolute monotheism, an insistence on righteousness, contempt for materialism and worldly power, love of the powerless. They often supported the kings but did not shrink from confronting authority and insisting on uncompromising justice. Among them were Amos, a humble shepherd who preached the superiority of righteousness to ritual; Jeremiah, who prophesied the destruction of Jerusalem as punishment for the people's idolatry; and Isaiah, who predicted the coming of a savior who would inaugurate a new day of universal peace and justice.

A characteristic story of the prophets is the confrontation between Elijah, perhaps the most famous prophet, and Ahab, king of Israel (r. 871–852 B.C.). Ahab coveted the vineyard of one Naboth, but Naboth refused Ahab's offer to buy it. Spurred on by his wife, Jezebel, Ahab trumped up charges against Naboth, who was unjustly stoned to death. Ahab then confiscated the vineyard. God sent Elijah to declare to Ahab that, as punishment for committing murder, "dogs will lick [Ahab's] blood"

**Map 2.2   Ancient Israel**   The Israelites settled in the Canaanite hill country west of the Jordan River and the Dead Sea after 1200 B.C. (*top map*). Control of Israelite territory after 928 B.C. was shared between two monarchies (*bottom map*): the kingdoms of Israel (conquered by the Assyrians in 722 B.C.) and Judah (conquered by the Babylonians in 598 B.C.).

and that of his family (1 Kings 21:19). In a remarkable scene, we witness not only Elijah's courage in confronting the king but also the king's surrender and repentance before Elijah's spiritual authority. Ahab (though not Jezebel) humbles himself and is spared, but his son and successor, King Ahaziah, who is equally wicked, is punished with a fatal injury. The Western tradition of civil disobedience owes much to the courage of the Hebrew prophets.

## Exile and Return, 598–ca. 400 B.C.

The prophets prepared the people of Judah for survival by correctly predicting ruin and exile and promising that divine providence would guarantee return. The tenacity of the Judeans in clinging to this message was remarkable. Indeed, it needed to be, for between 598 and 586 B.C. the Neo-Babylonians conquered Judah, destroying Jerusalem and the Temple. The cultural, political, and economic elite were deported to Babylon. Those who could, fled for Egypt. The dispirited remnant in Palestine shared their land with colonists from neighboring regions, with whom they intermarried and among whom their religion all but disappeared.

And that, given the usual fate of exiled and uprooted peoples in antiquity, should have been that. Yet not only did the Judeans in the Babylonian Captivity persevere in their religious loyalty; they actually returned to Palestine in large numbers.

The Neo-Babylonian rulers allowed Jewish deportees to continue to practice their religion. Jews* in Babylon were not slaves; rather they rented land on royal estates, and some became prosperous. Although some Babylonian Jews assimilated to local ways, many continued a Jewish religious life. Communal worship was observed in open places, perhaps with associated buildings. Some scholars argue that synagogues ("gatherings" in Greek), modest centers of prayer and study that have been the focus of Jewish worship ever since, first emerged in Babylon. It is also possible that the exiles put together the Torah in something like its current form. Elders led the community, while prophets continued to speak out: two examples are Ezekiel, who preached the restoration of the Temple, and the man known to us only as "Second Isaiah" (Isaiah 40–66). Second Isaiah emphasized the universal aspect of the god of Israel, who made empires rise and fall and would bring the exiles home from far-off Babylon.

The Temple in Jerusalem was rebuilt around 515 B.C., only seventy years after its destruction. This remarkable

**Israelite Seal**   This seal stone, which shows a roaring lion, was used by a man named Shema, an official of King Jeroboam of Israel. The stone was used to make an impression in hot wax, creating a seal on a document.   *(Reuben and Edith Hecht Collection, University of Haifa, Israel/Erich Lessing/Art Resource, NY)*

turn of events was possible partly because of the Persians, who conquered Babylon in 539 B.C. and proclaimed the freedom of the Jews to rebuild their Temple in Jerusalem. Still, Persian benevolence would not have been enough if the Judean elite had not kept the faith burning among the exiles.

Second Isaiah's message points to a second important development among the exiles of Judah. As striking as the return to Palestine was the survival of large numbers of Judeans as an unassimilated people outside of Judah—in other words, as Jews. For the first time, membership in a community of worship was divorced from residence. Jewish communities flourished in Babylon, Persia, and Egypt, but the members often chose not to become Babylonians, Persians, or Egyptians. From the sixth century B.C. on, a majority of Jews were living outside Palestine, and the Jewish Diaspora ("dispersion") became a permanent fact of history.

## The People of the Covenant

A rough equality among the people of Israel, limited government, and the rule of law under God were all fundamental Israelite political notions. Eventually, they would become fundamental political ideals for many in the West, and they would be applied not only to Israelites but to all people.

---

*Strictly speaking, the terms *Jew* and *Jewish* are anachronistic before the fifth century B.C.

According to Israelite belief, God made humans in his own image. Thus all individuals were equal in a fundamental sense; all were bound by God's law. A king who disobeyed this law was illegitimate. Indeed, Israel was ambivalent at best about the institution of kingship, which was tolerated as an evil made necessary only by the country's many armed enemies. God's covenant with the Hebrews was a religious contract with political consequences, rendering God the only true king of Israel. Far from being gods themselves or even God's representatives, Israel's kings were merely God's humble servants.

Israelite egalitarianism was restricted to men. Israelite women usually could not own or inherit property, as women could in Hammurabi's Babylon; or sue in court, as women could in pharaonic Egypt; or initiate a divorce, as women could in Classical Athens (see page 88). The powerful goddesses of other ancient cultures were absent in Israel. Women participated in the rituals of early Israelite religion and the original Temple (ca. 940–586 B.C.) but were segregated in a separate women's courtyard in the rebuilt Temple (ca. 515 B.C.–A.D. 79) and absent from Temple ritual. Indeed, the perspective of the Hebrew Bible is predominantly male. Consider just two examples. First, of the 1,426 names in the Hebrew Bible, 1,315 are male; only 111 women's names appear, about 9 percent of the total.[3] Second, only men and boys can bear the sign of the Lord's covenant with Israel—that is, circumcision.

Nevertheless, Israelite women enjoyed honor as mothers and partners in running the household. The Hebrew Bible states that woman (as exemplified by Eve, the first woman) was created as "a suitable partner" for man (Genesis 2:18, 20). Reproduction and hence motherhood assume great importance in the Hebrew Bible; the Lord enjoins humans to "be fruitful and multiply" (Genesis 1:28). The Bible also commands that children honor both their father and their mother: the two parents are equal in parental authority (Exodus 20:12).

The Hebrew Bible sometimes displays sympathy for and insights into the strategies that women used to counter the abuses of male power. Rebecca, for instance, thwarts her husband Isaac's plan to give his blessing to their son Esau. As the eldest, Esau was entitled to this honor, but Rebecca preferred her younger son Jacob, and she saw to it that he and not Esau obtained her husband's blessing.

Only about a half dozen women in the Hebrew Bible served as leaders of Israel, but that is more than in the literature of most other ancient cultures. Deborah (ca. 1125 B.C.), for example, a charismatic Israelite prophet, organizes an army that destroys the forces of a Canaanite commander. In a later book Esther, a Hebrew woman, becomes the wife of a Persian king whom the Bible calls Ahasuerus (probably Xerxes, r. 485–465 B.C.). Esther works ferociously at the Persian court to defeat a conspiracy to wipe out her people, and she saves them. The Book of Ruth (date uncertain) tells the story of a selfless and loyal woman, Ruth, who rescues her mother-in-law, Naomi, from ruin and poverty. The Bible celebrates Ruth as Naomi's "devoted daughter-in-law, who has proved better to you [Naomi] than seven sons." (See the box "Reading Sources: Ruth.")

Israelite culture prized women for their cunning, courage, and perseverance—qualities that allowed the people to survive. Military prowess was highly valued in men, but their inner qualities were appreciated as well. Schooled in defeat and exile, many Israelites came to the conclusion that "wisdom is better than weapons of war" (Ecclesiastes 9:18). Thus the Hebrew Bible stresses God's primary interest in goodness of soul: "The Lord does not see as man sees; men judge by appearances, but the Lord judges by the heart" (1 Samuel 16:7). The God of Israel prized righteousness above wealth, might, sacrifice, or ritual.

One might say that Israelite law reflected a similar tension between power and righteousness. On the one hand, just as the God of Israel was omnipotent and jealous, so the law of Israel was meant to be comprehensive and forceful. Capital punishment existed for murder, rape, incorrigible rebelliousness of a son against his parents, adultery by a married woman (both she and her lover were to be executed), a woman's loss of her virginity before marriage, and other offenses. Harsh punishment was mandated for Canaanite towns taken by siege: the entire population was to be killed so as not to corrupt Israel with their religious practices.

On the other hand, by taking intention into account, Israelite law echoed a note already present in Mesopotamia. The so-called Law of the Goring Ox, for instance, allowed a person to go unpunished for owning an ox that gores a person to death, unless the owner knew beforehand that the animal was dangerous. If the owner did know, however, the owner had to be put to death. Israelite law, moreover, demonstrated a belief in the sanctity of human life by prohibiting human sacrifice. An Israelite had to be ready in his or her heart (but *only* in his or her heart) to sacrifice his or her child to Yahweh, as Abraham was willing to sacrifice Isaac when Yahweh so commanded. After ascertaining Abraham's willingness to obey even to the point of sacrificing his son, Yahweh freed Isaac from the altar and supplied a ram as a substitute offering. Israelite monotheism thus rejected human sacrifice, as did the religions later derived from it.

## READING SOURCES    RUTH

*Some parts of the Hebrew Bible prohibit intermarriage. The Book of Ruth, however, praises marriage between Judean men and women from neighboring Moab (modern Jordan; see Map 2.2). This excerpt illustrates such unions, as it does the problem of food shortages, which were a special burden for widows.*

Once, in the time of the Judges when there was a famine in the land, a man [Elimelech] from Bethlehem in Judah went with his wife [Naomi] to live in Moabite territory. . . .

Elimelech died, and Naomi was left a widow with her two sons. The sons married Moabite women, one of whom was called Orpah and the other Ruth. [After ten years the sons died.] . . . Then Naomi, bereaved of her two sons as well as of her husband, got ready to return to her own country with her daughters-in-law, because she had heard in Moab that the LORD had shown his care for his people by giving them food. . . .

Naomi said to her daughters-in-law, "Go back, both of you, home to your own mothers. May the LORD keep faith with you, as you have kept faith with the dead and with me; and may he grant each of you the security of a home with a new husband." . . . Then Orpah kissed her mother-in-law and took her leave, but Ruth clung to her.

"Look," said Naomi, "your sister-in-law has gone back to her people and her God. Go, follow her." Ruth answered, "Do not urge me to go back and desert you. Where you go, I shall go, and where you stay, I shall stay. Your people will be my people, and your God my God. Where you die, I shall die, and there be buried. I solemnly declare before the LORD that nothing but death will part me from you." When Naomi saw that Ruth was determined to go with her, she said no more.

[They returned to Naomi's hometown, Bethlehem, in Judah.]

Naomi had a relative on her husband's side, a prominent and well-to-do . . . [man named] Boaz. One day Ruth the Moabite asked Naomi, "May I go to the harvest fields and glean [collect excess grain] behind anyone who will allow me?" "Yes, go my daughter," she replied. So Ruth went gleaning in the fields behind the reapers. [She met Boaz in his fields.] . . .

Boaz said to Ruth, "Listen, my daughter: do not go to glean in any other field. Do not look any farther, but stay close to my servant-girls. Watch where the men reap, and follow the gleaners; I have told the men not to molest you. Any time you are thirsty, go and drink from the jars they have filled." She bowed to the ground and said, "Why are you so kind as to take notice of me, when I am just a foreigner?" Boaz answered, "I have been told the whole story of what you have done for your mother-in-law since the death of your husband, how you left father and mother and homeland and came among a people you didn't know before. The LORD reward you for what you have done. . . ."

[Eventually, Boaz marries Ruth; their great-grandson would be Israel's greatest king, David.]

Source: Ruth 1:1, 3–6, 8–9, 14–18; 2:1–3, 8–12, in *The Oxford Study Bible: Revised English Bible with the Apocrypha.* © Oxford University Press and Cambridge University Press, 1989. Reprinted by permission of Cambridge University Press, Ltd., England.

## EARLY GREECE, TO CA. 725 B.C.

 THE Greeks founded the Western tradition in politics and philosophy. The ancient Greek genius was at its height in the era of the Greek city-states (ca. 700–300 B.C.), but it is already visible in the *Iliad°* and the *Odyssey°*, the epic poems of Homer (ca. 725 B.C.). Both are products of the first millennium B.C. Civilization, however, flourished in Greece a thousand years earlier, and Homer's works have roots in this earlier era. Most of what we know of this earlier period, called "Aegean° Greece" by scholars, is based on the discoveries of archaeologists. In particular, archaeology provides the evidence for the rise and fall of two monument-building, literate civilizations: the Minoans on the island of Crete and the Mycenaeans on the Greek mainland (see Map 2.3).

*Iliad* (IL-ee-ud)    *Odyssey* (ODD-uh-see)

**Aegean** (ih-JEE-un)

**"La Parisienne"** This masterpiece of Minoan art shows a priestess in a long robe, with her hair tied in a special knot. A fresco from Knossos, it was dubbed "the Parisian lady" because of its elegance. *(Historical Museum of Crete, Herakleion)*

## The Minoans and Early Greece, 3000–1375 B.C.

Europe's first civilization appeared in Greece, on the Aegean island of Crete° around 2000 B.C. From there, civilization spread to the Greek mainland.

Civilization came relatively late to Greece, but in comparison with Egypt and even western Asia, Greece is not a hospitable land. Mountainous, and watered by few rivers, it contains little cultivable farmland. Although pastureland and forest are more abundant, one-third of the country is entirely unproductive. Most of the farmland, moreover, is to be found in upland plains, which are divided by mountains, making it difficult to concentrate a large labor force to work the land efficiently. The south enjoys a mild Mediterranean climate but is quite dry. The north has a Balkan climate of hot summers and cold winters. The indented seacoast provides Greece with many harbors. Greece's geography influenced several recurring features of its history: contrasts between seafarers and mountaineers and between north and south, and the challenge of unifying so mountainous a terrain.

Agriculture preceded civilization in Greece. The first agricultural villages appeared shortly after 7000 B.C., bronze-making skills after 3000 B.C. After 3500 B.C. Greece became a supplier of raw materials for the new cities of western Asia. Both on the islands and the mainland, small towns appeared, sometimes fortified with stone walls, occasionally containing substantial stone and mud-brick structures. Between 3000 and 2400 B.C., people living on the Cycladic islands of the Aegean Sea produced exquisite marble sculptures and incised terracotta dishes.

Around 2000 B.C. civilization appeared on Crete. Its origins are hotly debated, but we know that it was literate because Cretan writing has survived. It consists of a syllabary, or system of simple syllables that form words, known as "Linear A." Although we know its language is not Greek, we do not know what it is. The island of Crete is located on the sea routes between the Greek mainland, Egypt, and Anatolia. The archaeological record contains many signs of trade and cultural contact between Cretans and nearby peoples, from one of whom, perhaps, the Minoans were descended. The evidence for Minoan civilization is concentrated in Crete's palaces—monumental structures that first appeared at various locations on the island around 2000 B.C. After destruction by earthquake, the palaces were rebuilt on an even grander scale, to flourish especially during the period from 1800 to 1550 B.C. Scholars call the palace-builders and their civilization "Minoan°," after King Minos of later Greek myth. He was supposed to have ruled a great sea empire from his palace at Knossos (see Map 2.3). What the Minoans called themselves remains a mystery.

The Minoan palaces were not merely royal residences but centers of administration, religion, politics, and economics. Minoan palace bureaucrats supervised a large sector of the economy, just as their counterparts

---

**Crete** (KREET)

**Minoan** (mih-NO-un)

did in Ugarit, Egypt, the Hittite kingdom, and other ancient societies. The largest Cretan palace, as well as the first to be excavated, Knossos offers a striking example of Minoan civilization. The main building at Knossos covers 3 acres, the associated structures an additional 2 acres. The palace was built around a large central court, 180 feet long by 82 feet wide, probably used for public ceremonies. A mazelike structure surrounded the court. The palace had enormous staterooms, residence quarters, storage rooms, artisans' workshops, and bathrooms, interconnected by corridors, ramps, and stairways. Light wells admitted daylight, and brightly colored frescoes decorated the walls. Cretan architects were aware of palace architecture elsewhere in the eastern Mediterranean and may have borrowed from it, but precisely who influenced whom remains an open question.

The palaces make clear that the Minoans exploited Crete's considerable natural wealth in agriculture and timber. Archaeological and linguistic evidence indicates a widespread Minoan trading network from the Levant to Sicily. A Minoan settlement flourished on the Aegean island of Thera, 70 miles north of Crete (see Map 2.3). This settlement was destroyed in 1626 (or possibly 1628) B.C. by one of the most violent volcanic eruptions in history. So huge a catastrophe produced climate changes for several years, evident in the pattern of tree rings in ancient wood. That is why scholars can offer so specific a date for Thera's eruption.

From the lack of fortifications around Cretan palaces and the small amount of arms and armor found in burial sites, it appears that the Minoans lived in relative peace. Minoan frescoes show that women as well as men played important roles in cult and ritual. The women portrayed by Cretan artists are often beautiful, bejeweled, and elegant, the men often graceful and athletic. We see, for example, acrobats practicing the sport of bull jumping. Landscapes and animals are frequently illustrated. A statuette of a priestess holding a snake in either hand depicts Minoan interest in the relationship between humans and the natural world. In short, Minoan civilization gives an impression of peace, prosperity, and happiness. No wonder we sense a somewhat lost-Eden quality about the violent and relatively sudden destruction of Minoan civilization. All of the palaces except Knossos were destroyed around 1550 B.C.; Knossos fell around 1375 B.C.

No shortage of theories has surfaced about the cause of the destruction, but the archaeological evidence strongly supports the notion of an invasion. But by whom? To find the answer, let us look to the Greek mainland.

**Palace of Knossos**   A paved ramp and (partially restored) portico are part of an entranceway to the palace. The tapered columns and combination of stone and timber are characteristic features of Minoan architecture.   *(Dmitrios Harissiadis/Benaki Museum)*

**Map 2.3    Aegean Greece**    The Minoan civilization (height: ca. 1800–1550 B.C.) and Mycenaean civilization (height: ca. 1400–1200 B.C.) flourished in turn in the Aegean region during the second millennium B.C. The center of Minoan civilization was the island of Crete. A mainland people, the Mycenaeans conquered Minoan Crete around 1550 B.C.

## The Mycenaeans, to ca. 1200 B.C.

A wave of destruction put an end to the Greek mainland's vigorous Copper Age (see page 10) around 2300 B.C. Centuries of relative poverty followed until, around 1700 B.C., signs of power and prosperity appear at a series of burial sites in central Greece and the Peloponnesus. The most dramatic are at Mycenae° (see Map 2.3), where the royal burials contain a treasure house of objects in gold and other precious metals. Many of the other cities in Greece that would later become famous, such as Athens and Thebes, were also thriving cities in this period.

The inhabitants of Mycenae, unlike the earlier inhabitants of the Greek peninsula, were Greek-speakers. They and the wider civilization they represent are called

Mycenaean°. Just when and how the Mycenaeans got to Greece are tangled questions. Some scholars imagine migration, others invasion. Some believe the Mycenaeans' ancestors arrived as early as 2300 B.C., whereas others think it was not until 1700 B.C., more than half a millennium later.

The Mycenaeans adopted and adapted technology, ideas, and art from their advanced neighbors in Crete, Egypt, Anatolia, and Syria-Palestine. The Mycenaeans traded with these neighbors. They also fought with them, for Mycenaean society was dominated by warrior-kings, raiders who exchanged booty to show off their wealth.

Around 1550 B.C. the mainland warriors achieved their greatest feat: the conquest of Crete. They destroyed most of the palaces but spared Knossos, which did not

**Mycenae** (my-SEE-nee)

**Mycenaean** (my-suh-NEE-un)

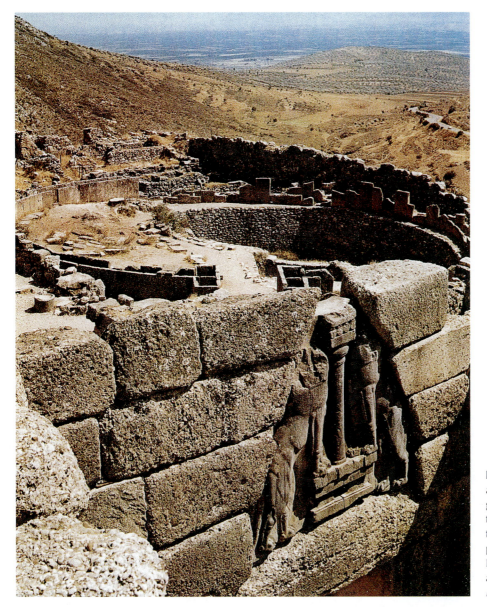

**Lion Gate at Mycenae**    Carved about 1250 B.C. above the main gate of the citadel's massive walls, the lions—flanking a column, their front paws resting on altars— probably represent royal authority. Inside the walls is Grave Circle B, a royal burial site.    *(Dmitrios Harissiadis/Benaki Museum)*

fall until about 1375 B.C. (we do not know the cause of that destruction). The warlike Mycenaeans had conquered the sophisticated Minoans. In turn, the Mycenaeans learned from their subjects and adopted a Minoan-style palace economy.

Mycenaean civilization was at its height between about 1400 and 1200 B.C. Kings lived in palaces whose storerooms were crammed with treasures. They traveled through their kingdoms on a network of good roads and could muster rowers and ships. Mycenaean artists excelled at potterymaking and fresco painting, gold inlay work and ivory carving. Mycenaean builders constructed palaces, fortifications, bridges, huge vaulted tombs, and sophisticated drainage works.

Palace officials supervised considerable economic activity, often in minute detail, including agriculture, pasturage, and artisanry. Women and children as well as men were included in the labor force. Our knowledge of the palace economy comes primarily from thousands of clay tablets inscribed by palace scribes around 1200 B.C. They are written in a script scholars call "Linear B," mostly an early form of Greek consisting of a combination of syllabary and ideograms (a system of symbols that stand for words or ideas).

Mycenaean merchants replaced Minoans in trade in the central and eastern Mediterranean. From Sicily to the Levant, they exported wine and scented oils and imported metals, ivory, and perhaps slaves. Mycenaean warriors engaged in activities ranging from raids and skirmishes to formal battles.

In the thirteenth century B.C., at the height of Mycenaean power, some unknown threat prompted the Mycenaean kings to fortify the palaces at Mycenae and elsewhere with stone walls. By 1200 B.C. most of the fortified sites had been destroyed. Afterward, only a few people continued to live in the old towns. It appears likely that Mycenaean Greece suffered from a combination of internal weakness and foreign invasion similar to that experienced by most of the eastern Mediterranean around 1250 to 1150 B.C., the era of the Sea Peoples (see page 34).

## Between Mycenae and the City-States, ca. 1100–725 B.C.

The era from the fall of Mycenae to the rise of the Greek city-states was long referred to as the Greek Dark Ages. But that gloomy term is used less often as archaeology increases our knowledge of the period from roughly 1100 to 800 B.C. The evidence does, however, suggest a considerable depopulation in Greece from the twelfth through the ninth century B.C. It seems that rich and poor alike were worse off than in Mycenaean times.

After the destruction of the palaces around 1200 B.C., Mycenaean culture continued to flicker before finally fading in the early eleventh century B.C. New peoples began to move into central and southern Greece around this time. They probably were the Dorians°, speakers of a Greek dialect who came from northern Greece. Their material culture was rougher and ruder than that of Mycenae's descendants; it boasts few distinctions besides the iron slashing sword and the long bronze fastener. The Dorians drove out or dominated the Mycenaean Greeks, turning much of central and southern Greece, including Crete, into Dorian centers. Among major settlements, only Athens maintained its independence. The city served as an asylum for Mycenaean refugees, many of whom migrated eastward around 1000 B.C. to the Aegean coast of Anatolia, which was destined to become an important center of Greek culture.

Greece from roughly 1100 to 800 B.C. was largely a poor and illiterate society of small towns and low-level agriculture and trade. Nevertheless, it produced notable painted pottery and preserved an oral tradition of poetry handed down from the Mycenaean era. After 800 B.C. a huge change came over Greece.

First of all, peace contributed to a sharp population rise, and the economy shifted from herding to farming, a more efficient source of food. Greek commerce, too, expanded, thanks in part to the impact of Phoenician traders.

Under pressure from rising population, Greeks founded colonies around the Mediterranean and the Black Sea beginning around 750 B.C. Meanwhile, trade and colonization inspired change at home. Dramatic new experiments in politics, warfare, and culture were attempted. It was the dawn of the era of the Greek city-state. We look at these changes in detail in Chapter 3. Here we focus on a milestone in literary artistry that heralded a new age: the epic poetry of Homer.

## Homer and History

Had ancient Greece produced a Bible, the *Iliad* and the *Odyssey* of Homer would have been its two Testaments. Only Hesiod°, a poet who lived around 700 B.C., had as much influence on later generations, but his poems (*Theogony* and *Works and Days*), though composed in the epic tradition, were shorter than Homer's and arguably less dramatic. But Greece did not have a Bible. Homer and Hesiod were poets, not priests. (As far as we know, the Greek world never had a priestly class comparable to that of Egypt or western Asia.) Although their poems inspired, moved, and educated the Greeks—a large part of a Greek boy's education consisted of learning to recite Homer from memory—they were not divine writ.

Homer was not a historian either. He was a bard, a professional singer of heroic poetry—of songs praising the deeds of the great. Heroic poetry consciously glorifies and magnifies the actions of its subjects.

Yet both archaeology and the evidence of inscriptions suggest that the story of the Trojan War is based on a kernel of truth. Troy really existed: it was a big, wealthy city, strategically located near the entrance to the Hellespont (or Dardanelles), the straits that lead toward the Black Sea. The king of Troy was attached politically to the Hittite empire, and his city had strong trading relations with the Mycenaean Greeks. The people of Troy probably spoke Luvian, a language related to Hittite. Troy was destroyed violently, possibly by Mycenaean warriors. Previously, around 1225 B.C. seemed the likeliest date for the destruction, but recent excavation argues for about 1200–1180 B.C.

---

**Dorians** (DOOR-ee-unz)

**Hesiod** (HEE-see-ud)

Most scholars today would date Homer to about 725 B.C. or later. Although Homer lived centuries after the end of Troy, he resided in an area whose culture had been affected by Troy and its neighbors. Homer lived in Ionia, a region of the central western coast of Anatolia, perhaps in the city of Smyrna. Homer was influenced by the earlier pre-Greek poets of Anatolia. A Luvian poem about Troy may have existed, and Homer could have drawn some of his material from it. In short, there might be more than a little history in Homer.

The author (or possibly authors) of the *Iliad* and the *Odyssey* worked in a continuous poetic tradition going back to the Mycenaean Age. Most scholars accept the theory that this tradition was oral, not written. Like oral poets elsewhere, Homer and his predecessors composed their poems as they sang them, making use of a stock of stories and formulaic expressions (such as the Greek equivalents of "swift-footed Achilles" and "grey-eyed goddess Athena"). In fact, Homer may have been illiterate.

Oral tradition gave Homer knowledge of a society that was long gone by his day. Although Homer's poems are studded with accurate details of Mycenaean palace life, the ideology of his characters generally reflects the beliefs of his own, post-Mycenaean society.

Both in Mycenaean times and in Homer's day, the Greeks were polytheists. The gods of Greece are similar in many ways to the gods of Sumer. They share the foibles and foolishness of humanity but are immortal and far more powerful than humans. The gods figure prominently in early Greek poetry, but they are less powerful than Yahweh, less immediate, and less interested in the inner life of men and women. Already emerging at the beginning of the Greek cultural tradition was the belief that became the hallmark of ancient Greece: that "man is the measure of all things," as the thinker Protagoras would declare in the fifth century B.C.

The Greek gods of the first millennium B.C. were worshiped in Mycenaean times—offerings to them are recorded on Linear B tablets. Because they were thought to live on Mount Olympus, a 9,500-foot-high peak in northern Greece (see Map 2.3), the gods were called the Olympians. Hesiod's *Theogony* tells the story of the Olympians' birth and their triumph over an older generation of deities. The "household" of the Olympians—the early Greek pantheon was conceived of as a noble's household—included Zeus°, a sky-god and the "father of gods and men," and his consort, Hera; Zeus's brother, Poseidon, god of the sea, earthquakes, and horses; Ares,

god of war; and Aphrodite, goddess of love. Also in the "household" were Zeus's children: Athena, goddess of wisdom and cunning; Hephaestus, god of craftsmen; Hermes, god of travelers and thieves; Apollo, god of disease and healing; and Artemis, goddess of the hunt, of maidens, and of childbirth.

Flawed and sometimes unpredictable, the Greek gods often seem childish, but the natural world they symbolized seemed equally inconstant to the ancients. The gods embody the values of a warrior society that put a premium on *aretê*°, or excellence, especially excellence in battle. The heroes in the *Iliad* and the *Odyssey* seek glory through military exploits. Homer's gods reward great warriors, but the gods insist on justice as well. Zeus punishes those who do evil—those who, for example, break oaths or give false judgments or violate the laws of hospitality. In the *Iliad*, the Trojan prince Paris sparks the Trojan War by abducting the beautiful Helen from her husband, the Greek king Menelaus, while he is a guest in Menelaus's household. In return, the Greeks attack Troy, a wealthy city in northwestern Anatolia. The gods destroy Troy as punishment for Paris's crime.

The *Iliad* and the *Odyssey* focus on the Trojan War and its aftermath. The *Iliad* is set in the tenth year of the conflict. The strain of fighting leads to a quarrel between Greek chieftains: Agamemnon, king of Mycenae and the leader of the expedition, and Achilles°, the greatest Greek warrior. The most prominent Trojans, King Priam and his eldest son, Hector, are less petty but will suffer the greater ruin. The *Odyssey* tells the story of the struggle of the Greek hero Odysseus° to return to Ithaca and to regain his kingship after a twenty-year absence, ten years in the war at Troy and ten years wandering homeward. It also focuses on the loyalty and ingenuity of Odysseus's wife, Penelope, who saves the household in her husband's absence, and the maturation of their son, Telemachus°, who helps his father regain his kingdom.

Homer puts as much emphasis on brains as on brawn; Odysseus, for example, is not just strong but also smart and cunning. And Homer's gods are no brutes; they believe in justice, hospitality, and respect for parents. Finally, although the Homeric poems focus on the upper classes—and primarily on men—the poems have a strain of sympathy for ordinary people and for women. Indeed, they show sympathy for failure. Homer's heroes court death and often obtain it. Unlike the psalmist of the Hebrew Bible, a Homeric hero walks alone "through the valley of the shadow of death" (Psalm 23:4); he has no

**Zeus** (ZOOS)

**aretê** (ah-reh-TAY)    **Achilles** (uh-KIL-eez)

**Odysseus** (oh-DIS-ee-us)    **Telemachus** (te-LEH-muh-kus) god to comfort or redeem him. He knows that the gods make human life hard and full of suffering. Human frailty, however, ennobles Homer's heroes.

Homer's princes are proud and jealous. In the *Iliad,* when Agamemnon is forced by divine command to return his "prize"—a girl captured in a raid—he demands in return the "prize" of Achilles, his greatest warrior—that is, Achilles' girl. Achilles' response is to sulk in his tent while the Trojans nearly defeat his fellow Greeks. In the *Odyssey,* a group of nobles lives off the absent Odysseus's estate, waiting to see which of them Odysseus's wife (and supposed widow) might marry. Odysseus's honor demands that he punish them by killing every last one. In both cases, Homer recognizes that the hero goes too far: Achilles' inaction leads to the death of his best friend, and ultimately to his own death; Odysseus's thirst for revenge leads to civil war.

## World of the Heroes

Homer focuses on the elite. Homeric warriors and their women hold aristocratic values and tend to look down on ordinary people. But society in Homer's day was more level and egalitarian. Except for a small number of traders and craft specialists who lived in towns, most people in the Greece of 725 B.C. lived in villages and hamlets. Most farmed or herded pigs, goats, or sheep, and most were free. The people of each community were called the *demos*°; the leading men, *basileis*°. *Basileis* means "kings," but it is more accurate to understand them as chiefs. No great difference of wealth existed between the basileis and ordinary free farmers.

Although the basileis took the lead in both government and war, the demos played a crucial role. Homer spotlights contests between aristocratic champions, but his vivid battle scenes also include large companies of ordinary men fighting in mass combat in close formation. And if the basileis dominated Homeric government, the demos had at least a small say.[4]

The basic instruments of government that would exist for centuries in Greece appear in the *Iliad* and the *Odyssey:* generals, orators, judges, a council, and an assembly. When making decisions about war and peace, a council of elder basileis consults an assembly of the warriors. In this arrangement we see a fundamental principle of Greek government: the political community should be composed of the warriors.

Let us turn now to the ideology of Homer's basileis, which would greatly influence later generations in antiq-uity. In the epics, the chiefs make friendships and exchange goods across international boundaries. Greek and Trojan chiefs kill each other on the battlefield but rarely hate each other. Indeed, some are bound by hereditary ties of guest-friendship and so decline to fight each other.

The main activity of Homer's basileis is warfare. The *Iliad* consists largely of a series of battlefield contests. Since women did not take part in battle, they are not presented as men's equals. Yet Homer rarely criticizes women in general, as some ancient Greek writers would in later centuries. Homer's women are weaker than men, but they are neither timid nor helpless. Penelope, for example, personifies female resourcefulness: by refusing to marry until she has finished weaving a shroud for Odysseus's elderly father, and then by unraveling every night what she has woven during the day, she puts the noble suitors off for years. She is as concerned with honor as any Homeric man. By refusing to accept an offer of marriage while Odysseus might still be alive, Penelope does honor to her own good name and to her husband's.

Homeric women play important roles in encouraging men or in bolstering men's courage by playing the foils to their doubts and dreads. In the *Iliad,* Hector overcomes his own fears of battle by hearing his wife, Andromache°, express *her* terror at the thought of his dying and leaving her a widow and their infant son an orphan. Moreover, by taking the burden of hearth and home on herself, Andromache allows Hector to define masculinity as making war.

Loyalty to the family played an important role in social relations. A person's obligations to kin included the duty to avenge crime or murder. Friendship, cemented by an exchange of gifts, was another important social institution. Even humble peasants prided themselves on hospitality.

Such values served Homeric society well. Although they would survive in later centuries, they would be challenged after 700 B.C. by the increasing emphasis on public life as the Greek city-state evolved.

## SUMMARY

THE first half of the first millennium B.C. witnessed dramatic developments among both the ancestors of the West and its founders. A new form of empire appeared. Multi-ethnic, far-flung, and claiming to be universal, such an empire would one

---

**demos** (DEE-mus)    **basileis** (bah-see-LAYS)        **Andromache** (an-DROM-eh-kee) day be brought into the Western tradition by Rome. The process began, however, among the West's ancestors in western Asia.

New military technology, the frank adoption of brutal and inhumane methods, and improvements in administration led to the creation of the Assyrian Empire, stretching from western Iran to Palestine and briefly even to Egypt. After short-lived hegemonies by Neo-Babylonians and Medes, the Persians established an empire that was larger, better organized, and more tolerant than the empire of the Assyrians. Heirs to Canaanite civilization of the second millennium B.C., the Phoenician city-states expanded across the Mediterranean Sea, less by military conquest than by trade and colonization.

The most important developments of the era, however, were not in commerce, weaponry, or imperialism but in new conceptions of the nature and meaning of human life. The Persians developed a new religion, Zoroastrianism, which emphasized ethics, dualism—that is, the conflict of good and evil with the eventual triumph of good—and redemption through a divine savior. The Israelites conquered Palestine and, even after losing it, held on to their identity by means of a tenacious belief in one god. They broke with tradition by insisting that their god was merciful and just. Omnipotent, God gave history meaning and direction. The purpose of life, in the Israelite view, was to serve God by acting righteously. The new religion laid the foundation for Judaism as well as Christianity and Islam. The Jews wrote down their religious and historical traditions in a book that, along with the Christian New Testament, proved to be the most influential single text in the history of the West: the Hebrew Bible.

We know little of the ideologies of the Minoan and Mycenaean civilizations of the second millennium B.C., but their economies and governments seem to have been similar to those of the other palace-run states of the eastern Mediterranean. Yet by the first millennium B.C., the Greeks, like the Persians and the Hebrews, had broken with tradition, but with a greater emphasis on the human than on the divine. Homer's epic poems, which took shape in approximately 725 B.C., focus on the fragile dignity of heroic human actions. Homer idealizes a society of aristocratic warriors seeking honor and glory. Although the Greek gods show favor to heroes, they display no transcendent interest in redeeming human souls. Men and women are doomed to die. Homer's legacy, therefore, was to glorify human heroism while recognizing the fleeting frailty of life. It was a legacy that raised as many questions as answers. In the middle centuries of the first millennium B.C., the Greeks would attempt to provide new solutions to Homer's problems. As we will see in the next chapter, their successes and failures in such diverse activities as politics and philosophy, war and art, literature and history, were the basis for much of Western civilization.

## ■ Notes

1. S. Insler, *The Gāthās of Zarathustra: Acta Iranica,* 8 (Leiden: E. J. Brill, 1975), p. 33.
2. Roland G. Kent, *Old Persian: Grammar, Texts, Lexicon* (New Haven, Conn.: American Oriental Society, 1950), p. 132.
3. Carol L. Meyers, "Everyday Life: Women in the Period of the Hebrew Bible," in *The Women's Bible Commentary,* ed. Carol A. Newsom and Sharon H. Ringe (Louisville, Ky.: Westminster/John Knox Press, 1992), p. 245.
4. Kurt A. Raaflaub, "Homer to Solon. The Rise of the *Polis:* The Written Sources," in *The Ancient Greek City-State: Symposium on the Occasion of the 250th Anniversary of the Royal Danish Academy of Science and Letters, July 1–4, 1992, Historisk-filosofiske Meddelelser* 67, The Royal Danish Academy of Sciences and Letters, ed. Mogens Herman Hansen (Copenhagen: Munksgaard, 1993), pp. 41–105.

## ■ Suggested Reading

Briant, Pierre. *From Cyrus to Alexander: The Persian Empire.* Translated by Peter T. Daniels. 2002. The fundamental introduction to the subject. Essential reading.

Dickinson, Oliver. *The Aegean Bronze Age.* 1994. Perhaps the best single introduction to a vast and fascinating subject.

Finley, M. I. *The World of Odysseus.* Rev. ed. 1978. A classic introduction to the Homeric poems; still good on society and ideology but out-of-date on historicity.

Markoe, Glenn. *Phoenicians.* 2000. An up-to-date introduction.

Oates, J. *Babylon.* Rev. ed. 1986. A well-illustrated survey, from the period of Sargon to the Hellenistic Greeks, with a section on Babylon's cultural legacy.

Saggs, H. W. F. *The Might That Was Assyria.* 1990. A readable introductory history celebrating the Assyrians' achievements.

Shanks, H., ed. *Ancient Israel: A Short History from Abraham to the Roman Destruction of the Temple.* 2d ed. 1999. Short, readable essays by scholars offering up-to-date introductions to the subject.

Wood, Michael. *In Search of the Trojan War.* 2d ed. 1998. A readable introduction to the new scholarship as of the mid-1990s.

**www.** **For a searchable list of additional readings for this chapter, go to college.hmco.com/students.**

# The Siege of Lachish

From the distance, it looks like one of the foothills that surround it. Up close, though, it can be clearly seen for what it is: Tel Lachish, the mound of the biblical city of Lachish. It is a link in the chain of evidence that tells one of the most remarkable stories in biblical history.*

Lachish was a great city, a royal fortress, and second only to Jerusalem in its importance to the kingdom of Judah (928–587 B.C.). In 701 B.C. the Assyrians under King Sennacherib (r. 704–681 B.C.) besieged Lachish and took it by force. The siege of Lachish is unique in early biblical history for the wealth of independent corroborating sources. In addition to reports in the Hebrew Bible are many Assyrian written documents. Furthermore, Sennacherib commemorated his victory by depicting the siege and recording the spoils in carved reliefs that he erected in his royal palace at Nineveh. Finally, the mound itself has been excavated, allowing a striking comparison of the archaeological and pictorial evidence of a siege in the biblical period.

Originally a Canaanite town, Lachish was fortified by the Israelite kings because of its strategic location. It sits southwest of Jerusalem in the Judean foothills, dominating the road between the Judean hills to the east and the Philistine coast to the west (see Map 2.2). By the reign of King Hezekiah of Judah (r. 715–686 B.C.), one of the most prominent kings of the House of David, Lachish was a large garrison city constructed on a monumental scale. It included inner and outer rings of thick walls, a massive gate complex, many houses and shops, and, in the center, a palace-fort surrounded by earthen ramps.

Having seen Assyria turn the kingdom of Israel into an occupied province, Hezekiah knew that he was facing the greatest power of the region. Nevertheless, he joined Egypt and the Philistine cities in a revolt soon after Sennacherib came to the throne in 704 B.C. Sennacherib responded by attacking the rebels in 701. The Hebrew Bible states: "In the fourteenth year of the reign of Hezekiah, Sennacherib king of Assyria attacked and took all the fortified cities of Judah" (2 Kings 18:13). We can read the results of the campaign in one of Sennacherib's inscriptions:

---

*In much of what follows about Lachish (LAH-kish), I rely on the discussion in David Ussishkin, *The Conquest of Lachish by Sennacherib* (Tel-Aviv: Tel-Aviv University, Institute of Archaeology, 1982).

"As to Hezekiah, the Jew, he did not submit to my yoke. I laid siege to 46 of his strong cities, walled forts and to the countless small villages in their vicinity, and conquered (them) by means of well-stamped (earth-) ramps, and battering-rams brought (thus) near (to the walls) (combined with) the attack by foot-soldiers, (using) mines, breeches as well as sapper work [that is, digging away foundations]." Hezekiah bowed to Assyrian power. He gave up territory (though not Jerusalem) and agreed to an increase in tribute, which now amounted to "30 talents of gold, 800 talents of silver, precious stones, antimony, large cuts of red stone, couches inlaid with ivory, elephant-hides, ebony-wood, boxwood and all kinds of valuable treasures, his own daughters, concubines, male and female musicians." So the Assyrian inscription records.

The Lachish reliefs (in Sennacherib's palace) offer a vivid picture of the attack on the city. Lachish was well fortified and well defended, but the Assyrians were experts in taking cities by storm. The reliefs show the camp of the attackers, Assyrian archers and slingers advancing on the city, battering rams and siege engines in action against the walls, flaming chariots thrown down by the defenders, and, after the city was taken, captives impaled on sharp stakes.

Look at the artist's reconstruction of an Assyrian assault on the city, based on the archaeological evidence. The soldiers are climbing a massive siege ramp that the Assyrians built against a "vulnerable" point in the city walls. The excavators of Lachish found the ramp, consisting of a level of stones cemented together over a core of boulders. It is the oldest siege ramp so far discovered in the ancient world. In and around the city the excavators found other evidence of the battle: hundreds of arrowheads, many sling stones, a number of pieces of bronze sheet mail used in armor, and what may be the crest of a helmet worn by one of the Assyrian spearmen shown attacking the city walls in the Lachish reliefs. Most dramatic, the excavators discovered about seven hundred skeletons, evidently civilians killed during the Assyrian attack and then buried in mass graves outside the city. Three of the individuals were trepanned—that is, they were operated on before death by removing a portion of their skulls. Perhaps this represents a last attempt, evidently futile, to save the lives of the wounded.

The Lachish reliefs also depict rows of captives and deportees marching toward Sennacherib on his throne.

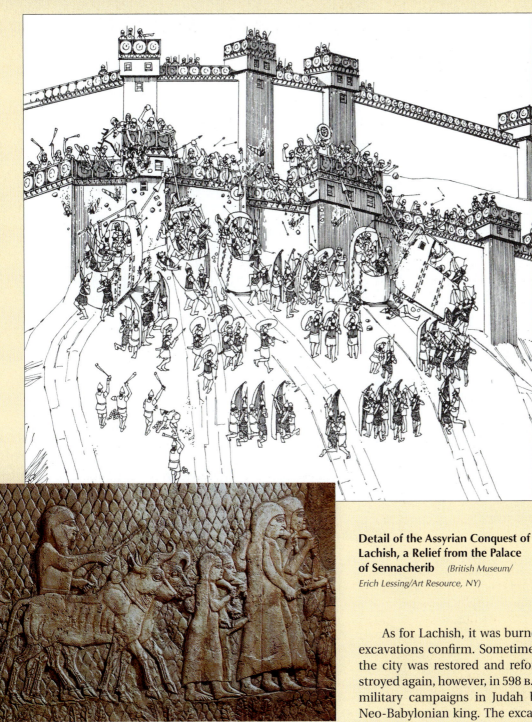

**Artist's Reconstruction of an Assyrian Assault on Lachish** *(Drawing by Gert le Grange, from David Ussishkin,* The Conquest of Lachish by Sennacherib *[Tel Aviv: Tel Aviv University, Institute of Archaeology, 1982], p. 123. Reproduced by permission.)*

**Detail of the Assyrian Conquest of Lachish, a Relief from the Palace of Sennacherib** *(British Museum/ Erich Lessing/Art Resource, NY)*

Look at this detail of the relief, showing a large Judean family leaving Lachish for exile. They are allowed to bring cattle with them, and a woman and child are permitted to ride on a wagon. The Assyrians claimed to have deported 200,150 people from Judah, of whom many men ended up as slave laborers working on Sennacherib's palace.

As for Lachish, it was burned to the ground, as the excavations confirm. Sometime in the seventh century the city was restored and refortified. Lachish was destroyed again, however, in 598 B.C., during the first of two military campaigns in Judah by Nebuchadrezzar, the Neo-Babylonian king. The excavators found a group of pottery sherds with ink inscriptions (called *ostraca*) in old Hebrew script, dating to just before that destruction. This unique set of documents in classical Hebrew writing consists of letters to a man named Yaush, the military governor of Lachish. They testify, among other things, to the worship of Yahweh, to the signal system linking the fortresses of Judah, and to the practices of the scribal profession. Once again, the city's misfortune has proved illuminating to students of the past.

# CHAPTER 3

# The Age of the Polis in Greece

## ca. 750–350 B.C.

IT is dawn. The light reveals a hillside in the city of Athens, a natural auditorium. Its rocky slopes, visible in the photograph opposite, would have been covered, beginning about 500 B.C., with wooden benches facing a platform cut into the rock. The six thousand men gathered there constitute a diverse group, ranging from farmers to philosophers, from dockyard workers to aristocrats. As they take their seats, these, the citizens of Athens, watch priests conducting prayers and offering a sacrifice. Then all eyes turn to the individual who mounts the platform—a herald. His booming voice asks the question that marks the start of business: "Who wishes to speak?" Someone rises to address the assembly. It is the first democracy in history—and the central laboratory in this great experiment in participation.

The assembly meeting recalls the defining features of what was, in its era, the characteristic political institution in much of Greece: the *polis* (plural, *poleis*). Usually translated as "city-state," the polis is better understood as "citizen-state." The polis was the product of communal activities—whether in the assembly, the military, or the theater—undertaken by its members: its citizens. Not every polis was a democracy, but every polis emphasized cooperative activities whose participants enjoyed at least a measure of equality. Every polis also sought a balance between the group and the individual, be that person the speaker, a military hero, or a freethinker.

Balance is a difficult state to achieve, however, and the equilibrium of the polis was frequently disturbed by tension and exclusion. Paradox marked the polis. Greek democracy failed to grant equal rights to women or immigrants, and it depended on slave labor. Relations among poleis were less often a matter of cooperation than of war. Although the Greeks created magnificent religious architecture, a portion of their intellectual elite came to the conclusion that the gods

Athenian Acropolis, with Pnyx Hill in foreground.
(Photo: Julia M. Fair)

were of little importance in explaining the universe. Whereas one leading polis, Sparta, was a paragon of militarism, obedience, and austerity, scorning the life of the mind, another, Athens, prided itself on freedom and cultural attainments. Yet the Greeks made the most even of such tensions, exploring them in literary genres—tragedy, comedy, history, and philosophy—that focused on the polis as a central theme. Creative tensions also marked Greek achievements in sculpture, painting, and architecture.

The era of the polis proved to be a defining moment in Western history. Although the Greeks of this era borrowed much from neighboring cultures, they were remarkably original. In the mid-first millennium B.C., the monotheistic religious heritage of the West first emerged among the Jews. During that same era, the Greeks founded the Western tradition in a broad range of culture, including politics; philosophy; literary genres such as comedy, tragedy, and history; and the visual and plastic arts of painting, sculpture, and architecture.

## QUESTIONS TO CONSIDER

- What was the Greek polis, and why was its development a defining moment in Western civilization?

- What was the nature of ancient Greek democracy?

- What were the differences between Athens and Sparta, and what did each contribute to the Western experiment?

- What were the limits of freedom and equality in the polis, and how did ancient Greek thinkers and writers explore those limits?

## TERMS TO KNOW

| | |
|---|---|
| polis | Pericles |
| Archaic Greece | Socrates |
| hoplite phalanx | Plato |
| Solon | Aristotle |
| Sappho | tragedy |
| Classical Greece | Herodotus |
| demokratia | Thucydides |

## SOCIETY AND POLITICS IN ARCHAIC GREECE, CA. 750–500 B.C.

HISTORIANS usually call the era in Greek history from roughly 750 to 500 B.C. the "Archaic period." In this context *archaic* refers to the style of sculpture in the two centuries before the "Classical period" (480–323 B.C.). Archaic Greece was a patchwork of hundreds of separate city-states, tribal leagues, and monarchies (see Map 3.1). Nevertheless, it displayed a distinctive style and outlook not only in art but also in politics, military arrangements, technology, economics, literature, and religion.

Although it was a period of paradox, the Archaic era laid the groundwork for much of lasting importance in Western civilization. Archaic Greece witnessed the simultaneous growth of individualism and a tight community spirit, the emergence of social cohesion despite a continual state of war, the coexistence of deep religious

piety and the West's first nontheistic philosophy. The Archaic period also saw the origin of characteristic Western types of governmental regimes—tyranny, oligarchy, and the first steps toward democracy—and of fundamental Western notions of citizenship and the rule of law.

### Agriculture, Trade, Colonization, and Warfare

An observer of ninth-century B.C. Greece would hardly have predicted greatness of that poor, illiterate society of small settlements and low-level trade. Yet, as we saw in the discussion of Homer in Chapter 2, everything began to change in Greece in the eighth century B.C. It was out of these changes that a new communal institution emerged: the polis°.

Change was a product of peace, which stimulated a sharp population rise. In response, the economy shifted

**polis** (PO-liss)

from herding to farming, a more efficient source of food. Seeking new agricultural land in the rocky Greek peninsula, farmers terraced hillsides and drained marshes. The typical agricultural unit was the family farm. Most farms were small and roughly equal in size, apparently a stimulus of social and political equality in Greece.

Greek commerce, too, was expanding. Shortly before 800 B.C., Greeks from the island of Euboea, perhaps following the example of Phoenician merchants and seafarers who had been casual traders in Greece for a century (see pages 44–45), established a trading post in Syria at Al-Mina on the mouth of the Orontes River, at the terminus of the chief caravan route from Mesopotamia (see Map 3.2). Shortly afterward, Euboeans established another trading post in the west, on an island in the Bay of Naples in Italy. In both east and west, Greek merchants sought iron and luxury goods. What they offered in return was probably silver, of which ancient Greece had rich deposits, and slaves.

From commerce it was but a short step to colonization in order to siphon off the extra mouths created by population growth. In colonization as in trade, the Greeks may have followed the example of the Phoenicians, who had begun establishing colonies probably in the ninth century B.C. Between about 750 and 500 B.C., the Greeks founded colonies throughout the Mediterranean and the Black Sea, planting nearly as many cities as already existed in Greece (see Map 3.2). Colonization in Italy and Sicily began in earnest around 750 B.C.; in the Chalcidice° in the northeast Aegean perhaps a generation later; in the Sea of Marmara about 680 B.C.; in North Africa around 630 B.C.; and in the Black Sea about 610 B.C. In the far west, Massalia (modern Marseilles) was established about 600 B.C. Southern Italy and Sicily, whose climate and landscape recalled the Aegean, were especially intense areas of Greek settlement, so much so that the Romans later called the region *Magna Graecia* ("Great Greece"). In the long run, Greek colonization proved to be of great importance for the spread of urban civilization westward, especially into Italy.

One important consequence of foreign contact was the introduction to Greece of the alphabet, borrowed from the Phoenicians. The first datable examples of the Greek alphabet were inscribed on pots in about 750 B.C. The alphabet spread rapidly and widely in the next century. Literacy underlay the achievements in poetry, philosophy, and the law that Archaic Greece has left behind. However, so few people at the time could read and write

| CHRONOLOGY | |
|---|---|
| ca. 750 B.C. | Greek colonization of Magna Graecia begins |
| ca. 725 B.C. | Sparta conquers Messenia |
| ca. 675 B.C. | Pheidon becomes tyrant of Argos |
| ca. 625 B.C. | Sappho active as poet |
| 594 B.C. | Solon is archon in Athens |
| ca. 560 B.C. | Pisistratus becomes tyrant of Athens |
| 508 B.C. | Cleisthenes begins reforms in Athens |
| 499 B.C. | Ionians revolt against Persia |
| 490 B.C. | Battle of Marathon |
| 480–479 B.C. | Persia invades Greece |
| 477 B.C. | Delian League founded |
| 460–429 B.C. | Pericles at peak of power |
| 458 B.C. | Aeschylus's *Oresteia* first performed in Athens |
| 431–404 B.C. | Peloponnesian War |
| 399 B.C. | Trial of Socrates |
| 395–386 B.C. | Corinthian War |
| 371 B.C. | Battle of Leuctra |

well that ancient Greek culture remained primarily an oral culture.

Another consequence of foreign contact was the introduction of new military technology, which the increase in wealth allowed the Greeks to adopt. Social changes, furthermore, fostered new tactics on the battlefield. The result was the hoplite phalanx°, a tightly ordered unit of heavily armed, pike-bearing infantrymen. The phalanx not only became the dominant military force in Archaic Greece, but, with relatively few changes in equipment and tactics, it remained supreme on land in Greece, western Asia, and other Mediterranean regions for centuries, until its defeat by a Roman army in 197 B.C.

---

Chalcidice (kal-SID-uh-see)

hoplite phalanx (HOP-lite FAY-lanks)

**Map 3.1   Archaic and Classical Greece**   The region of the Aegean Sea was the heartland of Greek civilization around 750 to 350 B.C. The mountainous terrain, rugged coastline, and numerous islands encouraged political fragmentation.

**Map 3.2    Phoenician and Greek Colonization**    Both the Phoenicians (beginning perhaps after 900 B.C.) and the Greeks (beginning around 750 B.C.) established numerous colonies on the coasts of the Mediterranean and Black Seas.

The phalanx emerged through a process of evolution rather than in a revolutionary leap. Before 800 B.C., single combat among the *basileis* (elite) appears to have decided battles. Around 800 to 750 B.C. armies began to include more men, fighting in close formation. Around 700 B.C. came new armaments. The result was the phalanx. The heavily armed infantryman (hoplite) of the fighting unit (phalanx) wore bronze armor on his shins and chest and a bronze helmet slit with a narrow opening for eyes and mouth. He carried a heavy wooden shield in his left hand. His weapons were a pike—a heavy, wooden, iron-tipped thrusting spear at least 9 feet long—and a short, iron stabbing sword.

The men of the phalanx were arranged in close ranks, normally four to eight deep. Soldiers stood together in line, each man's shield overlapping his neighbor's. Hoplite combat involved set battles—head-to-head, army-against-army, all-or-nothing affairs—rather than individual skirmishes or guerrilla raids. Too unwieldy for Greece's mountains, the phalanx fought only in the plains. Battle usually consisted of an initial charge, followed by a grueling contest. The men in the front line pounded the enemy with their pikes, while the men in the rear pushed forward. Finally, one side would give way and run. The victors stayed and erected a trophy.

Greek hoplite warfare rested on deep societal roots. Only independent men of means could afford hoplite armor. Thanks to the spread of the family farm, such men were common in Greece by around 700 B.C. Hoplites were amateur soldiers. Most were full-time farmers outside the fighting season, which lasted only for the summer months. The notion of the farmer-soldier, independent and free, would have a lasting impact on Western political thought. So would the warrior values of what became a way of life in Greece.

*Aretê°*, now translated as "excellence" or "virtue" but originally meaning "warrior prowess," was a central concept for the Greeks. In Homer a warrior fought mainly for personal and familial honor (see page 63). By around 650 B.C. aretê referred also to the community. According to the poet Tyrtaeus (ca. 650 B.C.), the ideal soldier not only fights bravely but "heartens his neighbor by his words."

---

**aretê** (ah-reh-TAY)

**Hoplites**    A detail from a Corinthian vase of 625 to 600 B.C. shows pike-wielding hoplites closed in battle over a fallen comrade. In this image as elsewhere, Greek artists rendered warriors seminude and fighting in small groups, but in reality hoplites went into battle wearing heavy armor and fought in large units.    *(Louvre © R.M.N./Art Resource, NY)*

Should he die, his death brings glory not only to his father but also to his city and his countrymen. Although the battlefield remained the favored arena for displays of aretê, the assembly or the council house became increasingly acceptable as an alternative.

Greek women did not serve as soldiers, but they were expected to encourage their men to fight and die for the city. Women were praised for bearing and raising sons to serve as future soldiers.

## Emergence of the Polis

Paradoxes abound in the origins of the polis. The polis was both a product of the changes of the eighth century B.C.

and a stimulus for change. As an urban settlement, the polis existed as early as the ninth or even the tenth century B.C., but its intense communal spirit did not emerge until around 700 B.C. In agriculture, the most important single profession, the prevalence of the family farm created a kind of rough social equality, which was reflected in a cultural emphasis on equality. Yet the polis was marked by social inequality as some grew rich on the profits of trade.

*Polis* came to denote not just a city but the community as a whole, corresponding roughly to a country or nation. One crude gauge of the centrality of the polis is the number, not to mention the significance, of words the Greeks derived from it: among them, *polites* (citizen), *politeia* (constitution), *politeô* (to govern), *ta politika* (politics), and *politikos* (politician).

Most poleis° were small, many less than 100 square miles in size. Athens was one of the largest. Its territory, known as Attica (see Map 3.3), covered 1,000 square miles (approximately the size of Rhode Island). At its height (ca. 430 B.C.) the population of Athens was about 400,000, but a typical polis contained only between 5,000 and 10,000 people. The philosopher Aristotle° (384–322 B.C.) wrote that an ideal polis should be small enough that the citizens know one another personally.

The polis consisted of two parts: the urban area, which usually was tiny, and the surrounding countryside, where most people lived. From the earliest times, the urban public space included both a defensible hill (preferably with a water supply), called a "high city" (*acropolis*°), and a "gathering place" (*agora*°), used as a marketplace and meeting place. At least one temple usually served as a focal point. After around 500 B.C. stone buildings, including council houses, theaters, covered porticoes, gymnasia, and baths, became increasingly common.

What distinguished the early polis, however, was not its buildings but its spirit. As the poet Alcaeus (b. ca. 630 B.C.) puts it, "Not houses finely roofed or the stones of walls well-built, nay nor canals and dockyards, make the polis, but men able to use their opportunity."

The Greeks came to call the polis a "common thing" (*koinon*). It was a shared commonwealth. It belonged to its people, not to a few nobles or to a king or a god. As early as about 700 B.C., important public documents were inscribed in stone. Acts of state were attributed not to a personified polis but to the community—for example, not to Thera but to "the Thereans," not to Sybaris but to "the Sybarites." The emphasis is on the plurality.

The emphasis was on equality as well. The early polis developed an ethos of measure and moderation. The ideal citizen was thought to be neither rich nor poor but of moderate means. Women were generally not considered citizens and were excluded from taking part in politics. Yet women's behavior was considered important to the polis. Laws against extravagant jewelry or unrestrained mourning (mourning the dead was considered women's work), for example, were put into place in some poleis.

In theory, all citizens were supposed to be roughly similar, but this was not always true in practice, as the politics of the early polis makes clear.

## Tyranny

Trade and colonization inspired change at home, for one thing, making increasing numbers of Greeks into seafarers. This was a critical development, for as the historian Thucydides° (ca. 455–397 B.C.) argues, a sea power tends to be more dynamic and innovative than a land power. Seafarers are likely to come into contact with new ideas and institutions. In antiquity, ships moved more quickly and cheaply than land transport; thus seafaring usually accelerated the rate of change.

One such change was Greece's growing wealth. To some extent, this wealth was general. The poet Hesiod (ca. 700 B.C.), for example, records the increasing size and prosperity of the class of free farmers. Some individuals, however, grew far wealthier than others. Yet many of these newly rich lacked the status of the *basileis,* the elite of landowning families who monopolized political power and honor. In order to claim a share, the newly rich seem to have made common cause with the independent farmers who staffed the hoplite phalanx. The result was tyranny.

*Tyrant,* a term borrowed from the East, possibly from Lydia (a wealthy kingdom in Anatolia), originally referred not to an arbitrary and oppressive ruler but rather to a champion of the people. Having overthrown a narrow and entrenched aristocracy, tyrants were popular at first. *Tyrant* did not become a pejorative word before roughly 550 B.C., when the people soured on the second and third generation of tyrants.

Greek tyranny began in Argos, a polis in the northeastern Peloponnesus°, around 675 B.C. (see Map 3.1). The first tyrant was an Argive named Pheidon. By 660 B.C. tyranny had spread to nearby Corinth. Over the course of the seventh and sixth centuries B.C., all the major Greek poleis except Sparta became tyrannies.

Sources of evidence for the first tyrannies are poor, and much about the tyrants is debated by scholars. Yet it does seem that in the seventh century B.C., wealthy men who had been denied political power rose on the shoulders of the hoplites and overthrew a narrow elite. They set up one-man rule, not in the name of the basileis, but on behalf of a much broader group: the prosperous farmers who fought in the phalanx.

Much of what the tyrants did, especially in the first generation, was popular and progressive. They stimulated the economy by founding colonies on trade routes,

---

poleis (PO-lays)   Aristotle (AR-is-tot-il)
acropolis (uh-CROP-uh-liss)   agora (AH-go-rah)

Thucydides (thoo-SID-uh-deez)
Peloponnesus (pel-uh-puh-NEE-suss)

standardizing weights and measures, and encouraging the immigration of skilled craftsmen from other poleis. Corinth under the tyrant Cypselus (r. ca. 657–625 B.C.), for example, became the wealthiest city in Greece by exporting agricultural produce. Tyrants built temples and instituted festivals, providing both jobs and leisure-time activities.

When tyrants passed power on to their sons, however, the second generation tended to rule oppressively. Buoyed by the discontent of the demos, the basileis regrouped and tried to take back power. Thrasybulus of Miletus (ca. 600 B.C.), one second-generation tyrant, advised accordingly: to maintain power, a tyrant should "lop off the tallest ears of grain"—that is, execute or exile aristocrats in order to deny leaders to the opposition. But the tide of discontent was not to be stopped. Few tyrannies lasted beyond the third generation, when they were overthrown and replaced by oligarchy (literally, "rule by the few") or, less often, by democracy (literally, "power of the people"). By 500 B.C. tyranny had disappeared from most of Greece.

## Sparta

Located in Laconia, a fertile valley in the south-central Peloponnesus, in the southern part of mainland Greece, Sparta seemed destined by geography for prosperity but not for glory. It was positioned not at a crossroads or beside a great harbor but rather by rugged mountains that might have left it isolated (see Map 3.1). Yet Sparta proved to be a powerful model of citizenship and constitutionalism, virtue and community, austerity and militarism.

The history of Sparta is not easy to write. Sparta was a closed military society, contemptuous of book learning, suspicious of foreigners, and secretive toward the outside world. Scholarship has lifted the veil a little, however. For example, Spartans believed that their unique system had been created at a stroke by the legendary lawgiver Lycurgus, who is supposed to have lived (according to the most common version) in the eighth century B.C. and whose charter for Sparta was a divine command. Nowadays, scholars argue for gradual innovations in Sparta rather than revolutionary change, for a process beginning around 650 B.C. and continuing for generations. And it is by no means clear that there ever was a Lycurgus. Let us consider the question of origins.

The foundations of Spartan society were laid around 650 B.C., when a three-part class system emerged. Helots°,

unfree laborers who worked the land for their masters, were at the lowest level. In the middle ranks were *perioikoi* (roughly, "neighbors"), who were free but under the thumb of the highest class. At the top stood Similars, who were the only full citizens. We do not know the number of helots, but we do know that they vastly outnumbered the other two classes.

Compared with individuals of the other classes, a Similar had a good life. If male and over age 30, he had the right to attend the assembly and to hold public office. Each male Similar, moreover, was given a basic allotment of land worked by helots, which freed him to fight. As the name implies, Similars were alike but not equal. Wealthy Similars owned more land than the basic allotment.

Although Sparta is remembered as a conservative society, the idea of a large group of men sharing power was radical in its day. When the system began around 650 B.C., Similars numbered about nine thousand. What gave them their clout and prestige? The Similars were probably hoplites, the backbone of Sparta's army.

In the mid-seventh century B.C., Sparta was even more dependent on its army than was the average polis; the reason is the helots. Most helots were Messenians, whose fertile territory had been conquered by Sparta in about 725 B.C. Although the Messenians were Greeks, they were forced to work for the conquerors. Sparta profited, but it now faced a security problem. The restive Messenian helots had to be policed, and a dramatic revolt sometime between 675 and 650 B.C. almost succeeded in expelling the Spartans. To keep Messenia, Sparta needed a crack army; to get that, it needed to train, support, and glorify its soldiers. The political and economic result was to make all Spartan hoplites into Similars.

Sparta was no democracy, however. The ancients classified the Spartan government as "mixed" because it distributed power among the Similars through a combination of monarchy, oligarchy (that is, rule by an elite few), and popular government. The assembly of Similars was the popular element in the regime, but its powers were limited. Real power was shared among those Similars who were kings, elders, and *ephors* (overseers), men generally belonging to a few wealthy families.

The elite did not lead lives of luxury, however, at least not after around 550 B.C., when austerity became the order of the day. Society was reordered to promote the discipline needed to keep control of the helots. For example, Spartans' diet was famous for its simplicity. The preferred food was a black broth of pork cooked in its own blood and spiced with salt and vinegar. To dis-

---

**helot** (HEL-ut)

courage consumption, Sparta issued no coins; the official "currency" consisted of heavy and clumsy iron skewers. Since the outside world was considered corrupt, Sparta engaged in little trade and admitted few foreigners to its territory—and those who were admitted were subject to periodic expulsion.

Whereas other poleis offered little or no formal public education, Sparta schooled its sons from childhood to be soldiers—a system known as the *agoge*° ("upbringing"). Limited to male Similars, the agoge created a life cycle unique in Greece. At birth babies were examined by public inspectors. Those who were considered deformed or unfit were "exposed"—that is, they were abandoned without food or shelter. The victims might die, but they might also be sold into slavery or even secretly adopted. (Other Greeks also practiced exposure of infants, but the choice was a family matter, not public policy.) Surviving children were raised at home up to the age of 7, at which point boys left the family to be boarded with a "herd" of their age mates. For the eleven years from age 7 to age 18, a boy went through rigorous training. On the theory that good soldiers should be strong and silent, boys learned only enough reading and writing for practical ends—for example, to transmit messages to and from military headquarters.

Many boys between the ages of 18 and 20 served in the *krypteia* (secret service), living secretly in the hills of Messenia, where they survived by hunting, foraging, and stealing. They spied on the ever rebellious Messenian helots, whom they could kill freely because every year Sparta declared war on helots. By age 20 all Similars had become hoplites, and they continued to serve in the army until age 60. Supported by helot labor, they devoted all their time to fighting and training the next generation.

Ironically, Sparta offered more opportunities outside the home to elite women than did other Greek states. For example, unlike most Greek girls, Spartan girls received a public education—limited, however, to physical training, which was thought to strengthen females for childbearing. Still, the sight of girls running, wrestling, and throwing the discus and javelin, which was common in Sparta, was unthinkable elsewhere in Greece. So was Sparta's unique recognition of the risks of maternity. Like Spartan men who died in battle, Spartan women who died in childbirth were allowed to have their names inscribed on their tombstones. All other Spartan burials were anonymous.

Spartan women were relatively more independent than women elsewhere in Greece. With the men con-

**Spartan Woman**    This bronze statuette (4¾ inches tall) from Laconia (CA. 530 B.C.) shows a woman running. Unlike other Greek women, elite Spartan women underwent physical education. Although their personal freedom was limited, women in Sparta suffered fewer restrictions than their counterparts in democratic Athens.    *(National Archaelogical Museum, Athens/Archaeological Receipts Fund)*

sumed by military training or warfare, women ran the day-to-day operations of life, controlling the helot farm-workers and servants, and raising the girls and the very small boys. Women married around age 20, men around 30. Newlyweds were supposed to spend only enough time together to produce offspring. Often left on their own without a husband's interference, and having been schooled in assertiveness by youthful physical training outdoors, Spartan women also had the advantage of being able to inherit property, unlike Athenian women. (See the box "Reading Sources: Spartan Women.")

Beginning around 550 B.C., Sparta used its military might to build up a network of alliances (dubbed the "Peloponnesian° League" by scholars) in the Peloponnesus and central Greece. It may seem paradoxical that a

---

**agoge** (ah-go-GAY)

**Peloponnesian** (pell-uh-puh-NEE-shun)

## READING SOURCES    SPARTAN WOMEN

*Spartan women were famous in antiquity for their remarkable freedom, but male observers differed as to whether the results were good or bad. In the following excerpts, Aristotle (384–322 B.C.) criticizes Spartan women, whereas Plutarch (ca. A.D. 50–120), a Greek scholar living in the Roman Empire, praises them.*

### Aristotle Complains

. . . The legislator [Lycurgus] wished the city as a whole to be hardy, and this is manifest in terms of the men; but he thoroughly neglected it in the case of the women, who live licentiously in every respect and in luxury. Wealth will necessarily be honored in a regime of this sort, particularly if they are dominated by women, as is the case of most stocks that are fond of soldiering and war. . . . This was the case with the Spartans, and many matters were administered by the women during the period of their [imperial] rule [405–371 B.C.]. And yet what difference is there between women ruling and rulers who are ruled by women? For the result is the same. . . .

Now this laxness concerning women appears to have arisen among the Spartans in a way that is quite reasonable. They spent much time away from their own land when they were at war. . . . As for the women, they say Lycurgus attempted to lead them toward the laws, but they were resistant, and he gave it up. . . . That what is connected with the women is not finely handled would seem not only to create an inappropriateness in the regime in its own terms, as was said earlier, but to contribute to their greed. For next to what has just been said, one must censure what pertains to the disparity in possessions. For it has happened that some of them possess too much property, and others very little; hence the territory has come into the hands of a few. . . . Indeed, nearly two-fifths of the entire territory belongs to women, both because many have become heiresses and because large dowries are given.

### Plutarch Counters

Aristotle claims wrongly that he [Lycurgus] tried to discipline the women but gave up when he could not control the considerable degree of license and power attained by women because of their husbands' frequent campaigning. . . . Lycurgus rather showed all possible concern for . . . [women] too. First he toughened the girls physically by making them run and wrestle and throw the discus and javelin. Thereby their children in embryo would make a strong start in strong bodies and would develop better, while the women themselves would also bear their pregnancies with vigour and would meet the challenge of childbirth in a successful, relaxed way. He did away with prudery, sheltered upbringing and effeminacy of any kind. He made young girls no less than young men grow used to walking nude in processions, as well as to dancing and singing at certain festivals with the young men present and looking on. . . .

There was nothing disreputable about the girls' nudity. It was altogether modest, and there was no hint of immorality. Instead it encouraged simple habits and an enthusiasm for physical fitness, as well as giving the female sex a taste of masculine gallantry, since it too was granted equal participation in both excellence and ambition.

---

Sources: Aristotle, *The Politics,* trans. Carnes Lord. Reprinted by permission of the publisher, The University of Chicago Press; Plutarch, "Life of Lycurgus," in *Plutarch on Sparta,* trans. Richard J. A. Talbert (Harmondsworth, England: Penguin, 1988), p. 24. Translation copyright © Richard J. A. Talbert. Reproduced by permission of Penguin Books Ltd.

 **For additional information on this topic, go to college.hmco.com/students.**

---

society that feared foreigners, as Sparta did, became the *hegemon*° (literally, "leader") of an extensive alliance system, but Sparta's fear made its leadership slow and careful. Sparta intervened in the wider world only to prevent threats from arising on the horizon, and usually only after a great deal of debate and with the utmost caution.

By around 500 B.C. all of the Peloponnesian poleis except Argos had alliances with Sparta, and in central Greece Thebes came aboard shortly thereafter. Allies swore "to follow Sparta wherever it may lead and to have

---

**hegemon** (HEJ-uh-mahn)

**Map 3.3    Attica**    Mountains and plains alternate in the 1,000-square-mile area of ancient Attica. The Long Walls connecting Athens with the port city of Piraeus were built around 450 B.C.

the same friends and enemies." Until its breakup in the aftermath of the Peloponnesian War (431–404 B.C.; see page 91), the Peloponnesian League was the dominant land power in Greece and, after the defeat of Persia in 480 B.C., in the entire eastern Mediterranean.

Sparta exemplified community spirit and respect for law. The people of Sparta, as the historian Herodotus° (ca. 485–425 B.C.) quotes a Spartan king, "are free . . . , but not entirely free; for they have a master, and that master is Law, which they fear." Sparta was also an exemplar of equality—limited equality, to be sure, but equality extended to a wider group than ever before in Greece. The notion of the Similars, moreover, contains the germ of the idea of the citizen: a free member of the political community who, unlike a subject, has rights as well as duties. Few other poleis could match the stability and sense of civic duty fostered by Sparta. In the realms of equality and citizenship, however, Sparta was eventually outstripped by Athens. In the realm of liberty, Athens wrote a new chapter in Western history.

## Early Athens

Around 650 B.C. the basileis of the Pedion, or Attic, Plain (see Map 3.3), who proudly called themselves the Eupatrids° ("well-fathered men"), ruled Athens. They served in one-year magistracies and afterward became life members of the Areopagus°, a council of elders named

---

**Herodotus** (he-ROD-uh-tus)

**Eupatrid** (YOO-pat-rid)    **Areopagus** (ar-ee-OP-uh-gus)

for its meeting place on the "hill of Ares." By its prestige, this aristocratic council held the lion's share of power, both in politics and in justice, for it also served as a court. The demos° (the people) met in an assembly. Probably from early times on, the assembly had, in theory, supreme lawmaking power as well as authority over war and peace, but voting was by shouting, and few people challenged Eupatrid wishes.

By 632 B.C. the aristocrats faced trouble in Athens as elsewhere because of corruption, economic change, and assertive hoplites. A failed attempt that year to establish a tyranny left the forces for change eager. In 621 B.C. a loose coalition opposed to Eupatrid rule forced a codification of the laws, which were then issued in writing. This Code of Draco°, named for its main drafter, was infamous for its harsh provisions (hence the adjective *draconian*); it was written, a later commentator suggested, "not in ink but blood." Yet Draco's Code seems only to have whetted an appetite for change. A wealthy non-Eupatrid elite of hoplites was emerging, grown rich exporting olive oil. Some were merchants; most were prosperous farmers. They now wanted political power. As for ordinary Athenians, they typically worked small family farms. Over the years, bad harvests and soil exhaustion had sent many into debt. Those who had pledged their land as collateral became known as *hektemoroi* ("sixth-parters"), probably because they owed one-sixth of their crops to their creditors. Other farmers sank even further into debt and had only themselves or their children as collateral. Some ended up as slaves, sometimes sold abroad. Because both rich and poor Athenians had grievances against the Eupatrids, revolution was in the air.

Enter Solon° (ca. 630–560 B.C.), who was appointed to the emergency position of sole *archon* (chief officer) for one year, probably 594 B.C. A Eupatrid who had become a merchant, Solon understood both the old and the new elite, and he was sympathetic to ordinary Athenians as well. As his surviving writings show, Solon was a moderate. He could have become tyrant, but he preferred to be a mediator; as such, he said, he "stood with a strong shield before both parties [the common people and the powerful] and allowed neither one to win an unfair victory."[1]

Solon's reforms were comprehensive, spanning both economics and politics. He helped ordinary people by the "shaking off of burdens," measures that abolished the institution of *hektemorage* and probably canceled some debts. He also abolished the practice of making loans on personal surety and set up a fund to redeem Athenians who had been sold into slavery abroad. By freeing the hektemoroi, Solon ensured Athens a large class of independent small farmers.

Solon's other economic reforms were aimed at encouraging Athenian trade. To foster the production of olive oil, a cash crop, he restricted all other agricultural exports. He changed Athenian weights, measures, and perhaps coins to conform to the most common Greek standard. The result was a commercial boom.

Solon made fundamental changes in Athenian government, too. He changed qualifications for office from birth to wealth, a boon to the non-Eupatrid elite. He established four census classes based on agricultural production. Most offices were reserved for men of property, but the poorest class, known as *thetes,* could participate in the assembly and courts. Solon probably established the Council of 400, which prepared the assembly's agenda. He is probably also responsible for regularizing council and assembly meetings and replacing the assembly's voice votes with the counting of hands.

Solon's moderation, respect for law, and liberation of the poor and downtrodden are milestones in Greek history. Yet Solon's reforms had an unexpected byproduct: the growth of slavery in Athens. Though booming, the Athenian economy lost its cheap labor when Solon freed debt slaves and hektemoroi. The solution was to buy slaves abroad and import them to Athens. At the time, the island city-state of Chios was the center of the slave trade in Greece (see Map 3.1). After Solon, Athens along with Chios developed one of history's first large-scale slave systems. Slaves worked in agriculture, crafts, trade, and elsewhere in the economy. Unlike helots, slaves could be bought and sold and were often uprooted, and the system was better policed than in earlier societies.

In the centuries after Solon, slavery grew widespread in Athens. Some slaves served in agriculture, some labored under miserable conditions in Athenian silver mines, and some were engaged in commerce or the military (where some rowers were slaves). Most, however, worked as domestics or in small workshops as, for example, metalworkers or furniture makers. The vast majority of slaves were non-Greek. Most were prisoners of war; some were victims of pirates or debtors from states where, unlike Athens, citizens might end up in debt slavery. Thrace (roughly, modern Bulgaria) and Anatolia were the main sources of slaves, but some slaves came from North Africa and other Mediterranean regions.

Living conditions for slaves were usually poor and those in the silver mines abysmal. Emancipation, how-

---

**demos** (DEE-mus)   **Draco** (DRAY-co)   **Solon** (SO-lun)

**Myth or Memory?**    The Monster of Troy vase pits Heracles and Hesione against a legendary monster whose skull (*upper right*) has recently been identified as a fossil giraffe. The scene, therefore, illustrates how the ancient Greeks used myth to recall prehistory.
*(Helen and Alice Colburn Fund, 63.420. Courtesy, Museum of Fine Arts, Boston)*

ever, was more common in Athens than in the American South before 1865. A few ex-slaves even rose to positions of wealth and power in Athens. A striking and unusual case is that of Pasion (d. 370 B.C.). Originally a slave employee of a banking firm, he bought his freedom and became the wealthiest Athenian banker of his day, as well as an Athenian citizen.

If free Athenians had any moral doubts about slavery, they went unrecorded. Yet there was much dissatisfaction with Solon's reforms, since his middle way satisfied neither Eupatrids nor champions of the free poor. After years of conflict, around 560 B.C. advocates of radical reform established a tyranny under Pisistratus° (ca. 600–528 B.C.). He and his sons held power for forty of the next fifty years.

Supported by the thetes, the Pisistratids exiled many Eupatrids and confiscated and redistributed their land. Pisistratus kept the façade of Solon's reforms while ensuring that loyal supporters held all key offices.

A stable regime, the tyranny witnessed prosperity at home and the expansion of Athenian influence abroad. Yet Pisistratus's dynasty lasted only two generations. A steadfast opponent of tyrants, Sparta deposed his son,

Hippias, in 510 B.C. Athens's elites by birth and wealth were ready to establish an oligarchy, but the way was open for an unexpected development: the emergence of popular government.

## THE CULTURE OF ARCHAIC GREECE

WHILE one trend in Archaic culture was communal solidarity, as reflected in the hoplite phalanx, another was the opposite: a growing elevation of individualism. Increased prosperity and mobility (social, geographic, and political) during the Archaic period encouraged the breakdown of old ties and left some people with a sense of their uniqueness. Archaic poetry and sculpture both demonstrate this new consciousness of the self.

Meanwhile, although most Archaic Greeks celebrated religion, a small group of thinkers expressed religious doubts. While monumental stone temples and international centers for divination were being erected to honor the pantheon of gods, Greek thinkers began to move away from divine and toward abstract and mechanistic explanations of the universe. Their defection marked the start of the Western philosophical tradition.

---

**Pisistratus** (pie-SIS-trah-tus)

## Revealing the Self: Lyric Poetry and Sculpture

Between approximately 675 and 500 B.C., the dominant Greek literary form was lyric poetry. This genre consisted of short poems written in a variety of styles but sharing a willingness to experiment, sometimes by revealing private feelings, sometimes by commenting on contemporary politics (as in the poetry of Tyrtaeus). Epic poetry, by contrast, was longer, grander in theme and tone, and less personal.

Homer never speaks directly about himself, and Hesiod reveals only a few personal details. In contrast, Archilochus° of Paros (ca. 700–650 B.C.), the earliest known of the lyric poets, flaunts the self. Born on the Cycladic island of Paros, Archilochus was the son, perhaps the illegitimate son, of a noble. He was a mercenary soldier (that is, he fought for pay for a foreign country) and a colonist before returning home and dying in a hoplite battle against a neighboring island. The varied subjects of Archilochus's poetry include love, travel, and war. Much of his poetry is satire, sometimes mocking and ironic, sometimes vicious and abusive. Archilochus takes a cynical and detached view of hoplite ideals, freely admitting that he once tossed away his shield to escape the battlefield: "And that shield, to hell with it! Tomorrow I'll get me another one no worse."[2]

Sappho° of Lesbos (ca. 625 B.C.) is also famous as a private poet, one who composed unmatched descriptions of intimate feelings, among them love for other women. Sappho is one of the few women poets of antiquity whose work has survived—very little, unfortunately, but enough to show that she was educated, worldly, and versed in politics. Like a modern experimental poet, she uses language self-consciously. Sappho's sensuality comes through in a description of her feelings at seeing a woman whose company she desires talking with a man: her heart shakes, her tongue is stuck, her eyes cannot see, her skin is on fire. "I am greener than grass," Sappho writes, "I feel nearly as if I could die."[3]

Sappho discusses female sexuality, a subject that Greek elite culture, dominated by males, tended to ignore. We know little about the sexuality of Greek women or of non-elite males. Among the male elite, romantic love in Archaic and Classical Greece was homosexual love or, to be precise, *pederasty* ("boy love"). The ideal relationship was supposed to involve a man in his twenties and a boy in his teens. The male elite was, strictly speaking, bisexual. By age 30, a man was expected to marry

**Athenian Kore**    This statue of a young woman (*kore*) exemplifies Archaic Greek sculpture's interest in the idealized human form. Note the slight smile, the carefully coifed hair, and the elaborate clothes. Influenced by contemporary Egyptian statues, Greek sculptors nonetheless created a new and original style.    *(Robert Frerck/Odyssey Productions)*

and raise a family. Perhaps bisexuality prevailed among elite females as well; Sappho, for example, eventually married and had a child.

Another sign of Archaic Greece's interest in the personal is the growing attention paid to the depiction of the human body, both in painting (most of the surviving examples are painted pottery) and in sculpture. Archaic artists displayed increasing skill and sensitivity in depicting the human form. The rich marble deposits in Greek soil gave sculptors promising material; baked clay (terra cotta) and bronze were other common sculptural media.

Early Archaic marble sculpture (seventh century B.C.) was strongly influenced by the way Egyptian sculpture

---

**Archilochus** (ar-KIL-uh-kus)    **Sappho** (SAF-foh)

represented the human body. Like Egyptian statuary, early Greek sculpture tended to be formal and frontal. But over the course of the seventh and sixth centuries B.C., Greek sculptors experimented with a greater variety of poses and with increasing realism in showing musculature and motion. This realism, however, was expressed within limits, for the favorite subject of Archaic sculptors was not ordinary people but idealized, beautiful youth. Typical sculptural forms were the naked young man (*kouros*) and clothed young woman (*kore*), which often served as grave markers or monuments. The goal was to show people not as they were but as they might be.

## Religious Faith and Practice

The Olympian gods who had been worshiped in the Mycenaean era survived in later ages, adapted to fit new political and social conditions. In the Archaic period, accordingly, the Olympian gods became gods of the polis.

Although the Olympians were revered throughout Greece, each polis had its patron deity: Apollo at Corinth, Hera at Argos and Samos, Athena at Athens and Sparta. Each polis also had its favorite heroes or demigods—for example, Theseus, the legendary founder of Athens, and Heracles (Hercules), a favorite of Dorian cities such as Sparta and Thebes. Devotees considered it important to build a "house"—that is, a temple—for the local patron god or at least for his or her statue. The first temples were built of wood; the earliest stone temple, a temple of Apollo at Corinth, was built around 550 B.C.

Temples were rectangular structures with long sides on the north and south, short sides on the east and west, a colonnade around all four sides, and a pitched roof. The columns were based loosely on those of Egyptian architecture. Greek temples faced east so sunlight would illuminate the interior, which consisted of two rooms: a small treasury, open to the west, and a larger main chamber, in which a statue of the deity stood. The interior decoration of the temple was simple. Outside, however, brownish red roof tiles, painted sculpture above the colonnade and in the pediments (the area between the gables and the front and rear doorways), and terra-cotta roof ornaments created a festive and lively effect. The bare white ruins seen today are misleading.

The emphasis on exterior rather than interior decoration in a Greek temple reflects the way the building was used. The main ceremony took place outside. A long altar stood in front of the temple and parallel to it. On feast days—and under the tyrants the number of such days was increased greatly, as a concession to the common people—temple priests would sacrifice animals (pigs, goats, lambs, and, less often, bulls) on the altar. Only the thighs would be burned for the gods. The rest of the meat would be boiled and distributed to worshipers.

As in other ancient cultures, so in Greece divination was an important element of religion. Divination was institutionalized in *oracles*, places where, it was believed, a god or hero might be consulted for advice. Of the various Greek oracles, that of Apollo at Delphi° (in central Greece) became the most prestigious and respected. At Delphi, Apollo spoke through the Pythia, a priestess who went into a trance. The utterances of Apollo at Delphi were famous among the Greeks for being ambiguous. Because different people might interpret them in different ways, Apollo could always be absolved after the fact if things did not turn out as the listener expected.

The oracle of Delphi was regularly consulted by poleis wishing to establish colonies. The oracle gave advice about the choice of location and the appropriate patron god or goddess, and it helped settlers draft new law codes. Delphi was also active in the search for new constitutions in the old poleis of Greece. Tradition says that Sparta based its government on a pronouncement of the Delphic oracle.

Archaic thinkers pondered the theme of divine justice. In Archaic literature we see less of the petty squabbling among the gods than in Homer and more of Zeus's majesty and justice. Although the wicked might seem to prosper, Zeus eventually punishes them or their descendants. "It never escapes him all the way when a man has a sinful spirit; and always, in the end, his judgment is plain," says Solon.[4]

Archaic writers delighted in portraying human emotions, but they had no confidence about the human ability to master emotions. In Archaic literature, people are weak and insignificant; their fortune is uncertain and mutable. Further, the gods are jealous of human success. People who aim too high are guilty of *hubris*—arrogance with overtones of violence and transgression. Hubris inevitably brings *nemesis*, "punishment" or "allotment." The safest course is for a person to be pious and humble.

So Archaic religion taught a humbling, even pessimistic, lesson. Yet religious teachings were not always heeded. The pages of Archaic history are full of people who aimed high and sought success with seemingly little worry and no dire consequences. In Ionia° (the territory of the Greek cities along the central western Anatolian coast; see Map 3.1), one group of Greek thinkers made a

---

**Delphi** (DEL-fye)
**Ionia, Ionian** (eye-OH-nee-uh, eye-OH-nee-un)

radical break with Archaic religion and invented speculative philosophy.

## The Origins of Western Philosophy

Abstract, rationalistic, speculative thinking emerged in Greece during the sixth century B.C. The first developments took place in Miletus°, an Ionian city. It is often said that the thinkers of Miletus (the Milesians) and their followers in other parts of Ionia invented philosophy. So they did, but we must be precise about what this means.

The Ionians were not the first to ask questions or tell stories about the nature and origins of the universe; virtually every ancient people did so. Nor did the Ionians invent science. They conducted no experiments. By 600 B.C., moreover, science—including mathematics, astronomy, medicine, and engineering—had been thriving for over two thousand years in Egypt and Mesopotamia, a heritage with which the Ionians were familiar and from which they borrowed.

The real importance of the Ionians is as pioneers of rationalism. They began the movement away from anthropomorphic or divine explanations and toward an abstract and mechanistic explanation of the universe. They themselves did not make a clear distinction between reason and revelation, but they made it possible for later Greek thinkers to do so. Later Greek philosophers were rarely (if ever) atheists, but they took for granted what the Ionians labored to establish: the primacy of human reason.

The Ionians saw themselves as students of nature—*physis* (from which the word *physics* is derived). Although they also commented on morality and politics, their interest in natural phenomena is what makes the Ionians significant. In their own day, the Ionians were called "wise men" (*sophoi*); to a later generation, they were "lovers of wisdom," *philosophoi* (from which *philosopher* comes).

Thales°, the first Milesian thinker, made a name for himself by successfully predicting a solar eclipse in 585 B.C. He is credited with founding Greek geometry and astronomy. Little survives of his writings or those of the other Milesians, but it is clear that he created the first general and systematic theory about the nature of the universe. According to Thales, the primary substance, the element from which all of nature was created, was water. He emphasized the mobility of water and its ability to nourish life.

A reply was not long in coming. Around 550 B.C. Anaximander of Miletus wrote the first known book of prose in Greek, expounding his own philosophy of nature. He attacked Thales for oversimplifying and for failing to do justice to the dynamism of nature. Anaximander accepted Thales' monist assumption—that all matter originated from one primary substance—but he called the substance "the unlimited" or "the undefined" rather than water. A third Milesian, Anaximenes, replied that the primary substance might be unlimited but it was not undefined. It was air, whose properties of condensation and rarefaction symbolized the dynamic and changing nature of things.

Humble as these theories might seem today, they represent a dramatic development: an open and critical debate among thinkers, each of whom was proposing an abstract and rational model of the universe. Many scholars have speculated about the origins of this development. Why Miletus? Why the sixth century B.C.? There are no sure answers, although certain influences have been suggested. Among them are Miletus's contacts on the trade routes with sophisticated Babylon, the proximity of Ionia to non-Greek peoples and the resulting Milesian appreciation of variety and complexity, and the search for law and order in contemporary Greek political life and its extension to the philosophical plane.

In its second generation early Greek philosophy moved to other Ionian cities and then migrated westward across the Mediterranean. Heracleitus° of Ephesus (ca. 500 B.C.) proposed fire as the primary substance. Although fire was ever changing, it had an underlying coherence. According to Heracleitus, this paradox nicely symbolized the nature of the universe. He summed up the importance of change by the aphorisms "All things flow" and "You cannot step into the same river twice." The universe witnessed a constant struggle of opposites, yet an essential unity and order prevailed. To describe this order, Heracleitus used the term *logos*. This key concept of Greek philosophy is difficult to translate; among other definitions, *logos* can mean "word," "thought," "reason," "story," or "calculation."

Heracleitus's contemporary, Pythagoras° of Samos, was both a rationalist and a religious thinker. On the one hand, Pythagoras was a mathematician who discovered the numerical ratios determining the major intervals of the musical scale—that is, the range of sound between high and low. It is less certain if, as tradition has it, he discovered the so-called Pythagorean theorem—that in a

---

**Miletus, Milesian** (my-LEE-tus, my-LEE-zhen)
**Thales** (THAY-leez)

**Heracleitus** (her-uh-CLY-tus)
**Pythagoras** (py-THAG-uh-russ)

right triangle the hypotenuse squared is equal to the sum of the squares of the other two sides.

On the other hand, Pythagoras believed that the purity of mathematics would improve the human soul. Just as he had imposed numerical order on the musical scale, so could philosophers understand the entire universe through number and proportion. The resulting knowledge was no mere academic exercise but a way of life. Pythagoras devoted himself to "observation" or "contemplation"—to *theoria* (from which *theory* comes).

In Croton in Magna Graecia (southern Italy), Pythagoras founded a religious community. Its members observed strict secrecy, but it appears that they abstained from meat because they believed in the kinship of all living things. They also believed in the reincarnation of the human soul, though not necessarily into a human body. Pythagoras is said to have stopped a man from beating a dog because he recognized from the barking that the dog was the reincarnation of a friend who had died.

The early Greek philosopher whose work is most fully preserved is Parmenides° of Elea in Magna Graecia. Parmenides (b. ca. 515 B.C.) completely distrusted the senses. He believed that reality was a world of pure being: eternal, unchanging, and indivisible, comparable to a sphere. To Parmenides, change was a mere illusion. Parmenides, therefore, is the first Western philosopher to propose a radical difference between the world of the senses and reality. This fundamental strain of Western thought would be taken up by Plato and his followers and then passed to Christianity.

To sum up, in philosophy as in so many other endeavors, the Archaic Greeks were great borrowers and even greater innovators who left a profound mark on later ages. By the late sixth century B.C., Archaic Greece was poised on the brink of a revolution that would give birth to the Classical period of Greek civilization.

# CLASSICAL GREECE

HE word *democracy* comes from the Greek word *demokratia*°, coined in Athens early in the fifth century B.C. *Demokratia* literally means "the power (*kratos*) of the people (*demos*)." A modern democracy is characterized by mass citizenship, elections, and representative government. Athenian *demokratia*, in contrast, was a direct democracy in which elections mattered

less than direct participation, citizenship was narrowly restricted, women were excluded from politics, resident aliens could almost never become citizens, and citizens owned slaves and ruled an empire. Modern democracies may cover a huge territory, but Athens encompassed only 1,000 square miles. Modern democracies tend to emphasize individual rights. Athens, in contrast, often placed the community first. In spite of these differences, Athenian *demokratia* established principles that are enshrined in democracy today: freedom, equality, citizenship without property qualifications, the right of most citizens to hold public office, and the rule of law.

The young democracy's greatest achievement was to spearhead Greece's victory over the Persian invaders in 480 B.C. After that victory, Athens became Greece's leading sea power. Yet Sparta remained the superior land power, and the two poleis were soon locked in a cycle of competition and war. The result nearly destroyed Athenian democracy. Even more serious, it undermined Greece's very independence.

## The Development of Demokratia, 508–322 B.C.

Tyranny often gave way to oligarchy—to government by wealthy men, both Eupatrids and non-Eupatrids. In Athens after Pisistratid rule, however, conditions were ripe for revolution. Solon had left a society of independent small farmers, while the Pisistratids had strengthened the ranks of immigrants and weakened the Eupatrids. Elite leaders nonetheless tried to establish an Athenian oligarchy. We may imagine strong popular opposition.

Ironically, a Eupatrid, a member of the Alcmeonid clan by the name of Cleisthenes° (d. ca. 500 B.C.), led the revolution. Originally Cleisthenes aimed to head the oligarchy, but his rivals shut him out of power. He turned then to the demos, whose leader he became. The watchwords of the day were *equality* and *mixing* (that is, mixing people from different regions of Attica in order to break down local, aristocratic power bases).

Frightened by the assertive populace, the oligarchs called for Spartan military assistance, but to no avail: Cleisthenes rallied the people to victory. The Athenian triumph proved, in Herodotus's opinion, "that equality is an excellent thing, not in one way only but in many. For while they were under a tyranny, [Athenians] were no better at fighting than any of their neighbors, but once they were rid of tyrants they became by far the best."[5]

Cleisthenes extinguished Eupatrid power once and for all by attacking its local bases of support. For example,

---

**Parmenides** (par-MEN-uh-deez)
**demokratia** (deh-mo-kra-TEE-uh)

**Cleisthenes** (KLICE-the-neez)

**Greek Trireme**    *Olympias* is a hypothetical reconstruction of an Athenian war galley of about 400 B.C. Rowed by 170 oarsmen arranged on three decks, the trireme fought by ramming an enemy ship with the bronze ram attached to its bow.    *(Courtesy of the Trireme Trust)*

he abolished the four traditional tribes and apportioned the people among ten new tribes. Immigrants and their descendants, who had been excluded from the old tribes, now joined natives in the new tribes. The tribes formed the basis of a new Council of 500 to replace Solon's Council of 400. The council was divided into ten tribal units, each serving as a kind of executive committee for one of the ten months of the civic year.

The centerpiece of the government was the assembly, some of whose members, emboldened by the new spirit of equality, now spoke up for the first time. The new Council of 500, like its predecessor, prepared the assembly's agenda, but assemblymen felt free to amend it. Only the Areopagus council remained a privileged preserve.

The last and most unusual part of the Cleisthenic system was ostracism, a sort of annual *un*popularity contest that received its name from the pieces of broken pottery (*ostraka*) on which the names of victims were chiseled. The "winner" was forced into ten years of exile, although his property would not be confiscated. Ostracism was meant to protect the regime by defusing factionalism and discouraging tyrants. Judging by Athens's consequent political stability, it worked.

In 508 B.C. the poorest Athenians had relatively little power in Cleisthenic government. But a change in conditions by the 450s made Athens even more democratic. During that period the oldest principle of Greek politics

came to the fore: Whoever fights for the state governs it. To counter the Persian threat against Greece in the 480s (see page 91), Athens built a great navy. The standard ship was a trireme°, an oared warship rowed by 170 men on three decks. The core of the rowers consisted of Athenian thetes. Just as hoplites supported new regimes in Greece after 700 B.C., so rowers supported new regimes in Greece after 500 B.C.

A second revolution occurred around 461 B.C., when Ephialtes (d. ca. 460 B.C.) and his young associate Pericles° (ca. 495–429 B.C.) targeted the last bulwark of privilege, the Areopagus. They stripped away the council's long-standing supervisory powers over the regime and redistributed those powers to the Council of 500 and the people's court. The decade of the 450s B.C. saw another innovation: payment for public service, specifically for jurors, who received a half-drachma (perhaps half a day's wages) for a day of jury duty. Eventually other public servants also received pay. Conservatives complained bitterly because they perceived, rightly, that state pay made political activity by poor people possible. State pay was, an Athenian said, "the glue of demokratia."

Demokratia became closely connected with Pericles, who inherited the constituency of Ephialtes after his assassination around 460 B.C. For much of the next

---

**trireme** (TRY-reem)    **Pericles** (PAIR-ih-kleez)

## READING SOURCES

# THE DEBATE ON DEMOCRACY

*Characters in Greek drama often discuss general principles. In this excerpt from Euripides' tragedy* The Suppliant Women *(ca. 420 B.C.), Theseus, legendary king of Athens, and a herald from Creon, tyrant of Thebes, debate the merits of democracy.*

**Herald**

What man is tyrant in this land? To whom / Must I give the word I bring from Creon, ruler / In Cadmus' country [Thebes] . . . ?

**Theseus**

One moment, stranger. / Your start was wrong, seeking a tyrant here. / This city is free, and ruled by no one man. / The people reign, in annual succession. / They do not yield the power to the rich; / The poor man has an equal share in it.

**Herald**

That one point gives the better of the game / To me. The town I come from is controlled / By one man, not a mob. And there is no one / To puff it up with words, for private gain, / Swaying it this way, that way. . . . /

The people is no right judge of arguments. / Then how can it give right guidance to a city? / A poor man, working hard, could not attend / To public matters, even if ignorance / Were not his birthright. When a wretch, a nothing, / Obtains respect and power from the people / By talk, his betters sicken at the sight.

**Theseus**

. . . Nothing / Is worse for a city than a tyrant. / In earliest days, before the laws are common, / One man has power and makes the law his own: / Equality is not yet. With written laws, / People of small resources and the rich / Both have the same recourse to justice. Now / A man of means, if badly spoken of, / Will have no better standing than the weak; / And if the little man is right, he wins / Against the great. This is the call of freedom: / "What man has good advice to give the city, / And wishes to make it known?" He who responds / Gains glory; the reluctant hold their peace. / For the city, what can be more fair than that?

Source: Adapted from Euripides, *The Suppliant Women*, trans. Frank Jones, in *Euripides IV: The Complete Greek Tragedies*, ed. David Grene and Richmond Lattimore. Reprinted by permission of the publisher, The University of Chicago Press.

thirty years, Pericles dominated Athenian politics. An aristocrat who respected the common people, an excellent orator who benefited from an education in philosophy, an honest and tireless worker, and a general who led in peace as well as war, Pericles was a political giant. Under his leadership, demokratia became firmly entrenched as the government and way of life in Athens.

Athenian democracy survived, with occasional oligarchic intrusions, for 150 years after Pericles' death. During those years it became more institutionalized and cautious, but it also became more thoroughly egalitarian.

### How Demokratia Worked

Unlike most modern democracies, Athenian demokratia was direct and participatory. Pericles once claimed that in Athens "people pay attention both to their own household and to politics. Even those occupied with other activities are no less knowledgeable about politics."[6] This is part boast, but only part. Large numbers of ordinary citizens at-

tended the assembly from time to time and held public office or served on the Council of 500 for a year or two. (See the box "Reading Sources: The Debate on Democracy.")

The instruments of government are easily sketched. The central institution was the assembly. Open to all male citizens over age 20, assembly meetings were held in the open air, on a hillside seating several thousand on benches (see the photograph on page 68). In the fourth century B.C. the assembly gathered a minimum of forty times per year, about once every ten days.

The assembly heard the great debates of the day. It made decisions about war and peace, alliance and friendship; it conferred honors and issued condemnations; it passed decrees relating to current issues and set up commissions to revise fundamental laws. In the assembly top orators addressed the people, but everyone, however humble, was theoretically entitled to speak.

The judicial branch consisted of courts, which, with a few exceptions, were open to all citizens, no matter how poor. Aristotle or a member of his school comments that "when the people have the right to vote in the courts, they control the constitution." Juries were large, commonly consisting of several hundred men chosen by lottery; small juries, it was felt, were easily bribed. After a preliminary hearing, cases were decided in a single day.

The executive consisted of the Council of 500 and some seven hundred public officials (also, under Athens's empire in the fifth century B.C., several hundred others living abroad). All male citizens over age 30 were eligible to serve. Most public officials were chosen by lottery, which put rich and poor, talented and untalented, on an equal footing. To guard against installing incompetents or criminals, all officials had to undergo a scrutiny by the council before taking office and an audit after the term. Most magistracies, moreover, were boards, usually of ten men, so even if a bad man managed to pass this scrutiny, he would be counterbalanced by his colleagues. Only generals and treasurers were chosen by election.

Athens had a relatively weak executive and no chief executive such as a president or prime minister. Generals and orators led assembly debates and sometimes exercised great influence, but ordinary people set the agenda and made the decisions by taking votes at each assembly meeting. On the local level, every deme (county) had an annually chosen executive and a deme assembly of all citizens.

So novel and populist a system of government has not been without critics, either in antiquity or today. Some have charged that the Athenian people were uneducated, emotional, and easily swayed by oratorical tricks. Others say that demokratia degenerated into mob rule after the death of Pericles. Still others complain about the lack of a system of formal public education, which denied many citizens equality of opportunity.

Another serious charge against Athenian demokratia is that it was democracy for a small elite only. Adult male citizens never accounted for more than one-tenth of the population, approximately 40,000 out of a total population—men, women and children, resident aliens, and slaves—of about 400,000. To become a citizen, a boy at age 18 had to prove that he was the legitimate son of a citizen father and a citizen maternal grandfather. Girls were never officially registered as citizens. Although the term *citizeness* existed, Athenian citizen women were usually referred to as "city women." As for resident aliens, whether male or female, they rarely attained citizenship.

In the fifth and fourth centuries B.C., Athens had a large population of foreigners. Some were transient. Others were officially registered resident aliens, or *metics*°. Metics came by the thousands from all over the Greek world and beyond. Some, like Aristotle (a native of a Greek colony in Macedonia°), were attracted by the city's schools of philosophy, but most came because of its unparalleled economic opportunities. Metics could not own land in Athens, and they had to pay extra taxes and serve in the Athenian military. Nevertheless, they prospered in Athenian commerce and crafts.

Athenian women were excluded from politics and played only a modest role in commerce as small retailers. In legal matters women were almost always required to be represented by a male guardian. Demokratia also promoted an ideal of the male as master of his household. Women were expected to be obedient and remain indoors.

Practice, however, was another matter. As Aristotle asks rhetorically, "How is it possible to prevent the wives of the poor from going out?" *Poor* is a synonym for *ordinary* in ancient Greek. Ordinary women could not stay at home because they had to run errands, draw water, and sometimes even help make ends meet. Ordinary houses, moreover, were small and cramped, and in the Mediterranean heat women could not stay inside all the time.

We occasionally get glimpses, sometimes more, of Athenian women resisting or working behind the scenes to correct male mistakes. An inheritance case reveals a woman go-between interceding among her quarreling male relations. Greek comedy shows women mocking male pretensions and establishing sisterly friendships. A woman who brought a large dowry into a marriage could use it and the threat of divorce to influence her husband (the dowry had to be returned to the woman's father or guardian if there was a divorce). In short, Athenian women had some access to the world outside the household and some influence within the household. There existed, nonetheless, a real disparity in power between men and women.

Athenian demokratia lacked many features of modern democracy, including a notion of universal human rights, the possibility for immigrants to become citizens, gender equality, the abolition of slavery, and public education. To its small citizen body, however, Athenian demokratia offered extraordinary freedom, equality, and responsibility, as well as a degree of participation in public life seldom equaled. Demokratia was a model of what democracy could be but not of who could take part.

## The Persian Wars, 499–479 B.C.

In 500 B.C. Sparta, hegemon of the Peloponnesian League, was the most prominent power of the Greek mainland. Across the Aegean Sea in Anatolia, the Greek city-states

---

**metic** (MEH-tik)

**Macedonia** (mah-suh-DOE-nee-uh)

**Amazon Queen**    This red-figure Athenian cup (ca. 440 B.C.) shows the Greek warrior Achilles about to slay the Amazon queen Penthesilea during the Trojan War, in which she fought on Troy's side. She was a symbol of feminine courage and beauty.    *(Staatliche Antikensammlungen und Glyptothek, Munich)*

had been under Persian rule for two generations, since Cyrus the Great's conquest in the 540s B.C. In 499 B.C., however, events began to unfold that not only would revolutionize that balance of power but also would throw the entire eastern Mediterranean into two hundred years of turmoil.

Led by Miletus, the Ionian Greek city-states rose in revolt against Persia in 499 B.C. Athens sent troops to help, but despite initial successes, Athens reconsidered the alliance and withdrew its forces. The Ionian coalition broke down thereafter and was crushed by Persia. Miletus was besieged and destroyed, but otherwise Persia was relatively lenient in Ionia.

Upstart Athens, however, could not go unpunished. In 490 B.C. Darius I sent a large naval expedition to Athens. About 25,000 infantrymen and 1,200 cavalrymen (with horses) landed at Marathon, some 24 miles from the city of Athens (see Map 3.3). Athens sent 10,000 men (including 1,000 allies) to defend Marathon, and a great battle ensued.

Persian overconfidence and the superiority of the Greek phalanx over Persia's loosely organized infantrymen won Athens a smashing victory. Persia suffered 6,400 casualties, Athens only 192. (The story, unconfirmed, that a messenger ran from the battlefield to the city of Athens with the news, "Rejoice, we conquer!" is the inspiration for the modern marathon race, a slightly

longer distance of about 26 miles.) After the battle, Athens experienced a burst of confidence that propelled it to power and glory.

Meanwhile, Persia sought a rematch. After Darius's death in 486, his son and successor, Xerxes, amassed a huge force of about a thousand ships and several hundred thousand soldiers and rowers, vastly outnumbering potential Greek opposition. Athens, under the leadership of Themistocles (ca. 525–460 B.C.), prepared by building a fleet of two hundred ships. Athens joined Sparta and twenty-nine other Peloponnesian poleis in the Hellenic League of defense, with Sparta in overall command. Most poleis either stayed neutral or, like Thebes and Argos, collaborated with Persia. The Greeks had over three hundred ships and about fifty thousand infantrymen.

Persia invaded Greece in 480 B.C. and won the opening moves. At the narrow pass of Thermopylae in central Greece (see Map 3.1), the Persians outflanked and crushed a small Spartan army, who died fighting to the last man, including their king, Leonidas. This sacrifice added to the Spartan reputation for courage but left the road south open. Abandoned by its defenders, Athens was sacked.

The tide then turned. The Greeks lured the Persian fleet into the narrow straits between Athens and Salamis. The Persians could not use their numerical superiority in this confined space, and the Greeks had the home advantage. The result was a crushing Persian defeat under

# The Enemy as Barbarian

Classical Greeks no longer regarded the enemy as honored rivals, as Homer's heroes had regarded Trojans. Rather, they looked down on the enemy as a barbarian. Greece's archenemies, the Persians, were portrayed as indulgent, effeminate, emotional, slavish, cruel, and dangerous. Consider the contrasting portraits of Persians and Greeks in these excerpts from the historian Herodotus's account of Persia's invasion of Greece in 480 B.C.

## The Persians

He [King Xerxes of Persia] then prepared to move forward to Abydos, where a bridge had already been constructed across the Hellespont from Europe to Asia. . . . It was here not long afterwards that the Greeks under Xanthippus the son of Ariphron took Artayctes the Persian governor of Sestos, and nailed him alive to a plank—he was the man who collected women in the temple of Protesilaus at Elaeus and committed various acts of sacrilege. This headland was the point to which Xerxes' engineers carried their two bridges from Abydos—a distance of seven furlongs. . . . The work was successfully completed, but a subsequent storm of great violence smashed it up and carried everything away. Xerxes was very angry when he learned of the disaster, and gave orders that the Hellespont should receive three hundred lashes and have a pair of fetters thrown into it. And I have heard before now that he also sent people to brand it with hot irons. He certainly instructed the men with the whips to utter, as they wielded them, the following words: "You salt and bitter stream, your master lays this punishment upon you for injuring him, who never injured you. But Xerxes the King will cross you, with or without your permission. No man sacrifices to you, and you deserve the neglect by your acrid and muddy waters"—a highly presumptuous way of addressing the Hellespont, and typical of a barbarous nation. In addition to punishing the Hellespont Xerxes gave orders that the men responsible for building the bridge should have their heads cut off. This unseemly order was duly carried out. . . .

## The Greeks

To the Spartan envoys . . . [the Athenians] said: "No doubt it was natural that the Lacedaemonians [Spartans] should dread the possibility of our making terms with Persia; nonetheless it shows a poor estimate of the spirit of Athens. Were we offered all the gold in the world, and the fairest and richest country the earth contains, we should never consent to join the common enemy and bring Greece into submission. There are many compelling reasons to prevent our taking such a course, even if we wish to do so: the first and greatest is the burning of the temples and images of our gods—now mere heaps of rubble. It is our bounden duty to avenge this desecration with all the power we possess—not to clasp in friendship the hand that wrought it. Again, there is the Greek nation—the common blood, the common language; the temples and religious ritual; the whole way of life we understand and share together—indeed, if Athens were to betray all this it would not be well done. We would have you know, therefore, if you did not already know it, that we will never make peace with Xerxes so long as a single Athenian remains alive."

## QUESTIONS

1. Find at least three examples in these passages of Persian barbarism.

2. By deciding to make war instead of negotiating peace, are the Athenians barbarians or civilized people?

3. Does Herodotus offer convincing proof that the Persians are more barbarous than the Greeks? Is he fair?

SOURCE: Herodotus, *The Histories*, translated by Aubrey de Sélincourt, revised by A. R. Burn (Penguin Classics 1954, rev. 1972), pp. 429, 550. Copyright © 1954. Reprinted by permission of Penguin Books Ltd.

the eyes of Xerxes himself, who watched the battle from a throne on a hillside near the shore.

Because their sea links to the Levant had been cut, Xerxes and the remainder of the Persian fleet left for home. Soon afterward the united Greek army under Spartan leadership defeated Persian forces on land at Plataea (just north of Attica; see Map 3.1) in 479 B.C. At about the same time, the Greek fleet defeated a reorganized Persian fleet off the Anatolian coast near Mycale. The victorious Greeks sailed the coast and liberated the Ionians. Not only did Persia fail to conquer the Greek mainland, but it also lost its eastern Aegean empire.

Greeks did not remember the invader fondly. After 480 they thought of Persians not merely as enemies but

## READING SOURCES

# PERICLES' FUNERAL ORATION

*The historian Thucydides reports that in the winter of 431–430 B.C., at the end of the first year of the Peloponnesian War (431–404 B.C.), Athens's leading politician, Pericles (ca. 495–429 B.C.), gave a speech at the public funeral of the Athenians who had died fighting that year. Pericles used the occasion to celebrate Athens's way of life.*

Our constitution does not copy the laws of neighboring states; we are rather a pattern to others than imitators ourselves. Its administration favors the many instead of the few; this is why it is called a democracy. . . .

Further, we provide plenty of means for the mind to refresh itself from business. We celebrate games and sacrifices all the year round, and the elegance of our private establishments forms a daily source of pleasure and helps to distract us from what causes us distress; while the magnitude of our city draws the produce of our world into our harbor, so that to the Athenian the fruits of other countries are as familiar a luxury as those of his own.

If we turn to our military policy, there also we differ from our antagonists. We throw open our city to the world, and never by alien acts exclude foreigners from any opportunity of learning or observing, although the eyes of an enemy may occasionally profit by our liberality, trusting less in system and policy than to the native spirit of our citizens; while in education, where our rivals from their very cradles by a painful discipline seek after manliness, at Athens we live exactly as we please, and yet are just as ready to encounter every legitimate danger. . . .

We cultivate refinement without extravagance and knowledge without effeminacy; wealth we employ more for use than for show, and place the real disgrace of poverty not in owning to the fact but in declining the struggle against it. . . .

In short, I say that as a city we are the school of Hellas; while I doubt if the world can produce a man, who where he has only himself to depend upon, is equal to so many emergencies, and graced by so happy a versatility as the Athenian.

Source: Reprinted by permission of The Free Press, a Division of Simon & Schuster, Inc., from *The Landmark Thucydides: A Comprehensive Guide to the Peloponnesian War*, by Robert B. Strassler. Copyright © 1996 by Robert B. Strassler.

as barbarians—that is, cultural inferiors. (See the box "Global Encounters: The Enemy as Barbarian.") At the same time, Greeks became more conscious of their own common culture.

## Struggles to Dominate Greece, 478–362 B.C.

The Greek unity forged by the struggle against Persia was fragile and short-lived. What followed was a constant struggle in diplomacy and war among city-states, usually arranged in leagues under hegemons.

Following the Greek victory over Persia, Athens expanded its power as hegemon of a new security organization. Founded on the island of Delos in the Aegean Sea, the so-called Delian League aimed both at protecting Greek lands and at plundering Persian territory. The number of allies grew from about 150 in 477 B.C. to about 250 in 431 B.C. at the height of the league.

Because they feared entanglement outside the Peloponnesus, most Spartans preferred to leave the Aegean to Athens. Some Spartans nonetheless watched with unease and jealousy as Athenian power boomed.

Afraid of the new titan, the major allied states rebelled, one by one, beginning with Thasos in 465 B.C., but Athens crushed each rebellion. Sometimes after surrender, rebels were executed and their wives and children sold into slavery. Allied complaints began to stir Sparta. A conflict between Greece's greatest land power, Sparta, and Greece's greatest sea power, Athens, started to look all but inevitable.

The Peloponnesian War, as this conflict is known today, came in 431 B.C. and lasted intermittently until 404 B.C. The war proved bloody and bitter. Battles between huge fleets, economic warfare, protracted sieges, epidemic disease, and ideological struggle produced a devastating war. It was clear that the Greeks could not maintain their unity against Persia; indeed, they appeared to be destroying themselves. (See the box "Reading Sources: Pericles' Funeral Oration.")

In this era both democratic Athens and oligarchic Sparta sought to promote their respective ideologies. Some

**Map 3.4    Greece in the Peloponnesian War**    During the long and bloody Peloponnesian War (431–404 B.C.), much of the Greek world was divided into two camps: one led by Sparta, the other by Athens.

unfortunate states became ideological battlegrounds, often at great cost of life. In Corcyra (modern Corfu; see Map 3.4), for example, bloody civil war marked a series of coups and countercoups in the 420s B.C.

Given Spartan supremacy on land and Athenian mastery of the sea, it is not surprising that the Peloponnesian War remained undecided for a decade and a half. The balance of power shifted only after an Athenian blunder, an expedition to conquer Sicily (415–413 B.C.) that became a quagmire and then a disaster, leading to total defeat and thousands of Athenian casualties. In the aftermath most of the Athenian empire rose in revolt. Persia re-emerged and intervened on Sparta's side—in return for Sparta's restoration of Ionia to Persia, an ironic counterpoint to Sparta's role in driving Persia from

Greece in 479. Athens, nevertheless, was sufficiently wealthy and plucky to hold out until 404 B.C.

Sparta won the Peloponnesian War, but establishing a new Greek order proved beyond its grasp. Spartans were soldiers, not diplomats; infantrymen, not sailors; and commanders, not public speakers. They made poor leaders. Sparta took over Athens's former empire and quickly had a falling-out with its allies, Persia, Corinth, and the Boeotian° city-states, especially Thebes.

In addition, Sparta suffered a vast decline in the number of citizens. The original nine thousand Similars of the seventh century B.C. had dropped to only about fif-

---

**Boeotia, Boeotian** (bee-O-shuh, bee-O-shun)

teen hundred in 371 B.C. The main problem seems to have been greed. Rich Spartans preferred to get richer by concentrating wealth in fewer hands rather than open the elite to new blood. Thousands of men could no longer afford to live as elite soldiers.

The result was military disaster. In 371 B.C. the Boeotian army crushed the Spartans at the Battle of Leuctra, killing a thousand men (including four hundred Similars) and a Spartan king. In the next few years Boeotia invaded the Peloponnesus, freed the Messenian helots, and restored Messenia to independence, after some 350 years of bondage. It was a fatal blow to Spartan power, but Boeotia, too, was exhausted and its main leaders, Epaminondas (d. 362 B.C.) and Pelopidas (403–364 B.C.), were dead. None of the Greek city-states had been able to maintain hegemony.

Nothing better demonstrates the fatal excess of individualism in Classical Greece and the absence of cooperative virtues than the wars of the city-states in the fourth century B.C. They accomplished nothing but leaving a weakened Greece prey to outsiders.

# THE PUBLIC CULTURE OF CLASSICAL GREECE

THE word *classical* means "to set a standard." The culture of Greece between 480 and 322 B.C. proved so influential in the later West that it may justly be called classical. Classical Greek culture was public culture. Poets were not inward-looking or alienated figures. Rather, to quote the Athenian playwright Aristophanes° (ca. 455–385 B.C.), they were "the teachers of men," who commented on contemporary public debate. (As the quotation might also suggest, men, especially citizens, dominated public life.) Dramas were performed in a state theater at state religious festivals. The philosopher Socrates° (469–399 B.C.) discussed philosophy in marketplaces and gymnasia. It was not private individuals but the public that was the major patron of sculpture and architecture.

Public life, accordingly, is the central theme of Classical Greek art and literature. In tragedy, for example, regardless of the particular hero or plot, the same character always looms in the background: the polis. The Classical historians Herodotus, Xenophon, and especially Thucydides focus on public affairs rather than private life. Classical philosophy ranged from biology to metaphysics, but politics was undoubtedly its central focus.

## Religion and Art

A hallmark of Classical culture is the tension between the religious heritage of the Archaic period and the worldly spirit of the Classical age. The Classical period was a time of prosperity, political debate, and military conflict. "Wonders are many on earth, and none more wondrous than man," said the Athenian tragedian Sophocles° (ca. 495–406 B.C.). Yet Sophocles was a deeply religious man who also believed that people were doomed to disaster unless they obeyed the laws of the gods. Sophocles mirrored a widespread debate, for he knew his countrymen well. He was not only a popular playwright but also a general, state treasurer, priest, and friend of Pericles.

Classical religion was less sure of itself than its Archaic predecessor. A few people even questioned the very existence of the gods, although most Greeks wanted religion to be adapted to the new age, not discarded altogether. Thus Athenian religion was tailored to the needs of a democratic and imperial city. In the 440s B.C., under Pericles' leadership, Athens embarked on a vast, ambitious, and expensive temple-building project, using Delian League funds and serving as a large public employment program. Temples were built in and around the city, most notably on the Athenian Acropolis. (See the feature "Weighing the Evidence: The Parthenon" on pages 102–103.)

To adapt religion to a new age, new cults also were introduced. The most popular was the worship of Asclipius, god of healing. Traditionally a minor figure and considered a son of Apollo, Asclipius became enormously popular in his own right beginning in the late fifth century B.C., perhaps in response to the high mortality of the Peloponnesian War. Outside Athens, large shrines to Asclipius at Epidauros (in the Peloponnesus) and Cos (an island off the Anatolian coast) became pilgrimage centers in the fourth century B.C. for ailing people in search of a cure.

Women played a major role in Classical Athenian religion. They were priestesses in more than forty major cults. They participated each year in many festivals, including several reserved only for women. One such festival, the Thesmophoria, a celebration of fertility held

---

Aristophanes (air-ih-STOF-uh-neez)
Socrates, Socratic (sock-ruh-TEEZ, suh-KRAT-ik)

Sophocles (sof-uh-KLEEZ)

**The Parthenon**    The temple of Athena Parthenos ("the Maiden") on the Athenian Acropolis, the Parthenon was dedicated in 438 B.C. One of the largest and most complex Greek temples, it was built of fine marble. The partially restored ruins symbolize the wealth, power, and greatness of Classical Greece.    *(William Katz/Photo Researchers)*

each autumn, featured a three-day encampment of women on a hillside in the city, right beside the Athenian assembly amphitheater. Women also attended public funeral orations in honor of soldiers who had died in battle. They probably attended plays as well.

Pericles was very much influenced by a woman, Aspasia°. She belonged to the small group of noncitizen women called *hetairai*, or courtesans (that is, prostitutes patronized by men of wealth and status). An educated woman from Miletus, Aspasia was for many years Pericles' mistress and bore him a son. Aspasia and Pericles gathered around them a glittering circle of thinkers and artists. Some say that Aspasia even influenced Pericles' political decisions.

In art, Classical sculptors completed the process begun by their Archaic forebears of mastering the accurate representation of the human body. In anatomical precision, Classical Greek sculpture was the most technically proficient sculpture the world had seen. Like Archaic

sculpture, it was not, however, an attempt to portray humans "warts and all" but rather an idealization of the human form.

## The Sophists and Socrates

Success in democratic politics required a knowledge of oratory. This demand was met in the late fifth century B.C. by the arrival in Athens of itinerant professional teachers of *rhetoric*, the art of speaking. They were known as Sophists° (from a word meaning "instruct" or "make wise"). Sicilian Greeks invented rhetoric around 465 B.C. by drawing up the rules of argument. For a fee—rarely small and sometimes astronomical—Sophists taught young Athenians the art of speaking. Their curriculum consisted not only of rhetoric but also of the rudiments of linguistics, ethics, psychology, history, and anthropology—in other words, any aspect of "human nature" that might help an aspiring politician. Within a

Aspasia (uh-SPAY-see-uh)

Sophist (SOF-ist)

few years most ambitious young Athenians of prosperous families were studying with Sophists.

At their best, Sophists sharpened young minds. Athenian tragedians, historians, and philosophers all benefited from sophistic teaching. Protagoras (b. ca. 485 B.C.), perhaps the best-known Sophist, summed up the spirit of the age in his famous dictum "Man is the measure of all things"—an appropriate credo for the interest in all things human that is apparent in Classical literature and art. There is, however, a more troubling side to the Sophists. As teachers of rhetoric, they taught respect for success, not for truth. Thus they acquired a reputation as word-twisters who taught men how to make "the weaker argument defeat the stronger."

Much to the distress of conservatives, Sophists drew a distinction between *nomos,* a word that means "law" or "convention," and *physis,* which means "nature." The distinction had revolutionary potential. In general, Sophists had little respect for the established order, or nomos. They considered it mere convention. A great man trained by a Sophist might rise above convention to realize the limitless potential of his nature, or physis. If he used his skill to overturn democracy and establish a tyranny, so much the worse for democracy. Indeed, the Sophists trained both unscrupulous democratic politicians and many of the oligarchs who launched coups d'état against Athenian democracy at the end of the fifth century B.C. As a result, *sophist* became a term of abuse in Athens and remains so to this day.

Classical Greek advances in rhetoric, therefore, were as problematic as they were brilliant. The Sophists had a wide-ranging effect on many different branches of thought. Consider, for example, the work of the philosopher Democritus° (b. ca. 460 B.C.), a native of the northern Greek polis of Abdera but a visitor to Athens. Democritus was not a Sophist, but he shared the common Sophistic notion that the reality of nature was far more radical than conventionally thought. He concluded that all things consisted of tiny, indivisible particles, which could be arranged and rearranged in an infinite variety of configurations. He called these particles *atoma,* "the uncuttable" (from which the word *atom* is derived).

The physicians of the Aegean island of Cos are known as Hippocratics, from Hippocrates° (b. ca. 460 B.C.), the first great thinker of their school. If they were not directly influenced by the Sophists, they shared similar habits of thought. Like the Sophists, the Hippocratics

were religious skeptics. They considered disease to be strictly a natural phenomenon in which the gods played no part. Hippocratic medicine was noteworthy for its methodology, which emphasized observation and prognosis (the reasoned prediction of future developments). The Hippocratics were the most rigorously naturalistic physicians to date, although no more successful in healing illness than earlier practitioners.

In the fifth century B.C. not all thinkers welcomed the conclusions of the Sophists. Perhaps their most notable critic, and the greatest of all fifth-century B.C. philosophers, was Socrates (469–399 B.C.). Unlike the Sophists, he charged no fees, had no formal students, and did not claim to teach any positive body of knowledge. His main virtue, he believed, was his awareness of his ignorance. Unlike the Sophists, most of whom were metics, Socrates was an Athenian citizen.

Socrates, however, resembled the Sophists in his intense interest in political theory. Like any good Athenian citizen, Socrates served in the military—as a hoplite during the Peloponnesian War. He had his doubts about democracy, which he criticized for inefficiency and for giving an equal voice to the uneducated. He preferred rule by a wise elite. Nonetheless, Socrates was too loyal an Athenian to advocate revolution.

Yet Socrates made many enemies because of his role as a self-styled "gadfly." He stung the pride of Athens's leaders by demonstrating their ignorance. Mistakenly considered a Sophist by the public because of his unconventional opinions, Socrates was tried, convicted, and executed in 399 B.C. by an Athenian court for alleged atheism and "corrupting the young." The Athenian public soon had second thoughts, and the trial of Socrates is usually considered one of history's great miscarriages of justice, as well as one of Athenian democracy's greatest blunders.

Socrates was trained in the Ionian natural philosophy tradition. He went beyond it, as the Roman thinker Cicero later said, by bringing philosophy "down from the heavens into the streets"; he changed the emphasis from the natural world to human ethics. Like most Greeks, Socrates believed that the purpose of life was the pursuit of aretê. Unlike his contemporaries, however, he did not consider aretê to be primarily excellence in battle or in public life but rather excellence in philosophy. One became good by studying the truth, which is part of what Socrates meant by his saying "Virtue (aretê) is knowledge." He also meant that no one who truly understood goodness would ever choose to do evil.

Teach people well, Socrates says, and they will behave morally. Socrates has gone down in history as an inspiring teacher despite his protestations of not teaching

---

**Democritus** (dee-MOCK-ruh-tus)
**Hippocrates, Hippocratics** (hih-POK-ruh-teez, hih-puh-KRAT-iks)

anything. His emphasis was not on research or writing, and in fact he refused to write anything down. He believed that truth can be found only in persons, not through books—that philosophy requires a thoughtful verbal exchange. His favorite technique was to ask people difficult questions. Pedagogy that relies on inquiry is still called the "Socratic method."

## Plato and Aristotle

Because Socrates never wrote anything down, we are dependent on others for our knowledge of him. Fortunately for us, he inspired students who committed his words and ideas to paper. Socrates' most distinguished student, and our most important source for his thought, was Plato° (427–348 B.C.), who in turn was the teacher of Aristotle (384–322 B.C.). Together, these three men laid the foundations of the Western philosophical tradition. They were thinkers for the ages, but each was also a man of his times.

Socrates grew up in confident Periclean days. Plato came of age during the Peloponnesian War, a period culminating in the execution of Socrates. Shocked and disillusioned, Plato turned his back on public life, although he was an Athenian citizen. Instead of discussing philosophy in public, Plato founded a private school in an Athenian suburb, the Academy. Plato held a low opinion of democracy, and when he did intervene in politics, it was not in Athens but in far-off Syracuse (in Sicily). Syracuse was governed by a tyranny, and Plato hoped to educate the tyrant's heir in philosophy—a vain hope, as it turned out.

In an attempt to recapture the stimulating give-and-take of a conversation with Socrates, Plato did not write straightforward philosophical treatises but instead dialogues or speeches. All of Plato's dialogues have more than one speaker, and in most the main speaker is named "Socrates." Sometimes this figure is the historical Socrates, sometimes merely a mouthpiece for ideas Plato wished to explore.

A voluminous writer, Plato is not easily summarized. The word that best characterizes his legacy, though, is *idealism*, of which Plato is one of Western philosophy's greatest exponents. Like Parmenides, Plato believed that the senses are misleading. Truth exists but is attained only by training the mind to overcome commonsense evidence. The model for Plato's philosophical method is geometry. Just as geometry deals not with this or that tri-

angle or rectangle but with ideal forms—with a pure triangle, a pure rectangle—so the philosopher could learn to recognize purity. A philosopher would not be misled by, for example, comparing aretê in Athens, Sparta, and Persia; a philosopher would understand the meaning of pure, ideal aretê. No relativist, Plato believed in absolute good and evil.

Philosophy is not for everyone, according to Plato. Only a few people have the necessary intelligence and discipline. In the *Republic*, a dialogue that is perhaps his best-known work, Plato demonstrates the nature of his idealism and its political consequences. He envisioned a society whose elite would study philosophy and attain enlightenment. They would understand the vanity of political ambition but would nonetheless accept the responsibility of governing the masses. Plato never makes clear precisely why they should assume this burden. It is possible he was enough of a traditionalist, in spite of himself, to consider a citizen's responsibility to the polis to be obvious. In any case, Plato's ideal state was one in which philosophers would rule as kings, benevolently and unselfishly.

Plato explored the details of such a state in the *Republic* and in other dialogues, particularly the *Laws*. It is not clear how wedded he was to specific details; indeed, some of them may have been meant merely to shock or to satirize. An overall picture emerges, however. The ideal state would be like a small polis: self-sufficient and closed to outside corrupt influences like Sparta, but committed to the pursuit of things intellectual like Athens. Society would be sharply divided into three classes—philosophers, soldiers, and farmers—with admission to each class based on merit rather than heredity. Poetry and drama would be strictly censored. Plato advocated public education and toyed with more radical notions: not only gender equality but also the abolition of the family and private property, institutions that he felt led to disunity and dissension. (See the box "The Continuing Experiment: Plato on Equality for Women.")

Plato's ideas have always been controversial but almost never ignored. Even in his own day, most people considered Plato far too radical. The writings of his great student Aristotle were more to contemporary tastes. Originally from Macedonia, Aristotle spent most of his life in Athens, first as a student at the Academy, then as the founder of his own school, the Lyceum°. Like Plato, Aristotle wrote dialogues, but none has survived. His main extant works are treatises, largely compilations by

---

**Plato** (PLAY-toe)

**Lyceum** (lie-SEE-um)

## Plato on Equality for Women

Plato (427–348 B.C.), in his masterpiece, *The Republic,* has Socrates argue for the radical idea that in a just society, men and women of what he calls the "guardian class" would have many of the same duties and privileges. These ideas seem to have had little practical effect, although Aristophanes pokes fun at such ideas in his comedy *Ecclesiazusae* (*Women in the Assembly*), ca. 392 B.C. The following fictional discussion between Socrates, who speaks first, and Glaucon (Plato's brother) reveals some of the details.

After we have completed the parts that men must play, we turn to those of women, especially as you call on me to do so.

For men of such a nature and education as we have described there is, in my opinion, no other right way to deal with wives and children than following the road upon which we started them. We attempted, in our argument, to establish the men as guardians of the flock.—Yes.

Let us then give them for the birth and upbringing of children a system appropriate to that function and see whether it suits us or not.—How?

Like this: do we think that the wives of our guardian watchdogs should join in whatever guardian duties the men fulfill, join them in the hunt, and do everything else in common, or should we keep the women at home as unable to do so because they must bear and rear their young, and leave to the men the labor and the whole care of the flock?

All things, he said, should be done in common, except that the women are physically weaker and the men stronger.

And is it possible, I asked, to make use of living creatures for the same purposes unless you give them the same upbringing and education?—It is not possible.

So if we use the women for the same tasks as the men, they must be taught the same things.—Yes.

Now we gave the men artistic and physical culture.—Yes.

So we must give both also to the women, as well as training in war, and use them for the same tasks.—That seems to follow from what you say.

Perhaps, I said, many of the things we are saying, being contrary to custom, would stir up ridicule, if carried out in practice in the way we are telling them.—They certainly would, he said. . . .

Is there anything better for a city than to have the best possible men and women?—Nothing.

And it is the arts and physical culture, as we have described them, which will achieve this?—Of course.

So the institution we have established is not only possible but also the best.—That is so.

The women then must strip for their physical training, since they will be clothed in excellence. They must share in war and the other duties of the guardians about the city, and have no other occupation; the lighter duties will be assigned to them because of the weakness of their sex.

### QUESTIONS

1. In what ways does Socrates propose to make women equal to men?

2. According to Socrates, why should men and women be equal?

3. How would most Greeks of his day have responded to his proposals?

SOURCE: G. M. A. Grube, trans., *Plato's Republic* (Indianapolis: Hackett, 1974), pp. 114, 118–119. Reprinted by permission of Hackett Publishing Company, Inc. All rights reserved.

students of his lecture notes. One of the most wideranging intellectuals, Aristotle had a voracious appetite for knowledge and for writing. His treatises embrace politics, ethics, poetry, botany, physics, metaphysics, astronomy, rhetoric, zoology, logic, and psychology.

Though influenced by Plato's idealism, Aristotle was a far more practical, down-to-earth thinker. His father had been a doctor, which may account for Aristotle's interest in applied science and in biology and the biological method. Unlike Plato, Aristotle placed great emphasis on observation and fieldwork and on classification and systemization.

Aristotle agreed with Plato about the existence of absolute standards of good and evil, but he emphasized the relevance of such standards to everyday life. Unlike Plato, Aristotle considered the senses important guides.

**Aristotle**   This bronze bust, found in a Roman-era villa in the Italian city of Herculaneum, is said to represent the great Classical philosopher. The statue has the dignified and pensive look betokening one of the giants of ancient Greek thought.   *(Alinari/Art Resource, NY)*

Change, he believed, was not an illusion but rather an important phenomenon. Aristotle's view of change was teleological—that is, he emphasized the goal (*telos* in Greek) of change. According to Aristotle, every organism changes and grows toward a particular end and is an integral and harmonious part of a larger whole. The entire cosmos is teleological, and each and every one of its parts has a purpose. Behind the cosmos was a principle that Aristotle called "the unmoved mover," the supreme cause of existence.

Aristotle defined an object's aretê as the fulfillment of its inherent function in the cosmos. The aretê of a horse, for example, was to be strong, fast, and obedient; the aretê of a rose was to look beautiful and smell sweet. As for the aretê of a human being, Aristotle agreed with Plato: only the philosopher achieved true aretê. As a pragmatist, however, Aristotle did not imagine philosophers becoming kings. Even so, he did not advocate democracy, which he considered mob rule. Instead, he advocated a government of wealthy gentlemen who had been trained by philosophers—not the best regime imaginable but, in Aristotle's opinion, the best one possible.

Aristotle believed that men had stronger capacities to make judgments than women and so should rule over them. He condemned states like Sparta that accorded power to women. (See the box "Reading Sources: Spartan Women" on page 78.) Hence Aristotle would be cited in later centuries to justify male dominance. Ironically, however, Aristotle was more enlightened on gender issues than most of his contemporaries. For example, he believed that since women played a crucial role in the family, they should receive education in morality.

Aristotle may be the single most influential thinker in Western history. His scientific writings not only were the most influential philosophical classics of Greek civilization, and of Roman civilization as well, but they remained so during the Middle Ages in the Arabic and Latin worlds. It took nearly two thousand years for serious rivals to challenge Aristotle's intellectual supremacy.

## Athenian Drama

Perhaps the greatest art form that emerged in the polis was drama. Modern comedy and tragedy find distant ancestors in the productions of Athens's theater of Dionysus, named for the god of unrestraint, liberation, and wine. Comedy and tragedy began in religious festivals honoring Dionysus (also known as Bacchus) but quickly became an independent forum for comment on public life. Ancient drama was poetry, not prose. Because it highlighted the relation of the individual to the community, drama proved to be the most suitable poetic medium for the ideology of the polis.

According to ancient tradition, tragedy was first presented at the Dionysian festival in Athens by Thespis in the 530s B.C. (hence the word *thespian* for "actor"). The first surviving tragedy dates from the 470s B.C., the first surviving comedy from the 420s B.C. A play in the fifth century B.C. consisted of a chorus (a group of performers working in unison) and three individual actors, who played all the various individual speaking parts. Plays were performed in an open-air theater on the south hillside of the Acropolis. Enormously popular, drama spread all over Greece, and eventually most poleis had a theater.

Classical Athenian tragedy was performed at the annual Dionysia in March. Each playwright would submit a trilogy of plays on a central theme, plus a raucous farce to break the tension afterward. Comedies, which were independent plays rather than trilogies, were performed both at the Dionysia and at a separate festival held in winter. Wealthy producers competed to outfit the most lavish and impressive productions. Judges would award

**Theater at Delphi**   Open to the air, an ancient Greek theater contained tiers of stone benches above a circular area where the action took place, behind which backdrops could be erected. The audience often had a view of stirring scenery that, at Delphi, included the temple of Apollo and the valley below.   *(Vanni/Art Resource, NY)*

prizes for the best plays—a typical reflection of Greek competitiveness.

*Tragedy* is not easy to define, except generally: a serious play with an unhappy ending. Perhaps a short tag from the playwright Aeschylus° can be said to sum up tragedy: *pathos mathei,* "suffering teaches." The essence of tragedy is what has been called the tragic sense of life: the nobility in the spectacle of a great man or woman failing but learning from failure. In *Oedipus the Tyrant* (ca. 428 B.C.) by Sophocles, for example, the hero unknowingly kills his father and unknowingly marries his mother. Oedipus cannot escape the consequences of his deeds, but he can react to his fate with dignity and heroism; he can try to understand it. Oedipus loses his power as tyrant and goes into exile, but he retains a degree of honor. He carries out his own punishment by blinding himself. As Aristotle observed, tragedy derives its emotional power from the fear and pity that it evokes and from the purification of the senses (*katharsis*) that it leaves in its aftermath.

The great period of Attic tragedy began and ended in the fifth century B.C. Aeschylus (525–456 B.C.), Sophocles (ca. 495–406 B.C.), and Euripides° (ca. 485–406 B.C.) were and are considered the three giant playwrights. Although other tragedians wrote plays, only the works of these three men (or, rather, a small fraction of their works)

have survived. Aeschylus was perhaps the most pious of the three. His plays—notably the trilogy of the *Oresteia* (the *Agamemnon,* the *Libation Bearers,* and the *Eumenides*), the only surviving tragic trilogy, dating from 458 B.C.—take as their central question the justice of Zeus. The subject is the myth of the House of Atreus—in particular, the murder of King Agamemnon by his much-wronged wife, Clytemnestra, and her murder in turn by their son, Orestes, avenging his father. Aeschylus casts this primitive saga into an epic of the discovery of justice. In fulfillment of the will of Zeus, Athena puts an end to vengeance killings and institutes the supposed first court of law: the court of the Areopagus in Athens.

Sophocles, too, was interested in divine justice. His tragedies focus on the relationship between the individual and the community. Heroic individuals have a spark of the divine in them, but their towering virtues are threats to ordinary people. In *Antigone* (ca. 442 B.C.), for example, the heroine refuses to compromise with injustice. Her late brother had committed treason, for which his corpse is denied burial—the standard Greek punishment. Antigone, however, insists on following a higher law, Zeus's law, which demands that all bodies be buried. Turmoil, disorder, and death ensue, but Antigone stays true to principle.

Of the three tragedians, Euripides is the least traditional and the most influenced by the Sophists. His plays reflect the disillusionment of the Peloponnesian War era.

**Aeschylus** (ESS-kih-luhs)   **Euripides** (yoo-RIP-uh-deez)

Euripides was more impressed by divine power than by divine justice. The central gods of Aeschylean drama are Zeus the father and Apollo the lawgiver, while Sophocles focuses on semidivine heroes, but Euripides' major deities are Dionysus and Aphrodite, goddess of erotic passion. In the *Bacchae* (406 B.C.), for example, an arrogant young king named Pentheus is punished for refusing to recognize the power of Dionysus (Bacchus). When he goes to the hills to spy on drunken women, called "Bacchae," who are worshiping the god, he ends up as their prisoner. Driven to frenzy by Dionysus, the women do not recognize the king. Indeed, Pentheus's own mother, one of the Bacchae, mistakes him for an animal and kills him.

The changes in tragedy from Aeschylus to Euripides reflect the changes in Athens as first imperial arrogance and then the Peloponnesian War took their moral toll. Aeschylus's confidence in the goodness of the community gives way first to a focus on the individual struggling to be good and then to a fundamental doubt about the possibility of goodness. The civic order, celebrated so confidently at the end of the *Oresteia* (458 B.C.), looks less certain in Sophocles' *Oedipus* (ca. 428 B.C.) and by the time of Euripides' *Bacchae* (406 B.C.) seems terrifyingly weak.

Comedy, too, was invented in Athens in the Classical period. Like tragedy, comedy offers a moral commentary on contemporary Athenian life. Unlike tragedy, which is usually set in the past and takes its characters from mythology, Athenian comedy (the so-called Old Comedy) is set in the present and pokes fun at politicians and public figures. Whereas tragedy is generally serious and sad, comedy is light, biting, and humorous.

The greatest writer of comedy in the fifth century B.C. was Aristophanes (ca. 455–385 B.C.). His extant plays are lively, ribald, even scatological, and full of allusions to contemporary politics. Aristophanes loved to show the "little guy" getting the better of the powerful and women deflating the pretensions of men. In *Lysistrata* (411 B.C.), his best-known play, he imagines the women of Greece stopping the Peloponnesian War by going on a sex strike, which forces the men to make peace.

## Historical Thought and Writing

Like drama, history flourished in the exciting intellectual atmosphere of classical Athens. Indeed, its two greatest historians, Herodotus (ca. 485–425 B.C.) and Thucydides (ca. 455–397 B.C.), are among the founders of history-writing in the West. This judgment is not meant to discount the contributions of, for example, the Hittites or

Hebrews, or the chronicles, inventories, and genealogies of early Greece. Herodotus and Thucydides, however, are more rationalistic than their predecessors, and their subject matter is war, politics, peoples, and customs—what we think of as the stuff of history-writing today. Indeed, the word *history* comes from a word used by Herodotus, *historiai*, meaning "inquiries" or "research."

The works of Herodotus (*The Histories*) and Thucydides (*The Peloponnesian War*) have unifying themes. The thread through *The Histories* is the cyclical rise and fall of empires. Herodotus sees the Persian Wars as merely one episode in a vast historical drama. Again and again, hardy, disciplined peoples conquered their neighbors, grew wealthy, were corrupted by a life of luxury, and were eventually conquered in turn. Success made people arrogant, driving them to commit injustices, which were eventually punished by Zeus. The breadth of Herodotus's vision is noteworthy. A native of Halicarnassus (a polis on the southwestern coast of Anatolia; see Map 3.4), Herodotus traveled widely, eventually settling in Athens. He wrote not only about Greeks but also about Persians, Egyptians, and a host of other peoples in Europe, Asia, and Africa. (See the box "Global Encounters: The Enemy as Barbarian" on page 90.)

Only a child at the time of the Persian Wars, Herodotus gathered information by interviewing older people in various countries as well as by checking what limited written public records existed. Herodotus also wrote about previous centuries and places he had not visited, but with uneven accuracy. He could rarely resist a good story, and alongside solid research are tall tales, unconfirmed accounts, and myths.

Thucydides, by contrast, prided himself on accuracy. He confined himself mainly to writing about an event that he had lived through and participated in: the Peloponnesian War. A failed Athenian general, Thucydides spent most of the Peloponnesian War in exile, carefully observing, taking notes, and writing.

Like Herodotus, Thucydides was influenced by the grandeur of Classical tragedy. He also shows the signs of the Sophist movement, especially in the finely crafted speeches he includes in his writing. Thucydides' great theme is the disastrous effect of war on the human soul. His case study, the Peloponnesian War, proved that war is a harsh teacher: it strips away the veneer of civilization and reveals the savagery of human nature. In Thucydides' opinion, Periclean Athens was a high point in the history of civilization. The strain of prolonged war, however, destroyed Athens's moral fiber as well as its empire.

## SUMMARY

WESTERN philosophy, science, politics, sculpture, painting, and literary genres such as comedy, tragedy, and history all emerged in Archaic and Classical Greece. The focus of ancient Greek life was the city-state, or polis. Though small, exclusive, often factionalized, and rarely capable of achieving unity in a large area, the polis may be unparalleled in its ability to foster individual creative genius. At the same time, the polis promoted the idea that public duty is more important than private advantage.

Paradox was the hallmark of the polis. The Greeks invented democracy while at the same time limiting the freedom of women and immigrants, oppressing slaves, and engaging in imperialism. Although the Greeks originated the concept that natural phenomena have natural causes, they nonetheless recognized the power of the irrational—be it divine whims or human emotions. With its democracy, freedom, and high culture, Athens stands for one aspect of the achievement of the polis; with its hierarchy, militarism, and austerity, Sparta stands for another.

Athens reached its peak under Pericles, whose leadership in the mid-fifth century B.C. ushered in a time of empire, prosperity, and cultural greatness. The major tragedians were all active, and the Sophist movement was at its most optimistic and progressive. Periclean Athens was unique, not only for the sheer concentration of talent but also for the sense that the state, the cultural elite, and the people were united in a common purpose.

Although later Greeks experienced a fall from that state of grace, they did not suffer any decline in creative achievement. The outbreak of the Peloponnesian War in 431 B.C. marked the beginning of a century in which Greek warfare was more brutal than before. Yet this century also delighted in the comedies of Aristophanes, devoured the history-writing of Herodotus and Thucydides, and debated the philosophy of Socrates, Plato, and Aristotle.

By the end of the fourth century B.C., as we shall see in Chapter 4, the polis would lose its independence to a powerful monarchy. In succeeding years, new cities in western Asia and Egypt would amass the wealth and power to challenge such old centers as Athens as cultural capitals. Yet the culture that flourished in the new sites was Greek culture. The polis lost its freedom but gained a central place in the legacy of the West.

### ■ Notes

1. Excerpt from a poem by Solon, quoted in Aristotle, *Constitution of Athens*, trans. Barry S. Strauss.
2. Charles Rowan Beye, *Ancient Greek Literature and Society*, 2d ed. (Ithaca, N.Y.: Cornell University Press, 1987), p. 78.
3. Ibid., p. 79.
4. Adapted from Richmond Lattimore, trans., *Greek Lyrics*, 2d ed. (Chicago: University of Chicago Press, 1960), p. 19.
5. Herodotus, *The Histories*, trans. Barry S. Strauss.
6. Thucydides, *The Peloponnesian War*, trans. Barry S. Strauss.

### ■ Suggested Reading

Biers, W. *The Archaeology of Ancient Greece: An Introduction.* 2d. ed. 1996. A clear presentation of the achievements and variety of archaeological excavation in Greece.

Boardman, John. *The Greeks Overseas: Their Early Colonies and Trade.* 4th ed. 1999. The standard introduction; authoritative, vivid, updated, and beautifully illustrated.

Cartledge, Paul. *The Spartans: The World of the Warrior-Heroes of Ancient Greece.* 2003. A lively and reliable introduction by a great expert on ancient Sparta.

Connolly, Peter, and Hazel Dodge. *The Ancient City: Life in Classical Athens and Rome.* 1998. Connolly's gorgeous illustrations and outstanding reconstructions distinguish this introduction to daily life in the two cities.

Hanson, Victor Davis. *The Wars of the Ancient Greeks.* 1999. A good introduction, especially to land warfare, by a leading military historian.

Martin, Thomas. *Ancient Greece from Prehistoric to Hellenistic Times.* 2000. A readable and scholarly introduction emphasizing politics and war.

Pomeroy, Sarah B. *Goddesses, Whores, Wives, and Slaves: Women in Classical Antiquity.* 1975. An overview of women in politics and society in Greece, the Hellenistic world, and Rome; still the best introduction to the subject.

Pomeroy, Sarah B., Stanley M. Burstein, Walter Donlan, and Jennifer Tolbert Roberts. *Ancient Greece: A Political, Social, and Cultural History.* 1999. A balanced introduction from the prehistoric to Hellenistic periods, with special emphasis on Classical Greece.

Strauss, Barry S. *Salamis: The Greatest Naval Battle of the Ancient World.* 2004. Opens a window onto Greece and Persia while telling a gripping story.

 **For a searchable list of additional readings for this chapter, go to college.hmco.com/students.**

# The Parthenon

The Parthenon, completed in 432 B.C., dominates both the skyline of Athens and the historical imagination of the West. The building's fine marble and Classical proportions symbolize the free, confident, and united society that one might expect of Periclean Athens, the world's first democracy (see the photograph on page 94). A close look, however, suggests a more complex story. The Parthenon's sculpture offers glimpses of the tensions behind the Classical façade.

The temple of Athena Parthenos ("the Maiden"), as the Parthenon is formally known, was a public project of Greece's wealthiest city-state, leading naval power, and premier democracy. Athenians spared no expense on its construction. Sculpture included a gold and ivory statue of the goddess Athena inside the temple and, on the outside, statuary in each pediment (the triangular space under the eaves) and sculptured reliefs running around the building above the exterior and interior colonnades.

So lavish a program of art demonstrated Athenian wealth but also served an educational purpose: to illustrate basic Athenian values. Because every Athenian male was expected to fight for the city when called on, militant competition is a central theme. Above the exterior colonnade, for example, ninety-two separate panels of relief sculpture depict gods and heroes fighting foes such as giants and centaurs.

See the detail from the south wall. It shows a fight between a human male and a centaur, a mythological creature who was half-man, half-beast. Both the man and the centaur are powerful, but the centaur is old and ugly, while the man is young and handsome. The man fights fairly, while the centaur makes a savage attack with arm and forelegs. The man belongs to a Greek people known as the Lapiths. According to myth, the centaurs attacked the Lapiths during a wedding celebration, but they were driven off by the Lapith men, led by the bridegroom and his Athenian friend, the hero Theseus.

**Centaur Struggling with Lapith, Parthenon Metope, South Side**

*(Courtesy of the Trustees of the British Museum)*

**Four Women in Procession, Parthenon Frieze, East Wall** *(The Louvre)*

To a real-life Athenian observer, the triumph of the Lapiths might have symbolized Athens's victory over the Persians. It was easy to make the connection because the Parthenon was a war monument as well as a temple. When the Persians invaded Athens in 480 B.C. they drove the Athenian people into exile and destroyed the temples on the Acropolis. After Greece's victory, the Athenians came home. But for forty years, they left the Acropolis empty as a reminder of Persian barbarism. Then Pericles sponsored a building program of new temples, of which the Parthenon was the grandest.

Delian League funds were diverted to pay for the new buildings, which raised controversy. Ironically, democratic Athens used allied money, earmarked for defense, to glorify itself. Some people considered that oppressive.

The sculpture above the interior colonnade is a continuous band, or frieze, around the four sides of the building, and it illustrates a procession. Warriors aplenty, primarily cavalrymen but also hoplites and charioteers, compose the lineup. Like the Lapith, the cavalrymen are depicted without clothes, and so they embody the ideal of strong bodies in the service of the polis.

Not all of the men in the interior frieze are warriors, though. Women, too, are depicted. See the detail from the east wall. Look at the four women shown here. The women are on foot, clothed and in solemn procession. The heavy folds of their robes, the hands held at their sides, and the expression on the one visible face all suggest calm and decorum.

From both of these pieces we may detect Athenian commonplaces about gender. Young women were expected to be maidenly, reserved, and modest. Their bodies were to be kept private. Young men were expected to be outgoing and assertive. Although men wore clothes in public, they exercised naked in gymnasia, wrestling grounds, and stadiums, competing in a healthy activity considered to be effective preparation for war.

The historian finds subtler messages in the two scenes. For example, however constrained the role of women, their very presence in the frieze is significant. Women were not permitted to attend the Athenian assembly, but they participated in the rituals and festivals that played so large a role in Athenian public life. Notice, for instance, the two girls shown in the back who are carrying ritual vessels.

Scholars disagree about the subject of the procession in the frieze. Most scholars argue that the subject is the Pan-Athenaic procession, held once every four years to honor Athena. The people depicted are said to be the people of Athens—a daring novelty, considering that all previous Greek temple sculpture was restricted to gods, heroes, and mythological figures. Some scholars view the scene as an illustration of a legend from the early history of Athens. In either case, one thing is clear: the Parthenon sculptures depict the Athenians the way they wanted to see themselves—as courageous, pious, and public-spirited.

# CHAPTER 4

# Alexander the Great and the Spread of Greek Civilization ca. 350–30 B.C.

THE young men in the pebble mosaic shown opposite wield ax and sword against the stag whom they are hunting. The artist, named Gnosis, was a master at rendering perspective and drama. Clearly, no expense was spared on the work, dated around 325 B.C. Both the vigor of the scene and the quality of the craftsmanship symbolize the spirit of a young man who was born in Pella, the Macedonian capital where the mosaic was displayed: that man was Alexander the Great. Alexander was a fearless warrior and one of the most brilliant generals in the history of the world. In just twelve years he conquered all the territory between Greece and India, as well as Egypt.

Alexander created new realities of power as king of Macedon° (r. 336–323 B.C.). A northeastern Greek kingdom that had previously been only a fringe power, Macedon rose meteorically under Alexander's father, Philip II (r. 359–336 B.C.), to become the leading military power in Greece. Philip was a brilliant and ambitious general, but Alexander outstripped him.

Alexander laid the foundations of a new Greek world: the world of the Hellenistic° period (323–30 B.C.), in which Hellenic, or Greek, language and civilization spread and were transformed. This era was distinct in many ways from the preceding Hellenic period (ca. 750–323 B.C.). In Hellenistic times, Macedonians and Greeks replaced Persians as the ruling people of Egypt and western Asia. Large numbers of Greek-speaking colonists moved south and east. Governed by Macedonian dynasties, Egypt and the Levant became integral parts

---

Macedonian (mah-seh-DOE-nee-un)    Macedon (MAH-seh-don)
Hellenistic (hel-len-IS-tik)

Stag Hunt, pebble mosaic from Pella.
(Pella Museum/Archaeological Receipts Fund)

105

of the Greek world and remained so until the Arab conquest in the seventh century A.D. Greek-speaking kingdoms thrived briefly as far east as modern Afghanistan and Pakistan. At times the new ruling elite was open to natives who learned Greek and adopted Greek ways, but more often natives were excluded and exploited.

Conquest put huge amounts of wealth into Greek hands. Alexander and his successors built great new cities: Antioch° in Syria, Pergamum° in Anatolia, Seleucia° in Mesopotamia, and, greatest of all, Alexandria in Egypt. Trade increased and expanded southward and eastward. In political life, individual cities continued to be important, but federal leagues (that is, unions of city-states) and monarchies ruled most of the Greek-speaking world.

Material and political expansion led to unanticipated cultural changes, which may be summarized as a turn inward. Frequently finding themselves among strange peoples, the Greeks sought comfort in new philosophies, religions, and modes of literary and artistic expression. Many of these new cultural forms emphasized people's emotions and intentions, not simply their actions. Science, meanwhile, flourished under royal patronage, as did the emerging discipline of literary criticism. The prestige of royal women tended to promote improvements in the overall status of Greek women.

Hellenistic Greeks boasted of having created one world—a common, or ecumenical (from the Greek *oikoumene*°, "inhabited") region. In truth, that world was complex. Native cultures flourished, while Greeks adapted and Hellenized a number of Egyptian and Asian deities.

Hellenistic Greek contact with one native culture in particular—Judaism—proved to have a lasting impact on the West. Under the impact of the Greeks, Judaism became more self-conscious and placed a greater emphasis on salvation, martyrdom, and individual study and prayer. Some Jews resisted Greek culture, others adopted it, and still others resolved to convert Greeks to Judaism. Reshaped by its contacts with the Greeks, Hellenistic Judaism was poised to transform Western religion.

---

Antioch (AN-tee-ock)    Pergamum (PUR-guh-mum)
Seleucia (seh-LOO-she-uh)    oikoumene (oy-koo-men-AY)

## QUESTIONS TO CONSIDER

- How did Macedon conquer both the Greek city-states and the Persian Empire, and what new states emerged as a result?
- How did Greek civilization spread during the Hellenistic era, and what distinguished it from the civilization of the preceding Classical period?
- What power did women, slaves, and native peoples have in Hellenistic society?
- What new philosophies, religions, and modes of literary and artistic expression were developed in the Hellenistic period?

## TERMS TO KNOW

| | |
|---|---|
| Macedon | Alexandria |
| Philip II | Antioch |
| Alexander the Great | Stoics |
| Hellenism | Epicureans |
| Ptolemies | mystery religions |
| Seleucids | Maccabees |
| Antigonids | |

# PHILIP AND ALEXANDER

THE Hellenistic world was founded by two conquerors: Philip II of Macedon (382–336 B.C.) and his son, Alexander III, known as Alexander the Great (356–323 B.C.). After a century of indecisive warfare among the Greek city-states, Philip swept south and conquered them in twenty years. In even less time Alexander conquered Egypt and all of western Asia as far east as modern India. The legacy of these impressive conquests was to spread Greek civilization and to change it, both of which consequences were revolutionary developments.

## The Rise of Macedon

Macedon was a border state, long weaker than its more advanced neighbors but capable of learning from them and ultimately of conquering them. Though rich in resources and manpower, Macedon lacked the relatively efficient organization of the polis. It included both tribal groups and scattered cities. Several dialects of Greek were spoken, some unintelligible to southern Greeks, who considered Macedonians "barbarians" (from the Greek *barbaros,* meaning "a person who does not speak Greek"). Ordinary Macedonians lived rough, sturdy lives, while the king and the royal court inhabited a sophisticated capital city, Pella, where they sponsored visits by leading Greek artists and writers. Philip confounded Greek stereotypes of Macedonian barbarism by turning out to be a brilliant soldier and statesman—a man of vast ambition, appetite, and energy. A hard drinker, vain, and a man with numerous wives and lovers, he was also an excellent orator and general. Philip's goals were to make himself dominant in Macedon and then, after neutralizing opposition in Greece, to conquer the Persian Empire, or at least its holdings in Anatolia. He accomplished all but the last.

The instrument of Philip's success was his army, a well-trained, professional, year-round force. Macedon, with its plains and horses, was cavalry country, and Philip raised cavalry to a new level of importance. In battle, the Macedonian phalanx would first hold the enemy phalanx until the cavalry could find a weak spot and break the enemy line. Then the phalanx would attack and finish the job. Macedonian hoplites carried extra-long pikes to keep the enemy at a distance. Philip also mastered the technology of siegecraft, raising it to a level unseen since Assyrian days (see page 41).

Philip used his army effectively. After capturing the lucrative gold mine of Mount Pangaeum in Thrace (the

| CHRONOLOGY | |
|---|---|
| 359–336 B.C. | Reign of Philip II of Macedon |
| ca. 342–292 B.C. | Life of playwright Menander |
| 338 B.C. | Greece falls to Philip at Battle of Chaeronea |
| 336–323 B.C. | Reign of Alexander the Great |
| 331 B.C. | Battle of Gaugamela completes Persian defeat |
| 322–275 B.C. | Wars of the Successors |
| 313 B.C. | Zeno founds Stoic philosophy in Athens |
| 312 B.C. | Seleucus I conquers Babylon |
| 304 B.C. | Ptolemy I king of Egypt |
| 294 B.C. | Museum founded in Alexandria |
| 276 B.C. | Antigonus Gonatas king of Macedon |
| 263 B.C. | Kingdom of Pergamum founded |
| ca. 246 B.C. | Parthia revolts from Seleucids |
| ca. 245 B.C. | Bactria gains independence |
| 244–222 B.C. | Reforms of Agis and Cleomenes in Sparta |
| ca. 225 B.C. | Eratosthenes of Cyrene calculates earth's circumference |
| 217 B.C. | Battle of Raphia brings Palestine under Ptolemies |
| 167–142 B.C. | Maccabean revolt in Judea |
| 146 B.C. | Antigonid Macedonia becomes a Roman province |
| 64 B.C. | Seleucid Syria becomes a Roman province |
| 30 B.C. | Ptolemaic Egypt becomes a Roman province |

region east of Macedon), he turned to the Greek city-states nearby. Olynthus, the most important, fell in 348 B.C. Led by the Athenian Demosthenes° (ca. 385–322 B.C.), the main Greek city-states prepared to make a stand.

---

**Demosthenes** (de-MOSS-thuh-neez)

Demosthenes was a superb orator, but his attempts to forge a unified force came too late. By 338 B.C., when an Atheno-Theban army met the Macedonians, Philip had already won over much of the Greek world through diplomacy, bribes, and threats. His complete military victory at Chaeronea in Boeotia was followed up with a lenient settlement in which all the Greeks except Sparta acknowledged Philip's hegemony (see Map 4.1). The Greeks would rebel against Macedon more than once but always in vain, until they fell under the even greater power of Rome. The polis would no longer decide the fate of the eastern Mediterranean.

In 336 B.C. Philip was murdered by a disgruntled courtier, and the invasion of the Persian Empire fell to his 20-year-old son, Alexander, the new king.

## Alexander the Conqueror

Alexander III of Macedon (r. 336–323 B.C.) is as famous in art as in literature, in romance as in history, in Iran and India as in Europe and America. Yet the evidence for the historical Alexander is almost as problematic as that for the historical Socrates or Jesus. After Alexander's untimely death at age 32, contemporaries wrote histories and memoirs, but none has survived. Several good historical accounts, based on earlier texts, are extant, but none was written less than three hundred years after Alexander's day. (See the box "Reading Sources: Virtues and Vices of Alexander the Great.") Alexander, moreover, was not only a legend in his own time but also a master propagandist. Many of the incidents of his life took place in remote regions or among a few individuals, and they tended to grow with the telling.

Still, Alexander's virtues are clear. He was charismatic, handsome, intelligent, and well educated; as a teenager he had Aristotle himself as a private tutor. Alexander was ruthless as well as cultured. He began his reign with a massacre of his male relatives, but he brought a team of Greek scientists along with him on his expedition through the Persian Empire. Although he destroyed peoples and places, Alexander founded twenty cities. One of those cities was born in 331 B.C., at the site of a fishing village in the northwestern part of Egypt's delta. Alexander and his advisers planned a great trading

**Alexander Mosaic**    This detail of a Roman-era mosaic from Pompeii shows Alexander the Great in battle, probably at Issus. Shining in his battle armor, Alexander is bareheaded, with a wide-eyed, intense gaze betokening his power. The larger scene includes the Persian king Darius, fleeing in his chariot.    *(Scala/Art Resource, NY)*

**Map 4.1   Conquests of Philip and Alexander**   Between 359 and 323 B.C., the armies of Macedon conquered first the Greek city-states and then the Persian Empire. Macedonian power extended from Greece and Egypt eastward to modern India.

center to replace Tyre, whose inhabitants had been killed or enslaved by the Macedonians who had stormed the town in 332 B.C. The new city, called Alexandria, later grew into the largest city in the Mediterranean.

For all his varied interests, Alexander was first and foremost a warrior. Battlefield commander of the Macedonian cavalry at age 18, he devoted most of the rest of his life to warfare. As a leader of men, Alexander was popular and inspiring, and he shared risks with his troops. He knew the value of propaganda and took pains to depict his expedition to the Greek city-states as a war of revenge for Persia's invasion of Greece in 480 B.C. instead of what it actually was: the onslaught of Macedonian imperialism. He loved the colorful gesture. He began his expedition to conquer Persia in 334 B.C. by sacrificing animals to the gods at Troy, a site evoking Homer's heroes.

On the eve of invasion, Persia vastly outnumbered Macedon on both land and sea. Darius III of Persia was rich; Alexander's treasury was virtually empty. The Macedonian expeditionary force was short on supplies. The peoples in Persia's multi-ethnic empire were restive, but so too were Alexander's Greek allies, the mainstay of his fleet. One of Darius's advisers proposed a naval campaign to raise a revolt in Greece and force the Macedonians home. How, then, did Alexander propose to conquer Persia?

The answer was the Macedonian army. Although Alexander invaded Anatolia with only about thirty-five thousand men, they were the fastest-marching, most experienced, and most skilled army in the eastern Mediterranean. If Persia would fight the Macedonians in a set battle, Alexander might be confident of victory—and it appeared that Persia would indeed fight. Persian elite

## READING SOURCES

# VIRTUES AND VICES OF ALEXANDER THE GREAT

*Writing in the second century A.D., four centuries after Alexander's death, the historian Arrian composed from earlier accounts what is now the best surviving history of Alexander. A military man himself, Arrian appreciated Alexander's skills but was not blind to his flaws.*

Alexander died in the 114th Olympiad, in the archonship of Hegesias at Athens [June 323 B.C.]. . . . He had great personal beauty, invincible power of endurance, and a keen intellect; he was brave and adventurous, strict in the observance of his religious duties, and hungry for fame. Most temperate in the pleasures of the body, his passion was for glory only, and in that he was insatiable. He had an uncanny instinct for the right course in a difficult and complex situation, and was most happy in his deductions from observed facts. In arming and equipping troops and in his military dispositions he was always masterly. Noble indeed was his power of inspiring his men, of filling them with confidence, and, in the moment of danger, of sweeping away their fear by the spectacle of his own fearlessness. When risks had to be taken, he took them with the utmost boldness, and his ability to seize the moment for a swift blow, before the enemy had any suspicion of what was coming, was beyond praise.

Doubtless, in the passion of the moment Alexander sometimes erred; it is true he took some steps towards the pomp and arrogance of the Asiatic kings: but I, at least, cannot feel that such errors were very heinous, if the circumstances are taken fairly into consideration. For, after all, he was young; the chain of his successes was unbroken, and, like all kings, past, present, and to come, he was surrounded by courtiers who spoke to please, regardless of what evil their word might do. On the other hand, I do indeed know that Alexander, of all the monarchs of old, was the only one who had the nobility of heart to be sorry for his mistakes.

Source: Arrian, *The Campaigns of Alexander,* trans. Aubrey de Sélincourt, rev. J. R. Hamilton (Harmondsworth, U.K.: Penguin, 1971), pp. 395–396.

**For additional information on this topic, go to college.hmco.com/students.**

---

ideology impelled the army to face the enemy head-on. Darius, moreover, was a new monarch and a usurper, and so under pressure to prove himself in the field. As expected, Macedon crushed the enemy. The war was decided in three great battles (see Map 4.1): at the Granicus River in Anatolia (334 B.C.), at Issus in Syria (333 B.C.), and at Gaugamela in Mesopotamia (331 B.C.). Darius fled into Iran and was deposed, assassinated, and replaced by a man whom Alexander captured and executed. By 328 B.C. Alexander's claim to be king of Persia was sealed with blood and iron.

Having conquered the Persian heartland, Alexander turned eastward. The last seven years of his career are marked by three themes. First is the continuing and, in Alexander's mind, apparently open-ended military campaign. He pushed his army not only into the eastern parts of the Persian Empire but beyond, into modern Pakistan, which had not been controlled by Persia since the early fifth century B.C. The Macedonians won a major victory there in 326 B.C. near the Hydaspes River (modern Jhelum River) over the army of King Porus, a force employing as many as two hundred elephants (see Map 4.1). Alexander's infantry suffered considerable casualties before inflicting enough wounds on the elephants to make them uncontrollable. Alexander prepared to continue eastward, perhaps as far as the Bay of Bengal, but his exhausted and homesick men had other plans. They mutinied beside the Hyphasis River (modern Beas River, near the modern Indo-Pakistani border) and forced Alexander finally to turn back. He reached Persia in late 325 B.C.

The second theme of Alexander's later career is his increasing despotism. After conquering Persia, Alexander turned on the Macedonian nobility, among whom he feared potential rivals, for Macedonian nobles had a tradition of rebelling against strong kings. The years after 330 B.C. were marked by conspiracy trials, purges, and assassinations. The most spectacular took place in 328 in Maracanda (modern Samarkand, located in Uzbekistan), where, after a drunken quarrel, Alexander murdered Cleitus, one of his senior commanders.

Another sign of Alexander's growing despotism was his demand for the trappings of Persian kingship. After

**Map 4.2   Hellenistic Kingdoms, Leagues, and City-States, ca. 240 B.C.**   After Alexander's death, his empire lost its political unity. Great new cities and kingdoms arose in the lands he had conquered.

conquering Persia, for example, he made independent-minded Greeks and Macedonians bow down before him. He required that the Greek city-states deify him. "If Alexander wishes to be a god, let him be," was the concise reply of the Spartans, but Alexander had set a precedent for both Hellenistic monarchs and Roman emperors.

The third theme of Alexander's later career is his novel policy of fusion. After returning from the Indian subcontinent, Alexander began training an army of thirty thousand Iranians and dismissed a large number of Macedonian troops. He forced his main commanders to marry Iranian women, just as he himself did. In 324 B.C. Alexander staged a grand banquet in Mesopotamia for nine thousand, at which he prayed for "concord and a partnership in rule between Greeks and Persians." Such actions were a sharp break with the traditional Greek belief in their national superiority. Aristotle, for example, had referred to the peoples of western Asia as fit only to be slaves. Alexander's policy probably owed less to ideal-

ism than to a desire for a new power base independent of the Macedonian nobility.

Alexander died in Babylon in June 323 B.C., a month before he turned 33, probably of malarial fever, although some contemporaries suspected poison and some historians have suggested drunkenness. Alexander did not designate a successor. His wife, pregnant at his death, would give birth to a son and heir, but he was shunted aside by the Macedonian generals, who began a long and bloody round of wars over the spoils of empire. It took approximately fifty years of fighting, from 322 to 275 B.C., to make clear that three large kingdoms—Macedon (under the Antigonid dynasty), Ptolemaic° Egypt, and the Seleucid° realm—would inherit most of Alexander's empire. The rest was divided among small kingdoms, federal leagues, and independent city-states (see Map 4.2).

---

**Ptolemaic** (tol-eh-MAY-ik)   **Seleucid** (seh-LOO-sid)

In the long run, Alexander's life was far more influential than his death. His conquests did nothing less than lay the foundations of the Hellenistic world. It is ironic to measure in such impersonal terms the achievements of one who, more than most people in history, exemplifies individual success. Whether it was exalting a savior or debunking a hero, much of Hellenistic culture centered on the myth of heroism that Alexander had engendered. Historians who insist that the individual is insignificant will rarely have a more challenging refutation than Alexander.

# THE HELLENISTIC KINGDOMS, 323–30 B.C.

VARIETY, flexibility, and the creation of a new elite to transmit Greek culture compose the Hellenistic political legacy. Hellenistic political units ranged from multi-ethnic kingdoms to small, ethnically homogeneous city-states (see Map 4.2). The Greek peninsula saw both a monarchy with republican pretensions and experiments in federalism and social revolution. In Asia and Egypt, a new ruling elite emerged consisting both of Greeks and Macedonians and of natives. Although the first group tended to dominate high office, natives were by no means excluded. The immigrants wanted land, wealth, or adventure. Their paths were smoothed by a new ideology that identified being Greek less with loyalty to an individual city than with participation in a common Greek civilization.

Although the Hellenistic world became relatively peaceful after 275 B.C., conflict among the kingdoms continued. Generally waged at a low level of intensity, with bribes and diplomacy as weapons, the conflict nonetheless sometimes broke out into major battles. A number of small states emerged in Anatolia, notably Pergamum, whose wealthy rulers were patrons of literature and art, and Galatia°, carved out by Celtic invaders from Europe.

## Colonialism, Greek Style

Many Greeks and Macedonians emigrated from home during the fourth and third centuries B.C., but we do not know how many. The few available statistics indicate a significant migration but not a mass exodus. By the sec-

**Clay Flask in Form of Black Boy**    This vase was made in the shape of a squatting figure in the late third century B.C. The subject shows the Hellenistic world's interest in black Africa, while the posture reveals the artist's search for an unusual pose.    *(Martin v. Wagner-Museum der Universität Würzburg)*

ond century B.C. the colonizing impulse had diminished in Greece and Macedon, but a large number of Jews left war-torn Palestine, particularly for Egypt. Ptolemaic Egypt and the Seleucid realm were also the most common destinations for Greek and Macedonian migrants.

Greek migrants could take advantage of a new definition of being Greek that had begun to emerge even before Alexander's conquests. Disappointed by the narrow and self-destructive localism of the Greek city-states, Isocrates° (428–338 B.C.), an Athenian teacher of rhetoric, sought a wider horizon. Isocrates redefined the meaning of Greek identity. He promoted the idea that Greece was not a collection of city-states but a civiliza-

---

**Galatia** (guh-LAY-shuh)

**Isocrates** (eye-SOCK-rah-teez)

tion. "The people we call Hellenes"—that is, Greeks—he wrote, "are those who have the same culture as us, not the same blood."[1]

The ideal of Greek culture made it easier for the migrants to maintain a Greek identity. For that matter, it was now possible for foreigners to become Greek by learning the Greek language and literature. The number of Hellenized foreigners was relatively small, yet their very existence marked a break from the Classical polis, where even a resident genius such as Aristotle could not obtain Athenian citizenship because he was not of Athenian descent.

The Greek language also served as a common denominator, along with Aramaic, both of which became the languages of trade in the eastern Mediterranean. To get a sense of the importance of Isocrates' redefinition of Hellenism, consider that one of the most famous Greek-speakers of all antiquity was Paul, the Christian apostle who was born a Jew in Tarsus, a city in southern Anatolia.

Immigrants sought to realize dreams of prosperity or adventure. Although agriculture was the main economic pursuit, trade, industry, finance, administration, and military service also offered opportunities. The large Ptolemaic bureaucracy needed administrators and tax collectors.

In the Ptolemaic and Seleucid realms, administration was a joint effort of both immigrants and natives. The Macedonian conquerors might have preferred to rely on Macedonians and Greeks, but their territories never attracted enough immigrants from "home" to make that possible. Besides, the new rulers needed both the goodwill and the local knowledge of the people whom they had conquered. Thus the upper echelons of government were dominated by Greek and Macedonian immigrants and their descendants, but native elites held government positions as well. Especially after about 200 B.C., some natives served the new rulers as administrators or soldiers, usually in low- or mid-level positions but sometimes in high office. Others worked in the traditional native administrative structures that survived largely intact in the new kingdoms—for example, as judges or village headmen or priests.

Consider, for example, soldiers. To create a permanent, hereditary military group living in the countryside, Ptolemy° I settled his soldiers on land allotments. Native Egyptians were excluded from the army at first but served as policemen. By the second century B.C., however, the dynasty turned to native Egyptians as a new

source of soldiers. In return for military service, natives now received land, tax breaks, and the right to call themselves Hellenes. Their Hellenism sometimes merely scratched the surface, but other times it went deeper.

An Egyptian named Plenis, a villager in middle Egypt in the late second century B.C., is a good example of this cultural cross-fertilization. Plenis was a tenant farmer on a royal estate and a priest in a local Egyptian cult. His horizon was not narrow, however. Like his father before him, Plenis served as a soldier in the Ptolemaic army. Plenis, moreover, could write Greek as well as Egyptian, and he even used a Greek name: Dionysius, son of Kephalas.

Temples, which often administered large estates, represented important sources of native power. Priests shaped local opinion and were in a position, therefore, both to enjoy considerable independence and to demand royal patronage. Both Ptolemies and Seleucids complied: from Babylon to Edfu, money poured into temple-building and renovation.

The Seleucids addressed the security needs of their far-flung realms by establishing over seventy colonies extending to central Asia. Some colonies were civilian, but most were military, composed of retired or reserve soldiers, mostly Greeks or Macedonians, but also including Jews and other non-Greek peoples. Colonists received land allotments. Greek-style public buildings were erected, and some cities were laid out according to a rectilinear grid reminiscent of the Classical polis. The gymnasium attained a great practical and symbolic importance as both the center of Greek culture and the preparatory school for entry into the elite. The Hellenistic gymnasium offered education in literature, philosophy, and oratory as well as athletics.

Some Seleucid colonies developed into flourishing cities. For example, Greek cities dominated the Syrian coastline and much of Anatolia until the coming of Islam in the seventh century A.D. Greek urbanization should not create the false impression, however, that the Seleucids were motivated by some civilizing mission. They were not. They established colonies to increase their power.

## Economic Expansion

Immigration and colonization were not the only sources of new economic opportunities. At the beginning of the Hellenistic era, Alexander turned the huge gold and silver reserves of Persia into coinage and released it onto the market virtually all at once. Although Alexander's action stimulated a rapid inflation lasting about seventy-five years, it also had the positive effect of greatly stimulating

**Ptolemy** (TOL-eh-mee)

**Tanagra Figurine**     A terra-cotta (baked clay) statuette of around 320 B.C. shows a modestly dressed woman wearing a hat and carrying a fan. Named for its place of manufacture in Greece, this popular style of figure demonstrates the Hellenistic taste for ordinary, household themes.     *(Staatliche Museen zu Berlin, Antikensammlung/Bildarchiv Preussischer Kulturbesitz)*

commerce. In particular, the economy of Hellenistic Egypt became highly monetarized, even on the village level. Barter continued to exist in Egypt, but the widespread presence of money served to increase the production and circulation of goods, helping to render Egypt an economic powerhouse. Another stimulus to trade was the creation of thriving new Hellenistic cities, especially Alexandria with its great harbors, canals, marketplaces, and infrastructure of banks, inns, courts, and shipbuilding facilities.

During Hellenistic times, trade and commerce tended to shift from Greece proper to Anatolia and Egypt (see Map 4.3). The island of Rhodes, located off the southwest tip of Anatolia, grew into a major trading center, especially for grain. This development was the result of excellent harbors; a location on the merchant routes between Asia, Africa, and southeastern Europe; and a superb fleet. The Rhodian aristocracy grew rich off taxes and duties, wisely reinvesting a portion of the profits in naval infrastructure (such as arsenals and dockyards) and in campaigns against pirates. Egypt, too, had many products to trade. Grain was the most important, but textiles, glass, papyrus (from which a kind of paper was produced; see the feature "Information Technology: Papyrus" on page 14), and luxury goods were also significant. Egyptian goods were sold throughout the Mediterranean. A network of canals connecting Alexandria to the Nile and the Red Sea beyond also made possible active trading with Sudan, Arabia, and India.

The Seleucid kingdoms controlled rich trade routes to Arabia, India, and central Asia. Commerce was facilitated by good roads, safe sea travel between the Persian Gulf and India, and a unified royal coinage. The Seleucids traded agricultural goods and manufactured products such as textiles, glassware, and metalwork for spices from India and Arabia. In the first century B.C. they even had trade contacts with China, whose silk garments reached the Mediterranean. The kingdom of Pergamum, which stretched inland from Anatolia's northwest coast, exported the agricultural products of the rich hinterland it controlled, as well as the local gray-blue building stone and, as an alternative to Egyptian papyrus, parchment.

Slavery was an important part of the Hellenistic social and economic scene. Although war and piracy were the main sources of enslavement, some people were born into slavery. In Sicily and southern Italy, slaves worked huge plantations, but eastern Mediterranean slaves were commonly found in the household or in administration, and in cities rather than in the countryside. Many unfree laborers worked on farms in Egypt and western Asia. Following the pre-Greek traditions of those

**Map 4.3   The Eastern Mediterranean, ca. 200 B.C.**   The great Hellenistic powers contended for control of this vibrant, turbulent, and prosperous region. Conflict centered on Palestine and the Aegean islands, the rulership of which frequently changed hands.

regions, they were generally tenant farmers tied to kings or potentates rather than outright slaves.

On some plantations conditions for slaves were harsh enough to lead to mass uprisings. It was not unusual, however, for domestic or administrative slaves to buy their freedom, sometimes using savings they were allowed to keep, sometimes borrowing money from the master or from friends. (See the box "Reading Sources: Macedonian Slaves Buy Their Freedom.") Greeks enslaved fellow Greeks, but often, it seems, with guilty consciences; they frequently made special efforts to help Greek slaves win their freedom. Even in bondage, therefore, Greeks had special privileges.

## Macedon and Greece

Macedon was the last of the three great Hellenistic kingdoms to emerge from civil war after Alexander's death.

Not until 276 B.C. was Antigonus Gonatas, grandson of Alexander's general Antigonus the One-Eyed, established firmly on the throne. His Antigonid° dynasty lasted about a century, when the conquering Romans made Macedon first a republic and then a Roman province.

True to the traditions of Macedon, the Antigonids projected an image of simplicity and toughness. Like Philip II and Alexander the Great, Antigonus immersed himself in the culture of the Greek city-states, partly because he admired it, partly because it brought him prestige. As a young man, Antigonus had studied the new school of Stoic philosophy in Athens (see page 128). As king, he devoted himself to the Stoic dictates of duty, describing his office as "noble servitude" and his diadem as a mere "rag." Antigonus shared the traditional Macedonian ambition to dominate the Greek city-states, but he faced

---

**Antigonid** (an-TIG-on-id)

## MACEDONIAN SLAVES BUY THEIR FREEDOM

*This marble inscription of either 280 or 235 B.C., from the city of Beroia in Macedonia, records the manumission of about a dozen slaves. Note that the slaves had to pay for their freedom, that they had to continue to serve their mistress, Attinas, for the rest of her life, and that they ran the risk of re-enslavement.*

In the reign of King Demetrios, seventh and twentieth year, month Peritios, in the priesthood of Apollonides the son of Glaukios. Payment for their freedom was made by Kosmas, Marsyas, Ortyx to Attinas, daughter of Alketas, for themselves and their wives, Arnion, Glauka, Chlidane, and for their children, both those now alive and any that may later be born, and for all their possessions, each fifty gold *staters* [coins]; and Spazatis for herself and her possessions paid gold *staters,* twenty-five of them. And for them if they remain with Attinas while Attinas lives and do whatever Attinas orders, and Attinas dies, they

may depart to wherever they wish. And it shall not be possible for Alketas nor Alketas' wife nor the descendants of Alketas nor Lareta to seize them or their wives or their children or Spazatis or to reduce [them] to slavery or to take away anything of their possessions on any pretext nor by another on their behalf. But if not, they shall be free and the one attempting to reduce them to slavery shall pay for each person one hundred gold *staters* and to the king another hundred for each person. And if anyone from their possessions takes [something], he shall pay double the value of that which he took from them. [But if] they do not remain and do not do whatever Attinas orders, they and [their] wives and their [children], while Attinas [lives, for the] one not doing [thus], his freedom shall be invalid. . . .

Source: Adapted from Stanley M. Burstein, *The Hellenistic Age from the Battle of Ipsos to the Death of Cleopatra VII* (Cambridge: Cambridge University Press, 1985), pp. 73–74.

rival powers. Besides Ptolemaic Egypt, there was the kingdom of Epirus in northwestern Greece and two new federal leagues in the south, the Aetolians° (north of the Corinthian Gulf) and the Achaeans° (in the Peloponnesus; see Map 4.3).

The federal leagues were more tightly organized than Classical Greek military leagues (such as the Peloponnesian League) and larger than the Boeotian League, a fourth-century B.C. federal alliance that had covered a relatively small territory. The new leagues permitted some participation by ordinary men but were dominated by the wealthy; they were not democracies.

Yet the leagues interest us as models of federalism that would one day influence the founders of the United States. The Aetolians, for example, practiced proportional representation by population in a federal council for constituent cities. The Achaeans successfully balanced local and federal authorities. Constituent cities kept their own constitutions while recognizing federal jurisdiction. The federal government consisted of a governing general (both president and commander-in-chief)

and ten subordinate magistrates, an executive council, and a general assembly.

Athens, less successful than Sparta in maintaining independence, repeatedly experienced Macedonian rule. Through a combination of war and diplomacy, however, Athens won periods of freedom from the late fourth to the mid-second century B.C., when Rome held sway over Greece. Athens remained a vibrant democracy until the late third century B.C., when the oligarchic upper classes finally won the upper hand for good.

Extremes of wealth and poverty, problems of debt, and class conflict challenged Hellenistic Greece. The decline of democracy enabled the wealthy to contribute less to the public good in taxes and to amass private fortunes. The result was sometimes class conflict, but the elite usually made just enough concessions to avoid full-scale revolution.

Sparta was an exception. In the late third century B.C. a social revolution was launched from above by Agis and Cleomenes, two Spartan kings working together. After defeat in the fourth century B.C., Sparta had become impoverished (see page 93). The reformers now offered debt relief, redistribution of land, and restoration of Classical Spartan austerity and equality. Popular in Sparta,

**Aetolians** (ay-TOL-ee-unz)    **Achaeans** (uh-KEE-unz)

the revolution threatened to spread elsewhere. Peloponnesian oligarchs called in Macedonian forces, which crushed Sparta in 222 B.C. and ended the revolution.

## Ptolemaic Egypt

The wealthiest, most sophisticated, and longest-lasting Hellenistic kingdom was Ptolemaic Egypt. One of Alexander's great generals, Ptolemy (d. 283 B.C.), became governor of Egypt in 323 B.C. and proclaimed himself king in 304 B.C. His dynasty lasted until Rome annexed Egypt in 30 B.C., after the suicide of the last of the line, Queen Cleopatra (see page 126). By contrast, Macedon was absorbed by Rome a century earlier, in 146 B.C.; Pergamum was annexed in 133 B.C.; and the Seleucid kingdom succumbed to Rome in 64 B.C.

Unlike the Antigonids, the Ptolemies did not pursue the simple virtues but rather gloried in wealth and grandeur. Ptolemy I showed the way to his successors when he had Alexander's funeral procession hijacked on its way to Macedonia and established a tomb and then a cult in the capital city, Alexandria—a Greek hero-shrine in the land of the pyramids. Ptolemy I made arrangements to have himself proclaimed "savior-god" after his death; his successors, less reticent, took divine honors while still alive.

The most important Ptolemaic borrowing, however, was the pharaonic tradition of royal intervention in the economy, which the Ptolemies combined with Greek customs of literacy and the use of money rather than barter. The result was a highly complex and profitable economy. Putting to use the science of the Museum, the great institute in Alexandria (see page 121), the Ptolemies sponsored irrigation and land reclamation projects, the introduction of new crops (for example, new varieties of wheat), and the greatly expanded cultivation of old ones (such as grapes for wine).

Most of the people of Egypt made their living in agriculture, either as independent small farmers or as tenants on large estates. Government enriched itself through taxes, rents, demands for compulsory labor, state monopolies (on such diverse items as oils, textiles, and beer), and various internal tolls and customs duties. The result was boom times under strong kings and queens in the third century B.C. Egypt became the most prosperous part of the Hellenistic world, and Alexandria became the wealthiest, most populous city in the Mediterranean, as well as its literary capital (see Map 4.3). In the second century B.C., however, continued economic prosperity was derailed by decline. Weak kings, bureaucratic corruption, inflation of the currency, and the end of Greek immigration created conditions for revolt.

Since pharaonic times, tendencies toward regional independence had bedeviled Egypt's government. The Ptolemaic period was no exception. Regional unrest stirred in the 240s B.C. and then mushroomed after the Battle of Raphia in 217 B.C., a struggle in Gaza between the Ptolemies and Seleucids for control of Palestine. The Ptolemies won, but only by enrolling thousands of Egyptians in the Macedonian phalanx, responding to a shortage of Greek mercenaries. Emboldened by their new military power, people in Upper Egypt soon broke into armed revolt against the government in far-off Alexandria. Rival kings appeared in the south, and unrest continued for about a century.

To advance their cause, the rebels inflamed anti-Greek sentiment. High taxes and regional rivalries, however, probably carried more weight than nationalism in the minds of most people. Although friction between immigrants and natives sparked from time to time, most Egyptians accepted the Ptolemies as pharaohs as long as they brought peace and prosperity. (See the box "Global Encounters: Egyptians Versus Greeks in a Temple.")

Nor did the Ptolemies allow national sentiment to stand in the way of reasserting their power. In 196 B.C., for example, Ptolemy V Epiphanes celebrated his coronation in full pharaonic ceremonial in Memphis. Egyptian priests commemorated the occasion in a decree written in Egypt's traditional language of kingship in a trilingual inscription (Greek, hieroglyphic, and demotic—ordinary—Egyptian). This inscription, discovered by French soldiers in 1798 and dubbed the Rosetta stone (named for the place where it was found), led to the modern European deciphering of hieroglyphics.

Despite the frictions, evidence points to native-settler cooperation, especially in the countryside, where intermarriage and bilingualism became common. Many an ordinary Greek became fully assimilated to Egyptian ways, and even wealthy, sophisticated, urban Greeks adopted a smattering of Egyptian customs. The Egyptian calendar, Egyptian names, and mummification were all in use. By 98 B.C. assimilation was evident in the cultural hybrid of a group of 18- and 19-year-old male youths who received traditional Greek military and literary training but prayed to Egypt's crocodile-god.

## Seleucids and Attalids

The kingdom founded by Alexander's general Seleucus° (ca. 358–281 B.C.) experienced shifting borders and inhabitants. The Seleucid kingdom began when Seleucus

---

**Seleucus** (suh-LOO-kus)

# Egyptians Versus Greeks in a Temple

This second-century B.C. papyrus, a petition to the authorities from a Greek worshiper of Serapis, provides insight into relations between Greeks and Egyptians in Hellenistic Egypt. It shows how Greeks lived in the temple at Memphis in order to worship Serapis, a Hellenized Egyptian god (see page 130). It also depicts violence and hostility across ethnic lines.

To Dionysius, general and one of the "friends" [of the king], from Ptolemy son of Glaucias, a Macedonian, one of those "held in detention" [that is, on a voluntary, religious retreat] for twelve years in the great Temple of Serapis in Memphis. As I have suffered grave injustice and my life has been frequently endangered by the temple cleaners whose names are listed below, I am taking refuge with you in the belief that in this way I would best secure justice. For on . . . [November 9, 161 B.C.] they came to the temple of Astarte, which is in the sanctuary, and in which I have been living "in detention" for the number of years mentioned above; some of them had stones in their hand and others sticks, and they tried to force their way in, in order to seize the opportunity to plunder the temple and to put me to death because I am a Greek, like men laying a plot against my life. But when I anticipated them and shut the door of the temple, and shouted to them to withdraw in peace, they did not go away even so. When Diphilus, one of the worshipers held "in de-

tention" by Serapis besides me, expressed indignation at their conduct in such a temple, they pushed him back, handled him very roughly and beat him up, so that their lawless brutality was clear for all to see. When these same men treated me in the same way in . . . [November 163], I immediately addressed a petition to you, but as I had no one to look after the matter further, they were let off scot-free and became even more arrogant. I therefore ask you, if you please, to order them to be brought before you, so that they may receive the punishment they deserve for all these misdeeds. Farewell.

## QUESTIONS

1. What is Ptolemy, son of Glaucias's complaint about? Is this the first time he has made such a complaint?

2. Why was Ptolemy unable to get justice before? What does this tell us about the way petitions were handled by the government?

3. Why were Ptolemy and Diphilus attacked? What does the attack indicate about Greek-Egyptian relations in second-century B.C. Egypt?

SOURCE: Adapted from M. M. Austin, *The Hellenistic World from Alexander to the Roman Conquest: A Selection of Ancient Sources in Translation* (Cambridge: Cambridge University Press, 1981), pp. 434–435. Reprinted with the permission of Cambridge University Press.

---

took Babylon in 312 B.C. and ended in 64 B.C. when Syria became a Roman province. Many territorial changes occurred in between. The first three kings ruled a domain stretching from the Aegean to Bactria° (modern Afghanistan), but by the early second century B.C. most of the Iranian Plateau and lands eastward had been lost. At its height, in the third century B.C., the Seleucid kingdom had three nerve centers: Ionia (in western Anatolia), with a capital at Sardis; Syria, with a capital at Antioch; and Babylonia, whose capital was Seleucia-on-the-Tigris (near modern Baghdad; see Map 4.2).

Unlike the compact Nile Valley, with its relatively homogeneous population, the far-flung and multi-ethnic Seleucid lands presented an enormous administrative

challenge. To govern such a conglomerate, the kings took over the Persian system of satraps (provincial governors), taxes, and royal roads and post (see page 46), to which they added an excellent army trained according to Macedonian traditions, a common coinage, and a Hellenistic ruler cult. The chief Seleucid innovation was the establishment of colonies. Greek and Macedonian soldiers and administrators dominated, but natives also filled bureaucratic slots.

The greatest Seleucid city was Antioch, which became one of the wealthiest and most luxurious of all eastern Mediterranean cities; only Ptolemaic Alexandria outstripped it. The intellectual and artistic capital of Greek Asia in Hellenistic times, however, was not Antioch but Pergamum, in northwestern Anatolia (see Map 4.3).

The rulers of Pergamum, the Attalid dynasty of kings, carved out a small kingdom that became indepen-

---

**Bactria** (BACK-tree-uh)

**Laocoön**   This famous statue group of the second or first century B.C. shows the Trojan priest Laocoön and his sons being strangled by snakes sent by the gods. The scene's emphasis on extreme emotion is typical of Hellenistic art. *(Scala/Art Resource, NY)*

dent of the Seleucids in 263 B.C. and fell into Roman hands in 133 B.C. The Attalids made Pergamum into a showplace of Greek civilization, a would-be second Athens. As in Athens, public building was focused on a steep acropolis. The upper city of Pergamum was laid out on hillside terraces rising to a palace and fortified citadel. One of the terraces housed the famous Pergamum Altar, a huge monument to an Attalid victory over the Celts, who first invaded Anatolia in 278 B.C. and whose advance the Attalids checked. They could not, however, stop the Celts from settling in central Anatolia, where they created their kingdom of Galatia.

Pergamum was famous for its sculptors and for a library second only to Alexandria's. Pergamene writers focused on scholarship, to the exclusion of poetry, perhaps as a result of the influence of Stoic philosophers, who disapproved of poetry's emotionalism.

## The Greco-Indian Interaction

The Seleucids' hold on Alexander's vast eastern domains turned out to be temporary. A new Persian dynasty, the Parthians°, achieved independence in the mid-third century B.C. and over the next century carved out an empire extending westward into Mesopotamia. But to the east, Bactria remained Greek, if not Seleucid. From the mid-third century B.C. an independent Greek Bactria prospered (see Map 4.2).

Vivid evidence of Greek colonization in Bactria comes from the site of Aï Khanum (its ancient name is unknown) in northern Afghanistan. This prosperous and populous city contained many reminders of Greece,

---

**Parthians** (PAR-thee-unz)

**A Greek-Influenced Indian Statue**  This figure of a *bodhisattva* ("enlightened one") belongs to the Gandharan school, which was heavily influenced by Hellenistic sculpture. The statue's proportions, facial features, and draped clothing particularly recall Hellenistic motifs, suggesting that it may be the work of a Greek sculptor.  *(Royal Ontario Museum)*

tury B.C., when the Persians settled Greek mercenaries there. Virtually no literary evidence survives, but monuments and, particularly, coins demonstrate Greco-Indian cultural interaction. For example, some coins from the second century B.C. show bilingual inscriptions in Greek and Indian languages. Their designs include a variety of Indian religious motifs, such as the lotus plant, symbol of Lakshmi, goddess of wealth and good fortune. Indians admired Hellenistic astronomy; one text goes so far as to say that Greek scientists should be "reverenced like gods."

The Hellenistic world seems to have intrigued King Asoka° (r. ca. 270–230 B.C.), who ruled almost the entire subcontinent, the largest empire in India to date. Asoka is best remembered as a religious reformer. A convert to Buddhism, he played a major role in its spread, which proceeded under the slogan of *dhamma*—that is, "morality" or "righteousness." One of his inscriptions records "victory" by dhamma, "where reigns the Greek king named Antiochus, and beyond the realm of Antiochus in the lands of the four kings named Ptolemy, Antigonus, Magas, and Alexander," which is generally thought to refer to embassies to the Hellenistic kingdoms.[2]

The envoys apparently found few converts, for it is difficult to find any trace of Buddhism in Hellenistic Greek culture, at least outside the Greco-Indian kingdoms. There one of the most powerful Greek rulers, Menander Soter Dikaios (r. ca. 155–130 B.C.), may have converted to Buddhism in the mid-second century B.C. But certain aspects of Indian religion—especially India's powerful currents of asceticism, mysticism, and monasticism—interested Greek intellectuals around the Mediterranean in Hellenistic and Roman times. Observers on Alexander's expedition, Hellenistic envoys, merchants, and philosophers in search of Eastern wisdom all served as conduits between East and West. One of the most influential was Megasthenes, a Seleucid ambassador to the court of Asoka's grandfather, who published his *Indika*, a description of India, around 300 B.C.

Yet the degree to which this interest influenced Greek and Roman culture is debatable. Although ancient writers mention Greek or Roman philosophers who were attracted by Indian culture, modern scholars tend to be cautious. The ancients had a weakness for tall tales and stories of exotic inspiration. Consider, for example, the following reports. Pyrrho of Elis, founder of the Hellenistic philosophical school of skepticism (see page 129), supposedly based his notion of the imperturbable sage

among them a gymnasium, theater, and library. A pillar in the gymnasium was inscribed in the mid-third century B.C. with 140 moral maxims from Delphi in Greece, over 3,000 miles away.

In the second century B.C. Bactrian kings extended their rule into the Indus River valley and the Punjab, a region with a modest Greek presence since the fifth cen-

**Asoka** (uh-SO-kuh)

on one Calanos, an Indian whom Pyrrho saw step calmly on a funeral pyre when Pyrrho was part of Alexander's expedition. Around A.D. 40 Apollonius of Tyana, a pagan religious thinker, is supposed to have traveled to India to study with its sages. Two centuries later the great Neo-Platonic philosopher Plotinus (A.D. 235–270) is reported to have traveled with the Roman emperor Gordian's army eastward, hoping in vain to reach India. Some scholars see Indian influence in Plotinus's mysticism and pantheism, but others dismiss these various reports.

Central Asian nomads overran Bactria in the late second century B.C. The Hellenistic kingdoms of India and Pakistan, however, survived until about the time of Christ, and some Greek communities lasted until the fifth century A.D. The Gandharan sculptors who flourished in a formerly Greek-ruled region in about A.D. 200 used Greek artistic techniques to depict Buddhist subjects, which might suggest the impact of Indian culture on the remaining Greek population.

# THE ALEXANDRIAN MOMENT

**B**Y the first century B.C. Alexandria was a city of half a million or more inhabitants. It was one of the largest, wealthiest, and most important cities in the world. The bulk of the people were Egyptian, but Greeks and Jews made up large minorities, and no one would have been surprised, in this cosmopolitan center, to see an Indian or a Celt, an Italian or a Persian.

The capital of Egypt, Alexandria was also perhaps the most important place where Greek culture was spread and transformed in the Hellenistic era. At the same time, it was a mix of ethnic cooperation and conflict. Underwater archaeologists, for example, looking for submerged parts of the city in Alexandria harbor, have found Egyptian sphinxes and obelisks as well as Greek statues. Written sources portray a picture of social change in the elite, an increase in leisure time, a growth in educational opportunities for both sexes, royal patronage of culture, and the value of even a limited knowledge of Greek literature as the ticket to advancement.

## The Anti-Epic Temperament

In 294 B.C. King Ptolemy I invited the deposed tyrant of Athens, Demetrius of Phalerum, to found an institution of culture in Alexandria. A writer himself, Ptolemy was no less sincere because the new foundation would bring him prestige and keep his engineers up to date on new

**Hellenistic Craftsmanship**    This cameo, known as the Farnese Plate, is a superb example of ancient gem production, and was probably made in Alexandria. The Nile (*far left*) and the other figures symbolize agricultural fertility.    *(G. Dagli Orti/ The Art Archive)*

technology for warfare and agriculture. Demetrius had studied with Aristotle's successor at the Lyceum, Theophrastus° (ca. 370–288 B.C.), a practical man interested in compiling and cataloging knowledge.

The new institution was called the Museum (literally, "House of the Muses," or the home of the female deities who inspired creativity). The Museum was a residence, study, and lecture hall for scholars, scientists, and poets. One of its key components was the Library, in its day the largest collection of Greek writing in the world. In the third century B.C.—at the height of the Ptolemaic kingdom—the Library contained 700,000 papyrus rolls, the equivalent of roughly 50,000 modern books. Its nearest competitor, at Pergamum, contained less than a third as many rolls.

The Library reflects the growth of the Hellenistic reading and writing public. As independence vanished, city-states converted their military training programs for 18- and 19-year-old men into educational programs in literature and philosophy. The names of over a thousand

---

**Theophrastus** (the-uh-FRAS-tus)

**Street Musicians**   The lively scene of a mixed group of young and old, male and female, recalls the jaunty mimes popular with the Hellenistic public. A mosaic from about 100 B.C., the artwork comes from a private villa in the Greco-Italian city of Pompeii.   *(Museo Nazionale, Naples)*

writers of the Hellenistic era survive, and after 300 B.C. anthologies, abridgments, and school texts multiplied.

Though modeled on Athens's Lyceum, the Museum represented a break from the public culture of the Classical period. The denizens of the Museum were an elite, dependent on royal patronage and self-consciously Greek and not Egyptian. At the Museum, culture was an object of study, not a part of civic life, as it had been in Classical Athens. A clever remark of Timon, a philosopher from the Peloponnesus who lived in the third century B.C., rings true: "In Egypt, land of diverse tribes, graze many pedants, fatted fowls that quarrel without end in the hen coop of the Muses."

Before we examine Alexandrian literature further, it is worth noting how greatly Hellenistic Athenian literature diverged from Classical culture. The greatest Hellenistic Athenian writer, a man famous throughout the

ancient world, was Menander° (ca. 342–292 B.C.). He was the master of a style of comedy called "New Comedy," as distinguished from the "Old Comedy" of Aristophanes, which had flourished a century earlier (see page 100). Where Old Comedy was raucous and ribald, New Comedy was restrained; where Old Comedy focused on public matters such as war and politics, New Comedy was domestic and private. New Comedy was typical of the turn away from public life in Hellenistic times.

Menander wrote over seventy plays, but only one complete work has survived, *Dyskolos* (*The Grouch*). There are also large excerpts from several other comedies as well as Roman imitations. Witty and fluent, Menander favored stock plots and stock characters: the

---

**Menander** (meh-NAN-der)

boastful soldier, the clever slave, the dashing but inept young man, the sweet maiden, and the old miser. Within those limitations, Menander created realistic and idiosyncratic characters. As a Hellenistic critic asked rhetorically: "O Menander and Life, which of you imitated the other?"

Like Menander, Alexandrian writers spurned public themes, but in Alexandria the characteristic literary figure was not the playwright but the critic. He was a professional man of letters, and he aimed at establishing a literary canon and standardizing the texts of the canonical authors. Adopted by the Romans, Alexandrian critical standards have influenced the West to this day.

Of the three greatest Alexandrian writers, two—Callimachus° (305–240 B.C.) and Apollonius° of Rhodes (b. ca. 295 B.C.)—worked at the Library; the third, Theocritus° (ca. 300–260 B.C.), probably lived on a stipend from the Ptolemies. Popular for centuries, Callimachus was probably the most influential, the complete Hellenistic poet. A native of Cyrene (see Map 4.2) who came to Alexandria as a schoolteacher, Callimachus found a position in the Library. There he composed a virtually universal history of all recorded Greek (and much non-Greek) knowledge.

A prolific writer, Callimachus generally preferred short to long poems: "Big book, big evil" was his maxim. Earlier Greek poets were usually austere and public-minded; Callimachus preferred the private, the light, and the exotic. "Don't expect from me a big-sounding poem," he writes. "Zeus thunders, not I."[3] Callimachus was expert at the pithy statement in verse—the epigram.

Another major Alexandrian writer was Callimachus's student Apollonius of Rhodes. Tradition claims that Apollonius retired to Rhodes after his epic poem *Argonautica*° (*Voyage of the Argo*) was poorly received. The subject is the legend of Jason and the heroes who travel on the ship *Argo* to Colchis, at the far end of the Black Sea, in pursuit of the Golden Fleece (the skin of a winged ram). With the help of the Colchian princess Medea, who falls in love with Jason, the heroes succeed and return home safely after numerous adventures.

The most striking thing about Apollonius is his doubt about the very possibility of heroism. Apollonius's Jason is no hero of old. Whereas Homer describes Odysseus as "never at a loss," Apollonius describes Jason as "helpless." Men move the action in the *Iliad* and the *Odyssey*; Jason

depends on a woman, Medea, for his success. Indeed, much of the *Argonautica* focuses on Medea and in particular on her love for Jason. With the exception of the works of Sappho, previous Greek poetry generally either ignored female eroticism or presented it in a hostile light. Apollonius's work illustrates both the improved status of women in Hellenistic ideology and the great interest of the age in the life of the emotions. All in all, the *Argonautica* is less a traditional epic than an anti-epic.

Like Callimachus, Theocritus, a native of Syracuse, wrote short, polished poetry. He composed thirty-one subtle and refined poems, conventionally known as idylls. The best known of the poems focus on country life. They are the first known pastoral poems; indeed, Theocritus probably invented the genre. Theocritus's pastorals explore nature, but always self-consciously, always with the city in mind. His peasants and shepherds are marvelously cultured, more like townspeople on an excursion than true rustics. Through his Roman admirers, Theocritus's love of nature has exerted a powerful hold on the Western literary imagination.

Outside the Museum, Alexandria had a lively popular culture, much of it Egyptian or influenced by Egyptian models. A glimpse of this culture is offered in the seven surviving mimes, or farces, of an obscure writer named Herondas or Herodas. Though written in literary Greek, they discuss commonplace subjects—shopping for shoes, tourism, lawsuits, and beatings at school—and titillating themes such as adultery and prostitution. Lively, bawdy, funny, and filled with the grit of everyday life in the third century B.C., they are a reminder of just how specialized the culture of the Museum was.

## Advances in Science and Medicine

The Ptolemies not only reaped practical benefits in military and agricultural technology from their Museum, but they also became the patrons of a flourishing period in the history of pure scientific inquiry. They unwittingly promoted a split between philosophy and science that has characterized much of Western culture since. Antigonid patronage of ethical and political philosophy helped keep Athens pre-eminent in those fields. In contrast, the study of science tended to shift to Alexandria. The rulers of Pergamum and, far to the west, Syracuse, a flourishing Hellenistic city in Sicily, were great patrons of science as well. Wealth, improved communications and literacy, continued warfare, and cross-fertilization between Greek and non-Greek traditions, especially Greek and Babylonian astronomy, were all catalysts of Hellenistic science.

---

**Callimachus** (kah-LIH-muh-kus)
**Apollonius** (ap-uh-LO-nee-us)
**Theocritus** (the-OCK-rih-tus)
*Argonautica* (ar-go-NAW-tih-kuh)

Some of the best-known figures of Hellenistic science were mathematicians. In his *Elements,* the Alexandrian Euclid (active ca. 300 B.C.) produced a systematic exposition of geometry that was hugely influential in both Western and Islamic civilizations. A Sicilian Greek, Archimedes° of Syracuse (287–212 B.C.), did original work on the geometry of spheres and cylinders, calculated the approximate value of pi (the ratio of a circle's circumference to its diameter), and made important discoveries in astronomy, engineering, optics, and other fields. Archimedes was as great an inventor as he was a theoretician. One of the most important of his innovations was the water snail, also known as Archimedes' screw—a device to raise water for irrigation. Invented by Archimedes during a stay in Egypt, the screw made it possible to irrigate previously barren land, as did the ox-driven water wheel, another Ptolemaic invention.

Advances in mathematics promoted advances in astronomy. Aristarchus of Samos (active ca. 275 B.C.) is known for his heliocentric hypothesis, which confounded tradition by having the earth revolve around the sun, instead of the sun around the earth. He was right, but Hellenistic astronomy lacked the data to prove his theory, so its rejection was not unreasonable at the time. Eratosthenes° of Cyrene (active ca. 225 B.C.) was saddled with the frustrating nickname of "Beta" (the second letter of the Greek alphabet) because he was considered second best in every branch of study. This "second best" nonetheless calculated through simple geometry an extraordinarily accurate measurement of the earth's circumference.

Hellenistic medicine thrived in Alexandria. Both Greece and Egypt had long-established medical traditions. Egyptian drugs, and possibly Egyptian doctors' knowledge of the eye as well as their emphasis on measurement, helped stimulate Alexandrian medical progress, as no doubt did the mere fact of cross-fertilization. The key to medical advance, however, was the dissection of human cadavers in Alexandria, a first in the history of science. In Greece, as in many ancient societies, religious tradition demanded that dead bodies not be mutilated. But in the frontier atmosphere of early Alexandria, this traditional taboo lost much of its force. Although Egyptians did not practice dissection, they did practice embalming, which may have helped Alexandrian Greeks overcome the prohibition against cutting open the human body. Ever supportive of research, the Ptolemies provided corpses to Greek scientists for dissection. Indeed, they had condemned criminals sent from prison for live dissection by scientists. The practice, only a short-lived experiment in the early third century B.C., outraged many writers in antiquity, just as today it would be considered an atrocity.

The leading scientific beneficiary was Herophilus° of Chalcedon (ca. 320–250 B.C.), a practicing physician in Alexandria. Among his achievements was the recognition (against Aristotle) that the brain is the center of the nervous system, a careful dissection of the eye, the discovery of the ovaries, and the description of the duodenum, which he named (*duodenum* is a Latin translation of a Greek word meaning "twelve fingers," describing the organ's length). In addition, Herophilus developed a detailed theory of the diagnostic value of measuring pulse rates.

Hellenistic technology has long fascinated and frustrated scholars. The great engineers invented both numerous engines of war and various "wonderworks" to amuse the royal court. Among the latter were mechanical puppets and steam-run toys. Given these advances, why did the Greeks achieve neither a scientific revolution, along the lines of the one begun in the early modern era by thinkers such as Copernicus and Galileo, nor an industrial transformation, such as was ushered in by the steam engine around A.D. 1800? Historians are not entirely sure but can venture a guess. Greek machine-making technology was not as sophisticated as that of eighteenth-century Europe. The prevalence of slavery in antiquity, moreover, discouraged the invention of labor-saving machines; steam was used only for playthings and gadgets. A related point is the elitist bias of Greek intellectual life. After Archimedes' death, for example, it was claimed that although he had written copiously on theoretical matters, he never bothered to write about his mechanical inventions because he considered them "ignoble and vulgar." (See the box "The Continuing Experiment: Archimedes' Experiment.")

Perhaps the most important point is the Greek attitude toward nature. Whereas Jews and Christians learned from the Bible that human beings have dominion over nature, thereby making possible the conclusion that it is appropriate to conquer nature, the Greeks thought in more restricted terms. They believed that nature set limits, that a virtuous person tried to follow nature, not subdue it. Thus Greek engineers were not inclined to make the revolutionary changes that their modern counterparts have promoted.

---

**Archimedes** (ar-kuh-MEE-deez)
**Eratosthenes** (er-uh-TOSS-the-neez)

**Herophilus** (her-AH-fih-lus)

## Archimedes' Experiment

Archimedes of Syracuse (ca. 287–212 B.C.) was the greatest mathematician of Greek antiquity and a notable inventor. In this crude but brilliant experiment, Archimedes proved that when an object is submerged in a fluid, it feels a buoyant force equal to the weight of the fluid that it has displaced. The anecdote is an intriguing reminder that although the ancient world did not have a Scientific Revolution like that of the early modern era, ancient scientists could conduct experiments.

[King Hiero of Syracuse asks Archimedes to test a gold crown, which, Hiero suspects, has been watered down with silver.]

The latter [Archimedes], while the case was still on his mind, happened to go to the bath, and on getting into a tub observed that the more his body sank into it the more water ran out over the tub. As this pointed out the way to explain the case in question, without a moment's delay, and transported with joy, he jumped out of the tub and rushed home naked, crying with a loud voice that he had found what he was seeking; for as he ran he shouted repeatedly in Greek, "Eureka, Eureka!" [you-REE-kuh] ("I have found it! I have found it!").

Taking this as the beginning of his discovery, it is said that he made two masses of the same weight as the crown, one of gold and the other of silver. After making them, he filled a large vessel with water to the very brim, and dropped the mass of silver into it. As much water ran out as was equal in bulk to that of the silver sunk in the vessel.

Then, taking out the mass, he poured back the lost quantity of water, using a pint measure, until it was level with the brim as it had been before. Thus he found the weight of silver corresponding to a definite quantity of water.

After this experiment, he likewise dropped the mass of gold into the full vessel and, on taking it out and measuring as before, found that not so much water was lost, but a smaller quantity: namely, as much less as a mass of gold lacks in bulk compared to a mass of silver of the same weight. Finally, filling the vessel again and dropping the crown itself into the same quantity of water, he found that more water ran over for the crown than for the mass of gold of the same weight. Hence, reasoning from the fact that more water was lost in the case of the crown than in that of the mass, he detected the mixing of silver with the gold, and made the theft of the contractor perfectly clear.

### QUESTIONS

1. What did Archimedes' experiment consist of, and what did it prove?

2. In what ways was Archimedes a practical man? In what ways was he an absent-minded professor?

3. Why did Archimedes carry out his experiment in a bath-house rather than a laboratory? What does this tell us about the conditions of science in ancient times?

SOURCE: Vitruvius, *The Ten Books of Architecture,* trans. Morris Hicky Morgan (Cambridge, Mass.: Harvard University Press, 1914), p. 254.

## Men and Women in Art and Society

Like Hellenistic literature, Hellenistic art attests to changing male attitudes toward women and toward gender issues. The portrait of Jason and Medea in Apollonius's *Argonautica* makes fun of masculine pretensions and celebrates the triumph of female intelligence. It also presents a sympathetic portrait of a woman's romantic desire for a man, as does Theocritus's work. In the Classical period, depictions of romantic love were generally restricted to male homoeroticism. Accordingly, statues of naked males were common, but women were almost always depicted clothed. Hellenistic sculpture, by contrast, affords many erotic examples of the female nude.

There are indications that the Hellenistic Greek male of the elite was much more willing than his Classical predecessor to see lovemaking as a matter of mutuality and respect. Classical vase-painting often depicts heterosexual lovemaking with a lusty and explicit mood. In contrast, in Hellenistic vase-painting the emphasis is more often on tenderness and domesticity. Hellenistic men wrote with sensitivity about satisfying a woman's needs and desires. The vogue for representations of Hermaphrodite°, the mythical creature who was half-female and half-male, may suggest a belief that the feminine was as important a part of human nature as the masculine.

---

**Hermaphrodite** (her-MAF-ro-dyte)

125

**Aphrodite of Cnidos** This 7½-foot-tall marble statue is a Roman copy of an original by Praxiteles (ca. 350–330 B.C.). Perhaps the most famous of Hellenistic female nudes, the statue was housed in a special shrine where it could be viewed in the round to accommodate all the interest it generated. *(Vatican Museums)*

Many a Hellenistic artist or writer seems to be as interested in emotion as in action and to focus on the inner as much as on the outer life. Hellenistic art often depicts women, children, and domestic scenes. Representations of warriors are as likely to focus on their unrestrained emotions as on their soldierly self-control.

Hellenistic women enjoyed small improvements in political and legal status and considerable improvements in economic and ideological status. A number of reasons explain these advances. First, Greek women, particularly in the elite, benefited from the spread of monarchy. For one thing, queens and princesses in royal courts had power and prestige that had been denied women in city-states. For another, under monarchy the notion of the loyal and prosperous subject replaced that of the independent citizen-warrior. Citizens in the Classical polis had been encouraged to be aggressive and exaggeratedly masculine to the point of hostility toward women. Subjects in Hellenistic monarchies were meant to cultivate the more passive and reflective virtues of legalism, obedience, and economic enterprise. Because Greek men associated these virtues with women, their respect for female qualities tended to increase. Also, in the new cities, as in many a frontier society, women were permitted to inherit and use property more often than in old Greece.

It was an era of powerful queens: Olympias, Alexander the Great's mother, played kingmaker after her son's death. Arsinoe II Philadelphus was co-ruler of Egypt with her husband (who was also her brother) for five years at the height of Ptolemaic prosperity around 275 B.C. The most famous Hellenistic woman, Cleopatra VII, was queen of Egypt from 51 to 30 B.C. Although she was the lover of two of the most powerful men in the world, the Romans Julius Caesar and Mark Antony, Cleopatra was no exotic plaything. Rather, she was a brilliant and ambitious strategist who nearly succeeded in winning a world empire for her family. (See the feature "Weighing the Evidence: Images of Cleopatra" on pages 134–135.)

Writers in the new Hellenistic cities often described freedom of movement for women. Theocritus and Herondas, for example, show women visiting a temple or a show. Nor did Hellenistic men, even in Athens, obey Pericles' injunction not to speak of women, even good women. In Hellenistic Athens, aristocratic fathers put up inscriptions in honor of their daughters who had participated in the cult of Athena. Although women generally continued to need a male guardian to represent them in public, in some situations, at least in Egypt (where the evidence is most plentiful), a woman could represent herself. A woman could petition the government on her

## READING SOURCES

# THE POWER OF HELLENISTIC WOMEN—AND ITS LIMITS

*These two inscriptions commemorate prominent women. The first, written about 218 B.C. in the city of Lamia, honors Aristodama of Smyrna. Note that although Aristodama is free to perform in public, her brother Dionysios probably traveled with her as her official guardian. The second inscription, from the city of Priene, perhaps in the first century B.C., recalls Phile, who funded an aqueduct and was rewarded with public office.*

### Aristodama

. . . With good fortune. Resolved [by the city] of the Lamians. Since Aristo[d]ama, daughter of Amyntas, a citizen of Smyrna in Io[nia], epic poetess, while she was in our city, gave several [public recitations] of her poems in which the nation of the Aetolians [and] the People's ancestors were worthily commemorated and since the performance was done with great enthusiasm, she shall be a proxenos [diplomatic representative] of the city and a benefactress, and she shall be given citizenship and the right to possess land and [a house] and the right of pasture and inviolability and security on land and sea in war and peace for herself and her descendants and their property for all time together with all other privileges that are given to other proxenoi and benefactors. And Diony[sios], her brother, and his descendants shall have the rights of a proxenos, citizenship, [inviolability]. . . .

### Phile

[Phil]e, daughter of Apollonios and wife of Thessalos, the son of Polydektes, having held the office of stephanephoros [magistrate], the first woman [to do so], constructed at her own expense the reservoir for water and the city aqueduct.

Source: Adapted from Stanley M. Burstein, *The Hellenistic Age from the Battle of Ipsos to the Death of Cleopatra VII* (Cambridge: Cambridge University Press, 1985), pp. 59, 86–87.

own behalf. Widows and mothers of illegitimate children could give their daughters in marriage or apprentice their sons. A few cities granted women citizenship and even permitted them to hold public office.

Some Hellenistic cities admitted women to the gymnasium, previously a male preserve. Heretofore only Sparta had promoted physical education for women, but by the first century A.D. women were even competing in the great Pan-Hellenic games. Gymnasia were also centers of education in music and reading. One consequence of growing literacy was the re-emergence of women poets and the first appearance of women philosophers in the West. Before dying at age 19, Erinna, who lived on the Aegean island of Telos during the late fourth century B.C., wrote the *Distaff*, a poem in memory of her childhood friend Baucis. This three-hundred-line poem, famous in antiquity, describes the shared experiences of girlhood. Hipparchia° of Maroneia (b. ca. 350 B.C.), like her husband, Crates of Thebes, studied Cynic philosophy. The Cynics, like another philosophical school, the Epicure-ans, supported a measure of equality between women and men. Hipparchia and Crates led an itinerant life as popular teachers and the Hellenistic equivalent of counselors or psychologists.

Much of the explanation for the relative freedom of elite women lies in the new economic power of this group. The new cities generally imposed fewer restrictions on women's economic roles than had Classical poleis such as Athens. In many cities women could sell land, borrow money, and decide whether their husbands could make loans or contracts on the strength of their dowries. Free women could manumit slaves as well. (See the box "Reading Sources: The Power of Hellenistic Women—and Its Limits.")

The role reversals of male and female in Hellenistic art and literature are indicators of genuine social change. Hellenistic women never attained the equality that sometimes exists between men and women today, but they did enjoy genuine though limited improvements in status. Men and women played new roles in a changed, complex world. The new Hellenistic philosophies and religions attempted to address that complexity.

---

**Hipparchia** (hih-PAR-kee-uh)

# THE TURN INWARD: NEW PHILOSOPHIES, NEW FAITHS

THE events of the Hellenistic era—emigration, a trend from independent city-states to monarchies and federal leagues, new extremes of wealth and poverty, and contact with foreign peoples and customs—all generated uncertainty. In response, Greek culture was spread and transformed. As literacy expanded, more Greeks than ever before could participate in cultural debate. New philosophies and religions arose to meet new spiritual concerns, generating ideas that would be influential for centuries.

The meeting of Jews and Greeks proved to be just as significant. Challenged by Greek conquest, Greek colonization, and their own migration to Greek lands, Jews alternately embraced Hellenism and engaged in resistance, both cultural and armed. In the process, first Judaism and then Hellenism were changed forever.

## Cynics, Stoics, Epicureans, and Skeptics

Although the polis lost its military and political preeminence in the fourth century B.C., philosophy continued to thrive. It was, however, much changed. With the city-state losing significance as a focus of loyalty, and with the Greek-reading public growing in size and geographic extent, Hellenistic philosophy paid less and less attention to politics. Moreover, as we have seen, Hellenistic science tended to become a separate discipline from philosophy. What was left as the primary subject of philosophy was ethics, the discovery of the best way to live. The essence of the good life, most philosophers agreed, was finding peace of mind, or freedom from troubles. Hellenistic philosophers won wide followings; indeed, for many people, primarily in the elite, philosophy became a way of life, even a religion.

Several competing philosophical schools emerged. The first to attract attention was Cynicism°. Never a widespread philosophy, Cynicism is nonetheless important as a precursor of the two most popular doctrines, Stoicism and Epicureanism. Finally, Skepticism rejected the main philosophies as mere dogmatism and proposed instead a commonsense attitude toward ethics.

The first Cynic was Diogenes° of Sinope (ca. 400–325 B.C.). An exile in Athens, Diogenes developed a philosophy that rejected all conventions. People find happiness, he decided, by satisfying their natural needs with simplicity. Accordingly, Diogenes chose a life of poverty. A beggar in rags, he delighted in shocking conventional morality. Famous for wit and shamelessness, he was nicknamed "Dog" (*kuon*) because the Greeks considered dogs to be shameless animals; his followers were called "Doglike" (*kunikoi*, whence the name *Cynic*).

Although he founded no school, Diogenes cast a wide shadow. Among those whom he indirectly influenced was Zeno (335–263 B.C.), who began one of the most important philosophical systems of antiquity: Stoicism°. Zeno came to Athens in 313 B.C. from Citium in Cyprus, a multi-ethnic city; he was possibly of Phoenician origin. Influenced by both Cynicism and Socratic philosophy, Zeno developed his own doctrines, which he taught in the *Stoa Poikile* ("Painted Porch," whence the name *Stoic*), a public building.

Like Plato and Aristotle, Zeno sought an absolute standard of good on which to base philosophical decisions. He found it in the divine reason (*logos*), which he considered the organizing principle of the universe and the guide to human behavior. The best life was a life in pursuit of wisdom—that is, a life of philosophy. Only that rare and forbidding figure, the Sage, could truly attain wisdom; ordinary people could merely progress toward it. What was required was study and the attempt to be free from all passion.

Stoicism may seem harsh. It is not surprising that *stoical* has come to describe austere indifference to pain. In some ways, however, Stoicism was comforting. First, freedom from passion was meant to bring peace of mind and happiness. Second, unlike Plato, the Stoics were empiricists—that is, they trusted the evidence of the senses, an attitude that they thought would inspire confidence and security. Third, the common share in divine logos entailed a common human brotherhood—led, to be sure, by a Greek-speaking elite. Fourth, because brothers have a duty to one another, the Stoics argued that a good person should play an active role in public life.

Like Hellenistic poets or portraitists, the Stoics emphasized the inner life. They believed that intentions matter. This Stoic belief was an important departure from Greek tradition, which tended to emphasize the outcome of an action, not its motivation. Stoicism also departed from traditional Greek localism, embracing a more cosmopolitan outlook. "This world is a great city, [and] has one constitution and one law," wrote Philo of Alexandria (30 B.C.–A.D. 45), a Stoic and a Jew. Many Stoics believed in a natural law or law of nations—that is,

---

**Cynicism** (SIN-uh-sizm)   **Diogenes** (dye-AH-juh-neez)     **Stoicism** (STO-ih-sizm)

that overarching and common principles governed international relations.

With its emphasis on duty and order, Stoicism became popular with Greek ruling elites, both Macedonian kings and their opponents in city-states and leagues. Stoicism would enjoy even greater success with the Romans, who found its strictures congenial to their own stern morality and who used its concept of a universal state to justify their empire. A great deal of Stoicism was later embraced by early Christian writers.

Epicurus (341–270 B.C.), an Athenian citizen, founded his philosophical school at around the same time as Zeno founded Stoicism. There were other similarities: both schools were empiricist and materialist (that is, they tended to trust the evidence of the senses), both sought peace of mind, and both inspired widespread followings. Epicurus, however, taught not in a public place but in a private garden. Whereas the Stoics encouraged political participation, the Epicureans counseled withdrawal from the rough-and-tumble of public life. "Calm" and "Live in hiding" are famous Epicurean° maxims.

Epicurus's materialism is based on the atomic theory of Democritus (see page 95). It envisions a thoroughly mechanistic universe in which the gods exist but play no active role in events. Individuals need fear neither fickle deities nor an unhappy afterlife because the soul is merely a combination of atoms that ceases to exist after death. What might be the purpose of life in such an unheroic universe? The answer was the avoidance of pain and the pursuit of pleasure. The latter component of Epicureanism was called hedonism (from *hedone*, Greek for "pleasure"), but not, as the word has come to mean today, indulgence in food, drink, or sex. Instead, Epicureans meant intellectual pleasure. Friendship and fraternity were Epicurean ideals—the private analogs, as it were, of Stoic brotherhood.

The Epicureans raised eyebrows and sometimes ire, occasionally suffering persecution by the state. They were accused of atheism and sensuality; to this day, *epicurean* connotes a fondness for luxury and pleasure. Classical Greek philosophy defined virtue as the highest good. The Epicurean emphasis on pleasure, even spiritual pleasure, seemed perverse to some. Yet Epicureanism was simple, sure of itself, and practical, and it offered both friendship and a sense of community. It became a popular philosophy, especially among the wealthy.

Skepticism° was founded by Pyrrho of Elis (ca. 360–270 B.C.), a Greek who traveled with Alexander to India. Like Stoics and Epicureans, Skeptics sought peace of mind. They rejected those thinkers' conclusions, however, on the grounds that they were dogmatic—that is, based not on positive proof but merely on opinion (*doxa*). Considering the senses unreliable, Skeptics rejected the commonsense approach of Stoics and Epicureans. They preferred to suspend judgment on the great philosophical questions (hence our term *skepticism* for a doubting state of mind). Whoever was able to do so could accept the customs of the community, avoid politics, and thereby obtain peace of mind.

## The Mystery Religions

The name "mystery religion" comes from the Greek word for "secret." A mystery religion initiated worshipers into secret teachings. Long a feature of Greek religion, the mystery religions—there were several different ones—grew very popular in Hellenistic times. Their rise is a sign of the decline of the traditional Greek religion of the Olympian gods.

The old Greek gods came under attack on every front in the Hellenistic era. First, the newly divinized kings stole the spotlight. Second, Hellenistic philosophers, like their Archaic and Classical predecessors, criticized the Olympians as primitive, unsophisticated, and immoral. A third attack came from science and scholarship. Around 300 B.C. Euhemerus of Messene wrote in his *Sacred Scripture* that Zeus, Ouranos, and Kronos were not divine beings but merely great kings of the past who were rewarded with deification, much as a Hellenistic monarch might be. Debunking the Olympians became a popular literary pastime.

The Olympians retained their temples, but the rituals seemed hollow and antiquarian. What was to replace them? Of the several new religious movements that marked the age, three stand out: the divinization of kings, the cult of Tyche (Fortune), and the mystery religions.

Under the Ptolemies and Seleucids, the ruler-worship that Alexander had demanded became standard procedure. Many subjects no doubt considered the divinity of their king or queen merely a patriotic formality. Others treated the divinized monarch as something like a patron saint who could intercede in heaven. The old Greek city-states, especially the democracies, bristled at ruler-worship. "To transfer to men the honor due to the gods," the Athenian playwright Philippides (active ca. 300 B.C.) wrote, "is to dissolve the democracy."

He might have said much the same about the Hellenistic cult of Tyche° (Fortune or Luck), often worshiped

---

**Epicurean** (eh-pi-kyuh-REE-un)    **Skepticism** (SKEP-tih-sizm)

**Tyche** (TOO-kay)

**A Cretan Dream Interpreter in Egypt**    A painted stele (ca. 200 B.C.) advertises the services of a Greek in Memphis near the Temple of Serapis, a Greco-Egyptian god. The inscription and pediment are Greek, while the pilasters, women, and sacred bull (facing an altar) are Egyptian.    *(Egyptian Museum, Cairo)*

as a goddess, sometimes as the protector of a particular city. The most famous example was the Tyche of Antioch, personified as a statue of a woman wearing the battlements of the city on her head as a kind of crown—a very popular statue, to judge by the many copies found around the Hellenistic world.

The mystery religions offered relief similar to that of the philosophical schools: ethical guidance, comfort, release from worries, reassurance about death, and a sense of unity. Consider the cult of Demeter at Eleusis, a town just outside the city of Athens. Demeter was the goddess of fertility. Her daughter, Persephone, supposedly spent half the year in the underworld, among the dead, but came back to earth each spring. As told to initiates, the myth symbolized the promise of a blessed afterlife. The precise details of the ritual remain unknown to this day. What is clear is that they included fasting, ritual bathing

in the sea, a procession, and a torch-lit ceremony in the great hall at Eleusis.

Various new mystery religions from outside Greece became more popular, particularly the Hellenized Egyptian cults of Serapis and of Isis. Created under Ptolemy I, Serapis° was meant to combine Osiris, the Egyptian god of the afterlife, with Apis, the god of the Nile flood. Serapis also suggested Pluto, the Greek god of the underworld. Hence it is an early example of the common Hellenistic practice of religious syncretism, or fusion. Despite its roots, Serapis-worship had little appeal to native Egyptians, but the god became popular in the Greek world as the patron of healing and sailing.

Another traditional Egyptian deity, Osiris's wife, Isis°, also became a popular Greek and, later, Roman

**Serapis** (SEH-ruh-pis)    **Isis** (EYE-sis)

**Bronze Coin with Menorah**   This issue of Mattathias Antigone (r. 40–37 B.C.), the last Hasmonean king, is an early example of the use of the seven-branched candelabrum as the symbol of the Jewish people. A similar candelabrum was used in the Temple of Jerusalem.   *(Erich Lessing/Art Resource, NY)*

goddess. Called the Goddess of Ten Thousand Names, Isis was said to symbolize all the female deities of antiquity. Hers was a cult of the afterlife and of the suffering but tender and loving mother; she was particularly popular among women. Thus, under Ptolemaic sponsorship, ancient Egyptian cults were recast and spread throughout the Greek-speaking world, circulating such notions as the suffering mother, the Last Judgment, and blessed eternal life after death. Early Christianity was much influenced by such Greco-Egyptian religious notions, but it was more directly the product of debate and ferment within Hellenistic Judaism.

## Hellenistic Judaism

Few consequences of Alexander's conquests had so lasting an impact as the mixing of Greeks and Jews. Even before Alexander took Judea from the Persians in 332 B.C., the two peoples were in occasional contact, but in the Hellenistic era, their fates became intertwined. The Greeks governed Judea and then lost it to a Jewish independence movement. Meanwhile, millions of Jews settled in Egypt, Syria, Anatolia, and Greece.

Changed by its contact with Greek culture, Hellenistic Judaism placed a greater emphasis on salvation,

martyrdom, and individual study and prayer. Jewish responses to Greek culture varied: they ranged from admiration to resistance to outreach—that is, the desire to convert Greeks to Judaism. In its creative ferment, Hellenistic Judaism proved to have a long-lasting impact on the West.

Hellenistic Judea was governed first by the Ptolemies until 200 B.C., then by the Seleucids, until the establishment of an independent Jewish state in 142 B.C., which came under Roman suzerainty in 63 B.C. The Greeks were not absentee rulers. Rather, they established a large number of Greek colonies in and around Judea, especially under the Seleucids. Many Jews, especially wealthy ones, adopted some degree of Greek culture. Not all of these so-called Hellenizers abandoned Judaism. Indeed, some reshaped Jewish traditions to appeal to a Greek audience. Yet some Hellenizers abandoned Jewish customs altogether for the Greek gymnasium, theater, and political institutions. With the help of the Seleucid king Antiochus IV Epiphanes (r. 175–163 B.C.), Jewish Hellenizers in 175 B.C. had Jerusalem proclaimed a Greek polis, renamed Antioch, like many a Seleucid city; they even built a gymnasium at the foot of the Temple Mount. In 167 B.C. they went further by outlawing Sabbath observance, prohibiting circumcision, and rededicating the Temple to Olympian Zeus.

The traditionalists, however, resisted. Aided by the political ineptitude of their opponents, who raised taxes, they rallied the Jewish masses into opposition. Soon a guerrilla revolt began in the countryside, led by the Hasmonean family, also known as the Maccabees, whose successes are celebrated today by Jews during the religious holiday of Hanukkah. The guerrilla movement developed into a disciplined armed uprising, which forced the Seleucids to tolerate an independent state under the Hasmonean dynasty. Religiously conservative at home, the state was expansionist abroad, conquering nearby territories such as the Galilee and forcing their inhabitants to convert to Judaism.

During the struggle over Hellenism, new elements of lasting significance became part of Judaism. First, the Jews developed a literature of spiritual resistance to the foreigner. This literature was apocalyptic—that is, it claimed to reveal dramatic, heretofore secret truths. Drawing on both biblical and Mesopotamian traditions, Jewish apocalyptic writing predicted a future cataclysm, when a royal redeemer would evict the foreigner and establish a new kingdom of Israel. The redeemer was often identified with another notion that first became popular in this era: the Messiah (literally, "anointed one"), someone anointed with oil signifying his election as king, a descendant of King David, who would save Israel. Another new aspect of Hellenistic Judaism was martyrdom, the notion of the holy sacrifice of one's life for a religious cause. There was also a growing belief in a final Judgment Day and resurrection, when God would raise the meritorious dead to live again on earth in their own bodies.

Hellenistic Judaism was far from monolithic. Various sects each proposed its own version of Judaism. Among these sects were the Sadducees° ("righteous ones"), a wealthy establishment group for whom the rituals of the Temple in Jerusalem were the heart of Judaism. Their opponents, the Pharisees° ("those who separated themselves"), insisted on the validity of the oral tradition of interpretation alongside the written law of the Hebrew Bible and the Temple rituals. The Pharisees proposed a kind of democratization of Judaism, emphasizing study and prayer in small groups. A third group was the Essenes°, generally identified with the Qumran° community in the Judean desert (see page 193). As for the Hellenizers, although some were merely status seekers, others sincerely wished to combine Jewish ethical monotheism with the cosmopolitan spirit of Hellenistic civilization. They wanted, in short, to bring Jewish teachings to non-Jews, or Gentiles ("the nations").

Most Jews of the Hellenistic era lived outside Judea. The Diaspora had spread into (among other places) Syria, Anatolia, the Greek mainland, and Egypt, where a strong Jewish presence during the Persian period grew even stronger, particularly in Alexandria. Jews served the Ptolemies as soldiers, generals, bureaucrats, and tax collectors. They also prospered in private enterprise. Jewish success, as well as their maintenance of a separate culture, led to hostility among ordinary Greeks and Egyptians. Such attitudes spawned the first anti-Semitic literature as well as sporadic violence that at times broke into riots and persecution. Yet there was also considerable admiration among Greek intellectuals for what they saw as Jewish virtue and antiquity.

Greek was the common tongue of Diaspora Jews. Between around 300 and 100 B.C. in Alexandria the Hebrew Bible was translated into Greek. Known as the Septuagint, or Seventy, from the number of translators who, legend has it, labored on the project, this text made the Bible accessible to a Jewish community increasingly unable to understand Hebrew or Aramaic. In later centuries the Septuagint became the Old Testament of Greek-speaking Christians.

Foreign conversions and immigration into the Diaspora began to change the meaning of the word *Jew*. The word came to mean less "inhabitant of Judea" than "practitioner of Judaism." In short, *Jew* came to denote as much a religion as a nation.

## SUMMARY

THE major legacy of the Hellenistic age was its culture. This Greek-speaking culture—which now extended across the Persian Empire and encompassed Egypt—was dominated by inhabitants of or immigrants from old Greece and their descendants. The broad-minded ideas of Isocrates smoothed the way for the Greeks of different city-states to unite in kingdoms but offered less hope to others. We must not lose sight, however, of the continued flourishing of native cultures in the multi-ethnic kingdoms of the Ptolemies and Seleucids. Although Greeks and Macedonians dominated these regimes, they never imposed homogeneity, either in politics or in culture.

The most important Greek cultural development of the age was a retreat from a complex of values associated with the citizen-warrior ideal of the Classical city-state. The polis came under the shadow of federal leagues and kingdoms; philosophers questioned the very point of political activity. The hero gave way to the antihero, often a man whose success was dependent on the kindness and love of a woman. The female nude became as important a subject for sculptors as the male nude. Hellenistic women were freer than their predecessors in their movement and their ability to hold property and have some say in public life.

Stoic philosophers were far more interested in intention (versus action) than were their Classical predecessors. Yet their interest in the subject pales before that of the Jews, new actors on the Greek stage. Judaism placed an emphasis on the interior dialogue between humans and the divine that was more radical than anything in the Greek tradition. Some Greeks admired Jewish ethics, but few were willing to accept Jewish laws and rituals. Greeks did, however, borrow from other native religions. Hellenistic religion, therefore, was an exception to the general Greek indifference to native culture. The common denominator of the new religious teachings was a close personal relationship with a savior-god who would guarantee comfort, peace, and eternal life after death.

---

**Sadducees** (SAJ-oo-seez)    **Pharisees** (FAIR-ih-seez)
**Essenes** (EH-seenz)    **Qumran** (koom-RAHN)

Ironically, these very doctrines brought their Greek adherents closer to Hellenistic Judaism, which preached righteousness and justice in this life and the hereafter through subordination to the truth of the one and only God. The Jewish doctrine of messianic kingship might even have reminded Greeks of their own ruler cults. Imperceptibly, Hellenic and Hebraic were drawing closer. Under the Roman successor state, which we examine in Chapters 5 through 7, Hellenism and Judaism would be combined in a new and powerful form: Christianity.

### ■ Notes

1. Isocrates, "Panegyricus," trans. H. I. Marrou, in *A History of Education in Antiquity,* trans. George Lamb (New York: Mentor Books/New American Library, 1956), p. 130.
2. Romila Thapar, *Aśoka and the Decline of the Mauryas* (Oxford: Oxford University Press, 1961), p. 256.
3. Quoted in Charles Rowan Beye, *Ancient Greek Literature and Society,* 2d ed. (Ithaca, N.Y.: Cornell University Press, 1987), p. 265.

### ■ Suggested Reading

Bosworth, A. B. *The Legacy of Alexander: Politics, Warfare, and Propaganda Under the Successors.* 2001. A study of the emergence of the Hellenistic kingdoms in the thirty years after Alexander's death.

Bowman, Alan K. *Egypt After the Pharaohs.* 1986. An excellent and highly readable introduction to the social history of the Ptolemaic and later periods.

Cohen, Shaye. *From the Maccabees to the Mishnah.* 1987. An excellent introduction by a distinguished scholar of Second Temple Judaism.

Grant, Michael. *From Alexander to Cleopatra: The Hellenistic World.* 1982. A lively and readable introduction; at its best on cultural history.

Green, P. *Alexander to Actium: An Essay in the Historical Evolution of the Hellenistic Age.* 1989. A collection of elegant essays synthesizing scholarship on a wide variety of topics in political, cultural, and social history.

Long, A. A. *Hellenistic Philosophy: Stoics, Epicureans, Sceptics.* 2d ed. 1986. A concise critical analysis of the main ideas and methods of thought of the major Hellenistic philosophers.

Shipley, Graham. *The Greek World After Alexander, 323–30 B.C.* 2000. A thorough, sophisticated, and learned introduction to the Hellenistic era; well versed in and prudent about recent scholarly controversies.

Wood, Michael. *In the Footsteps of Alexander the Great.* 1997. An engaging story that retraces Alexander's path today while it narrates his history; magnificent color photos of seldom-seen sites.

**For a searchable list of additional readings for this chapter, go to college.hmco.com/students.**

# Images of Cleopatra

"Cleopatra's nose: if it had been shorter, the whole face of the earth would have changed," wrote the French philosopher Blaise Pascal (1623–1662). He does Cleopatra an injustice. It was not a pretty face and classical features that enabled her to win the throne of Egypt (r. 51–30 B.C.), to obtain first Julius Caesar and then Mark Antony as ally and lover, and finally to come close to gaining control of the Roman Empire. Intelligence, daring, charm, and extraordinary diplomatic skill account for Cleopatra's success.

Let us consider the queen's manipulation of her public image—no mean task, given the fragility of Ptolemaic power in the first century B.C. Within Egypt the monarch had to satisfy several different ethnic groups. Most important were the Greeks and Macedonians—who dominated government, the military, and the economy—and the native Egyptian majority. Daughter of Ptolemy XII (r. 80–51 B.C.), Cleopatra was supposed to rule jointly with her brother, but they had a falling-out. She wrested the throne from him and then from another brother and thus had to assert her legitimacy. Also, Ptolemaic Egypt had to project an image of unity to the Romans, who were threatening to annex it as they had the other Hellenistic monarchies.

Cleopatra, like earlier Ptolemaic monarchs, met these challenges by presenting two faces to the world. To the Greeks and Romans she was a Hellenistic monarch; to the Egyptians she was an ancient pharaonic queen. Look first at the bronze coin of Cleopatra issued at Alexandria probably in the 30s B.C. The queen is shown as a young woman. Her hair, tied in a bun at the nape of her neck, is in the so-called melon style often seen in Hellenistic female portraits. She wears a diadem (royal headband), its ends hanging behind her neck. More commonly worn by Hellenistic kings than by queens, the diadem signifies Cleopatra's claim to authority.

So does the queen's profile. She is portrayed with a prominent chin, a large mouth, and a rugged nose. These features may not be the standard attributes of beauty, but they are precisely the features that mark coin portraits of Cleopatra's father. By emphasizing Cleopatra's physical similarity to her father, the portrait artist perhaps subtly suggests her right to sit on his throne.

The side of the coin not shown here is far from subtle: its legend states clearly in Greek, "Queen Cleopatra." The illustration is of an eagle and thunderbolt and a double cornucopia (horn of plenty) entwined with a diadem. The eagle and thunderbolt recall the Greek god Zeus, and the two cornucopias suggest fertility and prosperity. All are recurrent symbols of Ptolemaic royalty. The coin thus portrays Cleopatra as a Greek monarch, the worthy heir of her father. It would have been an effective image in Alexandria, a city dominated by Greeks and visited by Romans, but not in the countryside, especially south of the Nile Delta, in Upper Egypt, an area that was primarily Egyptian. Following dynastic custom, Cleopatra changed her image there.

In Upper Egypt earlier Ptolemies frequently had been represented in stone in traditional pharaonic style, and they were great restorers of ancient Egyptian temples and builders of new ones. Look at the sculptural relief from the temple of the Egyptian cow-goddess Hathor at Dendera in Upper Egypt. The temple was a monumental structure initiated and underwritten by Ptolemy XII. Cleopatra, his daughter, added an enormous relief on the outside of the rear wall. Carved into the stone are two persons carrying offerings for Egyptian deities. The persons are Cleopatra (*left*) and her son Ptolemy XV Caesar, who ruled with his mother from 44 to 30 B.C. Alleged to be the illegitimate son of Julius Caesar, Ptolemy XV was commonly known as Caesarion, or "little Caesar." At Dendera, however, he and his mother are shown neither as Romans nor as Greeks but as Egyptians.

**Bronze Coin of Cleopatra** *(Courtesy of the Trustees of the British Museum)*

Look closely at Cleopatra. She wears a long body-hugging robe. On her head is a royal headdress with symbols of the Egyptian gods: the lyre-shaped cow horns and sun-disk of Hathor, the tall plumes of Isis, and the ram's horn of Amon. Caesarion is shown as a pharaoh, wearing the double crown of Upper and Lower Egypt. Mother and son offer incense to the local deities. The small figure between Caesarion and Cleopatra is his *ka*, or soul.

Cleopatra's face is in profile but otherwise has very little in common with her portrait on the Alexandrian coin. Although the features are stylized pharaonic commonplaces, the shape of her head perhaps echoes the el-egant and graceful relief portraits of Hatshepsut (r. 1479–1457 B.C.), the most famous female pharaoh before Cleopatra.

Cleopatra commissioned other artworks and monuments in the native style in the Nile Valley. This was the custom of her dynasty, and Cleopatra had absorbed its traditions, but she stands second to none of the Ptolemies in shrewdness and subtlety. She was the only Ptolemaic monarch to learn to speak Egyptian, and she was the only one to come even close to gaining the upper hand over Rome. As the artifacts shown here indicate, she was able to put on an Egyptian face as easily as a Greek one, but she never lost sight of her true interests.

**Relief of Cleopatra and Caesarion** *(Erich Lessing/Art Resource, NY)*

# CHAPTER 5

# Rome, from Republic to Empire ca. 509–31 B.C.

Here is the Roman Forum. We are standing in the heart of the ancient city, under the arch of the emperor Septimius Severus, looking south toward two columns that once held statues of great citizens. Beyond them are the Sacred Way, Rome's oldest street, and the three elegant columns of the Temple of Castor and Pollux. In the background, beyond a market and vaulted warehouse, is the Palatine Hill. The photograph takes us from an arch celebrating military triumph to ruins evoking citizenship and piety, to a reminder of the everyday needs of the masses of Rome, and finally to a historic hill. On this hill shepherds founded the city of Rome, and on this hill, centuries later, emperors lived. We see, in short, the civic center of the city destined to give the Western world many of its fundamental ideas about government and empire. It is arguably the single most important public space in the history of the world.

The ancient Romans were a practical people. Virgil (70–19 B.C.), for example, the greatest Roman poet (see pages 179–180), celebrates not his countrymen's artistry or cultivation but rather their pragmatic accomplishments:

> For other peoples will, I do not doubt,
> still cast their bronze to breathe with softer features,
> or draw out of the marble living lines,
> plead causes better, trace the ways of heaven
> with wands and tell the rising constellations;
> but yours will be the rulership of nations,
> remember, Romans, these will be your arts:
> to teach the ways of peace to those you conquer,
> to spare defeated peoples, tame the proud.[1]

The Romans turned an Italian city-state into one of the largest empires in history, including all the countries of the Mediterranean

The Forum, Rome.
(Michael Yamshita/Woodfin Camp & Associates)

as well as large parts of western Asia and of northern and central Europe. By holding this empire for centuries and by promoting prosperity in every corner, Rome planted in what would become Britain, France, Germany, and Spain (among other places) the seeds of the advanced civilizations of the Mediterranean.

Rome is no less important for its influence on the Western civic tradition. Much of the modern vocabulary of politics, from *president* to *inauguration* to *forum,* can be traced back to Rome. After an early period of monarchy, Rome was for centuries a republic (Latin, *res publica,* literally "public thing") before becoming essentially a monarchy again under the Caesars. The Roman Republic mixed popular power with government controlled by wealthy landowners. The government was divided into three branches, which created a system of checks and balances that tended toward consensus. The result was efficiency and, for centuries, stability.

Roman politicians sought to control ordinary citizens but in some ways were more flexible than Greek democrats. Unlike Greece, Rome extended its citizenship to a large population, first throughout Italy and then across its entire empire. The modern nation-state with its mass citizenship owes much to Rome. Indeed, although Rome was not democratic, modern democracy—that is, popular government with a large population, whose officials are elected by the people—has roots in the Roman Republic as well as in the Greek city-state.

Fueled by fear, ambition, and greed, Roman expansion generated its own momentum. Rome's arrogance matched its success: in consolidating power over huge territories, the Romans committed atrocities, enslaved whole peoples, and destroyed cities with little provocation. Ironically, military success slowly undermined both Rome's political stability at home and the socioeconomic basis of its army. Meanwhile, the Romans showed great open-mindedness in borrowing from other societies, in particular from the Greeks, to whom the Republic owed great cultural debts. Also fascinating is the shrewdness and generosity with which the Romans shared their citizenship with the elites whom they had conquered, thereby winning their loyalty and strengthening Rome's grip on their territories.

Historians conventionally divide the Republic into three periods: Early (509–287 B.C.), Middle (287–133 B.C.), and Late (133–31 B.C.). This chapter begins with the origins of the city of Rome in the early first millennium B.C. and then traces the Republic from its foundation to its imperial conquests to its collapse under their weight. Success spoiled Rome. The unintended consequences of conquest on Rome's society, politics, and culture led to a revolution that, in the century beginning in 133 B.C., saw the Republic's downfall.

## QUESTIONS TO CONSIDER

- How was the Roman Republic governed, and to what degree did that government shape the later political tradition of the West?

- How much access to power did women, conquered peoples, and slaves have in Roman society?

- How did Rome acquire an empire that stretched from Britain to Iraq?

- What were the unintended consequences of conquest on Rome, and how did they lead to revolution that destroyed the Republic?

## TERMS TO KNOW

| | |
|---|---|
| Latin | triumph |
| Etruscans | legion |
| *res publica* | Gracchi |
| senate | Caesar |
| paterfamilias | Cicero |
| Punic Wars | Cato the Censor |

# BEFORE THE REPUBLIC, 753–509 B.C.

THE ancient Romans believed that their city was founded on April 21, 753 B.C., by Romulus, a descendant of refugees from the Trojan War. Although the name "Romulus" supplies a convenient etymology for "Rome," little stock can be placed in this story. Nevertheless, archaeology shows that Rome was already an important settlement by the eighth century B.C. A simple village of farmers and shepherds—a collection of huts—was established then on the Palatine Hill, one of the seven hills on which Rome would cluster and the place where tradition puts the settlement of 753 (see inset, Map 5.2, on page 150). But the first settlers on the hills of Rome came even earlier, around 1000 B.C., as pottery and graves show.

Archaeological evidence raises some basic questions: What were Rome's origins, and how did it grow? Are seeds of Roman greatness visible in its early history? By examining the data of archaeology and of those elements in ancient historiography that seem to be based on accurate tradition, we can answer these questions, at least in outline.

## Archaic Rome and Its Neighbors

Italy is a long peninsula, shaped roughly like a boot, extending about 750 miles from the Alps into the Mediterranean (see Map 5.1). In the far north, the high Alps provide a barrier to the rest of Europe. To the east, the Adriatic Sea separates Italy from modern Slovenia and Croatia; to the west, the Tyrrhenian Sea faces the large islands of Sardinia and Corsica (and the smaller but iron-rich island of Elba) and, beyond, the coasts of France and Spain. Off the "toe" of the Italian boot, and separated from the mainland by a narrow, 3-mile strait of water, is the large island of Sicily, rich farm country in ancient times. Sicily is only 90 miles from North Africa. In short, Italy is centrally located in the Mediterranean. It was both a target for conquerors and a springboard for conquest.

Italy contained some of the ancient Mediterranean's most fertile and metal-rich land. From the watershed of the Po and Adige Rivers in the north, the agriculturally rich plains of Etruria° (modern Tuscany), Latium° (the region of Rome), and Campania (the region of Naples) unfold southward down Italy's west coast. Although the Apennine° mountain range runs north-south along most

Etruria (ee-TROO-ree-uh)    Latium (LAY-shum)
Apennine (AP-puh-nine)

**CHRONOLOGY**

| | |
|---|---|
| 753–509 B.C. | Monarchy (traditional dates) |
| 509–287 B.C. | Early Republic |
| 449 B.C. | Law of the Twelve Tables |
| 338 B.C. | Latin League dissolved; Roman citizenship extended |
| 289 B.C. | First Roman coinage (traditional date) |
| 287–133 B.C. | Middle Republic |
| 264–146 B.C. | Punic Wars |
| 240 B.C. | First play produced at Rome |
| 197 B.C. | Rome defeats Macedonian phalanx |
| 146 B.C. | Rome destroys Carthage and Corinth |
| 133–31 B.C. | Late Republic |
| 133–121 B.C. | The Gracchi |
| 107–78 B.C. | Marius and Sulla |
| 73–71 B.C. | Spartacus's revolt |
| 66–62 B.C. | Pompey's eastern campaigns |
| 63 B.C. | Consulship of Cicero |
| 58–51 B.C. | Caesar conquers Gaul |
| 44 B.C. | Caesar assassinated |
| 31 B.C. | Antony defeated at Actium; Octavian in power |

of the Italian peninsula, they are low compared with the Alps and contain many passes, permitting the movement of armies.

A sensational recent archaeological discovery opens a window into second-millennium B.C. Italy. Poggiomarino is a prehistoric village consisting of houses that were built on oak pilings and separated by canals. The village, located on a river near Naples, was inhabited from around the 1500s B.C. to around 700 B.C. A masterpiece of prehistoric engineering, the village covered at least 7 acres and was a center of bronze production.

In the first millennium B.C., Italy was a hodgepodge of peoples and languages. They included the Etruscans in the north, Greek colonists in southern Italy and in Sicily,

ALPS

LIGURES

VENETI

ETRUSCANS

Mantua

Spina

Felsina
(Bologna)

Ravenna

Faesulae

Ligurian
Sea

Arno

Volaterrae

Arretium

ETRURIA

Perusia

UMBRI

PICENTES

Populonia

Clusium

Vetulonia

Elba

Volsinii

APENNINES

SABINES

Vulci

ETRUSCANS

Tiber

LIGURES

Tarquinii

Veii

Alalia

Caere

Rome

SAMNITES

APULI

Corsica

LATIUM

LATINS

Capua

CAMPANIA

Cumae

Neapolis (Naples)

MESSAPII

Puteoli

Herculaneum

OSCI

Pithecusae

Pompeii

Bay of Naples

Paestum

LUCANI

Tarentum

Gulf of
Tarentum

Sardinia

Sybaris

Tharros

SARDI

Tyrrhenian Sea

BRUTTII

Carales

MAGNA GRAECIA

Croton

Messana

Panormus

Mediterranean Sea

SICANI

SICULI

Sicily

Acragas
(Agrigentum)

Syracuse

Utica

Cape
Bon

Hippo Regius

Carthage

Malta

NORTH AFRICA

Adriatic Sea

ILLYRIA

### Latium

0 —— 15 Km.

0 —— 15 Mi.

Lake
Sabatinus

Tiber

Anio

Veii

Tibur

AEQUI

Aro

Gabii

Rome

Tusculum

Praeneste

HERNICI

Anagnia

Tiber

Ostia

Lake
Albanus

Mt. Albanus

Cora

Tyrrhenian
Sea

Lavinium

Lake
Nemorensis

Norba

Trerus

Ardea

VOLSCI

Satricum

Privernum

Antium

Roman territory, ca. 500 B.C.

Etruscans of Etruria

Expansion of Etruscans

Greeks

Carthaginians

*OSCI* Other peoples

**Etruscan Tomb Painting**   This wall painting from Tarquinia shows a married aristocratic couple at a banquet. The style of the figures is derived from Greek art, but the depiction of husband and wife dining on the same couch is characteristically Etruscan. *(National Museum, Tarquinia/Scala/ Art Resource, NY)*

and such mountain peoples as the Sabines and the Samnites. The Samnites spoke Oscan, an Indo-European language, as did the Campanians, who lived around Naples, and the Lucanians, who lived in south-central Italy. Both the Samnites and the Lucanians were warlike peoples who conquered their neighbors before finally being conquered by Rome. (See the feature Weighing the Evidence: From Poseidonia to Paestum on pages 170–171.)

Latium was home to a number of small Latin-speaking towns, one of them Rome. In the fifth century B.C. another important people arrived on the Italian scene: Celts (called Gauls by the Romans), large numbers of whom crossed the Alps and settled in northern Italy after roughly 500 B.C. Most of these various peoples spoke Indo-European languages, of which Latin, the language of the Romans (as well as other peoples of Latium), was one.

Rome's location in Italy was central and protected. Rome is located in Latium, which is about halfway down

**Map 5.1   Early Italy and Region of City of Rome**   Early Italy comprised a variety of terrain and peoples. Rome is located in the central Italian region of Latium. The Alps separate Italy from northern Europe. The Apennine mountain range runs almost the entire length of the Italian peninsula. Much of the rest of Italy is fertile plain.

the Italian peninsula. Located 15 miles inland on the Tiber°, the largest river on Italy's west coast, Rome had access to the sea. A midstream island makes Rome the first crossing place upstream from the Tiber's mouth, offering the Romans freedom of movement north and south. Yet strategically, Rome was protected. It was far enough from the sea to be safe from raiders and pirates. And its seven hills offered a natural defense—from nature as well as humans, because the Tiber often flooded its banks.

In the seventh century B.C. Archaic Rome (as the pre-Republican period is called) began to change from a large village into a city. In this era Rome saw its first stone houses, its first public building, and its first forum or civic center. In the sixth century B.C. streets, walls, drains, temples, and a racetrack followed. What caused the transformation? Perhaps the key factor was contact with Magna Graecia°, the Greek colonies to the south (see Map 5.1). Established in the eighth and seventh centuries B.C., the colonies transported westward the sophisticated urban civilization of the eastern Mediterranean.

More controversial is the impact on early Rome of its neighbors to the north, the Etruscans°. The twelve

Tiber (TY-ber)   **Magna Graecia** (MAG-nuh GREE-shuh)
Etruscans (ee-TRUS-kunz)

Etruscan city-states were organized in a loose confederation centered in Etruria. They grew rich from the mining of iron, copper, and silver, from piracy, from trade, and from a network of influential Etruscan emigrants throughout central Italy, probably including Rome's last three kings (traditionally dated 616–509 B.C.).

The Etruscans were brilliant, wealthy, and warlike. We know less about them than we would like, from their language, which is only partly understood, to their origins, which probably lay in Italy but possibly in Anatolia. Etruscan power extended to many places in central, northern, and even southern Italy. Many scholars argue that the Etruscans conquered pre-Republican Rome, but the evidence does not support that theory. Rather, an Etruscan nobleman, Lucius Tarquinius Priscus, migrated to Rome and was eventually elected king. Under him and his son (or perhaps grandson), Lucius Tarquinius Superbus, who was Rome's last king, Etruscan culture left an impact on Rome. For example, the Tarquins sponsored several building projects in Rome, including the great Temple of Jupiter on the Capitoline Hill in the center of Rome. But scholars disagree as to whether the Etruscan impact on Roman culture was superficial or deep.

At least we can be sure that the Etruscans were great artists and architects and very religious. They believed that it was possible to learn the will of the gods by interpreting the sight and sound of lightning and thunder and by carefully examining the internal organs, especially the liver, of sacrificial animals. Etruscan elite women had high status compared with their Greek or Roman counterparts. Etruscan women kept their own names, and Etruscan children bore the names of both parents. In addition, Etruscan elite women were permitted to attend athletic contests in spite of the presence of naked male athletes.

### The Roman Monarchy

Tradition says that Rome was ruled by seven kings before the foundation of the Republic. Although the number of kings may be a later invention, their existence is undoubted. In addition to traces of the monarchy in Republican institutions, there is archaeological proof: a form of the Latin word *rex* ("king"), for example, has been found inscribed on a Roman monument from the early sixth century B.C. The king's power, called *imperium* (from *imperare,* "to command"), was very great, embracing religious, military, and judicial affairs.

The king was advised by a council of elders, called the "fathers" (*patres* in Latin) or the "senate" (*senatus,* from *senex,* "old man"). In theory, the senate was primarily an advisory body, but in practice it was very powerful. Senators were the heads of the most important families in Rome, so the king rejected their advice at his peril. Romans spoke of the senate's *auctoritas,* a quasi-religious prestige.

Most senators were patricians°, as early Rome's hereditary aristocracy was known. The rest of the people, the bulk of Roman society, were called plebeians°. Plebeians were free; most were ordinary people, though some were wealthy. Patricians monopolized the senate and priesthoods, and they did not intermarry with plebeians.

The whole people, probably both patricians and plebeians, met in an assembly organized in thirty local units, or *curiae,* hence the name *curiate assembly.* Although the assembly's numbers were large, its powers were limited. Before becoming law, resolutions of the assembly required approval by the senate.

Early Rome was a class-based society, but it was open to foreigners. Among others, Etruscans, Sabines, and Latins—as the inhabitants of other Latin-speaking towns are called—came to settle in Rome. The Tarquins, whose family is traditionally said to have provided two kings of Rome, including the last, may have originally come from Corinth. Unlike Athenians, who tried to hide the presence of immigrants in their country by a myth of indigenous origins, Romans openly discussed their mixed roots. Foreigners at first had low status, but they gained equality around 550 B.C., for pragmatic purposes. Rome needed soldiers to fight its wars; in order to expand the body of loyal infantrymen, the immigrants were granted citizenship—a reform traditionally associated with King Servius Tullius (578–535 B.C.).

Servius probably introduced to Rome the hoplite phalanx (see page 73), with immigrants included in its ranks. The changes in the army contributed to the process that, within several generations of Servius's reform, took Rome from monarchy to republic.

## GOVERNMENT AND SOCIETY IN THE EARLY AND MIDDLE REPUBLICS, CA. 509–133 B.C.

TRADITION says that the Roman Republic was established in 509 B.C., when the kings were overthrown. Nowadays, scholars envision a long process rather than a single, dramatic upheaval. In either case, the new Republic was destined to have a

---

**patricians** (puh-TRIH-shunz)    **plebeians** (pleh-BEE-unz) unique influence on Western political institutions, so it is worth a close look.

The Republic differed from the monarchy in two basic ways. First, the Republic stood for liberty, which for the Romans meant both freedom from the arbitrary power of a king and freedom to participate in public affairs. Second, the Republic was a commonwealth, in Latin, *res publica*°, literally "public thing," as opposed to *res privata,* "private thing," as the Romans characterized monarchy. As a kingdom Rome belonged to the royal family, but as a republic it belonged to the Roman people. In theory, the Roman people were sovereign—that is, the people ruled the state.

But which people? This is a key question because the Romans did *not* embrace another principle that might seem to follow from liberty: equality. Rather, they believed in order, balance, and competition, all of which are central themes of Roman Republican history. Roman society and culture, moreover, were conservative. Once the young Republic had its new values in place, it tried to maintain those values over the centuries with little change. Nor did the Republic give up entirely on the old values of the monarchy. Rather, it continued some of those values.

## What Kind of Republic?

We know relatively little about the Early Republic (509–287 B.C.) but enough to know that it witnessed centuries of social and political conflict. The Middle Republic (287–133 B.C.) was a shorter and better-documented period of relative consensus at home and massive expansion abroad. Social and political conflict broke out again with a vengeance in the Late Republic (133–31 B.C.), ultimately rendering the Republic a deathblow.

The best and most even-handed ancient analyst of Roman politics is the historian Polybius° (ca. 200–118 B.C.). A Greek and former hostage who lived in Rome, Polybius observed his adopted city with an outsider's careful eye. Polybius argued that in the Middle Republic of his day, Rome was a "mixed constitution," balancing the power of the masses with the authority of the elite. The result was a strong and stable state.

Polybius divides Roman political institutions into three branches: executive, deliberative, and legislative. The American founders adopted a similar division, but they combined the legislative and deliberative functions and added a judicial branch. In Rome the executive branch also administered justice. Rome's executive branch was made up of magistrates—that is, public officials; the deliberative branch consisted of the Roman senate; and the legislative branch was composed of four different assemblies of the people.

Polybius argued that the assemblies were democratic, the senate oligarchic, and the magistrates a royal element. Not all historians agree. Polybius's critics say that he was misled by the democratic façade of Rome's assemblies. In the last analysis, they maintain, oligarchs controlled the state. They monopolized high office, rigged elections, dominated proceedings in the senate, set the course of cultural life, and controlled religion in a society that knew no separation of church and state.

Although these criticisms contain some truth, they overstate the case. Rome experienced real political competition and a real need to court the voters; all laws were debated, often fiercely, in public meetings; candidates for office ran ambitious campaigns, which suggests that the results were not rigged; the people's representatives could veto any action taken by public officials; and freed slaves became citizens, which was rarely true in a democratic Greek state such as Athens. Of course, the wealthy elite had considerable power, but that power was limited, which means that, as Polybius writes, the Roman political system was balanced and competitive.

In short, Rome was a mixed constitution. It was not always a stable society, however. Let us survey Rome's political institutions and then examine the conflicts of the Early Republic and the compromises that resolved them in the middle era. We will turn to the revolution that destroyed the Late Republic at the end of this chapter.

## Political Institutions

Executive power lay in the hands of Rome's powerful magistrates. They were elected and not chosen by lottery, as in Greek democracy. Election required campaigning, which in turn took money and connections. Magistracies were time-consuming jobs but offered no salary, unlike in Greek democracy. Thus only a wealthy few could afford to hold public office in Rome.

Eager for strong magistrates but afraid that power corrupts, Romans imposed the principles of *collegiality* and *annuality* on their officials. Every magistrate had one or more colleagues and held office for only one year. The chief magistrates were eventually called consuls, of which there were two. Each consul had the power to veto the other's actions. Like the former king, each consul had *imperium,* the power to issue commands and order punishments, including execution.

---

**res publica** (rays POO-blee-kuh)    **Polybius** (po-LIH-bee-us)

**A Clear Sign of Power**    The lictor, or official, depicted in this bronze statuette (ca. first century A.D.) accompanied Roman magistrates, who had *imperium,* the power to issue punishments resulting in execution. That power is visible in the fasces—an ax in a bundle of wooden rods bound with straps—that he holds.    *(Courtesy of the Trustees of the British Museum)*

From about 500 B.C. to about 300 B.C., other public offices were created to help the consuls as administration grew more complex. In addition, the Romans elected two censors, older men chosen once every few years for eighteen-month terms. At first their job was to supervise the census, the military register of citizens that recorded each man's property class. Later the censors became, as it were, supervisors of public morals, since they could punish "bad" citizens.

The Republic's government adapted flexibly to trying circumstances. In times of emergency, for example, the Republic turned power over to a single magistrate. The dictator, as he was called, made binding decisions, but he held office for only six months.

The Roman senate guided and advised the magistrates. During most of the Republic, the senate consisted of three hundred men, all former magistrates and each of whom served for life. Senators possessed great authority. They supervised public expenditures and were for all practical purposes in charge of foreign policy.

Only the assemblies of the people could make laws. There were four assemblies: the curiate assembly, the centuriate assembly, the council of the plebs, and the tribal assembly. Roman assemblies combined democratic and nondemocratic features. On the one hand, all decisions were made by majority vote, and only after speeches or campaigning. Assembly meetings were often preceded by public meetings, typically in the forum, which featured lively debate. Women, free noncitizens, and even slaves could attend. On the other hand, voting took place by groups, and those groups were unrepresentative. Furthermore, in contrast to Greece, assembly participants stood rather than sat down and received no salary for attendance.

Although the curiate assembly of the monarchy survived, in the Republic it had a largely ceremonial role. The centuriate assembly held real power: it elected magistrates, voted on laws and treaties, accepted declarations of war and peace, and acted as a court in cases of treason, homicide, and appeals of the magistrates' decisions. But this assembly was dominated by wealthy men, especially the equestrians, or cavalrymen. The poorest men, known as *proletarii* ("breeders"), often did not have even the chance to vote.

The two other assemblies were the council of the plebs and the tribal assembly. The tribal assembly eventually replaced the plebs and, in fact, became Rome's main legislative body in the third century B.C., outstripping the centuriate assembly in making laws. To understand the evolution and workings of the tribal assembly, we turn now to the class conflicts in Rome during the fifth through third centuries B.C.

## Conflict of the Orders

Social and political conflict severely tested the Roman state between 494 and 287 B.C. In the end, a more stable state was hammered out, led by a wider elite and offering a measure of popular power. As Rome reached a domestic political consensus, it presented a stronger military front to its enemies. By 300 B.C. Rome was ready to grow from local power to dominance in Italy and then the Mediterranean.

Tradition gives Rome only 136 patrician families in 509 B.C., but they dominated the Early Republic. The plebs, in contrast, comprised masses of peasants and a tiny number of men who, though wealthy, were not patricians. There were plebeian artisans, traders, and shopkeepers, but they made up only a small part of the population. The various plebeian groups each wanted to break patrician power. Wealthy plebeians wanted access to high office, from which they had been largely excluded. Ordinary plebeians demanded relief from debt, redistribution of land, and codification and publication of the law. For a century and a half, the two groups of plebeians made common cause, writing an important chapter in the history of political resistance.

Debt and hunger loomed large in the Early Republic. If a free man could not repay a loan, he had to work off what he owed, often for the rest of his life. Plebeians wanted this harsh system abolished. The average farm was too small to feed a family, so most peasants depended on public land for farming and grazing. Time and again throughout Republican history, however, public land was taken by the wealthy, who denied access to the poor. The only plebeian hope was to change the system.

The story of the plebs in the fifth century B.C. is one of solidarity. They organized themselves as a kind of state within the state, complete with their own assembly (the council of the plebs) and officials (the tribunes of the plebs). The decisions of the council of the plebs, called *plebiscita* (from which *plebiscite* comes), were binding only on the plebs; they did not receive the full force of law for over two hundred years. Yet the plebs did not retreat. On several occasions during the Early Republic, they resorted to secession: the plebs as a whole left the city, often for the Aventine Hill, where they stayed until their grievances were addressed (see inset, Map 5.2).

The ten tribunes°, elected annually by the plebs, were the people's champions. A tribune's house stood open to any plebeian who needed him, and he could not leave the city limits. Inside the city of Rome, a tribune also had the right to veto any act of the magistrates, assembly, or senate that harmed plebeians. In return, the plebs swore to treat the tribunes as sacrosanct and to lynch anyone who harmed them.

But the patricians struck back. They controlled important priesthoods and had many supporters in the military. Furthermore, the new tribal assembly, created around the same time as the council of the plebs, used a system of representation that heavily favored landowners such as patricians. The tribal assembly elected lower magistrates and, like the centuriate assembly, voted on laws and acted as a court of appeals.

Still, the plebeians pressed onward and forced concessions from the patricians, until finally the patricians retreated. They decided to neutralize the poor by meeting the main demands of the plebeian elite. The outcome was a new nobility that combined patricians and plebeians. The patricians had decided to compromise to keep most of their privileges. The personnel changed, but the elite maintained power in Rome.

The specific events in the patrician-plebeian conflict follow two lines of development: concessions to wealthy plebeians and concessions to poor ones. A key moment came in 449 B.C. with publication of the law code known as the "Twelve Tables," eventually, if not at first, on twelve bronze tablets in the Forum. By modern standards, the code was tough and primitive, but its very existence was a plebeian victory because published law was accessible and dependable. Unfortunately, the complex legal procedure remained a secret of the priests for another 150 years, which meant that no poor man could go to court without the help of a rich patron.

Continued plebeian pressure slowly yielded other gains through the fourth century B.C. Around 445 B.C. the patricians accepted patrician-plebeian intermarriage, but it took nearly another eighty years, until 367 B.C., until they agreed to plebeian consuls. That same year saw a debt-relief law, and further debt relief came in 326 B.C.

Finally, in 287 B.C., the patrician and plebeian orders were formally merged, and a law called the "lex Hortensia" made decisions of the council of the plebs and the tribal assembly binding on the whole community, including patricians. Rome's new, combined patrician-plebeian elite was based on wealth, not heredity. Most Romans were non-elite, but at least they had won something: debt relief, access to the published laws, increased power for their assembly, and, most important, protection from arbitrary power.

The problems of poverty continued, but during these same Early Republican years, the poor began to find another form of relief in the new land that Rome acquired through conquest.

**tribunes** (TRIB-yoonz)

**Shrine of a Wealthy Household**    This painting from Pompeii shows the spirit of the paterfamilias in a toga, which is wrapped around his head in keeping the Roman procedures of sacrifice. He is flanked by the spirits of departed ancestors. A snake symbolizes fertility.    *(Alinari/Art Resource, NY)*

## The Roman Household

Roman government was once thought to be nothing more than the maneuvering of a few powerful families. Today a more balanced picture of Rome's constitution prevails. Yet there remains no doubt that elite Roman families wielded great power.

The Latin word *familia* is broader in meaning than the English word *family*. Better translated as "household," it connotes slaves, animals, and property, as well as the members of a nuclear family and their ancestors or descendants. The familia was the basic unit of Roman society and a model of political authority. In theory, though not always in practice, the Roman household was an authoritarian institution governed by a male; thus the familia is an example of patriarchy.

The legal head of the familia was the *paterfamilias*°— the oldest living male, usually the father. According to

Roman law, the paterfamilias had supreme power within the household. Although he was supposed to call a council of senior male relatives to consult on major decisions, he was not required to follow their advice. He had the right to sell family members into slavery and the rarely used power to kill an errant wife or child. A son, no matter how old, was always legally subject to the authority of a living paterfamilias.

Roman respect for the paterfamilias stemmed from Roman esteem for ancestors, who were more important than in Greek culture. All patricians and some plebeians belonged to a *gens*° (plural, *gentes*), a kinship group that traced its ancestry back to a purported common ancestor. All Roman males had a personal and a family name, and patricians and elite plebeians also had a third (middle) name, indicating their gens—for example, Gaius Julius Caesar, whose personal name "Gaius" was followed by the gens name "Julius" and the familia name "Caesar."

In theory, the paterfamilias was the focus of power in the household, but practice was more complex. The sources are full of fathers who showed affection, love, and even indulgence toward their children. Moreover, Roman women usually married in their late teens and men in their late twenties. Given the low life expectancies, it was common for a man of 25 to have already buried his father. Many, perhaps even most, adult males were independent of a paterfamilias.

Unlike men, Roman women never became legally independent, even on the death of a paterfamilias. Instead of receiving a personal name, a daughter was called by the name of her father's gens. For example, Gaius Julius Caesar's daughter was called Julia; if Caesar had had a second daughter, she would have been Julia Secunda ("Julia the Second"). Although fathers were expected to support all male children, they had to support only the first of their daughters. In other words, they were free to "expose" additional daughters—that is, leave them in the open to die or, as was perhaps more likely, to be adopted or raised as a slave. A father also arranged a daughter's marriage and provided her with a dowry. In theory, again, the customs suggest a most severe relationship, but the evidence shows considerable father-daughter affection, including married daughters who sought advice or aid from their fathers.

Most women in early Rome married *cum manu*° (literally, "with hand")—that is, they were "handed over" to their husbands, who became their new paterfamilias.

---

**paterfamilias** (PAH-ter-fah-MIL-ee-us)

**gens** (junz)    **cum manu** (kum MAN-oo)

## READING SOURCES    THE RAPE OF LUCRETIA

*The historian Livy attributes the founding of the Roman Republic to outrage over the rape of the aristocratic woman Lucretia by Sextus Tarquinius, son of King Lucius Tarquinius Superbus. Though of dubious historicity, the story reveals a great deal about Roman attitudes toward gender, honor, and their political implications.*

A guest in Lucretia's house in her husband's absence, Sextus Tarquinius demands that she sleep with him.] But all in vain; not even the fear of death could bend her will. "If death will not move you," Sextus cried, "dishonor shall. I will kiss you first, then cut the throat of a slave and lay his naked body by your side. Will they not believe that you have been caught in adultery with a servant—and paid the price?" Even the most resolute chastity could not have stood against this dreadful threat.

[After being violated by Sextus Tarquinius, Lucretia summons her husband and father.] "In your bed, Collatinus, is the impress of another man. My body only has been violated. My heart is innocent, and death will be my witness. Give me your solemn prom-

ise that the adulterer shall be punished—he is Sextus Tarquinius. He it was who last night came as my enemy disguised as my guest, and took his pleasure of me. . . .

"What is due to him," Lucretia said, "is for you to decide. As for me, I am innocent of fault, but I will take my punishment. Never shall Lucretia provide a precedent for unchaste women to escape what they deserve." With these words she drew a knife from under her robe, drove it into her heart, and fell forward, dead.

Her father and husband were overwhelmed with grief. While they stood weeping helplessly, Brutus [aristocrat and family friend] drew the bloody knife from Lucretia's body, and holding it before him cried: "By this girl's blood—none more chaste till a tyrant wronged her—and by the gods, I swear that with sword and fire, and whatever else can lend strength to my arm, I will pursue Lucius Tarquinius Superbus, his wicked wife, and all his children, and never again will I let them or any other man be King in Rome."

Source: Livy, *The Early History of Rome,* trans. Aubrey de Sélincourt (Harmondsworth, U.K.: Penguin, 1971), pp. 98–99.

---

Even so, Roman wives and mothers had more prestige and freedom than their counterparts in Classical Greece. Legends of early Rome mention some who were peacemakers, negotiators, or catalysts of quarrels among men. (See the box "Reading Sources: The Rape of Lucretia.") Roman women regularly shared meals and social activities with their parents and were expected to take an interest in their husbands' political lives.

### Patrons and Clients

*Patron* (derived from *pater,* "father") means "defender" or "protector." *Client* means "dependent." Just as the Roman family was hierarchical, so Roman society consisted of pyramidal patron-client networks. Most patrons were in turn clients of someone more powerful; only a very few men stood at the top of the pyramid. To the Romans, justice meant not that patron and client treated each

other as equals but rather that they showed each other respect and fulfilled mutual obligations.

Various paths led to the status of client. A peasant in need of help on his farm might ask a wealthy neighbor to become his patron. A manumitted slave became the client of his former owner. A conquered foe became the client of the victorious general. The status of client or patron was hereditary.

Patron and client might help each other in various ways. A patron might provide a client with food or with property for a dowry. He might settle disputes or provide legal assistance. In return, a client owed his patron respect and service. He escorted his patron in public on important occasions—possession of a large clientele signified prestige and power. If his patron sought political office, the client voted for him and urged others to do so.

Cloaked in an elaborate language of goodwill, the patron-client relationship was considered a matter of *fides°* ("good faith" or "trustworthiness"). Romans spoke not of a client submitting to a patron's power but rather of a client "commending himself" to the patron's fides. A patron spoke not of his clients but of his "friends," especially if they were men of standing or substance.

A patron was supposed to put his clients before his kin by marriage; only blood or adoptive relations were to take precedence. According to the Twelve Tables, a patron who defrauded his client was accursed and subject to death with impunity.

Patronage played an important role in Roman domestic politics. A wealthy patron expected his humble clients to vote as he wished, but he abused them at his peril. If a man's clients grew discontented, they might find a new patron. Patronage was more straightforward in foreign affairs. Experience as patrons schooled Roman leaders in treating the peoples they conquered as clients, often as personal clients. Moreover, the Roman state sometimes took foreign countries into its collective fides—much as a patron did a client—thus allowing Rome to extend its influence without the constraints of a formal alliance.

## Religion and World-View

If we knew nothing about early Roman religion, we could deduce much about it from the familia and patronage. We could expect to find an emphasis on powerful fathers and binding agreements, and both are indeed present. The task of a Roman priest, whether an official of the state or an individual paterfamilias, was to establish what the Romans called the "peace of the gods." Roman cults aimed at obtaining the gods' agreement to human requests, at "binding" the gods—the Latin term for which is *religio.*

The earliest Roman religion was animistic—that is, it centered on the spirits that, the Romans believed, haunted the household and the fields and forests and determined the weather. The Lares, or spirits of departed ancestors, guarded the house, and the Penates watched over stored grain. The spirit of the hearth was Vesta, of the door Janus, of the rain and sun Jupiter (later identified with the Greek sky-god and the father-god Zeus), and of the crops and vegetation Mars (later identified with the Greek war-god Ares). The Romans believed that these spirits needed to be appeased—hence the contractual nature of their prayers and offerings. Over the years, as a result of Greek influence, anthropomorphism (that

**Bronze War God** This elegant fourth century B.C. Etruscan bronze, thought to represent Mars, the god of war, shows the metal breastplate worn by a warrior of that era. *(Scala/Art Resource, NY)*

is, the worship of humanlike gods and goddesses) replaced Roman animism.

Roman state religion grew out of house religion. Vesta, the hearth-goddess, became goddess of the civic hearth; Janus, the door-god, became god of the city's gates; Jupiter became the general overseer of the gods; and Mars became the god of war. When trade and conquest brought the Romans into contact with foreign religions, the Romans tended to absorb them. The senate

**fides** (FEE-days)

screened and sometimes rejected new gods, but by and large Roman polytheism was tolerant and inclusive.

The Republic sponsored numerous priestly committees, or colleges, to secure the peace of the gods. Originally restricted to patricians, most of the highest priesthoods were opened to plebeians by law in 300 B.C. Although some priesthoods were full-time jobs, most left the officeholder free to pursue a parallel career as a magistrate or a senator. The two most important priestly colleges were the augurs°, who were in charge of foretelling the future from omens and other signs, and the pontiffs, who exercised a general supervision of Roman religion. The chief pontiff, the *pontifex maximus*°, was the head of the state clergy. He was chosen by election. The pontiffs alone controlled the interpretation of the law until the fourth century B.C. The Romans allowed priests to interpret the law on the theory that an offense against humans was also an offense against the gods.

The system provided for only two colleges of priestesses: those of Ceres, goddess of fertility and death, and those of the Vestal Virgins. The six Vestals tended the civic hearth and made sure that its fire never went out. They served, as it were, as wives of the whole community, as guardians of the civil household. The Vestals were the only Roman women not under the authority of a paterfamilias. Chosen between the ages of 6 and 10 by the pontifex maximus, they had to remain virgins for thirty years or face death.

Roman ideology promoted simple and austere farmers' virtues—discipline, hard work, frugality, temperance, and the avoidance of public displays of affection even between spouses. Such virtues underlined the difference between the Republic and the kings, with their luxury and sophistication. At the same time, these virtues papered over class distinctions between rich and poor and so promoted stability.

Other Roman ideals included the supreme virtue of the household, *pietas*—devotion and loyalty to the familia, the gods, and the state. Household duties and gender obligations were defined clearly. Women were to be modest, upright, and practical. Men were to project *gravitas* ("weight" or "seriousness"), never lightness or levity. A serious man would display self-control and constancy, the ability to persevere against difficult odds. The masculine ideal was *virtus* (literally, "manliness"), which indicated excellence in war and government.

Roman men who attained virtus considered themselves entitled to the reward of *dignitas*, meaning not only public esteem but the tangible possession of a dignified position and official rank—in short, public office. The ultimate test of virtus, however, was in battle. Rome's wars supplied ample occasion to display it.

# FROM ITALIAN CITY-STATE TO WORLD EMPIRE, CA. 509–133 B.C.

AT the beginning of the Republic (ca. 509 B.C.), Roman territory comprised about 500 square miles. By 338 B.C. Rome controlled the 2,000 square miles of Latium and was moving north into Etruria and south into Samnite country. Three-quarters of a century later, in 265 B.C., Rome controlled all of the Italian peninsula south of an imaginary line from Pisae (modern Pisa) to Ariminum (modern Rimini), an area of about 50,000 square miles (see Map 5.2). By 146 B.C. Roman provinces included Sicily, Cisalpine Gaul (northernmost Italy), Sardinia, Corsica, and Spain (divided into two provinces). Once-great Carthage was the Roman province of Africa (roughly, modern Tunisia), and once-mighty Macedon was the province of Macedonia, whose governor was also effectively in charge of Greece. The Seleucid kingdom was free but fatally weakened. Rome was the supreme power between Gibraltar and the Levant. It was the greatest empire of the ancient West. How and why had Rome, from its humble beginnings as a local power, reached this breathtaking height?

## Republican Expansion: The Conquest of Italy, ca. 509–265 B.C.

Romans maintain that they conquered an empire without ever committing an act of aggression. When war was declared, a special college of priests informed the gods that Rome was merely retaliating for foreign injury. True, the Romans were frequently attacked by others, but often only after provocative behavior by Rome had left its rivals little choice.

Rome's early conquests reveal many of its lasting motives for expansion. No doubt lust for conquest played a part, as did fear and hatred of outsiders, but self-control and shrewdness were stronger Roman characteristics. Greed, particularly land-hunger, was a perennial theme. Sometimes a domestic political motive was at work, for foreign adventure was a convenient way of deflecting plebeian energies. Perhaps the most significant

---

augur (AW-ger)
**pontifex maximus** (PON-tih-fex MAX-ih-mus)

**Rome**

0 500 1000 M.
0 1500 3000 Ft.

FIELD OF MARS

Tiber

*Tiber Island*

CAPITOLINE MT.

QUIRINAL HILL

VIMINAL HILL

ESQUILINE MT.

Senate House

Forum

Temple of Jupiter

Regia

PALATINE MT.

CAELIAN MT.

Circus Maximus

AVENTINE MT.

Servian Wall

Hills of Rome

A L P S

Extent of Roman Italy by 218 B.C.

Aquileia

Verona

Po

Adige

Cremona

Placentia

Genua (Genoa)

CISALPINE GAUL

Bononia (Bologna)

Ariminum (Rimini)

Florentia (Florence)

Arno

Fanum Fortunae

Ancona

Pisae (Pisa)

*Ligurian Sea*

Arretium

UMBRIA

PICENUM

Castrum Truentinum

Populonia

ETRURIA

*Elba*

Saturnia

Castrum Novum

Tiber

Reate

Corfinium

Veii Rome

Appian Way

LATIUM

SAMNIUM

Arpinum

ILLYRIA

*Adriatic Sea*

*Corsica*

Aleria

APULIA

Barium

Beneventum

Venusia

Tarracina

Capua

CAMPANIA

Appian Way

Brundisium

Misenum

Neapolis (Naples)

Paestum

LUCANIA

Tarentum

CALABRIA

*Sardinia*

*Gulf of Tarentum*

Neapolis

BRUTTIUM

Thurii

Carales

*Tyrrhenian Sea*

Croton

*Mediterranean Sea*

Messana

Locri

Rhegium

Lilybaeum

*Sicily*

Syracuse

*Malta*

Utica

*Cape Bon*

Carthage

Hippo Regius

NORTH AFRICA

0 50 100 Km.
0 50 100 Mi.

Roman territory (full citizens)

Roman territory (citizens without suffrage)

Roman allies

Latin colonies

Carthaginian possessions

■ Greek cities

Major roads by 100 B.C.

## READING SOURCES   A ROMAN TRIUMPH

*The Roman triumph symbolizes the prestige flowing from military success in Rome; it also demonstrates the senate's attempt to control victorious generals. This description is drawn from the* Epitome of Zonaras, *a Byzantine historian of the twelfth century A.D. Zonaras drew his material on Rome from Plutarch (ca. A.D. 50–120) and Dio Cassius (second to third century A.D.).*

When any great success worthy of a triumph had been gained, the general was immediately saluted as imperator by the soldiers, and he would bind sprigs of laurel upon the *fasces* [bladed axes bundled in rods, carried as a symbol of authority] and deliver them to the messengers who announced the victory to the city. On arriving home he would assemble the senate and ask to have the triumph voted him. And if he obtained a vote from the senate and from the people, his title of *imperator* was confirmed. . . .

Arrayed in the triumphal dress and wearing armlets, with a laurel crown upon his head, and holding a branch in his right hand, he called together the people. After praising collectively the troops who had served with him, and some of them individually, he presented them with money and honored them also with decorations. . . . A large part of the spoils also was assigned to the soldiers who had taken part in the campaign. . . .

After these ceremonies the triumphant general would mount his chariot [with his children and relatives]. . . . A public slave . . . rode with the victor in the chariot itself, holding over him the crown of precious stones set in gold, and kept saying to him, "Look behind!" . . . Thus arrayed, they entered the city, having at the head of the procession the spoils and trophies and figures representing the captured forts, cities, mountains, rivers, lakes, and seas—everything, in fact, that they had taken. . . . When these adjuncts had gone on their way, the victorious general arrived at the Roman Forum, and after commanding that some of the captives be led to prison and put to death, he rode up to the Capitol. There he performed certain rites and made offerings and dined in the porticoes up there, after which he departed homewards towards evening, accompanied by flutes and pipes.

Source: Naphtali Lewis and Meyer Reinhold, eds., *Roman Civilization: Selected Readings,* vol. 1, *The Republic and the Augustan Age,* 3d ed., pp. 230–231. © 1990 by Columbia University Press. Reproduced with permission of Columbia University Press in the format Textbook via Copyright Clearance Center.

factors, however, were the personal ambitions of a warrior elite and the presence of conflict in early Italy.

Victory in battle promised both prestige and booty and the political success that might follow. Military achievement brought unique acclaim. For example, certain victorious generals were allowed to celebrate a triumph; no such ceremony rewarded the feats of peacemakers or distinguished judges or other public benefactors. The triumphant general rode a chariot through the city to the Temple of Jupiter on the Capitoline Hill. He was accompanied by his troops, by the spoils of victory including famous captives, and by the magistrates and senators. (See the box "Reading Sources: A Roman Triumph.")

The harsh reality of Italian politics also ruled against pacifism. Without the willingness to fight, Rome could never have maintained its freedom. Yet what began as a pragmatic response to present dangers hardened into a habit of meeting even remote threats with force. In the fourth century B.C., having gained control of Latium, Rome considered the Samnites of central and southern Italy to be a potential threat. In the third century B.C., once Rome controlled Italy, it felt threatened by Carthage. After Carthage, the threat of Macedon was squelched, and after Macedon, Seleucid Syria, and so on.

Though flexible and far-reaching, Roman diplomacy sometimes ended up in war. Rome made formal alliances with some states, granting protection in return for obedience and troops or ships when needed by Rome.

**Map 5.2   Roman Italy, ca. 265 B.C.**   Rome controlled a patchwork of conquered territory, colonies, and allied states in Italy, held together by a network of treaties and of roads. The city of Rome (*inset*) was built on seven hills beside the Tiber River.

Short of a formal commitment, however, Rome might accept a state "into its fides"—that is, treat the state as a client. The result was only a moral, and not a legal, commitment, which sometimes sufficed to frighten any would-be aggressor from harassing Rome's new friend. If not, Rome had to go into battle to prove its trustworthiness as a patron.

Military success requires tenacity, discipline, and flexibility—all qualities that Rome cultivated. Roman organizational ability and love of order made the Roman military camp a much more regular and systematic place than anything seen since Assyrian days. Beginning in the fourth century B.C., Rome began to reward its soldiers with regular pay; this and the distribution of conquered land improved morale. Two other points are even more significant: the willingness to utilize foreign military technology and the combination of generosity and firmness with which Rome treated its allies.

Borrowed from the Greeks in the sixth century B.C., the hoplite phalanx suited Rome on the relatively level ground of Latium but fared poorly in the rugged Apennines against the Samnites. Following a major defeat in 321 B.C., the Romans adopted with great success the Samnites' equipment and tactics.

Unlike the phalanx, which overpowered the enemy by fighting as one thickly massed unit, a Roman legion was flexible and adaptable. Legions were drawn up into three lines, thirty maniples ("handfuls"), and sixty centuries (literally "hundreds," although the number of men per century varied); each century was commanded by a centurion. A legion marched in a checkerboard pattern, leaving gaps in the lines. In battle each line closed its gaps as it attacked in turn. Unlike hoplites, who engaged the enemy at short range, legionnaires first threw their javelins at long range. Then, having broken the enemy's order, they charged and fought with sword and shield. The semi-independence of the maniples, each with its own commander and banner, created a more maneuverable army than that of the phalanx and one better suited for mountain fighting. When Rome's legions beat the Macedonian phalanx decisively in 197 B.C., military history entered a new era.

Rome was the leading power among the Latins, whom it led in an alliance known as the Latin League. Rome was first among equals, but the citizens of even the humblest Latin state had reciprocal rights of intermarriage and commerce with Romans and the right to become a citizen of another state by migrating there. Under Roman leadership the Latin League successfully defended Latium's borders against a series of enemies during the fourth and fifth centuries B.C. But eventually Rome had to confront a bitter two-year-long Latin revolt (340–338 B.C.).

The year 338 B.C. marked a turning point. Defeated peoples in the ancient world were often executed, deported, or enslaved. Victorious against the Latins, Rome, by contrast, pursued generosity. The Latin League was dissolved. Some of its member states were annexed, and their inhabitants became Roman citizens; others retained independence and alliance with Rome though no longer with one another. The non-Latin allies of the former rebels were also annexed by Rome, but they received the unique halfway status of "citizenship without suffrage." They shared the burdens of Roman citizenship but also all the rights except the vote; they also retained the right of local self-government. The settlement of 338 B.C. broke new ground by making it possible for Rome and its former allies and enemies to live together on the basis of relative equality.

The settlement also set a precedent for future Roman expansion. As Rome conquered Italy, a number of privileged Italian cities (called *municipia*) received the status of citizenship without suffrage. Others remained independent but were tied to Rome by perpetual alliance. Romans often annexed a portion of the land of these states.

If municipia were the carrots of Roman imperialism, the stick was a network of military roads and colonies crisscrossing Italy, allowing Rome to keep an eye on potential rebels. Roman roads allowed the swift movement of troops and linked the growing network of colonies. Colonies were established in strategically vital areas. The inhabitants, Roman and Latin, owed military service to Rome.

In later years, Italians would complain about treatment by Rome, but compared with inhabitants of Roman provinces outside Italy, they had a privileged status. Romans too would complain about allied demands for equality, but Rome received from its allies a huge pool of military manpower. The allies staffed the Roman armies that conquered the Samnites, Etruscans, and Gauls, all of whom came into the Roman orbit by the early third century B.C. Manpower abundance won Rome's war (280–276 B.C.) against the Greek general Pyrrhus° of Epirus (319–272 B.C.), an adventurer who intervened in southern Italy. Although Pyrrhus won battle after battle, he was unable to match Roman willingness to sustain thousands of casualties time and again. Pyrrhus's seeming victories, therefore, turned out to be defeats, which sent him home to Greece disappointed and left us with the expression "Pyrrhic victory."

---

**Pyrrhus** (PIR-us)

**The Appian Way**    Named for the censor Appius Claudius Caecus, who proposed its construction, Rome's first great road was built in 312 B.C. during the Samnite Wars. It originally ran 132 miles from Rome to Capua and was extended an additional 234 miles, probably by 244 B.C., to Brundisium, on Italy's southern Adriatic coast.    *(F. H. C. Birch/Sonia Halliday Photographs)*

As for Rome, by 265 B.C. it emerged as the ruler of all of Italy south of the Pisae-Ariminum line (see Map 5.2). One might say that Rome unified Italy, although Italy was less a unity than a patchwork of Roman territory and colonies and of diverse cities, states, and peoples each allied to Rome by separate treaties.

## Rome Versus Carthage: The Punic Wars, 264–146 B.C.

The conquest of Italy made Rome one of two great powers in the central Mediterranean. The other was Carthage°. Founded around 750 B.C. by Phoenicians from Tyre,

Carthage controlled an empire in North Africa, Sicily, Corsica, Sardinia, Malta, the Balearic Islands, and southern Spain. (The adjective *Phoenician* is *Punicus* in Latin, hence the term *Punic°* for *Carthaginian*.) Like Rome, Carthage was guided by a wealthy elite, but it was mercantile in character rather than agrarian. Rome was a land power, Carthage a sea power. Rome had virtually no navy. Carthage commanded a great war fleet, and its merchant ships dominated the western Mediterranean and played a major role in the east.

Carthage was an economic powerhouse. The Carthaginians exploited the mineral-rich mines of Spain. They were the first Mediterranean people to organize

---

**Carthage** (CAR-thidge)

**Punic** (PYOO-nik)

**Carthaginian Craftsmanship**   These pendants of male heads are made of colored glass and come from Carthage. The Phoenicians and their colonists excelled in glasswork as a medium for the production of luxury goods.   *(Erich Lessing/Art Resource, NY)*

large-scale plantations of slaves for the production of single crops. Even though the Romans zealously wiped out most of Carthaginian elite culture, they did make sure to preserve one Carthaginian classic: a multivolume work on agriculture by Mago. Translated from Punic into Latin by order of the senate, Mago's treatise had an enormous impact on Roman landowners, who, with the importation of massive numbers of slaves, adopted the plantation system in Italy (see pages 157–158).

Carthage boasted brilliant generals, especially in the Barca family, whose most famous member was Hannibal° (247–183 B.C.). Carthage might have been a handicapper's favorite at the outbreak of its long wars with Rome in 264 B.C., yet the end result was disaster for Carthage. A combination of Carthaginian weaknesses and Roman strengths accounts for the outcome.

Unlike Rome, Carthage did not have a citizen army. The commanders were Carthaginian, but most of the soldiers were mercenaries and of questionable loyalty. Unlike Rome, which treated its Italian allies well, Carthage showed contempt for its troops, who repaid the favor by revolting whenever they had the chance. Carthage fielded large armies but not as large as Rome's.

At the start of the Punic Wars, Rome had no navy or commanders to match the Barca family, but it proved adaptable, tenacious, and ruthless. To win the First Punic War (264–241 B.C.), for example, Rome not only built a navy but outlasted the enemy in a long and bloody conflict. After initially granting a mild peace treaty, Rome took advantage of later Carthaginian weakness to seize Sardinia and Corsica and to demand an additional indemnity.

Forced to give in to Rome's demands, Carthage decided to build a new and bigger empire in Spain, beginning in 237 B.C., under Barca family leadership. Han-

---

**Hannibal** (HAN-uh-bull)

nibal's father, the general Hamilcar Barca (d. 229 B.C.), had gone undefeated in the First Punic War and is said to have raised his son to seek a rematch. With Spain's rich deposits of silver and copper in its hands, Carthage once again posed a credible threat to Rome. In the mid-220s B.C., an ever watchful Rome challenged Carthaginian power in Spain through a Roman client there. The new Carthaginian commander, 27-year-old Hannibal Barca, was not to be cowed, however, and the Second Punic War ensued (218–201 B.C.).

Carthage was willing to risk war because Hannibal promised a quick, cheap, and easy victory. Because Carthage no longer had a fleet, the Romans felt secure in Italy; Hannibal surprised them by marching overland to Italy, making a dangerous passage across the Alps. A tactical genius, Hannibal reckoned that with his superior generalship, he could defeat the Romans in battle and cause them enormous casualties, and he was right. Hannibal's forces dominated the battlefield. Among his victories was the Battle of Cannae in Apulia (southeastern Italy), where, in 216 B.C., Carthage gave Rome the bloodiest defeat in its history, killing perhaps thirty thousand Romans.

But huge casualties alone could not bring Rome to its knees. Nor did all of Rome's allies revolt, as Hannibal had hoped. Most stood by Rome, which had treated them relatively well in the past and which now threatened rebels with reprisals. After Cannae, Rome's leadership followed a cautious strategy of harassment, delay, refusal to fight, and attrition. Hannibal was stymied by an enemy who lost battles but refused to surrender. In addition, Hannibal did not have the power to take the city of Rome.

In the meantime, Rome had bought valuable time to regroup. A new military star emerged: Publius Cornelius Scipio° (236–183 B.C.), a Roman who finally understood Hannibal's tactics and matched them. First Scipio conquered Carthage's Spanish dominions, and then he forced Hannibal back to North Africa for a final battle in 202 B.C. near Zama (in modern Tunisia). Scipio won the battle and gained the surname Africanus ("the African"). As for Hannibal, he played a prominent role in Carthaginian politics for about a decade, until Rome forced him into exile in Syria. In about 183 B.C., after taking part in the Seleucids' unsuccessful war against Rome, he committed suicide rather than face extradition to Rome.

The peace settlement of 201 B.C. stripped Carthage of its empire. Yet soon its economy rebounded, reviving old Roman fears of Carthage's political ambitions. In the

Third Punic War (149–146 B.C.), Rome mounted a three-year siege under the leadership of Scipio Aemilianus (185–129 B.C.), finally destroying the city of Carthage in 146 B.C. Approximately a century later, Carthage was resurrected as a Roman colony and became one of the empire's greatest cities. In the meantime, it was left desolate, its people killed or enslaved.

Rome emerged from the Punic Wars as the greatest power in the Mediterranean. It had acquired new provinces in Sicily, Sardinia, Corsica, Spain, and North Africa (where Carthage's former territory was annexed as the province of Africa). The road to further conquest seemed to lead in all directions.

## Victories in the Hellenistic East, ca. 200–133 B.C.

Most countries would have savored peace after an ordeal such as the Punic Wars, but Rome immediately leaped into a long conflict in Greece and Anatolia. Its aims were to weaken the power of Macedon, which it feared might threaten Rome one day, especially since the Macedonian king Philip V (r. 221–179 B.C.) had made an alliance with Hannibal after Cannae. Rome won a relatively quick and easy victory when in 197 B.C. the legions crushed the Macedonian phalanx at Cynoscephalae in central Greece (see Map 5.3).

Rome had hoped to impose a patron-client relationship on Greece and Macedon, thereby avoiding having to sustain a permanent military presence, but that hope failed. The independent-minded Greeks chafed at Roman domination. Several years of miscommunication and intrigue followed, only to lead to renewed wars. First the Seleucids, under the ambitious king Antiochus III (r. 223–187 B.C.), challenged Rome for hegemony on the Greek peninsula. It was in this war that Hannibal took a small, doomed part. Roman forces made short work of the enemy. Driven out not only from Greece but from Anatolia as well, the Seleucids in effect recognized Roman supremacy in the Mediterranean (188 B.C.).

Then came another two rounds of war that pitted Rome against Macedon and various Greek states (171–167 and 150–146 B.C.). Victorious in both wars, Rome deprived the Greeks and Macedonians of their independence. Wherever democracy had survived in Greece, it was replaced with oligarchy. In 146 B.C. Rome destroyed Corinth, one of Greece's wealthiest cities, as a warning against further rebellion. Greece then suffered Roman neglect and taxation for nearly two hundred years.

By annexing Carthage, Macedon, and Greece in the mid-second century B.C., Rome created a dynamic for expansion around the entire Mediterranean. Before the

---

**Scipio** (SIP-ee-o)

**Map 5.3  Roman Expansion, 264–44 B.C.**  Wars against Carthage, the major Greco-Macedonian powers, Gauls, Germans, North Africans, and other peoples brought Rome an empire on three continents.

### Map Legend

Roman territory in 264 B.C.
Roman territory added by 133 B.C.
Roman territory added by 44 B.C.
Parthian Empire in 44 B.C.
X  Major Battles

### Map Labels

ATLANTIC OCEAN

North Sea

Baltic Sea

Caspian Sea

Black Sea

Adriatic Sea

Mediterranean Sea

Red Sea

BRITAIN

GERMANY

GAUL

BELGICA

NARBONENSIS
Narbo
Lugdunum (Lyon)
Massilia (Marseille)

RAETIA

NORICUM

PANNONIA

ILLYRICUM

CISALPINE GAUL
Po

ALPS

ITALY
Arretium
Lake Trasimene 217 B.C.
Rome
Capua
Tarentum
Brundisium
Cannae 216 B.C.

CORSICA

SARDINIA

SICILY
Messana
Syracuse
Drepana 249 B.C.
Malta

BALEARIC IS.

New Carthage

NEARER SPAIN
Saguntum
Corduba (Cordoba)
Gades

FARTHER SPAIN
Numantia

Ebro

Rhine

Elbe

Vistula

Danube

Don

Dnieper

Dniester

Volga

BOSPORAN KINGDOM

DACIA

MOESIA

THRACE
Byzantium

MACEDONIA
Pydna 168 B.C.
Cynoscephalae 197 B.C.

EPIRUS

ACHAEA
Corinth
Athens

CRETE

RHODES

BITHYNIA AND PONTUS

GALATIA

CAPPADOCIA

ANATOLIA
Pergamum
ASIA
Ephesus

LYCIA

PAMPHYLIA

CILICIA
Tarsus

CYPRUS

CYRENAICA
Cyrene

AFRICA PROCONSULARIS
Carthage
Zama 202 B.C.

NUMIDIA

MAURETANIA

NORTH AFRICA

SAHARA

ARMENIA

CAUCASUS MTS.

PARTHIA
Ctesiphon
Seleucia
Carrhae 53 B.C.

SYRIA
Antioch
Damascus

JUDEA
Jerusalem
Petra

SINAI

EGYPT
Alexandria

Nile

Tigris

Euphrates

ARABIAN DESERT

### Scale

0        200        400 Mi.
0    200    400 Km.

**Luxurious Earrings**    A wealthy Roman woman might have been proud to wear these refined and expensive gold earrings, produced in a Greek city of southern Italy in about 200 B.C. Only 2 inches tall, each earring shows a dove standing on a small, garland-trimmed base.    *(Pair of earrings with pendant doves, Greek, Hellenistic period, 150–100 B.C.; Gold, garnet, and glass paste; L. 5.2 cm. Courtesy of the Museum of Fine Arts, Boston, Harriet Otis Cruft Fund, 68.5a.b)*

century was over, southern Gaul was annexed, and Rome had gained a foothold in Asia. The kingdom of Pergamum (northwestern Anatolia) had supported Rome throughout Rome's wars in the east. When Attalus III of Pergamum died without an heir in 133 B.C., he surrendered his kingdom to the Roman people, who made it into a province of Asia.

Two great Hellenistic states remained independent: the Seleucid kingdom, that is, Syria, and Ptolemaic Egypt. Roman ambassadors and generals frequently interfered in their affairs, however, and no one was surprised when, in the first century B.C., they too were annexed by Rome.

## The Socioeconomic Consequences of Expansion

Expansion led to enormous and unintended changes in Rome's society, economy, and culture. Already wealthy, the Roman elite now came into fabulous riches. Huge profits awaited the generals, patrons, diplomats, magistrates, tax collectors, and businessmen who followed Rome's armies. In Italy most profits were in the form of land; in the provinces wealth was found not only in land but also in slaves, booty, and graft. One of the worst grafters, Gaius Verres, governor of Sicily from 73 to 71 B.C., was prosecuted by Cicero (see page 167), then beginning his oratorical career, for allegedly extorting tens of thousands of pounds of silver from his province. But even Cicero skimmed off several thousand pounds of silver as governor of the province of Cilicia (southern Anatolia) from 51 to 50 B.C.

The first Roman coinage, traditionally dated to 289 B.C., facilitated commercial transactions. Previously, the Romans had made do with barter, uncoined bronze, and cast bronze bars, but now they imitated the workmanship and style of Greek coins. Equally prominent in the homes of wealthy Romans were Greek metalwork, jewelry, art objects, and other luxury goods. Conservatives bemoaned the decline of traditional Roman austerity, but they fought a hopeless rear-guard action.

Ordinary Romans needed no reminder of the virtues of austerity, for they did not share in the elite's profit from Roman expansion. Indeed, a century of intensive warfare—from the outbreak of the Punic Wars in 264 B.C. to the destruction of Carthage and Corinth in 146 B.C.—strained the lot of the Roman people to the breaking point. Hannibal's invasion left much of the farmland of southern Italy devastated and Italian manpower considerably reduced. Yet most people might have rebounded from these problems within a generation or two, if they had not faced other serious troubles.

Conscription had become the norm. The average term of military service between ages 17 and 46 was six years; the maximum term was twenty years. Because experienced legionnaires were at a premium, commanders were loath to release them from service. But the longer a man was away in the army, the harder it was for his wife and children to keep the family farm running. With help from a patron, they might be able to make do, though most patrons in fact added to the problem through the introduction to Italy of large-scale agricultural entrepreneurship. Those who sought wealth monopolized Italian farmland, imported huge numbers of slaves, and brought ruin on the free peasantry of Italy.

The last two centuries B.C. witnessed the transformation of Roman rural society from one of independent farmers to one in which slave labor played a major role. By the end of the first century B.C., Italy's slave population was estimated at two million to three million, about a third of the peninsula's total. Prisoners of war and conquered civilians provided a ready supply of slaves. Most worked in agriculture or mining, and their treatment was often abominable; the fewer house slaves were usually better off.

Wealthy Romans wanted to invest in large landed estates, or *latifundia*°, worked by slaves. These estates were either mixed farms (most often devoted to cultivating vines, olives, and grain) or ranches (establishments where animals were raised for meat, milk, and wool). One devotee of the latter was the prominent conservative Marcus Porcius Cato° (234–149 B.C.), known as Cato the Censor. Cato argued that there were only three ways to get rich: "pasturage, pasturage, and pasturage." All a would-be entrepreneur needed was land, which Rome had conquered a huge amount of in Italy. Called public land, Rome's new territory belonged to the Roman people, but an individual was legally entitled to claim about 320 acres as his own. Many entrepreneurs flouted the law, however, and grabbed much more than their fair share of public land. In addition, they often forced families of absent soldiers off private land, either by debt foreclosure or by outright violence. Sometimes families would leave the land for the city, but usually they stayed as tenants.

Before about 170 B.C., poor Romans were sometimes able to find land in colonies. By 170 B.C., however, Rome had established all the colonies in Italy that its security demanded, so this avenue of escape from poverty was closed. A displaced farmer who wanted to compete in the labor market would have found it difficult to underbid cheap slave labor. In any case, Roman ideology frowned on wage labor by citizens. Nor was it practical for a poor farmer to sue a wealthy patron who seized his land, because a plaintiff himself had to bring the accused into court.

The situation of the Italian peasantry was becoming increasingly miserable by the mid-second century B.C. As one modern scholar has put it, "In conquering what they were pleased to call the world, the Romans ruined a great part of the Italian people."[2]

## The Impact of Greece on Rome and Its Empire

Rome learned much from its new encounters with foreign peoples—and from none more than the Greeks. Wealthy Romans cultivated interests in Greek art, literature, rhetoric, and speculative thought; poor and rich alike enjoyed Greek drama. Before the mid-third century B.C. Roman literature was virtually nonexistent. An oral tradition of songs, ballads, and funeral oratory kept alive the deeds of the famous, for writing was generally restricted to commercial and government records and inscriptions. In short, the Romans conquered Italy without writing about it.

Contact with the Greek cities brought changes. Large numbers of Roman soldiers in Magna Graecia (southern Italy and Sicily) were introduced to comedy, tragedy, mimes, and sophisticated song lyrics, and many developed a permanent taste for them. It is no accident that the first production of a drama at Rome took place in 240 B.C., the year after the end of the First Punic War. Afterward, the annual production of such dramas became standard procedure.

No one could accuse the Romans of rushing headlong into a new age, however. The authorities continued to have their doubts about theater, which seemed excessively emotional and probably corrupt. They did not allow the building of a permanent theater in Rome until 55 B.C., insisting that the wealthiest city in the Mediterranean make do with makeshift wooden structures. Nor did the Roman elite readily become playwrights or poets. The first gentleman poet in Rome, Lucilius (180–102 B.C.), did not arrive until the second century B.C., and he was a Latin, not a Roman. His predecessors, the founders of Latin literature, were all of low social status; little of their work survives.

The two great early Latin playwrights are Titus Maccius Plautus (ca. 254–184 B.C.) and Publius Terentius Afer, today known as Terence (ca. 195–159 B.C.). Both of them wrote comedies on the model of the great Greek comic playwright Menander (see pages 122–123). Plautus was an Umbrian and a poor man who learned his Latin in Rome; Terence was a North African slave, educated and freed in Rome. Twenty-one plays by Plautus and six by Terence survive. Plautus's plays are generally earthy slapstick farces. They are invariably set in Greece, not Rome, in part out of escapism (many were written during the Second Punic War), in part out of the censorial demands of the Roman authorities. They nonetheless reveal much about Roman society. Terence's plays are more subtle than Plautus's, indicating the growing sophistication of Roman theatergoers.

Latin prose developed more slowly than did poetry and drama. The first histories by Romans, composed after the Second Punic War, were written in Greek, for Latin lacked the vocabulary or the audience for history. Cato the Censor was the first historian of Rome to write in Latin. His *Origines,* of which we have only remnants, recounted Roman history from the origin of the city to about 150 B.C. The earliest surviving Latin prose work is Cato's *On Agriculture.*

In the traditional education of a Roman aristocrat, parents and close family friends played the primary role. Although this practice continued, wealthy Romans in the second century B.C. began acquiring Greek slaves to

---

**latifundia** (lat-uh-FUN-dee-uh)    **Cato** (KAY-toe)

**The Round Temple**    This elegant, circular, Corinthian-columned structure in the Forum Boarium in Rome, built around 150 to 100 B.C., is the oldest surviving marble temple in the city. Greek in style, it is an example of Roman borrowing from sophisticated Hellenistic culture. *(Scala/Art Resource, NY)*

educate their sons in the Greek language and Greek literature. Soon Greek freedmen began setting up schools offering the same subjects. Before long, similar Latin grammar schools also opened.

One of the forms of Greek literature that appealed most to the practical-minded Romans was rhetoric. Roman orators studied Greek models, and many would say that they eventually outdid the Greeks. Cato was the first Roman to publish his speeches, and he also wrote a book on rhetoric. Both gave impetus to the spread of sophisticated rhetoric in Rome.

Scipio Aemilianus, conqueror of Carthage in 146 B.C., had a distinguished political and military career. He was also patron of a group of prominent statesmen and soldiers who shared his love of Hellenism. Among the writers whom they supported were the playwright Terence, the poet Lucilius, the historian Polybius, and the Stoic philosopher Panaetius (ca. 185–109 B.C.). The Stoic emphases on duty, wisdom, and world brotherhood appealed both to Rome's traditional ideology and to its more recent acquisition of empire. Yet not all Romans shared Scipio's admiration of Greek culture; Cato, for example, was famously ambivalent.

Cornelia, Scipio Aemilianus's mother-in-law, was an educated lover of Hellenism who wrote letters that existed several hundred years later as examples of elegant Latin prose. Her villa in the resort of Misenum on the Bay of Naples was well known for the distinguished guests whom she received there. When her husband, an outstanding statesman and general, died, Cornelia chose to remain a widow. One of the men who tried to change her mind was no less a figure than the king of Egypt. The widow spent her time managing her own estate and supervising the education of her two sons, the future tribunes Tiberius and Gaius Gracchus.

Although Cornelia's privileges were extraordinary, she is nonetheless a reminder of the opportunities that imperial expansion offered to wealthy Roman women. Marriage practices are one example of change. Few women were married *cum manu* anymore—that is, handed over by their fathers to their husbands. A woman's father or nearest male relative, not her husband, was most likely to be her paterfamilias, which meant that a husband's control over his wife's dowry was limited. The result was more freedom, at least for wealthy women.

Cornelia is also a reminder of the fundamental conservatism of Roman society. Although we know the years of birth and death of numerous elite Roman males of the second century B.C., we do not know Cornelia's. Nor did her literary interests entail any neglect of home and family. Cornelia bore twelve children, though only three of them lived to adulthood (such was the reality of infant mortality even for the wealthiest Romans).

# THE REVOLUTION FROM THE GRACCHI TO THE CAESARS, 133–31 B.C.

**A** CITIZEN of the Roman Republic in the mid-second century B.C. might have looked forward to a long and happy future for his country, unaware that the Republic—after 350 years of expansion—was about to begin a century of domestic and foreign unrest that would bring down the whole system. Why and how did the Republic collapse? More than a century of warfare weighed heavily on the ordinary people of Italy—the Romans and allied peasants whose farms were

ruined while they were off fighting. The Roman elite was bitterly divided over what to do about the problems of the peasants. One group wanted to redistribute land on behalf of the poor; another group had no sympathy for them.

By the Late Republic the city of Rome was crowded and populous: scholars estimate the number of inhabitants to have reached one million by the end of the first century B.C. The government had to take charge of the grain supply. But elite politicians exploited the issue for partisan purposes. Once before, during the struggle between the patrician and plebeian orders in the Early Republic, the elite had been similarly divided and had resolved its differences through compromise (see page 145). The Late Republic, however, was an age of individualism, sophistication, and cynicism. Ambitious nobles were no longer willing to subordinate themselves to the community. Thwarted from above, it was not long before competing armies of land-hungry peasants were marching across Italy.

## The Gracchi

Many Romans fretted over the military dimension of the agrarian crisis. In modern societies, draftees are often the poorest people. In Rome, military service was a prestigious activity, so a property qualification was imposed and the poor were not drafted. As fewer and fewer potential soldiers could afford to own property, however, during the second century it became necessary to reduce the property qualification several times. By 150 B.C. a conscript had to own property worth only 400 denarii—roughly a small house, a garden, and some personal belongings. If the peasantry continued its decline, Rome would either have to drop the property qualification for the military altogether or stop fielding armies. Clearly, something had to be done.

Into the breach stepped Tiberius Sempronius Gracchus° (d. 133 B.C.), one of the ten tribunes for the year 133 B.C. (See the box "Reading Sources: Tiberius Gracchus on Rome's Plight.") The son of Cornelia and a distinguished general and ambassador (whose name Tiberius shared), Tiberius belonged to the eminent Gracchi° family. He seemed an excellent spokesperson for a group of prominent senators who backed land reform. He proved, however, to be arrogant and overly ambitious. In pursuit of his goals, he deposed one of his fellow tribunes,

---

**Tiberius Gracchus** (ty-BEER-ee-us GRAK-us)
**Gracchi** (GRAK-eye)

# TIBERIUS GRACCHUS ON ROME'S PLIGHT

*In 133 B.C. Tiberius Gracchus proposed to confiscate from wealthy landowners public land possessed in excess of the legal limit and to redistribute it to poor Roman citizens. The proposal, and Tiberius's unorthodox methods of getting it passed into law, sparked a controversy that led to his murder. Plutarch (ca. A.D. 50–120) discusses Tiberius's motives and paraphrases one of his speeches.*

His brother Gaius recorded in one of his writings that when Tiberius on his way to Numantia [in Spain] passed through Etruria and found the country almost depopulated and its husbandmen and shepherds imported barbarian slaves, he [Tiberius] first conceived the policy which was to be the source of countless ills to himself and to his brother. But it was the people themselves who chiefly excited his zeal and determination with writings on the porticoes, walls, and monuments, calling on him to retrieve the public land for the poor.

. . . Tiberius, fighting for an honorable and just cause with an eloquence that would have dignified even a meaner cause, was formidable and invincible whenever, with the people crowding around . . . , he took his place and spoke in behalf of the poor. "The wild beasts that roam over Italy," he said, "have their dens, each has a place of repose and refuge. But the men who fight and die for Italy enjoy nothing but the air and light; without house or home they wander about with their wives and children. Their commanders lie when they exhort the soldiers in battle to defend sepulchers and shrines from the enemy, for not one of these many Romans has either hereditary altar or ancestral tomb; they fight and die to protect the wealth and luxury of others; they are styled masters of the world, and have not a clod of earth they can call their own."

Source: Plutarch, *Life of Tiberius Gracchus*, in Naphtali Lewis and Meyer Reinhold, eds., *Roman Civilization: Selected Readings*, vol. 1, *The Republic and the Augustan Age*, 3d ed., pp. 251–252. Copyright 1990 by Columbia University Press. Reproduced with permission of Columbia University Press in the format Textbook via Copyright Clearance Center.

Octavius, an opponent of reform, and thereby shocked and angered conservatives.

Tiberius's proposed law restored the roughly 320-acre limit to the amount of public land a person could own (plus an exception for a man with two sons, who was allowed to hold about 667 acres). A commission was to be set up to repossess excess land and redistribute it to the poor, in small lots that were to be inalienable—that is, the wealthy could not buy them back. The former landowners would be reimbursed for improvements they had made, such as buildings or plantings.

The proposal was moderate, but wealthy landowners repudiated it outright. Many senators suspected that Tiberius wanted to set himself up as a kind of superpatron, buoyed by peasant supporters. The senate was in fact more disturbed by Tiberius's methods than by the substance of his proposed law because those methods threatened the senate's power. In addition to deposing Octavius, Tiberius, when the bill became law, intervened in the senate's bailiwicks of foreign affairs and finances by earmarking tax receipts from the new province of Asia to finance land purchases. Finally, Tiberius broke with custom by running for a second consecutive term as tribune. While the tribal assembly prepared to vote on the new tribunes, some senators led a mob to the Forum and had Tiberius and three hundred of his followers clubbed to death.

This shocking event marked the first time in the Republic that a political debate was settled by bloodshed in Rome itself. The ancient sources agree that it was the beginning of a century of revolution. Tiberius's killers had not merely committed murder, but had attacked the traditional inviolability of the tribunes. Yet over the next century public violence grew as a weapon of politics in the Republic. The land commission went ahead with its work, even without Tiberius. His younger brother, Gaius° (d. 121 B.C.), ready to continue Tiberius's work, became tribune himself in 123 B.C. Gaius expanded Tiberius's coalition, adding to it supporters from the equestrian order and the urban populace, mainly composed of slaves and freedmen. He gave the plebs cheap grain at

Gaius (GUY-us)

subsidized prices. The equestrians were wealthy, landed gentry, similar to senators in most respects except for their failure to have reached the senate; they yearned for political power. A small but important group of equestrians was engaged in commerce and tax collection in the provinces. The senate regulated their activities through the so-called extortion courts, which tried corruption cases. Gaius staffed those courts with equestrians. Alluding to the new equestrian power, Gaius remarked, "I have left a sword in the ribs of the senate."

Gaius's ultimate aims are unclear, but one thing is certain: he posed a dangerous threat to the senate's power. He sponsored an extension of his brother's agrarian law, new colonies, public works, and relief for poor soldiers. Eventually Gaius ran aground on a plan to include the Italian allies as beneficiaries of agrarian reform—a farsighted notion but one unpopular with the Roman people, who were jealous of their privileges. Gaius was denied a third term as tribune in 121 B.C. (he had won a second the previous year). Soon his supporters engaged in violent scuffling with their opponents. The senate responded to his action by passing a declaration of public emergency, empowering the magistrates to use any means necessary to protect the state.

One of the consuls had Gaius and 250 of his followers killed. Another 3,000 Gracchans were executed soon thereafter. Within a few years the Gracchan land commission was abolished. It is estimated that approximately 75,000 citizens had been given land. The law, however, was amended to permit the resale of redistributed land, and with the wealthy poised to buy land back, the settlers' future was uncertain. The senatorial oligarchy was back in control.

Or so it seemed. In fact, Roman politics had become an unstable brew. In time, it became clear that the Gracchi had divided the political community into two loose groupings. On one side were the *optimates*° ("the best people"; singular, *optimas*), conservatives who asserted the rule of the senate against popular tribunes and the maintenance of the estates of the wealthy in spite of the agrarian crisis. On the other side were the *populares*° ("men of the people"; singular, *popularis*), who challenged the rule of the senate in the name of relief of the poor. The populares were not democrats. Like the optimates, they were Roman nobles who believed in hierarchy, but they advocated the redistribution of wealth and power as a way of restoring stability and strengthening the military.

## Marius and Sulla

By 100 B.C. Rome's agrarian crisis had become a full-scale military crisis, too. Roman armies under senatorial commanders fared poorly, both in Numidia (modern Algeria) and in southern Gaul against Germanic invaders (see Map 5.3). The situation was saved by an outsider to established privilege, an equestrian named Gaius Marius° (157–86 B.C.), the first member of his family to be elected consul, for 107 B.C. This "new man" proved to be a military reformer and a popularis. Marius made several moves to streamline and strengthen the Roman army: Camp followers were reduced in number, and individual soldiers were made to carry their own equipment. To meet the Germans, who attacked in overwhelming waves, maniples—the tactical subunits of a legion—were reorganized and combined into larger units called cohorts, rendering the army firmer and more cohesive. Most important, Marius abandoned altogether the property qualification for the military. As a result, Roman soldiers were no longer peasants doing part-time military service but rather landless men making a profession of the military.

Politically they became a force to be reckoned with. As an indispensable general, Marius demanded and won six elections to the consulship, unconstitutional though that was. Furthermore, after winning the wars in North Africa and Gaul, Marius championed his soldiers. In 100 B.C. he asked that land be distributed to them. The senate refused, but its victory was temporary. The poor recognized that only military leaders such as Marius desired to meet their need for land. As a result, ordinary Romans, who were all now eligible for the army, transferred their loyalty from the senate to their commander.

The Republic was weak, and it became weaker still as a result of two new wars. First, its Italian allies rose against Rome in a bloody and bitter struggle from 91 to 89 B.C. known as the "Social War"—that is, war with the *socii* ("allies"). The allies fought hard, and Rome, in order to prevail, had to concede to them what they had demanded at the outset: full Roman citizenship. The war wrought devastation in the countryside, further destabilizing the Republic. The other conflict of this period pitted Rome against Mithridates (120–63 B.C.), a rebellious king in northern Anatolia. Mithridates conquered Roman territory in western Anatolia and slaughtered the numerous Italian businessmen and tax collectors there. Once again a military man rose to save the day for Rome: Marius's rival and former lieutenant, Lucius Cornelius

---

**optimates** (op-tee-MAH-tayz)
**populares** (pah-poo-LAH-rayz)

**Marius** (MARRY-us)

Sulla° Felix (ca. 138–78 B.C.), consul for the year 88 B.C., patrician and optimas.

Yet Marius was jealous, and his troops and Sulla's fought over the issue of the command against Mithridates. Sulla's forces won the first round by marching on Rome, but after they departed for the east, Marius's men retook the city and settled scores. Victorious over Mithridates, Sulla returned to Italy in 83 B.C. and engaged in all-out civil war. Sulla defeated Marius's men in battle (minus Marius himself, who had died in 86), then sealed his victory with proscription. He had posted the names of his political opponents, as many as two thousand men. Their land was confiscated, their sons disenfranchised, and they were executed. Sulla settled his veterans, about eighty thousand men, on land in Italy from which he had expelled entire communities that had opposed him.

Having assumed the long-dormant office of dictator—but without a time limit on his tenure—Sulla attempted to restore the senatorial rule of pre-Gracchan days. To this end, he greatly weakened the tribunate and strengthened the senate, whose size he doubled, from about three hundred to about six hundred members.

The most long-lasting of Sulla's measures was his reform of the courts. He abolished trials before popular assemblies and equestrian-staffed courts. Criminal cases were now heard before one of seven standing courts, whose juries were composed of senators. Although later Roman criminal law evolved considerably, it was founded on Sulla's actions. Generally only wealthy people had access to the standing courts; alleged crimes involving ordinary people were heard before lesser magistrates.

Sulla retired in 79 B.C. and died a year later. His hope of restoring law and order under the senate died with him. Within ten years the old powers of the tribunes had been restored. Discontent smoldered among the men whose land Sulla had confiscated. Equally serious, many senators, aspiring to what Sulla had done and not to what he had said, pursued personal power, not the collective interests of the senate.

## Pompey and Caesar

New would-be Mariuses or Sullas now arose. The dominant leader of the seventies and sixties B.C. was the optimas Pompey° the Great (106–48 B.C.), a brilliant general and a supporter of Sulla. Young Pompey went from command to command: he put down an agrarian rebellion in Italy and a rebellion in Spain, cleared the Mediterranean of pirates, defeated Mithridates again, and added rich

**Bust of Julius Caesar**   This marble sculpture accurately conveys the conqueror's firmness of expression and perhaps his intelligence—but not his looks, since Caesar was bald.
*(Vatican Museums/Scala/Art Resource, NY)*

conquests to the empire in Anatolia, Syria, Phoenicia, and Palestine. In the fifties B.C. the tide began turning in favor of Gaius Julius Caesar° (100–44 B.C.), an even more gifted general and politician—indeed, perhaps one of history's greatest. A popularis, Caesar had family connections to Marius and his supporters. Caesar's career depended on his dazzling oratory, his boldness, and his sheer talent at war and politics. Caesar conquered Gaul, gained a foothold in Britain, and laid the foundations of Roman rule in Egypt (see Map 5.3).

While the elite of the Late Republic struggled to maintain order and secure power, ordinary people struggled for survival itself. Violence had become a way of life

---

**Sulla** (SUL-luh)   **Pompey** (POM-pee)

**Caesar** (SEE-zer)

# Spartacus's Slave Revolt

Spartacus's revolt was the third and most famous of three great slave rebellions that rocked Italy and Sicily between 135 and 71 B.C. The revolt itself was not a success; all of the slaves were either imprisoned or killed. But Spartacus terrified the Roman elite and became a powerful symbol of the struggle for freedom to all who were oppressed. This account, by the ancient writer Appian, illustrates his fight.

At about this same time, at the city of Capua in Italy, gladiators were being trained to fight in spectacles. Spartacus, a Thracian whom the Romans had imprisoned and then sold to be trained as a gladiator, had once fought as a soldier for the Roman army. He persuaded about seventy of the enslaved men to risk a break for freedom rather than to allow themselves to be put on display for the entertainment of others. Using force to overcome their guards, the men made their escape. The fugitives armed themselves with wooden clubs and daggers that they seized from travelers on the roads nearby, and then rushed to take refuge on Mount Vesuvius. Many fugitive slaves and even some free men from the surrounding countryside came to this place to join Spartacus. They began to stage bandit raids on nearby settlements. Spartacus had his fellow gladiators Oenomaus and Crixus as his two subordinate commanders. Since Spartacus divided the profits of his raiding into equal shares, he soon attracted a very large number of followers. . . .

[Spartacus wins victories in southern and northern Italy.] With the 120,000 men under his command, he began a march on Rome. So that traveling would be as light as possible, he torched all unnecessary supplies, killed all prisoners of war, and slaughtered all pack animals. Many deserters from the Roman army came to him, but he accepted none of them. The consuls made a stand against him in a place in the land of Picenum. Another great armed struggle took place here and the Romans were defeated again. Spartacus

changed his mind about an attack on Rome. He decided that he was not ready for an all-out battle and that his whole army was not yet properly armed for regular warfare. Moreover, so far no city had come over to his side, but only slaves, deserters, and the flotsam and jetsam of humanity. . . .

[After many successes and some defeats, Spartacus is forced into a final battle with a Roman army led by Crassus.] Since so many tens of thousands of desperate men were involved, the result was a protracted battle of epic proportions. Spartacus took a spear wound in his thigh. Collapsing on one knee, he held his shield up in front of him and fought off those who were attacking him, until he and the large number of men around him were finally surrounded and cut down. The rest of his army was thrown into disarray and confusion and was slaughtered in large numbers. The killing was on such a scale that it was not possible to count the dead. The Romans lost about a thousand men. The body of Spartacus was never found. When the survivors among Spartacus's men, who were still a large number, fled from the battle, they went up into the mountains, where they were pursued by Crassus's forces. Splitting themselves into four groups, they continued to fight until all of them had perished—all, that is, except six thousand of them, who were taken prisoner and crucified along the whole length of the highway that ran from Capua to Rome.

## QUESTIONS

1. Why do you think Spartacus attracted so many followers?

2. Why do you think Spartacus was able to defeat the Romans time and again? Why do you think he finally failed?

3. What evidence does the passage offer to show that Spartacus and his men were brave and determined?

in rural Italy. Many once-prosperous farmers, dispossessed peasants, and runaway slaves ended up as robbers or bandits. It was also an era of slave revolts, the most serious of which lasted from 73 to 71 B.C. under the leadership of Spartacus, a Thracian slave who had been a gladiator. An able commander, Spartacus beat nine separate Roman armies in two years before finally suffering

defeat. (See the box "The Continuing Experiment: Spartacus's Slave Revolt.") At the same time, Rome also faced major wars in Spain and Anatolia.

Roman women were sometimes pawns, sometimes partners in the political careers of Pompey and Caesar. In 80 B.C., for example, Pompey divorced his first wife to advance his career by marrying Aemilia, Sulla's step-daughter. Aemilia was not only married at the time but pregnant by her first husband. Soon after her divorce and remarriage, she died in childbirth. Caesar took many mistresses, among whom was the queen of Egypt, Cleopatra (see pages 134–135). Caesar had a penchant for certain Egyptian institutions, such as the Egyptian calendar, and he toyed with becoming a monarch himself, an inclination that Cleopatra perhaps encouraged. Another of Caesar's mistresses was Servilia, stepsister of Marcus Porcius Cato (Cato the Younger, 95–46 B.C.), great-grandson of the famous censor (see page 158). She was also the mother of Brutus, the man who would eventually help murder Caesar.

Pompey was an optimas, Caesar a popularis, but the two of them agreed that they, not the senate or the assemblies, should dominate Rome. Each man's ambition was more important to him than any political principles. In 60 B.C. they entered into a pact with a third ambitious noble, Marcus Licinius Crassus (d. 53 B.C.). Known today as the "First Triumvirate," this coalition amounted to a conspiracy to run the state. Their individual ambitions rebuffed by the senate, each man had an agenda that could be achieved by pooling resources in the triumvirate: for Pompey, ratification of his acts in the east and land for his veterans; for Caesar, who became consul for 59 B.C., a long period of command in Gaul and a free hand in his behavior there; for Crassus, a rebate for the tax collectors of Roman Asia, whom he championed, and eventually a command in Syria to make war on Parthia (the new Persian Empire).

Having achieved its goal, the triumvirate did not long survive, but its very existence shows how little the Republic now meant. Crassus died in an inglorious defeat at Carrhae in Syria in 53 B.C., tarnished further by the Parthians' successful capture of Roman legionary standards (see Map 5.3). Frightened by Caesar's stunning victories in Gaul, Pompey returned to the senatorial fold, now led by Cato the Younger. Cato and his supporters stood for the traditional rule of the senatorial oligarchy. In 49 B.C. they ordered Caesar to give up his command in Gaul, but instead Caesar marched on Italy with his army. Italy's northern boundary was marked by a tiny stream called the Rubicon; when Caesar defiantly crossed it, he declared, "The die is cast." Indeed it was, for civil war. Caesar swept to victory against the senate's army, led by Pompey, at Pharsalus in Greece in 48 B.C. Pompey fled but was assassinated. The complete destruction of the senate's forces took until 45 B.C.

The years of civil war took Caesar from Spain to Anatolia. During the fighting he showed the qualities that made him great: he was fast, tough, smart, adaptable, and

a risk-taker. He was a diplomat, too, offering mercy to any of his enemies who joined him. A talented writer, Caesar published two books about his military campaigns—*On the Gallic War* and *On the Civil War*—the latter appearing after his death. These works glorified Caesar's conquests and defended his decision to wage civil war. (See the box "Global Encounters: Caesar on the Gauls.")

Back in Rome, Caesar sponsored a huge number of reforms. His political goal was to elevate Italians and others at the expense of old Roman families. To achieve this, Caesar conferred Roman citizenship liberally, on all of Cisalpine Gaul (northernmost Italy) as well as on certain provincial towns. He enlarged the senate from six hundred to nine hundred, adding his supporters, including some Gauls, to the membership. Caesar sponsored social and economic reforms, too, including reducing debt and founding the first colonies outside Italy, where veterans and poor citizens were settled. He undertook a grand public building program in the city of Rome. Caesar's most long-lasting act was to introduce the calendar of 365¼ days, on January 1, 45 B.C. Derived from the calendar of Egypt, it is known as the Julian calendar.

Caesar did not hide his contempt for Republican constitutional formalities. By accepting a dictatorship for life he offended the old guard; by flirting with the title of king he infuriated them. With one eye toward avenging Crassus and another toward equaling the achievements of Alexander the Great, Caesar made preparations for a war against Parthia, but in vain. His career ended abruptly on March 15, 44 B.C. (the Ides of March by the Roman calendar), when sixty senators stabbed him to death. The assassination took place in the portico attached to the Theater of Pompey, in front of a statue of Pompey himself, where the senate was meeting that day. It had been eighty-nine years since the murder of Tiberius Gracchus.

The assassins called themselves Liberators, believing that they were freeing themselves from tyranny just as the founders of the Republic had done centuries before. Indeed, one of the chief conspirators, Marcus Junius Brutus (ca. 85–42 B.C.), claimed descent from Lucius Junius Brutus, traditional leader of the revolt against the Tarquins that was thought to have established the Republic. Like his co-conspirator Gaius Longinus Cassius (d. 42 B.C.), Brutus had been a magistrate, military officer, and provincial administrator.

The assassination of Caesar threw Rome back into turmoil. Civil war followed for the next thirteen years, first between the Liberators and Caesar's partisans and then between the two leading Caesarians. The final struggle pitted Mark Antony (Marcus Antonius, ca. 83–30 B.C.),

# Caesar on the Gauls

Julius Caesar (ca. 100–44 B.C.) advertised his achievements in conquering Gaul (58–51 B.C.) in his *Commentaries on the Gallic War*. The book focuses on battles and negotiations, but here Caesar discusses the society of the Gauls (also known as Celts). He depicts the inhabitants as superstitious and warlike.

In the whole of Gaul two types of men are counted as being of worth and distinction. The ordinary people are considered almost as slaves: they dare do nothing on their own account and are not called to counsels. When the majority are oppressed by debt or heavy tribute, or harmed by powerful men, they swear themselves away into slavery to the aristocracy, who then have the same rights over them as masters do over their slaves. Of the two types of men of distinction, however, the first is made up of the druids (priests), and the other of the knights.

The druids are involved in matters of religion. They manage public and private sacrifices and interpret religious customs and ceremonies. Young men flock to them in large numbers to gain instruction, and they hold the druids in great esteem. For they decide almost all disputes, both public and private: if some crime has been committed, if there has been murder done, if there is a dispute over an inheritance or over territory, they decide the issue and settle the rewards and penalties. If any individual or group of people does not abide by their decision, the druids ban them from sacrifices. This is their most severe punishment. Those who are banned in this way are counted among the wicked and criminal: everyone shuns them and avoids approaching or talking to them, so as not to suffer any harm from contact with them. . . .

Druids are not accustomed to take part in war, nor do they pay taxes like the rest of the people. . . . The principal doctrine they attempt to impart is that souls do not die but after death cross from one person to another. Because the fear of death is thereby set aside, they consider this a strong inducement to physical courage. Besides this, they debate many subjects and teach them to their young men—for example, the stars and their movements, the size of the universe and the earth, the nature of things, and the strength and power of the immortal gods.

The second class is that composed of the knights. When necessity arises and some war flares up—which before Caesar's arrival used to happen almost every year, so that they were either on the offensive themselves or fending off attacks—they are all involved in the campaign. Each man has as many retainers and dependents about him as is appropriate to his status in terms of his birth and resources. This is the sole form of power and influence they know.

The whole of the Gallic nation is much given to religious practices. For this reason those who are afflicted with serious illnesses and those who are involved in battles and danger either offer human sacrifice or vow that they will do so, and employ the druids to manage these sacrifices. For they believe that unless one human life is offered for another, the power and presence of the immortal gods cannot be propitiated.

## QUESTIONS

1. According to Caesar, who were the druids, and what did they do? How did they help the Gauls succeed as warriors? How did the druids differ from the knights?

2. What was the status of ordinary people in Gaul?

3. What do you think Caesar and his readers thought of the Gauls' practice of human sacrifice?

SOURCE: Julius Caesar, *Seven Commentaries on the Gallic War with an Eighth Commentary by Aulus Hirtius,* trans. Carolyn Hammond, pp. 126–128. Copyright © 1996 Oxford University Press. Reprinted by permission of Oxford University Press.

www. For additional information on this topic, go to college.hmco.com/students.

Caesar's chief lieutenant and the man who inherited his love affair with Cleopatra, against Octavian (Gaius Julius Caesar Octavianus, 63 B.C.–A.D. 14), Caesar's grandnephew and adopted son and heir to Caesar's name and his huge fortune. At first it looked as if Antony had the upper hand because Octavian was young and inexperienced, was not a general, and was cursed with poor health. Octavian was, however, a man of unusual cunning and prudence. His forces defeated Antony and Cleopatra at the naval battle of Actium (off northwestern Greece) in 31 B.C.; their suicides followed shortly. The Roman world held its breath to see how Octavian would govern it.

## The World of Cicero

Marcus Tullius Cicero° (106–43 B.C.) is one of the best-known figures of all antiquity. Like Marius, he was a wealthy equestrian from the central Italian town of Arpinum who, as consul (in 63 B.C.), became a "new man." Cicero was an optimas and defender of the senate, though ready for compromise with the equestrians, from whose ranks he himself had arisen. He made his name by successfully leading the opposition to Lucius Sergius Catilina, a down-and-out patrician who organized a debtors' revolt in Etruria; the army smashed the rebellion.

Cicero was intelligent, ambitious, and talented. As a young man he studied philosophy and oratory in Greece. As a result, he produced elevated and serious writings. Never as original as Plato or Aristotle, Cicero nonetheless was crucial in making the Latin language a vessel for the heritage of Greek thought. A prolific writer, Cicero produced over a hundred orations, of which about sixty survive; several treatises on oratory; philosophical writings on politics, ethics, epistemology (the study of the nature of knowledge), and theology; poetry, of which little survives; and numerous letters. After his death in 43 B.C., his immense correspondence was published, with little censored. The letters and speeches provide a vivid, detailed, and sometimes damning picture of politics.

Politics in the Late Republic was loud and boisterous. The elite prided itself on free speech and open debate. In senate deliberations, court cases, and public meetings in the Forum that preceded assembly votes, oratory—sometimes great oratory—was common. Few orators in history, though, have matched Cicero's ability to lead and mislead an audience by playing on its feelings. He knew every rhetorical trick and precisely when each was appropriate.

Because of increased freedom and greater educational opportunities, during the Late Republic it was possible for elite women as well as men to study oratory. Private tutors were common among the aristocracy, and girls often received lessons alongside their brothers. Girls sometimes also profited from a father's expertise. A particularly dramatic case is that of Hortensia, daughter of Quintus Hortensius Hortalus (114–50 B.C.), a famous orator and rival of Cicero. An excellent speaker herself, Hortensia defied tradition by arguing successfully in the

Roman Forum in 42 B.C. against a proposed war tax on wealthy women.

Cicero pilloried one elite woman who enjoyed considerable freedom: Clodia (b. ca. 95 B.C.). Sister of the notorious populist gang leader Clodius and wife of optimas politician Metellus Celer (d. 59 B.C.), Clodia moved in Rome's highest circles. Cicero accused her of poisoning her husband (the charge was unprovable). She is better remembered from the poems of Catullus (ca. 85–54 B.C.), where she is called Lesbia. In passionate and psychologically complex verse, Catullus describes the ups and downs of their affair, which Clodia eventually ended.

Ordinary people lacked the education and freedom to express themselves in the manner of a Catullus or Hortensia, but a less civilized means of expression was open to them: the political gang. Brawls and violence between the rival groups of Clodius, a supporter of Caesar, and Milo, a supporter of the senate, became increasingly common in the fifties B.C. As dictator, Caesar abolished the gangs.

Cicero's works provide evidence of a crucial development in the practice of Roman law. Often unheralded, what Cicero's contemporaries did was invent the notion of the legal expert, a person devoted to explaining and interpreting the law. Roman law needed interpretation because it was complex and intricate. Much of it was the work not of legislators but of magistrates, who issued annual statements setting forth how their courts would work. The result was unsystematic and sometimes contradictory and cried out for someone to make sense of it. Enter the jurisconsults, legal interpreters who emerged in the third and second centuries B.C. At first they had no special standing, but in the first century B.C. they became true jurists; their interpretations began to be considered authoritative. No earlier Mediterranean society had a professional class of legal experts, but no earlier society had faced issues as complicated and turbulent, or had grown to three million citizens, as the Roman Republic did in the mid-first century B.C. The Western tradition of legal science has its roots in Rome.

Rome's political system, unlike its legal system, did not adapt flexibly to changing circumstances. The disenfranchised of the Late Republic had reasonable goals: land for those who had fought for their country and admission to the senate of a wider group. Yet the old elite resisted both. Cicero's solution was to build on Sulla's reforms by uniting the senatorial and equestrian orders and by widening the Roman ruling class to include the elite of all Italy. The expanded ruling class could close ranks and establish *otium cum dignitate*, "peace with

**Cicero** (SIS-er-o)

respect for rank." Cicero's proposed new order was distinctly hierarchical.

In the turbulent times of the Late Republic, the Roman elite often turned to the Hellenistic philosophers. The poet Lucretius° (ca. 94–55 B.C.) describes the Epicurean ideal of withdrawal into the contemplative life in a long didactic epic called *On the Nature of Things*. Most elite Romans, however, including Cicero, preferred the activist philosophy of Stoicism (see page 128). Cicero put forth a generous view of human brotherhood. He argued that all people share a spark of divinity and are protected by natural law. Consequently, all persons have value and importance and should treat others generously. Such ideas would be influential in the new Roman Empire when, under the leadership of Augustus, fair treatment of provincials was a major theme. For Cicero, however, these ideas existed more as theory than as practice.

Cicero did not hide his lack of sympathy for his fellow citizens who were poor. In one speech he castigated "artisans and shopkeepers and all that kind of scum"; in a letter he complained about "the wretched half-starved populace, which attends mass meetings and sucks the blood of the treasury." Cicero also made his disdain for democracy clear: "The greatest number," he said, "should not have the greatest power."

Elitist as Cicero's views were, they were by no means extremist. Cassius, Brutus, and the other Liberators had little interest in even Cicero's limited compromises. Their stubbornness proved to be their downfall, for dispossessed peasants and ambitious equestrians transferred their loyalties to Julius Caesar and, later, to Augustus. One of Caesar's supporters, Sallust (86–ca. 34 B.C.), wrote biting and bitter works of history that indicted the greed and corruption of the optimates, whom he blamed for the decline of the Republic. In any case, peace was not restored, for the generation of Liberators was wiped out in renewed civil war, and a new generation emerged, weary for peace.

## SUMMARY

ROME was destined to provide Western civilization with many basic notions about government and empire, but Rome sprang from humble origins. A central Italian village at first, Rome was urbanized after contact with more sophisticated neighbors.

Lucretius (loo-CREE-shus)

Rome became a monarchy and then a republic. It practiced imperialism with almost unlimited success, but ultimately the weight of empire brought down first the social system and then the political regime.

The Republic was a mixed constitution. It combined popular power with control by an oligarchy. In its first centuries, the oligarchy displayed flexibility and wisdom. It proved able to accommodate not only the competitive instincts of the aristocracy and the recently rich but also the land-hunger of the common people. The old aristocracy of the patricians opened its ranks to the newly ambitious leaders of the plebeians and also made room in the government for popular representation. The ingrained hierarchy of the Roman social and cultural system helped keep politics stable.

The elite channeled popular energies into protecting the young Republic from its numerous rivals in central Italy. Rome consolidated its control of that region by wisely treating its allies with a mixture of firmness and generosity. By extending Roman citizenship, Rome gave them a stake in continued Roman hegemony. Having disposed of its nearest enemies, Rome mounted a quest for absolute security, a quest that led to conquest in Italy and the rest of the Mediterranean. Greed and ambition, as well as fear, were powerful motives of expansion.

Having defeated all opponents near and far, Rome seemed to have won absolute security by the mid-second century B.C. Yet its strength was deceptive. Contact with Greek culture liberated the Romans from ruder, peasant ways but also loosened previous restraints. A huge influx of slaves made acquisition of large estates profitable. The Italian peasantry was already weakened by conscription and the devastation of farmland, and the elite was arrogant from its military success. Thus it became easy for the strong to confiscate the land of the weak. The result was a growing and dangerous social instability with military and political ramifications. At the very moment of triumph, the Republic was in grave danger.

Members of the Roman elite, rather than displaying that talent for compromise that had made the Republic great, refused to share their wealth with the poor. The poor, however, got their revenge by throwing their support to new patrons, military leaders who raised private armies to win land for their followers and glory for themselves. By the first century B.C., the Republic had collapsed under the weight of political maneuvering, judicial murders, gang warfare, and civil war. The time was right for the last of the private commanders—Octavian—to recreate the Roman state under his leadership as Augustus, first of the emperors. In the next chapter we examine the world that he remade.

## Notes

1. *The Aeneid of Virgil,* trans. Allen Mandelbaum (Berkeley: University of California Press, 1971), pp. 160–161.
2. P. A. Brunt, *Social Conflicts in the Roman Republic* (New York: Norton, 1971), p. 17.

## Suggested Reading

Barker, H., and T. Rasmussen. *The Etruscans.* 1997. Excellent historical introduction and guidebook, written with gusto.

Beard, Mary, and Michael Crawford. *Rome in the Late Republic: Problems and Interpretations.* 2d ed. 1999. An unusual and innovative approach to the subject, emphasizing sociocultural and institutional analysis more than narrative.

Brunt, P. A. *Social Conflicts in the Roman Republic.* 1971. A fine, non-Marxist view of the importance of class conflict throughout Republican history.

Cornell, T. J. *The Beginnings of Rome: Italy and Rome from the Bronze Age to the Punic Wars (c. 1000–264 B.C.).* 1995. A readable and ambitious survey combining archaeological and literary evidence, often in support of iconoclastic conclusions.

Cornell, T. J., and J. Matthews. *Atlas of the Roman World.* 1982. A readable introduction to Roman history written by two scholars; the maps and photos are beautiful.

Crawford, Michael. *The Roman Republic.* 2d ed. 1993. The best short introduction; sophisticated, lively, and concise.

Dixon, Suzanne. *The Roman Family.* 1992. A good historical study in complexity; strongly aware of the difference between the myth and reality of the Roman family and nicely written.

Goldsworthy, Adrian. *Roman Warfare.* 2000. A concise and expert introduction.

Talbert, Richard A. *Barrington Atlas of the Greek and Roman World.* 2000. The most thorough, detailed, and scholarly atlas of this subject ever attempted.

Ward, A. M., F. M. Heichelheim, and C. A. Yeo. *A History of the Roman People.* 3d ed. 1998. The best introductory textbook; scholarly and readable.

**www.** For a searchable list of additional readings for this chapter, go to college.hmco.com/students.

# From Poseidonia to Paestum

Between them, the elegant Greek painting and the rough Roman bronze statue shown here sum up the history of the ancient city of Paestum. Paestum is located in southern Italy about 200 miles south of Rome. It was a port and commercial center in a rich agricultural region on the Gulf of Salerno. Founded as the Greek colony of Poseidonia around 600 B.C., Paestum ended up as a thriving Roman city after being conquered by the Romans in 273 B.C. In between (410–273 B.C.), Paestum was overrun and ruled by the Oscan-speaking Lucanian warriors of southern Italy. Somehow, no matter who ruled it or what it was called, Paestum managed to flourish. Its remains present a picture of the wealth, high civilization, and ethnic diversity of first-millennium B.C. Italy.

Look first at the painting from Greek-era Poseidonia of the man reclining on a couch. He wears a wreath and is holding a lyre in his right hand. He is one of ten men,

in a series of paintings, shown participating in a *sumposion,* or "wine party," a typical gathering of aristocratic Greek culture. (Ironically, we get our word *symposium,* or "academic meeting," from this ancient, alcoholic merrymaking.) His manicured beard and trim physique identify him as a member of the leisure class.

A superb example of ancient painting, it was discovered on the outskirts of Paestum in 1968 and dates to 480/470 B.C. It is part of one of five tomb paintings from the Tomb of the Diver, named after the painting, on the lid of the tomb, of a young man in the act of diving, perhaps a symbol of the journey into the underworld.

The artistic style, the clothing, and the sumposion are all Greek. Yet the practice of painting a tomb and the use of diving as a symbol of death are Etruscan in origin. Thus the paintings demonstrate the cultural mix of Greek Italy.

**A Guest Holding a Lyre (painting from Tomb of the Diver, Paestum)** *(Scala/Art Resource, NY)*

This sums up the experience of Poseidonia well, because the city grew rich as a commercial center between the Etruscans and the Greeks farther south. Poseidonia's Greekness is underlined by its excellent Doric temples; the ruins of these are among the best such ruins in the world today. Also of note is the Greek-style rectangular public space, with its central agora, three broad avenues, and thirty-two cross streets, as well as the strong walls.

Under the Lucanian conquerors, Poseidonia continued the traditions of tomb painting and cultural interchange. Many Lucanian tomb paintings from the town survive, and they illustrate a lively mix of Greek and Italic styles.

After Poseidonia was conquered by Rome in 273 B.C., it became known as Paestum and acquired the status of a Latin colony. As soldiers and sailors, the citizens of Paestum defended Roman interests in southern Italy. In return, and because they were Latin colonists, they enjoyed the privileges of free trade with Rome and intermarriage with Romans, as well as the more theoretical possibility of becoming Roman citizens by moving to Rome (but only after leaving a son in the colony). The citizens consisted of around five thousand Roman and Latin settlers as well as the local elite. Many non-elite inhabitants of Paestum no doubt lost land to the settlers.

Meanwhile, both the landscape and the politics of the city were transformed. The agora of Poseidonia became the forum of Paestum, on whose sides were built Roman-style buildings, including a council hall and a temple of Jupiter (like the temple on Rome's Capitoline Hill). Eventually Paestum would acquire an amphitheater and Roman baths.

Paestum also acquired a copy of a famous Roman work of art, the bronze statue of Marsyas, which is reproduced here. This statue dates to the mid-third century B.C. It was cast in imitation of a famous statue of Marsyas in Rome and erected at the center of Paestum on the west side of the forum.

For the Romans, Marsyas symbolized liberty. He was a character from Greek mythology and had been adopted by the prominent plebeian lineage of Marcius Rutilus to symbolize the victory of the plebeians in their struggle with the patricians.

The statue's right hand would have been raised in a gesture of authority. His calves are ringed by metal bands, like the legs of a slave, except that the chains of slavery have been broken off. For the citizens of Paestum, the statue celebrated their identification with Rome, their liberation from Lucanian rule, their privileged status as Latin colonists, and perhaps their freedom from economic need as landholders in a fertile territory.

**Marsyas (bronze statue, Paestum)**  *(Scala/Art Resource, NY)*

The statue of Marsyas is considered today to be one of the most important works of the new culture of an Italy dominated by Rome. But it is many other things as well: It symbolizes the combined plebeian-patrician elite of Rome and its success in extending Roman power throughout the peninsula. It demonstrates the continued importance of Greek culture, since Marsyas was a Greek character, but it also shows the flexibility with which the Roman elite adapted Greek symbols for its own purposes. And it reminds us of the willingness of the Romans to trample on local customs and impose Roman culture throughout Italy.

171

# CHAPTER 6

# Imperial Rome

## 31 B.C.–A.D. 284

THE imperial family of Rome walks in stately procession to a sacrifice: Livia, wife of Augustus, first of the emperors; his daughter, Julia; Julia's husband, Agrippa; and various cousins and in-laws and their children. They are formally dressed in togas and gowns, heads wreathed. The men and women gaze seriously; the boys and girls have impish looks, betraying thoughts of mischief as they hold their parents' hands. They are all carved in stone, one of several sculptured reliefs decorating the walls of a public monument in Rome. Dedicated on Livia's birthday in 9 B.C., the monument shown here illustrates the propaganda themes of the new regime, among them the happy family as symbol of peace after generations of civil war. The senate, which had commissioned the monument, called it the *Ara Pacis Augustae,* or "Altar of Augustan Peace."

Having made peace was no idle boast on Augustus's part. Not only did he end the Roman revolution, but he began a period of two hundred years of prosperity and stability in the Roman Empire. Augustus took advantage of Rome's war-weariness to create a new government out of the ruins of the Republic. Like the builders of the Early Republic's constitution, Augustus displayed the Roman genius for compromise. He had superb political instincts. Although he retained the final say, he shared a degree of power with the senate. He made financial sacrifices to feed the urban poor and distribute farms to landless peasants. He ended Rome's seemingly limitless expansion and stabilized the borders of the empire. He began to raise the provinces to a status of equality with Italy.

Ara Pacis (detail), Rome.
(Scala/Art Resource, NY)

**Augustus and the Principate, 31 B.C.–A.D. 68**

**The Roman Peace and Its Collapse, A.D. 69–284**

**Early Christianity**

The *pax Romana*° ("Roman peace"), at its height between A.D. 96 and 180, was an era of enlightened emperors, thriving cities, intellectual vitality, and artistic and architectural achievement in an empire of 50 million to 100 million people. Yet it was also an era of slavery. More positively, the Roman peace was a period of heightened spirituality. In the peaceful and diverse empire, ideas traveled from people to people, and the religious beliefs of an obscure sect from western Asia began to spread around the Mediterranean and into northern Europe. The new religion was Christianity.

After 180 Rome slowly passed into a grim period marked in turn by bad emperors, civil war, inflation, plague, invasion, and defeat. After reaching a nadir around 235 to 253, Rome's fortunes began to improve under a series of reforming emperors who would forge a stronger and vastly different empire.

## QUESTIONS TO CONSIDER

- How did Augustus lay the foundations of the new imperial government that would replace the Roman Republic? Why was he so successful?

- What was life like in the era of the Roman peace?

- How was the Roman Empire shaken by the crisis of the third century A.D., and how did it survive?

- What were the origins of Christianity in Palestine, and how did the new religion spread around the Roman world?

## TERMS TO KNOW

| | |
|---|---|
| Augustus | Tacitus |
| Principate | third-century crisis |
| Virgil | Jesus of Nazareth |
| Livia | Paul of Tarsus |
| Julio-Claudians | Christianity |
| pax Romana | rabbinic Judaism |
| Flavians | |

## AUGUSTUS AND THE PRINCIPATE, 31 B.C.–A.D. 68

N 31 B.C. Gaius Julius Caesar Octavianus (63 B.C.–A.D. 14), or Octavian, as Augustus was then known, stood at the top of the Roman world. His forces had defeated those of Mark Antony and Cleopatra at the Battle of Actium in northwestern Greece, whereupon his two chief enemies committed suicide. Few could have predicted the vision and statesmanship that Octavian now displayed. He spent the next forty-five years healing the wounds of a century of revolution. He did nothing less than lay the foundations of the prosperous two centuries enjoyed by the empire under the Roman peace (see Map 6.1).

### The Political Settlement

Octavian was both an astute politician and a lucky one. He was lucky in the length and violence of the civil wars. After Actium, most of his enemies were dead, so estab-

lishing the one-man rule that he claimed was necessary to restore stability was relatively easy. He was also lucky to live to be nearly 80—he had plenty of time to consolidate his rule. He was a cagey man and a sharp judge of others. Octavian learned the lesson of Caesar's greatest mistake. He understood that the Roman elite, however weakened, was still strong enough to oppose a ruler who flaunted monarchical power. To avoid a second Ides of March, therefore, Octavian was infinitely diplomatic.

Rather than call himself dictator, Octavian took the title of *princeps*° ("first citizen"), an old title of respect in the senate. From *princeps* comes *Principate*°, a term often used to describe the constitutional monarchy of the "Early Empire," the name that historians have given to the period from 31 B.C. to A.D. 192. Four years after Actium, in 27 B.C., the senate granted Octavian the honorific title *augustus,* symbolizing the augmentation, or increase, of his authority. He was also known as *Caesar* and *divi filius* ("son of a god"), which tied him to Julius Caesar. Another name, *imperator* ("commander" and, later, "emperor"), recalled the military might that Augustus (as we shall henceforth call him) could call on if needed.

---

pax Romana (PAHKS ro-MAHN-uh)

princeps (PRIN-keps)   Principate (PRIN-sih-pate)

In 27 B.C. Augustus proclaimed "the transfer of the state to the free disposal of the senate and the people"—that is, the restoration of the Republic. Remembering similar claims by Sulla and Julius Caesar, few Romans were likely to believe this, and few would have wanted the Republic restored in any case. They no doubt appreciated their ruler's tact, however. (See the box "Reading Sources: Augustus: The Official Story.")

Two strokes of genius marked the new regime. First, Augustus held power without monopolizing public offices. He held the civil authority of the tribunate without being a tribune and the military authority of provincial generals without holding a specific command. Generalships remained open to ambitious Romans as long as they accepted Augustus's power. Second, the new government divided the provinces between Augustus and the senate. To check any new would-be Caesar, Augustus kept for himself the frontier provinces, with the main concentration of armies, as well as grain-rich Egypt (which had been annexed as a Roman province after Actium). The local commanders were loyal equestrians who owed their success to Augustus. Most of the other provinces continued to be ruled as before by senators serving as governors.

Augustus wanted advice without dissent. He used the senate, or rather a committee of senators and magistrates, as a sounding board; the group evolved into a permanent advisory body. Ordinary senate meetings, however, what with informers and secret agents, lost their old freedom of speech. The popular assemblies fared even worse, as their powers were limited and eventually transferred to the senate. Nor would unruly crowds be tolerated. Augustus established the city of Rome's first police force and also stationed there his own personal guard. Called the praetorians°, or Praetorian Guard, the name used for a Roman general's bodyguard, the guard would play a crucial role in future imperial politics.

More important for the public good, Augustus established the first civil service, consisting of a series of prefectures—or departments—supervising, for example, the city watch, the grain supply, the water supply, the building of roads and bridges, tax collection, and the provisioning of the armies. Equestrians and freedmen were prominent in these prefectures and in provincial government, so they enthusiastically supported the Principate.

Although one may speak loosely of "imperial bureaucracy," neither Augustus nor his successors ever established a tight administrative grip on their far-flung empire. As in all ancient empires, Roman government

## CHRONOLOGY

| | |
|---|---|
| 31 B.C. | Octavian defeats Antony and Cleopatra at Actium |
| 27 B.C. | Augustus establishes Principate |
| 27 B.C.–A.D. 68 | Julio-Claudian dynasty |
| 19 B.C. | Death of Virgil |
| ca. A.D. 27–30 | Ministry of Jesus |
| ca. 67 | Death of Paul of Tarsus |
| 69–96 | Flavian dynasty |
| 70 | Temple in Jerusalem destroyed |
| 79 | Eruption of Vesuvius |
| 96–180 | The "Five Good Emperors" |
| ca. 117 | Death of Tacitus |
| 193–235 | Severan dynasty |
| ca. 200 | Mishnah and New Testament each completed |
| 212 | Almost all free inhabitants of empire awarded Roman citizenship |
| 235–284 | Period of military anarchy |

tended to be decentralized and limited. In an age in which few public officials received a salary, bribes were winked at.

## The Economic and Social Settlement

The old Roman ruling class made its peace with Augustus, but some never forgave him for ending their ancient privileges. The conservative historian Tacitus° (ca. A.D. 55–117) looked back wistfully to the Late Republic as a golden era of freedom, eloquence, and "the old sound morality." (See the box "Reading Sources: Augustus: A Skeptical View.") Even Tacitus, however, was forced to admit that most people in the Roman world welcomed and admired the Principate. The reason is simple: Augustus and his successors brought peace and prosperity after a century of disasters under the Late Republic.

---

**praetorians** (pre-TOR-ee-unz)

**Tacitus** (TASS-ih-tus)

**Legend:**

Roman Empire by death of Augustus, A.D. 14

Roman territory added by death of Hadrian, A.D. 138

Parthian territory conquered by Trajan, then lost, A.D. 114–117

Parthian Empire

X  Major battles

**Map 6.1  The Roman World in the Early Empire**  Many modern cities are built on the sites of Roman foundations, evidence of the immense extent of the Roman Empire at its height.

# AUGUSTUS: THE OFFICIAL STORY

*Not long before his death in A.D. 14, the emperor Augustus arranged for the display in Rome of two bronze tablets containing a record of his achievements. Copies of "the achievements of the Divine Augustus, by which he brought the world under the empire of the Roman people, and of the expenses which he bore for the state and people of Rome" were displayed around the empire. A complete copy survived in the Roman city of Ancyra in Anatolia (modern Ankara, Turkey).*

1. At the age of nineteen on my own responsibility and at my own expense I raised an army, with which I successfully championed the liberty of the republic when it was oppressed by the tyranny of a faction. . . .

3. I undertook many civil and foreign wars by land and sea throughout the world, and as victor I spared the lives of all citizens who asked for mercy. 2. [*sic*] When foreign peoples could safely be pardoned I preferred to preserve rather than eliminate them. 3. The Roman citizens who took the soldier's oath of obedience to me numbered about 500,000. I settled rather more than 300,000 of these in colonies or sent them back to their home towns after a period of service; to all these I assigned lands or gave money as rewards for their military service. . . .

20. I restored the Capitol and the theatre of Pompey, both works at great expense without inscribing my name on either. 2. I restored the channels of the aqueducts, which in several places were falling into disrepair through age, and I brought water from a new spring into the aqueduct called Marcia, doubling the supply. . . . 4. In my sixth consulship I restored eighty-two temples of the gods in the city on the authority of the senate, neglecting none that required restoration at the time. . . .

26. I extended the territory of all those provinces of the Roman people on whose borders lay peoples not subject to our government. . . .

27. I added Egypt to the empire of the Roman people. . . .

28. . . . I compelled the Parthians to restore to me the spoils and standards of three Roman armies and to ask as suppliants for the friendship of the Roman people. Those standards I deposited in the innermost shrine of the temple of Mars the Avenger. . . .

35. In my thirteenth consulship the senate, the equestrian order and the whole people of Rome gave me the title of Father of my Country, and resolved that this should be inscribed in the porch of my house and in the Curia Julia and in the Forum Augustum below the chariot which had been set there in my honor by decree of the senate. 2. At the time of writing I am in my seventy-sixth year.

Source: P. A. Brunt and J. M. Moore, eds., *Res Gestae Divi Augusti: The Achievements of the Divine Augustus* (Oxford: Oxford University Press, 1967), pp. 19–37. Reprinted by permission of Oxford University Press.

---

The Augustan period enjoyed affluence, especially in Italy; the other provinces caught up with Italy by the second century A.D. Agriculture flourished with the end of civil war. Italian industries became leaders in exports. Italian glass bowls and windowpanes, iron arms and tools, fancy silver eating utensils and candlesticks, and bronze statues and pots circulated from Britain to central Asia.

The perennial problem of the Late Republic had been land-hunger, which drove peasants into the arms of ambitious generals. Augustus kept his troops happy by compensating 300,000 loyal veterans with land, money, or both, often in new overseas colonies. At first he paid out these rewards from his own private sources; after A.D. 6, he made the rich pay via new taxes. The result kept the peace, but many nonsoldiers in Italy remained poor, as of course did the huge number of slaves.

As for the renegade commanders who had bedeviled the Late Republic, Augustus cut their potential power base by reducing the size of the army, gradually cutting the number of legions from over sixty to twenty-eight. The total size of the army, including light infantry and cavalry, was about 300,000. This reduction lightened Rome's tax burden but left Augustus with little room to expand the empire. In A.D. 9 Rome lost three legions to a native revolt against Rome's plan to extend its rule in Germany as far east as the Elbe River. Short of manpower, Augustus had to accept the Rhine River as Rome's new German frontier (see Map 6.1).

## READING SOURCES

## AUGUSTUS: A SKEPTICAL VIEW

*Tacitus, a member of the senatorial elite of the Early Empire, looked back longingly to the freedom of the Roman Republic. His* Annals *offer a scathing view of the early emperors, beginning with Augustus, whose reign he discusses briefly.*

Famous writers have recorded Rome's early glories and disasters. The Augustan Age, too, had its distinguished historians. But then the rising tide of flattery exercised a deterrent effect. The reigns of Tiberius, Gaius, Claudius, and Nero were described during their lifetimes in fictitious terms, for fear of the consequences; whereas the accounts written after their deaths were influenced by still raging animosities. So I have decided to say a little about Augustus, with special attention to his last period, and then go on to the reign of Tiberius and what followed. I shall write without indignation or partisanship: in my case the customary incentives to these are lacking.

The violent deaths of Brutus and Cassius left no Republican forces in the field. Defeat came to Sextus Pompeius in Sicily, Lepidus was dropped, Antony killed. So even the Caesarian party had no leader left except the "Caesar" himself, Octavian. He gave up the title of Triumvir emphasizing instead his position as consul; and the powers of a tribune, he proclaimed, were good enough for him—powers for the protection of ordinary people.

He seduced the army with bonuses, and his cheap food policy was successful bait for civilians. Indeed, he attracted everybody's goodwill by the enjoyable gift of peace. Then he gradually pushed ahead and absorbed the functions of the senate, the officials, and even the law. Opposition did not exist. War or judicial murder had disposed of all men of spirit. Upperclass survivors found that slavish obedience was the way to succeed, both politically and financially. They had profited from revolution, and so now they liked the security of the existing arrangement better than the dangerous uncertainties of the old regime. Besides, the new order was popular in the provinces. There, government by Senate and People was looked upon skeptically as a matter of sparring dignitaries and extortionate officials. The legal system had provided no remedy against these, since it was wholly incapacitated by violence, favoritism, and—most of all—bribery.

Source: Tacitus, *The Annals of Imperial Rome,* translated by Michael Grant (Penguin Classics, 1951; revised edition, 1971). Copyright © 1956, 1959, 1971 by Michael Grant Publications Ltd. Reprinted by permission of Frederick Warne & Company (Penguin Books UK).

Imperial defense remained a major issue. Strong Roman armies were a necessity along the hostile European frontier. On the friendlier border in western Asia and northern Africa, Augustus and his immediate successors set up client kingdoms, such as Judea and Armenia, to protect Roman territory. As for Parthia, Augustus compromised. He won no new territory but did achieve the symbolic victory of a return of the legionary standards lost by Crassus at Carrhae in 53 B.C.

Back in Rome the urban poor, many of them freedmen, enjoyed a more efficient system of free grain distribution under Augustus and a large increase in games and public entertainment—the imperial policy of "bread and circuses" designed to content the masses. Augustus also set up a major public works program, which provided jobs for the poor. He prided himself on having found Rome "a city of brick" and having left it "a city of marble."

To promote his ideology of renewal, Augustus sponsored social legislation embodying the old Republican virtues. He passed a series of laws encouraging marriage and childbearing and discouraging promiscuity and adultery. Such legislation was so flagrantly disobeyed that in 2 B.C. Augustus felt compelled to make an example of his own daughter, Julia (39 B.C.–A.D. 14), his only child, whose adulteries were the talk of Rome. As punishment she was banished to a barren islet.

Augustus's era marks the beginning of the classical period of Roman jurisprudence, during which the professionalism that had begun to mark Roman law in the Late Republic became a permanent fact. It was probably Augustus who established the practice, followed by later emperors, of granting a few distinguished jurists the exclusive right to issue legal opinions "on behalf of the princeps." He ensured, therefore, that experts guided the administration of justice. The first law school was opened in Rome under Augustus. Roman jurists, many of them provincials, adapted Roman law to the practices of the provinces. Although various provincial legal systems remained in use, the international system of Roman law was also used widely in the provinces.

In religion, too, Augustus was a legislator and reformer. He restored once-neglected cults and temples in order to appear as Rome's savior. He would probably

**Augustus of Prima Porta**    Named for the place where it was found, this statue (early first century A.D.) depicts an idealized and heroic Augustus. Scenes of victory, peace, and prosperity—symbols of the Principate—decorate his breastplate. Riding a dolphin, the Cupid at Augustus's feet recalls the Julian family's claim of descent from the goddess Venus. *(Alinari/Art Resource, NY)*

have approved when, after his death, he was deified, just as Julius Caesar had been. Even while he was still alive, Augustus was worshiped in the provinces as a god—in both the East, where the cult of Roma and Augustus grew in popularity, and the West, where centers of emperor-worship were established at the sites of Lyon and Cologne (see Map 6.1). The imperial cult, an important part of state propaganda until the empire became Christian in the fourth century A.D., was well underway.

Deification, whether formal or informal, was a heady brew, but Augustus deserved it more than most. He not only ended the Late Republican era of civil wars but established the Roman Empire on a completely new footing. Republican freedom was gone, but the emperor and bureaucrats brought stability. The peace of the Augustan Principate would last, with few interruptions, for two hundred years. Few people in history have created order so successfully.

## The Culture of the Augustan Age

Like *Periclean*, the adjective *Augustan*° has come to signify an era of literary and artistic flowering. In both periods strong elements of classicism shaped the arts—that is, an attempt to project fundamental, heroic, and idealized values, the values that the self-confident rulers of each epoch wished to promote. Both prose and poetry flourished in Augustus's empire. The emperor and his close adviser Maecenas° (d. 8 B.C.) were patrons of a number of important poets, chief among them Virgil° (70–19 B.C.) and Horace (65–8 B.C.). The historian Livy° (59 B.C.–A.D. 17), who wrote his history of Rome from the founding of the city to 9 B.C. under Augustus, also elicited the princeps's interest in his work. All three men contributed in their writings to the Augustan renewal and rededication of Rome.

In many ways Virgil speaks for his contemporaries. In the *Eclogues*—poems that, following an Alexandrian model (see page 122), have rustic settings—Virgil describes the miseries of the civil wars and the blessings of peace under Augustus. "A god created this peace for us; for he will always be a god to me," one character says. In the Fourth Eclogue, Virgil speaks of the birth of a child to usher in a restored Golden Age. At the Council of Nicaea in A.D. 325 (see page 212) and later, this poem was given a Christian interpretation. In the *Georgics*, Virgil describes the glories of Italian agriculture, which, thanks to Augustus, could be practiced peacefully again.

**Augustan** (aw-GUS-tin)    **Maecenas** (my-SEE-nus)
**Virgil** (VER-jill)    **Livy** (LIV-ee)

**Mosaic of the Doves**    This exquisite mosaic shows a number of doves drinking from or positioned around a gilded bronze basin on a marble pedestal. Derived from a Hellenistic work from Pergamum, this mosaic comes from a wealthy house in Pompeii.    *(Scala/Art Resource, NY)*

Virgil's masterpiece is an epic poem, the *Aeneid*°, "the story of Aeneas," the legendary Trojan founder of Rome, or at least of the Latin town from which Rome's founders eventually came. Legend also makes Aeneas the ancestor of Augustus. Thus the *Aeneid* indirectly celebrates Augustus, often considered Rome's second founder. The poem explores the pain and burden as well as the glory of empire.

If Virgil's work has the grandeur of marble, Horace's poems—*Odes, Epodes, Satires, Epistles,* and *Ars Poetica* (*Art of Poetry*)—are more like finely cut gems. They tend to be polished, complex, and detached. Like Virgil, Horace explores the themes of war and peace and praises Augustus. "With Caesar [Augustus] holding the lands, I shall fear neither turmoil nor violent death," declares one of the *Odes*. Both Horace and Virgil successfully adapted Greek models and, in the process, created something new. Few writers have had a greater influence on the later Western literary tradition.

Only 35 of the original 142 books of Livy's ambitious history have survived. Livy is both a master storyteller and a superb ironist. His anecdotes of Roman history are vivid and told in a grand rhetorical style. Livy is our major source for the Roman monarchy and Early Republic, although his account of early Rome is long on myth and short on fact. Nevertheless, Livy is not merely an entertaining stylist but a profound thinker on the meaning of history. He embroiders the facts and engages in frank, subjective judgments intended to inspire both patriotism and reflection on the ironies of history.

Another patron of writers in Augustus's circle was Messalla, himself an orator as well as a statesman. Love poetry was his special interest. Among the poets Messalla supported were Ovid, best known for works on love and mythology; Tibullus, an elegist; and his ward, Sulpicia. Although little survives of Sulpicia's work, more of her work exists than of any other Roman woman. She describes her passion for one Cerinthus: "a worthy man . . . at last a love . . . of such a kind that my shame, Gossip, would be greater if I kept it covered than if I laid it bare."[1]

Augustus and his entourage were also great patrons of the arts and of architecture, which they considered propaganda tools. They sponsored many major building projects throughout the empire, especially in Rome, which gained temples, a new Forum of Augustus, the Theater of Marcellus, the Baths of Agrippa, the Pantheon, and the Mausoleum of Augustus.

---

*Aeneid* (ee-NEE-id)

## The Julio-Claudians

Augustus and his successors presented the imperial household to the world as the ideal family, the very model of social order. Behind the walls of the palace, however, dwelt a troubled reality.

Augustus had only one child, Julia, from his first marriage, which ended in divorce. In 38 B.C. Augustus took as his second wife Livia° (58 B.C.–A.D. 29), who divorced her husband to marry Augustus even though she was pregnant with their second son. She did not bear Augustus children. Seeking a male successor, Augustus used Julia as a pawn in a game of dynastic marriage, divorce, and remarriage, but to no avail. Julia's first two husbands both predeceased her, as did two sons, each of whom Augustus had adopted. (In Rome it was common for a man without a birth son to adopt a son.) In the end, Augustus was forced to choose as successor, and adopt, a man he disliked, Tiberius° (42 B.C.–A.D. 37), Livia's elder son.

Livia was among the most powerful women in Roman history. One of Augustus's main advisers, she developed a reputation for intrigue, aimed, so gossip had it, at securing the succession for Tiberius. Livia's enemies accused her of poisoning many people, including Julia's husbands and sons; her own grandson, Germanicus (a brilliant general whose popularity threatened Tiberius's); and even Augustus himself, who died in bed after a short illness in A.D. 14.

From A.D. 14 to 68, Rome was ruled by other emperors from Augustus's family. The dynasty, known as the Julio-Claudians, consisted of Augustus's stepson Tiberius, great-grandson Caligula, grandnephew Claudius, and great-great-grandson Nero. For many elite Romans, this era was one of decadence, scandal, and oppression of the old nobility. Ordinary people, however, generally enjoyed the benefits of stable, effective, and peaceful government.

The reign of Tiberius (r. 14–37) was later remembered by the elite for its treason trials and murders. The senate complained as it steadily lost power to the princeps. The Roman masses grumbled because Tiberius cut back on games and building projects. But despite his shortcomings, Tiberius was a skilled and prudent administrator. He wisely drew back from war on the borders, reduced taxes and spending, and promoted honesty among provincial governors.

His successor, his nephew Gaius (r. 37–41), nicknamed Caligula° ("Baby Boots," after the boots he had worn as a little boy in his father's army camp), humiliated the senate. It was bad enough that he tried to have himself declared a living god. On top of that, he appointed his favorite horse not only high priest of a new cult in his honor but also a member of the senate. Caligula raised taxes and accused people of treason in order to confiscate property. He wanted to have his statue erected in the Temple at Jerusalem, and he would have done so, but he was assassinated first, the victim of a high-level conspiracy. After his death the senate debated restoring the Republic, but it was not to be.

Caligula's uncle, Claudius, was named emperor by the Praetorian Guard, which forced the senate to support him. Physically handicapped, Claudius (r. 41–54) was often the butt of jokes, but he was a man of substance: a historian, politician, and priest and someone fully versed in the cunning ways of his family. An activist emperor, he expanded the imperial offices with their powerful freedmen; oversaw the construction of an artificial harbor at Rome's silt-clogged port of Ostia; and conquered Britain, where Roman arms had not intervened since Julius Caesar's forays in 55 to 54 B.C.

Claudius's death may have been the result of poisoning by his wife, who was also his niece, Agrippina° the Younger (15–59); in any case, her son by a previous marriage, Nero, became emperor (r. 54–68). Nero's scandalous behavior rivaled Caligula's, and his treason trials outdid Tiberius's. After a great fire destroyed half of Rome in 64, Nero mounted a big rebuilding program and was accused of having started the fire just so that he could become famous as a builder. He found a scapegoat for the fire in the members of a small religious sect, the Christians, whom he persecuted. Ordinary Romans supported Nero because he gave them good government. He was unpopular with the senators and, more serious, with the army, because he failed to pay all his troops promptly. Confronted with a major revolt in 68, Nero committed suicide.

The next year, 69, witnessed Rome's first civil war in about a century. Three men claimed the imperial purple after Nero. A fourth, Vespasian° (Titus Flavius Vespasianus, r. 69–79), commander of the army quelling a revolt in the province of Judea, was able to make his claim stick. Peace was restored, but not the rule of Augustus's family. Vespasian founded a new dynasty, the Flavians° (r. 69–96), which was followed in turn by the Nervo-Trajanic (r. 96–138) and Antonine° (r. 138–192) dynasties. The ultimate tribute to Augustus may be that

---

**Livia** (LIV-ee-uh)   **Tiberius** (ty-BEER-ee-us)
**Caligula** (ca-LIG-yoo-luh)

**Agrippina** (a-grip-PIE-nuh)   **Vespasian** (ves-PAY-zhun)
**Flavians** (FLAY-vee-unz)   **Antonine** (AN-toe-nine)

**Agrippina the Younger**    This statue shows the mother of the emperor Nero praying. It is carved in basanite, a stone whose use is typical of the imperial Roman taste for art objects in exotic materials.    *(Courtesy, Mondadori Electa S.P.A.)*

his regime was stable enough to survive the extinction of his family.

## THE ROMAN PEACE AND ITS COLLAPSE, A.D. 69–284

MUCH about Rome in the second century A.D. appears attractive today. Within the multi-ethnic empire, opportunities for inhabitants to become part of the elite were increasing. The central government was on its way to granting Roman citizenship to nearly every free person in the empire, a process completed in the year 212. The emperors emphasized sharing prosperity and spreading it through the provinces. Italy was no longer the tyrant of the Mediterranean, but merely first among equals. To be sure, rebellions were crushed, but few people rebelled. This period, known as the *pax Romana,* or "Roman peace," seems particularly golden in contrast with what followed: the disastrous and disordered third century A.D., in which the empire came close to collapse but survived because of a radical and rigid transformation.

### The Flavians and the "Good Emperors"

The Flavian dynasty of Vespasian (r. 69–79) and his sons Titus (r. 79–81) and Domitian (r. 81–96) provided good government, and their successors built on their achievements. Unlike the Julio-Claudians, Vespasian hailed not from the old Roman nobility but from an Italian propertied family. A man of rough-and-ready character, Vespasian is supposed to have replied when Titus complained that a new latrine tax was beneath the dignity of the Roman government, "Son, money has no smell." Unlike his father and brother, Domitian reverted to frequent treason trials and persecution of the aristocracy, which earned him assassination in 96, although the empire as a whole enjoyed peace and sound administration under his reign.

The so-called Five Good Emperors are Nerva (r. 96–98), Trajan° (r. 98–117), Hadrian° (r. 117–138), and the first two Antonines, Antoninus Pius (r. 138–161) and Marcus Aurelius° (r. 161–180). They are in several ways examples of the principle of merit. Trajan, a Roman citizen born in Spain, was Rome's first emperor from outside Italy. Hadrian and Marcus Aurelius also came from Spain, and

---

**Trajan** (TRAY-jun)    **Hadrian** (HAY-dree-un)
**Marcus Aurelius** (MAR-kus o-REEL-ee-us)

Antoninus Pius from Gaul. Each of the Five Good Emperors except Marcus Aurelius adopted the most competent person, rather than the closest blood relative, as his son and successor, thus elevating duty over sentiment. Marcus Aurelius, a deeply committed Stoic, gave full vent to his sense of duty in his *Meditations,* which he wrote in Greek while living in a tent on the Danube frontier, where he fought long and hard against German raids. Antoninus was surnamed "Pius" (Dutiful) because he was devoted to his country, the gods, and his adoptive father, Hadrian.

The Five Good Emperors made humaneness and generosity the themes of their reigns. Trajan, for example, founded a program of financial aid for the poor children of Italy. They also went to great lengths to care for the provinces. These emperors not only commonly received petitions from cities, associations, and individuals in far-off provinces but answered them. Yet humaneness does not mean softness. Hadrian, for instance, ordered a revolt in Judea (132–135) suppressed with great brutality.

Like the Julio-Claudians, the Five Good Emperors advertised their wives to the world as exemplars of traditional modesty, self-effacement, and domesticity. In fact, they were often worldly, educated, and influential. Trajan's wife, Plotina, for example (d. 121 or 123), acted as patron of the Epicurean school at Athens, whose philosophy she claimed to follow. She advised her husband on provincial administration as well as dynastic matchmaking. Hadrian's wife, Sabina, traveled in her husband's entourage to Egypt (130), where her aristocratic Greek friend, Julia Balbilla, commemorated the trip by writing Greek poetry, which she had inscribed alongside other tourists' writings on the leg of one of two statues of Amenhotep III at Thebes, referred to in classical times as the "colossi of Memnon."

A darker side of the second-century empire was the problem of border defense. Augustus and the Julio-Claudians had established client kingdoms where possible, to avoid the expense and political dangers of raising armies. The emperors of the day tended to be more aggressive on the borders than their predecessors. They moved from client kingdoms to a new border policy of stationary frontier defense. Expensive fortification systems of walls, watchtowers, and trenches were built along the perimeter of the empire's border and manned with guards. A prominent example is Hadrian's Wall, which separated Roman Britain from the enemy tribes to the north. Stretching 80 miles, the wall required fifteen thousand defense troops.

The most ambitious frontier policy was that of Trajan, who crossed the Danube to carve out the new province of Dacia (modern Romania) and who used an excuse to invade Parthian Mesopotamia. He won battles as far away as the Persian Gulf, but he lost the war. As soon as his army left, Mesopotamia rose in revolt, followed by Germany. Trajan's reign marked the empire's greatest geographic extent, but Trajan had overextended Rome's resources. When he died, his successor, Hadrian, had to abandon Trajan's province of Mesopotamia (see Map 6.1).

## Prosperity and Romanization in the Provinces

Compared with a modern economy, the Roman economy was underdeveloped. Most people worked in agriculture, employed primitive technology, and lived at a subsistence level. Even so, the Roman Empire experienced modest economic growth during the first two centuries A.D. The chief beneficiaries were the wealthy few, but ordinary people shared in the economic expansion as well. In addition to stability and peace, several other

**Double Portrait, Pompeii**    This wall painting from a house joined to a bakery depicts a married couple, possibly the wealthy baker P. Paquius Proculus and his wife. The portraiture is realistic. The couple carry symbols of education: she holds wax tablets and a stylus (pen), while he grasps a sealed scroll.    *(Scala/Art Resource, NY)*

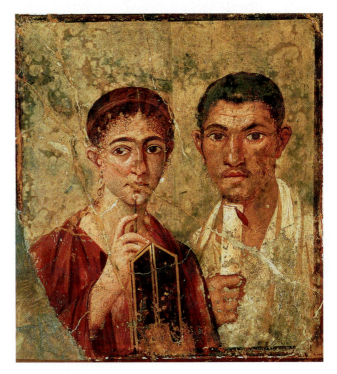

factors encouraged economic development. The western provinces witnessed the opening of new lands to agriculture, where improved techniques were applied. The growth of cities increased agricultural demand. Changes in Roman law aided commerce by making it easier to employ middlemen in business transactions. Travel and communications were relatively easy and inexpensive.

Trade boomed, as a recent archaeological discovery in the Italian city of Pisa° recalls. Nineteen Hellenistic and Roman ships were found at the site of the ancient harbor beginning in 1999. Several are merchant ships, both coastal freighters and small harbor craft. One of the ships was filled with amphoras (storage jars), still stacked in neat rows and filled with wine and sand. Both of those goods come from the region of the Bay of Naples, whose sand was used for concrete that could set underwater. The finds, which seem to date from the mid-second century A.D., offer a vivid picture of trade up and down the west coast of Italy. When the cargo was unloaded at Pisa, the ships probably picked up the local grain and marble, which was shipped in turn to Rome.

Rome was an economic magnet, but so, to a lesser extent, were all cities, and the second century A.D. was a great age of city life. New cities were founded far from the Mediterranean. They began as veterans' colonies, market towns, and even army camps, and some grew into cities of permanent importance in European history: Cologne (Colonia Claudia Agrippinensis), Paris (Lutetia Parisiorum), Lyon (Lugdunum), London (Londinium), Mérida (Emerita Augusta), Vienna (Vindobona), and Budapest (Aquincum).

Whether old or new, cities attracted large elite populations. The Principate was not a domain of country gentry but one in which ambitious people wanted to live in great cities, in emulation of the greatest city of the empire, Rome, which was by Augustus's day a city of perhaps a million people. In cities men competed for positions as magistrates, in imitation of the two consuls, or for seats on the local town council, often called a *curia*°, like the senate in Rome. Town councilors were called *decurions*° and known collectively as the *curial order*. Decurions played one-upmanship in sponsoring public buildings in the Roman style—one man endowing a new forum, another a triumphal arch, a third a library, a fourth an amphitheater, and so on. From Ephesus in Anatolia to Colchester in Britain, from Mainz in Germany to Leptis Magna in Libya, a Roman could

find familiar government institutions, architecture, and street plans. At Zeugma on the Euphrates River, for example, a city of seventy thousand people, aristocrats on Rome's eastern frontier lived in Italian-style villas decorated with classical frescoes and mosaics and adorned with bronze statues of the Greco-Roman gods.

Unlike men, women did not usually hold magistracies, but wealthy women of the empire could and did lavish money on public benefactions. Women endowed temples and synagogues, amphitheaters and monumental gateways, games and ceremonies. They were rewarded with wreaths, front-row seats, statues, priesthoods, and inscriptions honoring them as "most distinguished lady," "patron," and even "father of the city," to cite an extraordinary case from Roman Egypt.

The buildings were visible examples of Romanization, although the Romans did not use the term. If they had, it would have had a limited meaning because the emperors neither would nor could impose a lockstep cultural uniformity on their subjects. The empire was too big and ancient technology too primitive for that. The total population of the empire consisted of between 50 million and 100 million people, most of whom lived in the countryside. The small and largely urbanized Roman administration had little direct contact with most people. So, for example, only a minority of the inhabitants of the empire spoke Latin; in the East, Greek was the more common language of administration. Millions of people spoke neither Greek nor Latin. Celtic, Germanic, Punic, Berber, Coptic, Aramaic, and Syriac were other common languages in Roman domains. In short, the empire lacked the unity of a modern nation-state.

What, then, besides buildings and language might Romanization entail? One index has already been suggested: the participation of provincials in the central government, even as emperor. By around A.D. 200, for example, about 15 percent of the known Roman equestrians and senators came from North Africa. By this time the senate was no longer dominated by Italians but was representative of the empire as a whole.

Participation in government implies another index of Romanization—the extension of Roman citizenship outside Italy to magistrates, decurions, or even whole cities. Citizens took Roman names reflecting the emperor or promagistrate who had enfranchised them. Thus the provinces were full of Julii, Claudii, and Flavii, among others.

The spread of Roman customs is another measure of Romanization. For example, the gladiatorial shows that Romans loved became popular from Antioch to England. These combats advertised both Roman culture and

---

**Pisa** (PEE-zuh)  **curia** (KYOO-ree-uh)
**decurion** (day-KYOO-ree-un)

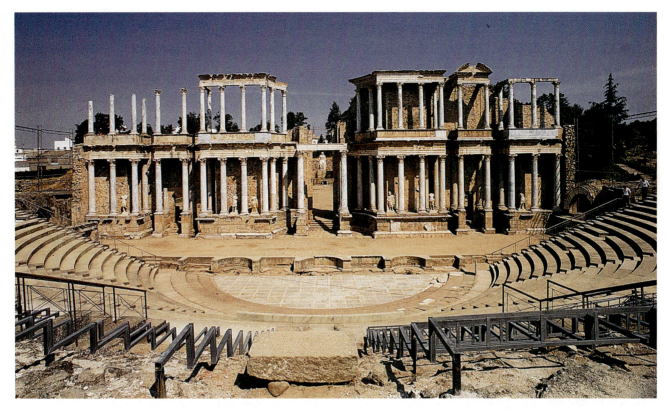

**Theater in Roman Spain**    This splendid structure at Mérida (ancient Augusta Emerita) was originally built in 24 B.C. and later reconstructed.    *(Vanni/Art Resource, NY)*

Roman brutality. (See the feature "Weighing the Evidence: Gladiators" on pages 200–201.)

By the same token, native customs might be adopted by Romans. Consider the case of Egypt, where, in the late 1990s, archaeologists discovered a vast Roman-era cemetery about 230 miles southwest of Cairo, in the Bahriya Oasis, Roman Egypt's wine country. The population was Romanized here. Yet the cemetery, with its dozens of gilded mummies from the first and second centuries A.D., shows the persistence of the mummification processes of the pharaohs.

Another ambiguous symbol of Romanization is found in A.D. 212. In a law known as the *Constitutio Antoniana,* the emperor Caracalla (r. 211–217) rendered nearly all of the free inhabitants of the empire Roman citizens. On the one hand, the law is a historical landmark. Near-universal Roman citizenship was a kind of halfway point between ancient empire and modern mass democracy. On the other hand, the *Constitutio Antoniana* was something of a gimmick. It was probably less an instrument of unification than of taxation, for citizens had a heavier tax burden than noncitizens.

The Roman army, by contrast, did promote Romanization. In antiquity as today, military service offered education and social mobility. Only citizens could join the legions; non-Romans served as auxiliaries. They received Roman citizenship after completing their regular term of service, twenty-five years, and with good reason: a Syrian or Gallic peasant, for example, who served in the Roman military would experience a way of life with old and deep roots in central Italy.

Non-Italians had, and took, the opportunity to rise high in the army or government. This was all to Rome's credit. Yet as Italians became a minority in the Roman army, and as ever larger numbers of frontier peoples were recruited, it became conceivable that someday the army might abandon its loyalty to Rome.

## Roman Law on Class and Marriage

Roman law is one of the ancient world's most influential and enduring legacies. Logical, practical, orderly, and—within the limits of a society of slaves and masters—relatively fair, Roman law has influenced the legal systems of most Western countries and many non-Western countries. The law governing Roman citizens was called *ius civile,* or "civil law." Originally this term covered a very broad range of legal matters, but in the empire its meaning was narrowed to private matters. Criminal law became a separate category.

The law helped Rome administer its empire. Roman law was not universal, and noncitizens continued to use their own laws for local matters, but the governors used Roman law to run their provinces, so local elites had to become familiar with it. Like so many Roman customs, the law was both hierarchical and flexible. Let us consider two areas in which the law affected daily life: class and marriage.

The law reflected Roman society's ingrained social inequality. Traditional special classes such as senators and equestrians survived, to be joined by the new distinction between citizens and noncitizens. Another important division cut across the citizen-alien distinction, that between *honestiores* (in general, the curial order) and *humiliores* (everyone else). Privileges previously inherent in citizenship, such as exemption from flogging by officials, now tended to be based on this new distinction, enshrined in private and criminal law.

The most basic legal distinction was that between free and slave—and the empire contained millions of slaves. A third category, ex-slaves or freedmen, also became increasingly important. Freedmen technically owed service to their former masters, who became their patrons, and most freedmen were humble. A few, however, grew rich in commerce or wielded enough power in imperial administration to lord it over even Roman aristocrats. The result was strong elite hostility toward freedmen, which is often reflected in Roman literature. Witness the stereotype of the vulgar freedman, embodied in Trimalchio in the *Satyricon°*, a novel by Petronius (first century A.D.). Trimalchio had more estates than he could remember and so much money that his wife counted it by the bushel-load.

As regards marriage, Roman family law was strict and severe in principle. In practice, however, it often proved pragmatic and even humane. Consider three cases: elite marriages, slave marriages, and soldiers' marriages.

As in the Late Republic, so in the Early Empire most Roman women married without legally becoming members of their husbands' families—or their children's. This gave women a degree of freedom from their husbands, but it left elite women, who owned property, with a problem: technically that property was controlled by their fathers or brothers. Yet society recognized a woman's

wish to leave her property to her children, and imperial law increasingly made it possible for her to do so—although the conservative Romans waited until the sixth century A.D. before abolishing completely the rights of greedy uncles. Another case is a mother's right to have a say in her children's choice of marriage partner. This maternal prerogative became accepted social practice even though Roman law gave women no such right.

Roman slaves married and had children, but they had to do so in the face of both legal and practical obstacles. Roman law gave slaves no right to marry, and it made slave children the property of the owner of the slave mother. Owners could and did break up slave families by sale. Even if a slave was freed, the law expressed far more concern with the continuing obligations of freedmen to their former masters than with the rights of slave families. Yet during the Early Empire cracks appeared in the wall of law that allowed slave families to slip through. (See the box "Reading Sources: Slaves with the Right Stuff.")

For example, although the law insisted that a slave be age 30 before being freed, it made an exception for an owner who wished to free a female slave younger than 30 in order to marry her. To take another example, the law conceded that slave children owed devotion and loyalty (*pietas*) to their slave parents.

Career soldiers from at least the time of Augustus on could not marry, probably on the grounds of military discipline. Yet many soldiers cohabited anyhow, often with noncitizen women in the areas where they served, and frequently children were the result. Not until the reign of Septimius Severus° (r. 193–211) were soldiers permitted to marry formally, and then only after twenty-five years of service. Yet not only had commanders permitted cohabitation for two centuries, but the law also made concessions now and then. For example, the Flavians gave soldiers a degree of freedom to make wills, which could allow them to leave property to illegitimate children. Various emperors gave groups of soldiers the privilege, on discharge, to legalize a marriage with a noncitizen, which ordinary Romans were not permitted to do.[2]

## The Culture of the Roman Peace

In Latin poetry the century or so after the death of Augustus is often referred to as the "Silver Age," a term sometimes applied to prose as well. The implication is that this period, though productive, fell short of the golden Augustan era. It might be fairer to say that the self-confidence of the Augustan writers did not last. As the permanence of monarchy became clear, many in the

---

*Satyricon* (suh-TEER-uh-con)

*Severus* (SEH-ver-us)

READING
SOURCES

## SLAVES WITH THE RIGHT STUFF

*In his book* On Agriculture, *Columella (first century* A.D.*) reveals Roman attitudes toward slaves, who he suggests need to be hardened for farmwork after the corruption of city life. He thinks of female slaves as breeding machines and as a restraining influence on male slaves. He opposes cruelty but not chains, if needed.*

A landowner must be concerned about what responsibility it is best to give each slave and what sort of work to assign to each. I advise that you not appoint a foreman from that type of slave who is physically attractive, and certainly not from the type who has been employed in the city, where all skills are directed toward increasing pleasure. This lazy and sleepy type of slave is accustomed to having a lot of time on his hands, to lounging around [waiting for his master at] the Campus Martius [playing fields], the Circus Maximus [race track], the theaters, the gambling dens, the snack bars, and the brothels, and he is always dreaming of these same foolish pleasures. If a city slave continues to daydream when he has been transferred to a farm, the landowner suffers the loss not just of the slave but actually of his whole estate. You should therefore choose someone who has been hardened to farm work from infancy, and who has been tested by experience. . . .

The foreman should be given a female companion both to keep him in bounds and also to assist him in certain matters. . . . He should not be acquainted with the city or the weekly market, except in regard to matters of buying and selling produce, which is his duty. . . .

. . . The foreman should not only be skilled in agricultural operations, but also be endowed with such strength and virtue of mind (at least as far as his slave's personality permits) that he may oversee men neither with laxity nor with cruelty. . . . There is no better method of maintaining control over even the most worthless of men than demanding hard labor. . . . After their exhausting toil, they will turn their attention to rest and sleep rather than fun and games. . . .

It should be an established custom for the landowner to inspect the slaves chained in the prison, to examine whether they are securely chained, whether their quarters are safe and well guarded, whether the foreman has put anyone in chains or released anyone from chains without his master's knowledge. . . .

A diligent master investigates the quality of his slaves' food and drink by tasting it himself. He examines their clothing, hand-coverings, and foot-coverings. He should even grant them the opportunity of registering complaints against those who have harmed them either through cruelty or dishonesty. . . . I have given exemption from work and sometimes even freedom to very fertile female slaves when they have borne many children, since bearing a certain number of offspring ought to be rewarded. For a woman who has three sons, exemption from work is the reward; for a woman who has more, freedom.

Source: Jo-Ann Shelton, *As the Romans Did: A Sourcebook in Social History*, 2d ed. Copyright © 1988, 1998 by Oxford University Press, Inc. Used by permission of Oxford University Press, Inc.

For additional information on this topic, go to college.hmco.com/students.

elite looked back to the Republic with nostalgia and bitterness. Silver Age writing often takes refuge in satire or rhetorical flourish. Writing under Trajan, for example, the historian Tacitus poured scorn on the Julio-Claudians and Flavians. Other Silver Age writers indulged in flattery and obsequiousness toward the emperor.

The Silver Age was an era of interest in antiquities and in compiling handbooks and encyclopedias; it was also an era of self-consciousness and literary criticism. In the first two centuries A.D., Roman writers came from an ever greater diversity of backgrounds and wrote for an ever wider audience, as prosperity and educational opportunities increased. Consider Lucian (ca. A.D. 115–185), an essayist and satirist. A native of Syria who probably spoke Aramaic before learning Greek, he served as an administrator in Roman Egypt.

Many writers of the era pursued public careers, which offered access to patronage. Tacitus, for instance, rose as high as proconsul of the province of Asia. Prominent literary families emerged, such as that of Pliny° the Elder (A.D. 23–79), an encyclopedic author on natural science, geography, history, and art; and his nephew,

**Pliny** (PLIH-nee)

Pliny the Younger (ca. A.D. 62–ca. 113), an orator and letter writer. The most notable literary family is that of Seneca° the Elder (ca. 55 B.C.–A.D. 40), a historian and scholar of rhetoric; his son, Seneca the Younger (ca. 4 B.C.–A.D. 65); and Seneca the Younger's nephew, the epic poet Lucan (A.D. 39–65).

Born in Cordoba, Spain, the younger Seneca moved at an early age to Rome, where he became a successful lawyer and wealthy investor. He was banished in A.D. 41 for alleged adultery with a sister of Caligula. Recalled in 49, he became tutor to the young Nero. When Nero became emperor in 54, Seneca became one of his chief advisers and helped bring good government to the empire. Seneca eventually fell out of favor, however, and was forced first into retirement and then, in A.D. 65, into suicide. He had been the major literary figure of his age, a jack-of-all-trades: playwright, essayist, pamphleteer, student of science, and noted Stoic philosopher.

A literary career was safer under the Five Good Emperors. Consider Tacitus and his contemporary, the poet Juvenal° (ca. A.D. 55–130). Juvenal's *Satires* are bitter and brilliant poems offering social commentary. He laments the past, when poverty and war had supposedly kept Romans chaste and virtuous. Amid "the woes of long peace," luxury and foreign ways had corrupted Rome, in his opinion. Critics often blame society's troubles on marginal groups. Juvenal, for example, launches harsh attacks on women and foreigners. Tacitus, too, is sometimes scornful of women.

Yet if he is biased on matters of gender, Tacitus is far from ethnocentric. Few historians have expressed graver doubts about the value of their country's alleged success. For example, Tacitus highlighted the simple virtues of the Germanic tribes, so different from the sophisticated decadence of contemporary Rome. Nostalgia for the Republic pervades his two greatest works, *The Histories*, which covers the civil wars of A.D. 69, and *The Annals* (only parts of which survive), chronicling the emperors from Tiberius through Nero. A masterpiece of irony and pithiness, Tacitus's style makes an unforgettable impression on the reader. (See the box "Reading Sources: Augustus: A Skeptical View" on page 178.)

Plutarch° (ca. A.D. 50–120), whose *Parallel Lives of Noble Greeks and Romans* later captured the imagination of Shakespeare, is probably the best-known pagan Greek writer of the first two centuries A.D. Like Livy, Plutarch emphasizes the moral and political lessons of history. A careful scholar, Plutarch found his true calling in rhetor-ical craftsmanship—polished speeches and carefully chosen anecdotes. As in Rome, rhetoric was the basis of much of Greek literary culture in this period.

Another star of Greek culture at this time was the physician Galen° of Pergamum (A.D. 129–?199). In his many writings, Galen was to medicine what Aristotle had been to philosophy: a brilliant systematizer and an original thinker. He excelled in anatomy and physiology and proved that the arteries as well as the veins carry blood. He was destined to have a dominant influence on European medicine in the Middle Ages.

## The Crisis of the Third Century, A.D. 235–284

Leaving the relative calm of the second century A.D. behind, the third-century Roman Empire descended into an ever widening spiral of crisis. Barbarian invasions, domestic economic woes, plague, assassinations, brigandage, urban decline—the list of Rome's problems is dramatic. The empire went "from a kingdom of gold to one of iron and rust," as Dio Cassius put it, summing up Roman history after the death of Marcus Aurelius in 180, when the seeds of crisis were sown.

Stability first began to slip away during the reign of the last of the Antonines, Marcus Aurelius's birth son, Commodus° (r. 180–192), a man with Nero's taste for decadence and penchant for terrorizing the senatorial elite. His predictable assassination led to civil war, after which Septimius Severus, commander of the Danube armies, emerged as the unchallenged emperor (r. 193–211). He founded the Severan dynasty, which survived until 235.

Severan reformers attempted to re-establish the empire on a firmer footing, but they only brought the day of crisis nearer. The main theme of Septimius's reign was the transfer of power—from the senate to the army and from Italy to the provinces. To extend the Roman frontier in North Africa and western Asia, Septimius expanded the army and improved the pay and conditions of service. These measures might have been necessary, but Septimius went too far by indulging in war with Parthia (197–199)—unnecessary war, because the crumbling Parthian kingdom was too weak to threaten Rome. What the war did accomplish, however, was to inspire the enemy's rejuvenation under a new Eastern dynasty, the Sassanids°.

The Sassanid Persians spearheaded increased pressure on Rome's frontiers. The Sassanids overran Rome's eastern provinces and captured the emperor Valerian himself in 260. (See the box "Global Encounters: Syria

---

Seneca (SEH-neh-kuh)   Juvenal (JOO-veh-nal)
Plutarch (PLOO-tark)

Galen (GAY-len)   Commodus (KOM-uh-dus)
Sassanid (SASS-uh-nid)

# Syria Between Rome and Persia

Rome and Persia fought three great battles in western Asia in A.D. 244, 252, and 260, all resounding victories for Persia under King Shapur I (r. ca. 241–272). In the first selection Shapur celebrates his success in an inscription carved in rock near Persepolis. The second selection provides a Greek view of what Syria's inhabitants endured when Shapur "burned, ruined and pillaged" in A.D. 252. It comes from the *Thirteenth Sibylline Oracle,* a verse commentary on contemporary events, purporting to be ancient prophecy.

## The Persian Inscription

I, the Mazda worshipping lord Shapur, king of kings of Iran and non-Iran, whose lineage is from the Gods. . . .

When at first we had become established in the empire, Gordian Caesar raised in all of the Roman Empire a force from the Goth and German realms and marched on Babylonia against the Empire of Iran and against us. On the border of Babylonia at Misikhe, a great "frontal" battle occurred. Gordian Caesar was killed and the Roman force was destroyed. And the Romans made Philip Caesar. Then Philip Caesar came to us for terms, and to ransom their lives, gave us 500,000 denars, and became tributary to us. . . .

And Caesar lied again and did wrong to Armenia. Then we attacked the Roman Empire and annihilated at Barbalissos a Roman force of 60,000 and Syria and the environs of Syria we burned, ruined and pillaged all. In this one campaign we conquered of the Roman Empire fortresses and towns . . . a total of 37 towns with surroundings.

In the third campaign when we attacked Carrhae and Urhai [Edessa] and were besieging Carrhae and Edessa Valerian Caesar marched against us. He had with him a force of 70,000. . . .

And beyond Carrhae and Edessa we had a great battle with Valerian Caesar. We made prisoner ourselves with our own hands Valerian Caesar and the others, chiefs of that army, the praetorian prefect, senators; we made all prisoners and deported them to Persis.

And Syria, Cilicia and Cappadocia we burned, ruined and pillaged. . . .

And men of the Roman Empire, of non-Iranians, we deported. We settled them in the Empire of Iran. . . .

We searched out for conquest many other lands, and we acquired fame for heroism, which we have not engraved here, except for the preceding. We ordered it written so that whoever comes after us may know this fame, heroism, and power of us.

## The Sibylline Oracle

. . . the evil Persians . . .

. . . the Persians, arrogant men . . .

. . . the arrow-shooting Persians . . .

Now for you, wretched Syria, I have lately been piteously lamenting; a blow will befall you from the arrow-shooting men, terrible, which you never thought would come to you. The fugitive of Rome will come, waving a great spear; crossing the Euphrates with many myriads, he will burn you, he will dispose all things evilly. Alas, Antioch, they will never call you a city when you have fallen under the spear in your folly; he will leave you entirely ruined and naked, houseless, uninhabited; anyone seeing you will suddenly break out weeping. . . .

Alas . . . they will leave ruin as far as the borders of Asia, stripping the cities, taking the statues of all and razing the temples down to the all-nourishing earth.

## QUESTIONS

1. According to Shapur's inscription, what were Rome's misdeeds toward Persia? According to the *Sibylline Oracle,* what were Persia's misdeeds toward Rome?

2. How did Persia retaliate, according to Shapur's inscription and according to the *Sibylline Oracle*? How and why do the two accounts differ?

3. Which account do you find more convincing? Why?

SOURCE: Inscription: Richard N. Frye, trans., *History of Ancient Iran* (Munich: C. H. Beck'sche Verlagsbuchhandlung, 1984), pp. 371–372. Reprinted by permission of Richard N. Frye. Oracle: D. S. Potter, trans., *Prophecy and History in the Crisis of the Roman Empire* (Oxford: Clarendon Press, 1990), p. 175.

**Hadrian's Wall** Built in A.D. 122–126, this extensive structure protected Roman England from raids by the tribes of Scotland. It represents the strategy of stationary frontier defense. *(Roy Rainford/Robert Harding Picture Library)*

Between Rome and Persia.") The caravan city of Palmyra (in Syria) took advantage of Rome's weakness to establish independence; its most famous leader was the queen Zenobia. Meanwhile, two Germanic tribes, the Franks and the Goths, hammered the empire from the northwest and northeast.

Fending off invasions at opposite fronts stretched Rome to the breaking point. To pay for defense, the emperors devalued the currency, but the result was massive inflation. As if this were not bad enough, a plague broke out in Egypt at midcentury and raged through the empire for fifteen years, compounding Rome's military manpower problems.

Assassinations and civil wars shook the stability of the government. Between 235—when the last Severan emperor, Severus Alexander, was murdered—and 284, twenty men were emperor, however briefly in some cases. Civilians suffered in the resulting disorder.

Yet the empire rebounded, which is a tribute to Roman resilience as well as a sign of the disunity and lack of staying power among the empire's enemies. Recovery began during the reign of Gallienus (r. 253–268), who ended the Frankish threat and nearly polished off the Goths. By 275 Aurelian (r. 270–275) had defeated the Goths and reconquered the eastern provinces, including Palmyra. Gallienus excluded senators from high military commands and replaced them with professionals. Moreover, he began a new, more modest policy of border defense. The Romans now conceded much of the frontier to the enemy and shifted to a defensive mode: fortified cities near the frontier served as bases from which to prevent deeper enemy penetration into Roman territory. They also concentrated mobile armies at strategic points in the rear, moving them where needed.

Gallienus's reforms pointed the way to imperial reorganization, but they remained to be completed by the two great reforming emperors at the end of the third century and the beginning of the fourth: Diocletian (r. 284–305) and Constantine (r. 306–337), subjects of the next chapter. When their work was done, the new Roman Empire of Late Antiquity might have been barely recognizable to a citizen of the Principate.

# EARLY CHRISTIANITY

INCREASING contact between Rome and its western provinces served to plant Roman cities, Roman law, and the Latin language (or its derivatives) in western Europe. As Rome in turn owed much to other Mediterranean peoples, it may be said that the Roman Empire was a vessel that transported ancient Mediterranean civilization to northern and western Europe. No feature of that civilization was to have a greater historical impact than the religion born in Tiberius's reign: Christianity.

Christianity began in the provincial backwater of Palestine among the Jews, whose language, Aramaic, was understood by few in Rome. It immediately spread to speakers of the two main languages of the empire, Greek and Latin, and the new movement addressed the common spiritual needs of the Roman world. By the reign of Diocletian, Christians had grown from Jesus's twelve original followers to perhaps millions, despite government persecution (see Map 6.2 on page 194). In the fourth century A.D., Christianity unexpectedly became the official religion of the entire Roman Empire, replacing polytheism—one of the most momentous changes in Mediterranean history. We turn to that change in the next chapter; here we consider the career of Jesus and the early spread of the Christian Gospel (literally, "Good Tidings"). But first, to set the stage, we look at other religions of the Roman Empire.

## Mystery Religions

The Romans were polytheists. They did not try to impose a single, unified religion on the empire. Instead, Romans were usually willing to admit new gods to their pantheon, as long as their worshipers took part in the patriotic emperor cult. Roman conservatism, moreover, engendered respect for other peoples' traditional faiths. Although Roman authorities had tried occasionally to expel these faiths from the city itself, the spread of new religions during the first three centuries A.D. proved irresistible. Besides Christianity and Judaism, the most important religions were Greek mystery cults, the cults of Isis and Mithras, and Manichaeism. These religions displayed a tendency toward syncretism, often borrowing rites, doctrines, and symbols from one another.

Greek mystery cults included the cults of Dionysus, the god of wine, and of Demeter, the goddess of grain, who was worshiped at annual ceremonies at Eleusis, a town outside Athens. The "mystery" consisted of secret rites revealed only to initiates. In the case of Demeter, the rites apparently had something to do with the promise of eternal life.

The cult of Isis° derived from the ancient Egyptians' worship of Isis (see page 26), her brother and husband, Osiris, and their son, Horus. Like the cult of Demeter, its central theme was eternal life, through the promise of resurrection achieved by moral behavior in this life. Isis, the "Goddess of Ten Thousand Names," was portrayed as a loving mother, and elements of Isis were later syncretized in the cult of the Virgin Mary. Her followers were known to march in colorful, and at times terrifying, parades through Roman streets, flagellating themselves as a sign of penitence.

Although men joined in the worship of Isis, the cult appealed particularly to women. The goddess's popularity crossed class lines; devotees ranged from slaves to one Julia Felix, whose estate at Pompeii included a garden shrine to Isis and Egyptian statuettes. By contrast, the worship of Mithras° was dominated by men, and especially by soldiers. Mithras, a heroic Persian god of light and truth, also promised eternal life. His worshipers believed that Mithras had captured and killed a sacred bull whose blood and body were the source of life. Accordingly, Mithraism focused on bull sacrifice carried out in a vaulted, cavelike temple called a *Mithraeum.* Initiates were baptized with bull blood and participated in various other rituals, among them a sacramental meal. Their moral code advised imitating the life of their hero.

Manichaeism° also originated in Persia, but later, in the third century A.D. Its founder, the Persian priest Mani, was martyred by conservative religious authorities. Manichaeism attempted to be the true synthesis of the religious beliefs of the period, recognizing not only Jesus but also Zoroaster and Buddha as prophets. The main tenet of Manichaeism was philosophical dualism, which emphasized the universal struggle between good (Light) and evil (Darkness). According to believers, the world had been corrupted by Darkness, but eventually the Light would return. In the meantime, good Manichaeans were to attempt to lead pure lives. Manichaeism was a powerful religious force for two centuries, and its believers were spread as far as India. The great theologian Augustine even flirted with it before becoming a Christian.

A new philosophy that developed in the same intellectual world as these Roman religions was Neo-Platonism°, which was founded by Plotinus° (A.D. 209–270). Using the works of Plato as a starting point, Plotinus

---

Isis (EYE-sis)  Mithras (MYTH-rus)
Manichaeism (MAN-ih-kee-izm)
Neo-Platonism (nee-oh-PLAY-ton-ism)
Plotinus (ploh-TIE-nus)

**Mithraeum**   This sculpted relief comes from an underground sanctuary along the Rhine frontier. It shows the hero-god Mithras sacrificing a bull, the central symbol of Mithraism. Actual bull sacrifices were carried out in temples known as Mithraea.   *(Private Collection)*

developed a philosophy in which the individual could first seek inner unity and then achieve oneness with the supreme unity of what Plotinus called the One or the Good. By this he meant an intangible and impersonal force that is the source of all values. Like the mystery cults, Plotinus's philosophy was difficult to understand, but it promised a kind of salvation. Neo-Platonism was destined to have a great influence on Western thought.

### Jesus of Nazareth

Christianity begins with Jesus. For all its historical importance, Jesus's life is poorly documented. The main source of information about it is the New Testament books of Matthew, Mark, Luke, and John. Jesus left no writings of his own. Early Christians, however, wrote a great deal. Between the second and fourth centuries A.D., Christians settled on a holy book consisting of both the Hebrew Bible, called the "Old Testament" by Christians, and a collection of writings about Jesus and his followers, called the "New Testament." The account of the Gospel according to Mark, probably the earliest Gospel, was most likely written about forty years after Jesus's crucifixion; several of the letters written by Paul of Tarsus (see page 196) date from the 40s A.D.; and the earliest non-Christian sources are later in date and are scanty. In 2002 some archaeologists thought that they had found new documentation of Jesus in the form of an ancient burial box supposed to have held the bones of Jesus's brother, James. But the box has been judged a fake by most experts.

No personality has generated as much discussion among Western scholars as has Jesus. Many would distinguish the Jesus of theology, the object of faith, from the Jesus of history, the figure who really lived in first-century Palestine. Recent work argues that the historical Jesus must be understood within the Judaism of his day. He was a product of the popular culture of the Palestinian countryside, a culture that was peasant and oral. Much of what the Gospels have to say about Jesus, some argue, must be rejected as later invention. These are controversial points, but many scholars would agree with one thing: we must be careful to avoid anachronism. By A.D. 200 two new religions had emerged, orthodox Christianity and rabbinic Judaism. The proponents of both religions claimed to be the rightful heirs of the biblical covenant. They engendered new perspectives that have colored the way Christians and Jews envisage the past before 200. The following account of Jesus seeks a middle ground among today's schools of interpretation.

Jesus was born a Jew. A speaker of Aramaic, he may also have known at least some Greek, widely spoken by both Jews and non-Jews in the several Hellenized cities of Palestine. To his followers, Jesus was Christ— "the anointed one" (from the Greek *Christos*), the man anointed with oil and thus marked as the king of Israel. They considered him the Messiah (from the Hebrew for "anointed one"), foretold in the Hebrew Bible, who would redeem the children of Israel and initiate the kingdom of heaven. The dynamism and popularity of his teachings led to a clash with Jewish and Roman authorities in Jerusalem, the capital city of Judea, and to his crucifixion. His mission began, however, in a corner of the Jewish world, in the northern region of Galilee°, where he lived in the town of Nazareth° (see inset, Map 6.2).

Jesus was probably born not long before the death in 4 B.C. of Herod, the Roman-installed client-king of Judea.

(The date of A.D. 1 for Jesus's birth, a mistaken calculation of Late Antiquity, does not accord with the data of the New Testament.) At around age 30, Jesus was baptized by the mysterious preacher John the Baptist. Soon afterward Herod Antipas, the Romans' client-king of Galilee, ordered the execution of John. John had preached that God's kingdom was about to arrive—a time of universal perfection and an end of misery. In preparation, sinful humankind needed to repent. Just how much influence John had on Jesus is a matter of debate, as is the question of John's relationship to the religious community of the Essenes°. Debate may be appropriate, for Judaism in the first century A.D. was in a state of creative disagreement. This era endorsed no one normative Judaism but rather a variety of Judaisms.

The Essenes lived apart from society in pursuit of a new covenant with God. The community at Qumran° in the Judean desert, whose history is documented in the Dead Sea Scrolls, ancient texts discovered in 1947, was probably Essene. The tenets of Qumran included frugality, sharing, participating in a sacred communal meal, and avoiding oath-taking. Adherents anticipated the coming of the Messiah and an end of days in which God would punish the wicked. Although Essene doctrine has much in common with early Christianity, early Christians did not withdraw from the world as the Essenes did but instead faced it.

There are both similarities and differences between Jesus's teaching and contemporary doctrines of Palestinian Judaism. The most popular group among Palestinian Jews, the Pharisees°, focused on the spiritual needs of ordinary folk (see page 132). The Pharisees believed that law was central to Judaism but argued that it could be interpreted flexibly, in light of the oral tradition that had grown up alongside the written text of the Hebrew Bible. The Pharisees emphasized charity toward the poor and spoke in parables—vivid allegories that made their teaching accessible.

Jesus argued similarly. Like the Pharisees, he strongly criticized the pillar of the Jewish establishment, the Sadducees°, the priests and wealthy men who saw the Temple at Jerusalem and its rites as the heart of Judaism. Also like the Pharisees, Jesus rejected the growing movement of the Zealots°, advocates of revolt against Roman rule, although there were Zealots among his followers. Yet Jesus was neither a Pharisee nor an Essene. His teaching went further than the Pharisees' in rejecting the need to

---

Galilee (GAL-uh-lee)   Nazareth (NAZ-uh-reth)

---

Essenes (ES-seenz)   Qumran (koom-RAHN)
Pharisees (FAIR-uh-seez)   Sadducees (SAD-yoo-seez)
Zealots (ZELL-ots)

**Map 6.2    The Expansion of Christianity to A.D. 200**    After its origin in Palestine, early Christianity found its main centers in the Greek-speaking cities of the Roman East. Missionaries such as Paul also brought the new faith to the Latin-speaking West, as well as to Ethiopia and Mesopotamia.

follow the letter of biblical law. Inward purity became the key principle, as reflected in Jesus's statement to his disciples (that is, his close followers): "Whoever does not accept the kingdom of God like a child will never enter it" (Mark 10:15). Only an adult could become expert in biblical law, but it is probably easier for a child than for an adult to attain spiritual innocence.

Jesus argued that the kingdom of God, which John the Baptist had said was coming soon, was actually already beginning to arrive. Moreover, Jesus said that he himself, acting through the direct order of God, could forgive sins. He emphasized the notion of God as a loving and forgiving father. He often spoke in parables and announced himself through miracles, particularly faith healing. He welcomed marginalized groups, including prostitutes and lepers.

Jesus's teaching is typified in the Sermon on the Mount, addressed to his many followers in Galilee. He praised the poor and the humble and scorned the pursuit of wealth instead of righteousness. He called for generosity and forgiveness, recalling the traditional Jewish golden rule—to treat others as one would like to be treated. He said that prayer, fasting, and acts of charity should be conducted in private, not in public, in order to emphasize purity of motive. He called on his followers to endure persecution in order to spread his teachings: "You are light for all the world," he told them.

Jesus spoke with conviction and persuasiveness—with "authority," as his followers said. In Galilee they greeted him as king. For some this was a purely spiritual designation; others planned an overthrow of Roman

**The Good Shepherd**   This ceiling painting comes from a Christian catacomb in Rome dating before A.D. 284. The pastoral image, common in the early church, recalls Christ's ministry. It symbolizes both his beneficence and his sacrifice, as well as his closeness to ordinary people.   *(Scala/Art Resource, NY)*

rule, although Jesus rejected that course of action. In any case, his teachings won him hostility from some Pharisees, who considered his claim to be able to forgive sins blasphemous, and from Sadducees stung by his criticisms. Neither group accepted Jesus as the Messiah. It should be emphasized, nevertheless, that most of Jesus's followers were Jewish.

Jesus challenged central authority by going to Jerusalem and teaching and healing in the Temple under the eyes of the priests whom he criticized. Nor did he confine his opposition to words: he drove merchants and moneychangers away from the Temple precincts by overturning their tables and perhaps even threatening them with a whip. Jesus attracted large crowds of followers, at least some of whom were armed. Sadducee authorities feared trouble, and so did the overlords of Judea, the Romans. The governor, Pilate (Pontius Pilatus), had already endured vehement Jewish objections to

the display in Jerusalem of an imperial medallion and of an inscription that seems to have asserted Augustus's divinity. Pilate had no need of further uproar. Temple police and Roman soldiers were called on to arrest Jesus quietly.

Jesus's subsequent trial and execution have always been controversial. The New Testament emphasizes the role of the Jewish leadership and the Jerusalem mob in Jesus's death. Written after the First Jewish Revolt (A.D. 66–70), however, the Gospels may reflect anti-Jewish sentiment in the empire. Crucifixion, the method used to execute Jesus, was a Roman penalty (the traditional Jewish method was stoning), and Jesus was executed by Romans, not Jews. Jesus probably appeared in informal and hurried proceedings before both the Jewish Council and Pilate. He suffered slow death by crucifixion on Golgotha (Calvary) Hill, just outside the city. It was a spring Friday, on the eve of the Passover festival, around A.D. 30.

## Paul of Tarsus

According to the Gospel writers, Jesus died on a Friday and rose from the dead on Sunday, an event commemorated by Christians at Easter. He is said to have then spent forty days on earth, cheering and commissioning his disciples in Galilee and working miracles, before finally ascending to heaven. Heartened, the disciples returned to Jerusalem and spread Jesus's teachings. They preached in synagogues, private households, and even the Temple, and to Greek-speaking as well as Palestinian Jews. Their movement spread in the thirties and forties A.D. throughout Palestine and into Syria. In Jerusalem Christians were known as Nazarenes—that is, followers of Jesus of Nazareth; it was at Antioch that they were first called "men of Christ" (*christianoi*).

The leaders of the movement were known as apostles, from the Greek *apostolos,* "one who is sent" and who enjoys the authority of the sender. The apostles believed that Jesus had sent them and given them authority. The apostles included Jesus's twelve original followers, or disciples. The most prominent disciple was Peter, a Galilean fisherman whom Jesus endowed with particular authority. After the crucifixion, Peter became a miracle-worker and leading apostle. According to a reliable tradition, he went to Rome, whose church he headed and where he died as a martyr in A.D. 64.

It was not clear at first that Christians would form a new religion separate from Judaism. Although the Sadducees and Jewish civil officials were hostile, Christians found much support among the Pharisees. Some Christians, however, contemplated a radical break; among them no one was more important than Paul of Tarsus (d. A.D. 67?).

Only Jesus himself played a greater role than Paul in the foundation of Christianity. A remarkable figure, Paul embodied three different and interlocking worlds. Born with the name of Saul, he was a Jew of the Diaspora from the southern Anatolian city of Tarsus. A learned Pharisee, Paul was a native speaker of Aramaic and knew Hebrew and Greek. His father was one of the few Jews to attain Roman citizenship, a privilege that Paul inherited. Paul's heritage speaks volumes about the variety of the Roman peace, and his religious odyssey speaks volumes more (see Map 6.2).

At first Paul joined in the persecution of the Christians, whom he considered blasphemous. Around A.D. 36, however, he claimed to see a blinding light on the road to Damascus, a vision of Jesus that convinced him to change from persecutor to believer. It was a complete turnaround, a *conversio* ("conversion"), to use the Latin word that would grow so important in years to come. Saul changed his name to Paul and became a Christian.

He also changed what being a Christian meant. The key to Paul's faith was not so much Jesus's life, although that was a model for Christian ethics, as it was Jesus's death and resurrection. Jesus's fate, Paul wrote, offered all humanity the hope of resurrection, redemption, and salvation. Paul retained his belief in Jewish morality and ethics but not in the rules of Jewish law. Following the law, no matter how carefully, would not lead to salvation; only faith in Jesus as Messiah would.

Such doctrines bespoke a break with Judaism, as did Paul's attitudes toward converts. Hellenistic Judaism had long reached out to Gentiles. Some became Jews. Others, scattered throughout the cities of the Roman Empire, were known as "God-fearers"—that is, they accepted the moral teachings of Judaism but refrained from following strict dietary laws, circumcision, and other Jewish rituals. Seneca the Younger, writing in the sixties, complains about the spread of Judaism: "The customs of this accursed race have gained such influence that they are now received throughout the world."[3]

The Jerusalem church baptized converts and considered them Jews, but Paul considered them not Jews but converts in Christ. For Pauline Christians, circumcision, dietary laws, and strict observance of the Sabbath were irrelevant. From the late forties to the early sixties A.D., Paul tirelessly undertook missionary journeys through the cities of the Roman East and to Rome itself. He aimed to convert Gentiles, and so he did, but many of his followers were Hellenized Jews and "God-fearers." Paul started Christianity on the road to complete separation from Judaism. Events over the next century widened the division. First, while Pauline churches prospered, departing ever more from Jewish customs, the Jerusalem church was decimated. Jewish authorities persecuted its leaders, and after Rome's suppression of the First Jewish Revolt and destruction of the Jerusalem Temple in A.D. 70, the rank and file of Palestinian Jews rallied to the Pharisees. Second, Jews and Christians competing for converts emphasized their respective differences. Third, although many Jews made their peace with Rome in A.D. 70, enough Jewish-Roman hostility remained to lead to uprisings in the Diaspora in 115 and to the Second Jewish Revolt in 132 to 135. Both were suppressed mercilessly by Rome, and Judaism became ever more stigmatized among Gentiles.

Bereft of the Temple at Jerusalem, Judaism nonetheless continued to prosper as a religion. Indeed, Jewish missionary activities continued, although they did not keep pace with the number of converts gained by Christianity. More striking is the emergence of the rabbis (the religious leaders of the Pharisees) as the mentors of Judaism. Popular among Jews, the rabbis also attracted the Romans because most rabbis opposed revolt. After both A.D. 70 and 135, the Romans made the rabbis responsible for Jewish self-government in Palestine. The rabbis left their mark on history, however, not in administration but in an intellectual movement. Continuing in the tradition of the Pharisees, the rabbis amplified the oral law—that is, they wrote interpretations of the Hebrew Bible that clarified the practice of Judaism. They developed the notion of the "dual Torah," elevating the oral law to equal authority with the written law of the Hebrew Bible. The notion legitimized the rabbis' enterprise, which made it possible for Judaism to evolve flexibly. The basic text of rabbinic Judaism is the Mishnah° (ca. A.D. 200), a study of Jewish law. In rabbinic Judaism lies the basis of the medieval and modern forms of the Jewish religion.[4]

## Expansion, Divergence, and Persecution

Although Jesus's mission was mainly in the countryside, early Christianity quickly became primarily an urban movement. Through missionary activity and word of mouth, the religion slowly spread. It was concentrated in the Greek-speaking East, but by the second century A.D. Christian communities dotted North Africa and Gaul and, beyond Roman boundaries, appeared in Parthian Iraq and in Ethiopia (see Map 6.2).

By around A.D. 200, an orthodox (Greek for "right-thinking") Christianity had emerged. Rooted in Judaism, it was nonetheless a distinct and separate religion that found most of its supporters among Gentiles. A simple "rule of faith," emphasizing the belief in one God and the mission of his son, Jesus, as savior, united Christians from one end of the empire to the other. Christianity attracted both rich and poor, male and female; its primary appeal was to ordinary, moderately prosperous city folk. Believers could take comfort from the prospect of salvation in the next world and in a caring community in the here and now. Christians emphasized charity and help for the needy, qualities all too often absent in Greco-Roman society. A Christian writer justly described a pagan's amazed comment on Christian behavior: "Look

how they love each other." Most early Christians expected Christ's return—and the inauguration of the heavenly kingdom—to be imminent.

Early churches were simple and relatively informal congregations that gathered for regular meetings. The liturgy, or service, consisted of readings from the Scriptures (the Old and New Testaments), teaching, praying, and singing hymns. Baptism was used to initiate converts. The Lord's Supper, a communal meal in memory of Jesus, was a major ritual. The most important parts of the meal were the breaking and distribution of bread at the beginning and the passing of a cup of wine at the end; these recalled the body and blood of Christ. As organizational structures emerged (see pages 212–213), churches in different cities were in frequent contact with one another, discussing common concerns and coordinating doctrine and practice.

Just as Jewish women were not rabbis, so early Christian women did not hold the priesthood. Jewish women, however, did hold office in the synagogue, and Christian women likewise served as deaconesses. Both endowed buildings and institutions. For example, consider the Italian Jewish woman Caelia Paterna, an office-holder honored by her congregation as "mother of the synagogue of the people of Brescia." Or the two Christian deaconesses, both slaves, whom Pliny the Younger tortured during his governorship of the Anatolian province of Bithynia° (ca. A.D. 110) in an attempt to extract information about the worrisome new cult. (See the box "The Continuing Experiment: Caesar and Christ.") Deaconesses played an active part in church charities and counseling and now and then preached sermons.

As Christianity spread, its troubles with the authorities deepened. For one thing, Christians met in small groups, a kind of assembly that conservative Romans had long suspected as a potential source of sedition. More troubling, however, was Christians' refusal to make sacrifices to the emperor. The Romans expected all subjects to make such sacrifices as a sign of patriotism. The only exception was the Jews, who were permitted to forgo the imperial cult because their ancestral religion prohibited them from worshiping idols. The Christians, however, were a new group, and the Romans distrusted novelty.

As a result, the emperors considered Christianity at best a nuisance and at worst a threat. Christians were tested from time to time by being asked to sacrifice to the

**Mishnah** (MISH-nuh)

**Bithynia** (buh-THIN-ee-uh)

# Caesar and Christ

The Romans valued law and order. They considered Christianity a threat to both because Christians refused to worship the emperor as a god. Yet the Romans wanted to avoid a full-scale persecution of Christianity because that, too, would disrupt public order. So they tried a policy of limited tolerance, as shown in this exchange of letters in about A.D. 110 between the governor of Roman Bithynia (northwest Anatolia), Pliny the Younger, and the emperor Trajan. Ultimately the policy failed.

### To the Emperior Trajan

It is a rule, Sir, which I inviolably observe, to refer myself to you in all my doubts; for who is more capable of guiding my uncertainty or informing my ignorance? Having never been present at any trials of the Christians, I am unacquainted with the method and limits to be observed either in examining or punishing them. Whether any difference is to be made on account of age, or no distinction allowed between the youngest and the adult; whether repentance admits to a pardon, or if a man has been once a Christian it avails him nothing to recant; whether the mere profession of Christianity, albeit without crimes, or only the crimes associated therewith are punishable in all these points I am greatly doubtful.

In the meanwhile, the method I have observed towards those who have been denounced to me as Christians is this: I interrogated them whether they were Christians; if they confessed it I repeated the question twice again, adding the threat of capital punishment; if they still persevered, I ordered them to be executed. For whatever the nature of their creed might be, I could at least feel no doubt that contumacy and inflexible obstinacy deserved chastisement. There were others also possessed with the same infatuation, but being citizens of Rome, I directed them to be carried thither.

. . . Those who denied they were, or had ever been, Christians, who repeated after me an invocation to the Gods, and offered adoration, with wine and frankincense, to your image, which I had ordered to be brought for that purpose, together with those of the Gods, and who finally cursed Christ, none of which acts, it is said, those who are really Christians can be forced into performing, these I thought it proper to discharge.

### Trajan to Pliny

The method you have pursued, my dear Pliny, in sifting the cases of those denounced to you as Christians is extremely proper. It is not possible to lay down any general rule which can be applied as the fixed standard in all cases of this nature. No search should be made for these people; when they are denounced and found guilty they must be punished; with the restriction, however, that when the party denies himself to be a Christian, and shall give proof that he is not (that is, by adoring our gods) he shall be pardoned on the ground of repentance, even though he may have formerly incurred suspicion. Accusations without the accuser's name signed must not be admitted in evidence against anyone, as it is introducing a very dangerous precedent, and by no means agreeable to the spirit of the age.

### QUESTIONS

1. What procedure does Pliny use against people denounced as Christians?

2. Why does Pliny consider distinctions by age? Why might he think that people who repent deserve a pardon?

3. Why does Trajan reject accusations without the accuser's name signed? What does he mean by "by no means agreeable to the spirit of the age"?

SOURCE: Pliny the Younger, *Letters,* trans. William Melmoth, rev. W. M. L. Hutchinson, Loeb Classical Library (Cambridge, Mass.: Harvard University Press, 1915), pp. 401–403, 407, slightly modified.

emperor; those who failed to do so might be executed, sometimes in the arena. More often, however, the Romans tacitly tolerated Christians as long as they kept their religion private. Christians could not proselytize in public places, put up inscriptions or monuments, or build churches. Christianity thus spread under severe restrictions, but spread it did, particularly in the cities of the East. The willingness of martyrs to die for the faith made a strong impression on potential converts. Although the number of Christians in the empire is not known, it is clear that by the late third century they were a significant and growing minority.

## SUMMARY

**B**ETWEEN the first century B.C. and the third century A.D., the Romans changed from a people who had come to destroy into a people who had come to fulfill. At the beginning of this period, the conquered provinces were oppressed by greedy bureaucrats and tax collectors, and Rome's imperial victories had nearly ruined the Italian peasantry. The Republic had collapsed under the weight of political maneuvering, judicial murders, gang skirmishes, and civil war.

A shrewd and sickly outsider, Octavian, confounded expectations by creating a new empire that would enjoy two centuries of stability; as Augustus, he served as its first emperor. Augustus reconciled the senatorial class by sharing a degree of power, but he guaranteed peace by keeping most of the armies in his own hand. He wisely reduced military spending and compromised with Rome's enemies to stabilize the frontiers. He solved the problem of rebellious soldiers by raising taxes to provide farms for veterans. Perhaps most important, he began a new policy toward the provinces, which were slowly raised to equality with Italy. In short, Augustus initiated the prosperous Roman peace, an era lasting until the third century A.D. To survive the crises of that century, it was necessary for Rome to maintain a bigger army supported by higher taxes collected by a larger bureaucracy—requirements that would shake the social, political, and cultural foundations of the empire, as Chapter 7 discusses.

Literature and the arts flourished in the peaceful period of the Early Empire. In the provinces, the Roman peace made possible an era of architectural and literary flowering. It was a prosperous era but not for everyone, as slavery remained widespread. Rome was a multi-ethnic empire whose inhabitants increasingly mixed with one another and exchanged ideas. None of these exchanges was more momentous than the emergence of several new religions, one of which would become in Late Antiquity the main religion of the Roman world: Christianity. Without the pax Romana of the Caesars, the Christian Gospel could not have been spread.

## ■ Notes

1. Mary R. Lefkowitz and Maureen B. Fant, trans., *Women's Life in Greece & Rome: A Source Book in Translation*, 2d ed. (Baltimore: Johns Hopkins University Press, 1992), p. 9.
2. This discussion of marriage and law owes much to Susanne Dixon, *The Roman Family* (Baltimore: Johns Hopkins University Press, 1992), pp. 36–60.
3. Seneca, *De Superstitione*, trans. Menachem Stern, in *Greek and Latin Authors on Jews and Judaism*, vol. 1 (Jerusalem: Israel Academy of Sciences and Humanities, 1976), p. 431.
4. On these points, see Lawrence H. Schiffman, *From Text to Tradition: A History of Second Temple and Rabbinic Judaism* (Hoboken, N.J.: Ktav Publishing House, 1991), pp. 1–16.

## ■ Suggested Reading

Adkins, Leslie, and Roy A. Adkins. *Handbook to Life in Ancient Rome*. 1998. An excellent reference book, arranged thematically, by two archaeologists.

Earl, D. C. *The Age of Augustus*. 1968. A beautifully illustrated introduction to government, society, and religion.

Fantham, Elaine, Helene Peet Foley, Natalie Boymel Kampen, Sarah B. Pomeroy, and H. A. Shapiro. *Women in the Classical World: Image and Text*. 1994. Chapters 10–13 provide an excellent introduction to the social and cultural history of women in the Roman Empire.

Köhne, Eckart, and Cornelia Ewigleben. *Gladiators and Caesars: The Power of Spectacle in Ancient Rome*. 2000. Originally written as an exhibition catalog, this well-illustrated collection of essays serves as a very good introduction to the subject.

Pagels, Elaine. *Beyond Belief: The Secret Gospel of Thomas*. 2003. Elegant and readable study of competing arguments and faiths within early Christianity.

Ramage, Nancy H., and Andrew Ramage. *Roman Art*. 3d ed. 2000. An excellent introductory text; especially good on the Roman Empire.

Wells, Colin. *The Roman Empire*. 2d ed. 1995. A sweeping, lively, and thoughtful overview of the subject from 44 B.C. to A.D. 235.

**For a searchable list of additional readings for this chapter, go to college.hmco.com/students.**

# Gladiators

Historians and novelists write about them, film makers portray them, revolutionaries salute them, and a few years ago television athletes claimed to be American updates of them. They are gladiators, literally men who carried a *gladius,* or sword. They fought to the death as entertainment, and they enraptured the Roman Empire.

Gladiators took part in so-called games or combat before large crowds. Armed with various specialized weapons, they fought each other and sometimes wild animals. Some unfortunates were thrust into fights with no weapons at all. The audience, seated in rank order, ranged from slaves to senators to the emperor himself. There was nothing tame about what they had come to see. Consider the word *arena,* referring to the site of the games. It literally means "sand," which is what covered the floor—and soaked up the blood.

Our fascination with the gladiator is nothing compared to the Romans'. Everybody in Rome talked about gladiators. At Pompeii, graffiti celebrated a star of the arena whom "all the girls sigh for." Jokes poked fun at gladiators, philosophers pondered their meaning, and literature is full of references to them.

Gladiatorial images decorated art around the empire, from mosaics to household lamps. Look at this mosaic from a Roman villa in Germany, one of several mosaic panels on the floor of the building's entrance hall, depicting scenes from the arena. The illustration shows a *retiarius,* or net-and-trident bearer, fighting a better-armed *secutor,* literally "pursuer," under the watchful eyes of a *lanista,* or trainer. As was typical, the retiarius wears no armor except for a shoulder piece protecting his left side. To defend himself against the dagger wielded by the secutor (in the mosaic, hidden behind the shield), the retiarius had to be fit enough to be able to keep moving. The difference between various types of gladiators would have been as obvious to a Roman as the difference between a catcher and a pitcher is to a baseball fan today.

As for the amphitheaters where gladiatorial combats took place, they were as common in Italy and the Roman Empire as skyscrapers are in a modern city. Look, for example, at this photograph of the amphitheater in the city of El Djem in modern Tunisia (the Roman province of Africa). Built of high-quality local stone in the third century A.D., the structure was meant to have sixty-four arches, but it was never completed. The openings in the floor permitted animals to be released into the arena. A large amphitheater like this one held at least thirty thousand spectators, and the largest amphitheater of all, the Flavian Amphitheater—or Colosseum—at Rome, seated around fifty thousand. Amphitheaters were less common in the East, but the fans there also were loyal, so the games went on—in theaters.

Most gladiators were condemned criminals, prisoners of war, or slaves bought for the purpose. The most famous slave gladiator was Spartacus, a Thracian. Along with seventy-seven other gladiators in the Italian city of Capua, Spartacus instigated a slave rebellion that attracted thousands and shook Italy for two years (73–71 B.C.). (See the box "The Continuing Experiment: Spartacus's Slave Revolt" on page 198.)

Yet some gladiators were free men who volunteered for a limited term of service. Once even the emperor Commodus (r. 180–192) served, to the disgust of other Roman nobles, who found the arena fascinating but low-class. The gladiator was part warrior, part athlete, part showman, and part butcher. Yet there was something of the pagan priest in the gladiator, too, for his was a solemn profession. Every gladiator took an oath to endure being burned, bound, beaten, and killed by the sword. They began each combat by greeting the official in charge (in Rome, the emperor) in this way: "We who are about to die salute you."

Students of the Romans find it hard to believe that they adored such a murderous sport, in which dozens and occasionally hundreds of men might die in a single day, to the roar of the crowds. Yet perhaps the arena makes us uncomfortable not so much because it is foreign but because it is familiar. Although we no longer flock to games in which men kill each other, we do go in droves to blood sports such as boxing, and we pack hockey rinks to watch men regularly give each other concussions. Modern people no longer kill animals in the arena for sport, but we hunt, fish, go on big-game safaris, watch cockfights, and, in Spain, kill bulls and occasionally get killed by them.

Besides, perhaps our discomfort reflects our instinctive understanding of the symbolism of the arena. The games were brutal, but so was the empire. Rome had brought peace to three continents, but it had done so by brandishing a sword, and it kept the peace by its readiness to fight. The arena kept Romans tough and warlike, or so an intellectual could argue, as does Pliny the Younger, who describes gladiatorial games:

**Roman Amphitheater, El Djem, Tunisia**
*(Adina Tovy/Robert Harding Picture Library)*

**Gladiator Mosaic, Nennig, Germany**
*(Bildarchiv Preussischer Kulturbesitz)*

[The games] inspired a glory in wounds and a contempt of death, since the love of praise and desire for victory could be seen, even in the bodies of slaves and criminals. (*Panegyric* 33)

Arguably the arena also contributed to public order. This was no small achievement, since the imperial army could not police a population of 50 million to 100 million, and few places had even the elementary police force that the city of Rome did. The violence that bloodied the amphitheater stepped into the breach by reminding criminals—or those defined as criminals—what punishment awaited them. Rob or kill, and you might end up in the arena. Refuse to worship the emperor, and you might be fed to the lions, as Christians were from time to time. Rebel against Rome, and you might find yourself on a chain gang building a new amphitheater, as tradition says thirty thousand prisoners of the First Jewish Revolt (A.D. 66–70) did. The result was the Colosseum.*

Occasionally pagan as well as Christian writers condemned gladiatorial games. Seneca the Younger (ca. 4 B.C.–A.D. 65), for example, criticized them for inciting greed, aggression, and cruelty. Yet so popular was Rome's theater of power that gladiators and their games were not abolished until around A.D. 400.

www. **For additional information on this topic, go to college.hmco.com/students.**

*The preceding two paragraphs lean heavily on the fine discussion in Colin Wells, *The Roman Empire*, 2d ed. (Cambridge, Mass.: Harvard University Press, 1995), pp. 248–255.

**201**

# CHAPTER 7

# The World of Late Antiquity 284–ca. 600

"SOLOMON, I have outdone you!" Tradition holds that the emperor Justinian (r. 527–565) uttered these words when he saw for the first time the magnificent Church of Hagia Sophia ("Holy Wisdom"), which he erected in Constantinople. Justinian's reign, words, and building provide an excellent entry into the late antique period. Justinian looked back to the biblical king Solomon in speaking of his church. The church itself is composed of two intersecting rectangular basilicas surmounted by a dome. Justinian's religious, military, and administrative policies were consistent with those of his predecessors for two centuries, and his legal reforms grew out of centuries of tradition. In many ways Justinian, perhaps Late Antiquity's greatest ruler, was a traditional Roman. But his church was unlike any building the Roman world had ever seen. Justinian's massive law code was more comprehensive and systematic than any of its predecessors. His military aspirations were audacious, as were his administrative plans. Justinian's reign points out the dynamic tensions of the late antique period: continuity and change, tradition and innovation, past and future.

Two centuries before Justinian the reigns of Diocletian (284–305) and Constantine (306–337) inaugurated a period that scholars now label "Late Antiquity." For many years educated people, often taking their lead from the elegant and influential *Decline and Fall of the Roman Empire* by the British historian Edward Gibbon (1737–1794), believed that, beset by insurmountable problems, the Roman Empire

Interior view of Hagia Sophia, the church of the "Holy Wisdom," built in Constantinople by Emperor Justinian between 532 and 537.
(Werner Forman/Art Resource, NY)

"fell" in the fifth century. With that fall, such a view insisted, the glories of classical civilization gave way to the gloom of the "Dark Ages." Today, on the contrary, specialists in the period from roughly 300 to 600 see vigor and achievement. They emphasize continuity and coherence over calamity and collapse. No one denies that the Roman world of 600 was different from the Roman world of 300. But recent scholarship stresses how the Romans themselves created a stable framework for change. No catastrophic time, place, or event marked the "fall of Rome."

From the time of its founding, the Roman Empire had suffered from various structural problems. In particular, the Roman world was vast geographically and diverse in its human and material resources. Changes were inevitable in such a world. This chapter identifies the most important changes that took place while the Roman Empire was evolving into its medieval European, Byzantine, and Muslim successors.

## QUESTIONS TO CONSIDER

- What were the most important reforms of Diocletian, Constantine, and their successors, and what roles did those reforms play in saving and transforming the empire?

- Who were the "barbarians," and what kinds of relations did Romans and barbarians have in Late Antiquity?

- How and why did the Catholic Church emerge in Late Antiquity?

- How did women and men, elites and ordinary people, urban dwellers and farmers, experience continuity and change in Late Antiquity?

## TERMS TO KNOW

| | |
|---|---|
| tetrarchy | monasticism |
| Edict of Milan | Visigoths |
| Arianism | Justinian |
| Council of Nicaea | Hagia Sophia |
| Monophysitism | Saint Augustine |
| papacy | Vulgate Bible |

# REBUILDING THE ROMAN EMPIRE, 284–395

THE third-century Roman Empire had lurched from crisis to crisis. Decisive action was needed if Rome was to survive. The chronic civil wars had to be brought to an end. The army needed to be reformed and expanded to meet new threats on the frontiers. And the economy had to be stabilized to bring in the revenue the government needed for administrative and military reforms. Rome was fortunate in raising up two rulers, Diocletian° and Constantine, with more than fifty years of rule between them, who understood the empire's problems and legislated energetically to address them. Although these rulers thought of themselves as traditional Romans, they actually initiated a far-reaching transformation of the Roman Empire.

## The Reforms of Diocletian (r. 284–305)

The son of a poor Dalmatian farmer, Diocletian rose through the ranks of the army until he attained a key position in the emperor's elite guards. When the emperor was murdered, the soldiers elevated Diocletian to the imperial office.

In about 293 Diocletian devised a regime that historians call the "tetrarchy°," or rule by four (see Map 7.1). He intended to address both the political instability of the Roman regime and the awesome size and complexity of the empire. First Diocletian decided to divide the empire into eastern and western halves and then selected an imperial colleague for himself. Ruling from Nicomedia and retaining the position of senior emperor, he took charge of the wealthy and militarily threatened eastern half of the empire. Diocletian and his colleague each selected a subordinate official who would eventually succeed to the imperial office. The advantage of the

---

**Diocletian** (dy-oh-KLEE-shun)

**tetrarchy** (teh-TRAR-kee)

tetrarchy was that it yielded four men of imperial rank who could lead armies and make decisions in political and administrative matters. Diocletian hoped that the tetrarchy would provide orderly succession to the imperial office and promote experienced, respected men.

Historians call the regime instituted by Augustus in 31 B.C. the "Principate" because the emperor pretended to be the "first citizen" and heir of the Republican magistrates, even though his real power depended on control of the army. By contrast, Diocletian abandoned all pretense of being a magistrate. Scholars call his regime the "Dominate," from the Latin *Dominus*, meaning "lord and master." Diocletian adopted Eastern, especially Persian, habits, such as wearing a gilded cloak and a jeweled diadem, sprinkling gold dust in his hair, sitting on an elevated throne, rarely appearing in public, and requiring those who approached to prostrate themselves before him. Diocletian succeeded in enhancing the prestige of the imperial office but did so at the price of making the emperor more remote from his subjects.

Given its size and problems, the Roman Empire was dramatically *under*governed. The empire had some fifty provinces, which varied greatly in size, population, wealth, strategic importance, and degree of Romanization, but the imperial administration was made up largely of aristocratic amateurs and numbered only a few hundred men when Diocletian ascended the throne. Rome had traditionally asked for relatively little from its empire—primarily taxes, military recruits, and loyalty. Local authorities generally did the tax collecting and military recruiting, with little interference from imperial agents.

Diocletian increased the number of officials and doubled the number of provinces by dividing old, large provinces into smaller ones. He then organized groups of provinces into thirteen dioceses and joined the dioceses into four prefectures. Diocletian subordinated each prefecture to a tetrarch and equipped each prefecture with a force of military, legal, financial, and secretarial officials headed by a praetorian prefect. By 350 the number of officers from the provincial to the prefectorial level had risen from a few hundred to thirty-five or forty thousand. Diocletian wished to fill the bureaucracy with trained administrators instead of with wealthy senators and equestrians, who viewed government service as a means of enriching themselves and advancing the interests of their families.

Diocletian also attended to Rome's military problems. His major initiative was an attempt to double the size of the army from about 300,000 to 600,000 men, although the final total ended up being only around 450,000. Diocletian also built new forts along the fron-

## CHRONOLOGY

| | |
|---|---|
| 284–337 | Reforms of Diocletian and Constantine |
| 300–400 | Origins and spread of Christian monasticism |
| 325–553 | First five ecumenical councils of the Christian church |
| 325–360 | Foundation and development of Constantinople |
| 350s–ca. 600 | Age of the Church Fathers |
| 370s–530s | Beginnings of the Germanic kingdoms inside the Roman Empire |
| 379–395 | Reign of Theodosius I, last emperor of a united empire |
| 408–450 | Reign of Theodosius II; consolidation of eastern Roman Empire |
| 410 | Visigoths sack Rome |
| 412–418 | Visigoths settle in Gaul |
| 430 | Vandals begin conquest of North Africa |
| 440–604 | Development of the Roman papacy |
| 450–600 | Anglo-Saxons settle in Britain |
| 476 | Last Roman emperor in the West deposed |
| 481–511 | Clovis founds Frankish kingdom |
| 493 | Beginning of Ostrogothic kingdom in Italy |
| 527–565 | Reign of Justinian I |

tiers and improved the roads that supplied frontier defenders. He began the systematic incorporation of barbarians into the army, a step that led to a blurring of the distinction between Romans and barbarians. Military service had long been attractive to people in the empire because it provided Roman citizenship as well as a secure income. After 212 almost every free man in the empire enjoyed automatic citizenship. As a result, mainly noncitizen barbarians living along the frontiers, whose only hope of citizenship was military service, found the army attractive. For a while the army tended to Romanize the barbarians, but as the proportion of barbarian

**Map 7.1  Diocletian's Division of the Roman Empire, 286** Diocletian divided the empire into eastern and western halves; each half was divided into two prefectures. Thus four regions, rulers, and bureaucratic administrations replaced the ineffective rule of one man.

Prefecture of Gaul
Prefecture of Italy
Prefecture of Illyricum
Prefecture of the East

ATLANTIC OCEAN

North Sea

Baltic Sea

BRITAIN

GERMANY

GAUL

Lyon

Rhine

Elbe

RAETIA

NORICUM

PANNONIA

DALMATIA

Adriatic Sea

Ravenna

Tiber

Rome

CISALPINE GAUL

Po

NARBONENSIS

Massilia

Rhône

Ebro

NEARER SPAIN

FARTHER SPAIN

CORSICA

SARDINIA

BALEARIC IS.

MAURETANIA

NORTH AFRICA

Carthage

NUMIDIA

SAHARA

Mediterranean Sea

SICILY

Syracuse

Brundisium

MACEDONIA

Corinth

Athens

MOESIA

DACIA

THRACE

Byzantium

Danube

Black Sea

CRIMEA

Don

Dnieper

Volga

Caspian Sea

ARMENIA

CAPPADOCIA

Tigris

Euphrates

SYRIA

Antioch

Damascus

JUDEA

Jerusalem

Petra

ARABIAN DESERT

Red Sea

Nile

EGYPT

Alexandria

LIBYA

Cyrene

CRETE

RHODES

CILICIA

Tarsus

ASIA

Smyrna

Pergamum

LYDIA

PHRYGIA

Nicomedia

CYPRUS

Line of division between east and west

400 Mi.

400 Km.

200

200

0

0

230 of 678

**Tetrarchy**    Ideal and reality are both evident in this sculpture of the tetrarchy. The rulers, depicted equal in size, embrace one another but also bare their weapons—to one another and to the world.    *(Scala/Art Resource, NY)*

soldiers and officers grew, the culture and ethos of the army began to change.

Diocletian's reforms were expensive and required a predictable income. Thus Diocletian attempted to regularize the tax system in the empire. The government conducted a census to identify all taxpayers and assessed the productive value of land. To address the mounting inflation of the third century, Diocletian issued in 302 the Edict of Maximum Prices, which froze the costs of goods. Since senators successfully defended their long-standing exemptions from taxes and the taxation of business ventures remained low, virtually the whole cost of the Roman system continued to fall on agriculture, in particular on small farmers. Diocletian's reform of the tax structure brought in more revenue, but it also caused hardships. A rising tax burden threatened those who were most vulnerable. And with more officials handling vastly greater sums of money, corruption ran rampant. Most people never saw the emperor, but they saw too much of his tax-gouging local minions. (See the box "The

Continuing Experiment: A Contemporary View of Diocletian's Reforms.")

The rationale behind Diocletian's reforms is easy to understand; their results were less easy to anticipate. The actions were costly in three unintended respects: moral, social, and economic. The emperors had always been military dictators, but Diocletian removed all pretense that they served at the behest of the Roman people. His frankness may have enhanced the aura of the imperial office, but it also loosened the ties between the ruler and his subjects. By reducing the official duties of the senatorial order, Diocletian alienated an influential group of about two thousand leading citizens. The enlarged imperial administration necessarily impinged on the autonomy of cities and their local leaders, for three centuries the key components of the imperial system. Finally, the expanded administration and army cost dearly in real cash. That cash had to be extracted from an empire that was in serious economic distress.

## The Reforms of Constantine (r. 306–337)

Diocletian's careful plans for the imperial succession collapsed almost immediately after his voluntary retirement in 305. When Diocletian's Western colleague (Constantius I) died in 306, his troops reverted to the hereditary principle and declared his son, Constantine, emperor. From 306 to 313 as many as six men claimed to be emperor somewhere in the empire. From 313 to 324 Constantine shared rule with one man, and from 324 to 337 he ruled alone over a reunited empire, although he made his sons subordinates in various parts of the empire. This compromise between the hereditary and tetrarchal systems persisted for the next two centuries.

Constantine had entered the imperial court as a young man in 293, when his father was made co-emperor, and he later served with his father in Britain and Gaul. He knew the system well and maintained the administrative structure that Diocletian had introduced. Constantine continued the eastward shift of power by creating a second imperial capital in the East. In 324 he selected an old Greek city, Byzantium°, and renamed it after himself, "Constantine's polis" or Constantinople (modern Istanbul). Byzantium's location, more than its size, wealth, or fame, recommended it. The city straddled military roads between the eastern and western halves of the empire, overlooked crucial trade lanes to and from the Black Sea region, and was well sited to respond to threats along both the Balkan and the eastern frontiers (see Map 7.1).

**Byzantium** (bizz-AN-tee-um)

# A Contemporary View of Diocletian's Reforms

Reformers always face severe challenges, and Diocletian was no exception. With the Roman Empire on the verge of fiscal, military, and administrative crisis, Diocletian needed to create new structures to protect his frontiers, generate additional revenues, and stabilize the economy. To accomplish these goals, he enacted a set of reforms that included doubling the size of the army and expanding and reorganizing the government (see pages 204–207). These reforms were not universally successful, as they resulted in economic dislocation and political alienation. This account by Lactantius (ca. 240–325), a hostile contemporary, highlights some of the criticisms of Diocletian's efforts.

While Diocletian, who was the inventor of wicked deeds and the contriver of evil, was ruining everything, he could not keep his hands even from God. This man, through both avarice and cowardice, overturned the whole world. For he made three men sharers in his rule; the world was divided into four parts, and armies were multiplied, each of the rulers striving to have a far larger number of soldiers than the emperors had had when the state was ruled by single emperors. The number of those receiving pay from the state was so much larger than the number of those paying taxes that, because of the enormous size of the assessments, the resources of the tenant farmers were exhausted, fields were abandoned, and cultivated areas were transformed into wildernesses. And to fill everything with fear, provinces were cut into bits; many governors and more minor offices lay like incubi over each region and every municipality, likewise many procurators of revenues, administrators, and deputy prefects. Very few civil cases came before all of these, but only condemnations and frequent confiscations, and there were not merely frequent but perpetual exactions of innumerable things, and in the process of exaction intolerable wrongs.

Whatever was imposed to maintain the soldiery might have been endured, but Diocletian, with insatiable avarice, would never permit the treasury to be diminished. . . . When by various iniquities he brought about enormously high prices, he attempted to legislate the price of commodities. Thus much blood was spilled, and nothing appeared on the market, and prices soared still higher. . . . In addition he had a certain endless passion for building, and made no small exactions from the provinces for maintaining laborers and artisans and for supplying wagons and whatever else was necessary for the construction of public works. Here basilicas, there a circus, here a mint, there a shop for making weapons, here a house for his wife, there one for his daughter.

## QUESTIONS

1. Bearing in mind that Lactantius was a Christian author who could not forgive Diocletian's brutal persecutions, do you think he was fair in assessing the emperor's efforts at reform?

2. Suppose you found a document in which Diocletian defended his reforms to Lactantius. What do you think it would say? What examples might Diocletian cite to prove that he had been successful?

3. How would you compare Diocletian's reforms with those of Constantine? Can you think of other examples of reforms that were well-intentioned and well-conceived but that nevertheless evoked opposition and controversy?

SOURCE: Lactantius, *On the Deaths of the Persecutors,* vii, in *Roman Civilization,* Volume 2: *The Empire,* ed. and trans. Naphtali Lewis and Meyer Reinhold. © 1990 by Columbia University Press. Reproduced with permission of Columbia University Press in the format Textbook via Copyright Clearance Center.

In financial affairs, too, Constantine's work echoed his predecessor's. He issued a new gold *solidus,* the principal money of account in the Roman Empire. This coin promoted monetary stability in the Mediterranean world for nearly a thousand years. Unfortunately, both a stable currency and Diocletian's price controls braked but could not stop the headlong rush of inflation.

In military affairs, Constantine believed that Rome's frontiers stretched too far to be held securely by garrisons, so he expanded the use of mobile field armies. These armies, recruited largely (as under Diocletian) from barbarians living along or beyond the frontiers, were stationed well inside the borderlands so that they could be mobilized and moved quickly to any threatened point. They were given their own command structures, under officers whom the Romans called "Masters of the Soldiers." The praetorian prefects were deprived of their military responsibilities and became exclusively civilian officials. The separation of civilian and military command made sense administratively and politically because it meant that no individual could combine the command of an army with the authority of a government post.

Whereas Diocletian will always be remembered for launching the last persecution of Christianity (303–305), Constantine legalized the new faith. Each man's motivation has evoked scholarly controversy. Diocletian was a Roman of conventional piety, who seems to have been convinced that the presence of Christian soldiers in his army offended the ancestral gods and denied victory to the Roman troops. Constantine's mother, Helena, was a devout Christian, and there were Christians in his father's court circle. In 312, while marching toward Rome to fight one of his rivals, Constantine believed that he saw in the sky a cross accompanied by the words "In this sign you shall conquer." Persuaded, Constantine put a chi-rho (from the first two letters of *Christos*, "Christ" in Greek) monogram on his sol-

**Chi-Rho**

diers' uniforms. He defeated his foe at the Milvian Bridge near Rome, and, certain that Christ had assured his victory, he and his Eastern colleague issued the Edict of Milan in 313, granting Christianity full legal status in the empire.

Diocletian's persecution had been harsh and systematic. He ordered churches to be closed and the Scriptures seized, arrested members of the clergy, and required all citizens to make a public act of sacrifice in a temple. Constantine did far more than merely stop the persecution or legalize Christianity. He granted the church tax immunities, exempted the clergy from military and civic obligations, and provided money to replace books and buildings that had been destroyed in the persecution. He and his mother sponsored the construction of impressive churches, such as Saint Peter's in Rome and the Church of the Holy Sepulcher over the traditional site of Christ's tomb in Jerusalem.

Scholars have long debated the strategic and political wisdom of Constantine's arrangements. Moving experienced troops away from the frontiers may have invited rather than deterred attacks. Recruiting barbarians into the field armies and leaving frontier defenses to barbarian auxiliaries may have created divided loyalties and conflicts of interest. Most Roman provincials had

**Old Saint Peter's**  Constantine I erected this huge five-aisled basilica over the presumed place of burial of the apostle Peter. This was the first Christian basilica erected over a saint's place of burial. The prominence of Peter, Rome, and the popes caused this church to be widely emulated. *(Scala/Art Resource, NY)*

not lived near soldiers. Now the soldiers and the veterans of the field armies became daily companions. One certain result of the reforms of Diocletian and Constantine was the militarization of Roman society—the transformation of the Roman Empire into a vast armed camp. The financial resources of that empire were now largely devoted to maintaining an expensive military establishment that was socially diverse and potentially politically volatile. Christians were still a minority of the population in Constantine's lifetime, so his legalization and patronage of the new faith may have been visionary but certainly offended the elites of his day.

Diocletian and Constantine responded with imagination to the third-century crisis. They created a new kind of rulership and a new type of imperial regime. Constantine erected a statue of himself in Rome that was more than 30 feet high; its head alone was about 8 feet tall. This statue is an indicator of the late antique imperial ideology. Constantine's size in stone serves to emphasize a distance that the viewer cannot articulate but cannot help feeling. The huge statue does not so much depict Constantine as proclaim emperorship. The majesty of Constantine and his long, productive reign, in conjunction with Diocletian's success and longevity, stands in stark contrast to the troubles of the third century. But we may ask, as contemporaries did, whether order was purchased at too high a price in terms of personal freedom.

## The Fourth-Century Empire: A Fragile Stability

Diocletian and Constantine considered themselves to be Roman traditionalists, but their wide-ranging reforms had actually introduced deep changes in the Roman system. When Constantine died in 337, the Roman Empire was more peaceful and stable than it had been throughout the crisis-ridden third century. But Rome's rulers were now more despotic; Rome's government was bigger, more intrusive, and more expensive; and Rome's military was larger and increasingly barbarian in composition. The open question in 337 was whether Rome would revert to the chaos of the third century or continue along the path marked out by the reforms of Diocletian and Constantine.

Succession to the imperial office remained a troubling issue despite the introduction of the tetrarchy. Constantine had employed a combination of the tetrarchal and dynastic systems. He had three subordinates, all of them his sons. They did not base their activities in the four prefectures, and they succeeded him jointly when he died. Constantine's sons had no heirs of their own, and when the last of them died in 361, the army turned to Julian (331–363), Constantine's nephew. Julian

was a great leader and a man who looked out for his troops. Nevertheless, people were trying to find a legitimate heir to Constantine, not merely a general who would reward the army. (See Table 7.1 for the succession of emperors in the eastern and western empires.)

### Table 7.1
### Roman Emperors from Diocletian to Justinian, 284–565

| East | West |
|---|---|
| Diocletian (284–305) | Maximian (285–305, 307–310) |
| | Constantius I (293–306) |
| Galerius (293–311) | |
| | Constantine I (306–337) |
| Maximinus (305–313) | Severus (306–307) |
| | Maxentius (307–312) |
| Licinius (308–324) | |
| Licincianus (317–323) | |
| | Crispus (317–325) |
| Constantius II (324–361) | Constantine II (317–340) |
| | Constans (333–350) |
| | Dalmatius (335–337) |
| Gallus (350–354) | |
| | Julian (355–363) |
| Julian (361–363) | Jovian (363–364) |
| Valens (364–378) | Valentinian I (364–375) |
| | Gratian (375–383) |
| | Maximus (383–387) |
| Theodosius I (379–395) | Valentinian II (383–392) |
| | Theodosius I (392–395) |
| Arcadius (395–408) | Honorius (395–423) |
| Theodosius II (408–450) | John (423–425) |
| Marcian (450–457) | Valentinian III (425–455) |
| Leo I (457–474) | Petronius Maximus (455) |
| | Avitus (455–456) |
| | Majorian (457–461) |
| | Libius Severus (461–465) |
| | Anthemius (465–472) |
| | Olybrius (472) |
| | Glycerius (473) |
| Leo II (474) | Julius Nepos (473–480) |
| Zeno (474–491) | Romulus Augustulus (475–476) |
| Anastasius (491–518) | |
| Justin I (518–527) | |
| Justinian I (527–565) | |

Julian ruled for only two years before he was killed fighting in Mesopotamia. Because Julian had no heirs, the army controlled the succession. The choice fell on Valentinian (r. 364–375) and his brother, Valens (r. 364–378). Valentinian ruled in the west, his brother in the east. Valentinian established a dynasty that ruled the Roman world for ninety-one years (364–455). In 378, when Valens was killed in battle, Valentinian's sons sent their brother-in-law, Theodosius° I (r. 379–395), who had risen through the military ranks in Spain, to the east to restore order.

Until his own death in 395 Theodosius was the most powerful man in the Roman world and, after his last brother-in-law died in 392, sole ruler. He enjoyed the confidence of the people and the army—the former because he was exceptionally competent and honest and the latter because he was an old military man and a superb general. He divided the empire between his two sons without dynastic or military challenge. His branch of the family lived on until the deaths of Theodosius II in the East in 450 and Valentinian III in the West in 455. Later rulers of the dynasty sometimes ruled alone, sometimes with chosen colleagues or subordinates. Dynastic and tetrarchal systems were thus blended effectively.

Following the reforms of Diocletian and Constantine, the army was supposed to protect the empire, not play a role in Roman politics. Events proved otherwise. In the 340s the Romans faced a renewed threat in the east from Persia, where an ambitious king sought to revive the glories of his ancestors. The Romans did not take this Persian threat lightly, for they knew that in the Persians they faced an old and formidable foe. In the west, Rome faced one serious challenge from the Visigoths (discussed later in this chapter). These military provocations inevitably enhanced the role of the army in public life and elevated military concerns over civilian ones. The presence of new threats contributed to the army's prominence in selecting emperors.

The fourth century did not witness the kind of intensive and sustained administrative reforms that characterized the reigns of Diocletian and Constantine. But emperors did introduce many modest measures, some of which had outcomes very different from those intended by their implementers. One example may stand for many.

During the reign of Valentinian I, a soldier raised to the imperial office by the army, the emperor wanted to make military careers more attractive and soldiers' lives more comfortable. To achieve these ends, Valentinian proposed providing soldiers with plots of land and seed grain. He aimed to supplement soldiers' pay, to tie them more securely to a particular region, and to make them more loyal to him. This creative idea complemented earlier military reforms.

Nonetheless, Valentinian's program angered the senators, who were still rich and influential. They agitated against the reform because, they said, the emperor was spending too much time worrying about the army, and he was depriving them of lands they desired. The senators also complained that the new program was expensive, and they were absolutely right. To pay for land and seed, Valentinian had to raise taxes.

Higher taxes were especially unpopular in the cities, where the burden of collecting them fell on the *decurions,* the main local officials who composed the town councils. From the time of Valentinian in the late fourth century, evidence points to a steady decline in loyalty to Rome among these provincial urban elites. Part of Rome's success under the Principate had been directly tied to the regime's ability to win over local elites all over the empire. Now a military reform whose rationale was clear and defensible actually provoked suspicion and disloyalty among senators and decurions.

When Theodosius died in 395, the Roman world still seemed reasonably secure. The families of Constantine and Valentinian had produced effective rulers. Scattered threats clouded the frontiers, but for the moment conditions appeared stable. Programs of institutional and economic reform continued apace, generally along the lines marked out by Diocletian and Constantine.

In the late fourth century, the empire may have numbered 50 million to 60 million inhabitants. Of these, not more than 5 million to 10 million lived in towns. Because Roman government was based on towns, the actual capacity of the Roman administration to keep track of, tax, coerce, and Romanize the population as a whole was limited. Nevertheless, as the Roman Empire became an increasingly militarized state, its towns were being dominated by central authorities as never before, and its rural population was being pressed hard by tax policies necessitated by larger civil and military structures. The reforms of Diocletian and Constantine continued to provide the framework within which these changes took place.

## THE CATHOLIC CHURCH AND THE ROMAN EMPIRE, 313–604

WHILE Rome's rulers were trying to stabilize the state during the fourth century, the empire was experiencing a dynamic process of religious change. The formerly small and persecuted communities of Christians were achieving majority status in the Roman

---

**Theodosius** (thee-oh-DOE-zhus)

world. The Christianization of the empire's population (see Map 7.2), first in towns and then in the countryside, and the emergence of the Catholic Church as a hierarchical, institutional structure were two of the greatest transformations of the ancient world. Many Christians, now able to practice their faith in public, discovered that they had sharp disagreements with one another on fundamental points of doctrine. Attempts to resolve those controversies entangled the church with the Roman authorities and strengthened the bishops of Rome. Moreover, numerous Christians—monks and nuns—sought a life of perfection away from the bustle of the world.

## Emperors, Bishops, and Heretics

Constantine discovered that his support of the church drew him into heated disputes over doctrine and heresy. *Heresy* comes from a Greek word meaning "to choose." Heretics are persons who choose teachings or practices that religious or state authorities deem wrong. The two greatest and most difficult heresies of Late Antiquity involved the central doctrines of Christianity: the deity of Jesus Christ himself and the relationship between his divine and human natures.

Christian belief holds that there is one God who exists as three distinct but equal persons: Father, Son, and Holy Spirit. But around 320 a priest of Alexandria, Arius° (ca. 250–336), began teaching that Jesus was the "first born of all creation." Christians had long been stung by the charge that their monotheism was a sham, that they really worshiped three gods. Arianism, as the faith of Arius and his followers is called, preserved monotheism by making Jesus slightly subordinate to the Father. Arianism won many adherents.

Constantine was scandalized by disagreements over Christian teachings and distressed by riotous quarrels among competing Christian factions. He dealt with religious controversies by summoning individual theologians to guide him and by assembling church councils to debate controversies and reach solutions. In 325 at Nicaea°, near Constantinople (see Map 7.2), the emperor convened a council of more than three hundred bishops, the largest council by far that had met up to that date. This was the first of many "ecumenical"—or all-world—councils in church history. The Council of Nicaea condemned Arius and his teachings. The bishops issued a creed, or statement of beliefs, which maintained that Christ was "one in being with the Father," co-equal and co-eternal.

Religious unity remained elusive, however. The Council of Nicaea's attempt to eliminate Arianism was unsuccessful in the short term. Constantius II (r. 337–361), Constantine's son and successor in the eastern half of the empire, was an avowed Arian, as were some later emperors. For more than forty years, Rome's rulers occasionally embraced a faith that had been declared heretical. It was during this time that the Visigothic priest Ulfilas entered the empire, was converted to Arian Christianity, and returned to spread this faith among his people. Arian Christianity spread widely among the barbarian peoples living along the empire's frontiers. By the time those people began to enter the empire in significant numbers (see pages 217–218), catholic Christianity had triumphed over Arianism, leaving the barbarians as heretics.

One emperor—Constantine's nephew Julian, called "the Apostate" by his Christian opponents—made a last-ditch attempt to restore paganism during his short reign (361–363). He did not resort to persecution but forbade Christians to hold most government or military positions or to teach in any school. Although Christianity had been legalized only in 313, by the 360s it was too well entrenched to be barred from the public sphere, and Julian's pagan revival died with him.

In the fifth century Monophysitism—literally "one-nature-ism"—emerged as a result of bitter quarrels between Christian thinkers in Alexandria and Antioch. Theologians were struggling to find a way to talk about the divine and human natures in Christ. Some emphasized one nature, some the other. Logically either proponent could have been called a Monophysite°, but true Monophysites stressed the divine over the human nature of Christ. In 451 the Eastern emperor Marcian called a new council at Chalcedon° to deal with the issue of Monophysitism. Like his predecessors, the emperor sought unity, and he was willing to let the theologians define the doctrines. At Chalcedon the theologians condemned the Monophysites and pronounced that Jesus Christ was true God and true man—that he had two authentic natures.

## The Institutional Development of the Catholic Church, ca. 300–600

The earliest Christian communities were urban and had three kinds of officials, whose customary titles in English are *bishop*, *priest*, and *deacon*. Deacons were clearly sub-

---

**Arius** (AIR-ee-us)    **Nicaea** (ny-SEE-uh)

**Monophysite** (muh-NAH-fizz-ite)
**Chalcedon** (KAL-seh-dun)

**Map 7.2    The Spread of Christianity to A.D. 600**    From its beginnings in Palestine (see Map 6.2 on page 194), Christianity, while still illegal, spread mainly in heavily urbanized regions. After Constantine legalized Christianity, the faith spread into every corner of the Roman world.

ordinate to the other two. They were responsible for charitable works and for arranging meetings. Bishops and priests presided at celebrations—most prominently the Eucharist (or Holy Communion, as it came to be called)—preached, and taught. Distinctions between bishops and priests developed over time. Depending on their relative size, towns would have many independent Christian groups, each headed by a priest. By about 200, as a sign of unity and authority, the eldest priest came to be called "overseer," the literal meaning of *bishop*. As more people converted, as the church acquired property, and as doctrinal quarrels began to cause divisions among the faithful, bishops began to be influential local officials. By the late fourth century, the bishops in the major cities of the empire were called *metropolitan bishops,* or sometimes *archbishops,* and they had responsibility for territories often called *dioceses*. In essence, the church was adapt-

ing to its own purposes the administrative geography of the Roman Empire.

From its earliest days the Christian community had espoused the doctrine of *apostolic succession*. In other words, just as Jesus had charged his apostles with continuing his earthly ministry, that ministry was passed on to succeeding generations of Christian bishops and priests through the ceremony of ordination. When one or more bishops laid their hands on the head of a new priest or bishop, they were continuing an unbroken line of clerics that reached back through the apostles to Jesus himself. The bishops of Rome coupled this general notion of apostolic succession with a particular emphasis on the original primacy of Peter, in tradition the leader of the apostles and the first bishop of Rome. The theory of "Petrine Primacy" was based on Matthew's Gospel (16:16–18), where Jesus founded his church on Peter, "the Rock," and conferred upon him the keys to the kingdom of heaven. The theory held that just as Peter had been the leader of the apostles, so the successors to Peter, the bishops of Rome, continued to be the leaders of the church as a whole. By the late fourth century the bishop of Rome was usually addressed as *papa*, or "pope" in English. The steadily growing importance of bishops everywhere was a marked feature of the age, and the growing authority of the bishop of Rome within the church is the most striking organizational process of the fourth and fifth centuries.

Christians in the Roman world frequently disagreed on matters of jurisdiction and theology. Attempts to resolve these controversies strengthened the ecumenical council as a regular organ of church government, increased the power of the papacy, and drew emperors more deeply into the public life of the church. In a series of laws issued between 378 and 381, Theodosius virtually outlawed the pagan cults, thereby making Christianity and Judaism the only legal religions, and required all Christians to believe as the bishop of Rome did, in the hope of imposing religious unity on battling groups of Christians. Unity under Roman leadership was essential, Theodosius said, because Peter had transmitted the unblemished faith directly to Rome and Peter's successors had preserved it there. The bishops of Rome took an ambivalent view of Theodosius's actions. On the one hand, they were glad to have the emperor's support. On the other hand, they did not wish for their authority or teaching to rest on imperial decrees. Theodosius's decree reflects the growing power of the bishop of Rome and demonstrates the degree to which the state and the church were becoming intertwined. The decree itself failed to achieve the unity Theodosius desired. Accordingly, in 381 he summoned another ecumenical council in Constantinople. This council again condemned Arianism, which thereafter declined in significance within the empire, although it remained vigorous among the barbarian peoples living along Rome's frontiers.

Ever since Nicaea, councils, with active participation by the emperors, had settled major disagreements in the church. Pope Leo I (r. 440–461) began to assert papal prerogatives. He had sent representatives to the Council of Chalcedon bearing his doctrinal formulation. Leo insisted that as the bishop of Rome, he had full authority to make decisions in doctrinal controversies. The emperor Marcian skillfully steered Leo's "Tome" to acceptance by the council, but to appease many Eastern bishops, who felt that too much authority was being claimed by the pope, the emperor also encouraged the council to assert that the bishop of Constantinople (or patriarch, as he

was often called) was second in eminence and power to the bishop of Rome. Leo, the greatest exponent of "Petrine Primacy" though not its originator, objected strenuously to the Council of Chalcedon's procedures. He disliked the prominent role of the emperor, complained that Eastern bishops had no right to challenge his doctrinal authority, and particularly opposed the elevation of Constantinople's status. Indeed, Leo said, Rome's position derived from its Petrine succession and not from imperial or conciliar decrees.

A generation later Pope Gelasius° I (r. 492–496) sent a sharply worded letter to the emperor Anastasius (r. 491–518), who had intervened in a quarrel between the Catholics and the still-numerous Monophysites. Gelasius protested the emperor's intervention. He told the emperor that the world was governed by the "power" of kings and by the "authority" of priests. Ordinarily, the pope said, the jurisdictions of kings and priests are distinct. In a controversy between them, however, priestly authority must have precedence, because priests are concerned with the salvation of immortal souls, whereas kings rule only mortal bodies. Gelasius was telling the emperor to stay out of theology, but he was implying much more. His opposition of the words *power*—meaning mere police power, the application of brute force—and *authority*—legitimacy, superior right—was of great importance. Gelasius elevated the church, with the pope at its head, above the whole secular regime, with the emperor at its head. Despite his lofty claims, Gelasius had no means of coercing emperors. Moreover, many clergy in the eastern Mediterranean refused to accept the idea that the pope had supreme authority in either doctrine or church government.

The pontificate of Pope Gregory I "the Great" (r. 590–604) exemplifies the position of the papacy as Late Antiquity drew to a close. Gregory was the scion of an old senatorial family. He had risen through several important positions in the Roman administration but then decided to abandon public life, sell off his family's property, and pursue a life of spiritual retreat. Soon, however, the Roman people elected him pope. His reputation for holiness was important to his election, but so too were his impeccable social credentials and wide political connections. Rome was threatened by the Lombards (a barbarian group that had entered Italy in the 560s), the local economy was in a shambles, and relations with the imperial government had been strained. Gregory did not wish to be elected pope, but given his conventional Roman sense of duty and obligation, he had little choice

---

**Gelasius** (juh-LAY-zee-us)

but to accept the office. Immediately he undertook dangerous diplomatic measures to ward off the Lombard threat. He also tried hard to improve relations with the emperor. And he put the local economy on reasonably sound footing. He reorganized the vast patrimonies of the church to place their products and revenues at the disposal of the Romans. In the absence of effective imperial administration in and around Rome, Gregory also began to attend to urban services and amenities, such as streets, aqueducts, and baths.

By 600, then, the bishop of Rome—the pope—viewed himself as the head of a universal, or catholic, church. Many members of the clergy disputed that view. Some simply disagreed with specific papal teachings. Others claimed that Jesus had given his authority equally to all the apostles and not uniquely to Peter and thus to Peter's successors. Emperors, too, rejected papal overreaching. After all, they had always claimed for themselves authority in all aspects of their subjects' lives, religious affairs included. By 600, however, there were no longer emperors in the West, and the Eastern rulers had few means of controlling the bishops of Rome. For their part, the bishops of Rome were gradually focusing their efforts on the western regions of the old Roman world.

The rise of the pope in the church as a whole was paralleled by the rise of bishops throughout the empire. By the last years of the fourth century, various ranking members of the social elite were everywhere entering the clergy and rising to its highest offices. This capture of the elite was the final, decisive factor in the triumph of Christianity.

The clergy was an outlet for the talents and ambitions of the elite. For some time senators had been excluded from military offices and reduced in civilian influence, and decurions were growing dissatisfied with public service. The *episcopal* office (that is, the office of bishop) was desirable to prominent men for many reasons. It was prestigious. Bishops wore distinctive clothing when officiating and were addressed by special titles—traditional Roman marks of respect. They had opportunities to control patronage in the way that prominent Romans always had done. They could intervene on behalf of individuals at the imperial court. They controlled vast wealth, as the generosity of pious Christians put more resources at their disposal. Communities elected their own bishops, and by the middle of the fifth century the dominant person in most towns was the bishop, not a civilian official. The bishops, however, were the same persons, from the same families, who had once dominated local society through civic service. The overall effect of these social changes was dramatic in the long run, but it happened very gradually.

The change from a secular to an ecclesiastical elite in Roman cities even led to alterations of the topography of the cities themselves. The elite usually financed local building projects, such as temples, basilicas, forums, and amphitheaters. Such benefactions declined sharply during the third century because of the uncertainty of the times. The fourth century at first saw little building on private initiative, but then came the construction of Christian cathedrals (a bishop's church, from *cathedra,* the chair or seat of the bishop's authority), episcopal residences, baptisteries, and local parish churches. Such buildings as a rule were not placed in the old city centers, which had associations with the pagan past. Instead, they were placed on the edges of populated districts. In the future these Christian centers served as poles around which ancient towns were reconfigured. The Roman elites built to show pride in their cities and to promote themselves. This did not change in Late Antiquity, but this time the elites were bishops or rich Christians, and the buildings were religious.

## The Rise of Christian Monasticism

For some men and women the call of the Gospel was radical. They yearned to escape the world and everything that might come between them and God. To do so, many of them embraced a new way of life—monasticism. Christian monks and nuns developed a theology and an institution that were among the most creative and long-lived achievements of Late Antiquity.

The practice of rigorous self-denial (*askesis*) was common to several religious and philosophical sects in antiquity—for example, the Pythagoreans and the Stoics—and was well known among the Jews in the time of Christ, as the Essenes show (see page 193). Ascetics believed that if they could conquer the desires of the body, they could commune with the supernatural beings who were greater and purer than humans encumbered by lust for food, drink, knowledge, sex, and adventure. Sometimes ascetic practices were adopted by tightly knit groups, sometimes by heroic solitaries.

The founder of Christian monasticism was a young Egyptian layman, named Anthony (d. 356). At age 19 Anthony gave away all his possessions and took up in the Egyptian desert a life of prayer and renunciation. His spiritual quest became famous, and many disciples flocked to him. Finally he decided to organize these seekers into a very loose community. His followers remained in solitude except for worship and meals. Anthony's form of monasticism is called *eremitic,* from the Greek *heremos,* or "desert," hence the word *hermit.*

## READING SOURCES

## MELANIA THE YOUNGER: THE APPEAL OF MONASTICISM TO WOMEN

*The appeal of monasticism was great for men and women, rich and poor, as the career of Melania (383–438) shows. She came from a wealthy Roman family but renounced her possessions and traveled widely in Italy, North Africa, Egypt, and Palestine, visiting holy men and women. This selection from her biography provides a glimpse of her life.*

Melania was foremost among the Romans of senatorial rank. Wounded by divine love, she had from earliest youth yearned for Christ, and longed for bodily chastity. Her parents, because they were illustrious members of the Roman senate and expected that through her they would have a succession of the family line, forcibly united her in marriage . . . when she was fourteen and her husband, seventeen. [After having two children, Melania persuaded her husband to join her in renouncing the world.] She bridled nature and delivered herself to death daily, demonstrating to everyone that woman is not surpassed by man in anything that pertains to virtue, if her decision is strong. She was by nature a gifted writer and wrote without mistakes in notebooks. She decided for herself how much she should write every day, and how much she should read in the canonical books and in the collections of homilies. Then she would go through the Lives of the fathers as if she were eating dessert. The blessed woman read the Old and New Testaments three or four times a year. The most holy fathers [Egyptian abbots] received her as if she were a man. In truth, she had been detached from the female nature, and had acquired a masculine disposition, or rather, a heavenly one.

Source: Elizabeth A. Clark, ed. and trans., *The Life of Melania the Younger*, vol. 14, *Studies in Women and Religion* (New York: Edwin Mellen Press, 1984), pp. 27–28, 35, 46, 53–54.

---

Pachomius° (290–346) created a more communal form of monastic life. A former Roman soldier, he was baptized a Christian in 313 and retired to the Egyptian desert, where he studied with a hermit. Eventually Pachomius founded a community of ascetics, which before long had grown to thousands of members. Perhaps because of his military background, or because his religious instincts favored order and unity, Pachomius wrote the first Rule, or code for daily living, for a monastic community. He organized most aspects of his community by designing a common life based on routines of private prayer, group worship, and work. By the time of his death, Pachomius led nine male and two female communities. Pachomius's pattern of monasticism is called *cenobitic*°, from the Greek for "common life." People living this common life were called *monks,* and the place where they lived was called a *monastery.* The head of the community was designated the *abbot,* a word meaning "father." In later times the term *abbess,* meaning "mother," was coined for the woman who led a female community, and a community of nuns came to be called a *convent.*

Monasticism spread from Egypt by means of texts such as the *Life of Anthony* (a late antique "bestseller"), collections of the wise sayings of famous desert abbots, and books written by persons who went to Egypt seeking a more perfect life—among whom were several prominent women. (See the box "Reading Sources: Melania the Younger: The Appeal of Monasticism to Women.") One attraction of monasticism among the devout was that it seemed to be a purer form of Christian life, uncorrupted by the wealth, power, and controversy of the hierarchical church. Many pious women embraced monasticism at least partly because they could not be ordained priests. Positions in monasteries, including that of abbess, provided responsible roles for talented women. Monasticism gave women a chance to choose a kind of family life different from the one available in households dominated by fathers and husbands.

Eremitic monasticism was prominent in Palestine and Syria and eventually throughout the Greek-speaking world. Eastern monasticism produced a great legislator in Basil (330–379), whose Rule was the most influential in the Orthodox Church (see page 231). Generally these monks assembled only for weekly worship and otherwise ate, prayed, and worked alone.

Eremitic monasticism arrived in the West in the person of Martin of Tours (336–397). Like Pachomius, Martin was a pagan Roman soldier who, after his military service, embraced both Christianity and asceticism. Even though he was elected bishop of Tours, Martin kept

---

**Pachomius** (pack-OH-mee-us)    **cenobitic** (sen-oh-BIT-ik)

to his rigid life of denial. Martin's form of monasticism influenced many in the western regions of the Roman world but set especially deep roots in Ireland. There the whole organization of the church was based on monasteries. At Kildare the abbess Brigid (d. 523) had more authority than the local bishop.

In the West cenobitic monasticism became the dominant pattern. Benedict of Nursia (480–545) abandoned his legal studies and a potential government career to pursue a life of solitary prayer in a mountain cave east of Rome. Benedict's piety attracted a crowd of followers, and in about 520 he established a monastery at Monte Cassino, 80 miles south of Rome. The Rule he drafted for his new community is marked by shrewd insights into the human personality. It emphasizes the bond of mutual love among the monks and obedience to the abbot. The Rule assigns the abbot wide powers but exhorts him to exercise them gently. The Rule allows monks a reasonable diet and decent, though modest, clothing. Although providing for discipline and punishment, the Rule prefers loving correction. In later centuries Benedict's Rule dominated monastic life.

Eremitic or cenobitic, East or West, monasticism was a conscious alternative and an explicit challenge to the civic world of classical antiquity. Monks and nuns did not seek to give their lives meaning by serving the state or urban communities. They went into remote places to serve God and one another. They sought not to acquire but to abandon. Spiritual wisdom was more important to them than secular learning, and they yearned for acknowledgment of their holiness, not recognition of their social status. Still, monasticism was sometimes controversial. Whereas many people admired and emulated these holy men and women, others disputed their claims to elite spiritual status.

At the dawn of Late Antiquity the church was persecuted and struggling. By the end of the period the church was rich and powerful, its leaders were prominent and prestigious, and in the monasteries, at least, its spiritual fervor was deep. This change was gradual but fundamental.

# THE RISE OF GERMANIC KINGDOMS IN THE WEST, CA. 370–530

THE years from the 370s to the 530s were decisive in the history of the Roman Empire in the West. When this period opened, the dynasty of Valentinian was firmly in control. When it closed, the western provinces of the empire had become a number of Germanic kingdoms, most of which maintained some formal relationship with the eastern Roman Empire. Roman encounters with the barbarians took many different forms, ranging from violent conflict to peaceful accommodation. The key point to understand is that although the barbarians supplanted Roman rule in the West, they did so slowly and often with Roman permission and assistance.

## Invasions and Migrations

Few images of the ancient world are more fixed in the popular imagination than the overrunning of the Roman Empire by hordes of barbarians who ushered in a dark age. The Romans inherited the word *barbarian* from the Greeks, who had divided the world between those who spoke Greek and those who did not. Barbarians were literally babblers, foreigners who spoke an unknown language. After the Romans granted citizenship to virtually everyone in the empire in 212, they adopted a Greek-style differentiation between Romans and barbarians. Technically the latter were merely foreigners, but in practice Romans thought barbarians inferior to themselves.

Individual groups of barbarians did invade the empire in various places at different times, but there was never a single, coordinated barbarian invasion of the Roman world that had well-formulated objectives. The Romans and barbarians did not face one another as declared enemies. Indeed, peaceful encounters outnumbered violent confrontations in the history of Romano-barbarian relations. The Romans had long traded with the barbarian peoples, carried out complicated diplomacy with them, and recruited them into their armies. Barbarian veterans were settled in most provinces of the empire.

If we cannot label one grand movement as "the barbarian invasions," we must also avoid the idea that the barbarians were naturally nomadic and migratory. Holding this view would tempt us to see the entry of the barbarians into the empire as one stage in a long process of human movement. Archaeological evidence collected to date makes it clear that the barbarians were settled agriculturists. They lived in villages, farmed the surrounding country, and raised livestock. If barbarians moved from one place to another, their movement must be explained with reference to specific developments and cannot be attributed to migratory habits.

Who were the barbarians? Linguists classify them as belonging to the Germanic branches of the Indo-European family of languages. The Germanic peoples can be differentiated from the Celts and Slavs with whom they shared much of central and eastern Europe, but apart from some minor linguistic variations, it is difficult to distinguish one Germanic group from another. What are we to make of the profusion of names offered

**Frankish Woman's Necklace**    This sixth-century "choker" necklace consists of brightly colored beads of glass, amber, amethyst, and rock crystal. The Franks were accomplished glassmakers, and this necklace provides some insight into women's taste.    *(Staatliche Museen zu Berlin, Museum für Vor- und Frühgeschichte/Bildarchiv Preussischer Kulturbesitz. Photo: Klaus Goken)*

to us by our sources: Franks, Saxons, Vandals, Visigoths, Ostrogoths, Lombards, Burgundians? The Romans referred to the Germanic peoples as tribes, but that does not mean that they were actually groups of related people. Every Germanic "tribe" was a confederation, and these confederations formed, dissolved, and re-formed many times. For example, the Visigoths who crossed the Danube in 376 included Visigoths proper and more than a half dozen other peoples. The confederations were formed either by powerful leaders who coerced less powerful people to join them or by groups of villages that banded together to protect themselves from aggressive neighbors. As a tribe was forming, its constituent peoples would intermarry and adopt the language, law, and lifestyle of the dominant group.

## Incorporating the Barbarians

The transformation of the western Roman Empire began as a result of an unexpected set of events involving the Huns, nomadic warriors from the central Asian steppes.

After plundering the frontiers of Persia and China for centuries, they turned west in search of booty and tribute. In 374 or 375 they fell on the Ostrogoths, who lived near the Black Sea, and frightened the Visigoths, who requested permission to cross the Danube and enter the empire.

Recent years had been difficult for the empire. Julian had fallen in battle with the Persians in 363, and dynastic quarrels were disturbing the West. The Romans thus delayed responding to the Visigoth request. Fearful of the Huns, the Visigoths crossed the Danube on their own and then asked if they might settle in the Balkans. Reluctantly, Valens° (r. 364–378) agreed but postponed permanent arrangements. While the central government considered how to deal with the Visigoths, local authorities sold them food at exorbitant prices and even traded dog meat for Gothic children, who were then enslaved. When the Visigoths revolted, Valens foolishly marched north to meet them with a small force. The Visigoths defeated his army and killed him at Adrianople in 378.

The history of the Visigoths thus presents an instructive example of Romano-Germanic relations. They had served as auxiliary troops entrusted with defending a stretch of the Danube frontier for a long time when they requested permission to enter the empire in 376. They did not cross the border as part of a massive invasion but because they were sorely threatened. In 382 Theodosius, whom we have met several times already, marched east to pacify the situation. He agreed to grant the Visigoths what they had been demanding: land to settle on and a Roman military title—that is, official status—for their king. A spokesman for Theodosius explained the emperor's motives: "Which is better: To fill Thrace with corpses or with farmers? To fill it with graves or with people? To travel through wilderness or cultivated land? To count those who have perished or those who are ploughing?" For decades barbarians had been settling inside the Roman frontiers, and they had served loyally in the army. Beginning in the fourth century, most high military officers in the Roman world were barbarians. The only peculiarity about the Visigoths' situation was that never before had the Romans admitted a whole people.

For about thirty years the Visigoths struggled to improve the terms of their settlements in the Balkans. Alaric°, the Visigothic king after 395, grew tired of unfulfilled promises and forced matters by attacking Italy. In 410 the Visigoths sacked Rome. The taking of the city for the first time in eight hundred years shocked the entire Roman world and has loomed large for centuries in people's ideas about the "fall" of the Roman Empire. Ac-

**Valens** (VAY-lenz)    **Alaric** (AL-uh-rik)

tually it was a ploy by Alaric to improve the terms of his already official status. Alaric died in 410, and his brother led the Visigoths north into southern Gaul. For good measure the new Visigothic king captured the Western emperor's sister, Galla Placidia, and forced her to marry him. However objectionable this act must seem, the Visigoths viewed it as a further demonstration of their loyalty to Rome and their determination to effect a satisfactory new treaty.

In 418 the Roman government gave in. A treaty permitted the Visigoths to settle in southern Gaul, with Toulouse as their base of operations. They were assigned the task of protecting the area from marauding bands of brigands. In return for their service, the Visigoths were given land allotments and a portion of Roman tax receipts as pay.

The Visigoths' treaty with Rome made theirs the first Germanic kingdom on Roman soil. From 418 to 451 the Visigoths' king, Theodoric I, served Rome loyally and earned the respect of the Gallo-Roman aristocrats among whom he ruled. Between 466 and 484 the Visigothic kingdom in Gaul reached its high point and continued to receive official recognition from Roman rulers. Southern Gaul, one of Rome's oldest provinces, gradually passed from the hands of the Roman bureaucracy and the local nobility into the control of the Visigoths. Nevertheless, from Constantine's first treaty with the Visigoths through the continuing recognition by the Romans of Visigothic kings, it was Roman policy more than Visigothic policy that determined the accommodation of this first Germanic kingdom within the framework of the western Roman Empire.

While they were dealing with the Visigoths, the Roman authorities realized that the Huns, who had settled in the Danube basin after driving the Visigoths into the empire, were a serious menace. They raided the Balkans, preyed on trade routes that crossed the region, and demanded tribute from the Eastern emperor. In 434 the fearsome warrior Attila murdered his brother and became sole ruler of the Huns. In return for a huge imperial subsidy, he agreed to cease raiding the Balkans. At the same time, a Roman general in Gaul concluded an alliance with the Huns in an attempt to use them to check the expansion of the Burgundians, an allied people who lived in the central Rhineland.

Together Attila and the Romans routed the Burgundians, but Attila realized the weakness of the Roman position in the West. He attacked Gaul in 451 and was stopped only by a combined effort of Romans, Visigoths, Burgundians, and Franks. Attila turned to Italy in 452, even approaching Rome, where Pope Leo I, not the emperor, convinced or bribed him to withdraw. Attila died in 454, and before another year was out, the short-lived Hunnic kingdom, largely Attila's personal creation, had vanished. (See the box "Global Encounters: Two Views of the Huns.")

## More Kingdoms: The End of Direct Roman Rule in the West

To meet threats in Gaul and elsewhere, the Romans had begun pulling troops out of Britain in the fourth century and abandoned the island to its own defense in 410. Thereafter, raiding parties from Scotland and Ireland, as well as seaborne attackers—called "Saxons" by contemporaries because some of them came from Saxony in northern Germany—ravaged Britain. The British continually appealed to the military authorities in Gaul for aid, but to no avail. Between 450 and 600 much of southern and eastern Britain was taken over by diverse peoples whom we call the "Anglo-Saxons." The newcomers jostled for position with the Celtic Britons, who were increasingly confined to the north and west of the island. Amid these struggles was born the legend of King Arthur, a Briton who defended his people and led them to victory. Gradually several small kingdoms emerged. Although Britain retained contacts with Gaul, the island had virtually no Roman political or institutional inheritance.

Valentinian III (r. 425–455) was born in 419 and became emperor of the West as a 6-year-old. Even when he came of age, his court was weakened by factional strife, and his regime was dominated by military men. After Valentinian, the western empire saw a succession of nonentities, the last of whom was deposed by Odoacer°, a Germanic general, in 476. Ruling in Italy, Odoacer simply sent the imperial regalia to Constantinople and declared that the West no longer needed an emperor. This is all that happened in 476, the traditional date for the "fall" of the Roman Empire.

After the vast coalition defeated the Huns in Gaul in 451, the remaining Roman authorities in the Paris region discovered that the Visigoths were expanding north of the Loire River into central Gaul. To check this advance, the Roman commander in Paris forged an alliance with the Franks. The Franks, long Roman allies, had been expanding their settlements from the mouth of the Rhine southward across modern Holland and Belgium since the third century.

The fortunes of the Frankish kingdom, indeed of all of Gaul, rested with Clovis. He became king of one group of Franks in 481 and spent the years until his death in 511 subjecting all the other bands of Franks to his rule. He

---

**Odoacer** (OH-doe-ace-er)

# Two Views of the Huns

The dread and disgust inspired by the Huns is well captured in the first passage, from the Roman historian Ammianus Marcellinus. The second passage, from a surviving fragment of the history of Priscus, shows the Huns in quite a different light.

**(a)**

From the moment of their birth they make deep gashes in their children's cheeks, so that when in due course hair appears its growth is checked by the wrinkled scars; as they grow older this gives them the unlovely appearance of beardless eunuchs. They have squat bodies, strong limbs, and thick necks, and are so prodigiously ugly and bent that they might be two-legged animals. Their shape, however disagreeable, is human. They have no use for seasoned food, but live on the roots of wild plants and the half-raw flesh of any animal, which they warm a little by placing it between their thighs and the backs of their horses. They have no buildings to shelter them. They wear garments of linen or of the skins of field-mice stitched together. Once they have put their necks into some dingy shirt they never take it off or change it until it rots and falls to pieces. They have round caps of fur on their heads, and protect their hairy legs with goatskins. They are ill-fitted to fight on foot, and remain glued to their horses, hardy but ugly beasts, on which they sometimes sit like women to perform their everyday business and they even bow forward over their beasts' narrow necks to enjoy a deep and dreamy sleep.

**(b)**

[The Roman ambassadors] came upon a very large village in which the dwelling of Attila was said to be more notable than those elsewhere. It had been fitted together with highly polished timbers and encircled with a wooden palisade, conceived not for safety but for beauty. Next to the king's dwelling that of Onegisus [chief minister to Attila] was outstanding, and it also had a circuit of timbers but was not embellished with towers in the same way as Attila's. Not far from the enclosure was a large bath. . . . Maidens came to meet Attila as he entered this village, advancing before him in rows under fine white linen cloths stretched out to such a length that under each cloth, which was held up by the hands of the women along either side, seven or even more girls walked. There were many such formations of women under the linen cloths, and they sang Scythian songs. When he [Attila] came near the house of Onegisus, the wife of Onegisus came out with a host of servants, some bearing dainties and others wine, greeted him and asked him to partake of the food which she had brought for him with friendly hospitality. To gratify the wife of his intimate friend, he ate sitting on his horse, the barbarians accompanying him having raised the silver platter up to him. Having also tasted the wine, he went on to the palace, which was higher than the other houses and situated on a high place.

## QUESTIONS

1. How do these two accounts differ in tone, emphasis, and details?

2. Leaving aside the question of whether these accounts are true, what impressions do you think they would have made on the Romans? What impressions were they intended to make?

3. How do the public rituals of the Huns compare with those of the Romans?

Sources: Excerpt (a): Ammianus Marcellinus, *The Later Roman Empire* (A.D. *354–378*), 31.2, ed. and trans. Walter Hamilton (Harmondsworth, U.K.: Penguin, 1986), pp. 411–412. Excerpt (b): Priscus, Fragment 8, in C. D. Gordon, *The Age of Attila: Fifth-Century Byzantium and the Barbarians* (Ann Arbor: University of Michigan Press, 1961), pp. 84–85.

---

gained the allegiance of the Frankish people by leading them to constant military victories that brought territorial gains, plunder, and tribute. The greatest of Clovis's successes came in 507, when he defeated the Visigoths and drove them over the Pyrenees into Spain.

Clovis was popular, not only with the Franks but also with the Gallo-Roman population, for three reasons. First, Clovis and the Romans had common enemies: Germanic peoples still living beyond the Rhine and pirates who raided the coast of Gaul. Second, whereas most of the Germanic peoples were Arian Christians, the majority of the Franks passed directly from paganism to Catholicism. Thus Clovis and the Gallo-Romans had a shared faith that permitted Clovis to portray his war against the Visigoths as a kind of crusade against heresy. Third, Clovis eagerly sought from Constantinople formal recognition

**Map 7.3   The Germanic Kingdoms, ca. 530**   By 530 the western provinces of the Roman Empire (compare Map 6.1 on page 176) had evolved into Germanic kingdoms. Just as Roman provincial boundaries had changed numerous times, the existence and extent of Germanic kingdoms were also impermanent.

and titles, appeared publicly in the dress of a Roman official, and practiced such imperial rituals as distributing gold coins while riding through crowds. The Frankish kingdom under Clovis's family—called "Merovingian°," from the name of one of his semilegendary ancestors—became the most successful of all the Germanic realms.

Several early Germanic kingdoms were short-lived. The Burgundian kingdom, which had once prompted the Romans to ally with the Huns, was swallowed up by the Franks in the 530s. The Vandals, who crossed the Rhine in 406 and headed for Spain, crossed to North Africa in 429 (see Map 7.3). They were ardent Arians, who persecuted the Catholic population. They refused imperial offers of a treaty on terms similar to those accepted by other Germanic peoples. And they constantly plundered the islands of the western Mediterranean and the Italian coast, even sacking Rome in 455. Roman forces from Constantinople eliminated the Vandals in 534.

The Ostrogoths, allies who had been living in Pannonia since the 370s as subjects of the Huns, began to pose a threat to the eastern empire after Attila's death. In 493 the emperor decided to send them to Italy to remove Odoacer, who had earned the displeasure of the Roman administration by laying hands on the sentimentally significant land of Italy—and doing so on his own initiative instead of the emperor's directive. The government at Constantinople was familiar with the Ostrogoths' king, Theodoric, because he had been a hostage there for several years. The emperor also wished to remove the Ostrogoths from the Danube basin. Sending Theodoric to Italy seemed like a way to solve two problems simultaneously.

Theodoric ousted Odoacer quickly enough and set up his capital in Ravenna°, the swamp-surrounded and virtually impregnable city that had sheltered the imperial administration for much of the fifth century. Through the force of his personality, and by a series of marriage

---

**Merovingian** (mehr-oh-VIN-jun)

**Ravenna** (rah-VEN-nuh)

**Amalasuntha, Daughter of Theodoric**    This ivory plaque (ca. 530) depicts Amalasuntha in the way that Roman consuls and emperors had long been depicted on their assumption of office. Since the late fifth century empresses had been depicted this way, too. Amalasuntha projects an image of legitimacy. Compare her appearance with that of Theodora on page 226.    *(Kunsthistorisches Museum, Vienna)*

alliances, Theodoric became the dominant ruler in western Europe. In Italy he promoted peace, stability, and good government. Still, Theodoric had two strikes against him. First, he and his people were Arians. Second, although the population of Italy was accustomed to having an imperial court dominated by barbarians and to having Germanic military men in Gaul as the real powers in the state, they had never been directly ruled by a barbarian, and some of them could not accept Theodoric. By the 520s Theodoric grew increasingly suspicious and dictatorial.

When Theodoric died, his daughter Amalasuntha (498–535) served as regent for her son Athalaric from 526 to 534 and then briefly served as queen. A contemporary said that she was beautiful and well educated. Clearly she favored the Romans in Italy and promoted cultural fusion. For this she evoked the keen hatred of the staunch Goths, who deposed and then murdered her. Her death was Justinian's pretext to launch the Gothic Wars (535–554), which put an end to the Ostrogothic kingdom.

By the 530s the western Roman Empire had vanished, the conclusion of a process initiated by the entry of the Visigoths into the Balkans in 376. Of all the peoples who had contested for a share of Rome's legacy, only the Franks in Gaul, the Visigoths in Spain, and the Anglo-Saxons in Britain had created durable political entities. Most of two prefectures with their several dozen provinces had turned into a small number of kingdoms (see Map 7.3).

Why did the Roman government perish in the West? Beginning with Diocletian, Rome's best rulers were resident in and concerned mainly about the East. The Visigoths and other peoples were settled in their own kingdoms on Roman soil instead of being enrolled in and dispersed among Roman army units. Also during Diocletian's rule, the army was increasingly Germanized, and Germanic military men gained high offices in the state. Those leaders often dominated imperial courts and negotiated the series of treaties that submitted former provinces to barbarian peoples. Provincial elites had long been accustomed to having prominent Germans in their midst. The new situation was not unusual to them. Churchmen readily embraced the Catholic Franks and tolerated Arians, such as the Visigoths, when they promoted peace and good government without abusing the Catholic population.

## Old and New in the West

The Germanic kingdoms had a great deal in common with one another and very much resembled the late Roman Empire, which had been their common tutor. Each realm was led by a king who usually appeared in two distinct guises. To his people, the king was the military leader. The essential bond of unity among each Germanic people was loyalty to the leader, who repaid his followers in booty, tribute, land, legal protection, and military security. To the Romans, the king appeared as an ally and magistrate. Almost all Germanic kings bore Roman titles such as *consul* or *patrician,* and in these officially conferred titles resided the authority necessary to govern Roman populations. The kings also succeeded to a long line of Germanic Masters of the Soldiers, the title of the highest military officers in a prefecture. Each monarchy was led by a dynasty—for example, the Merovingians among the Franks—that was pre-eminent in wealth and possessed a sacral aura not unlike that of the Roman emperors.

The most common local officials were counts, a combined civilian-military position that made its first appearance in the fifth century. Initially a direct representative of the emperor, a count had financial, judicial, and military responsibilities. Local notables, usually great landowners, initially resented counts but gradually aspired to the office. Kings were careful to promote important locals, both Romans and their own people, to the office of count.

Local administration remained based in cities and towns. Taxes continued to be paid to royal governments throughout the sixth century. Provincial populations did not find this policy odd or unjust. Their taxes had always gone primarily to pay for the Roman military establishment, and the monarchies were the heirs of that establishment. Latin persisted as the language of administration. Until the end of Late Antiquity, notaries continued to draw up wills, records of land transactions, and legal documents of all kinds. Law codes issued by the Germanic kingdoms were largely adaptations of Roman provincial law. In other words, the legal conditions under which most people lived stayed pretty much the same. In sum, people's daily lives changed surprisingly little as a result of the replacement of Roman provinces by Germanic kingdoms.

# THE ROMAN EMPIRE IN THE EAST, 395–565

HE creation of the tetrarchy at the end of the third century had separated the eastern and western halves of the Roman Empire administratively. In theory, there was only one empire, ruled by one senior emperor, but in practice the Eastern and Western courts followed different policies in many areas,

notably in their relations with the Germanic peoples. Fundamental cultural differences also distinguished East from West. The East was more populous, more heavily urbanized, and more prosperous. The eastern Mediterranean was Greek in culture and livelier intellectually than the West. From Diocletian in the third century to Justinian in the sixth, the eastern Roman Empire evolved slowly along the path marked out by its first great reformers. Moreover, the eastern empire survived as the western empire was being parceled out into kingdoms.

## Constantinople and Its Rulers

Constantius II (r. 337–361), Constantine's son and his successor in the East, began making Constantinople a truly imperial city. He gave "New Rome" its own senate and urban magistrates, placing the city on an equal constitutional footing with Rome. Constantinople did not have an ancient aristocracy, so Constantius had to create a senatorial order. This he did by recruiting some Romans and promoting prominent and cultivated persons from cities in the eastern half of the empire, thereby forging bonds between the capital and its hinterland. Constantius and his successors also built palaces, public buildings, and churches to give the city a truly imperial character (see Map 7.4).

With the exception of the founder, the ablest members of the dynasty of Valentinian ruled in the East. The greatest of these was Theodosius II (r. 408–450), who enjoyed the longest imperial reign in Roman history. Through skillful diplomacy and the occasional application of force, he managed to keep the eastern empire free of serious Germanic incursions and the Persians at bay in Mesopotamia. To protect his capital on the landward side, he built massive walls, whose ruins are impressive even today. He promoted learning in the city and both added and beautified important buildings. Theodosius and his family made the new capital a real intellectual center.

Born in 401, Theodosius ascended the throne as a child. Throughout his life the two greatest influences on him were his sister, Pulcheria (399–453), and his wife, Athenais-Eudoxia (ca. 400–460). Theodosius's moderate religious policy owed much to his wife, while his deep personal piety seems attributable to his sister. Pulcheria achieved the appointment and dismissal of imperial officers, guided foreign policy, and patronized scholars and churchmen. Only rarely do surviving sources permit us to observe the activities of imperial women. The cases of Pulcheria and Eudoxia hint at how much we do not know.

**Map 7.4   Constantinople in Late Antiquity**   Protected by the sea, the Golden Horn, and its massive landward walls, Constantine's new city was an impregnable fortress for a thousand years. Note how the city was equipped with palaces, forums, wide thoroughfares, and other urban amenities.   *(Source: The Cambridge Illustrated History of THE MIDDLE AGES, edited by Robert Fossier, translated by Janet Sondheimer. Copyright © 1989. Used by permission of Cambridge University Press.)*

Theodosius's greatest achievement was his law code of 438. The most comprehensive collection of Roman law yet produced, this code brought together all Roman laws issued since Constantine and arranged them in systematic fashion. The principal Germanic kingdoms were established just after the Theodosian code was issued. From this text, and from the Roman institutional structures that employed it, the barbarians were taught the rule of law and regulations for the conduct of daily affairs.

## The Emperor Justinian (r. 527–565)

After Theodosius II died in 450, the eastern empire endured seventy-seven years of rule by military men who lacked the culture, vision, or administrative capacity of their predecessors. But they preserved the empire and kept its government functioning. It was from these rough soldiers that Justinian emerged to become the greatest ruler of Late Antiquity, one of the greatest of all Rome's

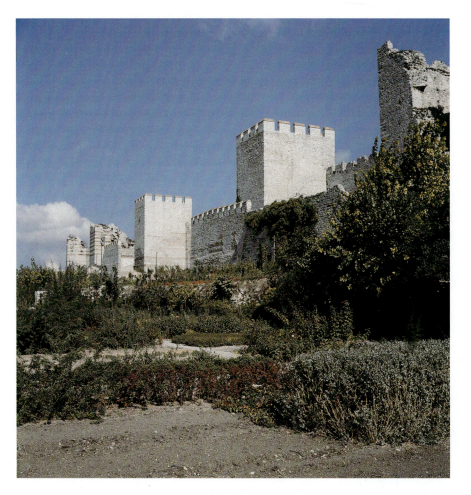

**Theodosian Walls**    By 413 Theodosius II had erected a massive set of walls, extending more than four miles, to protect Constantinople on the landward side. The wall system consisted of a double set of walls with brick facings and rubble-filled interiors. The main walls (shown here) were about 35 feet high with towers about every 240 feet.    *(Sonia Halliday Photographs)*

emperors. (See the feature "Weighing the Evidence: The Ravenna Mosaics" on pages 236–237.)

Justinian was born in an Illyrian village (Croatia, today), entered the army, and secured high office under his illiterate uncle Justin, who had likewise risen from the peasantry to the imperial office (r. 518–527). Despite growing up in rural military camps, Justinian showed a wide range of interests and abilities. He surrounded himself with remarkable people and gave them considerable latitude. In 525 he flouted convention by marrying the actress Theodora (ca. 497–548). A woman of intelligence, imagination, and great courage, Theodora was one of Justinian's key advisers. Contemporaries believed that she guided the emperor's religious policy. She certainly spent lavishly on charitable activities, not least on homes for former prostitutes. Justinian also identified and promoted such previously obscure figures as the gifted general Belisarius°, the administrative genius

John the Cappadocian, and the greatest legal mind of the age, Tribonian°. He entrusted two mathematicians, Anthemius° of Tralles and Isidore of Miletus, with the task of designing the Church of Hagia Sophia, which remains his principal monument.

Almost immediately on assuming the throne, Justinian put John the Cappadocian to work reforming an administration that had been little altered in two centuries despite vast changes in the scope of the empire. John worked particularly to secure tighter control of provincial administrators, to ensure a steady flow of tax revenue, and to eliminate official corruption. Tribonian and a commission were assigned the task of producing the first comprehensive collection of Roman law since that of Theodosius II in 438. Between 529 and 533 Justinian's code was issued in three parts. The *Code* was a systematically organized collection of all imperial legislation. The

---

**Belisarius** (bel-uh-SAR-ee-us)

**Tribonian** (tree-BONE-ee-un)
**Anthemius** (an-THEE-mee-us)

**Theodora**    This magnificent sixth-century mosaic from Ravenna (it is one of a pair; see page 237) depicts the empress Theodora in all her power and majesty.    *(Scala/Art Resource, NY)*

*Digest* was a collection of the writings of the classical Roman jurists, the legal philosophers of the Early Empire. The *Institutes* was a textbook for law students. (See the box "Reading Sources: Basic Principles of Roman Law.") Justinian's code is the most influential legal collection in human history. It summarizes a thousand years of legal work, remained valid in the eastern empire until 1453, and has subsequently influenced almost every legal system in the modern world.

Not long after undertaking his legal and administrative reforms, Justinian launched an ambitious attempt to reunite the empire by reconquering its lost western provinces. Belisarius retook Africa from the Vandals and Italy from the Ostrogoths. Justinian also landed an army in Spain in an unsuccessful attempt to wrest Iberia from the Visigoths.

Justinian's ability to sustain major campaigns in the West was limited by the need to ward off constant threats in the East. The empire faced new enemies—Bulgars and Slavs—in the Balkans and a resurgent old foe—the Persians—in Mesopotamia. Costly treaties and humiliating subsidies bought a string of cease-fires but no definitive settlements in these areas. The emperor's campaigns were so expensive that his administrative reforms wound up looking like contrivances to make more money for the emperor to waste. In 532 violent mobs coursed through the streets of Constantinople demanding the dismissal of John the Cappadocian and other imperial agents. Justinian almost fled, but Theodora persuaded him to put down the riot. In 542 the Mediterranean world was visited by the most devastating plague in centuries, one more blow to the empire.

Justinian's religious policy also met with sharp opposition. A genuinely pious man, Justinian legislated frequently on behalf of the church and, along with Theodora, practiced generous charitable benefactions. Still, by both

READING
SOURCES
# BASIC PRINCIPLES OF ROMAN LAW

*Roman law is distinguished not only by its particular rules but also by its approach to the subject of law as a whole. These words are from the beginning of Justinian's Institutes, his textbook for law students.*

Justice is an unswerving and perpetual determination to acknowledge all men's rights. Learning in the law entails knowledge of God and man, and mastery of the difference between justice and injustice. . . . The commandments of the law are these: live honorably; harm nobody; give everyone his due. There are two aspects to the subject: public and private. Public law is concerned with the organization of the Roman state, while private is about the well-being of individuals. [Private law] has three parts, in that it is derived from the law of nature, of all peoples, or of the state. The law of nature is the law instilled by nature in all creatures. It is not merely for mankind but for all creatures of the sky, earth and sea. From it comes intercourse between male and female, which we call marriage; also the bearing and bringing up of children. Observation shows that other animals also acknowledge its force. The law of all peoples and the law of the state are distinguished as follows. All peoples with laws and customs apply law which is partly theirs alone and partly shared by all mankind. The law which each people makes for itself is special to its own state. It is called "state law," the law peculiar to that state. But the law which natural reason makes for all mankind is applied the same everywhere. It is called the "law of all peoples" because it is common to every nation. The law of the Roman people is also partly its own and partly common to all mankind. . . . The name of a particular state, Athens for example, is used to identify its state law. Similarly we refer to the law of the Roman people as the Roman state law. By contrast, the law of all peoples is common to all mankind. The reality of the human condition led the peoples of the world to introduce certain institutions. Wars broke out. People were captured and made slaves contrary to the law of nature. By the law of nature all men were initially born free. Nearly all the contracts come from this law of all peoples: sale, hire, partnership, deposit, loan, and many others. Next, our law is either written or unwritten. . . . Written law includes acts, plebeian statutes, resolutions of the senate, imperial pronouncements, magistrates' edicts, and answers given by jurists. . . . Law comes into being without writing when a rule is approved by use. Long-standing custom founded on the consent of those who follow it is just like legislation. . . . The law of nature, which is observed uniformly by all peoples, is sanctioned by divine providence and lasts forever, strong and unchangeable. The law which each state establishes for itself is often changed either by tacit consent of the people or by later legislation.

Source: Peter Birks and Grant McLeod, ed. and trans., *Justinian's Institutes*, 1.1–2, pp. 37–39. Cornell University Press, 1987. Reprinted by permission of the publisher.

**For additional information on this topic, go to college.hmco.com/students.**

personal conviction and a sense of official duty, Justinian desired religious unity. Justinian was mildly Monophysite, and his wife was enthusiastically so. Justinian tried again and again to find a compromise that would bring all parties together. His church council of 553 assembled amid high hopes, but his proposed doctrinal compromises alienated the clergy in Syria, Egypt, and Rome.

To create a monument equal to his lofty vision of the empire, Justinian sought out Anthemius and Isidore. He charged the two great mathematicians to design a church that would represent the place where heaven and earth touched. Regular meetings in this place of the emperor, the patriarch, and the people gave repeated symbolic confirmation of the proper ordering of the state. There is no evidence that Justinian dictated the form of his church—the Church of Hagia Sophia°—but the fact that he did not turn to any of the city's regular builders suggests that he was not looking for a traditional basilica.

Hagia Sophia was the largest Christian church until the construction of Saint Peter's in Rome (1503–1614). The building begins with a square just over 100 feet on a

**Hagia Sophia** (AYE-yuh so-FEE-yuh)

**Hagia Sophia, Exterior View**    The column-like "minarets" (towers from which faithful Muslims were called to prayer, erected by the Turks after their capture of the city in 1453) are the only significant change in the appearance of Justinian's massive church. Its weighty but austere exterior belies the grace and elegance of its interior space (see page 202).    *(David Lomax/Robert Harding Picture Library)*

side, 70 feet above which are four great arches. Two of the arches are solid and form the nave walls of the church; the other two give way to semicircular continuations of the nave. Above the main square is a dome that seems to float on the blaze of light that pours through its windows. The inside is a riot of color, achieved by marble fittings in almost every imaginable hue and by the mysterious play of light and shadow. The effect of the whole is disorienting. The space in most basilicas is ordered, controlled, elegant. The space in Hagia Sophia is horizontal and vertical, straight and curved, square and round. The inside is by turns dark and light, purple and green, red and blue. It is indeed as if one has entered a realm that is anchored to this world but gives access to another.

It is appropriate that in assessing his church, Justinian should have looked backward to Solomon, the Hebrew king who built Jerusalem's Temple. In almost all respects Justinian was a traditional, backward-looking ruler. His concern for the administrative minutiae of his empire would have made perfect sense to Diocletian. His combination of military and diplomatic initiatives would have been appreciated by Theodosius I, whose namesake, Theodosius II, would have admired Justinian's legal code. In his religious policies, especially his quest for unity, Justinian drew from a deep well of imperial precedent. Even in his attempt to restore direct rule in Rome's former western provinces, Justinian showed himself a traditionalist.

# SOCIETY AND CULTURE IN LATE ANTIQUITY

DURING these centuries of the ascendancy of the eastern Roman Empire, and the splintering of the western, the daily lives of men and women of every social class changed relatively little in terms of power relationships and economic opportunities. Nevertheless, provincial elites, members of the clergy, and barbarians gained unprecedented influence. Ordinary farmers, the overwhelming majority of the population, experienced changes in their legal status but not in their material well-being. Secular intellectual life lost most of its vitality, but a vibrant Christian culture flourished in the writings of the Church Fathers. Christianity added yet another element to the diversity that always characterized the Roman world.

## Social Hierarchies and Realities

Roman society had long been hierarchical, and from Republican times Rome had been governed by a hereditary class. Although the members of this class affected a style of life that set them apart, they were never a closed caste. First, they did not reproduce themselves very effectively. About two-thirds of the Roman aristocracy was replaced every century—a typical pattern in premodern societies. This turnover created significant opportunities for social mobility. Second, just as the empire had been born in a social transformation that brought the Italian aristocracy into the Roman governing class, so Late Antiquity was characterized by a transformation that brought provincial elites and barbarians into the framework of power. Paradoxically, social change was always masked as social continuity, because when new men reached the top, they tried to embrace the culture and values of those whom they had replaced.

Three ideals guided the lives of elite men: *otium, amicitia,* and *officium. Otium,* "leisure," meant that the only life worth living was one of withdrawal in which the finer things in life—literature especially—could be cultivated. *Amicitia,* "friendship," implied several things. It could mean the kinds of literary contacts that the thousands of surviving letters from Late Antiquity reveal. Friendship also could mean patronage. The doorstep of every noble household was crowded every morning with hangers-on who awaited their patron's small offerings and any commands as to how they might do his will. *Officium,* "duty," was the sense of civic obligation that Roman rulers communicated to the provincial upper classes.

Aristocrats governed in both public and private ways, which are almost impossible to differentiate. Though gradually excluded from key military and administrative posts, nobles did not lose their influence. They used their wealth to win or reward followers, bribe officials, and buy verdicts. In towns decurions controlled local market privileges, building trades, police forces, fire brigades, and charitable associations. Their public and private means of persuasion and intimidation were immense. In the West, in the growing absence of an imperial administration, Roman public power did not so much "decline and fall" as find itself privatized and localized. Patronage and clientage in Roman society had a benevolent dimension, but they also revealed the raw realities of power.

In Roman society power was everything, and those who lacked power were considered "poor," regardless of their financial status. On this reckoning, much of the urban population was poor because they lacked access to the official means of coercion and security that the notables enjoyed. Merchants, artisans, teachers, and others were always vulnerable because their social, political, or economic positions could change at a moment's notice. They lacked the influence to protect themselves.

Most citizens of the late antique world can be classed as farmers, but this categorization is misleading because it lumps together the greatest landowners and the poorest peasants. Late Antiquity saw a trend in the countryside that continued into the Middle Ages: freedom and slavery declined simultaneously. Many small, independent farmers, probably people who had long been the clients of local grandees, handed over their possessions—*commended* them is the technical term—and received back the use of them in return for annual rents in money or in kind. They became *coloni,* "tenants." Their patrons promised to protect them from lawsuits and from severe economic hardship. More and more, these coloni were bound to their places of residence and forced to perform services or pay fees that marked their status as less than fully free. At the same time, many landlords who could no longer afford to house, feed, and equip slaves gave them their freedom and elevated them to the status of coloni. Probably the day-to-day lives of the great mass of the rural population and their position at the bottom of the social hierarchy changed very little.

Women's lives are not as well known to us as men's. "Nature produced women for this very purpose," says a Roman legal text, "that they might bear children and this is their greatest desire." Ancient philosophy held that women were intellectually inferior to men, science said they were physically weaker, and law maintained that they were naturally dependent. In the Roman world women could not enter professions, and they had limited rights in legal matters. Christianity offered women opposing models. There was Eve, the eternal temptress through whom sin had fallen on humanity, and then there was Mary, the virginal mother of God. The Bible also presented readers with powerful, active women, such as Deborah and Ruth, and loyal, steadfast ones, such as Jesus's female disciples. Amid this varied popular and learned opinion, we can still detect some possibilities for independent and influential activity on the part of women.

Girls usually did not choose their marriage partners. Betrothals could take place as early as age 7 and lawful marriages at 12. Most marriages took place when the girl was around 16; husbands were several years older. A daughter could reject her father's choice only if the intended man was unworthy in status and behavior. Women could inherit property from their fathers and retained some control over their marital dowries. Divorce was possible but only in restricted cases. A divorced woman who had lost the financial security provided by her husband and father was at a distinct disadvantage legally and economically unless she had great wealth.

Christianity brought some interesting changes in marriage practices. Since the new faith prized virginity and celibacy, women now had the option of declining marriage. The church at Antioch supported three thousand virgins and widows. Christian writers tried to attract women to the celibate life by emphasizing that housework was drudgery. Christianity required both men and women to be faithful in marriage, whereas Roman custom had permitted men, but not women, to have lovers, prostitutes, and concubines. Christianity increased the number of days when men and women had to abstain from sex. Ancient cultures often prohibited sexual intercourse during menstruation and pregnancy, but Christianity added Sundays and many feast days as forbidden times. Further, Christianity disapproved of divorce, which may have accorded women greater financial and social security, although at the cost of staying with abusive or unloved husbands.

Traditionally women were not permitted to teach in the ancient world, although we do hear of women teachers such as Hypatia of Alexandria (355–415), renowned for her knowledge of philosophy and mathematics. Some Christian women, such as Melania, were formidably learned. (See the box "Reading Sources: Melania the Younger: The Appeal of Monasticism to Women" on page 216.) Until at least the sixth century the Christian church had deaconesses who had important responsibilities in the in-struction of women and girls. Medical knowledge was often the preserve of women, particularly in areas such as childbirth, sexual problems, and "female complaints."

Christianity also affected daily life. Churchmen were concerned that women not be seen as sex objects. They told women to clothe their flesh, veil their hair, and use jewelry and cosmetics in moderation. Pious women no longer used public baths and latrines. Male or female, Christians thought and lived in distinctive new ways. All Christians were sinners, and so all were equal in God's eyes and equally in need of God's grace. Neither birth, wealth, nor status was supposed to matter in this democracy of sin. Theological equality did not, however, translate into social equality.

The church also introduced some new status distinctions. Holiness became a badge of honor, and holy men and women became Late Antiquity's greatest celebrities. After their death they were venerated as saints. Sanctuaries were dedicated to them, and people made pilgrimages to their tombs to pray and seek healing from physical and spiritual ailments. Miracle stories became popular. Thus in some ways Christianity produced a society the likes of which the ancient world had never known, a society in which the living and the dead jockeyed for a place in a hierarchy that was at once earthly and celestial. But in other ways Christianity reoriented traditional Roman patron-client relations so that client sinners in this world were linked to sanctified patrons in heaven.

## The Quest for a Catholic Tradition

By the middle of the fifth century the Nicene Creed, first spelled out in 325, had taken definitive shape; it is still recited regularly in many Christian churches. With the Council of Nicaea we see the first clear evidence that people were striving for a *catholic* form of Christianity. This Greek word means "universal." Strictly speaking, catholic Christianity would be the one form professed by all believers. A fifth-century writer said that the catholic faith was the one believed "everywhere, all the time, by everyone." It is no accident that the Catholic Church grew up in a Roman world steeped in ideas of universality. The most deeply held tenet of Roman ideology was that Rome's mission was to civilize the world and bend it to Roman ways.

One intriguing development in Late Antiquity is the emergence of several Christian communities claiming fidelity to a universal, or catholic, tradition. The Latin Christian church in the West clung tightly to the doctrinal formulations of Nicaea and Chalcedon and took its

**Sarcophagus of Junius Bassus**    Junius Bassus, prefect of Rome, died in 359 and was laid to rest in this splendid sarcophagus (from the Greek "body eater"). Three points are important: First, as members of the Roman elite became Christian, they could afford to employ the finest craftsmen. Second, as Christianity became legal, it could search for artistic expression. Third, these Old and New Testament scenes proclaim Christ's divinity but, in an age of intense theological quarrels, glide over his humanity.    *(Hirmer Verlag München)*

bearings from Latin church writers. In the eastern Mediterranean writers tended to use the word *Orthodox,* which means "right believing" but also carries clear implications of catholicism, or "universality." The Orthodox Church centered primarily on the emperors and patriarchs, used Greek, and followed Greek Christian writers. The Coptic Church in Egypt was Monophysite, followed the teachings of the patriarchs of Alexandria, and used the Coptic language. The Jacobite Church, a mildly Monophysite, Syriac-speaking group, was originally strong in Syria, from which it spread to Mesopotamia and beyond. Each of these churches produced a literature, an art, and a way of life that marked its members as a distinct community. These traditions did not reflect the emergence of something new in Late Antiquity so much as a Christian reinterpretation of very old cultures and ideals. Each of these traditions exists today.

Christianity drew much from the pagan and Jewish environments within which it grew, but its fundamental inspiration was the collection of writings called in modern times the Bible. In antiquity this material was called *ta hagia biblia* or *sacra biblia,* meaning "the holy books."

It was understood to be a collection of sacred writings, and the individual items in that collection had different meanings. From the second century, Christian writers began trying to define a canon, a definitive list of genuine Old and New Testament scriptures. It was widely recognized that without an official, standardized set of Christian writings, there could be no uniformity of Christian belief. This process of determining authentic Scripture was not completed until the middle of the fifth century.

While the search was underway for an authoritative list of books, it was also necessary to try to get uniform versions of the books that were being pronounced canonical. The Greek East used the Greek version of the Old Testament and the Greek New Testament. But that version was unsuitable in the West, where Latin was the principal tongue. Late in the fourth century Pope Damasus° commissioned Jerome (331–420), a man who had renounced his wealth for a life of monasticism and scholarship, to prepare a Latin version based on a new translation of the Hebrew Scriptures and Greek New

**Damasus** (DAM-uh-sus)

Testament. Jerome's version was called the "Vulgate Bible" because it was the Bible for the "people" (*vulgus*) who knew Latin.

The development of a scriptural canon paralleled the elaboration of a creedal statement that would set down precisely what Christians believed. As we have seen, the Councils of Nicaea and Constantinople defined the nature of the Trinity, and Chalcedon formulated the relationship between the human and divine natures of Christ. There were also debates about the nature of the priesthood, the structure and authority of the church, and the problem of human free will. Practical questions came up, too. How could Christians fulfill the moral demands of their faith while living in a world whose values were often at odds with church teachings?

Answers to these kinds of questions were provided by a group of Greek and Latin writers who are called the "Church Fathers" and whose era is called "patristic" (from *patres*, the Latin word for "fathers"). In versatility and sheer output they have few rivals at any time. Their intellectual breadth was matched by their elegant style and trenchant reasoning.

Many Christian writers addressed the problems of moral living in the world. In his treatise *On Duties*, Ambrose of Milan (339–397) attempted to Christianize the public ethos that Cicero had spelled out many years before in his book of the same name. Cicero talked of citizens' obligations to one another and to the law and the need for those in power to be above reproach in the conduct of their personal lives. Ambrose reinterpreted these obligations as duties that Christians owed to one another because of their common worship of God.

Pope Gregory I wrote *The Pastoral Rule* to reformulate Cicero's and Ambrose's ideas in ways that made them relevant to society's Christian leaders, the clergy. John Chrysostom° (347–407), a patriarch of Constantinople and one of the most popular and gifted preachers of Late Antiquity (his name means "golden tongued"), bitterly castigated the immorality of the imperial court and aristocracy: by setting a bad example, they endangered the souls of their subjects.

Boethius° (480–524) illustrates contemporary themes well. Descended from one of Rome's oldest families, he held high offices but eventually earned the enmity of Theodoric the Ostrogoth, who imprisoned and executed him. He was a prolific writer, whose Latin translations of Greek philosophical texts bequeathed those writings to the Middle Ages. In his most famous book, *The Consolation of Philosophy*, written while he was in prison,

Boethius describes how the soul could rise through philosophy to a knowledge of God. Once again we see the classical and the Christian blended in a new synthesis.

## Saint Augustine and the Christian Tradition

The most influential Christian thinker after Saint Paul was Augustine of Hippo (354–430). Augustine was born in North Africa to a pagan father and a Christian mother. His family was of modest means, but at great sacrifice they arranged for him to receive the best education available. He embarked on a career as a professor of rhetoric. Once he had established himself, he moved on to Rome and then to Milan, which in the fourth century was the unofficial Western capital. Augustine fell under the spell of Ambrose and embraced the Christianity that his mother, Monica, had been urging on him throughout his life. Later Augustine chronicled his quest for truth and spiritual fulfillment in his *Confessions*, a classic of Western literature. (See the box "Reading Sources: The Moment of Augustine's Spiritual Awakening.") In 395 Augustine became a bishop and until his death served the North African community at Hippo, and the wider Christian world, with a torrent of writings.

Not a systematic thinker, Augustine never set out to provide a comprehensive exposition of the whole of Christian doctrine. Instead, he responded to problems as they arose. Crucial among these were the relationship between God and humans, the nature of the church, and the overall plan of God's creation.

In the early fifth century some people believed that they could achieve salvation by the unaided operation of their own will. Augustine responded that although God did indeed endow humankind with free will, Adam and Eve had abused their will to rebel against God. Ever since that first act of rebellion, a taint, called by theologians "original sin," predisposed all humans to continual rebellion, or sin, against God. Only divine grace can overcome sin, and only by calling on God can people receive grace. Here was a decisive break with the classical idea of humanity as good in itself and capable of self-improvement, perhaps even perfection, in this world. According to Augustine, all people are sinners, in need of God's redemption.

Some North African heretics taught that sacraments celebrated by unworthy priests are invalid. Augustine believed that the validity of the church's sacraments—those ritual celebrations that are considered to be channels for the communication of grace, of God's special aid and comfort to the faithful—does not depend on the personal merit of the minister. A priest or a bishop acts in God's place and through divine grace. Therefore, faith

---

**Chrysostom** (KRIH-sus-tum)    **Boethius** (bow-EE-thee-us)

# THE MOMENT OF AUGUSTINE'S SPIRITUAL AWAKENING

*In this passage Augustine relates the moment of his conversion and abandonment of his former life. Notice the roles of God, books, his old friend Alypius, and his devoted mother, Monica.*

So that I might pour out all these tears and speak the words that came with them I rose up from Alypius and went further away that I might not be embarrassed even by his presence. This was how I felt and he realized it. No doubt I had said something or other, and he could feel the weight of my tears in the sound of my voice. And so I rose to my feet, and he, in a state of utter amazement, remained in the place where we had been sitting. I flung myself down on the ground somehow under a fig tree and gave free rein to my tears; they streamed and flooded from my eyes. . . . And in my misery I would exclaim: "How long, how long this 'tomorrow and tomorrow'? Why not now? Why not finish this very hour with my uncleanness?"

So I spoke, weeping in the bitter contrition of my heart. Suddenly a voice reaches my ears from a nearby house. It is the voice of a boy or a girl (I don't know which) and in a kind of singsong the words are constantly repeated: "Take it and read it. Take it and read it." At once my face changed and I began to think carefully of whether the singing of words like these came into any kind of game which children play, and I could not remember that I had ever heard anything like it before. I checked the force of my tears and rose to my feet, being quite certain that I must interpret this as a divine command to me to open the book and to read the first passage which I should come upon. For I had heard this about Anthony: He had happened to come in when the Gospel was being read, and as though the words read were spoken directly to himself, he had received the admonition: "Go, sell your possessions, and give to the poor. You will then have treasure in heaven. Afterward, come back and follow me" [Matthew 19:21]. And by such an oracle he had been converted to you.

So I went eagerly back to the place where Alypius was sitting, since it was there that I had left the book of the Apostle [Paul] when I rose to my feet. I snatched up the book, opened it, and read in silence the passage on which my eyes first fell: "Not in carousing and drunkenness, not in sexual excess and lust, not in quarreling and jealousy. Rather, put on the Lord Jesus Christ and make no provisions for the desires of the flesh" [Romans 13:13–14]. I had no wish to read further; there was no need to. For immediately I had reached the end of this sentence, it was as though my heart was filled with a light of confidence and all the shadows of my doubt were swept away.

Before shutting the book I put my finger or some other marker in the place and told Alypius what had happened. By now my face was perfectly calm. Alypius in his turn told me what had been going on in himself. He asked me to see that passage which I had read. . . . He was strengthened by the admonition. . . . The next thing we do is go inside and tell my mother. How happy she is! We describe to her how it all took place, and there is no limit to her joy and triumph . . . for she saw that with regard to me you had given her so much more than she used to ask for when she wept so pitifully before you. . . . I was now standing on that rule of faith just as you had shown me to her in a vision so many years before.

Source: St. Augustine, *The Confessions of St. Augustine*, trans. Rex Warner, pp. 182–183. Copyright © 1963 by Rex Warner, renewed © 1991 by F. C. Warner. Used by permission of Dutton Signet, a division of Penguin Group (USA) Inc.

in God is paramount. The church is thus a community of acknowledged sinners led by the clergy in a quest for eternal salvation. To Augustine, God alone is perfect. Clergy, rulers, and churches are all human institutions, all more or less good in particular circumstances.

To many adherents of the traditional Roman religion, the sack of Rome by the Visigoths in 410 was repayment for Rome's abandonment of its traditional gods. To refute them, Augustine wrote the most brilliant and difficult of all his works, *The City of God*. This book is a theology of history. Augustine sees time not as cyclical—the traditional classical view—but as linear. Since the creation of the world, a plan has been in operation—God's plan—and that plan will govern all human activity until the end of time. History is the struggle between those who call on divine grace, who are redeemed, who are citizens of the City of God, and those who keep to the ways of the world, who persist in sin, who live in the earthly city. One may observe the unfolding of the divine plan by seeing how much of the earthly city has been redeemed at any given time.

Even though the Roman Empire was officially Christian, Augustine refused to identify his City of God with it. Nor would he say that the church and the City of God were identical. What he did say was that the sack of Rome was a great irrelevance because many kingdoms and empires had come and gone and would continue to do so, but only the kingdom of God was eternal and, in the long run, important. To a Roman people whose most cherished belief held that the world would last exactly as long as Rome's dominion, Augustine's dismissal of Rome's destiny sounded the death knell of the classical world-view.

Augustine also addressed the problem of education. He regarded salvation as the goal of life but realized that people have to carry on with their ordinary occupations. He also knew that almost the entire educational establishment was pagan in design and content. Education was confined mainly to the elite, who sought schooling partly to orient themselves within their cultural tradition and partly to gain employment, often in the imperial or urban service. This education had three mainstays. Latin or Greek grammar—rarely both—was the first. Augustine, for instance, knew little Greek, and by the sixth century few people in the East knew Latin. The second mainstay of education was rhetoric, once the art of public speaking but now, increasingly, literary criticism. The third was dialectic, or the art of right reasoning. In Late Antiquity public schools were fast disappearing as the need for them slipped away. But the church still needed educated persons, so it provided schools in cathedrals and monasteries.

In a treatise entitled *On Christian Doctrine*, Augustine expressed some ideas about education that proved influential for a millennium. He argued that everything a person needs to know to achieve salvation is contained in the Bible. But the Bible, written in learned language, is full of difficult images and allusions. How is an ordinary person to learn what he or she needs to know in order to master this great book of life? Only by getting some schooling, and that education would inevitably be in the classical languages and literatures. To express his attitude toward that schooling, Augustine used the image of "spoiling the Egyptians," borrowed from the account of the Hebrews' Exodus from Egypt, when they took with them whatever they could use. Augustine's attitude toward classical learning was that it was useful only to the extent that it equipped individuals to read the Bible,

to understand it, and to seek salvation. Classical culture had no intrinsic merit. It might give pleasure, but it was equally likely to be a distraction or a temptation to immorality.

The Italian writer Cassiodorus° (ca. 485–580) gave this Augustinian interpretation of the classical heritage its definitive statement in his treatise *On Divine and Human Readings*. After the fall of the Ostrogothic kingdom, whose king Theodoric he had served loyally, Cassiodorus retired and set up a school of Christian studies. His treatise served as a kind of annotated bibliography and curriculum of the major writings on school subjects, such as grammar, rhetoric, and dialectic, and on biblical commentary. For centuries, schools organized on Augustine's and Cassiodorus's model did an estimable job of preparing the clergy to carry out their functions.

## SUMMARY

WHEN the late antique period opened, Rome's vast and diverse empire was beset with innumerable political, military, and economic problems. The classical culture that had evolved over centuries in the Mediterranean world seemed to have lost much of its vigor and appeal. But energetic rulers such as Diocletian and Constantine undertook half a century of intense military, economic, and administrative reform that put the empire on firm footings while simultaneously changing forever the basic nature of the Roman state.

By 600 the Roman Empire still survived, but it was confined to the eastern Mediterranean, where it would persist for another millennium. In the West Rome's former provinces had evolved into a series of barbarian kingdoms. Each of those kingdoms retained significant features of the governmental systems of the provinces in which they arose. Whether in the East or in the West, military men led a world whose culture was less civilian than in early imperial times. But the militarization of public life in Late Antiquity preserved the eastern empire and created a stable framework for the transition from empire to kingdoms in the West.

In 300 barbarians were a worrisome threat along the northern frontiers of the empire. By 600 barbarians had created, from Britain to Spain, a succession of kingdoms, the most successful of which owed great debts to Rome. The barbarians did not appear suddenly in Late Antiq-

---

**Cassiodorus** (cass-ee-oh-DOR-us)

uity. Rome knew these people and had traded, fought, and allied with them for centuries. The barbarians did not come to destroy Rome but to join it, to benefit from it, to learn its ways. The creation of the barbarian kingdoms was in many ways one of Rome's most creative political acts.

In 300 the Christian church was suffering persecution. By 600 the church spanned the old Roman world. A hierarchy of sophisticated leaders ably governed the church. Christianity had absorbed what it could of ancient culture, and the church had adapted Roman institutions. Prominent families had once governed Roman towns and provinces through urban institutions. The bishops and patriarchs who governed late antique towns via their church offices often came from those same families or families just like them. The Church Fathers addressed some of the most fundamental problems of human existence in correct, sometimes elegant and moving, Greek and Latin.

The late antique world was fully embroiled in a process of evolution. That evolution would go on. In the West kingdoms would appear and disappear, but the basic political structure of the European Middle Ages would be the kingdom. The eastern Roman Empire would shed more and more of its Roman heritage and turn into a regime we call "Byzantine." But the Byzantines themselves always insisted that they were Romans. The lands of North Africa and the Middle East that had long but tenuous relations with Rome would produce a new political order under the followers of the prophet Muhammad. But that world, too, would owe much to its Roman predecessor, while also inheriting some of the Roman world's old and deep divisions. In 600 the basic building blocks of the West were in place: Greco-Roman culture and institutions, Judeo-Christian religious beliefs, and barbarian peoples. In the world we call "medieval," those building blocks would be assembled in new configurations.

## ■ Suggested Reading

Bowersock, G. W., P. Brown, and O. Grabar, eds. *Late Antiquity: A Guide to the Post-Classical World.* 1999. Though basically an encyclopedia, this masterful volume contains long entries on all the major topics and up-to-date essays on big themes.

Brown, Peter. *The World of Late Antiquity.* 1971. A sprightly and beautifully illustrated interpretation of cultural crosscurrents by the most gifted interpreter of Late Antiquity.

Clark, Gillian. *Women in Late Antiquity: Pagan and Christian Lifestyles.* 1993. A first-ever attempt to capture the lives of late antique women in all respects.

Liebeschuetz, J. H. W. G. *The Decline and Fall of the Roman City.* 2001. A remarkable assessment of all aspects of urban change from the fourth to the seventh century .

Markus, Robert. *The End of Ancient Christianity.* 1990. This stimulating and beautifully written book explores the changing meanings of sacred and secular in the period from 400 to 600.

**For a searchable list of additional readings for this chapter, go to college.hmco.com/students.**

# The Ravenna Mosaics

*Propaganda.* The word has unsavory connotations. It suggests that someone is trying to convince someone else to do or to believe what is wrong. Actually the word means only "things to be propagated," a message to be gotten out. The message itself may be good or bad, true or false.

When we think of propaganda, we must consider both the message and the medium in which it is conveyed. In antiquity, governments had several means of getting their messages out. Almost all the means were public, visible, striking.

Mosaics are among the most spectacular art forms of Late Antiquity, and in the churches of Ravenna they attained the summit of their propagandistic power. A mosaic is a picture formed by the intricate arrangement of thousands of tiny bits (called *tesserae*) of glass, stone, or metal. An artist created a rough sketch of the intended picture and then laid out the tesserae to conform to the sketch. Next the artist applied wet plaster to a small section of the surface, usually a wall or a floor, that was to receive the picture and then embedded that section's tesserae into the plaster. This process was repeated until the mosaic was completed. The result was a durable art form of great beauty and visual interest. In the picture on the opposite page, you can see the tesserae and even some of the sparkle produced by the effect of sunlight and candlelight reflecting off the mosaic.

Mosaics were sometimes placed in private homes by the very wealthy, but more often they were put in conspicuous public places. Churches commonly received them in Late Antiquity. As more of society became Christian, aristocrats in particular were happy to spend lavishly to adorn their places of worship with beautiful decorations. Masses of people saw those decorations, reflected on who had financed them, and pondered the meaning of the images themselves.

The greatest patron of all was the emperor. By putting up any work of art, the emperor proclaimed his power and influence. His reach was vast even if he never left Constantinople. Nothing shows this better than the Ravenna mosaics erected by Justinian.

Let us recall the situation. The Arian Ostrogoths had taken over Italy in 493. Ruling from Ravenna, they claimed to be imperial allies and representatives. Down to 535 there were strains between Ravenna and Constantinople, and in that year Justinian launched the twenty-year-long Gothic Wars. During and after the wars, churches were erected as symbols of the imperial restoration.

The mosaic pictured here is located on the left-hand side of the apse, above and behind the altar, in the Church of San Vitale in Ravenna. Its central figure is the emperor Justinian. Immediately opposite it is another mosaic (partially reproduced on page 226) focusing on the empress Theodora. San Vitale was a monument to the defeat of the Arian Goths. Any worshiper who raised his or her eyes from the altar saw immediately both Justinian and Theodora. These images made a powerful statement in a city that had been ruled by a Gothic king for thirty-three years. Justinian was leaving no doubt about who was in charge. Consider, too, the prominence accorded to Theodora. Justinian really did view her as a partner in his rule.

That the emperor and empress were in charge is indicated in several distinct ways. They are slightly larger and are standing in front of their attendants. They are not quite like the other humans shown in the mosaic. They wear crowns and rich purple—that is to say, imperial—garments. They present gifts: he a gold paten holding the eucharistic bread and she a golden chalice containing the eucharistic wine. Thus the emperor and empress are represented as the donors of the church and as the guarantors of authentic worship.

Justinian tried throughout his reign to promote *homonoia* ("concord"). He tried to reconcile many political and religious factions. Notice the figure to Justinian's left (your right), over whose bald head you can read MAXIMIANUS. This man was the archbishop of Ravenna, a close ally of the emperor and the person responsible both for eradicating Arianism and for reconciling Arians. His prominent position next to the emperor, and the fact that he alone is named, assured everyone of the correct doctrinal position. And in case anyone needed a further reminder, Maximianus holds in his hand the cross of Christ: there would be no more Arian subordination of the second person of the Trinity to the first.

We may note one more piece of propaganda. Look at the man standing to the left of Justinian and slightly behind him—between Justinian and Maximianus. This is Julianus Argentarius, a wealthy layman who was in all things the emperor's agent in Ravenna. He helped to finance and oversaw the construction of not only San Vitale but also several other churches in Ravenna. His presence signifies *homonoia*, the traditional concord between the emperor and the elite throughout the empire. Relations between the court and the Italian elite had been very strained under the Ostrogoths. Julianus's presence signaled that all was well once again. Vanity played a role, too. Julianus paid for the art, so he had himself included in it.

The Church of San Vitale was itself a propaganda statement. Theodoric was buried in a grand octagonal tomb. Justinian's builders chose an octagonal form for San Vitale. This church is also a sepulcher—a shrine for the remains of Saint Vitalis, an early Ravenna Christian who was martyred for the true faith.

In a world without the modern mass media, the media of antiquity served well to broadcast messages to people who understood their real and symbolic language. Recall the image on a Hellenistic coin (page 134). Look again at the statue of the tetrarchs (page 207). Cassiodorus once said that Rome was "a forest of statues." Every one of them was a propaganda statement.

---

**www.** For additional information on this topic, go to college.hmco.com/students.

**Justinian and His Courtiers, Apse Mosaic, San Vitale, Ravenna** *(Scala/Art Resource, NY)*

# CHAPTER 8

# Early Medieval Civilizations 600–900

THE Great Mosque of Cordoba, erected by Abd ar-Rahman in 786–787, at first glance appears much like a late antique building: elegant columns, arches arranged in arcades, rectangular space. But this is a *mosque,* an Islamic house of worship, and it was built in Spain, one of Rome's oldest provinces. We saw in Chapter 7 that Spain had fallen to the Visigoths in the sixth century and that Justinian had been unable to reconquer the region. Between 711 and 716 an army of Arabs and North African tribesmen overwhelmed Spain and inaugurated seven centuries of Islamic rule on the Iberian Peninsula. A time traveler transported to the Mediterranean world of 600 would almost certainly have predicted only two heirs to Rome: the eastern empire and the kingdoms of the barbarian West. It is extremely unlikely that our intrepid wanderer would have foreseen one of the most dramatic developments in the history of Western civilization: the rise of the Arabs and their Islamic faith.

In this chapter three areas and histories engage our attention: the Islamic East, the Byzantine Empire, and the Latin West. For each, the seventh century was an era of dramatic change, the eighth century a period of reform and consolidation, and the ninth century a time of upheaval. A new imperial tradition developed in all three areas. Muslims, Orthodox Christians, and Catholics all believed themselves to be chosen by God, and their rulers defined themselves as God's earthly agents. In all three realms the interaction of local traditions and the Roman past produced new forms of central government that would prove influential for centuries. Commercial ties began to transform the Mediterranean world into a community of peoples who needed to balance mutual interests with bitter rivalries.

The Great Mosque serves as a remarkable reminder of how much changed—and how much remained the same—in the early Middle Ages. Arches and arcades graced classical architecture for more than

The Great Mosque of Cordoba was erected by Abd ar-Rahman in 786–787.
(Christopher Rennie/Robert Harding Picture Library)

239

a millennium. But Cordoba's arches are horseshoe shaped, a minor innovation. The arches incorporate alternating bands of red and cream-colored stone. These shapes and colors may be local traditions, an imitation of the Roman aqueduct at Mérida, Byzantine imports, or Syrian characteristics. The building is basilican in shape. In a basilica the space is oriented to the area where officials presided—to an altar when the basilica is a church. In a mosque the space is oriented to the *qibla* wall—the wall facing Mecca, the birthplace of Muhammad and Islam. The elements of the Great Mosque were old, but the overall effect was new.

The period from 600 to 900 is commonly called the "early Middle Ages." What does this term mean? In the seventeenth century a Dutch scholar wrote of the *Medii Aevi,* the "Middle Times" that lay between antiquity and the dawning modern world. The name stuck. As a label for the post-Roman world, "Middle Ages" (whose adjectival form is "medieval") has become traditional. The fact that we no longer talk of an abrupt and catastrophic "fall" of the Ro-

man Empire means that we no longer use the word *medieval* in negative ways.

### QUESTIONS TO CONSIDER

- What were the most important factors in the rise of the Arab peoples and the Islamic faith?
- Why did a distinctive civilization that can be called "Byzantine" emerge?
- In what ways were the Frankish and Anglo-Saxon kingdoms successful?
- What were the chief similarities among the early medieval civilizations? the chief differences?

### TERMS TO KNOW

| | |
|---|---|
| Muhammad | Papal States |
| Five Pillars of Islam | Charlemagne |
| Quran | vassal |
| caliphate | Carolingian Renaissance |
| iconoclasm | manor |
| Orthodoxy | |

## THE ISLAMIC EAST

ANCIENT writers took little notice of the Arabs, who inhabited much of the area from the Arabian peninsula to the Euphrates River. Around 600 the prophet Muhammad (570–632) appeared among them preaching a faith old in its basic elements but new in its formulation. With unprecedented spiritual and military fervor, converts to that new faith conquered territories from Spain to the frontiers of China. Slowly, they built an imperial system with a coherent government and ideology. At the same time, cultural elites began forging a new civilization out of the ethnic, religious, and historical diversity of that vast realm.

### Arabia Before Muhammad

The Arab world in the early seventh century was large and turbulent. Long dominated by the Roman and Persian Empires, the region had no stable, large-scale political

entities. People belonged to close-knit clans, or extended families, that in varying associations formed tribes. In theory, tribes were groups of people tracing descent from a known ancestor; in reality—and in this, Arab and Germanic peoples were alike—tribes were complex groups of relatives, allies, and political or economic clients.

As complex as its political situation was the region's ethnic and religious composition. The Roman world was overwhelmingly Christian, although there were many kinds of Christians. The Persian realm was officially Zoroastrian, but it had Jewish, Christian, Manichaean, and Buddhist minorities. The Arabs themselves were generally pagans, but Arabia had Jewish and Christian minorities.

The Arab East was also economically intricate and fragile. Bedouins° (Arabs who were nomadic pastoralists) provided for their own needs from their herds of sheep and goats, from small-scale trading in towns, and from regular raids on one another and on caravans. Some farmers worked the land, but in many areas soils were

---

**bedouins** (BED-oo-inz)

too poor and rain was too infrequent to support agriculture. Cities supported traders who carried luxury goods, such as spices, incense, and perfumes, from the Indian Ocean region and southern Arabia along caravan routes to the cities of the eastern Mediterranean. These traders formed the economic and political elite of Arabia, and they led the tribes. Mecca, dominated by the powerful tribe of the Quraysh°, was the foremost city of Arabia, but competition among cities and tribes was fierce.

A solution to the competition among tribes and towns for control of trade routes was the institution of *harams*°, or sanctuaries—places where contending parties could settle disputes peacefully. Mecca was one of the chief harams in Arabia, and its founding was attributed to the Israelite patriarch Abraham and one of his sons, Ishmael. The focus of the sanctuary was the black stone shrine known as the Kaaba°, founded by Abraham, according to Arab tradition. For centuries people from all over Arabia had made pilgrimages to Mecca, to the Kaaba, supposedly following Abraham's example.

## The Prophet and His Faith

Muhammad was born in 570 to a respectable though not wealthy or powerful clan of the Quraysh tribe. His father died before he was born, his mother shortly afterward, leaving Muhammad under the care of his grandparents and an uncle. Like many young Meccans, he entered the caravan trade. By the time he was 20, Muhammad had such a reputation for competence and moral uprightness that he became financial adviser to a wealthy Quraysh widow, Khadija° (555–619). Though older than Muhammad, she became his wife in 595, and they had a loving marriage until her death.

From his youth Muhammad was a man of spiritual insight. In 610 he received the first of many revelations that commanded him to teach all people a new faith that called for an unquestioned belief in one god, Allah, and a deep commitment to social justice for believers. Muhammad began teaching in Mecca, but he converted few people outside his own circle; his wife was his first convert. Some Meccans were envious of Muhammad. Others feared that his new faith and new god might call into question the legitimacy of the shrines in Mecca and jeopardize the traditional pilgrimages to the Kaaba and the trade that accompanied them. By 619 Muhammad's well-connected wife and uncle were dead, and his position was precarious.

**Quraysh** (KOOR-aysh)  **haram** (HAR-ahm)
**Kaaba** (KAH-bah)  **Khadija** (KAH-dee-ah)

### CHRONOLOGY

| | |
|---|---|
| 570–632 | Life of Muhammad |
| 597 | Pope Gregory I sends missionaries to England |
| 610–641 | Reign of Heraclius in Byzantium |
| 622 | Hijra |
| 632–733 | Muslim conquests |
| 661–750 | Umayyad caliphate |
| 664 | Council of Whitby |
| 711–716 | Muslim conquest of Spain |
| 717–802 | Isaurian dynasty at Byzantium |
| 726–787, 815–842 | Byzantine iconoclasm |
| 750 | Founding of Abbasid caliphate |
| 751 | Lombard conquest of Ravenna |
| 755–774 | Frankish conquest of Lombards |
| 755–756 | Foundation of Papal States |
| 757–796 | Reign of Offa of Mercia |
| 768–814 | Reign of Charlemagne |
| 780s–860s | Carolingian Renaissance |
| 786–809 | Reign of Harun al-Rashid |
| 800 | Imperial coronation of Charlemagne |
| 843 | Treaty of Verdun creates three Frankish kingdoms |
| 867–886 | Reign of Basil I |

At this juncture citizens from Medina, a smaller trading community wracked by dissension among pagan Arabs, Jews, and followers of Muhammad, asked Muhammad to establish a haram there. In the summer of 622 small groups of Muhammad's disciples made their way to Medina, and in September Muhammad joined them. His journey from Mecca to Medina, the *hijra*°, marks the beginning of a new era, symbolized to this day in the Arab world by a calendar that dates "In the year of the Hijra."

**hijra** (HEEZH-rah)

**Map 8.1    Arab Conquests to 733**    This map vividly illustrates the spectacular gains by the Arabs in the time of Muhammad, under the first caliphs, and under the Umayyads. Later slow, steady gains in Africa, central Asia, and India expanded the empire even farther. Muslim conquest did not at first mean widespread conversion to Islam; Egypt, for example, was not majority Muslim before the tenth century.

Although Muhammad was fully in control in Medina, Mecca remained the focus of his attention. In addition to his sentimental attachment to Mecca, its political and economic importance were critical to his emerging desire to convert all of Arabia. His followers began attacking Meccan caravans and battled with the Meccans several times in the 620s. In 630 Muhammad and many of his followers returned to Mecca in triumph. Muhammad left the Quraysh in control, and he retained the Kaaba as a focus of piety. After making local arrangements, he returned to Medina and set about winning over the bedouins of the Arabian desert. By the time Muhammad died in 632, he had converted most of Arabia (see Map 8.1).

To what exactly had Muhammad and his followers converted? At the most basic level, people were asked to surrender completely to Allah, the one true God—that is, they were asked to make *al-Islam*, "the surrender." Those who surrendered became *Muslims* and joined the *umma muslima°*, a completely new kind of community in which membership depended only on belief in Allah and acceptance of Muhammad as Allah's prophet. No longer were one's duties confined to a particular clan, tribe, or town. All members of the umma were understood to have personal and communal responsibility for all other members. Because of the experience of the hijra, Islam was a religion of exile, of separation from the ordinary world, and of reliance on God.

The basic teachings of Islam are traditionally described as "Five Pillars": (1) the profession of faith, "There is no God but Allah and Muhammad is His Prophet"; (2) individual prayer five times daily, plus group prayer at noon on Friday in a *mosque,* a Muslim house of prayer; (3) the sunup-to-sundown fast for one month per year; (4) the donation of generous alms to the poor; and (5) a

---

**umma muslima** (OO-mah MOOSE-lee-mah)

**Dome of the Rock**    This magnificent mosque in Jerusalem (built in 691–692) is the third-holiest shrine of Islam—after the Kaaba in Mecca and the Prophet's mosque in Medina. Muslims believe that Muhammad ascended to heaven from this spot.    *(Michael Holford)*

pilgrimage to Mecca at least once in a person's lifetime. These pillars are still the central requirements of Islam.

In the early decades the pillars sustained a faith that stressed strict monotheism and practices that affirmed Islam and built up a sense of community. At certain times of the day all Muslims everywhere bowed in prayer, with their heads facing toward Mecca. Everyone paid alms, creating thereby a feeling of solidarity among all members of the umma. Mecca itself and the experience of pilgrimage were central to all Muslims. Originally there was no elaborate theology, intricate doctrinal mysteries, creed, or clergy. Men called *imams* led the Friday prayers in the mosque and usually offered sermons that applied Muslim teaching to the issues of the day, but Islam involved no ordained priesthood as in Judaism or Christianity and no hierarchy as in the Christian churches.

Muhammad communicated God's teaching to his followers, always insisting that he was transmitting a direct, verbal revelation and not offering his own interpretations. That revelation came in the form of "recitations" that make up the *Quran°*, the Scriptures of Islam. Not long after Muhammad's death his closest followers arranged the recitations into 114 *Suras,* or chapters. The Quran contains legal and wisdom literature like the Hebrew Scriptures and moral teaching like the Christian New Testament. It also prescribes regulations for diet

**Quran** (koo-RAHN)

## READING SOURCES

## THE MESSAGE OF THE QURAN

*The Quran consists of 114 Suras, literally the "steps" (we might say chapters) by which one rises to knowledge of Allah. The earliest versions of the Quran were equipped with a running commentary. The first four extracts here illustrate the simplicity and elegance of Muslim prayer and the absolute transcendence of Allah. The last two extracts demonstrate the profound sense of religious continuity that marked Muhammad's teaching.*

### Sura 1

In the name of Allah, Most Gracious, Most Merciful. / Praise be to Allah, the Cherisher and Sustainer of worlds; / Most Gracious, Most Merciful. / Master of the Day of Judgment. / Thee do we worship and Thine aid we seek. Show us the straight way, the way of those on whom Thou hast bestowed Thy grace, Thou whose portion is not wrath, and who do not go astray.

### Sura 4.171

O People of the Book! Commit no excesses in your religion, nor say of Allah anything but truth. Christ Jesus the son of Mary was a messenger of Allah . . . so believe in Allah and in His messengers. Say not "Trinity" . . . for Allah is One God. Glory be to Him for He is exalted above having a son. To Him belong all things in the heavens and on earth.

### Sura 3.84

Say ye: We believe in Allah, and the revelation given to us, and to Abraham, Ismail, Isaac, Jacob and the descendants (children of Jacob), and that given to Moses and to Jesus and that given to all prophets from their Lord, but we make no difference between one and another of them, and we bow to Allah.

### Sura 2.87

We gave Moses the book and followed him up with a succession of messengers; We gave Jesus the son of Mary clear signs and strengthened him with the Holy Spirit.

### Sura 48

If the People of the Book rely upon Abraham, let them study his history. His posterity included both Israel and Ismail. Abraham was a righteous man of Allah, a Muslim, and so were his children. Abraham and Ismail built the Kaaba as the house of Allah and purified it, to be a centre of worship for all the world: For Allah is the God of all peoples.

### Sura 56

God's truth is continuous, and His prophets from Adam, through Noah and Abraham, down to the last of the prophets, Muhammad, form one brotherhood. Of Imran father of Moses and Aaron sprang a woman, who devoted her unborn offspring to Allah. That child was Mary the mother of Jesus. Her cousin was the wife of the priest Zakariya, who took charge of Mary. To Zakariya, in his old age, was born a son Yahya, amid prodigies: Yahya was the herald of Jesus the son of Mary and was known as John the Baptist.

Source: *The Meaning of the Holy Qur'an,* new edition with revised translation, commentary, and newly compiled comprehensive index by Abdullah Yusuf Ali (Beltsville, Md.: Amana Publications, 1988), pp. 14, 40, 51, 55–56, 134–135.

and for personal conduct. For example, the Quran forbids alcohol and gambling, censures luxury and ostentation, and imposes strict sexual restraints on both men and women. (See the box "Reading Sources: The Message of the Quran.")

Initially the Quran was interpreted rather freely within the umma, doubtless because there was no clergy to impose a uniform interpretation. After the Prophet's death, some people felt the need for an authoritative teaching—as early Christians had felt the need for a canon of Christian scripture and teaching—and their efforts resulted in the collections called the *sunna,* which means roughly "good practice"—that is, the words and customs of Muhammad himself. Crucial in the development of the sunna were the *hadith,* the "sayings" of the Prophet, the comments he sometimes made about how God's revelation was to be understood and applied. Extant compilations of the sunna date from the ninth century, and scholars are not sure what portion of them derives authentically from the age of the Prophet.

## The Arab Conquests

Muhammad's death brought a crisis. Who or what was to succeed him? In 632 the Meccan elite chose Abu Bakr as *caliph°*, or "successor to the Prophet." Abu Bakr was elderly, an early convert to Islam, and a former secretary to Muhammad. He and his three successors down to 661 (Umar, Uthman, and Ali) were all Meccans, relatives of the Prophet by marriage, and early converts. Islamic tradition calls them the "Rightly Guided Caliphs."

Abu Bakr left his successor, Umar, a united Arabia (see Map 8.1), no small feat in that fractious world. Umar began the lightning conquests by the Arabs of much of the Roman and Persian Empires. He initiated the policy of granting choice positions in the expanding caliphate, the Arab empire, to old converts and of ranking them according to precedence in conversion. As the old elite divided up the new provinces of the caliphate, some of them became *emirs* (governors), and others became lower administrators. Arab administrators then collected from all conquered people personal taxes and land taxes. Converts to Islam paid only land taxes. Arab settlers paid no taxes and received salaries from the taxes paid by others.

Umar was murdered by a slave in 644, leaving his successor, Uthman, a huge empire to administer. A great centralizer, Uthman chose emirs, regulated the finances of the provinces, and authorized the preparation of the definitive text of the Quran. In attempting to preserve the advantages of the old Meccan elite, Uthman alienated many people, particularly in Egypt, Syria, and Iraq, who had benefited from conquest and who guarded jealously their newfound local wealth and power. Uthman was murdered in 656 and replaced by Ali, Muhammad's son-in-law, whose goal was to create a truly Islamic government by emphasizing the religious side of the caliph's office as the leader of the umma. Ali was in turn killed by a disillusioned follower in 661. Years later some Muslims looked back to Ali as the true model for the caliph. These Muslims formed the *Shi'a,* the "Party of Ali."

When Ali was killed, the caliphate passed to Mu'awiya°, a Meccan who was the governor of Syria and commander of the finest army in the Arab world. That army ensured Mu'awiya's position. From 661 to 750 the Umayyads°, as Mu'awiya's family is called, built many of the caliphate's institutions.

The Umayyads instituted greater centralization. This involved the introduction of a unified coinage, the Arabization of the administration (granting all key positions to Arabs), and taking tight control of provincial government and taxation. The Umayyads moved the capital of the caliphate to Damascus in their own power base of Syria, more centrally located than the old towns of Mecca and Medina and closer to the militarily active zones in eastern Iran and along the Byzantine frontier in Syria. In addition, the Umayyads presided over the final territorial expansion of the caliphate (see Map 8.1). To the west, the caliph's forces took North Africa and Spain and conducted raids deep into Gaul. In the east, though stymied by unsuccessful sieges against Constantinople, campaigns moved the frontier against the Byzantine Empire into the mountains of southern Anatolia and, farther east, established nominal authority as far as the Indus River valley.

Rome's empire expanded for 350 years, but the caliphate reached its zenith in scarcely 100. How can we account for the astonishingly rapid creation of such a vast empire? External factors were important. Byzantium and Persia had financially and militarily weakened themselves in a series of wars that ended just as the caliphate of Umar commenced. Moreover, the Byzantine and Persian states were exceedingly diverse, and the Arab armies dismantled them piecemeal. Both old empires, but especially the Byzantine, had deep religious divisions. Coptic Egypt and Jacobite Syria, for example, willingly yielded to the Arabs, who demanded taxes and submission but otherwise left them alone. The Byzantines and Persians tended to depend on static frontier garrisons and large armies that could not be quickly mobilized and moved long distances. The Arabs rarely risked great pitched battles. They preferred a gradually expanding military frontier gained by numerous lightning strikes.

Internal factors were more significant, however. For centuries, raiding and plundering had been a way of life in Arabia, but because Islam forbade Muslims from raiding other Muslims, a new outlet for traditional violence was needed. The Prophet himself had believed firmly in the need to expand the faith, and his successors shared that belief. Muslim ideology divided the world into the "House of Islam" and the "House of War." In the House of Islam the justice of Allah reigned supreme. In the House of War *jihad,* or holy war, was the rule. Christians and Jews, as fellow "Peoples of the Book"—sharers in a scriptural tradition reaching back to Abraham—were spared the choice of conversion or death, but "infidels" were expected to submit and convert. The Arab conquests were carefully planned and directed to channel violence out of Arabia, to populate much of western Asia with loyal Muslims, and to reward members of the umma.

caliph (KAY-lif)    Mu'awiya (MOO-ah-wee-uh)
Umayyads (OO-my-ahdz)

## The Abbasid Revolution

Despite their military and administrative successes, the Umayyads were not popular. Many people resented their bureaucratic centralization. Such resentment was acute in areas heavily populated by recent converts, who had always disliked the old Arabian elites, and in frontier provinces, where Arab immigrants along with local converts desired autonomy. The secular nature of Umayyad rule also offended those pious Muslims who expected a high standard of personal morality from their rulers. The opposition came to a head in a series of rebellions that culminated in the naming of a rival caliph, Abu'l Abbas, in 749. In 750 he defeated his Umayyad opponent.

The Abbasids° reigned until the thirteenth century. Initially, especially in the caliphate of Harun al-Rashid° (r. 786–809), they brought the Islamic world its first golden age. Harun's reign was marked by political stability, economic prosperity, and cultural achievements. Abbasid successes are attributable to political acumen and ideological restructuring.

With their frontier origins, the Abbasids were sympathetic to the caliphate's provincial populations. Thus they created a more international regime. Non-Arabs and recent converts felt toward Islam, the Prophet, and the Prophet's family a loyalty that they would not grant to the old Arabian potentates who had led and initially benefited from the Arab conquests. The Abbasid polity was based on the idea of the fundamental equality of all believers, old or new, Arab or not.

Members of the Abbasid family received some key government posts, as did Iranians and other non-Arabs. Most important, however, local persons got more choice positions than Meccan or Syrian aristocrats. The capital of the caliphate was moved from Syria to Iraq, but to avoid favoring any existing group or region, the Abbasids built a new city, Baghdad, which they called "the navel of the universe." By addressing regional and ethnic sensitivities in an effective way, they were able to maintain, even extend, the centralized state of the Umayyad period.

The daily business of governing was usually in the hands of the *wazir*, who headed the administration, advised the caliph, and often exercised a powerful formative influence on the caliph's children and heirs. The first caliphs chose administrators from loyal Arabs and from experienced Christian subjects. Under the Umayyads the regime was Arabized. Then under Harun al-Rashid the government became international, professional, and hereditary. The chief agency of government was the treasury, which had separate branches dealing with Muslim alms, land and poll taxes paid by subjects, and land taxes paid by converts. Alone among early medieval governments, the caliphate could draw up annual budgets. Alongside the treasury in exerting power was a prestigious group of palace servants. They did not hold major offices, but their informal influence on the caliph and his family was great. The army was another prominent body within the state.

The central government had several links to the provinces. In addition to controlling the army and provincial governorships, the caliph employed a network of regular envoys and spies. The court, especially under the Abbasids, drew able young men from all over into the service of the caliph and created hopes among provincial elites that they, too, might be chosen. In every district and city there were judges, or *qadi*°, to oversee the application of Islamic law. Qadi were under the authority of the caliph.

The death of Harun in 809 sparked a century of problems. Intense family rivalries touched both the succession to the caliphate and the possession of key provincial positions. The bureaucracy became an increasingly influential pressure group, and the palace servants began to foment intrigues. The army became more and more a professional body comprising non-Arabs, especially Turks, hired from the frontiers and beyond because Arabs, enjoying their salaries, declined to serve. The parallel with the Germanization of the late Roman army is striking. The army, the bureaucracy, and the courtiers all had different and conflicting interests and did not hesitate to press their own advantages. Religious divisions persisted, even intensified. Many felt that the Abbasids had not gone far enough in erecting a truly Islamic regime, but some felt that the caliphs had gone too far in claiming both the political and religious authority of the Prophet. Whole regions took advantage of Abbasid leniency in granting local autonomy and began to fall away. After the early tenth century the Abbasid caliphs had little effective power.

## The Emergence of Islamic Culture

Two currents are apparent in the culture of the Islamic East: One is the elaboration of religious thought; the other is the assimilation of multiple cultural heritages. Both were influenced by the spread of Islam that mixed

---

**Abbasids** (uh-BASS-idz)
**Harun al-Rashid** (hah-ROON al-rah-SHEED)

---

**qadi** (KAH-dee)

Greek, North African, Iranian, Turkish, and even Hindu elements into a culture already rich with Arab, Christian, and Jewish ingredients.

Muslims assembled for prayer in mosques, the often beautiful buildings usually modeled on the original mosque in Medina. The worshipers—with men and women in separate areas—arrayed themselves in parallel rows and were led in prayer by an imam. In time the imams started offering interpretations of the Quran, and collections of these interpretations began to circulate. Similarly, Muslim judges began to issue opinions on how the Quran and sunna might be applied to the daily lives of believers. Teachers in mosque schools also were influential. Together these authority figures, collectively the *ulama,* developed a body of religious thought. Lacking elaborate theology and creeds, Islamic religious thought pertains to practice and allegiance more than ideas. The point is less to *know* Islam than to *live* it.

The late ninth and early tenth centuries saw the emergence of a religious split in the Islamic world that persists to this day. The opposing groups are Shi'ite and Sunni Muslims. Shi'ites believe that caliphs should be chosen only according to strict standards of moral and spiritual worthiness. Further, they insist that the only way to ensure such worthiness is to choose caliphs from the line of Ali, the fifth caliph, husband of Muhammad's daughter Fatima and, in 661, a victim of assassination. Moreover, they believe that the whole ulama should measure up to Shi'ite standards. Sunni Muslims, always the vast majority, proclaim that only they adhere to the sunna, the "good practice" of Muhammad himself. Sunnis accept the legitimacy of the whole line of Umayyad and Abbasid caliphs and the teachings of the ulama.

In 832 an Abbasid caliph endowed the "House of Wisdom," an academy for scholars in Baghdad (compare Charlemagne's palace school; see pages 262–264), and from this point on Muslim scholars had the leisure and wherewithal to begin tackling the corpus of Greek thought, especially the scientific writers. The earliest Arab scholars sought mainly to master the learning of the past. Greek, Persian, and Indian works were collected and translated, manuscripts were copied, and libraries were built. Muslims showed little interest in the *literary* heritage of antiquity, the ancient legacy that was so important and controversial to Christian scholars.

So we may ask: Was the Islamic caliphate part of the West or not? Was it brother, or cousin, to the emerging Byzantine and Latin worlds? From the vantage point of 900, the answer we might give to those questions—"largely Western"—differs from the answer we might give today—"largely Eastern." In later chapters we will see how the Islamic world became less Western and more Eastern.

## THE BYZANTINE EMPIRE

THE century after Justinian's death in 565 was difficult for the eastern Roman Empire. Attacks by Persians, Bulgars, and Muslims; riots and rebellions; plagues and famines; and some weak rulers put the empire in a perilous position. Two fundamental changes transformed the eastern Roman Empire into a new civilization that we call "Byzantine°," from "Byzantium," the ancient Greek name for the capital city, Constantinople. In external affairs the empire experienced a sharp geographic contraction until it stabilized into the shape it would hold into the thirteenth century. In internal affairs the empire changed both its basic administrative structures and its cultural orientation.

### External Changes

In 600 the empire still laid claim, along the southern and eastern shores of the Mediterranean, to most of the lands that Rome had ruled for centuries. But in the East the empire had been suffering recurrent losses to Persia. In 610 Heraclius°, a gifted ruler, ascended the throne. Between 622 and 629 Heraclius campaigned brilliantly and recovered almost everything that had been lost. But he faced a cruel irony. When the Arab expansion began under Umar, Heraclius's empire was militarily and financially exhausted. As the seventh century wore on, Arabs captured Syria, Palestine, and Mesopotamia and began a centuries-long push into Anatolia. Eventually they even threatened the capital, Constantinople.

In the Balkans Heraclius and his successors fought constant battles, with mixed results. They checked the advance of the Slavic peoples, who had been expanding southward for some years. The Slavic advance was partly generated by social and political forces among the Slavs themselves and partly a result of pressure from the Avars and Bulgars. These peoples, who were related to the Huns, had begun penetrating into the Danube basin in the late sixth century. The empire tried hard, with varying success, to check their forward march.

Where the West was concerned, Heraclius and his successors were powerless to stop the Arab advance in

---

**Byzantine** (BIZZ-un-teen)    **Heraclius** (her-ACK-lee-us)

**Greek Fire** Invented in the seventh century by Callimachus, a Syrian engineer, Greek fire was a mixture formed from petroleum, sulfur, saltpeter, and lime that ignited on contact with water. It was first used to repel the Muslim siege of Constantinople in 678. *(Institut Amatller d'Art Hispanic)*

North Africa and Spain. In Italy imperial control was confined to a few outposts around Rome, Ravenna, and Sicily. Generally Italy was too far away and strategically insignificant to attract much attention from the imperial government.

By around 700 the empire was assuming the basic geographic shape it would hold for centuries. (See the box "Global Encounters: Byzantium Views Its Neighbors.") In contrast to the vast lands once ruled by Rome, the empire was now confined to the eastern Balkans and western Anatolia. Then in 717 Leo III "the Isaurian°" (Leo was actually Syrian, but later legends made him a resident of Isauria in Anatolia), became emperor in a moment of acute crisis. Arab armies had seized much of Anatolia and had laid siege to Constantinople. The city would surely have fallen had it not been for the "Greek fire" that made it impossible for the attacking navy to operate beneath the seaward walls. Leo repulsed the attack and then ruled successfully until 741. He was followed by his able and charismatic son, Constantine V (r. 741–775). Constantine held the line in Anatolia and enjoyed decades of military success along the Balkan frontier.

In Italy alone Isaurian policy was unsuccessful. When Justinian reconquered Italy from the Ostrogoths (see page 226), his armies devastated the region and left it poor and weak. Into the gap stepped the Lombards, who gradually built a kingdom in the north of Italy—Lombardy still bears their name—and set up a series of duchies in the center and south of Italy. The Byzantines prudently dedicated their resources to holding their Balkan and Anatolian frontiers, but this strategy left their subjects in Italy clamoring for aid. Eventually the popes put themselves at the head of a movement in Italy that turned to the Franks for protection. In 755 and 756 the Frankish king marched to Italy, defeated the Lombards, and donated the territories he seized from them to the pope. On the one hand, this inaugurated the "Papal States," the ever changing set of lands in Italy whose current remnant is Vatican City. On the other hand, this military encounter put an end to effective Byzantine control in Italy, except for the areas around Naples and Sicily. In 827 Muslims seized Sicily, and in the ensuing decades they subjected southern Italy to continuous raids and occasional conquests.

Constantine V's promising son, Leo IV (r. 775–780), survived him only briefly. He left a 6-year-old heir, Con-

___
**Isaurian** (eye-SOAR-ee-un)

# Byzantium Views Its Neighbors

Early in the seventh century the emperor Maurice (r. 582–602) wrote a book called *Strategikon,* a manual of military strategy. Included in Maurice's book is the following section on some of the peoples surrounding Byzantium. The selection invites us to reflect on racial and ethnic stereotyping and on Romano-Byzantine intelligence-gathering capabilities.

The Scythian nations are one in their mode of life and in their organization, which is primitive and includes many peoples. Of these peoples only the Turks and Avars concern themselves with military organization. The nation of the Turks is very numerous and independent. They are not versatile or skilled in most human endeavors. The Avars are scoundrels, devious, and very experienced in military matters.

These nations have a monarchical form of government, and their rulers subject them to cruel punishments for their mistakes. Governed not by love but by fear, they steadfastly bear labors and hardships. They are very superstitious, foul, faithless, possessed by an insatiate desire for riches. They scorn the oath, do not observe agreements, and are not satisfied by gifts. They are fickle, avaricious and, composed of so many tribes as they are, have no sense of kinship or unity with one another.

The light-haired races [Franks and Lombards] place great value on freedom. They are bold and undaunted in battle. Daring and impetuous as they are, they consider any timidity and even a short retreat as a disgrace. They calmly despise death as they fight violently in hand-to-hand combat either on horseback or on foot. Whether on foot or on horseback, they draw up for battle not in any fixed measure and formation, or in regiments or divisions, but according to tribes, their kinship with one another, and common interest. Often when things are not going well and their friends have been killed, they will risk their lives fighting to avenge them.

Either on horseback or on foot they are impetuous and undisciplined in charging, as if they were the only people in the world who are not cowards. They are disobedient to their leaders. They despise good order, especially on horseback. They are easily corrupted by money, greedy as they are. They are hurt by suffering and fatigue. Although they possess bold and daring spirits, their bodies are pampered and soft, and they are not able to bear pain calmly. They are hurt by heat, cold, rain, lack of provisions, especially of wine, and postponements of battle.

The nations of the Slavs and Antes live in the same way and have the same customs. They are both independent, absolutely refusing to be enslaved or governed. They are populous and hardy, readily bearing heat, cold, rain, nakedness, and scarcity of provisions. They are kind and hospitable to travelers in their country. Their women are more sensitive than any others in the world. Owing to their lack of government and their ill feeling toward one another, they are not acquainted with an order of battle. They are completely faithless and have no regard for treaties, which they agree to more out of fear than by gifts. They are always at odds with each other, and nobody is willing to yield to another.

## QUESTIONS

1. On what specific grounds can you compare and contrast Byzantine views of these three groups of peoples?

2. Do you think that the information Maurice provides would have been useful to commanders in the field?

3. How much of this information strikes you as sheer stereotype and how much as empirical observation?

SOURCE: George T. Dennis, trans., *Maurice's Strategikon: A Handbook of Byzantine Military Strategy* (Philadelphia: University of Pennsylvania Press, 1984), pp. 116, 119–120, 120–122. Reprinted by permission of the University of Pennsylvania Press.

stantine VI, and a remarkable widow, Irene (ca. 752–803), as regent for her son. Irene was a skilled politician, but under her the army grew restive because she preferred to make treaties, sometimes on unfavorable terms, than to send troops into the field. She did not trust the military's loyalty. Moreover, Irene had to contend with a foolish son who spent his time trysting with ladies of the court rather than attending to his official duties. In 797 Irene had him blinded, ironically in the very palace chamber where she had given birth to him. This was not a barbaric act in the Byzantine way of thinking. By mutilating Constantine VI, she merely rendered him unfit to rule: Roman ideology held that only a physically perfect person could reign; the alternative would have been to murder him. In any case, Irene's credibility sank to nothing, and in 802 she was deposed by a wily old soldier, Nicephorus° (r. 802–811).

Nicephorus (nye-SEFF-for-us)

**Map 8.2    The Byzantine Empire in the Eighth and Ninth Centuries**    After suffering tremendous territorial losses to the barbarians and Arabs, the Byzantine Empire transformed its military, institutional, and cultural structures to create a regime that lasted until it was conquered by Crusaders in 1204. This map shows the *themes*, Byzantium's major institutional innovation.

**Coin of Empress Irene** This gold *nomisma* of the Empress Irene was struck between 797 and 802. The text reads "Irene, Empress." Note the craftsmanship of the Byzantine moneyers. *(Courtesy of the Trustees of the British Museum)*

Whether in some ideal situation Nicephorus might have been successful is impossible to say. His problems came from two fearsome foes. In Anatolia he faced the redoubtable and aggressive Harun al-Rashid, and in the Balkans he contended with the clever Bulgarian Khan Krum° (r. ca. 803–814). Nicephorus got a break when Harun died in 809, but he fell in battle with Krum, who gruesomely made a drinking cup out of his skull. The Isaurian reputation for invincibility died on that battlefield.

For two generations Byzantium suffered through short reigns, usurpations, political unrest, and military reverses. In 867 a rough soldier, Basil I (r. 867–886), seized the throne and, like Heraclius and Leo III before him, reversed the fortunes of the state. He established a new dynasty, the "Macedonian," and for the first time in years won important military victories. Faced as they were by worthy foes in both Anatolia and the Balkans, the Byzantines, the heirs of the Romans, might have vanished from history. But capable leaders emerged just often enough, especially in the eighth century, to preserve a state that, even in a vastly reduced shape, carried the Roman legacy into the future.

## Internal Changes

Even as its territory was shrinking, Byzantium undertook military and administrative reforms, revised its laws, and refocused its culture, particularly its religious practices. In the early Middle Ages a distinctive "Byzantium" emerged in place of Rome.

Leo and Constantine, the Isaurians, are reminiscent of Diocletian and Constantine, or of Justinian. They energetically brought to completion military reforms that had been pursued intermittently since the late sixth century. These reforms amounted to a major administrative change. For centuries Rome had recruited, trained, and paid professional troops out of tax revenues; they even used tax revenues to settle barbarian soldiers in their midst. Leo and Constantine put the finishing touches on a new "theme" system.

Men from frontier regions were now recruited and settled on farms in military districts called *themes*. All themes, whether land-based army ones or sea-based naval ones, were under the command of a leader who was simultaneously the civil and military chief of his theme. The farmer-soldiers did not pay taxes on their farms but discharged their obligation to the state by personal service. Some standing troops were retained, mainly around the capital, but henceforth the thematic armies (see Map 8.2) formed the backbone of the Roman system.

The new system was less of a drain on the state treasury than the old one. Lower tax revenues were needed, and, correspondingly, so were fewer bureaucrats to collect the money. The empire was smaller than in the past and needed a different kind of army: smaller squadrons concentrated near the threatened frontier regions in Anatolia and the Balkans rather than large armies that were expensive to maintain and cumbersome to transport over long distances.

The Isaurians undertook other reforms, too. Leo issued the *Ecloga*°, the first major revision and updating of Roman law since Justinian's. Issuing a law code was a matter of pride and a clear representation of power and authority. But the *Ecloga* was "a selection of laws," an abridgment whose purpose was to provide a simplified code adapted to the empire's new circumstances.

Leo and Constantine also instituted far-reaching reforms in imperial administration, which had changed little in centuries. Roman bureaucracy had consisted of a few large departments headed by officials with immense responsibilities and power. The revised Byzantine system

---

**Krum** (KROOM)

*Ecloga* (ECK-low-guh)

was characterized by a profusion of departments under officers who had little real power or sway. The emperor neutralized the bureaucrats by drawing them from all social classes, paying them well, and giving them pompous titles and lots of public recognition, all the while dividing their responsibilities, curbing their influence, and making them dependent on himself. The Byzantine government was never a breeding ground for factional squabbles as in the caliphate.

Byzantine culture came to be increasingly defined by the church. The massive Arab conquests that stripped Byzantium of so much territory also removed the ancient patriarchates of Alexandria, Jerusalem, and Antioch from effective contact with Constantinople. Often in the past the empire had been disturbed by severe theological quarrels generated by the differing views held in the several patriarchates. These disputes had been disruptive, but they had also prompted a great deal of learned religious writing. Now, deprived of this stimulus, Byzantium turned inward.

Inside the smaller Byzantine Empire, monasticism gradually assumed a more prominent place in religious life. So many members of elite families sought to become monks that the Isaurians actually tried to limit entry into the religious life. Byzantine monks tended to be deeply learned, intensely critical of the patriarchs of Constantinople—whom they regarded as worldly and political—and opposed to imperial interference in the church. In Theodore of Studion (759–826) Byzantine monasticism found its greatest reformer and legislator since Basil, four centuries earlier (see page 216).

In 726 Emperor Leo III embarked on a bold new religious policy: iconoclasm. For centuries a beautiful and inspiring religious art had been emerging that troubled the emperor. Leo, a man of simple but fervent piety, believed that the presence of religious images, called "icons," in churches and public places was offensive to God. Moreover, Leo was convinced that the military disasters suffered by the empire in recent years were attributable to divine displeasure at the violation of Moses's prohibition of "graven images." Accordingly, he and his son banned religious images. They and some of their more enthusiastic followers even destroyed a few of them. Hence they were called "iconoclasts," which means "image breakers." Iconoclasm was officially proclaimed by a church council in 754, repudiated by another council in 787, proclaimed again in 815, and then definitively rejected in 843.

Although it might seem like an odd and local dispute, iconoclasm had several important consequences in its own time and reveals important aspects of emerging Byzantium to the modern observer. Iconoclasm was categorically rejected as heretical by the popes. This

difference drove a sharp wedge between Eastern and Western Catholics. The debates over iconoclasm finally sharpened Byzantine thinking on the role and function of art in religious life. To this day the icon plays a more prominent role in religious devotion in the East than in the West. Moreover, the battle over iconoclasm evoked some of the most sophisticated Greek religious writing since Late Antiquity. Writers such as John of Damascus (675–749) and Theodore of Studion wrote learned treatises

**Saint Peter**    A rare pre-iconoclastic icon from Mount Sinai: Peter is depicted as a late antique magistrate—wise and distinguished—not as a simple fisherman. The medallions depict Christ in the center, Mary on the right, and John the Evangelist on the left. In a late antique depiction of a consul, the images would have had the emperor in the center, the empress on the right, and the co-consul on the left. *(Alexandria-Michigan-Princeton Archeological Expedition to Mount Sinai/Roger Wood/Corbis)*

in defense of religious art that drew on Greek patristic writing (see page 232) and on ancient Greek philosophy in ways that sharply differentiated Byzantine and Western religious thought.

As the Byzantines turned more and more deeply into their own traditions, they exposed other differences between themselves and the West. Some of these were important, such as the dispute over the so-called *filioque*. In the East people taught and believed that the Holy Spirit proceeded "from the Father." In the West people said that the Holy Spirit proceeded "from the Father *and from the Son*" (*filioque* in Latin). Greek monks shaved the front of their heads, whereas Western monks shaved a circlet on the top. The Greek church used leavened (with yeast) bread in worship, whereas the Western church used unleavened bread. Taken together these differences amounted to a sharpening of the divide between Christian groups whom we may now label "Orthodox" and "Roman Catholic." Neither group wished to see a division in the Christian world, but physical separation and independent cultural evolution were producing two different traditions based, paradoxically, on a single late antique Christianity.

With its new geographic shape and its Orthodox faith, Byzantium was at once something old and something new. In official Byzantine ideology, the Roman Empire had always been one and inseparable. It is interesting to ask how familiar Augustus Caesar would have found the empire of Constantine V. With its indebtedness to classical and Christian traditions, there can be no question that Byzantium was a part of the West. But in its comparatively modest size, its constantly threatened frontiers, and its Orthodox traditions, Byzantium was going to have a somewhat different future than the portions of the West situated inside Rome's former western provinces. It is worth noting, too, that as was the case in the Muslim world, the seventh and ninth centuries were acutely tumultuous in Byzantium, whereas the eighth was marked by consolidation and achievement.

# CATHOLIC KINGDOMS IN THE WEST

**I**N the Latin West the seventh century also was marked by challenges, the eighth century by innovation and accomplishment, and the ninth century by new threats and in some areas near collapse. The social and political heritages of both the Germanic and the Roman past interacted with Christianity and the church to produce the third early medieval civilization: Catholic Europe. Crucial to these developments were the evangelization of the countryside, the growth of an ecclesiastical hierarchy, the shift of papal interests away from the Mediterranean world toward western Europe, and the evolving relationship between royal governments and the Catholic Church.

## The Struggles of Visigothic Spain

After their defeat at Clovis's hand in 507, the Visigoths were never able to re-establish dynastic continuity. As a result, Spain witnessed rebellions and usurpations more frequently than any other area in the West. In addition to internal struggles, Spain faced external threats from the Franks, the Ostrogoths in Italy, the Byzantines, and finally the Muslims.

The accomplishments of the Visigothic king Leovigild° (r. 568–586) seem remarkable given the state of Spain on his accession. He nearly unified the country, and he established a capital (Toledo) and a seat of government—which the Visigoths had been lacking since they lost Toulouse in 507. Leovigild was a good general and a charismatic leader who understood the value of enhancing the royal office. He wore royal vestments, sat on a throne, and issued coins with his own image and name. Leovigild's greatest problem was the Arianism of the Visigothic minority in the midst of the Catholic population. An Arian himself, he tried hard to convert Catholics to Arianism but failed. In 589, under King Reccared (r. 586–601), the Visigoths officially embraced Roman Catholicism.

The conversion of the Visigoths permitted close cooperation between the church and the monarchy and placed the resources of the church at the disposal of the king as he attempted to unite and govern the country. The career of Archbishop Isidore of Seville (560–636) is a prime indicator of those resources. He came from an old Hispano-Roman family, received a fine education, and wrote histories, biblical commentaries, and a learned encyclopedia. By the mid-seventh century, economic prosperity, a high degree of assimilation between Goths and Hispano-Romans, and a brilliant culture marked the high point of Visigothic Spain. The succession problem, however, was never overcome, and a stable central government was beyond reach.

In 711 Muslims from North Africa invaded Spain. Within five years Berbers (native North Africans and recent converts to Islam who were led by Arabs) completed the conquest of much of the Iberian Peninsula, except for the northwest. In 716 the caliph at Damascus introduced an emir who ruled from Cordoba. The emirate of Cordoba struggled to make good its authority over all of Spain but

---

**Leovigild** (lee-OH-vuh-gild)

**A Mother Hen and Her Chicks** This delightfully frivolous object may have been a gift from Pope Gregory I to the Lombard queen Theudelinda. It helps us to appreciate the aesthetic tastes of the barbarians. *(Cathedral Treasure, Monza/Scala/Art Resource, NY)*

failed to do so. Christians in the rugged mountains of the northwest—the region called Asturias°—could not be dislodged, and the Muslims' part of Spain—known as al-Andalus°—was plagued by the same divisions as the Islamic East: Arab factions against other Arab factions, Arabs against non-Arab Muslims, and Muslims against non-Muslims. Secure in mountainous Asturias (see Map 8.3 on page 259), Christian kings built a capital at Oviedo and, in the ninth century, launched attacks against al-Andalus. For six hundred years this conflict between Christians and Muslims was the chief dynamic of Spanish history.

## Italy and the Papal States

In 600 the Italian political scene was crowded. Several Germanic groups, several Byzantine outposts, and the popes were all contending for power. By the late eighth century the Franks dominated northern Italy, the popes had created a state in the center, and the Byzantines clung to Naples and Sicily, much of which they lost to Muslims in the ninth century.

As we have seen, the Lombards conquered most of the Italian peninsula after the Gothic Wars. Neither numerous nor united, the Lombards were also Arians. Although the Lombard kings converted to Catholicism by 680, formed a strong government, and issued the most sophisticated Germanic law code, they always faced a dilemma. The kings had not systematically organized the conquest of Italy. From their capital at Pavia they dominated the Po Valley, but other Lombards settled elsewhere and created independent duchies. Kings were weakened because they did not control the duchies and because between Lombardy and the duchies lay Rome and Ravenna, which were nominally Byzantine.

The strongest Lombard king of the eighth century, Aistulf° (r. 749–757), decided to risk the consequences of attacking Ravenna and Rome. He conquered the former but caused the pope to turn to Pippin III, the king of the Franks, for aid and protection. Pippin came to Italy, defeated Aistulf, and forced him to give to the pope all the lands he had taken from Rome and Ravenna. A few years later Aistulf's successor reopened hostilities in central Italy. In 774 Charlemagne, Pippin's son and successor, defeated the Lombards, deposed their king, and took the Lombard crown for himself.

The Franks guaranteed to the popes undisputed possession of a substantial territory in central Italy. This first Papal State was the culmination of three processes. First, as Roman imperial power declined in Late Antiquity, bishops often became the effective leaders of their towns. This position brought them power and prestige but also burdens. The popes found themselves responsible for Rome's food and water supply, the upkeep of its public buildings, and local charitable services. To pay for these functions, the popes began to organize the efficient bureaucratic administration of the patrimonies, the lands of the Roman church.

Second, the popes took the lead in protecting many people in central Italy, whether they lived on the patri-

---

**Asturias** (ahs-TOUR-ee-ahs)   **al-Andalus** (al-AHN-dah-loose)      **Aistulf** (ICE-tulf) monies or not, thus preserving their purses from Byzantine taxes and their souls from heresy. This effort, too, forged bonds between the popes and the Italians.

Third, eighth-century Rome spawned a justification for papal temporal rule. According to the *Donation of Constantine,* a document written in Rome (probably in the 760s), when Constantine departed Rome for the East in the 320s, he allegedly gave to the pope the authority to rule Rome and the whole West. In reality, no pope ever made such grandiose claims, and no concrete claims were ever based on the *Donation.* But the existence of the document signals a crucial progression from protection to direct rule. From the beginning, however, the Papal States were vulnerable and required a protector.

## The Fate of the British Isles

Britain was less thoroughly Romanized, more quickly abandoned by the Romans, and more deeply influenced by Germanic peoples than any other locality in the West. Around 600 the small Anglo-Saxon kingdoms created in the sixth century took the first steps toward converting to Christianity, transforming Britain into England, and joining England inseparably to the European world (see Map 8.3). And another history was unfolding in the British Isles, that of the Celtic peoples in the north and west of Britain itself and in Ireland.

The Celts—Britain's inhabitants before the Romans invaded in the first century—were related to peoples who lived in a broad band from Anatolia to Ireland and Spain. The Anglo-Saxons confined the British Celts to the western regions of Cornwall and Wales and to the northern area of Scotland. Ireland, seemingly beyond reach, had almost no Roman or Anglo-Saxon imprint.

The period between 600 and 900 saw only the faint beginnings of consolidation in the Celtic realms, where the development of the Catholic Church preceded large-scale political organization. Each Celtic region produced an elaborate mythology connected with heroic missionaries who supposedly brought the Christian faith in Late Antiquity. The best-known stories swirl around Ireland's Saint Patrick (390?–461?). The son of a Roman official in the north of Britain, Patrick was captured by pirates, enslaved in Ireland, freed, and eventually made a priest; he then returned to Ireland as a missionary. From his base at Armagh°, Ireland's first bishopric, Patrick and his successors spread Christianity, and a vigorous monasticism, throughout the island. Historical, too, is the Irish aristocrat Columba (521–597), who, after his family lost a great battle, migrated in 563 to the isle of Iona off the coast of Scotland.

From his monastery on Iona, Columba and his successors began the evangelization of the native Picts in Scotland.

Among the most successful Anglo-Saxon kingdoms were Wessex, Northumbria, and Mercia. Each had a reasonably large population and territory and opportunities for expansion. Wessex, for example, spread south and west into Devon, Cornwall, and Wales; Northumbria, which stretched along the North Sea coast, spread west to the Irish Sea and north into lowland Scotland (see Map 8.3). These kingdoms had ambitious rulers whose wars provided booty, land, and glory for old followers and new recruits. English kings quickly adopted symbolic aspects of rule to legitimize their authority and enhance their prestige. Archaeologists have found fine scepters and coins bearing early kings' names. The kings of Northumbria presided in a magnificent wooden hall, and their movements were preceded and announced by banners.

Relations with the church were important also. Two issues proved crucial: the conversion to Christianity and the development of an ecclesiastical hierarchy. In 597 Pope Gregory I sent a small band of missionaries under a Roman monk named Augustine (d. 604) to King Aethelbert of Kent, whose Christian wife, Bertha, had prepared the ground for the newcomers. From their base of operations at Canterbury in southeastern England, Augustine and his successors had limited success spreading Christianity, but a new field of influence was opened to them when Aethelbert's daughter married a king of Northumbria and took missionaries to her new home. Monks from Iona, as noted, were already introducing Christianity into central and lowland Scotland. When later Northumbrian kings turned to Iona for missionaries and bishops, Roman and Celtic Christianity came face-to-face in Northumbria.

The Christianity brought from Ireland did not differ in fundamental ways from the Roman Christianity imported at Canterbury. Indeed, the Irish were Roman Catholics. But Ireland had been isolated from the centers of Christian life since Late Antiquity, and its church had developed a number of distinctive local customs. For example, the two traditions used different calendars and thus celebrated Easter—the commemoration of the resurrection of Jesus Christ and the central celebration of the Christian year—on different days. In 664 a Northumbrian king called a church council at the monastery of Whitby, whose abbess was the former royal princess Hilda (614–680), a champion of Celtic customs. (See the box "Reading Sources: Two English Holy Women: Hilda and Leoba.") At Whitby, Roman and Irish representatives debated their positions. The king, choosing the universal over the particular, decided for Rome.

In 668 the pope sent to England a new archbishop of Canterbury, Theodore (r. 668–690). He was a Syrian monk

---

**Armagh** (ARR-mah)

## READING SOURCES

# TWO ENGLISH HOLY WOMEN: HILDA AND LEOBA

*These passages reveal some of the opportunities available to highborn women who embraced the religious life. Hilda, abbess of Whitby, was of royal descent and involved herself in many of the great events of her day. Leoba, of noble birth, joined a significant monastery in Wessex but later, and quite unusually, migrated to the continent, where she joined forces with the famous missionary Boniface.*

Hilda] led her life in two equal parts, the first thirty-three years devoted to secular occupations and the second even more nobly devoted to the Lord in monastic life. She was indeed nobly born, the daughter of Hereric, a nephew of King Edwin. . . . When, having abandoned her secular garb, she decided to serve God alone, she went away to the land of the East Angles, whose king was a relative, from where she aimed to travel to Gaul and live as an exile for the Lord's sake where her sister Hereswith, mother of king Aldwith of the East Angles, was already living. But Bishop Aidan called her home and gave her land for a monastery. . . . Later she undertook to found a monastery at Whitby . . . and there she taught righteousness, mercy, purity, and other virtues, but above all peace and charity. . . . So great was her discretion that not only common people but even kings and princes used to come and ask her advice. . . . Those who submitted to her leadership had to study the scriptures . . . and five men from this monastery became bishops.

[Leoba's] mother consecrated her and handed her to Mother Tetta (abbess of Wimbourne and sister of an English king) to be taught the sacred sciences. . . . The girl, therefore, grew up and was taught with such care by the abbess and all the nuns that she had no interests other than the monastery and the pursuit of sacred knowledge. She took no pleasure in aimless jests and wasted no time on girlish romances but, fired by the love of Christ, fixed her mind always on reading or hearing the Word of God. Whatever she heard or read she committed to memory, and put all that she learned into practice. . . . Boniface sent messengers to Tetta asking him to send Leoba . . . for Leoba's reputation for learning and holiness had spread far and wide and her praise was on everyone's lips. . . . When she came, the man of God [Boniface] received her with the deepest reverence, holding her in great affection, not so much because she was related to him on his mother's side as because he knew that by her holiness and wisdom she would confer many benefits by her word and example. . . . He gave her the monastery at a place called Bischofsheim, where there was a large community of nuns. These were trained according to her principles in the discipline of monastic life and made such progress in her teaching that many of them became superiors of others, so that there was hardly a convent of nuns in that part that did not have one of her disciples as abbess.

Sources: Hilda: Adapted from Venerabilis Baedae, *Historiam Ecclesiasticam Gentis Anglorum,* 4.21, ed. Charles Plummer (Oxford: Oxford University Press, 1896), pp. 252–254 (translated by T. Noble); Leoba: Thomas F. X. Noble and Thomas Head, eds., *Soldiers of Christ: Saints and Saints' Lives from Late Antiquity and the Early Middle Ages* (University Park: Pennsylvania State University Press, 1995), pp. 264–266.

who had traveled widely in the East, lived for a time in Rome, gained great experience in church administration, and acquired a reputation for both learning and discretion. The church in England was in an administrative shambles. Working tirelessly, Theodore built up a typical Roman ecclesiastical structure, introduced authoritative Roman canon law for the church, and promoted Christian education. Theodore laid the foundations for a unified English church that contributed to the eventual political unification of England.

Ecclesiastical peace led to the flourishing of monastic life. Monasteries played two important roles in this period. First, they led the way in bringing Christianity to ordinary people. Despite early gains among kings and nobles, Christianity had barely begun to penetrate the countryside. Second, monks maintained international connections, ranging from Ireland to Rome, that attached England to the major intellectual currents of the day and enabled the English to make their own contributions.

**Lindisfarne Gospels: Opening Page of the Gospel According to Matthew** In the last years of the seventh century in the north of England, scribes and painters produced this exquisite book, which combines the artistic styles of the Mediterranean and Celtic worlds. *(British Library)*

After Theodore's school at Canterbury, the most important early center of learning was in Northumbria. There English, Irish, Frankish, and Roman currents flowed together in the monasteries of Lindisfarne, Wearmouth, and Jarrow and in the cathedral school of York. British schools produced some of the most beautiful illuminated manuscripts—books whose texts are adorned with gorgeous paintings—of the early Middle Ages.

The greatest product of this intellectual tradition was Bede (673–735). When he was 7, his parents placed him in the monastery at Wearmouth. He soon transferred to neighboring Jarrow and spent the rest of his life there. Bede was a teacher of genius, an erudite scholar, and a superb Latin stylist. His *Ecclesiastical History of the English People,* the most important source for English history from the fifth century to the eighth, did much to identify the Anglo-Saxons as a single English people. His biblical commentaries remained influential all over Europe for centuries. His studies of temporal reckoning popularized the use of A.D. dating, which replaced a bewildering array of local systems.

The career of King Offa of Mercia° (r. 757–796) shows the trends in early Britain. His ancestors were pagans, but he was a patron of the church, convener of councils, and recipient of papal envoys. He dominated all of Britain and was the first to call himself "King of the English." He issued a law code, reformed Mercia's institutions, and signed England's first international trade agreement—with Charlemagne.

After Offa's death, Viking raiders (see page 265) destroyed whatever unity had been achieved. For two generations local rulers struggled just to survive, and in 865 a Viking army launched a conquest of the whole country. In 871 Alfred the Great (r. 871–899) ascended the throne of Wessex, won a series of military victories, rallied the English, and began the slow reconquest of northern and eastern England from the Vikings. Alfred promoted intellectual recovery, church reform, and political stability. After half a century of chaos, Alfred revived the centralizing and unifying work of his eighth-century predecessors and laid the foundations for the English state of the tenth and eleventh centuries.

Britain's integration into the wider world is revealed by a seventh-century ship burial unearthed near Sutton Hoo (in East Anglia) in 1939. The ship, either a grave for or a memorial to an unknown king, had been hauled up onto the land, filled with treasures, and buried. The array of goods found at Sutton Hoo is astonishing. The hull contained Byzantine silver, represented by spoons and a large dish; Frankish gold, in the form of dozens of coins, jewelry, and personal adornments from many places; and pots, beakers, and other domestic items of varied provenance. The artistic decorations on these items demonstrate influences ranging from the Mediterranean to the Rhineland, Scandinavia, and Ireland.

## THE CAROLINGIAN EMPIRE

CLOVIS and the Franks created the most effective of the early Germanic kingdoms. During the seventh century that kingdom, too, experienced difficulties but did not disappear. Just as Roman aristocrats had borne the ancient heritage into the

**Mercia** (MUR-sha)

Middle Ages, so now a Frankish family, called "Carolingian" from the name of its greatest member, Charlemagne, assembled the talent and resources of the Frankish realm in a new way. Charlemagne reformed his government and church, patronized learning, and resurrected the western empire. Early medieval civilization reached its culmination in the work of Charlemagne and his dynasty.

## The Rise of the Carolingian Family, 600–768

When Clovis died in 511, he divided his realm among his sons, and thereafter several kingdoms coexisted. The Merovingian royal families feuded constantly, sought to expand at one another's expense, and drew local aristocracies into their battles. Trade and intellectual life declined, and some regions that had been conquered in the sixth century slipped away.

Nevertheless, the *idea* of a single kingdom of the Franks persisted. Kings and aristocrats in the small kingdoms competed for leadership of the realm as a whole. The flourishing culture of late antique Gaul was largely gone, but a creative Christian monastic culture was growing up in all parts of the Frankish kingdom. Monks began accomplishing the difficult task of converting the countryside to Christianity. The seventh century, in other words, was a time when the late antique regime was slowly changing into the medieval regime.

Central to this development was the rise to prominence of the Carolingians. The family appeared in history just after 600 and thereafter monopolized the office of mayor of the palace (sort of a prime minister) to the king in Austrasia° (the easternmost kingdom; see Map 8.3). The Carolingians were the boldest and wealthiest family in Austrasia, perhaps in the Frankish world. Within two generations they unified the Frankish realm and increased their own power.

The Carolingians used several methods to accomplish their ends. They formed alliances with powerful noble families in many regions. They waged war against the enemies of the Franks to restore the territorial integrity of the kingdom. Charles Martel (d. 741), Charlemagne's grandfather, led the Frankish forces that put an end to Arab raiding in Gaul, defeating a large force near Poitiers in 733. With booty from their wars, tribute from conquered peoples, spoils taken from recalcitrant opponents, and even lands seized from the church, the Carolingians attracted and rewarded more and more followers until no one was a match for them. The Carolingians also allied themselves very early with leading churchmen, both episcopal and monastic. They aided missionaries in the

**Austrasia** (aw-STRAY-zhuh)

**Map 8.3    The Carolingian World**    The territory over which Charlemagne exerted direct or indirect control was vast. The areas beyond the Rhine and Danube, never part of the Roman Empire, became under the Carolingians a permanent part of Western civilization. The Treaty of Verdun (see inset), signed by Charlemagne's grandsons in 843, was the first and most important of many divisions of the Carolingian Empire that eventually led to the emergence of France and Germany.

work of converting central Germany, thereby expanding Frankish influence in that area.

For years the Carolingians were content with the office of mayor of the palace. Then in 749 Pippin III (son of Charles Martel) decided to send envoys to the pope to ask whether it was right that the person who had all the power in the land of the Franks was not the king. The pope responded that this situation ran counter to the divine plan. Accordingly, in 751 the last Merovingian king was deposed, and Pippin was elected in his place (r. 751–768). Pippin had prepared his usurpation very carefully with his Frankish supporters, but he appealed to the pope to make it appear that he had become king with divine approval and not by crude seizure. Hard-pressed by the Lombards in Italy, the pope probably gave Pippin the answer he wanted primarily to enlist him as an ally. Three years later the pope visited the Frankish kingdom, where he crowned and anointed Pippin and his sons, including Charlemagne. (The practice of anointing the head of a ruler with holy oil, which renders the recipient sacred, dates back to the kings of Israel. The head and hands of Catholic bishops also were anointed. The anointing of rulers and churchmen persisted throughout the Middle Ages and into the modern world.) The pope also forbade the Franks ever to choose a king from a family other than the Carolingians and received from their new favorites a promise of aid in Italy.

## The Empire of Charlemagne, 768–814

Charlemagne (Carolus Magnus, "Charles the Great" in Latin) was a huge man, and his stature has grown in European history and legend. Like all great leaders, Charlemagne (r. 768–814) was complex. He spoke and read Frankish, Latin, and some Greek but never learned to write. He promoted Christian morality but perpetrated unspeakable brutalities on his enemies and enjoyed several concubines. Many battles were fought in his name, but he rarely accompanied his armies and fought no campaigns that are remembered for strategic brilliance. Determination and organization were the hallmarks of his forty-six-year reign.

0 150 300 Km.

0 150 300 Mi.

Asturias Kingdom
Frankish Kingdom, 768
Areas conquered by Charlemagne
Tributary peoples
Byzantine territories

**TREATY OF VERDUN, 843**

KINGDOM OF LOUIS THE GERMAN

Aachen

Verdun

Paris

Strasbourg

*TRIBUTARY PEOPLES*

KINGDOM OF CHARLES THE BALD

KINGDOM OF LOTHAIR

PAPAL STATES

Rome

0 200 400 Km.

0 200 400 Mi.

*Iona* SCOTLAND

Armagh

Jarrow

IRELAND Dublin

NORTHUMBRIA

York

DANISH MARCH

WALES

MERCIA

EAST ANGLIA

Utrecht

SAXONY 804

CORNWALL

DEVON

WESSEX

ESSEX

Canterbury

KENT

SUSSEX

FLANDERS

Aachen

Fulda

AUSTRASIA

Mainz

*Rhine*

TRIBUTARY

Echternach

Rouen

Paris

*Danube*

BRITTANY

NEUSTRIA

Orléans

ALEMANNIA

BAVARIA 788

SLAVIC

Tours

Poitiers

BURGUNDY

ISTRIA

PEOPLES

AQUITAINE

Lyon

Milan

VENETIA

Venice

Oviedo

Pavia

*Rhône*

Bordeaux

GASCONY

LOMBARDY

Ravenna

DALMATIA

ASTURIAS

Roncesvalles

Aniane

*Ebro*

Marseille

Lérins

PAPAL STATES

DUCHY OF SPOLETO

UMAYYAD SPAIN

SPANISH MARCH 811

Spoleto

Rome

Barcelona

CORSICA

Monte Cassino

DUCHY OF BENEVENTO

Toledo

Salerno

Cordoba

BALEARIC IS.

SARDINIA

BYZANTINE EMPIRE

SICILY

It took until the mid-780s for Charlemagne to assess and understand his world (see Map 8.3). His first major achievement was the articulation of a new ruling ideology in the Latin West. In capitularies°—royal executive orders—of 789, Charlemagne required all males to swear an oath of allegiance to him, and he compared himself to a biblical king in his responsibility to admonish, to teach, and to set an example for his people. He referred to the people of his realm as a "New Israel," a new chosen people. Interestingly, this chosen people was not exclusively Frankish. No distinctions were to be made among Franks or Bavarians or Saxons. Everyone was to be equal in allegiance to the king and in membership in a sort of Augustinian City of God.

Einhard (ca. 770–840), Charlemagne's friend and biographer, reports that Augustine's *City of God* (see page 233) was the king's favorite book. The king understood it to mean that two opposing domains contended for power on earth: a City of God consisting of all right-thinking Christians—the "New Israel"—and a City of Man consisting of pagans, heretics, and infidels. This idea is similar to the Islamic umma (see page 242). To Charlemagne and his advisers, it was obvious that as God was the sole legitimate ruler in heaven, Charlemagne was the sole legitimate and divinely appointed ruler on earth.

Modern readers may think that Charlemagne had crossed a boundary between church and state. It is crucial to understand that to Charlemagne, as to his Muslim and Byzantine contemporaries, no such boundary existed. Church (or religion) and state were complementary attributes of a polity whose end was personal salvation, not military security or personal fulfillment. Charlemagne's ideological legacy was twofold. On the one hand, it created possibilities for bitter struggles later in the Middle Ages between secular rulers and ecclesiastical powers about the leadership of Christian society. On the other hand, it made it hard to define the state and its essential purposes in other than religious terms.

The most disputed event in the reign of Charlemagne was his imperial coronation in Rome on Christmas in 800. It is important to separate how this event happened from what it meant to the participants. In April 799 some disgruntled papal bureaucrats and their supporters attacked Pope Leo III (r. 795–816) in an attempt to depose him. Leo was saved by an ally of Charlemagne and then traveled all the way to Saxony, where the king was camped with his army. Charlemagne agreed to restore the pope to Rome and, as his ally and protector, to investigate those who had attacked him. No real offenses could be proved against the pope, who appeared publicly in Rome to swear that he had done nothing wrong. Everything was handled to avoid any hint that the pope had been put on trial. When Charlemagne went to Saint Peter's Basilica on Christmas Day, he prayed before the main altar. As he rose from prayer, Pope Leo placed a crown on his head, and the assembled Romans acclaimed him as emperor.

Debate over this coronation arises from a remark of Einhard, who said that if Charlemagne had known what was going to happen, he would not have gone to church that day, even though it was Christmas. Einhard's point was not that Charlemagne did not wish to be emperor. For at least fifteen years, prominent people at the Carolingian court had been addressing Charlemagne in imperial terms in letters, treatises, and poems. Moreover, some were saying that because of Irene's usurpation (see page 249), the imperial throne was vacant—implying that a woman could not truly rule. What Einhard did mean was that Charlemagne saw himself as a Frankish and Christian emperor, not as a *Roman* emperor. The imperial office dignified his position as leader of the Frankish "Israel." Charlemagne did not wish to be beholden to the pope or to the Romans.

Charlemagne's policies did not change after his coronation. He continued his program of legal and ecclesiastical reform and put the finishing touches on some military and diplomatic campaigns. In 806 he divided his empire among his three legitimate sons. Two of them died, so in 813 he made Louis his sole heir and successor. Charlemagne outlived most of the friends and companions of his youth and middle age. He outlived four wives and many of his children. Old and alone, ill and lame, he died in early 814.

Charlemagne's legacy was great. He brought together the lands that would become France, Germany, the Low Countries, and northern Italy and endowed them with a common ideology, government, and culture. He provided a model that Europeans would look back to for centuries as a kind of golden age. His vast supra-regional and supra-ethnic entity, gradually called "Christendom," drew deeply on the universalizing ideals of its Roman, Christian, and Jewish antecedents but was, nevertheless, original. With its Roman, Germanic, and Christian foundations, the Carolingian Empire represented the final stage in the evolution of the Roman Empire in the West.

## Carolingian Government

Charlemagne accomplished much through the sheer force of his personality and his boundless energy. But he also reformed and created institutional structures. These helped him to carry out his tasks, guaranteed a measure

---

**capitularies** (kuh-PITCH-u-lar-eez)

of permanence to his reforms, and created government patterns that lasted in many parts of Europe until the twelfth century.

The king (or emperor—the offices differed little in practical importance) was the heart of the system. In theory, the king ruled by God's grace and did not have to answer for his conduct to any person. In reality, the king necessarily sought consensus through a variety of means. The king controlled vast lands, which gave him great wealth of his own and also the means to reward loyal followers. By controlling appointments to key positions, the king required men to come to him for power, wealth, and prestige.

The Eastern contemporaries of the Carolingians relied on large numbers of carefully trained, paid civil servants. In contrast, the Carolingians employed a limited number of men who were tied to them by bonds of familial and personal allegiance. The Carolingian court included several ceremonial officers and a domestic staff, all desirable positions. For example, the constable, an officer in charge of transporting the royal entourage, was usually a great aristocrat; the real work of the office was carried out by underlings. The treasurer was the keeper of the king's bedchamber, where the royal treasure chest was kept. Several chaplains, whose primary duty was to see to the spiritual needs of the court, kept official records. The queen controlled the domestic staff and the stewards who managed the royal estates.

Local government was mainly entrusted to counts. About six hundred counts, and several times that number of minor officials, managed the empire. As in Merovingian times, the counts were administrative, judicial, and military officials. Most came from prominent families, and the office increased the wealth and importance of its holders. Counts had to promulgate and enforce royal orders and preside in regular sessions of local courts. They got one-third of the fines, so the zealous pursuit of justice was in their interest.

The royal court and the localities were linked in several ways. Under Charlemagne and his successors it became usual for all major officers, whether secular (counts and their subordinates) or ecclesiastical (bishops and abbots), to be *vassals* of the king. Vassals solemnly pledged loyalty and service to the king. Vassalage drew on both Roman and Germanic customs. Patron-client ties had always been socially and politically important among the Romans, and the allegiance of warriors to a chief was a key Germanic bond. But by connecting personal loyalty with public office, Charlemagne created something essentially new. Only a few thousand men, a tiny fraction of the total population, were vassals at any time. They constituted the political and social elite.

Another connection between the king and his local agents was the assembly that met in various places once or twice a year. In theory, all free men could attend these gatherings, which sometimes had separate secular and

**Model of Charlemagne's Palace at Aachen**   In the foreground is the octagonal chapel and throne room of Charlemagne's palace at Aachen. It is joined by galleries to the residential quarters in the background. Construction was begun in 788. The models for these buildings were found in Rome, Trier, and Ravenna.   *(Römisch-Germanisches Zentralmuseum)*

ecclesiastical sessions, to advise the king on matters of great importance, such as war and peace or legal reforms. In practice, only the vassals had the means or the interest to ensure their presence. Most of the great Carolingian reforms were formulated in these assemblies by cooperation between the king and his most important subjects. The assemblies served to defuse dissension, but the king also brought his power to bear locally by traveling widely. The monarchy possessed estates all over the heartlands of the kingdom, and the royal entourage often moved from one place to another. Monasteries and cathedrals provided hospitality to the king. As the royal party traveled about the realm, they were able to check on local conditions and to compel local officials to comply with royal wishes.

In 788 Charlemagne began to build a palace at Aachen°, and in the last twenty years of his life he usually resided there (see Map 8.3). The later Carolingian rulers all tended to have fixed residences, as did the Byzantines and the Abbasids. In adopting fixed residences and elaborate court rituals, the Carolingians may have been returning to Roman precedents or copying their contemporaries to appear as sophisticated as they. Elegant courts and intricate rituals project an aura of grandeur that enhances people's respect for their rulers. It is no accident that a key innovation of Charlemagne's reign coincided with his permanent residence in Aachen. In the late 780s he began to send out pairs of roving inspectors, or *missi dominici*°, envoys of the lord king. Their function was to see that royal orders were being observed, that counts were dispensing justice honestly, and that persons of power were not oppressing the powerless.

## The Carolingian Renaissance

Charlemagne's reforms culminated in a revival of learning that scholars have named the "Carolingian Renaissance" (*renaissance* is French for "rebirth"). Charlemagne's fundamental ideas are revealed by the constant use in contemporary sources of words such as *rebirth, renewal, reform,* and *restoration.* Charlemagne, his advisers, and his successors looked back for inspiration to Christian and papal Rome, to Saint Peter and Constantine, and to the Church Fathers. To them the rebirth of Western society as a "New Israel" was equivalent to the theological rebirth of an individual in baptism. The Carolingians were the driving force behind intellectual growth in their era, and in all areas they subordinated learning to their ideological program.

To accomplish his objectives, Charlemagne required every cathedral and monastery to establish a school. (See the box "The Continuing Experiment: Charlemagne's Efforts at Educational Reform.") To set up and run those schools, he summoned to his court many of the most able and influential intellectual figures of the day, among them Franks, such as his biographer Einhard, grammar teachers from Italy, and Visigothic theologians from the Spanish border. His most famous recruit was the Anglo-Saxon Alcuin° (735–804), the most learned man of his day and the heir of Bede and of the brilliant culture of Northumbria.

Much of the work of Alcuin and his associates was devoted to producing textbooks and to teaching elementary knowledge. Charlemagne was convinced that people needed to be taught the basic truths of Christianity if he were to accomplish his task of leading them to salvation. A massive effort was thus undertaken to copy manuscripts of the Bible and the writings of the Latin Church Fathers. These books, the essential resources for the whole program, needed to be disseminated as widely as possible. The process of copying was facilitated by a new script, Caroline minuscule. (See the feature "Weighing the Evidence: The Manuscript Book" on pages 272–273.)

It is significant that Charlemagne could attract Alcuin from York, the most renowned school in the West, to head his palace school, just then forming. Alcuin recognized that Charlemagne could place more resources at his disposal than anyone else and had the will to do so. Alcuin also saw the long-term benefits that would come from his work. Alcuin's pupils spread out in the next generation to create a network of schools that went right on multiplying across the ninth century. That is a powerful legacy. And Alcuin did more than just teach. He wrote learned works and poetry and was for twenty years Charlemagne's most trusted adviser.

With his plan, personnel, and schools in place, Charlemagne took many concrete steps. He secured from Rome a copy of the authoritative canon law of the church. In 789, after some years of study by his court scholars, this law was issued for his whole kingdom. In about 786 Charlemagne got from the pope a *sacramentary,* a service book for worship in cathedral churches, and, again after a period of examination, this was imposed throughout the kingdom. Charlemagne sought an authoritative copy of the *Rule of St. Benedict,* and after study and commentary, this Rule was imposed on all monasteries in the kingdom.

---

Aachen (AH-ken)
*missi dominici* (MISS-ee doe-MEE-nee-kee)

Alcuin (AL-kwin)

# Charlemagne's Efforts at Educational Reform

Charlemagne equated the rebirth of Western society with spiritual renewal, so he addressed his major reforms to the church and its leaders. In about 789 Charlemagne sent letters like this one to every bishop and ordered them to transmit the letters to the churches and monasteries in their territories, for it was in those institutions that schools were to be found. Christianity is a faith of books, and of the Bible above all. Charlemagne was trying to reform the church and Christian practices, and to achieve his goals he saw a need to attend to a basic program of education. Proper schooling, he believed, would produce proper behavior.

Be it known to your devotion, which is most pleasing to God, that we, together with our faithful men, have considered it to be useful that the bishoprics and monasteries entrusted by the favor of Christ to our control . . . ought to be zealous in the cultivation of learning and in teaching those who by the gift of God are able to learn, according to the capacity of each individual. Thus just as the observance of the rule [that is, the guidelines observed in a monastery] imparts grace and order to their conduct, so also zeal in teaching and learning may do the same for their sentences, so that those who desire to please God by living rightly should not neglect to please him also by speaking correctly. For although conduct may be better than knowledge, nevertheless knowledge precedes conduct. In the past few years letters were often sent to us from several monasteries in which it was stated that the brethren who dwelt there offered on our behalf sacred and pious prayers. We have noticed in most of these letters both correct thoughts and uncouth expressions, because what pious devotion dictated faithfully to the mind,

the tongue, uneducated on account of the neglect of study, was not able to express without error. So we began to fear that perhaps, as the skill in writing was less, so also the wisdom for understanding the Holy Scriptures might be much less than it ought to be. For we all know well that, although errors of speech are dangerous, far more dangerous are errors in understanding. Therefore, we exhort you not only to avoid neglecting the study of literature, but also with most humble mind, pleasing to God, to study earnestly so that you may be able more easily and correctly to penetrate the mysteries of the divine Scriptures. Since, moreover, images, tropes, and similar figures are to be found in the sacred pages, no one doubts that each one will in reading them understand the spiritual sense more quickly if previously he shall have been fully instructed in letters. Such men are to be chosen for this work who have both the will and ability to learn and the desire to instruct others. For we desire you to be devout in mind, learned in discourse, chaste in conduct, and eloquent in speech.

## QUESTIONS

1. Charlemagne's "renaissance" was obviously to be built on the learning of the clergy. What were his arguments for this? Was this a wise foundation?

2. Why would Charlemagne have thought that "knowledge precedes conduct"?

3. In Charlemagne's time, or any other, is basic education a good place to begin reforming society as a whole? Why or why not?

SOURCE: Adapted from Dana C. Munro, *Translations and Reprints from the Original Sources of European History,* vol. 6 (Philadelphia, 1899), pp. 12–16.

---

Secular reforms mirrored religious ones. Orders regularized the management of all royal estates. Charlemagne attempted to update local law codes and to make them as uniform as possible. Not since Rome had governments possessed either the interest in or the means to promote such centralization. It is striking that in the eighth century the caliphate, the Byzantine Empire, and the Carolingian Empire were engaged in similar centralizing activities.

Versatility was a hallmark of Carolingian learning. Various scholars excelled at poetry, history, and biography. Biblical studies and theology attracted a lot of attention. One figure who personifies the Carolingian Renaissance is the Visigoth Theodulf° (ca. 760–821). He came to court in about 790 and served thereafter as a missus, royal adviser, abbot of several monasteries, and bishop of Orléans. He issued important legislation for his diocese. He was the foremost Old Testament expert of his day and the only one who knew Hebrew. He wrote the official Frankish response to Byzantine iconoclasm. He

---

**Theodulf** (THEE-oh-dulf)

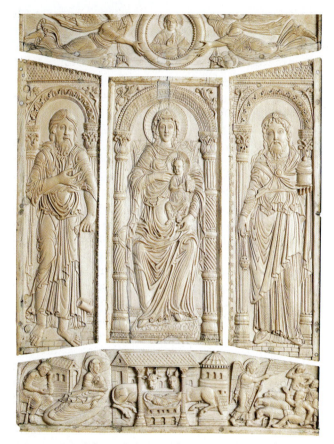

**Ivory Cover of the Lorsch Gospels**  In 810 the monks at Lorsch produced a Gospel book and probably its covers, too. This cover (front or back? scholars are not sure) is now in London. It depicts an enthroned Mary with Jesus on her lap, flanked by Zacharias and his son, John the Baptist. The ivory carving is of such exquisite quality that scholars long refused to believe that this was not a late antique work.  *(V&A Picture Library)*

also composed theological treatises, many letters, and dozens of poems. At Germigny° he designed a church that is a masterpiece of early Carolingian architecture.

Carolingian art is a crowning glory of the age. The manuscripts decorated under Charlemagne's patronage and then, for three generations, under the patronage of his descendants and of prominent churchmen show versatility, respect but not awe for the past, and innovation. Several distinct currents inspired and informed Carolingian art. Most prominent were the animal and geometric decorative motifs of Irish and Anglo-Saxon art; the elegance, formality, and sense of composition of classical art; basic elements of style from Byzantine painting; actual scenes from papal Rome; and the mysteries of

**Germigny** (JHER-mee-nee)

Christian theology. Every element was borrowed, but the finished product was new.

Architecture shows the same trends. Charlemagne's palace complex at Aachen has parallels in imperial Constantinople, papal Rome, and Ostrogothic Ravenna. Workers and building materials were fetched from all over the empire. From 768 to 855, 27 cathedrals were built along with 417 monasteries and 100 royal residences. For basic buildings the Carolingians adapted the basilica. The classical basilica was a horizontal building, but the Carolingians, by altering the western end and façade (the "westworks"), added the dimension of verticality. In Romanesque and Gothic architecture this innovation would have a long career (see pages 345–348).

## The Fragmentation of Charlemagne's Empire, 814–887

The Carolingian Empire did not outlive the ninth century. Rome's empire lasted much longer, as did Byzantium's and Islam's. All of these realms were fatally weakened by similar problems, but those problems arose more quickly and acutely in the Carolingian world than elsewhere. By the end of the ninth century small political entities had replaced the unified Carolingian Empire.

Size and ethnic complexity contributed to the disintegration of the empire. The empire included many small regions—Saxony, Bavaria, Brittany, and Lombardy, for example—that had their own resident elites, linguistic traditions, and distinctive cultures, which had existed before the Carolingians came on the scene and persist to this day. The Merovingian and Carolingian periods were basically a unifying intrusion into a history characterized by regional diversity. The Carolingians made heroic efforts to build a common culture and to forge bonds of unity, but the obstacles were insuperable.

Another key issue in the breakup of the Carolingian Empire was political and dynastic. The Carolingians regularly tried to create subkingdoms for all their legitimate sons while preserving the imperial title for one of them. This was a creative attempt to concede limited autonomy to particular regions by means of local kingships—for instance, in Bavaria, Italy, and Aquitaine—while preserving the "Augustinian" unity of the empire as a whole. Unfortunately, younger sons rarely yielded to their older brothers, and the bonds of loyalty among cousins, nephews, and grandchildren grew weak. Frequent divisions of the empire, or of segments of it, placed local nobilities in the difficult position of changing their allegiance frequently and of jeopardizing their offices and landholdings.

In the Treaty of Verdun in 843 (see inset, Map 8.3) the three grandsons of Charlemagne—Charles the Bald,

Louis the German, and Lothair—divided the empire into three realms: the West Frankish, the East Frankish, and the Middle Kingdoms. After fierce battles among the brothers, each appointed forty members to a study commission that traversed the empire to identify royal properties, fortifications, monasteries, and cathedrals so that an equitable division of these valuable resources could be made. Each brother needed adequate resources to solidify his rule and to attract or hold followers. The lines drawn on the map at Verdun did not last even for a generation.

Slowly large West Frankish and East Frankish Kingdoms emerged, swallowing the Middle Kingdom, and created a framework for the future France and Germany. But they had to compete with many smaller entities. Some of these—in Italy, the Rhineland, and southern France—were old and distinctive regions that recaptured their former independence. Others were essentially new creations, born in the absence of firm Carolingian control. Newcomers also appeared on the scene, most prominently Scandinavian and Slavic principalities.

Before the ninth century, Scandinavia had known only small-scale political units under local chieftains and their trusted followers. Economic and political pressure from the Carolingians gradually began to push both Denmark and Norway in the direction of greater political consolidation. A single Danish monarchy has a continuous history from the late ninth century, and Norway's monarchy dates from the early tenth.

To the east of the Carolingian Empire lay a vast swath of Slavic lands. The Carolingians fought, allied, and traded with these peoples for decades. Charlemagne destroyed the Avar khanate in the Danube basin in campaigns between 788 and 804. By the middle of the ninth century the princes of Great Moravia dominated the region and played a complicated diplomatic game between the East Frankish rulers and the Byzantine emperors. To the east of the Moravians, the Bulgarians profited from the Avar and then the Carolingian collapse to expand their kingdom. For two centuries the Bulgarians dominated the northern Balkans and threatened Byzantium.

The most durable consequence of this political restructuring along the eastern frontier of the Frankish world was religious. In 863, on an invitation from Moravia and in hopes of countering the Franks, the Byzantine emperor sent the missionaries Cyril° (826–869) and Methodius° (805–884) into eastern Europe. The emperor hoped to erect an Orthodox union of his own realm, the southern Slavs, and the newly converted Bulgarians. Likewise he was seeking a diplomatic bulwark between the Bulgarians in the East and the Franks in the West. Unfortunately for Byzantium, Cyril and Methodius agreed with the pope to introduce Roman Catholic Christianity in return for the pope's permission to use the Slavonic language in worship. Cyril and Methodius were formidable linguists who created a religious literature in "Church Slavonic" that went far toward creating a new cultural realm in central Europe.

Finally a new wave of attacks and invasions contributed decisively to the fragmentation of the Carolingian Empire. In the middle decades of the ninth century, Muslims, Vikings, and Magyars wreaked havoc on the Franks.

Based in North Africa and the islands of the western Mediterranean, Muslims attacked Italy and southern France. The Byzantines lost Sicily to raiders from North Africa in 827 and found themselves seriously challenged in southern Italy. In the 840s Muslims raided the city of Rome. These same brigands preyed on trade in the western Mediterranean and even set up camps in the Alps to rob traders passing back and forth over the mountains.

"From the fury of the Northmen, O Lord, deliver us," was a plaintive cry heard often in ninth-century Europe. Those Northmen were Vikings, mainly Danes and Norwegians, seeking booty, glory, and political opportunity. Most Viking bands were formed by leaders who had lost out in the dawning institutional consolidation of the northern world. Some were opportunists who sought to profit from the weakness of Carolingian, Anglo-Saxon, and Irish rule. In the mid-ninth century, Vikings began settling and initiated their own state-building activities in Ireland, England, northwestern France ("Normandy"—the region of the Northmen), and Rus (early "Russia").

Magyars, relatives of the Huns and Avars who had preceded them into eastern Europe, were accomplished horsemen whose lightning raids, beginning in 889, hit Italy, Germany, and even France. East Frankish Carolingians tried to use the Magyars as mercenaries against the troublesome Moravians. In the end, the Magyars destroyed the incipient Moravian state and raided with impunity.

All of these attacks were unpredictable and caused local regions to fall back on their own resources rather than look to the central government. Commerce was disrupted everywhere. Schools, based in ecclesiastical institutions, suffered severe decline. The raids represented a thousand pinpricks, not a single deadly sword stroke. Yet their collective effect amounted to despair and disruption on a massive scale.

Even though the Carolingian Empire itself disintegrated, the idea of Europe as "Christendom," as a single political-cultural entity, persisted. The Latin Christian culture promoted by Carolingian schools and rulers set the tone for intellectual life until the twelfth century.

---

**Cyril** (SEER-ul)  **Methodius** (meth-oh-DEE-us)

**Oseberg Ship**    Discovered in 1880, the Oseberg ship was buried in Norway in (probably) the tenth century. The ship may have belonged to a king and contained the remains of Queen Asa. It is 70 feet long and 16 feet wide. Its crew would have been thirty to forty men. *(University Museum of National Antiquities, Oslo)*

Likewise, Carolingian governing structures were inherited and adapted by all of the successor states that emerged in the ninth and tenth centuries. In these respects the Carolingian experience paralleled the Roman, and the Islamic and Byzantine, too. A potent, centralizing regime disappeared but left a profound imprint on its heirs. For hundreds of years Western civilization would be played out inside the lands that had been Charlemagne's empire and between those lands and their Byzantine and Muslim neighbors.

# EARLY MEDIEVAL ECONOMIES AND SOCIETIES

THE economic and social history of the early Middle Ages provides additional evidence of the similarities among the three early medieval civilizations, while also revealing differences. Overall the world remained rural, society was hierarchical, and women were excluded from public power. Although broad political frameworks changed, the lives of most people changed rather little.

## Trade and Commerce

In the simplest terms, trade is a mechanism for exchanging goods from one person or group to another. There are many such exchange mechanisms. The Roman government, for example, moved large amounts of goods from the center of the empire to the frontiers to supply its armies. Roman, Byzantine, and Islamic governments raised taxes in one place, bought goods in another, and then consumed their purchases someplace else. Tribute and plunder were also effective exchange mechanisms, as were diplomatic gifts: a caliph, for example, sent Charlemagne an elephant.

The most common exchanges were intensely local, but several major trading networks operated during the early Middle Ages. In the East, Mesopotamia was linked by rivers to the Persian Gulf, East Africa, and southern Asia; by land and sea to Byzantium; and by land and rivers to the Black Sea region, Slavic Europe, and the Baltic. Byzantines traded mainly by sea. The whole Mediterranean was open to them, and from the Black Sea they received the products of the Danube basin. The Muslim world was fundamentally a land empire that had relatively poor roads and primitive wheeled vehicles, so transport considerations were crucial: a caravan of some five hundred camels could move only one-fourth to one-half the cargo of a normal Byzantine ship.

The West had many trade routes. The Rhône-Saône river system carried goods, as did the land routes through the Alpine passes. The North and Baltic Seas were the hubs of a network that linked the British Isles, the whole of the Frankish north (by means of its rivers), the Rhineland, Slavic Europe, Byzantium, and the Muslim world. The Danube was also a major highway. The major trade networks intersected at many points. Despite religious and ideological differences, Rome's three heirs regularly traded with one another. Recent research has documented hundreds of east-west and north-south contacts across the early medieval period.

Food and other bulk goods never traveled very far because the cost was prohibitive. Most towns were supplied with foodstuffs by their immediate hinterlands, so the goods that traveled long distances were portable and valuable. Cotton and raw silk were transported to the Mediterranean, where they were made into cloth in, respectively, Egypt and Byzantium. Paper and pottery were transported around the caliphate. Asian spices and perfumes were avidly sought everywhere. The Byzantines traded in silk cloth, fine ivories, delicate products of the gold- and silversmiths' art, slaves, and naval stores. Byzantium, with its large fleet, usually controlled the Black and Mediterranean Seas. Reduced in prosperity, the empire could no longer dictate trade terms to subject peoples and competed badly with the Muslims. Trade in the West was partly in high-value luxury goods but mainly in ordinary items such as plain pottery, raw wool, wool cloth, millstones, weapons, and slaves.

## Town and Countryside

To think of the ancient world is to think of cities, but to think of the medieval world is to envision forests and fields. Actually 80 to 90 percent of people in antiquity lived in rural settings, and in the early Middle Ages the percentage was not much higher. What changed was the place occupied by towns in the totality of human life. Fewer government functions were based in towns, cultural life was less bound to the urban environment, and trade in luxuries, which depended on towns, declined.

Towns in the West lost Roman governmental significance but often survived as focal points of royal or, more often, ecclesiastical administration. A cathedral church

required a large corps of administrators. Western towns were everywhere attracting *burgs*, new settlements of merchants, just outside their centers. Because Vikings frequently raided these burgs, their existence was precarious. Few Western towns were impressive in size or population. Rome may have numbered a million people in the time of Augustus, but only about thirty thousand lived there in 800. Paris had perhaps twenty thousand inhabitants at that time. These were the largest cities by far in Catholic Europe.

In the Byzantine East, apart from Constantinople, the empire had a more rural aspect after the Muslims took control of the heavily urbanized regions of Syria, Egypt, and parts of Anatolia in the seventh century. The weakening of the caliphate in the second half of the ninth century was a spur to renewed urban growth in the Byzantine Empire. In provincial cities population growth and urban reconstruction depended heavily on military conditions: cities threatened by Arabs or Bulgarians declined.

The Arabs were great city-builders. Baghdad—four times larger in area than Constantinople, with a million residents to the latter's 400,000—was created from scratch. The most magnificent city in the West was Cordoba, the capital of Muslim Spain. Its population may have reached 400,000, and its Great Mosque, begun in 786, held 5,500 worshipers, more than any Latin church except Saint Peter's. The city had 900 baths, 1,600 mosques (Rome had about 200 churches), 60,000 mansions, and perhaps 100,000 shops. Its libraries held thousands of books, while the largest Carolingian book collections numbered a few hundred.

Agriculture nevertheless remained the most important element in the economy and in the daily lives of most people in all three realms. Farming meant primarily the production of cereal grains, which provided diet staples such as bread, porridge, and beer. Regions tended to specialize in the crops that grew most abundantly in local circumstances. For example, olives and grapes were common in the Mediterranean area, whereas cereals predominated around the Black Sea and in central Gaul. Animal husbandry was always a major part of the rural regime. English sheep provided wool and meat. In Frankish and Byzantine regions pigs, which were cheap to raise, supplied meat, but for religious reasons pork was almost absent in the Muslim East—Islam adopted the Jewish prohibition against it.

A key development in the Frankish West was the appearance of a bipartite estate, sometimes called a "manor." On a bipartite estate, one part of the land was set aside as a reserve (or *demesne*°), and the rest was

demesne (duh-MEEN)

**Labors of the Months**   From a ninth-century West Frankish manuscript, this picture illustrates the labors of the various months of the year. How many of them can you figure out? How do these compare with farm labors where you live?   *(Österreichische Nationalbibliothek)*

divided into tenancies. The reserve, consuming from one-quarter to one-half of the total territory of the estate, was exploited directly for the benefit of the landlord. The tenancies were generally worked by the peasants for their own support. The bipartite estate provided the aristocrats with a livelihood while freeing them for military and government service.

Estates were run in different ways. A landlord might hire laborers to farm his reserve, paying them with money exacted as fees from his tenants. Or he might require the tenants to work a certain number of days per week or weeks per year in his fields. The produce of the estate might be gathered into barns and consumed locally or hauled to local markets. The reserve might be a

separate part of the estate, a proportion of common fields, or a percentage of the harvest. The tenants might have individual farms or work in common fields. Although the manor is one of the most familiar aspects of European life throughout the Middle Ages, large estates with dependent tenants also were evolving in the Byzantine and Islamic worlds.

## Social Patterns

Most of the surviving medieval records were written by elite members of society and reveal little about the middle and lower orders of society. Nevertheless, certain similarities are evident in the social structures of all levels in all three societies. The elites tended to be large landholders, to control dependent populations, and to have access to government offices. There were regional differences, too. Scholars ranked higher in Byzantium and the caliphate than in the West; churchmen, especially bishops, were powerful in Christian societies but had no counterparts in Muslim ones. Literature, surely reflecting social realities, portrays the cultivated Muslim gentleman in the Abbasid period. This social type, marked by learning, good manners, and a taste for finery, does not appear in Byzantium or in the West until the twelfth century.

The middling classes show some disparities among the regions. Merchants, for example, often rose through the social ranks to become great aristocrats in Muslim society. Islamic society often evinced great mobility because of its restless, expanding nature and because Islamic ideology rejected distinctions in the umma. In Byzantium traditional Roman prejudices against merchants and moneymaking activities persisted. Thus rich merchants whose wealth gave them private influence frequently lacked public power and recognition. In the West merchants were neither numerous nor powerful in the Carolingian period. In some towns, moreover, commerce was in the hands of Jews, always outsiders in a militantly Christian society. (See the box "Reading Sources: The Status of Carolingian Jews.")

Merchants were not the only people occupying the middle rungs of the social ladder. All three societies, in fact, possessed both central elites and provincial elites. Service at the Carolingian, Byzantine, or Abbasid court counted for more than service in a provincial outpost. It was one thing to be abbot of a great monastery and quite a different thing to preside over a poor, tiny house. The thematic generals in Byzantium were lofty personages; their subordinates held inferior positions. The vassals of a Carolingian king formed a real aristocracy, but vassals' vassals were of decidedly lower rank.

Degrees of freedom and local economic and political conditions shaped the lives of peasants. In all three societies some farmers were personally free and owed no cash or labor services to anyone but the central government. In areas such as Abbasid Iraq ordinary free farmers led a comfortable life. In the Frankish world most peasants existed outside the dawning manorial system. They were free, and if they lived in areas of good land and political security, such as the Paris basin, their lives most likely were congenial. Byzantine peasants, though free, often lived in areas of military danger, and in some parts of the Balkans they eked out a living from poor soils. Highly taxed and perpetually endangered, they may have

viewed their freedom as small compensation for their economic and personal insecurity. All peasants were alike in their subjection to political forces over which they had no control.

At the bottom of the social scale everywhere were slaves. Christianity did not object to slavery in general but forbade the enslavement of Christians. Islam likewise prohibited Muslims from enslaving other Muslims. Slaves, therefore, tended to be most common in pagan societies—Scandinavia, for example—or in frontier regions where neighboring pagans could be captured and sold. There were more slaves in the Muslim world than in Byzantium, which had, in turn, more than the West.

Women were bound to the same social hierarchies as men. Predictably enough, women had few formal, public roles to play. Their influence, however great, tended to function in the private sphere, rarely revealed to us by sources that stem from the public realm of powerful men. Aristocratic women had opportunities and power that were denied ordinary women. Irene ruled at Byzantium as empress. Frankish and Anglo-Saxon queens were formidable figures in their realms. Carolingian queens managed the landed patrimony of the dynasty—dozens of huge estates with tens of thousands of dependents. The combination of a lack of evidence and the rigorous exclusion of women from public life in the Islamic world means that virtually no Muslim women emerge as distinct personalities in the early Middle Ages.

The conversion of England to Christianity was fostered by women. Most convents had aristocratic abbesses who presided over complex enterprises and often schools. In the Frankish world aristocratic women secured some learning, and one, Dhuoda, wrote in 841 a manual of advice for her son that conveys biblical and patristic teachings as well as practical wisdom. The Frankish convent at Chelles was a renowned center for the copying of manuscripts. Some Anglo-Saxon nuns owned ships and invested in commercial activities to support their convents. Almost all aspects of the cloth industry were in women's hands.

One example of the problems in the evidence concerning women relates to church roles. Women could not hold priestly office, and although deaconesses served at Hagia Sophia in the sixth century, they disappeared soon after and had long before vanished in the West. Religious power could come from personal sanctity as well as holding office. One study of some 2,200 saints from the early Middle Ages finds only about 300 females. It was hard for women to gain recognition as saints. And if a woman became a saint, her holiness was inevitably described either as "manly"—an extreme ascetic was praised for having the strength and courage of a man—or as

# THE STATUS OF CAROLINGIAN JEWS

*In 826 or 827 Archbishop Agobard of Lyon wrote this protest to the emperor Louis the Pious because the emperor had issued legislation favorable to the Jewish minority in general and to Jewish merchants in particular. Agobard's anti-Semitism is probably typical for the period and serves to indicate the precarious position of the Jews in the militantly Christian Frankish empire.*

I commit myself to your goodness and patience as I inform you of what is ruinous to pass over in silence. There came Gerric and Frederick who were preceded by Evrard, your missi [envoys] in fact, yet not doing your will completely but rather acting on behalf of another. They showed themselves to be terrible to the Christians and mild to the Jews, especially in Lyon, where they set up a persecuting faction against the Church and they goaded the church to many groans, sighs, and tears.

When the Jews first arrived, they gave me a message in your name and another one to the man who rules the district of Lyon in place of the count; [this message] ordered him to offer aid to the Jews against me. We absolutely did not believe that such messages as these issued from your judgment, although they were read out in your sacred name and sealed with your ring. The Jews began to rage with a certain odious insolence, threatening that we would be afflicted with every sort of injury by the agents whom they had obtained to take vengeance upon Christians. After them, Evrard arrived and repeated the same thing and said that your majesty was truly angry with me because of the Jews. Then the aforementioned agents arrived, holding in their hands a tax code and a capitulary of sanctions which we do not believe exists by your command. Consequently, certain of our priests whom they threatened by name, did not dare to show their faces. We suffered these things from the Jews' supporters and for no other reason but that we preached to Christians that they should not sell Christian slaves to them; that they should not allow these Jews to sell Christians to Spain nor to possess them as paid domestics lest Christian women celebrate the Sabbath with them, work on Sundays, eat with them during Lent, and their paid servants eat meat on these

days; and that no Christian should buy meats sacrificed and butchered by Jews and sell them to other Christians; and that they should not drink their wine or other things like this. . . .

. . . It is absolutely necessary that your pious solicitude know how the Christian faith is being harmed by the Jews in certain ways. For when they lie to simple Christians and boast that they are dear to you because of the patriarchs; that they enter and leave your sight with honor; that most excellent people desire their prayers and blessings and confess that they wished they had the same author of the law as the Jews; when they say that your counselors are aroused against us for their sake, because we forbid Christians from drinking their wine; when, in trying to claim this, they boast that they have received from Christians many, many pounds of silver from the sale of wine and cannot find out, after running through the canons, why Christians should abstain from their food and drink; when they produce commands signed with golden seals in your name and containing words which, in our opinion, are not true; when they show people women's clothes as if they were sent to their wives by your kinsmen or matrons of the palaces; when they expound upon the glory of their forefathers; when they are permitted, contrary to the law, to build new synagogues—[when all this occurs] it even reaches the point when naive Christians say that the Jews preach to them better than our priests. And this was particularly true when the aforementioned agents ordered that the markets that usually occur on Saturdays should be moved lest [the Jews'] Sabbatism be impeded, and they let [the Jews] choose on which days they had to go to market from then on, claiming that this suited the utility of the Christians because of the Sunday vacation.

Source: *Agobardi Lugdunensis Opera Omnia*, Opusculum XI, trans. W. L. North, ed. L. Van Acker, Corpus Christianorum. *Continuatio Mediaevalis* 52, pp. 191–195. Copyright © 1981. Permission granted by Brepols Publishers, Turnhout (Belgium).

**For additional information on this topic, go to college.hmco.com/students.**

beautiful, virginal, and domestic—in other words, with female stereotypes.

The domestic sphere is another difficult realm to enter. The Quran permitted a man to have up to four wives if he could care for them and would treat them equitably. A Muslim woman, however, was given her dowry outright, and multiple marriages may have meant that relatively more Muslim women could gain a measure of security. In Byzantium and the West, families rarely arranged marriages for more than one or two daughters. Others remained single or entered convents. Women at all social levels tended to pass from the tutelage of their fathers to that of their husbands. In antiquity a suitor usually paid a fee, or "bride price," to his prospective wife's father and then endowed his wife with a "morning gift," money or possessions of her own. Gradually this practice changed to a system whereby a bride's father paid a dowry to her future husband. Thus a wife who was cast aside could be left impoverished, for in most places the law did not permit her to inherit land if she had brothers. Females were such valuable property in the marriage market that rape was an offense not against a girl but against her father. A man could divorce, even kill, his wife for adultery, witchcraft, or grave robbing and then marry again. A woman could usually gain a divorce only for adultery, and she could not remarry. For the vast majority of women, daily life was hedged about with legal limitations and personal indignities.

## SUMMARY

WE have traced three parallel histories in the development of early medieval civilizations. The first one is chronological. In the Arab, Byzantine, and Latin worlds, the seventh century was an age of rapid, dynamic change, the eighth century a time of consolidation and reform, and the ninth century a period of renewed challenges.

The second history is political, religious, and ideological. Three different peoples built large imperial states. Each state fashioned a central government that focused on a powerful leader who was seen as a specially chosen agent of God. Each state erected a system of rule that tied a government capital to its outlying regions. In the Muslim and Byzantine worlds that system was highly bureaucratic; in the Carolingian Empire the system was more amateur and personal. A religion—Islam, Orthodoxy, or Roman Catholicism—provided the glue that held each society together and defined the mission of its govern-

ment. The cultural life of each area was inspired mainly by an attempt to integrate a powerful religious message with older intellectual traditions.

The third history concerns the fate of these imperial realms. In the Islamic and Latin worlds large states broke down to leave many smaller heirs. In each instance, changes in the caliber of leadership, unpredictable foreign attacks, and the sheer diversity of the polity pulled the large state apart. The Byzantine Empire, much smaller than the Roman Empire had been, managed to defend its territory, but that territory was greatly reduced from former times.

We began this chapter by imagining what Rome's legacy might be. Islam and the caliphate emerged as surprising elements, while Byzantium and the Carolingian worlds followed more predictable courses. In the next chapter we ask what happened after about 900. This time the surprising element will be found in the West. Though battered in 900, western Europe was on the verge of an astonishing period of growth and development.

## ■ Suggested Reading

Becher, Matthias. *Charlemagne.* 2003. Brief yet detailed, up-to-date, and readable; by a distinguished German historian.

Berkey, Jonathan P. *The Formation of Islam: Religion and Society in the Near East, 600–1800.* 2003. Compact yet comprehensive and readable; equipped with fine "Suggestions for Further Reading," this book is now the place to start on the Islamic world.

Bitel, Lisa M. *Women in Early Medieval Europe, 400–1100.* 2002. Entertaining and informative, this is the first comprehensive treatment of early medieval women.

Brown, Peter. *The Rise of Western Christendom.* 2d ed. 2003. A verbal feast, now fully documented, this book presents a stimulating assessment of the place of Christianity in the rise of Western culture.

Denny, Frederick M. *An Introduction to Islam.* 2d ed. 1994. By far the most accessible, readable account of the Islamic faith; the book covers all periods but is helpful for the early centuries.

McCormick, Michael. *Origins of the European Economy: Communications and Commerce AD 300–900.* 2001. A stupendous achievement, this richly detailed book is *the* starting point for an understanding of the early medieval commercial economy.

Whittow, Mark. *The Making of Orthodox Byzantium, 600–1025.* 1996. Lively, readable, controversial, and engaging, this book challenges standard views.

**For a searchable list of additional readings for this chapter, go to college.hmco.com/students.**

# The Manuscript Book

How long do you think it would take you to copy this whole textbook by hand? We know that it took about a year for two skilled monastic scribes to copy a Bible. Every medieval book was literally a manuscript (from *manuscriptum*, "written by hand"). Manuscripts contain important texts but are also revealing artifacts in their own right.

Codicology and paleography are the primary manuscript sciences. *Codicology,* the study of books as physical objects, investigates the materials and techniques used to make them. *Paleography,* the study of handwriting, seeks to read texts and to date and localize surviving books.

Depicted here is a *folio* ("page") of the Dagulf Psalter, named for the Carolingian scribe who wrote it in 795 on Charlemagne's orders as a gift for Pope Hadrian I (r. 772–795). The rich and powerful often used books as gifts. A psalter is a collection of the 150 biblical psalms and other canticles (songs or prayers derived from the Bible and used for worship). Can you make out the Latin words INCIPIUNT CANTICI at the very top of the page? They mean "Here begin the canticles." The text is the Canticle of the Prophet Isaiah (Isaiah 12:1–6). Its title is CANTICUM ESAIE PROP[H].

Cathedrals and monasteries usually had *scriptoria,* "writing offices," where scribes and illuminators worked with bookmakers to produce manuscripts. Manuscripts were made from parchment, or animal skin. According to an old legend, in the second century B.C. the Egyptians cut off the supply of papyrus to the kingdom of Pergamum, forcing the Pergamenes to use animal hides to make writing material. Be that as it may, the English word *parchment* derives from the Latin name for this writing material: *pergamenum.* By the sixth century A.D. parchment had supplanted papyrus as the primary writing material in most of Europe.

Parchment was made by soaking an animal's hide in a caustic lye solution for three to six weeks to remove fat, hair, and blemishes. The hide was then scraped vigorously, washed, rubbed smooth with ashes or pumice, and then stretched on a frame to dry. The finest parchment, called *vellum,* was made from the hides of calves, lambs, or kids. It was almost white in color and nearly translucent. Most parchment was not so fine.

When the parchment was dry, the bookmaker cut and lined it—notice how straight and even the lines are in the picture. Then he took four sheets of parchment, laid them down together, and folded them, placing the fold at the left, to form a booklet of sixteen pages called a "quire" (see the drawing). Because the two sides of a piece of parchment differ in color (the "hair side," or outside, is usually darker than the "flesh side," or inside) the quires were arranged so that hair sides faced hair sides and flesh sides faced flesh sides. A manuscript consisted of many quires sewn together. The smallest surviving manuscript is 2 by 3 inches; the largest is about 19 by 36 inches. The larger the pages, the more costly was the book. One huge Bible produced in Bede's Northumbria required the hides of five hundred sheep.

The first page of the first quire was numbered 1[r] and 1[v], or 1 recto and 1 verso, meaning 1 "right side" and 1 "turned side." The second sheet was numbered 2[r] and 2[v]. Today book pages are numbered 1, 2, 3, and so on, and books always start with an odd-numbered page on the right side—an inheritance from medieval manuscripts.

Scribes and illuminators received the prepared quires. Scribes wrote text onto the parchment. Illuminators added beautiful pictures or designs. You have on pages 248, 257, 268, 278, 286, 297, 300, 311, 322, 337, and 372 examples of the magnificent illuminations painted into some medieval books. Most books, however, had no such images at all.

Now you are ready to learn some paleography. We have already deciphered the first two lines of the folio shown here. These lines are written in a "display script." For visual appeal and to facilitate reference, scribes often used different handwriting, colors, or both to highlight first letters, first words, or first lines. Books, including the one you are reading, maintain this tradition. The huge writing—can you make out CONFITE?—marks the beginning of Isaiah's text. It continues, on line four, with *bor tibi dne qnm ira.* Line five carries on with *tus es mihi. conversus.* Look at line six: *est furor tuus&consolatusesme.* Can you make out the letters yourself? These words mean, "I will confess to you, O Lord, for you were angry with me, but you turned your anger away and brought me consolation."

Several things bear notice here. First, the main script is Caroline minuscule, the new script that accompanied Charlemagne's educational reforms. Because of its clarity, it is the basis for many modern typefaces. Compare the letters in the picture with the ones you are reading.

**The Dagulf Psalter**   (*Österreichische Nationalbibliothek*)

**A Quire**

Second, notice the frequent recourse to abbreviation. Writing was time- and space-consuming, prompting the development of elaborate systems of abbreviation. Can you see, in line four, the letters *dne* with a strike over them, and then the letters *qnm,* also with a strike? In this case the words expand to *domine* and *quoniam.* Look at line two, where you see *prop*[h], shorthand for *Prophetae* ("Prophet"). Also notice the ampersands in lines six, eight, nine, and ten. They stand for *et,* Latin for "and." Note, too, how the last words in line six run together.

Third, in antiquity texts had neither breaks between words nor punctuation. As non–Latin-speakers learned to write the language, however, they usually put breaks between the words to facilitate understanding. You can see that most of this text has breaks, except in line six. In lines one, eight, and ten, you can also see a rather curious symbol: ;. It is a full stop, or period.

What else might you learn from a manuscript? Handwriting and systems of abbreviation are distinctive, and specialists use them to date and localize manuscripts. Because parchment was prepared in different ways, some manuscripts can be dated or placed by an analysis of their parchment. Inks differed in chemistry and appearance and thus help to date and localize books as well. Styles of illumination and forms of images can also be localized or traced from one scriptorium to another. By knowing when, where, and by whom books were written or illuminated, historians can reconstruct the life and work of intellectual centers that were scattered long ago.

It is estimated that a medieval manuscript without illuminations was worth one year's wages for an ordinary working person. Would you spend a year's wages on a book?

# CHAPTER 9

# The Expansion of Europe in the High Middle Ages 900–1300

THE picture to the left represents one small section of the Bayeux Tapestry, a narrative account—in words and illustrations—of the conquest of England in 1066 by Duke William of Normandy. This scene is an apt introduction to the central theme of this chapter: expansion.

This section of the 230-foot-long tapestry depicts William setting sail for England. William had already gained greater authority in the duchy of Normandy than any duke before him. Now he was about to press his claim to the throne of England. He gathered soldiers from all over western France and boldly crossed the English Channel. Leaving nothing to chance, he transported horses, too, as you can see in the picture.

One group of Normans conquered England, while another seized control of southern Italy. Still other Normans played a decisive role in the period's most prominent manifestation of expansion: the Crusades. Meanwhile, certain Scandinavians settled Iceland and Greenland to the west, while others founded the first state on Russian soil. Spanish Christians pushed back the Muslims in Iberia. From the Baltic to the Balkans, Slavic rulers founded new states and pressed hard against their neighbors. German rulers crossed the Alps into Italy, French kings reached the Pyrenees, and English monarchs pushed into Wales, Scotland, and Ireland. Seldom has Europe's political geography expanded so dramatically as during the High Middle Ages.

Between 900 and 1300 Europe's population began one of its longest periods of sustained growth. People brought more land under cultivation, introduced new crops, and made agriculture more efficient. Villages, towns, and cities grew in number and size. Trade expanded in every material and in every direction.

Bayeux Tapestry (ca. 1077), depicting the fleet of William the Conqueror of Normandy sailing to England in 1066.
(Michael Holford)

Europe witnessed the re-emergence of centralizing monarchies in France, England, and Spain. Some new realms, such as Denmark and Hungary, built strong central governments. And an explosion of new states occurred along the frontiers of the old Carolingian Empire.

The "West" began taking on a more *western European* character. The Crusades complicated relations between Christian Europeans and Muslims, and both the Crusades and increasing religious differences alienated western Europe from Byzantium, and Roman Catholics from Orthodox believers. The center of Western civilization became more and more anchored to northwestern Europe. And that same western Europe was expanding to influence lands in Scandinavia and the Slavic world that had played no role at all in the West's classical, Mediterranean phase. The High Middle Ages repeatedly posed the question: Where is the West?

**QUESTIONS TO CONSIDER**

- What were the main causes of the economic, political, and military expansion of Europe during the High Middle Ages?
- What basic problems confronted rulers who wished to expand the power and influence of central governments?
- How did the Catholic Church both help and hinder political development?
- What basic factors contributed to the rise, persistence, and eventual decline of the crusading movement?

**TERMS TO KNOW**

| | |
|---|---|
| guilds | Magna Carta |
| lay investiture | Parliament |
| communes | Reconquista |
| Papal Monarchy | Crusades |
| feudal revolution | |

## ECONOMIC EXPANSION

THE economic expansion of Europe is manifest in many kinds of evidence that are more often qualitative than quantitative. Medieval people did not keep the kinds of records of births, deaths, population, or business activity that modern states routinely accumulate. Literary anecdotes can be revealing, of course, but they are no substitute for hard data. After about 1000 every available indicator points to a growing population and an expanding scale and sophistication of economic activity.

### The Growing Population

The population of Europe began rising slowly in the Carolingian period and may have doubled between 1000 and 1200. Scattered bits of evidence suggest that the total population of western Europe grew from around 30 million in 1000 to 55 million or 60 million in 1200. In the thirteenth century population growth gradually slowed.

In a few regions where family size can be estimated, fertile marriages were producing on the average 3.5 children in the tenth century and from 6 to 7 in the twelfth. People were also living longer than their forebears. Studies of aristocrats, high clergy, and soldiers show that a surprising 40 percent of them were over 40 years old. Male life expectancy was surely longer than female because of the dangers of childbirth, always the great killer of women in the premodern world. The general trend is clear: more babies being born, more infants living into adulthood, more adults living longer.

Everywhere in Europe new land was brought into cultivation. More than half of the French documents relating to land in the twelfth century mention *assarting,* the bringing of previously untilled land under the plow. Thousands of acres of forest were felled. Marshes were reclaimed from the sea. Some 380,000 acres were drained along the western coast of France and probably twice that amount in both Flanders and England. This activity is inexplicable without assuming a growing number of mouths to feed.

Agriculture benefited from a warmer and drier climate through this whole period. Not a single vegetable blight was recorded. Food was more abundant and more nutritious. Animals were increasingly reared for their meat, and higher meat consumption meant more protein in the diet. Beans and other legumes, also rich in protein, were more widely cultivated. Fine grains such as wheat replaced poorer cereals—ryes and spelts—in many areas. People of every class and region were almost certainly eating better and living longer and healthier lives.

## Technological Gains

The eleventh century was a decisive period in the spread of new technologies in Europe. Innovations occurred in agriculture, transportation, mining, and manufacturing. Agricultural changes came first as a rising population created an increased demand for food that could be met only by new practices. By the late twelfth century an acre of farmland in a fertile region was probably yielding a crop three to four times larger than in the Carolingian era. Given the combination of more land under cultivation and more yield per acre, the overall gains in the food supply were enormous.

The increases can be accounted for in several ways. Horses were more frequently used as draft animals. They were more expensive to acquire than oxen but no more costly to feed, and they did, in a day, a third or half again as much work. For much less "fuel" horses could haul loads farther and faster than oxen. Thus fewer people could, with horses, cultivate more land than their predecessors managed with oxen. In addition, they could cultivate the land more frequently and increase yields because more seed would fall on more finely plowed soil. The dissemination of the horse collar made possible the expanded use of horses—older forms of harnesses suitable for the low-slung, broad-shouldered ox would have choked a horse.

Plows, too, were improved. The light wooden scratch plow used by the Romans was satisfactory for the thin soils of the Mediterranean region but barely disturbed the heavy soils of northern Europe. The invention of a heavy wheeled plow with an iron coulter (or plowshare) and a moldboard was a real breakthrough. The iron plowshare cut deep furrows, and then the moldboard turned and aerated the soil. This heavy plow allowed farmers to exploit good soils more fully without exhausting the ground too rapidly. This plow seems to have been introduced into Carolingian Europe from the Slavic world, but it was not widely adopted before the eleventh century.

Wider adoption of nitrogen-fixing crops, such as peas and some kinds of beans, retarded soil exhaustion

## CHRONOLOGY

| | |
|---|---|
| 862 | Founding of Kiev |
| 870–930 | Settlement of Iceland |
| 962 | Imperial coronation of Otto I |
| 987 | Accession of Hugh Capet in France |
| 988 | Kievan Rus accept Orthodox Christianity |
| 1016 | Conquest of England by Cnut |
| 1066 | Norman Conquest of England |
| 1072–1085 | Pontificate of Gregory VII |
| 1078 | Decree against lay investiture |
| 1085 | Spanish reconquest of Toledo |
| 1086 | *Domesday Book* |
| 1095–1099 | First Crusade |
| 1122 | Concordat of Worms |
| 1171 | Henry II of England invades Ireland |
| 1176 | Battle of Legnano |
| 1198–1216 | Pontificate of Innocent III |
| 1202–1204 | French drive English out of Normandy |
| 1203 | Fourth Crusade |
| 1212 | Battles of Bouvines and Las Navas de Tolosa |
| 1215 | Magna Carta |
| 1265 | First Parliament in England |
| 1294–1303 | Quarrel between Boniface VIII and Philip IV |
| 1295 | Model Parliament |

and also put more protein in the diet. Leaving land fallow was another means of avoiding soil exhaustion. In the early Middle Ages this meant setting aside about half of the arable land every year (the two-field system) or working the land intensively for a few years and then moving on. By the twelfth century three-field schemes of crop rotation were common.

Under the three-field system, two-thirds of the arable land saw nearly constant use. The amount of an estate under cultivation rose from 50 to 67 percent. Crop rotation brought other benefits as well. Horses ate oats, but (except in a few places such as Scotland) medieval people generally did not. If farmers wished to use horses, they had to dedicate some of their land to growing oats. A three-field rotation allowed some flexibility. Finally the alternation of winter crops (wheat and rye), spring crops (oats, barley, and legumes), and fallow ensured against a single season of unusually harsh weather.

Surplus produce was intended mainly for the growing towns. To supply that market, improvements in transportation were necessary. Kings often passed laws to secure the safety of highways, and popes three times (in 1097, 1132, and 1179) threatened highwaymen—robbers who preyed on travelers—with excommunication. Landlords required their dependents to maintain roads and bridges. Many stone bridges were constructed in France

**Heavy Wheeled Plow**    The improved plow, the horse collar, and the cooperative labors of many peasants in preparing the fields led to an agricultural boom in the European countryside. *(Bibliothèque nationale de France)*

between 1130 and 1170 because wooden bridges were so vulnerable to fire. Indeed, fire destroyed the bridge at Angers (in western France) five times between 1032 and 1167.

Transport improved not only because of safer roads but also thanks to better vehicles. Documents and pictures in manuscripts agree that the old two-wheeled cart, drawn by oxen, began giving way to the sturdy four-wheeled, horse-drawn wagon. Because greater quantities of foodstuffs could be moved farther and faster, urban communities could be supplied from larger areas. This was a crucial factor in enabling cities to grow and in providing urban residents with a predictable and diverse range of foods.

Evidence from several parts of Europe points to the years after 925 as the beginning of real growth in the mining industry. Notable improvements occurred in both the quarrying of stone and the extraction of metals. Mines were not deep because people lacked the means to keep the shafts and galleries free of water. Still, the exploitation of surface and near-surface veins of ore—principally iron but also tin and silver—intensified, to supply the increased demand for plowshares, tools, weapons, construction fittings, and coins. Stone quarrying, the most common form of mining in the Middle Ages, benefited directly from more efficient stone saws and indirectly from improvements in transport. Better techniques in stonecutting, construction, and conveyance help to explain, for example, the increase in the number of England's stone religious buildings from sixty to nearly five hundred in the century after 1050.

## Forms of Enterprise

Agricultural specialization became common. People began to cultivate intensively those crops that were best suited to local conditions. The area around Toulouse, for example, concentrated on herbs from which blue and yellow dyes were made. The central regions of France focused on cereal grains, while the Bordeaux and Burgundy regions emphasized the grapes that produced

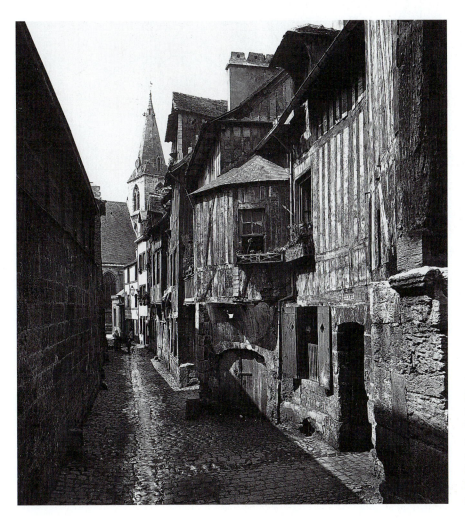

**Twelfth-Century Timbered House, Rouen, France**   The house at the center of this picture was destroyed in World War II after holding its place for nearly eight hundred years. It shows one of the many uses of timber, and its narrow street gives an authentic feel of a medieval town.   *(Roger-Viollet/ Getty Images)*

**Map 9.1   European Resources and Trade Routes, ca. 1100**   In an age of expansion, some products were consumed locally, but many others were transported over longer and longer distances. Commercial connections expanded, too, creating several interlocking networks.

wine. Northern Germany specialized in cattle raising; northern England favored sheep.

Agricultural specialization helps to explain the growth in trade everywhere (see Map 9.1). For certain commodities local trade continued to flourish. Italian wines and olive oil, for example, were not produced for far-off markets; they tended to move from countryside to town within a region. The same was true of French or English grains. However, French wines were much prized throughout Europe, especially in England, and certain products, such as English wool and Flemish cloth, were carried far and wide. Salt fish from the Baltic found its way all over the continent. Lumber was routinely traded across the Mediterranean to the wood-poor Muslim world. Spain was a source of warhorses. Southern Europe supplied the northern demand for spices, oranges, raisins, figs, almonds, and other exotic foodstuffs. Caen, in Normandy, sent shiploads of its beautifully colored and textured stone to England for the construction of churches and monasteries. Rising population, higher productivity, and greater prosperity added up to a larger volume of goods moving farther and more frequently.

The lumber industry reveals many facets of medieval economic activity. Before the twelfth century wood was the main building material, and even later it yielded to stone mainly for the church and aristocracy. But wood could be used for more than construction. For example, the Venetian shipyards needed about twenty oaks, twenty towering pines, and fifty or so beeches to make a ship. In the early twelfth century the Venetians were making about ten vessels a year, twice the number they had been building two centuries earlier. Whether for ships or for homes, the demand for wood grew steadily.

Wood exemplifies the expansion and interconnectedness of the medieval economy and society. Forests were essential to daily life, providing the wood for houses, fences, and fuel in villages and towns. Animals, especially pigs, were grazed at the edges of the forest to permit as much land as possible to be dedicated to food crops. Wild animals were hunted in the forest. For aristocrats hunting was as much for sport as for food. For poorer rural people, however, wild game made up a significant part of the regular diet. The forest was also a plentiful source of fruits, nuts, and honey. Thus the decision to cut down a stand of trees was a serious one.

## The Roles of Cities and Towns

All over Europe towns grew impressively in size and importance. Table 9.1 shows the growth of three Italian cities. Such growth also occurred in cities in Flanders,

**Table 9.1**
**Population Increases in Italian Cities, 1200–1300**

| City | 1200 | 1300 | Percentage Increase |
|---|---|---|---|
| Florence | 15,000 | 96,000 | +640% |
| Siena | 19,000 | 52,000 | +274% |
| Pisa | 20,000 | 38,000 | +190% |

*Source:* Adapted from Malcolm Barber, *The Two Cities: Medieval Europe, 1050–1320* (London: Routledge, 1992), p. 270.

such as Bruges and Ghent, and in Paris, London, and other cities that were becoming national capitals. Ghent expanded its city walls five times between 1160 and 1300, a sure sign of growth even in the absence of population figures. Similar forces were operating in the countryside. In 1100 about 11 fortified villages surrounded Florence, but by 1200 the city was ringed by 205 such villages.

For the first time since late antiquity, cities were becoming centers for many activities. Governments, which required larger staffs of trained personnel, settled in towns. The towns of Italy and Flanders, though not national capitals, ruled over extensive hinterlands. Schools and eventually universities (see pages 339–340) were urban institutions. Mercantile, industrial, and legal organizations were located in towns. Ecclesiastical organization was always urban based. Towns began to compete with royal and aristocratic courts as literary centers, and cathedrals, the great buildings of the age, were exclusively urban.

One distinctive urban phenomenon was the rise of guilds. In 1200, for example, Paris had one guild of merchants and four or five craft or trade associations. By 1270 the city had 101 craft or trade guilds, and by 1292 the number had risen to 130.

The guilds had many functions. Their main purpose was economic: to regulate standards of production, to fix prices, and to control membership in their respective trades. But as towns grew larger and more impersonal, these associations of people engaged in similar occupations fostered a sense of belonging, a feeling of community. Members tended to live in the same areas and to worship together in a parish church. Growing wealth in general, coupled with fierce local pride, produced building competitions whose results are still visible in the huge neighborhood churches that survive in most European towns. The guilds indulged in elaborate festivals and celebrations, which sometimes turned into drunken debauches despite being held to honor saints. The guilds

## READING SOURCES — TWO VIEWS OF MEDIEVAL MARKETS

*Europe's expanding commerce induced rulers to foster conditions favorable to trade but provoked serious concerns in the minds of moralists. In the first of these documents Germany's emperor Frederick Barbarossa (r. 1152–1190) takes steps to promote a fair at Aachen. In the second the distinguished theologian Humbert of Romans (1194–1277) criticizes and satirizes the new economy.*

### Frederick Promotes

Since the royal palace of Aachen excels all provinces and cities in dignity and honor . . . it is fitting and reasonable that we . . . should fortify that same place with lavish gifts of liberty and privileges as if with walls and towers. We have therefore decreed that there should be held twice a year the solemn and universal fairs of Aachen. And this we have done on the advice of the merchants. . . . We have given this liberty to all merchants, that they may be quit and free of toll throughout the year at these fairs in this royal place, and they may buy and sell goods freely just as they wish. No merchant nor any other person may take a merchant to court for payment of debt during these fairs, nor take him there for any business that was conducted before the fairs began. . . . And all people coming to, or staying at, or going from the fairs shall have peace for their persons and goods. And lest the frequent changing of coins, which are sometimes light and sometimes heavy, redound to the hurt of so glorious a place . . . we have ordered money to be struck there of the same purity, weight, and form, and in the same quantity, and to be kept to the same standard. . . . Whoever out of boldness decides to oppose our decree, or by temerity to break it, shall be in our mercy and will pay a hundred pounds of gold to our court.

### Humbert Protests

Though markets and fairs are terms often used indiscriminately, there is a difference between them, for fairs deal with larger things, occasionally, and to them come men from afar. But markets are for lesser things, the daily necessities of life, and they are held weekly and only people near at hand come. Hence markets are usually morally worse than fairs. They are held on feast days and men thereby miss the divine office and sermon . . . sometimes too they are held in graveyards and other holy places. Frequently you will hear men swearing there "By God I will not give you so much for it," or "By God I will not take a smaller price." . . . Sometimes the lord is defrauded of market dues, which is perfidy and disloyalty . . . sometimes quarrels happen and violent disputes . . . drinking is occasioned. . . . Thus the legend runs of a man who, entering an abbey, found many devils in the cloister but in the market place found only one. This filled him with wonder. But it was told to him that in the cloister all is arranged to help souls to God, so many devils are required to lead monks astray, but in the market place, since each man is a devil to himself, only one other demon suffices.

Source: Slightly adapted from Roy C. Cave and Herbert H. Coulson, *A Source Book for Medieval Economic History* (New York: Bruce, 1936), pp. 120–121, 113. Reprinted by permission of Biblio & Tannen.

---

were also mutual assurance societies. That is, they assisted colleagues who fell on hard times, saw to the funeral expenses of members, and provided for widows and orphans.

The guilds had a damaging impact on women. As more economic activity came under the umbrella of the guild structures, women were more systematically excluded from guild membership. Usually women could become guild members only as wives or widows. They could not open economic enterprises of their own, although they were workers in many trades. Despite a growing, diversifying economy, women were increasingly denied opportunities, although later centuries would find women establishing their own guilds.

## Commercial Growth and Innovation

Towns were focal points in commercial networks. The basic trade routes and networks had existed since Carolingian times, but a novelty of the twelfth century was the emergence of the Champagne fairs as a meeting point for the commerce of north and south. Since the early Middle Ages, a few locations hosted permanent fairs, and many places sponsored occasional fairs. By the middle of the twelfth century, however, the spices, silks, and dyes of the Mediterranean, the wool of England, the furs and linens of Germany, and the leather products of Spain began to be sold in a series of six fairs held in the Champagne region of France from spring to autumn.

At any time of year, travel was difficult and costly. Few dared to venture across the Alps in the winter, and the northern seas, especially the passage around Denmark, were treacherous in cold weather. Even in the relatively calm Mediterranean, the Venetians refused to send out their trading fleet between November and March. Overland trade was impeded by snow, rain, mud, and highwaymen. Governments tried to restrain robbers, but no one could change the weather.

Seaborne trade expanded. The stern rudder, better sails, the compass (in use by 1180), and better navigational charts facilitated sea travel, as did the growing use of larger ships. An Italian fleet sailed to Flanders in 1277, and within a few years the old overland trade routes, and with them the Champagne fairs, began a decline that was not reversed until the invention of the railroad in the nineteenth century. (See the box "Reading Sources: Two Views of Medieval Markets.")

## Changing Economic Attitudes

As medieval society generated more wealth and populations concentrated in cities, people who were relatively well-off became more conscious of those who were less fortunate. Moralists began to argue that the poor were a special gift of God to the rich, who could redeem their own souls by generous charitable benefactions. Most towns established schemes of poor relief. But the numbers of poor people grew so rapidly, particularly in large towns, that helping seemed hopeless, and some gave up trying. Hospitals, for example, began to refuse abandoned babies for fear that they would be deluged with them.

Efforts to alleviate the condition of the poor constituted one ethical concern of medieval thinkers, but two issues attracted even more attention. First, theologians and lawyers alike discussed the "just price," the price at which goods should be bought and sold. Christian teaching had long held that it was immoral to hoard food during a famine or knowingly to sell a damaged item. But what was the correct price in ordinary circumstances? A theological view, often dismissed as unrealistic, held that items could be sold for only the cost of the materials in them and the labor absolutely necessary to produce them. A commercial view, often dismissed as immoral, insisted that a fair price was whatever the market would bear, regardless of costs or consequences. A working consensus held that a just price was one arrived at by bargaining between free and knowledgeable parties.

The other ethical issue concerned usury, the lending of money at interest. Christian writers were always hostile to commercial enterprise, and they had plenty of biblical warrant for their view. Psalm 15 warned that no one can be blameless "who lends his money at usury." Luke's Gospel admonished Christians to "give without expecting to be repaid in full." Luke actually forbade the profit that makes most commercial enterprises possible. In the twelfth century churchmen began to be much more assiduous in their condemnations of usury, a practice that had been winked at for centuries.

Prohibitions against usury in twelfth-century Europe (a society in full economic expansion) produced some remarkably inventive ways to get around the prohibitions. One person might agree to sell another person an item at a certain price and then buy it back on a fixed date at a higher price. Exchange rates between currencies could be manipulated to mask usurious transactions. Gradually thinkers began to defend usury on the grounds that a person who lent money incurred a risk and deserved to be compensated for that risk.

Investment demands credit, and credit requires some payback for the lender. Even in the face of deep hostility, credit mechanisms spread in thirteenth-century Europe. They were held up to minute scrutiny by theologians and popular preachers and were found to be evidence of man's sinfulness, acquisitiveness, greed. But all these practices persisted, fueled by the expansion of the European economy, and began putting individual profit alongside community interest at the heart of social and economic thought.

## THE HEIRS OF THE CAROLINGIAN EMPIRE: GERMANY, ITALY, AND FRANCE

THE scope of political and institutional life expanded everywhere between 900 and 1300. In 900 the Carolingian Empire was collapsing. By 1300 France had emerged as a large, stable kingdom, and Italy had turned into several reasonably coherent regional entities. One might have predicted these post-Carolingian outcomes from the pre-Carolingian experience of these two areas. The most surprising political development within the old Carolingian lands, indeed within Europe as a whole, was Germany's rise to a premier position in the tenth century and then its long, slow decline. The states that evolved out of the Carolingian Empire faced common challenges: the achievement of territorial integrity; the growing responsibility of the central government; complicated political relations among kings, aristocrats, and churchmen; and the elaboration of new ideas about the state and its responsibilities.

## Germany and the Empire, 911–1272

From the ninth century to the present, no state in Europe has been less stable territorially and politically than Germany and the German Empire. Time after time the Germans confronted new possibilities and challenges. An investigation of three questions in particular will help us comprehend German history after the Carolingians. First, what role did dynastic instability play in German history? Second, what rules governed political development in the German lands? Third, how did the German rulers regulate relations with the leaders of the church?

When the Treaty of Verdun (see page 264) assigned an East Frankish kingdom to Louis the German in 843, it created something essentially new. Frankish rulers had long claimed authority over some of the lands that eventually became Germany, but before 843 no unified kingdom had ever existed in the territories east of the Rhine River (see Map 9.2). The Carolingians tried hard to impose common institutions on the diverse regions running from Saxony in the north to Bavaria in the south, but they faced immense difficulties in doing so. The lands had no tradition of common or unified rule. There was no single "German" people; Saxons thought of themselves as Saxon, for example, not as German. Roman culture had barely penetrated into German lands, and Christian culture was recent and fragile. "Germany" had—has—no natural frontiers. Germany was, finally, the most thoroughly rural area of the Carolingian world.

After the last East Frankish Carolingian died in 911, the dukes, or leaders, of Germany's major regions chose one of their number as king. In 919 they did so again, their choice this time falling on Duke Henry of Saxony. Henry and his successors, each of whom was named Otto, ruled capably until 1024, when Henry II died without an heir. This time the German dukes turned to a distantly related family, the Salians. The Salian family died out in the middle of the twelfth century and was replaced by the Staufer, who ruled until 1250. Then, after twenty-two years without a recognized ruler, the Germans elected a member of the Habsburg family. This record of frequent dynastic change might be contrasted

| Rulers of Medieval Germany |
| --- |
| **Saxons** |
|   Henry I (919–936) |
|   Otto I (936–973) |
|   Otto II (973–983) |
|   Otto III (983–1002) |
|   Henry II (1002–1024) |
| **Salians** |
|   Conrad II (1024–1039) |
|   Henry III (1039–1056) |
|   Henry IV (1056–1106) |
|   Henry V (1106–1125) |
| **Staufer** |
|   Conrad III (1138–1152) |
|   Frederick Barbarossa (1152–1190) |
|   Henry VI (1190–1197) |
|   Frederick II (1212–1250) |

with the situation in France (see pages 292–295), where one family reigned from 987 to 1328. Our task now is to see how this dynastic instability affected the course of German history.

Who were these dukes, and why were they so influential? German romantic tradition regarded them as the heroic leaders of distinct ethnic communities, the so-called Tribal Duchies. In fact, the dukes were the descendants of local rulers introduced by the Carolingians. They were wealthy and powerful; they contested with kings for control of the bishops and abbots in their duchies; and sometimes they managed to make vassals out of the lower ranks of the aristocracy in their territories, effectively denying kings connections with these people. In sum, the dukes were extremely jealous of their independence.

At the beginning of Saxon (Ottonian) rule, Germany comprised five duchies: Saxony, Franconia, Lorraine, Swabia, and Bavaria. When the Ottonians came to power, they concentrated on using both force and strategic alliances to attempt to control one or more of these duchies. Hoping to win new territories and distract troublesome aristocrats, the Ottonians began Germany's centuries-long drive to the east, into Slavic Europe. In 955 Otto I gained power and prestige when he led a combined German force to victory against the Magyars at Lechfeld.

The Ottonians also tried to control the church, especially bishops and abbots, to gain the allegiance of powerful and articulate allies. In 962 Otto I, who had begun

**Map 9.2    Germany and Its Duchies, ca. 1000–1200**
The chief political dynamic in Germany was a contest for power between the kings and the dukes. The duchies emerged in the ninth and tenth centuries and outlived one dynasty of kings after another.

expanding into Italy in 952, was crowned emperor in Rome by the pope. Why did he seek to revive the Carolingian imperial office? The imperial title conferred two benefits on the German kings: it gave them immense prestige and power that owed nothing to the dukes, and it raised the possibility of securing huge material resources in Italy, where, as emperors, they did not have to share power the way they did in Germany. The marriage of Otto II to a Byzantine princess was a sign of Germany's growing stature. Their son, Otto III, sponsored a brilliant court, patronizing writers and painters. When he died in 1002, Germany was the pre-eminent land in Europe.

The eleventh century and early twelfth century brought dramatic changes to Germany. The Salians, distant relatives of the Ottonians, mounted the throne in 1024, opening opportunities for political disruption. When the second Salian ruler, Henry III, died in 1056, he left behind a 6-year-old heir and a decade of civil war. Military expansion virtually ceased, and powerful aristocrats struggled with one another and with their kings. Chief

**Henry IV, Duchess Matilda of Tuscany, and Abbot Hugh of Cluny**    The embattled Henry IV here implores Matilda, a tremendously wealthy landowner and ally of Pope Gregory VII, to intercede with the pope. The powerful abbot of Cluny looks over the scene protectively. Written documents do not portray women's power as vividly as this image does.    *(Vatican Library, Rome)*

among these aristocrats were the dukes, who had chafed under Ottonian and Salian efforts to control them.

When Henry IV came of age in 1066, he faced opposition on all sides, controlled no duchies, was not yet emperor, and had lost much of his father's control of the church. When he tried to make church appointments in the traditional way, he encountered the fierce opposition of the newly reformed papacy in the person of Pope Gregory VII (r. 1073–1085). Gregory was brilliant, proud, and inflexible—and determined to bend Henry to his will. Their battles inaugurated the so-called investiture controversy, which lingered on until 1122, when both of the original foes were long dead. (See the box "Reading Sources: The Issues in the Investiture Controversy.")

What was the investiture controversy, how had it come about, and what impact did it have on Germany? In the middle of the eleventh century a group of ardent church reformers appeared in Rome. Committed to improving the moral and intellectual caliber of the clergy

all over Europe, they targeted the chief impediment to reform: the control of church appointments by laymen—or "lay investiture," as they called it. This brought the reformers into direct conflict with the Salians, who, like Charlemagne and the Ottonians before them, believed that they reigned supreme in the "City of God." These German rulers stood, in their own view, nearest to God in a great hierarchy; the clergy occupied the rungs beneath them in human society. Thus the king was God's specially chosen agent on earth, and the higher clergy were the king's natural helpers in governing the realm. To the reformers, the proper organization of society was just the opposite: the clergy, with the pope at its head, stood nearest to God, with secular monarchs subordinate to the church.

When these reformers challenged royal supremacy on ideological grounds, the particular quarrel over the appointment of churchmen mushroomed into a general struggle for leadership in Christian society. In Germany

## READING SOURCES    THE ISSUES IN THE INVESTITURE CONTROVERSY

*These two documents illustrate the range of issues involved in the conflict between the emperor Henry IV and Pope Gregory VII. The first excerpt is from a long letter written by Henry in 1076. The second is a decree issued by Gregory in 1078.*

### Henry Denounces the Pope

Henry, king not by usurpation but by the holy ordination of God, to Hildebrand, not now pope but false monk:

Such greeting as this you have merited through your disturbances, for there is no rank in the church on which you have brought, not honor but disgrace, not blessing but curse. To mention only a few notable cases, you have dared to assail the holy rulers of the church, archbishops, bishops, and priests, and you have trodden them underfoot like slaves ignorant of what their master is doing; . . . you have regarded them as knowing nothing, yourself as knowing all things. . . .

We have endured all this in our anxiety to save the honor of the apostolic see, but you have mistaken our humility for fear and have ventured to attack the royal power conferred on us by God, and threatened to divest us of it. As if we had received our kingdom from you! As if the kingdom and empire were in your hands, not God's! For our Lord Jesus Christ did call us to the kingdom. . . . You have assailed me who, though unworthy of anointing, have nevertheless been anointed to the kingdom and who, according to the traditions of the holy fathers, are subject to the judgment of God alone. . . . The true pope Peter exclaims "Fear God, honor the king." But you, who do not fear God, dishonor me, His appointed one. . . .

You, therefore, damned by this curse and by the judgment of all our bishops and ourselves, come down and relinquish the apostolic chair which you have usurped. I, Henry, king by the grace of God, together with all our bishops, say to you: "Come down, come down, to be damned throughout all eternity."

### Gregory Strikes Back

Inasmuch as we have learned that, contrary to the ordinances of the holy fathers, the investiture of churches is, in many places, performed by lay persons, and that from this cause many disturbances arise in the church by which the Christian religion is degraded, we decree that no one of the clergy shall receive the investiture of a bishopric, abbey, or church from the hand of an emperor, or king, or of any layperson, male or female. If anyone shall presume to do so, let him know that such investiture is void by apostolic authority, and that he himself shall lie under excommunication until fitting satisfaction shall have been made.

Source: Slightly adapted from James Harvey Robinson, *Readings in European History*, vol. 1 (Boston: Ginn, 1904), pp. 279–281, 275.

---

the struggle between Henry IV and Gregory VII became a pretext for ducal and aristocratic opposition to the king. Even though the kings could not control the dukes, they had sometimes wrest the naming of bishops from them. Meanwhile, Henry expended time and resources in Italy trying in vain to control Rome and the pope.

The Concordat of Worms°, concluded in 1122 between Henry V (r. 1106–1125) and Pope Calixtus II (r. 1119–1124), brought the investiture controversy to an end. The decree stipulated that episcopal (bishopric) elections should be free and conducted according to church law. Only after a man had been duly elected bishop could a king, or emperor, invest him with the symbols and offices of secular authority. The Concordat was a blow to the German political system as it had existed for centuries. When Otto III died in 1002, Germany was powerful and confident. When Henry V died in 1125, Germany was weak, disunited, and searching for new bases of authority.

With the accession of Frederick Barbarossa ("Red Beard") in 1152, a new family, the Staufer, consolidated its hold on the German throne. Frederick, whose base was in Swabia, patiently worked to get the other dukes to recognize his overlordship, even though he was powerless to demand payments or services from them. His plan was slowly to build up the idea that the king was the highest lord in the land (a plan that his French and English contemporaries used effectively). In 1158 Frederick

---

**Worms** (VORM)

summoned representatives of the major northern and central Italian cities to demand full recognition of his regalian, or ruler's, rights. These included military service; control of roads, ports, and waterways; administration of tolls, mints, fines, vacant fiefs, and confiscated properties; appointment of magistrates; construction of palaces; and control of mines, fisheries, and saltworks. No German king had ever possessed these kinds of rights before. Frederick's attempts to control northern Italy resulted in the creation of the Lombard League, a union of Italian cities that inflicted a humiliating defeat on German forces at Legnano° in 1176.

Frederick also struggled for more than twenty years to get the popes to recognize his claim to the imperial office, which he viewed as a source of prestige and as a legitimation of his right to rule Italy. When he spoke of his "Holy Roman Empire," he meant that his power came, on the one hand, from God himself and, on the other hand, from the Romans via Charlemagne. Theory did not match reality, however, and the papacy was able to thwart virtually all his political initiatives. The handsome, energetic, and athletic Frederick accomplished much, and he might have done more had he not drowned in Anatolia in 1190 while on his way to the Third Crusade.

Frederick's successor, Henry VI (r. 1190–1197), ruled for only a short time and left behind an infant son, Frederick II (r. 1212–1250). Frederick II had been born in Sicily. His mother, Constance, had no standing in Germany and little influence in Italy. Accordingly, she placed her son under the tutelage of Pope Innocent III. By the time Frederick came of age, he so despaired of governing Germany that he conceded the "Statute in Favor of the Princes," which lodged royal power in ducal hands in return for a vague acknowledgment of his overlordship. Frederick concentrated his own efforts in Italy, where he sought to institute a sophisticated regime based on Byzantine and Norman (see page 291) models. Although he made good progress, he faced constant opposition from the popes, who were unwilling to trade a German ruler with interests in Italy for an essentially Italian ruler with interests in Germany. When Frederick II died in 1250, effective central authority in both Germany and Italy collapsed. After twenty-two years of weak or contested rule, the German dukes turned to Rudolf of Habsburg whose descendants remained influential in German politics until the early twentieth century. Neither the Habsburgs nor any subsequent German emperors restored the position held by the Ottonians.

An understanding of Germany's fate requires that we return to the questions with which we began this discussion. One wonders: Might a long-lived dynasty have made a difference? Germany was not without great rulers: Otto I, Otto III, Frederick Barbarossa, and even Frederick II were the equals of any contemporary ruler. But repeated changes of ruling family in the context of a fragile political regime provided repeated opportunities for fragmentation. The German monarchy had a very limited territorial base and, compared with these kings' Carolingian predecessors and their French and English contemporaries, they possessed unimpressive government institutions. The kings themselves were dukes, and as such their areas of truly effective control were usually limited to one duchy. The Saxons were based in the north, the Salians in the center, and the Staufer in the south. Thus continuity of rule was constantly threatened by huge dynastic, institutional, and geographical challenges.

Was the Italian venture a mistake? Germany's involvement with Italy and the imperial title has occasioned no end of controversy. To some, royal involvement in Italy signals a failure to deal imaginatively with Germany itself. To others, the quest for prestige, power, and money in Italy was actually a creative solution to the monarchy's relative impotence in Germany. There was, of course, always a danger that Italy itself would become the prime object of the German ruler's attention, as actually happened under Frederick II. In the end the struggle for control of Italy brought Germany's rulers two unforeseen consequences. First, since the imperial title had to be obtained in Rome from the pope, the papacy was handed an unprecedented opportunity to meddle in German politics. That opportunity evolved from an initial request for protection, through periodic demands for political concessions, to a claim that the pope actually had the right to decide whether a particular individual was morally fit to be crowned emperor. Second, leading Italian cities were not content to be ruled by the Germans. The dramatic German defeat at Legnano is representative of the ongoing challenges and provocations to German authority.

With its promise, undoubted achievements, and yet ultimate failure, Germany is the political mystery of medieval Europe. In turning now to other regions of Europe, we will continue to explore the roles dynasty, geography, institutions, and ideology played there.

## The Varying Fortunes of Italy

The history of Italy has always been played out in three regions: north, central, and south. The Carolingians and the Germans after them laid a heavy hand on northern Italy. In the center of the peninsula the Papal States was the key player. Outsiders always dominated the south, but their identities changed often.

---

**Legnano** (len-YAN-oh)

**Map 9.3    The Communal Movement in Italy**    Beginning in the late eleventh century, many towns in northern Italy, some in the central regions, and a very few in the south erected communal forms of government. This distribution reflects the relative wealth of north and south and the power of the popes in the center. North of the Alps only Flanders and northern France experienced comparable communal movements.

As we have seen, German attempts to impose their authority on northern Italy met with limited success. One key obstacle to German rule was the communal movement (see Map 9.3), the most dynamic element on the Italian scene. Two conditions help to explain the rise of communes. The first relates to economic expansion. In the early eleventh century Italian towns began to rid the Mediterranean of Muslim pirates. By 1100 Italian merchants could trade anywhere in the Mediterranean world with confidence.

The second contributing factor relates to political developments in Italian towns. The Carolingians governed towns through resident counts, and German emperors tried to maintain this system. The powers of the counts tended to be weak, however, so the Germans also relied on bishops, who were, in Italy as in Germany, key props to the system of imperial rule. But bishops and counts were not alone in holding urban power. Since the late tenth century both bishops and counts had been granting fiefs to local men in order to strengthen their own authority and to procure defenses for the towns. Gradually these men, whose lands made them wealthy in the expanding economy, moved into the towns and, in turn, gave fiefs to other men in the countryside. These lords were wealthy and jealous of their power.

Communes were sworn associations of the local nobility—these landed lords—and their vassals. Commune members swore to uphold one another's rights and called themselves the *popolo*, or "people," although the people as a whole had nothing to do with the early communes. A commune accorded a high degree of participation to its members in choosing leaders and in coming together in an assembly that voted on matters of common concern. The leaders of the early communes were usually called *consuls*—a deliberate attempt to evoke the Roman past. Usually elected for a single year, the consuls varied in number from four to twenty in different cities. The consuls proposed matters to an assembly for ratification. By the 1140s every significant city in northern and central Italy had a commune.

The communes did not necessarily originate as attempts to make cities independent. Frequently, however, as communal governments became more established and confident, that is what they did. One by one, cities either refused to recognize papal or imperial overlordship or else renegotiated the terms under which they would acknowledge the rule of their historic masters. The working out of this ongoing relationship was a major development in the history of the Italian cities in the twelfth century.

Although each Italian commune constituted an entity unto itself, a fairly coherent evolution is evident. By the late twelfth century the consular communes were still governed by oligarchies of men whose wealth and power came from land, trade, and industry. Guild interests, however, gained in prominence at the expense of the landed groups among whom the communal movement had arisen, and ordinary workers began to clamor for participation. The communes were becoming increasingly volatile and violent.

One solution to this potential crisis was the introduction of the *podestà*°, a sort of city manager chosen by the local oligarchy. The podestà often came from the outside, served for a set period (usually six months or a year), and underwent a careful scrutiny at the conclusion of his term. He was expected to be competent not only at ordinary administration but also at military leadership, so that he could police the city as well as defend it. He brought with him a group of seasoned officials as subordinates. Normally he could not be a property owner in the town, marry into local society, or dine privately with any citizen. By the middle of the thirteenth century some podestàs were becoming virtual professional administrators. One man, for example, was elected sixteen times in nine cities over a period of thirty-four years, four times in Bologna alone.

The Italian commune was a radical political experiment. Everywhere else in medieval Europe power was thought to radiate downward—from God, the clergy, the

emperor, the king. In a commune power radiated upward from the popolo to its leaders. For several centuries the Italian city was arguably the most creative institution in the Western world. When Frederick Barbarossa tried to introduce tight imperial control, the future of northern and central Italy hung in the balance. But his defeat at the hands of the Lombard League at Legnano in 1176 left the Italian cities free to continue their distinctive political evolution.

Although some communes emerged in central Italy—even, briefly, in Rome in the 1150s—the key power in this region was the papacy, and the main political entity was the Papal States. In the political turmoil of the tenth and eleventh centuries, the papacy lost a great deal of territory. Throughout the twelfth and thirteenth centuries, therefore, a basic objective of papal policy was to recover lost lands and rights. This quest to restore the territorial basis for papal power and income helps explain why the popes so resolutely opposed German imperial influence in Italy.

The most striking development pertaining to the papacy is the expansion of its institutions. Gradually there emerged what historians have long called the "Papal Monarchy." This term is meant to characterize a church whose power was increasingly centralized in the hands of the popes. In Rome the pope presided over the *curia*, the papal court. The College of Cardinals, potentially fifty-three in number, formed a kind of senate for the church. They elected the popes (by majority after 1059 and by a two-thirds majority after 1179), served as key advisers, headed the growing financial and judicial branches of the papal government, and often served as legates. Legates were papal envoys, some of whom were sent to particular people or places provisionally, to communicate a message or to conduct an investigation, and some of whom were more like resident ambassadors who represented the pope on a continuing basis. Lateran Councils met often and gathered the clergy from all over Europe to legislate for the church as a whole. The hierarchical structure of the church became more visible as ecclesiastical business tended to accumulate in Rome.

| Important Popes During the High Middle Ages |
| --- |
| Gregory VII (1073–1085) |
| Urban II (1088–1099) |
| Innocent III (1198–1216) |
| Boniface VIII (1294–1303) |

---

**podestà** (poe-des-TAH)

High medieval popes also reserved to themselves certain jurisdictional and coercive prerogatives. Only popes could officially canonize a saint, a powerful reservation of rights against local communities. Popes could excommunicate persons—that is, exclude them from the sacraments of the church and the community of Christians. This was a form of social death in that excommunicated persons could not eat, converse, or socialize with others. Popes could lay a territory under interdict. This decree forbade all religious services except baptisms and burials and was designed to bring maximum pressure to bear on a particular individual. Finally, popes could invoke the inquisition. Despite horror stories about the inquisition, this was a judicial mechanism fully rooted in Roman law and widely used in the medieval West. Basically, an inquisition involved churchmen taking sworn testimony in an attempt to discover heresy.

Who were the popes? What were they like? Most of them had been cardinals with years, if not decades, of experience in the government of the church. Many of the twelfth- and thirteenth-century popes were lawyers, which may explain, in part, their dedication to institutional and legal reforms. Not a single pope from this period has been canonized as a saint. One Englishman was elected; the rest were Roman, Italian, or French. Most were noblemen.

Institutions were important, but personalities mattered, too. Innocent III (r. 1198–1216), for example, was the most powerful man ever to hold the papal office. He came from a minor Italian noble family, received early training in theology and law, and entered the papal administration while in his twenties. His entire life was dedicated to promoting the legal prerogatives of the papacy and the moral improvement of Christian society. As a young man Innocent wrote *On the Contempt of the World,* in which he expressed his hope for a life of peace and contemplation. As an older man he hurled legal thunderbolts at the greatest public figures of the day.

From the ninth century on, the region south of Rome was contested among Byzantines, North African Muslims, and local potentates. In 1026 Norman pilgrims bound for the Holy Land landed in southern Italy, where local people invited them to enlist in the fight against the Muslims. By the 1040s the original Normans had been joined by many more who were seeking land and adventure. Initially opposed to the Normans, the papacy later allied with their leader as a counterweight against the Germans.

From his capital at Palermo, Roger II, also known as "Roger the Great" (r. 1130–1154), ruled a complex state that blended Byzantine, Lombard, and Norman structures. In Italy, as in England (see page 296), the Normans

**Coronation of Roger II in Sicily, 1130**    Roger's coronation by Jesus Christ makes a powerful ideological statement: he owes his office to no earthly power. The cultural crosscurrents of Sicily are visible: Roger is depicted more like a Byzantine emperor than a Western king. The inscriptions above his head ("Rogerios Rex") and next to Christ's are in Greek, not Latin. Beside Christ's head are the customary Greek abbreviations **IC** (the first and last letters of **I**esu**S**) and **XP,** for **ChR**istos. (The original surely contains the full XP symbol.) *(Scala/Art Resource, NY)*

showed a genius for adaptation. Perched advantageously at the juncture of the Latin, Greek, and Arab worlds, the Norman court was more advanced in finance and bureaucratic administration than any of its European contemporaries. No one forgot for a moment, however, that the Normans were primarily great warriors. A chronicler said of the Normans, "They delight in arms and horses."

When the male Norman line died out, its heiress, Constance, married Henry VI of Germany (Barbarossa's son) and gave birth to Frederick II. For two generations the papacy struggled to break German control of southern Italy. Once the popes had defeated Frederick II, they decided to look for more pliant allies in the south. They invited a succession of French and Spanish princes to assume the Crown, thus touching off long-standing rivalries in the area. A profusion of outsiders always dominated southern Italy.

## Capetian France, 987–1314

When the Treaty of Verdun created the West Frankish Kingdom in 843, no one knew what the future of France might be. Referring to France's tremendous diversity, the twentieth-century French leader Charles de Gaulle once quipped, "It is impossible to govern a country with 325 kinds of cheese." During the late ninth century and much of the tenth, the area suffered cruelly from constant waves of Viking attacks and from repeated failures of the Carolingian family to produce adult heirs to the throne. Chroniclers often quoted the lament of King Solomon: "Woe to thee, O land, whose king is a child." At the end of the tenth century, however, the Carolingians were replaced by the Capetians°, the family of Hugh Capet (r. 987–996). The Capetians ruled France for more than three hundred years—an impressive achievement in light of the repeated failure of German dynasties. The first key issue we must pursue pertains to the power and prestige of the monarchy. Then, bearing in mind de Gaulle's joke, we explore how a large but very complex group of territories was assembled into a kingdom. Finally we look at the nature of government in medieval France and the principles on which that government rested.

From the very beginning the Capetian kings of France sought to preserve the royal office, increase its prestige, and consolidate its political base. Hugh Capet inaugurated the tradition of crowning his son as his successor during his own lifetime. This meant that when the old king died, a new king was already in place and the nobility could not easily meddle in the succession. Robert II (r. 996–1031) displayed the "royal touch," a ceremony in which the king was believed to be able to cure people of scrofula (a common respiratory ailment) by touching them. No French nobleman, no matter how powerful, ever laid claim to such miraculous powers. Louis VII (r. 1137–1180) began to make elegant tours of the country to put himself, his office, and his sparkling entourage on display.

The Capetians were heirs of the dukes of Paris. This meant that initially they controlled no more than Paris

| The Capetian Kings of France |
| --- |
| Hugh Capet (987–996) |
| Robert II (996–1031) |
| Henry I (1031–1060) |
| Philip I (1060–1108) |
| Louis VI (1108–1137) |
| Louis VII (1137–1180) |
| Philip II (1180–1223) |
| Louis VIII (1223–1226) |
| Louis IX (1226–1270) |
| Philip III (1270–1285) |
| Philip IV (1285–1314) |

and its immediate region. They contested for control of this region with a number of ambitious and aggressive families. Louis VI (r. 1108–1137) systematically ground down all his local opponents and made his area, the Ile de France, one of the best-governed regions in all of France. Capetian kings also capitalized on their control of the old, rich, prestigious, and centrally located city of Paris. The kings promoted the shrine of Saint Denis, the legendary first bishop of Paris, as a kind of "national" shrine for France. The kings also controlled about two dozen bishoprics and some fifty monasteries in northern France. This power base gave the kings unrivaled opportunities to extend their influence and, in turn, to build up a cadre of loyal and articulate supporters. Although French kings provoked a few battles with the papacy, France experienced no investiture controversy.

For more than a century Hugh Capet and his successors steadily turned the French monarchy into a prestigious office on solid, if local and limited, political foundations. During the reigns of Louis VI and Louis VII the two great dynamics of high medieval French history come into view: First, the territory ruled by France's kings expanded enormously. Second, the kings finally overwhelmed the territorial princes after a centuries-long struggle.

France's territorial expansion was tightly connected to military success. The background to French military success is complicated. In the late eleventh and early twelfth centuries one family of French magnates, the counts of Anjou° (see Map 9.4), acquired control over a good deal of western France by marriage, diplomacy, and intimidation. Then Geoffrey of Anjou married the heiress of the duchy of Normandy, whose father, William the Conqueror, we will meet later. A bit later Geoffrey's

---

**Capetians** (kuh-PEE-shunz)

**Anjou** (ahn-JHOU)

**Map 9.4    French Territorial Principalities, ca. 1200**    As the Carolingian West Frankish Kingdom (see Map 8.3, page 259) broke down and feudal bonds proliferated, many territories arose under counts and dukes. Their struggles to impose control locally and to fight off royal supervision animated French history.

son and heir married Duchess Eleanor of Aquitaine, the recently divorced wife of Louis VII of France. In 1154 Henry of Anjou, as a result of incredibly complicated political and matrimonial alliances, became King Henry II of England, but he still retained control of about 60 percent of France.

For several generations the kings of France hammered away at this Angevin° Empire. Henry of Anjou's four sons were viciously jealous of one another, and the French kings exploited their rivalries to weaken Angevin

Angevin (AN-juh-vin)

authority in western and southwestern France. When one of Henry's sons, King John of England, absconded with the fiancée of a vassal of King Philip II (r. 1180–1223), the king of France, Philip summoned John to court to answer for his conduct. John's refusal to appear led to war in 1202. By1204 Philip had won a resounding victory and control over a substantial portion of western France. The English and French kings came to blows over their competing claims to French territory several more times in the thirteenth century. Each time the French won, including a major victory over an allied English and German army at Bouvines° in 1214.

Southeastern France was gained by wars of a different kind. In the last decades of the twelfth century several cities in the southeast became hotbeds of the Albigensian° heresy—an important religious movement (see page 328). Some Catholic locals and many churchmen urged the kings to undertake military action against the heretics. The French kings were prudent and bided their time until they had the resources to deal with this turbulent region. Under Louis VIII (r. 1223–1226) and Louis IX (r. 1226–1270) the French monarchy finally extended its authority to France's Mediterranean coast.

The chief political dynamic in France was the contest for power between the kings and the territorial princes (see Map 9.4). At stake was the monarchy's ability to introduce effective rule into the lands won in all those battles. Who were the territorial princes? They were locally powerful magnates, rather like the German dukes, most of whose ancestors had been officials appointed by the Carolingians. But whereas Germany comprised five major duchies, France had a dozen or more territorial principalities. In the tumultuous circumstances of the tenth and eleventh centuries some individuals and families had been remarkably successful in building castles, reducing the local population to subjection, and gathering into their own hands the powers that the Carolingian kings had once exercised in their localities. (See the feature "Weighing the Evidence: The Medieval Castle" on pages 314–315.)

Ironically, the territorial princes also faced localized rivalries for power and influence. Countless individuals built castles, brutally subjected local peasants, and became lords. Sometimes these individuals were the vassals of the territorial princes—say, the dukes of Normandy or the counts of Anjou—and sometimes they had vassals of their own. In the Carolingian world the number of vassals was small, their fidelity reasonably solid, and their services reliable. By 1100 the number of vassals was immense, their fidelity was constantly shifting, and they tended to provide only local military service. Scholars

call this shift from effective Carolingian government to myriad local lordships a "feudal revolution."

For the kings of France to re-create central government, they had to overcome the disruptive tendencies of this revolution and then consolidate institutions. Under Louis VI and Louis VII some of the most powerful men in the realm visited court and swore allegiance to the Crown. Under Philip II and Louis IX the Capetians gradually turned this ceremonial obedience into effective subjection, just as Frederick Barbarossa had tried but failed to do in Germany.

In the twelfth and thirteenth centuries the Capetians followed a few basic policies to increase their ability to govern. They circumvented the local lords as much as possible. When they won military victories, the kings did not dole out the seized lands to lords as new fiefs but instead kept them in their own hands, or in the hands of family members as *appanages*. What is more, the kings introduced into these lands local officials, called bailiffs or provosts, who were of modest social background, had no personal ties to their assigned regions, often had some schooling in law, and were intensely loyal to the kings. By the time of Louis IX, officials called *enqueteurs*° were sent around the country to inspect the work of bailiffs and provosts. Such roles had been unheard-of since the Carolingian *missi dominici* (see page 262). Louis also began to issue *ordonnances*, what we might call executive orders, that were binding on all the land under the king's control. These precepts are reminiscent of Carolingian capitularies (see page 260).

If in 1000 France was a land of innumerable tiny lordships, then by 1300 it was the best-governed kingdom in Europe. Indicative of France's position is the outcome of two battles between King Philip IV (r. 1285–1314) and Pope Boniface VIII (r. 1294–1303). First Philip attempted to tax the French clergy, and then he sought to bring a bishop before his court. Boniface angrily objected to Philip's intervention in ecclesiastical affairs. But things had changed drastically since the fateful confrontation between Henry IV and Gregory VII. Boniface had to back down.

The Welsh humorist Walter Map (1140–1209) provides this assessment of France in his day:

> The emperor of Byzantium and the king of Sicily may boast about their gold and silken cloth, but they have no men who can do more than talk, men incapable of war. The Roman emperor or, as they say, the emperor of the Germans, has men apt in arms and warlike horses, but no gold, silk or any other wealth. . . . The king of England lacks nothing and possesses every-

---

Bouvines (BOO-veen)    Albigensian (al-buh-JEN-see-un)    enqueteur (on-KEH-tur) thing, men, horses, gold, silk, jewels, fruits and wild beasts. And we in France have nothing except bread, wine and joy.[1]

Walter comically underestimates the resources of the French. In 1300 theirs was the largest, richest, and best-governed kingdom in Europe. French culture and language were increasingly dominant. In Louis IX the Capetian family actually produced a saint of the Catholic Church—Saint Louis. Considering France's situation in 900, and compared with Germany's in 1300, these were impressive achievements.

## THE BRITISH ISLES

I N the British Isles expansion had three dimensions: the tremendous growth of the English government, England's relentless push into the Celtic world, and the emergence of states in the Celtic world. England, about the size of Alabama, is smaller than France or Germany and more homogeneous in population, culture, and language than either of them, or than Italy. Building effective governance in England was, therefore, a somewhat easier task than it was elsewhere. Nevertheless, England faced some acute dynastic, military, and political crises. Moreover, England shared an island with two Celtic neighbors, Wales and Scotland, whose inhabitants were close kin to the people of England's neighboring island, Ireland (see Map 9.5). For better or worse, the fates of the English and Celtic inhabitants of the British Isles are inseparable.

### Viking and Norman Invasions in England

Alfred (r. 871–899; see page 257) heroically rallied the English against the Vikings, and his descendants ruled England for more than a century. They gradually rolled back the frontier of the "Danelaw," the areas of eastern and northern England controlled by Viking settlers (mainly Danes, hence the name). Alfred and his successors built strong central institutions. All free men in the realm owed

**Map 9.5   Northern and Eastern Europe, ca. 1200**   Apart from Germany, the core states of Europe emerged inside the former Roman frontiers or right alongside them. After 900 an arc of new states emerged, from the Celtic realms and Iceland in the west, to Scandinavia in the north, to the western, southern, and eastern Slavs in eastern Europe.

allegiance to the king and could in principle be called to the militia, or *fyrd°*. The great men of the realm attended meetings of the royal council, or *witan°*, which was partly a court of law and partly a deliberative, consultative body. The king could issue writs—executive orders rather like Carolingian capitularies. The Danegeld— literally "money for the Danes"—was originally collected solely in times of danger and then slowly transformed into a regular tax. All of England was divided into shires, and each shire had a royally appointed officer the *shire-reeve* (or sheriff).

Late in the tenth century English leadership failed in the face of a severe threat from a new generation of Vikings. The powerful king of Denmark, Swein Forkbeard, conquered England in 1014, but survived his conquest by only two years. His son Cnut then ruled from 1016 to 1035, at which point power passed to Cnut's sons.

Cnut did not match the stereotype of the wild and woolly barbarian. He was simultaneously king of Denmark and England, and for a time of Norway, too. He wed his daughter to Emperor Henry III and himself to Emma, the widow of the last English king. He was cultured, Christian, and an acquaintance of the pope.

When Cnut's sons died in 1042 without heirs, the English nobles called over from Normandy Edward, called "the Confessor," the son of the last English king. Edward, who was unusually pious, had taken a vow of chastity. Because he was not going to have an heir, claimants to the English throne began jockeying for position. Edward seems to have promised his throne to William, the duke of Normandy. Most of the English nobles preferred Harold of Wessex, one of their number. In Norway Harald Sigurdson (who became known as Hardrada, or "Hard-Ruler") prepared to make a claim as Cnut's rightful heir.

When Edward died, the English elected Harold, and immediately he learned that Hardrada had invaded. He marched to meet the Norse challenger and won an impressive victory at Stamford Bridge, only to learn that William had meanwhile landed in the south. Foolishly Harold rushed south to meet William, without resting or reinforcing his troops. At Hastings William defeated Harold, and England was his for the taking.

Amid these frequent changes in rulers one thing remained constant: the smooth functioning of the Anglo-Saxon state. It is no surprise that neither Cnut nor William, known as "the Conqueror" (r. 1066–1089), desired to dismantle or replace the old English institutions. But William had won England by conquest, and he did introduce some changes. He turned most of the estates

| Important Kings of England |
| --- |
| Alfred (871–899) |
| Ethelred II (978–1016) |
| Cnut (1016–1035) |
| Edward the Confessor (1042–1066) |
| Harold of Wessex (1066) |
| William I (the Conqueror) (1066–1089) |
| William II (1089–1100) |
| Henry I (1100–1135) |
| Stephen I (1135–1154) |
| Henry II (1154–1189) |
| Richard I (1189–1199) |
| John (1199–1216) |
| Henry III (1216–1272) |
| Edward I (1272–1307) |

in England into fiefs and distributed them among some 180 of his most loyal followers. Each of these vassals held his fief in return for a fixed quota of soldiers for the royal army. To raise the approximately five thousand soldiers required by William, each of his vassals had to create vassals of his own. The technical name for this process of vassals creating vassals is *subinfeudation*. In 1087 William exacted the Salisbury Oath, which established the principle of liege homage°, according to which the king was the final lord of all vassals. To avoid creating compact territorial principalities on the French model, William scattered his vassals' holdings around the kingdom. Finally, to learn as much as he could about his new kingdom, and about the fiefs he had assigned to his followers, William conducted a massive survey of England that resulted in 1086 in the *Domesday Book*, named for the Day of Judgment, against which there was no appeal. No comparable survey of any state was accomplished until the American census of 1790.

## The Development of English Law and Government

William was succeeded by two of his sons in turn, William II (r. 1089–1100) and Henry I (r. 1100–1135). Henry's only son drowned in a shipwreck, and the English nobles would accept neither his daughter Matilda as their queen nor her husband Geoffrey of Anjou as their king. Owing to William's conquest and settlement, most

---

**fyrd** (FEERD)    **witan** (WHIT-un)

**liege homage** (LEEGE AHM-idge)

of the English elite were in fact Normans, and the Normans and Angevins were old foes. Consequently, the English turned in 1135 to a French prince, Stephen of Blois, who was a grandson of William the Conqueror through a daughter. Stephen I died childless in 1154 and bequeathed his kingdom to Henry of Anjou, the son of Geoffrey and Matilda, who ruled as Henry II (r. 1154–1189).

Henry was as much a French prince as an English king. From his father, mother, and wife (Eleanor of Aquitaine; see page 293), he had inherited a large part of France and was much preoccupied with his continental realm. He constantly battled his four sons for control of these vast French holdings. Two of these sons eventually became king. Richard I, also known as "Richard the Lionhearted" (r. 1189–1199), was a dashing prince who spent only ten months in England, preferring to pass his time on crusade or campaigning in France. John (r. 1199–1216) was defeated by France's Philip II, inducing contemporaries to mock him as "John Lackland" and "John Softsword."

On the surface it looks as though dynastic turmoil and military adventures make up the central themes of England's history. But just as Viking and Norman rulers built on the solid foundations of the Anglo-Saxon state, so the Anglo-Normans and Angevins retained and expanded those very foundations. They refined the financial machinery of the English government, the Exchequer, named for the checkerboard table on which the accounts were reckoned. They vastly improved the judicial institutions. Henry I began to send itinerant justices around the realm. He brought the royal court, with its swift, fair, and competent justice, within the reach of most people, and he made royal justice more attractive than the justice available in local lords' courts. Henry II expanded the work of the courts and created an extensive system of writs. These documents, available to almost anyone, had the effect of transferring cases into the royal courts. This expansion of the work of the royal courts led to the emergence of a common law in England—a law common to all people, courts, and cases.

Henry II used the sworn inquest to learn about his realm. He conducted an inquest of knights' service to find out what service vassals owed to which people. He conducted an inquest of sheriffs to learn how the sheriffs were performing their jobs and replaced those found shirking their responsibilities. This action is the context for the Robin Hood stories about the cruel sheriff of Nottingham and the kind king who looks out for the people. Finally the Anglo-Norman and Angevin kings employed in their government "men raised from the dust," as one aristocratic contemporary contemptuously called them. These were men from the middling ranks of society, per-

**Swift and Certain Justice**    This picture from about 1130 depicts some of the forty-four thieves hung by Sheriff Ralph Basset in 1124. As a common law spread throughout England, criminals were more likely to be caught and punished. *(The Pierpont Morgan Library, New York/Art Resource, NY)*

haps with some training in law, who were loyal to the king and advanced his interests against the aristocrats, who were intensely jealous of their own rights and privileges.

England's relations with the church fell somewhere between Germany's and France's in both intensity and outcome. Anglo-Saxon kings generally enjoyed cordial relations with the church on a traditional Carolingian model. William the Conqueror controlled the church with an iron hand but introduced reforms and reformers who were acceptable to Rome. Perhaps Gregory VII left William alone because he did not wish to fight on too many fronts simultaneously. Archbishop Anselm of Canterbury and Henry I had a quarrel that lasted several years, but they finally mended their differences in a settlement that anticipated the terms of the Concordat of Worms.

## READING SOURCES

## SELECTIONS FROM THE MAGNA CARTA

*When the English barons forced King John to sign the Magna Carta in 1215, they had very practical grievances and concrete priorities. The following selections from the charter's sixty-three articles are representative of the kinds of issues involved in the barons' dispute with the king. Note the absence of flowery rhetoric and grandiose statements of philosophical principles.*

1. Know that we in the first place have granted to God and by this our present charter have confirmed, for us and for our heirs in perpetuity, that the English church shall be free, and shall have its rights undiminished and its liberties unimpaired.

2. If any of our earls or barons, or others holding of us in chief by knight service shall die, and at his death his heir be of full age and owe relief [a payment for an heir to succeed to a fief], he shall have his inheritance on payment of the ancient relief. . . .

4. The guardian of the land of such an heir who is under age shall not take from the land more than the reasonable revenues, customary dues and services, and that without destruction or waste of men or goods. . . .

7. After her husband's death, a widow shall have her marriage portion and her inheritance at once and without any hindrance; nor shall she pay anything for her dower, her marriage portion, or her inheritance which she and her husband held on the day of her husband's death; and she may stay in her husband's house forty days after his death, within which period her dower shall be assigned to her.

8. No widow shall be compelled to marry so long as she wishes to live without a husband, provided that she gives security that she will not marry without our consent if she holds of us, or without the consent of the lord of whom she holds, if she holds of another. . . .

12. No scutage [tax] or aid is to be levied in our realm except by the common counsel of our realm, unless it is for the ransom of our person, the knighting of our eldest son, or the first marriage of our eldest daughter. . . .

16. No man shall be compelled to perform more service for a knight's fee or any other free tenement than is due from it. . . .

38. Henceforth no bailiff shall put anyone on trial by his own unsupported allegation, without bringing credible witnesses to the charge.

39. No free man shall be taken or imprisoned or disseised [dispossessed] or outlawed or exiled or in any way ruined, nor will we go or send against him, except by the lawful judgment of his peers or by the law of the land.

Source: J. C. Holt, *Magna Carta* (Cambridge: Cambridge University Press, 1969), pp. 317, 319, 321, 323, 327. Reprinted with the permission of Cambridge University Press.

**www.** **For additional information on this topic, go to college.hmco.com/students.**

---

Henry II was always anxious to extend the influence of his courts. In 1164 he decided that "criminous clerks," or members of the clergy who had committed a crime, should be judged in royal courts. The archbishop of Canterbury, Thomas Becket (ca. 1118–1170), protested that clerics could be tried only in church courts. Although the two sides came to a reconciliation, a band of overly zealous knights murdered Becket, believing that they were doing the king's bidding. In fact, the crime so outraged the church and the public that Henry had to back down on criminous clerks and give up some authority to Rome. Despite these religious quarrels, however, England experienced no investiture controversy.

John's conflict with the church resulted in far more dramatic changes for England. The loss of Normandy had been costly in terms of prestige and resources. In difficult circumstances John got into a row with Pope Innocent III because he refused to admit to England the pope's candidate for archbishop of Canterbury. John had already had minor scrapes with ecclesiastical officials because of his exploitation of the church's revenues. Eventually he submitted because Innocent had laid England under interdict and John needed the pope's support for his planned war against Philip II of France. True to his nickname "Softsword," John lost at Bouvines (see page 294) and thus ended his quarrel with Rome.

With John's inglorious defeat and shameful capitulation, the barons of England had had enough. These barons (a general name for the upper ranks of English society) were increasingly upset that an expanding royal government limited their influence. In 1215 a large group of disgruntled barons forced King John to sign the Magna Carta, or "Great Charter" (so called because it was written on an unusually large sheet of parchment). This document required the king to respect the rights of feudal lords, not abuse his judicial powers, and consult his "natural" advisers—that is, the barons. (See the box "Reading Sources: Selections from the Magna Carta.")

John tried to wiggle out of the Magna Carta, but he died in 1216, leaving only a minor heir, and the barons exacted many concessions from the regency government. When Henry III came of age in 1234, he struggled to win a limited application of the Magna Carta. The barons, on the contrary, wanted a voice in devising royal policy, especially military policy, in light of recent defeats. They also wished to have some say in naming the king's closest advisers and in controlling the work of the king's agents, especially judges. This tension between king and barons led to several meetings of the royal court, often called *parliaments,* a French word meaning, roughly, "talking together." (The genuine ancestors of England's historic Parliament met in 1265 and 1295.) Initially these meetings had no fixed rights or procedures, no set group of attendees, and no defined role. The kings viewed them as clever political devices to win support for royal policies. The barons viewed them as opportunities to play a real role in a government that had been marginalizing them. In retrospect we can see that the English were groping to find a way to build consultation into their system.

The reign of Edward I (1272–1307) sums up the achievements of England's rulers in the High Middle Ages. Like his predecessors, Edward instituted sworn inquests to ascertain his rights and resources. He issued numerous statutes, laws that bear comparison with Louis IX's *ordonnances* (see page 294)—which earned him the nickname "the English Justinian." He worked skillfully with the newly emerging Parliament. And like other English rulers before him, Edward balanced political and military accomplishments, bravely fighting for years on the Welsh and Scottish frontiers.

## The Celtic Realms

When the Romans appeared on the scene, Celtic peoples could be found in virtually every region from Ireland to Anatolia. Most Celts were absorbed by more numerous and powerful Germanic and Slavic peoples. It was in the British Isles that the most durable and distinctive Celtic regions evolved into Ireland, Wales, and Scotland. Two essential dynamics characterized each of these regions.

First, tiny political entities gradually turned into larger kingdoms. Second, relations between England and the Celtic realms were everywhere decisive in the historical development of the latter (see Map 9.5).

In each of the Celtic realms the movement toward greater unity was opened by the efforts of powerful, ambitious leaders to subjugate numerous well-entrenched local potentates, many of whom had expanded their power during the period of Viking invasions. In Ireland Brian Boru (r. 976–1014) became the first ruler to exercise real authority over most of the island. In Wales Rhodri the Great (d. 898) and Howell the Good (d. 950) were the first rulers to gain at least nominal authority over the whole of the land. Although disunity is a continuous theme of Scottish history, the centuries after the reign of Kenneth MacAlpin (843–858) reveal the slow creation of a national tradition.

The course of development in the Celtic lands was disrupted by the English in the eleventh and especially the twelfth centuries. The Norman Conquest of England brought adventurers to the frontiers of Wales and Scotland. Sometimes these continental knights advanced with the support of William the Conqueror and his sons, but more often they looked to wild frontier regions for opportunities to escape tight control. In Wales some Normans allied with various local princes who resented the growing power of the Welsh kings. Prince Grufydd ap Cynan° (d. 1137) then turned to King Henry I in 1114 and promised allegiance if Henry would aid him in his quest to establish his authority throughout Wales. From that time forward, the actual power of Welsh rulers varied greatly, and English kings usually claimed some authority over the region. Scottish kings managed to enlist a good many Norman knights into their service, but this recruitment effort angered the English kings and clouded the lines of allegiance in Northumbria, where many of those knights had been sent in the first place. Civil disturbances in Ireland induced King Rory O'Connor (r. 1156–1186) to turn to King Henry II of England for mercenaries to help him establish his power. But by 1171 Henry had invaded Ireland himself and inaugurated the complicated English involvement that persists to this day.

Edward I of England intervened repeatedly in the Celtic world. In 1277 he invaded Wales with the intention of totally subduing the Welsh. He built immense castles, whose ruins are still impressive today. Edward also made his son the Prince of Wales—still the title of the heir to the British throne. Between 1100 and 1260 England and Scotland went to war four times, and Edward resolved to

**Grufydd ap Cynan** (GRIFF-ith op KY-nun)

**Howell the Good**    This picture of Howell, from a manuscript of his laws, depicts him wearing a crown, holding a scepter, and sitting on a tufted throne that looks like a palace. These are key symbols of rule.    *(The National Library of Wales)*

put an end to this struggle by annexing Scotland. The Scots, however, rallied to the standard of Robert Bruce (r. 1306–1329), a dashing knight who was, ironically, of Norman extraction. Robert managed to free Scotland for centuries.

## THE GROWTH OF NEW STATES

The proliferation of new states constitutes one of the most remarkable examples of expansion in high medieval Europe. In Spain Christian rulers waged a steady war of reconquest against the Islamic caliphate of Cordoba that led to the emergence of the kingdoms of Portugal, Castile, and Aragon. In Scandinavia mighty leaders built durable kingdoms in Denmark, Norway, and Sweden. Local rulers created a band of new Slavic states running from the Baltic to the Balkans, from Poland to Bulgaria. To the east of those Slavic realms, around the city of Kiev, the Scandinavian Rus founded the first state on Russian soil. Between 900 and 1300 the geographic range of Europe's political entities more than doubled.

### Reconquista and Kingdom Building in Spain

Historians perceive two driving forces in the rich and colorful history of medieval Spain. One is the bloody experience of several centuries of war along an expanding frontier. The other is the constant interplay within the Iberian Peninsula of three vibrant cultures: Christian,

**Map 9.6    The Christian Reconquista of Muslim Spain**    From slow beginnings in the ninth century to the epochal Battle of Las Navas de Tolosa (1212), the Christians in Spain pushed back the Muslim frontier and built durable states behind it.    *(Source: David Nicholas, The Evolution of the Medieval World. Copyright © 1992. Used by permission of Longman Group UK.)*

Jewish, and Muslim. We describe the first of these forces in this chapter and the second in the next.

The emirate of Cordoba (see page 253) began breaking up after 1002, and the weakness of the tiny successor realms afforded an unprecedented opportunity to the Christians living in the north of the peninsula. King Sancho I (r. 1000–1035) of Navarre launched an offensive against the Muslims. This war, carried on intermittently until the fifteenth century, came to be called the *Reconquista*°, the "Reconquest."

Before Sancho died, he divided his realm among his sons; thus the kingdoms of Aragon and Castile arose alongside Navarre. Alfonso I (r. 1065–1109) of Castile really advanced the Reconquista. In 1085 his forces captured the Muslim stronghold and old Visigothic capital of Toledo, an important moral and strategic victory. Alfonso's military successes owed much to the dashing warrior Rodrigo Díaz de Vivar, known as "El Cid" ("the Lord," from the Arabic *sayyid*). Rodrigo, a gifted but slightly unscrupulous mercenary, fought for both Muslims and Christians. The Reconquista was moving on three fronts (see Map 9.6). In the east the emerging kingdom of Aragon-Catalonia advanced along the Mediterranean coast. In the center León-Castile pressed hard against al-Andalus. In the west the nascent kingdom of Portugal became a factor in Iberian politics. Rodrigo's successes, and the reconquest of Toledo, led the retreating Muslims to summon aid in the 1150s from militant North African Muslims. The Christian advance temporarily stopped.

In the early thirteenth century Pope Innocent III stirred up crusading zeal and lent encouragement to

---

**Reconquista** (ray-con-KEE-stuh)

clerics and nobles in Spain who wished to reopen hostilities against the Muslims. In 1212 a combined Castilian-Aragonese army won a decisive victory at Las Navas de Tolosa, south of Toledo. The victory of Las Navas de Tolosa was a great turning point in Spanish history. The outcome of the Reconquista, which did not conclude until the fifteenth century, was never again in doubt.

Twelfth-century Spanish kings, especially in Castile, imposed hereditary rule and exacted oaths of allegiance from their free subjects. The kings tried to force powerful nobles to become their vassals. They were more successful on the military frontier than back in their homelands because in the war zones nobles could be assigned new fiefs carved out of recent conquests. Kings profited from the Reconquista to enhance their status and power.

In the thirteenth century Spain produced kings of genius, especially James I of Aragon (r. 1213–1276) and Ferdinand III (r. 1217–1252) and Alfonso X (r. 1252–1284) of Castile. These rulers were pious men, genuinely inspired by the ideal of the Crusades (discussed later in this chapter) and zealous in the promotion of the church. They also were hardheaded rulers. James turned Aragon-Catalonia into the greatest naval power of the western Mediterranean and a formidable economic power. Ferdinand and Alfonso derived great prestige from their successful wars. Those wars provided a flow of booty and

**Alfonso the Wise**    The Spanish king Alfonso X, depicted here in a thirteenth-century manuscript from Spain, is judging his Muslim and Christian subjects. Alfonso's reputation for impartiality was important in his culturally diverse realm.    *(Biblioteca Nacional, Madrid)*

a supply of lands to reward the Castilian nobles who spent their energy on the frontier rather than on attacking the king. These kings built strong central governments. Increasingly they used professional officers in key government posts and dispatched roving officials from the court to check on local rulers. Alfonso issued a major law book for the whole of Castile. These laws were based on Roman law and emphasized royal power. The Cortes, a representative assembly made up primarily of urban notables, began forging an alliance between the king and the towns. Iberia was not united in the thirteenth century, but it had evolved into four coherent blocks: a small and impotent Muslim region in Valencia and Granada, and three vibrant kingdoms centered on Portugal, Castile, and Aragon.

## Scandinavia

Europe's expanding map saw new states in Scandinavia, the Roman name for the lands that became Denmark, Norway, and Sweden. Although the faint beginnings of political consolidation in Denmark can be traced to the Carolingian period, actual development of the states of Scandinavia dates from the tenth and eleventh centuries. Overseas expansion played one key role in northern political development. Another was the slow achievement of political unity by kings who had to overcome powerful local interests (see Map 9.5).

The sea, not the land, is the great fact of Scandinavian history. Norway has more than 1,000 miles of coastline, and no point in Denmark is more than 35 miles from the sea. Scandinavia did not offer opportunities for large, land-based kingdoms or empires, but the sea provided Scandinavians with a wide scope for activities.

More than any other people of the north, the Vikings capitalized on the sea as a highway. Vikings were raiders, of course, but also settlers. Much of northeastern England, the Danelaw, was settled by Northmen. In 911 the Norwegian Rollo and his followers settled what became Normandy in northern France. Between 870 and 930 many Norwegians and some Danes settled Iceland and a little later established bases in Greenland. In 862 a Swedish force, accustomed to raiding and trading along the rivers of what would become Russia, established a base at Novgorod. Raiders, traders, and settlers, the Scandinavians fostered the expansion of Europe.

Because the sea made exit from Scandinavia so easy, and because the whole region had absolutely no tradition of unified government, kings had a hard time establishing their power. Essentially kings were war leaders with loyal bands of followers. Territorial states were thus built up as powerful leaders persuaded or forced more and more men to join them. Denmark's was the first of the northern monarchies to emerge in the early tenth century. Norway's monarchy arose a little later in the tenth century, but for much of the eleventh century Norway was under Danish control. As the Danes fell more and more under German influence in the eleventh century, Norway managed to break free. Sweden's monarchy was the last to emerge in the northern world; it was not fully stable until the twelfth century, but by 1300 it had become the most powerful.

Christianity came rather late to Scandinavia, with the first missionaries entering the region in the ninth century and widespread conversion ensuing in the eleventh. Norway's King Olaf (r. 1016–1028), affectionately remembered as Saint Olaf, was the first northern king who actively promoted Christianization. Scandinavian kings viewed the church as a useful adjunct to their power. They cooperated in creating bishoprics on the assumption that members of the high clergy would be educated, talented allies in the process of building central governments. Ironically, the church was a stabilizing force in Scandinavia during the very years when the investiture controversy wreaked havoc in Germany.

## The Slavic World

In eastern Europe, between the Elbe and Dnieper° Rivers, lived numerous peoples customarily called Slavs. Their languages were once much alike but differentiated over time. Partly because of language differences and partly because of the areas in which these people settled, scholars divide them into western, southern, and eastern Slavs. These peoples were never conquered by the Romans, assimilated few influences from the classical world, and received Christianity later than western Europe. Still, as states began emerging in eastern Europe, they exhibited many of the same problems that older and more westerly states had encountered: shifting frontiers, clashes between ambitious rulers and powerful nobles, and outside military and cultural influences (see Map 9.5).

The first western Slavic state was Great Moravia, created in the 830s by capable dukes while the Carolingian Empire was experiencing civil wars. As we saw earlier (see page 265), the Moravian leaders invited the missionaries Cyril and Methodius to their realm, thereby beginning the establishment of Christianity in eastern Europe. Moravia's early promise was cut short in 906 by the Magyars. Also in the late ninth century the Přemysl° dynasty

---

**Dnieper** (NEE-per)    **Přemysl** (PURR-em-ih-sill)

**Twelfth-Century Polish Castle**   This reconstruction of a castle shows it to have been a combination of earthworks and wooden stockades. Such castles, common in western Europe in the tenth and eleventh centuries, afforded protection to people from a wide area and permanent dwellings to a few.   *(CAF Warsaw/Sovfoto)*

forged a kingdom in Bohemia that lasted through the Middle Ages, although for long periods it was under German domination.

The greatest of the western Slavic states was Poland. In the 960s and 970s Duke Mieszko° (d. 992) unified a substantial territory and received Christianity from Rome. The first action created the Polish state, and the second anchored Poland firmly within the orbit of the Latin West. Mieszko's descendants, the Piast dynasty of kings, ruled until Boleslav III divided the kingdom among his three sons in 1138. For more than two centuries Polish development was retarded as weak rulers contested for

power with local magnates, who themselves were successfully subordinating both peasants and men of middling status.

The creation of a Hungarian state played a decisive role in dividing the western and southern Slavs. The Magyars were disruptive raiders from the 880s until their defeat by Otto I in 955. After that disaster the Magyars concentrated on building a state within the Danube basin, the home base from which they had launched their raids. The Magyars, who were related to the Huns and Avars, blended with the local Slavs. King (later Saint) Stephen (r. 997–1038), who received Christianity from Rome, was the real founder of Hungary. Like Poland, Hungary was attached to the Latin West. Stephen's

---

Mieszko (mee-ESH-koe)

family, the Arpads, ruled in Hungary for centuries. They built ruling centers at Buda and Esztergom, created an impressive territorial organization, and promoted the growth of the church. They also expanded in almost every direction.

The southern Slavs built a band of states that extended across the Balkans. The first, reaching back to the seventh century, was Bulgaria. The Bulgars were a Turkic people who first led and then merged into the local Slavic population. The first Bulgarian state lasted until the early eleventh century, when the Byzantines, who had suffered many defeats at Bulgarian hands, destroyed it. By the late twelfth century, when Byzantium itself had weakened, a new Bulgarian state emerged, but its rulers never had the firm control that their predecessors had wielded. Under Khan Boris (r. 852–879) Bulgaria made the momentous decision to accept Orthodox Christianity from Constantinople instead of Roman Catholicism, despite the pope's best efforts.

To the west of Bulgaria lay Serbia, a region dominated until the fourteenth century by Bulgaria and Byzantium. Perhaps because of constant outside threats, Serbia made little progress toward internal unity. The region accepted Orthodox Christianity. To the west of Serbia lay Croatia, a land formed when two originally independent areas, Dalmatia on the Adriatic coast and Croatia itself, were joined together in the early tenth century. Through much of the tenth and eleventh centuries, Croatia managed to preserve itself and evade the clutches of Hungary, Byzantium, and Venice. By 1107, however, Croatia was incorporated by Hungary as a more or less autonomous region. Croatia, owing to Italian and Hungarian influence, became Roman Catholic.

The creation of the major eastern Slavic state is shrouded in mystery and legend. It seems that in 862 a Swedish Viking named Rurik and his followers, called Varangians, established or seized a trading camp at Novgorod. A few years later Oleg (r. 879–912) took over Kiev and made it his base of operations. Thus was founded Kievan Rus, a state that, like Hungary and Bulgaria, began with an outside, elite leadership over a local Slavic majority. Kievan Rus lasted until the Mongols destroyed it in 1240.

Kiev was ruled by grand dukes who pursued four basic policies. They created a vast trading network that linked Germany, Scandinavia, Byzantium, and the caliphate. They shared power with regional nobles who built up several important towns of their own. They received Orthodox Christianity from Constantinople in 988. And, finally, they struggled to defend Kiev, indeed Rus territory as a whole, from wave after wave of invaders from the eastern steppes.

Eventually Kievan Rus was destroyed by the Mongols. These were a loose coalition of pastoral nomads from Mongolia (lands lying east of the Caspian Sea and north of China) and Turkic soldiers. The charismatic leader Jenghiz Khan (1154–1227) turned the Mongols into an invincible fighting force. He and his successors built an empire stretching from China to eastern Europe. In 1221 the Mongols began their attacks on Rus, and in 1240 Kiev fell.

Jenghiz Khan's empire was divided into several khanates on his death, with Rus dominated by the Golden Horde, so called because of the splendid golden tent from which they ruled. The Mongols accorded subject people considerable autonomy, but they demanded heavy taxes

**Virgin of Vladimir**   The holiest icon of Russia, once the miraculous protector of the city of Vladimir and later of Moscow, this image was painted in Constantinople in 1131. Rus, and later Russian, icons tended to follow Byzantine traditions very closely.   *(Scala/Art Resource, NY)*

# The Mongol Khan Writes to the Pope

Alarmed, like many of his contemporaries, by the Mongol onslaught, Pope Innocent IV (r. 1243–1254) sent missionaries to try to convert the Mongol khan Guyuk to Christianity. Large groups of Mongols had only recently converted to Christianity. Innocent not only did not get the answer he was hoping for, but he must have been shocked by Guyuk's haughty reply in 1246.

We, by the power of the eternal heaven, Khan of the great Ulus [compare the Islamic umma; see page 242], Our Command: This is a version sent to the great pope that he may know and understand in the Muslim [actually, Persian] tongue, what has been written. If he reaches you with his own report, You, who are the great pope, together with all the princes, come in person to serve us. You have also said that supplication and prayer have been offered by you, that I might find a good entry into baptism. This prayer of yours I have not understood. Other words which you have sent me: "I am surprised that you have seized all the lands of the Magyar [i.e., Hungarians] and the Christians. Tell us what their fault is." These words of yours I have also not understood. The eternal God has slain and annihilated these lands and peoples, because they have neither adhered to Chingis [Jenghiz] Khan, nor to the Khagan, both of whom have been sent to make known God's command, nor to the command of God. Like your words, they also were impudent, they were proud and they slew our messengers. How could anybody seize or kill by his own power contrary to the command of God?

Though you likewise say that I should become a trembling Nestorian [probably the only form of Christianity well known to the Mongols] Christian, worship God, and be an ascetic, how do you know whom God absolves, in truth to whom He shows mercy? How do you know that such words as you speak are with God's sanction? From the rising of the sun to its setting, all the lands have been made subject to me. Who could do this contrary to the command of God?

Now you should say with a sincere heart: "I will submit and serve you." You yourself, at the head of all the princes, come at once to serve and wait upon us! At that time I shall recognize your submission.

If you do not observe God's command, and if you ignore my command, I shall know you as my enemy. Likewise, I shall understand you. If you do otherwise, God knows what I know.

## QUESTIONS

1. How does Guyuk try to convince Innocent that he and he alone has God's favor?

2. Do you think that Guyuk was, literally or figuratively, diplomatic?

3. Suppose that we had Innocent's response to Guyuk [we do not]. What might he have said in reply?

Source: Christopher Dawson, *Mission to Asia.* Copyright © 1980. Reprinted by permission of Sheed & Ward Limited.

and occasionally carried out brutal raids to remind everyone who was in control. Through their domination of trade, the Mongols weakened the urbanization and commerce built up by Kievan Rus. Throughout the West, people were alarmed by the Mongol onslaught. (See the box "Global Encounters: The Mongol Khan Writes to the Pope.")

When Charlemagne was crowned emperor in 800, only Bulgaria existed as a state in the vast lands of eastern Europe. But the overriding trends of the era inexorably swept into that region. Three centuries later those lands were home to several small states and also to some impressively large and successful ones. The Slavic world was thoroughly pagan in 800 and largely Christian by 1200. State building and Christianization in eastern Eu-

rope represent two significant examples of European expansion in the High Middle Ages.

## THE CRUSADES, 1095–1291

IN 1096 an army of Christian knights who called themselves pilgrims left Europe to liberate the Holy Land from the Muslim "infidel." (This was the first of many crusades, so called because the warriors were *crucesignati*, "signed by the cross.") By the late eleventh century Europe was a fortress that had marshaled its resources for an attack on the world around it. Europe's expanding population, economic dynamism, political consolidation, and buoyant optimism made possible not only the First Crusade but also many more over two centuries.

## The Background: East and West

With the accession in 867 of the Macedonian dynasty in the person of Basil I, the Byzantine Empire experienced a period of vigorous, successful rule that lasted until 1025. Although the Macedonians fostered striking cultural achievements, carried out significant administrative reforms, and established the kind of tight control of the church that had been so elusive in the iconoclastic era (see page 252), they were primarily great soldiers. Along the Balkan frontier the Macedonian rulers kept both the Bulgarians and Kievan Rus at bay while also neutralizing many smaller Slavic principalities. Basil II (r. 976–1025), called "the Bulgar Slayer," wore down Bulgaria in a series of relentless campaigns. In the West the Macedonians maintained an effective diplomacy with Venice that permitted lucrative commercial opportunities in the Adriatic. In the East the Macedonian rulers profited from the gradual dissolution of the Abbasid caliphate by expanding their frontier in Anatolia.

By contrast, throughout the ninth and tenth centuries the ability of the caliphs in Baghdad to control their vast empire declined precipitously. Egypt and North Africa escaped Baghdad's control almost completely, and religious strife between Sunni and Shi'ite Muslims further destabilized the Islamic state.

After Basil II's death in 1025, Byzantium suffered a long period of short reigns and abrupt changes in policy. Great aristocratic families in Anatolia slipped from imperial control. In the capital factional squabbling swirled around the imperial court, and in the person of Patriarch Michael Cerularius (r. 1043–1058) the church sought to break out from two centuries of domination. When in 1054 Cerularius and Pope Leo IX (r. 1049–1054) quarreled so bitterly over ecclesiastical customs that they excommunicated each other, the traditionally cooperative papal-Byzantine religious diplomacy gave way to a deep schism between the Catholic and Orthodox Churches that still exists. Religious tensions were complicated when the staunchly anti-Byzantine Normans began creating their kingdom in southern Italy.

It was in these divisive circumstances that the Seljuk Turks appeared on the eastern frontier of Anatolia. Bands of Turks, peoples from central Asia, had been serving the caliphs as mercenaries since the ninth century. With new leaders at their head, and with both the caliphate and the empire distracted, the Turks broke into

Anatolia with a vengeance. In 1071 at Manzikert a skirmish between Byzantine and Turkish soldiers turned into a rout in which Byzantium lost an army, an emperor, and the Macedonian reputation for military prowess.

Ever since the emergence of the Turkish threat in the early eleventh century, the Byzantines had been seeking mercenary help. The imperial defeat at Manzikert made their search more urgent and led to appeals to the West. Some troops were rounded up but not enough, so in 1095 Emperor Alexius Comnenus (r. 1081–1118) sent envoys to ask Pope Urban II (r. 1088–1099) to support a plea for mercenary help against the Turks.

To most people in western Europe, the Turkish threat to Byzantium mattered little. What *did* alarm Westerners was Turkish attacks on pilgrims to Jerusalem. The popes saw in the plight of the Byzantines and of Western pilgrims some opportunities to manifest their leadership of the church. The papacy also wanted very much to heal the Roman-Orthodox rift. The popes, therefore, placed a high value on aiding the Byzantines.

Moreover, a crusade was perfectly consonant with the ethos of the knights of western Europe. Knights were born and trained to fight. The literature of the age glorified war and warriors. But churchmen had for some years been advancing an ideal of Christian knighthood that stressed fighting God's enemies. In the late tenth century there arose, first in France and then in many other places, peace movements called the "Peace of God" or the "Truce of God." These movements sought to prevent war in certain seasons, such as around Christmas and Easter, and on certain days of the week, chiefly Sunday. Peace movements also attempted to outlaw fighting near churches, protect noncombatants, and soften the treatment of enemies and captives. Together the movements induced knights to fight non-Christians outside Europe. Along with religious zeal, a quest for fame and fortune motivated many young men whose political prospects at home were limited.

## The "Pilgrimage" to Jerusalem

Pope Urban II received Alexius's envoys in 1095 and then left Italy for France. He was actually a fugitive because Henry IV controlled Rome. In November at Clermont, Urban delivered a rousing speech to a vast Christian assembly. He ignored the Eastern emperor's appeal for aid and instead promised salvation to soldiers who would enlist in a great struggle to free the Holy Land. The crowd acclaimed his words with a shout of "God wills it!" (See the box "The Continuing Experiment: Pope Urban's Call for the First Crusade.")

# Pope Urban's Call for the First Crusade

The decision to launch the Crusades was based on a variety of factors. Muslim Turks were fighting with the Byzantines, Arab Muslims were reported to be harassing Christian pilgrims, and Spanish Christians were fighting Muslims in Iberia. The popes were beginning to assert leadership in the church and wished, by helping the Byzantines, to heal the rift between the Eastern and Western churches. In November 1095, with a speech at Clermont in France (several slightly different versions of which survive), Pope Urban II launched the Crusades. What he intended to accomplish may never be known for sure. The consequences of his actions are clear: over two centuries the Crusades cost many lives, worsened relations between Catholic and Orthodox Christians, and devastated Muslim-Christian relations.

Oh, race of Franks, race from across the mountains, race chosen and beloved by God set apart from all nations by the situation of your country, as well as by your Catholic faith and the honor of Holy Church! To you our discourse is addressed, and for you our exhortation is intended. We wish you to know what a grievous cause has led us to your country, what peril, threatening you and all the faithful, has led us to your country.

From the confines of Jerusalem and the city of Constantinople a horrible tale has gone forth and very frequently has been brought to our ears; namely that a race from the kingdom of the Persians, an accursed race, a race utterly alienated from God, has invaded the lands of those Christians and has depopulated them by the sword, pillage, and fire; it has led away a part of the captives into its own country and a part it has destroyed by cruel tortures; it has either destroyed the churches of God or appropriated them for the rites of its own religion. They circumcise the Christians, and the blood of the circumcision they either spread on the altars or pour into the vases of the baptismal font. When they wish to torture people by a base death, they perforate their navels, and, dragging forth the end of the intestines, bind it to a stake; then with flogging they lead the victim around until his guts have gushed forth. Others they bind to a post and pierce with arrows. Others they compel to extend their necks and attempt to cut through their necks with a single blow of a sword. What shall I say of the abominable rape of the women? To speak of it is worse than to be silent. The kingdom of the Greeks is now dismembered by them and deprived of territory so vast in extent that it cannot be traversed in a march of two months.

On whom, therefore, is the task of avenging these wrongs incumbent if not upon you? You upon whom above other nations God has conferred remarkable glory in arms, great courage, bodily energy, and the strength to humble those who resist you. Let the deeds of your ancestors move you and incite your minds to manly achievements. Let the Holy Sepulcher of the Lord, which is possessed by unclean nations, especially move you, and likewise the holy places which are now treated with ignominy and irreverently polluted. Oh, most valiant warriors and descendants of invincible ancestors, be not degenerate, but recall the valor of your ancestors.

However, if you are hindered by love of children, parents, and wives remember what the Lord says in the Gospel: "He that loves father or mother more than me is not worthy of me." Let none of your possessions detain you, no solicitude for your family affairs, since this land you inhabit, shut in on all sides by the sea and mountain peaks, is too narrow for your large population and furnishes scarcely enough food. Hence it is that you murder and devour one another. Let therefore hatred depart from among you, let your quarrels end. Enter upon the road to the Holy Sepulcher; wrest that land from the wicked races and subject it to yourselves.

When Pope Urban had said these and many similar things he so influenced to one purpose those who were present that they cried out, "God wills it."

## QUESTIONS

1. What appeals to reason, emotion, and self-interest does Urban make in this speech?

2. Why might Urban describe the Christians as a "race chosen and beloved by God"? How does this compare with his description of Muslims?

3. Did the Crusades unfold according to Urban's intentions?

SOURCE: *Urban's Speech at Clermont in the Version of Robert the Monk,* in A. C. Krey, *The First Crusade* (1921; repr., Gloucester, Mass.: Peter Smith, 1958), pp. 30–32 (somewhat abridged).

By 1096 four large armies, which eventually swelled to perhaps a hundred thousand men—mostly French knights, with a smattering of troops from other parts of Europe—assembled under the leadership of the pope's legate. The forces were to rendezvous at Constantinople, where they seem to have expected a cordial imperial welcome and all necessary assistance. Alexius, however, took a rather different view, for several reasons. First, a ragtag band of ordinary people preceding the Crusaders had torn through the Balkans like a plague of locusts. Second, the crusading armies themselves sorely taxed the imperial authorities, who spent a lot of time and money arranging their passage from the frontier of Hungary to the gates of Constantinople. Finally, Alexius wanted mercenaries to fend off Turks in Anatolia, not armed pilgrims intent on liberating Palestine (see Map 9.7).

After receiving nominal promises of loyalty and the return or donation of any lands captured, Alexius moved the Crusaders into Anatolia. Almost immediately the Latin army defeated a Turkish force, thus earning a valuable, though short-lived, reputation for invincibility. The troops then entered Syria and laid siege to Antioch, which did not fall until 1098. At this point rivalries among the Crusaders came into the open. One force went to the frontier of Armenia and carved out a principality. One of the ubiquitous Normans kept Antioch for himself. The main army pressed on to Jerusalem and, after a short but fierce siege, conquered it in July 1099. A Muslim historian describes the scene:

> In the Masjid [Mosque] al-Aqsa the Franks slaughtered more than 70,000 people, among them a large number of Imams and Muslim scholars, devout and ascetic men who had left their homelands to live lives of pious seclusion in the Holy Place. The Franks stripped the Dome of the Rock [the Mosque of Umar, near the al-Aqsa mosque, pictured on page 243] of more than forty silver candelabra, each of them weighing 3,600 drams [almost 40 pounds], and a great silver lamp weighing forty-four Syrian pounds, as well as a hundred and fifty smaller candelabra and more than twenty gold ones, and a great deal more booty.[2]

**Map 9.7  The Crusades, 1096–1270**    The long-standing Western interest in the Holy Land is vividly illustrated by the Crusades. Note the numerous routes taken, lands traversed, destinations attained, and points of cultural encounter.

## READING SOURCES

## AN ARAB PERSPECTIVE ON THE FIRST CRUSADE

*The Muslim historian Ibn al-Athir (1160–1233) provides several interesting perspectives on the First Crusade in his work* The Perfect History. *The Baldwin with whom this account opens is not historical; perhaps he is a composite of the many Baldwins then active in the West. Nevertheless, al-Athir's depiction of the crudeness of Roger of Sicily is interesting, as are his incidental revelations of Christian-Muslim cooperation and of divisions in the Islamic world.*

Baldwin, their king, assembled a great army and sent word to Roger [of Sicily] saying: "I have assembled a great army and now I am on my way to you, to use your bases for my conquest of the African coast. Thus you and I shall become neighbors." Roger called together his companions and consulted them about these proposals. "This will be a fine thing for them and for us!" they declared, "for by this means these lands will be converted to the Faith." At this Roger raised one leg and farted loudly, and swore that it was of more use than their advice. "Why?" "Because if this army comes here it will need quantities of provisions and fleets of ships to transport it to Africa, as well as reinforcements from my own troops. Then, if the Franks succeed in conquering this territory they will take it over and will need provisioning from Sicily. This will cost me my annual profit from the harvest. If they fail they will return here and be an embarrass-

ment to me here in my own domain. As well as this Tamim [the emir of Tunisia in North Africa] will say that I have broken faith with him and violated our treaty, and friendly relations and communications between us will be disrupted. As far as we are concerned, Africa is always there. When we are strong enough we will take it."

He summoned Baldwin's messenger and said to him: "If you have decided to make war on the Muslims your best course will be to free Jerusalem from their rule and thereby win great honour. I am bound by certain treaties and promises of allegiance with the rulers of Africa." So the Franks made ready to attack Syria.

Another story is that the Fatimids [local rulers] of Egypt were afraid when they saw the Seljuqids extending their empire through Syria as far as Gaza, until they reached the Egyptian border and Atziz [a general] invaded Egypt itself. They therefore sent to invite the Franks to invade Syria and so to protect Egypt from the Muslims [the Fatimids, although militantly Muslim, were regarded as heretics by other Muslims]. But God knows best.

Source: Francesco Gabrieli, *Arab Historians of the Crusades*, pp. 3–4. Selected and translated from the Arabic sources by E. J. Costello. Copyright © 1969 by the University of California Press. Reprinted by permission of the University of California and the University of California Press.

Godfrey of Bouillon, leader of the troops that had "liberated" Jerusalem, was named "Advocate of the Holy Sepulcher" and became ruler of the Christians in the East. He lived only a short time, however, and was replaced by his brother, Baldwin, as king of Jerusalem in 1100.

Judged on its own terms, the First Crusade was a success. The Holy Land was retaken from the infidel, and the pilgrim routes were passable once more. Entirely uncertain, however, were the prospects of the crusader states, the future course of Western relations with Byzantium, and the reaction of the Islamic world once it recovered from its initial shock. (See the box "Reading Sources: An Arab Perspective on the First Crusade.")

## The Later Crusades

Crusading was intended to protect the Holy Land and keep open the pilgrim routes to Jerusalem. The creation of the small crusader states in the hostile environment of Syria and Palestine made continued crusading almost inevitable. In 1144 the tiny crusader state at Edessa on the Armenian frontier fell to a Muslim army. Although the news saddened Europeans, it took immense efforts by the papacy and other religious leaders to launch another crusade. Finally Conrad III of Germany and Louis VII of France agreed to lead it, but because neither would willingly submit to the other's authority, the Second Crusade accomplished little. Its one achievement was an

**Saladin Routs the Franks**    This vivid image of Saladin defeating the Franks—that is, the Crusaders—at the Battle of Hattin (1187) comes from a thirteenth-century history by Matthew Paris. In this battle the Franks lost an army and their relic of the true cross and shortly afterward lost control of Jerusalem. These shocking defeats precipitated the Third Crusade.    *(Courtesy, Master and Fellows of Corpus Christi College Library, Cambridge)*

accident. In 1147 an army of English, French, and Flemish soldiers who were proceeding to the Holy Land by sea put in on the Iberian coast and captured Lisbon. This opened a new front in the Reconquista and laid the foundations for the later kingdom of Portugal (see Map 9.7).

The papacy called for the Third Crusade when Saladin° (1138–1193), a powerful local leader typical of the disintegrating Abbasid caliphate, recaptured Jerusalem in 1187. It is a measure of the force of the crusading ideal that the greatest crowned heads of the day—Frederick Barbarossa, Philip II, and Richard the Lionhearted—answered the call. It must be said, however, that only Frederick did so enthusiastically. Frederick died en route in 1190, while Philip returned home in 1191 and Richard in 1192. Because neither Richard nor Philip would stay in Palestine to fight Saladin, this crusade merely won access to Jerusalem for pilgrims.

_____

**Saladin** (sah-lah-DEEN)

Disappointed with the results of the Third Crusade, Innocent III began calling for another crusade immediately on his election in 1198. Popular preachers summoned an army, once again largely French, and the pope and the Fourth Crusade's military leaders engaged the Venetians to construct a fleet of war and transport ships. In less than eighteen months they produced 50 galleys and 450 transports, a tribute to the awesome capabilities of the Venetian shipyards.

Ships, however, were expensive, and the Venetians drove hard bargains. When too few Crusaders and too little money appeared, the Venetians suggested that the Crusaders could discharge some of their debt by recapturing from the Hungarians the formerly Venetian port of Zara on the Dalmatian coast. This idea outraged the pope, but he could do little about it. Then into the camp of the Crusaders came a pretender to the Byzantine throne, who promised that if the Crusaders would help him to claim his patrimony, he would contribute to the cost of the Crusade. The Venetians urged the indebted Crusaders to accept this offer, and, to the horror of Innocent III, the Fourth Crusade turned to Constantinople.

Once in Constantinople the Crusaders learned that their new ally had few friends in the Byzantine capital, but the venture hardly collapsed. The Venetians saw an opportunity to expand business opportunities in the East, and the soldiers welcomed a chance to plunder the Mediterranean's greatest city and to avenge what they regarded as a century of Byzantine perfidy. Thus the Fourth Crusade captured not Jerusalem but Constantinople. Until 1261, the Eastern and Western churches were reunited under papal leadership, and substantial tracts of the Balkans fell to Western knights under a "Latin emperor" of Constantinople.

In later decades popes began to take a more active role in planning crusades. No pope wanted to lose control of a crusade as Innocent had done, and all popes saw that the liberation of Jerusalem required a solid base of operations in the eastern Mediterranean. Egypt was the objective of the Fifth (1218–1221) and Sixth (1248–1250) Crusades. Despite a few victories, the Crusaders could not win a secure base. No further crusades to the East were organized in the thirteenth century. In 1291 Acre, the last Crusader stronghold, fell, and the original crusading era ended.

During the crusading period the Holy Land was not the sole object of Crusaders' attentions. In about 1140 the pope preached a crusade against the Normans in southern Italy, and several popes in the thirteenth century, fearful of imperial encroachment, preached crusades against the Staufer dynasty in Italy. In 1147 the papacy authorized a crusade in the Baltic that opened nearly four centuries of German expansion into the pagan Slavic lands to the east of Saxony. In 1208 Innocent III proclaimed a crusade against the Albigensians in southwestern France.

## A Balance Sheet

Why did the Crusades end? There are several reasons. By the late thirteenth century more violence was being directed inward against heretics and political foes of the papacy than outward against the alleged enemies of Christendom itself. As rulers became more sophisticated and controlled more territory, they had less interest in the intangible benefits of crusading, such as prestige. Whereas the cities of Italy once needed to open up Mediterranean ports, now they wished to secure comparative advantage over one another. The Christian ideals of poverty, charity, and service were incompatible with warfare. Literary images provide another insight into the decline of the Crusades. After 1300 we are less likely to read about a Christian knight fighting honorably for God and king than about a gentleman of manners seeking the favor of a fair lady.

Crusading was brutal. Soldiers and their clerical companions spent years away from their homes and families, endured scorching Mediterranean heat, and suffered shortages of food and basic supplies. The vulnerable crusader states never received enough settlers to be viable communities, and consequently intermarriage with locals was common and gradually produced a hybrid culture that was neither European nor Middle Eastern. Warfare was constant on all sides. When Crusaders conquered a town, they executed many locals. When Muslims recaptured a town, they did the same. The tremendous enthusiasm evident in 1095 could not be sustained over two centuries.

A balance sheet for the crusading movement as a whole reveals more losses than gains. The Crusades exported many violent men from Europe, but it is not clear that Europe became a less violent place. As might be expected, the Crusades devastated relations between Christian Europe and the Muslim world. The Fourth Crusade mortally wounded Byzantium and worsened the already tense standoff between the Catholic and Orthodox Churches. Crusading zeal was directed deliberately against heretics and coincidentally against Jews. The Jewish populations of several towns were massacred on the eve of the First and Second Crusades. The Crusades did not create anti-Semitism, but they aggravated it. Some women, particularly in France, from which the majority of all Crusaders came, may have enjoyed momentary benefits in terms of control of land, wealth, and people while their husbands were away. But the long-term trend in feudal society was disadvantageous to women, and the Crusades did not change that. Finally, the Crusades may have done as much to disrupt Mediterranean trade as to promote it. Italian urban rivalries took the place of Latin-Muslim-Byzantine ones. That a single new product, the apricot, entered Europe in the crusading era seems small reward for such a huge effort.

## SUMMARY

BETWEEN 900 and 1300 Western civilization experienced a long period of dramatic, sustained expansion. In the early Middle Ages, Rome's three heirs—western Europe, Byzantium, and the Islamic caliphate—were poised in a rough equilibrium. By the High Middle Ages, western Europe had seized the upper hand thanks to a strong economy, political centralization, and Europe's first concerted attempt to reverse the tide of Islamic conquests.

Several factors contributed to Europe's economic growth. The population rose steadily. People everywhere brought new land under cultivation, adopted better agricultural techniques, and improved transportation systems. Greater efficiencies in agriculture promoted urban growth, as some people were freed from farming to undertake commercial and artisanal pursuits. Never before had Europe's economy grown so rapidly.

Governments expanded their power in most parts of Europe. Rulers in England, France, and Spain drew on both precedent and the innovative spirit of the present to create effective centralized institutions. In the Celtic, Scandinavian, and Slavic worlds dynamic new states emerged. In Italy durable urban governments dotted the landscape, while the Roman church expanded its governing structures and the popes assumed a leading position in European society. A German kingdom arose where none had existed before, became briefly the greatest state in Europe, and then collapsed under the weight of innumerable problems.

European rulers faced a variety of problems in enlarging or consolidating their states. England, Spain, and Hungary all expanded at the expense of their neighbors. England, again, as well as France, Denmark, and Norway, expanded by extending control over local magnates. England, France, Hungary, and Spain developed the strongest government institutions.

Several states failed to consolidate their power. The German emperors were challenged by local rulers and buffeted by the investiture controversy. Their dream of a unified German state faded away. Poland could not survive dynastic divisions and a Mongol attack. The largest European state, Kievan Rus, was wiped from the map by an expansionary power from the East, the Mongols.

Europe's economic dynamism, increasing political stability, military might, and militant Christianity came together to produce the Crusades. Around 900 Europe was suffering attacks from Vikings, Muslims, and Magyars. Vikings and Magyars were incorporated into Europe, but from 1100 to 1300 Europe retaliated against the Muslim world. The Crusades embittered relations between Latin Christians, on the one hand, and Orthodox Christians and Muslims, on the other. But the crusading movement stands for the history student as perhaps the key indicator of the expansive nature of late medieval Europe.

Europeans of the High Middle Ages did more than just plant fields, pass laws, and fight wars. They lived in increasingly complex social structures, broadened their range of religious experiences, invented two new architectural styles, created a novel intellectual institution (the university), and wrote literary masterpieces. We will turn to all these creative—and expanding—realms of human endeavor in the next chapter.

## ■ Notes

1. Walter Map, *De nugis curialum*, 5.5, in John H. Mundy, *Europe in the High Middle Ages* (London: Longman, 1973), p. 387.
2. Slightly adapted from the *Gesta Francorum*, trans. August C. Krey, in *The First Crusade* (Princeton, N.J.: Princeton University Press, 1921), p. 257.

## ■ Suggested Reading

Bartlett, Robert. *The Making of Europe: Conquest, Colonization and Cultural Change, 950–1350.* 1993. An engaging account of the expansion and "Europeanization" of Europe.

Bisson, Thomas, ed. *Cultures of Power: Lordship, Status, and Process in Twelfth-Century Europe.* 1995. The thirteen sparkling essays in this book cover much of Europe and attempt to explain how power was actually wielded in a society in which states were just emerging.

Bloch, Marc. *Feudal Society.* Translated by L. A. Manyon. 2 vols. 1964. This best-known book by one of this century's greatest historians seeks to explain the total history of the post-Carolingian world in terms of the ideals and practices of feudalism.

Moore, Robert I. *The First European Revolution.* 2000. A distinguished historian offers the first comprehensive, synthetic treatment of the High Middle Ages in fifty years. Stimulating and readable.

Reynolds, Susan. *Fiefs and Vassals.* 1994. Brilliant, controversial, and difficult, this massive book challenges many long-standing ideas about feudalism.

———. *Kingdoms and Communities in Western Europe, 900–1300.* 2d ed. 1997. After exploring the kinds of legal notions that guided medieval community building, this lively book turns to communities themselves, ranging from the parish to the kingdom.

Riley-Smith, Jonathan, ed. *The Oxford Illustrated History of the Crusades.* 1997. A set of essays with lavish illustrations that explores almost every aspect of the Crusades and the world that produced them.

For a searchable list of additional readings for this chapter, go to college.hmco.com/students.

# The Medieval Castle

Storybook castles, in the manner of Disneyland, figure prominently in almost everyone's idea of the Middle Ages. The reality was different. Medieval castles were generally small, stark, and uncomfortable, not beautiful and romantic.

Castles represent a stage in the history of both dwellings and fortifications. Initially, castles were private, residential, and military. A consideration of these three elements will place the castle in historical context and illustrate what historians learn from the impressive ruins that dot the landscape of Europe and the crusader states.

The first medieval castles were constructed in the tenth century. The French word *château* (from the Latin *castellum*) means "great house," signifying the castle's residential purpose. Powerful aristocrats erected castles not just as their principal dwellings but also as a base for securing and extending their social and political influence. From his castle a lord could dominate the surrounding region. The castle also sheltered the lord's immediate dependents temporarily in the event of an attack and his military retainers more or less permanently.

A few castles were built exclusively for military purposes. In 1110 Crusaders captured a strategic plateau rising 2,000 feet above the main road from inner Syria to the Mediterranean. Between 1142 and 1205 Crusaders continually expanded the fortifications of the castle pictured here, the "Krak des Chevaliers" (from Syriac *karka*, meaning "fortress," and the Old French word for "horsemen"). This castle fell to Muslim attackers in 1271. The techniques of fortification developed in the crusader East influenced castle building in Europe.

The medieval city of Murviedro, Spain, takes its name from the Latin *mures veteres* (old walls). In 1871 the city was given back its ancient name, Sagunt. The hilltop above ancient Saguntum (attacked by Hannibal, thus affronting the Romans and providing a pretext for the Second Punic War between Rome and Carthage; see page 155), reveals fortifications from the prehistoric, Carthaginian, Roman, Visigothic, and Muslim periods. The most spectacular visible remains date from the Muslim period, between 900 and 1098, when El Cid captured the site.

Castles took many forms. From 900 to 1200 the "motte and bailey" castle was the most common. A lord commanded his dependents to dig a circular ditch and heap the dirt into a mound (the motte). The ditch, together with a wooden palisade—a fencelike wall—was the bailey. A wooden tower was often built atop the mound. Some castles included an elaborate series of mounds, ditches, and wooden walls—look at the picture of the Polish motte and bailey castle on page 304—but usually these structures were quite simple.

As siege techniques improved (catapults could hurl projectiles weighing 600 pounds), the wooden building of the bailey began to be replaced by stone. By 1150 or 1200, stone towers (*donjons*, from the Latin *dominium* for "lordship") were only the inner portion—the "keep"—of a more complicated structure of walls, towers, and gates. It was not unusual for walls to be 75 or 100 feet high. Because of the growing power of bombarding engines, castle walls often had to be made thicker. Towers built at 40- or 50-foot intervals projected beyond the walls so that defenders armed with bows and arrows could fire at attackers along the length of a castle wall. Look at the spacing of the towers in the castles pictured here. At Krak des Chevaliers we see one of the earliest examples of a double ring of walls. Two walls made it more difficult for attackers to take the keep and permitted defenders to battle invaders from inside both the inner and the outer walls.

To allow people to enter and leave, castles had gate towers, usually with two gates, one on the outside and one on the inside. Intricate systems of winches, cranks, and counterweights regulated the raising and lowering of the gates. Speedy operation was essential. Some castles had small "sally-ports" from which soldiers could make a rapid dash to attack a besieging enemy.

When possible, lords sited their castles on the edges of cliffs because fewer sides were open to assault and a garrison of modest size could defend the remaining walls. Krak sits on an impressive natural site. The fortress of Murviedro, perched on a hilltop, commands the surrounding territory. Rulers and conquerors from Roman to modern times have exploited this dominating site. To walls and natural defenses were sometimes added ditches.

Much can be learned from the number of castles in a particular area. The presence of numerous small castles across the countryside suggests an extreme decentralization of power in that place and time. Remains of several hundred castles have been found in France alone; and England in 1100 boasted a castle every 10 miles. Conversely, areas with only a few large, strategically sited castles were likely subject to greater central control. Careful mapping of the known locations of castles can

**Krak des Chevaliers, Syria, ca. 1200** (Michael Jenner/Robert Harding Picture Library)

**Muslim Fortress of Murviedro, Valencia, Spain, Eleventh Century** (Institut Amatller d'Art Hispanic)

tell historians a great deal about the structure of social and political relationships.

Castles both contributed and responded to developments in military technology, such as more powerful catapults. Stone castles proliferated as Europe grew wealthier and as quarrying technology improved. Castles grew larger as monarchies rather than private individuals built them. Like cathedrals, massive state-funded castles tended to be built by professionals rather than by local laborers.

Both fortifications and magnificent dwellings have existed in Western civilization for millennia. From about 900 to 1200 the castle met the needs of a politically dominant warrior aristocracy for a private residence with military significance. In later centuries, the castle, as a château, retained its private and residential nature but lost much of its military character to garrisoned fortresses in the service of kings and princes.

 **For additional information on this topic, go to college.hmco.com/students.**

# CHAPTER 10

# Medieval Civilization at Its Height 900–1300

LOOKING down the nave of Chartres Cathedral, built between 1192 and 1220, produces a number of somewhat contradictory sensations. The size and verticality; the play of light and dark; the amazing array of shapes, corners, and angles—all are a bit mysterious. They were meant to be. At the same time there is a logically ordered geometric elegance to the building that is plain to see. And this was intended, too.

The cathedral at Chartres aptly symbolizes the range of historical currents dominant in high medieval Europe. We saw in Chapter 9 that Europe was expanding economically, politically, and militarily. Like its greater context, this building is very large; the cathedrals built in the burgeoning cities of the twelfth and thirteenth centuries were larger than any that had been built since Justinian erected Hagia Sophia. The bishops of Chartres expended most of their considerable income—Chartres lies in France's richest grain-growing region—for some twenty years to build this church. Literally dozens of these great buildings were going up at the same time all over Europe, providing employment for thousands of ordinary workers and numerous master craftsmen. Nobles and townsfolk donated windows and other fixtures to the building, making the building itself an expression of the period's more complex society.

Chartres Cathedral is an excellent example of the Gothic style in architecture, medieval Europe's supreme architectural achievement. Gothic is one of two major stylistic innovations of this period. The other is Romanesque, a style that reached the summit of its beauty and power in the early twelfth century just as Gothic was about to appear. This change in architectural styles parallels others in the High Middle Ages. The Carolingian focus on grammar, on the most basic

Nave of Chartres Cathedral, looking east.
(Éditions Gaud)

literary skills, gave way to an interest in logic. Intellectual problems that had in the past been solved by appeals to scriptural or patristic authority were now addressed by human reason. This produced a new style of intellectual endeavor called "Scholasticism." Monasteries and cathedrals housed schools in the Carolingian world, but by the thirteenth century the university had emerged as a higher kind of cultural institution.

Latin remained the dominant language of scholars, but almost everywhere the vernacular spoken languages were becoming graceful and effective tools for written communication. Religious themes were still foremost in writings of all kinds, but adventures, romances, and other works dedicated to secular themes were gaining in prominence. The Christian tradition still undergirded intellectual life, but that tradition was now spurred on to new heights of insight and expression by encounters with long-lost Greek texts and with the writings of Jewish and Muslim intellectuals. Look where you will, cultural life was richer and more complex than ever before.

The previous chapter concentrated on the economic foundations of society and on the ways in which people organized themselves politically. This chapter begins by introducing the increasingly complex social structures within which people lived and then turns to a study of what those people thought, said, and built.

## QUESTIONS TO CONSIDER

- Into what principal social groups were the people of high medieval Europe organized?

- What role did logic play in spurring intellectual development and in contributing to the growth of Scholasticism?

- Why did some spiritual movements result in heresy, while others ended in new religious orders?

- What cultural achievements mark the High Middle Ages as a period of crowning achievement?

## TERMS TO KNOW

| | |
|---|---|
| Cluny (Cluniacs) | Hildegard of Bingen |
| Bernard of Clairvaux | Thomas Aquinas |
| chivalry | summa |
| Francis of Assisi | Romanesque |
| Dominic de Guzman | Gothic |
| canon law | |

## THE TRADITIONAL ORDERS OF SOCIETY

AFTER centuries of various experiments with ordering social relations after the end of the Roman Empire in the West, a new social order had evolved by 900 that was distinctively medieval. Alfred the Great (r. 871–899) of England once said that a kingdom needed "men of prayer, men of war, and men of work." In the tenth century two French bishops wrote lengthy works exploring this same theme. This three-way division reveals the way the elite looked at the world. It provided neat places for the clergy, warrior-aristocrats, and peasants. The clergy and the nobility agreed that they were superior to the "workers," but fierce controversies raged over whether ultimate leadership in society belonged to the "prayers" or the "fighters."

By the time this tripartite view of society was fully established in the West, it had begun to fit social realities less well. It excluded townspeople, who were becoming ever more important. Town residents worked for a living, of course, but only farmers were considered "workers." Alfred and the bishops did not speak about women, and they consciously excluded minorities, chiefly Jews. To form a full picture of Europe's increasingly intricate social relations, we begin with contemporary theoretical pronouncements and then look for the people whom the theoreticians neglected.

## Those Who Pray: The Clergy

As the church promoted its own vision of the tripartite ordering of society, it assigned primacy to the prayers—its own leaders. Within the clergy, however, sharp disagreements arose over whether the leading prayers were the monks in the monasteries or the bishops in their cathedrals. Whereas in the Carolingian world the clergy served occasionally as an avenue of upward social mobility for talented outsiders, in the High Middle Ages church offices were usually reserved for the younger sons of the nobility. The church was always hierarchical in organization and outlook, so the increasingly aristocratic character of the church's leadership tended to reinforce those old tendencies.

In the aftermath of the Carolingian collapse, a great spiritual reform swept Europe. It began in 910 when Duke William of Aquitaine founded the monastery of Cluny° in Burgundy on land that he donated (see Map 9.4, page 293). At a time when powerful local families dominated almost all monasteries, Cluny was a rarity because it was free of all lay and episcopal control and because it was under the direct authority of the pope. Cluny's abbots were among the greatest European statesmen of their day and became influential advisers to popes, French kings, German emperors, and aristocratic families.

In the tradition of the Carolingian monastic reforms, Cluny placed great emphasis on liturgical prayer. The monks spent long hours in solemn devotions and did little manual work. Because Cluniac prayer was thought to be especially efficacious, nobles all over Europe donated land to Cluny and placed local monasteries under Cluniac control. Many independent monasteries also appealed to Cluny for spiritual reform. By the twelfth century hundreds of monasteries had joined in a Cluniac order. Individual houses were under the authority of the abbot of Cluny, and their priors had to attend an annual assembly. Although the majority of houses reformed by Cluny were male, many convents of nuns also adopted Cluniac practices.

Cluny promoted two powerful ideas. One was that the role of the church was to pray for the world, not to be implicated deeply in it. The other was that freedom from lay control was essential if churches were to concentrate on their spiritual tasks.

The same spiritual forces that motivated the Cluniacs inspired Bishop Adalbero of Metz in 933 to promote the restoration of Benedictine practices in the dilapidated Lorraine monastery of Gorze°. Customs at Gorze resem-

---

Cluny (CLUE-nee)    Gorze (GORTZ-eh)

### CHRONOLOGY

| | |
|---|---|
| **ca. 900** | *Beowulf* |
| **910** | Foundation of Cluny |
| **940–1003** | Gerbert of Aurillac |
| **960–1028** | Fulbert of Chartres |
| **d. 970** | Roswitha of Gandersheim |
| **1000–1088** | Berengar of Tours |
| **ca. 1033–1109** | Anselm of Canterbury |
| **ca. 1050–1150** | Emergence of the Romanesque |
| **1079–1142** | Peter Abelard |
| **1184** | Waldensians declared heretics |
| **1090–1153** | Bernard of Clairvaux |
| **1098** | Foundation of Cîteaux |
| **1098–1179** | Hildegard of Bingen |
| **ca. 1100** | *Song of Roland* |
| **1135–1183** | Chrétien de Troyes |
| **1170–1221** | Dominic de Guzman |
| **ca. 1177–1213** | Mary of Oignies |
| **1181–1226** | Francis of Assisi |
| **1194–1253** | Clare of Assisi |
| **1208** | Albigensian Crusade launched |
| **1210–1280** | Mechtild of Magdeburg |
| **1225–1274** | Thomas Aquinas |
| **1265–1321** | Dante Alighieri |

bled those at Cluny, and they spread widely in Lorraine, Germany, and England. The Gorze reform was well received by kings and nobles; its aim was not so much to withdraw from the world as to improve it. Monks from the Gorze and Cluniac traditions bitterly condemned clerical immorality and inappropriate lay interference in the church. They preached against clerical marriage and simony, the buying and selling of church offices.

Reformers in the more ascetic eremitic tradition (see page 215) desired more profound changes. They criticized the monastery at Cluny, saying that it had become too opulent and successful, and the monastery at Gorze

**Reconstruction of Cluny**
A view of the monastic complex at Cluny in the early twelfth century. Note the basilica (the largest church in Europe until the sixteenth century), the cloister (to the left, actually south, of the basilica, with its dormitory in the foreground and refectory opposite the basilica), and the workshops. *(Based on a drawing from* Cluny des Églises et la Maison du Chef d'Ordre, *by R. J. Conant. Courtesy, Medieval Academy of America)*

because it seemed too immersed in worldly affairs. A desire to build new communities according to their vision of the apostolic church, featuring a life of poverty, self-denial, and seclusion, captivated the ascetics. Thus the eleventh and early twelfth centuries saw a proliferation of both male and female experiments in eremitic monasticism. Other Europeans believed that the apostolic calling demanded not only an austere regimen of personal renunciation but also an active life of Christian ministry. Cathedral clergy, called canons, in particular, adapted the Rule of Saint Augustine so that they could live a communal life and also carry out priestly duties.

The greatest critics of the Cluniac tradition, and the real monastic elite of the early twelfth century, were the Cistercians. In 1098 Abbot Robert left his Burgundian monastery of Molesme° because he believed it had abandoned the strict teachings of Saint Benedict. He founded a new monastery at Cîteaux° in Burgundy. This house was to follow the Benedictine Rule literally and to refuse all secular entanglements: lands, rents, and servile dependents. So rigorous and poor was the community that it

struggled until a charismatic young Burgundian nobleman named Bernard (1090–1153) joined in 1112. Three years later Bernard left to found a daughter house at Clairvaux, of which he remained abbot for the rest of his life. Through his writing, preaching, and personal example, Bernard dominated the religious life of Europe in his lifetime. By the end of the twelfth century there were about five hundred Cistercian (from the Latin for *Cîteaux*) monasteries in Europe, and Bernard's own Clairvaux had seven hundred monks. Initially the Cistercians wished to be an order of adult men. They successfully avoided admitting young boys, but by 1200 they had authorized about one hundred convents of Cistercian nuns.

And it was not just the Cistercians and the traditional Benedictines who attracted women. The twelfth century saw many new communities of women from England to eastern Europe. The age's growing prosperity and population contributed both potential nuns and healthy endowments, but the key factor was that women were responding to the spiritual forces of the age in the same way men were.

With the monastic clergy gaining so much in prestige and visibility, the episcopal clergy countered with its

Molesme (MOE-lem)  Cîteaux (SEE-toe)

own view of society. Surely, the bishops agreed, spiritual, moral, and intellectual improvement were desirable. Likewise, it was time to end the grossest examples of lay interference in the church. But precisely because so many bishops came from great families and were so well connected, they were less inclined to be rigid about the line of demarcation between lay and clerical responsibilities. In Germany, for example, the king's chapel recruited young noblemen to train them as clerics and to inculcate in them the policies and ethos of the court. Many of these chaplains were appointed to bishoprics and then advanced the king's interests in their new ecclesiastical areas of authority. They were often men of spiritual depth and resented what they regarded as monastic carping about their worldliness. By the middle of the twelfth century bishops, and finally popes, had imposed on the church a view that monks belonged in their monasteries and that bishops should lead society.

It was always the special responsibility of the clergy to look after the moral order of society. In the turbulent world of gentlemen warriors, the church had its own ideas about what a perfect "fighter" should do. The English bishop and scholar John of Salisbury (d. 1180), reflecting on knighthood in the twelfth century, concluded that it existed "to protect the church, to attack infidelity, to reverence the priesthood, to protect the poor, to keep the peace, to shed one's blood and, if necessary, to lay down one's life for one's brethren."

Turning large numbers of violent young men into servants of the church was a tall order for the clergy, and they had only limited success. One strategy that worked was the creation of military orders. The Palestine-based Knights of St. John, or Hospitallers, and Knights of the Temple, or Templars, are the major examples, but others existed in Spain and Germany. The Hospitallers started near Jerusalem as a foundation under Benedictine auspices dedicated to charitable works and care of the sick. They evolved into a monastic order using a version of the Rule of Saint Benedict and devoted themselves to the defense of pilgrims to the Holy Land. The Templars were men living under religious rule and sworn to protect the small states created by the Crusaders (see pages 310–312). These military orders measured up very well to the clergy's idea of what a perfect knight should be.

The clergy could also regulate disputes in society. For example, when a community was divided by a difficult conflict that demanded resolution, it might turn to the *ordeal*—a judicial procedure that sought divine judgment by subjecting the accused to a physically painful or dangerous test. An accused person might walk a certain distance carrying hot iron or plunge a hand into a boiling cauldron to pluck out a pebble. The resulting wounds would be bandaged for a set time and then examined. If they were healing, the person was considered innocent; if festering, guilty. The clergy officiated at ordeals until the papacy forbade their participation in 1215.

Clergymen were also the conservators of the shrines where people gained special access to the holiness of the saints. The clergy wrote and preached about the miracles of the saints, and stories circulated through the church about relics, or artifacts associated with these martyrs. The shrines where relics were preserved attracted pilgrims seeking healing from illness, injury, or misfortune. The clergy thus played unique roles in forming and nurturing communities in the world and in interceding for this world with God in the next.

## Those Who Fight: The Nobility

In recent years scholars have spilled a sea of ink trying to define the medieval nobility. The matter is important because even though the nobility constituted only a small minority of the total population, nobles were and expected to be the ruling class. To appreciate their crucial role, we need to consider the shape of the nobility and the nobles' lifestyle and ethos.

In English the word *noble* can be either an adjective or a noun. More commonly, it is an adjective, as in a "noble sentiment" or a "noble deed." Before the twelfth century the Latin *nobilis* was almost exclusively an adjective. The word pertained to certain desirable personal qualities. Then, gradually, the word became a noun and pertained to a certain kind of person.

What kind of person? In the ideal case a noble was a well-born, cultivated, office-holding soldier. In the earlier Middle Ages many men held offices without necessarily being considered noble. Virtually all free men were expected to be soldiers, but few of them ranked as nobles. It was in the century or so following the feudal revolution (see page 294) that these distinct elements were fused into a single social order.

In a world in which lords were everywhere extending their power, military prowess became more valuable. At the same time the need for horses and for more expensive arms and armor made it almost impossible for ordinary freemen to be soldiers. Likewise, ambitious lords who wished to expand their influence, and who were often, in an expanding economy, more prosperous than their forebears, were looking for ways to use their resources to gain followers. These trends came together as lords granted to their followers either military gear or lands, which would generate the income necessary to

**Courtly Love**    This manuscript illumination from Heidelberg shows a fair lady arming her knight for battle, probably for a tournament, as other ladies watch from the walls above. In the age of chivalry, war could be bloody and brutal—or it could be romantic.    *(Heidelberg, University Library/akg-images)*

and through many centuries, there was nothing systematic about how services were obtained or discharged.

Contemporary sources often call vassals "knights." Knights rarely boasted high birth or venerable ancestry. Nor were they initially officeholders appointed by kings or emperors. Moreover, they were not wealthy and could not sustain the kind of lavish lifestyle that one might expect from nobles. Across the eleventh and twelfth centuries knights saw their status change, in part because they aped the behavior of the nobles, who themselves accepted the necessity of military ability.

All over Europe, especially where royal power was ineffective, both knights and nobles secured tighter control of peasant labor. This process provided knights and nobles with the money to build castles and to acquire fine possessions. As governments expanded their competence, these nobles and knights often held high offices, or if they did not, they pressured kings to concede such offices to them. Lords also tended to gather their lands into coherent blocks and to name themselves after the castles they built on their lands. Families also began to produce genealogies tracing their ancestry to relatives in the distant past, and to kings if at all possible. At the same time families began to practice primogeniture—that is, reserving their lands, castles, and titles to the *primus genitus,* or "firstborn" son.

This allotment of the choicest inheritances to a shrinking group turned loose a large number of younger sons. Many of them entered the clergy, a tendency that helps to explain the rising aristocratic character of the church. It should be emphasized right away, however, that this was not a punishment. Sons were not "dumped" on the church. Clerical careers were prestigious and relatively comfortable. But more numerous than clerics were the young men who were without an estate and who lacked the means to secure a bride and to form a family of their own. It was from these men that vast crusading armies were recruited. These were also the men who traipsed about Europe looking for fame and fortune, or failing that, a lord to serve. Many of these "young" men were 30 or 40 years old. They were called young because they had not yet established themselves.

By 1200 the nobility was a group identified by the profession of arms, the holding of office, a consciousness of family traditions, and an elevated lifestyle. A specific ethos—chivalry—belonged to the nobility. Today chivalry is often thought of as either an elaborate code of conduct regulating relations between the sexes or the value system behind the literary image of dashing knights in shining armor saving damsels in distress from fire-breathing dragons. Actually its very name derives from *cheval,* French

obtain arms and horses. We call those followers "vassals" and the lands they obtained "fiefs°." Vassalage became a widespread institution all over Europe, and fief-holding became a normal accompaniment to vassalage. By contrast, in the Carolingian world vassalage was unusual and rarely connected with fief-holding.

Vassals and fiefs bring to mind the concept of *feudalism* or the term *feudal system.* As we saw in Chapter 9, England, France, and to a lesser degree Germany and Italy, were in some respects feudal realms. That is, lords, right up to the king, secured some personal and political services from vassals in return for material rewards, often landed estates called "fiefs." Today historians are reluctant to use the term *feudal system* because across Europe

**fief** (FEEF)

for "horse," the classic conveyance of a knight, or *caballarius* in Latin. Chivalry began as the code of conduct for mounted warriors.

Chivalry highly esteemed certain masculine, militant qualities. Military prowess was the greatest of chivalric virtues. A knight who was not a great warrior was useless. Literature of the time exalts the knight who slays fearsome beasts or the hero who single-handedly overwhelms impossible numbers of the enemy. Openhanded generosity was another key virtue. The truly noble person engaged in sumptuous display to manifest his power, to show concern for his dependents, and to enlarge his entourage. Medieval literature is full of rich banquets and stunning presents. In Anglo-Saxon England the king was called "the giver of rings." Knights were obsessed with their honor, their reputations. They sought glory, the better to win a lord or a bride or, if a lord already, to attract followers.

Chivalry also involved loyalty, the glue that held feudal society together. But we must take into account statements such as the following by a twelfth-century English historian, William of Malmesbury: "They [knights] are faithful to their lords, but swift to break faith. A breath of ill fortune and they are plotting treachery, a bag of money and their mind is changed." Knights, especially the "young," were loyal to their lords when they could be, but fundamentally they were loyal to themselves.

What role was left to noblewomen in a world of chivalry and lordship? By the late eleventh century three developments adversely affected the position of aristocratic women. First, the elaboration of the chivalric ethos defined most key social and political roles as military and "manly" and thereby excluded women. By the middle of the twelfth century it was rare for a woman to hold a castle and unheard-of for one to ride to arms. Second, the consolidation of lineages by aristocratic families accompanied a moral campaign by the church to promote monogamous, unbreakable marriages. This situation subordinated women's freedom in the marriage market to the dynastic and patrimonial demands of great families. Third, the spread of lordship, with its intricate network of personal and proprietary relationships based on military service, tended to deprive women of independent rights over land.

But every rule has its exceptions. As noble families married off fewer of their daughters to noblemen, "extra" daughters accounted in part for the dramatic increase in the number and size of convents. Convents of aristocratic nuns were places where women could be highly educated and almost entirely in control of their own affairs. Matilda, daughter of the German empress Adelaide,

was abbess of Quedlinburg, mistress of vast estates in northern Germany, and a dominant figure in German politics. But knights looking for brides would often marry the younger daughters of noblemen, because if they could establish a household, any children born of that marriage could lay claim to the noble lineage of their maternal grandfathers.

Less predictably, Gaita, wife of a Norman prince in Italy, fought in helmet and armor alongside her husband, as did Duchess Agnes of Burgundy. And let us reflect on the career of Adela of Blois (ca. 1067–1137). She was the daughter of William the Conqueror, the wife of a powerful French count, and the mother of King Stephen I of England (see page 297). In addition to regularly accompanying her husband as he administered his county, Adela founded monasteries, promoted religious reform, hosted Pope Paschal II, helped to reconcile her brother Henry I with the archbishop of Canterbury (thus averting an English investiture controversy), issued formal legal judgments, held fairs, and skillfully negotiated the aristocratic politics of western France after her husband's death. Adela is unusual because we know so much about her. In other words, noblewomen in high medieval society may often have led interesting, active lives, but there are few surviving records to document this.

## Those Who Work: The Peasants

The peasants were the "workers" in the tripartite model. An extremely diverse segment of society, "peasants" ranged from slaves to free persons of some means. Except in frontier zones, where victims were available and religious scruples diminished, slaves declined dramatically in numbers during the tenth and eleventh centuries (as illustrated by the shift in meaning of the classical Latin *servus* from "slave" to "serf"). Serfs, persons bound to the soil, constituted the majority of the peasants, although their legal and social statuses differed considerably from place to place. In the twelfth century serfdom was disappearing in France even as its terms were hardening in central and eastern Europe. Serfdom was a mixture of economic, legal, and personal statuses. The serf could be flogged in public, could be set upon by dogs, was excluded from many judicial proceedings, required approval to contract a marriage, and was denied the right to bear arms.

The tenth and eleventh centuries were decisive in the reshaping of rural society. As lordships of all kinds and sizes formed in the countryside, they drew communities of people. Castles were critical. Powerful men generally sited their castles in close proximity to wood, water, and iron. Sometimes a monastery, rural church, or grave-yard also attracted a castle or else grew up near one and helped to anchor a site. (See the feature "Weighing the Evidence: The Medieval Castle" on pages 314–315.)

People from a fairly wide area settled in the vicinity of the castle. Many, originally free, commended them-selves to the local lord by handing over their properties and receiving them back in return for rents or personal services. Other people fell into dependent status through military or economic misfortune. What eventually emerged was the manor, an institution best described as a power-ful lord controlling the lives of an often large number of dependents. He required payments and services from them and regulated their ordinary disputes. His control was simultaneously public and private.

A minor castellan, or lord of a castle, might control only a small manor and would probably be the vassal of a great lord. A powerful landed lord, on the other hand, would generally control many manors and would often give some of them to retainers as fiefs. In other words, the reorganization of the countryside affected the nobil-ity and the peasantry and created parallel sets of vertical bonds of association: feudal lords and vassals entered into political bonds; lords and peasants entered into economic bonds.

The structure of individual manors, and the dues owed by peasants, varied tremendously across Europe. Certain trends were fairly consistent, however. As the economy expanded, as trade brought more and different products into Europe, and as a more consciously aristo-cratic lifestyle spread, the nobility began to want dispos-able cash. Thus in many places corvées° (labor services) were commuted into cash payments. Peasants were re-quired to pay rent from their own holdings instead of working on the lord's lands. But lords still needed provi-sions, so they sometimes split peasant payments into cash and kind. Old forms of service could be wholly re-tained, involving many days per year of work on the lord's demesne, the portion of the manor the lord re-served for his own benefit. In such cases the lord could still extract money from his peasants by requiring them to use his mill and oven and then charging them gristing and kilning fees.

The trend everywhere, however, was for labor ser-vices to diminish. In one region in northern France, twelfth-century peasants owed only three corvées of two days' each per year for harvesting and haymaking. Else-where, peasants might still be required to haul crops to market or to keep roads, bridges, and buildings in repair.

**corvée** (KOR-vay)

On many estates where the menfolk had been largely freed from corvées, the women might still have to work in the lord's house washing laundry, sewing, plucking fowl, cooking, minding dogs, and tending to other house-hold chores.

In the expanding economy of the eleventh and twelfth centuries, the peasants grew more prosperous, and their lords constantly sought new ways to extract the fruits of that prosperity. Peasants thus began to band to-gether to demand that "customs" be observed. These customs were more or less formal agreements spelling out the terms under which work and fees would be arranged. In general life improved for the peasants in terms of both legal status and living conditions.

The European village was a key product of the tenth and eleventh centuries. People who originally gathered together around a castle for security and livelihood be-gan to form a durable human community. Their church and graveyard helped to reinforce the community by tying together the living and the dead and by giving the village a sense of memory and continuity. Peasants gen-erally worked only 250 to 270 days per year, so they had a good deal of time for festivals and celebrations. Births, baptisms, betrothals, and deaths provided opportunities for the community to come together and affirm its mu-tual ties. Market days and sessions of the lord's court also assembled the village. Villagers needed to cooperate in many of the operations of daily life. They shared tools, plow teams, and wagons. They performed their corvées together. The peasants experienced much less social dif-ferentiation than the nobility, and so less tension.

The status of women in peasant society tended to be, in legal theory and in daily reality, the same as that of men at a time when the status of aristocratic women was fragile. Marriage contracts from northern Italy show that brides often entered marriages with a complement of valuable tools. This suggests that peasant women re-tained some control over their own personal property and also reminds us that the huge gains in rural produc-tivity were almost certainly attributable in part to the work and ingenuity of women. (See the box "Reading Sources: The Furnishings of a Welsh Household.")

## Those Left Out: Townspeople and Jews

The tripartite model excluded two important groups of people. The first neglected group consisted of the in-creasingly numerous citizens of Europe's growing towns. Obviously people in towns worked, but the prejudices of the aristocracy were rural, so the only "workers" deemed necessary to the smooth functioning of the social order

## READING SOURCES

# THE FURNISHINGS OF A WELSH HOUSEHOLD

*This passage from the laws of Howell the Good (d. 950) concerns the distribution of household property in case of divorce. The aim was to achieve a nearly even split. Notice the kinds of objects a house might hold and who got what.*

The husband shall have all the pigs, the wife the sheep. The husband shall have all the horses and mares, the oxen and cows, bullocks and heifers; the wife shall have the goats. . . . All the vessels for milk, except one pail, are the wife's; all the dishes, except one meat dish, are the husband's. One cart and yoke are the wife's. All the jars and drinking vessels are the husband's. Of the bedding, the husband shall have all the bedclothes which are beneath, the wife those which are above. The husband shall have the cauldron, the pillow, the winnowing sheet, the coulter, the wood axe, the gimlet [hole-borer], the flog, all the sick-les except one, and the gridiron. The wife shall have the pan and the tripod, the broadaxe and the sieve, the ploughshare, the flax and the seed of the flax, and the precious things except gold and silver. If there are any of these (gold or silver) they are to be divided in two equal parts. The products of the loom shall be divided in two equal parts, both linens and woolens. The husband shall have the barn and the grain and whatever is above or in the ground, and the hens and the geese and one cat. The wife shall have the meat that is salted and the cheese that is fresh . . . and the vessel of butter . . . and the ham . . . and as much of the flour as she can carry. Each of them shall have his or her personal clothing, except the cloaks, which shall be divided.

Source: Ian F. Fletcher, ed. and trans., *Latin Redaction A of the Law of Hywel* (Aberystwyth, Wales: Center for Advanced Welsh and Celtic Studies, 1986), pp. 58–59.

---

were farmers. In the second group were Europe's principal religious minority, the Jews. Jews could be found almost everywhere, although they constituted only about 1 percent of the population as a whole and, outside of Rome and parts of Spain, formed no single community numbering more than 1,500 to 2,000.

The central factor in the growth of towns was the rise in the productivity and profitability of medieval agriculture. For the first time in history a regular and substantial farm surplus could support an urban population that did not produce its own food. Increased local exchange, coupled with the relentless growth of a money economy, meant there were fortunes to be made and cash to be spent. Some of that cash was spent on luxury and exotic products that increasingly became the objects of far-flung commercial networks. A good part of the cash was spent by rural nobles, who earned it from rents, booty, and the profits of the private exercise of public power. When those nobles moved into towns, they created opportunities for merchants, craftsmen, day laborers, domestic servants, and professional people such as notaries and lawyers. This was particularly true in Europe's most heavily urbanized regions: Flanders, southern France, and northern Italy. The key point is that the growth of the medieval city and of its human community began in the medieval countryside.

Town society was hierarchical, but its structures were new, ill defined, and flexible. Rich men built up bands of followers who supported them in urban politics, protected their neighborhoods, and occasionally raided the houses of their enemies in the next neighborhood. Relatives, friends, neighbors, people from a common rural district, or those engaged in similar trades tended to worship together in particular churches, observe certain festivals, and look after one another's families.

In the rapidly changing world of the tenth and eleventh centuries, towns provided numerous opportunities for women. In urban industries such as clothmaking, tanning, laundering, and brewing, women sometimes managed and even owned enterprises. Apart, perhaps, from finance and the law, distinctions between male and female roles were not as sharp in towns as in rural areas.

If urban men and all women stood in an ambiguous relationship to the ideals of the male, rural, aristocratic elite, we can hardly imagine what it must have been like for Jews. Jewish communities had existed in most European towns since antiquity. Then, because the Byzantine and Islamic worlds vacillated between persecution and

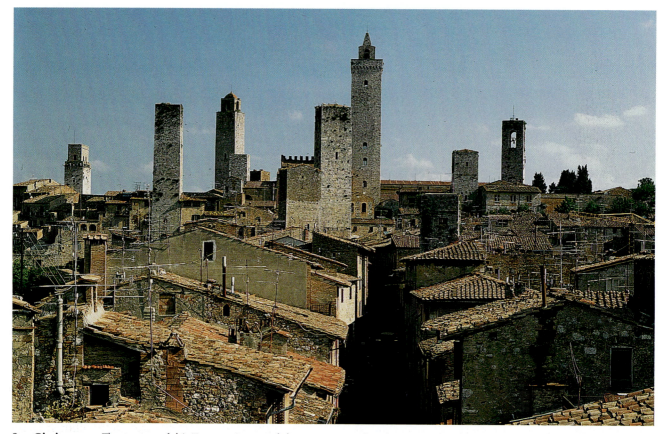

**San Gimignano**    The towers of this Tuscan city reveal the concentrated and competitive nature of power in the Italian communes. Most of these towers date from around 1300.    *(Scala/Art Resource, NY)*

toleration, many Jews migrated to western Europe, with the largest numbers settling in northern France and the German Rhineland. The Jewish community in England formed only around 1100. Paris had northern Europe's largest Jewish community, perhaps two thousand people in the twelfth century. Many cities had Jewish populations numbering two hundred to three hundred, but groups of forty or fifty were common. Although some Jews in Italy, Spain, and Germany owned farms and vineyards, most Jews settled in cities, where they could live and worship in community with other Jews. Urban clusters also provided strength in numbers for people who could at any moment fall victim to persecution and whose power was not based on landholding.

Three of the most important developments in high medieval Europe were disastrous for Jews. First, the growth of the European economy, with its attendant urban and commercial expansion, brought countless Christians into the practice of trade, an occupation dominated by Jews since Late Antiquity. As Jews were excluded from commercial opportunities, they were more and more con-

fined to moneylending. Jews had been moneylenders before the economic surge of the High Middle Ages, but the expanding economy made financial operations more widespread than ever before. Given that, as we saw in Chapter 9, Christian moralists considered handling money to be the Devil's work, the visibility of Jews as moneylenders brought them much criticism, although they were never alone in this practice.

The second phenomenon that adversely affected Jews was the reform of the church. With so much attention being paid to the proper Christian life and the correct organization of the church, it was inevitable that more attention would be directed to the one prominent group in Western society that was not Christian.

Third, the Crusades unleashed vicious attacks on Jews. As crusading armies headed east in 1096, they visited unspeakable massacres on the Jewish communities of several German towns. This awful process was repeated on the eve of the Second Crusade in 1146–1147 and again just before the third in 1189. Popular frenzy identified the Jews as Christ-killers and equated them with Muslims as the enemies of Christianity. In fact, and despite grotesque and groundless stories about Jews kidnapping and ritually killing Christian children, Jews everywhere wished to live in peace with their Christian neighbors and to be left alone to observe their distinctive religious, dietary, and social customs.

The Jews were not without sympathetic champions, however. From the time of Gregory I (r. 590–604), the papacy urged peaceful coexistence and prayers for Jewish conversion. In the twelfth and thirteenth centuries popes forcefully reminded Christians that while converting Jews was highly desirable, Jews were to be tolerated and left in peace. The Carolingians protected the Jews, and some kings in succeeding centuries repeated or even expanded upon Carolingian legislation. Spanish Jews were taken under royal protection in reconquered areas in 1053, and Henry IV took German Jews under his protection in 1084. In England and France Jews enjoyed royal protection until the late twelfth century. Jews frequently served as royal advisers in Spain and were often entrusted with sensitive diplomatic missions elsewhere.

Despite such policies, Jews were vulnerable to attack at almost any time from people who simply disliked them or who owed them money. But in 1181 Philip II of France, always on the lookout for income, had his henchmen arrest Jews and confiscate their possessions. In 1182 he expelled them from the royal demesne. Across the thirteenth century French kings accorded the Jews less and less protection and often abused them financially. In 1306 Philip IV expelled the Jews from France after confiscating their goods. In England the story is much the same. The impecunious Henry II laid crushing taxes on the Jews in 1171. In 1189 in London and in 1190 in York, massive riots stirred by false rumors raged against the Jewish populations. In 1290 Edward I seized Jewish possessions and expelled Jews from the country. Royal protection of German Jews was reasonably effective until the death of Frederick II in 1250, after which time local princes often repudiated debts to Jewish lenders and appropriated Jewish property.

# SOCIAL AND RELIGIOUS MOVEMENTS, CA. 1100–1300

TWELFTH- and thirteenth-century Europe witnessed several social movements unlike any that had occurred before. Spurred by increasingly intrusive governments, economic dislocation, and spiritual turmoil, they involved large numbers of people; cut across lines of gender, wealth, status, and occupation;

and appeared in many places. Most of these movements had cohesive beliefs, even ideologies, and well-determined goals. They are the first large-scale social movements in European history.

## Heretics and Dissidents

The canon lawyer Gratian (see page 335) defined *heresy* as a situation in which "each man chooses for himself the teaching he believes to be the better one"—that is, he ignores official doctrines. For Gratian and his like-minded contemporaries, faith was not an individual matter. Unity of belief was crucial in a catholic ("universal") Christian Europe. In the twelfth century, the church reacted ever more strictly to challenges to its teachings or to its exclusive right to teach. The effort by the church to define its law, theology, and bureaucratic procedures with greater precision drew lines more sharply than ever before between what was and was not acceptable.

Heretics did not see themselves as secessionists from the true church. Quite the contrary, they saw themselves as its only representatives. Church teachings always encountered a degree of popular skepticism. Not everyone believed, for example, that Jesus was born of a virgin or that he was true God and true man. But such doubts had not previously led to mass defections. Before the middle of the twelfth century, challenges to the church came from men—as far as we can tell the ringleaders were all men—who saw themselves as inspired reformers.

Tanchelm° of Antwerp preached between 1100 and 1115 in the Netherlands. He scandalized the mainstream by calling churches brothels and clerics whores. He rejected the sacraments and the payment of tithes. Although Tanchelm was radical and pugnacious, his ideas constituted a fairly coherent program of criticism. Like many others, he was concerned about the immorality and wealth of the church. But Tanchelm and his followers went even further. The heretic distributed his nail and hair clippings as relics of a sort, and in a bizarre public ceremony he "married" a statue of the Virgin Mary. Across the twelfth century church orthodoxy was challenged by others whose influence seems to have been local. What is interesting is how numerous, and similar, they all were.

Coherent movements of much larger proportions emerged later in the century. In 1173 Waldo, a rich merchant of Lyon, decided to sell all his property, give the proceeds to the poor, and embrace a life of poverty and preaching. Waldo was motivated by the same quest for the apostolic life that had animated the eremitic movement of the eleventh century. But there was a difference:

**Tanchelm** (TANK-elm)

he was a layman. Waldo attracted many followers (known as Waldensians), and in 1179 Pope Alexander III (r. 1159–1181) scrutinized him closely, found his beliefs to be essentially correct, and approved his vow of poverty. But the pope commanded Waldo to preach only when invited to do so by bishops. The bishops, jealous about their own power, extended no such invitations.

Waldo and his "Poor Men of Lyon" went right on preaching and in 1184 were formally declared heretics. Until this point it was not their ideas so much as their appropriation of a clerical duty, preaching, that had set the church against them. From this time on, however, the Waldensians became more radical in their attacks. In about 1204 one group of Waldensians was reconciled to the Catholic Church, but the majority, who had spread all over southern France and Italy, into Germany, and as far away as Poland, remained estranged. Waldensian communities exist to this day.

The most serious of the popular heretical movements was Catharism (from the Greek *katharos,* meaning "pure"). Because there were numerous Cathars near the southern French town of Albi, the whole movement is sometimes called "Albigensian." In fact, Cathars could be found all over Europe, although they did cluster in northern Italy and southern France. Cathars were the religious descendants of Mani (see page 191), a third-century Persian who taught an extreme dualism that featured polarities in almost all things: good-evil, love-hate, flesh-spirit. Extreme Cathars abstained from flesh in all ways: they were vegetarians and renounced sexual intercourse so as not to produce offspring—that is, more flesh. Probably radiating from Bulgaria, Cathar ideas had spread widely in the West by the 1140s. Catharism attracted many converts when Nicetas, the Cathar bishop of Constantinople, visited northern Italy and southern France between 1166 and 1176. People of every station joined the new church, which, in its own view, was the only true church.

The Catholic Church sent isolated preachers against the Cathars, but with little success. In 1198 and 1203, Pope Innocent III organized systematic preaching tours in southern France, but these, too, lacked solid results, and in 1208 the pope's legate was murdered by a supporter of the count of Toulouse, who was sympathetic to the Cathars. The killing led to the launching of the Albigensian Crusade, a loosely structured military action that lasted into the 1260s. Although the crusade itself was largely over by the 1220s, violence against Albigensians sputtered for decades: a massacre in 1244 and inquisitorial campaigns in 1246 and again in 1256 to 1257. Isolated resisters struggled on into the fourteenth century.

Albigensians denounced the clergy of their day as rich and corrupt. These teachings attracted urban dwellers who resented the wealth and pretensions of the clergy—the same people who followed Waldo. Nobles may have been drawn to the movement because it gave them opportunities to take possession of extensive tracts of church lands, something the investiture controversy had denied them. In addition, embracing Catharism may have been a way for nobles to resist the increasing encroachment of the government of far-off Paris. The Albigensians also attracted many women. Unlike the Catholic Church, which denied clerical, preaching, and teaching offices to women, the heretical sects tended to permit women to hold leading roles.

The Albigensians, like the Waldensians, were driven by the same spiritual zeal and desire for ecclesiastical reform that moved many of their contemporaries. They differed from other would-be reformers in that they did not seek to reform the Catholic Church from within but departed from it or insisted that they alone represented it. Thus these heretical movements marked the first serious challenge to the ideology of a uniformly "catholic" Christendom since Late Antiquity. (See the box "Reading Sources: Pronouncements of the Fourth Lateran Council on Heresy.")

## Reform from Within: The Mendicant Orders

Traditional monastic orders continued to win adherents, but their interpretation of the apostolic life meant ascetic withdrawal from the world, not pastoral work and preaching. Laymen who wished both to embrace poverty and to preach fell under the suspicion of the ecclesiastical authorities. Early in the thirteenth century a new movement arose, the mendicants (literally, beggars). Mendicants were men who aimed to preach, to be poor, and to create formal but noncloistered religious orders. Though similar to the heretics in many ways, they submitted willingly to ecclesiastical authority.

The mendicant phenomenon began when Francis of Assisi° (1181–1226), the son of a rich Italian merchant, decided to renounce the wealth and status that were his birthright. He carried out his renunciation in a most public display before the bishop of Assisi in 1206. Francis had gradually grown tired of a life of ease and luxury, but he also experienced a blinding moment of spiritual insight when, by chance, his eyes fell on the passage in the Scriptures in which Christ commanded the rich young ruler, "Go, sell all you have, and follow me." Francis stripped himself naked so that "naked he might follow the naked Christ."

For a few years Francis wandered about Italy begging for his meager sustenance, repairing churches, car-

---

**Assisi** (uh-SEE-zee)

READING SOURCES

# PRONOUNCEMENTS OF THE FOURTH LATERAN COUNCIL ON HERESY

*By 1215 the papacy had become alarmed at the number and strength of the heretical movements in Europe, and it began to take strong measures to counter the dissidents.*

3. Convicted heretics shall be handed over for due punishment to their secular superiors, or the latter's agents. If they are clerks [members of the clergy], they shall first be degraded [lose their clerical rank]. The goods of the layman thus convicted shall be confiscated; those of the clergy shall be applied to the churches from which they drew their stipends. . . . If a temporal lord neglects to fulfil the demand of the church that he purge his land of the contamination of heresy, he shall be excommunicated by the metropolitan and other bishops of the province. If he fails to make amends within a year, it shall be reported to the Supreme Pontiff, who shall pronounce his vassals absolved from fealty to him and offer his land to Catholics. . . . Catholics who assume the cross and devote themselves to the extermination of heretics shall enjoy the same indulgence and privilege as those who go to the Holy Land. . . .

7. Further we add that every archbishop and bishop, in person or by his archdeacon or other suitable and trustworthy persons, shall visit each of his parishes, in which there are said to be heretics, at least once a year. And he shall compel three or more men of good reputation, or even, if need be, the whole neighborhood, to swear that, if any of them knows of any heretics or of any who frequent secret conventicles or who practise manners and customs different from those common amongst Christians, he will report them to the bishop; and, unless they clear themselves of the accusation, or if they relapse into their former mischief, they shall receive the canonical punishment.

Source: Henry Bettenson, *Documents of the Christian Church,* 2d ed. (London: Oxford University Press, 1963), p. 133.

---

ing for the sick, and preaching repentance to all who would listen. By 1210 he had attracted many followers, and together they set out to see Innocent III to win approval. After considering the matter for a while, Innocent decided to approve the new order of friars (that is "brothers," from the Latin *fratres*) as long as they would accept monastic tonsure—a ritual haircut signifying submission—profess obedience to the pope, and swear obedience to Francis. The pope was genuinely won over by Francis himself, but he also sensed that by permitting the formation of the Franciscan order, he could create a legitimate and controllable repository for the explosive spiritual forces of the age.

Francis prepared a simple Rule based on his understanding of the scriptural ideals of poverty, preaching, and service. Alarmed by the vagueness of the first Rule and by the extraordinary influx of new members, the papal curia in 1223 prevailed on Francis to submit a revision that stressed order, a hierarchy of officials, and a novitiate—a regularized period of training for new members. Somewhat disappointed by this regulated formality, Francis withdrew more and more from the world and lived reclusively in the hills near Assisi.

After Francis died, the issues of property, power, education, and ordination provoked deep controversies within his order. Usually called "Franciscan," Francis's order is technically the "Friars Minor." The movement had begun among laymen, but over time more Franciscan brothers became ordained priests. Franciscans established schools in most great cities, and by the middle of the thirteenth century some of Europe's greatest intellects were Franciscans. This prominence, like the sacramental power of ordination, was a kind of wealth that Francis had wished to avoid. The real issue of wealth, however, turned on the possession of property. Francis had aimed for both personal and corporate poverty. In the 1230s papal legislation had alleviated strict poverty by permitting the order to acquire property to support its work. Nevertheless, the issue of property continued to spark controversy among the Franciscans.

Of the nine or ten mendicant orders that developed, the other major one was the Dominican, a product of very different experiences than the Franciscan. Its founder, Dominic de Guzman (1170–1221), was the son of a Spanish nobleman. He became a priest and later a cathedral canon. While traveling, he saw firsthand the Albigensian

**The Confirmation of the Rule of Saint Francis, 1223** This painting by Giotto di Bondone (1265–1337) depicts Pope Honorius III confirming the much-revised version of Francis's Rule, first approved by Innocent III in 1210. Giotto, one of the greatest medieval painters, pioneered the use of geometric perspective. *(Scala/Art Resource, NY)*

heresy in southern France, and in 1206 he went to Rome to seek permission to preach against the heretics. The Albigensian Crusade began in 1208, but Dominic's methods were those of persuasion, not coercion.

Albigensian criticisms of the ignorance, indifference, and personal failings of the clergy could never be applied to Dominic and his fellow preachers. Dominic and his followers were supported enthusiastically by the bishop of Toulouse, who saw how useful these zealous preachers of unblemished lives could be. In 1215 Dominic, with his bishop's assistance, attempted to form a new order, but by that time Rome had forbidden the creation of new orders for fear of heresy or uncontrollable diversity. Thus Dominic's "Order of Preachers" (the proper name

for the "Dominicans") adopted the Rule of Saint Augustine, which many communities of cathedral canons had been using since the eleventh century.

In 1217 Dominic presided at the first general meeting of the order. The Dominicans decided to disperse, some going to Paris, some (including Dominic) to Rome, some to other cities in Europe. Henceforth the order saw its mission as serving the whole church. Dominican schools were set up all over Europe, and the order acquired a reputation for learning and scholarship. The Dominicans were voluntarily poor, but the order was never rent by a controversy over property as the Franciscans were. Dominic's was a vision of personal, not corporate, poverty. Likewise, as a preaching order, the Dominicans had to be learned and ordained. Franciscan misgivings on these issues did not touch them.

Both the Franciscan and Dominican orders reflected a widespread desire to emulate the apostolic life of the early church by poverty and preaching. Both submitted to legitimate authority. Francis's religious vision of charity and service was the product of a heartfelt need for repentance and renewal. This concern for the soul often caused Franciscans to serve as missionaries. Dominic set out to save the church from its enemies. He desired preachers who were sufficiently learned that they could combat the errors of heretics. Both men saw the need for

exemplary lives. Francis was a more charismatic figure than Dominic, and his apostolate to the urban poor was more compelling. By 1300 Franciscan houses outnumbered Dominican by 3 to 1. The mendicants were the greatest spiritual force in high medieval Europe.

## Communities of Women

The religious forces that attracted men drew women as well. Traditional orders, however, tended to be hostile toward women. Cluniacs and Cistercians struggled to keep women out of their ranks. The wandering preachers

**The Parting of Mary from the Apostles**    Duccio di Buoninsegna lived from the middle of the thirteenth century to 1318 or 1319. He did his finest work in Siena, including a huge altarpiece, one of whose panels depicts the touching scene of Mary taking leave of the apostles just before her death. Note the clever way Duccio has arranged the figures and how he balances Saint Paul, standing in the doorway, with Mary, reclining on the bed.    *(Scala/Art Resource, NY)*

## READING SOURCES

# NEW ORDERS FOR WOMEN: CLARES AND BEGUINES

*These excerpts, from the prologue to Clare's Rule and from a document detailing the origins of the Beguines, illustrate the initiative of women in the new religious orders. Observe, too, how the women's submission to authority relieved them from suspicion of heresy or insubordination.*

### Clare's Rule

Clare, the unworthy servant of Christ and the little plant of the most blessed Francis, promises obedience and reverence to the Lord Pope Innocent [III] and his canonically elected successors, and to the Roman Church. And, just as at the beginning of her conversion, together with her sisters she promised obedience to the Blessed Francis, so now she promises his successors to observe that same obedience inviolably, and the other sisters shall always be obliged to obey the successors of Blessed Francis and Sister Clare and other canonically elected abbesses who succeed her.

### The Beguines

Those ladies of good memory, Joanna and her sister Margaret, successive countesses of Flanders and Hai-nault, noticed that the region was greatly abounding in women for whom, because of their own position or that of their friends, suitable marriages were not possible, and they saw that the daughters of respectable men, both nobles and commoners, wished to live chastely, but could not easily enter a monastery because of the great number of these girls and the poverty of their parents, and that respectable and noble but impoverished damsels had to go begging or shamefully support themselves or seek support from their friends, unless some solution could be found. Then by divine inspiration, as it is piously believed, having first obtained the advice and consent of respectable men of the diocese and elsewhere, in various parts of Flanders they set up certain spacious places which are called Beguinages, in which the aforesaid women, girls, and damsels were received, so that living in common therein, they might preserve their chastity, with or without taking vows, and where they might support and clothe themselves by suitable work, without shaming themselves or their friends.

Source: Emilie Amt, *Women's Lives in Medieval Europe* (New York: Routledge, 1993), pp. 236, 264.

---

of the twelfth century, without exception, acquired women as followers, but the usual results were either segregation of the women in cloisters or condemnation of the whole movement.

In 1212 Francis attracted the aristocrat Clare of Assisi (1194–1253), who was fleeing from an arranged marriage. She wanted to live the friars' life of poverty and preaching, and Francis wanted to assist her. Aware that the sight of women begging or preaching would be shocking, in 1215 he gave Clare and his other female followers their own rule. Clare became abbess of the first community of the "Poor Clares." Though cloistered and forbidden to preach, the Clares lived lives of exemplary austerity and attracted many adherents.

Beguines° were communities of women who lived together, devoted themselves to charitable works, but did not take vows as nuns. The Beguine movement grew from the work in Nivelles, near Liège°, of Mary of Oignies° (ca. 1177–1213). She was drawn to the ideals of voluntary poverty and service to others. So strong was the pull that she renounced her marriage, gave away all her goods, worked for a while in a leper colony, and thought of preaching against the Cathars. Instead, she formed a community.

Groups of Beguines appeared all over the Low Countries, western Germany, and northern France. This was the first exclusively women's movement in the history of Christianity. Beguines sometimes vowed poverty and sometimes did not. They sometimes cloistered themselves into communities and sometimes taught and served the poor and outcast. They neither challenged the officials and teachings of the church nor demanded a right to preach. As laywomen, they did not give rise to scandal as noncloistered nuns would have. They were

---

**Beguines** (BAY-geenz)

**Liège** (lee-EZHE)    **Oignies** (OWN-yeese)

content to have power over their own lives and communities but not seek a voice in the wider world around them. (See the box "Reading Sources: New Orders for Women: Clares and Beguines.")

Thirteenth-century Europe knew more female than male mystics, and female mysticism tended to focus on Jesus, especially on His presence in the Eucharist. This is the first religious devotion that can be shown to have been more common to women than to men. Most of the mystics were either nuns or Beguines. As the clergy was defining its own prerogatives more tightly, and excluding women more absolutely from the exercise of formal public power, female communities provided a different locus for women's activity.

Women who spent their lives in community with other women reveal, in their writings, none of the sense of moral and intellectual inferiority that was routinely attributed to women by men and often by women themselves. Women who were in direct spiritual communion with God acquired, as teachers, mediators, and counselors in their communities, power that they simply could not have had outside those settings.

# LATIN CULTURE: FROM SCHOOLS TO UNIVERSITIES

THE dynamism so evident in the economic, social, and political life of Europe is just as apparent in cultural life. As in the late antique and Carolingian periods, courts and churches were the greatest patrons of artists and authors. But in this age of expansion the number and geographic spread of such patrons increased dramatically. By 1150 the church comprised 50 percent more bishoprics and about three times as many monasteries as it had in 900. In 1300 monarchies reigned in many places—Scandinavia and the Slavic world, for example—where none had existed in 900. In addition to an increase in the sheer amount of cultural activity, the years between 900 and 1300 also witnessed innovations. Logic replaced grammar at the heart of the school curriculum. Latin letters remained ascendant, but literature in many vernacular (native) languages began to appear in quantity and quality. Romanesque art and architecture were fresh and original interpretations of their Carolingian ancestors. Europe's incipient urbanization produced the first stirrings of a distinctively urban culture. In one of those cities, Paris, a new kind of academic institution emerged—the university—which was arguably the period's greatest legacy to the modern world.

## The Carolingian Legacy

Cultural life depends on both creative geniuses and generous patrons. Political dislocation and constant attacks in the ninth and tenth centuries initially deprived schools and masters of the Carolingian patronage that they had enjoyed for a century or more. The Carolingians left firm enough foundations in a few centers for intellectual life to continue, but the scale of activity between 900 and 1050 was smaller than before. Three examples serve to capture the spirit of the age that set the stage for the High Middle Ages.

Gerbert of Aurillac° (940–1003) was the most distinguished intellect of his age. He left his home in Aquitaine to study in Spain and Italy before settling in Reims, in northern France, where he was a teacher and then briefly a bishop. He attracted the attention of the emperor Otto III and spent some time at the German court, earning appointments as abbot of Bobbio, bishop of Ravenna, and, finally, pope. Gerbert followed Carolingian tradition in being a collector of manuscripts and critic of texts, but he departed from older traditions in his interest in mathematics and in his study of logic—the formal rules of reasoning that, in the Western tradition, trace back over many thinkers to Aristotle (see pages 96–98).

Fulbert of Chartres° (960–1028), Gerbert's finest pupil, elevated the cathedral school of Chartres to the paramount place in academic Europe. Fulbert wrote letters in elegant Latin and composed fine poems. He carried on his master's literary interests more than his scientific ones, and well into the twelfth century Chartres remained a major center of literary studies.

Another figure of interest is the aristocratic German nun Roswitha of Gandersheim (d. 970). She wrote poems on saints and martyrs, as well as a story about a priest who sold his soul to the devil. In her mature years, Roswitha wrote Latin plays in rhymed verse based on the Roman writer Terence. In these plays she refashioned tales from Roman and biblical history to convey moral truths.

## The Study of Law

Law was a field of major innovation. The increasing sophistication of urban life demanded a better understanding of law. The growing responsibilities of the church called for orderly rules, and the church's frequent quarrels with secular rulers demanded careful delineations of

---

**Gerbert of Aurillac** (DJAIR-bear of OR-ee-ak)
**Fulbert of Chartres** (FULL-bear of SHART)

334

**Map 10.1  Europe, ca. 1230**  By the early thirteenth century the European states that would exist into modern times were clearly visible, although each would continue to undergo changes. To gain a sense of the evolution of Europe, compare this map with Maps 6.1, 7.3, and 8.3.

rights and responsibilities. Governments issued more laws and regulations than at any time since antiquity.

In about 1012 Burchard, the bishop of Worms, produced a collection of canon law that was influential for more than a century and heightened reformers' awareness of the law of the church. By midcentury scholars studying canon law in Italy and France helped to promote the papal view of reform. In Bologna (see Map 10.1) Irnerius° (d. ca. 1130), a transplanted German and protégé of Emperor Henry V, began teaching Roman law from the law code of Justinian (see pages 225–226). This legal work culminated in the publication in 1140 of the *Decretum* of the Bolognese monk Gratian°. The most comprehensive and systematic book of canon law yet written, Gratian's work remained authoritative for centuries.

Throughout the twelfth century canon lawyers studied and wrote commentaries on Gratian's *Decretum.* These legists are called "decretists." Gratian had systematically collected earlier papal *decretals* (official pronouncements), but popes continued to issue them. Several collections of these new decretals were prepared in the thirteenth century, and the scholars who studied these later decrees are called "decretalists." The church thus produced a vast corpus of law and legal commentary.

Law was by no means confined to the church. England was precocious in creating a common law, a single law applied uniformly in its courts. But English law was based on the careful accumulation of legal decisions—or precedents—and not on the routine application of the provisions of a law code. There were many law codes elsewhere. Alfonso X of Castile issued the *Siete Partidas,* a comprehensive law code largely reliant on Roman law. Prince Iaroslav (d. 1054) is reputed to have issued the first version of the laws of Kievan Rus. Iaroslav's laws were written in Old Russian, but they drew heavily on the laws and legal traditions of neighboring peoples. Byzantine law was revised under the Macedonian dynasty.

## Greek, Arab, and Jewish Contributions

Norman and German settlement in southern Italy and Sicily, the Reconquista in Spain, the Crusades, and the creation of Italian communities in many Mediterranean cities brought European thinkers face-to-face with the intellectual traditions of Classical Greece, Islam, and medieval Judaism. Between 1100 and 1270 almost the whole corpus of Aristotle's writings, virtually unknown in the West for a millennium, became available. Arab commentaries on Aristotle, as well as Jewish philosophical and theological works, began to circulate. The presence of all these texts and currents of thought was decisive in expanding the range and raising the level of Western thought.

Prior to about 1100 only a few of Aristotle's writings, primarily some of his early writings on logic, had been available in the West. Gradually scholars recovered Aristotle's full treatment of logic, then his scientific writings, and finally his studies of ethics and politics. Aristotle's books posed a number of problems for Christian scholars. If knowledge is a good thing and good things are gifts of God, how did a pagan get so smart? Is it possible that faith is unnecessary to knowledge? What relationship exists between faith and reason? Aristotle taught that the universe is eternal and mechanistic. His thought left no room for creation or for the continuing role of a Creator. For Christian thinkers Aristotle asked questions that demanded answers: Were the Scriptures true? Did God create the world as Genesis said? Did God continue to intervene in this world?

Between 750 and 900, mainly in Iran, a group of Arabic-speaking Christians began translating into Arabic the Greek texts of Aristotle as well as the more than fifteen thousand pages of commentary on Aristotle that had been produced between about A.D. 100 and 600. These translators were Monophysite Christians chased out of Syria by the emperor Heraclius when he conquered the area from the Persians (see page 247). This flood of material inspired generations of Arab scholars to tackle the thought of the man often called simply "the Philosopher."

Two major Arab thinkers were particularly influenced by the vast Aristotelian corpus. Ibn-Sina (980–1037), called Avicenna° in the West, was drawn to the fundamental problem of how to understand the relationship between objects that exist in the world and the knowledge of those objects that is formed and held in the human mind. (See the box "Global Encounters: The Making of an Arab Scholar.") Ibn Rushd (1126–1198), called Averroes°, wrote no fewer than thirty-eight commentaries on the works of Aristotle, and at least fifteen of these were translated into Latin in the thirteenth century. Among many contributions, Averroes particularly tried to clarify the relationship between truths acquired through the exercise of reason and truths that depend on divine revelation. Although his exact meaning remains controversial, his contemporaries and many later scholars understood him to teach the "double truth": Truths about the natural world are more or less accessible to everyone depending on a person's intellectual ability. Revealed truths, however, are available only to the most enlightened.

Spain and northern France were both important centers of Jewish thought. In Spain some Jewish thinkers

---

**Irnerius** (ear-NAIR-ee-us)    **Gratian** (GRAY-shun)    **Avicenna** (ah-vih-SENN-uh)    **Averroes** (uh-VERR-oh-eese)

# The Making of an Arab Scholar

These excerpts from the engaging life of Avicenna (980–1037) reveal not only his remarkable intellectual attainments but also his ongoing encounter with Greek thought. Avicenna was deeply influenced by Aristotle, and, in turn, his writings influenced Jewish and Christian writers who were also coming to grips with the greatest of Greek philosophers. His writings on medicine were authoritative until the seventeenth century.

My father was from Balkh and moved from there to Bukhārā [now Turkmenistan] . . . where I was given teachers of the Quran and polite letters [literature, especially poetry]. By the time I was ten years old I had mastered the Quran and so much of polite letters as to provoke wonderment. My father decided to send me to a certain grocer who knew Indian arithmetic so that I could learn it from him. Then Abu Abdallah al-Natili, who claimed to be a philosopher, came to Bukhārā. My father lodged him in our house in the hope that I would learn something from him. Before he came I was studying jurisprudence . . . and I was one of the best pupils. Then, under the guidance of al-Natili, I began to study the *Isagogue* [a commentary on some of Aristotle's works]. Thus I learned from him the broad principles of logic, but he knew nothing of the subtleties. Then I began to read books and study commentaries on my own until I mastered logic. I also read the geometry of Euclid. Then I passed on to the *Almagest* [Ptolemy's second-century astronomical treatise]. Eventually I busied myself with the study of the [treatises] and other commentaries on physics and metaphysics [subjects treated at great length by Aristotle and by Avicenna's Arab predecessors, especially al-Farabi], and the doors of knowledge opened before me. Then I took up medicine and began to read books written on this subject. Medicine is not one of the difficult sciences, and in a very short time I undoubtedly excelled in it, so that physicians of merit studied under me. At the same time I carried on debates and controversies in jurisprudence. At this point I was sixteen years old.

I resumed the study of logic and all parts of philosophy. During this time I never slept a whole night through and I did nothing but study all day long. Whenever I was puzzled by a problem . . . I would go to the mosque, pray, and ask the Creator of All to reveal to me that which was hidden from me and to make easy for me that which was difficult. Then at night I would return home, put a lamp in front of me, and set to work reading and writing.

I returned to the study of divine science. I read the book called *Metaphysics* [by Aristotle], but could not understand it, the aim of its author remaining obscure for me. I read the book forty times, until I knew it by heart, but I still could not understand its meaning or its purpose. Then one afternoon I happened to be in the market of the booksellers, and a crier was holding a volume in his hand and shouting the price. I bought it and found that it was Abu'l Nasr al-Farabi's book explaining the meaning of the *Metaphysics*. I returned to my house and made haste to read it. Immediately the purposes of this book became clear to me because I already knew it by heart. I was very happy at this, and the next day I gave much alms to the poor in thanksgiving to Almighty God.

In my neighborhood there lived a man who asked me to write him an encyclopedic work on all the sciences. I compiled the *Majmū* for him and named it after him. In it I dealt with all sciences other than mathematics. I was then twenty-one years old.

## QUESTIONS

1. In what academic subjects was Avicenna particularly interested?

2. In what ways was Avicenna's education like and unlike that received by students in Europe?

3. How did faith and reason play complementary roles in Avicenna's education?

Source: Bernard Lewis, ed., *Islam: From the Prophet Muhammad to the Capture of Constantinople*, vol. 2 (New York: Harper and Row, 1974), pp. 177–181.

 **For additional information on this topic, go to college.hmco.com/students.**

also grappled with Aristotle. Solomon ibn Gebirol (1021–1070), called Avicebron°, wrote *The Fountain of Life*, a treatise that attempted to reconcile Aristotle with the Jewish faith by finding a role for God in communicating knowledge to every human mind. The greatest of all medieval Jewish thinkers, Moses ben Maimon (1135–1204), called Maimonides°, wrote *A Guide for the Perplexed*. The perplexed he had in mind were those who had trou-

---

**Avicebron** (uh-VIH-sih-bron)

**Maimonides** (my-MON-uh-deez)

**Muslim Scholars in a Garden**    From a thirteenth-century Iraqi manuscript, this picture
shows literary men in a pleasure garden. Beasts are driving a water wheel to refresh them,
and a lute player accompanies their poetry with music.    *(Bibliothèque nationale de France)*

ble reconciling the seemingly opposed claims of reason
and faith. Maimonides taught a doctrine very close to
Averroes's double truth.

Solomon ben Isaac (1040–1105), called Rashi, was
educated in Jewish schools in the Rhineland and then set
up his own school in Troyes°. He became the most
learned biblical and Talmudic scholar of his time, indeed
one of the wisest ever. The Talmud was a detailed and
erudite commentary on the scriptural studies of the ancient rabbis. It existed in two collections made in the
fifth century, one in Palestine and one in Babylon. Later
in the twelfth century Rashi's grandsons carried on his
work and earned great fame on their own. Christian

scholars who wished to know the exact meaning of passages in the Bible sometimes consulted them.

From Persia to Spain to France, then, countless
thinkers were engaged in serious reflection on the mechanics of knowing, the nature of reality, the relationship
between reason and faith, and the meaning and significance of revelation. In the years just around 1100 Latin
Christian scholars began to encounter this torrent of
thought and writing.

## The Development of Western Theology

Carolingian schools had focused on grammar—that is,
on the basic foundations of language. Gradually logic
supplanted grammar at the center of both intellectual
interests and school curricula. Problems inside Europe

---

**Troyes** (TWAH)

initiated this shift, but soon the external influences we just described increased its scope. Eventually the wider application of logic produced a new intellectual style and also evoked bitter criticisms.

Berengar (ca. 1000–1088), master of the school of Tours, wrote a treatise that denied Christ's presence in the Eucharist—the Communion bread and wine received by Catholics and Orthodox Christians in the celebration of the mass. This position was heretical. Ordinarily churchmen would have refuted Berengar simply by quoting various passages from the Scriptures or from the writings of the Church Fathers, along with conciliar pronouncements about the consecrated elements. The evidence, however, was ambiguous. Berengar's claim was finally proved false, at least to the satisfaction of his opponents, by Lanfranc, archbishop of Canterbury during the reign of William the Conqueror. Lanfranc used Aristotelian logical argumentation to dispose of Berengar's heretical arguments.

Anselm (ca. 1033–1109), Lanfranc's successor as archbishop of Canterbury, developed an ingenious logical proof for the existence of God. The French theologian and philosopher Peter Abelard (1079–1142) used logic to reconcile apparent contradictions in the Scriptures and in the writings of the Church Fathers. We must not suppose that Anselm and Abelard were skeptics. Anselm's motto was "Faith seeking understanding." For him logic was the servant of divine truth. He would have agreed completely with Abelard's assessment that "faith has no merit with God when it is not the testimony of divine truth that leads us to it, but the evidence of human reason."

For conservatives such as Bernard of Clairvaux (see page 320) and Hildegard of Bingen (1098–1179), however, faith and immediate divine inspiration were primary. To them logical approaches to divine truth were the height of arrogance. Hildegard—well educated, musically gifted, and knowledgeable in medical matters—was perhaps the most profound psychological thinker of her age. More than anyone before her, Hildegard opened up for discussion the feminine aspects of divinity. She, like Bernard, believed that God was to be found deep within the human spirit, not in books full of academic wrangling.

The future lay with Anselm and Abelard, however. Anselm was the most gifted Christian thinker since Augustine. He wrote distinguished works on logic, and his theological treatise *Why God Became Man* (ca. 1100) served for three hundred years as the definitive philosophical and theological explanation of the incarnation of Christ, the central mystery of the Christian faith.

Peter Abelard was a more colorful figure. He argued rudely and violently with all his teachers, though in the end he was probably more intelligent than any of them.

He rose to a keener understanding of Aristotle than anyone in centuries, and he developed a sharper sense of both the power and the limitations of language than anyone since the Greeks. He concerned himself with ethics, too, and was one of the first writers to see intention as more important than simple action.

Abelard seduced and then secretly married Heloise, one of his pupils and the daughter of an influential Paris churchman. Heloise's relatives castrated Abelard for his refusal to live openly with his wife. Abelard then arranged for Heloise to enter a convent, and he joined a monastic community, where he continued writing and teaching. The two carried on a voluminous correspondence that reveals Heloise as a first-rate philosophical thinker and one of her age's most knowledgeable connoisseurs of Classical literature. Some of Abelard's more imaginative ideas earned him formal ecclesiastical condemnations in 1121 and 1140. He popularized the schools of Paris, however, and attracted to them promising scholars from all over Europe.

Abelard and several of his contemporaries engaged in one of the first widespread intellectual debates in Western history, the quarrel over "universals." *Universal* is the philosophical name for a concept that applies to more than one seemingly related object. The dispute over universals went to the heart of people's understanding of reality, their sense of the limitations of human reason, and their awareness of problems of language.

To illustrate: May we agree that you are reading a book right now? May we further agree that the book you are reading is not identical to any other book on your bookshelf? And may we go one step further and agree that no book on your bookshelf is exactly like any other book on that shelf? So, why do we call all of these objects books? "Book" is here the universal that we are trying to understand.

A medieval "realist," whose thought may be traced back to Plato, would say that there is a concept, let us call it "bookness," that exists in our minds before we ever encounter any particular object that we label a book. Just as no book is ever identical to any other, so too no specific book is a perfect representation of that concept "bookness." The concept is fully real, and all representations of it in the world are mere hints, suggestions of a more perfect reality.

A medieval "nominalist," on the contrary, would say that "book" is merely a name (*nomen* in Latin, whence nominalism) that we apply to objects that we deem to bear sufficient similarity to one another that they can be adequately captured by one name. But only each particular book is fully real.

Problems aplenty surround the quarrel over universals: Is reality purely an intellectual proposition, or is reality a quality of existence in the world? How does the mind acquire knowledge of the universal? How does the mind know to which objects to apply the universal? What specific differences exist between objects to which the same name is applied?

With the emergence of the problem of universals, we enter fully into a new intellectual approach that has long been called "Scholasticism." This word has come to have many different meanings, but at the most basic level it describes a movement that attempted to show that Christian theology is inherently rational, that faith and reason need not be contradictory or antithetical. Scholasticism also implies a certain systematization of thought. Gratian's attempt to organize all of canon law rationally and systematically was a Scholastic exercise. Twelfth-century biblical scholars tried to produce a single, systematic commentary on the Bible. In 1160 Peter Lombard produced the *Four Books of Sentences,* a comprehensive treatment of all of Christian theology.

Thomas Aquinas (1225–1274) was the greatest of the Scholastics, the most sensitive to Greek and Arab thought, and the most prolific medieval philosopher. A Dominican friar, Thomas was educated at Naples, Cologne, and Paris. Apart from brief service at the papal court, he spent the years after 1252 teaching and writing in Paris. His two most famous works are the *Summa Contra Gentiles* and the *Summa Theologiae.* A *summa* is an encyclopedic compendium of carefully arrayed knowledge on a particular subject. One might think of Gratian's and Peter Lombard's works as precursors to the great summas of the thirteenth century. Thomas's first summa addresses natural truth—that is, the kinds of things that any person can know through the operation of reason. His second summa is a summation of the revealed truths of the Christian faith.

Thomas's works are distinctive for two reasons. First, no one before him had so rigorously followed the dialectical method of reasoning through a whole field of knowledge, not just a particular problem. For thousands of pages Thomas poses a question, suggests answers, confronts the answers with objections, refutes the objections, and then draws a conclusion. Then he repeats the process. Second, Thomas carefully distinguishes between two kinds of truths. On the one hand are *natural truths,* truths (even theological ones) that anyone can know (or so Thomas thought)—for example, that God exists. On the other hand are *revealed truths,* truths that can be known (if not understood) only through faith in God's revelation—for example, the Trinity or the incarnation of Christ. Thomas maintains that natural and revealed truths simply cannot contradict one another because God is ultimately the

source of both. If a natural truth—for example, Aristotle's contention that the world is eternal—appears to contradict a revealed truth, the natural truth is wrong. Thomas was accused by some contemporaries of applying reason too widely, and after his death some of his ideas were condemned by the church. But he actually steered a middle path between intellectual extremes. In this respect Thomas was like Maimonides and Averroes.

## The University

In the early decades of the twelfth century students gathered wherever famous teachers might be found. Such teachers—figures like Peter Abelard—clustered in a few centers, and the students congregated there as well. The last decades of the twelfth century saw a swarm of masters and students in Paris. Like members of secular guilds (see page 281), the masters organized. The University of Paris was the result of their efforts. By 1300 universities had formed elsewhere in France, as well as in Italy, England, and western Germany.

Several forces drove masters to organize. They wanted to negotiate with the bishop's chancellor, the traditional head of all schools in an episcopal city. They wanted to regulate the curriculum that students followed and to prescribe the requirements for entry into their own ranks. They also desired to set the fees to be charged for instruction. By 1209 the bishop of Paris, the pope, and the king of France had granted formal recognition to the university.

In Bologna the university developed a little differently. Here the students came primarily to study law, after already acquiring a basic education. These law students were usually older and more affluent than students elsewhere, and foreign to Bologna. Consequently, in Bologna the university arose from a guild of students who united to set standards in fees and studies and to protect themselves against unscrupulous masters.

Universities were known for certain specializations: Paris for arts and theology, Bologna for law, Salerno in Italy and Montpellier in France for medicine, Oxford for mathematical and scientific subjects. Still, the basic course of study was similar. At Paris a young scholar came to the city, found lodgings where he could, and attempted to find a master who would guide him through the arts curriculum. These boys might be in their early teens or several years older, depending on their earlier educations and financial resources. The arts course, which was the prerequisite to all higher faculties, usually lasted from four to six years. The bachelor's degree was a license to teach, but a bachelor who wished to teach in a university needed to go on for a master's degree. The master's degree required at least eight years of study (including the baccalaureate years), which culminated in a public oral examination. Some masters went on to become doctors in theology, law, or medicine. A doctorate required ten to fifteen years of study. Medieval academicians were immensely learned.

Student life was difficult. In many ways students were always foreigners. Although their presence in a town enhanced its prestige, townspeople exploited them by charging exorbitant prices for food and rent. Students' own behavior was not always above reproach. There was surely some truth in the frequently lodged charge that students were noisy, quarrelsome, given to drinking, and excessively fond of prostitutes. England's Oxford and Cambridge were unique in always providing residential colleges for students; Paris got one later, and the mendicants often established houses of study. Typically, though, students were on their own.

Students had to work very hard. The arts curriculum demanded a thorough acquaintance with all the famous texts of grammar, logic, and rhetoric. Higher studies added more Aristotle, particularly his philosophical writings. In theology the students had to master the Scriptures, the principal biblical commentaries from patristic times to the present, and the *Four Books of Sentences*. In medicine the ancient writings of Galen and Hippocrates were supplemented by Arab texts as well as by observation and experimentation.

The basic method of teaching provides yet another definition of Scholasticism—that is, the method of studying in the schools. The teacher started by reciting a short piece of a set text, carried on with the presentation and discussion of many authoritative commentaries on that text, and concluded with his own explanations. The teacher then presented another passage of the set text and repeated the whole process. This education focused on standard books and accepted opinions and required students to remember large amounts of material. The curriculum nevertheless produced thinkers of prodigious originality.

In principle, universities were open to free men, but in practice they were restricted to those who had the means to attend them. Women were not accepted at universities, either as students or as teachers. It was generally thought, by men, that learning made women insubordinate. Lacking the required education, women were denied entry into the learned professions of theology, law, and medicine, despite the fact that many rural and some urban medical practitioners were women. Nevertheless, women commonly possessed and transmitted knowledge of both folk remedies and scientific medicine. Trota

of Salerno, who probably lived in the twelfth century, wrote a knowledgeable treatise, *On the Care of Women*. (See the box "The Continuing Experiment: Women and Medicine in Twelfth-Century Salerno.") Documents from medieval Naples record the names of twenty-four women surgeons between 1273 and 1410. How these women were educated is utterly unknown.

## THE VERNACULAR ACHIEVEMENT

A MAJOR achievement of high medieval civilization, from Iceland to Kievan Rus, was the appearance of rich literatures in native tongues. Vernacular, from the Latin *vernaculus,* meaning "homeborn" or "domestic," is the name for the languages other than Latin—say, English or French. Although Latin remained the language of the clerical elite, writers of vernacular prose and poetry produced some of the greatest works in Western literature.

### Literatures and Languages

The number of people who could speak, read, or write Latin was always a minority in western Europe, just as native Greek-speakers were a minority in Byzantium. As Latin, beginning in Late Antiquity, slowly evolved into the Romance (from Roman) languages, people who used what eventually became French, Italian, and Spanish had some advantages over the people in Celtic, Germanic, or Slavic lands, where the languages bore no obvious relationship to Latin. Persons who spoke Old French in their towns and villages would have had an easier time learning Latin than people who spoke Irish or Polish. Nevertheless, vernacular literatures began to appear at roughly the same time all over Europe, between about 800 and 1000.

Of course, many writers continued to use Latin for several centuries. University scholars continued to compose their learned treatises in the ancient tongue, but now often in a style that was less ornate than before. Most law books and public documents were still in Latin, but in a "vulgar" Latin that was reasonably close to the vernacular in areas where Romance languages were spoken. Technical manuals—on farming and animal husbandry, on warfare and armaments, or on law and government—were prepared in Latin, too, but again in a style that was far more accessible than that of their ancient models. Popular literature—poetry, history and biography, and romance and adventure—was still often written in Latin. Some of this material was serious, but some breathed a

# Women and Medicine in Twelfth-Century Salerno

Late in the twelfth century an anonymous author compiled three lengthy medical texts into one that came to be called the "Trotula." The second of these treatises, "On the Cures of Women," was almost certainly written by a woman named Trota. For centuries scholars argued that a woman could not have written the widely disseminated Trotula because women could neither study nor teach in the Salerno schools. Absolutely nothing is known about Trota herself, but her text presents an intriguing question: How was she able to acquire vast learning in the Greek, Arab, and Persian medical traditions? Perhaps Trota "practiced" medicine. Whatever the case, most of her text involves either physical appearance or problems connected with menstruation and childbirth. Trota's treatise put her ahead of her time, but just maybe there were other women like her, concealed by ignorance and prejudice.

There are some women who, when they come to their time of menstruation, have either no or very few menses. For these, we proceed thus. Take root of the red willow with which large wine jars are tied and clean them well of the exterior bark, and, having pulverized them, mix them with wine or water and cook them, and in the morning give them in a potion when it has become lukewarm.

To those giving birth with difficulty we give aid in this manner. We should prepare a bath and we put the woman in it, and after she leaves let there be a fumigation of spikenard and similar aromatic substances. For strengthening and for opening the birth canal, let there be sternutatives [substances that induce sneezing] of white hellebore well ground into a powder. For just as Copho [a twelfth-century Salerno medical teacher] says, the organs are shaken and the uterus ruptures and thus the fetus is brought out and comes out.

For making the face red, take root of red and white bryony and clean it and chop it finely and dry it. Afterward, powder it and mix it with rose water, and with cotton or a very fine cloth we anoint the face and it induces redness. For the woman having a naturally white complexion, we make a red color if she lacks redness, so that with a kind of fake or cloaked whiteness a red color will appear as if it were natural.

For freckles of the face which appear by accident, take root of bistort and reduce it to powder, and cuttlefish bones and frankincense, and from all these things make a powder. And mix with a little water and smear it, rubbing, on the (face) in the morning . . . until you have removed the freckles.

An ointment for whitening the face. Take two ounces of the very best white lead, let them be ground; afterward let them be sifted through a cloth, and that which remains in the cloth, let it be thrown out. Let it be mixed in with rainwater and let it cook until the consumption of the water, which can be recognized when we see it almost completely dried out. Then let it be cooled. And when it is dried out and cooled, let rose water be added, and again boil it until it becomes hard and thick, so that from it very small pills can be formed. And when you wish to be anointed, take one pill and liquefy it in the hand with water and then rub it well on the face, so that the face will be dried. Then let it be washed with pure water, and this will last for eight days.

## QUESTIONS

1. Does it make sense that a medical treatise by a woman would emphasize issues of particular concern to women?

2. Why do you suppose that scholars long refused to believe that a woman could have written this book?

3. Do you detect in Trota's writing evidence of experimental, empirical science?

SOURCE: Monica H. Green, ed. and trans., *The Trotula: A Medieval Compendium of Women's Medicine* (Philadelphia: University of Pennsylvania Press, 2001), pp. 117–119, 139, 141, 163. Reprinted by permission of the University of Pennsylvania Press.

light and carefree spirit. The anonymous German known as the Archpoet (d. 1165) wrote poems about drinking and womanizing. These lines are typical of his work:

> In the public house to die
> Is my resolution;
> Let wine to my lips be nigh
> At life's dissolution:

> That will make the angels cry,
> With glad elocution
> "Grant this drunkard, God on high,
> Grace and Absolution!"[1]

No less insouciant were the authors of biting satires such as the anonymous *The Gospel According to the Silver Marks*, which parodies the wealth and greed of the papal curia.

# Paper

Today paper is so common and so plentiful that we scarcely give it a moment's notice. The words you are reading right now are printed on paper. Chances are, you have paper of several kinds, sizes, thicknesses, and colors around your desk. But paper was not always so familiar. In Europe paper was not widely used before 1300 and did not supplant parchment as a writing material until about 1600. Where did paper come from? What is it, exactly, and how is it made? Why is it important?

The Chinese invented paper, probably in the second century B.C. For two or three centuries, however, the Chinese did not discern paper's possibilities as a writing material. Instead, they used it as a wrapping material, for personal hygiene—rather like a tissue—and for clothing. By A.D. 100 the Chinese had adopted paper as their preferred writing material. For centuries thereafter they kept the papermaking process a closely guarded secret.

Legend has it that in 751 the Arabs learned the art of papermaking from some Chinese prisoners of war in Samarkand and carried the knowledge westward into the caliphate. Until perhaps 1200 the Arabs kept the secret from contemporary Christians, largely because they were able to sell paper in Mediterranean ports at hugely profitable prices. The oldest surviving Western paper document is the 1102 will of Adelaide of Sicily, the widow of King Roger I. Gradually Christians in Sicily and Spain, places with intense Muslim-Christian contacts, learned how to make paper. By the thirteenth century there were a number of papermaking centers in Italy, southern France, and Spain. By 1500 the paper industry was flourishing all over Europe.

Paper takes its name from papyrus, the writing material common in antiquity but largely replaced by parchment (see page 272) in the early Middle Ages. Paper and papyrus are, however, utterly different. Papyrus was made from the inner bark of the papyrus plant, whereas the Chinese originally made paper from pulpy plants such as flax or hemp. Gradually the Chinese learned to make paper from rags, or discarded textiles. The Arabs learned how to make rag paper and communicated this knowledge to the Christian West. Today most paper is made from wood pulp.

A medieval papermaker put rags and water in a cauldron and repeatedly stirred and beat the contents, sometimes over heat, until a thick, gooey film formed on the surface. The papermaker then dragged a square or rectangular metal frame with tiny perforations in it through the thick mixture. When he pulled out the frame, it had a thin coating of the fluid, known as the "deckel." After the deckel was dry, he peeled it off the frame and placed it on a sheet of felt. Another felt cloth was then placed on top of the deckel, followed by another deckel, another felt cloth, and so forth, until the pile was perhaps a foot high. Using a mechanical press, the papermaker removed excess moisture

---

But after 1200 this fresh spirit was largely confined to writings in the vernacular. For after that year Latin was rarely used as the language for serious, original literary compositions. (See the feature "Information Technology: Paper.")

The literary masterpieces of the High Middle Ages are almost entirely written in vernacular languages. The epic poem *Beowulf* is the first classic of English literature. We do not know who wrote it or when it was written. Scholars formerly assigned it to the eighth century, but they now usually place it later, in the ninth or possibly the tenth century. The story focuses on three great battles fought by the hero, Beowulf°. The first two are against the monster Grendel and Grendel's mother, who have been harrying the kingdom of an old ally of Beowulf's family; the third is against a dragon. *Beowulf* is a poem of adventure and heroism, of loyalty and treachery. It treats lordship, friendship, and kinship. Themes of good and evil resound throughout. The poem is barely Christian but nevertheless deeply moral. It speaks, in a mature, vigorous, and moving language, to and for the heart of a warrior society.

*Beowulf* is the best-known Anglo-Saxon work but by no means the only one. One of the Viking attacks that led to the undoing of Ethelred II was commemorated in *The Battle of Maldon*. Several volumes of elegiac and lyric poetry, mostly on religious themes, also survive. And Anglo-Saxon writers produced chronicles, legal materials and charters, and at least one large collection of homilies.

Some fragments of poetry in Old French survive from the ninth century, but the great *chansons de gestes* ("songs of deeds," or celebrations of the great) appeared in the eleventh century. Undoubtedly they were transmitted

---

Beowulf (BAY-oh-wolf)

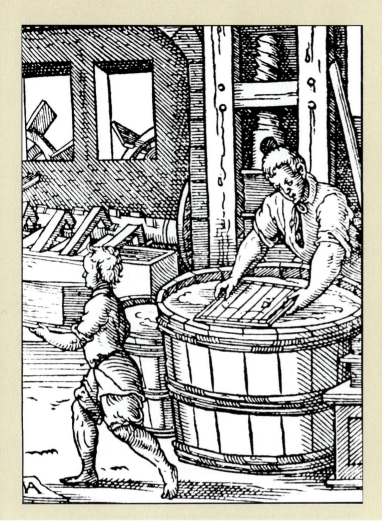

from the pile of deckels and felt. He then hung up the deckels—now paper—to dry. Finally he "sized" the sheets, coating them with animal glue so that they would accept ink without smudging.

Paper's historical importance may be considered from several points of view. Paper provides an exceptionally good example of a technology that the West learned from other people, and it illustrates how technologies can travel long distances. The wider use of paper promoted business firms dedicated to selling notebooks, tablets, and fine single sheets. Written documents ranging from personal letters to public records became more numerous once a cheaper writing material became more readily available. One scholar suggests that alphabetization became widespread only after the existence of paper made the arranging of disposable slips feasible. When printing (about which you will learn in Chapter 12; see page 414) was introduced into Europe, the possibility arose of quickly making multiple copies of a given book or document. Parchment was too expensive for this purpose. Thus the more rapid dissemination of books and ideas that marks the transition from the medieval to the modern world was facilitated by the fortunate conjunction of paper and printing.

**Woodcut by Jost Amman, the Oldest Illustration of Papermaking** Note the vat, frame, and press. The printer's assistant ("devil") is carrying away deckels to dry. *(From Jules Heller,* Papermaking *[New York: Watson-Guptill Publications, 1978]. Reproduced with permission.)*

orally for a long time before they were written down. The best is the *Song of Roland,* written around 1100. In 778 as Charlemagne's army was returning from Spain, Basques raided the baggage train and killed Count Roland. By 1100 this obscure event, long kept alive in oral traditions, had been transformed into a heroic struggle between Charlemagne and his retinue and an army of countless thousands of "paynim," who are crude caricatures of Muslims.

Like *Beowulf,* the *Song of Roland* is a story about loyalty and treachery, bravery in the face of insuperable odds, and the kindness and generosity of leaders. Both take us into a man's chivalric world, where females are all but absent. The two works do not show us personal hopes, fears, or motivations. What pours forth is the communal ethos and the dominant values of the elite, male social group. Although *Beowulf* is lightly clothed in Christianity, the *Song of Roland* is thickly vested in the faith.

The heroic epic tradition that *Beowulf* and the *Song of Roland* represent did not disappear as the Middle Ages unfolded, but literary energies were applied in new directions. Southern France, in the middle and late twelfth century, added something new to Western literature: the love lyrics of the troubadours. This poetry, composed by both men and women, profoundly influenced an age and created the literary movement that has long been called "courtly love." Chivalry was initially a code for men interacting with other men. In the world of courtly love, chivalry became an elaborate set of rules governing relations between men and women.

Courtly love had several sources. The classical poet Ovid (43 B.C.–?A.D. 17), who wrote *The Art of Love,* a manual of seduction, was one. Another was the lyrical poetry of Muslim Spain. Ironically, feudal values such as loyalty and service played a critical role as men became, in effect, love vassals. Platonic ideas made some contribution, too, particularly the notion that any love in this world could be only a pale imitation of real love. The courtly poets sang of *fin'amours,* a pure love in contrast to the mere lust of the masses. A lover cherished an unattainable lady. He would do anything for the merest display of pleasure or gratitude on her part, as we see in these lines from Bernart de Ventadorn, court poet of the counts of Toulouse in the late twelfth century:

> Down there, around Ventadorn, all my friends
> have lost me, because my lady does not love me;
> and so, it is right that I never go back there again,
> because always she is wild and morose with me.
> Now here is why the face she shows me is gloomy and
>     full of anger:
> because my pleasure is in loving her and I have settled
>     down to it.
> She is resentful and complains for no other reason.[2]

Male troubadours placed women on pedestals and, in ballads, worshiped them from afar. Women troubadours took a different line. Women's poems were more realistic, human, and emotionally satisfying. Castellozza° (b. ca. 1200), the southern French wife of a Crusader, idealized not at all when she wrote these lines:

> Friend, if you had shown consideration,
> meekness, candor and humanity,
> I'd have loved you without hesitation,
> but you were mean and sly and villainous.

And she did not assign the active role exclusively to the man:

> Handsome friend, as a lover true
> I loved you, for you pleased me,
> But now I see I was a fool,
> for I've barely seen you since.[3]

Count William IX of Poitou° (1071–1127) was among the first of the troubadours, and his daughter, Eleanor of Aquitaine, brought the conventions of this poetry and point of view to the French and Angevin courts. She and her daughters were the greatest literary patrons of the late twelfth century. The wives of kings and nobles who were frequently away from home maintained stunning courts and cultivated vernacular literature.

The courtly literature of northern France owed much to the troubadour tradition of the south but broke new ground in both forms and content. The romance and the lay were the chief new forms. Both drew on Classical literature, the heroic Germanic past, and the Arthurian legends of the Celtic world to create stories of love and adventure. The romance usually develops a complex narrative involving several major characters over a long time. The lay is brief and focuses on a single incident. The most famous twelfth-century writer of romance was Chrétien de Troyes (1135–1183), the court writer of Marie of Champagne, the daughter of Eleanor of Aquitaine. The greatest writer of lays was Marie de France, who wrote at the Angevin court in the 1170s.

The romances and lays explore the contradictions and tensions in a variety of human relationships. Loyalty and honor make frequent appearances. Lancelot, a paragon of knightly virtue, desperately loves his lord Arthur's wife, Guinevere. What is he to do? How can he be loyal to his lord, to his love, and to himself? What will he do when a single course of action brings both honor and dishonor? In the epics speeches are made to swords, to horses, or sometimes to no one in particular; the points being made are universalized. In the romances credible human beings struggle to resolve powerful and conflicting emotional and moral dilemmas.

Slavic literatures began with the missionaries Cyril and Methodius (see page 265), who developed both a language, Church Slavonic, and a script, Glagolitic. The Glagolitic script was modified into the Cyrillic, which was adopted by all the Slavic peoples who embraced Orthodoxy and remains in use today. The earliest writing in the Slavic languages was religious: biblical translations, saints' lives, and selections from the Church Fathers. Historical writings and imaginative literature, such as the *Tale of Igor*, made their appearance in Kievan Rus in the twelfth century. The latter work, a semilegendary account of Prince Igor and his many battles, is reminiscent of the *chansons des gestes.*

The Scandinavians who settled Iceland produced a diverse literature. They created law books, detailed accounts of their settlements, and a mighty saga tradition. *Saga* means "things said," and it is almost certainly the case that the greatest sagas were oral tales long before they were written down between about 1150 and 1350. Sagas fall into two categories: Historical sagas blend fact and fiction to praise the deeds of the great heroes of the Viking age. Family sagas mix history and myth to relate the stories of the great families who settled Iceland.

France led the way in the production of vernacular literature, but French models did not inspire slavish imitation. This is seen most clearly in the work of the master of all vernacular writers, Dante Alighieri° (1265–1321).

---

**Castellozza** (KAHS-teh-lohtz-eh)  **Poitou** (PWAH-too)

**Dante Alighieri** (DAHN-tay ah-lih-GYAIR-ee)

Dante began as a poet in *la dolce stil nuova,* "the sweet new style," which came from France and captivated Italians. But he moved beyond it in many ways. Dante was a man of extraordinarily wide learning and reading. He served Florence in public capacities and became an exile amid political strife. He wrote a long treatise in defense of the empire—or, really, against the secular rule of the church. But he is best known for one of the masterpieces of world literature, *The Divine Comedy.*

The secret of the *Comedy's* success is not easy to grasp. It is a long and difficult poem, but it is also humorous, instructive, and moving. In an exquisitely beautiful Italian, Dante took the most advanced theology and philosophy of his time, the richest poetic traditions, a huge hoard of stories, many contemporary events, and a lot of common sense and wove them into an allegorical presentation of the journey of the whole human race and of the individual lives of all people.

Accompanied by the Roman poet Virgil (see page 179), Dante travels through Hell and Purgatory, commenting along the way on the condition of the people he meets. Then, because Virgil is a pagan and only Dante's true love can accompany Dante into paradise, Beatrice, the love of Dante's youth, joins him for a visit to Heaven. The poet's central metaphor is love; the love he feels for Beatrice symbolizes the love God feels for the world. Dante canvasses humanity from the pits of Hell, which he reserved for traitors, to the summit of Paradise, where a man inspired by pure love might, despite his sinfulness, dare to look into the face of God.

Although the romances and lays were by no means the exclusive preserve of the elite, very little is known about popular literature. Two exceptions are the mystery play and women's devotional writing. Mystery plays made their first appearance in the eleventh century. The liturgy of the church, which formally re-enacted the life of Christ, was confined to the clergy. But this limitation did not prevent troupes of actors from staging, on church porches or village greens, scenes from the life of Christ in simple, direct language. By the twelfth and thirteenth centuries guilds in many towns sponsored the production of plays commemorating the Christian mysteries. Such plays served as both a form of popular entertainment and a device for teaching elementary Christian ideas. The female religious movements of the age gave rise to prose and verse works in various vernaculars. Mechtild of Magdeburg (1210–1280), a German Beguine, wrote *The Flowering Light of Divinity,* a mystical, allegorical account of the marriage between God and a spiritual woman. The vernaculars opened avenues of expression to women, who were normally denied Latin learning.

## Innovations in Architecture

*Romanesque,* "in the Roman style," is a term that was coined in the nineteenth century to characterize the architecture and, to a lesser extent, the painting of the period between the waning of Carolingian art and the full emergence of Gothic art in the late twelfth century. Today scholars view the Romanesque style as a transition between Carolingian and Gothic.

At several places in Ottonian Germany, a return of political stability led to the construction of churches. Ducal dynasties and women of the imperial family were among the most generous patrons. Pride in their Carolingian inheritance and their new imperial dignity led the Germans to a distinctive architectural style marked by very thick walls, alternating piers and columns in the nave, and galleries. As this architectural style spread all over Europe in the eleventh century, it produced true Romanesque, a style that differed from Roman and Carolingian styles mainly in the greater internal height and space made possible by vaulting (see Figure 10.1). To the rectangular elegance of the classical basilica and the height of the Carolingian westworks (see page 264), Romanesque builders added a refined verticality.

Among the distinctive features of Romanesque churches were their wall paintings and frescoes, sculpture, reliquaries, pulpits, and baptisteries—in short, their exuberant decoration and ornament. Europe's growing wealth and sophistication, and the pride of the church's aristocratic patrons, are very much in evidence. Especially in

**Figure 10.1    The Structure of Romanesque Architecture**
The basic structural element of Romanesque architecture was the barrel vault, which, when two were joined at right angles, formed a groin vault. These vaults produced great height and strength but gave buildings a massive, fortresslike appearance.
*(Source: Anne Shaver-Crandell,* The Middle Ages. *Copyright © 1982 Cambridge University Press. Reprinted with permission of Cambridge University Press.)*

**Barrel vault**          **Groin vault**

**Romanesque Exterior, Saint Sernin, Toulouse**    This fortresslike church (ca. 1080–1120) was paid for by the offerings of pilgrims on their way to shrines in Spain. Its massive walls and numerous colonnades are typical of Romanesque architecture. The form of the building suggests the cross of Christ. For the interior of this church, see the facing page.    *(Jean Dieuzaid, Toulouse)*

the south of France, the façades of Romanesque churches provided space for sculpture. The tympanum above the doors, a space seen by all who entered, was a favored location. Large-scale sculpture made a comeback after its almost total absence in the early Middle Ages.

It is surely no coincidence that Gothic art and architecture emerged just as the West was absorbing the rediscovery of Euclid's mathematical writings and applying the intensely ordered logic of Aristotle to everything from legal problems to theological mysteries. One of the most familiar images of the Middle Ages is the inspiringly beautiful Gothic cathedral. It is thus ironic that the word *Gothic* first appeared in the sixteenth century as a term of deri-

sion for what was then regarded as an outmoded style so ugly that only the horrible conquerors of Rome, the Goths, could have been responsible for it. The name stuck, but today it simply identifies a period in European architecture, sculpture, and painting that began in the middle of the twelfth century and that in some places lasted until the early sixteenth century.

Gothic is a French invention. It was Abbot Suger° (1085–1151) of Saint-Denis, a monastery outside Paris, who, in rebuilding his basilica beginning in 1135, con-

---

**Suger** (SOO-jhay)

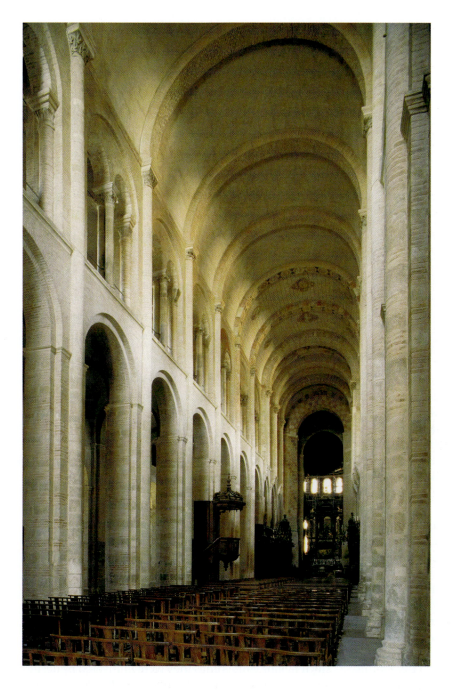

**Romanesque Interior, Saint Sernin, Toulouse**   The interior space of Saint Sernin is elegant, high, and well-ordered. But its typical Romanesque effect—from "barrel" vaulting—is that of a tunnel. Massive piers support the gallery and roofing above.   *(Éditions Gaud)*

sciously sought a new style. He desired to achieve effects of lightness, almost weightlessness, in the stonework of his church and to admit large amounts of light to create a dazzling and mysterious aura on the inside. The Bible often uses images of light to refer to God, and Suger wished to give expression to those images in the house of God for which he was responsible.

Suger produced something startlingly original by combining a number of elements that had long been in use—three in particular: A *pointed arch* is more elegant than a round one; it also permits the joining of two arches of identical height but different widths, which, in turn, permits complex shapes and sizes (see Figure 10.2). The *ribbed vault* is lighter and more graceful than the

**Figure 10.2    The Structure of Gothic Architecture**    The adoption of pointed arches, an import from the Islamic world, let Gothic builders join structures of identical height but different widths (something that barrel and groin vaulting could not do; see Figure 10.1 on page 345). The resulting structures were high, light, airy, and visually interesting. *(Source: Anne Shaver-Crandell,* The Middle Ages. *Copyright © 1982 Cambridge University Press. Reprinted with permission of Cambridge University Press.)*

barrel and groin vaults characteristic of Romanesque architecture; it also exerts less stress and facilitates experimentation with shapes. Finally, *point support*—basically, the support of structural elements at only certain points—permits the replacement of heavy, stress-bearing walls with curtains of stained glass. The points of support might be massive internal piers or intricate skeletal frameworks, called *buttresses,* on the outside of the church.

These three elements—pointed arch, ribbed vault, and point support—produce a building that is characterized by verticality and translucency. Everything seems to spring upward, and stone surfaces appear so frequently punctured by light as almost to disappear altogether. The desired, and achieved, effect is one of harmony, order, and mathematical precision.

The Gothic style soon spread in central and northern France. The cathedral of Notre-Dame of Paris was built beginning in the 1150s, and the royal portal at Chartres Cathedral was reconstructed after 1145. Gothic churches could be huge. The interior of Notre-Dame, for example, is 493 feet long and 107 feet high. To avoid a sense of sheer mass, Gothic builders used triple or quadruple elevations inside the buildings and took advantage of point support to pierce the walls at frequent intervals with stained glass windows. Exterior surfaces were broken up with windows, sculptures, colonnades, and towers. No opportunity was missed to create visual interest and complexity. (See the feature "Weighing the Evidence: Stained Glass" on pages 350–351.)

The thirteenth century was the most mature period for French Gothic architecture and also the time when Gothic spread most widely throughout Europe. Its popularity may be attributed to the superiority of French masons and stonecutters and also to the tremendous prestige of French culture. By 1300 distinctive Gothic traditions shaped the urban landscape in almost all parts of Europe from Iceland to Poland.

## SUMMARY

COMPARISONS between the Europe of 900 and the Europe of 1300 are instructive both as reminders of what had happened and as suggestions of what was to come. In 900 Carolingian Europe was being attacked on every side. By 1300 Europe was vastly larger than in Carolingian times; not only was its geography greater, but it also had expanded in economic, political, military, and cultural terms.

Europe's traditional social orders—the "three Estates" as they would later be called—came fully into view after 900. Described by contemporaries as prayers, fighters, and workers, these orders accounted for some but not all of the major groups. The clergy was more numerous and more diverse in structure than ever before. Women played important roles as nuns, writers, and reformers. The nobility was more tightly organized into lineages, and an aristocratic ethos, chivalry, characterized noble lifestyles. Some peasants gained in personal freedom, others lost; some grew more prosperous and comfortable, others lived in want and misery. The townsfolk of an expanding Europe constituted a growing and increasingly important group that was never a part of the society of rural gentlemen warriors. Minorities, chiefly Jews, enjoyed some new opportunities in the High Middle Ages but also suffered attacks and prejudice.

Large-scale social movements appeared for the first time in Western history. These movements were generally religious. Sometimes they were motivated by desires to reform the church, and sometimes they arose from a longing for the primitive, pristine days of Christianity. A few of the movements, the Waldensians and Albigensians, for example, would end up as heresies. Other groups, the mendicants above all others, managed to accommodate themselves to the church and thus lent it their energy and insight. For the first time women played important roles in the new religious movements.

As Europe expanded, Latin Christendom encountered long-lost Classical learning as well as Arab and Jew-

**Gothic Exterior, Notre-Dame, Paris**   In this view of Notre-Dame from the south side (from the Left Bank of the Seine) you can see (*on the left*) the triple elevation of the Gothic nave, the transept (crossing) with its huge yet delicate rose window, and (*on the right*) the choir with its flying buttresses.   *(David R. Frazier/Photo Researchers)*

ish thought. The cultural life of the traditional intellectual centers—monastic and cathedral schools—was immeasurably enriched by these cultural meetings and mixings. Gradually European intellectual life was so stimulated that a new approach to scholarship—Scholasticism—and a new kind of institution—the university—ensued.

While Latin remained the language of lecture hall and courtroom, vernacular languages took their place alongside the ancient tongue. Impressive literatures in prose and verse arose from Iceland to Kievan Rus. Tales of love and adventure predominated in vernacular literatures, but inspiring moral and religious works appeared, too. Women contributed in many languages. In addition to those literatures, the high medieval period saw first Romanesque and then Gothic architecture.

As the fourteenth century dawned, people all over Europe had reasons to be both hopeful and anxious. They were, in fact, at the start of one of the most turbulent and creative periods in Western history, a period when crisis after crisis would afflict the expanded Europe and the spectacular achievements of the High Middle Ages.

### ■ Notes

1. John Addington Symonds, *Wine, Women and Song: Medieval Latin Students' Songs* (reprint, New York: Cooper Square, 1966), p. 69.
2. Frederick Goldin, *Lyrics of the Troubadours and Trouvères: An Anthology and a History* (New York: Doubleday, 1973), p. 135.

*(continued on page 352)*

# Stained Glass

To walk into one of Europe's great churches is to enter a realm of mystery and beauty produced by the play of light—the brilliant light of the morning sun, the softer glow of the evening sun, the muted tones of a cloudy day—on thousands of square feet of colored glass. This mystery and beauty were created intentionally in Europe in the High Middle Ages. But the magnificent surviving medieval windows are not important solely for their beauty. Their images provide unique and crucial insights into religious and secular life.

Pictured here are two thirteenth-century cathedral windows. The one from Canterbury depicts that city's great bishop and martyr, Thomas Becket. A large window at Chartres depicts Saint Lubin, a sixth-century bishop of the city who was the patron saint of the town's inn and tavern keepers, and Noah, according to the Bible the first planter of grapevines. Here, in a window donated by the vintners guild, we see barrels of wine being hauled to market.

Many of Canterbury's windows represent aspects of the life of the murdered archbishop. The one pictured here shows Thomas as a bishop, not as a martyr. He is wearing a miter, the traditional headgear of a bishop. He also wears a *pallium,* a white wool band sent to a new archbishop by the pope. Becket's vestments are green, the most common liturgical color of the religious year (others were white, purple, and red). This window, then, would have served to remind people of their beloved bishop as he was in life, not martyrdom.

In Chartres wine was important to the church because of its use in mass, and it was also a staple of the local economy. Accordingly, the vintners are portrayed in twenty-three of this window's forty-one panels. By comparison, most guilds are depicted only once in the windows they donated. These windows remind us, as they reminded contemporaries, of how these magnificent buildings fitted into the daily life of their communities. Religious devotions and secular preoccupations blended in one spot.

Glass is made by heating silica, found naturally in sand, flint, and quartz, to a very high temperature and then fusing the molten silicate with a borate or phosphate often obtained from ashes produced by burning natural substances. Colored glass was made by adding metal oxides to the molten mixture. Iron oxide produced red, copper oxide produced green, and cobalt produced blue. Such glass, called "pot glass," tended to be opaque, obviously unsuitable for windows. To achieve greater translucency, glassmakers made "flashed glass" by fusing at low temperatures a layer of colored liquid to the surface of a panel of clear glass. Although fine glass vessels were made in a number of places, notably in Venice and the Rhineland, the large sheets of colored glass used for church windows were commonly manufactured in Lorraine and Normandy.

To make a stained glass window, a master glazier first drew a cartoon—a sort of rough draft—on a flat board, or perhaps on a piece of parchment. He then cut pieces of colored glass into various irregular shapes according to his design. To produce facial features, folds in garments, or other details, the glazier painted the inner sides of the colored glass pieces with dark-colored paints and then fired them at low temperatures to produce an enamel-like effect. You can see this patina on Thomas's face. Once the glazier had all his pieces cut and placed, he joined them together by means of lead strips that were **H** shaped. If you look closely, you can see the pieces of glass, lead stripping, and painted details in the images on these pages. The whole picture was then fitted into a metal frame and mounted in a window opening.

Documents first mention the use of glass in church windows in the sixth century. The oldest surviving fragments of stained glass date from the ninth century, and the oldest complete windows from around 1100. With large Romanesque churches, and even more with the huge Gothic churches, came opportunities to use more and more glass. First the greater height of Romanesque buildings meant that tall windows could be placed high up in the nave walls. Then the structural innovations of Gothic architecture that removed stress, and hence stone, from the walls permitted them to become vast expanses of glass. Chartres Cathedral has 176 windows. Many high medieval churches had windows more than 50 feet high.

So far we have looked at *how* medieval Europeans created stained glass and incorporated it into their greatest churches. But *why* did they undertake such time-consuming and costly decoration? Suger, the scholarly twelfth-century abbot of Saint-Denis outside Paris who rebuilt his basilica in the Gothic style, spoke of the spiritual force of his new glass windows:

> When . . . the loveliness of the many-colored gems has called me away from external cares . . . then it seems

**Canterbury, Thirteenth-Century Window:
Thomas Becket** *(Sonia Halliday Photographs)*

**Chartres, Thirteenth-Century Window:
Story of Saint Lubin** *(© Clive Hicks)*

to me that I see myself dwelling in some strange region of the universe which neither exists entirely in the slime of the earth nor entirely in the purity of heaven; and that, by the grace of God, I can be transported from this inferior to that higher world.*

In the Greek philosophers, the Bible, and the Church Fathers, light always represents one way of imagining the unimaginable reality of God. For Suger and his contemporaries the luminous effect of stained glass suggested the very presence of God.

Earthquakes, fires, and wars have destroyed most of the glass that was installed in the Middle Ages. Today's visitor to Europe views more or less valid nineteenth-

century reconstructions, except at Canterbury in England and Chartres in France, where almost all of the original glass survives. Usually medieval churches were laid out on an east-west axis. The western façade was normally pierced by tall "lancet" windows and by a single "rose" window (look at the southern rose window of Notre-Dame on page 349). These windows typically portrayed scenes from the life of Christ and/or the Virgin Mary. The northern aisle windows usually contained Old Testament scenes, the southern windows New Testament scenes.

Stained glass played a key role, alongside sculpture, preaching, and churchyard dramas, in communicating the faith to ordinary people. Seldom has a teaching tool been so beautiful. Scholars also speak of stained glass as "painting with glass." Indeed, the art form most like stained glass is painting, especially the painting of illuminations on the pages of manuscripts.

*Suger, *De rebus in administratione sua gestis*, ed. E. Panofsky, 2d ed. (Princeton, N.J.: Princeton University Press, 1979), pp. 63–65.

351

3. Meg Bogin, *The Women Troubadours* (New York: Norton, 1976), p. 69.

## ■ Suggested Reading

Bony, Jean. *French Gothic Architecture of the Twelfth and Thirteenth Centuries.* 1983. Huge, clearly presented, and magnificently illustrated, this is a browser's book as well as a sustained essay by a master of his subject.

Bouchard, Constance B. *Strong of Body, Brave and Noble: Chivalry and Society in Medieval France.* 1998. A superb summation of the social and cultural history of the medieval aristocracy.

Bynum, Caroline Walker. *Jesus as Mother: Studies in the Spirituality of the High Middle Ages.* 1982. A collection of sparkling essays by a major historian that makes the feminine in religious thought accessible, even central, to any discussion of medieval religion.

Colish, Marcia. *Medieval Foundations of the Western Intellectual Tradition.* 1997. The first original and comprehensive history of medieval thought in a generation.

Grundmann, Herbert. *Religious Movements in the Middle Ages.* 1995. Translated into English sixty years after its appearance in German, this book has lost none of its interest or explanatory power.

Jaeger, C. Stephen. *Ennobling Love: In Search of a Lost Sensibility.* 1999. A beautiful and moving interpretation of the love literature of the High Middle Ages and of its philosophical and theological dimensions.

Lambert, Malcolm. *Medieval Heresy: Popular Movements from the Gregorian Reform to the Reformation.* 3d ed. 2002. Brilliant and readable, this book is the best history of medieval heresy ever written and one of the best books on medieval religion generally.

Southern, R. W. *Scholastic Humanism and the Unification of Europe.* 1995. A truly brilliant overview of twelfth-century culture by its greatest twentieth-century student.

---

**For a searchable list of additional readings for this chapter, go to college.hmco.com/students.**

Questa e lentrata et luscita della generale biccherna del chomuo
disiena fatta altempo de saui huomini thomme di nostro ditu
ra chamarlengho per uno anno chominando adi pmo digiennaio 1436
et finito adi ultimo didicebre 1437. et dichecho di sogino. misser baldassarre

I N the fourteenth century, Europeans sang an old Franciscan hymn, "Day of Wrath, Day of Burning." Its verses described the fear and disorder that would accompany the end of the world and God's judgment of the saved and the damned. That hymn could well have been in the mind of the painter of the facing illustration. When countless Europeans, such as these poor souls beneath the winged angel of death, fell victim to epidemic disease, many people thought they knew why. The illustrator seems to believe it was God's judgment against sinners, including these gamblers sickened by the angel's plague-tipped arrows. The flood, fire, and pestilence that ravaged late medieval Europe were thought to be premonitions of the breakdown of the world and a time of judgment.

The late Middle Ages (ca. 1300–1500) are often described as a period of continued crisis and decline that put an end to the growth and expansion of the previous three centuries. In truth, however, the years of crisis in the fourteenth and early fifteenth centuries gave way to a dramatic economic, social, and political recovery in the fifteenth century. The cultural and intellectual changes that accompanied the crisis and recovery are the focus of Chapter 12, "The Renaissance."

Military, political, religious, economic, and social crises burdened Europe in the fourteenth and early fifteenth centuries. Between 1337 and 1453 France and England fought a war that touched most of the states of western Europe. The Hundred Years' War, as it has come to be known, was fought primarily over English claims to traditionally French lands. Problems were not confined to England and France. Aristocrats in many parts of Europe challenged the hereditary rights of their rulers. In the towns of Germany and Italy patrician classes

Painted cover for a fifteenth-century government account book from Siena, Italy, showing symbols of death—arrows, a scythe, and a horse—to carry the angel of death from place to place. (Staatliche Museen zu Berlin, Preussischer Kulturbesitz Kunstgewerbemuseum/Bildarchiv Preussischer Kulturbesitz. Photo: Mues-Funke)

# Crisis and Recovery in Late Medieval Europe 1300–1500

**The Crisis of the Western Christian Church**

**War and the Struggle over Political Power, 1300–1450**

**Economy and Society**

**The Consolidation of the Late Medieval Governments, 1450–1500**

moved to reduce the influence of artisans and laborers in government, instituting oligarchies or even aristocratic lordships in place of more democratic governments.

Questions of power and representation also affected the Christian church as ecclesiastical claims to authority came under attack. Secular governments challenged church jurisdictions. Disputed papal elections led to the so-called Great Schism, a split between rival centers of control in Rome and Avignon (a city in what is now the south of France). In the aftermath of the crisis, the papacy was forced to redefine its place in both the religious life and the political life of Europe.

A series of economic and demographic shocks worsened these political and religious difficulties. Part of the problem was structural: the population of Europe had grown too large to be supported by the resources available. Famine and the return of the plague in 1348 sent the economy into long-term decline. In almost every aspect of political, religious, and social life, then, the fourteenth and early fifteenth centuries marked a pause in the growth and consolidation that had characterized the earlier medieval period.

Yet out of the crises a number of significant changes emerged. By 1500 the European population and economy were again expanding. England and France emerged strengthened by military and political conflicts. And the consolidation of the Spanish kingdoms, the Ottoman Empire, and the states of eastern Europe altered the political and social makeup of Europe. None of the transformations could have been predicted in 1300 as Europe entered a religious, political, and social whirlwind.

## QUESTIONS TO CONSIDER

- How did the Great Schism change the church and the papacy?
- What forces worked to limit the power of rulers in the fourteenth and early fifteenth centuries?
- What was the impact of the Black Death?
- How did the political makeup of Europe in 1500 differ from that in 1300?

## TERMS TO KNOW

| | |
|---|---|
| Babylonian Captivity of the Papacy | Hundred Years' War |
| | Joan of Arc |
| Great Schism | Black Death |
| conciliarists | Hanseatic League |
| Council of Constance | Spanish Inquisition |
| Jan Hus | Golden Bull |

# THE CRISIS OF THE WESTERN CHRISTIAN CHURCH

**E**ARLY in the fourteenth century the Christian church endured a series of crises that instigated a debate about the nature of church government and the role of the church in society. First the popes and their entourages abandoned their traditional residences in central Italy and moved to Avignon, an imperial enclave in the south of modern France. Then, in the wake of a disputed election, two and later three rivals claimed the papal throne. Simultaneously, the church hierarchy faced challenges from radical reformers who wished to change it. At various times all the European powers became entangled in the problems of the church. By the mid-fifteenth century the papacy realized that it needed a stronger, independent base. Papal recovery in the fifteenth century was predicated on political power in central Italy.

## The Babylonian Captivity, 1309–1377

The Christian church was in turmoil as a result of an attack on Pope Boniface VIII (r. 1294–1303) by King Philip IV (r. 1285–1314) of France. The king attempted to kidnap Boniface, intending to try him for heresy because of the pope's challenges to the king's authority within his own kingdom. The outstanding issues revolved around the powers of the pope and the responsibilities of the clergy to political leaders. It was, in fact, largely because of tensions with the northern kingdoms that the French archbishop of Bordeaux° was elected Pope Clement V (r. 1305–1314). Clement chose to remain north of the Alps in order to seek an end to warfare between France and England and to protect, to the extent possible, the wealthy religious order of the Knights of the Temple, or Templars (see page 321), which Philip was in the process of suppressing. Clement also hoped to prevent the king from carrying through his threatened posthumous heresy trial of Boniface. After the death of Boniface it was clear that the governments of Europe had no intention of recognizing papal political authority as absolute.

Clement's pontificate marked the beginning of the so-called Babylonian Captivity, a period during which the pope resided almost continuously outside of Italy. In 1309 Clement moved the papal court to Avignon, on the Rhône River in a region that was still part of the Holy Roman Empire—the name that by the fourteenth century was given to the medieval empire whose origin reached back to Charlemagne. His successor, Pope John XXII (r. 1316–1334), set the tone for the brilliant papal court. To celebrate the marriage of his grandniece in 1324, for example, he ordered a wedding feast during which the numerous guests consumed 4,012 loaves of bread, 8¾ oxen, 55¼ sheep, 8 pigs, 4 boars, and vast quantities of fish, capons, chickens, partridges, rabbits, ducks, and chickens. The repast was topped off with 300 pounds of cheese, 3,000 eggs, and assorted fruits. The guests washed down this feast with about 450 liters of wine.

The papacy and its new residence in Avignon became a major religious, diplomatic, and commercial center. The size of the court changed as dramatically as its venue: although the thirteenth-century papal administration required only two hundred or so officials, the bureaucracy in Avignon grew to about six hundred. It was not just the pope's immediate circle that expanded the population of Avignon. Artists, writers, lawyers, and merchants from across Europe were drawn to the new center of administration and hub of patronage. Kings, princes, towns, and ecclesiastical institutions needed representatives at the papal court. Papal administrators continued to intervene actively in local ecclesiastical affairs, and the pope's revenues from annates (generally a portion of the first year's revenues from an ecclesiastical office granted by papal letter), court fees, and provisioning charges continued to grow.

Bordeaux (bor-DOE)

## CHRONOLOGY

| | |
|---|---|
| 1303 | Pope Boniface VIII attacked at Anagni and dies |
| 1305 | Election of Pope Clement V |
| 1309 | Clement V moves papal court to Avignon; beginning of Babylonian Captivity |
| 1337 | Beginning of Hundred Years' War between England and France |
| 1348–1351 | Black Death |
| 1356 | German emperor issues Golden Bull |
| 1378 | Great Schism |
| 1381 | English Rising |
| 1397 | Union of Kalmar unites Denmark, Norway, and Sweden |
| 1410 | Battle of Tannenberg |
| 1414–1417 | Council of Constance |
| 1415 | Battle of Agincourt |
| 1420 | Treaty of Troyes |
| 1431 | Execution of Joan of Arc |
| 1438 | Pragmatic Sanction of Bourges |
| 1453 | End of the Hundred Years' War Ottoman Turks conquer Constantinople |
| 1469 | Marriage of Ferdinand and Isabella unites kingdoms of Aragon and Castile |
| 1480 | Ivan III ends Tatar overlordship of Moscow |
| 1485 | Tudor dynasty established in England |
| 1492 | Spanish conquest of Granada Jews expelled from Spanish lands Columbus commissioned to discover new lands |
| 1494 | Charles VIII invades Italy |

Not everyone approved of this situation. It was the Italian poet and philosopher Francesco Petrarch (1304–1374) who first referred to the Avignon move as a "Babylonian Captivity of the papacy." Recalling the account in the Hebrew Bible of the exile of the Israelites and New

<table>
<tr><td>

**READING SOURCES**

</td><td>

# SAINT CATHERINE OF SIENA AND THE AVIGNON PAPACY

</td></tr>
</table>

*Catherine Benincasa (1347–1380) joined the Dominican order at age 16. Renowned for her piety and spirituality, she used her influence to pressure the popes to return to Rome and reform the church. This letter to Pope Gregory XI was probably dictated (Catherine was illiterate) in 1376.*

My soul longs with inestimable love that God in His infinite mercy will take from you each passion and all tepidity of heart and will reform you into another man by rekindling in you an ardent and burning desire, for in no other way can you fulfill the will of God and the desires of all His servants. Alas, my sweetest Babbo [literally "Daddy"], pardon my presumption in what I have said and am saying—the sweet and primal Truth forces me. This is His will, Father; He demands this of you. He demands that you require justice in the multitude of iniquities committed by those nourished and sheltered in the garden of the Holy Church; He declares that beasts should not receive men's food. Because He has given you authority and because you have accepted it, you ought to use your virtue and power. If you do not wish to use it, it might be better for you to resign what you have accepted; it would give more honor to God and health to your soul.

In addition, His will demands that you make peace with all Tuscany where now you have strife. Receive all your wicked and rebellious sons whenever you can peacefully do so—but punish them as a father would an offending son. . . . [T]hat which appears impossible to you is possible to the sweet goodness of God who has ordained and willed that it be so. Beware, as you hold your life dear, that you are not negligent in this nor treat lightly the works of the Holy Spirit. . . . You can have peace by avoiding the perverse pomps and delights of the world and by preserving God's honor and the Holy Church's rights.

Source: Robert Coogan, *Babylon on the Rhone: A Translation of Letters by Dante, Petrarch, and Catherine of Siena on the Avignon Papacy* (Potomac, Md.: Studia Humanitatis, 1983), p. 115.

Testament images of Babylon as the center of sin and immorality, he complained of

> [an] unholy Babylon, Hell on Earth, a sink of iniquity, the cesspool of the world. There is neither faith, nor charity, nor religion, nor fear of God, nor shame, nor truth, nor holiness, albeit the residence . . . of the supreme pontiff should have made it a shrine and the very stronghold of religion.[1]

To Petrarch and others the exile of the papacy epitomized all that was wrong with the church. Many people renowned for their piety, including women such as Saint Catherine of Siena and Saint Bridget of Sweden, appealed to the pope to return to simpler ways and to Rome, his episcopal city. (See the box "Reading Sources: Saint Catherine of Siena and the Avignon Papacy.")

## The Great Schism, 1378–1417

In 1377 Pope Gregory XI (r. 1370–1378) bowed to critics' pressure and did return to Rome. He was shocked by what he found: churches and palaces in ruin and the city violent and dangerous. By the end of 1377 he had resolved to retreat to Avignon, but he died a few months later. In a tumultuous election during which the Roman populace entered the Vatican Palace and threatened to break into the conclave itself, the cardinals finally elected a compromise candidate acceptable to both the French cardinals and the Roman mob. Urban VI (r. 1378–1389) may have been electable, but he was also violent, intemperate, and eager to reduce the privileges of the clerical hierarchy. In response, the French cardinals questioned the legitimacy of the election, which they came to believe had been conducted under duress. Within months they deposed Urban and elected in his place a French cardinal who took the name Clement VII (r. 1378–1394). Urban responded by denouncing the cardinals and continuing to rule in Rome. The church now had two popes.

After some hesitation Western Christians divided into two camps, initiating the Great Schism°, a period of almost forty years during which no one knew for sure who was the true pope. This was a deadly serious issue for all.

**Schism** (SKIZ-em)

**Gregory XI Returns to Rome**
This highly stylized painting conveys the hopes of European Christians when Gregory XI returned from Avignon in 1377. Saint Catherine of Siena, who had pleaded for the pope's return, is seen in the foreground.
*(Scala/Art Resource, NY)*

The true pope had the right to appoint church officials, decide important moral and legal issues, and allow or forbid taxation of the clergy by the state. Each side found ready supporters among the states of Europe; however, support for one pope or the other often had more to do with political rivalries than with religious convictions. The two sides largely mirrored the political tensions in Europe. France and those governments most closely allied with it—Burgundy, Savoy, Naples, Scotland, and Castile—tended to support Clement, who eventually resettled in Avignon. The English, together with most Italian governments, the German Empire, Scandinavia, Hungary, Portugal, and Poland, supported Urban, the pope in Rome.

The crisis gave impetus to new discussions about church government: Should the pope be considered the sole head of the church? Debates within the church followed lines of thought already expressed in the towns and kingdoms of Europe. Representative bodies—the English Parliament, the French Estates General, the Swedish Riksdag°—already claimed the right to act for the realm, and in the city-states of Italy ultimate authority was thought to reside in the body of citizens. Canon lawyers and theologians similarly argued that authority resided in the whole church, which had the right and duty to come together in council to correct and reform the church hierarchy. Even the most conservative of these "conciliarists" agreed that the "universal church" had the right to respond in periods of heresy or schism. More radical

**Riksdag** (RIX-dog)

conciliarists argued that the pope as bishop of Rome was merely the first among equals in the church hierarchy and that he, like any other bishop, could be corrected by a gathering of his peers—that is, by an ecumenical council.

The rival popes found themselves under increased pressure to end the schism. The issue seemed on its way to resolution when the two parties agreed to meet in northern Italy in 1408. In the end, though, the meeting never took place, and in retrospect many doubted whether either party had been negotiating in good faith. In exasperation the cardinals, the main ecclesiastical supporters of the rival popes, called a general council in Pisa, which deposed both popes and elected a new one. Since the council lacked the power to force the rivals to accept deposition, the result was that three men now claimed to be the rightful successor of Saint Peter. Conciliarists, by themselves, could not mend the split in the church.

Resolution finally came when the Holy Roman emperor Sigismund (r. 1411–1437) forced the diplomatically isolated third papal claimant, John XXIII (r. 1410–1415), to call a general council of the church. The council, which met from 1414 to 1417 in the German imperial city of Constance, could never have succeeded without Sigismund's support. At one point he forced the council to remain in session even after Pope John had fled the city in an attempt to end deliberations.

## Heresy and the Council of Constance, 1414–1418

Sigismund hoped that a council could help him heal deep religious and civil divisions in Bohemia, the most important part of his family's traditional lands (see Map 11.3). Bohemia and its capital, Prague, were Czech-speaking. But Prague was also the seat of the Luxemburg dynasty of German emperors and the site of the first university in German or Slavic lands. Religious and theological questions quickly became entangled with the competing claims of Czech and German factions. The preaching and teaching of the Czech reformer Jan Hus (ca. 1370–1415) were at the center of the debate. As preacher in the Bethlehem Chapel in Prague from 1402 and eventually as rector of the university, Hus was the natural spokesman for the non-German townspeople in Prague and the Czech faction at the university. His criticisms of the church hierarchy, which in Prague was primarily German, fanned into flames the smoldering embers of Czech national feeling. It was Sigismund's hope that a council might clarify the orthodoxy of Hus's teachings and heal the rift within the church of Bohemia.

The council's response to the theological crisis was based on the church's experience with heresy over the previous forty years, primarily the teachings of John Wyclif (1329–1384). In the 1370s Wyclif, an Oxford theologian and parish priest, began to criticize in increasingly angry terms the state of the clergy and the abuses of the church hierarchy. By 1387 his ideas had been declared heretical and his followers were hunted out. Wyclif's most dangerous criticism was his denial of the priest's indispensable position as an intermediary between God and believers. Wyclif believed that the church could be at once a divine institution and an earthly gathering of individuals. Thus, in his opinion, individual Christians need not unquestioningly obey the pronouncements of the church hierarchy. Final authority lay only in the Scriptures, insisted Wyclif, who sponsored the first translations of the Bible into English. He gathered about himself followers called "Lollards," who emphasized Bible reading and popular piety; some even supported public preaching by women. According to one disciple, "Every true man and woman being in charity is a priest."[2] Because of their attacks on the ecclesiastical hierarchy, Lollards were popular among the nobility of England, and especially at the court of Richard II during the 1390s. In the first two decades of the fifteenth century, however, their influence waned.

Wyclif's influence continued on the Continent, especially in the circle of Jan Hus and the Czech reformers. While Hus disagreed with some of Wyclif's more radical ideas, he also attacked clerical power and privileges. By 1403 the German majority in the university had condemned Hus's teaching as Wycliffite, thus initiating almost a decade of struggle between Czechs and Germans, Hussites and Catholics. This was the impasse that Sigismund hoped the Council of Constance could settle. Accordingly, he offered a suspicious Hus a safe conduct pass to attend the council. When Hus arrived, it became clear that the councilors and Hus himself were in no mood to compromise. The council revoked the pledge of safe conduct and ordered Hus to recant his beliefs. He refused. The council condemned him as a heretic and burned him at the stake on July 6, 1415.

Far from ending Sigismund's problems with the Bohemians, the actions of the council provided the Czechs with a martyr and hero. The execution of Hus provoked a firestorm of revolution in Prague. Czech forces roundly defeated an imperial army sent in to restore order. The Hussite movement gathered strength and spread throughout Bohemia. Moderate Hussites continued Hus's campaign against clerical abuses and claimed the right to receive both the bread and the wine during the sacrament of Communion. Radical Hussites argued that the true church was the community of spiritual men and women; they had no use for ecclesiastical hierarchy of any kind. The German emperors were unable to defeat a united Hussite movement. In 1433 a new church council and moderate Hussites negotiated an agreement that allowed the Hussites to continue some of their practices, including receiving both bread and wine at Communion, while returning to the church. Radical Hussites refused the compromise, and the war dragged on until 1436. Bohemia remained a center of religious dissent, and the memory of Hus's execution at a church council would have a chilling effect on discussions of church reform during the Reformation in the sixteenth century.

## The Reunion and Reform of the Papacy, 1415–1513

To most of the delegates at the Council of Constance, the reunion and reform of the papacy were more important than the issue of heresy. And as we will see, the crisis of the schism brought in its aftermath a transformed Christian church.

After initially agreeing to abdicate if his rivals did the same, John changed his mind and fled from Constance. Sigismund recaptured him and returned him to the council, where he was deposed. Pope Gregory XII (r. 1406–1415), the Roman pope, realizing he had lost all his support, resigned—after himself calling the council, as a rightful pope should do. Benedict III (r. 1394–1417), the pope in Avignon, refused to resign and he also was deposed. Finally, in 1417, the council elected a Roman nobleman as Pope Martin V (r. 1417–1431).

The council justified its actions in what was perhaps its most important decree, *Haec sancta synodus* ("This sacred synod"): "This sacred synod of Constance . . . declares . . . that it has its power immediately from Christ, and that all men, of every rank and position, including even the pope himself are bound to obey it in those matters that pertain to the faith."[3] Popes could no longer expect to remain unchallenged if they made claims of absolute dominion, and ecclesiastical rights and jurisdictions increasingly were matters for negotiation.

Critics agreed that the pope no longer behaved like the "Servant of the Servants of Christ" but instead acted like the "Lord of Lords." Cardinals claimed to represent the church at large as counterweights to papal abuse, but as the nobility of the church, they and other members of the hierarchy required the income from multiple offices to maintain their presence at the papal court. Both the cardinals and the popes viewed any reforms to the present system as potential threats to their ability to function. The council, however, recognized the need for further reforms. A second reform council met at Basel

**Pope Martin Receiving the Crown from a Council**    Delegates to the Council of Constance stated that even the pope had to accept the decrees of a council sitting for the whole church.    *(From* Chronik des Konstanzen Konzils, *1414–1418. Courtesy, Rosgartenmuseum, Constance)*

from 1431 to 1449, but with modest results. The council again tried to reduce papal power, but this time it received little support from European governments.

Because of the continuing conciliarist threat, the papacy needed the support of the secular rulers of Europe. Thus the papacy was forced to accept compromises on the issues of reform, on ecclesiastical jurisdictions and immunities, and on papal revenues. Various governments argued that it was they, and not the pope, who should be responsible for ecclesiastical institutions and jurisdictions within their territories.

Lay rulers focused on several issues. They wanted church officials in their territories to belong to local families. They wanted ecclesiastical institutions to be subject to local laws and administration. And by the 1470s it was clear that they wanted to have local prelates named as cardinal-protectors. These were not churchmen who could serve the church administration in Rome; rather they functioned as mediators between local governments and the papacy. The most famous of these new political cardinals was Thomas Wolsey of England (ca. 1470–1530), who was an important supporter of King Henry VII and chancellor of England under Henry VIII.

The reunited papacy had to accept claims it would have staunchly opposed a century earlier. One of the most important of these was the Pragmatic Sanction of Bourges of 1438. The papacy was unable to protest when the French clergy, at the urging of the king, abolished papal rights to annates, limited appeals to the papal court, and reduced papal rights to appoint clergy within France without the approval of the local clergy or the Crown. Similar concessions diminished church authority throughout Europe. Perhaps the most momentous was a bull (official papal document) issued in 1478 by Pope Sixtus IV (r. 1471–1484) that allowed Ferdinand and Isabella of Aragon and Castile to institute a church court, the Spanish Inquisition, under their own auspices (see page 387).

With reduced revenues from legal fees, annates, and appointments, the popes of the fifteenth century were forced to derive more and more of their revenue and influence from the Papal States. By 1430 the Papal States accounted for about half of the annual income of the papacy. Papal interests increasingly centered on protecting the papacy's influence as a secular ruler of a large territory in central Italy. Thus the papacy had to deal with many of the same jurisdictional, diplomatic, and military challenges that faced other medieval governments.

## WAR AND THE STRUGGLE OVER POLITICAL POWER, 1300–1450

A LAWYER who served King Philip IV of France (r. 1285–1314) observed that "everything within the limits of his kingdom belongs to the lord king, especially protection, high justice and dominion."[4] Royal officials in England and France generally believed that "liberties"—that is, individual rights to local jurisdictions—originated with the king. These ideas were the result of several centuries of centralization of political power in royal hands. At almost the same time, however, an English noble challenged royal claims on his lands, saying, "Here, my lords, is my warrant," as he brandished a rusty long sword. "My ancestors came with William the Bastard [that is, William the Conqueror, in 1066] and

conquered their lands with the sword, and by the sword I will defend them against anyone who tries to usurp them."[5] The views of the royal lawyer and the feisty earl exemplify the central tension over power in the late Middle Ages. The struggle over political power was played out in the context of the Hundred Years' War, which affected not just England and France but also most of western Europe, especially Italy. In England and France the crisis led to strengthened monarchies. In Italy, however, public power resided more and more in local entities.

### England, France, and the Hundred Years' War, 1337–1453

In the twelfth and thirteenth centuries centralization of royal power in England and France had proceeded almost without interruption. In the fourteenth century matters changed in both countries. Questions of the nature of royal power, common responsibility, and hereditary rights to rule challenged the power of the English and French monarchs.

In England fears arising from the growing power of the English crown and the weakness of a gullible king brought issues to a head during the reign of Edward II (r. 1307–1327). By the early fourteenth century, resident justices of the peace (JPs) were replacing the expensive and inefficient system of traveling justices. In theory, the JPs were royal officials doing the king's bidding, but this was often not the case in reality. These unpaid local officials were modestly well-to-do gentry who were often clients of local magnates. Justices were known to use their offices to carry out local vendettas and feuds and to protect the interests of the wealthy and powerful.

The barons, the titled lords of England, were interested in controlling more than just local justices. Fearing that Edward II would continue many of the centralizing policies of his father, the barons passed reform ordinances in 1311 limiting the king's right to wage war, leave the realm, grant lands or castles, or appoint chief justices and chancellors without the approval of Parliament, which they dominated. Special taxes or subsidies were to be paid to the public Exchequer rather than into the king's private treasury. Some of these ordinances were later voided, but the tradition of parliamentary consent remained a key principle of English constitutional history.

The baronial influence grew because Edward II was a weak and naive king, easily influenced by court favorites. After a humiliating defeat at the hands of the Scots at the Battle of Bannockburn (1314), his position steadily deteriorated until he was deposed in 1327 by a coalition of barons led by his wife, Queen Isabella. After a short re-

## FRENCH AND ENGLISH SUCCESSION IN THE FOURTEENTH CENTURY

**Philip IV of France** (r. 1285–1314)

**Charles of Valois**

**Louis X** (r. 1314–1316)

**Philip V** (r. 1316–1322)

**Charles IV** (r. 1322–1328)

**Isabella**

**Edward II of England** (r. 1307–1327)

**Philip VI of France** (r. 1328–1350)

**John I** (r. 1316)

**Edward III of England** (r. 1327–1377)

**John II** (r. 1350–1364)

gency, their son Edward III (r. 1327–1377), assumed the throne. He was a cautious king, ever aware of the violence and rebelliousness of the baronage.

French kings seemed significantly more powerful in the early fourteenth century. A complex succession crisis, however, made clear the limits of French kingship. In 1328 the direct Capetian line, which had sired the kings of France since the election of Hugh Capet in 987, finally died out. The last Capetians did produce daughters, but by the fourteenth century many argued that according to custom the French crown should pass through the male line only. Thus the French nobility selected as king Philip of Valois (Philip VI; r. 1328–1350), a cousin of the last king through the male line (Charles IV; r. 1322–1328). He was chosen in preference to the daughters of the last Capetian kings and, more significantly, in preference to King Edward III of England, whose mother, Isabella, was the daughter of King Philip IV (r. 1285–1314).

Controversy over succession was just one of the disputes between the French and English. An even longer-standing issue was the status of lands within France that belonged to the English kings. In 1340, climaxing a century of tensions over English possessions in France, Edward III of England formally claimed the title "King of France," and the Hundred Years' War was on.

The war was marked by quick English raids and only occasional pitched battles. With a population of about 16 million, France was far richer and more populous than England. On at least one occasion the French managed to field an army of over 50,000; the English mustered only 32,000 at most. These armies were easily the largest ever assembled by a medieval European kingdom.

In almost every engagement the English were outnumbered. Their strategy, therefore, was to avoid pitched battles except on the most advantageous terms. Edward III engaged in extremely destructive raids, hoping to lure the French into ill-considered attacks. The English stole what they could, destroyed what they could not steal, and captured enemy knights to hold for ransom.

The war can be divided into four stages. The first stage (1337–1360) was characterized by a rapid series of English assaults and victories. The few pitched battles, including Crécy (1346) and Poitiers (1356), show how Edward's strategy worked (see Map 11.1). In these cases the English gathered their forces in careful defensive positions and took advantage of an individualistic French chivalric ethos according to which, in the words of one knight, "who does the most is worth the most." The key to the English defensive position was the use of long-bowmen and cannon. As French knights labored up a hill in a vain attempt to reach the English lines, they were met with withering fire. The longbow was developed in Wales, and the English perfected its use in numerous border wars with the Scots. Arrows from the longbow had more penetrating power than a bolt from a crossbow, and the longbow could be fired much more rapidly. Gunpowder and cannon probably arrived in the West from China in the late thirteenth century. Both the French and the English adopted firearms. Although there is a debate over how effective they were, when used in combination with the longbow, they effectively disrupted and scattered advancing troops.

In the second stage of the war (1360–1396), French forces responded more cautiously to the English tactics

**1337**
**(before the Battle of Crécy)**

- English holdings
- French holdings
- Extent of English holdings after Treaty of Paris, 1259

ENGLAND
Southampton
Calais
FLANDERS
PONTHIEU
English Channel
NORMANDY
CHAMPAGNE
Paris
Seine
BRITTANY
MAINE
ANJOU
Loire
HOLY ROMAN EMPIRE
TOURAINE
BURGUNDY
POITOU
AUVERGNE
AQUITAINE
Bordeaux
Garonne
DAUPHINÉ
Rhône
Saint-Sardos
GASCONY
LANGUEDOC
Toulouse
SPAIN
Mediterranean Sea
0 100 Km.
0 100 Mi.

**1360**
**(after the Battle of Poitiers)**

- English holdings
- French holdings
- ✕ Major battles

ENGLAND
Calais
FLANDERS
Crécy 1346 ✕
English Channel
Rouen
NORMANDY
CHAMPAGNE
Paris
Seine
BRITTANY
MAINE
ANJOU
Loire
HOLY ROMAN EMPIRE
TOURAINE
BURGUNDY
Poitiers 1356 ✕
POITOU
AUVERGNE
AQUITAINE
Bordeaux
Garonne
DAUPHINÉ
Rhône
GASCONY
LANGUEDOC
Toulouse
SPAIN
Mediterranean Sea
0 100 Km.
0 100 Mi.

**ca. 1429**
**(after the siege of Orléans)**

- English holdings
- French holdings
- Burgundian lands allied with England to 1435
- ✕ Major battle

ENGLAND
Calais
HOLY ROMAN EMPIRE
Agincourt 1415 ✕
FLANDERS
English Channel
Rouen
Reims
NORMANDY
CHAMPAGNE
Paris
Seine
Domrémy
BRITTANY
Orléans
MAINE
ANJOU
Loire
Bourges
TOURAINE
DUCHY OF BURGUNDY
COUNTY OF BURGUNDY
POITOU
AUVERGNE
AQUITAINE
Bordeaux
Garonne
Rhône
DAUPHINÉ
GASCONY
LANGUEDOC
Toulouse
SPAIN
Mediterranean Sea
0 100 Km.
0 100 Mi.

**1453**
**(end of war)**

- English holdings
- French holdings
- Burgundian lands reconciled with France after 1435
- ✕ Last battle

ENGLAND
Calais
BRABANT
FLANDERS
English Channel
LUXEMBOURG
HOLY ROMAN EMPIRE
NORMANDY
Paris
CHAMPAGNE
Seine
BRITTANY
MAINE
ANJOU
Loire
DUCHY OF BURGUNDY
COUNTY OF BURGUNDY
TOURAINE
POITOU
AQUITAINE
Castillon-sur-Dordogne 1453 ✕
AUVERGNE
Bordeaux
Garonne
Rhône
DAUPHINÉ
GASCONY
LANGUEDOC
Toulouse
SPAIN
Mediterranean Sea
0 100 Km.
0 100 Mi.

*The author of this chronicle—probably the most complete account of the English peasant revolt of 1381—seems to have been an eyewitness to the dramatic events in London. Like most literate people, the chronicler seems more comfortable with the attitudes and opinions of civil officials and landlords than with the concerns of the "rabble."*

Wherefore the commons rose against [the royal] commissioner sent to investigate [rebellious acts in the region] and came before him to tell him that he was a traitor to the king and the kingdom and was maliciously proposing to undo them by the use of false inquests taken before him. Accordingly they made him swear on the Bible that never again would he hold such sessions nor act as a justice in such inquests. They proposed to kill all the lawyers, jurors and royal servants they could find. . . .

[The rebels came to London, where they executed several royal servants. They, and possibly their leader, Wat Tyler, forced the king to agree to allow them to deal "with all the traitors against him."] And they required that henceforth no man should be a serf nor make homage or any type of service to any lord, but should give four pence for an acre of land. They asked also that no one should serve any man except at his own will and by means of a regular covenant. . . .

[In a confused melée during a meeting with King Richard, Tyler was stabbed.] Wat spurred his horse, crying to the commons to avenge him, and the horse carried him some four score [eighty] paces and then he fell to the ground half dead. And when the commons saw him fall, and did not know for certain how it happened, they began to bend their bows and to shoot. Therefore the king himself spurred his horse, and rode out to them, commanding them that they should all come before him at the field of St. John of Clerkenwell [a few hundred yards from where Tyler was wounded].

Afterwards, when the king had reached the open fields, he made the commons array themselves on the west side. . . . [The mayor of London had Wat Tyler] carried out to the middle of Smithfield [a market area on the edge of town] . . . and had him beheaded. . . . And so ended his wretched life. But the mayor had his head set on a pole and carried before him to the king, who still remained on the field. . . . And when the commons saw that their chieftain, Wat Tyler, was dead in such a manner, they fell to the ground there among the corn, like beaten men, imploring the king for mercy for their misdeeds. And the king benevolently granted them mercy.

Source: *The Anonimalle Chronicle,* in R. B. Dobson, *The Peasant's Revolt of 1381,* pp. 123, 125, 128, 161, 166–167. Reprinted by permission of Macmillan Ltd. Copyright © 1970 by The Macmillan Press Ltd.

and slowly regained much of the territory they had lost. But during this stage, the disruptions and expenses of war placed a huge burden on both French and English society. In the confusion and unrest following the French disaster at Poitiers in 1356, Étienne Marcel, provost (director) of the merchants of Paris, mobilized a protest movement designed to reduce royal and aristocratic power. This revolution seemed too radical to conservative townspeople in the provinces, and Marcel's only allies were bands

**Map 11.1    England and France in the Hundred Years' War**
The succession of maps depicts both why hit-and-run tactics worked for the English early in the war and why the English were ultimately unable to defeat the French and take control of all of France.

of rebellious countrymen roaming the region around Paris. These rebels, and eventually Marcel himself, were isolated and then defeated by aristocratic armies.

England was soon rocked by unrest as well. The Rising of 1381 is often called the Peasants' Revolt, despite the fact that townsfolk as well as peasants participated. Already England seethed with unrest as a result of the plague (see pages 371–372) and landlord claims for traditional dues. But the final straw was a poll tax levied to pay for the war. Commoners responded with violent protests. The heart of the uprising was a revolt by rural peasants and artisans in the southeast, primarily in Kent and Essex. Popular armies led by Wat Tyler (d. 1381) converged on London in June 1381. Tyler was murdered during a dramatic meeting with Richard II outside London, and a reaction against the rebels quickly ensued. (See the box "Reading Sources: The Rising of 1381.")

The rest of Richard's reign was anything but tranquil. Recognizing the dangers of noble influence, Richard tried to insulate himself from the peers of the realm by choosing advisers from the lesser nobility and the middle classes as well as from the peerage. The result was increasing tensions with the peers and charges that Richard's rule was tyrannical. Simmering discontent boiled over, and leaders of the peers captured Richard and forced him to abdicate in 1399. Parliament then elected as king Henry IV (r. 1399–1413), the first ruler from the House of Lancaster. Richard died in prison under mysterious circumstances in 1400.

A fateful shift occurred in the third stage of the war (1396–1422). King Charles VI (r. 1380–1422) of France suffered bouts of insanity throughout his long reign, which made effective French government almost impossible. The English king Henry V (r. 1413–1422) renewed his family's claim to the French throne. At Agincourt in 1415 the English (led by Henry himself) again enticed a larger French army into attacking an English position fortified by longbows and cannon. By the terms of the Treaty of Troyes (1420), Charles VI's son (the future Charles VII) was declared illegitimate and disinherited; Henry married Catherine, the daughter of Charles VI, and he was declared the legitimate heir to the French throne. A final English victory seemed assured, but both Charles VI and Henry V died in 1422, leaving Henry's infant son, Henry VI (r. 1422–1461), to inherit both thrones.

The kings' deaths ushered in the final stage of the Hundred Years' War (1422–1453), the French reconquest. In 1428 military and political power seemed firmly in the hands of the English and the great aristocrats. Yet in a stunning series of events the French were able to reverse the situation.

**The Battle at Agincourt**    The English victory at Agincourt marked the high point of English influence in France. Once again English archers defeated a larger, mounted force.

*(The Granger Collection, New York)*

# THE INQUISITION OF JOAN OF ARC

*An important question at the trial of Joan of Arc was whether her acts had any authoritative value: Did the voices she heard originate with God or the Devil? The judges wanted to demonstrate to their own satisfaction that Joan was one of "the sowers of deceitful inventions" of which the Gospels warned. They fully expected that external signs could reveal hidden truths.*

The following memorandum is a summation of the commission's case against the maid.

You said that you wore and still wear man's dress at God's command and to His good pleasure, for you had instruction from God to wear this dress, and so you put on a short tunic, jerkin, and hose with many points. You even wear your hair cut above the ears, without keeping about you anything to denote your sex, save what nature has given you. . . . The clergy declare that you blaspheme against God, despising Him and His sacraments, that you transgress divine law, Holy Scripture and the canons of the Church, that you think evil and err from the faith, that you are full of vain boasting, that you are given to idolatry and worship of yourself and your clothes, according to the customs of the heathen.

You have declared that you know well that God loves certain living persons better than you, and that you learned this by revelation from St. Catherine and St. Margaret; also that those saints speak French, not English, as they are not on the side of the English. And since you knew that your voices were for your king, you began to dislike the Burgundians.

Such matters the clergy pronounce to be a rash and presumptuous assertion, a superstitious divination, a blasphemy uttered against St. Catherine and St. Margaret, and a transgression of the commandment to love our neighbors.

And you have said . . . that you know that all the deeds of which you have been accused in your trial were wrought according to the command of God and that it was impossible for you to do otherwise. . . . Wherefore the clergy declare you to be schismatic, an unbeliever in the unity and authority of the Church, apostate and obstinately erring from the faith. . . . [The inquisitor admonished her,] "You have believed in apparitions lightly, instead of turning to God in devout prayer to grant you certainty; and you have not consulted prelates or learned ecclesiastics to enlighten yourself: although, considering your condition and the simplicity of your knowledge, you ought to have done so."

Source: W. P. Barrett, trans., *The Trial of Jeanne d'Arc* (New York: Gotham House, 1932), pp. 331–338.

**For additional information on this topic, go to college.hmco.com/students.**

In 1429, with the aid of the mysterious Joan of Arc (d. 1431), the French king, Charles VII, was able to raise the English siege of Orléans° and begin the reconquest of the north of France. Joan was the daughter of prosperous peasants from an area of Burgundy that had suffered under the English and their Burgundian allies. Like many late medieval mystics, she reported regular visions of divine revelation. Her "voices" told her to go to the king and assist him in driving out the English. Dressed as a man, she was Charles's most charismatic and feared military leader. With Joan's aid, the king was crowned in the cathedral at Reims, the traditional site of French coronations. Joan was captured during an audacious attack on Paris itself and eventually fell into English hands. Because of her "unnatural dress" and her claim to divine guidance, she was condemned and burned as a heretic in 1431. (See the box "Reading Sources: The Inquisition of Joan of Arc.") A heretic only to the English and their supporters, Joan almost instantly became a symbol of French resistance. Pope Calixtus III reversed the condemnation in 1456, and Joan was canonized in 1920. The heretic became Saint Joan, patron of France.

Despite Joan's capture, the French advance continued. By 1450 the English had lost all their major centers except Calais°. In 1453 the French armies captured the fortress of Castillon-sur-Dordogne° in what was to be

Orléans (or-lay-OHN)

Calais (Ca-lay)
Castillon-sur-Dordogne (kas-ti-YON sir dor-DON-ya)

the last battle of the war (see Map 11.1). There was no treaty, only a cessation of hostilities.

The war touched almost every aspect of life in western Europe: political, religious, economic, and social. It ranged beyond the borders of France as Scotland, Castile, Aragon, and German principalities were at various times drawn into the struggle. French and English support for rival popes prevented early settlement of the Great Schism in the papacy (see pages 358–360). Further, the war caused a general rise in the level of violence in society. As Henry V casually observed, "War without fire is as bland as sausages without mustard."[6] And because of the highly profitable lightning raids, this war was never bland. During periods of truce many soldiers simply ranged through France, pillaging small towns and ravaging the countryside. Others went in search of work as mercenaries, especially in Germany, Poland, and Italy. Truces in France did not necessarily mean peace in Europe.

## Italy

Compared with France and England, fourteenth- and fifteenth-century Italy was a land of cities. In northern Europe a town of over 20,000 or 30,000 people was unusual; only Paris and London boasted more than 100,000 people in the fourteenth century. Yet at one time or another in the late Middle Ages, Milan, Venice, Florence, and Naples all had populations near or exceeding 100,000, and countless other Italian towns boasted populations of well over 30,000. Unlike northern European states with their kings or emperors, however, the Italian peninsula lacked a unifying force. The centers of power were in Italy's flourishing cities. Political life revolved around the twin issues of who should dominate city governments and how cities could learn to coexist peacefully.

By the late thirteenth century, political power in most Italian towns was divided among three major groups. First was the old urban nobility that could trace its wealth back to grants of property and rights from kings, emperors, and bishops in the tenth and eleventh centuries. Second was the merchant families who had grown wealthy in the twelfth and thirteenth centuries as Italians led the European economic expansion into the Mediterranean. Third, challenging these entrenched urban groups, were the modest artisans and merchants who had organized trade, neighborhood, or militia groups and referred to themselves as *popolo,* or "people." Townspeople gathered together in factions based on wealth, family, profession, neighborhood, and even systems of clientage that reached back into the villages from which many of them had come. "War and hatred have so multiplied among the Italians,"

observed one Florentine, "that in every town there is a division and enmity between two parties of citizens."

Riven with factions, townspeople often would turn control of their government over to a *signor*°, a "lord" or "tyrant," often a local noble with a private army. Once firmly in power, the tyrant often allowed the government to continue to function as it had, requiring only that he control all major political appointments. The process might appear democratic, but it represented a profound shift in power. The transformation was clear in Mantua, where, according to one chronicler, "[Pinamonte Bonacolsi (d. 1293)] usurped the lordship of his city and expelled his fellow-citizens and occupied their property. . . . He was feared like the devil."[7] In the case of Milan, the noble Viscontis° used support from the emperor Henry VII (r. 1308–1313) to drive their opponents out of the city. Eventually granted Milan and its territories as a duchy, the Viscontis, and later their Sforza successors, made marriage alliances with the French crown and created a splendid court culture. In a series of wars between the 1370s and 1450s, the dukes of Milan expanded their political control throughout most of Lombardy, Liguria, and, temporarily, Tuscany. The Viscontis maintained control of the city and much of the region of Lombardy until the last scion of the family died in 1447.

The great republics of Venice and Florence escaped domination by signori, but only by undertaking significant constitutional change. In both republics political life had been disrupted by the arrival of immigrants and by the demands of recently enriched merchants and speculators for a voice in government. In 1297, reacting to increased competition for influence, the Venetian government enacted a reform that would come to be known as the "Closing of the Grand Council." The act enlarged to about eleven hundred the number of families eligible for public office, but its eventual effect was to freeze out subsequent arrivals from ever rising to elite status. The Venetian patriciate became a closed urban nobility. Political, factional, and economic tensions were hidden beneath a veneer of serenity as Venetians developed a myth of public-spirited patricians who governed in the interests of all the people, leaving others free to enrich themselves in trade and manufacture.

In Florence the arguments over citizenship and the right of civic participation disrupted public life. Violent wealthy families, immigrants, and artisans of modest background were cut off from civic participation. A series of reforms culminating in the Ordinances of Justice of

---

**signor** (sin-YOUR)   **Viscontis** (vis-KON-tees)

1293 to 1295 restricted political participation in Florence to members in good standing of certain merchant and artisan guilds. Members of violence-prone families were defined as *Magnate* (literally, "the powerful") and disqualified from holding public office. In spite of the reforms, political power remained concentrated in the hands of the great families, whose wealth was based primarily on banking and mercantile investments. These families used their political influence and economic power to dominate Florentine life.

There were short-lived attempts to reform the system and extend the rights of political participation to include the more modest artisans and laborers. The most dramatic was in 1378 when the Ciompi°, unskilled workers in Florence's woolen industry, led a popular revolution hoping to expand participation in government and limit the authority of the guild masters over semiskilled artisans and day laborers. They created new guilds to represent the laborers who had no voice in government. Barely six weeks after the Ciompi insurrection, however, wealthy conservatives began a reaction suppressing, exiling, or executing the leaders of the movement and eventually suppressing the new guilds. Political and economic power was now even more firmly in the grip of influential patricians.

Following a crisis in 1434 brought on by war and high taxes, virtual control of Florentine politics fell into the hands of Cosimo de' Medici, the wealthiest banker in the city. From 1434 to 1494, Cosimo; his son, Piero; his grandson, Lorenzo; and Lorenzo's son dominated the government in Florence. Although the Medicis were always careful to pay homage to Florentine republican traditions, their control was virtually as complete as that of the lords of towns such as Ferrara and Milan.

Indeed, by the middle of the fifteenth century little differentiated the republics—Florence and Venice—from cities such as Milan and Mantua, where lords held sway. Although Florentines maintained that they intervened to protect Florentine and Tuscan "liberty" when the Viscontis of Milan threatened Tuscany and central Italy, their interests went beyond simple defense. Relations among the great cities of Milan, Venice, Florence, Rome, and Naples were stabilized by the Peace of Lodi and the creation of the Italian League in 1454. In response to endemic warfare in Italy and the looming threat of the Ottoman Turks in the eastern Mediterranean (see page 381), the five powers agreed to the creation of spheres of influence that would prevent any one of them from expanding at the expense of the others.

Ciompi (CHOMP-ee)

**The Journey of the Magi** The story of the journey of the Magi to Bethlehem to find the baby Jesus seemed a perfect image of the power and wisdom of rulers. This painting (a detail) of the Magi was commissioned for the private chapel of Cosimo de' Medici, the de facto ruler of Florence. *(Palazzo Medici Riccardi, Florence/Scala/Art Resource, NY)*

The limits of these territorial states became clear when King Charles VIII of France invaded Italy in 1494 to assert his hereditary claim to the kingdom of Naples. The French invasion touched off a devastating series of wars called the Habsburg-Valois Wars (1496–1559). French claims were challenged by the Habsburg emperors and also by the Spanish, who themselves made claims on southern Italy and much of Lombardy. The cost of prolonged warfare kept almost all governments in a state of crisis. Unrest brought on by the invasion even allowed

Pope Alexander VI (r. 1492–1503) to attempt to create a state for his son, Cesare Borgia° (1475–1507), in central Italy.

In Florence the wars destroyed the old Medici-dominated regime and brought in a new republican government. Anti-Medici efforts were initially led by the popular Dominican preacher Girolamo Savonarola (1452–1498). In the constitutional debates after 1494, Savonarola argued that true political reform required a sweeping purge of the evils of society. Gangs of youth flocked to his cause, attacking prostitutes and homosexuals. Many of his followers held "bonfires of vanities," burning wigs, silks, and other luxuries. In 1498, when his followers had lost influence in the government, Savonarola was arrested, tortured, and executed.

In spite of republican reforms, new fortresses, and a citizen militia, the Florentine government was unable to defend itself from papal and imperial armies. In 1512 the Habsburg emperor restored Medici control of Florence. The Medicis later became dukes and then grand dukes of Tuscany. The grand duchy of Tuscany remained an independent, integrated, and well-governed state until the French Revolution of 1789. Venice also managed to maintain its republican form of government and its territorial state until the French Revolution, but like the grand dukes of Tuscany, the governors of Venice were no longer able to act independently of the larger European powers.

The Habsburg-Valois Wars ended with the Treaty of Cateau-Cambrésis° in 1559, which left the Spanish kings in control of Milan, Naples, Sardinia, and Sicily. Thus the Spanish dominated Italy, but without the centralizing control typical of England and France. Venice, Tuscany, the Papal States and even lesser republics and principalities retained significant influence, as Italy remained a land of regional governments.

# ECONOMY AND SOCIETY

AFTER nearly three centuries of dramatic growth, Europe in 1300 was seriously overpopulated, with estimates ranging from about 80 million to as high as 100 million. In some parts of Europe, population would not be this dense again until the late eighteenth century. Opportunities dwindled because of overpopulation, famine, war, and epidemic, which also brought changes in trade and commerce. As the population began to decline, this trend, along with deflation and transformed patterns of consumption, affected agriculture, which was still the foundation of the European economy. Recovery from all these crises altered the structure and dynamics of families, the organization of work, and the culture in many parts of Europe.

## Plague and Demographic Crisis

People in many parts of Europe were living on the edge of disaster in 1300. Given the low level of agricultural technology and the limited amount of land available for cultivation, it became increasingly difficult for the towns and countryside to feed and support the growing population. The nature of the problem varied from place to place.

Growing numbers of people competed for land to farm and for jobs. Farm sizes declined throughout Europe as parents tended to divide their land among their children. Rents for farmland increased as landlords found that they could play one land-hungry farmer against another. Competition for jobs kept wages low, and when taxes were added to high rents and low wages, many peasants and artisans found it difficult to marry and raise families. Thus, because of reduced opportunities brought on by overpopulation, poor townspeople and peasants tended to marry late and have small families.

More dramatic than this crisis of births were the deadly famines that occurred in years of bad harvests. The great famine of 1315 to 1322 marks a turning point in the economic history of Europe. Wet and cold weather repeatedly ruined crops in much of northern Europe. Food stocks were quickly exhausted, and mass starvation followed. People died so quickly, English chroniclers reported, that survivors could not keep up with the burials. At Ypres, in Flanders, 2,800 people (about 10 percent of the population) died in just six months. And shortages continued. Seven other severe famines were reported in the south of France or Italy during the fourteenth century.

If Europe's problem had merely been one of famine brought on by overpopulation, rapid recovery should have been possible. But the difficulties of overpopulation were exacerbated by war and plague. As noted previously, the devastation of cities and the countryside was a common tactic in the Hundred Years' War. It was also typical of the local wars in parts of Spain, Germany, and especially Italy. The destruction of trees and vineyards and the theft of livestock made it difficult for rural populations to survive. Then, in 1348, the Black Death, or "the great Mortality" as contemporaries called it, struck Europe.

---

**Borgia** (BOR-zheh)
**Cateau-Cambrésis** (kah-toe kam-bray-SEE)

Today there is no consensus as to what caused the Black Death. In the early twentieth century, after the bacillus that causes bubonic plague was identified by French and Japanese physicians in Hong Kong, it was assumed that bubonic plague was the cause. Subsequently, there have been controversial claims that DNA fragments of bubonic plague have been found in mass graves. Yet bubonic plague usually travels slowly and infects a relatively small portion of a given population. By contrast, the Black Death seemed to race across Europe, wiping out entire families and infecting whole cities. Because of this evidence, some historical epidemiologists have speculated that the cause may actually have been anthrax or a "hemorrhagic plague" similar to the Ebola virus.

Although the historical identification of the Black Death remains controversial, contemporaries had little doubt about where the disease came from. Genoese traders, they believed, contracted the plague in Caffa, on the Black Sea coast. Infected sailors carried the disease south into Egypt and west into Sicily, then on to Genoa and Venice. From there it followed established trade routes first into central Italy; later to the south of France, the Low Countries, and England; and finally, through the North and Baltic Seas, into Germany and the Slavic lands to the east (see Map 11.2).

Mortality rates varied, but generally 60 percent or more of those infected died. In the initial infestation of 1348 to 1351, 25 to 35 percent of Europe's population may

**Map 11.2    The Progress of the Black Death**    The Black Death did not advance evenly across Europe; rather, as is clear from the dates at which it struck various regions, it followed the main lines of trade and communication.

have died. In some of Europe's larger cities the death rate may have been as high as 60 percent. In Florence, for example, the population probably declined from about 90,000 to about 50,000 or even less. And the nearby town of Siena likely fared even worse, with the town and its suburbs losing 55 percent of their people. The shock and disruption were immense. Governments in some towns simply ceased to function at the height of the epidemic. Chroniclers reported that no one could be found to care for the sick or bury the dead. Although abandonment of the sick was probably more a fear than a reality, the epidemic nonetheless significantly disrupted daily life.

Just as areas were rebounding from the initial outbreak of the plague, it returned between 1360 and 1363, and then for three centuries thereafter almost no generation could avoid it. It has been calculated that in central Italy, where the best records are available, the plague returned on average every eleven years between 1350 and 1400. Less is known about the plague in Muslim lands and in the eastern Mediterranean, but the situation seems to have been similar to the European experience. Because the plague tended to carry off the young, the almost generational return of the disease accounts for the depressed population levels found in many parts of Europe until the late fifteenth century and in western Asia until the late seventeenth or eighteenth century.

Lacking an understanding of either contagion or infection, fourteenth-century doctors depended on traditional theories inherited from the Greeks, especially the work of Galen°, to treat the plague. In Galenic medicine good health depended on the proper balance of bodily and environmental forces; it could be upset by corrupt air, the movement of planets, and even violent shifts in emotions. Yet in the fifteenth and sixteenth centuries, as the rhythms of the infestations became clearer, towns and, later, territorial governments perceived the contagious nature of the disease. Officials instituted increasingly effective quarantines and embargoes to restrict the movement of goods and people from areas where the plague was raging. Some argue that this innovative effort at public health regulation probably explains the disappearance of the plague from western Europe by the early eighteenth century. (See the box "The Continuing Experiment: Plague and Public Health.")

Alongside medical theory, however, another class of explanations developed. Taking a lead from miracle stories in which Jesus linked illness and sin, many Christians considered the Black Death a signal of the Last Judgment, or at least a sign of the severe judgment of God on a sin-

ful world. Given that view, a traditional, and logical, religious response was to urge various moral reforms and penitential acts, such as charitable gifts, special prayers, and holy processions. (See the feature "Weighing the Evidence: A Painting of the Plague" on pages 390–391.) Many Muslim theologians also concluded that "the plague is part of Allah's punishment." Women were often thought to be a source of moral pollution and hence one of the causes of God's wrath. In Muslim Egypt, women were ordered off the streets; in Christian Europe prostitutes were driven out of towns.

A movement of penitents called "flagellants" arose in Hungary and spread quickly into Germany and across France and the Low Countries. In an imitation of Christ's life and sufferings, they sought to atone in their own bod-

**Flagellant Procession**    Ritual punishments like the one shown in this manuscript illumination were intended to be part of a general reform of individuals and society. *(Bayerische Staatsbibliothek)*

# Plague and Public Health

Europeans did not have a clear understanding of the Black Death and its causes. Yet as these public decrees from Venice demonstrate, they were careful to take whatever steps they could to help control the spread of the disease and treat its victims. These first experiments in public health would ultimately lead to institutions like today's local departments of health or the national Centers for Disease Control and Prevention.

### [May 11, 1400]

Since it has become known that a ship on which many are sick or have died has come to Venice from Ragusa [now Dobrovnik on the coast of Bosnia] . . . and that Ragusa is highly contagious with plague, and since . . . when an epidemic was evident in our city and Ragusa was healthy, Ragusans never allowed Venetians or their ships to enter Ragusan territories . . . it is only right that we should establish the same provisions they have that . . . those from countries filled with corruption should not bring their excesses to Venice. . . .

### [September 27, 1413]

Everyone must search out and remove suspicious materials because they may generate all manner of infection in living areas. This is especially true in our city since it is built on marshes. . . . For some time now dyeing has been done with woad and *sanguine* [a clay-based red dye] which our distinguished physicians consider mortally putrefied and capable of corrupting the air. . . . Thus, be it known that no one of whatever rank after next March can . . . dye with woad or sanguine within the boundaries of the city unless outside in areas that look out on the marshes. . . .

### [August 28, 1423]

Almost every year our city of Venice is infected with a pestiferous disease and this only happens because a host of outsiders from places filled with this pestiferous disease come to Venice. . . . It would be good and right for Venice to do what other communities and lordships do since they do not allow persons from regions and localities infested with the disease to come into their regions and localities. Be it known, therefore, that from next April 1424, the Lords and Colleges [i.e., the government of Venice] whenever they hear that any city is infected with disease, may decree . . . that citizens and residents of such pestiferous cities or localities may not come to Venice. . . . Further, the government shall have the right to have a hospital built on the Lido of San Nicolai . . . in which the prior or prioress [of the hospital] . . . must receive those who are sick [because of the pestilence] and provide them with whatever is necessary. . . . And since our city is often infected with this illness by sea because of persons sick with the pestilence who often come to Venice on warships and merchant ships and then disappear [into the city], . . . it is ordered that all ship owners [Venetian or foreign], . . . if there are any sick persons on board when they arrive in Venice, must place these sick persons in the hospital as soon as they reach port.

## QUESTIONS

1. What did the Venetians think caused this mortality? Does there seem to be more than one source of illness?

2. The hospital built at San Nicolai was one of the first plague hospitals in Europe. What seems to be the reason the Venetians built it?

SOURCE: *Venezia e la peste* (Venice: Marsilio, 1980), pp. 364–365 (translated by Duane Osheim). Reprinted by permission of Duane Osheim.

---

ies for the sins of the world. Following an ancient Christian tradition, they ritually beat (flagellated) themselves between the shoulders with metal-tipped whips. Through their processions and sufferings, these pilgrims hoped to bring about a moral and religious transformation of society. The arrival of flagellants was often an occasion for an end of feuds and political violence within a community. But their arrival just as often was an occasion for political and even religious unrest. Authorities recognized the flagellants and the leaders of the religious riots as dangerous and drove them from towns.

In a quest for a purer, truly Christian society, the flagellants brought suspicion on all those who were not Christian or who were otherwise suspect. Some parts of Europe witnessed murderous attacks on outsiders, especially lepers and Jews, who were suspected of spreading the contagion in an attempt to bring down Latin Christendom. These attacks probably have more to do with tensions and fears already existing in parts of Europe than with the provocations of the flagellants. Like many other anti-Semitic myths, the rumors of wells poisoned by Jews seemed to arise in the south of France and spread in their most virulent forms to German towns along the Rhine. In Strasbourg attacks on Jews preceded the arrival of the plague. Except in a few districts, officials opposed attacks on Jews, lepers, and heretics. Doctors and churchmen often observed that Jews were unlikely culprits, since the plague claimed Jewish as well as Christian victims.

It was a commonplace among contemporary chroniclers that "so many did die that everyone thought it was the end of the world." Yet it was the very young, the elderly, and the poor—those least likely to pay taxes, own shops, or produce children—who were the most common victims. And even in towns such as Florence, where mortality rates were extraordinarily high, recovery from the initial epidemic was rapid. Government offices were closed at most for only a few weeks; markets reopened as soon as the death rate began to decline; and within two years tax receipts were back at preplague levels. Below the surface, however, famine, warfare, plague, and population decline fueled the economic and social transformations of the late Middle Ages.

## Trade and Agriculture

In the aftermath of plague, the economy of Europe changed in a number of profound ways. Disruptions brought on by population decline were accompanied by changes in the basic structure of economic life. In particular, Italy's domination of the European economy was challenged by the growth of trade and manufacturing in many other parts of Europe. Further, Italian bankers came to face competition from equally astute local bankers.

Discussions of the economy must begin with Italy because it was the key point of contact between Europe and the international economy. In 1300 Italian merchants sold woolens produced in Flanders and Italy to Arab traders in North Africa, who sold them along the African coast and as far south as the Niger Delta. The Italians used the gold that they collected in payment to buy spices and raw materials in Byzantium, Egypt, and even China. They resold these highly prized goods in the cities and at regional fairs of northern Europe. Italian traders also sold spices, silks, and other luxuries throughout Europe, from England to Poland.

Because of their expertise in moving bullion and goods and their ready sources of capital, Italian merchants, such as the Ricciardis of Lucca who flourished in England, were ideal bankers and financial advisers to the popes

and European rulers, who appreciated sources of ready capital. In time of war rulers tended to trade the rights to various revenues to Italian bankers, who had cash at hand. Merchants from Cremona, Genoa, Florence, and Siena forged commercial agreements with the kings of France, Aragon, and Castile, and with the papacy.

The most powerful bank in fifteenth-century Europe was the Medici bank of Florence. Founded in 1397 by Giovanni de' Medici° (1360–1429), the bank grew quickly because of its role as papal banker. Medici agents transferred papal revenues from all parts of Europe to Rome and managed papal alum mines, which provided an essential mineral to the growing cloth industry. Cosimo de' Medici° (1389–1464), Giovanni's son and successor, transformed the enterprise into a series of bilateral partnerships with easily controlled junior partners in other parts of Europe. In this way he avoided the problem of supervision and control that plagued other banks, whose partners were equal and free to speculate and invest as they wished.

The dramatic career of the Frenchman Jacques Coeur (1395?–1456) demonstrates that by the mid-fifteenth century, Italian merchants were not the only Europeans who understood international trade. After making a fortune trading in southern France, Coeur managed the French royal mint and became the financial adviser of King Charles VII (r. 1422–1461). He put the French monarchy back on a solid financial footing after the Hundred Years' War, becoming in the process the wealthiest individual in France. Not surprisingly, his wealth and influence earned him jealous enemies, who tried to bring him down with outrageous claims: he was accused of murdering the king's mistress, trading with Muslims, and stealing royal funds. In 1451 his property was confiscated, and he was jailed for a short time. He later led a papal expedition against the Turks in the Aegean, where he died.

By 1500 Italians faced increased competition from local merchants throughout Europe. From as early as the late thirteenth century, trade along the North and Baltic Seas in northern Europe was dominated by the Hanseatic League, an association of over a hundred trading cities centered on the German city of Lübeck. By the late fourteenth and early fifteenth centuries, the Hansa towns controlled grain shipments from eastern Europe to England and Scandinavia. The league's domination waned in the second half of the fifteenth century, however, as Dutch, English, and even southern German merchants gained shares of the wool, grain, and fur trades. Towns in the east-

---

**Giovanni de' Medici** (joe-VAHN-nee day-MAY-di-chi)
**Cosimo de' Medici** (CAW-see-moe day-MAY-di-chi)

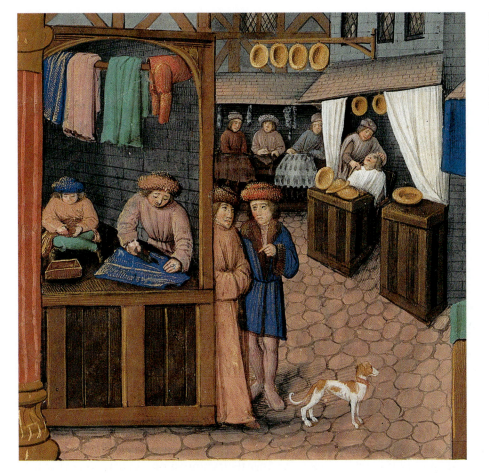

ern Baltic found that their interests no longer coincided with those of the towns in western Germany that made up the Hanseatic League. Wroclaw° (in modern Poland) signaled the nature of the change when it resigned from the league in 1474 to expand trade connections with the southern German towns.

In contrast to the Hanseatic League of towns, merchants in southern Germany adopted Italian techniques of trade, manufacture, and finance to expand their influence throughout central Europe. German merchants regularly bought spices in the markets of Venice and distributed them in central and eastern Europe. By the fifteenth century the townspeople of southern Germany also produced linen and cotton cloth, which found ready markets in central and eastern Europe.

The Fugger° family of Augsburg in southern Germany, the most prosperous of the German commercial families,

exemplifies the variety of activities undertaken by south German merchants. Hans Fugger (1348–1409) moved to Augsburg from a nearby village in the 1360s and quickly established himself as a weaver and wool merchant. By the 1470s Hans's grandson, Jacob Fugger (1459–1525), was a dominant figure in the spice trade and also participated in a number of unusually large loans to a succession of German princes. The Fuggers became leaders in the Tyrolean silver-mining industry, which expanded dramatically in the late fifteenth century. And in the early sixteenth century they handled all transfers of money from Germany to the papacy. Jacob Fugger's wealth increased fourfold between 1470 and 1500. The Fuggers were indispensable allies of the German emperors. Jacob himself ensured the election of Charles V as Holy Roman emperor in 1519, making a series of loans that allowed Charles to buy the influence that he needed to win election.

As wealthy as the great merchants were, in most parts of Europe prosperity was still tied to agriculture and the production of food grains. In northern and western

**Wroclaw** (VROT-swav)    **Fugger** (FOO-ger)

Europe foodstuffs were produced on the manorial estates of great churchmen and nobles. These estates were worked by a combination of farmers paying rents, serfs who owed a variety of labor services, and day laborers who were hired during planting and harvesting. In the face of a decimated population, landlords and employers found themselves competing for the reduced number of laborers who had survived the plague. In 1351 the English crown issued the Statute of Laborers, which pegged wages and the prices of commodities at preplague levels. According to the statute, regulation was necessary because laborers "withdrew themselves from serving great men and others unless they have living [in food] and wages double or treble of what they were [before the plague]." This statute and similar ones passed in other parts of Europe were dead letters. So long as population levels remained low, landowners were unable to keep wages low and rents high.

Cloth manufacture, not agriculture, was the part of the European economy that changed most dramatically in the late Middle Ages. First in Flanders, then later in England, Germany, and the rest of Europe, production shifted from urban workshops to the countryside. Industries in rural areas tended to be free of controls on quality or techniques. Rural production, whether in Flanders, England, or Lombardy, became the most dynamic part of the industry.

Rural cloth production, especially in southwestern Germany and parts of England, was organized through the putting-out system. Merchants who owned the raw wool contracted with various artisans in the city, suburbs, or countryside—wherever the work could be done most cheaply—to process the wool into cloth. Rural manufacture was least expensive because it could be done as occasional or part-time labor by farmers, or by their wives or children, during slack times of the day or season. Because production was likely to be finished in the countryside (beyond guild supervision), the merchant was free to move the cloth to wherever it could most easily and profitably be sold; guild masters had no control over price or quality.

Two other developments also changed the woolen trade of the fifteenth century: the rise of Spain as an exporter of unprocessed wool and the emergence of England, long recognized as a source of prime wool, as a significant producer of finished cloth. Spain was an ideal region for the pasturing of livestock. By the fifteenth century highly prized Spanish wool from merino sheep was regularly exported to Italy, Flanders, and England. By 1500 over three million sheep grazed in Castile alone, and rev-

enues from duties on wool formed the backbone of royal finance.

In England, in contrast, economic transformation was tied to cloth production. During the fifteenth century England reduced its export of its high-quality raw wool and began instead to export its own finished cloth. In 1350 the English exported just over 5,000 bolts of cloth. By the 1470s exports had risen to 63,000 bolts, and they doubled again by the 1520s. The growth of cloth exports contributed enormously to the expansion of London. During the fourteenth and fifteenth centuries English commerce became increasingly controlled by London merchant-adventurers. Soon after 1500 over 80 percent of the cloth for export passed through the hands of the Londoners. This development, coupled with the rise of London as a center of administration and consumption, laid the foundation for the economic and demographic growth that would make London the largest and most prosperous city in western Europe by the eighteenth century.

All these patterns of economic change in the fifteenth century challenged customs and institutions by admitting new entrepreneurs into the marketplace. But Europe was still a conservative society in which social and political influence was more prized than economic wealth. Patricians in many European towns acted to dampen competition and preserve traditional values. Great banking families such as the Medicis of Florence tended to avoid competition and concentrations of capital. They did not try to drive their competitors out of business because the leaders of rival banks were their political and social peers. In northern Europe, governments in towns such as Leiden restricted the concentration of resources in the hands of the town's leading cloth merchants. Their aim was to ensure full employment for the town's laborers, political power for the guild masters, and social stability in the town.

Full employment was not just for men. Although men had controlled the guilds and most crafts in the thirteenth and early fourteenth centuries, women's guilds existed in several European cities, including Paris and Cologne. In Italy some women could be found among the more prosperous crafts. Women often practiced their trades in the context of the family. In Cologne, for instance, women produced the linen yarn and silk cloths that their husbands sold throughout Europe. Speaking of the silkmakers of Cologne, a report noted that "the women are much more knowledgeable about the trade than are the men." Unlike southern Europe, where women had no public roles, some northern towns apparently allowed women's guilds to protect their members' activities as artisans and

**Women at Work**    Although guild records tend to ignore the contributions of women, many women worked in their husbands' shops. In this miniature a woman is selling jewelry. Widows often managed the shops they inherited.    *(Bibliothèque nationale de France)*

even peddlers. Because they often worked before marriage, townswomen in northern Europe tended to marry at a later age than did women in Italy. Many women earned their own marriage dowries. Since they had their own sources of income and often managed the shop of a deceased husband, women could be surprisingly independent. They were consequently under less pressure to remarry at the death of a spouse. Although their economic circumstances varied considerably, up to a quarter of the households in northern towns such as Bern and Zurich were headed by women. Many of them were widows, but many others, perhaps a third, were women who had never married.

The fifteenth century brought new restrictions to women's lives. In England brewing ale had been a highly profitable part-time activity that women often combined with the running of a household. Ale was usually produced in small batches for household use, and whatever went unconsumed would be sold. The introduction of beer changed matters. Because hops were added as a preservative during brewing, beer was easier to produce, store, and transport in large batches. Beer brewing became a lucrative full-time trade, reducing the demand for the alewife's product and providing work for men as brewers. At the same time the rights of women to work in urban crafts and industries were reduced. Wealthy fathers became less inclined to allow wives and daughters to work outside the home. Guilds banned the use of female laborers in many trades and severely limited the rights of widows to supervise their spouses' shops. For reasons that are not entirely clear, journeymen—employees of guild masters who themselves hoped to become masters—

objected to working alongside women. These complaints may have come from workers who realized that their status as employees was permanent instead of a temporary stage before promotion to master. By the early sixteenth century journeymen in Germany considered it "dishonorable" for a woman, even the master's wife or daughter, to work in a shop.

Despite the narrowing of economic opportunities for women, the overall economic prospects of peasants and laborers improved. Lower rents and increased wages in the wake of the plague meant a higher standard of living for small farmers and laborers. Before the plague struck in 1348, most poor Europeans had subsisted on bread or grain-based gruel, consuming meat, fish, and cheese only a few times a week. A well-off peasant in England had lived on a daily ration of about two pounds of bread and a cup or two of oatmeal porridge washed down with three or four pints of ale. Poorer peasants generally drank water except on very special occasions. After the plague laborers were more prosperous. Adults in parts of Germany may have consumed nearly a liter of wine, a third of a pound of meat, and a pound or more of bread each day. Elsewhere people could substitute an equivalent portion of beer, ale, or cider for the wine. Hard times for landlords were good times for peasants and day laborers.

Landlords in England responded to the shortage of labor by converting their lands to grazing in order to produce wool for the growing textile market. In parts of Italy landlords invested in canals, irrigation, and new crops in order to increase profits. In eastern Germany and Poland landlords were able to take advantage of political and social unrest to force tenants into semi-free servile status. This so-called second serfdom created an impoverished work force whose primary economic activity was in the lord's fields, establishing commercial grain farming. Increasingly in the second half of the century grains cultivated in Poland and Prussia found their way to markets in England and the Low Countries. Europe east of the Elbe River became a major producer of grain, but at a heavy social cost.

The loss of perhaps a third of the urban population to the plague had serious consequences in the towns of Europe. Because of lower birthrates and higher death rates, late medieval towns needed a constant influx of immigrants to expand or even to maintain their populations. These immigrants did not find life in the cities easy, however. Citizenship in most towns was restricted to masters in the most important guilds, and local governments were in their hands, if not under their thumbs. In many towns citizens constructed a system of taxation that worked to their own economic advantage and fell heavily on artisans and peasants living in territories controlled by the towns. Unskilled laborers and members of craft guilds depended for their economic well-being on personal relationships with powerful citizens who controlled the government and the markets. Peace and order in towns and in the countryside required a delicate balance of the interests of the well-to-do and the more humble. When that balance was shattered by war, plague, and economic depression, the result was often a popular revolt, such as the Ciompi insurrection of 1378 in Florence and the Rising of 1381 in England.

## THE CONSOLIDATION OF THE LATE MEDIEVAL GOVERNMENTS, 1450–1500

**B**Y 1500 it seemed that the French royal lawyer's claim that all within the kingdom belonged to the king was finally accepted. With the exception of Italy and Germany, strong central governments recovered from the crises of war and civil unrest that wracked the fourteenth and fifteenth centuries. The Hundred Years' War and the resulting disorganization in France and England seemed to strike at the heart of the monarchies. But through the foundation of standing armies and the careful consolidation of power in the royal court, both countries seemed stronger and more able to defend themselves in the second half of the century. And as the Italians learned in the wars following the French invasion of 1494, small regional powers were no match for the mighty monarchies.

### France, England, and Scandinavia

In France recovery from a century of war was based on a consolidation of the monarchy's power. A key to French military successes had been the creation of a paid professional army, which replaced the feudal host and mercenary companies of the fourteenth century. Charles VII created Europe's first standing army, a cavalry of about eight thousand nobles under the direct control of royal commanders. Charles also expanded his judicial claims. He and his son, Louis XI (r. 1461–1483), created new provincial *parlements*, or law courts, at Toulouse°, Grenoble°, Bordeaux, and Dijon°. They also required that local

---

**Toulouse** (too-LOOZ)     **Grenoble** (greh-NO-bul)
**Dijon** (dee-ZHON)

laws and customs be registered and approved by the parlements.

A second key to maintaining royal influence was the rise of the French court as a political and financial center. Through careful appointments and judicious offers of annuities and honors, Charles VII and Louis XI drew the nobility to the royal court and made the nobles dependent on it. "The court," complained a frustrated noble, "is an assembly of people who, under the pretense of acting for the good of all, come together to diddle each other; for there's scarcely anyone who isn't engaged in buying and selling and exchanging . . . and sometimes for their money we sell them our . . . humanity."[8] One of Louis XI's advisers noted that Charles VII never had revenues greater than 18,000 francs in a single year but that Louis collected 4.7 million. By 1500 France had fully recovered from the crisis of war and was once again a strong and influential state.

The fate of the English monarchy was quite different. Henry VI (r. 1422–1461) turned out to be weak-willed, immature, and prone to bouts of insanity—inherited, perhaps, from his French grandfather, Charles VI (see page 366). The infirmity of Henry VI and the loss of virtually all French territories in 1453 led to factional battles known as the Wars of the Roses—the red rose symbolized Henry's House of Lancaster, the white the rival House of York. Edward of York eventually deposed Henry and claimed the Crown for himself as Edward IV (r. 1461–1483). He faced little opposition because few alternatives existed. English public life was again thrown into confusion, however, at Edward's death. The late king's brother, Richard, duke of Gloucester, claimed the protectorship over the 13-year-old king, Edward V (r. April–June 1483), and his younger brother. Richard seized the boys, who were placed in the Tower of London and never seen again. He proclaimed himself king and was crowned Richard III (r. 1483–1485). He withstood early challenges to his authority but in 1485 was killed in the Battle of Bosworth Field, near Coventry, by Henry Tudor, a leader of the Lancastrian faction. Henry married Elizabeth, the surviving child of Edward IV. Symbolically at least, the struggle between the rival claimants to the Crown appeared over.

Like his predecessor, Edward IV, Henry VII (r. 1485–1509) recognized the importance of avoiding war and taxation. Like the French kings, he created a patronage network of local officials to secure allies for his dynasty. Royal power, however, was not based on a transformation of the institutions of government. Following Edward's example, Henry controlled local affairs through the traditional system of royal patronage. He also imitated Edward in emphasizing the dignity of the royal office. Though

careful with his funds, he was willing to buy jewels and clothing if they added to the brilliance of his court. As one courtier summed up his reign, "His hospitality was splendidly generous. . . . He knew well how to maintain his majesty and all which pertains to kingship." Henry solidified ties with Scotland and Spain by marrying his daughter, Margaret Tudor, to James IV of Scotland and his sons, Arthur and (after Arthur's death) Henry, to Catherine of Aragon, daughter of the Spanish rulers Ferdinand and Isabella.

The English monarchy of the late fifteenth century departed little from previous governments. The success of Henry VII was based on several factors: the absence of powerful opponents; lower taxation thanks to twenty-five years of peace; and the desire, shared by ruler and ruled alike, for an orderly realm built on the assured succession of a single dynasty.

In the fourteenth and fifteenth centuries the Scandinavian kingdoms of Denmark, Sweden, and Norway lay open to economic and political influences from Germany. German merchants traded throughout the area and completely controlled access to the important port of Bergen in Norway. German nobles sought to influence northern political life, especially in Denmark. The Scandinavian aristocracy, however, especially in Denmark, remained wary of German interests. Alert to outside pressures, Scandinavian elites tended to marry among themselves and forge alliances against the Germans.

Public authority varied greatly across Scandinavia. In Norway, Denmark, and Sweden the power of the king was always mediated by the influence of the council, made up of the country's leading landowners. Power was based on ownership or control of lands and rents. All the Scandinavian countries were home to a significant class of free peasants, and they were traditionally represented in the Riksdag in Sweden and the Storting in Norway, popular assemblies that had the right to elect kings, authorize taxes, and make laws. Scandinavians spoke similar Germanic languages and were linked by close social and economic ties. Thus it is not surprising that the crowns of the three kingdoms were joined during periods of crisis. In 1397 the dowager queen Margaret of Denmark was able to unite the Scandinavian crowns by the Union of Kalmar, which would nominally endure until 1523.

## Eastern Europe and Russia

Two phenomena had an especially profound effect on the governments of eastern Europe. One was the emergence of a newly important ruling dynasty. The other was the decline of Mongol, or Tatar, influence in the region. Since

**Saint Vitus Cathedral**    The construction of Saint Vitus cathedral in the flamboyant late Gothic style was part of Emperor Charles IV's program to transform Prague into the leading city of east-central Europe.    *(Werner Neumeister, photographer)*

the thirteenth century much of eastern Europe had been forced to acknowledge Tatar dominion and pay annual tribute. Now the Tatar subjugation was challenged and finally ended.

As in much of Europe, political power was segmented and based on personal relationships between family members, communities, clients, and friends. Life in the East was further complicated by the mix of languages, cultures, and religions. Native Catholic and Orthodox populations were further diversified in the fourteenth century by the arrival of Muslims in the Balkans and Ashkenazi Jews throughout most of the region. Escaping growing persecution, the Ashkenazim migrated to Poland, Lithuania, and Ruthen-

ian lands (parts of modern Russia), where they lived under their own leaders and followed their own laws.

This mix of cultures and religions played a role in the growth of new states. Under the pretext of converting their pagan neighbors to Christianity, the mostly German Teutonic Knights sought to expand eastward against the kingdom of Poland and the Lithuanian state. They were thwarted, however, by a profound dynastic shift. In 1386 Grand Duke Jagiello (r. 1377–1434) of Lithuania converted to Catholic Christianity and married Hedwig, the daughter and heir of King Louis of Poland (r. 1370–1382). The resulting dynastic union created a state with a population of perhaps six million that reached from the Baltic nearly to the Black Sea. Polish-Lithuanian power slowed and finally halted the German advance to the east. Most serious for the Teutonic Knights was their defeat in 1410 at Tannenberg, in Prussia, by a Polish-Lithuanian army led by Jagiello's cousin, Prince Vytautus of Lithuania. The Polish-Lithuanian union was only dynastic. The descendants of Jagiello, called Jagiellonians, had no hereditary right to rule Poland, and the Lithuanians opposed any Polish administrative influence in their lands. Yet because of Jagiellonian power, the Poles continued to select them as kings. At various times Jagiellonians also sat on the thrones of Bohemia and Hungary.

Poland and Lithuania remained more closely tied to western Europe than to the Russian East. They tended to be Catholic rather than Orthodox Christians. They wrote in a Roman rather than a Cyrillic script. And their political institutions resembled those of western Europe. Polish nobles managed to win a number of important concessions, the most significant being freedom from arbitrary arrest and confinement. This civil right was secured in Poland well before the more famous English right of habeas corpus. It was during this period, and under the influence of the Polish kings, that Cracow emerged as the economic and cultural center of Poland. Cracow University was founded in 1364 in response to the foundation of Prague University by the emperor Charles IV in 1348. After the dynastic union of Poland and Lithuania, Polish language and culture increasingly influenced the Lithuanian nobility. This union laid the foundation for the great Polish-Lithuanian commonwealth of the early modern period.

Lithuania had never been conquered by the Tatars, and its expansion contributed to the decline of Tatar power. The rise of Moscow, however, owed much to the continuing Tatar domination. Since the Mongol invasions in the thirteenth century, various towns and principalities of Kievan Rus had been part of a Tatar sphere of influence. This primarily meant homage and payment of an annual tribute.

A key to the emergence of Moscow occurred when Ivan I (r. 1328–1341), Prince of Moscow, was named Grand Prince and collector of tribute from the other Russian princes. Not for nothing was he called "the Moneybag." It was during this same period that the head of the Russian Orthodox Church was persuaded to make his home in Moscow. And in 1367 the princes began to rebuild the Kremlin walls in stone.

The decisive change for Moscow, however, was the reign of Ivan III (r. 1462–1505). By 1478 Ivan III, called "Ivan the Great," had seized the famed trading center of Novgorod. Two years later he was powerful enough to re-

nounce Mongol overlordship and refuse further payments of tribute. After his marriage to an émigré Byzantine princess living in Rome, Ivan began to call himself "Tsar" (Russian for "Caesar"), implying that in the wake of the Muslim conquest of Constantinople, Moscow had become the new Rome.

## The Ottoman Empire

The eastern Mediterranean region was a politically tumultuous area in the fourteenth century, when the Ottoman Turks were first invited into the Balkans by the hard-pressed Byzantine emperor. Early in the fifteenth century the Turks were only one, and perhaps not even the greatest, of the Balkan threats to the Byzantine Empire and the other Balkan states (see Map 11.3). Hungarians, Venetians, and Germans also competed for influence in this volatile area. Individuals and groups added to the turmoil by expediently switching their political allegiances and even their religions. In the 1420s, for example, as the Turks and the Hungarians fought for influence in Serbia, the Serbian king moved easily from alliance with one to alliance with the other. Elites often retained their political and economic influence by changing religion. The Christian aristocracy of late-fifteenth-century Bosnia, for example, was welcomed into Islam and instantly created a cohesive elite fighting force for the Turks. Conversely, as Turkish power in Albania grew, one noble, George Castriota (d. 1467), known by his Turkish name Skanderbeg, reconverted to Christianity and became a leading figure in the resistance to the Turks. Only after his death were the Turks able to integrate Albania into their empire.

An Ottoman victory over a Christian crusading army at Varna, on the Black Sea coast, in 1444 changed the dynamics and virtually sealed the fate of Constantinople. It was only a matter of time before the Turks took the city. When Mehmed° II (r. 1451–1481) finally turned his attention to Constantinople in 1453, the siege of the city lasted only fifty-three days. Turkish artillery breached the walls before a Venetian navy or a Hungarian army could come to the city's defense. The destruction of the last vestiges of the Roman imperial tradition that reached back to the emperor Augustus sent shock waves through Christian Europe and brought forth calls for new crusades to liberate the East from the evils of Islam. It also stirred anti-Christian feelings among the Turks. The rise of the Ottoman Turks transformed eastern Europe and led to a profound clash between Christian and Muslim civilizations.

---

**Mehmed** (MEH-met)

**Map 11.3    Turkey and Eastern Europe**    With the conquest of Constantinople, Syria, and Palestine, the Ottoman Turks controlled the eastern Mediterranean and dominated Europe below the Danube River. The Holy Roman emperors, rulers of Italy, and kings of Spain had to be concerned about potential invasions by land or by sea.

After the fall of Constantinople the Turks worked to consolidate their new territories. Through alliance and conquest Ottoman hegemony extended through Syria and Palestine and by 1517 to Egypt. Even the Muslim powers of North Africa were nominally under Turkish control. In short order they expanded to the west and north, seizing Croatia, Bosnia, Dalmatia, Albania, eastern Hungary, Moldavia, Bulgaria, and Greece. Turkish strength was based on a number of factors. The first was the loyalty and efficiency of the sultan's crack troops, the Janissaries. These troops were young boys forcibly taken from the subject Christian populations, trained in the Turkish language and customs, and converted to Islam. Although they functioned as special protectors of the Christian community from which they were drawn, they were separated from it by their new faith. Because the Turkish pop-ulation viewed them as outsiders, they were particularly loyal to the sultan.

The situation of the Janissaries underlines a secondary explanation for Ottoman strength: the unusually tolerant attitudes of Mehmed, who saw himself not only as the greatest of the *ghazi* (crusading warriors who were considered the "instruments of Allah") but also as emperor, heir to Byzantine and ancient imperial traditions. Immediately after the conquest of Constantinople he re-populated the city with Greeks, Armenians, Jews, and Muslims. Mehmed especially welcomed Sephardic Jews from Spain and Portugal to parts of his empire. Thessalonica (Salonika), for example, was second only to Amsterdam as a Sephardic Jewish center until the community was destroyed in World War II. Religious groups in the cities lived in separate districts centered on a church or

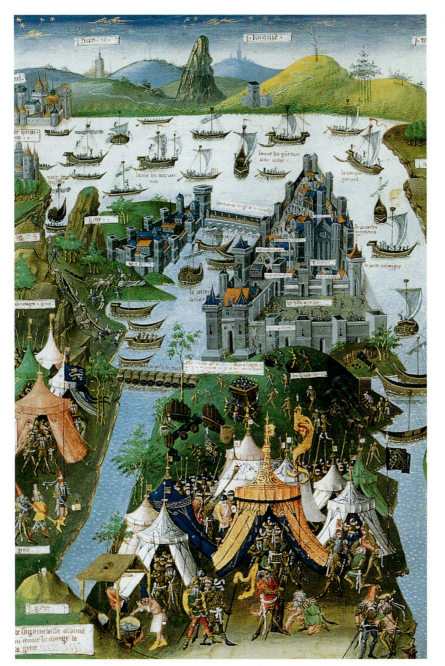

**The Siege of Constantinople**    The siege of Constantinople by the Turks required the attackers to isolate the city both by sea and by land. This miniature from the fifteenth century shows the Turkish camps, as well as the movements of Turkish boats, completing the isolation of the city. *(Bibliothèque nationale de France)*

synagogue, and each religious community retained the right to select its own leaders. (See the box "Global Encounters: A Disputation.") Mehmed made Constantinople the capital of the new Ottoman Empire. And by building mosques, hospitals, hostels, and bridges, he breathed new life into the city, which he referred to as Istanbul—that is, "the city." In the fifty years following the conquest, the population of the city grew an extraordinary 500 percent, from about 40,000 to over 200,000, making it the largest city in Europe, as it had been in Late Antiquity.

At a time when Christian Europe seemed less and less willing to tolerate non-Christian minorities, the Ottoman Empire's liberal attitude toward outsiders seemed striking. Muslims and non-Muslims belonged to the same trade associations and traveled throughout the empire. Mehmed had no qualms about making trade agreements with the

# A Disputation

Konstantin Mihailovic, a Serb by birth, was captured by the Turks during the conquest of Constantinople in 1453. He later served with the Turks until he returned to the Christian forces in 1463. His description of a typical Turkish disputation, or debate, taking place in the presence of the sultan or another dignitary is an interesting example of how the Muslim, Jewish, and Christian peoples of the Balkans tried to understand one another.

The masters and scribes have among themselves this custom: they arrange their deliberations before the highest lord after the emperor. . . . And then they begin to argue one against the other, speaking mostly about the prophets. Some [of these Turkish scribes] recognize Our Lord Jesus Christ as a prophet, and others as an archprophet, alongside God the Creator of Heaven and earth. And also the Lord, from the time when the Mohammedan faith began, created eight hundred camels, like invisible spirits, which go around every night and gather evil *Busromane* [i.e., the Muslim, or the Chosen People of God] from our [Muslim] graves and carry them to *kaur* graves [the Kaury are "the Confused People," i.e., the Christians]; and then gather good kaury and carry them to our graves. And now the good kaury will stand with our Busroman council and the evil Busromane will stand with the kaur council on Judgment Day before God. For [a pious one] says . . . , "The Christians have a faith but have no works." Therefore Mohammed will lead the Busromane to Paradise and Jesus will order the Christians to hell. Moses will sorrow for the Jews that they have not been obedient to him. . . . He [one of the scribes] spoke in this way:

"Elias and Enoch are both in body and soul in paradise; but before Judgment Day they must die. But Jesus both in body and in soul is in heaven. He is the only one who will not die a death but will be alive forever and ever. Mohammed both in body and soul was in heaven, but remained with us on earth." And then the masters began to dispute, one in one way and one in another, and there were many words among them. And having raised a cry one against another, they began to throw books at one another. [Then the official in charge of the disputation] . . . told them to cease this disputation and he ordered that food be brought them according to their custom and they gave them water to drink, since they do not drink wine. And then, having eaten their fill, they gave thanks to God, praying for the souls of the living and the dead and for those who fight against the kaury or Christians.

## QUESTIONS

1. Like many people, the scribes in the debate are aware that good and evil behavior is not the special preserve of one people. How do they explain that individuals will be punished or rewarded for their deeds?

2. Christian theologians traditionally considered Muslims to be heretics who could not be saved. How do these debaters evaluate Christians?

SOURCE: Konstantin Mihailovic, *Memoirs of a Janissary,* translated by Benjamin Stolz. Copyright © 1975. Reprinted by permission of Michigan Slavic Publications.

Italian powers in an attempt to consolidate his control. And in Serbia, Bulgaria, Macedonia, and Albania he left in place previous social and political institutions, requiring only loyalty to his empire.

Mehmed had to tread carefully, though, because the Turks had a number of powerful enemies. Serious problems, for example, surfaced during the reign of Mehmed's son, Bayazid° (r. 1481–1512). Following Turkish tradition, Mehmed had not chosen a successor but let his sons fight for control. Normally the successful claimant achieved the throne by doing away with his closest relatives. Bayazid's brother, Jem, however, fled into the protective custody of Christian powers, where he spent the rest of his life. In times of crisis kings and popes would threaten to foment rebellion in Ottoman lands by releasing him. Bayazid also had to worry about the Mamluk Turks, who controlled Egypt and Syria, and the new Safavid dynasty in Persia. Although both were Muslim, they were willing to join with various Christian states to reduce the power of the Ottomans. Only in the second decade of the sixteenth century, after Bayazid's son, Selim (r. 1512–1520), had defeated the Persians and the Mamluks, were the Ottomans finally safe from attack from the east or south.

---

Bayazid (bay-a-ZEED)

## The Union of Crowns in Spain

While expanding across the Mediterranean, the Turks came in contact with the other new state of the fifteenth century, the newly unified kingdom of Spain. As in Poland-Lithuania, the Spanish monarchy was only a dynastic union. In 1469 Ferdinand, heir to the kingdom of Aragon and Catalonia, married Isabella, daughter of the king of Castile. Five years later Isabella became queen of Castile, and in 1479 Ferdinand took control of the kingdom of Aragon. This union of Crowns eventually would lead to the creation of a united Spain, but true integration was still a distant dream in 1469.

The permanence of the union was remarkable because the two kingdoms were so different. Castile was a much larger and more populous state. It had taken the lead in the Reconquista, the fight begun in the eleventh century to reclaim Iberia from Muslim rule. As a result, economic power within Castile was divided among the groups most responsible for the Reconquista: military orders and nobles. The military orders of Calatrava, Santiago, and Alcantara were militias formed by men who had taken a religious vow similar to that taken by a monk, with an added commitment to fight against the enemies of Christianity. In the course of the Reconquista, the military orders assumed control of vast districts. Lay nobles who aided in the Reconquista also held large tracts of land and proudly guarded their independence.

Castile's power stemmed from its agrarian wealth. During the Reconquista Castilians took control of large regions and turned them into ranges for grazing merino sheep, producers of the prized merino wool exported to the markets of Flanders and Italy (see page 376). To maximize the profits from wool production, the kings authorized the creation of the Mesta, a brotherhood of sheep producers. The pastoral economy grew to the point that by the early sixteenth century Castilians owned over three million sheep.

Economic power in Castile lay with the nobility, but political power rested with the monarch. Because the nobility was largely exempt from taxation, nobles ignored the Cortes°, the popular assembly, which could do little more than approve royal demands. The towns of Castile were important only as fortresses and staging points for militias rather than as centers of trade and commerce.

The kingdom of Aragon was dramatically different. The center of the kingdom was Barcelona, an important trading center in the Mediterranean. In the fourteenth and fifteenth centuries the kings of Aragon concentrated their efforts on expanding their influence in the Mediterranean, especially south of France and Italy. By the middle of the fifteenth century the Aragonese empire included the kingdom of Naples, Sicily, the Balearic° Islands, and Sardinia.

The power of the Aragonese king, in sharp contrast to the Castilian monarchy, was limited because the Crown was not unified. The ruler was king in Aragon and Navarre but only count in Catalonia. Aragon, Catalonia, and Valencia each maintained its own Cortes. In each area the traditional nobility and the towns had a great deal more influence than did their counterparts in Castile. The power of the Cortes is clear in the coronation oath taken by the Aragonese nobility: "We who are as good as you and together are more powerful than you, make you our king and lord, provided that you observe our laws and liberties, and if not, not."[9] The distinction between Aragon and Castile could not be stronger.

Initially the union of the crowns of Aragon and Castile did little to unify the two monarchies. Nobles fought over disputed boundaries, and Castilian nobles felt exploited by Aragonese merchants. Trade duties and internal boundaries continued to be disputed. The two realms even lacked a treaty to allow for the extradition of criminals from one kingdom to the other. Castilians never accepted Ferdinand as more than their queen's consort. After the death of Isabella in 1504 he ruled in Castile only as regent for his infant grandson, Charles I (r. 1516–1556). "Spain" would not emerge in an institutional sense until the late sixteenth century.

Nonetheless, the reign of Isabella and Ferdinand marked a profound change in politics and society in the Iberian kingdoms and in Europe in general. Ferdinand and Isabella married their daughter Joanna, to Philip of Habsburg in 1496 to draw the Holy Roman Empire into the Italian wars brought on by the French invasion (see pages 369–370). The marriage of their daughter Catherine of Aragon to Prince Arthur of England in 1501 was designed to obtain yet another ally against the French. Those two marriages would have momentous consequences for European history in the sixteenth century.

The reign of Ferdinand and Isabella is especially memorable because of the events of 1492. In January of that year a crusading army conquered Granada, the last Muslim stronghold in Iberia. In March Ferdinand and Isabella ordered the Jews of Castile and Aragon to convert or leave the kingdom within four months. In April Isabella

---

**Cortes** (cor-TEZ)

**Balearic** (ba-LEER-ik)

**Ferdinand and Isabella Interrogating a Jew**   Jews in Spain and many other parts of Europe were considered to be under the specific jurisdiction of local rulers. Jews and their converso relatives turned to the king and queen in 1492 when Jews faced the order to convert or leave the kingdom. *(Museo de Zargoza)*

issued her commission authorizing Christopher Columbus "to discover and acquire islands and mainland in the Ocean Sea" (see pages 440–441).

The conquest of Granada and the expulsion of the Jews represented a radical shift in the Spanish mentality. Until the beginning of the fifteenth century Spain maintained a level of religious tolerance unusual in Christendom. In the fourteenth century perhaps 2 percent of the population of Iberia was Jewish, and the Muslim population may have been as high as 50 percent. The various groups were inextricably mixed. The statutes of the Jewish community in Barcelona were written in Catalan, a Spanish dialect, rather than in Hebrew. *Maranos,* Jewish converts to Christianity, and *moriscos,* Muslim converts, mixed continuously with Christians and with members of their former religions. It was difficult at times to know which religion these converts, or *conversos,* actually practiced. One surprised northern visitor to Spain remarked that one noble's circle was filled with "Christians, Moors, and Jews and he lets them live in peace in their faith."

This tolerant mingling of Christians, Muslims, and Jews had periodically occasioned violence. All three communities, in fact, preferred clear boundaries between the groups. In 1391, however, a series of violent attacks had long-lasting and unfortunate effects on Iberian society. An attack on the Jews of Seville led to murders, forced conversions, and suppression of synagogues throughout Spain. In the wake of the assault, large portions of the urban Jewish population either converted to Christianity or moved into villages away from the large commercial cities. The Jewish population in Castile may have declined by a fourth. Although the anti-Jewish feelings were expressed in religious terms, the underlying cause was anger over the economic prominence of some Jewish or converso families. After 1391 anti-Jewish feeling increasingly became racial. As one rebel said, "The converso remains a Jew and therefore should be barred from public office."[10]

Hostility and suspicion toward Jews grew throughout the fifteenth century until Ferdinand and Isabella concluded that the only safe course was to order all Jews to accept baptism. Jews who would not convert would have to leave the kingdom within four months. The order was signed on March 31, 1492, and published in late April after an unsuccessful attempt by converso and Jewish leaders to dissuade the monarchs from implementing it.

Many Jews could not dispose of their possessions in the four months allowed and so chose to convert and remain. But it is estimated that about ten thousand Jews left Aragon and that even more left Castile. Many moved to Portugal and then to North Africa. Some went east to Istanbul or north to the Low Countries. A number of others moved to the colonies being established in the New World in the vain hope of avoiding the Inquisition, which was already underway when the expulsion order was issued (see below). In 1504 the expulsion order was extended to include all Muslims.

The economic and social costs of the expulsion were profound. Not every Muslim or Jew was wealthy and cultured, but the exiles did include many doctors, bankers, and merchants. Spanish culture, long open to influences from Muslim and Jewish sources, became narrower and less willing to accept new ideas. After the expulsion a chasm of distrust opened between the "Old Christians" and the "New Christians"—that is, those newly converted. As early as the first decades of the fifteenth century, some religious orders had refused to accept "New Christians." They required that their members demonstrate *limpieza de sangre,* a purity of blood. By 1500 the same tests of blood purity became prerequisites for holding most religious and public offices. Thus by the end of the fifteenth century the Iberian kingdoms had created more powerful, unified governments, but at a terrible cost to the only portion of Christendom that had ever practiced religious tolerance.

Complaints that led to the expulsion arose from a variety of sources. The fact that many of the most important financiers and courtiers were Jews or conversos bred jealousies and tensions among the communities. All three religious communities favored distinct dress and identifying behaviors. Old Christians seemed concerned that many of the conversos might reconvert to Judaism, and the fear of reconversion, or "judaizing," led many to advocate the institution of the Spanish Inquisition.

Inquisitions were well known in many parts of Europe, but the Spanish Inquisition was unique because in 1478 Pope Sixtus IV placed the grand inquisitor under the direct control of the monarchs. Like most Christian rulers, Ferdinand and Isabella believed that uniform Christian orthodoxy was the only firm basis for a strong kingdom. Inquisitors attacked those aspects of converso tradition that seemed to make the conversos less than fully Christian. They were concerned that many conversos and maranos had converted falsely and were secretly continuing to follow Jewish or Muslim rituals—a fear that some recent scholars have argued was unfounded.

Because its administration, finances, and appointments were in Spanish, not papal, hands, the Spanish Inquisition quickly became an important instrument for the expansion of state power. Many inquisitors used their offices to attack wealthy or politically important converso families not just to drive them from public life but also to fill the royal treasury, which was where the estates of those judged guilty wound up. "This inquisition is as much to take the conversos' estates as to exalt the faith," concluded one despairing conversa woman.[11]

## The Limits of Consolidation: Germany

The issue of central versus local control played a key role in German affairs as well. The Holy Roman Empire of the late Middle Ages was dramatically different from the empire of the early thirteenth century. Emperors generally were unable to claim lands and preside over jurisdictions outside Germany. And within Germany power shifted eastward. Imperial power had previously rested on lands and castles in southwestern Germany. These strongholds melted away as emperors willingly pawned and sold traditional crown lands in order to build up the holdings of their own families. Emperor Henry VII (r. 1308–1313) and his grandson, Charles IV (r. 1347–1378), for example, liquidated imperial lands west of the Rhine in order to secure the House of Luxemburg's claims to the crown of Bohemia and other lands in the east. The Habsburgs in Austria, the Wittelsbachs in Bavaria, and a host of lesser families staked out power bases in separate parts of the empire. As a result, Germany unraveled into a loose collection of territories. And more seriously, the power of each emperor depended almost entirely on the wealth and power of his dynastic lands.

The power of regional authorities in the empire was further cemented by the so-called Golden Bull of 1356, the most important constitutional document of late medieval German history. In it Charles IV declared that henceforth the archbishops of Cologne, Mainz, and Trier, plus the secular rulers of Bohemia, the Rhenish Palatinate, Saxony, and Brandenburg, would be the seven electors responsible for the choice of a new emperor. He further established that the rulers of these seven principalities should have full jurisdictional rights within their territories. The Golden Bull acknowledged the power of regional princes, but it did nothing to solve the inherent weakness of an electoral monarchy. Between 1273 and 1519 Germany elected fourteen emperors from six different dynasties, and only once, in 1378, did a son follow his father. The contrast between Germany and the monarchies of Iberia, France, and England is striking. By 1350 Germany had no hereditary monarchy, no common legal system, no common coinage, and no representative assembly. Political power rested in the hands of the territorial princes.

Territorial integration was least effective in what is now Switzerland, where a league of towns, provincial knights, and peasant villages successfully resisted a territorial prince. The Swiss Confederation began modestly enough in 1291 as a voluntary association to promote regional peace. By 1410 the confederation had conquered most of the traditionally Habsburg lands in the Swiss areas. By the 1470s the Swiss had invented the myth of

William Tell, the fearless woodsman who refused to bow his head to a Habsburg official, as a justification for their independent and anti-aristocratic traditions. Though still citizens of the Holy Roman Empire, the Swiss maintained an independence similar to that of the princes. Their expansion culminated with the Battle of Nancy in Lorraine in 1477, when the Swiss infantry defeated a Burgundian army and killed Charles the Bold, the duke of Burgundy. From then on "turning Swiss" was a common threat made by German towns and individuals who hoped to slow territorial centralization.

## SUMMARY

THE Europe of 1500 was profoundly different from the Europe of two centuries earlier. The religious, political, and economic crises of the fourteenth and early fifteenth centuries seemed about to destroy the progress of the previous centuries. But the recovery of the second half of the fifteenth century was nearly as dramatic as the preceding disasters.

In the aftermath of schism and conciliar reform, the church also was transformed. Because of conciliar challenges to papal authority, popes had to deal much more carefully with the governments of Europe. They found themselves vulnerable to pressures from the other European powers. Recognizing that, in the end, popes could count on support only from those areas they controlled politically, the papacy became an Italian regional power.

The economy had grown more complex in the wake of the plague and demographic change. New patterns of trade and banking and new manufacturing techniques spread throughout Europe. As important as simple recovery was the fact that the new economy was now more firmly rooted in northern Europe. Italian merchants and bankers faced stiff competition from local counterparts throughout Europe.

Recovery was equally dramatic for the kings of France and England, the princes and despots of Germany, and the rulers of eastern Europe. After the Hundred Years' War and challenges from aristocrats, townsmen, and peasants, governments grew stronger as kings, princes, and town patricians used royal courts and patronage to extend their control. Military advances in the fifteenth century, such as the institution of standing armies, gave the advantage to larger governments. This was as true in Hungary as it was in France.

Yet recovery among the traditional Western powers was largely overshadowed by the emergence of the tsars in Moscow and the rise of the Ottoman and Spanish Empires. These three emergent powers upset the political and diplomatic balance in Europe and would dominate politics and diplomacy in the next century.

In addition to their obvious political power, most of these states—from Spain to Scandinavia to the Ottoman Empire—became adept at using art, literature, and history to explain and magnify their courts and confirm their places in history and society. This was certainly true of the papacy, and over the course of the fifteenth century it became true of other governments as well. It is to the role of culture that we turn in the next chapter.

## ■ Notes

1. Quoted in Guillaume Mollat, *The Popes at Avignon, 1305–1378* (London: Thomas Nelson, 1963), p. 112.
2. Quoted in Mary Aston, *Lollards and Reformers: Images and Literacy in Late Medieval Religion* (Ronceverte, W.V.: Hambledon, 1984), p. 60.
3. Quoted in Francis Oakley, *The Western Church in the Later Middle Ages* (Ithaca, N.Y.: Cornell University Press, 1979), pp. 65–66.
4. Quoted in Charles T. Wood, *Joan of Arc and Richard III* (New York: Oxford University Press, 1988), pp. 56–57.
5. Quoted in Michael T. Clanchy, "Law, Government, and Society in Medieval England," *History* 59 (1974): 75.
6. A. Buchon, *Choix des Chroniques* (Paris, 1875), p. 565, as quoted in John Gillingham and J. C. Holt, eds., *War and Government in the Middle Ages* (Totowa, N.J.: Barnes & Noble, 1984), p. 85.
7. Salimbene de Adam, quoted in John Larner, *Italy in the Age of Dante and Petrarch, 1215–1380* (New York: Longman, 1980), p. 141.
8. Quoted in Peter Shervey Lewis, *Later Medieval France: The Polity* (New York: Macmillan, 1968), p. 15.
9. Quoted in Angus MacKay, *Spain in the Middle Ages: From Frontier to Empire, 1000–1500* (London: Macmillan, 1977), p. 105.
10. Quoted in Angus MacKay, "Popular Movements and Pogroms in Fifteenth-Century Spain," *Past & Present* 55 (1972): 52.
11. Haim Beinart, ed., *Records of the Trials of the Spanish Inquisition in Ciudad Real,* vol. 1, trans. Duane Osheim (Jerusalem: Israel Academy of Sciences and Humanities, 1974), p. 391.

## ■ Suggested Reading

Bennett, Judith, and Amy Froide, eds. *Singlewomen in the European Past.* 1999. The medieval essays in this collection are especially good on working women.

Cohn, Samuel K., Jr. *The Black Death Transformed.* 2002. The most recent study of the plague in medieval Europe. In a closely argued analysis, Cohn concludes that the Black Death was not bubonic plague.

Duffy, E. *Saints & Sinners: A History of the Popes*. 1997. An excellent introduction to the papacy by a leading historian. The sections on the late Middle Ages are clear and balanced.

Dyer, C. *Making a Living in the Middle Ages: The People of Britain, 850–1520*. 2002. A masterful and accessible survey of the economic history of England that is especially good on rural life.

Guenée, B. *States and Rulers in Later Medieval Europe*. Translated by Juliet Vale. 1985. The best general introduction to the nature of government in the late Middle Ages. It introduces recent trends in historical research.

Inalcik, H. *The Ottoman Empire: The Classical Age, 1300–1600*. 1973. A general discussion of the growth of the Ottoman state by Turkey's best medieval historian.

Keen, Maurice H. *English Society in the Later Middle Ages, 1348–1500*. 1990. A general introduction to late medieval England that covers culture and religion as well as politics.

Nicholas, D. *The Transformation of Europe, 1300–1600*. 1999. A comprehensive survey of politics and society in Europe between 1300 and 1600; includes coverage of Scandinavia and the Slavic lands as well as northwestern Europe.

Oakley, Francis. *The Western Church in the Later Middle Ages*. 1979. The best general history of the church in the late Middle Ages. Oakley gives superior treatments of the Great Schism and conciliarism.

Warner, Marina. *Joan of Arc: The Image of Female Heroism*. 1981. An excellent and quite readable book that emphasizes the conflicting religious and political opinions about "the Maid."

**For a searchable list of additional readings for this chapter, go to college.hmco.com/students.**

# A Painting of the Plague

Writers who survived the coming of pestilential disease in 1348 described a world of terror in which things seemed changed forever. Look at this painting, *St. Sebastian Interceding for the Plague-Stricken,* created by the Flemish artist Josse Lieferinxe between 1497 and 1499. One dying man seems to be falling terrified to the ground, while a female bystander in the background screams in alarm. Images of Christ, Saint Sebastian (pierced by arrows), a devil, and a priest seem to indicate that something terrifying and undreamed-of is happening. But what exactly was the terror, and what had changed?

The art of the later Middle Ages is an extremely valuable source for understanding social and religious values. As you look at *St. Sebastian Interceding for the Plague-Stricken,* the first step is to understand what men and women in the fourteenth and fifteenth centuries thought about death. After 1400 European Christians often depicted the universality of death in paintings showing the Dance of Death. The motif varies, but typically Death grasps the hands of men and women, rich and poor, noble and peasant, and leads them away. Deathbed scenes were another popular motif. In the late Middle Ages most people believed that at death the good and evil acts committed by an individual were tallied in the Book of Life and the person was either granted eternal life, first in Purgatory and then Paradise, or consigned to eternal suffering in Hell. Judgment scenes often depict the Virgin Mary or another saint pleading before God or contending with the Devil or demons over the souls of the dying.

It was essential for people to prepare for a good death. Individuals studied the *artes moriendi,* or "arts of dying." A lingering, painful illness was often interpreted as an opportunity for penitential suffering that would benefit the soul. At the point of death, the dying person could confess and receive absolution for sins and the last sacraments of the church. From that moment on, he or she needed to maintain a calm faith, free from fear. Salvation and eternal life depended on avoiding further sin, especially the questioning of God's forgiveness and mercy. Death was a public event. Clergy, family, religious societies, even neighbors helped the dying person to avoid losing faith at the end. The person might pray, "Virgin Mary, Mother of God, I have placed my hope in you. Free my soul from care, and from Hell, and bitter death."*

The concept of a good death is critical to understanding the European response to the plague. To be sure, individuals rarely look forward to death, then or now. Numerous writers and chroniclers lamented the suddenness of death and the lack of priests to hear confessions. Individuals who were healthy in the morning might be dead by nightfall. The suddenness, the lack of time to prepare for a good death, heightened the dread that accompanied the onset of the illness.

Medieval Christians turned to saints to represent them before God at the point of death and to stop the onslaught of the plague. Three patron saints were especially popular. The Virgin Mary was often shown using her cloak to shelter towns and individuals from arrows carrying pestilence. Saint Roch, himself a victim of the plague, was thought to intercede and protect those who prayed in his name. And Saint Sebastian, an early Christian martyr slain with arrows (later understood as symbols of death caused by the plague), was thought to be an especially effective patron during epidemics. In times of plague, people went on pilgrimages to local shrines dedicated to these or local saints, carried images of the saints in processions, and built churches and chapels in honor of the saints in thanks for deliverance from the plague.

With these issues in mind, what do we see in Lieferinxe's painting? The painting portrays an outbreak of the plague. We note first the body of the dead person, carefully shrouded. Ideally the dead, like the corpse here, were taken to a church and given a Christian burial. But chroniclers often reported that so many died, and died so quickly, that no one could be found to bury them properly. In many towns the dead were gathered on carts and hauled to gaping common graves outside the towns. We can see one such cart leaving the castle in the background. In a series of images, then, Lieferinxe shows what mattered most to people. In the foreground is the shrouded body attended by a priest and other clerics bearing a cross. This person experienced a good death. In contrast, the man who has fallen behind the body is suffering a bad death, one that caught him unaware. He is the object of the concern and grief of those near him. In the sky just above the castle walls, a white-robed angel and a horned, ax-wielding demon contend over the souls of the dead and dying. At the top of the painting Christ listens to the prayers of Saint Sebastian. The painting thus portrays the impact and horror of plague

*Quoted in Philippe Ariès, *The Hour of Our Death* (New York: Knopf, 1981), p. 108.

**Lieferinxe: St. Sebastian Interceding for the Plague-Stricken** *(The Walters Art Museum, Baltimore)*

and also the way Christians were expected to respond to it.

Returning to our original question, we can conclude that the terror of epidemic plague was not entirely like a modern panic. Medieval people saw the Black Death, its ghastly devastation, and its only possible solution or meaning in terms of traditional religious values: the true terror was to be caught unaware.

 **For additional information on this topic, go to college.hmco.com/students.**

# CHAPTER 12

# The Renaissance

**T**HE painting on the left, *School of Athens* by Raphael (1483–1520), was commissioned for the Stanze°, the papal apartments in the Vatican. At the center Plato and Aristotle advance through a churchlike hall, surrounded by the great thinkers and writers of the ancient world. But Raphael portrayed more than just ancient wisdom. The figure of Plato is, in fact, a portrait of Leonardo da Vinci. A brooding Michelangelo leans on a marble block in the foreground. In a companion painting on the opposite wall, Raphael depicted a gathering of the greatest scholars of Christendom. In this way he brought together Christian and classical, writers and artists, and captured the entire cultural reform plan of the Renaissance.

The revival these paintings celebrate was a response to the religious, social, economic, and political crises discussed in the previous chapter. Italians, and later Europeans generally, found themselves drawn to imitate Roman literature, ethics, and politics. The ideas of antiquity seemed to offer an opportunity to perfect the theological ideas about moral and political life current in the earlier Middle Ages.

Renaissance Italians wrote of themselves and their contemporaries as having "revived" arts, "rescued" painting, and "rediscovered" classical authors. They even coined the phrases "Dark Ages" and "Middle Ages" to describe the period that separated the Roman Empire from their own times. They believed that their society saw a new age, a rebirth of culture. And to this day we use the French word for "rebirth," *renaissance,* to describe the period of intense creativity and change from 1300 to 1500 not just in Italy but in all of Europe.

---

**Stanze** (STAN-zay)

Raphael, *School of Athens* (detail). Raphael created this classical setting by using the technique of linear perspective.
(Scala/Art Resource, NY)

**Humanism and Culture in Italy, 1300–1500**

**The Arts in Italy, 1250–1550**

**The Spread of the Renaissance, 1350–1536**

**The Renaissance and Court Society**

This view comes to us primarily from the work of the nineteenth-century Swiss historian Jacob Burckhardt. In his book *The Civilization of the Renaissance in Italy* (1860) he argued that Italians were the first individuals to recognize the state as a moral structure free from the restraints of religious or philosophical traditions. Burckhardt believed that individuals are entirely free. Their success or failure depends on personal qualities of creative brilliance rather than on family status, religion, or guild membership. Burckhardt thought he saw in Renaissance Italy the first signs of the romantic individualism and nationalism that characterized the modern world.

In fact, as brilliant as Renaissance writers and artists were, they do not represent a radical shift from the ideas or values of previous medieval culture. As we have seen, there were no "Dark Ages." Although the culture of Renaissance Europe was in many aspects new and innovative, it had close ties both to the ideas of the High Middle Ages and to traditional Christian values.

How, then, should we characterize the Renaissance in Europe? The Renaissance was an important cultural movement that aimed to reform and renew by imitating what the reformers believed were classical and early Christian traditions in art, education, religion, and political life. Italians, and then other Europeans, came to believe that the social and moral values, as well as the literature, of classical Greece and Rome offered the best formula for changing their own society for the better. This enthusiasm for a past culture became the vehicle for changes in literature, education, and art that established cultural standards that were to hold for the next five hundred years.

## QUESTIONS TO CONSIDER

- How did Europeans try to use classical values to reform their world?
- What was "new" about Renaissance art?
- In what ways did humanism outside Italy differ from Italian humanism?
- How did European rulers use Renaissance art and culture?

## TERMS TO KNOW

| | |
|---|---|
| Renaissance | linear perspective |
| humanism | Leonardo da Vinci |
| Petrarch | Sistine Chapel |
| civic humanism | Gutenberg |
| *On the Donation* | Thomas More |
| *of Constantine* | Erasmus |
| Machiavelli | |

## HUMANISM AND CULTURE IN ITALY, 1300–1500

ITALIANS turned to models from classical antiquity in their attempts to deal with current issues of cultural, political, and educational reform. A group of scholars who came to be known as humanists began to argue the superiority of the literature, history, and politics of the past. As humanists discovered more about ancient culture, they were able to understand more clearly the historical context in which Roman and Greek writers and thinkers lived. And by the early sixteenth century their debates on learning, civic duty, and the classical legacy had led them to a new vision of the past and a new appreciation of the nature of politics.

### The Emergence of Humanism

Humanism initially held greater appeal in Italy than elsewhere in Europe because the culture in central and northern Italy was significantly more secular and more urban than the culture of much of the rest of Europe. Members of the clergy were not likely to dominate government and education in Italy. Quite the reverse: Boards dominated by laymen had built and were administering the great urban churches of Italy. Religious hospitals and charities were often reorganized and centralized under government control. In 1300 four cities in Italy (Milan, Venice, Florence, and Naples) had populations of about 100,000, and countless others had populations of 40,000 or more. By contrast, London, which may have had a population of 100,000, was the only city in England with more than 40,000 inhabitants. Even the powerful Italian aristocracy tended to live at least part of the year in towns and conform to urban social and legal practices.

Differences between Italy and northern Europe are also apparent in the structure of local education. In northern Europe education was organized to provide clergy for local churches. In the towns of Italy education was much more likely to be supervised by town governments to provide training in accounting, arithmetic, and the composition of business letters. Public grammar masters taught these basics, and numerous private masters and individual tutors were prepared to teach all subjects. Giovanni Villani, a fourteenth-century merchant and historian, described Florence in 1338 as a city of about 100,000 people in which perhaps as many as 10,000 young girls and boys were completing elementary education and 1,000 were continuing their studies to prepare for careers in commerce. Compared with education in the towns of northern Europe, education in Villani's Florence seems broad-based and practical.

Logic and Scholastic philosophy (see page 339) dominated university education in northern Europe in the fourteenth and fifteenth centuries but had less influence in Italy, where education focused on the practical issues of town life rather than on theological speculation. Educated Italians of this period were interested in the *studia humanitatis,* which we now call humanism. By *humanism,* Italians meant rhetoric and literature—the arts of persuasion. Poetry, history, letter writing, and oratory based on standardized forms and aesthetic values consciously borrowed from ancient Greece and Rome were the center of intellectual life. In general, fourteenth-century Italians were suspicious of ideological or moral programs based on philosophical arguments or religious assumptions about human nature.

Italian towns were the focus of theorizing about towns as moral, religious, and political communities. Writers wanted to define the nature of the commune—the town government. Moralists often used "the common good" and "the good of the commune" as synonyms. By 1300 it was usual for towns to celebrate the feast days of their patron saints as major political as well as religious festivals. And town governments often supervised the construc-

## CHRONOLOGY

| | |
|---|---|
| 1304–1314 | Giotto paints Arena Chapel in Padua |
| 1345 | Petrarch discovers Cicero's letters to Atticus |
| 1348–1350 | Boccaccio, *The Decameron* |
| 1393–1400 | Chaucer, *The Canterbury Tales* |
| 1401 | Ghiberti wins competition to cast baptistery doors, Florence |
| 1405 | Christine de Pizan, *The Book of the City of the Ladies* |
| 1427 | Unveiling of Masaccio's *Trinity* |
| 1434 | Van Eyck, *The Arnolfini Wedding* |
| 1440 | Valla, *On the Donation of Constantine* |
| 1440s | Da Feltre establishes Villa Giocosa in Mantua |
| 1450s | Gutenberg begins printing with movable metal type |
| 1460 | Gonzaga invites Mantegna to Mantua |
| 1475 | Pope Sixtus IV orders construction of Sistine Chapel |
| 1494 | Dürer begins first trip to Venice |
| 1511 | Michelangelo, *David* Erasmus, *The Praise of Folly* |
| 1513 | Machiavelli, *The Prince* |
| 1516 | More, *Utopia* |
| 1527 | Castiglione, *The Book of the Courtier* |

tion and expansion of cathedrals, churches, and hospitals as signs of their wealth and prestige.

Literature of the early fourteenth century tended to emphasize the culture of towns. The most famous and most innovative work of the fourteenth century, *The Decameron* by Giovanni Boccaccio° (1313–1375), pondered moral and ethical issues, but in the lively context of Italian town life. Boccaccio hoped the colorful and irreverent descriptions of contemporary Italians, which make his *Decameron* a classic of European literature, would

---

**Giovanni Boccaccio** (jo-VAH-nee bo-KAH-chi-o)

also lead individuals to understand both the essence of human nature and the folly of human desires. The plot involves a group of privileged young people who abandon friends and family during the plague of 1348 to go into the country, where on successive days they mix feasting, dancing, and song with one hundred tales of love, intrigue, and gaiety. With its mix of traditional and contemporary images, Boccaccio's book spawned numerous imitators in Italy and elsewhere. Many credit him with popularizing a new, secular spirit. But the point too often missed by Boccaccio's imitators was, as he himself said, that "to have compassion for those who suffer is a human quality which everyone should possess."

The majority of educated Italians in the early fourteenth century, such as Boccaccio, were not particularly captivated by thoughts of ancient Rome. Italian historians chose to write the histories of their hometowns. Most, including Giovanni Villani of Florence, were convinced that their towns could rival ancient Rome. Theirs was a practical world in which most intellectuals were men trained in notarial arts—the everyday skills of oratory, letter writing, and the recording of legal documents.

### Early Humanism

The first Italians who looked back consciously to the literary and historical examples of ancient Rome were a group of northern Italian lawyers and notaries who imitated Roman authors. These practical men found Roman history and literature more stimulating and useful than medieval philosophy. Writers such as Albertino Mussato of Padua (1262–1329) adopted classical styles in their poetry and histories. Mussato used his play *The Ecerinis* (1315) to tell of the fall of Can Grande della Scala, the tyrannical ruler of Verona (d. 1329), and to warn his neighbors of the dangers of tyranny. From its earliest the classical revival in Italy was tied to issues of moral and political reform.

This largely emotional fascination for the ancient world was transformed into a literary movement for reform by Francesco Petrarch (1304–1374), who popularized the idea of mixing classical moral and literary ideas with the concerns of the fourteenth century. Petrarch was the son of an exiled Florentine notary living at the papal court in Avignon. Repelled by the urban violence and wars he had experienced on his return to Italy, Petrarch was highly critical of his contemporaries: "I never liked this age," he once confessed. He criticized the papacy in Avignon, calling it the "Babylonian Captivity" (see pages 356–358); he supported an attempt to resurrect a republican government in Rome; and he believed that im-

itation of the actions, values, and culture of the ancient Romans was the only way to reform his sorry world.

Petrarch believed that an age of darkness—he coined the expression "Dark Ages"—separated the Roman world from his own time and that the separation could be overcome only through a study and reconstruction of classical values: "Once the darkness has been broken, our descendants will perhaps be able to return to the pure, pristine radiance."[1] Petrarch's program, and in many respects the entire Renaissance, involved first of all a reconstruction of classical culture, then a careful study and imitation of the classical heritage, and finally a series of moral and cultural changes that went beyond the mere copying of ancient values and styles.

Petrarch labored throughout his life to reconstruct the history and literature of Rome. He learned to read and write classical Latin. While still in his twenties he discovered, reorganized, and annotated fragments of Livy's *Roman History*, an important source for the history of Republican Rome. His work on Livy was merely the first step. In the 1330s he discovered a number of classical works, including orations and letters by Cicero, the great philosopher, statesman, and opponent of Julius Caesar (see page 167). Cicero's letters to his friend Atticus were filled with gossip, questions about politics in Rome, and complaints about his forced withdrawal from public life. They create the portrait of an individual who was much more complex than the austere philosopher of medieval legend.

Petrarch's humanism was not worldly or secular; he was and remained a committed Christian. He recognized the tension between the Christian present and pagan antiquity. "My wishes fluctuate and my desires conflict, and in their struggle they tear me apart," he said.[2] Yet he prized the beauty and moral value of ancient learning. He wrote *The Lives of Illustrious Men*, biographies of men from antiquity whose thoughts and actions he deemed worthy of emulation. To spread humanistic values he issued collections of his letters, written in classically inspired Latin, and his Italian poems. He believed that study and memorization of the writings of classical authors could lead to the internalization of the ideas and values expressed in those works, just as a honeybee drinks nectar to create honey. He argued that the ancient moral philosophers were superior to the Scholastic philosophers, whose work ended with the determination of truth, or correct responses. "The true moral philosophers and useful teachers of the virtues," he concluded, "are those whose first and last intention is to make hearer and reader good, those who do not merely teach what virtue and vice are but sow into our hearts love of the best . . .

## READING SOURCES

# PETRARCH RESPONDS TO HIS CRITICS

*Many traditional philosophers and theologians criticized humanists as "pagans" because of their lack of interest in logic and theology and their love of non-Christian writers. In this letter defending humanistic studies Petrarch explains the value of Cicero's work to Christians.*

Cicero] points out the miraculously coherent structure and disposition of the body, sense and limbs, and finally reason and sedulous activity. . . . And all this he does merely to lead us to this conclusion: whatever we behold with our eyes or perceive with our intellect is made by God for the well-being of man and governed by divine providence and counsel. . . . [In response to his critics who argued for the superiority of philosophy he adds:] I have read all of Aristotle's moral books. . . . Sometimes I have become more learned through them when I went home, but not better, not so good as I ought to be; and I often complained to myself, occasionally to others too, that by no facts was the promise fulfilled which the philosopher makes at the beginning of the first book of his Ethics, namely, that "we learn this part of philosophy not with the purpose of gaining knowledge but of becoming better." . . . However, what is the use of knowing what virtue is if it is not loved when known? What is the use of knowing sin if it is not abhorred when it is known? However, everyone who has become thoroughly familiar with our Latin authors knows that they stamp and drive deep into the heart the sharpest and most ardent stings of speech by which those who stick to the ground [are] lifted up to the highest thoughts and to honest desire. . . .

Cicero, read with a pious and modest attitude, . . . was profitable to everybody, so far as eloquence is concerned, to many others as regards living. This was especially true in [Saint] Augustine's case. . . . I confess, I admire Cicero as much or even more than all whoever wrote a line in any nation. . . . If to admire Cicero means to be a Ciceronian, I am a Ciceronian. I admire him so much that I wonder at people who do not admire him. . . . However, when we come to think or speak of religion, that is, of supreme truth and true happiness, and of eternal salvation, then I am certainly not a Ciceronian, or a Platonist, but a Christian. I even feel sure that Cicero himself would have been a Christian if he had been able to see Christ and to comprehend His doctrine.

Source: Petrarch, "On His Own Ignorance and That of Many Others," in *The Renaissance Philosophy of Man,* ed. Ernst Cassirer, Paul Oskar Kristeller, and John H. Randall, pp. 86, 103, 104, 114, 115. Reprinted by permission of the publisher, The University of Chicago Press.

**For additional information on this topic, go to college.hmco.com/students.**

and hatred of the worst."[3] (See the box "Reading Sources: Petrarch Responds to His Critics.")

## Humanistic Studies

Petrarch's articulation of humanism inspired a broad-based transformation of Italian intellectual life that affected discussions of politics, education, literature, and philosophy. His style of historical and literary investigation of the past became the basis for a new appreciation of the present.

Petrarch's program of humanistic studies became especially popular with the wealthy oligarchy who dominated political life in Florence. The Florentine chancellor Coluccio Salutati° (1331–1406) and a generation of young intellectuals who formed his circle evolved an ideology of civic humanism. Civic humanists wrote letters, orations, and histories praising their city's classical virtues and history. In the process they gave a practical and public meaning to the Petrarchan program. Civic humanists argued, as had Cicero, that there was a moral and ethical value intrinsic to public life. In a letter to a friend, Salutati wrote that public life is "something holy and holier than idleness in [religious] solitude." To another he added, "The active life you flee is to be followed both as an exercise in virtue and because of the necessity of brotherly love."[4]

Coluccio Salutati (ko-LOO-chi-o sal-you-TAH-tee)

**Isabella d'Este** As part of the program to revive ancient Roman practices, Italian rulers had medals struck containing their own images. This image of Isabella was meant to celebrate the woman herself and the fact that her husband held the imperial office of marquis. *(Kunsthistorisches Museum, Vienna/ Erich Lessing/Art Resource, NY)*

More than Petrarch himself, civic humanists desired to create and inspire men of virtue who could take the lead in government and protect their fellow citizens from lawlessness and tyranny. In the early years of the fifteenth century civic humanists applauded Florence for remaining a republic of free citizens rather than falling under the control of a lord, like the people of Milan, whose government was dominated by the Viscontis (see page 368). In his *Panegyric on the City of Florence* (ca. 1405) Leonardo Bruni (ca. 1370–1444) recalled the history of the Roman Republic and suggested that Florence could re-create the best qualities of the Roman state. To civic humanists, the study of Rome and its virtues was the key to the continued prosperity of Florence and similar Italian republics.

One of Petrarch's most enthusiastic followers was Guarino of Verona (1374–1460), who became the leading advocate of educational reform in Renaissance Italy. After spending five years in Constantinople learning Greek and collecting classical manuscripts, he became the most successful teacher and translator of Greek literature in Italy. Greek studies had been advanced by Manuel Chrysoloras (1350–1415), who, after his arrival from Constan-

tinople in 1397, taught Greek for three years in Florence. Chrysoloras was later joined by other Greek intellectuals, especially after the fall of Constantinople to the Turks in 1453. Guarino built on this interest.

Guarino emphasized careful study of grammar and memorization of large bodies of classical history and poetry. He was convinced that through a profound understanding of Greek and Latin literature and a careful imitation of the style of the great authors, a person could come to exhibit the moral and ethical values for which Cicero, Seneca, and Plutarch were justly famous. Although it is unclear whether Guarino's style of education had such results, it did provide a thorough education in literature and oratory. In an age that admired the ability to speak and write persuasively, the new style of humanistic education pioneered by Guarino spread quickly throughout Europe. The elegy spoken at Guarino's funeral sums up Italian views of humanistic education as well as the contribution of Guarino himself: "No one was considered noble, as leading a blameless life, unless he had followed Guarino's courses."

Guarino's authority spread quickly. One of his early students, Vittorino da Feltre (1378–1446), was appointed tutor at the Gonzaga court of Mantua. Like Guarino, he emphasized close literary study and careful imitation of classical authors. But the school he founded, the Villa Giocosa°, was innovative because he advocated games and exercises as well as formal study. In addition, Vittorino required that bright young boys from poor families be included among the seventy affluent students normally resident in his school. Vittorino was so renowned that noblemen from across Italy sent their sons to be educated at the Villa Giocosa.

Humanistic education had its limits, however. Leonardo Bruni of Florence once composed a curriculum emphasizing literature and moral philosophy for a young woman to follow. But, he suggested, there was no reason to study rhetoric: "For why should the subtleties of . . . rhetorical conundrums consume the powers of a woman, who never sees the forum? . . . The contests of the forum, like those of warfare and battle, are the sphere of men."[5] To what extent did women participate in the cultural and artistic movements of the fourteenth and fifteenth centuries? Was the position of women better than it had been previously? The current of misogyny—the assumption that women were intellectually and morally weaker than men—continued during the Renaissance, but it was not unopposed.

---

**Giocosa** (jo-KO-sa)

During the fifteenth century many women did learn to read and even to write. Religious women and wives of merchants read educational and spiritual literature. Some women needed to write in order to manage the economic and political interests of their families. Alessandra Macinghi-Strozzi° of Florence (1407–1471), for example, wrote numerous letters to her sons in exile describing her efforts to find spouses for her children and to influence the government to end their banishments.

Yet many men were suspicious of literate women. Just how suspicious is evident in the career of Isotta Nogarola of Verona (b. 1418), one of a number of fifteenth- and sixteenth-century Italian women whose literary abilities equaled those of male humanists. Isotta quickly became known as a gifted writer, but men's response to her work was mixed. One anonymous critic suggested that it was unnatural for a woman to have such scholarly interests and accused her of equally unnatural sexual interests. Guarino of Verona himself wrote to her warning that if she was truly to be educated, she must put off female sensibilities and find "a man within the woman."[6]

The problem for humanistically educated women was that society provided no acceptable role for them. A noblewoman such as Isabella d'Este° (see page 420), wife of the duke of Mantua, might gather humanists and painters around her at court, but it was not generally believed that women themselves could create literary works of true merit. When women tried, they were usually rebuffed and urged to reject the values of civic humanism and to hold instead to traditional Christian virtues of rejection of the world. In other words, a woman who had literary or cultural interests was expected to enter a convent. That was a friend's advice to Isotta Nogarola. It was wrong, he said, "that a virgin should consider marriage, or even think about that liberty of lascivious morals."[7] Throughout the fifteenth and early sixteenth centuries some women in Italy and elsewhere in Europe learned classical languages and philosophy, but they became rarer as time passed. The virtues of humanism were public virtues, and Europeans of the Renaissance remained uncomfortable with the idea that women might act directly and publicly.

## The Transformation of Humanism

The fascination with education based on ancient authorities was heightened by the discovery in 1416, in the Monastery of Saint Gall in Switzerland, of a complete manuscript of Quintilian's *Institutes of Oratory*, a first-

Macinghi-Strozzi (ma-CHIN-ghee STRO-tzi)
d'Este (duh-ES-tay)

**Women and Culture**   This painting of Saint Barbara from the early fifteenth century shows a typical Flemish interior with a woman reading. It was not unusual for well-to-do women to read even if they could not write.   *(Museo de Prado/Institut Amatller d'Art Hispanic)*

century treatise on the proper education for a young Roman patrician. The document was found by Poggio Bracciolini° (1380–1459), who had been part of the humanist circle in Florence. The discovery was hardly accidental. Like Petrarch, the humanists of the fifteenth century scoured Europe for ancient texts to read and study. In searching out the knowledge of the past, these fifteenth-century humanists made a series of discoveries that changed their understanding of language, philosophy, and religion. Their desire to imitate led to a profound transformation of knowledge.

A Florentine antiquary, Niccolò Niccoli (1364–1437), coordinated and paid for much of this pursuit of "lost" manuscripts. A wealthy bachelor, Niccolò spent the fortune he had inherited from his father by acquiring ancient statuary, reliefs, and, most of all, books. When he died, his collection of more than eight hundred volumes of Latin and Greek texts became the foundation of the humanist library housed in the Monastery of San Marco in Florence. Niccolò had specified that all his books "should be accessible to everyone," and humanists from across Italy and the rest of Europe came to Florence to study his literary treasures. Niccolò's library prompted Pope Nicholas V (r. 1447–1455) to begin the collection that is now the Apostolic Library of the Vatican in Rome. The Vatican library became a lending library, serving the humanist community in Rome. Similar collections were assembled in Venice, Milan, and Urbino. The Greek and Latin sources preserved in these libraries allowed humanists to study classical languages in a way not possible before.

The career of Lorenzo Valla (1407–1457) illustrates the transformation that took place in the fifteenth century as humanism swept Europe. Valla was born near Rome and received a traditional humanistic education in Greek and Latin studies. He spent the rest of his life at universities and courts lecturing on philosophy and literature. Valla's studies had led him to understand that languages change with time—that they, too, have a life and a history. In 1440 he published a work called *On the Donation of Constantine*, which purported to record the gift by the emperor Constantine (r. 311–337) of jurisdiction over Rome and the western half of the empire to the pope when the imperial capital was moved to Constantinople (see page 207). In the High and late Middle Ages the papacy used the document to defend its right to political dominion in central Italy. The donation had long been criticized by legal theorists, who argued that Constantine had no right to make it. Valla went further and attacked the legitimacy of the document itself. Because of its language and form,

he argued, it could not have been written at the time of Constantine:

> Through his [the writer's] babbling, he reveals his most impudent forgery himself. . . . Where he deals with the gifts he says "a diadem . . . made of pure gold and precious jewels." The ignoramus did not know that the diadem was made of cloth, probably silk. . . . He thinks it had to be made of gold, since nowadays kings usually wear a circle of gold set with jewels.[8]

Valla was correct; the *Donation* was an eighth-century forgery.

Valla later turned his attention to the New Testament. Jerome (331–420) had put together the Vulgate edition of the Bible in an attempt to create a single accepted Latin version of the Hebrew Bible and the New Testament (see page 232). In 1444 Valla published his *Annotations on the New Testament.* In this work he used his training in classical languages to correct Jerome's standard Latin text and to show numerous instances of mistranslations. His annotations on the New Testament were of critical importance to humanists outside Italy and were highly influential during the Protestant Reformation.

The transformation of humanism exemplified by Valla was fully expected by some Florentines. They anticipated that literary studies would lead eventually to philosophy. In 1456 a young Florentine began studying Greek with just such a change in mind. Supported by the Medici rulers of Florence, Marsilio Ficino° (1433–1499) began a daunting project: to translate the works of Plato into Latin and to interpret Plato in light of Christian doctrine and tradition.

Ficino believed that Platonism, like Christianity, demonstrated the dignity of humanity. He wrote that everything in creation was connected along a continuum ranging from the lowliest matter to the person of God. The human soul was located at the midpoint of this hierarchy and was a bridge between matter and God. True wisdom, and especially experience of the divine, could be gained only through contemplation and love. According to Ficino, logic and scientific observation did not lead to true understanding, for humans know logically only what they can define in human language; individuals can, however, love things, such as God, that they are not fully able to comprehend.

Ficino's belief in the dignity of man was shared by Giovanni Pico della Mirandola° (1463–1494), who proposed to debate with other philosophers nine hundred

---

**Poggio Bracciolini** (PO-joe bra-chi-o-LEE-nee)

**Ficino** (fi-CHI-no)
**Giovanni Pico della Mirandola** (joe-VAH-nee PIH-ko del-ah mi-RAHN-do-la)

theses dealing with the nature of man, the origins of knowledge, and the uses of philosophy. Pico extended Ficino's idea of the hierarchy of being, arguing that humans surpassed even the angels in dignity. Angels held a fixed position in the hierarchy, just below God. In contrast, humans could move either up or down in the hierarchy, depending on the extent to which they embraced spiritual or worldly interests. Pico further believed that he had proved that all philosophies contain at least some truth. He was one of the first humanists to learn Hebrew and to argue that divine wisdom could be found in Jewish mystical literature. Along with others, he studied the Jewish Cabala, a collection of mystical and occult writings that humanists believed dated from the time of Moses. Pico's adoption of the Hebrew mystical writings was often controversial in the Jewish community as well as among Christians.

Pico's ideas were shared by other humanists, who contended that an original divine illumination—a "Pristine Theology," they called it—preceded even Plato and Aristotle. These humanists found theological truth in what they believed was ancient Egyptian, Greek, and Jewish magic. Ficino himself popularized the *Corpus Hermeticum* (the Hermetic collection), an amalgam of magical texts of the first century A.D. that was mistakenly thought to be the work of an Egyptian magician, Hermes Trismagistos. They assumed Hermes wrote during the age of Moses and Pythagoras. Like many mystical writings of the first and second centuries, Hermetic texts explained how the mind could influence and be influenced by the material and celestial worlds.

Along with exploring Hermetic magic, many humanists of the fifteenth and sixteenth centuries investigated astrology and alchemy. All three systems posit the existence of a direct, reciprocal connection between the cosmos and the natural world. In the late medieval and Renaissance world astrological and alchemical theories seemed reasonable. By the late fifteenth century many humanists assumed that personality was profoundly affected by the stars and that the heavens were not silent regarding human affairs. It was not by accident that for a century or more after 1500 astrologers were official or unofficial members of most European courts.

Interest in alchemy was equally widespread though more controversial. Alchemists believed that everything was made of a primary material and that therefore it was possible to transmute one substance into another. The most popular variation, and the one most exploited by hucksters and frauds, was the belief that base metals could be turned into gold. The hopes of most alchemists, however, were more profound. They were convinced that they could unlock the explanation of the properties of the whole cosmos. On a personal and religious level, as well as on a material level, practitioners hoped to make the impure pure. The interest in understanding and manipulating nature that lay at the heart of Hermetic magic, astrology, and alchemy was an important stimulus to scientific investigations and, ultimately, to the rise of modern scientific thought.

## Humanism and Political Thought

The humanists' plan to rediscover classical sources meshed well with their political interests. "One can say," observed Leonardo Bruni, "that letters and the study of the Latin language went hand in hand with the condition of the Roman republic." Petrarch and the civic humanists believed that rulers, whether in a republic or a principality, should exhibit all the classical and Christian virtues of faith, hope, love, prudence, temperance, fortitude, and justice. A virtuous ruler would be loved as well as obeyed. The civic humanists viewed governments and laws as essentially unchanging and static. They believed that when change does occur, it most likely happens by chance— that is, because of fortune (the Roman goddess Fortuna). Humanists believed that the only protection against chance is true virtue, for the virtuous would never be dominated by fortune. Thus, beginning with Petrarch, humanists advised rulers to love their subjects, to be magnanimous with their possessions, and to maintain the rule of law. Humanistic tracts of the fourteenth and fifteenth centuries were full of classical and Christian examples of virtuous actions by moral rulers.

The French invasions of Italy in 1494 (see pages 369–370) and the warfare that followed called into question many of the humanists' assumptions about the lessons and virtues of classical civilization. Francesco Guicciardini° (1483–1540), a Florentine patrician who had served in papal armies, suggested that, contrary to humanistic hopes, history held no clear lessons. Unless the causes of separate events were identical down to the smallest detail, he said, the results could be radically different. An even more thorough critique was offered by Guicciardini's friend and fellow Florentine, Niccolò Machiavelli (1469–1527). In a series of writings Machiavelli developed what he believed was a new science of politics. He wrote *Discourses on Livy*, a treatise on military organization, a history of Florence, and even a Renaissance play titled *The Mandrake Root*. He is best remembered, however, for *The Prince* (1513), a small tract numbering fewer than a hundred pages.

---

**Francesco Guicciardini** (fran-CHES-ko gwih-char-DI-nee)

**Machiavelli** In this portrait Machiavelli is dressed as a government official. After being exiled from Florence by the Medici, he wrote to a friend that each night when he returned from the fields he dressed again in his curial robes and pondered the behavior of governments and princes.
*(Scala/Art Resource, NY)*

Machiavelli felt that his contemporaries paid too little heed to the lessons to be learned from history. Thus in his discourses on Livy he comments on Roman government, the role of religion, and the nature of political virtue, emphasizing the sophisticated Roman analysis of political and military situations. A shortcoming more serious than ignorance of history, Machiavelli believed, was his contemporaries' ignorance of the true motivations for people's actions. His play *The Mandrake Root* is a comedy about the ruses used to seduce a young woman. In truth, however, none of the characters is fooled. All of them, from the wife to her husband, realize what is happening but use the seduction to their own advantage. In the play Machiavelli implicitly challenges the humanistic assumption that educated individuals will naturally choose virtue over vice. He explicitly criticizes these same assumptions in *The Prince*. Machiavelli holds the contrary view: that individuals are much more likely to respond to

fear and that power rather than rhetoric makes for good government.

Machiavelli's use of the Italian word *virtù* led him to be vilified as amoral. Machiavelli deliberately chose a word that meant both "manliness" or "ability" and "virtue as a moral quality." Earlier humanists had restricted *virtù* to the second meaning, using the word to refer to upright qualities such as prudence, generosity, and love. Machiavelli tried to show that in some situations these "virtues" could have violent, even evil, consequences. If, for example, a prince was so magnanimous in giving away his wealth that he was forced to raise taxes, his subjects might come to hate him. Conversely, a prince who, through cruelty to the enemies of his state, brought peace and stability to his subjects might be obeyed and perhaps even loved by them. A virtuous ruler must be mindful of the goals to be achieved—that is what Machiavelli really meant by the phrase often translated as "the ends justify the means."

Machiavelli expected his readers to be aware of the ambiguous nature of virtue—whether understood as ability or as morality. "One will discover," he concludes, "that something which appears to be a virtue, if pursued, will end in his destruction; while some other thing which seems to be a vice, if pursued, will result in his safety and his well-being."[9]

Like Guicciardini, Machiavelli rejected earlier humanistic assumptions that one needed merely to imitate the great leaders of the past. Governing is a process that requires different skills at different times, he warned: "The man who adapts his course of action to the nature of the times will succeed and, likewise, the man who sets his course of action out of tune with the times will come to grief."[10] The abilities that enable a prince to gain power may not be the abilities that will allow him to maintain it.

With the writings of Machiavelli humanistic ideas of intellectual, moral, and political reform came to maturation. Petrarch and the early humanists believed fully in the powers of classical wisdom to transform society. Machiavelli and his contemporaries admitted the importance of classical wisdom but also recognized the ambiguity of any simplistic application of classical learning to contemporary life.

## THE ARTS IN ITALY, 1250–1550

TOWNSPEOPLE and artists in Renaissance Italy shared the humanists' perception of the importance of classical antiquity. Filippo Villani (d. 1405), a wealthy Florentine from an important business family, wrote that artists had recently "reawakened

**Giotto's Naturalism**    Later painters praised the naturalistic emotion of Giotto's painting. In this detail from the Arena Chapel, Giotto portrays the kiss of Judas, one of the most dramatic moments in Christian history. *(Scala/Art Resource, NY)*

a lifeless and almost extinct art." In the middle of the fifteenth century the sculptor Lorenzo Ghiberti concluded that with the rise of Christianity "not only statues and paintings [were destroyed], but the books and commentaries and handbooks and rules on which men relied for their training." Italian writers and painters themselves believed that the recovery of past literary and artistic practices was essential if society was to recover from the "barbarism" that they believed characterized the recent past.

The Renaissance of the arts is traditionally divided into three periods. In the early Renaissance artists imitated nature; in the middle period they rediscovered classical ideas of proportion; in the High Renaissance artists were "superior to nature but also to the artists of the ancient world," according to the artist and architect Giorgio Vasari (1511–1574), who wrote a famous history of the eminent artists of his day.

## The Artistic Renaissance

The first stirrings of the new styles can be found in the late thirteenth century. The greatest innovator of that era was Giotto° di Bondone of Florence (ca. 1266–1337). Although Giotto's background was modest, his fellow citizens, popes, and patrons throughout Italy quickly recognized his skill. He traveled as far south as Rome and as far north as Padua painting churches and chapels. According to later artists and commentators, Giotto broke with the prevailing stiff, highly symbolic style and introduced lifelike portrayals of living persons. He produced paintings of dramatic situations, showing events located in specific times and places. The frescoes of the Arena Chapel in Padua (1304–1314), for example, recount episodes in the life of Christ.

---

**Giotto** (JO-toe)

**The Doors of Paradise**    Ghiberti worked on panels for the baptistery from 1403 to 1453. In his representations of scenes from the Old Testament he combined a love of ancient statuary with the new Florentine interest in linear perspective.
*(Baptistery of San Giovanni, Florence/Scala/Art Resource, NY)*

In a series of scenes leading from Christ's birth to his crucifixion, Giotto situates his actors in towns and countryside in what appears to be actual space. Even Michelangelo, the master of the High Renaissance, studied Giotto's painting. Giotto was in such demand throughout Italy that his native Florence gave him a public appointment so that he would be required by law to remain in the city.

Early in the fifteenth century Florentine artists devised new ways to represent nature that surpassed even the innovations of Giotto. The revolutionary nature of these artistic developments is evident from the careers of Lorenzo Ghiberti (1378–1455), Filippo Brunelleschi°

(1377–1446), and Masaccio° (born Tomasso di ser Giovanni di Mone, 1401–ca. 1428). Their sculpture, architecture, and painting began an ongoing series of experiments with the representation of space through linear perspective. Perspective is a system for representing three-dimensional objects on a two-dimensional plane. It is based on two observations: (1) as parallel lines recede into the distance, they seem to converge; and (2) a geometric relationship regulates the relative sizes of objects at various distances from the viewer. Painters of the Renaissance literally found themselves looking at their world from a new perspective.

---

**Brunelleschi** (broon-eh-LES-key)

**Masaccio** (ma-SAH-cho)

# Brunelleschi's Dome

The construction of a dome over the Cathedral of Santa Maria del Fiore in Florence was acknowledged to be one of the most influential accomplishments of the Renaissance, combining Florentine and medieval traditions of building with ideas based on a study of the past. A dome, with a diameter of about 180 feet and weighing 2,500 tons, was impossible to build using traditional construction methods. Filippo Brunelleschi solved the problem of supporting the double domes during construction by using a complex pattern of brickwork, such that each layer of the dome was locked into and braced by the preceding layer. As important as the technical innovations were, historians are interested in the significance given to Brunelleschi's achievement by his fellow Florentines. This late-fifteenth-century portrait makes clear how Florentines understood his accomplishment and by extension how they thought the old and the new had to be combined.

And [Filippo Brunelleschi] decided that while he looked at the sculpture of the ancients . . . to rediscover the fine and highly skilled method of building and the harmonious proportions of the ancients and how they might, without defects, be employed with convenience and economy. Noting the great and complex elements making up these matters—which had nevertheless been resolved—did not make him change his mind about understanding the methods and means they used. . . . He saw ruins—both standing and fallen down for some reason or other—which had been vaulted in various ways. He considered the methods of centering the vaults and other systems of support, how they could be dispensed with and what method had to be used, and when—because of the size of the vault or for other reasons—

armatures could not be used. . . . In many places [Filippo] had excavations made in order to see the junctures of the membering of the buildings and their type—whether square, polygonal, completely round, oval or whatever. When possible they estimated the height [by measuring] from base to base for the height and similarly [they estimated the heights of] the entablatures and roofs from the foundations. . . . [Filippo was called to a meeting to discuss the proposed vaulted dome of Florence's new cathedral.] That the vault had to be supported with centering was taken for granted by all the masters except Filippo. . . . [He was asked to demonstrate his system in the construction of a chapel.] And so he did. . . . Fixed at the lowest side is a cane or pole that circles upward, gradually narrowing as the cane or pole presses constantly on the bricks . . . on the unfixed side until it is enclosed. . . . Finally after other experiments . . . , he was asked about the procedure [for vaulting] such a great thing without centering, with a double vault and a lantern appropriate to such a large building. . . . Filippo reasoned orally with great conscientiousness and precision, and finally he was requested to put down in writing the method of keeping it steady and firm so that it would not slip.

## QUESTIONS

1. What seems to have been the significance for Brunelleschi of studying the ancients?

2. What does this story tell us about the relationship between artist (or architect) and patron?

Source: Antonio di Tuccio Manetti, *The Life of Brunelleschi,* ed. Howard Saalmon and trans. Catherine Enggass, published at University Park by The Pennsylvania State University Press, 1970, pp. 50, 52, 66, 68, 70. Copyright © 1970 by The Pennsylvania State University. Reproduced by permission of the publisher.

In 1401 Ghiberti won a commission to design door panels for the baptistery of San Giovanni in Florence. He was to spend the rest of his life working on two sets of bronze doors on which were recorded the stories of the New Testament (the north doors) and the Old Testament (the east doors). Ghiberti used the new techniques of linear perspective to create a sense of space into which he placed his classically inspired figures. Later, in the sixteenth century, Michelangelo remarked that the east doors were worthy to be the "Doors of Paradise," and so they have been known ever since.

In the competition for the baptistery commission, Ghiberti had beaten the young Filippo Brunelleschi, who, as a result, gave up sculpture for architecture and later left Florence to study in Rome. While in Rome he is said to have visited and measured surviving examples of classical architecture—the artistic equivalent of humanistic literary research. According to Vasari, he was capable of "visualizing Rome as it was before the fall." Brunelleschi's debt to Rome is evident in his masterpiece, Florence's foundling hospital. Built as a combination of hemispheres and cubes and resembling a Greek stoa or an arcaded Roman basilica, the long, low structure is an example of how profoundly different Renaissance architecture was from the towering Gothic of the Middle Ages. But his experience in Rome was also critical to his famous plan for constructing a dome over the Cathedral of Santa Maria del Fiore in Florence. (See the box "The Continuing Experiment: Brunelleschi's Dome.")

In the first decade of the fifteenth century, many commentators believed that painting would never be as innovative as either sculpture or architecture. They knew of no classical models that had survived for imitation. Yet the possibilities in painting became apparent in 1427 with the unveiling of Masaccio's *Trinity* in the Florentine Church of Santa Maria Novella. Masaccio built on revolutionary experiments in linear perspective to create a painting in which a flat wall seems to become a recessed chapel. The space created is filled with the images of Christ crucified, the Father, and the Holy Spirit.

In the middle years of the fifteenth century, artists came to terms with the innovations of the earlier period. In the second half of the fifteenth century, however, artists such as the Florentine Sandro Botticelli° (1445–1510) added a profound understanding of classical symbolism to the technical innovations of Masaccio and Brunelleschi. Botticelli's famous *Primavera* (*Spring,* 1478), painted for a member of the Medici family, is filled with Neo-Platonic symbolism concerning truth, beauty, and the virtues of humanity.

The high point in the development of Renaissance art came at the beginning of the sixteenth century in the work of several masters throughout Italy. Artists in Venice learned perspective from the Florentines and added their own tradition of subtle coloring in oils. The works of Italian artists were admired well beyond the borders of Italy. Even Sultan Mehmed II of Constantinople valued Italian painters. (See the box "Global Encounters: Gentile Bellini Travels to Meet the Turkish Sultan.")

The work of two Florentines, Leonardo da Vinci (1452–1519) and Michelangelo Buonarroti (1475–1564), best exemplifies the sophisticated heights that art achieved early in the sixteenth century. Leonardo, the bastard son of a notary, was raised in the village of Vinci outside of Florence. Cut off from the humanistic milieu of the city, he desired above all else to prove that his artistry was the

Botticelli (bot-ti-CHEL-ee)

equal of his formally schooled social superiors. In his notebooks he confessed, "I am fully conscious that, not being a literary man, certain presumptuous persons will think they may reasonably blame me, alleging that I am not a man of letters."[11] But he defended his lack of classical education by arguing that all the best writing, like the best painting and invention, is based on the close observation of nature. Close observation and scientific analysis made Leonardo's work uniquely creative in all these fields. Leonardo is famous for his plans, sometimes prophetic, for bridges, fortresses, submarines, and airships. There seemed to be no branch of learning in which he was not interested. In painting he developed chiaroscuro, a technique for using light and dark in pictorial representation, and showed aerial perspective. He painted horizons as muted, shaded zones rather than with sharp lines. "I know," he said, "that the greater or less quantity of air that lies between the eye and the object makes the outlines of that object more or less distinct."[12] It was Leonardo's analytical observation that had the greatest influence on his contemporaries.

Michelangelo, however, was widely hailed as the capstone of Renaissance art. In the words of a contemporary, "He alone has triumphed over ancient artists, modern artists and over Nature itself." In his career we can follow the rise of Renaissance artists from the ranks of mere craftsmen to honored creators, courtiers who were the equals of the humanists—in fact, Michelangelo shared Petrarch's concern for reform and renewal in Italian society. We can also discern the synthesis of the artistic and intellectual transformations of the Renaissance with a profound religious sensitivity.

The importance of Michelangelo's contribution is obvious in two of his most important works: the statue *David* in Florence and his commissions in the Sistine Chapel of the Vatican in Rome. From his youth Michelangelo had studied and imitated antique sculpture, to the point that some of his creations were thought by many actually to be antiquities. He used his understanding of classical art in *David* (1501). Florentines recalled David's defeat of the giant Goliath, saving Israel from almost certain conquest by the Philistines. *David* thus became a symbol of the youthful Florentine republic struggling to maintain its freedom against great odds. As Vasari noted, "Just as David had protected his people and governed them justly, so whoever ruled Florence should vigorously defend the city and govern it with justice."[13]

Michelangelo was a committed republican and Florentine, but he spent much of his life working in Rome on a series of papal commissions. In 1508 he was called

## Gentile Bellini Travels to Meet the Turkish Sultan

Giovanni and Gentile Bellini were two of the leading Renaissance artists in Venice. Their fame spread throughout the Mediterranean and resulted in this unusual cultural meeting in 1479. A portrait of the emperor Mehmed II by Gentile now hangs in the National Gallery in London.

Some portraits having been taken to Turkey to the Grand Turk [the sultan] by an ambassador, that emperor was so struck with astonishment that, although the Mohammedan laws prohibit pictures, he accepted them with great goodwill, praising the work without end, and what is more, requesting that the master himself be sent to him. But the Senate, considering that Giovanni could ill support the hardships, resolved to send Gentile his brother, and he was conveyed safely in their galleys to Constantinople, where being presented to Mehmed [II], he was received with much kindness as an unusual visitor. He presented a beautiful picture to the prince, who admired it much, and could not persuade himself to believe that a mortal man had in him so much of the divinity as to be able to express the things of nature in such a lively manner. Gentile painted the Emperor Mehmed himself from life so well that it was considered a miracle, and the emperor, having seen many specimens of his art, asked Gentile if he had the courage to paint himself; and Gentile having answered "Yes," before many days were over he finished a lifelike portrait by means of a mirror, and brought it to the monarch, whose astonishment was so great that he would have it a divine spirit dwelt in him. And had not this art been forbidden by the law of the Turks, the emperor would never have let him go. But either from fear that people would murmur, or from some other cause, he sent for him one day, and having thanked him, and given him great praise, he bade him to ask whatever he would and it should be granted him without fail. Gentile modestly asked for nothing more than that he would graciously give him a letter of recommendation to the Senate and Lords of Venice. His request was granted in as fervent words as possible, and then, loaded with gifts and honors, and with the dignity of a cavalier, he was sent away. Among the other gifts was a chain of gold of two hundred and fifty crowns weight, worked in the Turkish manner. So, leaving Constantinople, he came safely to Venice, where he was received by his brother Giovanni and the whole city with joy, every one rejoicing in the honors which Mehmed had paid him. When the Doge and Lords [of Venice] saw the letters of the emperor, they ordered that a provision of two hundred crowns a year should be paid him all the rest of his life.

### QUESTIONS

1. What seems to be the role of Renaissance art and artists in Venetian and Turkish diplomacy?

2. How does the relationship between the sultan and Gentile Bellini compare to the relationship between Christine de Pizan and the duke of Burgundy (see the box on page 412)?

SOURCE: *Stories of the Italian Renaissance from Vasari,* arranged and translated by E. L. Seeley (London and New York, 1908), pp. 135–137.

---

by Pope Julius II (r. 1503–1513) to work on the ceiling of the Sistine Chapel. Michelangelo spent four years decorating the ceiling with hundreds of figures and with nine scenes from the Book of Genesis, including the famous *Creation of Adam.* In the late 1530s, at the request of Pope Clement VII (r. 1523–1534), he completed *The Last Judgment,* which covers the wall above the altar. In that painting the techniques of perspective and the conscious recognition of debts to classical culture recede into the background as the artist surrounds Christ in judgment with saints and sinners. In the hollow, hanging skin of flayed Saint Bartholomew we can detect a psychological self-portrait of an artist increasingly concerned with his own spiritual failings.

Michelangelo's self-portrait reminds us that the intellectual content of the artist's work is one of its most enduring traits. He was a Platonist who believed that the form and beauty of a statue are contained, buried, in the stone itself. The artist's job is to peel away excess material and reveal the beauty within. As he noted in one of his poems, sculpting is a process not unlike religious salvation:

Just as by carving . . . we set
Into hard mountain rock
A living figure
Which grows most where the stone is most removed;
In like manner, some good works . . .
Are concealed by the excess of my very flesh.[14]

**The Pietà**   Michelangelo sculpted three versions of Mary holding the crucified Jesus. This late, unfinished work reveals Michelangelo's desire to show the suffering of Christ. *(Scala/Art Resource, NY)*

## Art and Patronage

The religious passion of Michelangelo's poetry indicates one of the reasons that art was so popular in Renaissance Italy. Art, like poetry, provided symbols and images through which Italians could reason about the most important issues of their communities. Italians willingly spent vast sums on art because of its ability to communicate social, political, and spiritual values.

Italy in the fourteenth and fifteenth centuries was unusually wealthy relative to the towns and principali-

ties of northern Europe. Despite the population decline caused by plague and the accompanying economic dislocations, per person wealth in Italy remained quite high. Because of banking, international trade, and even service as mercenaries, Italians, and particularly Florentines, had money to spend on arts and luxuries. Thus the Italians of the Renaissance, whether as public or private patrons, could afford to use consumption of art as a form of competition for social and political status.

It was not just the elite who could afford art. Surprisingly modest families bought small religious paintings, painted storage chests, and decorative arts. Moralists advised families to buy small paintings of the Virgin Mary or the baby Jesus. Families also bought small paintings of saints considered special to their town or family. Wealthy and modest families alike bought brightly decorated terra-cotta pitchers, platters, and plates. Decorative arts were a critical social marker for families at all levels. (See the feature "Weighing the Evidence: Renaissance Marriage Chests" on pages 426–427.) Thus the market for art steadily increased in the fourteenth and fifteenth centuries, as did the number of shops and studios in which artists could be trained.

Artists in the modern world are accustomed to standing outside society as critics of conventional ideas. In the late Middle Ages and Renaissance, artists were not alienated commentators. In 1300 most art was religious in subject, and public display was its purpose. Throughout Europe art fulfilled a devotional function. Painted crucifixes, altarpieces, and banners were often endowed as devotional or penitential objects. The Arena Chapel in Padua, with its frescoes by Giotto, was funded by a merchant anxious to pay for some of his sins.

In the late Middle Ages and Renaissance, numerous paintings and statues throughout Italy (and much of the rest of Europe) were revered for their miraculous powers. During plague, drought, and times of war people had recourse to the sacred power of the saints represented in these works of art. (See the feature "Weighing the Evidence: A Painting of the Plague" in Chapter 11, pages 390–391.) The construction of the great churches of the period was often a community project that lasted for decades, even centuries. The city council of Siena, for example, voted to rebuild its Gothic Cathedral of Saint Mary, saying that the Blessed Virgin "was, is and will be in the future the head of this city" and that through veneration of her "Siena may be protected from harm." Accordingly, although the subject of art was clearly and primarily religious, the message was bound up in the civic values and ideas of the fourteenth and fifteenth centuries.

**Men and Women Playing Cards**    This fresco painted in the early fifteenth century in Milan is typical of the art used to decorate the homes of the wealthy. It depicts one of the pastimes of noble families.    *(Scala/Art Resource, NY)*

The first burst of artistic creativity in the fourteenth century was paid for by public institutions. Communal governments built and redecorated city halls to house government functionaries and to promote civic pride. Most towns placed a remarkable emphasis on the beauty of the work. Civic officials often named special commissions to consult with a variety of artists and architects before approving building projects. Governments, with an eye to the appearance of public areas, legislated the width of streets, height limits, and even the styles of dwelling façades.

The series of paintings called the *Good Government of Siena* illustrates the use of art to communicate political ideas. Painted in the first half of the fourteenth century

by Ambrogio Lorenzetti° (ca. 1300–1348), *Good Government* combines allegorical representations of Wisdom and the cardinal virtues on one wall with realistic street scenes of a well-ordered Siena on an adjacent wall. Across from the scenes of good government are its opposite, graphic representations of murder, rape, and general injustice and mayhem. In this ambitious work, with its specific scenes and unmistakable tone, the government broadcast a clear political message in realistic brushstrokes. The popular preacher San Bernardino of Siena (1380–1444) reinforced the point of Lorenzetti's painting: "To see Peace depicted is a delight and so it is a

---

**Ambrogio Lorenzetti** (am-BROH-jo loh-ren-ZET-ee)

shame to see War painted on the other wall." And Bernardino's sermon reminded listeners of the conclusions they should draw: "Oh my brothers and fathers, love and embrace each other . . . give your aid to this toil which I have undertaken so gladly, to bring about love and peace among you."[15]

Public art in Florence was often organized and supported by various guild organizations. Guild membership was a prerequisite for citizenship, so guildsmen set the tone in politics as well as in the commercial life of the city. Most major guilds commissioned sculpture for the Chapel of Or San Michele, a famous shrine in the grain market (its painting of the Virgin Mary was popularly thought to have wonderworking powers) and seat of the Guelf Party, the city's most powerful political organization. Guilds took responsibility for building and maintaining other structures in the city as well. Guildsmen took pride in creating a beautiful environment, but as the clothmakers' decision to supervise the baptistery shows, the work reflected not only on the city and its patron saint but also on the power and influence of the guild itself.

The princes who ruled outside the republics of Italy often had similarly precise messages that they wished to communicate. Renaissance popes embarked on a quite specific ideological program in the late fifteenth century to assert their dual roles as spiritual leaders of Christendom and temporal lords of a central Italian state (see pages 421–423). Rulers such as the Este dukes of Ferrara and the Sforza dukes of Milan constructed castles within their cities or hunting lodges and villas in the countryside and adorned them with pictures of the hunt or murals of knights in combat—scenes that emphasized their noble virtues and their natural right to rule.

By the mid-fifteenth century patrons of artworks in Florence and most other regions of Italy were more and more likely to be wealthy individuals. Many of the patrons who commissioned and oversaw artists were women. Women paid for the construction of convents and chapels. In many cases their patronage can simply be understood as an extension of their families, but in many other cases it was not. One woman who had lived for years as a concubine of a merchant in Florence used her dead lover's bequest to commission a painting titled *Christ and the Adultress,* making clear that even women in her situation could hope for God's mercy.

Republics, in which all families were in principle equal, initially distrusted the pride and ambition implied by elaborate city palaces and rural villas. By the middle of the fifteenth century, however, such reserve was found in none but the most conservative republics, such as

Venice and Lucca. Palaces, gardens, and villas became the settings in which the wealthy could entertain their peers, receive clients, and debate the political issues of the day. The public rooms of these *palazzos* were decorated with portraits, gem collections, rare books, ceramics, and statuary. Many villas and palaces included private chapels. In the Medici palace in Florence, for example, the chapel is the setting for a painting of the Magi (the three wise men who came to worship the infant Jesus) in which the artist, Benozzo Gozzoli (1420–1498), used members of the Medici family as models for the portraits of the Magi and their entourage (see the painting on page 369). The Magi, known to be wise and virtuous rulers, were an apt symbol for the family that had come to dominate the city.

Artists at princely courts were expected to work for the glory of their lord. Often the genre of choice was the portrait. One of the most successful portraitists of the sixteenth century was Sofonisba Anguissola° (1532–1625). Anguissola won renown as a prodigy because she was female and from a patrician family; one of her paintings was sent to Michelangelo, who forwarded it to the Medici in Florence. Since women would never be allowed to study anatomy, Anguissola concentrated her talents on portraits and detailed paintings of domestic life. Later she was called to the Spanish court, where the king, queen, and their daughter sat for her. She continued to paint after her marriage and return to Italy. Even in her nineties she welcomed painters from all parts of Europe to visit and discuss techniques of portraiture.

## THE SPREAD OF THE RENAISSANCE, 1350–1536

B Y 1500, the Renaissance had spread from Italy to the rest of Europe. Well beyond the borders of the old Roman Empire, in Prague and Cracow, for example, one could find a renewed interest in classical ideas about art and literature. As information about the past and its relevance to contemporary life spread, however, the message was transformed in several important ways. Outside Italy, Rome and its history played a much less pivotal role. Humanists elsewhere in the West were interested more in religious than in political reform, and they responded to a number of important local interests. Yet the Renaissance notion of renewal based on a deep understanding and imitation of the past remained at the center of the movement. The nature of

**Anguissola** (an-GWIS-so-lah)

the transformation will be clearer if we begin by considering the nature of vernacular literatures before the emergence of Renaissance humanism.

## Vernacular Literatures

The humanistic movement was not simply a continuation of practical and literary movements. The extent of its innovation will be clearer if we look briefly at the vernacular literatures (that is, written in native languages, rather than Latin) of the fourteenth and fifteenth centuries.

As in Italy, fourteenth-century writers elsewhere were not immediately drawn to classical sources. Boccaccio's work, for example, influenced another vernacular writer, Geoffrey Chaucer (ca. 1343–1400), the son of a London burgher, who served as a diplomat, courtier, and member of Parliament. In addition to the pervasive French influence, Chaucer read and studied Boccaccio. Chaucer's most famous work, *The Canterbury Tales,* consists of stories told by a group of thirty pilgrims who left the London suburbs on a pilgrimage to the shrine of Saint Thomas Becket at Canterbury Cathedral. The narrators and the stories themselves describe a variety of moral and social types, creating an acute, sometimes bitter, portrait of English life. The Wife of Bath is typical of Chaucer's pilgrims: "She was a worthy woman all her life, husbands at the churchdoor she had five." After describing her own marriages she observes that marriage is a proper way to achieve moral perfection, but it can be so only if the woman is master.

Although Chaucer's characters present an ironic view of the good and evil that characterize society, Chaucer's contemporary, William Langland (ca. 1330–1400), took a decidedly more serious view of the ills of English life. Whereas Boccaccio and Chaucer all told realistic tales about life as it truly seemed to be, Langland used the traditional allegorical language (that is, symbolic language in which a place or person represents an idea) of medieval Europe. In *Piers Plowman* Langland writes of people caught between the "Valley of Death" and the "Tower of Truth." He describes the seven deadly sins that threaten all of society and follows with an exhortation to do better. Both Chaucer and Langland expected that their audiences would immediately recognize commonly held ideas and values.

Despite the persistence of old forms of literature, new vernacular styles arose, although they still dealt with traditional values and ideas. Throughout Europe many writers directly addressed their cares and concerns. Letters like those of the Paston family in England or Alessandra Macinghi-Strozzi in Italy described day-to-day affairs of business, politics, and family life. Letters dictated and sent by Saint Catherine of Siena and Angela of Foligno offered advice to the troubled. Small books of moral or spiritual writings were especially popular among women readers in the fourteenth and fifteenth centuries, among them *The Mirror for Simple Souls* by Marguerite of Porete (d. 1310). Though Marguerite was ultimately executed as a heretic, her work continued to circulate anonymously. Her frank descriptions of love, including God's love for humans, inspired many other writers in the fourteenth and fifteenth centuries. Less erotic but equally riveting was the memoir of Margery Kempe, an alewife from England, who left her husband and family, dressed in white (symbolic of virginity), and joined other pilgrims on trips to Spain, Italy, and Jerusalem.

One of the most unusual of the new vernacular writers was Christine de Pizan (1369–1430), the daughter of an Italian physician at the court of Charles V of France. When the deaths of her father and husband left her with responsibility for her children and little money, she turned to writing. From 1389 until her death, she lived and wrote at the French court. She is perhaps best known for *The Book of the City of the Ladies* (1405). In it she added her own voice to what is known as the *querelle des femmes,* the "argument over women." Christine wrote to counter the prevalent opinions of women as inherently inferior to men and incapable of moral judgments. She argued that the problem was education: "If it were customary to send daughters to school like sons, and if they were then taught the natural sciences, they would learn as thoroughly and understand the subtleties of all the arts and sciences as well as sons." Christine described in her book an ideal city of ladies in which prudence, justice, and reason would protect women from ignorant male critics. (See the box "Reading Sources: Christine de Pizan Describes Her Life as a Writer.")

All these vernacular writings built on popular tales and sayings as well as on traditional moral and religious writings. Unlike the early humanists, the vernacular writers saw little need for new cultural and intellectual models.

## The Impact of Printing

The spread of humanism beyond Italy was aided greatly by the invention of printing. In the fifteenth century the desire to own and to read complete texts of classical works was widespread, but the number of copies was severely limited by the time and expense of hand-copying, collating, and checking manuscripts. Poggio Bracciolini's letters are filled with complaints about the time and expense of reproducing the classical manuscripts he had

## READING SOURCES

## CHRISTINE DE PIZAN DESCRIBES HER LIFE AS A WRITER

*Christine de Pizan (1364–1430) was brought by her Italian father to the court of King Charles V of France. Her situation was unusual in that her father and her husband both encouraged her interests in poetry and literature. She wrote poems, letters, and books and is especially famous for her writings in defense of women's intellectual and moral status. In this excerpt she describes her situation and explains how a writer of either sex could make a living.*

[M]y husband] died in the bloom of youth at thirty-four years of age, and I, at twenty-five, was left with the responsibility of three small children and a large household. . . . I was not able to get full and precise information on the state of his affairs. For it is customary for married men not to discuss financial matters in detail with their wives. . . . As my youth was already largely behind me, as were most of my outside obligations, I returned to the way of life that suited me best: seclusion and quiet. In my solitude, there came back to me some remnants of Latin and the beauteous sciences, along with sayings from the authors and rhetorical pieces I had heard my beloved father and husband recite but, in my frivolity, had remembered quite poorly. Despite the fact that my nature inclined me to learning from my earliest years, my duties as a married woman kept me otherwise occupied, as did the burdens of frequent childbearing. . . . So I turned to the path of study, towards which I was inclined by nature and constellation. . . . I began with the ancient histories from the beginnings of the world, then the history of the Hebrews, the Assyrians, and the early kingdoms, proceeding from one to the other and coming to the Romans, the French, the Britons, and several other historians, and then to what scientific learning I was able to grasp in the time available for study. Next I took up the works of the poets, my knowledge increasing all the while. . . . I began to write short pieces in a lighter vein, and like the workman who perfects his technique by practicing, I learned more and more new things through the study of diverse disciplines, and refined my style with greater subtleness and the use of nobler material. Between the year 1399, when I began writing, and the present 1405, I have composed fifteen principal works. . . . Now the most venerable and powerful Prince Philip, Duke of Burgundy, brother of [King] Charles the Wise, had in his benevolence extended his affection to me after he became familiar with some of my works, which I had only recently sent to him because I considered them unworthy to be opened in his presence. In recognition of the constancy of my application rather than of any great subtlety found in what I wrote, he praised and remunerated me generously, and graciously took my son into his service. Moreover, he deigned to pay me the great honor of asking me in person to record as an example for all posterity the noble life and deeds of the said wise king.

Source: Charity Cannon Willard, ed., *The Writings of Christine de Pizan.* Copyright © 1994. Reprinted by permission of Persea Books, Inc. (New York).

---

discovered. One copy he had commissioned was so inaccurate and illegible as to be nearly unusable. Traveling to repositories and libraries was often easier than creating a personal library. It was rarely possible for someone who read a manuscript once to obtain a complete copy to compare with other works.

The invention of printing with movable lead type changed things dramatically. (See the feature "Information Technology: The Print Revolution.") Although block printing had long been known in China and was a popular way to produce playing cards and small woodcuts in Europe, only with the creation of movable type by Johann Gutenberg in the 1450s did printing become a practical way to produce books. Between 180 and 200 copies of the so-called Gutenberg Bible were printed in 1452 and 1453. It was followed shortly by editions of the Psalms. By 1470 German printing techniques had spread to Italy, the Low Countries, France, and England. It has been estimated that by 1500 a thousand presses were operating in 265 towns (see Map 12.1). The output of the early presses was extremely varied, ranging from small devotional books and other popular and profitable literature to com-

**Map 12.1   The Spread of Printing**   Printing technology moved rapidly along major trade routes to the most populous and prosperous areas of Europe. The technology was rapidly adopted in peripheral areas as well as in highly literate centers such as the Low Countries, the Rhine Valley, and northern Italy.

plete editions of classical authors and their humanistic and theological texts.

Printing allowed for the creation of agreed-upon standard editions of works in law, theology, philosophy, and science. Scholars in different parts of the European world could feel fairly confident that they and their colleagues were analyzing identical texts. Similarly, producing accurate medical and herbal diagrams, maps, and even reproductions of art and architecture was easier. Multiple copies of texts also made possible the study of rare and esoteric

literary, philosophical, and scientific works. An unexpected result of the print revolution was the rise of the printshop as a center of culture and communication. The printers Aldus Manutius (1450–1515) in Venice and Johannes Froben (d. 1527) in Basel were humanists. Both invited humanists to work in their shops editing their texts and correcting the proofs before printing. Printshops became a natural gathering place for clerics and laymen. Thus they were natural sources of humanist ideas and later, in the sixteenth century, of Protestant religious programs.

# The Print Revolution

For more than five thousand years, from the dawn of civilization in Mesopotamia and Egypt, people in the West wrote by hand. Imperial decrees, sacred Scriptures, commercial transactions, private letters—all required the skills of a select group of scribes, clerks, or monks. In Korea and China, however, mechanical printing using carved wooden blocks had been introduced by A.D. 750. Movable type, using characters made of baked clay, was invented in China in the eleventh century. But the Chinese continued to prefer block printing well into the modern period. Written Chinese consists of thousands of ideographic characters, and the labor of creating, organizing, and setting so many different bits of type made it much simpler to cut individual pages from a single wooden block. European languages, which can be written with fewer than a hundred characters, were much better adapted to printing with movable, reusable type.

It appears that Mongol armies brought examples of Chinese printing to western Asia and Europe at the end of the thirteenth century. (The Venetian Marco Polo reported seeing paper money during his travels to the East in the late thirteenth century.) In the early fourteenth century Europeans began using block printing techniques to produce religious images, short prayers, and even decks of playing cards. As with Chinese printing, European block printing was a slow and expensive process for printing large numbers of varied texts. The print revolution had to wait another century, until the innovations of the German goldsmith Johann Gutenberg (ca. 1399–1468).

Gutenberg drew on his knowledge of metallurgy to devise a lead-tin-copper alloy that could be cast into durable, reusable type. His crucial invention was a type mold consisting of a flat strip of metal—stamped in the same way a coin is minted, leaving the impression of a single letter—inserted in the bottom of a rectangular brass box held together by screws. Molten metal was poured into it, producing a single piece of type. An experienced type founder could produce up to six hundred pieces of type a day. No wooden-block carver could approach that rate. Gutenberg then adapted the screw press commonly used to produce linen, paper, and wine to make a printing press. He followed the example of Flemish painters by adding linseed oil to the ink to make it thick enough to adhere uniformly to the metal type.

In 1455 the Gutenberg Bible was published in Mainz, Germany—but not by Gutenberg. After years of costly experimentation, Gutenberg was forced to turn over his equipment and newly printed Bibles to his partner and creditor, the wealthy merchant and moneylender Johann Fust.

The new technology, which enabled printers to create a thousand or more copies in a single print run, was highly efficient. Simple printed school texts cost only a quarter of the price of hand-copied texts. The leading bookseller in the university town of Bologna managed to stock ten thousand copies of texts, treatises, and commentaries. By 1500 even street singers sold printed copies of their songs.

Gutenberg's invention was revolutionary because, for the first time, the same information and ideas were available

## Humanism Outside Italy

As the influence of the humanist movement extended beyond Italy, the interests of the humanists changed. Although a strong religious strain infused Italian humanism, public life lay at the center of Italian programs of education and reform. Outside Italy, however, moral and religious reform formed the heart of the movement. Northern humanists wanted to renew Christian life and reinvigorate the church. Critics of the church complained that the clergy were wealthy and ignorant and that the laity were uneducated and superstitious. To amend those failings, northern humanists were involved in building educational institutions, in unearthing and publishing texts by Church Fathers, and in chronicling local customs and history. The works of the two best-known humanists, Thomas

More and Desiderius Erasmus, present a sharp critique of contemporary behavior and, in the case of Erasmus, a call to a new sense of piety. The religious views of Erasmus were so influential that northern humanism has generally come to be known as "Christian humanism."

The intellectual environment into which humanism spread from Italy had changed significantly since the thirteenth century. The universities of Paris and Oxford retained the status they had acquired earlier but found themselves competing with a host of new foundations. Like Paris, almost all had theological faculties dominated by Scholastically trained theologians. Nevertheless, the new foundations often had chairs of rhetoric, or "eloquence," which left considerable scope for those who advocated humanistic learning. These new universities, from Cracow (1367) to Uppsala in Sweden (1477), also

**A French Printshop** The production of a book took many skills. This sixteenth-century illumination shows the entire process. On the left one man works the press while a second prepares to ink a press. On the right we see the scholar with a manuscript (*rear*), a compositor selecting type as he checks the text in a book, and finally a second scholar checking the broadsides produced by the press. *(Giraudon/Art Resource, NY)*

throughout Europe at virtually the same time. The great Venetian printer Aldus Manutius (1450–1515) produced over 120,000 volumes, many in the new, smaller, easily portable "octavo" format—about 6 by 9 inches. Books from the Aldine Press and other humanistic publishers played a decisive role in spreading humanism to parts of Europe where manuscript books were difficult to acquire.

Moreover, book owning was no longer the exclusive preserve of scholars. This was all the more true because printers included on their lists works in vernacular languages, not just the ancient classics. Perhaps half of the books produced by most publishers were small prayer books and short selections of Bible stories or saints' lives printed in vernacular languages. The popularity of these texts affected the languages themselves. William Caxton (1422–1492), for example, began printing books in English in 1472. His pioneering work helped standardize modern English, just as the publication of Martin Luther's German translation of the Bible in 1522 would standardize modern German. The advent of printing had other far-reaching consequences: it promoted the increase of literacy throughout Europe, and in the sixteenth century printed books and pamphlets would become a prime vehicle for Protestants and Catholics to spread religious ideas and protests.

By the eighteenth century printed books had changed the nature of popular culture. Myths, folk songs, and popular histories were traditionally passed by word of mouth, often changing in the telling to fit the time and place. Once they appeared in print, they could no longer be performed and refashioned, only recited. Printing not only changed the way information was transmitted but also changed the information itself.

reflected the increased national feeling in various regions of Europe. The earliest university in the lands of the German Empire, the Charles University in Prague (1348), was founded at the request of emperor Charles IV, whose court was in Prague. The foundation of a new university at Poszony (1465) by Johannes Vitéz was part of a cultural flowering of the Hungarian court at Buda. A supporter of King Matthias Corvinus, Vitéz corresponded with Italian humanists, collected manuscripts, and tried to recruit humanist teachers to come to Buda. The universities in Vienna (1365), Aix (1409), Louvain (1425), and numerous other cities owed their foundations to the pride and ambition of local rulers.

The humanists associated with the new universities were often educated in Italy, but they brought a new perspective to their work. Humanists in Sweden wrote histories of the Goths, celebrating the contributions of Germans to European culture. Polish humanists wrote similarly, in one case trying to define where in eastern Europe one could draw the line between Europe and Asia.

Humanists on faculties of law at French universities used humanistic techniques of historical and linguistic study. Italian-trained French lawyers introduced what came to be called the "Gallican style" of jurisprudence. Because legal ideas, like language, changed over time, they argued that Roman law had to be studied as a historically created system and not as an abstract and unchanging structure. Humanists like Guillaume Budé (1468–1540) moved from the study of law to considerations of Roman coinage, religion, and economic life in order to better understand the formation of Roman law. The desire to understand the law led other humanist-legists to add the study of society in ancient Gaul to their work on Rome, and then to examine the law of other societies as well.

The new universities often became centers of linguistic studies. Humanistic interest in language inspired the foundation of "trilingual" colleges in Spain, France, and the Low Countries to foster serious study of Hebrew, Greek, and Latin. Like Italian humanists, other humanists believed that knowledge of languages would allow students to understand more clearly the truths of Christianity. Typical of this movement was the archbishop of Toledo, Francisco Jiménez de Cisneros (1436–1517), who founded the University of Alcalá in 1508 with chairs of Latin, Greek, and Hebrew. He began the publication of a vast new edition of the Bible, called the "Polyglot ("many tongue") Bible" (1522) because it had parallel columns in Latin, Greek, and, where appropriate, Hebrew. Unlike Valla, Jiménez intended his translations not to challenge the Vulgate but merely to clarify its meaning. The university and the Bible were part of an effort to complete the conversion of Muslims and Jews and to reform religious practices among the old Christians.

To these humanists, the discovery and publication of early Christian authors seemed critical to any reform within the church. Jacques Lefèvre d'Étaples° (1455–1536) of France was one of the most famous and influential of these humanistic editors of early Christian texts. After 1500 he concentrated on editing the texts of the early Church Fathers. The true spirit of Christianity, he believed, would be most clear in the works and lives of those who had lived closest to the age of the apostles. Christian humanists inspired by Lefèvre became key players in the later Reformation movements in France. Lefèvre's faith in the value of classical languages was shared by John Colet (1467–1519) of England, founder of St. Paul's School in London. He instituted a thorough program of teaching Latin and Greek aimed at creating scholars who would have access to the earliest Christian writings.

Tensions between the humanists and the advocates of Scholastic methods broke out over the cultural and linguistic studies that formed the heart of the humanist program. Taking to heart the humanistic belief that all philosophies and religions, not just Christianity, contained universal moral and spiritual truths, Johannes Reuchlin° (1455–1522) of Württemberg embarked on a study of the Cabala. Johannes Pfefferkorn, a Dominican priest and recent convert from Judaism, attacked Reuchlin's use of Jewish traditions in the study of Christian theology. Sides were quickly drawn. The theological faculties of the German universities generally supported Pfefferkorn. The human-

ists supported Reuchlin. In his own defense Reuchlin issued *The Letters of Illustrious Men,* a volume of correspondence he had received in support of his position. This work gave rise to one of the great satires of the Renaissance, *The Letters of Obscure Men* (1516), written by anonymous authors and purporting to be letters from various narrow-minded Scholastics in defense of Pfefferkorn. Although the debate arose over the validity of Hebraic studies for Christian theology and not over humanistic ideas of reform or wisdom, it indicates the division between the humanists and much of the Scholastic community. Many people initially misunderstood the early controversies of the Protestant Reformation as a continuation of the conflicts between humanists and Scholastic theologians over the uses of Hebrew learning.

## Thomas More and Desiderius Erasmus

The careers of two humanists in particular exemplify the strength—and the limits—of the humanistic movement outside Italy: Sir Thomas More (1478–1535) of London and Desiderius Erasmus (1466–1536) of Rotterdam. Their careers developed along very different paths. More was educated at St. Anthony's School in London and became a lawyer. He translated Lucan and wrote a humanistic history of Richard III while pursuing his public career. He is most famous for his work *Utopia* (1516), the description of an ideal society located on the island of Utopia (literally, "nowhere") in the newly explored oceans. This powerful and contradictory work comprises two volumes. Book I is a debate over the moral value of public service between Morus, a well-intentioned but practical politician, and Hythloday, a widely traveled idealist. Morus tries to make the bureaucrat's argument about working for change from within the system. Hythloday rejects the argument out of hand. Thomas More himself seems to have been unsure at that time about the virtues of public service. He was of two minds, and the debate between Morus and Hythloday reflects his indecision. As part of his critique of justice and politics in Europe, Hythloday describes in Book II the commonwealth of Utopia, in which there is no private property but strict equality of possessions, and, as a result, harmony, tolerance, and little or no violence.

Since the publication of *Utopia* debates have raged about whether More, or anyone, could ever really hope to live in such a society. Some scholars have questioned how seriously More took this work—he seems to have written the initial sections merely to amuse friends. Yet whatever More's intentions, Utopia's society of equality, cooperation, and acceptance continues to inspire social commentators.

Ironically, More, like his creation Morus, soon found himself trying to work for justice within precisely the sort

---

**Lefèvre d'Étaples** (le-FEV-ra du-TAHP-le)
**Reuchlin** (RYE-klin)

of autocratic court that Hythloday criticized. Not long after the completion of *Utopia* More entered the service of King Henry VIII (r. 1509–1547), eventually serving as chancellor of England. As a staunch Catholic and royal official More never acted on utopian principles of peace and toleration. He was, in fact, responsible for the persecution of English Protestants in the years before the king's break with Rome (see page 479). More's opposition to Henry's divorce and repudiation of papal authority, and his refusal to acknowledge Henry as the head of the English church, led him to resign his offices. He was eventually imprisoned and beheaded. More's writing was a stinging critique of political values. He implied that society could be reformed, yet in the period after 1521 his humanism and his vision of Utopia had no influence on his own public life.

Unlike More, who was drawn to the power of king and pope, Erasmus always avoided working for authorities. Often called the "Prince of Humanists," he was easily the best-known humanist of the early sixteenth century. He was born the illegitimate son of a priest in the Low Countries. Forced by relatives into a monastery, he disliked the conservative piety and authoritarian discipline of traditional monastic life. Once allowed out of the monastery to serve as an episcopal secretary, he never returned. He lived and taught in France, England, Italy, and Switzerland. Of all the humanists it was Erasmus who most benefited from the printing revolution. The printer Aldus Manutius invited him to live and work in Venice, and he spent the last productive years of his life at Johannes Froben's press in Basel. He left the city only when Protestant reformers took control of the city government.

Over a long career Erasmus brought out repeated editions of works designed to educate Christians. His *Adages*, first published in 1500, was a collection of proverbs from Greek and Roman sources. The work was immensely popular, and Erasmus repeatedly issued expanded editions. He tried to present Greek and Roman wisdom that would illuminate everyday problems. *The Colloquies* was a collection of popular stories, designed as primers for students, that taught moral lessons even as they served as examples of good language. His ironic *Praise of Folly* (1511) was dedicated to Thomas More. An oration by Folly in praise of folly, it is satire of a type unknown since antiquity. Folly's catalog of vices includes everyone from the ignoramus to the scholar. But more seriously Erasmus believed, as Saint Paul had said, that Christians must be "fools for Christ." In effect, human existence is folly. Erasmus's Folly first made an observation that Shakespeare would refine and make famous: "Now the whole life of mortal men, what is it but a sort of play in which . . . [each person] plays his own part until the director gives him his cue to leave the stage."[16]

Erasmus's greatest contributions to European intellectual life were his edition of and commentaries on the New Testament. His was a critical edition of the Greek text and a Latin translation independent of the fourth-century Latin Vulgate of Jerome. Unlike Jiménez, Erasmus corrected parts of the Vulgate. He rejected the authority of tradition, saying, "The sin of corruption is greater, and the need for careful revision by scholars is greater also, where the source of corruption was ignorance."[17] What was revolutionary in his edition was his commentary, which emphasized the literal and historical recounting of human experiences. Erasmus's Bible was the basis of later vernacular translations of Scripture during the Reformation.

Underlying Erasmus's scholarly output was what he called his "Philosophy of Christ." Erasmus was convinced that the true essence of Christianity was to be found in the life and actions of Christ. Reasonable, self-reliant, truly Christian people did not need superstitious rituals or magic. In his *Colloquies* he tells of a terrified priest who during a shipwreck promised everything to the Virgin Mary if only she would save him from drowning. But, Erasmus observed, it would have been more practical to start swimming!

Erasmus believed that a humanistic combination of classical and Christian wisdom could wipe away violence, superstition, and ignorance. Unlike More, Erasmus never abandoned the humanistic program. Yet his philosophy of Christ, based on faith in the goodness and educability of the individual, was swamped in the 1520s and 1530s by the sectarian claims of both Protestants and Catholics. Although Erasmus's New Testament was influential in the Reformation, his calls for reforms based on tolerance and reason were not.

## Renaissance Art in the North

In the early fifteenth century, while Brunelleschi and Masaccio were revolutionizing the ways in which Italian artists viewed their world, artists north of the Alps, especially in Flanders, were making equally striking advances in the ways they painted and sculpted. Artistic innovation in northern Europe began with changes tied closely to the world of northern courts; only later did artists take up the styles of the Italian Renaissance. Northerners took Italian Renaissance art and fit it to a new environment.

Northern art of the late fourteenth and fifteenth centuries changed in two significant ways. In sculpture the long, austere, unbroken vertical lines typical of Gothic sculpture gave way to a much more complex and emotional style. In painting Flemish artists moved from ornate, vividly colored paintings to experiments with ways to create a sense of depth. Artists strove to paint and

The influence of Renaissance styles in the north of Europe dates from the reign of the French king Francis I (r. 1515–1547), when Italian artists in significant numbers traveled north. Francis invited Italian artists to his court—most notably Leonardo da Vinci, who spent his last years in France. The most influential of the Italian-style creations in France was doubtless Francis's château Fontainebleau, whose decorations contained mythologies, histories, and allegories of the kind found in the Italian courts. Throughout the sixteenth century Italianate buildings and paintings sprang up throughout Europe.

Perhaps the most famous artist who traveled to Italy, learned Italian techniques, and then transformed them to suit the environment of northern Europe was Albrecht Dürer of Nuremberg (1471–1528). Son of a well-known goldsmith, Dürer became a painter and toured France and Flanders learning the techniques popular in northern Europe. Then in 1494 he left Nuremberg on the first of two trips to Italy, during which he sketched Italian landscapes and studied the work of Italian artists, especially in Venice. What he learned in Italy, combined with the friendship of some of Germany's leading humanists, formed the basis of Dürer's works, which blended northern humanistic interests with the Italian techniques of composition and linear perspective. Dürer worked in charcoal, watercolors, and paints, but his influence was most widely spread through his numerous woodcuts covering classical and contemporary themes. His woodcut *Whore of Babylon*, prepared in the context of the debate over the reform of the church, is based on sketches of Venetian prostitutes completed during his first visit to Italy.

Numerous other artists and engravers traveled south to admire and learn from the great works of Italian artists. The engravings they produced and distributed back home made the southern innovations available to those who would never set foot in Italy. In fact, some now lost or destroyed creations are known only through the copies engraved by northern artists eager to absorb Italian techniques.

## THE RENAISSANCE AND COURT SOCIETY

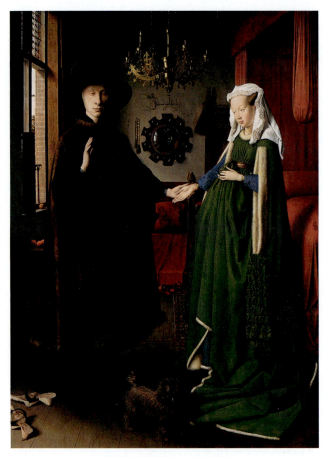

**Van Eyck: The Arnolfini Wedding**    Careful observation of people and places was typical of the new art of both northern and southern Europe. Van Eyck seems to have re-created this scene to the smallest detail. His own image appears in the mirror on the wall.    *(Reproduced by Courtesy of the Trustees, The National Gallery, London)*

THE educational reforms of the humanists and the innovations in the arts between 1300 and 1550 provided an opportunity for rulers and popes alike to use culture to define and celebrate their authority. Art, literature, and politics merged in the brilliant life of the Renaissance Italian courts, both secular

sculpt works that more faithfully represented reality. The sculptures of Claus Sluter (1350–1406), carved for a family chapel of the Burgundian dukes at Champmol, captured a lifelike drama unlike the previous Gothic sculpture. Court painters such as Jan van Eyck (ca. 1390–1441), in miniatures, portraits, and altar paintings, also moved away from a highly formalized style to a careful representation of specific places. In van Eyck's portrait of the Italian banker and courtier Giovanni Arnolfini and his bride, the image of the painter is reflected in a small mirror behind the couple, and above the mirror is written, "Jan van Eyck was here, 1434." Whereas Italians of the early fifteenth century tried to re-create space through linear perspective, the Flemish used aerial perspective, softening colors and tones to give the illusion of depth.

## The Elaboration of the Court

The courts of northern Italy took an interest in the cultural and artistic innovations of the Renaissance artists and humanists inspired by classical civilization, and they closely imitated many of the values and new styles that were developing in the courts of northern Europe, such as the court of Burgundy. Throughout Europe attendance at court became increasingly important to members of the nobility as a source of revenue and influence. Kings and the great territorial lords were equally interested in drawing people to their courts as a way to influence and control the noble and the powerful.

Rulers in most parts of Europe instituted monarchical orders of knighthood to reward allies and followers. The most famous in the English-speaking world was the Order of the Garter, founded in 1349 by King Edward III. The orders were but one of the innovations in the organization of the court during the fourteenth and fifteenth centuries. The numbers of cooks, servants, huntsmen, musicians, and artists employed at court jumped dramatically in the late Middle Ages. In this expansion the papal court was a model for the rest of Europe. The popes at Avignon in the fourteenth century already had households of nearly six hundred persons. If all the bureaucrats, merchants, local officials, and visitors who continually swarmed around the elaborate papal court were also counted, the number grew even larger.

Courts were becoming theaters built around a series of widely understood signs and images that the ruler could manipulate. Culture was meant to reflect the reputation of the ruler. On important political or personal occasions, rulers organized jousts or tournaments around themes drawn from mythology. The dukes of Milan indicated the relative status of courtiers by inviting them to participate in particular hunts or jousts. They similarly organized their courtiers during feasts or elaborate entries into the towns and cities of their realms.

The late fourteenth and fifteenth centuries were periods of growth in the political and bureaucratic power of European rulers. The increasingly elaborate and sumptuous courts were one of the tools that rulers used to create a unified culture and ideology. At the court of the Gonzagas in Mantua, one of the most widely known of the fifteenth-century courts, the manipulation of Renaissance culture for political purposes was most complete.

## The Court of Mantua

The city of Mantua, with perhaps 25,000 inhabitants in 1500, was small compared with Milan or Venice—the two

**Portrait of a Black Man**   Albrecht Dürer sketched this portrait in the early sixteenth century, most likely in a commercial center such as Venice or Nuremberg. By that time it was common to show one of the three Magi as black, but such depictions, unlike Dürer's drawing here, were rarely based on portrait studies.   *(Graphische Sammlung, Albertina, Vienna)*

and papal. To understand fully the Renaissance and its importance in the history of Europe, we need to examine the uses of culture by governments, specifically investigating the transformation of European ideas about service at court during the fourteenth and fifteenth centuries. We will take as a model the politics and cultural life at one noble court: the court of the Gonzaga family of Mantua. Then we will see how the Renaissance papacy melded the secular and religious aspects of art, culture, and politics in its glittering court in Rome. Finally, we will discuss the development of the idea of the Renaissance gentleman and courtier made famous by Baldassare Castiglione°, who was reared at the Gonzaga court.

---

**Castiglione** (ka-stil-ee-OH-nee)

cities with which it was most commonly allied. Located in a rich farming region along the Po River, Mantua did not have a large merchant or manufacturing class. Most Mantuans were involved in agriculture and regional trade in foodstuffs. The town had been a typical medieval Italian city-state until its government was overthrown by the noble Bonacolsi family in the thirteenth century. The Bonacolsis in turn were ousted in a palace coup in 1328 by their former comrades, the Gonzagas, who ruled the city until 1627.

The Gonzagas faced problems typical of many of the ruling families in northern Italy. The state they were creating was relatively small, their right to rule was not very widely recognized, and their control over the area was weak. The first step for the Gonzagas was to construct fortresses and fortified towns that could withstand foreign enemies. The second step was to gain recognition of their right to rule. In 1329 they were named imperial vicars, or representatives in the region. Later, in 1432, they bought the title "marquis" from the emperor Sigismund for the relatively low price of £12,000—equivalent to a year's pay for their courtiers. By 1500 they had exchanged that title for the more prestigious "duke."

Presiding over a strategic area between the Milanese and Venetian states, the Gonzagas maintained themselves through astute diplomatic connections with other Italian and European courts and through service as well-paid mercenaries in the Italian wars of the fifteenth and sixteenth centuries. Marquis Lodovico (d. 1478) served the Venetians, the Milanese, the Florentines, and even the far-off Neapolitans. With considerable understatement, Lodovico concluded, "We have worn armor for a long time."

The family's reputation was enhanced by Gianfrancesco° (d. 1444) and Lodovico, who brought the Renaissance and the new court style to Mantua. By 1500 as many as eight hundred or more nobles, cooks, maids, and horsemen may have gathered in the court. Critics called them idlers, "who have no other function but to cater to the tastes of the Duke." It was under the tutelage of the Gonzagas that Vittorino da Feltre created his educational experiment in Villa Giocosa, which drew noble pupils from throughout Italy. It would be hard to overestimate the value for the Gonzagas of a school that attracted sons of the dukes of Urbino, Ferrara, and Milan and of numerous lesser nobles. The family also called many artists to Mantua. Lodovico invited Antonio Pisano, called Pisanello (ca. 1415–1456), probably the most famous court artist of the fifteenth century. Pisanello created a series of frescoes on Arthurian themes for the Gonzaga palace. In these frescoes Lodovico is portrayed as a hero of King Arthur's Round Table.

The Gonzagas are best known for their patronage of art with classical themes. Leon Battista Alberti redesigned the façade of the Church of Sant'Andrea for the Gonzagas in the form of a Roman triumphal arch. The church, which long had been associated with the family, became a monument to the Gonzaga court just as the Arch of Constantine in Rome had celebrated imperial power a thousand years earlier. In the 1460s Lodovico summoned Andrea Mantegna (1441–1506) to his court. Trained in Padua and Venice, Mantegna was at that time the leading painter in northern Italy. His masterwork is the *Camera degli Sposi* (literally, "the room of the spouses"), completed in 1474. It features family portraits of Lodovico Gonzaga and his family framed in imitations of Roman imperial portrait medallions. One scene shows Lodovico welcoming his son, a newly appointed cardinal, back from Rome—proof to all of the new status of the Gonzagas.

The Gonzaga court, like most others, was both public and private. On the one hand, finances for the city, appointments to public offices, and important political decisions were made by the men who dominated the court. On the other hand, as the prince's domestic setting, it was a place where women were expected to be seen and could exert their influence. Women were thus actively involved in creating the ideology of the court. Through the patronage of classical paintings, often with moral and political messages, wives of princes helped make the court better known and more widely accepted throughout Italy and Europe.

The arrival of Isabella d'Este (1494–1539) at court as the wife of Francesco Gonzaga marked the high point of the Renaissance in Mantua. Isabella had received a classical education at Ferrara and maintained an interest in art, architecture, and music all her life. As a patron of the arts, she knew what she wanted. (See the box "Reading Sources: Isabella d'Este Orders Art.") Isabella was also an accomplished musician, playing a variety of string and keyboard instruments. She and others of the Gonzaga family recruited Flemish and Italian musicians to their court. By the end of the sixteenth century Mantua was one of the most important musical centers of Europe. One festival brought twelve thousand visitors to the city. Later it would be in Mantua that Claudio Monteverdi (1567–1643) wrote works that established the genre of opera.

In the fourteenth century Petrarch had complained that however enjoyable feasting in Mantua might be, the place was dusty, plagued by mosquitoes, and overrun with frogs. By the end of the fifteenth century the Gonzagas had secured for themselves and their city a prominent place on the Italian, and the European, stage.

---

**Gianfrancesco** (jan-fran-CHES-ko)

READING
SOURCES

## Isabella d'Este Orders Art

*Isabella d'Este, the marchioness of Mantua, created one of the foremost collections of Renaissance art in sixteenth-century Italy. As a result of her quest to acquire representative works by the leading artists of the period, she left an unparalleled collection of letters. In the following directive to Pietro Perugino she describes what she expects from a painting she had commissioned from him.*

Master Perugino, painter, [shall] make a painting on canvas 2½ braccia [5 feet] high and 3 braccia [6 feet] wide, and the said Pietro, the contractor, is obliged to paint on it a certain work of Lasciviousness and Modesty (in conflict) with these and many other embellishments, transmitted in this instruction to the said Pietro by the said Marchioness of Mantua, the copy of which is as follows:

Our poetic invention, which we greatly want to see painted by you, is the battle of Chastity against Lasciviousness, that is to say, Pallas [Athena] and Diana fighting vigorously against Venus and Cupid. And Pallas should seem almost to have vanquished Cupid, having broken his golden arrow and cast his silver bow underfoot; with one hand she is holding him by the bandage which the blind boy has before his eyes, and with the other she is lifting her lance and about to kill him. . . . And to give more expression and decoration to the picture, beside Pallas I want to have the olive tree sacred to her, with a shield leaning against it bearing the head of Medusa, and with the owl, the bird peculiar to Pallas, perched among the branches. And beside Venus I want her favorite tree, the myrtle, to be placed, but to enhance the beauty, a fount of water must be included, such as a river or the sea, where fauns, satyrs and more cupids will be seen, hastening to the help of Cupid, some swimming through the river, some flying, and some riding upon white swans, coming to join such an amorous battle. . . .

I am sending you all these details in a small drawing so that with both the written description and the drawing you will be able to consider my wishes in this matter. But if you think that perhaps there are too many figures in this for one picture, it is left to you to reduce them as you please, provided that you do not remove the principal basis, which consists of the four figures of Pallas, Diana, Venus and Cupid. If no inconvenience occurs I shall consider myself well satisfied; you are free to reduce them, but not to add anything else. Please be content with this arrangement.

Source: David S. Chambers, *Patrons and Artists in the Italian Renaissance* (London and New York: Macmillan, 1970), pp. 136–138. Reproduced with permission of Palgrave Macmillan.

## The Renaissance Papacy

The issues of power and how it is displayed had religious as well as secular dimensions. After its fourteenth- and fifteenth-century struggles over jurisdiction, the papacy found itself reduced in many respects to the status of an Italian Renaissance court. But popes needed to defend their primacy within the church from conciliarists, who had argued that all Christians, including the pope, were bound to obey the commands of general councils. The ideological focus of the revived papacy was Rome.

The first step in the creation of a new Rome was taken by Pope Nicholas V (r. 1446–1455), a cleric who had spent many years in the cultural environment of Renaissance Florence. Hoping to restore Rome and its church to their former glory, Nicholas and his successors patronized the arts, established a lively court culture, and sponsored numerous building projects. Nicholas was an avid collector of ancient manuscripts that seemed to demonstrate the intellectual and religious primacy of Rome. He invited numerous artists and intellectuals to the papal court, including the Florentine architect and writer Leon Battista Alberti (1404–1472). On the basis of his research in topography and reading done in Rome, Alberti wrote his treatise *On Architecture* (1452), the most important work on architecture produced during the Renaissance. It was probably under Alberti's influence that Nicholas embarked on a series of ambitious urban renewal projects in Rome, which included bridges, roads, and a rebuilt Saint Peter's Basilica.

The transformation of Rome had an ideological purpose. As one orator proclaimed, "Illuminated by the light of faith and Christian truth, [Rome] is destined to be the firmament of religion . . . , the secure haven for Christians."[18] Thus the papal response to critics was to

**Giving of the Keys to Saint Peter**    Pietro Perugino's painting of Saint Peter receiving from Christ the keys to "bind and loose" on earth and in heaven illustrates the basis of papal claims to authority within the Christian church. This is the central message of the decorative plan of the Sistine Chapel.    *(Scala/Art Resource, NY)*

note that Rome and its government were central to political and religious life in Christendom. By reviving the style and organization of classical antiquity, the church sought to link papal Rome to a magnificent imperial tradition reaching back to Augustus and even to Alexander the Great. To papal supporters only one authority could rule the church. Early tradition and the continuity of the city itself, they assumed, demonstrated papal primacy.

One particular monument in Rome captures most vividly the cultural, religious, and ideological program of the papacy: the Sistine Chapel in the Vatican Palace. The chapel is best known for the decoration of the ceiling by the Florentine artist Michelangelo (see pages 406–407) and for the striking images in his painting of the Last Judgment. The chapel, however, was commissioned by Pope Sixtus IV in 1475. It was to be an audience chamber in which an enthroned pope could meet the representatives of other states. In addition, it was expected that the college of cardinals would gather in the chapel for the election of new popes.

The decorations done before Michelangelo painted the ceiling reflect the intellectual and ideological values that Sixtus hoped to transmit to the churches and governments of Christendom. Along the lower sidewalls are portraits of earlier popes, a feature typical of early Roman churches. More significant are two cycles of paintings of the lives of Moses and Christ, drawing parallels between them. To execute the scenes Sixtus called to Rome some of the greatest artists of the late fifteenth century: Sandro Botticelli, Domenico Ghirlandaio°, Luca Signorelli°, and Pietro Perugino°. The works illustrate the continuity of the Old Testament and New Testament and emphasize the importance of obedience to the authority of God. The meaning is most obvious in Perugino's painting of Saint Peter receiving the keys to the Kingdom of Heaven from Christ. The allusion is to Matthew 16:18: "Thou art Peter and upon this rock I shall build my church." The keys are the symbol of the claim of the pope, as successor to Saint Peter, to have the power to bind and loose sinners and their punishments.

Directly across from Perugino's painting is Botticelli's *The Judgment of Corah,* which portrays the story of the opponent who challenged the leadership of Moses and Aaron while the Israelites wandered in the wilderness. Corah and his supporters, according to Numbers 16:33,

---

**Ghirlandaio** (gear-lan-DIE-yo)    **Signorelli** (seen-yor-EL-lee)
**Perugino** (peh-roo-JEE-no)

fell live into Hell. Various popes recalled the fate of Corah and the rebels. The pope was bound to oppose the council, Pope Eugenius argued, "to save the people entrusted to his care, lest together with those who hold the power of the council above that of the papacy they suffer a punishment even more dire than that which befell Corah."[19]

The effects of Renaissance revival were profound. Rome grew from a modest population of about 17,000 in 1400 to 35,000 in 1450. By 1517 the city had a population of over 85,000, five times its population at the end of the Great Schism. The papal program was a success. Rome was transformed from a provincial town to a major European capital, perhaps the most important artistic and cultural center of the sixteenth century. Visitors to the Sistine Chapel, like visitors to the papal city itself, were expected to leave with a profound sense of the antiquity of the papal office and of the continuity of papal exercise of religious authority. Because the building and decorating were being completed as the Protestant Reformation was beginning in Germany, some historians have criticized the expense of the political and cultural program undertaken by the Renaissance popes. But to contemporaries on the scene, the work was a logical and necessary attempt to strengthen the church's standing in Christendom.

## Castiglione and the European Gentleman

Renaissance ideas did not just spread in intellectual circles. They also were part of the transformation of the medieval knight into the early modern "gentleman." In 1528 Baldassare Castiglione (1478–1529) published *The Book of the Courtier*. The work, which describes the ideal behavior of a courtier, was based on Castiglione's own distinguished career serving in Italian courts. Set at the court of Urbino, the book chronicles a series of fictional discussions over the course of four nights in March 1507. Among the participants are the duchess of Urbino, Elizabeth Gonzaga; her lady-in-waiting; and a group of humanists, men of action, and courtiers. In four evenings members of the circle try to describe the perfect gentleman of court. In the process they debate the nature of nobility, humor, women, and love.

Castiglione describes, in many respects, a typical gathering at court, and the discourses reflect contemporary views of relations between men and women. The wives of princes were expected to be organizers of life at court but also paragons of domestic virtues. Thus in this book the women organize the discussion, and the men discuss. Although the women direct and influence the talk by jokes and short interventions, they cannot afford to dominate the debate: "[Women] must be more circumspect, and more careful not to give occasion for evil being said of them . . . for a woman has not so many ways of defending herself against false calumnies as a man has."[20]

The topics of such discussions were not randomly chosen. Castiglione explains that he wished "to describe the form of courtiership most appropriate for a gentleman living at the courts of princes." Castiglione's popularity was based on his deliberate joining of humanistic ideas and traditional chivalric values. Although his topic is the court with all its trappings, he tells his readers that his models for the discussion were Greek and Latin dialogues, especially those of Cicero and Plato. As a Platonist he believed that all truly noble gentlemen have an inborn quality of "grace." It has to be brought out, however, just as Michelangelo freed his figures from stone. Castiglione held that all moral and courtly virtues exist in tension with their opposites: "no magnanimity without pusillanimity." With numerous examples of good and bad in the world, wisdom can be revealed only through careful imitation, for like the classical authors favored by humanists, Castiglione advises, "He who lacks wisdom and knowledge will have nothing to say or do."[21]

What struck Castiglione's readers most was his advice about behavior. Francesco Guicciardini of Florence once remarked, "When I was young, I used to scoff at knowing how to play, dance, and sing, and other such frivolities. . . . I have nevertheless seen from experience that these ornaments and accomplishments lend dignity and reputation even to men of good rank."[22] Guicciardini's comment underlines the value that readers found in Castiglione's work. Grace may be inbred, but it must be brought to the attention of those who control the court. Courtiers should first of all study the military arts. They have to fight, but only on occasions when their prowess will be noticed. Castiglione adds practical advice about how to dress, talk, and participate in music and dancing: never leap about wildly when dancing as peasants might, but dance only with an air of dignity and decorum. Castiglione further urges the courtier to be careful in dress: the French are "overdressed"; the Italians too quickly adopt the most recent and colorful styles. Reflecting political as well as social realities, Castiglione advises black or dark colors, which "reflect the sobriety of the Spaniards, since external appearances often bear witness to what is within."

According to Castiglione, the courtier must take pains "to earn that universal regard which everyone covets." Too much imitation and obvious study, however, lead to affectation. Castiglione counsels courtiers to carry themselves with a certain diffidence or unstudied naturalness (*sprezzatura°*) covering their artifice. Accomplished courtiers

---

sprezzatura (spretz-ah-TU-ra)

**Federigo da Montefeltro's Studiolo**
The duchy of Urbino was a showpiece of Renaissance court life and was the eventual locale for Castiglione's *Book of the Courtier*. It owed much of its fame to Duke Federigo da Montefeltro. Federigo's study is decorated with an expensive inlaid wooden design. Its illusion of great space and the expense of its construction were meant to celebrate Federigo's wealth and power.    *(Scala/Art Resource, NY)*

should exhibit "that graceful and nonchalant spontaneity (as it is often called) . . . so that those who are watching them imagine that they couldn't and wouldn't even know how to make a mistake." Thus Castiglione's courtier must walk a fine line between clearly imitated and apparently natural grace.

Castiglione's book was an immediate success and widely followed even by those who claimed to have rejected it. By 1561 it was available in Spanish, French, and English translations. The reasons are not difficult to guess. It was critical for the courtier "to win for himself the mind and favour of the prince," and even those who disliked music, dancing, and light conversation learned Castiglione's arts "to open the way to the favour of princes." Many of the courtly arts that Castiglione preached had been traditional for centuries. Yet Castiglione's humanistic explanations and emphasis on form, control, and fashion had never seemed so essential as they did to the cultured gentlemen of the courts of the Renaissance and early modern Europe.

## SUMMARY

THE Renaissance was a broad cultural movement that began in Italy in response to a series of crises in the early fourteenth century. It was a cultural and ideological movement based on the assumption that study and imitation of the past was the best method for reform and innovation in the future. Neither the thoughtful world of Petrarch nor the courtly world of Castiglione, however, sparked the origins of modern individualism or introduced a culture radically different from the medieval past. Between 1300 and 1500, however, Europe experienced profound cultural innovation in literature, political and social thought, and art. The attitudes toward the past and ideas about education formed in this period became the model of European cultural life for the next two hundred years. The cultural values of modern Europe were those inherited from the Renaissance.

The impulse for change arose from the belief, shared by thinkers from Petrarch to Machiavelli, that there was a great deal to be learned from study of the Roman past. This was the basis for humanistic innovations in language, history, and politics. Even revolutionary thinkers such as Lorenzo Valla and Niccolò Machiavelli began with the study of classical literature and history. The same transformation is evident among the artists. Early in the fifteenth century Florentines who experimented with perspective were intent on recovering lost Roman knowledge, and Michelangelo was praised not only for mastering but for surpassing Roman norms.

Issues of reform and renewal were less tied to public life outside of Italy. Moral and spiritual issues were more important. Yet the same movement from imitation to transformation is evident. Erasmus and Dürer assimilated the best of the new art and culture from Italy, but in

*The Praise of Folly* and in Dürer's woodcuts the use of past ideas and models was neither simple nor direct.

The integration of art, literature, and public life was most evident in the ways that art was used by governments. The Gonzaga court and the papacy clearly recognized the value of artistic and literary works as vehicles for explaining and justifying power and influence. The beauty of Mantegna's painting and the power of Michelangelo's frescoes do not obscure their messages about power and authority.

Innovation depended on the study of the past. As humanists came to know more fully the art and history of Greece and Rome, they recognized the extent to which classical culture represented only one source of legal, historical, or moral understanding. Europeans' recognition of other, often competing, traditions would be tested in the sixteenth century, when they came face-to-face with a previously unknown world.

## ◼ Notes

1. Quoted in J. B. Trapp, ed., *Background to the English Renaissance* (London: Gray-Mills Publishing, 1974), p. 11.
2. Quoted in N. Mann, *Petrarch* (Oxford: Oxford University Press), p. 67.
3. Petrarch, "On His Own Ignorance and That of Many Others," in *The Renaissance Philosophy of Man*, ed. Ernst Cassirer, Paul Oskar Kristeller, and John H. Randall (Chicago: University of Chicago Press, 1948), p. 105.
4. Quoted in Benjamin G. Kohl and Ronald G. Witt, *The Earthly Republic* (Philadelphia: University of Pennsylvania Press, 1978), p. 11.
5. Quoted in M. L. King, *Women of the Renaissance* (Chicago: University of Chicago Press, 1991), p. 194.
6. Quoted ibid., p. 222.
7. Quoted ibid., p. 198.
8. K. R. Bartlett, *The Civilization of the Italian Renaissance* (Lexington, Mass.: D. C. Heath, 1992), p. 314.
9. Quoted in *The Portable Machiavelli*, ed. and trans. Peter Bondanella and Mark Musa (New York: Penguin, 1979), p. 128.
10. Quoted ibid., p. 160.
11. Quoted in *The Notebooks of Leonardo da Vinci*, ed. J. P. Richter, vol. 1 (New York: Dover, 1883 and 1970), p. 14.
12. Quoted ibid., p. 129.
13. Giorgio Vasari, *The Lives of the Artists*, trans. George Bull (Baltimore: Penguin, 1965), p. 338.
14. Julia Bondanella and Mark Musa, eds., *The Italian Renaissance Reader* (New York: Meridian Books, 1987), p. 377.
15. I. Origo, *The Merchant of Prato: Francesco di Marco Datini, 1335–1410* (New York: Knopf, 1957), pp. 155–156.
16. Quoted in A. Rabil, Jr., *Renaissance Humanism: Foundations, Forms, and Legacy*, vol. 2 (Philadelphia: University of Pennsylvania Press, 1988), p. 236.
17. Quoted ibid., p. 229.
18. Raffaele Brandolini, quoted in Charles L. Stinger, *The Renaissance in Rome* (Bloomington: Indiana University Press, 1985), p. 156.
19. Quoted in Leopold D. Ettlinger, *The Sistine Chapel Before Michelangelo* (Oxford: Oxford University Press, 1965), p. 105.
20. Quoted in R. M. San Juan, "The Court Lady's Dilemma: Isabella d'Este and Art Collecting in the Renaissance," *Oxford Art Journal* 14 (1991): 71.
21. Unless otherwise noted, quotes from Castiglione are from Baldassare Castiglione, *The Book of the Courtier*, trans. George Bull (Baltimore: Penguin, 1967).
22. Quoted in R. W. Hanning and D. Rosand, eds., *Castiglione: The Ideal and the Real in Renaissance Culture* (New Haven, Conn.: Yale University Press, 1983), p. 17.

## ◼ Suggested Reading

Brown, Alison. *The Renaissance*. 2d ed. 1999. An excellent short introduction to Renaissance art and culture designed for those with little or no background in the field.

Burke, Peter. *The European Renaissance: Centres and Peripheries*. 1998. A broad account of Renaissance cultural movements in Europe.

———. *The Fortunes of the Courtier: The European Reception of Castiglione's Cortegiano*. 1995. A well-written survey of the influence of Castiglione's ideas.

Goldthwaite, Richard. *Wealth and the Demand for Art in Italy, 1300–1600*. 1993. A thoughtful essay about the social and economic influences on the creation and patronage of art.

Goodman, A., and A. Mackay, eds. *The Impact of Humanism*. 1990. A volume of basic surveys of the arrival of Italian humanistic ideas in the various lands of Europe.

Hale, John R. *The Civilization of Europe in the Renaissance*. 1994. A beautifully written survey of the culture of Europe in the fifteenth to seventeenth centuries.

King, M. L. *Women of the Renaissance*. 1991. A survey of the social, economic, and cultural experience of women during the Renaissance.

Stinger, Charles L. *The Renaissance in Rome*. 1985. An engaging survey of the vibrant cultural life at the papal court and in the city during the Renaissance.

Welch, E. S. *Art and Society in Italy, 1350–1500*. 1997. A well-written, well-illustrated discussion of the social context in which artists worked.

Witt, R. G. *"In the Footsteps of the Ancients": The Origins of Humanism from Lovato to Bruni*. 2000. The definitive work on European humanism and the cultural connections between Italy and France.

**For a searchable list of additional readings for this chapter, go to college.hmco.com/students.**

# Renaissance Marriage Chests

The image here shows a marriage procession, including a servant carrying a large chest, or *cassone*. The picture is self-referential, since it was painted on the front of just such a cassone. We know that the painter of this image was Lo Scheggia (1406–1486), the younger brother of Masaccio, and that he was recording a popular story of a marriage between the Bardi and Buondelmonte families of Florence. Lo Scheggia's work exhibits many of the characteristics we associate with Renaissance style. But historians often want to evaluate more than just painting technique. Historians of material culture are interested in the objects themselves and in the meanings that contemporaries gave to the possession and exhibition of them. To understand this we need to know when and where cassoni were produced, why individuals prized them, and what the study of this image from a cassone can tell us about life in Renaissance Italy.

These highly practical chests were used by all but the poorest members of society. In houses that lacked closets, cabinets, and other kinds of storage space, everything was kept in wooden chests. Larger chests were used to store clothing, bedding, jewelry, and even weapons. Smaller chests were used for money, account books, and documents. Many of these chests had secret compartments where, for example, a businessman might keep his most sensitive documents. The most important chests made up the furnishings of the master of the house's bedroom. In a Renaissance palace the master's bedroom was also the room where he met with important allies and family members and conducted his most important business.

Cassoni took on new meaning between the late fourteenth and early sixteenth centuries. During that time it was common for a groom to commission a matched set of chests: one for himself and the second to hold the fine clothes and jewelry that were part of his wife's dowry. These chests were decorated inside and out with scenes from classical mythology, medieval romances, and other popular stories. Classical Roman figures such as Lucretia, who sacrificed her life to maintain her virtue, were common subjects. Some chests celebrated the virtues of chastity or fortitude—virtues thought to be essential in a proper wife. Thus cassoni came to represent the taste, wealth, and social status of the families involved.

**Lo Scheggia: The Bardi-Buondelmonte Wedding** *(Alberto Bruschi di Grassina Collection, Florence/Bridgeman Art Library International)*

With these thoughts in mind, let us look closely at Lo Scheggia's cassone painting. The first thing we should notice is the procession at the left of the picture. We see a man accompanying a woman dressed in black into a house. The two are followed by others leading a horse (a sign of nobility) and carrying bedclothes and the chest. The procession testifies to the very public completion of the marriage process, which often stretched over months, if not years. It began with an engagement, followed by a promise of marriage, then a symbolic exchange of rings and physical consummation of the marriage, usually at the bride's home. The marriage was finalized by a procession to the groom's home. This procession celebrated publicly the alliance between the two families, as well as their standing in the community. Everyone noted carefully what and how much was carried in the procession, which was an indication of the size of the bride's dowry. The decoration of the marriage chest(s) in some way reflected the families involved.

What does the cassone image by Lo Scheggia indicate? The bride is the key to the story. Typically a wealthy bride wore bright new clothes and jewelry, but this bride is dressed in black. The image tells a story not unlike that of Romeo and Juliet. The families of the bride and groom, Lionora de' Bardi and Ippolito Buondelmonte, had been enemies for generations. Despite this fact, the two were in love. We can read the tale of their love in three scenes from right to left. In the first scene on the right, Ippolito is caught in Lionora's house. He refuses to declare his love for her because he wants to protect her reputation. In the middle scene Lionora, dressed as a widow, interrupts Ippolito's trial and declares her love for him. By dressing as a widow, she symbolically declares that they have already made their wedding vows and are, in fact, married. The authorities accept her declaration, and in the final scene on the left, the marriage is made public. Ippolito leads Lionora in a marriage procession, complete with wedding chest, to their new home. According to tradition, their marriage ended the feud between the two families.

We do not know who commissioned this chest. Nonetheless, we can now step back and speculate a bit about what Florentines might have noticed when they viewed the procession in which this cassone was carried through the streets of Florence. The image of the wedding couple and the servants carrying expensive dowry items, as well as the chest itself, testify to the importance of the families involved. In a community such as Florence, where certain families were at the center of politics and public life, this image no doubt reminded those watching the procession of the power of prominent families and their critical role in maintaining civic peace.

veyotlipan.

oncã qn
qmaca q̃

# CHAPTER 13

# European Overseas Expansion to 1600

**H**ERNÁN Cortés's° march in 1519 through the Valley of Mexico toward Tenochtitlán°, the Aztec capital, was recorded not only in Spaniards' journals but also by local witnesses. In the native portrayal shown here, an elegantly garbed Mexica leader brings food and supplies to Cortés. Behind the adventurer are his own Spanish soldiers and his native allies. Many native peoples saw the Spanish as their defenders against the Aztecs, their harsh, recently arrived overlords. The woman standing next to Cortés is Malintzin° (who later adopted the Spanish name Doña Marina). She was an Aztec noblewoman traded by her stepfather to the Maya and eventually given to Cortés. As a translator and interpreter, she was an essential ally during the conquest of Mexico.

The image, with its baskets of bread, meats, and fodder, is part of a pictograph telling the story of Cortés in the Nahuatl° language of the Mexica peoples. The arrival of the Spanish began a cultural exchange between the Spanish and the peoples of the Americas that was more complex than even they initially imagined. The picture captures the contradictory aspects of European contact with Asia and the Americas. Europeans called it discovery, but they were entering sophisticated, fully functioning political and cultural worlds. Doña Marina's presence also reminds us of a more general truth—that without allies, pilots, and interpreters among the native peoples, Europeans would have been lost both in the New World and in the Old.

Cortés's meeting with the Mexica peoples was part of a program of European overseas expansion that began in the last decade of the fifteenth century and would eventually carry Europeans to every part

---

Cortés (kor-TEZ)    Tenochtitlán (teh-NOCK-tit-lan)    Malintzin (ma-LIN-tzin)
Nahuatl (na-HWAT-luh)

---

Cortés—shown with Doña Marina—is greeted by local leaders during the march to Tenochtitlán.    (Trans. no. V/C 31[2]. Courtesy Department of Library Sciences, American Museum of Natural History)

**The European Background, 1250–1492**

**Portuguese Voyages of Exploration, 1350–1515**

**Spanish Voyages of Exploration, 1492–1522**

**Spain's Colonial Empire, 1492–1600**

**The Columbian Exchange**

of the world. It would change how Europeans thought of themselves and how they understood their own connections to the rest of the world. Their expansion unified the "Old World" continents of Asia, Africa, and Europe with a "New World"—the Americas and the islands of the Pacific. Accounts of contacts between the Old World and the New are influenced, perhaps more than any other episode of Western history, by the perspectives of the writers and the readers.

Those who focus on the transfer of European religion and culture view exploration and settlement as marking the creation of a new world with new values. However, the descendants of the native peoples who greeted the newly arriving Europeans—the Amerindians and the Aborigines, Maori, and Polynesians of the Pacific islands—remind us that the outsiders brought modern warfare and epidemic diseases that virtually destroyed indigenous cultures.

Spain sent its explorers west because the Portuguese already controlled the eastern routes to Asia around the African coast and because certain technological innovations made long open-sea voyages possible. Thus, as those who celebrate European expansion have said, the story includes national competition, the development of navigational techniques, and strategic choices.

Finally, the Europeans overthrew the great empires of the Aztecs and the Inca, but the transfer of

European culture was never as complete as the Europeans thought or expected. As our image suggests, the language and customs of the conquered peoples, blanketed by European language and law, survived, though the lands colonized by the Europeans would never again be as they had been before their encounter with the Old World.

## QUESTIONS TO CONSIDER

- Why was it the Portuguese who pioneered European exploration of sea routes to Asia?
- How were the Spanish able to conquer the populous and sophisticated empires they entered?
- In what ways did European nations exploit the lands and trade routes they found?
- What changes did European expansion bring to the Old World and the New?

## TERMS TO KNOW

Prince Henry "the Navigator"
plantation system
Vasco da Gama
trading-post empire
Treaty of Tordesillas
Ferdinand Magellan
Aztecs
Inca
Hernán Cortés
Doña Marina
Council of the Indies
encomienda
Bartolomé de Las Casas
Columbian Exchange

## THE EUROPEAN BACKGROUND, 1250–1492

BY 1400 Europeans already had a long history of connections with Africa and Asia. They regularly traded with Arabs in North Africa, traveled through the Muslim lands on the eastern edge of the Mediterranean, and eventually reached India, China, and beyond. After 1400, however, Europeans developed the desire and the ability to travel overseas to distant lands in Africa and Asia. Three critical factors behind the exploratory voyages of the fifteenth and early sixteenth cen-

turies were technology, curiosity and interest, and geographic knowledge. A series of technological innovations made sailing far out into the ocean less risky and more predictable than it had been. The writings of classical geographers, myths and traditional tales, and merchants' accounts of their travels fueled popular interest in the East and made ocean routes to the East seem safe and reasonable alternatives to overland travel.

### Lands Beyond Christendom

Medieval Europeans knew there were lands to their west. Irish monks and Norse settlers traveled there. Indeed, by the late ninth century Norse sailors, primarily Norwegians, had constructed boats combining oars and sails with strong-keeled hulls, which they used to travel to Iceland, Greenland, and eventually Vinland—the coast of Labrador and Newfoundland. The Norse traveled in families. A woman named Gudridr gave birth to a son in North America before returning to Iceland and eventually going on a pilgrimage to Rome. Although the settlements in North America and Greenland ultimately failed, the Norse were followed by English, French, and Spanish fishermen who regularly visited the rich fishing grounds off North America.

The Greeks and Romans had cultivated contacts with the civilizations of Asia and Africa, and despite the nation-building focus of the Middle Ages, interest in the lands beyond Christendom had never been lost. In the thirteenth and fourteenth centuries European economic and cultural contacts with these lands greatly increased. The rising volume of trade between Europe and North Africa brought with it information about the wealthy African kingdoms of the Niger Delta. The Mongols in the thirteenth century allowed European merchants and missionaries to travel along trade routes extending all the way to China, opening regions formerly closed to them by hostile Muslim governments.

Trade in the Mediterranean also kept Christians and Muslims, Europeans and North Africans in close contact. Europeans sold textiles to Arab traders, who carried them across the Sahara to Timbuktu, where they were sold for gold bullion from the ancient African kingdoms of Ghana and Mali, located just above the Niger River. European chroniclers recorded the pilgrimage to Mecca of Mansa Musa, the fabulously wealthy fourteenth-century emperor of Mali. Italian merchants tried unsuccessfully to trade directly with the African kingdoms, but Muslim merchants prevented any permanent contact.

Europeans enjoyed more successful trade connections farther east. The discovery in London of a brass shard inscribed with a Japanese character attests to the breadth of connections in the early fourteenth century. After the rise of the Mongols, Italian merchants regularly traveled east through Constantinople and on to India and China. By the fourteenth century they knew how long travel to China might take and the probable expenses along the way. European intellectuals also maintained an interest in the lands beyond Christendom. They had read the late classical and early medieval authors who described Africa, the Indies, and China.

The work of the greatest of the classical geographers, Ptolemy° of Alexandria (ca. A.D. 127–145), was known only

Ptolemy (TOL-eh-mee)

## CHRONOLOGY

| | |
|---|---|
| ca. 1400 | Portuguese reach Azores |
| 1444 | Prince Henry "the Navigator" discovers Cape Verde Islands |
| 1487 | Dias becomes first European to sail around Cape of Good Hope |
| 1492 | Columbus reaches New World |
| 1494 | Treaty of Tordesillas |
| 1497 | Da Gama sails to India around Cape of Good Hope<br>Cabot sights Newfoundland |
| 1501 | Vespucci concludes Columbus discovered a new continent |
| 1507 | Waldseemüller issues the first map showing "America" |
| 1510 | Portuguese capture Goa |
| 1513 | Balboa becomes first European to see Pacific Ocean |
| 1519–1522 | Magellan's expedition sails around the world |
| 1519–1523 | Cortés conquers the Aztecs, destroys Tenochtitlán |
| 1533 | Pizarro conquers Cuzco, the Inca capital |
| 1534 | Cartier discovers St. Lawrence River |
| 1542 | Charles V issues "New Laws" |
| 1545 | Spanish discover Potosí silver mines |

indirectly until the early fifteenth century, but medieval thinkers read avidly and speculated endlessly about the information contained in the works of authors from Late Antiquity. For instance, one author reported that snakes in Calabria, in isolated southern Italy, sucked milk from cows and that men in the right circumstances became wolves—the earliest mention of werewolves. By the twelfth century fictitious reports circulated widely in the West of a wealthy Christian country in the East or possibly in Africa. Chroniclers at that time talked of Prester John, who some thought was a wealthy and powerful descendant of the Magi, the wise men from the East who Scripture says visited the baby Jesus. The legend of the kingdom of

READING SOURCES

## SIR JOHN MANDEVILLE DESCRIBES PRESTER JOHN

*The Travels of Sir John Mandeville is said to have been the work of an English cleric. In fact, Travels was probably written before 1350 in France or the Low Countries. The book, which combines pilgrimage accounts, ancient geographic lore, and contemporary ideas about "marvels," was immediately a "bestseller." It helped to create popular expectations in the minds of travelers to Asia and the New World. His description of Prester John's kingdom typifies knowledge of the wider world in the late Middle Ages.*

This emperor, Prester John, holds a vast, great land, and has many great cities and good towns in his realm, and many large and diverse isles. . . . This Prester John has many kings and many islands and many different peoples of diverse conditions under him. And this land is very good and rich, but not so rich as is the land of the great Khan. For the merchants do not often come there in search of merchandise, as they do in the land of the great Khan, for it is too far to travel. And on the other part, in the Isle of Cathay [China], men find all manner of things that are necessary—cloths of gold and silk, spices and all manner of goods. And therefore although men find greater markets in the land of Prester John, nonetheless men dread the long way and the great peril of the sea in those parts.

For in many places the sea is made up of rocks of adamant that attract iron. Therefore no ships pass that have either bonds or nails in them. . . . And also they dread the long way. And therefore they go to Cathay, for it is nearer. And yet it is not so near for a man must travel eleven or twelve months by sea and land from Genoa or Venice before he comes to Cathay. And yet the land of Prester John is further and requires more perilous journeys. . . . In that desert there are many wild men that are hideous to look at; they are horned and they do not speak but grunt like pigs. And there are also very many wild hounds. And there are many parrots that they call *psittakes* in their language. And they speak without any training and salute men who go through the desert and speak naturally as if they too were men.

Source: Adapted from *The Travels of Sir John Mandeville* (London: Macmillan, 1900; New York: Dover, 1964), pp. 178–181. Citations are to the Dover edition.

Prester John probably reflects some knowledge of the Christian groups living near the shrine of Saint Thomas in India or the kingdom of Ethiopia. In the fifteenth century European Christians looked to Prester John for aid against the rising Turkish empire. (See the box "Reading Sources: Sir John Mandeville Describes Prester John.")

Tales of geographic marvels are epitomized by *The Travels of Sir John Mandeville*, a book probably written in France but purporting to be the observations of a knight from St. Albans, just north of London. Mandeville says that he left England in 1322 or 1323 and traveled to Constantinople, Jerusalem, Egypt, India, China, Persia, and Turkey. Sir John describes the islands of wonders, inhabited by dog-headed humans, one-eyed giants, headless men, and hermaphrodites. Less fantastically, Mandeville reports that the world could be, and in fact had been, circumnavigated. He adds that the lands south of the equator, the Antipodes°, were habitable.

More reliable information became available in the thirteenth century, largely because of the arrival of the Mongols. Jenghiz Khan° and his descendants created an empire that reached from eastern Hungary to China (see page 305). This *pax Mongolica,* or area of Mongol-enforced peace, was a region in which striking racial and cultural differences were tolerated. In the 1240s and 1250s a series of papal representatives traveled to the Mongol capital at Karakorum near Lake Baikal in Siberia. The letters of these papal ambassadors, who worked extensively to gain converts and allies for a crusade against the Turks, were widely read and greatly increased accurate knowledge about Asia. Other missionaries and diplomats journeyed to the Mongol court, and some continued farther east to India and China. By the early fourteenth century the church had established a bishop in Beijing°.

Italian merchants followed closely on the heels of the churchmen and diplomats. The pax Mongolica of-

---

Antipodes (an-TIP-o-deez)

Jenghiz Khan (JEN-gus KAHN)     Beijing (bay-JING)

fered the chance to trade directly in Asia and the adventure of visiting lands known only from travel literature. In 1262 Niccolo and Maffeo Polo embarked from Venice on their first trip to China. On a later journey they took Niccolo's son, Marco (1255–1324). In all they spent twenty-four years in China. Marco dictated an account of his travels to a Pisan as they both languished as prisoners of war in a Genoese jail in 1298. It is difficult to know how much of the text represents Marco's own observations and how much is chivalric invention by the Pisan. Some modern commentators have even speculated that Marco himself never traveled to China. His contemporaries, however, had no doubts. The book was an immediate success even among Venetians, who could have exposed any fraud. Christopher Columbus himself owned and extensively annotated a copy of Marco Polo's *Travels,* which combines a merchant's observations of ports, markets, and trade with an administrator's eye for people and organizations.

By 1300 a modest community of Italians had settled in China. By the late thirteenth and fourteenth centuries Italian traders were traveling directly to the East in search of Asian silks, spices, pearls, and ivory. They and other European merchants could consult the *Handbook for Merchants* (1340) compiled by the Florentine Francesco Pegalotti°, which described the best roads, the most hospitable stopping points, and the appropriate freight animals for a trip to the East. Fragmentary reports of Europeans in the Spice Islands (also known as the Moluccas), Japan, and India indicate that many Europeans other than merchants traveled simply for the adventure of visiting new lands.

### Navigational Innovations

The invention of several navigational aids in the fourteenth and fifteenth centuries made sailing in open waters easier and more predictable. Especially important was the fly compass, consisting of a magnetic needle attached to a paper disk (or "fly"). The simple compass had been invented in China and was known in Europe by the late twelfth century, but because it was not initially marked off in degrees, it was only a rudimentary aid to navigation. By 1500 astrolabes and other devices enabling sailors to use the positions of the sun and stars to assist in navigation had also become available. An astrolabe allowed sailors to measure the altitude of the polestar in the sky and thereby calculate the latitude, or distance north or south of the equator, at which their ship was sailing. Still,

until the general adoption of charts marked with degrees of latitude, most navigators relied on the compass, experience, and instinct—dead reckoning.

The most common Mediterranean ship of the late Middle Ages was a galley powered by a combination of sails and oars. Such a vessel was able to travel quickly and easily along the coast, but it was ill-suited for sailing the open seas. Throughout the Mediterranean shipbuilders experimented with new designs, and during the fifteenth century the Portuguese and Spanish perfected the caravel and adapted the European full-rigged ships. (See the feature "Weighing the Evidence: The Ships of Exploration" on pages 458–459.) Large, square sails efficiently caught the wind and propelled these ships forward, and smaller triangular sails (lateens) allowed them to tack diagonally across a headwind, virtually sailing into the wind.

By the 1490s the Portuguese and Spanish had developed the ships and techniques that would make long open-sea voyages possible. What remained was for Europeans, especially the Portuguese and Spanish, to conclude that such voyages were both necessary and profitable.

### The Revolution in Geography

The situation changed significantly over the course of the fourteenth century. With the conversion of the Mongols to Islam, the breakdown of Mongol unity, and the subsequent rise of the Ottoman Turks, the highly integrated and unusually open trade network fell apart. The caravan routes across southern Russia, Persia, and Afghanistan were abruptly closed to Europeans. Western merchants once again became dependent on Muslim middlemen.

The reports of travelers, however, continued to circulate long after the trade routes shut down, contributing to a veritable revolution in geography in the decades before the Portuguese and Spanish voyages.

In 1375 Abraham Cresques°, a Jewish mathematician from the Mediterranean island of Majorca, produced what has come to be known as the *Catalan World Atlas.* He combined the traditional medieval *mappa mundi* (world map) with a Mediterranean *portolan.* The mappa mundi often followed the O-T form—that is, a circle divided into three parts representing Europe, Africa, and Asia, the lands of the descendants of Noah. Jerusalem—the heart of Christendom—was always at the center of the map. What the map lacked in accuracy, it made up in symbolism. The portolan, in contrast, was entirely practical. Sailors valued it because of its accurate outline of coasts, complete with sailing instructions and reasonable

---

**Pegalotti** (peg-ah-LOW-tee)

**Cresques** (KRESK)

**Hereford Mappa Mundi**    Like other medieval illustrations of Eastern lands, this thirteenth-century map combines known fact with myth. The top section locates the city of Samarcand (modern-day Samarkand, Uzbekistan). At the bottom, next to a mythical bird-person, a pelican feeds its young with its own blood.    *(The Dean and Chapter of Hereford and the Hereford Mappa Mundi Trust)*

portrayals of ports, islands, and shallows along with general compass readings. The *Catalan World Atlas* largely holds to the portolan tradition but has more correct representations of the lands surrounding the Mediterranean.

In the fifteenth century, following Ptolemy's suggestions, mapmakers began to divide their maps into squares marking lines of longitude and latitude. This format made it possible to show with some precision the contours of various lands and the relationships between landmasses. Numerous maps of the world were produced in this period. The culmination of this cartography was a globe constructed for the city of Nuremberg in 1492, the very year Columbus set sail. From these increasingly accurate maps it has become possible to document the first exploration of the Azores, the Cape Verde Islands, and the western coast of Africa.

After his voyages Columbus observed that maps had been of no use to him. True enough. But without the accumulation of knowledge by travelers and the mingling of that knowledge with classical ideas about geography, it is doubtful whether Columbus or the Portuguese seaman Vasco da Gama would have undertaken—or could have found governments willing to support—the voyages that so dramatically changed the relations between Europe and the rest of the world.

# PORTUGUESE VOYAGES OF EXPLORATION, 1350–1515

PORTUGAL, a tiny country on the edge of Europe, for a short time led the European overseas expansion. Portuguese sailors were the first Europeans to perfect the complex techniques of using the winds and currents of the South Atlantic, especially along the western coast of Africa (see Map 13.1). Portugal's experience reflects the range of options open

**Winter Wind Patterns**

**Ocean Currents**

**Map 13.1    Winds and Currents**    Winds and ocean currents move in giant clockwise and counterclockwise circles that limit the directions in which ships can sail efficiently. It was impossible, for example, for the explorers to sail directly south along the entire western coast of Africa.

to Europeans as they extended their influence into new areas. As the Portuguese moved down the African coast, and later as they tried to compete commercially in Asia, they adapted traditional Mediterranean cultural and commercial attitudes to fit the new environment in which they found themselves. In some areas the Portuguese created networks of isolated naval and trading stations to control the movement of goods. In other areas they attempted to create substantial colonies, inhabited by Portuguese settlers. In still other areas they introduced

**Map 13.2  World Exploration, 1492–1535**   The voyages of Columbus, da Gama, and Magellan charted the major sea-lanes that became essential for communication, trade, and warfare for the next three hundred years.

plantation slavery to create commercial products for the international market. Spain and the other European states would use these same strategies in Asia and the New World as they expanded their economic and political interests overseas.

## The Early Voyages

Portugal, like other late medieval European states, hoped that exploration and expansion would lead to "gold and Christians." The search for Christians was accelerated in the fifteenth century by the growing power of the Ottoman Turks. Europeans increasingly desired an alliance with the mythical Christian kingdoms of the East to open a second front against the militant Turks. Further, rediscovering the "lost" Christians and reclaiming Jerusalem fed Christian expectations that they were living in the last days before Christ's return.

For the Portuguese, facing the Atlantic and insulated from a direct Turkish threat, the lure of gold was always mixed with their religious motives. The nearest source of gold was well known to late medieval Christians: the African kingdoms of the Niger Delta. The problem for European traders and their governments was that commercial contacts with this wealthy region remained controlled by the Muslim Berber merchants of North Africa. The Portuguese and Spanish hoped to break the monopoly by taking control of the North African coast or by means of a flanking movement along the western coast of Africa.

Actual exploration of the Atlantic had begun long before Europeans recognized the extent of the Turkish threat. By 1350 the Madeiras and the Canaries, groups of islands off the western coast of Africa, regularly were included on European maps. By about 1365 Portuguese, Spanish, and probably French sailors were visiting the Canary Islands. By 1400 the Azores°, a chain of islands one-third of the way across the Atlantic, were known and from early in the fifteenth century were routine ports of call for Portuguese ships (see Map 13.2). These voyages were no mean feat, calling for sophisticated ocean sailing out of sight of land for weeks at a time.

In the second decade of the fifteenth century the Portuguese expansion began in earnest with the capture of the Muslim port of Ceuta° on the coast of Morocco. From then on, the Portuguese, led by Prince Henry "the Navigator" (1394–1460), younger son of King John I (r. 1385–1433), moved steadily down the western coast of Africa. Contemporaries reported that Prince Henry was intent on reaching the "River of Gold"—that is, the Gold Coast of Africa and the Niger Delta. To accomplish this, he directed efforts to colonize the Canaries (which eventually were lost to the Spanish), the Azores, and Madeira°, the largest of the Madeira Islands. He also sponsored a series of expeditions down the African coast, reaching Senegal and the Cape Verde Islands by 1444. The Portuguese quickly established trading stations in the region and soon were exporting gold and slaves to Lisbon.

The islands off the coast of Africa were uninhabited, except for the Canaries, which the Portuguese tried unsuccessfully to keep from the Spanish. Thus the Portuguese could not merely plant trading communities within a larger population, for the Azores and Madeira had no native population. As a result, by the early 1440s the Portuguese were bringing sheep, seed, and peasants to these hitherto unoccupied islands, and the Crown was granting extensive lordships to encourage reluctant nobles to relocate to the Azores. The islanders survived largely by exporting sheep and grain to Iberia.

A significant transformation occurred on Madeira in the 1440s, when the Portuguese introduced sugar cane to the island. Sugar production was capital- and labor-intensive. A great many workers were needed to cut the cane, and expensive mills and lengthy processing were required to extract and produce sugar. On Madeira most of the work was done by Portuguese peasants. But when the Portuguese extended sugar cultivation to the newly discovered and colonized Cape Verde Islands in the 1460s, they found that Portuguese peasants would not work voluntarily in the sultry equatorial climate. Soon the Portuguese introduced a slave-based plantation system to maximize production and profits.

Slaves imported from the Black Sea areas had been used in agriculture since the introduction of sugar cultivation into the Mediterranean in the thirteenth century. The Portuguese had been trading in slaves along the western coast of Africa since the 1440s—the date from which black slaves appear in Lisbon. African slaves, along with slaves from northern and eastern Europe, could be found in Italy and throughout the Mediterranean in the fifteenth century, most often as domestics or laborers in small enterprises. Not since Roman times, however, had slave-based industries developed on the scale of the Portuguese sugar plantations. Sugar production in the New World would be modeled on the plantation system perfected by the Portuguese on their island colonies in the Atlantic.

---

**Azores** (AY-zorz)    **Ceuta** (say-OO-tuh)

**Madeira** (ma-DEER-uh)

## The Search for a Sea Route to Asia

Until the middle of the fifteenth century the Niger Delta remained the focus of Portuguese interest. Only after securing control of the western coast of Africa did the Portuguese look seriously at sailing around Africa and discovering a sea route to Asia.

The fifteenth-century sailors who first tried to sail down the coast of Africa faced enormous difficulties. Water and wind currents tend to move in clockwise and counterclockwise circles against which it is difficult for a sail-powered ship to make progress (see Map 13.1). Winds near the equator generally blow from the east; farther north and south, the westerlies prevail. Some zones, in certain seasons, are pockets of stillness—called doldrums—with few breezes to propel ships. A navigator had to find winds and currents moving in the direction he wished to travel. Sailing directly from port to port was virtually impossible.

Knowledge of winds and currents allowed Bartholomeu Dias (1450?–1500) to explore the coast of southern Africa in 1487. He followed the traditional Portuguese routes until southeasterly winds forced him to sail south and west, almost to the Brazilian and Argentine coasts. Then he was able to ride the westerlies well past the southern tip of Africa, where he turned north. On his return he sighted what he called the "Cape of Storms," later renamed the "Cape of Good Hope" by the Portuguese king. Dias had perfected the techniques for searching out currents in the Southern Hemisphere and opened the way to India.

A decade after Dias's return from the Cape of Good Hope, Vasco da Gama (1460?–1524) set sail on a voyage that would take him to Calicut on the western coast of India (see Map 13.2). Using the information gathered from countless navigators, travelers, and even spies sent into East Africa, da Gama set sail in 1497 with four square-rigged, armed caravels and over 170 men. He had been provided with maps and reports that indicated what he might expect to find along the eastern coast of Africa. He also carried textiles and metal utensils, merchandise of the type usually traded along the western coast of Africa. This was a trading mission and in no sense a voyage of discovery.

Da Gama followed established routes beyond the Cape of Good Hope and into the Indian Ocean. He traveled up the coast until he reached Malindi in Mozambique, where he secured an Arab pilot who taught him the route to Calicut. Although the goods the Portuguese traders presented were not appropriate for the sophisticated Asian market, da Gama did manage to collect a cargo of Indian spices, which he brought back to Portugal, arriving in 1499. From that pioneering voyage until the Portuguese lost their last colonies in the twentieth century (Goa, 1961; Mozambique, 1975), Portugal remained a presence in the Indian Ocean.

## The Portuguese in Asia

Trade in the Indian Ocean was nominally controlled by Muslims, but in fact a mixture of ethnic and religious groups—including Muslims, Hindus, Chinese, Jains, and Nestorian Christians—participated in the movement of cottons, silks, and spices throughout the region. There were numerous small traders, as well as prosperous long-distance merchants with connections reaching into Central Asia, Africa, and China.

Less than a century before Vasco da Gama's arrival, the Chinese seaman Zheng He° made a series of voyages into the Indian Ocean. In 1405 he led a huge armada of 317 ships and over 27,000 sailors on an expedition designed to expand the trade and political influence of Ming China. He would make six subsequent trips before a new emperor, intent on concentrating his resources on China's internal development, ended the ventures. With the retreat of the Chinese, trade returned to its previous patterns.

The hodgepodge of trade reflected the political situation. Vasco da Gama's arrival coincided with the rise of the Moguls, Muslim descendants of Jenghiz Khan. By 1530 they had gained control of most of northern India, and during the sixteenth century their influence increased in the south. The wealth and security of the Moguls depended on landed power. They generally left traders and trading ports to themselves. Throughout the sixteenth century the Moguls remained tolerant of India's religious, cultural, and economic diversity. Neither Muslim nor Hindu powers initially considered the Portuguese an unusual threat.

Asians may not have worried much about the Portuguese because at first there were so few of them. Vasco da Gama arrived with only three ships. And the subsequent fleet of Pedro Alvares Cabral carried only fifteen hundred men. In the 1630s, after more than a century of emigration, probably no more than ten thousand Portuguese were scattered from modern Indonesia to the east coast of Africa. In addition to government officials, Portuguese settlers were likely to be petty traders, local merchants, and poorly paid mercenaries.

The problem for the Portuguese was that their numbers were so few and their trade goods had so little value

---

**Zheng He** (JUNG HUH)

**Portuguese in India**    This watercolor by a Portuguese traveler shows the varied peoples and customs and the great wealth to be found in India. Europeans were fascinated by all that seemed different from their own world.    *(Biblioteca Casanatense, Rome. Photo: Humberto Nicoletti Serra)*

in sophisticated, highly developed Asian markets. In most cases they bought spices, textiles, and dyes with gold and silver brought from mines in central Europe and the New World. In response to this difficult situation, they created a seaborne "trading-post empire"—an empire based on control of trade rather than on colonization. It was, in fact, a model that fit well with their crusading experience in North Africa and their desire to push back Muslim control.

Portugal's commercial empire in the East was based on fortified, strategically placed naval bases. As early as Vasco da Gama's second expedition in 1502, the Portuguese bombarded Calicut and defeated an Arab fleet off the coast of India. This encounter set the stage for Portugal's most important imperial strategist, Alfonso d'Albuquerque (1453–1515), governor-general of Portuguese colonies in India. He convinced the monarchy that the key to dominance in the region was the creation of fortified naval bases commanding the Bay of Bengal

and thereby controlling access to the coveted Spice Islands. (See the box "Reading Sources: Albuquerque Defends the Portuguese Empire.") By 1600 the Portuguese had built a network of naval bases that reached from Mozambique and Mombasa on the east coast of Africa to Goa on the west coast of India and the island of Macao off southeastern China (see Map 13.2).

The Portuguese established a royal trading firm, the Casa da India, to manage the booming market in cinnamon, ginger, cloves, mace, and a variety of peppers. Although their control was far from total, the Portuguese did become significant exporters of spices to Europe. More significant was the creation of the Portuguese Estado da India, or India office, to oversee Portuguese naval forces, administer ports, and regulate maritime trade. Under the Portuguese system all merchants were expected to acquire export licenses and to ship products through Portuguese ports. Asians often found it more convenient to cooperate than to resist, and most agreed to pay for

## ALBUQUERQUE DEFENDS THE PORTUGUESE EMPIRE

*In this letter of 1512 to the king of Portugal, Alfonso d'Albuquerque, the governor-general of Portugal's colonies in India, informs the king of conditions in the East, explains his strategy, and defends himself against his critics.*

The first time the Muslims entered Goa, we killed one of their captains. They were greatly grieved by the [Portuguese] capture of Goa and there is great fear of Your Highness among them. You must reduce the power of [the Muslim] rulers, take their coastal territories from them and build good fortresses in their principal places. Otherwise you will not be able to set India on the right path and you will always have to have a large body of troops there to keep it pacified. Any alliance which you may agree with one or other Indian king or lord must be secured, Sire, because otherwise you may be certain that, the moment your back is turned, they will at once become your enemies.

What I am describing has now become quite usual among them. In India there is not the same punctiliousness as in Portugal about keeping truth, friendship and trust, for nobody here has any of these qualities. Therefore, Sire, put your faith in good fortresses and

order them to be built; gain control over India in time and do not place any confidence in the friendship of the kings and lords of this region because you did not arrive here with a just cause to gain domination of their trade with blandishments and peace treaties. Do not let anybody in Portugal make you think that this is a very hard thing to achieve and that, once achieved, it will place you under great obligation. I tell you this, Sire, because I am still in India and I would like people to sell their property and take part in this enterprise that is so much to your advantage, so great, so lucrative and so valuable. . . .

In a place where there is merchandise to be had and the Muslim traders will not let us have precious stones or spices by fair dealing, and we want to take these foods by force, then we must fight the Muslims for them. If, on the other hand, they see us with a large body of troops, they do us honor, and no thought of deceit or trickery enters their heads. They exchange their goods for ours without fighting and they will abandon the delusion that they will expel us from India.

Source: T. F. Earle and J. Villiers, eds., *Albuquerque: Caesar of the East,* p. 109. Copyright © 1990 by Aris and Phillips. Reprinted by permission of the publisher.

export licenses and trade through Portuguese ports. They even found it expedient to ship in European-style vessels and to use Portuguese as the language of commerce.

## SPANISH VOYAGES OF EXPLORATION, 1492–1522

SPANISH overseas expansion seems a logical continuation of the centuries-long Reconquista (see pages 300–303). In 1492 Castile was finally able to conquer the last Muslim kingdom of Granada and unify all of Iberia, with the exception of Portugal, under a single monarchy. Initially, in 1479, the Spanish kingdoms had agreed to leave the exploration and colonization of the African coast to the Portuguese, yet they watched nervously as the Portuguese expanded their African contacts. Portuguese successes led Castilians to con-

centrate their efforts on what came to be called the "Enterprise of the Indies"—that is, the conquest and settlement of Central and South America.

The sailing and exploring necessary to compete with the Portuguese produced critical information about ocean winds and currents and facilitated later voyages. They also established the basic approaches that the Spanish would follow in their exploration, conquest, and colonization of the lands where they dropped anchor.

### The Role of Columbus

The story of the enterprise begins with Christopher Columbus (1451–1506), a brilliant seaman, courtier, and self-promoter who has become a symbol of European expansion. Columbus, however, was not a bold pioneer who fearlessly did what no others could conceive of doing. He benefited from long-standing interests in the world beyond European shores.

Columbus was born into a modest family in Genoa and spent his early years in travel and in the service of the Castilian and Portuguese crowns. His vision seems to have been thoroughly traditional and medieval. He knew the medieval geographic speculations inherited from Arab and ultimately Classical Greek sources. Medieval seafarers did not fear a flat earth; rather, the concern was whether a ship could cover the vast distances necessary to sail west to Asia. Studying information in *Imago Mundi°* (*Image of the World,* 1410), by the French philosopher Pierre d'Ailly° (1350–1420), Columbus convinced himself that the distance between Europe and Asia was much less than it actually is. D'Ailly's estimate put the east coast of Asia within easy reach of the western edge of Europe. "This sea is navigable in a few days if the wind is favorable," d'Ailly concluded.

D'Ailly's theories seemed to be confirmed by the work of the Florentine mathematician Paolo Toscanelli°. Columbus knew of Toscanelli's calculations and even revised them downward. From his own study he concluded that the distance from the west coast of Europe to the east coast of Asia was about 5,000 miles, instead of the actual 12,000. Columbus's reading of traditional sources put Japan in the approximate location of the Virgin Islands. (It is not surprising that Columbus remained convinced that the Bahamas were islands just off the coast of Asia.) When Amerindians told him of Cuba, he concluded that it "must be Japan according to the indications that these people give of its size and wealth."[1]

On the basis of first-century descriptions Columbus assured Spanish authorities that King Solomon's mines were only a short distance west of his newly discovered islands. In addition to finding the gold of Solomon, Columbus expected that by sailing farther west he could fulfill a series of medieval prophecies that would lead to the conversion of the whole world to Christianity. This conversion, he believed, would shortly precede the Second Coming of Christ. In Columbus's own view, then, his voyages were epochal not because they were ushering in a newer, more empirical world but because they signaled the fulfillment of history, God's plan for redemption.

Columbus's enthusiasm for the venture was only partially shared by the Spanish monarchs, Ferdinand and Isabella. Vasco da Gama had been well supplied with a flotilla of large ships and a crew of over 170 men, but Columbus sailed in 1492 with three small vessels and a crew of 90. Da Gama carried extra supplies and materials for trade and letters for the rulers he knew he would meet. Colum-

bus had nothing similar in his sea chest. His commission did authorize him as "Admiral of Spain" to take possession of all he should find, but royal expectations do not seem to have been great.

Yet on October 12, about ten days later than he had expected, Columbus reached landfall on what he assumed were small islands in the Japanese chain. He had actually landed in the Bahamas. Because Columbus announced to the world that he had arrived in the Indies, the indigenous peoples have since been called "Indians" and the islands are called the "West Indies." (See the box "Reading Sources: Christopher Columbus Describes His Discoveries.")

Columbus reported to the Spanish monarchs that the inhabitants on the islands were friendly and open to the new arrivals. He described a primitive, naked people eager, he believed, to learn of Christianity and European ways. Indeed, the Tainos, or Arawaks, whom he had misidentified, did live simple, uncomplicated lives. The islands easily produced sweet potatoes, maize, beans, and squash, which along with fish provided an abundant diet. Initially these people shared their food and knowledge with the newcomers, who they seem to have thought were sky-visitors.

The Spanish, for their part, praised the Tainos. The visitors generally believed that they had discovered a compliant, virtuous people who, if converted, would be exemplars of Christian virtues to Europeans. Columbus himself observed:

> They are very gentle and do not know what evil is; nor do they kill others, nor steal; and they are without weapons. They say very quickly any prayer that we tell them to say, and they make the sign of the cross, †. So your Highnesses ought to resolve to make them Christians.[2]

The Spanish authorities changed their opinion quickly. The settlers Columbus left at his fortress set an unfortunate example. They seized food stocks, kidnapped women, and embarked on a frenzied search for gold. Those who did not kill one another were killed by the Tainos.

During succeeding voyages, Columbus struggled to make his discoveries the financial windfall he had promised the monarchs. He was utterly unable to administer this vast new land. He quickly lost control of the colonists and was forced to allow the vicious exploitation of the island population. He and other Spanish settlers claimed larger and larger portions of the land and required the Indians to work it. Islands that easily supported a population of perhaps a million natives could not support those indigenous peoples and the Spanish newcomers and still provide exports to Spain. Scholars have estimated that the

---

*Imago Mundi* (i-MAHG-o MUN-di)    **d'Ailly** (die-YEE)
**Toscanelli** (toss-ka-NELL-ee)

## READING SOURCES

## CHRISTOPHER COLUMBUS DESCRIBES HIS DISCOVERIES

*Columbus's hopes for success depended on maintaining the goodwill of Ferdinand and Isabella. Columbus wrote this letter toward the conclusion of his first voyage, which he believed might secure his rights to lordship over all the new territories he found. He took pains to make clear that what he had found was what one would expect to find on the edge of Asia.*

In conclusion, to speak only of what has been accomplished on this voyage, which was so hasty, their highnesses can see that I give them as much gold as they may need, if their highnesses will render me very slight assistance; moreover, spice and cotton, as much as their highnesses shall command; and mastic [yellow resin necessary for various adhesives], as much as they shall order to be shipped and which, up to now, has been found only in Greece, in the island of Chios, and the Seignory [of Venice] sells it for what it pleases; and also wood, as much as they shall order to be shipped, and slaves, as many as they shall order to be shipped and who will be from the idolaters. And I believe that I have found rhubarb and cinnamon [essential ingredients for medicines], and I shall find a thousand other things of value, which people I have left here will have discovered, for I have not delayed at any point and in truth I shall have done more, if the ships had served me as reason demanded.

Source: Cecil Jane, ed. and trans., *The Voyages of Christopher Columbus*, part 1 (London: Argonaut Press, 1930), p. 16.

native population of the islands may have fallen to little more than thirty thousand by 1520, largely because of diseases (see pages 453–454). By the middle of the sixteenth century the native population had virtually disappeared.

Columbus remained convinced that he would find vast fortunes just over the horizon. But he found neither the great quantities of gold he promised nor a sea passage to Asia. With the islands in revolt and his explorations seemingly going nowhere, the Spanish monarchs stripped Columbus of his titles and commands. Once he was returned to Spain in chains. Even after his final transatlantic trip, he continued to insist that he had finally found either the Ganges° River of India or one of the rivers that according to the Hebrew Bible flow out of the earthly paradise. Although Columbus died in 1506 rich and honored for his discoveries, he never gained all the power and wealth he had expected. He remained frustrated and embittered by the Crown's refusal to support one more voyage, during which he expected to find the mainland of Asia.

In 1501, after sailing along the coast of Brazil, the Florentine geographer Amerigo Vespucci° (1451–1512) drew the obvious conclusion from the information collected by Columbus's explorations. He argued that Columbus had discovered a new continent unknown to the classical world. These claims were accepted by the German mapmaker Martin Waldseemüller°, who in 1507 honored Amerigo's claim by publishing the first map showing "America."

### Columbus's Successors

Columbus's explorations set off a debate over which nations had the right to be involved in trade and expansion. Portuguese claims were based on a papal bull of 1481, issued by Pope Sixtus IV (r. 1471–1484), that granted Portugal rights to all lands south of the Canaries and west of Africa. After Columbus's return, the Spaniards lobbied one of Sixtus's successors, Alexander VI (r. 1492–1503), whose family, the Borgias, was from the kingdom of Aragon. In a series of bulls Pope Alexander allowed the Spanish to claim all lands lying 400 miles or more west of the Azores. Finally, in the Treaty of Tordesillas° (1494), Spain and Portugal agreed that the line of demarcation between their two areas should be drawn 1,480 miles west of the Azores. The treaty was signed just six years before Pedro Alvares Cabral (1467–1520) discovered the coast of Brazil. Thus the Spanish unwittingly granted the Portuguese rights to Brazil.

**Ganges** (GAN-jeez)
**Amerigo Vespucci** (ah-MARE-ih-go ves-POO-chi)

**Waldseemüller** (vald-SAY-mill-er)
**Tordesillas** (tor-day-SEE-yas)

**Colonial Seaport**    Travelers to the new world tried to convey what they saw as important about the lands they visited. In this image, the artist emphasizes a mercantile harbor and its connection to the interior.    *(The Pierpont Morgan Library/Art Resource, NY)*

Adventurers and explorers worried little about the legal niceties of exploration. Even as Columbus lay dying in 1506, others, some without royal permission, sailed up and down the eastern coasts of North and South America. Amerigo Vespucci traveled on Spanish vessels as far as Argentina, while Spanish explorers sailed among the islands of the Caribbean and along the coast of the Yucatán Peninsula. Vasco Nuñez de Balboa° (1475–1519) crossed the Isthmus of Panama in 1513 and found the Pacific Ocean exactly where the natives living in the region said it would be.

The most important of the explorations that Columbus inspired was the voyage undertaken by Ferdinand Magellan in 1519 (see Map 13.2). Although his motives are unclear, Magellan (1480?–1521) may have planned to complete Columbus's dream of sailing to the Indies. By the 1510s mariners and others understood that the Americas were a new and hitherto unknown land, but they did not know what lay beyond them or what distance separated the Americas from the Spice Islands of Asia. After sailing along the well-known coastal regions of South America, Magellan continued south, charting currents and looking for a passage into the Pacific. Late in 1520 he beat his way through the dangerous straits (now the Strait of Magellan) separating Tierra del Fuego° from the mainland. These turbulent waters marked the boundary of the Atlantic and Pacific Oceans. It took almost four months to travel from the straits to the Philippines. The crew suffered greatly from scurvy and a shortage of water and at times had to eat the rats aboard ship to survive. One crew member reported, "We ate biscuit, which was no longer biscuit, but powder of biscuit swarming with worms, for

---

**Vasco Nuñez de Balboa** (VAS-ko NOON-yez day bal-BO-a)

**Tierra del Fuego** (ti-AIR-ah del foo-WAY-go)

they had eaten the good."[3] Nevertheless, Magellan managed to reach the Philippines by March 1521. A month later he was killed by natives.

Spanish survivors in two remaining ships continued west, reaching the Moluccas, or Spice Islands, where they traded merchandise that they had carried along for a small cargo of cloves. A single surviving ship continued around Africa and back to Spain, landing with a crew of 15 at Cádiz in September 1522, after a voyage of three years and the loss of four ships and 245 men. Magellan completed and confirmed the knowledge of wind and ocean currents that European sailors had been accumulating. One of his sailors wrote of him, "More accurately than any man in the world did he understand sea charts and navigation."[4] The way was now open for the vast expansion of Europeans and European culture into all parts of the world.

Spanish adventurers were not the only ones to follow in Columbus's wake. The French and the English concentrated their explorations farther north. Building on a tradition of fishing off the coast of Newfoundland, English sailors under the command of John Cabot (1450?–1499?) sighted Newfoundland in 1497, and later voyages explored the coast as far south as New England. Cabot initiated an intense period of English venturing that would lead to an unsuccessful attempt to found a colony on Roanoke Island in 1587 and eventually to a permanent settlement at Jamestown in 1607. French expeditions followed Cabot to the north. In 1534 Jacques Cartier° (1491–1557) received a royal commission to look for a northern passage to the East. He was the first European to sail up the St. Lawrence River and began the process of exploration and trading that would lead to a permanent presence in Canada beginning in the early seventeenth century. But British and French settlements in the New World came later. The sixteenth century belonged to the Spanish.

# SPAIN'S COLONIAL EMPIRE, 1492–1600

**S**PANISH penetration of the New World was a far cry from the model of the Portuguese in Asia. The Spaniards established no complex network of trade and commerce, and no strong states opposed their interests. A "trading-post empire" could not have worked in the New World. To succeed, the

Spaniards needed to colonize and reorganize the lands they had found.

Between 1492 and 1600 almost 200,000 Spaniards immigrated to the New World. "New Spain," as they called these newly claimed lands, was neither the old society transported across the ocean nor an Amerindian society with a thin veneer of Spanish and European culture. To understand the history of New Spain it is essential to grasp what it replaced, and how: the Spaniards overthrew two major civilizations and created new institutions in the wake of conquest. The whole story is not conquest and extermination—many of the Spanish attempted to secure fair treatment for the indigenous peoples who were now part of the Spanish Empire.

## The Americas Before the European Invasion

The Spaniards and later their European peers entered a world vastly different from their own. It was a world formed by two momentous events—one geological, the other anthropological. The first was the creation of the continents of North and South America. The Americas, along with Africa and the Eurasian landmass, were once part of a single supercontinent. The breakup of this supercontinent left the Americas, Africa, and Eurasia free to evolve in dramatically different ways. The continental breakup occurred millions of years ago, long before the appearance of human beings and many other forms of mammalian life.

The second momentous event was the peopling of the Americas. Some migrants may have come over the seas. Most, though, arrived thanks to a temporary rejoining of the Americas to the Eurasian landmass by land and ice bridges that allowed Asians to cross over what is now the Bering Strait to the Americas in the period between 30,000 and 10,000 B.C. Their timing had a great impact. They arrived in the Americas long before the beginnings of the Neolithic agricultural revolution, which involved the domestication of numerous plants and animals. The agricultural revolution in the Americas occurred around 3000 B.C., perhaps six thousand years after similar developments in the Old World. The peoples of the Americas created complex societies, but those societies lacked large domesticated meat or pack animals (the llama was the largest), iron, other hard metals, and the wheel.

Nonetheless, by the time of Columbus's arrival, relatively populous societies were living throughout North and South America. Population estimates for the two continents range from 30 million to 100 million—the lower figure is probably more accurate. North America saw the development of complex Mound Builder societies in the

---

**Cartier** (kar-ti-YAY)

**Tenochtitlán**   The Aztec capital was built on an island. Its central temples and markets were connected to the rest of the city and the suburbs on the lakeshore by numerous canals. The city and its surrounding market gardens seemed to the Spanish to be floating on water.   *(The Newberry Library, Chicago)*

East and along the Mississippi River and pueblo societies in the deserts of the American Southwest. But the greatest centers of Amerindian civilization were in central and coastal Mexico and in the mountains of Peru.

In the late fifteenth century, as the cultural collision approached, the two most powerful centers were the empires of the Aztecs and the Inca. When the collection of tribes now known as the "Aztec" (or Mexica) peoples appeared in central Mexico in the early fourteenth century, they found an already flourishing civilization concentrated around the cities and towns dotting the Valley of Mexico. Through conquest the Aztecs united the many Nahuatl-speaking groups living in the valley into a confederation centered in Tenochtitlán, a city of perhaps 200,000 people built on an island in Lake Texcoco (see Map 13.3). In early-sixteenth-century Europe only London, Constantinople, and Naples would have been as large as the Aztec capital. It literally rose out of the water of Lake Texcoco. Only Venice could have equaled the sight.

The whole valley supported an unusually high population of about a million. Using canals along the edge of the lake and other canals in Tenochtitlán itself, merchants easily moved food, textiles, gold and silver ornaments, jewels, and ceremonial feathered capes into the city markets. Spaniards later estimated that fifty thousand or more people shopped in the city on market days.

Religion was integral to the Aztecs' understanding of their empire. They believed that the world was finite and that they lived in the last of five empires. It was only regular human sacrifice to Huitzilopochtli° that allowed the world to continue: the hearts of victims were necessary to sustain their god, to ensure that the sun would rise each morning. Thus life for the Aztecs required a relentless parade of death.

Tenochtitlán was the center of an imperial culture based on tribute. Towns and villages under Aztec control

**Huitzilopochtli** (wheat-zeel-oh-POSHT-lee)

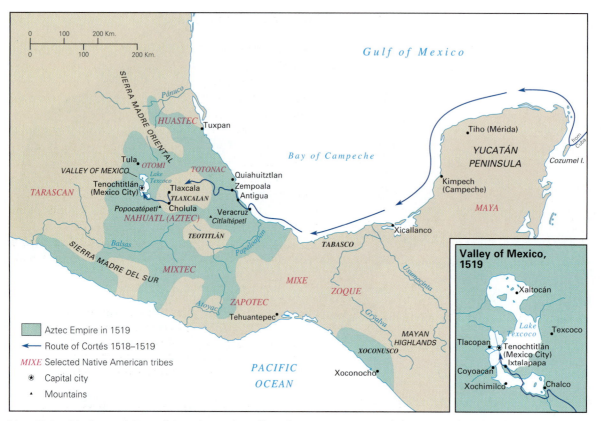

**Map 13.3 Mexico and Central America** The Valley of Mexico was a populous region of scattered towns, most of which were part of the Aztec Empire. As Cortés marched inland from Vera Cruz toward the valley, he passed through lands that for generations had been in an almost constant state of war with the Aztecs.

owed ongoing allotments of food and precious metals to the Aztecs. To emphasize that Aztec power and dominance were complete, the Aztecs not only collected vast quantities of maize, beans, squash, and textiles but demanded payment in everything down to centipedes and snakes. The most chilling tribute, however, was in humans for sacrifice. When the wars of expansion that had provided prisoners came to an end, the Aztecs and their neighbors fought "flower wars"—highly ritualized battles to provide prisoners to be sacrificed. Five thousand victims were sacrificed at the coronation of Moctezuma° II (r. 1502–1520) in 1502. Even more, reportedly twenty thousand, were sacrificed at the dedication of the great temple of Huitzilopochtli in Tenochtitlán.

Aztec society maintained a perpetual state of war with the peoples beyond the mountains that ringed the Valley of Mexico—especially the people along the Caribbean

coast. Given this constant state of war, plus the heavy burdens in tribute placed on the nearby subject cities, it is no wonder that the Aztecs were obsessed by the contingencies of life. At the end of each calendar cycle of fifty-two years, all fires in the empire were extinguished until fire-priests ascertained that the world would continue. And the Aztec world did continue until August 1523 (see page 449).

The other great Amerindian empire of the fifteenth century, the empire of the Inca, was also of recent origin. During the fifteenth century the Inca formed efficient armies and expanded their control beyond the central highlands of Peru. Fifteen thousand miles of roads and a sophisticated administrative system allowed the Inca to create a state that extended from modern-day Ecuador to Chile (see Map 13.4). As they expanded, they demanded political control and tribute but seem to have been tolerant of local traditions and language. The Inca perfected systems of irrigation and bridge-building initiated by ear-

**Moctezuma** (mok-teh-ZOO-ma)

**Aztec Warrior**    This watercolor, by a Mexican artist who was trained in European painting, depicts a pre-Aztec ruler. The dress and the stone-edged sword would have been typical of the Aztecs, too.    *(Bibliothèque nationale de France)*

lier inhabitants of the region. The empire, centered on the city of Cuzco high in the mountains of Peru, was able to sustain a population that may have reached 10 million by the end of the fifteenth century.

Human sacrifice, though not unknown to the Inca people, was not an essential part of their religious life. Their state was unsettled, however, by increasingly harsh tax exactions. Under the Inca system the title Paca Inca, or "Great Inca," was inherited by the eldest son of the ruler's principal wife. The ruler's wealth, however, was retained by the rest of his family, who maintained the court as if the ruler still lived. Thus each new ruler needed money to finance the creation of an entirely new court, and taxes were not only high but continuously climbing.

Both great Amerindian empires, despite their brilliance, rested on uneasy conquests. Subject groups would be willing allies for any invader.

## The Spanish Conquests

Hernán Cortés (1485–1546) was ambitious to make something of himself in the New World. Of a poor but aristocratic background from the Extremadura region of southwestern Spain, he had gone to the West Indies in 1504 to seek his fortune in the service of the governor of Cuba. The governor gave him a commission to lead an expeditionary force to investigate reports of a wealthy and prosperous mainland Indian civilization. From the beginning Spanish authorities seem to have distrusted Cortés's aims. In fact, he departed hastily from Cuba to evade formal notification that the governor had revoked his commission because of insubordination.

Cortés landed in Mexico at the site of the city he would name Vera Cruz ("True Cross") early in 1519 with

**Map 13.4    The Inca Empire**    The Inca Empire was accessible from Spanish strongholds in Mexico only by sea. Spanish exploration and domination brought the destruction of Inca mountain citadels and the transfer of administrative power to the new Spanish city of Lima on the coast.

a tiny command of five hundred men, sixteen horses, eleven ships, and a few pieces of artillery. Aided by a devastating outbreak of smallpox and Amerindian peoples happy to shake off Aztec control, Cortés and his troops managed to destroy the network of city-states dominated by the Aztecs of Tenochtitlán in two years and lay claim to the Valley of Mexico for the king of Spain. The manner in which Cortés explained and justified his mission can serve as a model against which to measure the adventures of other sixteenth-century Europeans in the Americas.

Cortés, like Machiavelli (see pages 401–402), believed in the power of truly able leaders (men of *virtù*) to overcome chance through bold acts. Even so, an attempt to capture a city of 200,000 with an army of 500 appears more foolhardy than bold. Cortés seems to have attempted it simply because he found himself with very little choice. With his commission revoked by the governor of Cuba, Cortés arrived on the mainland as a rebel against both the governor of Cuba and the king of Spain. He burned his ships in Vera Cruz harbor, making clear to all his men that there was no turning back. Much of what he did and said concerning the great Aztec Empire was an attempt to justify his initial act of insubordination and win back royal support. He quickly found allies among native groups who, for their own reasons, wished to see the Aztec Empire destroyed. The allied forces moved toward Tenochtitlán.

Cortés was greatly aided by fortune in the form of Malintzin, a Mexica woman who after her conversion to Christianity called herself Doña Marina (ca. 1501–1550). Malintzin was Cortés's interpreter and, later, his mistress. Without her, one of Cortés's followers recalled, "we could not have understood the language of New Spain and Mexico." Her story illustrates many of the complex interactions at play in sixteenth-century Mexico. Born a noble Aztec, she was sold by her stepfather and mother, ending up in the hands of the Maya. They gave her, along with twenty other women, to Cortés. Knowing both the Maya and Mexica languages, and quickly learning Spanish, she was the one person who could mediate between Spaniard and native. She changed her name to the Spanish Doña Marina and was baptized as a Christian. After bearing Cortés a son, she finished her life in Spain as the wife of a Spanish gentleman. Like many of the natives who felt no affection for the Aztecs of Tenochtitlán, she did not find it difficult to aid the Spaniards.

Despite the help of Malintzin and Spaniards who had previously lived with the natives, the meeting of Aztecs and Spaniards demonstrated the breadth of the chasm separating the Old World and the New. At first the Aztec king Moctezuma was unconcerned about the coming of the Spaniards. Later he seems to have attempted to buy them off. And finally he and his successors fought desperately to drive them out of Tenochtitlán. The Aztecs' indecision was caused in large part by the fact that in neither words nor gestures did the two groups speak the same language. Hearing that the Spaniards were on the march, Moctezuma sent ambassadors bearing gold, silver, and other costly gifts, which they presented in a most humble fashion to the Spaniards. To a modern ear the gifts sound like (and have often been interpreted to be) desperate attempts to buy off the invaders. To Cortés, or any European or Asian resident of the Old World, such gifts were a sign of submission. But to Moctezuma and most Amerindians the giving of gifts with great humility by otherwise powerful and proud people could be a show of wealth and status. Seen in that light, Moctezuma's lavish gifts and apparent humility were probably meant to demonstrate the superiority of his civilization, and Cortés's acceptance of the gifts seemed to indicate his recognition of his own inferior status.

Spaniards later claimed that Moctezuma was confounded by the sudden appearance of these peoples from the East. Cortés himself reported to the king of Spain that when he first met Moctezuma, the Aztec leader said, "We have always held that those who descended from [the god Quetzalcoatl°] would come and conquer this land and take us as his vassals." Later Spaniards explained that the Aztecs believed that Quetzalcoatl, the serpent-god symbolically conquered by Huitzilopochtli, had traveled to the east, promising one day to return and reclaim his lands, thus ending Aztec rule. The Spaniards believed that Moctezuma's ambivalence toward them was rooted in his belief in that myth.

Neither story holds up in light of the evidence. There is no surviving preconquest source for Moctezuma's supposed confession, and the myth of the return of Quetzalcoatl was first recorded in Spanish, not Mexica, sources long after the conquest. In truth, neither Cortés nor historians can satisfactorily explain in Western terms Moctezuma's initial response to the Spaniards. Cortés took the Aztec leader captive in 1521 and began what would be a two-year battle to take control of the capital and its empire. Although weakened by the arrival of smallpox and other virulent Old World diseases, the Aztecs continued to fight even as more and more of the subject peoples joined the Spanish besiegers. The Spaniards cut off food and water to Tenochtitlán, but still the Aztecs fought.

---

**Quetzalcoatl** (ket-zahl-coh-AH-tal)

Different understandings of the rules of war, different traditions of diplomacy, and different cultures prevented the Aztecs and Cortés from reaching any understanding. The peoples of the Valley of Mexico tried to take captives to be sacrificed in temples. The Spaniards, to Aztec eyes, killed indiscriminately and needlessly on the battlefield. Cortés later complained of the Aztecs' refusal to negotiate: "We showed them more signs of peace than have ever been shown to a vanquished people." Thus, to end a war that neither side could resolve in any other way, in August 1523 Cortés and his allies completely destroyed the garden city of Tenochtitlán.

Cortés's recurring insubordination was an unfortunate model. His own lieutenants later rebelled against his control and attempted to create their own governments as they searched for riches and El Dorado, a mythical city of gold. Later adventurers marched throughout the North American Southwest and Central and South America following rumors of hidden riches. Using private armies and torturing native peoples, veterans of Cortés's army and newly arrived speculators hoped to find wealth that would allow them to live like nobles on their return to Spain. Like Cortés, they claimed to be acting for the monarchy and the church, but in fact they expected that success would justify their most vicious acts.

Francisco Pizarro° (1470–1541) was the most successful of the private adventurers. Poor and illegitimate at birth, he arrived in the Americas ambitious for riches and power. After serving in Balboa's army, participating in several slaving expeditions, and helping to found Panama City, Pizarro was prosperous but still not wealthy. Rumors of Inca wealth filtered through to Central America. Pizarro and a partner resolved in 1530 to lead an expedition down the west coast of South America in search of the Inca capital. Benefiting from disorganization caused by a smallpox epidemic and ensuing civil war, Pizarro was able to find local sympathizers.

Like Cortés, he used numerous Indian allies in his most important battles. Aided by Amerindians eager to throw off Inca domination, he captured and executed the Paca Inca and conquered the capital of Cuzco by 1533. He later built a new capital on the coast at Lima (see Map 13.4), from which he worked to extend his control over all of the old Inca Empire. Pizarro and his Spanish partners seized vast amounts of gold and silver from the Inca. The Spanish eventually found silver mines at Potosí°, which would be a critical source of revenue for the Spanish monarchy. Resistance to Spanish rule continued

---

**Pizarro** (pih-ZAR-o)    **Potosí** (po-to-SEE)

into the 1570s, when the last of the independent Inca strongholds was finally destroyed.

## Colonial Organization

The Spanish crown needed to create a colonial government that could control the actions of its headstrong adventurers and create an orderly economy. Although the Spaniards proclaimed that they would "give to those strange lands the form of our own [land]," the resulting political and economic organization of the new Spanish possessions was a curious mixture of old and new.

The head of the administration was the monarchy. As early as the reigns of Ferdinand and Isabella, Spanish monarchs had tried to curb the excesses of the explorers and conquerors who traveled in their name. Isabella initially opposed the enslavement of Amerindians and any slave trade in the new lands. Further, the monarchs promoted a broad-based debate about the rights of Amerindians and the nature of religious conversion. It was royal policy that native rights, even the right not to become Christian, were to be protected. Mexicans had to accept missionaries, but they did not have to convert. Royal control, however, was limited by the sheer distance between the court and the new provinces. It could easily take two years for a royal response to a question to arrive at its destination. Things moved so slowly that as one viceroy ruefully noted, "If death came from Madrid, we should all live to a very old age." Given the difficulties of communication, the powers of local administrators had to be very broad.

By 1535 Spanish colonial administration was firmly established in the form it would retain for the next two hundred years. The king created the Council of the Indies, located at court, eventually in Madrid, which saw to all legal and administrative issues pertaining to the new possessions. The new territories themselves were eventually divided into the viceroyalty of Mexico (primarily Central America and part of Venezuela) and the viceroyalty of Peru.

In Spain, Castilian conquerors completely dominated newly won lands, but in New Spain royal administrators created Indian municipalities, or districts, in which Spaniards had no formal right to live or work. Government in these municipalities remained largely in the hands of preconquest native elites. Throughout the sixteenth century, official documents in these communities continued to be written in Nahuatl, the Aztec language. These native communities were, however, fragile. Colonists and local administrators often interfered in the hope of gaining

# An Inca Nobleman Defends His Civilization

Felipe Guaman Poma was born into a noble Inca family with a long history of service first to the Inca kings and later to the Spanish administrators. Although Guaman Poma became a Christian and adapted to Spanish rule, he appealed to the king of Spain in 1613 to intervene on behalf of the Indian peoples. In this section he describes the evils he has seen and suggests how the king could remedy them.

The aforementioned priests . . . do not act like the blessed priests of Saint Peter. . . . Rather, they give themselves over to greed for silver, clothing, and things of the world. . . . [They] ask for Indians to carry to market their wine, peppers, coca, and maize. Some have Indians bring mountain wine and coca down from the high plains to the hot lowlands. Being highland people, they die from fever and chills. . . . [They] have thread spun and woven, oppressing the widows and unmarried women, making them work without pay. . . . And in this [dealing with the priests] the Indian women become notorious whores. . . . [They] clamor to involve themselves too much in judicial matters. . . . As a result they enter into disputes and initiate petitions and are bad examples for the pueblo [i.e., village]. . . . They treat them so imperiously and thereby destroy the Indians of this kingdom.

The ancient [Andean] priests . . . acted devoutly and gave good example, as with the virgins and nuns of the temples. And so the rest [of the Indians] submitted to their justice and law. They were Christians in everything but their idolatry.

Because of such damage and so many complaints lodged against them, these fathers and pastors should be appointed on an interim basis—for a year at a time if he is good; and if he is not, may he not remain a single day. He should be at least fifty years old because a child's or a young man's follies are not good. . . . They should be proven and tested for academic preparation as well as for humility, charity, love and fear of God and justice, and for knowledge of the Quechua [or] Aymara languages of the Indians, needed to reach them, confess them, and preach the Gospel and sermons [to them].

They should be examined by the reverend fathers . . . who are great scholars and preachers in the world. Those [who pass the examinations] should be sent to Your Lordship and to the head viceroy for appointment as interim pastors, posting a guaranteed bond. With this they will lose their arrogance; they will obey your lordship.

In the time of the conquest of a province there was only one priest in charge of instruction; . . . he demanded no silver and only enough to eat. Thus these first ones were exemplary saints. They . . . did not pretend to be a bishop or a magistrate. Thus [the people] converted to God giving themselves over to peace and to the royal Crown.

## QUESTIONS

1. What are the complaints about the behavior of Christian priests? What do these complaints imply about the place of a priest in a village?

2. What role does Guaman Poma expect priests to play in a village?

3. What are the benefits Guaman Poma expects villagers to receive from Spanish administrators?

SOURCE: Kenneth Mills and William B. Taylor, eds., *Colonial Latin America: A Documentary History* (Wilmington, Del.: Scholarly Resources, 1998), pp. 158–163.

---

control. (See the box "Global Encounters: An Inca Nobleman Defends His Civilization.")

## The Colonial Economy

The problem that most plagued the government was the conquerors' desire for laborers to work on the lands and in the mines that they had seized. From Columbus's first visit the Spanish adopted a system of forced labor developed in Spain. A colonist called an *encomendero*° was offered a grant, or *encomienda*°, of a certain number of people or tribes who were required to work under his direction. The Spanish government expected that the encomendero was to be a protector of the conquered peoples, someone who would Christianize and civilize

---

encomendero (en-co-men-DARE-o)
encomienda (en-co-mi-EN-da)

them. In theory, Indians who voluntarily agreed to listen to missionaries or to convert to Christianity could not be put under the control of an encomendero. If they refused, however, the Spaniards believed they had the right of conquest. In many areas encomenderos allowed life to continue as it had, simply collecting traditional payments that the preconquest elites had claimed. In other cases, where the subject peoples were forced into mining districts, the conditions were brutal. The treatment of native peoples was "more unjust and cruel," one reformer concluded, "than Pharaoh's oppression of the Jews."

The pressures exerted by the encomenderos were worsened by the precipitous fall in the indigenous population. Old World diseases such as smallpox and measles swept through peoples with no previous exposure to them (see pages 453–454). In central Mexico, where we know most about population changes, the preconquest population was at least 10 million to 12 million and may have been twice that. By the mid-sixteenth century, the native population may have declined to just over 6 million, and it probably plunged to less than 1 million early in the seventeenth century before beginning to grow again.

A large population was essential to the Spanish and the Portuguese when they introduced the Old World plantation system to the New World. The Caribbean islands and Brazil were ideal for the production of sugar—a commercial crop in great demand throughout Europe. At first plantations and mines were worked by Amerindians, but when their numbers shrank, the Spanish and Portuguese imported large numbers of slaves from Africa.

Africans had participated in the initial stages of the conquest. Some had lived in Spain and become Christian; indeed, Amerindians called them "black whitemen." Most Africans, however, were enslaved laborers. African slaves were in Cuba by 1518; they labored in the mines of Honduras by the 1540s. After the 1560s the Portuguese began mass importations of African slaves into Brazil to work on the sugar plantations. It has been estimated that 62,500 slaves were brought into Spanish America and 50,000 into Brazil during the sixteenth century. By 1810, when the movement to abolish the slave trade began to gather momentum, almost 10 million Africans had been involuntarily transported to the New World to work the fields and mines on which the colonial economy depended.

**Caribbean Sugar Plantation**
The production of sugar from cane was easily industrialized and centralized. Missing from this depiction of the process are the supervisors who would have overseen the slaves at every step.    *(Courtesy of the John Carter Brown Library at Brown University)*

The conquerors had hoped to find vast quantities of wealth that they could take back to the Old World. In the viceroyalty of Mexico the search for El Dorado remained largely unsuccessful. The discovery in 1545 of the silver mines at Potosí in Peru, however, fulfilled the Spaniards' wildest dreams. Between 1550 and 1650 the Spanish probably sent back to Spain 181 tons of gold and 16,000 tons of silver, one-fifth of which was paid directly into the royal treasury.

The tonnage of precious metals was so great that the French scholar Jean Bodin° (see page 534) held this infusion of wealth responsible for the rampant inflation that disrupted the European economy in the late sixteenth century. Although Bodin overestimated the European-wide effect of the precious metals on prices, the flood of silver and gold did have a significant impact on the Continent. The treasure represents one-quarter of the income of King Philip II of Spain in the 1560s and made him the richest monarch in Europe. The New World bonanza funded Spanish opposition to the Protestant Reformation and Spain's attempts to influence the politics of most of its neighbors. And the Spanish coins, the *reales*° and *reales a ocho*° (the "pieces of eight" prized by English pirates), became the common coin of European traders and even Muslim and Hindu traders in the Indian Ocean. In a world with limited commercial credit, the Spanish treasure allowed for the beginnings of a truly integrated system of world trade.

## The Debate over Indian Rights

To most conquerors the ruthless pursuit of wealth and power needs little justification, but the more thoughtful among the Spaniards were uneasy. "Tell me," demanded Friar Antonio Montesinos° in 1511, "by what right or justice do you hold these Indians in such cruel and horrible slavery? By what right do you wage such detestable wars on these people who lived idly and peacefully in their own lands?"[5]

Initially the conquerors claimed the right to wage a just war of conquest if Amerindians refused to allow missionaries to live and work among them. Later, on the basis of reports of human sacrifice and cannibalism written by Columbus and other early explorers, Europeans concluded that the inhabitants of the New World rejected basic natural laws. Juan Gines de Sepulveda°, chaplain of

King Charles I of Spain, argued in 1544 that the idolatry and cannibalism of the Indians made them, in Aristotle's terms, natural slaves—"barbarous and inhuman peoples abhorring all civil life, customs and virtue." People lacking "civil life" and "virtue" clearly could not be allowed self-government. Other writers commented that nakedness and cannibalism were both signs of the lack of "civility" among the Amerindians. Sepulveda implied that Indians were merely "humanlike," not necessarily human.

Franciscan and Dominican missionaries were especially vocal opponents of views such as Sepulveda's. To these missionaries the Indians initially seemed innocent and ideal subjects for conversion to the simple piety of Christ and his first apostles. In their eyes Indians were like children who could be converted and led by example and, where necessary, by stern discipline. The simple faith of the newly Christian native peoples was to be an example, the missionaries believed, for the lax believers of old Europe. These mendicants saw themselves as advocates for Indians; they desired to protect the natives from the depredations of the Spanish conquerors and the corruptions of European civilization.

The most eloquent defender of Indian rights was Bartolomé de Las Casas (1474–1566), a former encomendero who became a Dominican missionary and eventually bishop of Chiapas in southern Mexico. Las Casas passionately condemned the violence and brutality of the Spanish conquests. In a famous debate with Sepulveda, Las Casas rejected the "humanlike" argument. "All races of the world are men," he declared. All are evolving along a historical continuum. It was wrong, he added, to dismiss any culture or society as outside or beyond natural law. Like all other peoples, Indians had reason. That being the case, even the most brutal could be civilized and Christianized, but by conversion, not coercion. In the view of Las Casas, the argument for natural slavery was indefensible.

King Charles accepted Las Casas's criticisms of the colonial administration. In 1542 he issued "New Laws" aimed at ending the virtual independence of the most adventurous encomenderos. He further abolished Indian slavery and greatly restricted the transfer of encomiendas. (See the box "The Continuing Experiment: The New Laws of Charles V.") We should have no illusion, however, that these measures reflected a modern acceptance of cultural pluralism. The very mendicants who protected the Indians assumed that Westernization and Christianization would quickly follow mercy. When it did not, as during revolts in the 1560s, the mendicants themselves sometimes reacted with a puzzled sense of anger, frustration, and betrayal.

---

**Bodin** (bo-DAN)   **reales** (re-AL-es)
**reales a ocho** (re-AL-es a O-cho)
**Montesinos** (mon-teh-SEE-nos)
**Juan Gines de Sepulveda** (HWAN HE-nays de se-PUL-ve-da)

# The New Laws of Charles V

**I**n 1542 Emperor Charles V attempted to respond to the excesses committed by Spaniards in the Americas. Spanish colonists had been given rights over native peoples with the understanding that the Spaniards were to instruct the Amerindians in the Christian religion. The colonists quickly turned the Indians into slaves, however. The results of Charles's laws were bittersweet, since they did put a stop to many excesses but fell far short of a tolerant understanding of other cultures and peoples.

Whereas one of the most important things in which the Audiencias [law courts] are to serve us is in taking very special care of the good treatment of the Indians and preservation of them, We command that the said Audiencias enquire continually into the excesses or ill treatment which are or shall be done to [the Indians] by governors or private persons. . . . The Audiencias must not allow that in suits between Indians, or with them, there be ordinary proceedings at law [that is, costly and expensive litigation], nor dilatory expedients, as is wont to happen through the malice of some advocates and solicitors, but that they be determined summarily [that is, briefly as in a small claims court], observing their usages and customs, unless they be manifestly unjust; and that the Audiencias take care that this be so observed by the other, inferior judges. Item. We ordain and command that from henceforth for no cause of war or any other [cause] whatsoever, though it be under the title of rebellion, nor by ransom nor in any other manner can an Indian be made a slave, and we will [i.e., command] that they be treated as our vassals of the Crown of Castile since such they are. . . . Also, we command that with regard to the burdening of the said Indians, the Audiencias take especial care that they be not made to bear burdens, or in case that in some parts this cannot be avoided that it be in such a manner that no risk of life, health and preservation of the said Indians may ensue from an immoderate burden. . . . Moreover, we command that from all those persons who hold Indians without proper title, having entered into possession of them by their own authority, such Indians be taken away and be placed under our Royal Crown. Item. We ordain and command that our said Presidents and Auditors [i.e., royal officials] take great care that the Indians who in any of the ways above mentioned are taken away . . . be very well treated and instructed in the matters of our holy Catholic faith, and as our free vassals. . . . They are also to provide that they be governed with justice in the way and manner that the Indians who are under our Royal Crown are at present governed in New Spain.

## QUESTIONS

1. What are the wrongs that Charles V hopes to remedy?
2. What are the limits on the freedoms of the Indians?

Source: Lewis Hanke, ed., *History of Latin American Civilization,* vol. 1 (Boston: Little, Brown, 1973), pp. 108–111.

 **For additional information on this topic, go to college.hmco.com/students.**

---

## THE COLUMBIAN EXCHANGE

**T**HE conquerors, adventurers, and traders who completed the expansion begun by the voyages of Christopher Columbus and Vasco da Gama profoundly altered the Old World and the New. A system of world trade had been in place before 1492, but now, as the Spanish proclaimed, Europe and especially Spain were at the center of economic and political life. As the Spanish and other Europeans moved throughout the world, they carried with them religions, ideas, people, plants, animals, and diseases—forever uniting the Old World and the New. This blending of cultures is known as the "Columbian Exchange."

### Disease

Columbus and those who followed him brought not only people to the New World but also numerous Old World diseases. "Virgin-soil" epidemics—that is, epidemics of previously unknown diseases—are invariably fierce. Although the New World may have passed syphilis to Spain, from which it quickly spread throughout the Old World, diseases transferred from the Old World to the New were much more virulent than syphilis. Smallpox spread from

Cuba to Mexico as early as 1519. It was soon followed by diphtheria, measles, trachoma, whooping cough, chickenpox, bubonic plague, malaria, typhoid fever, cholera, yellow fever, scarlet fever, amoebic dysentery, influenza, and some varieties of tuberculosis. Disease served as the silent ally of the conquerors. At critical points during the conquest of Tenochtitlán, smallpox was raging in the Aztec population. The disease later moved along traditional trade networks. An epidemic shortly before Pizarro's expedition to Peru carried off the Paca Inca and may have contributed to the unrest and civil war that worked to the advantage of the invaders.

Lacking sources, historians cannot trace accurately the movement of epidemic diseases or their effects on New World populations, yet many archaeologists and historians remain convinced that Old World diseases moved north from Mexico and ravaged and disrupted Amerindian populations in eastern North America long before the arrival of European immigrants. In most of the New World 90 percent or more of the native population was destroyed by wave after wave of previously unknown afflictions. Explorers and colonists did not enter an empty land but rather an *emptied* one.

It was at least partially because of disease that both the Spanish and the Portuguese needed to import large numbers of African slaves to work their plantations and mines. With the settlement of southeastern North America, plantation agriculture was extended to include the

**Images of the New World**    A mix of fact and fiction characterized many early images of the New World. The text below this illustration claims that these natives share everything, even wives; that they are cannibals; and that they have no government. The woodcut seems to justify Spanish domination.    *(Spencer Collection, New York Public Library/Art Resource, NY)*

**Gardening in Spanish Mexico**    This closed Spanish-style garden is a mix of the old and the new. Workers use both a Spanish hoe and an indigenous spade to cultivate new plants introduced by the Spanish.    *(Biblioteca Nacional, Madrid/Institut Amatller d'Art Hispanic)*

production of tobacco and later cotton. As a result of the needs of plantation economies and the labor shortages caused by epidemics, African slaves were brought in by the thousands, then hundreds of thousands. In the Caribbean and along the coasts of Central and South America, the Africans created an African Caribbean or African American culture that amalgamated African, European, and American civilizations.

## Plants and Animals

It became increasingly clear to the Spaniards that the New World had been completely isolated from the Old. The impact of Old World peoples on native populations was immediately evident to all parties. But scholars have recently argued that the importation of plants and animals had an even more profound effect than the arrival of Europeans. The changes that began in 1492 created "Neo-Europes" in what are now Canada, the United States, Mexico, Argentina, Australia, and New Zealand. The flora and fauna of the Old World, accustomed to a relatively harsh, competitive environment, found ideal conditions in the new lands. Like the rabbits that overran the Canary Islands and eventually Australia, Old World plants and animals multiplied, driving out many New World species.

The most important meat and dairy animals in the New World today—cattle, sheep, goats, and pigs—are imports from Europe. Sailors initially brought pigs or goats aboard ship because they were easily transportable sources

of protein. When let loose on the Caribbean islands, they quickly took over. The spread of horses through what is now Mexico, Brazil, Argentina, the United States, and Canada was equally dramatic. To the list of domesticated animals can be added donkeys, dogs, cats, and chickens. The changes these animals brought were profound. Cattle, pigs, and chickens quickly became staples of the New World diet. Horses enabled Amerindians and Europeans to travel across and settle on the vast plains of both North and South America.

The flora of the New World was equally changed. Even contemporaries noted how Old World plants flourished in the New. By 1555 European clover was widely distributed in Mexico—Aztecs called it "Castilian grass." Other Old World grasses, as well as weeds such as dandelions, quickly followed. Domesticated plants, including apples, peaches, and artichokes, spread rapidly and naturally in the hospitable new environment. Early in the twentieth century it was estimated that only one-quarter of the grasses found on the broad prairies of the Argentine pampas were native before the arrival of Columbus. Studies of plant life in California, Australia, and New Zealand offer much the same results. The Old World also provided new and widely grown small grains such as oats, barley, and wheat.

The exchange went both ways. Crops from the New World also had an effect on the Old. By the seventeenth century maize (or American corn), potatoes, and sweet potatoes had significantly altered the diets of Europe and Asia and supported the dramatic population growth that invigorated Italy, Ireland, and Scandinavia. With the addition of the tomato in the nineteenth century, much of the modern European diet became dependent on New World foods. The new plants and new animals, as well as the social and political changes initiated by the Europeans, pulled the Old World and the New more closely together.

## Culture

One reason for the accommodation between the Old World and the New was that the Europeans and Amerindians tended to interpret conquest and cultural transformation in the same way. The peoples living in the Valley of Mexico believed that their conquest was fated by the gods and that their new masters would bring in new gods. The Spaniards' beliefs were strikingly similar, based on the revelation of divine will and the omnipotence of the Christian God. Cortés, by whitewashing former Aztec temples and converting native priests into white-clad Christian priests, was in a way fulfilling the Aztecs' expectations about their conqueror.

Acculturation was also facilitated by the Spanish tendency to place churches and shrines at the sites of former Aztec temples. The shrine of the Virgin of Guadalupe° (on the northern edge of modern Mexico City), for example, was located on the site of the temple of the goddess Tonantzin°, an Aztec fertility-goddess of childbirth and midwives. The shrine of Guadalupe is a perfect example of the complex mixture of cultures. The shrine initially appealed to *creoles*—people of mixed Spanish and Mexican descent. In the seventeenth century and after, it came to symbolize the connection of poor Mexicans to Christianity and was a religious rallying point for resisting state injustices.

The colonists tended to view their domination of the New World as a divine vindication of their own culture and civilization. During the sixteenth century they set about remaking the world they had found. In the century after the conquest of Mexico, Spaniards founded 190 new cities in the Americas. Lima, Bogota, and many others were proudly modeled on and compared with the cities of Spain. In 1573 King Philip II (r. 1556–1598) established ordinances requiring all new cities to be laid out on a uniform grid with a main plaza, market, and religious center. The new cities became hubs of social and political life in the colonies. In these cities religious orders founded colleges for basic education much like the universities they

had organized in the Old World. In the aftermath of conquest there were schools to teach Spanish, the liberal arts, and trades to the Amerindian population. By mid-century, however, the urban colleges were primarily for the mestizo and Spanish population. In 1551 the Crown authorized the first universities in the New World. The universities in Mexico City and Lima mirrored the great Spanish university in Salamanca, teaching law and theology to the colonial elites. Colonists attempted to re-create in all essentials the society of Spain.

The experience of the Spanish and Portuguese in the sixteenth century seemed confirmed by the later experiences of the French and English in the seventeenth century. In seventeenth-century New England the English Puritan John Winthrop concluded, "For the natives, they are nearly all dead of smallpox, so as the Lord hath cleared our title to what we possess."[6] A seventeenth-century French observer came to a similar conclusion: "Touching these savages, there is a thing that I cannot omit to remark to you, it is that it appears visibly that God wishes that they yield their place to new peoples."[7] Political philosophers believed that in the absence of evidence that the indigenous people were improving the land, the rights to that land passed to those who would make the best use of it. Thus colonists believed that they had divine and legal sanction to take and to remake these new lands in a European image.

## SUMMARY

As we have seen, there was never a time when Europeans were unaware of or unconcerned about the outside world. Yet the expansion begun by the Portuguese along the coast of Africa and then on to India began a fateful expansion of European economic, political, and cultural influence. For the Portuguese and later for the Spanish, the voyages were almost never adventures of discovery. By rumor and careful reading they had ideas about what they would find. Nonetheless, they were faced with challenges that led them to adapt their Mediterranean and European ways of organization. The Portuguese developed a trading-post system to control trade in Asia. In the New World the Spanish developed a system of law and administration that transformed the world they had found. Further, the Europeans developed a system of plantation slavery that spread throughout the New World.

The expansion of Europe was not the movement of highly developed commercial economies into underde-

---

**Guadalupe** (gwa-da-LOO-peh)     **Tonantzin** (to-NAN-tzin) veloped areas. In Asia the Portuguese and later the Dutch and English were a military presence long before they were an economic one. In the New World, even as the Spanish conquered peoples and changed their languages, governments, and religions, many aspects of Amerindian culture survived in the local Indian municipalities.

Modern historians considering decolonization, economic revolutions in many parts of Asia, and multiculturalism have been changing their thinking about European expansion in the fifteenth century. They have made us very aware of what was lost during the violent and tragic conquests that were part of European expansion. It is impossible to say whether the economic and technical benefits of the amalgamation of the Old World and the New outweigh the costs.

The economic, political, and cultural changes brought about by the conquest created a hybrid culture. But even those who celebrate the transformation of the New World would probably agree with the conclusions of a Native American in the Pacific Northwest: "I am not sorry the missionaries came. But I wish they had known how to let their news change people's lives from the inside, without imposing their culture over our ways."[8] Tolerance, however, was not a hallmark of Western societies. Europeans were incapable of allowing others to change "from the inside." The inability to understand and tolerate others was to be a key to the strife created by the other great event of the sixteenth century—the movement to reform church and society.

## ■ Notes

1. Quoted in William D. Phillips, Jr., and Carla Rahn Phillips, *The Worlds of Christopher Columbus* (Cambridge: Cambridge University Press, 1992), p. 163.
2. Quoted ibid., p. 166.
3. Quoted in J. H. Parry, ed., *The European Reconnaissance: Selected Documents* (New York: Harper & Row, 1968), p. 242.
4. Quoted in Alfred W. Crosby, *Ecological Imperialism: The Biological Expansion of Europe, 900–1900* (Cambridge: Cambridge University Press, 1986), p. 125.
5. Quoted in Mark A. Burkholder and Lyman L. Johnson, *Colonial Latin America* (Oxford: Oxford University Press, 1990), p. 29.
6. Quoted in Crosby, p. 208.
7. Quoted ibid., p. 215.
8. Quoted in Maria Parker Pascua, "Ozette: A Makah Village in 1491," *National Geographic* (October 1991), p. 53.

## ■ Suggested Reading

Burkholder, Mark A., and Lyman L. Johnson. *Colonial Latin America.* 1990. A thorough introduction to the conquest and colonization of Central and South America by the Spanish and Portuguese.

Clendinnen, Inga. *Aztecs: An Interpretation.* 1991. A dramatic, beautifully written essay on the Aztecs that shows how daily life, religion, and imperialism were linked.

Crosby, A. W. *Ecological Imperialism: The Biological Expansion of Europe, 900–1900.* 1986. A discussion of how migrating peoples carried plants, animals, and diseases; includes excellent maps and illustrations.

Curtin, P. *The Tropical Atlantic in the Age of the Slave Trade.* 1991. An introductory pamphlet that is an excellent first work for students interested in the history of slavery and the movement of peoples from Africa to the New World.

Friedman, John Block, and Kristen Mossler Figg, eds. *Trade, Travel, and Exploration in the Middle Ages.* 2000. This encyclopedia includes discussions of the earliest stage of European expansion, especially contacts with Asia.

Mills, Kenneth, and William B. Taylor, eds. *Colonial Latin America: A Documentary History.* 1998. This engaging collection of primary documents and short essays also includes unique discussions of contemporary maps and drawings.

Phillips, J. R. S. *The Medieval Expansion of Europe.* 1988. The best survey of European interest in and knowledge of the world beyond Christendom; especially good on European travelers to the East in the thirteenth century.

Phillips, William D., Jr., and Carla Rahn Phillips. *The Worlds of Christopher Columbus.* 1992. Though written for a popular audience, this is an excellent survey of Columbus and his voyages and an up-to-date summary of recent work on Columbus, maritime technology, and Spanish colonial interests.

Scammell, Geoffrey. *The First Imperial Age: European Overseas Expansion, 1400–1715.* 1989. As the title implies, this is an introductory survey of European colonial interests through the early eighteenth century, with the Spanish and Portuguese explorations discussed in the context of later French and English experiences.

Subrahmanyam, S. *The Portuguese Empire in Asia, 1500–1700: A Political and Economic History.* 1993. A thoughtful introduction to Portuguese expansion by a renowned Indian economic historian.

For a searchable list of additional readings for this chapter, go to college.hmco.com/students.

# The Ships of Exploration

Historians are quite certain that Christopher Columbus sailed to the New World in three ships—two caravels and a nao. But what is a caravel? And how does it differ from a nao? We generally assume that caravels are smaller and more maneuverable, but how can we know? The short answer is we cannot know for sure; we are not quite certain what these words mean. And, of course, this leads to a larger problem. How can we visualize objects described in our sources? If we cannot truly understand naval technology, how can we evaluate its impact on the exploration of the New World or on the dominion over the seas by European navies? Unless we can see what they were describing, we are limited to our imaginations.

An important source for historians is surviving examples of early modern ships. Historians can examine ships preserved and displayed in museums throughout Europe to evaluate changes in construction and rigging (the arrangement of sails) and to date the important innovations that led to the creation of the great European sailing ships. The most famous may be the *Mary Rose*, a Tudor warship salvaged in 1982 from the waters off Portsmouth, England, through the financial patronage of Charles, Prince of Wales. The most dramatic is doubtless the *Vasa*, a brilliantly preserved Swedish warship that sank as it left Stockholm on its maiden voyage early in the seventeenth century.

But the least pretentious and yet undoubtedly the most important is the Mataro model—the earliest known example of naval technology by perhaps 150 years. In the second half of the fifteenth century this model was hung as a votive offering in the Church of Saint Simon de Mataro near Barcelona, Spain. It was common for people to leave votive offerings in shrines, churches, and chapels. The sick and injured often left realistic wax images of their afflicted body parts after they had recovered. Sometime after 1450 a shipwright or a sailor made this model, apparently of a specific ship, which was then hung in the church, probably in thanks for the completion of a difficult voyage. In 1929 the model was deposited in the Prince Henrik Museum in Rotterdam, where it can still be seen today.

Since the offering was for the safety of a specific ship, it seems likely that the builder made the model as exact as possible. This is extremely important, since we have no blueprints, no complete written descriptions, nor any other archaeological remains from this critical period just

**Mataro Model Ship, Fifteenth Century**
*(Maritiem Museum, Rotterdam)*

before Columbus sailed. The few artists who did include ships in their works were not sailors and so did not include the details that would allow us to understand how ships were built. In this respect the model is quite different. It is just over 4 feet long and just under 2 feet wide, which would correspond to a ship measuring about 80 feet by 33 feet. What can we learn about ships and naval technology from this model?

The line drawing shown at right, based on the Mataro model, shows how the boat's hull was attached to its frame. This seemingly simple task documents a critically important change in construction. Small boats can be con-

**The Construction of a Fifteenth-Century Ship's Hull** *(S. F. Manning)*

Stem apron
(To provide a landing
for back-fastening of
wales and planking
against the stem.)

Second wale

First wale

First frame
futtock

Floor timbers

Stern post apron

SFM

structed by tying the exterior shell together and then fitting interior supports to the inside. This is still the most efficient way to make small boats. But shell-building does not work for large ships. We know that by sometime in the sixteenth century, builders no longer used shell-building techniques. Construction of large ships began with a skeleton or frame to which the shell was added. Such ships could be larger, could hold more cargo, and, most significantly, could carry heavy deck guns. Size and firepower were critical to European naval power. The Mataro model indicates an early move toward the newer style of construction. As the drawing suggests, in the middle of the fifteenth century, construction began with a partial skeleton—a keel at the bottom with several ribs toward the midsection. The shell was then tied to the frame, and extra supports were added.

Small boats tended to be open. As ships got larger and hauled more and more cargo, supplies, and weapons over greater distances, builders added decking and sheltered areas above the deck—the forecastle and poop deck. Examination of the model shows how decking and superstructure were added to a boat that was still partially a shell construction. Notice the line of small timbers protruding from the hull. They represent the beams on which the deck and superstructure could be added. Since the skeletal structure was incomplete on this transitional vessel, this was the best way to tie deck and superstructure into the structure of the boat.

The Mataro ship model cannot answer all historians' questions. It is critical to know how many masts and what sorts of sails powered the ship. When the model was discovered in the 1920s, it had three crude masts made from twigs with the bark still on them. These had clearly been added at a later date. The model initially had at least two masts, but we cannot tell whether they carried only lateen sails (which made Mediterranean boats highly maneuverable) or the much more efficient combination of square sails with a single small lateen. (Large lateen sails could not be handled by a small crew and were virtually unmanageable in heavy weather.) It would be useful to know what our model builder understood about sails and rigging in the mid-fifteenth century. Yet the careful study of the Mataro model and the continued search for other archaeological remains may reveal more fully what contemporaries had in mind when they tell us that Columbus sailed with a nao and two caravels.

# CHAPTER 14

# The Age of the Reformation

EL Greco's *The Burial of the Count de Orgaz* encapsulates the hopes and contradictions of the age of the Reformation. El Greco ("the Greek") first learned to paint on the island of Crete, then studied and worked in Venice and Rome before settling in Spain. This painting expresses the medieval Christian understanding of a good death. We see a saintly knight surrounded by clergy and witnesses as his soul (in the form of a cloud-wrapped body) is commended to Christ. But El Greco (1541–1614) painted during a period of social, political, and religious turmoil, when medieval assumptions about the nature of salvation were being challenged by religious reformers.

If we look more closely at the painting, we can see what El Greco and Roman Catholic Christians wished to emphasize. The two figures holding the count's body are Saint Stephen, the first Christian martyr, and Saint Augustine, perhaps the most important of the early Church Fathers. They represent the continuity of the Christian tradition. But just as important is the heavenly hierarchy of saints and angels reaching from the count upward to Christ. At the very top are Saint John and Saint Mary, who are interceding with Christ for the count's soul. The hierarchy of saints and intercessors so vividly painted by El Greco represents one of the clearest differences between the two contending visions of Christian life and society. Most reformers rejected the idea that salvation depended on the intervention of others, no matter how saintly. Salvation was a simpler process. The hierarchy of saints and angels depicted by El Greco seemed unnecessary.

The crisis of the Reformation began with a challenge to the religious authority of the papacy. Debates over the power and authority of the church that raged during this period, however, did not occur in

El Greco: *The Burial of the Count de Orgaz*. This traditional chapel painting shows the close connection between the earthly and celestial realms in traditional Catholic Christianity.   (Institut Amatller d'Art Hispanic)

**The Reformation Movements, ca. 1517–1545**

**The Empire of Charles V (r. 1519–1556)**

**The English Reformation, 1520–1603**

**France, Scandinavia, and Eastern Europe, 1523–1560**

**The Late Reformation, ca. 1545–1600**

a political vacuum. Support for the old church was an issue of state that profoundly affected the exercise of political authority in the Holy Roman Empire. In England and Scandinavia, in contrast, monarchs viewed the church as a threat to strong royal government, and reformers soon found themselves with royal patrons. Elsewhere, especially in eastern Europe, no strong central governments existed to enforce religious unity, and so a variety of Christian traditions coexisted.

By the second half of the sixteenth century political and religious authorities concentrated their energies on a process of theological definition and institutionalization that led to the formation of the major Christian religious denominations we know today. They created Roman Catholic, Anglican, Reformed (Calvinist), and Lutheran churches as clearly defined confessions, with formally prescribed religious beliefs and practices.

An important aspect of the reform movement was the emphasis on individual belief and religious participation. Far from freeing the individual, however, the Christian churches of the late sixteenth century all emphasized correct doctrine and orderliness in personal behavior. Although early Protestants rejected a system that they accused of oppressing the individual, the institutions that replaced the old church developed their own traditions of control.

The increased moral control held by churches accompanied and even fostered the expansion of state power that would characterize the late sixteenth and seventeenth centuries.

---

### QUESTIONS TO CONSIDER

- Why did the reformers seek to establish entirely new churches outside the Roman Catholic Church?

- What political factors limited Charles V's ability to respond to the religious crisis?

- What principal Protestant traditions emerged during the sixteenth century, and how did they differ from the Roman Catholic Church?

- What were the guiding principles of Catholic reform?

- How did social and political interests affect the Reformation?

---

### TERMS TO KNOW

| | |
|---|---|
| Martin Luther | Charles V |
| justification by faith | Henry VIII |
| *sola scriptura* | Act of Supremacy (1534) |
| Huldrych Zwingli | Society of Jesus |
| John Calvin | Ignatius Loyola |
| Anabaptists | *Index of Prohibited Books* |
| Augsburg Confession | Council of Trent |

---

## THE REFORMATION MOVEMENTS, CA. 1517–1545

IN 1517 Martin Luther, a little-known professor of theology in eastern Germany, launched a protest against practices in the late medieval church. Luther's criticisms struck a responsive chord with many of his contemporaries and led to calls for reform across much of Europe. All the reformers, even the most radical, shared with Luther a sense that the essential sacramental and priestly powers claimed by the late

medieval church were illegitimate. These reformers initially had no intention of forming a new church; they simply wanted to return Christianity to what they believed was its earlier, purer form. Although their various protests resulted in the creation of separate and well-defined religious traditions, the differences among the reformers became clear only in the second half of the sixteenth century. Thus it is appropriate to speak of "Reformation movements" rather than a unified Protestant Reformation.

We call the men and women who joined these new churches "Protestants," but the reformers tended to think of themselves as "evangelical reformed Christians." The word *evangelical* derived from *evangel* (literally, "good news"), the New Testament Gospel. They were evangelical in the sense that they believed that authority derived from the Word of God, the Bible. They were reformed Christians because their aim was to restore Christianity to the form they believed it exhibited in the first centuries of its existence.

## The Late Medieval Context

Although reformers claimed religious life was in decline before the Reformation, medieval Christianity was, in fact, flourishing. Questions of an individual's salvation and personal relationship to God and to the Christian community remained at the heart of religious practice and theological speculation. Nominalist theologians, the leading thinkers of the late Middle Ages, rejected the key assumption of previous Scholastics—that moral life was circumscribed by universal ideas and generally applicable rules. In the words of William of Ockham (ca. 1285–1347), "No universal reality exists outside the mind." Truth was to be found in daily experience or in revealed Scripture, not in complex logical systems. At the heart is Ockham's method—known as "Ockham's razor"—the observation that what can be explained simply "is vainly explained by assuming more."

Nominalist theologians dismissed ponderous systems of logic, but they held on to the traditional rituals and beliefs that tied together the Christian community. They believed in a holy covenant in which God would save those Christians who, by means of the church's sacraments and through penitential acts, were partners in their own salvation. Foremost among the penitential acts was the feeding of "Christ's Poor," especially on important feast days. The pious constructed and supported hospices for travelers and hospitals for the sick. Christians went on pilgrimages to shrines such as the tomb of Saint Thomas Becket in Canterbury or the Church of Saint James of Compostela in Spain. They also built small chapels, called chantry chapels, for the sake of their own souls. To moralists work itself was in some sense a penitential and ennobling act.

The most common religious practice of the late Middle Ages was participation in religious brotherhoods. Urban brotherhoods were usually organized around a craft guild or neighborhood; rural brotherhoods were more likely to include an entire village or parish. Members vowed to attend monthly meetings, to participate in processions on feast days, and to maintain peaceful and charitable relations with fellow members.

## CHRONOLOGY

| | |
|---|---|
| **1513–1517** | Fifth Lateran Council meets to consider reform of the Catholic Church |
| **1517** | Luther makes public his "Ninety-five Theses" |
| **1518** | Zwingli is appointed people's priest of Zurich |
| **1520** | Pope Leo X condemns Luther's teachings |
| **1521** | Luther appears at the Diet of Worms |
| **1524–1525** | Peasant revolts in Germany |
| **1527** | Imperial troops sack Rome |
| **1530** | Melanchthon composes the Augsburg Confession summarizing Lutheran belief |
| **1534** | Calvin flees Paris / Loyola founds the Society of Jesus |
| **1535** | Anabaptist community of Münster is destroyed |
| **1536** | Calvin arrives in Geneva and publishes *Institutes of the Christian Religion* |
| **1545–1563** | Council of Trent meets to reform Catholic Church |
| **1555** | Emperor Charles V accepts the Peace of Augsburg |
| **1559** | Parliament passes Elizabethan Act of Supremacy and Act of Uniformity |

The most typical religious feast was that of *Corpus Christi* (the "Body of Christ"). The feast celebrated and venerated the sacrament of the mass and the ritual by which the bread offered to the laity became the actual body of Christ. Corpus Christi was popular with the church hierarchy because it emphasized the role of the priest in the central ritual of Christianity. The laity, however, equated Corpus Christi with the body of citizens who made up the civic community.

Kingdoms, provinces, and towns all venerated patron saints who, believers thought, offered protection from natural as well as political disasters. At the pinnacle were royal saints such as Edward of England, Louis of France, and Olaf of Norway. Festivals in honor of the saints were major events in towns or kingdoms. The most revered saint in the late Middle Ages was the Virgin Mary, the mother of Jesus. The most popular new pilgrimage shrines in the north of Europe were dedicated to the Virgin. It was she, townspeople believed, who protected them from invasion, plague, and natural disasters. In such a society it was impossible to distinguish between religion and society, church and state.

Women played a prominent role in late medieval religious life. Holy women who claimed any sort of moral standing often did so because of visions or prophetic gifts such as knowledge of future events or discernment of the status of souls in Purgatory. Reputations for sanctity provided a profound moral authority. The Italian Blessed Angela of Foligno° (ca. 1248–1309) had several visions and became the object of a large circle of devoted followers. She was typical of a number of late medieval religious women who on the death of a spouse turned to religion. They tended to gather "families" around them, people whom they described as their spiritual "fathers" or "children." They offered moral counsel and boldly warned businessmen and politicians of the dangers of lying and sharp dealings. "Oh my sons, fathers, and brothers," counseled Angela, "see that you love one another . . . [and] likewise unto all people."[1]

In the late Middle Ages religious houses for women probably outnumbered those for men. For unmarried or unmarriageable (because of poverty or disabilities) daughters, convents provided an economical, safe, and controlled environment. Moralists denounced the dumping of women in convents: "They give [unmarriageable daughters] to a convent, as if they were the scum and vomit of the world," Saint Bernardino of Siena (1380–1444) concluded. The general public, however, believed that well-run communities of religious women promoted the spiritual and physical health of the general community. In a society in which women were not allowed to control their own property and, except among the nobility, lacked a visible role in political and intellectual life, a religious vocation may have had a compelling appeal. At the least it permitted women to define their own religious and social relationships. Well-to-do or aristocratic parents also appreciated the fact that the traditional gift that accompanied a daughter entering a religious house was much smaller than a dowry.

Some women declined to join convents, which required vows of chastity and obedience to a Rule and close male supervision. They could be found among the many pilgrims who visited local shrines, the great churches of Rome, or even the holy city of Jerusalem. Many other women chose to live as anchoresses, or recluses, in closed cells beside churches and hospitals or in rooms in private homes. Men and women traveled from all parts of England seeking the counsel of the Blessed Julian of Norwich (d. after 1413), who lived in a tiny cell built into the wall of a parish church.

The most controversial group of religious women were the Beguines, who lived in communities without taking formal vows and often with minimal connections to the local church hierarchy. By the early fifteenth century Beguines were suspect because clerics believed that these independent women rejected traditional religious cloistering and the moral leadership of male clergy; consequently, it was thought, they were particularly susceptible to heresy. Critics maintained that unsupervised Beguines held to what was called the "Heresy of the Free Spirit," a belief that one who had achieved spiritual perfection was no longer capable of sin. Fantastic rumors of sexual orgies, spread by fearful clerical opponents, quickly brought suspect women before local church authorities. Although some Beguines may have held such a belief in spiritual perfection, the majority certainly did not. Even so, they were feared by an ecclesiastical hierarchy that distrusted independence.

A more conservative movement for renewal in the church was the Brothers and Sisters of the Common Life, founded by the Dutchman Geert Groote° (1340–1384). A popular preacher and reformer, Groote gathered male and female followers into quasi-monastic communities at Deventer in the Low Countries. Eventually a community of Augustinian canons was added at Windesheim. Brothers and Sisters of the Common Life supported themselves as book copyists and teachers in small religious schools. Members of these communities followed a strict, conservative spirituality that has come to be known as the *devotio moderna*, or "modern devotion." Although they called themselves "modern," their piety was traditional. Their ideas are encapsulated in *The Imitation of Christ*, a popular work of traditional monastic spirituality written by Thomas à Kempis (ca. 1380–1471), a canon of Windesheim. They advocated the contrary ideals of fourteenth-century religious life: broader participation by the laity and strict control by clerical authorities.

Religious life in the late medieval period was broadly based and vigorous. Theologians, laypeople, and popular preachers could take heart that they were furthering their own salvation and that of their neighbors. Thus the Reformation of the sixteenth century involved more than simple moral change.

---

**Foligno** (fo-LIN-yo)

**Geert Groote** (HIRT HROW-ta)

**Crowning with Thorns**    Late medieval Christians meditated on Christ's sufferings and preferred images like this one that shows a tortured Christ living in their own time.
*(Courtesy, Augustiner Chorherrenstift, Herzogenburg. Photo: Fotostudio Wurst Erich)*

## Martin Luther and the New Theology

Martin Luther (1483–1546) eventually challenged many of the assumptions of late medieval Christians. He seemed to burst onto the scene in 1517, when he objected to the way in which papal indulgences—that is, the remission of penalties owed for sins—were being bought and sold in the bishopric of Brandenburg. Luther's father, a miner from the small town of Mansfeld, had hoped that his son would take a degree in law and become a wealthy and prestigious lawyer. Luther chose instead to enter a monastery and eventually become a priest.

Throughout his life Luther seems to have been troubled by a sense of his own sinfulness and unworthiness. According to late medieval theology, the life of a Christian was a continuing cycle of sin, confession, contrition, and penance, and the only way to achieve salvation was to have confessed all one's sins and at least begun a cycle of penance at the time of one's death. Christians lived in

fear of dying suddenly, unconfessed. The purchase of indulgences, membership in penitential brotherhoods, ritualized charity, and veneration of popular saints were seen as ways to acquire merit in the eyes of God.

Luther came to believe that the church's requirement that believers achieve salvation by means of confession, contrition, and penance made too great a demand on the faithful. Instead, Luther said, citing the New Testament, salvation (or justification) was God's gift to the faithful. Luther's belief is known as "justification by faith." Acts of charity were important products resulting from God's love, but in Luther's opinion, they were not necessary for salvation. Late in his life Luther explained how he came by these ideas:

Though I lived as a monk without reproach, I felt that I was a sinner before God with an extremely disturbed conscience. I could not believe that he was placated by my [acts of penance]. I did not love, yes, I hated the righteous God who punishes sinners. At last, by the mercy of God, I gave context to the words, namely, "In it the righteousness of God is revealed, as it is written, 'He who through faith is righteous shall live.'" There I began to understand that the righteous lives by a gift of God, namely by faith. Here I felt that I was altogether born again and had entered paradise itself through open gates.[2]

Although Luther recalled a sudden, dramatic revelation, it now seems clear that his insight developed slowly over the course of his academic career and during his defense of his teachings. Nonetheless, his recollection conveys a sense of the novelty of his theology and suggests why his attack on the late medieval church proved to be so much more devastating than the complaints of earlier critics.

Others had complained of impious priests, an unresponsive bureaucracy, and a church too much involved in matters of government, but the theology that Luther developed struck at the doctrinal foundations of the church itself. Luther separated justification from acts of sanctification—from the good works or charity expected of all Christians. In Luther's theology the acts of piety so typical of the medieval church were quite unnecessary for salvation because Christ's sacrifice had brought justification once and for all. Justification came entirely from God and was independent of human works. Luther argued that the Christian was at the same time sinner and saved, so the penitential cycle and careful preparation for a "good death" were, in his opinion, superfluous.

Luther also attacked the place of the priesthood in the sacramental life of the church and, by extension, the power and authority a church might claim in public life. The church taught that, through the actions of ordained priests, Christ was really present in the bread and wine of the sacrament of Holy Communion. Luther agreed that the sacrament transformed the bread and wine into the body and blood of Christ, but he denied that priests had a role in the transformation. Priests, in Luther's view, were not mediators between God and individual Christians. John Wyclif and Jan Hus (see page 360) had argued against the spiritual authority of unworthy priests. Luther, however, challenged the role of all clergy, and of the institutional church itself, in the attainment of salvation. Thus he argued for a "priesthood of all believers."

In the years before 1517 Luther's views on salvation and his reservations about the traditional ways of teaching theology attracted little interest outside his own university. Matters changed, however, when he questioned the sale of indulgences. Indulgences were often granted as rewards for pilgrimages or for noteworthy acts of charity or sacrifice. The papacy frequently authorized the sale of indulgences to pay various expenses. Unscrupulous priests often left the impression that purchase of an indulgence freed a soul from Purgatory. After getting no response to his initial complaints, Luther made his "Ninety-five Theses" public. He probably posted his document on the door of the Wittenberg Castle church, the usual way to announce topics for theological debates. His text created a firestorm when it was quickly translated and printed throughout German-speaking lands. His charges against the sale of indulgences encapsulated German feelings about unworthy priests and economic abuses by the clergy. Luther was acclaimed as the spokesman of the German people.

In a debate with a papal representative in Leipzig in 1519, Luther was forced to admit that in some of his positions he agreed with the Czech reformer Jan Hus, who had been burned at the stake as a heretic in 1415. In the Leipzig debate and in hearings the following year, Luther responded to his critics and tried to explain more fully the nature of the changes he advocated. Three tracts were especially important. In *Address to the Christian Nobility of the German Nation* Luther urged the princes to reject papal claims of temporal and spiritual authority. (See the box "Reading Sources: Martin Luther's Address to the Christian Nobility of the German Nation.") In *On the Babylonian Captivity of the Church* he argued for the principle of *sola scriptura*—that is, church authority had to be based on biblical teachings. In *On Christian Freedom* he explained clearly his understanding of salvation: "A Christian has all he needs in faith and needs no works to justify him." Luther was speaking of spiritual freedom from unnecessary ritual, not social or political freedom. This distinction would later be crucial to Luther's opposition to political and economic protests by peasants and artisans.

In 1520 Pope Leo X (r. 1513–1521) condemned Luther's teachings and gave him sixty days to recant. Luther refused to do so and publicly burned the papal letter. In 1521 Emperor Charles V called an imperial diet, or parliament, at Worms to deal with the religious crisis. Charles demanded that Luther submit to papal authority. Luther, however, explained that religious decisions must be based on personal experience and conscience, as both were informed by a study of Scripture:

> Unless I am convicted by the testimony of Scripture or by clear reason, for I do not trust either in the Pope or in councils alone, since it is well known that they have often erred and contradicted themselves, I cannot and will not retract anything, for it is neither safe nor right to go against conscience. I cannot do otherwise, here I stand, may God help me. Amen.[3]

READING
SOURCES

## MARTIN LUTHER'S ADDRESS TO THE CHRISTIAN NOBILITY OF THE GERMAN NATION

*Luther wrote this tract to the rulers of Germany to explain the nature of his conflict with the church over ecclesiastical authority. In this excerpt he outlines his disagreements with the system of clerical status and immunities that had grown throughout the Middle Ages.*

The Romanists have very cleverly built three walls around themselves. In the first place, when pressed by the temporal power, they have made decrees and declared that the temporal power had no jurisdiction over them, but that on the contrary, the spiritual power is above the temporal. In the second place, when the attempt is made to reprove them with the Scriptures, they raise the objection that only the Pope may interpret the Scriptures. In the third place if threatened with a council, their story is that no one may summon a council but the Pope.

Let us begin by attacking the first wall. It is pure invention that the Pope, bishops, priests, and monks are called the spiritual estate while princes, lords, craftsmen, and peasants are the temporal estate. This is indeed a piece of deceit and hypocrisy: all Christians are truly of the spiritual estate. The Pope or bishop anoints, shaves heads, ordains, consecrates, and prescribes garb different from that of the laity, but he can never make a man into a Christian or into a spiritual man by so

doing. He might well make a man into a hypocrite or a humbug and a blockhead, but never a Christian or a spiritual man. Therefore a priest in Christendom is nothing else but an officeholder. As long as he holds his office, he takes precedence; where he is deposed, he is a peasant or a townsman like anybody else.

The second wall is still more loosely built and less substantial. The Romanists want to be the only masters of Holy Scripture, although they never learn a thing from the Bible their life long. Besides, if we are all priests, and all have one faith, one gospel, one sacrament, why should we not also have the power to test and judge what is right or wrong in matters of faith?

The third wall falls of itself, when the first two are down. When the Pope acts contrary to the Scriptures, it is our duty to stand by the Scriptures and to reprove him and to constrain him, according to the word of Christ. The Romanists have no basis in Scripture for their claim that the Pope alone has the right to call or to confirm a council. This is just their own ruling, and it is only valid so long as it is not harmful to Christendom or contrary to the laws of God.

Source: Martin Luther, *Three Treatises*, in *The American Edition of Luther's Works* (Philadelphia: Fortress Press, 1970), pp. 10–22. Copyright © 1943 Muhlenberg Press. Used by permission of Augsburg Fortress.

---

The emperor and his allies stayed firmly in the papal camp (see Map 14.1), and the excommunicated Luther was placed under an imperial ban—that is, declared an outlaw. As Luther left the Diet of Worms, friendly princes took him to Wartburg Castle in Saxony, where they could protect him. During a year of isolation at Wartburg, Luther used Erasmus's edition of the Greek New Testament as the basis of a translation of the New Testament into German , which became an influential literary as well as religious work.

### The Reformation of the Communities

Luther challenged the authority of the clerical hierarchy and called on laypeople to take responsibility for their own salvation. His ideas spread rapidly in the towns and

countryside of Germany because he and his followers took advantage of the new technology of printing. (See the feature "Weighing the Evidence: A Reformation Woodcut" on pages 494–495.) Perhaps 300,000 copies of his early tracts were published in the first years of the protest. Luther's claim that the Scriptures must be the basis of all life and his appeal to the judgment of the laity made sense to the men and women in towns and villages, where councils of local people were accustomed to making decisions based on ideas of the common good. It is also true that townspeople and villagers saw religious and civic life as being inextricably interconnected. For them the notion of a religiously neutral act was unthinkable.

The impact of Luther's ideas quickly became evident. If the active intercession of the clergy was not necessary for the salvation of individuals, then, according to Luther's

Map 14.1    **Reform in Germany, 1517–1555**    The pattern of religious reform in Germany was complex. Although some territorial princes, such as the dukes of Bavaria, rejected the reform, most free towns, particularly those in the southwest, adopted it.

followers, there was no reason for the clergy to remain unmarried and celibate, nor for men and women to cloister themselves in monasteries and convents. Also, maintained Luther's partisans, the laity's participation in the sacrament of the Eucharist need not be restricted. Thus the priest must distribute wine to the congregants along with the bread. With the spread of Luther's ideas came the end of a very visual part of clerical power. Because Luther's followers believed that penitential acts were not prerequisites for salvation, they tended to set aside the veneration of saints and give up pilgrimages to the shrines and holy places all over Europe.

Many historians have referred to the spread of these reform ideas as the "Reformation of the Common Man." In Strasbourg, Nuremberg, Zurich, and other towns ideas about the primacy of the Bible and attacks on clerical priv-ilege were spread by "people's priests." These individuals were hired by the town government to preach and teach, and to care for the souls in the community. Many of the most famous reformers initially gained a following through preaching. The message seems to have spread especially quickly among artisan and mercantile groups, which put pressure on town governments to press for reform. Agitation was often riotous. One resident of Augsburg exposed himself during a church service to protest what he believed was an evil and idolatrous service. Women on both sides of the reform stepped out of traditional roles, in which they were seen as subservient. For instance, a "common man" was understood to be the sturdy bulwark of the sacred community, but a "common woman" was a prostitute. Even women tended to accept these stereotypes. Nonetheless, aristocratic women such as Margaret of Angoulême° in France (see pages 482–483) supported and protected reformers. Other women wrote tracts advocating reform or defending the old order, and still others used shovels and rakes to defend religious values.

The process of reform in Zurich is instructive. In 1519 the people's priest of Zurich was Huldrych Zwingli° (1484–1531), son of a rural official from a nearby village. After a university education he became a typical late medieval country priest, right down to his publically acknowledged mistress. Yet after experiences as a military chaplain and an acquaintance with the humanist writings of Erasmus, Zwingli began to preach strongly biblical sermons. In 1522 he defended a group of laymen who protested by breaking the required Lenten fast. Later in the same year he requested episcopal permission to marry. Early in 1523 he led a group of reformers in a public debate over the nature of the church. The city council declared in favor of the reformers, and Zurich became in effect a Protestant city.

Unlike Luther, Zwingli believed that reform should be a communal movement—that town governments should take the lead in bringing reform to the community. Zwingli explained that the moral regeneration of individuals was an essential part of God's salvation. In the years following 1523 the reformers restructured church services, abolishing the mass. They also removed religious images from churches and suppressed monastic institutions. Zwingli further disagreed with Luther about the nature of the sacrament of Holy Communion. Whereas Luther, like Catholic theologians, accepted that Christ was truly present in the bread and wine, Zwingli argued that Christ's presence was merely spiritual—that the bread and wine only signified Christ. This disagreement created within the reform movement a division that made a common response to papal or imperial pressure difficult.

The reform message spread from towns into the countryside, but often with effects that the reformers did not expect or desire. Luther thought his message was a spiritual and theological one. Many peasants and modest artisans, however, believed that Luther's message of biblical freedom carried material as well as theological meaning.

In many parts of Germany villagers and peasants found themselves under increasing pressure from landlords and territorial princes. Taking advantage of changed economic and political conditions, these lords were intent on regaining claims to ancient manorial rights, on suppressing peasant claims to use common lands, and on imposing new taxes and tithes. Like townspeople, peasants saw religious and material life as closely connected.

Angoulême (ohn-goo-LEM)    Zwingli (SVING-lee)

**Peasant Freedom**    The German peasants believed that Luther's call for individual freedom of conscience included economic and political freedom. Their revolt of 1524 and 1525 struck terror into the hearts of German rulers. As this woodcut indicates, the peasant army was lightly armed. Many carried only tools such as pitchforks, flails, and scythes. *(Title page of an anonymous pamphlet from the Peasants' War, 1525)*

They argued that new tithes and taxes not only upset tradition but violated the Word of God. Using Luther's argument that authority should be based on the Scriptures, peasants from the district of Zurich, for example, petitioned the town council in 1523 and 1524, claiming that they should not be required to pay tithes on their produce because there was no biblical justification for doing so. Townsmen rejected the peasants' demand, noting that although the Bible did not stipulate such payments, it also did not forbid them. Accordingly, the peasants should make them "out of love"—that is, because they were traditional.

Demands that landlords and magistrates give up human ordinances and follow "Godly Law" soon turned to violence. Peasants, miners, and villagers in 1524 and 1525 participated in a series of uprisings that began on the borderlands between Switzerland and Germany and spread throughout southwestern Germany, upper Austria, and even northern Italy. Bands of peasants and villagers, perhaps a total of 300,000 in the empire, revolted against their seigneurial lords or even their territorial overlords.

Luther initially counseled landlords and princes to redress the just grievances. As reports of riots and increased violence continued to reach Wittenberg, however, Luther condemned the rebels as "mad dogs" and urged that they be suppressed. Territorial princes and large cities quickly raised armies to meet the threat. The peasants were defeated and destroyed in a series of battles in April 1525. When it became clear that the reformers were unwilling to follow the implications of their own theology, villagers and peasants lost interest in the progress of the reform. As a townsman of Zurich commented, "Many came to a great hatred of the preachers, where before they would have bitten off their feet for the Gospel."[4]

## John Calvin and the Reformed Tradition

The revolts of 1524 and 1525 demonstrated the mixed messages traveling under the rubric "true" or "biblical" religion. In the 1530s the theological arguments of the reformers began to take on a greater clarity, mostly because of the Franco-Swiss reformer John Calvin (1509–1564). Calvin had a humanistic education in Paris and became a lawyer before coming under the influence of reform-minded thinkers in France. In 1534 he fled from Paris as royal pressures against reformers increased. He arrived in Geneva in 1536, where he would remain, except for a short exile, until the end of his life.

Because of Geneva's central location and the power of Calvin's theology, it quickly came to rival Wittenberg as a source of Protestant thought. Reformed preachers moved easily from Geneva to France, Scotland, England, and the Low Countries, carrying with them Calvin's ideas about salvation and the godly. Until the end of his life Calvin was a magnet drawing people interested in reform.

The heart of Calvin's appeal lay in his formal theological writings. In 1536 he published the first of many editions of the *Institutes of the Christian Religion*, which was to become the summa of Reformed theology. In it Calvin laid out a doctrine of the absolute power of God and the complete depravity and powerlessness of humanity.

Like Luther, Calvin viewed salvation as a mysterious gift from God. Yet Calvin differed from Luther in a crucial aspect. Salvation was by grace, but it was part of a progressive sanctification. This was a critical difference, for Luther did not believe that human behavior could be transformed. We are, he said, "simultaneously justified and sinners." By contrast, Calvin believed that there could be no salvation "if we do not also live a holy life." Thus the religious behavior of the individual and the community was an essential gift of justification. As a result, Calvin believed that it was the church's duty to promote moral progress. Public officials were to be "vicars of God." They had the power to lead and correct both the faithful and the unregenerate sinners who lived in Christian communities. In his years in Geneva Calvin tried to create a "Christian Commonwealth," but Geneva was far from a theocracy. Calvin's initial attempts to create a Christian community by requiring public confession and allowing church leaders to discipline sinners were rejected by Geneva's city council, which exiled Calvin in 1538.

On his return in 1541 he sought to institute church reforms modeled on those he had observed in the Protestant city of Strasbourg. Calvin's Reformed church hierarchy was made up of four offices: preachers, teachers, deacons, and elders. Preachers and teachers saw to the care and education of the faithful. Deacons, as in the early church, were charged with attending to the material needs of the congregation. Elders—the true leaders of the Genevan church—were selected from the patriciate who dominated the civil government of the city. Thus it makes as much sense to speak of a church governed by the town as a town dominated by the church. The elders actively intervened in education, charity, and attempts to regulate prostitution. Consistories, or church courts, made up of preachers and community elders who enforced community moral and religious values, became one of the most important characteristics of Reformed (Calvinist) communities.

Most reformers accepted a commonplace medieval idea that since salvation depended on God's gift of grace, God in effect "predestined" some people to be saved. They differed on whether this meant that God predestined others to damnation. Luther argued that Christians could never know why some people were saved and others were not. Calvin, however, believed that God's power was such that "eternal life is foreordained for some, eternal damnation for others."

Calvin suggested that the elect, those predestined for salvation, would benefit from "signs of divine benevolence," an idea that would have a profound impact on the Calvinist understanding of the relationship of wealth to spiritual life. Calvin believed that good works and a well-ordered society were the result of God's grace. By the seventeenth century many followers of Calvin in Europe's commercial centers believed that the elect had a duty to work in the secular world and that wealth accumulated in business was a sign of God's favor. It was an idea nicely adapted to the increasingly wealthy society of early modern Europe.

That connection between salvation and material life, however, lay in the future. The aspect of election that most interested Calvin was the creation of a truly Christian community by the elect. To accomplish this, Reformed churches—that is, those that took their lead from Zwingli and Calvin, purged themselves of any manifestation of "superstition." Like Zwinglians, they rejected the idea that Christ was really present in the sacrament of Holy Communion. They rejected the role of saints. They removed from their churches and destroyed paintings and statuary that they believed were indications of idolatry.

Reformed churchmen reacted promptly and harshly to events that seemed to threaten either church or state. The most famous episode involved the capture, trial, and execution of Michael Servetus (1511–1553), a Spanish physician and radical theologian who rejected traditional doctrines such as the Trinity and specifically criticized many of Calvin's teachings in the *Institutes*. After corresponding with Servetus for a time, Calvin remarked that if Servetus were in Geneva, "I would not suffer him to get out alive." After living in various parts of Europe, Servetus eventually did come anonymously to Geneva. He was recognized and arrested. Calvin was as good as his word. After a public debate and trial Servetus was burned at the stake for blaspheming the Trinity and the Christian religion. Calvin's condemnation of Servetus was all too typical of Christians in the sixteenth century. Lutherans, Calvinists, and Catholics all believed that protection of true religion required harsh measures against the ignorant, the immoral, and the unorthodox. All too few would have said, as the humanist reformer Sebastion Castellio did, "To burn a heretic is not to defend a doctrine, but to burn a man."[5]

**Iconoclasm**    Calvinists believed that Christians had to live in communities in which "true religion" was practiced. Iconoclasts (image smashers) cleansed churches of all paintings and statuary that might lead people back to the worship of idols—that is, the medieval cult of saints. This illustration shows just how organized iconoclasm really was.    *(The Fotomas Index, U.K.)*

# The Hutterite Community

Peter Riedemann (1506–1556), a founding member of the Hutterites, was captured and imprisoned several times for his Anabaptist beliefs. In his Confession of Faith, written as an explanation to his jailers, Riedemann lays out a vision of the simple Christian community that still remains central to Hutterites and Moravians throughout the world. The confession begins with an explanation of the Apostles' Creed, then discusses the nature of salvation and the structure of the Christian community. This excerpt highlights some of the distinctive features of the Hutterites.

## Community of Goods

All believers have fellowship in holy things, that is, in God. . . . Just as Christ has nothing for himself, . . . no members of Christ's body should possess any gift for themselves or for their own sake. . . . Community of goods applies to both spiritual and material gifts. All of God's gifts, not only the spiritual but also the temporal, have been given so that they not be kept but be shared with each other. Therefore, the fellowship of believers should be visible not only in spiritual but also in temporal things. . . .

## Separation from the World

God has chosen this church for himself and separated the members from all peoples, so that they might serve him with one mind and heart. . . . We have left the gatherings of profane and impure people, and we wish that everyone would do the same. . . . If some will not repent and will not keep the true ordinances of God, but remain in sin, we must let them go their way and leave them to God.

## Warfare

Christ . . . has prepared a kingdom for himself . . . therefore all worldly warfare in this kingdom has come to an end. . . . Therefore Christians should not take part in war, nor should they use force for the purpose of vengeance.

## Church Discipline

Paul says, "Put away the evil that is among you" [I Corinthians 5:13]. . . . That is why we admonish one another, warning and rebuking each other persistently. . . . A different method is used for major sins. . . . Such a person is separated from the church without admonition. . . . When a person is banned, we have no fellowship with him and nothing to do with him so that he may become ashamed . . . in the hope that the sinner will be moved to return all the more quickly to God. If that does not happen, the church remains pure and is innocent of his sin. . . . When a person is excluded, we have no fellowship with that person until there is true repentance, . . . until he has received from the church the good report of a truly repentant life.

## Adornment

First, we say with Peter that the adornment of Christians does not consist in outward show, such as jewelry, fine clothing, or similar trappings. . . . The only thing they should learn from the children of the world is diligence. In order to please each other, worldly people are diligent to dress and to adorn themselves to the very utmost in accordance with the fashion of the land in which they live. . . . Christians should adorn themselves . . . so as to please God, who dwells in heaven.

## QUESTIONS

1. What is the justification for the communal sharing of all goods?

2. In what ways does Riedemann suggest that Christians should differ from the rest of the world?

3. How can a community enforce its discipline?

Source: *Peter Riedemann's Hutterite Confession of Faith*, ed. and trans. John J. Friesen, pp. 119–123, 152–155. Herald Press, Scottsdale, PA 15683. All rights reserved.

 For additional information on this topic, go to college.hmco.com/students.

## The Radical Reform of the Anabaptists

Michael Servetus was but one of a number of extremists who claimed to be carrying out the full reform implied in the teachings of Luther, Zwingli, and Calvin. Called "Anabaptists" (or "rebaptizers" because of their rejection of infant baptism) or simply "radicals," they tended to take biblical commands more literally than the mainline reformers. They represented a broad social movement dominated by peasants and modest townspeople. They were more interested in behavior and community standards than in learned theological arguments. They believed that only adults should be baptized, and then only after confession of sin. They believed that Christians should live apart in communities of the truly redeemed. Thus they refused to take civil oaths or hold public office, for to do so would be to compromise with unreformed civil society.

The earliest of the radicals allied themselves with the rebels of 1524 and 1525. Thomas Müntzer (1490–1525) was an influential preacher who believed in divine revelation through visions and dreams. His visions told him that the poor were the true elect and that the end of the world was at hand. An active participant in the uprisings of 1525, Müntzer called on the elect to drive out the ungodly. After the defeat of the rebels, he was captured and executed by the German princes.

Other radicals, such as the revolutionaries who took control of the northern German city of Münster, rejected infant baptism, adopted polygamy, and proclaimed a new "Kingdom of Righteousness." The reformers of Münster instituted the new kingdom in the city by rebaptizing those who joined their cause and expelling those who opposed them. They abolished private property rights in Münster and instituted new laws concerning morality and behavior. Leadership in the city eventually passed to a tailor, Jan of Leiden (d. 1535), who proclaimed himself the new messiah and lord of the world. The Anabaptists were opposed by the prince-bishop of Münster, the political and religious lord of the city. After a sixteen-month siege, the bishop and his allies recaptured the city in 1535. Besieging forces massacred men, women, and children. Jan of Leiden was captured and executed by mutilation with red-hot tongs.

With the destruction of the Münster revolutionaries in 1535, the Anabaptist movement turned inward. Under leaders such as Menno Simons (1495–1561), who founded the Mennonites, and Jakob Hutter (d. 1536), who founded the Hutterian Brethren, or Hutterites, they rejected their predecessors' violent attempts to establish truly holy cities. To varying degrees they also rejected connections with civil society, military service, and even civil courts. They did, however, believe that their own communities were exclusively of the elect. They tended to close themselves off from outsiders and enforce a strict discipline over their members. The elders of these communities were empowered to excommunicate or "shun" those who violated the groups' precepts. Anabaptist communities have proved unusually durable. Hutterite and Mennonite communities continue to exist in western Europe, North America, and parts of the former Soviet Union. (See the box "The Continuing Experiment: The Hutterite Community.")

Like Luther, all of the early reformers appealed to the authority of the Bible in their attacks on church tradition. Yet in the villages and towns of Germany and Switzerland, many radicals were prepared to move far beyond the positions Luther had advocated. When they did so, Luther found himself in the odd position of appealing for vigorous action by the very imperial authorities whose previous inaction had allowed his own protest to survive.

## THE EMPIRE OF CHARLES V (R. 1519–1556)

LUTHER believed that secular authorities should be neutral in religious matters. In his eyes the success of the early Reformation was simply God's will:

> I simply taught, preached and wrote God's Word; otherwise I did nothing. And while I slept or drank Wittenberg beer with my friends, the Word so greatly weakened the Papacy that no prince or emperor ever inflicted such losses on it.[6]

Luther's belief in the Word of God was absolute, yet he must have known, even as he drank his beer, that the Holy Roman emperor could have crushed the reform movements if he had been able to enforce imperial decrees. But attempts to resolve religious conflict became entangled with attempts to hold together the family lands of the Habsburg emperor and with political rivalries among the various German princes. The eventual religious settlement required a constitutional compromise that preserved the virtual autonomy of the great princes of Germany. Charles had dreamed of using his imperial office to restore and maintain the political and religious unity of Europe. The political realities of sixteenth-century Europe, however, made nobles afraid of the emperor even when he tried to preserve the unity of the church.

### Imperial Challenges

Emperor Charles V (r. 1519–1556) was the beneficiary of a series of marriages that, in the words of his courtiers, seemed to re-create the empire of Charlemagne (see Map 15.1, page 506). From his father, Philip of Habsburg, he inherited claims to Austria, the imperial crown, and Burgundian lands that included the Low Countries and the county of Burgundy. Through his mother, Joanna, the daughter of Ferdinand and Isabella of Spain, Charles

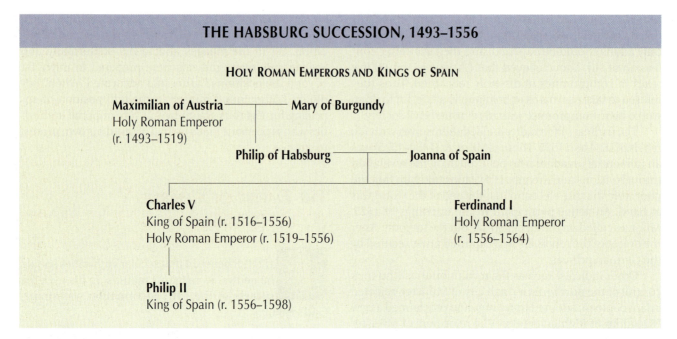

## THE HABSBURG SUCCESSION, 1493–1556

### HOLY ROMAN EMPERORS AND KINGS OF SPAIN

**Maximilian of Austria** ———— **Mary of Burgundy**
Holy Roman Emperor
(r. 1493–1519)

**Philip of Habsburg** ———— **Joanna of Spain**

**Charles V**
King of Spain (r. 1516–1556)
Holy Roman Emperor (r. 1519–1556)

**Ferdinand I**
Holy Roman Emperor
(r. 1556–1564)

**Philip II**
King of Spain (r. 1556–1598)

became heir to the kingdoms of Castile, Aragon, Sicily, Naples, and Spanish America. During the Italian wars of the early sixteenth century Charles's holdings in Italy expanded to include the duchy of Milan and most of the rest of Lombardy. By 1506 he was duke in the Burgundian lands, in 1516 he became king of Aragon and Castile, and in 1519 he was elected Holy Roman emperor. Every government in Europe had to deal with one part or another of Charles's empire. His chancellor enthused, "[God] has set you on the way towards a world monarchy, towards the gathering of all Christendom under a single shepherd."

Charles seems to have sincerely desired such a world monarchy, but he faced challenges in each of the areas under his control. In Castile, for example, grandees, townspeople, and peasants felt they had grounds for complaint. They objected that taxes were too heavy and that Charles disregarded the Cortes and his natural advisers, the old nobility. But most of all they complained that too many of his officials were foreigners whom he had brought with him from his home in Flanders. Protests festered in the towns and villages of Castile and finally broke out into a revolt called the *Comunero* (townsmen's or citizens') movement. Between 1517 and 1522, when religious reform was making dramatic advances in Germany, many of the most important towns of Spain were in open rebellion against the Crown. Charles's forces eventually took control of the situation, and by 1522 he had crushed the Comuneros. But in the critical years between 1522 and 1530 he was careful to spend much of his time in his Spanish kingdoms.

Charles's claims in Italy, as well as in the Pyrenees and the Low Countries, brought him into direct conflict with the Valois kings of France. In the critical 1520s the Habsburgs and the Valois fought a series of wars (see page 369). Charles dramatically defeated the French at Pavia in northern Italy in 1525, sacked and occupied Rome in 1527, and became the virtual arbiter of Italian politics. The volatile situation in Italy made for cynical alliances. In the course of the struggle the Catholic Francis I of France, whose title was "the Most Christian King," found it to his advantage to ally himself with Charles's most serious opponents, the Protestants and the Turks. Francis demonstrated the truth of Machiavelli's dictum that private virtues play a small role in political and diplomatic life. The Habsburg-Valois Wars dragged on until, in exhaustion, the French king Henry II (r. 1547–1559) and the Spanish king Philip II (r. 1556–1598) signed the Treaty of Cateau-Cambrésis in 1559 (see page 370).

Charles was not the only ruler to claim the title "emperor" and a succession reaching back to the Roman Empire. After the conquest of Constantinople in 1453, the sultan of the Ottoman Turks began to refer to himself as "the Emperor." After consolidating control of Constantinople and the Balkans, Turkish armies under the command of the emperor Suleiman (r. 1520–1566), known as "the Magnificent," resumed their expansion to the north and west. After capturing Belgrade, Turkish forces soundly defeated a Hungarian army at the Battle of Mohács in 1526. Charles appealed for unity within Christendom against

**The Capture of Belgrade, 1521**    During the sixteenth century Ottoman Turks dominated the Balkans militarily and were a significant force in European diplomacy. They were masters of coordinated attacks combining artillery and infantry.    *(Österreichische Nationalbibliothek)*

the threat. Even Martin Luther agreed that Christians should unite during invasion.

Suleiman's army besieged Vienna in 1529 before being forced to retreat. The Turks also deployed a navy in the Mediterranean and, with French encouragement, began a series of raids along the coasts of Italy and Spain. The Turkish fleet remained a threat throughout the sixteenth century. The reign of Suleiman marked the permanent entry of Turkey into the European military and diplomatic system. Turkish pressure was yet another reason Charles was unable to deal with German Protestants in a direct and uncompromising way. (See the box "Global Encounters: Duels Among Europeans and Turks.")

## German Politics

The political configuration of Germany had an ongoing influence on the course of religious reform. In 1500 Germany was much less centralized than France or England. The emperor's claims in most areas amounted to the

right to collect modest taxes on households and individuals, a court of high justice, and the authority to proclaim imperial truces. Yet the empire lacked a unified legal system, and the emperor himself had only one vote on the imperial council. In many respects political centralization and innovation were characteristics of individual territories, not of the empire as a whole. The power of the emperor depended on his relations with the towns and princes of Germany.

In the first years after Luther issued his "Ninety-five Theses," he was defended by the elector Frederick of Saxony, who held a key vote in Charles's quest for election as Holy Roman emperor. As long as Frederick protected Luther, imperial officials had to proceed against the reformer with caution. When Luther was outlawed by the imperial Diet of Worms in 1521, Frederick and many other princes and towns refused to enforce the edict against him and his followers unless their own grievances against the emperor and their complaints about the church were taken up at the same time. At the Diet of

# Duels Among Europeans and Turks

Augier Ghislain De Busbecq (1522–1592), a Flemish diplomat in the service of Ferdinand I of Austria (who became Emperor Ferdinand I after the abdication of Charles V), was twice sent to Constantinople as ambassador. Understanding the Turks and their interests was critical for the Germans as attacks by the Turks in eastern Europe prevented the empire from either suppressing the German Protestants or pressing German claims against the French. The following selection is part of a letter written from Constantinople in 1560. In it Busbecq discusses violence among the Turks and contrasts it with Europeans' behavior.

The mention I made a while ago of matters in the confines of Hungary, gives me occasion to tell you, what the Turks think of duels, which among Christians are accounted a singular badge of personal valor. There was one Arstambey, a sanjack [district official], who lived on the frontier of Hungary, who was very much famed as a robust person [Arsta signifies a lion in Turkey]. He was an expert with the bow; no man brandished his sword with more strength; none was more terrible to his enemy. Not far from his district there also dwelt one Ulybey, also a sanjack, who was jealous of the same praise. And this jealousy (initiated perhaps by other occasions) at length occasioned hatred and many bloody combats between them. It happened thus, Ulybey was called to Constantinople, upon what occasion I know not. When he arrived there, the Pashas [governors] had asked many questions of him in the Divan [court] concerning other matters. At last they demanded how it was that he and Arstambey

came to fall out. To put his own cause in the best light, he said that once Arstambey had laid an ambush and wounded him treacherously. Which he said Arstambey need not have done, if he would have shown himself worthy of the name he bears because Ulybey often challenged him to fight hand to hand and never refused to meet him on the field. The Pashas, taking great offense, replied, "How dare you challenge a fellow soldier to a duel? What? Was there no Christian to fight with? Do both of you eat your emperor's bread? And yet, you attempt to take one another's life? What precedent did you have for this? Don't you know that whichever of you had died, the emperor would have lost a subject?" Whereupon, by their command, he was carried off to prison where he lay pining for many months. And at last, with difficulty, he was released, but with the loss of his reputation.

It is quite different among us Christians. Our people will draw their swords many times against each other before they ever come in sight of a public enemy, and unfortunately, they count it a brave and honorable thing to do. What should one do in such a case? Vice has usurped the seat of virtue and that which is worthy of punishment is counted noble and glorious.

## QUESTIONS

1. What does Busbecq believe is the great strength of Turkish society?

2. What most distinguishes the Turkish empire from Christendom?

SOURCE: *The Four Epistles of A. G. Busbequius Concerning His Embassy to Turkey* (London: J. Taylor & J. Wyat, 1694), pp. 196–198.

---

Speyer in 1526, delegates passed a resolution empowering princes and towns to settle religious matters in their territories as they saw it. In effect, this resolution legitimated the reform in territories where authorities chose to follow the new teachings and presaged the final religious settlement in Germany.

German princes took advantage of the emperor's relative powerlessness and made choices reflecting a complex of religious, political, and diplomatic issues. Electoral Saxony and ducal Saxony, the two parts of the province of Saxony, split over the issue of reform. Electoral Saxony,

Luther's homeland, was Lutheran. Ducal Saxony was strongly Catholic. Especially in the autonomous towns many decisions about religion were often made with one eye on the choices made by neighbors and competitors.

Some rulers acted in ways that were even more consciously cynical and self-serving. The grand master of the religious order of the Teutonic Knights, Albrecht von Hohenzollern (1490–1568), who controlled the duchy of Prussia, renounced his monastic vows. Then, at the urging of Luther and other reformers, he secularized the order's estates (that is, he transferred them from church to private ownership), which then became East Prussia, hereditary lands of the Hohenzollern family. In other territories rulers managed to claim the properties of suppressed religious orders. Even when, as in the case of Count Philip of Hesse (1504–1567), much of the revenue from secularization was used to create hospitals and an organized system of charity, the reforming prince was still enriched.

Some rulers found their personal reservations about Luther reinforced by their fears of popular unrest. Luther's call for decisions based on personal conscience seemed to the dukes of Bavaria, for example, to repudiate princely authority and even to provoke anarchy. In the confused and fluid situation of the 1520s and 1530s, imperial interests were never the primary issue.

### The Religious Settlement

With the fading of the Turkish threat on Vienna in 1529, Charles V renewed his pressure on the German principalities at a meeting of the imperial diet at Augsburg in 1530. It was for this diet that Philip Melanchthon (1497–1560), Luther's closest adviser, prepared the Augsburg Confession, which would become the basic statement of the Lutheran faith. Melanchthon hoped that the document would form the basis of compromise with Catholic powers, but that possibility was rejected out of hand by the imperial party. Charles aimed to affirm his strength in Germany by forcing the princes to end the reform movement and enforce bans on Luther's teachings.

The Protestant princes responded by forming the League of Schmalkalden. At first the founders of the league claimed that they were interested in protecting Lutheran preaching, but the league quickly developed as a center of opposition to imperial influence in general. Eventually Charles and a group of allied princes managed to defeat the league at the Battle of Mühlberg in 1547. The emperor was unable to continue pressure on the Protestants, however, because he had depended on the support of some Protestant princes in his battles with the league. As a result, even after military defeat, the Protestant princes were able to maintain religious autonomy. In the religious Peace of Augsburg of 1555, the emperor formally acknowledged the principle that sovereign princes could choose the religion to be practiced in their territories—*cuius regio, eius religio* ("whose territory, his religion"). There were limits, however: leaders had only two choices—remain under papal authority or adopt the Augsburg Confession outlined by Melanchthon. Reformed churches associated with Zwingli or Calvin were not legally recognized (see Map 14.2).

Shortly after the settlement, Charles abdicated his Spanish and imperial titles. Exhausted by years of political and religious struggle, he ceded the imperial crown to his brother, Ferdinand (r. 1556–1564). He transferred his possessions in the Low Countries, Spain, Italy, and the New World to his son, Philip II (r. 1556–1598). Charles had believed his courtiers when they had compared his empire to that of the ancient Romans. He had accepted that his duty as emperor was to unite Christendom under one law and one church. But in no part of his empire did he ever command the authority that would have allowed him to unite his lands politically, let alone to re-establish religious unity. Following his abdication Charles retired to a monastery in Spain, where he died in 1558.

## THE ENGLISH REFORMATION, 1520–1603

THE Reformation in England is often called a monarchical Reformation. In contrast with Germany, where reform occurred in spite of imperial opposition, in England the Crown instituted the reform. As in Germany, however, institutional change in the church followed from both secular issues and reform ideas. In England an initially hostile monarch began to tolerate reform when he perceived the papacy as an unbiblical, tyrannical force blocking essential state policy. Although reformers were active in England, their success depended entirely on royal support. And by the middle of the sixteenth century, it was royal interest in compromise that brought a settlement that left England a curious hybrid of reformed and traditional religious practices.

### Henry VIII and the Monarchical Reformation

England was closely tied to Germany. Since the twelfth century large numbers of German merchants had lived and traded in England, and Cologne was home to a considerable English community. Anglo-German connections became especially significant during the Reformation. Reformers from Wittenberg and other Protestant towns had contact with English merchants from London who traded and traveled on the Continent. One reformer, William Tyndale (ca. 1494–1536), served as a bridge between the Continent and England. He had a humanistic education in classical languages and began working on a translation of the Bible in the 1520s. Forced to flee London by the church hierarchy, he visited Luther in Wittenberg before settling in Antwerp, where he completed his

**Map 14.2  Catholics and Protestants in 1555**  At the time of the Peace of Augsburg, Christendom in western Europe was divided into three major groups. Lutheran influence was largely confined to parts of Germany and Scandinavia, while Calvinist influence was strong in Switzerland, Scotland, the Low Countries, and parts of France. Most of the West remained within the Roman Catholic Church.

English New Testament. By 1526 copies of his translation and his religious tracts flooded England. By the 1520s Lutheran influence was noticeable in London and Cambridge. There is still debate about just how strong this early influence was. To some extent the ground may have been prepared for the reformers by the few surviving Lollards (see page 360), who tended to be literate and were an ideal market for Tyndale's English Bible and his numerous reformist tracts. But religious brotherhoods, lay piety, and traditional forms of penance remained an important part of religious life. If reform was to succeed, it required support from the king.

Henry VIII (r. 1509–1547) began his reign as a popular and powerful king. Handsome, athletic, and artistic, he seemed to be the ideal ruler. Henry took an interest in theology and humanistic culture. At first he was quite hostile to Luther's reform ideas and wrote *Defense of the Seven Sacraments,* which earned him the title "Defender of the Faith" from a grateful Pope Leo X. Throughout his life Henry remained suspicious of many Protestant ideas, but he led the initial phase of the break with the papacy because of his political problems with the highly orthodox Holy Roman emperor Charles V. The first phase of the English Reformation was thus monarchical.

Henry VII had initiated closer relations with Spain when he married his eldest son, Arthur, Prince of Wales, to Ferdinand of Aragon's daughter, Catherine. After Arthur's death the future Henry VIII was married to his brother's widow in 1509. Henry VIII later tried to further the Anglo-imperial alliance when he arranged a treaty by which the emperor Charles V, who was Catherine of Aragon's nephew, agreed to marry Henry's daughter, Mary Tudor. But by the late 1520s the Anglo-imperial alliance fell apart when Charles, responding to Spanish pressures, renounced the proposed marriage and instead married a Portuguese princess.

Henry's relations with Charles were further hampered by what the English called "the King's Great Matter"—that is, his determination to divorce Catherine. Recalling the unrest of the Wars of the Roses (see page 379), Henry believed that he needed a son to ensure that the Tudors could maintain control of the English crown. By 1527 Henry and Catherine had a daughter, Mary, but no living sons. Henry became convinced that he remained without a male heir because, by biblical standards, he had committed incest by marrying his brother's widow. As Leviticus 20:21 says, "If a man takes his brother's wife, it is impurity; they shall remain childless." Henry desired an annulment. Unfortunately for him, Leo X's successor, Pope Clement VII (r. 1523–1534), was a virtual prisoner of imperial troops who had recently sacked Rome and

taken control of most of Italy. As long as Charles supported Catherine of Aragon and his forces occupied Rome, a papal annulment was out of the question.

The king's advisers quickly divided into two camps. Sir Thomas More, humanist writer (see pages 416–417), royal chancellor and staunch Catholic, urged the king to continue his policy of negotiation with the papacy and his efforts to destroy the growing Protestant party. Until his resignation in 1532, More led royal authorities in a vigorous campaign against the dissemination of the newly translated Tyndale Bible and against the spread of Protestant ideas. More was opposed and eventually ousted by a radical party of Protestants led by Thomas Cranmer (1489–1556) and Thomas Cromwell (1485?–1540), who saw in the king's desire for a divorce an effective wedge to pry Henry out of the papal camp. Cromwell, who eventually replaced More as chancellor, advised the king that the marriage problem could be solved by the English clergy without papal interference.

Between 1532 and 1535 Henry and Parliament took a number of steps that effectively left the king in control of the church in England. Early in 1533 Cranmer was named archbishop of Canterbury. Later that year Parliament ruled that appeals of cases concerning wills, marriages, and ecclesiastical grants had to be heard in England. In May an English court annulled the king's marriage to Catherine. Four months later Henry's new queen, Anne Boleyn, gave birth to a daughter, Elizabeth.

After the split began, the king started to seize church properties. Parliamentary action culminated in the passage of the Act of Supremacy in 1534, which declared the king to be "the Protector and only Supreme Head of the Church and the Clergy of England." Henry meant to enforce his control by requiring a public oath supporting the act. Sir Thomas More refused to take the oath and was arrested, tried, and executed for treason. In some respects Parliament had acted as an instrument of reform, in the manner of the German and Swiss town councils that moderated debates over church reform. In England, however, Parliament and perhaps a majority of the laity perceived this reform primarily as a political issue.

Cromwell and Cranmer had hoped to use "the King's Great Matter" as a way to begin a Lutheran-style reform of the church. But, though separated from the papal party, Henry remained suspicious of religious change. He complained of radicals who "do wrest and interpret and so untruly allege [novel understandings of Scripture] to subvert and overturn as well the sacraments of Holy Church as the power and authority of princes and magistrates." Between 1534 and Henry's death in 1547, neither the Protestant nor the Catholic party was able to gain the

**Reform of the Old Church**   This woodcut shows the Protestant understanding of the reforms of Edward VI, the removal of Catholic paraphernalia, and Edward's patronage of the Bible and Holy Communion.   *(Courtesy, Brown University Library)*

upper hand at court or at Canterbury. Substantive changes in the English church would be made by Henry's children.

## Reform and Counter-Reform Under Edward and Mary

Prince Edward, Henry's only surviving son in 1547, was born to Henry's third wife, Jane Seymour. He was only 10 years old when his father died. By chance Edward Seymour, who was Prince Edward's uncle, and the Protestant faction were in favor at the time of Henry's death. Seymour was named duke of Somerset and Lord Protec-

tor of the young King Edward VI (r. 1547–1553). Under Somerset the Protestants were able to make significant changes in religious life in England. Edward completed the "dissolution of the monasteries"—the process of confiscating properties belonging to chapels and shrines—that his father had begun. In an act of great symbolic meaning, priests were legally allowed to marry; many had already done so. Finally, Archbishop Cranmer introduced the first edition of the English *Book of Common Prayer* in 1549. The publication updated some late medieval English prayers and combined them with liturgical and theological ideas taken from Luther, Zwingli, and

Calvin. In its beautifully expressive English, it provided the laity with a primer on how to combine English religious traditions with reform theology. Later, continental Protestants were named to teach theology at Oxford and Cambridge. If Edward had not died of tuberculosis in 1553, England's reform would have looked very much like the movement in Switzerland and southern Germany.

Protestant reformers attempted to prevent Mary Tudor (r. 1553–1558), Henry's Catholic daughter, from claiming the throne, but Mary and the Catholic party quickly took control of the court and the church. Mary immediately declared previous reform decrees to be void. Cardinal Reginald Pole (1500–1558), who had advocated reform within the Catholic Church, became the center of the Catholic restoration party in Mary's England. Pole rooted out Protestants within the church. More than eight hundred gentlemen, clerics, and students fled England for Protestant havens on the Continent. Some officials, including Cranmer, chose to remain and paid with their lives. In all, three hundred Protestants, mostly artisans and laborers, were tried and executed by church courts, earning the queen her nickname, "Bloody Mary."

The policies of the queen brought about an abrupt return of the English church to papal authority. Most of the English quickly and easily returned to traditional Roman religious practices. Statues were removed from hiding and restored to places of honor in churches and chapels. Although conclusive evidence is lacking, the queen's initial successes may indicate that the Reformation was not broadly supported by the people. In fact, the restoration of Catholicism by Mary might have worked had the queen not died after little more than six years on the throne. At her death the final settlement of the reform in England was far from certain.

**The Queen in Parliament** This image was meant to show the willingness of Parliament to support the queen, a key element of the Elizabethan Settlement. *(Bibliothèque nationale de France)*

## The Elizabethan Settlement

Queen Elizabeth (r. 1558–1603), daughter of Anne Boleyn, succeeded to the throne at the death of her half sister. The reign of Elizabeth was one of the most enigmatic and successful of English history. At home she managed to gain control of the various political and religious factions in the country, and abroad she exploited the rivalries of a variety of international powers to her own advantage. She seems to have clearly recognized the necessity of striking a balance between opposing forces.

Her first pressing task was to effect a religious settlement. Early in her reign she twice left church services at the elevation of the bread by the priest. Since in Catholic thought it was this action of the priest that made Christ present in the bread, she was indicating symbolically her opposition to a purely Catholic understanding of the sacraments. In the next few years she continued to work for the restoration of many features of her father's and her half brother's reforms. In 1559 the new Act of Supremacy and an Act of Uniformity reinstituted royal control of the English church and re-established uniform liturgical and doctrinal standards. The *Book of Common Prayer* composed by Cranmer was brought back, and final changes were made in the liturgy.

Protestants had hoped for a complete victory, but the "Elizabethan Settlement" was considerably less than that. Although figures are lacking, it is likely that a large portion of the English population did not support a return to Henry's and Edward's reforms. After making clear her significant differences with Rome, Elizabeth confounded her most fervent Protestant supporters by offering a number of concessions to Anglo-Catholics. She remained celibate, and she ordered the Anglican clergy to do the same—although she could do little to prevent clerical marriage. More important, she and her closest advisers allowed a great variety of customs and practices favored by Anglo-Catholics. These matters, the queen's supporters argued, were not essential to salvation, and thus individuals could be allowed to choose. Many of the prayers in the *Book of Common Prayer,* for example, seemed "papist" to the most radical Protestants. Similarly, many of the traditional clerical vestments and altar furnishings remained unchanged. Elizabeth probably knew that the Protestants had no alternative but to support her and thus felt free to win back the support of the Anglo-Catholics.

Toward the end of Elizabeth's reign Richard Hooker (1554–1600) published his *Laws of Ecclesiastical Polity,* which provides an excellent description of the Anglican (English) Church born of the Elizabethan Settlement. England, Hooker maintains, had its own way of handling religious affairs. Theologically it represented a middle ground between the traditions cultivated by the Roman church and the more radically biblical religion favored by the Lutherans of Germany and the Calvinists of Switzerland. The Church of England moderated Luther's and Calvin's absolute reliance on Scriptures with history and tradition. In areas where tradition was strong, processions and other pre-Reformation traditions continued to animate village life. In other areas more austere reformed practices were likely to predominate.

## FRANCE, SCANDINAVIA, AND EASTERN EUROPE, 1523–1560

IN England and in the empire of Charles V, the success of the new religious reforms depended greatly on the political situation. It would be naive to conclude, as Luther claimed, that "the Word did everything." Yet this complex religious reform movement cannot be reduced to the politics of kings and princes. The issues will be clearer if we survey politics and reform in the rest of Europe, noting whether and to what extent the new ideas took root. In France, for example, the widespread, popular support of the old religion limited the options of the country's political leaders. Similarly, in northern

Europe religious reform was an issue of both popular feeling and royal politics.

### France

Luther's work, and later the ideas of the urban reformers of southwestern Germany and Switzerland, passed quickly into France. Geneva is in a French-speaking area close to the French border. It, like Strasbourg, was easy for French Protestants to reach. Perhaps because of France's proximity to the Calvinists in French-speaking Switzerland or because of the clarity and power of Calvin's *Institutes,* French Protestants, known as Huguenots, were tied more closely to the Calvinists of Geneva than to the Lutherans of Germany.

It is difficult, however, to know how many French Christians were Protestants. At the height of the Reformation's popularity Protestants probably represented no more than 10 percent of the total population of France. It has been estimated that Protestant congregations numbered about 2,100 in the 1560s—in a country that had perhaps 32,000 traditional parishes. Protestants seem to have comprised a diverse mix that included two of the three most important noble families at court: the Bourbon and Montmorency families. Clerics interested in moral reform and artisans who worked at new trades, such as the printing industry, also made up a significant portion of the converts. Perhaps reflecting the numerous printers and merchants in their numbers, Protestants tended to be of higher than average literacy. The Protestant population was spread throughout the country. Protestants were particularly well represented in towns and probably constituted a majority in the southern and western towns of La Rochelle, Montpellier, and Nîmes. Paris was the one part of the realm in which they had little influence, and their absence in the capital may have been their undoing.

The conservative theologians of the Sorbonne in Paris were some of Luther's earliest opponents. They complained that many masters at the University of Paris were "Lutheran." As early as 1523 Parisian authorities seized and burned books said to be by Luther. But as in Germany, there was no clear understanding of who or what a Lutheran was. The Sorbonne theologians were also suspicious of a number of "pre-reformers," including the humanistic editor Jacques Lefèvre d'Étaples (1455–1536; see page 416), who late in life had come to an understanding of justification quite like Luther's. Others were clerics intent on religious reform within the traditional structures. Unlike Luther and the French Protestants, these pre-reformers did not challenge the priests' relationship to the sacra-

**The Great Cauldron**  In dramatic images, this French woodcut shows the Protestant expectation that the Bible carried down by the Holy Spirit will overturn the whole cauldron of false images and errors that supported the old church. *(Bibliothèque nationale de France)*

ments. They were interested in the piety and behavior of churchmen. They never challenged the role of the clergy in salvation. King Francis's own sister, Margaret of Angoulême (1492–1549), gathered a group of religious persons, including several reformers, at her court. (See the box "Reading Sources: The Conversion of Jeanne d'Albret.") But Margaret herself urged that theology be left to scholars; she believed that the laity should stick to simple pieties. Like Margaret, most French Christians had no clear sense that Protestant teachings required a complete break with medieval Christian traditions.

Like previous French kings, Francis I (r. 1515–1547) hoped to extend royal jurisdictions in France and make France an international power. Engaged in the seemingly intractable wars with the Habsburgs, Francis generally ignored religious questions. In 1525 he was taken captive in the wake of a military disaster at Pavia in Lombardy. He was held prisoner for nearly a year, during which time conservatives at the Sorbonne and in Paris moved actively against suspected Protestants. Francis was not initially opposed to what seemed to be moral reform within the church. His own view was that the king's duty was to preserve order and prevent scandal, and at first carrying out that duty meant protecting reformers whom the conservative militants persecuted. The king feared disorder more than he feared religious reform.

## THE CONVERSION OF JEANNE D'ALBRET

*Jeanne d'Albret (1528–1572) was the niece of King Francis I and the mother of Henry of Navarre, the future Henry IV. In this letter, written in 1555 to Viscount Gourdon, a Huguenot supporter, she explains the pressures on her to remain Catholic and why she chose to become Protestant. After her conversion, her court became a center of the Huguenot movement.*

I am writing to tell you that up to now I have followed in the footsteps of the deceased Queen, my most honored mother—whom God forgive—in the matter of hesitation between the two religions. The said Queen [was] warned by her late brother the King, François I of good and glorious memory, my much honored uncle, not to get new doctrines in her head so that from then on she confined herself to amusing stories. Besides, I well remember how long ago, the late King, my most honored father, surprised the said Queen when she was praying in her rooms with the ministers Roussel and Farel, and how with great annoyance he slapped her right cheek and forbade her sharply to meddle in matters of doctrine. He shook a stick at me which cost me many bitter tears and has kept me fearful and compliant until after they had both died. Now that I am freed by the death of my said father two months ago, a reform seems so right and so necessary that, for my part, I consider that it would be disloyalty and cowardice to God, to my conscience and to my people to remain any longer in a state of suspense and indecision. It is necessary for sincere persons to take counsel together to decide how to proceed, both now and in the future. Knowing that you are noble and courageous and that you have learned persons about you, I beg you to meet me.

Source: Adapted and reprinted by permission of the publishers from Nancy L. Roelker, trans., *Queen of Navarre: Jeanne d'Albret, 1528–1572* (Cambridge, Mass.: Harvard University Press, 1968), p. 127. Copyright © 1968 by Nancy L. Roelker.

On October 18, 1534, however, Francis's attitude changed when he and all Paris awoke to find the city littered with anti-Catholic placards containing, in the words of the writers, "true articles on the horrible, great and insufferable abuses of the Papal Mass." The response of the Parisians was outrage. They attacked foreigners, especially those who by dress or speech seemed "Lutheran"—that is, German or Flemish. Several months later Francis led a religious procession through Paris in honor of the Blessed Sacrament. The "Affair of the Placards" changed Francis's ideas about the sources of disorder. Opposition to traditional religious practices became more difficult and more dangerous. John Calvin himself was forced to leave Paris, and eventually France, because he feared persecution. Between 1534 and 1560 some ten thousand Protestants fled France, many joining Calvin in Geneva.

By the middle of the sixteenth century it was clear that neither Protestant nor Catholic factions would be able to control religious and political life in France. Francis I died in 1547, and the stage was set for a series of destructive factional struggles over religion and political power that would continue for the rest of the century (see Chapter 15).

## Scandinavia

All of Scandinavia became Lutheran. Initial influences drifted north from Germany, carried by Hanseatic merchants and students who had studied at the universities of northern Germany. Yet the reform in Sweden and Denmark even more than in England was monarchical. In both Scandinavian kingdoms the kings began with an attack on the temporal rights and properties of the church. Changes in liturgy and practice came later as reformers gained royal protection.

Since 1397 all Scandinavia had been united in theory in the Union of Kalmar (see page 379). But early in the sixteenth century the last pretenses of unity were shattered. Christian I of Denmark (r. 1513–1523) invaded Sweden and captured Stockholm, the capital. So great was his brutality that within a few years Gustav Vasa, a leading noble, was able to secure the loyalty of most of the Swedes and in 1523 was elected king of Sweden. Gustav's motto was "All power is of God." Like Henry VIII of England, Gustav (r. 1523–1560) moved carefully in an attempt to retain the loyalty of as many groups as possible. Although he never formally adopted a national confession of faith, the Swedish church and state gradually took on a more Lutheran character. In an effort to secure royal finances, the Riksdag, or parliament, passed the Vasteras Ordinances, which secularized ecclesiastical lands and authorized the preaching of the "Pure Word of God." Olaus Petri (1493–1552), Sweden's principal reform preacher, was installed by royal order in the cathedral of Stockholm.

In Denmark the reformers also moved cautiously. Frederick I (r. 1523–1533) and his son, Christian III (r. 1534–1559), continued the policy of secularization and control that Christian I had initiated. Danish kings seemed interested in reform as a diplomatic means of attack on the Roman church. It seems that in Denmark the old religion simply suffered from a sort of royal indifference. The kings tended to support reformers as a way to attack the political power of the bishops. The Danes finally accepted the Augsburg Confession, which was becoming the most widely accepted exposition of Lutheran belief, in 1538. The transformation of practice proceeded slowly over the next decades.

In the frontier regions of Scandinavia—Finland, Iceland, and Norway—the reform was undertaken as a matter of royal policy. Initially only a handful of local reformers introduced and proselytized the new theology and practice. In many regions resistance to the Reformation continued for several generations. One valley hidden in the mountains of western Norway continued to follow the old religion for three centuries after its contacts with Rome had been severed.

### Eastern Europe

In some respects there was less opposition to the expansion of Protestantism in eastern Europe. The result was the creation of a unique religious culture. The church hierarchy was not in a position to enforce orthodoxy. Some rulers were indifferent to religious debates, as were the Muslim Ottoman Turks, who controlled much of eastern Hungary and what is now Romania. Other rulers whose societies already contained Orthodox and Catholic Christians, as well as Muslims and Jews, offered toleration because they could ill afford to alienate any portion of their subject populations.

Protestant ideas initially passed through the German communities of Poland and the trading towns along the Baltic coast. But in the 1540s Calvinist ideas spread quickly among the Polish nobles, especially those at the royal court. Given the power and influence of some of the noble families, Catholics were unable to suppress the various secret Calvinist congregations. During the first half of the sixteenth century Protestantism became so well estab-

lished in Poland that it could not be rooted out. Throughout the sixteenth century Protestantism remained one of the rallying points for those opposed to the expansion of royal power.

The situation was much the same in Hungary and Transylvania. Among German colonists, Magyars, and ethnic Romanians there were numerous individuals who were interested first in Luther's message and later in Calvin's revisions of the Reformed theology. The situation was exacerbated after the Turkish victory at Mohács in 1526, which destroyed the traditional political and religious elite of Hungary. Because no one could hope to enforce uniformity, some cities adopted a moderate Lutheran theology, and others followed a Calvinist confession. By the 1560s the Estates (representative assemblies) of Transylvania had decreed that four religions were to be tolerated—Catholic, Lutheran, Reformed (Calvinist), and Unitarian. Further, when various radical groups migrated from the west in search of toleration, they were able to create their own communities in Slavic and Magyar areas.

The Reformation was to have virtually no influence farther to the east, in Russia. The Orthodox Church in Russia was much more firmly under government control than was the church in the West. The Russian church followed the traditions of the Greek church, and Western arguments over justification made little sense in Orthodox churches. Given the historic suspicion of the Orthodox churches toward Rome, the Russians were more tolerant of contacts with the Protestants of northern Europe, but there would be no theological innovation or reform in sixteenth-century Russia.

## THE LATE REFORMATION, CA. 1545–1600

IN the first half of the sixteenth century Catholics applied the term *Lutheran* to anyone who was anticlerical. As Francesco Guicciardini (1483–1540), a papal governor in central Italy, remarked:

I know of no one who loathes the ambition, the avarice, and the sensuality of the clergy more than I. . . . In spite of all this, the positions I have held under several popes have forced me, for my own good, to further their interests. Were it not for that, I should have loved Martin Luther as much as myself—not so that I might be free of the laws based on Christian religion as it is generally interpreted and understood;

but to see this bunch of rascals get their just deserts, that is, to be without vices or without authority.[7]

Guicciardini's remarks catch both the frustration many Christians felt toward the traditional church and the very real confusion over just what it was that Luther had said. In parts of Germany by the late 1520s and across Europe by the 1550s, political and religious leaders attempted to explain to the people just what *Lutheran, Reformed (Calvinist),* and *Catholic* had come to mean. It was only in the second half of the sixteenth century that these terms came to have any clarity. After the middle of the sixteenth century it was true that along with theological and political changes, the Reformation represented a broad cultural movement.

The profound changes that began in the sixteenth century continued into the seventeenth. People began to sort out what it meant to belong to one church instead of to another. Central governments supported religious authorities who desired religious uniformity and control over individual Christians. In all parts of Europe, religious behavior changed. Both Protestants and Catholics became more concerned with the personal rather than the communal aspects of Christianity. After the sixteenth century the nature of Christianity and its place in public life, whether in Protestant or in Catholic countries, differed profoundly from Christianity in the Middle Ages.

## Catholic Reform, 1512–1600

Historians commonly speak of both a movement for traditional reform and renewal within the Catholic Church, and a "Counter-Reformation," which was a direct response to and rejection of the theological positions championed by the Protestants. It is certainly true that one can categorize certain acts as clearly challenging the Protestants. However, to do so is to miss the point that the energetic actions of the Roman Catholic Church during the sixteenth century both affirmed traditional teachings and created new institutions better fitted to the early modern world.

The idea of purer, earlier church practices to which the "modern" church should return had been a commonplace for centuries. The great ecumenical Council of Constance early in the fifteenth century had called for "reform in head and members" (see page 361). In 1512, five years before Luther made his public protests, Pope Julius II (r. 1503–1513) convened another ecumenical council, the Fifth Lateran Council (1513–1517), which was expected to look into the problems of nonresident clergy, multiple benefices, and a host of other issues. This tradition of moral reform was especially strong in Spain, Portugal, and Italy, lands whose political rulers were either indifferent or opposed to Protestant reforms.

The desire for reform along traditional lines was deeply felt within the Catholic Church. In the wake of the sack of Rome by imperial troops in 1527, one Roman cardinal, Bishop Gian Matteo Giberti° of Verona (1495–1543), returned to his diocese and began a thoroughgoing reform. He conducted visitations of the churches and other religious institutions in Verona, preached tirelessly, worked hard to raise the educational level of his clergy, and required that priests live within their parishes. Giberti believed that morally rigorous traditional reform and renewal could counter the malaise he perceived. Other reforming bishops could be found throughout Catholic Europe.

New religious foundations sprang up to renew the church. The Spanish mystic Teresa of Avila (1515–1582) reflected the thinking of many when she lamented, "No wonder the Church is as it is, when the religious live as they do." Members of the new orders set out to change the church through example. The Florentine Filippo Neri (1515–1595) founded the Oratorian order, so named because of the monks' habit of leading the laity in prayer services. Filippo was joined in his work by Giovanni Palestrina (ca. 1525–1594), who composed music for the modest but moving prayer gatherings in Rome. Palestrina's music combined medieval plainchants with newer styles of polyphony, creating complex harmonies without obscuring the words and meaning of the text. The popularity of the Oratorians and their services can be measured in part by the fact that oratories, small chapels modeled on those favored by Filippo, remain to this day important centers of the musical life in the city of Rome.

The Catholic reform of the sixteenth century, however, was better known for its mystical theology than for its music. In Italy and France, but especially in Spain, a profusion of reformers chose to reform the church through austere prayer and contemplative devotions. Teresa of Avila, who belonged to a wealthy converso family (see pages 386–387), led a movement to reform the lax practices within the religious houses of Spain. Famed for her rigorous religious life, her trances, and her raptures, Teresa animated a movement to reform the order of Carmelite nuns in Spain. Because of her writings about her mystical experiences she was named a "Doctor of the Church," a title reserved for the greatest of the church's theologians. (See the box "Reading Sources: Saint Teresa of Avila on Rapture and Mortification.")

The most important of the new religious orders was the Society of Jesus, or Jesuits, founded in 1534 by Ig-

---

**Giberti** (ji-BARE-ti)

**A Marian Shrine**    Shrines, such as this one in Regensburg dedicated to the Virgin Mary, remained important centers of Catholic piety. As we see here, shrines drew large crowds made up of individuals and religious groups who came in search of spiritual and physical healing. *(Foto Marburg/Art Resource, NY)*

natius Loyola (1491–1556). A conservative Spanish nobleman, Loyola was wounded and nearly killed in battle. During a long and painful rehabilitation he continuously read accounts of the lives of the saints. After recovering he went on a pilgrimage and experienced a profound conversion.

Loyola initially meant to organize a missionary order directed at converting the Muslims. The structure of his order reflected his military experience. It had a well-defined chain of command leading to the general of the order and then to the pope. To educate and discipline the members, Loyola composed *Spiritual Exercises,* emphasizing the importance of obedience. He encouraged his followers to understand their own attitudes, beliefs, and even lives as less important than the papacy and the Roman church. If the church commands it, he concluded, "I will believe that the white object I see is black." He prohibited Jesuits from holding any ecclesiastical office that might compromise their autonomy. After papal approval of the order in 1540, the Jesuits directed their

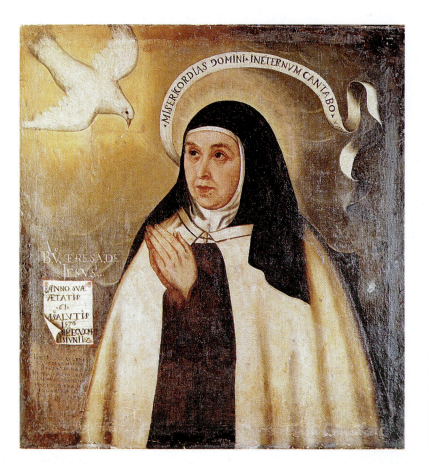

**A Mystical Reformer**  Saint Teresa of Avila came from a converso family. She believed that renewal within the Christian church would come through mysticism, prayer, and a return to traditional religious practices. She founded a reformed Carmelite order of nuns to further religious renewal in Spain. *(Institut Amatller d'Art Hispanic)*

activities primarily to education in Catholic areas and re-conversion of Protestants.

Throughout Europe Jesuits gained fame for their work as educators of the laity and as spiritual advisers to the political leaders of Catholic Europe. In the late sixteenth and early seventeenth centuries they were responsible for a number of famous conversions, including that of Christina (1626–1689), the Lutheran queen of Sweden, who abdicated her throne in 1654 and spent the rest of her life in Rome. Jesuits were especially successful in bringing many parts of the Holy Roman Empire back into communion with the papacy. They have rightly been called the vanguard of the Catholic reform movement.

Catholic reformers were convinced that one of the reasons for the success of the Protestants was that faithful Christians had no clear guide to orthodox teachings. The first Catholic response to the reformers was to try to separate ideas they held to be correct from those they held to be incorrect. Successive popes made public lists of books and ideas that they considered to be in error. The lists were combined into the *Index of Prohibited Books* in 1559. The

climate of suspicion was such that the works of humanists such as Erasmus were prohibited alongside the works of Protestants such as Martin Luther. In times of religious tensions, the *Index* could be vigorously enforced. In general, however, it did little to inhibit the circulation of books and ideas. It was finally suppressed in 1966.

During the first half of the sixteenth century Catholics joined Protestants in calls for an ecumenical council that all believed would solve the problems dogging the Christian church. But in the unsettled political and diplomatic atmosphere that lasted into the 1540s, it was impossible to find any agreement about where or when a universal council should meet. Finally, in 1545, at a time when the hostilities between the Valois and Habsburgs had cooled, Pope Paul III (r. 1534–1549) was able to convene an ecumenical council in the city of Trent, a German imperial city located on the Italian side of the Alps.

It is difficult to overemphasize the importance of the Council of Trent. It marked and defined Roman Catholicism for the next four hundred years. Reformers within the Catholic Church hoped that it would be possible to

READING
SOURCES

## SAINT TERESA OF AVILA ON RAPTURE AND MORTIFICATION

*Teresa de Jesus (1515–1582) was a mystic, reformer, and tireless defender of women's spirituality. Religious authorities were initially suspicious of the daughter of an important converso family, fearing both Judaizing and spiritual teaching by a woman. She was, however, immensely influential. She led a reform movement within the Carmelite order, wrote hundreds of letters of spiritual advice, and analyzed carefully the nature of prayer and meditation. This letter, written in 1577 to her brother, is typical of the counsel she offered to those who sought her guidance.*

You must understand that for these last eight days I have been in such a state. . . . Just before I wrote to you, my raptures came on again; and this gives me great trouble, because they sometimes happen in public, and while I am at matins [the first church service of the morning]. To resist is not sufficient, nor can they be concealed. I am so ashamed that I could hide myself I know not where. I earnestly beg of God to deliver me from having them in public; and do you also pray for me, for they are attended with many inconveniences, and it seems to me that prayer does not consist in having them at all. On those days I am almost like one drunk: . . . it is painful to attend to anything more than to what the soul wishes.

I believe I have already given you an answer as to what you said about remaining [after a rapture], as if nothing had happened. . . . I remember now that I sent you an answer, for I have received a great number of letters since I read yours: and even now I have to write so many answers, that I can hardly find time to send this off. At other times, the soul continues in such a state, that she cannot return to herself for many days, and she seems to resemble the sun, whose rays give heat, and yet the sun is not seen: thus it appears as if the soul dwelt somewhere else, and animated the body without being in it, because some faculty is suspended.

When you cannot recollect yourself properly in the time of prayer, or when you are desirous of doing something for our Lord, I send you this hair-shirt, which will powerfully revive your love. . . . But I recommend this mortification with some fear. As you are of a sanguine temperament, anything might heat your blood; but yet the pleasure is so great which is produced by doing something for God (even should it be a mere nothing, like this is), that I earnestly wish you to try this penance. When the winter is over, you shall do a little more, for I intend taking care of you. Write, and tell me how you like this "trifling!" mortification [remembering what our Lord suffered for us]. . . . I cannot help smiling, to see how you send me sweetmeats, delicacies, and money, and I send you a hair-shirt!

Source: Slightly adapted from *The Letters of Saint Teresa*, trans. John Dalton (London: Thomas Baker, 1893), pp. 154–155, 158, 159.

---

create a broadly based reform party within the church and that the council would define theological positions acceptable to the Protestants, making reunion possible. Unfortunately for the reformers, conservatives quickly took over the papal-controlled council.

The Council of Trent sat in three sessions between 1545 and 1563. The initial debates were clearly meant to mark the boundaries between Protestant heresy and the orthodox positions of the Catholic Church. In response to the Protestant emphasis on the Scriptures, the council said that the church always recognized the validity of traditional teaching and understanding. Delegates rejected the humanists' work on the text of the Bible, declaring that the Latin Vulgate edition compiled by Jerome in the late fourth century was the authorized text. In response to the widely held Protestant belief that salvation came through faith alone, the council declared that good works were not merely the outcome of faith but prerequisites to salvation. The council rejected Protestant positions on the sacraments, the giving of wine to the laity during Holy Communion, the marriage of clergy, and the granting of indulgences.

Protestant critics often point to these positions as evidence that the work of the council was merely negative. To do so, however, is to ignore the many ways in which the decrees of the council were an essential part of the creation of the Roman Catholic Church that would function for the next four centuries. The delegates at Trent generally felt that the real cause behind the Protestant movement was the lack of leadership and supervision within the church. Many of the acts of the council dealt with that issue.

First, the council affirmed apostolic succession—the idea that the authority of a bishop is transmitted through a succession of bishops, ultimately leading back through the popes to Saint Peter. Thus the council underlined the ultimate authority of the pope in administrative as well as theological matters. The council ordered that local bishops should reside in their dioceses; that they should establish seminaries to see to the education of parish clergy; and that, through regular visitation and supervision, they should make certain that the laity participated in the sacramental life of the church. In the final sessions of the council the nature of the Roman Catholic Church was summed up in the Creed of Pius IV, which like the Lutheran Augsburg Confession expressed the basic position of the church.

## Confessionalization

The labors of the Jesuits and the deliberations of the Council of Trent at midcentury proved that reconciliation be-

**The Gesu in Rome**    This church is the center of the Jesuit order and the burial place of Saint Ignatius Loyola. Its baroque architecture set the tone for many later buildings in Rome and for many new Catholic churches elsewhere.    *(Scala/Art Resource, NY)*

tween the Protestant reformers and the Catholic Church was not possible. Signs of the separation include the flight of several important Protestant religious leaders from Italy in the late 1540s and the wholesale migration of Protestant communities from Modena, Lucca, and other Italian towns to France, England, and Switzerland. These actions signify the beginnings of the theological, political, and social separation of "Protestant" and "Catholic" in European society. Further, the states of Europe saw themselves as the enforcers of religious uniformity within their territories. It is from this time forward that denominational differences become clearer.

The theological separation was marked in a number of concrete and symbolic ways. Churches in which both bread and wine were distributed to the laity during the sacrament of Holy Communion passed from Catholic to Protestant. Churches in which the altar was moved forward to face the congregation but the statuary was retained were likely to be Lutheran. Churches in which statues were destroyed and all other forms of art were removed were likely to be Reformed (Calvinist), for Calvin had advised that "only those things are to be sculpted or painted which the eye is capable of seeing; let not God's majesty, which is far above the perception of the eyes, be debased through unseemly representations."[8] Even matters such as singing differentiated the churches. Although the Calvinist tradition tended to believe that music, like art, drew the Christian away from consideration of the word, Luther believed that "next to the Word of God, music deserves the highest praise." Lutherans emphasized congregational singing and the use of music within the worship service. Countless pastors in the sixteenth and seventeenth centuries followed Luther in composing hymns and even theoretical tracts on music. This tradition would reach its zenith in the church music of Johann Sebastian Bach (1685–1750), most of whose choral works were composed to be part of the normal worship service.

Music had played an important role in Catholic services since well before the Reformation. It was really architecture that distinguished Catholic churches from Protestant churches in the late sixteenth and seventeenth centuries. In Rome the great religious orders built new churches in the baroque style (see page 533). Baroque artists and architects absorbed all the classical lessons of the Renaissance and then went beyond them, sometimes deliberately violating them. Baroque art celebrates the supernatural, the ways in which God is not bound by the laws of nature. Whereas Renaissance art was meant to depict nature, baroque paintings and sculpture seem to defy gravity. The work celebrates the supernatural power

and splendor of the papacy. This drama and power are clear in the construction of the Jesuit Church of the Gesù° in Rome and even more so in Gianlorenzo Bernini's (1598–1680) throne of Saint Peter, made for Saint Peter's Basilica in the Vatican. The construction of baroque churches, first in Spain and Italy but especially in the Catholic parts of Germany, created yet another boundary between an austere Protestantism and a visual and mystical Catholicism.

## The Regulation of Religious Life

Because of the continuing religious confusion and political disorder brought on by the reforms, churchmen, like state officials, were intent on maintaining religious order within their territories by requiring what they understood to be the practice of true Christianity. In an ironic twist, both Protestant and Catholic authorities followed much the same program. In both camps regulation of religion became a governmental concern. Religious regulation and state power grew at the same time. This true religion was much less a public and communal religion than medieval Christianity had been. Medieval Christians had worried greatly about public sins that complicated life in a community. In the age of confessionalization theologians—both Protestant and Catholic—became preoccupied with the moral status and interior life of individuals. Sexual sins and gluttony now seemed more dangerous than economic sins such as avarice and usury. Even penance was understood less as a "restitution" that would reintegrate the individual into the Christian community than as a process of coming to true contrition for one's sins.

The changed attitude toward penance made the sense of Christian community less important and left individuals isolated and more subject to the influence of the church and secular authorities. In all parts of Europe officials were consumed with the control and supervision of the laity.

All of the major religious groups in the late sixteenth century emphasized education, right doctrine, and social control. In Catholic areas it was hoped that a renewed emphasis on private confession by the laity would lead to a proper understanding of doctrine. During this period Charles Borromeo, archbishop of Milan (1538–1584), introduced the private confessional box, which isolated priest and penitent from the prying ears of the community. This allowed confessors the time and opportunity to instruct individual consciences with care. As early as the

---

**Gesu** (jeh-SUE)

**The Holy Household**    One of the most popular ideas among Protestants was that true religion should be taught and preserved in the Christian family, presided over by the father. The detail in this painting shows not only the interior of a Flemish home but also the role of the father and the symbolic importance of meals eaten together.    *(The Shakespeare Birthplace Trust)*

1520s some Lutheran princes had begun visitations to ensure that the laity understood basic doctrine.

Churchmen in both Protestant and Catholic areas used catechisms—handbooks containing instruction for the laity. The first and most famous was by Luther himself. Luther's *Small Catechism* includes the Lord's Prayer, Ten Commandments, and Apostles' Creed, along with simple, clear explanations of what they mean. More than Catholic rulers, Protestant rulers used church courts to enforce discipline within the community. Churchmen began to criticize semireligious popular celebrations such as May Day, harvest feasts, and the Feast of Fools, whose origins lay in popular myths and practices that preceded Christianity. Such observances were now scorned for en-

couraging superstition and mocking the social and political order with, for example, parodies of ignorant clergy and foolish magistrates.

Religious authorities were also concerned by what seemed to be out-of-control mysticism and dangerous religious practices, especially among women. The impact of the Reformation on the status of women has often been debated. The Protestant position is that the Reformation freed women from the cloistered control of traditional convents. Further, the Protestant attack on state-controlled prostitution reduced one of the basest forms of exploitation. To the realists who argued that young, unmarried men would always need sexual outlets, Luther replied that one cannot merely substitute one evil practice for another. Critics of the Reformation counter that a convent was one of very few organizations that a woman could administer and direct. Women who took religious vows, Catholics point out, could engage in intellectual and religious pursuits similar to those enjoyed by men. The destruction of religious houses for women, Catholics argue, destroyed one of the few alternatives that women had to life in an authoritarian, patriarchal society.

In fact, in the late sixteenth and early seventeenth centuries both Protestant and Catholic authorities viewed with suspicion any signs of religious independence by women. In the first years of the Reformation some women did leave convents, eager to participate in the reform of the church. Early in the 1520s some women wrote tracts concerning the morality of the clergy. And for a time women served as deacons in some Reformed (Calvinist) churches. Yet like the female witches discussed in Chapter 15, these religious women seemed somehow dangerous. Lutheran and Calvinist theologians argued that a woman's religious vocation should be in the Christian care and education of her family. And even the most famous of the sixteenth- and seventeenth-century female Catholic mystics were greeted with distrust and some hostility. Religious women in Catholic convents were required to subordinate their mysticism to the guidance they received from male spiritual advisers. Calvinist theologians exhibited similar suspicions toward the theological and spiritual insights of Protestant women. For the laity in general and for women in particular, the late Reformation brought increased control by religious authorities.

## SUMMARY

**D**URING the age of the Reformation Europe experienced a number of profound shocks. The medieval assumption of a unified Christendom in the West was shattered. No longer could Europeans assume that at heart they held similar views of the world and the place of individuals in it. Charles V had begun his reign with hopes for one law, one faith, and one empire. He ended it by dividing his empire and retiring to a monastery.

The Protestant challenge did not simply attack the institutional structure or the moral lapses as previous heretical movements had done. The early Protestant reformers rejected the penitential system that was at the heart of the medieval church. Peasants and artisans argued that Luther's message of Christian freedom liberated them from both economic and spiritual oppression.

Both Protestant and peasant rejected the traditions of the late Middle Ages.

Monarchies and republics throughout Europe came to view religious institutions and religious choices as matters of state. Many of the small states of Germany, Scandinavia, and the territories that now form Latvia and Estonia became Lutheran. Many of the Swiss cantons, parts of the Low Countries, and Scotland became Reformed (Calvinist). England followed its own course forming the Anglican Church. Spain, Portugal, Italy, France, and the rest of the Low Countries and Germany remained part of the reformed and rejuvenated Roman Catholic Church. Poland and Hungary were religiously mixed, with a strong Reformed church influence among the aristocracy. Much of the rest of eastern Europe followed no clear pattern. When faced with theological challenges and cries for moral reform, governments reacted in ways that offered religious change and bolstered the claims of secular authorities. In England and Sweden calls for reform resulted in the secularization of church property, which put vast new sources of wealth in the hands of the kings. In the towns of Germany and Switzerland governments redoubled their efforts to regulate religion and moral life. In Catholic countries the church hierarchy extended its control over the religious life of the laity. Thus both Reformation and Counter-Reformation brought about a significant strengthening of religious and secular authorities.

Ironically, the reforms that Luther and other Protestants advocated on the basis of individual study and conscience led to new confessional beliefs and a conviction that right religion was a matter of state interest. Religious power, which to some extent had been a matter of personal conscience and local community, became an issue to be decided by the aggressive states of Europe.

## ■ Notes

1. Angela of Foligno, *The Book of Divine Consolation of the Blessed Angel of Foligno,* trans. Mary G. Steegmann (New York: Cooper Square Publishers, 1966), p. 260.
2. Martin Luther, *Works,* vol. 34 (Philadelphia: Muhlenberg Press, 1960), pp. 336–337.
3. Quoted in Steven Ozment, *The Age of Reform, 1250–1550* (New Haven, Conn.: Yale University Press, 1980), p. 245.
4. Quoted in Robert W. Scribner, *The German Reformation* (London: Macmillan, 1986), p. 32.
5. Quoted in Carter Lindberg, *The European Reformations* (New York: Blackwell Publishers, 1996), p. 269.
6. Quoted in Euan Cameron, *The European Reformation* (Oxford: Clarendon Press, 1991), pp. 106–107.

*(continued on page 496)*

# A Reformation Woodcut

Erhard Schön's 1533 woodcut "There Is No Greater Treasure Here on Earth Than an Obedient Wife Who Desires Honor" and other broadsheets like it informed and amused Europeans of all walks of life in the late fifteenth and sixteenth centuries. Schön's image of a henpecked husband and his wife followed by others would have been instantly recognizable to most people. Accompanying texts clarified the message implied in the woodcut itself. But how may we, centuries later, "read" this message? How does the modern historian analyze Schön's broadsheet to investigate popular ideas about social roles, religion, and politics? What do this and similar broadsheets tell us about popular responses to the social and religious tumults of the sixteenth century?

Look at the simple and clear lines of the woodcut. They give a clue about the popularity of broadsheets. They were cheap and easy to produce and were printed on inexpensive paper. Artists would sketch an image that an artisan would later carve onto a block. A printer could produce a thousand or more copies from a single block. Even famous artists such as Albrecht Dürer (see page 418) sold highly profitable prints on religious, political, and cultural themes.

Almost anyone could afford broadsheets. Laborers and modest merchants decorated their houses with pictures on popular themes. In the middle of the fifteenth century, before the Reformation, most images were of saints. It was widely believed, for example, that anyone who looked at an image of Saint Christopher would not die on that day.

During the political and religious unrest of the sixteenth century, artists increasingly produced images that referred to the debates over religion. Schön himself made his living in Nuremberg producing and selling woodcuts. He and other artists in the city were closely tuned to the attitudes of the local population. One popular image was titled "The Roman Clergy's Procession into Hell."

Schön's "Obedient Wife" reflects a fear shared by both Protestants and Catholics: the rebellious nature of women. Evidence suggests that women in the late fifteenth and sixteenth centuries may have been marrying at a later age and thus were likely to be more independent-minded than their younger sisters. The ranks of single women were swollen by widows and by former nuns who had left convents and liberated themselves from male supervision. Thus it was not difficult for men in the sixteenth century to spot women who seemed dangerously free from male control.

Let us turn again to the woodcut, to see what worried villagers and townspeople and how Schön depicted their fears. Notice the henpecked husband. He is harnessed to a cart carrying laundry. Both the harness and the laundry were popular images associated with women's duties. During popular festivals German villagers often harnessed unmarried women to a plow to signify that they were shirking their duty by not marrying and raising children. Doing the laundry was popularly thought to be the first household chore that a powerful wife would force on her weak-kneed husband. Countless other images show women, whip in hand, supervising foolish husbands as they pound diapers with a laundry flail. "Woe is me," says the poor man, all this because "I took a wife." As if the message were not clear enough, look at what the woman carries in her left hand: his purse, his sword, and his pants. (The question "Who wears the pants in the family?" was as familiar then as it is now.) But the woman responds that he is in this position not because of marriage but because he has been carousing: "If you will not work to support me, then you must wash, spin, and draw the cart."*

The figures following the cart are commenting on the situation. The young journeyman is asking the maiden at his side, "What do you say about this?" She responds coyly, "I have no desire for such power." The woman dressed as a fool counsels the young man never to marry and thus to avoid anxiety and suffering. But an old man, identified as "the wise man," closes the procession and ends the debate. "Do not listen to this foolish woman," he counsels. "God determines how your life together will be, so stay with her in love and suffering and always be patient."

If we think about this woodcut's images and text, we can understand the contrary hopes and fears in sixteenth-century Germany. Like the young woman, the Christian wife was expected to eschew power either inside or outside the home. Martin Luther concluded that

---

*Keith Moxey, *Peasants, Warriors and Wives: Popular Imagery in the Reformation* (Chicago: University of Chicago Press, 1989), pp. 108–109; includes a translation of portions of the text in the broadsheet.

**"There Is No Greater Treasure Here on Earth Than an Obedient Wife Who Desires Honor,"**
**Erhard Schön**   *(Schlossmuseum, Gotha)*

"the husband is the head of the wife even as Christ is head of the Church. Therefore as the Church is subject to Christ, so let wives be subject to their husbands in everything" (Ephesians 5:23–24). Authority was to be in the hands of husbands and fathers. But if the good wife was required to avoid power, the good husband was expected to follow Luther's precepts for the Christian family. As the wise old man observes, the husband must be a loving and forgiving master.

Schön's woodcut and others similar to it should remind you of the "argument over women" discussed in Chapter 12 (see page 411). The words of the wise man

and the young maid bring to mind Christine de Pizan's *Book of the City of the Ladies* when they urge love and understanding, but their hopefulness is undercut by the power and immediacy of the image. As the broadsheet clearly demonstrates, suspicion of women characterized even the most simple literature of Reformation Europe.

**For additional information on this topic, go to college.hmco.com/students.**

7. Francesco Guicciardini, *Maxims and Reflections (Ricordi)*, trans. Mario Domandi (Philadelphia: University of Pennsylvania Press, 1965), p. 48.

8. Quoted in Lindberg, p. 375.

## ■ Suggested Reading

Bennedict, Philip. *Christ's Churches Purely Reformed: A Social History of Calvinism.* 2002. A magisterial survey of the Reformed (Calvinist) tradition that emphasizes the dynamics of religious communities.

Bireley, Robert. *The Refashioning of Catholicism: A Reassessment of the Counter Reformation.* 1999. A well-written survey that places the Roman Catholic Church in the context of political, social, and religious developments between 1450 and 1600.

Cameron, Euan. *The European Reformation.* 1991. The best recent history of the Reformation, emphasizing the common principles of the major reformers.

Dickens, Arthur G. *The English Reformation.* 1991. A classic, clear discussion of English religion, emphasizing the popular enthusiasm for reform, which Dickens believes was connected to the earlier Lollard movements.

Haigh, Christopher, ed. *The English Reformation Revised.* 1987. A collection of essays criticizing Dickens's thesis on the popular basis of reform in England; the introduction is especially useful for following what is still an important debate over reform.

Hillerbrand, Hans J., ed. *The Oxford Encyclopedia of the Reformation.* 1996. An essential source on almost all topics of sixteenth-century history; the entries are accessible and up-to-date.

McGrath, Alister E. *A Life of John Calvin: A Study in the Shaping of Western Culture.* 1990. An excellent biography emphasizing the denitive role of Calvin's religious thought.

Oberman, Heiko. *Luther: Man Between God and the Devil.* 1989. A brilliant, beautifully written essay connecting Luther to prevailing late medieval ideas about sin, death, and the Devil.

Oberman, Heiko, Thomas Brady, and James Tracy, eds. *Handbook of European History, 1400–1600: Late Middle Ages, Renaissance, and Reformation.* 1994–1995. A collection of excellent introductory studies of political, religious, and social life.

Pettegree, Andrew, ed. *The Reformation World.* 2000. A demanding but very comprehensive survey of the most recent work on the Reformation.

**For a searchable list of additional readings for this chapter, go to college.hmco.com/students.**

# CHAPTER 15

# Europe in the Age of Religious Wars 1560–1648

THREE well-dressed gentlemen stand over a mutilated body; one of them holds up the severed head. Elsewhere sword-wielding men engage in indiscriminate slaughter, even of babies. Corpses are piled up in the background. This painting memorializes the grisly events of August 24, 1572. A band of Catholic noblemen accompanied by the personal guard of the king of France had hunted down a hundred Protestant nobles, asleep in their lodgings in and around the royal palace, and murdered them in cold blood. The king and his counselors had planned the murders as a preemptive political strike because they feared that other Protestant nobles were gathering an army outside Paris. But the calculated attack became a general massacre when ordinary Parisians, overwhelmingly Catholic and believing they were acting in the king's name, turned on their neighbors. About three thousand Protestants were slain in Paris over the next three days.

This massacre came to be called the Saint Bartholomew's Day Massacre for the Catholic saint on whose feast day it fell. Though particularly horrible in its scope, the slaughter was not unusual in the deadly combination of religious and political antagonisms it reflected. Religious conflicts were by definition intractable political conflicts since virtually every religious group felt that all others were heretics who could not be tolerated and must be eliminated. Rulers of all faiths looked to divine authority and religious institutions to uphold their power.

In the decades after 1560 existing political tensions contributed to instability and violence, especially when newly reinforced by religious differences. Royal governments continued to consolidate authority, but resistance to royal power by provinces, nobles, or towns accustomed to independence now might have a religious sanction.

The Saint Bartholomew's Day Massacre.
(Musée Cantonal des Beaux-Arts, Lausanne)

**Economic Change and Social Tensions**

**Imperial Spain and the Limits of Royal Power**

**Religious and Political Conflict in France and England**

**Religious and Political Conflict in Central and Eastern Europe**

**Writing, Drama, and Art in an Age of Upheaval**

Warfare over these issues had consumed the Holy Roman Empire in the first half of the sixteenth century. The conflict had now spilled over into France and the Netherlands and threatened to erupt in England. In the early seventeenth century the Holy Roman Empire once again was wracked by a war simultaneously religious and political in origin. Regardless of its roots, warfare itself had become more destructive than ever before thanks to innovations in military technology and campaign tactics. Tensions everywhere were also worsened by economic changes, especially soaring prices and grinding unemployment.

A period of tension, even extraordinary violence, in political and social life, the era of the late sixteenth and early seventeenth centuries was also distinguished by great creativity in some areas of cultural and intellectual life. The plays of Shakespeare, for example, mirrored the passions but also reflected on the dilemmas of the day and helped to analyze Europeans' circumstances with a new degree of sophistication.

---

## QUESTIONS TO CONSIDER

- How did ordinary people cope with the economic stresses of these decades?

- In what ways was the most powerful state of the era—Spain—exceptional among western European monarchies, and in what ways was it typical of them?

- Why did war break out again in the Holy Roman Empire, and what was the significance of the conflict?

- In what ways do the literature and art of this period reflect the political, social, and religious tensions of the age?

---

## TERMS TO KNOW

| | |
|---|---|
| price revolution | Elizabeth I |
| gentry | Puritans |
| Philip II | Thirty Years' War |
| the Armada | Peace of Westphalia |
| Huguenots | Ivan IV, the "Terrible" |
| Edict of Nantes | baroque |

---

# ECONOMIC CHANGE AND SOCIAL TENSIONS

RELIGIOUS strife, warfare, and economic change disrupted the everyday lives of whole communities as well as individuals in the late sixteenth and early seventeenth centuries. Wars were devastating to many areas of western Europe and contributed to especially severe economic decline in parts of the Low Countries (the Netherlands), France, and the Holy Roman Empire. But other factors, most notably a steady rise in prices, also played a role in the dramatic economic and social changes of the century after 1550. A series of economic changes altered power relations in cities, in the countryside, and in the relationship of both to central governments. Ordinary people managed their economic difficulties in a variety of ways: they sought new sources of work; they protested against burdensome taxes; sometimes they found scapegoats for their distress among their neighbors.

## Economic Transformation and the New Elites

The most obvious economic change was an unrelenting rise in prices, which resulted in the concentration of wealth in fewer and fewer hands. Sixteenth-century observers attributed rising prices to the inflationary effects of the influx of precious metals from Spanish territories in the New World. Historians now believe that European causes may also have helped trigger this "price revolution." Steady population growth caused a relative shortage of goods, particularly food, and the result was higher prices. Both the amount and the effect of price changes were highly localized, depending on factors such as the structure of local economies and the success of harvests. Between 1550 and 1600, however, the price of grain may have risen between 50 and 100 percent, and sometimes more, in cities throughout Europe—including eastern Europe, the breadbasket for growing urban areas to the west. Wages did not keep pace with prices; historians estimate that wages lost between one-tenth and one-fourth of their value by the end of the century. The political and religious struggles of the era thus took place against a background of increasing want, and economic distress was often expressed in both political and religious terms.

These economic changes affected the wealthy as well as the poor. During this period monarchs were making new accommodations with the hereditary aristocracy—with the Crown usually emerging stronger, if only through concessions to aristocrats' economic interests. Underlying this new symbiosis of monarchy and traditional warrior-nobles were the effects of the widespread economic changes. These changes would eventually blur lines between the old noble families and the new elites and would simplify power relationships within the state. Conditions in the countryside, where there were fewer resources to feed more mouths, grew less favorable. But at the same time, more capital became available to wealthy urban or landholding families to invest in the countryside, by buying land outright on which to live like gentry or by making loans to desperate peasants. This capital came from profits from expanded production and trade and was also an effect of the scarcity of land as population and prices rose. Enterprising landholders raised ground rents wherever they could, or they converted land to the production of wool, grain, and other cash crops destined for distant markets.

As a result, a stratum of wealthy, educated, and socially ambitious "new gentry," as these families were called in England, began growing and solidifying. Many of the men of these families were royal officeholders. Where the practice existed, many bought titles outright or were granted nobility as a benefit of their offices. They often lent money to royal governments. The monumental expense of wars made becoming a lender to government, as well as to individuals, an attractive way to live off personal capital.

No one would have confused this up-and-coming gentry with warrior-aristocrats from old families, but the social distinctions between them are less important (to us) than what they had in common: legal privilege, the security of landownership, a cooperative relationship with the monarchy. Monarchs deliberately favored the new gentry as counterweights to independent aristocrats.

City governments also changed character as wealth accumulated in the hands of formerly commercial families. Town councils became dominated by successive generations of privileged families, now more likely to live from landed than from commercial wealth. By the beginning of the seventeenth century traditional guild control of government had been subverted in many places. Towns became more closely tied to royal interests by means of the mutual interests of Crown and town elites.

## CHRONOLOGY

| | |
|---|---|
| 1556–1598 | Reign of Philip II |
| 1558–1603 | Reign of Elizabeth I |
| 1559 | Act of Supremacy (England) |
| 1562–1598 | Religious wars in France |
| 1565 | Netherlands city councils and nobility ignore Philip II's law against heresy |
| 1566 | Calvinist "iconoclastic fury" begins in the Netherlands |
| 1567 | Duke of Alba arrives in the Netherlands |
| 1571 | Defeat of Turkish navy at Lepanto |
| 1576 | Sack of Antwerp |
| 1579 | Union of Utrecht |
| 1588 | Defeat of Spanish Armada |
| 1589–1610 | Reign of Henry IV |
| 1598 | Edict of Nantes (France) |
| 1609 | Truce between Spain and the Netherlands is declared |
| 1618–1648 | Thirty Years' War |
| 1620 | Catholic victory at Battle of White Mountain |
| 1621 | Truce between Spain and the Netherlands expires; war between Spain and the Netherlands begins |
| 1629 | Peace of Alais |
| 1631 | Swedes under Gustav Adolf defeat imperial forces |
| 1635 | Peace of Prague |
| 1640–1653 | "Long Parliament" in session in England |
| 1648 | Peace of Westphalia |

The long medieval tradition of towns serving as independent corporate bodies had come to an end.

## Economic Change and the Common People

The growth of markets around Europe and in Spanish possessions overseas, as well as population growth within

Europe, had a marked effect on patterns of production and the lives of artisans and laborers. Production of cloth on a large scale for export, for example, now required huge amounts of capital—much more than a typical guild craftsman could amass. Cloth production was increasingly controlled by new investor-producers with enormous resources and access to distant markets. These entrepreneurs bought up large amounts of wool and hired it out to be cleaned, spun into thread, and woven into cloth by wage laborers in urban workshops or by pieceworkers in their homes. Thousands of women and men in the countryside around urban centers helped to support themselves and their families in this way.

The new entrepreneurs had sufficient capital entirely to bypass guild production. In towns guilds still regulated most trades but could not accommodate the numbers of artisans who sought to join them. Fewer and fewer apprentices and journeymen could expect to become master artisans. The masters began to treat apprentices virtually as wage laborers, at times letting them go during slow periods. The household mode of production, in which apprentices and journeymen had worked and lived side by side with the master's family, also began to break down, with profound economic, social, and political consequences.

One of the first reflections of the dire circumstances faced by artisans was an attempt to reduce competition at the expense of the artisans' own mothers, sisters, daughters, and sons. Increasingly, widows were forbidden to continue practicing their husbands' enterprises, though they headed from 10 to 15 percent of households in many trades. Women had traditionally learned and practiced many trades but rarely followed the formal progress from apprenticeship to master status. A woman usually combined work of this kind with household production, with selling her products and those of her husband, and with bearing and nursing children. Outright exclusion of women from guild organization appeared as early as the thirteenth century but now began regularly to appear in guild statutes. In addition, town governments tried to restrict women's participation in work such as selling in markets, which they had long dominated. Even midwives had to defend their practices, even though as part of housewifery women were expected to know about herbal remedies and practical medicine. Working women thus began to have difficulty supporting themselves if single or widowed and difficulty supporting their children. In the changing position of such women we can see the distress of the entire stratum of society that they represent.

Wealth in the countryside was also becoming more stratified. Population growth caused many peasant farms to be subdivided for numerous children, creating tiny plots that could not support the families who lived on them. Countless peasants lost what lands they had to wealthy investors—many of them newly wealthy gentry—who lent them money for renting more land or for purchasing seed and tools, and then reclaimed the land when the peasants failed to repay. Other peasants were simply unable to rent land as rents rose. To survive, some sought work as day laborers on the land of rich landlords or more prosperous farmers. But with the shrinking opportunities for farming, this option became less feasible. Many found their way to cities, where they swelled the ranks of the poor. Others, like some of their urban counterparts, coped by becoming part of the newly expanding network of cloth production, combining spinning and weaving with subsistence farming. However, one bad harvest might send them out on the roads begging or odd-jobbing; many did not long survive such a life.

In eastern Europe peasants faced other dilemmas, for their lands had a different relationship to the wider European economy. The more densely urbanized western Europe, whose wealth controlled the patterns of trade, sought bulk goods, particularly grain, from eastern Germany, Poland, and Lithuania. Thus there was an economic incentive for landowners in eastern Europe to bind peasants to the land just as the desire of their rulers for greater cooperation had granted the landlords more power. Serfdom now spread in eastern Europe, while precisely the opposite condition—a more mobile labor force—grew in the West.

## Coping with Poverty and Violence

The common people of Europe did not submit passively to either the economic difficulties or the religious and political crises of their day. Whatever their religion, common people took the initiative in attacking members of other faiths to rid their communities of them. Heretics were considered to be spiritual pollution that might provoke God's wrath, and ordinary citizens believed that they had to eliminate heretics if the state failed to do so. Common people, as well as elites and governments, were thus responsible for the violence that sometimes occurred in the name of religion.

Ordinary people fought in wars not only from conviction but also from the need for self-defense and from economic choice. It was ordinary people who defended the walls of towns, dug siege works, and manned artillery batteries. Although nobles remained military leaders, armies consisted mostly of infantry made up of common people, not mounted knights. Women were part of armies, too. Much of the day-to-day work of finding food and firewood, cleaning guns, and endlessly repairing inadequate clothing was done by women looking after their husbands and lovers among the troops.

Many men joined the armies and navies of their rulers because, given the alternatives, the military seemed a reasonable way of life. Landless farm hands, day laborers, and out-of-work artisans found the prospect of employment in the army attractive enough to outweigh the dangers of military life. Desertion was common; nothing more than the rumor that a soldier's home village was threatened might prompt a man to abandon his post. Battle-hardened troops could threaten their commanders not only with desertion but with mutiny. A mutiny of Spanish soldiers in 1574 was a well-organized affair, for example, somewhat like a strike. Occasionally mutinies were brutally suppressed; more often they were successful and troops received some of their back wages.

Townspeople and country people participated in riots and rebellions to protest their circumstances when the situation was particularly dire or when other means of action had failed. The devastation of religious war led to both peasant rebellions and urban uprisings. Former

soldiers, prosperous farmers, or even noble landlords whose economic fortunes were tied to peasant profits might lead rural revolts. Urban protests could begin spontaneously when new grievances worsened existing problems. In 1585 food riots in Naples were provoked not simply by a shortage of grain but also by a government decision to raise the price of bread during the shortage. Rebels sometimes seized property—for example, they might distribute looted bread among themselves—and occasionally killed officials. Their protests rarely generated lasting political change and were usually brutally quashed.

Governments at all levels tried to cope with the increasing problem of poverty by changing the administration and scale of poor relief. In both Catholic and Protestant Europe caring for the poor became more institutionalized and systematic, and more removed from religious impulses. In the second half of the sixteenth century, governments established public almshouses and poorhouses to dispense food or to care for orphans or the destitute in towns throughout Catholic and Protestant Europe. Initially these institutions reflected an optimistic

**Soldiers and Civilians**    This contemporary painting of a military camp illustrates the presence of women and even children among the troops. Common people were the majority of combatants in wartime.    *(Kunsthistorisches Museum, Vienna/Art Resource, NY)*

vision of an ideal Christian community attentive to material want. But by 1600 the charitable distribution of food was accompanied by attempts to distinguish "deserving" from "undeserving" poor, by an insistence that the poor work for their ration of food, and even by an effort to compel the poor to live in almshouses and poorhouses.

These efforts were not uniformly successful. Begging was outlawed by Catholic and Protestant city governments alike, but never thoroughly suppressed. Catholic religious orders and parishes often resisted efforts at regulating their charitable work—even when they were imposed by Catholic governments. Nonetheless, the trend was clear. From viewing poverty as a fact of life and as an occasional lesson in Christian humility, European elites were beginning to see it as a social problem. And they saw the poor as people in need of control and institutional discipline.

## The Hunt for Witches

Between approximately 1550 and 1650 Europe saw a dramatic increase in the persecution of women and men for witchcraft. Approximately one hundred thousand people were tried and about sixty thousand executed. The surge in witch-hunting was closely linked to communities' religious concerns and also to the social tensions that resulted from economic difficulties.

Certain types of witchcraft had long existed in Europe. So-called black magic of various kinds—one peasant casting a spell on another peasant's cow—had been common since the Middle Ages. What now made the practice seem particularly menacing, especially to elites, were theories linking black magic to Devil worship. Catholic leaders and legal scholars began to advance such theories in the fifteenth century, and by the late sixteenth century both Catholic and Protestant elites viewed a witch not only as someone who might cast harmful spells but also as a heretic.

The impetus for most individual accusations of witchcraft came from within the communities where the "witch" lived—that is, from common people. Usually targeted were solitary or unpopular people whose difficult relationships with fellow villagers made them seem likely sources of evil. Often such a person had practiced black magic (or had been suspected of doing so) for years, and the villagers took action only when faced with a community crisis, such as an epidemic.

The majority of accused witches were women. Lacking legal, social, and political resources, women may have been more likely than men to use black magic for self-protection or advancement. Women's work often made them vulnerable to charges of witchcraft since families'

food supplies and routine medicines passed through women's hands. The deaths of young children or of domestic animals, such as a milk cow, were among the most common triggers for witchcraft accusation. The increase in poverty during the late sixteenth and early seventeenth centuries made poor women frequent targets of witch-hunts. It was easier to find such a woman menacing—and to accuse her of wrongdoing—than to feel guilty because of her evident need.

Both Christian dogma and humanistic writing portrayed women as morally weaker than men and thus more susceptible to the Devil's enticements. Writings on witchcraft described Devil worship in sexual terms, and the prosecution of witches had a voyeuristic, sexual dimension. The bodies of accused witches were searched for the "Devil's mark"—a blemish thought to be Satan's imprint. In some regions women accounted for 80 percent of those prosecuted and executed. A dynamic of gender stereotyping was not always at work, however; in other regions prosecutions were more evenly divided between men and women, and occasionally men made up the majority of those accused.

Because they were often prompted by village disasters or tragedies, individual accusations of witchcraft increased in these decades in response to the crises that beset many communities. In addition, isolated accusations often started localized frenzies of active hunting for other witches. Dozens of "witches" might be identified and executed before the whirlwind subsided. These more widespread hunts were driven in part by the anxieties of local elites about disorder and heresy and were facilitated by contemporary legal procedures that they applied. These procedures permitted lax rules of evidence and the use of torture to extract confessions. Torture or the threat of torture led most of those accused of witchcraft to "confess" and to name accomplices or other "witches." In this way a single initial accusation could lead to dozens of prosecutions. In regions where procedures for appealing convictions and sentences were fragile or nonexistent, witch-hunts could expand with alarming speed. Aggressive hunts were common, for example, in the small principalities and imperial cities of the Holy Roman Empire, which were largely independent of higher political authority. (See the box "Reading Sources: A City Official Worries About Witch-Hunting.")

The widespread witch-hunts virtually ended by the late seventeenth century, in part because the intellectual energies of elites shifted from religious to scientific thought. The practice of witchcraft continued among common folk, although accusations of one neighbor by another never again reached the level of these crisis-ridden decades.

READING
SOURCES

## A CITY OFFICIAL WORRIES ABOUT WITCH-HUNTING

*In this letter written in 1629, the chancellor to the prince-bishop of the German city of Würzburg confides to a friend his doubts about the wisdom of zealous witch-hunting. Note that he mentions the deaths of many young people and many members of the elite. The persecutions seem to have taken on a life of their own. Note that the chancellor's revulsion at the effects of witch-hunting have not yet led him to reject the whole notion of witchcraft, however.*

As to the affair of the witches . . . it has started up afresh, and no words can do justice to it. Ah, the woe and misery of it—there are still four hundred in the city, high and low, of every rank and sex . . . so strongly accused that they may be arrested at any hour. It is true that, of the people of my Gracious Prince here, some out of all the offices and faculties must be executed: clerics, elected councilors and doctors, city officials . . . several of whom [you] know. There are law students to be arrested. The Prince-Bishop has over forty students who are soon to be pastors; among them thirteen or fourteen are said to be witches. . . . The notary of our Church consistory, a very learned man, was yesterday arrested and put to the torture. In a word, a third part of the city is surely involved. The richest, most attractive, most prominent of the clergy are already executed. A week ago a maiden of nineteen was executed, of whom it is everywhere said that she was the fairest in the whole city, and was held by everybody a girl of singular modesty and purity. . . . To conclude this wretched matter, there are children of three or four years . . . who are said to have had intercourse with the Devil. I have seen put to death children of seven, promising students of ten, twelve, fourteen and fifteen. Of the nobles—but I cannot and must not write more of this misery. . . .

P.S. Though there are many . . . terrible things happening it is beyond doubt that, at a place called the Fraw-Rengberg, the Devil in person, with eight thousand of his followers, held an assembly and celebrated mass before them all. . . . There took place not only foul but most horrible and hideous blasphemies, whereof I shudder to write.

Source: Alan C. Kors and Edward Peters, eds., *Witchcraft in Europe, 1100–1700: A Documentary History* (Philadelphia: University of Pennsylvania, 1972), pp. 251–252. Reprinted by permission of the University of Pennsylvania Press.

## IMPERIAL SPAIN AND THE LIMITS OF ROYAL POWER

To contemporary observers, no political fact of the late sixteenth century was more obvious than the ascendancy of Spain. Philip II (r. 1556–1598) ruled Spanish conquests in the New World as well as wealthy territories in Europe, including the Netherlands and parts of Italy. Yet imperial Spain did not escape the political, social, and religious turmoil of the era. Explosive combinations of religious dissent and political disaffection led to revolt against Spain in the Netherlands. This conflict revealed the endemic tensions of sixteenth-century political life: nobles, towns, and provinces trying to safeguard remnants of medieval autonomy against efforts at greater centralization—with the added complications of economic strain and religious division. The revolt also demonstrated the material limits of royal power, since even with treasure from the American conquests pouring in, Philip could at times barely afford to keep armies in the field. As American silver dwindled in the seventeenth century, Philip's successors faced severe financial and political strains even in their Spanish domains.

### The Revolt of the Netherlands

Philip's power stemmed in part from the far-flung territories he inherited from his father, the Habsburg king of Spain and Holy Roman emperor Charles V: Spain, the Low Countries (the Netherlands), the duchy of Milan, the kingdom of Naples, the conquered lands in the Americas, and the Philippine Islands in Asia. (Control of Charles's Austrian lands had passed to his brother, Ferdinand, Philip's uncle; see Map 15.1.) Treasure fleets bearing precious metals from the New World began to reach Spain regularly during Philip's reign. Spain was now the engine powering a trading economy unlike any that had existed

**Map 15.1  The Spanish Habsburgs and Europe, ca. 1556**  Philip II's control of territories in northern Italy permitted the overland access of Spanish troops to the Netherlands and heightened the Spanish threat to France. Lands bordering the western Mediterranean made the sea a natural sphere of Spanish influence as well. Habsburg lands in central Europe were controlled after 1556 by Charles V's brother Ferdinand and his descendants.

Lands ruled by the Spanish Habsburgs

Lands ruled by the Austrian Habsburgs

Boundary of the Holy Roman Empire

Spanish military corridor ("Spanish Road")

Major battles

**The City of Antwerp**    Antwerp, in the southern Netherlands, was the point of sale for Portuguese spices brought around Africa from India; the selling and transshipping center for Baltic goods, including timber, fur, and grain; and the source for manufactured goods such as cloth.    *(Musées royaux des Beaux-Arts de Belgique)*

in Europe before. To supply its colonies Spain needed timber and other shipbuilding materials from the hinterlands of the Baltic Sea. Grain from the Baltic fed the urban populations of Spain (where wool was the principal cash crop) and the Netherlands, while the Netherlands, in turn, was a source of finished goods, such as cloth. The major exchange point for all of these goods was the city of Antwerp in the Netherlands, the leading trading center of all of Europe by 1550.

The Netherlands were the jewel among Philip's European possessions. These seventeen provinces (constituting mostly the modern nations of Belgium and the Netherlands) had been centers of trade and manufacture since the twelfth century. In the fourteenth and fifteenth centuries they had enjoyed political importance and a period of cultural innovation under the control of the dukes of Burgundy. By the time Philip inherited the provinces from his father, a sort of federal system of government had evolved to accommodate the various centers of power. Each province had an assembly (Estates)

in which representatives of leading nobility and towns authorized taxation, but each also acknowledged a central administration in Brussels that represented Philip. Heading the council of state in Brussels was a governor-general, Philip's half sister, Margaret of Parma.

Philip's clumsy efforts to adjust this distribution of power in his favor pushed his subjects in the Netherlands into revolt. Though conscientious to a fault, Philip was a rigid, unimaginative man. Born and raised in Spain, he had little real familiarity with the densely populated, linguistically diverse Netherlands, and he never visited there after 1559. Early in Philip's reign, tensions in the Netherlands arose over taxation and Spanish insistence on maintaining tight control. Bad harvests and commercial disruptions occasioned by wars in the Baltic region in the 1560s depressed the Netherlands' economy and made it difficult for the provinces to pay taxes demanded by Spain. When the Peace of Cateau-Cambrésis° of 1559

---

**Cateau-Cambrésis** (kah-toe kam-bray-SEE)

**Philip II in 1583** Dressed in the austere black in fashion at the Spanish court, Philip holds a rosary and wears the Order of the Golden Fleece, an order of knighthood, around his neck. At age 56 Philip has outlived four wives and most of his children. *(Museo del Prado, Madrid)*

brought an end to the long struggle between the Habsburgs and the Valois° kings of France, the people of the Netherlands had reason to hope for lower taxes and reduced levels of Spanish control, yet neither was forthcoming. Indeed, Philip had named to the council of state officials who were Spaniards themselves or had close ties to the Spanish court, bypassing local nobles who had fought for Philip and his father before 1559 and who expected positions of influence in his government.

Philip only added to the economic and political discontent by unleashing an invigorated repression of heresy. Unlike his father, Philip directed the hunt for heretics not just at lower-class dissenters but also at well-to-do Calvinists—followers of the French Protestant religious reformer John Calvin—whose numbers were considerable. Punishment for heresy now included confiscation of family property along with execution of the individ-

ual. By 1565 municipal councils in the Netherlands were routinely refusing to enforce Philip's religious policies, believing that urban prosperity—as well as their personal security—depended on restraint in the prosecution of heresy. Leading nobles also stopped enforcing the policies on their estates.

Encouraged by greater tolerance, Protestants by 1566 had begun to hold open-air meetings and attract new converts in many towns. In a series of actions called the "iconoclastic fury," townsfolk around the provinces stripped Catholic churches of the relics and statues deemed idolatrous by Calvinist doctrine. At the same time, reflecting the economic strain of these years, some townsfolk rioted to protest the price of bread. One prominent nobleman warned Philip, "All trade has come to a standstill, so that there are 100,000 men begging for their bread who used to earn it . . . which is [important] since poverty can force people to do things which otherwise they would never think of doing."[1]

In early 1567 armed bands of Calvinist insurgents seized two towns in the southern Netherlands by force of arms in hopes of stirring a general revolt that would secure freedom of worship. Margaret of Parma quelled the uprisings by rallying city governments and loyal nobles, now fearful for their own property and power. But by then, far away in Spain, a decision had been made to send in the Spanish duke of Alba with an army of ten thousand men.

Alba arrived in August 1567 and, to bolster his own shaky standing at the Spanish court, acted more like a conqueror than a peacemaker. He billeted troops in friendly cities, established new courts to try rebels, arrested thousands of people, executed about a thousand rebels (including Catholics as well as prominent Protestants), and imposed heavy new taxes to support his army. Thus Alba repeated every mistake of Spanish policy that had triggered rebellion in the first place.

Margaret of Parma resigned in disgust and left the Netherlands. Protestants from rebellious towns escaped into exile, where they were joined by nobles who had been declared traitors for resisting Alba's extreme policies. The most important of these was William of Nassau°, prince of Orange (1533–1584), whose lands outside the Netherlands, in France and the Holy Roman Empire, lay beyond Spanish reach and so could be used to finance continued warfare against Spain. A significant community with military capability began to grow in exile.

In 1572 ships of exiled Calvinist privateers known as the "Sea Beggars" began preying on Spanish shipping and coastal fortresses from bases in the northern provinces.

---

**Valois** (val-WAH)

**Nassau** (NAS-saw)

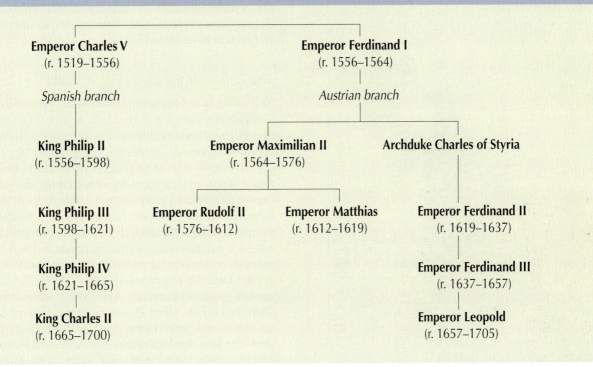

## THE SPANISH AND AUSTRIAN HABSBURGS, 1556–1700

Emperor Charles V (r. 1519–1556)

Emperor Ferdinand I (r. 1556–1564)

*Spanish branch*

*Austrian branch*

King Philip II (r. 1556–1598)

Emperor Maximilian II (r. 1564–1576)

Archduke Charles of Styria

King Philip III (r. 1598–1621)

Emperor Rudolf II (r. 1576–1612)

Emperor Matthias (r. 1612–1619)

Emperor Ferdinand II (r. 1619–1637)

King Philip IV (r. 1621–1665)

Emperor Ferdinand III (r. 1637–1657)

King Charles II (r. 1665–1700)

Emperor Leopold (r. 1657–1705)

These provinces, increasingly Calvinist, became the center of opposition to the Spanish, who concentrated their efforts against rebellion in the wealthier southern provinces. Occasionally the French and English lent aid to the rebels.

The war in the Netherlands was a showcase for the new and costly technology of warfare in this period. Many towns were (or came to be, as a consequence of the revolt) equipped with "bastions," newly designed walled defenses that could resist artillery fire; such cities could not be taken by storm. Where bastions had been built, military campaigns consisted of grueling sieges, skirmishes in surrounding areas for control of supplies, and occasional pitched battles between besiegers and forces attempting to break the siege. Vast numbers of men were required both for effective besieging forces and for garrisoning the many fortresses that controlled the countryside and defended access to major towns.

In an attempt to supply the Netherlands with seasoned veterans and materiel from Spain and Spanish territories in Italy, the Spanish developed the "Spanish Road," an innovative string of supply depots where provisions could be gathered in advance of troops marching to the Netherlands (see Map 15.1). Maintaining its large armies, however, taxed Spain's resources to the breaking point. Even with American silver at hand, Philip could at times barely afford to keep armies in the field. Inevitably, large numbers of troops also exhausted the countryside, and both soldiers and civilians suffered great privations. On occasion Spanish troops reacted violently to difficult conditions and to delayed pay (American treasure dwindled badly between 1572 and 1578). In 1576 Spanish troops sacked the hitherto loyal city of Antwerp and massacred about eight thousand people. This event was bitterly remembered afterward as the "Spanish Fury."

The massacre prompted leaders in the southern provinces to raise their own armies to protect themselves against the Spanish. Late in 1576 they concluded an alliance with William of Orange and the northern rebels. But the northern and southern provinces were increasingly divided by religion, and their differences were skillfully exploited by Philip's new commander, Margaret's son Alexander Farnese°, duke of Parma. With galleons from America filling the king's coffers again, Parma wooed the Catholic elites of the southern provinces back into loyalty to Philip, in return for promises to respect their provincial liberties and safeguard their property from troops.

Farnese (far-NAY-zee)

Map 15.2 legend:
- United Provinces as of 1609
- Spanish Netherlands
- Truce line, 1609

**Map 15.2 The Netherlands, 1559–1609** The seventeen provinces of the Netherlands were strikingly diverse politically, economically, and culturally. Like his father, Philip was, technically, the ruler of each province separately—that is, he was count of Flanders, duke of Brabant, and so forth.

In 1579 the northern provinces united in a defensive alliance, the Union of Utrecht°, against the increasingly unified south. Parma's forces could not surmount the natural barrier of the Rhine River that bisects the Low Countries (see Map 15.2) or meet the increasing costs of siege warfare in waterlogged terrain, particularly as Spain diverted money to conflicts with England in 1588 and France after 1589. In 1609 a truce was finally concluded between Spain and the northern provinces. This truce did not formally recognize the "United Provinces" as an independent entity, though in fact they were. The modern nations of Belgium (the Spanish provinces) and the Netherlands are the distant result of this truce.

The independent United Provinces (usually called, simply, the Netherlands) was a fragile state, an accident of warfare at first. But commercial prosperity began to emerge as its greatest strength. Much of the economic

activity of Antwerp had shifted north to Amsterdam in the province of Holland because of fighting in the south and a naval blockade of Antwerp by rebel ships. Philip's policies had created a new enemy nation and had enriched it at his expense.

## The Failure of the Invincible Armada

The revolt of the Netherlands had lured Spain into wider strategic involvement, particularly against England. Spain and England had a common foe in France and common economic interests, and Philip had married Mary Tudor, the Catholic queen of England (r. 1553–1558). Even after Mary's death and the accession of her Protestant half sister, Queen Elizabeth (r. 1558–1603), Spanish-English relations remained cordial. Relations started to sour, however, when Elizabeth began tolerating the use of English ports by the rebel Sea Beggars and authorizing attacks by English privateers on Spanish treasure fleets. In response Spain supported Catholic resistance to Elizabeth within England, including plots to replace her on the throne with her Catholic cousin, Mary, Queen of Scots. Greater Spanish success in the Netherlands, raids by the Spanish and English on each other's shipping, and Elizabeth's execution of Mary in 1587 prompted Philip to order an invasion of England. A fleet (*armada*) of Spanish warships sailed in 1588.

"The enterprise of England," as the plan was called in Spain, represented an astounding logistical effort. The Armada was supposed to clear the English Channel of English ships in order to permit an invading force—troops under Parma in the Netherlands—to cross on barges. The sheer number of ships required for the undertaking—about 130—meant that some, inevitably, were slower supply ships, or vessels designed for the more protected waters of the Mediterranean. The English also had the advantage in arms, since they had better long-range artillery and better-trained gunners.

When the Armada entered the Channel on July 29, the English harassed the Spanish with artillery from a distance without sustaining much damage themselves. Parma could not get his men readied on their barges quickly enough once the fleet's presence in the Channel had been confirmed by messenger, nor could the fleet protect itself while waiting offshore. On the night of August 7 the English launched eight fire ships—burning vessels set adrift to deliver arson—into the anchored Spanish fleet. At dawn on the next day, they attacked the weakened fleet off Gravelines°, sank many ships, and dispersed what remained. (See the box "Reading Sources: Secret Dispatches from the Venetian Ambassador in Spain.")

---

Utrecht (OO-trekt)

Gravelines (grahv-LEEN)

*Because it so heavily depended on its trading empire, Venice closely monitored developments at foreign courts. The Venetian ambassador at the Spanish court sent these reports back about the Spanish Armada. Note that the most sensitive material (in italics here) was sent in code. What differences do you notice between the encoded dispatches and the others? What seems to be the ambassador's attitude toward Philip and his invincible fleet? What can you learn from these dispatches about how fast and how accurately news traveled in sixteenth-century Europe?*

### April 30, 1588

Day by day we are expecting news that the Armada has sailed. It has drawn down the river to Belem at the mouth of the port, three miles from Lisbon. The blessing of the standard [flag] was performed with great pomp and many salvos of artillery. . . . Here in all the churches they make constant prayers; and the king himself is on his knees two or three hours every day before the sacrament. Everyone hopes that the greater the difficulties, humanly speaking, the greater will be the favor of God.

### June 4, 1588

The Armada set sail from Lisbon at length on the twenty-ninth of last month, a Sunday. . . . They are now waiting the news of its arrival at Corunna to embark more troops, and then to sail. I have from time to time reported the great preparations which have been made; but we here must expect news of its progress from other quarters now, unless the peace is effected in Flanders.

### July 12, 1588

*The wiser wonder what can induce the king to insist, quite against his natural temper, that the Armada shall give battle to the English, who are known to be awaiting the attack with eager courage, and so they surmise that, over and above the belief that God will be on his side, two motives urge the king to this course; first, that he has some secret understandings which will fail if there is any delay; secondly, that these expenses of a million of gold a month cannot be supported for long, and so he has resolved to try his fortune. . . .*

### August 20, 1588

Don Bernardino de Mendoza [the Spanish ambassador in France] announces from France, in letters of the second of August, that the Armada has given battle to the English, sunk some of their ships, won a great victory and passed on to join the duke of Parma; but the report is so confused, and that ambassador is so accustomed to deceive himself, that they are waiting confirmation of the news. . . .

### September 6, 1588

*The bad news received in dispatches from the duke of Parma, and dated the tenth of August . . . pain the king and the court all the more that they were unexpected, and moreover quite contrary to the news sent by [Mendoza], who by three different couriers had confirmed . . . that [the Armada] had sunk many of the enemy and was on the point of effecting a junction with the Duke of Parma. . . . It is a blessing that the bad news did not reach Spain while the king was suffering from fever, for though His Majesty professes to allow no occurrence to disturb his equanimity, yet this war moves him in such a way as to prove clearly that on other occasions he was only acting and that now he is unable to do so, perhaps because this war is entirely conducted by himself alone and that it should not succeed brings to light all his anxiety.*

Source: *The Pursuit of Power: Venetian Ambassadors' Reports on Turkey, France and Spain in the Age of Philip II, 1560–1600*, by James C. Davis, editor and translator. English translation copyright © 1970 by James C. Davis. Reprinted by permission of HarperCollins Publishers, Inc.

**www** For additional information on this topic, go to college.hmco.com/students.

---

The Battle at Gravelines was the first major artillery battle by sailing ships and helped set the future course of naval warfare. It was a disaster for Philip's hopes and for thousands of sailors and soldiers in Spanish pay. Many of the surviving ships sank in bad weather or were forced into hostile harbors as the Armada sailed for home around the northern tip of the British Isles (see Map 15.1). Less than half of Philip's great fleet made it back to Spain.

## Successes at Home and Around the Mediterranean

Despite his bountiful overseas empire and his preoccupation with the Netherlands, many of Philip's interests still centered on the Mediterranean. Spain and the kingdom of Naples had exchanged trade for centuries. Newer ties had been forged with the duchy of Milan and the city-

**The Battle of Lepanto**    On October 7, 1571, vessels of the Holy League (Spain, Venice, and the papacy) defeated the Ottoman fleet off the coast of Greece. It was the last great battle between galleys—the oared warships that had dominated Mediterranean waters since ancient times. The Ottomans never again contested for power in the western Mediterranean, but they rebounded to eclipse Venice in the east.    *(Courtesy, National Maritime Museum)*

state of Genoa, whose bankers were financiers to the Spanish monarchy. It was in his kingdoms of Spain and their Mediterranean sphere of interest that Philip made his power felt more effectively, though not without effort.

Philip's father, Charles V, had tried to secure the western Mediterranean against the Turks and their client states along the African coast, but it was under Philip that the Turkish challenge in the western Mediterranean receded. The Spanish allied temporarily with the papacy and Venice—both were concerned with Turkish naval power in the Mediterranean—and their combined navies inflicted a massive defeat on the Turkish navy at Lepanto, off the coast of Greece, in October 1571 (see Map 15.1). The Turks remained the leading power in the eastern Mediterranean, but their ability to threaten Spain and Spanish possessions in the West was over.

To Philip and his advisers, the Turks represented a potential internal threat as well, since it was feared that they might incite rebellion among his Muslim subjects. These were the nominally Christian descendants of the Muslims of Granada, who had been conquered by the Spanish in 1492. Called *moriscos,* they had been forced

to convert to Christianity in 1504 or be expelled from Spain. Yet no serious effort had been made to teach them Christian beliefs in their own language (Arabic), and they had not been assimilated into Spanish society. Philip inaugurated a new wave of persecution and provoked a massive rebellion by the moriscos that began on Christmas Day in 1568. The revolt took two years to suppress. After it was crushed, the moriscos of Granada were forcibly exiled and dispersed farther north in Spain.

Philip's power in each of his Spanish kingdoms was limited by the traditional privileges of towns, nobility, and clergy. In Aragon, for example, he could raise revenues only by appealing to local assemblies, the Cortes°. Philip made significant inroads into Aragonese independence by the end of his reign, however. Noble feuds and peasant rebellions in Aragon during the 1580s provided a pretext for sending in veteran troops from the Netherlands campaigns to establish firmer royal control. Philip was successful in the long run in Aragon, as he had not been in the Netherlands, because he used ade-

**Cortes** (core-TEZ)

quate force but tempered it afterward with constitutional changes that were cleverly moderate. He cemented the peace by appearing in Aragon in person, in the words of a contemporary, "like a rainbow at the end of a storm."[2]

In Castile, the arid kingdom in the center of the Iberian Peninsula, the king was able to levy taxes with greater ease but only because of concessions that gave nobles undisputed authority over their peasants. Philip established his permanent capital, Madrid, and his principal residence, the Escorial, there. The Spanish Empire became more and more Castilian as the reign progressed, with royal advisers and counselors increasingly drawn only from the Castilian elite. Yet the rural economy of Castile was stunted by the dual oppression of landholders and royal tax collectors.

Philip also invaded and annexed Portugal in 1580, temporarily unifying the Iberian Peninsula. The annexation was ensured by armed force but had been preceded by careful negotiation to guarantee that Philip's claim to the throne—through his mother—would find some support within the country. When Philip died in 1598, he was old and ill, a man for whom daily life had become a painful burden. His Armada had been crushed; the Netherlands had slipped through his fingers. Yet he had learned from his mistakes and had been more successful, by his own standards, in other regions that he ruled.

### Spain in Decline, 1600–1648

Spain steadily lost ground economically and strategically after the turn of the century. Imports of silver declined. The American mines were exhausted, and the natives forced to work in them were decimated by European diseases and brutal treatment. Spain's economic health was further threatened by the very success of its colonies: local industries in the Americas began to produce goods formerly obtained from Spain. The increasing presence of English, French, and Dutch shipping in the Americas provided colonists with rival sources for the goods they needed. Often these competitors could offer their goods more cheaply than the Spanish, for Spanish productivity was low and prices were high because of the inflationary effects of the influx of precious metals.

Spain renewed hostilities with the United Provinces in 1621, after the truce of 1609 had expired. Philip IV (r. 1621–1665) also aided his Habsburg cousins in the Thirty Years' War in the Holy Roman Empire (see page 523). Squeezed for troops and revenue for these commitments, other Spanish territories revolted. The uprisings reflected both economic distress and unresolved issues of regional autonomy. Castile bore the brunt of the financial support of the state. The chief minister to Philip IV, Gaspar de Guzmán, Count Olivares° (1587–1645), was an energetic Castilian aristocrat determined to distribute the burdens of government more equitably among the various regions of Spain. His policies provoked rebellions in Catalonia and Portugal.

In Catalonia, a province of the kingdom of Aragon, the revolt began as a popular uprising against the billeting of troops. At one point Catalan leaders invited French troops to defend them and solemnly transferred their loyalty to the French king in the hope that he would respect their autonomy. Spain resumed control only in 1652, after years of military struggle and promises to respect Catalan liberties.

In Portugal a war of independence began in 1640, also launched by popular revolt. The Spanish government tried to restore order with troops under the command of a leading Portuguese prince, John, duke of Braganza. The duke, however, was the nearest living relative to the last king of Portugal, and he seized this opportunity to claim the crown of Portugal for himself. Although war dragged on until 1668, the Portuguese under John IV (r. 1640–1656) succeeded in winning independence from Spain.

As a result of these uprisings, Count Olivares resigned in disgrace in 1643. In 1647 upheaval would shake Spain's Italian possessions of Sicily and Naples. By mid-century Spain had lost its position as the pre-eminent state in Europe.

## RELIGIOUS AND POLITICAL CONFLICT IN FRANCE AND ENGLAND

I̅N the second half of the sixteenth century France was convulsed by civil war that had both religious and political causes. Although a temporary resolution was achieved by 1598, the kingdom was still divided by religion and by military and political challenges to royal authority. England, in contrast, was spared political and religious upheaval in the second half of the century, in part because of the talents and long life of its ruler, Elizabeth I. But in the seventeenth century constitutional and religious dissent began to reinforce each other in new ways and dramatically threatened royal power.

---

**Olivares** (oh-lih-VAR-ez)

## The French Religious Wars, 1562–1598

Civil war wracked France from 1562 until 1598. As in the Netherlands, the conflicts in France had religious and political origins and international ramifications. The French monarch, like Philip, was unable to monopolize military power. In 1559 the king of France, Henry II (r. 1547–1559), had concluded the Peace of Cateau-Cambrésis with Philip II, ending the Habsburg-Valois Wars, but had died in July of that year from wounds suffered at a tournament held to celebrate the new treaty. His death was a political disaster. Great noble families vied for influence over his 15-year-old son, Francis II (r. 1559–1560). The queen mother, Catherine de' Medici° (1519–1589), worked carefully and intelligently to balance the nobles' interests. She gained greater authority when, in late 1560, the sickly Francis died and was succeeded by his brother, Charles IX—a 10-year-old for whom Catherine was officially the regent. But keeping the conflicts among the great courtiers from boiling over into civil war proved impossible.

In France, as elsewhere, noble conflict invariably had a violent component. Noblemen carried swords and daggers and were accompanied by armed entourages. Although they relied on patronage and army commands from the Crown, the Crown depended on their services. Provincial landholdings, together with the royal offices they enjoyed, afforded enough resources to support private warfare, and the nobles assumed the right to wage it.

In addition, religious tension was rising throughout France. (Henry II had welcomed the 1559 treaty in part because he wanted to turn his attention to "heresy.") Public preaching by and secret meetings of Protestants (known as "Huguenots°" in France) were causing unrest in towns. At court members of leading noble families—including the Bourbons, who were princes of royal blood—had converted to Protestantism and worshiped openly in their rooms in the palace. In 1561 Catherine convened a national religious council, known as the Colloquy of Poissy°, to reconcile the two faiths. When it failed, she chose provisional religious toleration as the only practical course and issued a limited edict of toleration in the name of the king in January 1562.

The edict led only to further unrest. Ignoring its restrictions, Protestants armed themselves, while townspeople of both faiths insulted and attacked one another at worship sites and religious festivals. In March 1562 the armed retainers of a Catholic duke killed a few dozen Protestants gathered in worship at Vassy°, near one of the duke's estates. The killing, in bringing the military power of the nobility to bear on the broader problem of religious division, sparked the first of six civil wars. In some ways the initial conflict was decisive. The Protestant army lost the principal pitched battle of the war in December 1562. This defeat checked the growth of the Protestant movement by reducing the appeal of the movement to nobles. The peace edict granted in 1563 curtailed the reach of the Huguenot movement; the limited rights granted to Protestants in the Crown's edict made it difficult for Protestants in towns—where the vast majority of them lived—to worship. But if the Protestants were not powerful enough to win, neither were they weak enough to be decisively beaten.

The turning point most obvious to contemporaries came a decade later. The Protestant faction was still represented at court by the Bourbon princes and by the very able and influential nobleman Gaspard de Coligny°, related to the Bourbons by marriage. Coligny was pressing the king for a war against Spain in order to aid Protestant rebels in the Netherlands. Opposed to entanglement in another war against Spain and alarmed by rumors of Huguenot armies massing outside Paris, Charles IX (r. 1560–1574) and his mother authorized royal guards to murder Coligny and other Protestant leaders on August 24, 1572—Saint Bartholomew's Day. Coligny's murder touched off a massacre of Protestants throughout Paris and, once news from Paris had spread, throughout the kingdom.

The Saint Bartholomew's Day Massacre revealed the degree to which religious differences had strained the fabric of community life. Neighbor murdered neighbor in an effort to rid the community of heretical pollution; bodies of the dead, including Coligny's, were mutilated. Gathered in the south of France, the remaining Huguenot forces vowed "never [to] trust those who have so often and so treacherously broken faith and the public peace."[3] Huguenot writers published tracts arguing that royal power was by nature limited and that rebellion was justified against tyrants who overstepped their legitimate authority.

Further war produced the inevitable truces and limited toleration, but many Catholics also renounced reconciliation. Some noblemen formed a Catholic league to fight in place of the weakened monarchy. Charles's brother, Henry III (r. 1574–1589), was another king of limited abilities. Middle-aged, Henry had no children. The heir to his throne was the Protestant Henry of Navarre, and the

---

de' Medici (day MAY-di-chi)  **Huguenots** (HEW-guh-nots)
**Poissy** (pwa-SEE)

**Vassy** (vah-SEE)
**Gaspard de Coligny** (gas-PAR duh koh-leen-YEE)

## THE FRENCH SUCCESSION, 1515–1715

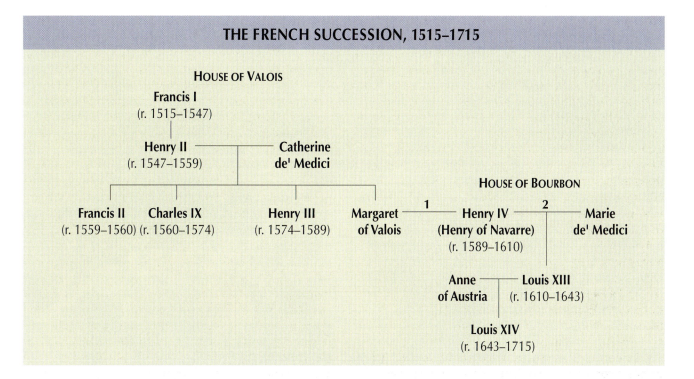

HOUSE OF VALOIS

**Francis I**
(r. 1515–1547)

**Henry II** ———— **Catherine**
(r. 1547–1559)         **de' Medici**

HOUSE OF BOURBON

**Francis II**    **Charles IX**         **Henry III**      **Margaret**    1    **Henry IV**    2    **Marie**
(r. 1559–1560) (r. 1560–1574)        (r. 1574–1589)     **of Valois**         **(Henry of Navarre)**         **de' Medici**
                                                                       (r. 1589–1610)

**Anne** ———— **Louis XIII**
**of Austria**         (r. 1610–1643)

**Louis XIV**
(r. 1643–1715)

assumption of the throne by a Protestant was unimaginable to the zealous Catholic faction at court and to many ordinary Catholics. By the end of Henry III's reign, the king had almost no royal authority left to wield. He was forced to cooperate with first one of the warring parties and then another. In December 1588 he resorted to murdering two courtiers who led the ultra-Catholic faction; in turn he was murdered by a priest in early 1589.

Henry of Navarre, the Bourbon prince who became Henry IV (r. 1589–1610), had to fight for his throne. He faced Catholic armies now subsidized by Philip II of Spain, an extremist Catholic city government in Paris, and subjects who were tired of war but mainly Catholic, and he could count on only meager support from Protestants abroad. Given these obstacles, the politically astute Henry agreed to convert to Catholicism.

After his conversion in 1593, the wars continued for a time, but after thirty years of civil strife many of Henry's subjects believed that only rallying to the monarchy could save France from chaos. Nobles grew increasingly disposed, for both psychological and practical reasons, to cooperate with the Crown. Service to a successful king could be a source of glory, and Henry was personally esteemed because he was a talented general and brave, gregarious, and charming. The nobility forced the citizens of Paris and other cities to accept Henry's authority.

The civil war period thus proved to be an important phase in the incremental accommodation of the nobility to the power of the state.

In April 1598 Henry granted toleration for the Huguenot minority in a royal edict proclaimed in the city of Nantes°. The Edict of Nantes was primarily a repetition of provisions from the most generous edicts that had ended the various civil wars. Nobles were allowed to practice the Protestant faith on their estates; townspeople were granted more limited rights to worship in selected towns in each region. Protestants were also guaranteed rights of self-defense—specifically, the right to maintain garrisons in about two hundred towns. About half of these garrisons would be paid for by the Crown. (See the box "The Continuing Experiment: Tolerating Religious Diversity: The Edict of Nantes.")

The problem was that the Edict of Nantes, like any royal edict, could be revoked by the king at any time. Moreover, the provision allowing Protestants to keep garrisoned towns reflected concessions to Protestant aristocrats, who could support their followers by paid garrison duty. It also reflected the assumption that living peacefully amid religious diversity might prove to be impossible. Thus, although Henry IV ended the French religious wars, he

**Nantes** (NAHNT)

**The Entry of Henry IV into Paris After the Religious Wars**    The king is depicted here as the magnanimous victor, and the residents of the city are shown as both submissive and grateful.    *(Réunion des Musées Nationaux/Art Resource, NY)*

had not solved the problem of religious and political division within France.

### The Consolidation of Royal Authority in France, 1598–1643

During Henry IV's reign, France recovered from the long years of civil war. Population and productivity began to grow; the Crown encouraged internal improvements to facilitate commerce. Henry's chief minister, Maximilien de Béthune°, duke of Sully° (1560–1641), increased royal revenue by nibbling away at traditional local self-

---

Béthune (bay-TOON)    Sully (soo-LEE)

government and control of taxation. He succeeded in creating a budget surplus and in extending mechanisms of centralized government.

Yet Henry's regime was stable only in comparison with the preceding years of civil war. The power of the great nobility had not been definitively broken. Moreover, the king had agreed to a provision, known as the *paulette* (named for the functionary who first administered it), that allowed royal officeholders not merely to own their offices but also to pass on those offices to their heirs in return for the payment of an annual fee. Primarily a device to raise revenue after decades of civil war, the paulette also helped cement the loyalty of royal bureaucrats at a critical time, particularly that of the royal

# Tolerating Religious Diversity: The Edict of Nantes

**H**enry IV of France proclaimed this edict of toleration in 1598 in order to end all pretext for civil war over the issue of religion. The Edict of Nantes ensured that Catholicism would remain pre-eminent but tried also to guarantee the rights of Protestants within France. The effort at toleration proved very fragile, however. Some of the privileges granted Protestants were withdrawn by Henry's son, and the entire edict was revoked in 1685 by Henry's grandson. Full civil equality for Protestants and Jews in France was not achieved until almost two hundred years after Henry's edict.

Henry, by the grace of God king of France . . . to all to whom these presents come, greeting: . . .

We have, by this perpetual and irrevocable edict, established and proclaimed. . . . First, that the recollection of everything done by one party or the other [in the later civil wars] . . . and during all the preceding period of troubles, remain obliterated and forgotten, as if no such things had ever happened.

We ordain that the Catholic Apostolic and Roman religion shall be restored and reestablished in all places and localities of this our kingdom . . . where the exercise of the same has been interrupted, . . . forbidding very expressly all persons, of whatsoever estate, quality, or condition, from troubling, molesting, or disturbing ecclesiastics in the celebration of divine service, in the enjoyment or collections of tithes, fruits or revenues of their benefices. . . .

And in order to leave no occasion for troubles or differences between our subjects, we . . . herewith permit, those of the said religion called Reformed [Protestants] to live and abide in all the cities and places of this our kingdom . . . without being annoyed, molested, or compelled to do anything in the matter of religion contrary to their consciences. . . .

We very expressly forbid to all those of the said religion its exercise, either in respect to ministry, regulation, discipline, or the public instruction of children . . . otherwise than in the places permitted and granted by the present edict. . . .

We also forbid all our subjects . . . from carrying off by force or persuasion, against the will of their parents, the children of the said religion, in order to cause them to be baptized or confirmed in the Catholic Apostolic and Roman Church; and the same is forbidden to those of the said religion called Reformed. . . .

Books concerning the said religion called Reformed may not be printed and publicly sold, except in cities and places where the public exercise of the said religion is permitted.

We ordain that there shall be no difference . . . made in respect to the said religion, in receiving pupils to be instructed in universities, colleges, and schools; nor in receiving the sick and poor into hospitals, retreats, and public charities.

## QUESTIONS

1. In what ways and to what degree does the edict establish mutual toleration of the two religions?

2. What barriers to civil and religious peace does the edict seem to anticipate?

SOURCE: James Harvey Robinson, *Readings in European History,* vol. 2 (Boston and New York: Ginn, 1906), pp. 183–185.

---

judges of the supreme law court, the Parlement of Paris, who had recently agreed to register the Edict of Nantes only under duress. However, the paulette made royal officeholders largely immune from royal control since their posts were now in effect property, like the landed property of the traditional nobility.

In 1610 a fanatical Catholic assassinated Henry IV. Henry's death brought his 9-year-old son, Louis XIII (r. 1610–1643), to the throne with Louis's mother, Marie de' Medici, serving as regent. Marie was disgraced when her unpopular leading minister—resented for monopo-lizing patronage—was assassinated with Louis's approval in 1617.

Four years later Louis faced a major rebellion by his Huguenot subjects in southwestern France. Huguenots felt that Louis's recent marriage to a Spanish princess and other ominous policies meant that royal support for toleration was wavering. Certain Huguenot nobles initiated fighting as a show of force against the king. The wars persisted, on and off, for eight years, as the French royal troops, like the Spanish in the Netherlands, had difficulty breaching the defenses of even small fortress towns. The main Huguenot stronghold was the well-fortified port city of La Rochelle, which had grown wealthy from European and overseas trade. Not until the king took the city, after a siege lasting more than a year and costing thousands of lives, did the Protestants accept a peace on royal terms.

The Peace of Alais° (1629) reaffirmed the policy of religious toleration but rescinded the Protestants' military and political privileges. It was a political triumph for the Crown because it deprived French Protestants of the means for further rebellion while reinforcing their dependence on the Crown for religious toleration. Most of the remaining great noble leaders began to convert to Catholicism.

The Peace of Alais was also a personal triumph for the king's leading minister, who crafted the treaty and who had directed the bloody siege that made it possible. Armand-Jean du Plessis° (1585–1642), Cardinal Richelieu°, came from a provincial noble family and rose in the service of the queen mother. He was admired and feared for his skill in the political game of seeking and bestowing patronage—a crucial skill in an age when elites received offices and honors through carefully cultivated relationships at court. His control of many lucrative church posts gave him the resources to build up a large network of clients. He and the king—whose sensitive temperament Richelieu handled adeptly—formed a lasting partnership that had a decisive impact not only on French policy but also on the entire shape of the French state.

Richelieu favored an aggressive foreign policy to counter what he believed still to be the greatest threat to the French crown: the Spanish Habsburgs. When war resumed between the Netherlands and Spain after their truce expired in 1621 (see page 526), Richelieu sent troops to attack Spanish possessions in Italy. In the 1630s, with the king's full confidence, he superintended large-scale fighting against Spain in the Netherlands itself, as well as in Italy, and he began subsidizing Swedish and German Protestant armies fighting the Habsburgs in Germany.

Richelieu's policies were opposed by many people, who saw taxes double, then triple, in just a few years. Many courtiers and provincial elites favored keeping a tenuous peace with Spain, a fellow Catholic state, and objected to alliances with German Protestants. They were alarmed by the increasing taxes and by the famine, disease, and, above all, the revolts that accompanied the peasants' distress. Their own status was also directly

threatened by Richelieu's monopoly of royal patronage and by his creation of new offices, which diluted and undermined their power. In 1632, for example, Richelieu created the office of *intendant*. Intendants had wide powers for defense and administration in the provinces that overrode the established bureaucracy.

By 1640 Richelieu's ambitious foreign policy seemed to be bearing fruit. The French had won territory along their northern and eastern borders by their successes against Habsburg forces. But when Richelieu and Louis XIII died within five months of each other, in December 1642 and May 1643, Richelieu's legacy was tested. Louis XIII was succeeded by his 5-year-old son, and the warrior-nobility, as well as royal bureaucrats, would waste little time before challenging the Crown's new authority.

## Precarious Stability in England: The Reign of Elizabeth I, 1558–1603

England experienced no civil wars during the second half of the sixteenth century, but religious dissent challenged the stability of the monarchy. In Elizabeth I (r. 1558–1603), England—in stark contrast to France—possessed an able and long-lived ruler. Elizabeth was well educated in the humanistic tradition and was already an adroit politician at the age of 25, when she acceded to the throne at the death of her Catholic half sister, Mary Tudor (r. 1553–1558).

Elizabeth faced the urgent problem of reaching a policy of consensus in religious matters. Her father, Henry VIII (r. 1509–1547), had broken away from the Catholic Church for political reasons but had retained many Catholic doctrines and practices. A Calvinist-inspired Protestantism had been prescribed for the Church of England by the advisers of Henry's successor, Elizabeth's young half brother, Edward VI (r. 1547–1553). True Catholicism, such as Mary had tried to reimpose, was out of the question. The Roman church had never recognized Henry VIII's self-made divorce and thus regarded Elizabeth as a bastard with no right to the throne.

Elizabeth adopted a cleverly moderate solution and used force, where necessary, to maintain it. In 1559 Parliament passed a new Act of Supremacy, which restored the monarch as head of the Church of England. Elizabeth dealt with opposition to the act by arresting bishops and lords whose votes would have blocked its passage by Parliament. Elizabeth and most of her ministers, all moderate realists, were willing to accept some flexibility in personal belief. For example, the official prayer book in use in Edward's day was revised to include elements of both traditional and radical interpretations of Commu-

---

**Alais** (ah-LAY)  **du Plessis** (doo pleh-SEE)
**Richelieu** (RISH-el-yeuh)

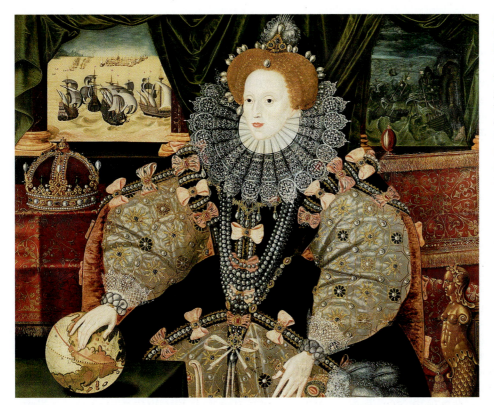

**Elizabeth I: The Armada Portrait**
Both serene and resolute, Elizabeth is flanked by "before" and "after" glimpses of the Spanish fleet; her hand rests on the globe in a gesture of dominion that also memorializes the circumnavigation of the globe by her famous captain, Sir Francis Drake, some years before.

*(By kind permission of Marquess of Tavistock and Trustees of Bedford Estate)*

nion. But church liturgy, clerical vestments, and, above all, the hierarchical structure of the clergy closely resembled Catholic practices. The Act of Uniformity required all worship to be conducted according to the new prayer book. Although uniformity was required in worship, Elizabeth was careful, in her words, not to "shine beacons into her subjects' souls."

Catholicism continued to be practiced, especially by otherwise loyal nobility and gentry in the north of England, who worshiped privately on their estates. But priests returning from exile beginning in the 1570s, most newly imbued with the proselytizing zeal of the Counter-Reformation (the Catholic response to the Protestant Reformation), practiced it more visibly and were zealously prosecuted for their boldness. In the last twenty years of Elizabeth's reign, approximately 180 Catholics were executed for treason, two-thirds of them priests. (By 1585 being a Catholic priest in itself was a crime.)

In the long run, the greater threat to the English crown came from the most radical Protestants in the realm, known (by their enemies initially) as Puritans. Puritanism was a broad movement for reform of church practice along familiar Protestant lines: an emphasis on Bible reading, preaching, and private scrutiny of conscience; a de-emphasis on institutional ritual and cleri-

cal authority. Most Puritans had accepted Elizabeth's religious compromise for practical reasons but grew increasingly alienated by her insistence on clerical authority and her refusal to change any elements of the original religious settlement. A significant Presbyterian underground movement began to form among them. Presbyterians wanted to dismantle the episcopacy—the hierarchy of priests and bishops—and to govern the church instead with councils, called "presbyteries," that included lay members of the congregation. Laws were passed late in the queen's reign to enable the Crown to prosecute more easily, and even to force into exile, anyone who attended "nonconformist" (non-Anglican) services.

The greatest challenge Elizabeth faced from Puritans came in Parliament, where they were well represented by many literate gentry. Parliament met only when called by the monarch, and in theory members could merely voice opinions and complaints. Initiating legislation and prescribing policy were beyond its purview. However, only Parliament could vote taxes. Further, since it had in effect helped constitute royal authority by means of the two Acts of Supremacy, Parliament's supposedly consultative role had been expanded by the monarchy itself. During Elizabeth's reign, Puritans capitalized on Parliament's enlarged scope, using meetings to press for further religious reform. In 1586 they went so far as to introduce bills calling for an end to the episcopacy and the Anglican prayer book. Elizabeth had to resort to imprisoning one Puritan leader to end debate on the issue and on Parliament's right to address it.

Also during Elizabeth's reign, efforts at English expansion in the New World began, in the form of unsuccessful attempts at colonization and successful raids on Spanish possessions. However, the main focus of her foreign policy remained Europe itself. Elizabeth, like all her forebears, felt her interests tightly linked to the independence of the Netherlands, whose towns were a major outlet for English wool. Philip II's aggressive policy in the Netherlands increasingly alarmed her, especially in view of France's weakness. She began to send small sums of money to the rebels and allowed their ships access to southern English ports, from which they could raid Spanish-held towns on the Netherlands' coast. In 1585, in the wake of the duke of Parma's successes against the rebellions, she committed troops to help the rebels.

Her decision was a reaction not only to the threat of a single continental power dominating the Netherlands but also to the threat of Catholicism. From 1579 to 1583 the Spanish had helped the Irish fight English domination and were involved in several plots to replace Elizabeth with her Catholic cousin, Mary, Queen of Scots. These threats occurred as the return of Catholic exiles to England peaked. The victory over the Spanish Armada in 1588 was quite rightly celebrated, for it ended any Catholic threat to Elizabeth's rule.

The success against the Armada has tended to overshadow other aspects of Elizabeth's foreign policy, particularly with regard to Ireland. Since the twelfth century an Anglo-Irish state dominated by great princely families had been loosely supervised from England, but most of Ireland remained under the control of Gaelic chieftains. Just as Charles V and Philip II attempted to tighten their governing mechanisms in the Netherlands, so did Henry VIII's minister, Thomas Cromwell, streamline control of outlying areas such as Wales and Anglo-Ireland. Cromwell proposed that the whole of Ireland be brought under English control partly by the established mechanism of feudal ties: the Irish chieftains were to pay homage as vassals to the king of England.

Under Elizabeth this legalistic approach gave way to virtual conquest. Elizabeth's governor, Sir Henry Sidney, appointed in 1565, inaugurated a policy whereby Gaelic lords, by means of various technicalities, could be entirely dispossessed of their lands. Any Englishman capable of raising a private force could help enforce these dispossessions and settle his conquered lands as he saw fit. This policy provoked stiff Irish resistance, which was viewed as rebellion and provided the rationale for further military action, more confiscations of lands, and more new English settlers. Eventually the Irish, with Spanish assistance, mounted a major rebellion, consciously Catholic and aimed against the "heretic" queen. The rebellion gave the English an excuse for brutal suppression and massive transfers of lands to English control. The political domination of the Irish was complete with the defeat, in 1601, of the Gaelic chieftain Hugh O'Neill, lord of Tyrone, who had controlled most of the northern quarter of the island. Although the English were unable to impose Protestantism on the conquered Irish, to Elizabeth and her English subjects the conquests in Ireland seemed as significant as the victory over the Spanish Armada.

The English enjoyed relative peace at home during Elizabeth's reign. However, her reign ended on a note of strain. The foreign involvements, particularly in Ireland, had been very expensive. Taxation granted by Parliament more than doubled during her reign, and local taxes further burdened the people. Price inflation related to government spending, social problems caused by returned unemployed soldiers, and a series of bad harvests heightened popular resentment against taxation. Despite her achievements, therefore, Elizabeth passed two problems on to her successors: unresolved religious tensions and financial instability. Elizabeth's successors would also find in Parliament an increasing focus of opposition to their policies.

## Rising Tensions in England, 1603–1642

In 1603 Queen Elizabeth died, and James VI of Scotland, the Protestant son of Mary, Queen of Scots, ascended to the English throne as James I (r. 1603–1625). Religious tensions between Anglicans and Puritans were temporarily quieted under James because of a plot, in 1605, by Catholic dissenters. The Gunpowder Plot, as it was called, was a conspiracy to blow up the palace housing both king and Parliament at Westminster. Protestants of all stripes once again focused not on their differences but on their common enemy, Catholics.

Financial problems were James's most pressing concern. Court life became more elaborate and an increasing drain on the monarchy's resources. James's extravagance was partly to blame for his financial problems, but so were pressures for patronage from courtiers. Added to the debts left from the Irish conflicts and wars with Spain were new military expenses as James helped defend the claims of his daughter and her husband, a German prince, to rule Bohemia (see page 525).

**Criticism of Monopolies**    Holders of royally granted monopolies were bitterly resented by English consumers and tradespeople alike, as this contemporary print reveals. The greedy beast pictured here controls even ordinary commodities such as pins, soap, and butter.    *(Courtesy of the Trustees of the British Museum)*

To raise revenue without Parliament's consent, James relied on sources of income that the Crown had enjoyed since medieval times: customs duties, wardship (the right to manage and liberally borrow from the estates of minor nobles), and the sale of monopolies, which conveyed the right to be sole agent for a particular kind of goods. To rebuild his treasury James increased the number of monopolies for sale and even created a new noble title—baronet—which he sold to socially ambitious commoners.

The monopolies were widely resented. Merchants objected to the arbitrary restriction of production and trade; common people found that they could no longer afford certain ordinary commodities, such as soap. Resentments among the nobility were sharpened, and general criticism of the court escalated, as James indulged in extreme favoritism of certain courtiers, including the corrupt George Villiers° (1592–1628), duke of Buckingham, who served as the king's first minister.

When James summoned Parliament to ask for funds in 1621, Parliament used the occasion to protest court corruption and the king's financial measures. The members revived the medieval procedure of impeachment and removed two royal ministers from office. In 1624, still faced with expensive commitments to Protestants abroad and in failing health, James again called Parliament, which voted new taxes but also openly debated the wisdom of the king's foreign policy.

Tensions between Crown and Parliament increased under James's son, Charles I (r. 1625–1649). One reason was the growing financial strain of foreign policy as well as the policies themselves. Charles declared war on Spain and supported the Huguenot rebels in France. Many wealthy merchants opposed this aggressive foreign policy because it disrupted trade. In 1626 Parliament was dissolved without granting any monies, in order to stifle its objections to royal policies. Instead, Charles levied a forced loan and did not hesitate to imprison gentry who refused to lend their money to the government.

Above all, Charles's religious policies were a source of controversy. Charles was personally inclined toward "high church" practices: an emphasis on ceremony and sacrament reminiscent of Catholic ritual. He also was a believer in Arminianism, a school of thought that rejected the Calvinist notion that God's grace cannot be earned, and hence emphasized the importance of the sacraments and the authority of the clergy. Charles's attempt to fashion the Church of England into an instrument that would reflect and justify royal claims to power put him on a collision course with gentry and aristocrats who leaned toward Puritanism.

Charles's views were supported by William Laud° (1573–1645), archbishop of Canterbury from 1633 and thus leader of the Church of England. He tried to impose changes in worship, spread Arminian ideas, and censor opposing views. He also challenged the redistribution of church property, which had occurred in the Reformation of the sixteenth century, and thereby alienated the gentry on economic as well as religious grounds.

Charles's style of rule worsened religious, political, and economic tensions. Cold and intensely private, he did not inspire confidence or have the charm or the political skills to disarm his opponents. His court was ruled by formal protocol, and access to the king was highly restricted—a serious problem in an age when proximity to the monarch was a guarantee of political power.

Revenue and religion dominated debate in the Parliament of 1628–1629, which Charles had called, once

---

**Villiers** (VIL-yerz)

**Laud** (LAWD)

again, to get funds for his foreign wars. In 1628 Parliament presented the king with a document called the Petition of Right, which protested his financial policies as well as arbitrary imprisonment. (Seventeen members of Parliament had been imprisoned for refusing loans to the Crown.) Though couched conservatively as a restatement of customary practice, the petition in fact claimed a tradition of expanded parliamentary participation in government. Charles dissolved Parliament in March 1629, having decided that the money he might extract was not worth the risk.

For eleven years Charles ruled without Parliament. When he was forced by necessity to summon it again in 1640, the kingdom was in crisis. Royal finances were in desperate straits, even though Charles had pressed collection of revenues far beyond traditional bounds. In 1634, for example, he had revived annual collection of "ship money"—a medieval tax levied on coastal districts to help support the navy during war. England, however, was not at war at that time, and the tax was levied not only on seaports but on inland areas, too.

The immediate crisis in 1640—and the reason for Charles's desperate need for money—was a rebellion in Scotland. Like Philip II in the Netherlands, Charles tried to rule in Scotland through a small council of men who did not represent the local elite. Worse, he also tried to force his "high church" practices on the Scots. The Scottish Church had been more dramatically reshaped during the Reformation and now was largely Presbyterian in structure. The result of Charles's policies was riots and rebellion. Unable to suppress the revolt in a first campaign in 1639, Charles was forced to summon Parliament to obtain funds to raise a more effective army.

But the Parliament that assembled in the spring of 1640 provided no help. Instead, members questioned the war with the Scots and other royal policies. Charles's political skills were far too limited for him to re-establish a workable relationship with Parliament under the circumstances. Charles dissolved this body, which is now known as the "Short Parliament," after just three weeks. Even more stinging than Charles's dissolution of the Parliament was the lack of respect he had shown the members: a number of them were harassed or arrested. Mistrust fomented by the eleven years in which Charles had ruled without Parliament thus increased.

Another humiliating and decisive defeat at the hands of the Scots later in 1640 made summoning another Parliament imperative. Members of the "Long Parliament" (it sat from 1640 to 1653) took full advantage of the king's predicament. Charles was forced to agree not to dissolve or adjourn Parliament without the members' consent and to summon Parliament at least every three

years. Parliament abolished many of his unorthodox and traditional sources of revenue and impeached and removed from office his leading ministers, including Archbishop Laud. The royal commander deemed responsible for the Scottish fiasco, Thomas Wentworth, earl of Strafford, was executed without trial in May 1641.

The execution of Strafford shocked many aristocrats in the House of Lords (the upper house of Parliament), as well as some moderate members of the House of Commons. Meanwhile, Parliament began debating the perennially thorny religious question. A bare majority of members favored abolition of Anglican bishops as a first step in thoroughgoing religious reform. Working people in London, kept apprised of the issues by the regular publication of parliamentary debates, demonstrated in support of that majority. Moderate members of Parliament, in contrast, favored checking the king's power but not upsetting the Elizabethan religious compromise.

An event that unified public and parliamentary opinion at a crucial time—a revolt against English rule in Ireland in October 1641—temporarily eclipsed these divisions and once again focused suspicion on the king. The broad consensus of anti-Catholicism once again became the temporary driving force in politics. Fearing that Charles would use Irish soldiers against his English subjects, Parliament demanded that it have control of the army to put down the rebellion. In November the Puritan majority introduced a document known as the "Grand Remonstrance," an appeal to the people and a long catalog of parliamentary grievances against the king. It was passed by a narrow margin, further setting public opinion in London against Charles. The king's remaining support in Parliament eroded in January 1642 when he attempted to arrest five leading members on charges of treason. The five escaped, and the stage was set for wider violence. The king withdrew from London, unsure he could defend himself there, and began to raise an army. In mid-1642 the kingdom stood at the brink of civil war.

# RELIGIOUS AND POLITICAL CONFLICT IN CENTRAL AND EASTERN EUROPE

THE Holy Roman Empire enjoyed a period of comparative quiet after the Peace of Augsburg halted religious and political wars in 1555. The 1555 agreement, which permitted rulers of the various states within the empire to impose either Catholicism or Lutheranism in their lands, proved to be a workable solution, for a time, to the problem of religious division. By the early seventeenth century, however, fresh causes of instability brought about renewed fighting. One factor was the rise of Calvinism, for which no provision had been necessary in 1555. Especially destabilizing was the drive by the Austrian Habsburgs to reverse the successes of Protestantism both in their own lands and in the empire at large and to solidify their control of their diverse personal territories. The result was a devastating conflict known as the Thirty Years' War (1618–1648).

Like conflicts elsewhere in Europe, the Thirty Years' War reflects religious tensions, regionalism versus centralizing forces, and dynastic and strategic rivalries between rulers. The war was particularly destructive because of the size of the armies and the degree to which army commanders evaded control by the states for which they fought. As a result of the war, the empire was eclipsed as a political unit by the regional powers that composed it. Meanwhile, a Polish state resembling the Habsburg territories in its regional diversity remained the dominant state in northeastern Europe. But it would soon face challenges, particularly from a powerful new state being crafted in Russia.

## Fragile Peace in the Holy Roman Empire, 1556–1618

The Austrian Habsburgs ruled over a diverse group of territories in the Holy Roman Empire, as well as northwestern Hungary (see Map 15.3). On his abdication in 1556, Emperor Charles V granted Habsburg lands in central Europe to his brother, Ferdinand (see the chart on page 509), who had long been the actual ruler there in Charles's stead. On Charles's death in 1558, Ferdinand was duly crowned emperor.

Though largely contiguous, Ferdinand's territories comprised independent duchies and kingdoms, each with its own institutional structure, and included speakers of Italian, German, and Czech, plus a few other languages. The non-German lands of Bohemia (the core of the modern Czech Republic) and Hungary had been distinct kingdoms since the High Middle Ages. Both states bestowed their crowns by election and had chosen Ferdinand, the first Habsburg to rule them, in separate elections in the 1520s and 1530s. Most of Hungary was now under Ottoman domination, but Bohemia, with its rich capital, Prague, was a wealthy center of population and culture.

Unlike the Netherlands, these linguistically and culturally diverse lands were still governed by highly decentralized institutions. Moreover, unlike their Spanish cousins, the Austrian Habsburgs made no attempt to impose religious uniformity in the late sixteenth century. Ferdinand was firmly Catholic but tolerant of reform efforts within the church. Both he and his son, Maximilian II (r. 1564–1576), believed that an eventual reunion of the Catholic and Protestant faiths might be possible. During his reign Maximilian worked to keep religious peace in the empire as a whole and granted limited rights of worship to Protestant subjects within his ancestral lands (separate territories more or less equivalent to modern Austria in extent). Catholicism and many strands of Protestantism flourished side by side in Maximilian's domains, above all in Hungary and, especially, Bohemia, which had experienced its own religious reform movement under Jan Hus in the fifteenth century.

Maximilian's son, Rudolf II (r. 1576–1612), shared the religious style of his father and grandfather. He was an energetic patron of the arts and humanist education and sponsored the work of scientists. Yet Rudolf was a weak leader politically and was challenged by his brother and ambitious cousins for control both of Habsburg lands and the empire itself. Meanwhile, the resurgence of Catholicism in the wake of the Council of Trent (1545–1563) had begun to shift the religious balance. Members of the Jesuit order arrived in Habsburg lands in the reign of Maximilian. Tough-minded and well trained, they established Catholic schools and became confessors and preachers to the upper classes. Self-confident Catholicism emerged as one form of cultural identity among the German-speaking ruling classes, and thus as a religious impetus to further political consolidation of all the Habsburg territories.

Resurgent Catholicism was evident, too, in the empire as a whole, where certain princes were confident they might now eliminate Protestantism, as their ancestors had failed to do. In the face of this challenge, certain Protestant princes formed a defensive pact known as the Evangelical Union in 1608. In response Catholic princes formed an alliance, the Holy League, the next year. A major war between the two alliances over a disputed territory was narrowly averted the following year. Like the English under Elizabeth, Habsburg subjects and peoples in the empire had enjoyed a period of calm in political and religious matters. Now, as in England, the stage was set for conflict of both kinds.

## The Thirty Years' War, 1618–1648

The Thirty Years' War was touched off in 1618 by a revolt against Habsburg rule in the kingdom of Bohemia. Bohemia was populous and prosperous; Rudolf II had made its bustling capital, Prague, his imperial capital. Its powerful and diverse Protestant community had wrested formal recognition of its right to worship from Rudolf and his younger brother, Matthias (r. 1612–1619).

**NORWAY**

**SWEDEN**

**FINLAND**

**SCOTLAND**
Edinburgh •

*North Sea*

**RUSSIA**

**ESTONIA**

**LIVONIA**

*Baltic Sea*

**IRELAND**
Dublin •

**DENMARK**

*JUTLAND*

**ENGLAND**

*SCHLESWIG*

Copenhagen •

Gdansk
(Danzig) •

**PRUSSIA**

Vilna •

London •

**UNITED PROVINCES**
Amsterdam •

Lübeck •
Hamburg •
**MECKLENBURG**

**POMERANIA**

**BRANDENBURG**
Berlin •

*Vistula*

**POLAND-LITHUANIA**

Warsaw •

*Dniester*

Essen •
Cologne •
**SPANISH NETHERLANDS**
Antwerp •

Magdeburg •

**SAXONY**

**SILESIA**

*Rhine*

Paris •

**UPPER PALATINATE**

**LOWER PALATINATE**
Metz •

**BOHEMIA**
Prague •

*MORAVIA*

*Elbe*

Nantes •

*Loire*

**BAVARIA**
Augsburg •

Salzburg •

**AUSTRIA**

Vienna •

*Danube*

Buda •
• Pest

*MOLDAVIA*

*BESSARABIA*

**FRANCE**

**FRANCHE-COMTÉ**

Zurich •
**SWITZERLAND**
Geneva •

*TYROL*
Trent •

*STYRIA*

*CARINTHIA*

**HUNGARY**

*TRANSYLVANIA*

**SAVOY**

*PIEDMONT*

Milan •
**GENOA**

**REPUBLIC OF VENICE**
Venice •

*CARNIOLA*

*CROATIA*

*SLAVONIA*

Belgrade •

**SERBIA**

*WALLACHIA*

**SPAIN**

*Ebro*

**TUSCANY**

**PAPAL STATES**

*BOSNIA HERZEGOVINA*

*Adriatic Sea*

**MONTENEGRO**

*CORSICA*
(To Genoa)

Rome •

**NAPLES**
Naples •

**BULGARIA**

Constantinople •

*Black Sea*

*BALEARIC IS.*

*SARDINIA*

*O T T O M A N   E M P I R E*

*Aegean Sea*

Palermo •

*SICILY*

Athens •

*CRETE*
(To Rep. of Venice)

*Mediterranean Sea*

**SWEDEN**

**DENMARK**

**BREMEN**

WISMAR

**POMERANIA**

**VERDEN**

**Legend:**
- Austrian Habsburg lands
- Spanish Habsburg lands
- Other German states
- Swedish lands by 1648
- Ottoman Empire and Tributary States
- Boundary of Holy Roman Empire

0 150 300 Km.
0 150 300 Mi.

**Map 15.3   Europe During the Thirty Years' War, 1618–1648**   The Thirty Years' War was fought largely within the borders of the Holy Roman Empire. It was the result of conflicts within the empire as well as the meddling of neighbors for their own strategic advantages.

Matthias was quickly succeeded by his cousin Ferdinand II (r. 1619–1637), who was the ideal Counter-Reformation prince and unlikely to honor these agreements. Educated by the Jesuits, Ferdinand sincerely believed that reimposing Catholicism was his Christian duty; he once stated that he would "sooner beg than rule over heretics."[4] He had virtually eliminated Protestantism, by persuasion as well as by compulsion, in the small duchy in southern Austria he had governed before assuming the throne.

Ferdinand would not tolerate the political independence of nobles and towns in Bohemia or the religious pluralism that independence defended. As Philip II had done in the Netherlands, Ferdinand appointed a regency council to govern in his name. That council enforced unpopular policies: the right to build new Protestant churches was denied, Bohemian crown lands were given to the Catholic Church, and non-Catholics were barred from serving in government.

On May 23, 1618, delegates to a Protestant assembly that had unsuccessfully petitioned Ferdinand to end his violations of earlier guarantees marched to the palace in Prague where the royal officials met. After a confrontation over their demands, the delegates "tried" the officials on the spot for treason and, literally, threw them out of the palace window. The incident became known as the "Defenestration of Prague" (from the Latin *fenestra*, or "window"). (The officials' lives were saved only because they fell into a pile of refuse in the moat.) The rebels proceeded to set up their own government.

This upstart Bohemian government officially deposed Ferdinand and elected a new Protestant king in 1619: Frederick, elector of the Palatinate and a Calvinist prince. His election had implications for the Holy Roman Empire as a whole because his role as leader of the territories in west-central Germany called the Lower and Upper Palatinate conveyed the right to be one of the seven electors who chose the emperor.

Emboldened by these events, Protestant subjects in other Habsburg lands asked for guarantees of freedom of worship similar to those enjoyed by Protestants in Bohemia. Other princes saw their chance to make political gains. For example, rival claimants to Habsburg rule in Hungary took up arms against Ferdinand.

The revolt in Bohemia set off a wider war because foreign rulers also felt their interests to be involved. The English king, James I, supported Frederick because Frederick was married to his daughter. Spain's supply routes north from Italy to the Netherlands passed next to Frederick's lands in western Germany. France's first interest was its rivalry with Spain; thus France kept its eye on the border principalities that were strategically important to Spain. In addition, France desired to keep Protestant as well as Catholic princes within the empire strong enough to thwart Austrian Habsburg ambitions. Thus, from the outset, the war was a conflict not only over the Habsburgs'

**The Defenestration of Prague**
This contemporary print memorializes the events of May 23, 1618. Bohemian Protestants tried two imperial officials for violating agreements that safeguarded their religious liberties. The two officials and their secretary were thrown out of the windows of Prague castle. *(Corbis)*

power in their own lands but also over the balance of religious and political power in the empire and in Europe (see Map 15.3).

Ferdinand secured aid from the Catholic duke of Bavaria and from his cousin, King Philip III (r. 1598–1621) of Spain, by promising them Frederick's lands in the Palatinate. By the fall of 1620 a Catholic army was closing in on Bohemia. On November 8, on a hillside near Prague, the Catholic force faced a Bohemian army that had received little aid from its Protestant allies. The Battle of White Mountain was a complete Catholic victory.

Despite the rout, fighting did not cease but instead became more widespread. The truce between Spain and the Netherlands, established in 1609, expired in 1621, and the nearby Lower Palatinate, now in Spanish hands, offered a staging point for Spanish forces and thus threatened the peace in that corner of the empire. Claiming to be a Protestant champion, the Protestant king of Denmark, Christian IV (r. 1588–1648), who was also duke of Holstein in northern Germany, sought to conquer additional German territory. His goals were to gain greater control over profitable German Baltic seaports and to defend himself against any Catholic attempt to seize northern German territory. Christian received little help from fellow Protestants, however. The Dutch were busy with Spain, the English were wary of fighting after Frederick's defeat, and Denmark's regional rivals, the Swedes, were uninterested in furthering Danish ambitions in the Baltic.

The confusing blend of politics and religion that motivated the Protestant rulers was also evident on the Catholic side. When imperial forces defeated Christian's armies in 1626, Catholic princes became alarmed at the possibility of greater imperial power in northern Germany. Led by the duke of Bavaria, they arranged a truce that resulted in Denmark's withdrawal from the fighting on relatively generous terms. At the same time, Protestants outside Bohemia saw the potential consequences of imperial victory and took up arms. As his armies defeated Christian, Ferdinand issued new edicts that in effect voided the religious settlement in place since 1555. His victorious armies brutally enforced his edicts wherever they passed.

Christian's rival, Gustav Adolf, king of Sweden (r. 1611–1632), now assumed the role of Protestant leader. An innovative military leader, Gustav Adolf hoped to gain territory along the Baltic seacoast, but personal aggrandizement also was one of his goals. His campaigns were capped by a victory over an imperial army at Breitenfeld°,

in Saxony, in 1631. After he was killed in battle in 1632, however, the tide turned in favor of Ferdinand's forces. A decisive imperial victory over a combined Swedish and German Protestant army at Nördlingen° in 1634 led to the Peace of Prague (1635), a general peace treaty favorable to Catholics.

The Peace of Prague brought only a temporary peace, however, because Ferdinand died shortly thereafter and French involvement increased now that other anti-Habsburg forces had been eclipsed. France tried to seize imperial territory along its own eastern border and generously subsidized continued fighting within the empire by channeling monies to Protestant princes and mercenaries there. The fighting dragged on. By the end of the Thirty Years' War order had disintegrated so completely in the wake of the marauding armies that both staunchly Catholic rulers and firmly Protestant ones allied with religious enemies to safeguard their states.

A comprehensive peace treaty became possible when France withdrew its sponsorship of the fighting in order to concentrate on its conflict with Spain. The French wanted only a workable balance of power in the empire, which was achieved once they and their allies convincingly defeated imperial forces in 1645. More urgent to the French was the continued rivalry with the Spanish Habsburgs for control of territory along France's eastern and northern borders and in Italy. A defeat by France in the Spanish Netherlands in 1643 had convinced Spain to concentrate on that rivalry, too, and fighting between them continued separately until 1659. Negotiations for peace had begun in 1643 among war-weary states of the empire and resulted in a group of agreements known as the Peace of Westphalia° in 1648.

## The Effects of the War

The Thirty Years' War ruined the economy and decimated the population in many parts of the empire and had long-term political consequences for the empire as a whole. One reason for the war's devastation was a novel application of firepower to warfare that increased both the size of armies and their deadly force in battle. This was the use of volley fire, the arrangement of foot soldiers in parallel lines so that one line of men could fire while another reloaded. This tactic, pioneered in the Netherlands around the turn of the century, was further refined by Gustav Adolf of Sweden. Gustav Adolf amassed large numbers of troops and increased the rate of fire so that a virtually continuous barrage was maintained. He

---

**Breitenfeld** (BRIGHT-un-feld)

**Nördlingen** (NERD-ling-un)    **Westphalia** (west-FAIL-yuh)

**The Horrors of War** This painting by a seventeenth-century artist depicts an attack on a supply convoy by opposing troops. Control of supplies to feed and equip the increasing numbers of troops was one of the most important aspects of warfare. *(Staatsgalerie Aschaffenburg [Schloss], Bayerische Staatsgemäldesammlungen/ Godwin Alfen-ARTOTHEK)*

also used maneuverable field artillery to protect the massed infantry from cavalry charges.

Following Gustav Adolf's lead, armies of all the major states adopted these new offensive tactics. But defensive expertise—as in holding fortresses—also remained important, and pitched battles, such as at Nördlingen in 1634, still tended to be part of sieges. The costs in resources and human life of this kind of warfare reached unheard-of dimensions. Popular printed literature and court drama both condemned the horrors of the war.

Where fighting had been concentrated, as in parts of Saxony, between one-third and one-half of the inhabitants of rural villages and major towns may have disappeared. Many starved, were caught in the fighting, or were killed by marauding soldiers. The most notorious atrocity occurred in the aftermath of the siege of Magdeburg° in 1631. After the city surrendered to besieging Catholic

forces, long-deprived soldiers ate and drank themselves into a frenzy, raped and killed indiscriminately, and set fires that destroyed the town. Some victims of war migrated to other regions in search of peaceful conditions and work. Some joined the armies in order to survive. Others formed armed bands to fight off the soldiers or to steal back enough goods to live on.

Compounding these effects of war were the actions of armies hired by enterprising mercenary generals for whom loyalty to the princes who paid them took a back seat to personal advancement. They contracted to provide, supply, and lead troops and thus were more willing than the princes would have been to allow troops to live "economically" on plunder. States thus managed to field large armies but had not yet evolved the mechanisms fully to fund, and thus control, them.

The Peace of Westphalia, which ended fighting in the empire, was one of the most important outcomes of the war. The various treaties composing the peace effectively

---

**Magdeburg** (MAHG-duh-boorg)

put an end to religious war in the empire. Calvinism was recognized as a tolerated religion. The requirement that all subjects must follow their ruler's faith was retained, but some leeway was allowed for those who now found themselves under new rulers.

In political matters the treaties reflected some of the recent successes of the Swedes by granting them territory on the Baltic coast. France gained the important towns of Metz, Toul, and Verdun on its eastern border. Spain formally recognized the independence of the Netherlands.

The most important political outcome of the peace was a new balance of power in the empire. Most of the major Catholic and Protestant rulers extended their territories at the expense of smaller principalities and cities. The son of Frederick, Protestant king of Bohemia, received back the smaller of the two Palatine territories that his father had held. The Upper Palatinate—as well as the right to be a new elector of the emperor—was given to the powerful duke of Bavaria. The principalities within the empire were acknowledged, in the peace, to be virtually autonomous, both from the emperor and from one another. In addition, the constitution of the empire was changed to make it very difficult for one prince or a group of princes to disrupt the peace in their own interests. As a result, the agreements at Westphalia were the beginning of one hundred years of peace within the Holy Roman Empire.

Another outcome was that the Habsburgs, though weakened as emperors, were strengthened as rulers of their own hereditary lands on the eastern fringes of the empire. Except in Hungary, Protestantism—and its contrary political baggage—had been eliminated early in the wars, and the peace did not alter these circumstances. The Habsburgs moved their capital back to Vienna from Prague, and the government of their hereditary lands gained in importance as administration of the empire waned.

## Stability and Dynamism in Eastern Europe

On the southern frontier of Austrian Habsburg lands, the empire of the Ottoman Turks continued to control southeastern Europe in the late sixteenth and early seventeenth centuries. The Ottoman state had reached the practical limits of its expansion with the conquests of Suleiman I (r. 1520–1566), known to Europeans as "the Magnificent." Sporadic fighting between the Ottomans and the Habsburgs continued in Hungary, which the Ottomans largely controlled, but the fighting there was secondary to the Ottomans' rivalry with the Safavid rulers of Persia. The Ottomans succeeded in extending their territory eastward into modern Iraq, Azerbaijan, and Georgia at Safavid expense. Despite the Ottomans' many commitments and a succession of weak rulers, their presence in southeastern Europe remained secure, partly because they respected the cultural and religious diversity of their Christian subjects. Aristocratic and regional independence were factors, too: Christian princes, particularly in the Hungarian borderlands, found distant Turkish overlords more palatable than closer Habsburg ones. The naval defeat at Lepanto in 1571 (see page 512) had been a setback for the Ottomans, but they quickly rebuilt their fleet and re-established supremacy in the eastern Mediterranean.

Ottoman power was a constant presence in European affairs, but a more dynamic state in the late sixteenth century was the newly proclaimed empire in Russia (see Map 15.4). Through the late Middle Ages Muscovite princes had accumulated land and authority as they vied for pre-eminence with other principalities after the decline of Kievan Rus (modern Ukraine). Ivan III (r. 1462–1505) absorbed neighboring Russian principalities and ended Moscow's subservience to Mongol overlords. He then took the title of "Tsar," Russian for "Caesar." In 1547 his grandson, Ivan IV (r. 1533–1584), was officially proclaimed "Tsar of All the Russias" and became the first ruler to routinely use the title. For Russians this title placed Ivan IV in higher esteem than the neighboring Polish-Lithuanian and Swedish kings.

Ivan's use of the title reflects his imperial intentions, as he continued Moscow's push south, into lands that were once part of Kievan Rus, and east, against the Tatar states of Astrakhan, Kazan, and Sibir (Siberia). Within his expanding empire Ivan ruled as an autocrat. The practice of gathering tribute money for Mongol overlords had concentrated many resources in the hands of Muscovite princes. Ivan was able to bypass noble participation and intensify the centralization of government by creating ranks of officials loyal only to him. Part of his authority stemmed from his personality. He was willing, perhaps because of mental imbalance, to use ruthless methods—including torture and the murder of thousands of subjects—to enforce his will.

Ivan came to be called "the Terrible," from a Russian word meaning "awe-inspiring." Although a period of disputed succession to the throne known as the "Time of Troubles" followed Ivan's death in 1584, the foundations of the large and cohesive state he had built survived until a new dynasty of rulers was established in the seventeenth century.

Checking Russian expansion to the west was the commonwealth of Poland-Lithuania, a large, multi-ethnic state at the height of its power (see Map 15.4). The duchy

Map 15.4 **Two Empires in Eastern Europe, ca. 1600** Poland-Lithuania dominated the Baltic coast and its productive hinterland in the sixteenth century, but it would face increasing challenges for control of its eastern territories by the expanding Russian state.

of Lithuania had conquered the territories known as Ruthenia (comprising most of modern Belarus and Ukraine) in the fourteenth century. Then in 1386 a marriage had brought the duchy of Lithuania and the kingdom of Poland under a joint ruler. Like the union of Castile and Aragon in Spain, the union of Poland and Lithuania was initially only dynastic. But two hundred years later, in 1569, they were brought under a single set of institutions by the Treaty of Lublin. Even so, the two states retained distinct traditions. Poles spoke Polish, a Slavic language, and were primarily Catholic, although there were also large minorities of Protestants, Orthodox Christians, and Jews in Poland. Lithuanians, whose language was only distantly related to the Slavic languages, were mostly Catholic as well, although Orthodox Christianity predominated among the Ruthenians, who spoke a Slavic language related to both Russian and Polish. Poland-Lithuania was unusual among European states in that religious toleration was a long-standing practice and was even enshrined in law in 1573.

Valuable resources such as grain, timber, and other naval stores passed through Polish-controlled ports on the Baltic Sea on their way to western Europe. Poland itself also became an increasingly important source of grain for Spanish, French, and English cities. Russia and Sweden, however, challenged Polish control of the lucrative Baltic coast. Polish forces were able to defeat efforts by Ivan the Terrible to control Livonia (modern Latvia), with its important port of Riga°, and briefly placed a Polish claimant on the Russian throne during the Time of Troubles. They were not as successful against the Swedes, who, under the expansionist Gustav Adolf, took Riga and the Baltic coast to its north in 1621 (as part of the same drive for Baltic territory that lay behind his involvement in the Thirty Years' War). The Turks also were a constant threat to Poland-Lithuania on its southern border.

In addition to the foreign challenges it faced by virtue of its geography, Poland-Lithuania had internal weaknesses. It was a republic of the nobility, with a weak elected king at its head. (The elective crown was a tradition that had developed over centuries when the throne had been contested by rival claimants from within Poland or from other states.) The great nobles, whose fortunes increased with the grain trade, ran the affairs of state through the national parliament, the Sejm°, as well as local assemblies and various lifelong offices. They drastically limited the ability of the Crown to tax and to grant new titles of nobility, as was the practice throughout Europe. These limitations meant that the king could not re-

ward and reinforce the loyalty of wealthy gentry or the small numbers of urban elites so that they might be a counterweight to noble power. Limited funds also meant that the Polish crown would be hard put to defend its vast territories later in the seventeenth century.

## WRITING, DRAMA, AND ART IN AN AGE OF UPHEAVAL

**B**OTH imaginative literature and speculative writing, such as political theory, bear the stamp of their times. In the late sixteenth and early seventeenth centuries, political speculation often concerned questions of the legitimacy of rulers and of the relationship of political power to divine authority—urgent problems in an age when religious division threatened the very foundations of states. Authors and rulers alike often relied on still-prevalent oral modes of communication to convey their ideas. Indeed, some of the greatest literature and some of the most effective political statements of the period were presented as drama and not conveyed in print. Nevertheless, literacy continued to spread and led to greater opportunities for knowledge and reflection. The medium of print became increasingly important to political life. In the visual arts, the dramatic impulse was wedded to religious purposes to create works that conveyed both power and emotion.

### Literacy and Literature

Traditional oral culture changed slowly under the impact of the spread of printing, education, and literacy. Works of literature from the late sixteenth and early seventeenth centuries incorporate material from traditional folktales, consciously reflecting the coexistence of oral and literate culture. In *Don Quixote*°, by Spain's Miguel de Cervantes° (1547–1616), the title character and his companion, Sancho Panza, have a long discussion about oral and literate traditions. The squire Panza speaks in the style that was customary in oral culture—a rather roundabout and repetitive style, which enabled the speaker and listener to remember what was said. Much of the richness of *Don Quixote* is due to the interweaving of prose styles and topical concerns from throughout Cervantes' culture—from the oral world of peasants to the refined world of court life. Yet the perspective that enabled Cervantes to accomplish this rich portrayal came

---

**Riga** (REE-guh)   **Sejm** (SAME)

**Quixote** (key-HO-tay)   **Cervantes** (sair-VAHN-tayz)

from his own highly developed literacy and the awareness of language that literacy made possible.

The spread of education and literacy in the late sixteenth century had a dramatic impact on attitudes toward literature and on literature itself. The value of education—particularly of the continuing humanist recovery of ancient wisdom—was reflected in much of the literature of the period. Writers found in humanistic education a vision of what it meant to be cultivated and disciplined men of the world. This vision provided the beginnings of a new self-image for members of the warrior class.

It is customary to regard the French author Michel de Montaigne° (1533–1592) as the epitome of the reflective—and, more important, the *self*-reflective—gentleman. Montaigne was a judge in the parlement (law court) of Bordeaux. In 1570 he resigned from the court and retired to his small château, where he wrote his *Essais* (from which we derive the word *essays*), a collection of short reflections that were revolutionary in both form and content. Montaigne invented writing in the form of a sketch, an "attempt" (the literal meaning of *essai*) that enabled him to combine self-reflection with formal analysis.

Montaigne's reflections range from the destructiveness of the French civil wars to the consequences of European exploration of the New World. Toward all of these events and circumstances, Montaigne was able to achieve an analytic detachment remarkable for his day. For example, he noted an irony in Europeans labeling New World peoples "savages," given Europeans' seemingly endless and wanton violence against those "savages" and one another. (See the box "Global Encounters: Montaigne Discusses Barbarity in the New World and the Old.") Owing to the spread of printing and literacy, Montaigne had—in addition to his own effort and the resources of leisure—a virtually unparalleled opportunity to reflect on the world through reading the wide variety of printed texts available to him. For the first time it was possible for a leisured lay reader to consider and compare different events, values, and cultures.

Montaigne's essays also reveal a distancing from himself. This distancing was another result of literacy—not simply the ability to read and write but the capacity to enjoy long periods of solitude and reflection in the company of other solitary, book-bound voices. Montaigne's works mark the beginning of what we know as the "invention" of private life, in which an individual is known more by internal character and personality traits than by social role and past behavior.

Montaigne (mon-TEN-yuh)

The works of the great English poet and playwright William Shakespeare (1564–1616) are still compelling to us because of the profundity of the questions he asked about love, honor, and political legitimacy, but he asked these questions in terms appropriate to his own day. One of his favorite themes—evident in *Hamlet* and *Macbeth*—is the legitimacy of rulers. He was at his most skilled, perhaps, when exploring the contradictions in values between the growing commercial world he saw around him and the older, seemingly more stable world of feudal society. Subtle political commentary distinguishes Shakespeare's later plays, written near and shortly after the death of Queen Elizabeth in 1603, when political and economic problems were becoming increasingly visible and troublesome. Shakespeare explored not only the duties of rulers but also the rights of their subjects. In *Coriolanus* he portrays commoners as poor but neither ignorant nor wretched; they are in fact fully rational and capable of analyzing their situation—perhaps more capable, Shakespeare hints, than their ruler is. The play is safely set in ancient Rome, but the social and political tensions it depicts clearly applied to the Elizabethan present.

Shakespeare, Cervantes, and other writers of their day were also representatives of what were starting to be self-consciously distinct national literatures. The spread of humanism added a historical dimension to their awareness of their own languages and to their distinct subject matter: each one's own society and its past. This kind of self-consciousness is evident in Shakespeare's historical plays, such as *Henry V* and *Richard II*. In *Richard II* he depicts the kingdom in terms that reflect the Elizabethan sense of England as a separate and self-contained nation:

> This royal throne of kings, this scept'red isle,
> This earth of majesty, this seat of Mars,
> This other Eden, demi-paradise,
> This fortress built by Nature for herself
> Against infection and the hand of war,
> This happy breed of men, this little world,
> This precious stone set in the silver sea . . .
> This blessed plot, this earth, this realm, this
>    England . . .
> (*Richard II*, act 2, sc. 1, lines 40–50)[5]

## The Great Age of Theater

Shakespeare's extraordinary career was possible because his life coincided with the rise of professional theater. In the capitals of England and Spain professional theaters first opened in the 1570s. Some drama was produced at court or in aristocratic households, but most

# Montaigne Discusses Barbarity in the New World and the Old

In one of his most famous essays, the French jurist and essayist Michel de Montaigne (1533–1592) ironically compares the customs of Native Americans with the customs of his own society. Information about Native Americans came from published reports of European voyages and from news of individual Native Americans who had journeyed (usually forcibly) to Europe. Europeans' encounters with peoples in the New World gave Montaigne a vantage point from which to criticize his own society.

They have their wars with [other] nations, to which they go quite naked, with no other arms than bows or wooden spears. . . . It is astonishing that firmness they show in their combats, which never end but in slaughter and bloodshed; for, as to routs and terror, they know nothing of either.

Each man brings back as his trophy the head of the enemy he has killed. . . . After they have treated their prisoner well for a long time with all the hospitality they can think of . . . they kill him with their swords. This done, they roast him and eat him in common and send some pieces to their absent friends.

I am not sorry that we notice the barbarous horror of such acts, but am heartily sorry that . . . we should be so blind to our own. I think there is more barbarity . . . in tearing by tortures and the rack a body still full of feeling, in roasting a man bit by bit, having him bitten and mangled by dogs (as we have not only read but seen within fresh memory . . . among neighbors and fellow citizens, and what is worse, on the pretext of piety and religion).

Three of these men (were brought to France) . . . and [someone] wanted to know what they had found most amazing. . . . They said that in the first place they thought it very strange that so many grown men, bearded, strong and armed who were around the king . . . should submit to obey a child [the young French king]. . . . Second (they have a way in their language of speaking of men as halves of one another), they had noticed that there were among us men full and gorged with all sorts of good things, and that their other halves were beggars at their doors, emaciated with hunger and poverty; and they thought it strange that these needy halves could endure such injustice.

## QUESTIONS

1. What practices in the two cultures is Montaigne commenting on in this excerpt?

2. In what ways does he find Native American culture admirable by comparison to his own? What aspects of his own culture is he criticizing?

3. How are contemporary events and conditions reflected in Montaigne's remarks?

SOURCE: Donald M. Frame, trans., *The Complete Essays of Montaigne* (Stanford, Calif.: Stanford University Press, 1948), pp. 153, 155–159. Reprinted by permission of the publisher.

---

public theaters drew large and very mixed audiences, including the poorest city dwellers. Playwrights, including Shakespeare, often wrote in teams under great pressure to keep acting companies supplied with material. The best-known dramatist in Spain, Lope de Vega° (1562–1635), wrote more than fifteen hundred works on a wide range of topics. Although religious themes remained popular in Spanish theater, as an echo of medieval drama, most plays in England and Spain treated secular subjects and, as in *Coriolanus,* safely disguised political commentary.

Over time theater became increasingly restricted to aristocratic circles. In England Puritan criticism of the "immorality" of public performance drove actors and playwrights to seek royal patronage. The first professional theater to open in Paris, in 1629, as political and religious turmoil quieted, quickly became dependent on Cardinal Richelieu's patronage. Inevitably, as court patronage grew in importance, the wide range of subjects treated in plays began to narrow to those of aristocratic concern, such as family honor and martial glory. These themes are depicted in the works of the Spaniard Pedro Calderón° (1600–1681), who wrote for his enthusiastic patron, Philip IV, and of the Frenchman Pierre Corneille° (1606–1684), whose great tragedy of aristocratic life, *Le Cid,* was one of the early successes of the seventeenth-century French theater.

Drama's significance as an art form is reflected in its impact on the development of music: the opera, which weds drama to music, was invented in Italy in the early

---

**Lope de Vega** (LOW-pah day VAY-guh)

**Calderón** (kall-day-ROHN)    **Corneille** (kore-NAY)

seventeenth century. The first great work in this genre is generally acknowledged to be *Orfeo* (*Orpheus*, 1607) by Claudio Monteverdi° (1567–1643). Opera, like drama, reflected the influence of humanism in its secular themes and in its emulation of Greek drama, which had used both words and music. The practice of music itself changed under the dramatic impulse. Monteverdi was the first master of a new musical style known as "monody," which emphasizes the progression of chords. Monodic music is inherently dramatic, creating a sense of forward movement, expectation, and resolution.

## Sovereignty in Ceremony, Image, and Word

Whether produced on a public stage or at court or in a less formal setting, drama was a favored method of communication in this era because people responded to and made extensive use of the spoken word. Dramatic gesture and storytelling to get a message across were commonplace and were important components of politics.

What we might call "street drama" was an ordinary occurrence. When great noble governors entered major towns, such as when Margaret of Parma entered Brussels, a solemn yet ostentatious formal "entry" was often staged. The dignitary would ride through the main gate, usually beneath a canopy made of luxurious cloth. The event might include staged tableaux in the town's streets, with costumed townspeople acting out brief symbolic vignettes, such as David and Goliath, and it might end with an elaborate banquet. A remnant of these proceedings survives today in the ceremony by which distinguished visitors are given "the keys to the city," which, in the sixteenth century, really were functional.

Royalty made deliberate and careful use of dramatic ceremony. Royal entries into towns took on an added weight, as did royal funerals and other such occasions. These dramas reinforced political and constitutional assumptions in the minds of witnesses and participants. Thus over time we can see changes in the representations of royal power. In France, for example, the ritual entry of the king into Paris had originally stressed the participation of the leading guilds, judges, and administrators, symbolizing their active role in governing the city and the kingdom. But in the last half of the sixteenth century the procession began to glorify the king alone. Speculation about and celebration of power, as well as dramatic emotion, also occurred in the visual arts—most notably in painting and architecture, in the style now known as "baroque°." Baroque style was a new kind of visual language that could project power and grandeur and simultaneously engage viewers' senses. (See the feature "Weighing the Evidence: Baroque Art" on pages 536–537.)

The very fact that rulers experimented self-consciously with self-representation suggests that issues pertaining to the nature and extent of royal power were profoundly important and far from settled. Queen Elizabeth I had the particular burden of assuming the throne in a period of great instability. Hence she paid a great deal of attention to the image of herself that she conveyed in words and authorized to be fashioned in painting. Elizabeth

**An Image of Royalty**   This dramatic painting of Charles I on horseback was executed by the baroque artist Anthony Van Dyck in about 1633. It was one of several paintings of himself and the royal family that Charles commissioned from Van Dyck. This painting was originally hung at the end of a long gallery in one of the royal palaces, next to similarly triumphal images of Roman emperors.   *(The Royal Collection © 2003, Her Majesty Queen Elizabeth II)*

---

**Monteverdi** (mon-tay-VAIR-dee)   **baroque** (ba-ROKE)

## READING SOURCES

# ELIZABETH I ADDRESSES HER TROOPS

*The day after English ships dispersed the Spanish Armada in 1588, Elizabeth addressed a contingent of her troops. She used the opportunity to fashion an image of herself as a warrior above all but also as the beloved familiar of her people, unafraid of potential plots against her. Note her willingness to portray herself as androgynous—that is, embodying both female and male qualities.*

My loving people, we have been persuaded by some that are careful of our safety, to take heed how we commit ourselves to armed multitudes, for fear of treachery. But I assure you, I do not desire to live to distrust my faithful and loving people. Let tyrants fear. I have always so behaved myself that, under God, I have placed my chiefest strength in the loyal hearts and good will of my subjects; and therefore I am come amongst you, as you see, at this time, not for my reaction or disport, but being resolved, in the midst and heat of the battle, to live or die amongst you all, to lay down for my God, and for my kingdom, and for my people, my honor and my blood, even in the dust. I know I have the body of a weak and feeble woman, but I have the heart and the stomach of a king, and of a king of England too, and think foul scorn that Parma or Spain, or any prince of Europe should dare to invade the borders of my realm; to which, rather than any dishonor shall grow by me, I myself will take up arms, I myself will be your general, judge, and rewarder of every one of your virtues in the field.

Source: J. E. Neale, *Queen Elizabeth I* (New York: Anchor, 1957), pp. 308–309.

styled herself variously as mother to her people and as a warrior-queen (drawing on ancient myths of Amazon women). She made artful use of the image of her virginity to buttress each of these images—as the wholly devoted, self-sacrificing mother (which, of course, had religious tradition behind it) or as an androgynous ruler, woman but doing the bodily work of man. (See the box "Reading Sources: Elizabeth I Addresses Her Troops.")

More formal speculation about constitutional matters also resulted from the tumult of the sixteenth and seventeenth centuries. As we have seen, the Protestant faction in France advanced an elaborate argument for the limitation of royal power. Alternative theories enhancing royal authority were offered, principally in support of the Catholic position though also simply to buttress the beleaguered monarchy itself. The most famous of these appeared in *The Six Books of the Republic* (1576), by the legal scholar Jean Bodin° (1530–1596). Bodin was a Catholic but offered a fundamentally secular perspective on the purposes and source of power within a state. His special contribution was a vision of a truly sovereign monarch. Bodin offered a theoretical understanding that is essential to states today and is the ground on which people can claim rights and protection from the state—namely, that there is a final sovereign authority. For Bodin that authority was the king. He recognized that in practice royal power was constrained by limitations, but he was intrigued more by the theoretical grounding for royal authority than by its practical application.

Contract theory devised by French Protestants to legitimize resistance to the monarchy had to be abandoned when Henry IV granted toleration to the Huguenots in 1598. In England theoretical justification of resistance to Charles I was initially limited to invoking tradition and precedent. Contract theory, as well as other sweeping claims regarding subjects' rights, would be more fully developed later in the century.

Bodin's theory of sovereignty, however, was immediately echoed in other theoretical works, most notably that of Hugo Grotius° (1583–1645). A Dutch jurist and diplomat, Grotius developed the first principles of modern international law. He accepted the existence of sovereign states that owed no loyalty to higher authority (such as the papacy) and thus needed new principles to govern their interactions. His major work, *De Jure Belli ac Pacis* (*On the Law of War and Peace,* 1625), was written in response to the turmoil of the Thirty Years' War. Grotius argued that relations between states could be based on

---

**Bodin** (bo-DAHN)

**Grotius** (GROW-shus)

respect for treaties voluntarily reached between them. In perhaps his boldest move he argued that war must be justified, and he developed criteria to distinguish just from unjust wars.

## Summary

THE late sixteenth and early seventeenth centuries were an era of intense struggle over political and religious authority. Rulers everywhere, through a variety of expedients, tried to buttress and expand royal power. They were resisted by traditional centers of power, such as independent-minded nobles. But they were also resisted by the novel challenge of religious dissent, which empowered subjects both to claim a greater right to question authority and to risk more in their attempts to oppose it. In some areas of Europe, such as the Holy Roman Empire, the struggles reached some resolution. In other areas, such as England, decades of bloody conflict still lay ahead.

On the whole these conflicts did little to improve the lives of ordinary people since for the most part victorious elites decided matters of religion and governance in their own interests. In addition, the difficult economic circumstances of these decades meant that working people, desperate for a secure livelihood, rioted or took up arms out of economic as well as religious concerns.

Yet however grim the circumstances people faced, the technology of print and the spread of literacy helped spur speculative and creative works by providing the means for reflection and the audiences to receive and appreciate it. Ironically, the increased importance and grandeur of court life, though a cause of political strain, resulted in a new wave of patronage for art, literature, and drama. Some of the works we still value portray the splendid ambience of royal courts. Other works, such as Shakespeare's plays, both reflect and reflect on the tensions and contradictions in the society of the day: for example, the importance of the stability provided by royal authority as opposed to the dignity and wisdom of ordinary people, who had no claim to power at all.

### ■ Notes

1. Geoffrey Parker, *The Dutch Revolt* (London: Penguin, 1985), p. 288, n. 5.
2. Quoted in A. W. Lovett, *Early Habsburg Spain, 1517–1598* (Oxford: Oxford University Press, 1986), p. 212.
3. Quoted in R. J. Knecht, *The French Wars of Religion, 1559–1598* (London: Longman, 1989), p. 109.
4. Quoted in Jean Berenger, *A History of the Habsburg Empire, 1273–1700,* trans. C. A. Simpson (London and New York: Longman, 1990), p. 239.
5. *The Riverside Shakespeare*, ed. G. Blakemore Evans, 2d ed. (Boston: Houghton Mifflin, 1997), p. 855. Copyright © 1997 by Houghton Mifflin Company. Reprinted by permission of the publisher.

### ■ Suggested Reading

Berenger, Jean. *A History of the Habsburg Empire, 1273–1700,* trans. C. A. Simpson. 1990. A detailed treatment of Habsburg rule in the Holy Roman Empire and in their own principalities. Considers economic and cultural changes as well as political ones.

Bonney, Richard. *The European Dynastic States, 1494–1660.* 1991. A rich survey of the period that is solid on eastern as well as western Europe. Written from an English point of view, it does not consider England as part of Europe.

Eagleton, Terry. *William Shakespeare.* 1986. A brief and highly readable interpretation of Shakespeare that emphasizes the tensions in the plays caused by language and by ideas from the new world of bourgeois commercial life.

Edwards, Philip. *The Making of the Modern English State.* 2001. A readable survey of political and religious developments in England that incorporates much new scholarship.

Holt, Mack P. *The French Wars of Religion, 1562–1629.* 1995. An up-to-date synthesis that evaluates social and political context while not slighting the importance of religion.

Lynch, John. *Spain, 1516–1598: From Nation-State to World Empire.* 1991. A survey covering the reign of Philip II by a leading scholar of Spanish history.

Parker, Geoffrey. *The Military Revolution.* 1988; and Black, Jeremy. *A Military Revolution?* 1991. Two works that disagree about the nature and extent of the changes in military practices and their significance for military, political, and social history. Black tries to refute claims of a dramatic military "revolution."

Parker, Geoffrey. *The Dutch Revolt.* 2d ed. 1985. The best survey of the revolt available in English.

Wiesner, Merry. *Women and Gender in Early Modern Europe.* 1993. Discusses all aspects of women's experience, including their working lives.

For a searchable list of additional readings for this chapter, go to college.hmco.com/students.

# Baroque Art

If today you were to walk through the cathedral in the Belgian city of Antwerp and notice this painting, titled *The Raising of the Cross,* it might not strike you as remarkable. The crucifixion of Jesus is a frequent subject of religious painting, after all. But let us look at the image more carefully. First of all, this is a portrayal not of Jesus on the cross but rather of the *raising* of the cross. In other words, it captures a moment of action, not its aftermath. The frame of the painting is filled with action as well. The figures on the left and at the center support the cross and push it up. At the bottom right we see figures straining at ropes as they pull the cross upright. Our eye is drawn to the movement in the painting partly by the use of light, which floods the figure of Jesus. We also note the unexpected diagonal position of the crucified figure, and we survey the image in order to make sense of it.

This is a dynamic painting, and simultaneously an emotionally engaging one. We encounter Jesus not as a static, perhaps already dying, figure on the cross, but at the very moment of his crucifixion. There is also a striking similarity between the figure of Jesus and those of the men who are working hard to accomplish his crucifixion: they are all men, whose muscled bodies are more alike than not. The human pathos of the moment is brought to life.

The image you see before you is one of three panels in a triptych, or three-paneled altarpiece. The left-hand panel depicts Saint John, the Virgin Mary, and others witnessing Jesus's crucifixion. The panel on the right shows a Roman officer watching over his soldiers as they crucify two thieves. Whereas most triptychs of the period contained three unrelated images, here the panels combine to form a single story of the crucifixion.

This altarpiece was executed in 1610 by the influential painter Peter Paul Rubens (1577–1640), a native of Antwerp, in the southern Netherlands. Rubens was one of the great masters of what came to be called the baroque style. Baroque techniques were pioneered in the late sixteenth century in Italy, first in church design, and spread slowly, with many regional variations, especially throughout Catholic Europe, during the seventeenth century. The origin of the term *baroque* has been debated; it may have come from the Portuguese *barroco,* used to describe irregularly shaped pearls. The term as applied to the arts was initially derogatory, denoting distortion, illogic, and irregularity. Baroque painting was distinguished by the dramatic use of color and shading and by the dynamic energy of figures. Baroque artists based their work on Renaissance achievements in representing the human form in a convincing three-dimensional space. But with the strong use of light, movement, and more robust and realistic human figures, these artists enhanced the drama and emotional impact of what they depicted.

Like baroque artists, baroque architects modified the precision, symmetry, and orderliness of Renaissance architecture to produce a sense of greater dynamism in space. Baroque churches, for example, were impressively grand and monumental yet emotionally engaging at the same time. Façades and interiors were both massive and, through the clever use of architectural and decorative components, suggestive of movement. A good example of this is the work of Gianlorenzo Bernini° (1598–1680), who designed the portico outside Saint Peter's Basilica in Rome, as well as the highly ornate bronze canopy over the altar inside the basilica. Dramatic illusion in the interior of buildings—such as painting a chapel ceiling with figures receding as if ascending to heaven—was a common device in baroque architecture. One of the primary purposes of baroque architecture and art was to create simultaneously a display of power and an invitation to sensory experience. Baroque art encouraged piety that was not only emotionally involved, and thus satisfying, but also awe-inspired. In this way it reflected the aims of the Counter-Reformation church, whose leaders were among its most important patrons.

Peter Paul Rubens's early training in Italy shaped him as an artist and established his secondary career as a diplomat. Throughout his life he undertook diplomatic missions for the Habsburg viceroys in the Spanish Netherlands, gaining artistic commissions wherever he went. Rubens's subject matter varied widely, including church design and decoration, portraiture, and landscape painting, reflecting the fact that baroque art also had important secular applications. Indeed, magnificent baroque palaces symbolized the wealth and power of the elites (see the photos on pages 545 and 554).

Rulers began to employ artists as portrait painters, such as Rubens's pupil Anthony Van Dyck (1599–1641), whose painting of Charles I of England appears on page 533. Because portraits have become so common, we

---

**Bernini** (bare-NEE-nee)

**Rubens: The Raising of the Cross**
*(Onze Lieve Vrouwkwerk, Antwerp Cathedral,
Belgium/Peter Willi/Bridgeman Art Library)*

cannot fully appreciate how arresting this image would have been in its day. Like Rubens's *Raising of the Cross,* Van Dyck's image of Charles was a novel rendering of familiar elements. The image of a ruler on horseback was well known, but it had never been exploited as fully by English monarchs as it had been by rulers on the Continent. This large portrait of the king was designed to be hung at the end of a long palace corridor so that, from a distance, a courtier would have the illusion of actually seeing the king riding proudly through a triumphal arch. This effect was similar to that achieved by artists who painted church ceilings with receding angels and cherubs, giving the faithful the illusion of gazing up toward heaven.* Compare this portrait with the much more stilted one of Elizabeth I on page 519. It is striking how effective the technical and stylistic innovations of baroque art and architecture were in expressing secular as well as spiritual power.

---

*This discussion draws on the work of Roy Strong, *Van Dyck: Charles I on Horseback* (New York: Viking, 1972), pp. 20–25.

THE portrait of King Louis XIV of France as a triumphant warrior, to the left, was one of hundreds of such images of the king that decorated his palace at Versailles and other sites around his kingdom—where they made his subjects aware of his presence, regardless of whether he was in residence. Louis is dressed as a Roman warrior, and his power is represented by a mixture of other symbols—Christian and pagan, ancient and contemporary. An angel crowns him with a victor's laurel wreath and carries a banner bearing the image of the sun. In his hand Louis holds a marshal's baton—a symbol of military command—covered with the royal emblem of the fleur-de-lys°. In the background, behind the "Roman" troops following Louis, is an idealized city.

These trappings symbolized the significant expansion of royal power during Louis's reign. He faced down the challenges of warrior-nobles, suppressed religious dissent, and tapped the nation's wealth to wage a series of wars of conquest. A period of cultural brilliance early in his reign and the spectacle of an elaborate court life crowned his achievements. In his prime, his regime was supported by a consensus of elites; such harmony was made possible by the lack of institutional brakes on royal authority. However, as his attention to symbolism suggests, Louis's power was not unchallenged. By the end of the Sun King's reign the glow was fading: France was struggling under economic distress brought on by the many wars fought for his glory and had missed opportunities for commercial success abroad. Elites throughout France who had once accepted, even welcomed, his rule became trenchant critics, and common people outright rebels.

---

**fleur-de-lys** (flur–duh–LEE)

Louis XIV in Roman armor, by the contemporary artist Charles Le Brun. (Scala/Art Resource, NY)

# Europe in the Age of Louis XIV ca. 1640–1715

After the Thirty Years' War, vigorous rulers in central and eastern Europe undertook a program of territorial expansion and state building that led to the dominance in the region of Austria, Brandenburg-Prussia, and Russia. The power of these states derived, in part, from the economic relationship of their lands to the wider European economy. In all the major states of continental Europe, princely governments were able to monopolize military power for the first time, in return for economic and political concessions to noble landholders. In England, by contrast, the Crown faced rebellion by subjects claiming religious authority and political legitimacy for their causes. Resistance to the expansion of royal authority, led by Parliament, resulted in the execution of the king and the establishment of a short-lived republic, the Commonwealth. Although the monarchy was restored, the civil war had long-term consequences for royal power in England.

The seventeenth century also witnessed a dynamic phase of European expansion overseas, following on the successes of the Portuguese and the Spanish in the fifteenth and sixteenth centuries. Eager migrants settled in the Americas in ever increasing numbers, while forced migrants—enslaved Africans—were transported by the thousands to work on the profitable plantations of European colonizers. Aristocrats, merchants, and peasants back in Europe jockeyed to take advantage of—or to mitigate the effects of—the local political and economic impact of Europe's expansion.

---

### QUESTIONS TO CONSIDER

- How did Louis XIV successfully expand royal power in France?

- What were the long-term consequences of the English civil war?

- What economic and political interests led to war in eastern Europe?

- How did the expansion of international trade and colonization affect European states and communities?

---

### TERMS TO KNOW

| | |
|---|---|
| Louis XIV | Treaty of Carlowitz |
| absolutism | Brandenburg-Prussia |
| mercantilism | Cossacks |
| Parliament | Peter the Great |
| Oliver Cromwell | Dutch East India Company |
| Glorious Revolution | plantation system |

---

## FRANCE IN THE AGE OF ABSOLUTISM

**A**BSOLUTISM is a term often used to describe the extraordinary concentration of power in royal hands achieved by the kings of France, most notably Louis XIV (r. 1643–1715), in the seventeenth century. Louis continued the expansion of state power begun by his father's minister, Cardinal Richelieu (see page 518). The extension of royal power, under Louis as well as his predecessor, was accelerated by the desire to sustain an expensive and aggressive foreign policy. The policy itself was partly traditional—fighting the perpetual enemy, the Habsburgs, and seeking military glory—and partly new—expanding the borders of France. Louis XIV's successes in these undertakings made him both envied and emulated by other rulers: the French court became a model of culture and refinement. But increased royal authority was not accepted without protest: common French people as well as elites dug in their heels.

### The Last Challenge to Absolutism: The Fronde, 1648–1653

Louis came to the throne as a 5-year-old child in 1643. Acting as his regent, his mother, Anne of Austria (1601–1666), had to defuse a serious challenge to royal authority during her son's minority. Together with her chief minister and personal friend, Cardinal Jules Mazarin°

---

**Mazarin** (mah-zah-RAHN)

(1602–1661), she faced opposition from royal bureaucrats and the traditional nobility as well as the common people.

Revolts against the concentration of power in royal hands and against the exorbitant taxation that had prevailed under Louis's father began immediately. In one province a group of armed peasants cornered the intendant and forced him to agree to lower taxes; elsewhere provincial parlements tried to abolish special ranks of officials, especially the intendants, created by Richelieu. In 1648, after several more years of foreign war and the financial expedients to sustain it, the most serious revolt began, led by the Parlement° of Paris and the other sovereign law courts in the capital.

The source of the Parlement's leverage over the monarchy was its traditional right to register laws and edicts, which amounted to judicial review. Now the Parlement, as a guardian of royal authority, attempted to extend this power by debating and even initiating government policy. The sovereign courts sitting together drew up a reform program abolishing most of the machinery of government established under Richelieu and calling for consent to future taxation. The citizens of Paris rose to defend the courts when royal troops were sent against them in October.

Mazarin was forced to accept the proposed reform of government, at least in theory. He also had to avert challenges by great nobles for control of the young king's council. Civil war waxed and waned around France from 1648 to 1653. The main combatants were conventionally ambitious great nobles, but reform-minded urban dwellers often made common cause with them, to benefit from their military power. Meanwhile, middling nobles in the region around Paris began to devise a thoroughgoing reform program and to prepare for a meeting of the Estates General—a representative assembly—to enact it.

These revolts begun in 1648 were derided with the name "Fronde°," which was a popular children's game. However, the Fronde was not child's play; it constituted a serious challenge to the legacy of royal government as it had developed under Richelieu. It ended without a noteworthy impact on the growth of royal power for several reasons. First, Mazarin methodically regained control of the kingdom through armed force and artful concessions to individual aristocrats, who were always eager to trade their loyalty for the fruits of royal service. Meanwhile, the Parlement of Paris, as well as many citizens of the capital, welcomed a return to royal authority when civil war caused starvation as well as political unrest.

Moreover, the Parlement of Paris was a law court, not a representative assembly. Its legitimacy derived from

Parlement (par-luh-MAWNH)    Fronde (FRAWND)

## CHRONOLOGY

| | |
|---|---|
| 1602 | Dutch East India Company formed |
| 1607 | Jamestown colony founded in Virginia |
| 1608 | Champlain founds Quebec City |
| 1613 | Michael becomes first Romanov tsar in Russia |
| 1620 | Pilgrims settle at Plymouth (Massachusetts) |
| 1642–1648 | Civil war in England |
| 1643 | Louis XIV becomes king of France |
| 1648–1653 | Fronde revolts in France |
| 1649 | Execution of Charles I |
| 1649–1660 | English Commonwealth |
| 1659 | Peace of the Pyrenees |
| 1660 | Monarchy restored in England |
| 1661 | Louis XIV assumes full control of government |
| 1672–1678 | Dutch War |
| 1682 | Peter the Great becomes tsar of Russia |
| 1685 | Edict of Nantes revoked |
| 1688 | Glorious Revolution |
| 1699 | Treaty of Carlowitz |
| 1700–1721 | Great Northern War |
| 1701–1714 | War of the Spanish Succession |
| 1713 | Peace of Utrecht |
| 1715 | Death of Louis XIV |

its role as upholder of royal law, and it could not, over time, challenge the king on the pretext of upholding royal tradition in his name. Parlementaires tended to see the Estates General as a rival institution and helped quash the proposed meeting of representatives. Above all, they wanted to avert reforms such as the abolition of the paulette, a fee guaranteeing the hereditary right to royal office (see page 516).

Unlike in England, there was in France no single institutional focus for resistance to royal power. A strong-willed and able ruler, as Louis XIV proved to be, could obstruct or override challenges to royal power, particularly when he satisfied the ambitions of aristocrats and those bureaucrats who profited from the expansion of royal power. Moreover, the young Louis had been traumatized by the uprisings of the Fronde and grew up determined never to allow another such challenge to his absolute sovereignty.

## France Under Louis XIV, 1661–1715

Louis XIV fully assumed control of government at Mazarin's death in 1661. It was a propitious moment. The Peace of the Pyrenees in 1659 had ended in France's favor the wars with Spain that had dragged on since the end of the Thirty Years' War. As part of the peace agreement, Louis married a Spanish princess, Maria Theresa. In the first ten years of his active reign Louis achieved a degree of control over the mechanisms of government unparalleled in the history of monarchy in France or anywhere else in Europe. Louis was extremely vigorous and proved a diligent king. He put in hours a day at a desk while sustaining the ceremonial life of the court, with its elaborate hunts, balls, and other public events.

Louis did not invent any new bureaucratic devices but rather used existing ranks of officials in new ways that increased government efficiency and further centralized control. He radically reduced the number of men in his High Council, the advisory body closest to the king, to include only three or four great ministers of state affairs. This intimate group, with Louis's active participation, handled all policymaking. The ministers of state, war, and finance were chosen exclusively from non-noble men of bourgeois background whose training and experience fitted them for such positions. Jean-Baptiste Colbert° (1619–1683), perhaps the greatest of them, served as minister of finance and supervised most domestic policy from 1665 until his death. He was from a merchant family and had served for years under Mazarin.

Several dozen other officials, picked from the ranks of up-and-coming lawyers and administrators, drew up laws and regulations and passed them to the intendants for execution at the provincial level. Sometimes these officials at the center were sent to the provinces on short-term supervisory missions. The effect of this system was to bypass many entrenched provincial bureaucrats, particularly those known as tax farmers. Tax farmers were freelance businessmen who bid for the right to collect taxes in a region in return for a negotiated fee they paid to the Crown. The Crown, in short, did not control its

**Colbert** (coal-BEAR)

own tax revenues. The money Louis's regime saved by the more efficient collection of taxes (revenues almost doubled in some areas) enabled the government to streamline the bureaucracy: dozens of the offices created over the years to bring cash in were bought back by the Crown from their owners.

The system still relied on the bonds of patronage and personal service—political bonds borrowed from aristocratic life. Officials rose through the ranks by means of service to the great, and family connection and personal loyalty still were essential. Of the seventeen different men who were part of Louis XIV's High Council during his reign, five were members of the Colbert family, for example. In the provinces important local families vied for minor posts, which at least provided prestige and some income.

Further benefits of centralized administration can be seen in certain achievements of the early years of Louis's regime. Colbert actively encouraged France's economic development. He reduced the internal tolls and customs barriers, which were relics of medieval decentralization—for example, the right of a landholder to charge a toll on all boats along a river under his control. He encouraged industry with state subsidies and protective tariffs. He set up state-sponsored trading companies—the two most important being the East India Company and the West India Company, established in 1664.

*Mercantilism* is the term historians use to describe the theory behind Colbert's efforts. This economic theory stressed self-sufficiency in manufactured goods, tight control of trade to foster the domestic economy, and the absolute value of bullion. Both capital for development—in the form of hard currency, known as bullion—and the amount of world trade were presumed to be limited in quantity. Therefore state intervention in the form of protectionist policies was believed necessary to guarantee a favorable balance of payments.

This static model of national wealth did not wholly fit the facts of growing international trade in the seventeenth century. Nevertheless, mercantilist philosophy was helpful to France. France became self-sufficient in the all-important production of woolen cloth, and French industry expanded notably in other sectors. Colbert's greatest success was the systematic expansion of the navy and merchant marine. By 1677 the navy had increased almost sixfold, to 144 ships. By the end of Louis XIV's reign the French navy was virtually the equal of the English navy.

Colbert and the other ministers began to develop the kind of planned government policymaking that we now take for granted. Partly by means of their itinerant supervisory officials, they tried to formulate and execute policy based on carefully collected information. How many men of military age were available? How abundant was this year's harvest? Answers to such questions enabled not only the formulation of economic policy but also the deliberate management of production and services to achieve certain goals—above all, the recruitment and supply of the king's vast armies.

Beginning in 1673 Louis tried to bring the religious life of the realm more fully under royal control, claiming for himself—with mixed success—some of the church revenues and powers of ecclesiastical appointment that still remained to the pope. Partly to bolster his position with the pope, he also began to attack the Huguenot community in France. First he offered financial inducements for conversion to Catholicism. Then he took more drastic steps, such as destroying Protestant churches and quartering troops in Huguenots' homes to force them to convert. In 1685 he declared that France would no longer abide any Protestant community, and he revoked the Edict of Nantes. A hundred thousand Protestant subjects—including some six hundred army and navy officers—refused even nominal conversion to Catholicism and chose to emigrate.

Meanwhile, Louis faced resistance to his claims against the pope from within the ranks of French clergy. These churchmen represented a movement within French Catholicism known as Jansenism, after Cornelius Jansen, a professor of theology whose writings were its inspiration. Jansenists practiced an austere style of Catholic religiosity that, in its notions about human will and sinfulness, was akin to some Protestant doctrine. Louis was suspicious of Jansenism because its adherents included many of his political enemies, particularly among families of parlement officials. Louis was wary of any threat to the institutional—or symbolic—unity of his regime, such as Protestants and Jansenists represented. At the end of Louis's long reign another pope obligingly declared many Jansenist doctrines to be heretical as part of a compromise agreement with Louis on matters of church governance and finance. Louis's efforts to exert greater control over the church had brought him modest practical gains, but at the price of weakening the religious basis of his authority in the eyes of many sincere Catholics.

By modern standards the power of the Crown was still greatly limited. The "divine right" of kingship, a notion formulated by Louis's chief apologist, Bishop Jacques Bossuet° (1627–1704), did not mean unlimited power to rule; rather it meant that hereditary monarchy was the

**Bossuet** (BOS-soo-way)

divinely ordained form of government, best suited to human needs. *Absolutism* was not ironfisted control of the realm but rather the successful focusing of energy, loyalties, and symbolic authority in the Crown. The government functioned well in the opening decades of Louis's reign because his role as the focal point of power and loyalty was both logical, after the preceding years of unrest, and skillfully exploited. Much of the glue holding together the absolutist state lay in informal mechanisms such as patronage and court life, as well as in the traditional hunt for military glory—all of which Louis amply supplied.

## The Life of the Court

An observer comparing the lives of prominent noble families in the mid-sixteenth and mid-seventeenth centuries would have noticed striking differences. By the second half of the seventeenth century, most sovereigns or territorial princes had the power to crush revolts, and the heirs of the feudal nobility had to accommodate themselves to the increased power of the Crown. The nobility relinquished its former independence but retained economic and social supremacy and, as a consequence, considerable political clout. Nobles also developed new ways to symbolize their privilege by means of cultural refinement. This process was particularly dramatic in France as a strong Crown won out over a proud nobility.

One sign of Louis's success in marshaling the loyalty of the aristocracy was the brilliant court life that his regime sustained. No longer able to wield independent political power, aristocrats lived at court whenever they could. There they endlessly jostled for patronage and prestige—for commands in the royal army and for honorific positions at court itself. (See the box "Reading Sources: A Courtier Criticizes the King.") A favored courtier might, for example, participate in the elaborate daily *lever* (arising) of the king; he might be allowed to hand the king his shirt—a demeaning task, yet a coveted one for the attention by the king that it implied and guaranteed. Courtiers now defended their honor with private duels, not warfare, and more routinely relied on elegant ceremonial, precise etiquette, and clever conversation to demarcate their political and social distinctiveness. (See the feature "Weighing the Evidence: Table Manners" on pages 570–571.)

As literacy became more widespread and the power of educated bureaucrats of even humble origin became more obvious, nobles from the traditional aristocracy began increasingly to use reading and writing as a means to think critically about their behavior—in the case of men, to re-imagine themselves as gentlemen rather than warriors. Noblewomen and noblemen alike began to reflect

## READING SOURCES

# A COURTIER CRITICIZES THE KING

*Louis de Rouvroy, duke of Saint-Simon (1675–1755), was a favored courtier but one critical of Louis XIV on a number of counts. In this excerpt from his memoirs, Saint-Simon evaluates the character of the king and criticizes his reliance on men of bourgeois background for his leading ministers. As a member of the traditional aristocracy, Saint-Simon certainly had a reason for disliking this policy. However, this testimony does have the ring of unbiased authenticity in some important respects.*

[The king's] ministers, general, mistresses and courtiers learned soon after he became their master that glory, to him, was a foible rather than an ambition. They therefore flattered him to the top of his bent, and in so doing, spoiled him. Praise, or better, adulation . . . were the only road to his favour and those whom he liked owed his friendship to choosing their moments well and never ceasing in their attentions. That is what gave his ministers their power, for they had endless opportunities of flattering his vanity, especially by suggesting that he was the source of all their ideas. . . .

He was well aware that though he might crush a nobleman with the weight of his displeasure, he could not destroy him or his line, whereas a secretary of state or other such minister could be reduced together with his whole family to those depths of nothingness from which he had been elevated. . . . Therein lay the reason for the watchful, jealous attitude of his ministers, who made it difficult for the King to hear any but themselves, although he pleased to think that he was an easy man to approach.

Nevertheless, in spite of the fact that the King had been so spoiled with false notions of majesty and power, that every other thought was stifled in him, there was much to be gained from a private audience, if it might be obtained, and if one knew how to conduct oneself with all the respect due to his dignity and habits. Once in his study, however prejudiced he might be . . . he would listen patiently, good-naturedly, and with a real desire to be informed. You could see that he had a sense of justice and a will to get at the truth. . . . It is therefore enough to make one weep to think of the wickedness of an education designed solely to suppress the . . . intelligence of that prince, and the insidious poison of barefaced flattery which make him a kind of god in the very heart of Christendom.

Source: Louis, duc de Saint-Simon, *Versailles, the Court and Louis XIV*, ed. Lucy Norton (New York: Harper and Row, 1966), pp. 248–251. Reprinted by permission of the Estate of Lucy Norton.

---

on their new roles in letters, memoirs, and the first novels. A prominent theme of these works is the increasing necessity for a truly private life of affection and trust, with which to counterbalance the public façade necessary to an aspiring courtier. The most influential early French novel was *The Princess of Cleves* by Marie-Madeleine Pioche de la Vergne (1634–1693), best known by her title, Madame de Lafayette. Mme. de Lafayette's novel treats the particular difficulties faced by aristocratic women who, without military careers to bring glory and provide distraction, were more vulnerable than men to gossip and slander at court and more trapped by their arranged marriages.

Louis XIV's court is usually associated with the palace he built at Versailles°, southwest of Paris. Some of the greatest talent of the day worked on the design and construction of Versailles from 1670 through the 1680s. It became a masterpiece of luxurious but restrained baroque style—a model for royal and aristocratic palaces throughout Europe for the next one hundred years.

Before Louis's court in his later years withdrew to Versailles, it traveled among the king's several châteaux around the kingdom, and in this itinerant period of the reign, court life was actually at its most creative and productive. These early years of Louis's personal reign were the heyday of French drama. The comedian Jean-Baptiste Poquelin, known as Molière° (1622–1673), impressed the young Louis with his productions in the late 1650s and was rewarded with the use of a theater in the main royal palace in Paris. Like Shakespeare earlier in the century, Molière explored the social and political tensions of his day. He satirized the pretensions of the aristocracy, the social climbing of the bourgeoisie, and the self-righteous piety of clerics. Some of his plays were banned from performance, but most were not only tolerated but extremely

---

**Versailles** (vare-SIGH)

**Molière** (mole-YARE)

**The Château of Versailles**  This view of the central section of the palace is taken from the gardens. The reflecting pools you see here are on the first level of an immense terraced garden that, to someone exiting the château, seems to stretch to the horizon. The apparent openness of the king's residence (notice the rows of floor-length windows on the ground floor) is in stark contrast to a fortified castle and was a dramatic statement of a new kind of royal power.  *(Château de Versailles, France/Peter Willi/The Bridgeman Art Library)*

popular with the elite audiences they mocked. Their popularity is testimony to the confidence of Louis's regime in its early days.

Also popular at court were the tragedies of Jean Racine° (1639–1699), who was to the French theater what Shakespeare was to the English: the master of poetic language. His plays, which treat familiar classical stories, focus on the emotional and psychological lives of the characters and often stress the unpredictable, usually unhappy, role of fate, even among royalty. The pessimism in Racine foreshadowed the less successful second half of Louis's reign.

### The Burdens of War and the Limits of Power

Wars initiated by Louis XIV dominated the attention of most European states in the second half of the seventeenth century. Louis's wars sprang from traditional causes: the importance of the glory and dynastic aggrandizement

of the king and the preoccupation of the aristocracy with military life. But if Louis's wars were spurred by familiar concerns about territorial and economic advantage, they were far more demanding on state resources than any previous wars.

In France and elsewhere the size of armies grew markedly. And with the countryside still smarting from the rampaging armies of the Thirty Years' War, so did the need for greater management of troops. Louis XIV's victories in the second half of the century are partly traceable to his regime's attention to the bureaucratic tasks of recruitment, training, and supply, which together constituted another phase of the "military revolution." The new offensive tactics developed during the Thirty Years' War (see page 526) changed the character of armies in ways that demanded more resources for training. A higher proportion of soldiers became gunners, and their effectiveness lay in how well they operated as a unit. Armies began to train seriously off the field of battle because drill and discipline were vital to success. France was the

---

**Racine** (rah-SEEN)

**Map 16.1    Territorial Gains of Louis XIV, 1667–1715**    Louis's wars, though enormously expensive for France, produced only modest gains of territory along France's eastern and northern frontiers.

first to provide its soldiers with uniforms, which boosted morale and improved discipline. The numbers of men on the battlefield increased somewhat as training increased the effectiveness of large numbers of infantry, but the total numbers of men in arms supported by the state at any time increased dramatically once the organization to support them was in place. Late in the century France kept more than 300,000 men in arms when at war (which was most of the time).

Louis's first war, in 1667, reflects the continuing French preoccupation with Spanish power on French frontiers. Louis invoked rather dubious dynastic claims to demand from Spain lands in the Spanish Netherlands and the large independent county on France's eastern border called the Franche-Comté° (see Map 16.1). After a

**Franche-Comté** (FRAWNSH–con-TAY)

brief conflict, the French obtained only some towns in the Spanish Netherlands by the terms of the Treaty of Aix-la-Chapelle. Louis had already begun to negotiate with the Austrian Habsburgs over the eventual division of Spanish Habsburg lands, for it seemed likely that the Spanish king, Charles II (r. 1665–1700), would die without an heir. So, for the moment, Louis was content with modest gains at Spain's expense, confident that he would get much more in the future.

Louis's focus then shifted to a new enemy, the Dutch. The Dutch had been allied with France since the beginning of their existence as provinces in rebellion against Spain. The French now turned against the Dutch for reasons that reflect the growth of the international trading economy: Dutch dominance of seaborne trade. The French at first tried to offset the Dutch advantage in trade with tariff barriers against Dutch goods. But confidence in the

French army led Louis's generals to urge action against the vulnerable Dutch lands. "It is impossible that his Majesty should tolerate any longer the insolence and arrogance of that nation," rationalized the usually pragmatic Colbert in 1670.[1]

The Dutch War began in 1672, with Louis personally leading one of the largest armies ever fielded in Europe—perhaps 120,000 men. At the same time, the Dutch were challenged at sea by England. The English had fought the Dutch over trade in the 1650s; now Louis secretly sent the English king, Charles II, a pension to secure an alliance against the Dutch.

At first the French were spectacularly successful against the tiny Dutch army. However, the Dutch opened dikes and flooded the countryside, and what had begun as a rout became a soggy stalemate. Moreover, the Dutch were beating combined English and French forces at sea and were gathering allies who felt threatened by Louis's aggression. The French soon faced German and Austrian forces along their frontier, and by 1674 the English had joined the alliance against France as well.

Nonetheless, the French managed to hold their own, and the Peace of Nijmegen° in 1678 gave the illusion of a French victory. Not only had the French met the challenge of an enemy coalition, but Spain ceded them further border areas in the Spanish Netherlands as well as control of the Franche-Comté.

Ensconced at Versailles since 1682, Louis seemed to be at the height of his powers. Yet the Dutch War had in fact cost him more than he had gained. Meeting the alliance against him had meant fielding ever increasing numbers of men. Internal reforms in government and finance ended under the pressure of paying for war, and old financial expedients of borrowing money and selling privileges were revived. Other government obligations, such as encouraging overseas trade, were neglected. Colbert's death in 1683 dramatically symbolized the end of an era of innovation in the French regime.

Louis's unforgiving Dutch opponent, William of Orange, king of England from 1689 to 1702, renewed and stirred up anti-French alliances. The war, now known as the Nine Years' War, or King William's War, was touched off late in 1688 by French aggression—an invasion of Germany to claim an inheritance there. In his ongoing dispute with the pope, Louis seized the papal territory of Avignon° in southern France. Boldest of all, he helped the exiled Catholic claimant to the English crown mount an invasion to reclaim his throne.

A widespread war began with all the major powers—Spain, the Netherlands, England, Austria, the major German states—ranged against France. The French also carried the fighting abroad by seizing English territory in Canada. As with the Dutch War, the Nine Years' War was costly and, on most fronts, inconclusive. This time, though, there was no illusion of victory for Louis. In the Treaty of Ryswick (1697) Louis gave up most of the territories in Germany, the Spanish Netherlands, and northern Spain that he managed to occupy by war's end. Avignon went back to the pope, and Louis relinquished his contentious claim to papal revenues. The terrible burden of war taxes combined with crop failures in 1693 and 1694 caused widespread starvation in the countryside. French courtiers began to criticize Louis openly.

The final major war of Louis's reign, called the War of the Spanish Succession, broke out in 1701. In some ways it was a straightforward dynastic clash between France and its perennial nemesis, the Habsburgs. Both Louis and Habsburg Holy Roman emperor Leopold I (r. 1657–1705) hoped to claim for their heirs the throne of Spain, left open at the death in 1700 of the last Spanish Habsburg, Charles II. Leopold represented the Austrian branch of the Habsburg family (see page 509), but Charles II bequeathed the throne to Louis's grandson, Philip of Anjou°, by reason of Louis's marriage to the Spanish princess Maria Theresa. Philip quickly proceeded to enter Spain and claim his new kingdom. War was made inevitable when Louis renounced one of the conditions of Charles's will: Philip's accession to the throne of Spain, Louis insisted, did not preclude his becoming king of France as well. This declaration was an act of sheer belligerence, for Philip was only third in line for the French throne. The Dutch and English responded to the prospect of so great a disruption of the balance of power in Europe by joining the emperor in a formal Great Alliance in 1701. The Dutch and English also wanted to defend their colonial interests since the French had already begun to profit from new trading opportunities with the Spanish colonies.

Again the French fought a major war on several fronts on land and at sea. Again the people of France felt the cost in crushing taxes worsened by harvest failures. Major revolts inside France forced Louis to divert troops from the war. For a time it seemed that the French would be soundly defeated, but they were saved by the superior organization of their forces and by dynastic accident: unexpected deaths in the Habsburg family meant that the Austrian claimant to the Spanish throne suddenly

---

**Nijmegen** (NIME-ay-gehn)    **Avignon** (ah-veen-YOHN)

**Anjou** (ahn-ZHOO)

was poised to inherit rule of Austria and the empire as well. The English, more afraid of a revival of unified Habsburg control of Spain and Austria than of French domination of Spain, quickly called for peace negotiations.

The Peace of Utrecht in 1713 resolved long-standing political conflicts and helped to set the agenda of European politics for the eighteenth century. Philip of Anjou was recognized as Philip V, the first Bourbon king of Spain, but on the condition that the Spanish and French crowns would never be worn by the same monarch. To maintain the balance of power against French interests, the Spanish Netherlands and Spanish territories in Italy were ceded by a second treaty in 1714 to Austria, which for many decades would be France's major continental rival. The Peace of Utrecht also marked the beginning of England's dominance of overseas trade and colonization. The French gave to England lands in Canada and the Caribbean and renounced any privileged relationship with Spanish colonies. England was allowed to control the highly profitable slave trade with Spanish colonies.

Louis XIV had added small amounts of strategically valuable territory along France's eastern border (see Map 16.1), and a Bourbon ruled in Spain. But the costs in human life and resources were great for the slim results achieved. Moreover, the army and navy had swallowed up capital that might have fueled investment and trade; strategic opportunities overseas were lost, never to be regained. Louis's government had been innovative in its early years but remained constrained by traditional ways of imagining the interest of the state.

# ENGLISH CIVIL WAR AND ITS AFTERMATH

**I**N England, unlike in France, a representative institution—Parliament—became an effective, permanent brake on royal authority. The process by which Parliament gained a secure role in governing the kingdom was neither easy nor peaceful, however. As we saw in Chapter 15, conflicts between the English crown and its subjects, culminating in the Crown-Parliament conflict, concerned control over taxation and the direction of religious reform. Beginning in 1642 England was beset by civil war between royal and parliamentary forces. The king was eventually defeated and executed, and for a time the monarchy was abolished altogether. It was restored in 1660, but Parliament retained a crucial role in governing the kingdom—a role that was confirmed when,

in 1688, it again deposed a monarch whose fiscal and religious policies became unacceptable to its members.

## Civil War and Regicide, 1642–1649

Fighting broke out between the armies of Charles I and parliamentary armies in the late summer of 1642. The Long Parliament (see page 522) continued to represent a broad coalition of critics and opponents of the monarchy, ranging from aristocrats concerned primarily with abuses of royal prerogative to radical Puritans eager for thorough religious reform and determined to defeat the king. Fighting was halfhearted initially, and the tide of war at first favored Charles.

In 1643, however, the scope of the war broadened. Charles made peace with Irish rebels and brought Irish troops to England to bolster his armies. Parliament in turn sought military aid from the Scots in exchange for promises that Presbyterianism would become the religion of England. Meanwhile, Oliver Cromwell (1599–1658), a Puritan member of the Long Parliament and a cavalry officer, helped reorganize parliamentary forces. The eleven-hundred-man cavalry trained by Cromwell and known as the "Ironsides," supported by parliamentary and Scottish infantry, defeated the king's troops at Marston Moor in July 1644. The victory made Cromwell famous.

Shortly afterward Parliament further improved its forces and created the New Model Army, rigorously trained like Cromwell's Ironsides. Sitting members of Parliament were barred from commanding troops; hence upper-class control of the army was reduced. This army played a decisive role not only in the war but also in the political settlement that followed the fighting.

The New Model Army won a convincing victory over royal forces at Naseby in 1645. In the spring of 1646 Charles surrendered to a Scottish army in the north. In January 1647 Parliament paid the Scots for their services in the war and took the king into custody. In the negotiations that followed, Charles tried to play his opponents off against one another, and, as he had hoped, divisions among them widened.

Most members of Parliament were Presbyterians, Puritans who favored a strongly unified and controlled state church along Calvinist lines. They wanted peace with the king in return for acceptance of the new church structure and parliamentary control of standing militias for a specified period. They did not favor expanding the right to vote or other dramatic constitutional or legal change. These men were increasingly alarmed by the rise of sectarian differences and the actual religious freedom that

**Oliver Cromwell**    Cromwell had seen his own family's income decline under the weight of Charles I's exactions. Elected to Parliament in 1628 and again in 1640, he also brought a long-standing religious zeal to his public life. His opposition to the "tyranny and usurpation" of the Anglican Church hierachy first prompted him to criticize royal government.    *(In the collection of the Duke of Buccleuch and Queensberry KT)*

many ordinary people were claiming for themselves. With the weakening of royal authority and the disruption of civil war, censorship was relaxed, and public preaching by ordinary men and even women who felt divinely inspired was becoming commonplace.

Above all, Presbyterian gentry in Parliament feared more radical groups in the army and in London who had supported them up to this point but who favored more thoroughgoing reform. Most officers of the New Model Army, such as Cromwell, were Independents, Puritans who favored a decentralized church, a degree of religious toleration, and a wider sharing of political power among men of property, not just among the very wealthy gentry. In London a well-organized artisans' movement known as the "Levellers" favored universal manhood suffrage, law reform, better access to education, and decentralized churches—in short, the separation of political power from wealth and virtual freedom of religion. Many of the rank and file of the army were deeply influenced by Leveller ideas.

In May 1647 the majority in Parliament voted to offer terms to the king and to disband the New Model Army—without first paying most of the soldiers' back wages. This move provoked the first direct intervention by the army in politics. Representatives of the soldiers were chosen to present grievances to Parliament; when this failed, the army seized the king and, in August, occupied Westminster, Parliament's meeting place. Independent and Leveller elements in the army debated the direction of possible reform to be imposed on Parliament. (See the box "The Continuing Experiment: The Putney Debates.")

In November Charles escaped from his captors and raised a new army among his erstwhile enemies, the Scots, who were also alarmed by the growing radicalism in England. Civil war began again early in 1648. Although it ended quickly with a victory by Cromwell and the New Model Army in August, the renewed war further hardened political divisions and enhanced the power of the army. The king was widely blamed for the renewed bloodshed, and the army did not trust him to keep any agreement he might now sign. When Parliament, still dominated by Presbyterians, once again voted to negotiate with the king, army troops under Colonel Thomas Pride prevented members who favored Presbyterianism or the king from attending sessions. The "Rump" Parliament that remained after "Pride's Purge" voted to try the king. A hasty trial ensued, and Charles I was executed for "treason, tyranny and bloodshed" against his people on January 30, 1649.

## The Interregnum, 1649–1660

A Commonwealth—a republic—was declared. Executive power resided in a council of state. The House of Lords having been abolished, legislative power resided in the one-chamber Rump Parliament. Declaring a republic proved far easier than running one, however. The execution of the king shocked most English and Scots and alienated many elites from the new regime. The legitimacy of the Commonwealth government would always be in question.

The tasks of making and implementing policy were hindered by the narrow political base on which the government now rested. Excluded were the majority of the reformist gentry who had been purged from Parliament. Also excluded were the more radical Levellers; Leveller leaders in London were arrested when they published tracts critical of the new government. Within a few years

# The Putney Debates

In October 1647 representatives of the Leveller movement in the army ranks confronted Independents—largely comprising the officer corps—in formally staged debates in a church at Putney, outside London. In this exchange, the Leveller representative, Thomas Rainsborough, advocates universal manhood suffrage, whereas Cromwell's fellow officer, Henry Ireton, argues for a more restricted franchise. The staging of the debates reflects the importance of the army in deciding the scope of constitutional change in England at this moment of extraordinary political fluidity. Even more important were the views that were aired at the debates, which had in common the assertion that government should exist only by the consent of the governed. These ideas became reality very slowly. The poorest men (and all women) did not get the vote in Britain until the twentieth century.

**Rainsborough:** . . . Really I think that the poorest he that is in England hath a life to live as the greatest he; and therefore truly, sir, I think it's clear, that every man that is to live under a government ought first by his own consent to put himself under that government; and I do think that the poorest man in England is not at all bound in a strict sense to that government that he hath not had a voice to put himself under; and I am confident that, when I have heard the reasons against it, that something will be said to answer those reasons, insomuch that I should doubt whether I was an Englishman or no, that should doubt of these things.

**Ireton:** . . . I think that no person hath a right to an interest or share in the disposing of the affairs of the kingdom, and in determining or choosing those that shall determine what laws we shall be ruled by here, no person hath a right to this that hath not a permanent fixed interest in this kingdom, and those persons together are properly the represented of this kingdom, who taken together, and consequently are to make up the represented of this kingdom, are the representers, who taken together do comprehend whatsoever is of real or permanent interest in the kingdom, and I am sure there is otherwise (I cannot tell what), otherwise any man can say why a foreigner coming in amongst us, or as many as will be coming in amongst us, or by force or otherwise settling themselves here, or at least by our permission having a being here, why they should not as well lay claim to it as any other. We talk of birthright. Truly birthright there is thus much claim: men may justly have by birthright, by their very being born in England, that we should not seclude them out of England. That we should not refuse to give them air and place and ground, and the freedom of the highways and other things, to live amongst us, not any man that is born here, though he in birth, or by his birth there come nothing at all that is part of the permanent interest of this kingdom to him. That I think is due to a man by birth. But that by a man's being born here he shall have a share in that power that shall dispose of the lands here, and of all things here, I do not think it a sufficient ground, but I am sure if we look upon that which is the utmost, within man's view, of what was originally the constitution of this kingdom, upon that which is most radical and fundamental, and which if you take away, there is no man hath any land, any goods, you take away any civil interest, and that is this: that those that choose the representers for the making of laws by which this state and kingdom are to be governed, are the persons who taken together, do comprehend the local interest of this kingdom; that is, the persons in whom all land lies, and those in corporations in whom all trading lies. This is the most fundamental constitution of this kingdom, and which if you do not allow, you allow none at all.

## QUESTIONS

1. On what grounds does Henry Ireton argue for restricting the right to participate in government? How does he counter Rainsborough's more sweeping claim that all men should be governed only with their own consent?

2. What social, religious, economic, and political conditions prevalent in seventeenth-century England help us to explain the origins of these ideas?

3. In what ways might the Putney debates have been important, even though the ideas aired in them were not enacted, in the main, for centuries to come?

many disillusioned Levellers would join a new religious movement called the Society of Friends, or Quakers, which espoused complete religious autonomy. Quakers declined all oaths or service to the state, and they refused to acknowledge social rank.

Above all, the new government was vulnerable to the power of the army, which had created it. In 1649 and 1650 Cromwell led expeditions to Ireland and Scotland, partly for sheer revenge and partly to put down resistance to Commonwealth authority. In Ireland Cromwell's forces acted with shameful ruthlessness. English control there was strengthened by more dispossession of Irish landholders, which also served to pay off the army's wages. Meanwhile, Parliament could not agree on systematic reforms, particularly the one reform Independents in the army insisted on: more broadly based elections for a new Parliament. Fresh from his victories, Cromwell led his armies to London and dissolved Parliament in the spring of 1652.

In 1653 a cadre of army officers drew up the "Instrument of Government," England's first and only written constitution. It provided for an executive, the Lord Protector, and a Parliament to be based on somewhat wider male suffrage. Cromwell was the natural choice for Lord Protector, and whatever success the government of the Protectorate had was due largely to him.

Cromwell was an extremely able leader who was not averse to compromise. Although he had used force against Parliament in 1648, he had worked hard to reconcile the Rump Parliament and the army before marching on London in 1652. He believed in a state church, but one that allowed for control, including choice of minister, by local congregations. He also believed in toleration for other Protestant sects, as well as for Catholics and Jews, as long as no one disturbed the peace.

As Lord Protector, Cromwell oversaw impressive reforms in law that testify to his belief in the limits of governing authority. For example, contrary to the practice of his day, he opposed capital punishment for petty crimes. The government of the Protectorate, however, accomplished little given Parliament's internal divisions and opposition to Cromwell's initiatives. The population at large still harbored royalist sympathizers; after a royalist uprising in 1655, Cromwell divided England into military districts and vested governing authority in army generals.

In the end the Protectorate could not survive the strains over policy and the challenges to its legitimacy. When Cromwell died of a sudden illness in September 1658, the Protectorate did not long survive him. In February 1660 the decisive action of one army general en-

**Popular Preaching in England**    Many women took advantage of the collapse of royal authority to preach in public—a radical activity for women at the time. This print satirizes the Quakers, a religious movement that attracted many women. *(Mary Evans Picture Library)*

abled all the surviving members of the Long Parliament to rejoin the Rump. The Parliament summarily dissolved itself and called for new elections. The newly elected Parliament recalled Charles II, son of Charles I, from exile abroad and restored the monarchy. The chaos and radicalism of the late civil war and "interregnum"—the period between reigns, as the years from 1649 to 1660 came to be called—now spawned a conservative reaction.

## The Restoration, 1660–1685

Charles II (r. 1660–1685) claimed his throne at the age of 30. He had learned from his years of uncertain exile and from the fate of his father. He did not seek retribution but rather offered a general pardon to all but a few rebels (mostly those who had signed his father's death warrant), and he suggested to Parliament a relatively tolerant religious settlement that would include Anglicans as well as Presbyterians. He was far more politically adept than his father and far more willing to compromise.

That the re-established royal government was not more tolerant than it turned out to be was not Charles's doing but Parliament's. During the 1660s, the "Cavalier" Parliament, named for royalists in the civil war, passed harsh laws aimed at religious dissenters. Anglican orthodoxy was reimposed, including the re-establishment of bishops and the Anglican *Book of Common Prayer*. All officeholders and clergy were required to swear oaths of obedience to the king and to the established church. As a result, hundreds were forced out of office and pulpits. Holding nonconformist religious services became illegal, and Parliament passed a "five-mile" act to prevent dissenting ministers from traveling near their former congregations. Property laws were tightened and the criminal codes made more severe.

The king's behavior in turn began to mimic prerevolutionary royalist positions. Charles II began to flirt with Catholicism, and his brother and heir, James, openly converted. Charles promulgated a declaration of tolerance that would have included Catholics as well as nonconformist Protestants, but Parliament would not accept it. Anti-Catholic feeling still united all Protestants. In 1678 Charles's secret treaties with the French became known (see page 547), and rumors of a Catholic plot to murder Charles and reimpose Catholicism became widespread. No evidence of any plot was ever unearthed, although thirty-five people were executed for alleged participation. Parliament focused its attention on anti-Catholicism, passing the Test Act, which barred all but Anglicans from public office. As a result, the Catholic James was forced to resign as Lord High Admiral.

When Parliament moved to exclude James from succession to the throne, Charles dissolved it. A subsequent Parliament, worried by the specter of a new civil war, backed down. But the legacy of the civil war was a potent one. First, despite the harsh laws, to silence all dissent was not possible. After two decades of religious pluralism and broadly based political activity, it was impossible to reimpose conformity; well-established communities of various sects and self-confidence bred vigorous resistance. The clearest reflection of the legacy of events was the power of Parliament. Though reluctant to press too far, Parliament had tried to assert its policies against the desires of the king.

Nevertheless, by the end of his reign Charles was financially independent of Parliament, thanks to increased revenue from overseas trade and secret subsidies from France, his recent ally against Dutch trading rivals. This financial independence and firm political tactics enabled Charles to regain, and retain, a great deal of power. If he had been followed by an able successor, Parliament might have lost a good measure of its confidence and independence. But his brother James's reign and its aftermath further enhanced Parliament's power.

## The Glorious Revolution, 1688

When James II (r. 1685–1689) succeeded Charles, Parliament's royalist leanings were at first evident. James was granted customs duties for life and was also given funds to suppress a rebellion by one of Charles's illegitimate sons. James did not try to impose Catholicism on England as some had feared, but he did try to achieve toleration for Catholics in two declarations of indulgence in 1687 and 1688. However admirable his goal—toleration—he had essentially changed the law of the realm without Parliament's consent and further undermined his position with heavy-handed tactics. When several leading Anglican bishops refused to read the declarations from their pulpits, he had them imprisoned and tried for seditious libel. However, a sympathetic jury acquitted them.

James also failed because of the coincidence of other events. In 1685, at the outset of James's reign, Louis XIV of France had revoked the Edict of Nantes. The possibility that subjects and monarchs in France and, by extension, elsewhere could be of different faiths seemed increasingly unlikely. Popular fears of James's Catholicism were thus heightened early in his reign, and his later declarations of tolerance, though benefiting Protestant dissenters, were viewed with suspicion. In 1688 not only were the Anglican bishops acquitted but the king's second wife, who was Catholic, gave birth to a son. The birth raised the specter of a Catholic succession.

In June 1688, to put pressure on James, leading members of Parliament invited William of Orange, husband of James's Protestant daughter, Mary, to come to England. William mounted an invasion that became a rout when James refused to defend his throne. James simply abandoned England and went to France. William called Parliament, which declared James to have abdicated and offered the throne jointly to William and Mary. With French support James eventually invaded Ireland in 1690—bound for Westminster—but was defeated by William at the Battle of Boyne that year.

The substitution of William (r. 1689–1702) and Mary (r. 1689–1694) for James, known as the "Glorious Revolution," was engineered by Parliament and confirmed its power. Parliament presented the new sovereigns with a

Declaration of Rights upon their accession and, later that year, with a Bill of Rights that defended freedom of speech, called for frequent Parliaments, and required subsequent monarchs to be Protestant. The effectiveness of these documents was reinforced by Parliament's power of the purse. Parliament's role in the political process was ensured by William's interests in funding his ambitious military efforts, particularly the Netherlands' ongoing wars with France.

The issues that had faced the English since the beginning of the century were common to all European states: religious division and elite power, fiscal strains and resistance to taxation. Yet the cataclysmic events in England—the interregnum, the Commonwealth, the Restoration, the Glorious Revolution—had set it apart from other states. Consequently, the incremental assumption of authority by a well-established institution, Parliament, made challenge of the English monarchy more legitimate and more effective.

# New Powers in Central and Eastern Europe

BY the end of the seventeenth century three states dominated central and eastern Europe: Austria, Brandenburg-Prussia, and Russia. After the Thirty Years' War the Habsburgs' dominance in the splintering empire waned, and they focused on expanding and consolidating their power in their hereditary possessions. Brandenburg-Prussia, in northeastern Germany, emerged from obscurity to rival the Habsburg state. The rulers of Brandenburg-Prussia had gained lands in the Peace of Westphalia, and astute management transformed their relatively small and scattered holdings into one of the most powerful states in Europe. Russia's new stature in eastern Europe resulted in part from the weakness of its greatest rival, Poland, and the determination of one leader, Peter the Great, to assume a major role in European affairs. Sweden controlled valuable Baltic territory through much of the century but eventually was also eclipsed by Russia as a force in the region.

The internal political development of these states was dramatically shaped by their relationship to the wider European economy: they were sources of grain and raw materials for the more densely urbanized West. The development of and the competition among states in central and eastern Europe were closely linked to developments in western Europe.

## The Consolidation of Austria

The Thirty Years' War (see pages 523–528) weakened the Habsburgs as emperors but strengthened them in their own lands. The main Habsburg lands in 1648 were a collection of principalities comprising modern Austria, the kingdom of Hungary (largely in Turkish hands), and the kingdom of Bohemia (see Map 16.2). In 1714 Austria acquired the Spanish Netherlands, which were renamed the Austrian Netherlands. Although language and ethnic differences prevented an absolutist state along French lines, Leopold I (r. 1657–1705) instituted political and institutional changes that enabled the Habsburg state to become one of the most powerful in Europe through the eighteenth century.

Much of the coherence that already existed in Leopold's lands had been achieved by his predecessors in the wake of the Thirty Years' War. The lands of rebels in Bohemia had been confiscated and redistributed among loyal, mostly Austrian, families. In return for political and military support for the emperor, these families were given the right to exploit their newly acquired land and the peasants who worked it. The desire to recover population and productivity after the destruction of the Thirty Years' War gave landlords further incentive to curtail peasants' autonomy, particularly in devastated Bohemia. Austrian landlords throughout the Habsburg domains provided grain and timber for the export market and foodstuffs for the Austrian armies, while elite families provided the army with officers. This political-economic arrangement provoked numerous serious peasant revolts, but the peasants were not able to force changes in a system that suited both the elites and the central authority.

Although Leopold had lost much influence within the empire itself, an imperial government made up of various councils, a war ministry, financial officials, and the like still functioned in his capital, Vienna. Leopold worked to extricate the government of his own lands from the apparatus of imperial institutions, which were staffed largely by Germans more loyal to imperial than to Habsburg interests. In addition, Leopold used the Catholic Church as an institutional and ideological support for the Habsburg state.

Leopold's personal ambition was to re-establish devout Catholicism throughout his territories. Acceptance of Catholicism became the litmus test of loyalty to the Habsburg regime, and Protestantism vanished among elites. Leopold encouraged the work of Jesuit teachers and members of other Catholic orders. These men and women helped staff his government and administered religious life down to the most local levels.

**Baroque Splendor in Austria**   The Belvedere Palace (whose name means "beautiful view") was built near Vienna as the summer residence of the great aristocratic general Prince Eugene of Savoy, who had successfully led Habsburg armies against the Turks and had reaped many rewards from Leopold and his successors. The palace shares many features in common with Louis XIV's palace of Versailles (see page 545).   *(Erich Lessing/Art Resource, NY)*

Leopold's most dramatic success, as a Habsburg and a religious leader, was his reconquest of the kingdom of Hungary from the Ottoman Empire. Since the mid-sixteenth century the Habsburgs had controlled only a narrow strip of the kingdom. Preoccupied with countering Louis XIV's aggression, Leopold did not himself choose to begin a reconquest. His centralizing policies, however, alienated nobles and townspeople in the portion of Hungary he did control, as did his repression of Protestantism, which had flourished in Hungary. Hungarian nobles began a revolt, aided by the Turks, aiming for a reunited Hungary under Ottoman protection.

The Habsburgs emerged victorious in part because they received help from the Venetians, the Russians, and especially the Poles, whose lands in Ukraine were threatened by the Turks. The Turks overreached their supply lines to besiege Vienna in 1683. When the siege failed, Habsburg armies slowly pressed east and south, recovering Buda, the capital of Hungary, in 1686 and Belgrade (modern Serbia) in 1688. The Danube basin lay once

again in Christian hands. The Treaty of Carlowitz ended the fighting in 1699, after the first conference where European allies jointly dictated terms to a weakening Ottoman Empire. Austria's allies had also gained at the Ottomans' expense: the Poles recovered the threatened Ukraine, and the Russians gained a vital foothold on the Black Sea.

Leopold gave land in the reclaimed lands to Austrian officers who he believed were loyal to him. The traditions of Hungarian separatism, however, were strong, and the great magnates—whether they had defended the Habsburgs against Turkish encroachment or guarded the frontier for Turkish overlords—retained their independence. The peasantry, as elsewhere, suffered a decline in status as a result of the Crown's efforts to ensure the loyalty of elites. In the long run Hungarian independence weakened the Habsburg state, but in the short run Leopold's victory over the Turks and the recovery of Hungary itself were momentous events, confirming the Habsburgs as the pre-eminent power in central Europe.

## The Rise of Brandenburg-Prussia

Three German states, in addition to Austria, gained territory and stature after the Thirty Years' War: Bavaria, Saxony, and Brandenburg-Prussia. By the end of the seventeenth century the strongest was Brandenburg-Prussia, a conglomeration of small territories held, by dynastic accident, by the Hohenzollern family. The two principal territories were electoral Brandenburg, in northeastern Germany, with its capital, Berlin, and the duchy of Prussia, a fief of the Polish crown along the Baltic coast east of Poland proper (see Map 16.2). In addition, the Hohenzollerns ruled a handful of small principalities near the Netherlands. The manipulation of resources and power that enabled these unpromising lands to become a powerful state was primarily the work of Frederick William, known as "the Great Elector" (r. 1640–1688).

Frederick William used the occasion of a war to effect a permanent change in the structure of government. He took advantage of a war between Poland and its rivals, Sweden and Russia (described in the next section), to win independence for the duchy of Prussia from Polish overlordship. When his involvement in the war ended in 1657, he kept intact the general war commissariat, a combined civilian and military body that had efficiently directed the war effort, bypassing traditional councils and representative bodies. He also used the standing army to force the payment of high taxes. Most significantly, he established a positive relationship with the Junkers°, hereditary landholders, which ensured him both revenue and loyalty. He agreed to allow the Junkers virtually total control of their own lands in return for their agreement to support his government—in short, they surrendered their accustomed political independence in exchange for greater economic and social power over the peasants who worked their lands.

Peasants and townspeople were taxed, but nobles were not. The freedom to control their estates led many nobles to invest in profitable agriculture for the export market. The peasants were serfs who received no benefits from the increased productivity of the land. Frederick William further enhanced his state's power by sponsoring state industries. These industries did not have to fear competition from urban producers because the towns had been frozen out of the political process and saddled with heavy taxes. Though an oppressive place for many Germans, Brandenburg-Prussia attracted many skilled refugees, such as Huguenot artisans fleeing Louis XIV's France.

Bavaria and Saxony, in contrast to Brandenburg-Prussia, had vibrant towns, largely free peasantries, and weaker aristocracies but were relative nonentities in international affairs. Power on the European stage depended on military force. Such power, whether in a large state like France or in a small one like Brandenburg-Prussia, usually came at the expense of the people.

## Competition Around the Baltic: The Decline of Poland and the Zenith of Swedish Power

The rivers and port cities of the Baltic coast were conduits for the growing trade between the Baltic hinterland and the rest of Europe. In 1600 a large portion of the Baltic hinterland lay under the control of Poland-Lithuania, a vast and diverse state at the height of its power, but one that would prove an exception to the pattern of expanding royal power in the seventeenth century. Wars in the middle of the century were extremely destructive in regard not only to lives and property but also, unlike in neighboring Prussia, to the coherence of the state as well.

Internal strains began to mount in Poland-Lithuania in the late sixteenth century. The spread of the Counter-Reformation, encouraged by the Crown, created tensions with both Protestant and Orthodox subjects in the diverse kingdom. The greatest source of political instability was the power of landholding nobles, whose fortunes grew as Poland became the granary of western Europe. Impoverished peasants were bound to the land, and lesser gentry, particularly in the Ruthenian lands of Lithuania, were shut out of political power by Polish aristocrats. In Ukraine communities of Cossacks, nomadic farmer-warriors, grew as Polish and Lithuanian peasants fled harsh conditions to join them. The Cossacks had long been tolerated because they served as a military buffer against the Ottoman Turks to the south, but now Polish landlords wanted to reincorporate the Cossacks into the profitable political-economic system they controlled.

In 1648 the Polish crown faced revolt and invasion that it could not fully counter. The Cossacks led a major uprising, which included Ukrainian gentry as well as peasants. The Cossacks held their own against the Polish armies. Meanwhile, the Crown's efforts to reach a peace agreement were blocked by the noble landlords against whom the revolt had been directed. In 1654 the Cossacks tried to assure their autonomy by transferring their allegiance to Moscow. They became part of a Russian invasion of Poland-Lithuania that by the next year had engulfed much of the eastern half of the dual state. At the same time, Poland's perennial rival, Sweden, seized central Poland in a military campaign marked by extreme brutality. Many

---

**Junkers** (YUNG-kurz)

**Map 16.2  New Powers in Central and Eastern Europe, to 1725**  The balance of power in central and eastern Europe shifted with the strengthening of Austria, the rise of Brandenburg-Prussia, and the expansion of Russia at the expense of Poland and Sweden.

Polish and Lithuanian aristocrats continued to act like independent warlords and cooperated with the invaders to preserve their own local power.

Operating with slim resources, Polish royal armies eventually managed to recover much territory—most important, the western half of Ukraine (see Map 16.2). But the invasions and subsequent fighting were disastrous. These wars were afterward referred to as "the deluge," and with good reason. The population of Poland declined by as much as 40 percent, and vital urban economies were in ruins. The Catholic identity of the Polish heartland had been a rallying point for resistance to the Protestant Swedes and the Orthodox Russians, but the religious tolerance that had distinguished the Polish kingdom and had been mandated in its constitution was now abandoned. In addition, much of its recovery of Lithuanian territory was only nominal.

The elective Polish crown passed in 1674 to the military hero Jan Sobieski° (r. 1674–1696), known as "Vanquisher of the Turks" for his role in raising the siege of Vienna in 1683. Given Poland's internal weakness, however, Sobieski's victories in the long run helped the Ottomans' other foes—Austria and Russia—more than they helped the Poles. Moreover, though a brilliant tactician, he was a master of an increasingly outmoded form of warfare that was almost wholly reliant on cavalry. He was unable to force reforms that would have led to increased royal revenue and a more up-to-date royal army. After his death Poland would be vulnerable to the political ambitions of its more powerful neighbors. Augustus II of Saxony (r. 1697–1704, 1709–1733) dragged Poland back into war, from which Russia would emerge the clear winner in the power struggle in eastern Europe.

The Swedes, meanwhile, had successfully vied with the Poles and other competitors for control of the lucrative Baltic coast. Swedish efforts to control Baltic territory began in the sixteenth century, first to counter the power of its perennial rival, Denmark, in the western Baltic. It then competed with Poland to control Livonia (modern Latvia), whose principal city, Riga, was an important trading center for goods from both Lithuania and Russia. By 1617, under Gustav Adolf, the Swedes gained the lands to the north surrounding the Gulf of Finland (the most direct outlet for Russian goods), and in 1621 they displaced the Poles in Livonia itself. Swedish intervention in the Thirty Years' War came when imperial successes against Denmark both threatened the Baltic coast and created an opportunity to strike at Sweden's old enemy. The Treaty of Westphalia (1648) confirmed Sweden's earlier gains and added control of further coastal territory, mostly at Denmark's expense.

The port cities held by Sweden were profitable but simply served to pay for the costly wars necessary to seize and defend them. Indeed, Sweden's efforts to hold Baltic territory were driven by dynastic and strategic needs as much as economic objectives. The ruling dynasty struggled against Denmark's control of western Baltic territory in order to safeguard its independence from the Danes, who had ruled the combined kingdoms until 1523. Similarly, competition with Poland for the eastern Baltic was part of a dynastic struggle after 1592. Sigismund Vasa, son of the king of Sweden, had been elected king of Poland in 1587 but also inherited the Swedish throne in 1592. Other members of the Vasa family fought him successfully to regain rule over Sweden and extricate Swedish interests from Poland's continental preoccupations. Although Sigismund ruled Poland until his death in 1632, a Vasa uncle replaced him on the Swedish throne in 1604.

The one permanent gain that Sweden realized from its aggression against Poland in the 1650s was the renunciation of the Polish Vasa line to any claim to the Swedish crown. Owing to its earlier gains, Sweden reigned supreme on the Baltic coast until the end of the century, when it was supplanted by the powerful Russian state.

## Russia Under Peter the Great

The Russian state expanded dramatically through the sixteenth century under Ivan IV and weathered the period of disputed succession known as the "Time of Troubles" (see pages 528–530). The foundations of the large and cohesive state laid by Ivan enabled Michael Romanov° to rebuild autocratic government with ease after being chosen tsar in 1613.

The Romanovs were an eminent aristocratic family related to Ivan's. Michael (r. 1613–1645) was selected to rule by an assembly of aristocrats, gentry, and commoners who were more alarmed at the civil wars and recent Polish incursions than at the prospect of a return to strong tsarist rule. Michael was succeeded by his son, Alexis (r. 1645–1676), who presided over the extension of Russian control to eastern Ukraine in 1654 following the wars in Poland and developed an interest in cultivating relationships with the West.

Shifting the balance of power in eastern Europe and the Baltic in Russia's favor was also the work of Alexis's son, Peter I (r. 1682–1725), "the Great." Peter accomplished this by military successes against his enemies and by

**Sobieski** (so-BYESS-key)

**Romanov** (ROH-man-off)

**Peter the Great**    This portrait by a Dutch artist captures the tsar's "westernizing" mission by showing Peter in military dress according to European fashions of the day.
*(Rijksmuseum-Stichting, Amsterdam)*

forcibly reorienting Russian government and society toward involvement with the rest of Europe.

Peter was almost literally larger than life. Nearly 7 feet tall, he towered over most of his contemporaries and had physical and mental energy to match his size. He set himself to learning trades and studied soldiering by rising through the ranks of the military like a common soldier. He traveled abroad to learn as much as he could about western European economies and governments. He wanted the revenue, manufacturing output, technology and trade, and, above all, up-to-date army and navy that other rulers enjoyed. In short Peter sought for Russia a more evolved state system because of the strength it would give him.

Immediately on his accession to power, Peter initiated a bold series of changes in Russian society. His travels had taught him that European monarchs coexisted with a privileged but educated aristocracy and that a brilliant court life symbolized and reinforced their authority. So he set out to refashion Russian society in what amounted

to an enforced cultural revolution. He provoked a direct confrontation with Russia's traditional aristocracy over everything from education to matters of dress. He elevated numerous new families to the ranks of gentry and created an official ranking system for the nobility to encourage and reward service to his government.

Peter's effort to reorient his nation culturally, economically, and politically toward Europe was most apparent in the construction of the city of St. Petersburg on the Gulf of Finland, which provided access to the Baltic Sea (see Map 16.2). In stark contrast to Moscow, dominated by the medieval fortress of the Kremlin and churches in the traditional Russian style, St. Petersburg was a modern European city with wide avenues and palaces designed for a sophisticated court life.

Although Peter was highly intelligent, practical, and determined to create a more productive and better-governed society, he was also cruel and authoritarian. Peasants already were bearing the brunt of taxation, but their tax burden worsened when they were assessed arbitrarily by head and not by output of the land. The building of St. Petersburg cost staggering sums in both money and workers' lives. Peter's entire reform system was carried out tyrannically; resistance was brutally suppressed. Victims of Peter's oppression included his son, Alexis, who died after torture while awaiting execution for questioning his father's policies.

Peter faced elite as well as populist rebellions against the exactions and the cultural changes of his regime. The most serious challenge was the revolt in 1707 of the Cossacks in the Don River region against the regime's tightened controls. (See the box "Reading Sources: Resistance to Peter the Great.") A major reason for the high cost of Peter's government to the Russian people was his ambition for territorial gain—hence his emphasis on an improved, and costly, army and navy. Working side by side with workers and technicians, many of whom he had recruited while abroad, Peter created the Russian navy from scratch. At first ships were built in the south to contest Turkish control of the Black Sea. Later they were built in the north to secure and defend the Baltic. Peter also modernized the Russian army by employing tactics, training, and discipline he had observed in the West. He introduced military conscription and munitions plants. By 1709 Russia was able to manufacture most of the up-to-date firearms its army needed.

Russia waged war virtually throughout Peter's reign. Initially with some success, he struck at the Ottomans and their client state in the Crimea. Later phases of these conflicts brought reverses, however. Peter was spectacularly successful against his northern competitor, Sweden, for control of the weakened Polish state and the Baltic

## READING SOURCES

## RESISTANCE TO PETER THE GREAT

*Many of Peter's subjects resisted his policies, including nobles who despised the enforced cultural changes and peasants who chafed under his more traditional demand of heavy taxes. This letter from July 1705 reflects the efforts of one group of resisters, city dwellers from Astrakhan, a port on the Caspian Sea, to join forces with the Cossacks of the Don River region to their west. Many citizens of Astrakhan had been at odds with the tsars over church reforms since the seventeenth century. Note that their objections to Peter's cultural reforms, which included European dress and other matters of style (such as being clean-shaven and using tobacco), are thus couched in religious terms. What other concerns does this document reveal? Why might the citizens of Astrakhan have forged an alliance with the Cossacks?*

To [the Chief] and to all the Don Cossack Host, we . . . all the city folk of Astrakhan . . . send our greetings. We wish to inform you of what has happened in Astrakhan on account of our Christian faith, because of beard-shaving, German dress, and tobacco; how we, our wives and our children were not admitted into churches in our old Russian dress; how men and women who entered the holy church had their clothes shorn and were expelled and thrown out. . . . Moreover, in the last year, they imposed on us and collected a [new] tax: one ruble "bath money" apiece; and they also ordered us to pay [a certain tax] per seven feet of cellar space. . . . The [local governor] together with other men in authority, colonels and captains, took away all of our firearms and wanted to kill us. . . . They also took away from us, without orders, our bread allowance and forbade that it be issued to us. We endured all this for a long time. [At last,] after taking counsel among ourselves . . . moved by our great distress, for we could endure it no more to be in danger of losing our Christian faith, we resisted: we killed some of them and have put some others in prison. You, the Cossack [Chief] and all the Host of the Don, please deliberate among yourselves and stand up together with us to defend the Christian faith, and send a message about your decision to us at Astrakhan. We are awaiting you . . . and we rely upon you.

Source: Alfred J. Andrea and James H. Overfield, *The Human Record: Sources of Global History,* vol. 2: *Since 1500,* 2d ed. (Boston: Houghton Mifflin, 1994), pp. 168–169.

---

Sea. The conflicts between Sweden and Russia, known as the Great Northern War, raged from 1700 to 1709 and, in a less intense phase, lasted until 1721. By the Treaty of Nystadt in 1721, Russia gained its present-day territory in the Gulf of Finland near St. Petersburg, plus Livonia and Estonia. These acquisitions gave Russia a secure window on the Baltic and, in combination with its gains of Lithuanian territory earlier in the century, made Russia the preeminent Baltic power, at Sweden's and Poland's expense.

## THE EXPANSION OF OVERSEAS TRADE AND SETTLEMENT

BY the beginning of the seventeenth century competition from the Dutch, French, and English was disrupting the Spanish and Portuguese trading empires in Asia and the New World. During the seventeenth century European trade and colonization expanded and changed dramatically. The Dutch not only became masters of the spice trade but broadened the market to include many other commodities. In the Americas a new trading system linking Europe, Africa, and the New World came into being with the expansion of tobacco and, later, sugar production. French and English colonists began settling in North America in increasing numbers. By the end of the century trading and colonial outposts around the world figured regularly as bargaining chips in disagreements between European states. More important, overseas trade had a crucial impact on life within Europe: on patterns of production and consumption, on social stratification, and on the distribution of wealth.

### The Growth of Trading Empires: The Success of the Dutch

By the end of the sixteenth century the Dutch and the English were making incursions into the Portuguese-controlled spice trade with areas of India, Ceylon, and

**Map 16.3 Dutch Commerce in the Seventeenth Century** The Dutch supplanted Portuguese control of trade with Asia and dominated seaborne trade within Europe.

the East Indies. Spain had annexed Portugal in 1580, but the drain on Spain's resources from its wars with the Dutch and French prevented Spain from adequately defending its enlarged trading empire in Asia. The Dutch and, to a lesser degree, the English rapidly supplanted Portuguese control of this lucrative trade (see Map 16.3).

The Dutch were particularly well placed to be successful competitors in overseas trade. They already dominated seaborne trade within Europe, including the most important long-distance trade, which linked Spain and Portugal—with their wine and salt, as well as spices, hides, and gold from abroad—with the Baltic seacoast, where these products were sold for grain and timber produced in Germany, Poland-Lithuania, and Scandinavia. The geographic position of the Netherlands and the fact that the Dutch consumed more Baltic grain than any other area, because of their large urban population, help to explain their dominance of this trade. In addition, the Dutch had improved the design of their mer-

chant ships to maximize their profits. By 1600 they were building the *fluitschip* (flyship) to transport cargo economically; it was a vessel with a long, flat hull, simple rigging, and cheap construction.

The Dutch were successful in Asia because of institutional as well as technological innovations. In 1602 the Dutch East India Company was formed. The company combined government management of trade, typical of the period, with both public and private investment. In the past groups of investors had funded single voyages or small numbers of ships on a one-time basis. The formation of the Dutch East India Company created a permanent pool of capital to sustain trade. After 1612 investments in the company were negotiable as stock. These greater assets allowed proprietors to spread the risks and delays of longer voyages among larger numbers of investors. In addition, more money was available for warehouses, docks, and ships. The English East India Company, founded in 1607, also supported trade, but more modestly. It had

**Dutch Strength at Sea**    This painting by the Dutch artist Van der Velde the Younger celebrates a Dutch victory over a combined French and English fleet in 1673. The Dutch had fought their primary commercial rivals, the English, during the 1650s and had built up their fleet of warships in response. Like most major sea battles of the era, this one was fought close to home, off the Dutch coast near the sea-lanes to Amsterdam.    *(HarperCollins Publishers/The Art Archive)*

one-tenth the capital of the Dutch company and did not use the same system of permanent capital held as stock by investors until 1657. The Bank of Amsterdam, founded in 1609, became the depository for the bullion that flowed into the Netherlands with the flood of trade. The bank established currency exchange rates and issued paper money and instruments of credit to facilitate commerce.

A dramatic expansion of trade with Asia resulted from the Dutch innovations, so much so that by 1650 the European market for spices was glutted, and traders' profits had begun to fall. To control the supply of spices, the Dutch seized some of the areas where they were produced. The Dutch and English further responded to the oversupply of spices by diversifying their trade. The proportion of spices in cargoes from the East fell from about 70 percent at midcentury to just over 20 percent by the century's end. New consumer goods such as tea, coffee, and silk and cotton fabrics took their place. The demand of ordinary people for inexpensive yet serviceable Indian cottons grew steadily. Eventually the Dutch and the English, alert for fresh opportunities in the East, entered the local carrying trade among Asian states. Doing so enabled them to make profits even without purchasing goods, and it slowed the drain of hard currency from Europe—

currency in increasingly short supply as silver mines in the Americas were depleted.

## The "Golden Age" of the Netherlands

The prosperity occasioned by the Netherlands' "mother trade" within Europe and its burgeoning overseas commerce helped foster social and political conditions unique among European states. The concentration of trade and shipping sustained a healthy merchant oligarchy and also an extensive and prosperous artisanal sector. Disparities of wealth were smaller here than anywhere else in Europe. The shipbuilding and fishing trades, among others, supported large numbers of workers with a high standard of living for the age.

The Netherlands appeared to contemporaries to be an astonishing exception to the normal structures of politics. Political decentralization in the Netherlands persisted. The Estates General (representative assembly) for the Netherlands as a whole had no independent powers of taxation. Each of the seven provinces retained considerable autonomy. Wealthy merchants in the Estates of the province of Holland, in fact, constituted the government for the entire nation for long periods because of

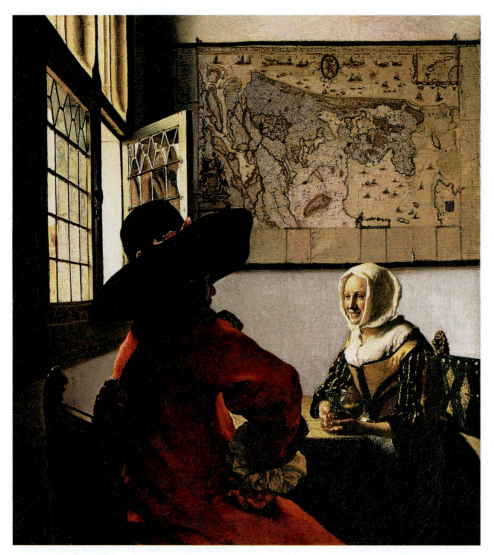

**Vermeer: The Soldier and the Laughing Girl**    This is an early work by one of the great artists of the Dutch "Golden Age." Dutch art was distinguished by its treatment of common, rather than heroic, subjects. The masterful use of light and perspective in paintings such as this one would not be equaled until the invention of photography.    *(Copyright The Frick Collection, New York)*

Holland's economic dominance. The head of government was the executive secretary, known as the pensionary, of Holland's Estates.

Holland's only competition in the running of affairs came from the House of Orange, aristocratic leaders of the revolt against Spain (see pages 508–510). They exercised what control they had by means of the office of *stadholder*°—a kind of military governorship—to which they were elected in individual provinces. Their principal interest was the traditional one of military glory and self-promotion. Therein lay a portion of their influence, for they continued to lead the defense of the Netherlands against Spanish attempts at reconquest until the Peace of Westphalia in 1648 and against French aggression after 1672. Their power also came from their status as the only counterweight within the Netherlands to the dominance of Amsterdam's (in Holland) mercantile interests. Small towns dependent on land-based trade or rural areas dominated by farmers and gentry looked to the stadholders of the Orange family to defend their interests.

**stadholder** (STAHT-hole-der)

As elsewhere, religion was a source of political conflict. The stadholders and the leading families of Holland, known as regents, vied for control of the state church. Pensionaries and regents of Holland generally favored a less rigid and austere form of Calvinism than did the stadholders. Their view reflected the needs of the diverse urban communities of Holland, where thousands of Jews, as well as Catholics and various Protestants, lived. Foreign policy was also disputed: Hollanders desired peace in order to foster commerce, whereas stadholders willingly engaged in warfare for territory and dynastic advantage.

These differences notwithstanding, Dutch commercial dominance involved the Netherlands in costly wars throughout the second half of the century. Between 1657 and 1660 the Dutch defended Denmark against Swedish ambitions in order to safeguard the sea-lanes and port cities of the Baltic. More costly conflicts arose because of rivalry with the more powerful England and France. Under Cromwell the English attempted to close their ports to the Dutch carrying trade. In 1672 the English under Charles II allied with the French, assuming that together they could destroy Dutch power and perhaps even divide the Netherlands' territory between them. The Dutch navy, rebuilt since Cromwell's challenge, soon forced England out of the alliance.

Owing largely to the land war with France, the Estates in Holland lost control of policy to William of Nassau (d. 1702), prince of Orange after 1672. William drew the Netherlands into his family's long-standing close relationship with England. Like other members of his family before him, William had married into the English royal family: his wife was Mary, daughter of James II.

Ironically, after William and Mary assumed the English throne, Dutch commerce suffered more in alliance with England than in its previous rivalry. William used Dutch resources for the land war against Louis XIV and reserved for the English navy the fight at sea. By the end of the century Dutch maritime strength was being eclipsed by English sea power.

## The Growth of Atlantic Colonies and Commerce

In the seventeenth century the Dutch, the English, and the French joined the Spanish as colonial and commercial powers in the Americas. The Spanish colonial empire, in theory a trading system closed to outsiders, was in fact vulnerable to incursion by other European traders. Spanish treasure fleets were themselves a glittering attraction. In 1628, for example, a Dutch captain seized the entire fleet. But by then Spain's goals and those of its competitors had begun to shift. The limits of an economy based on the extraction, rather than the production, of wealth became clear with the declining output of the Spanish silver mines during the 1620s. In response the Spanish and their Dutch, French, and English competitors expanded the production of the cash crops of tobacco, dyestuffs, and, above all, sugar.

The European demand for tobacco and sugar, both addictive substances, grew steadily in the seventeenth century. The plantation system—the use of forced labor to produce cash crops on vast tracts of land—had been developed on Mediterranean islands in the Middle Ages by European entrepreneurs, using slaves procured in Black Sea ports by Venetian and Genoese traders. Sugar production by this system had been established on Atlantic islands, such as the Cape Verde Islands, using African labor, and then in the Americas by the Spanish and Portuguese. Sugar production in the New World grew from about 20,000 tons in 1600 to about 200,000 tons by 1770.

In the 1620s, while the Dutch were exploiting Portuguese weakness in the Eastern spice trade, they were also seizing sugar regions in Brazil and replacing the Portuguese in slaving ports in Africa. The Portuguese were able to retake most of their Brazilian territory in the 1650s. But the Dutch, because they monopolized the carrying trade, were able to become the official supplier of slaves to Spanish plantations in the New World and the chief supplier of slaves as well as other goods to most other regions. (See the box "Global Encounters: Journal of a Dutch Slave Ship.") The Dutch were able to make handsome profits dealing in human cargo until the end of the seventeenth century, when they were supplanted by the British.

The Dutch introduced sugar cultivation to the French and English after learning it themselves in Brazil. Sugar plantations began to supplant tobacco cultivation, as well as subsistence farming, on the Caribbean islands the English and French controlled. Beginning in the late sixteenth century English and French seamen had seized island territories to serve as provisioning stations and staging points for raids against or commerce with Spanish colonies. Some island outposts had expanded into colonies and attracted European settlers—some, as in North America, coming as indentured servants—to work the land. Sugar cultivation, though potentially more profitable than tobacco, demanded huge outlays of capital and continual supplies of unskilled labor, and it drastically transformed the settlements' characters. Large plantations owned by wealthy, often absentee landlords and dependent on slave labor replaced smaller-scale independent farming. The most profitable sugar colonies were, for the French, the islands of

**Sugar Manufacture in Caribbean Colonies**  Production of sugar required large capital outlays, in part because the raw cane had to be processed quickly, on-site, to avoid spoilage. This scene depicts enslaved workers operating a small sugar mill on the island of Barbados in the seventeenth century. In the background a press crushes the cane; in the foreground the juice from the cane is boiled down until sugar begins to crystallize.  *(Mary Evans Picture Library)*

Martinique° and Guadeloupe° and, for the English, Barbados° and Jamaica.

Aware of the overwhelming Spanish territorial advantage in the New World, and yet still hoping for treasures such as the Spanish had found, the English, French, and Dutch were also eager to explore and settle North America. From the early sixteenth century on, French, Dutch, English, and Portuguese seamen had fished and traded off Newfoundland. By 1630 small French and Scottish settlements in Acadia (near modern Nova Scotia) and on the St. Lawrence River and English settlements in Newfoundland were established to systematically exploit the timber, fish, and fur of the north Atlantic coasts.

In England rising unemployment and religious discontent created a large pool of potential colonists, some of whom were initially attracted to the Caribbean. The

Martinique (mar-tih-NEEK)
Guadeloupe (gwah-dah-LOO-puh)
Barbados (bar-BAY-dose)

first of the English settlements to endure in what was to become the United States was established at Jamestown, named for James I, in Virginia in 1607. ("Virginia," named for Elizabeth I, the "Virgin Queen," was an extremely vague designation for the Atlantic coast of North America and its hinterland.)

The Crown encouraged colonization, but a private company similar to those that financed long-distance trade was established to organize the enterprise. The directors of the Virginia Company were London businessmen. Investors and would-be colonists purchased shares. Shareholders among the colonists could participate in a colonial assembly, although the governor appointed by the company was the final authority.

The colonists arrived in Virginia with ambitious and optimistic instructions. They were to open mines, establish profitable cultivation, and search for sea routes to Asia. But at first they struggled merely to survive. (See the box "Reading Sources: The Disappointments of the Virginia Colony.") The indigenous peoples in Virginia, un-

# Journal of a Dutch Slave Ship

These excerpts from a journal kept by the captain of the Dutch ship *St. Jan* record a 1659 slave-trading voyage that began in Africa and ended on Curaçao, a Dutch island colony in the Caribbean.

The 8th [of March]. We arrived with our ship on Saturday before Arda [in modern Benin] to take on board the surgeon's mate, and tamarinds as refreshment for the slaves. We set sail the next day to continue our voyage to Rio Reael.

The 22nd [of May]. We weighed anchor again and sailed out of the Rio Reael. . . . We acquired there in trade two hundred and nineteen slaves, men and women, boys as well as girls; and we set our course for [islands in the Gulf of Biafra] in order to seek food for the slaves, because nothing was to be had in Rio Reael.

The 26th ditto. On Monday we arrived [on the islands]. We spent seven days there looking but barely obtained enough for the slaves' daily consumption; therefore we decided to sail [up a nearby river] to see whether any food could be found there.

The 29th [of June]. On Sunday we decided to continue our voyage because there was also little food [up the river mouth] for the slaves because of the heavy rain which we had daily and because many slaves were suffering from dysentery caused by the bad food supplied to us at [St. George del Mina, a Dutch fort established to serve the slave trade]. . . .

The 11th [of August]. We lay sixteen days at Cape Lopez [modern Gabon] in order to take on water and firewood. Among the water barrels some forty were taken apart to be repaired because our cooper died . . . [and] we had no one who could repair them.

The 24th [of September]. On Friday we arrived at the island of Tobago [in the Caribbean] where we took on water and also bought some bread for our crew because for three weeks they have had no rations.

The 1st of November. We lost our ship on the reef [east of Curaçao] and our crew fled in the boat immediately. There was no chance to save the slaves because we had to abandon the ship on account of heavy surf.

The 4th ditto. We arrived with the boat at . . . Curaçao. The [governor] dispatched two sloops to retrieve the slaves from the shipwreck. One of the sloops was taken by a pirate together with eighty-four slaves.

## QUESTIONS

1. Note the dates in the captain's journal. How much time was devoted to trade and provisioning in Africa? How much time to the transatlantic journey?

2. The voyage seems to have been very poorly planned, particularly regarding provisioning. Is this a fair interpretation of the document?

3. A companion document reveals that 110 of the 219 captive men, women, and children died during the voyage across the Atlantic. Note the fate of those who were still alive by journey's end. Why was a pirate able to escape with so many of the slaves?

SOURCE: Charles T. Gehring and J. A. Schiltkamp, eds., *New Netherlands Documents,* vol. 17 (Interlaken, N.Y.: Heart of the Lakes Publishing, 1987), pp. 128–131. Used by permission from the *New Netherland Project,* The New York State Library.

For additional information on this topic, go to college.hmco.com/students.

---

like those in Spanish-held territories, were not organized in urbanized, rigidly hierarchical societies that, after conquest, could provide the invaders with a labor force. Indeed, much of the local native population was quickly wiped out by European diseases. The introduction of tobacco as a cash crop a few years later saved the colonists economically—although the Virginia Company had already gone bankrupt and the Crown had assumed control of the colony. With the cultivation of tobacco, the Virginia colony, like the Caribbean islands, became dependent on forced, eventually slave, labor.

Among the Virginia colonists were impoverished men and women who came as servants indentured to those who had paid their passage—that is, they were bound by contract to pay off their debts by several years of labor. Colonies established to the north, in what was called "New England," also drew people from the margins of English society. Early settlers there were religious

## READING SOURCES

## THE DISAPPOINTMENTS OF THE VIRGINIA COLONY

*In this letter sent to the Virginia Company back in London in 1608, Captain John Smith (1580–1631) explains somewhat angrily that the colony cannot produce the profits that the investors had hoped for. He notes the folly of carrying boats west over the fall line of the Virginia rivers—where, it had been assumed, they might sight the Pacific Ocean as the Spaniards had done in Panama. He reports no sign of the colony of Sir Walter Raleigh, which vanished after being planted in North Carolina in 1585. He also notes the difficulties of mere survival, let alone extracting wealth.*

I have received your letter, wherein you write that . . . we feed you but with ifs and ands and hopes, and some few proofs . . . and that we must expressly follow your instructions sent by Captain Newport [the commander of the supply ship], the charge of whose voyage . . . we cannot defray.

For the quartered boat to be borne by the soldiers over the falls, Newport had 120 of the best men. . . . If he had burned her to ashes, one might have carried her in a bag, but as she is, five hundred cannot, to a navigable place above the falls. And for him, at that time to find in the South Sea a mine of gold, or any of them sent by Sir Walter Raleigh, at our consultation I told them was as likely as the rest. . . . In their absence I followed the new begun works of pitch and tar, glass, [potash, and lumber], whereof some small quantities we have sent you. But if you rightly consider, what an infinite toil it is in Russia and [Sweden], where the woods are proper for naught else [and where] there be the help of both man and beast . . . yet thousands of those poor people can scarce get necessaries to live. . . .

From your ship we had not provision in victuals worth twenty pound, and we are more than two hundred to live upon this. . . . Though there be fish in the sea, fowls in the air, and beasts in the woods . . . they are so wild and we so weak and ignorant, we cannot much trouble them.

Source: Philip L. Barbour, ed., *The Complete Works of Captain John Smith (1580–1631)*, vol. 2 (Chapel Hill: University of North Carolina Press, 1986), pp. 187–189.

---

dissidents. The first to arrive were the Pilgrims, who arrived at Plymouth (modern Massachusetts) in 1620. They were a community of religious Separatists who had originally immigrated to the Netherlands from England for freedom of conscience.

Following the Pilgrims came Puritans escaping escalating persecution under Charles I. The first, in 1629, settled under the auspices of another royally chartered company, the Massachusetts Bay Company. Among their number were many prosperous Puritan merchants and landholders. Independence from investors in London allowed them an unprecedented degree of self-government once the Massachusetts Bay colony was established.

Nevertheless, the colonies in North America were disappointments to England because they generated much less wealth than expected. Shipping timber back to Europe proved too expensive, although New England forests did supply some of the Caribbean colonists' needs. The fur trade became less lucrative as English settlement pushed the Native Americans who did most of the trapping west and as French trappers to the north encroached on the trade. Certain colonists profited enormously from the tobacco economy, but the mother country did so only moderately because the demand in Europe for tobacco never grew as quickly as the demand for sugar. The English settlements did continue to attract more migrants than other colonizers' outposts. By 1640 Massachusetts had some fourteen thousand European inhabitants. Through most of the next century the growth of colonial populations in North America would result in an English advantage over the French in control of New World territory.

The French began their settlement of North America at the same time as the English, in the same push to compensate for their mutual weakness vis-à-vis the Spanish (see Map 16.4). The French efforts, however, had very different results, owing partly to the sites of their settlements but mostly to the relationship between the mother country and the colonies. The French hold on territory was always tenuous because of the scant num-

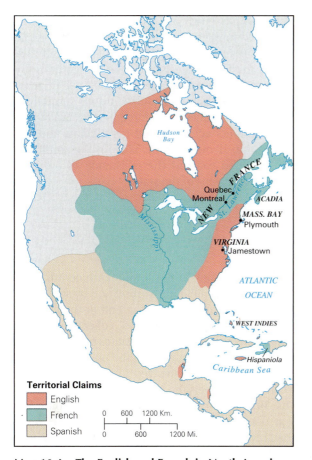

**Map 16.4    The English and French in North America, ca. 1700**  By 1700 a veritable ring of French-claimed territory encircled the coastal colonies of England. English-claimed areas, however, were more densely settled and more economically viable.

St. Lawrence River and founded Quebec City (1608). He convinced the royal government, emerging from its pre-occupations with religious wars at home, to promote the development of the colony. French explorers went on to establish Montreal, farther inland on the St. Lawrence (1642), and to explore the Great Lakes and the Mississippi River basin (see Map 16.4).

Such investment as the French crown was able to attract went into profitable trade, mainly in furs, and not into the difficult business of colonization. French trappers and traders who ventured into wilderness areas were renowned for their hardiness and adaptability, but they did not bring their families and establish settled, European-style towns. Quebec remained more of a trading station, dependent on shipments of food from France, than a growing urban community. Added to the commercial dimension of New France was the church's interest: much of the energy of French colonization was expended by men and women of religious orders—the "Black Robes"—bringing their zeal to new frontiers. By the middle of the seventeenth century all of New France had only about three thousand European inhabitants.

The seeming weakness of the French colonial effort in North America was not much noticed at the time. French and English fishermen, trappers, and traders competed intensely, and the French often reaped the greater share of profits, owing to their closer ties with Native American trading systems. Outright battles occasionally erupted between English and French settlements. But for both England and France the major profits and strategic interests in the New World lay to the south, in the Caribbean. The Dutch experience reveals the degree to which North America, for all colonial powers, was of secondary importance to the plantation profits farther south. In 1624 the Dutch founded a trading center, New Amsterdam, at the site of modern-day New York City. Fifty years later they relinquished New Amsterdam—the cornerstone of their northern enterprise—to the English in return for recognition of the Dutch claims to sugar-producing Guiana (modern Suriname°) in South America.

Consequently, by far the largest group of migrants to European-held territories in the Americas were forced migrants: African men and women sold into slavery and transported across the Atlantic to work the plantations established by Europeans. A conservative estimate is that approximately 1.35 million Africans were forcibly transported as slave labor to the New World during the seventeenth century.

ber of colonists who could be lured from home. There seems to have been less economic impetus for colonization from France than from England. And after the French crown took over the colonies, any religious impetus evaporated, for only Catholics were allowed to settle in New France. Moreover, control by the Crown forced a traditional hierarchical political organization on the French colonies. A royal governor directed the colony, and large tracts of land were set aside for privileged investors. Thus North America offered little to tempt French people of modest means who were seeking a better life.

The first successful French colony was established in Acadia in 1605. This settlement was an exception among the French efforts because it was founded by Huguenots, not by Catholics. A few years later the explorer Samuel de Champlain (1567?–1635) navigated the

---

**Suriname** (SIR-ih-nam)

## The Beginning of the End of Traditional Society

Within Europe the economic impact of overseas trade was profound. Merchants and investors in a few of Europe's largest cities reaped great profits. Mediterranean ports such as Venice, once the heart of European trade, did not share in the bonanza from the new trade with Asia or the Americas. Atlantic ports such as Seville, through which most Spanish commerce with the New World flowed, and, above all, Amsterdam began to flourish. The population of Amsterdam increased from about 30,000 to 200,000 in the course of the seventeenth century.

All capital cities, however, not just seaports, grew substantially during the 1600s. Increasing numbers of government functionaries, courtiers and their hangers-on, and people involved in trade lived and worked in capital cities. These cities also grew indirectly from the demand such people generated for services and products, ranging from fashionable clothing to exotic foodstuffs. For the first time cities employed vast numbers of country people. Perhaps as much as one-fifth of the population of England passed through London at one time or another, creating the mobile, volatile community so active in the English civil war and its aftermath.

The economy became more productive and flexible as it expanded, but social stratification intensified. Patterns of consumption in cities reflected the economic gulfs between residents. Most people could not afford to buy imported pepper or sugar. Poverty increased in cities, even in vibrant Amsterdam, because cities attracted people fleeing rural unemployment with few skills and fewer resources. As growing central governments heaped tax burdens on peasants, many rural people were caught in a cycle of debt; the only escape was to abandon farming and flock to cities.

Peasant rebellions occurred throughout the century as a result of depressed economic conditions and heavy taxation, reflecting the expansion of royal power and expensive royal military ambitions. Some small-scale revolts involved direct action, such as seizing the tax collector's grain or stopping the movement of grain to the great cities. Urban demand often caused severe food shortages in rural areas in western Europe, despite the booming trade in grain with eastern Europe via the Baltic.

The typical peasant revolt in western Europe during the seventeenth century, however, was directed against escalating taxation. Tax rebellions often formed spontaneously, perhaps as tax officials passed through a village, but they were not mere chaotic gatherings of rabble. Country folk were accustomed to defending themselves as communities—against brigands and marauding soldiers, for example. Local gentry or prosperous farmers who ordinarily fulfilled the function of local constable led such revolts from time to time, convinced that they represented the legitimate interests of the community against rapacious officials higher up. The scale of peasant violence meant that thousands of troops sometimes had to be diverted from a state's foreign wars. As a matter of routine, soldiers accompanied tax officials and enforced collection all over Europe. Thus, as the ambitions of rulers grew, so too did the resistance of ordinary people to the exactions of the state.

## SUMMARY

THE beginning of the seventeenth century was marked by religious turmoil and by social and political upheaval. By the end of the century, the former had faded as a source of collective anxiety, and the latter was largely resolved. States troubled by religious and political turmoil or on the political margins early in the century had evolved into secure and dynamic centers of power: the Netherlands, the Habsburg domains, Brandenburg-Prussia, and Russia. Following the most powerful monarchy in Europe, France, most states had moved from internal division—with independent provinces and aristocrats going their own way—to greater coherence. This stability was both cause and consequence of rulers' desires to make war on an ever larger scale. By the end of the century only those states able to field massive armies were competitive on the European stage. The Netherlands, a stark exception to the pattern of centralized royal control, began more closely to resemble other states under the pressure of warfare by century's end.

At the beginning of the century, overseas trade and colonization had been the near monopoly of Spain and Portugal. At the end of the century the English, French, and Dutch had supplanted the Iberian states in controlling trade with Asia and were reaping many profits in the Americas, especially from the extension of plantation agriculture. Beneath all these developments lay subtle but significant economic, social, and cultural shifts. One effect of the increased wealth generated by overseas trade and the increased power of governments to tax their subjects was a widening gulf between rich and poor. New styles of behavior and patterns of consumption highlighted differences between social classes. Long-term effects of overseas voyages on Old World attitudes, as well as fundamental changes in world-views that were paving the way for modern science, would have a revolutionary impact on Europeans and their cultures.

## ■ Notes

1. Quoted in D. H. Pennington, *Europe in the Seventeenth Century,* 2d ed. (London: Longman, 1989), p. 508.

## ■ Suggested Reading

Collins, James B. *The State in Early Modern France.* 1995. An up-to-date synthesis by one of the leading scholars of French absolutism.

Howard, Michael. *War in European History.* 1976. A general study of warfare emphasizing the relationship between war making and state development.

Ingrao, Charles. *The Habsburg Monarchy, 1618–1815.* 1994. A treatment of the Austrian Habsburgs that stresses the distinctiveness of the Habsburg state.

Kishlansky, Mark. *A Monarchy Transformed.* 1996. The most recent full scholarly treatment of political events in England.

Musgrave, Peter. *The Early Modern European Economy.* 1999. A recent survey of the scholarship on the expanding European economy.

Oakley, Stewart P. *War and Peace in the Baltic, 1560–1790.* 1992. An excellent survey of the Baltic region in the early modern period.

Pennington, D. H. *Europe in the Seventeenth Century.* 2d ed. 1989. A general history of the century.

Riasanovsky, Nicolas V. *A History of Russia.* 6th ed. 2000. A reliable and readable survey of Russian history from medieval times; includes an extensive bibliography of major works available in English.

Schama, Simon. *The Embarrassment of Riches: An Interpretation of Dutch Culture in the Golden Age.* 1997. An innovative study of Dutch culture that explores the social and psychological tensions created by its growing wealth in the seventeenth century.

Wolf, Eric R. *Europe and the People Without History.* 1982. A survey of European contact with and conquest of peoples after 1400; includes extensive treatments of non-European societies and detailed explanations of the economic and political interests of the Europeans.

**For a searchable list of additional readings for this chapter, go to college.hmco.com/students.**

# Table Manners

If you were to sit down in a fancy restaurant, order a juicy steak, and then eat it with your bare hands, other diners would undoubtedly stare, shocked by your bad manners. It has not always been the case that table manners meant very much—were able to signal social status, for example. It was not always the case that table manners existed at all in the sense that we know them. How did they evolve? How did they come to have the importance that they do? And why should historians pay any attention to them?

Imagine that you have been invited to dinner at a noble estate in the year 1500. As you sit down, you notice that there are no knives, forks, and spoons at your place, and no napkins either. A servant (a young girl from a neighboring village) sets a roast of meat in front of you and your fellow diners. The lords and ladies on either side of you hack off pieces of meat with the knives that they always carry with them, and then they eat the meat with their fingers. Hunks of bread on the table in front of them catch the dripping juices.

One hundred fifty years later, in 1650, dinner is a much more "civilized" meal. Notice the well-to-do women dining in this engraving by the French artist Abraham Bosse (1602–1676). The table setting, with tablecloths, napkins, plates, and silverware, is recognizable to us. The lady at the extreme right holds up her fork and napkin in a somewhat forced and obvious gesture. These diners have the utensils that we take for granted, but the artist does not take them for granted: they are intended to be noticed by Bosse's elite audience.

In the seventeenth century aristocrats and gentry signaled their political and social privilege with behavior that distinguished them from the lower classes in ways their more powerful ancestors had found unnecessary. Historians have called this the invention of civility. As we have seen, proper courtesy to one's superiors at court was considered essential. It marked the fact that rituals of honor and deference were increasingly taking the place of armed conflict as the routine behavior of the upper classes. Also essential, however, were certain standards of physical privacy and delicacy. Something as seemingly trivial as the use of a fork became charged with symbolic significance. As the actual power of the aristocrats was circumscribed by the state, they found new expressions of status. Since the sixteenth century new kinds of manners had been touted in handbooks,

reflecting changes that already had occurred at Italian courts. During the seventeenth century these practices became more widespread and opened up a gulf between upper- and lower-class behavior.

Some of the new behaviors concerned bodily privacy and discretion. A nobleman now used a handkerchief instead of his fingers or coat sleeve, and he did not urinate in public. The new "rules" about eating are particularly interesting. Why did eating with a fork seem refined and desirable to aristocrats trying to buttress their own self-images? As any 3-year-old knows, eating with a fork is remarkably inefficient.

Using a fork kept you at a distance—literal and symbolic—from the animal you were eating. Napkins wiped away all trace of bloody juices from your lips. Interestingly, as diners began to use utensils, other eating arrangements changed in parallel ways. Sideboards had been in use for a long time, but pieces of meat were now discreetly carved on the sideboard and presented to diners in individual portions. The carcass was brought to the sideboard cut into roasts instead of unmistakably whole, and it was often decorated—as it is today—to further disguise it.

The new aristocrat was increasingly separated from the world of brute physical force, both in daily life and on the battlefield. In warfare brute force was no longer adequate. Training, discipline, and tactical knowledge were more important and heightened the significance of rank, which separated officers from the vast numbers of common soldiers (see page 545). Aristocrats now lived in a privileged world where violence—except for an occasional duel—was no longer a fact of life. Their new behavior codes signaled their new invulnerability to others. Above all, they worked to transform a loss—of the independence that had gone hand in hand with a more violent life—into a gain: a privileged immunity to violence.

Specific manners became important, then, because they were symbols of power. The symbolic distance between the powerful and the humble was reinforced by other changes in habits and behavior. A sixteenth-century warrior customarily traveled on horseback and often went from place to place within a city on foot, attended by his retinue. A seventeenth-century aristocrat was more likely to travel in a horse-drawn carriage. The presence of special commodities from abroad—such as sugar—in the seventeenth century created further possibilities for signaling status.

**Table Manners of the Upper Class in the Seventeenth Century** *(Courtesy of the Trustees of the British Museum)*

It is interesting to note that other personal habits still diverged dramatically from what we would consider acceptable today. Notice the large, stately bed in the same room as the dining table in Bosse's engraving. Interior space was still undifferentiated by our standards, and it was common for eating, talking, sleeping, and estate management all to go on in a single room. The grand bed is in the picture because, like the fork, it is a mark of status. Like virtually everything else, what is "proper" varies with historical circumstance.

571

# CHAPTER 17

# A Revolution in World-View

THE year is 1649. Queen Christina of Sweden welcomes us with her gaze and her gesture to witness a science lesson at her court. Her illustrious instructor, the French philosopher René Descartes, clutches a compass and points to an astronomical drawing. The young queen, twenty-three years old at the time, was already well known as a patron of artists and scholars. Christina had invited Descartes to her court because of his achievements in physics and philosophy. This painting depicts the fact that during Christina's lifetime, new theories in the field of astronomy revolutionized the sciences and required new definitions of matter to explain them. Descartes earned famed both for his novel theories about matter and for his systematic approach to the application of human reason to understanding the universe. This painting celebrates both Descartes's work and Christina's sponsorship of it.

The revolution within the sciences had been initiated in the sixteenth century by the astronomical calculations and hypotheses of Nicholas Copernicus, who posited that the earth moves around the sun. The work of the Italian mathematician and astronomer Galileo Galilei, as well as others, added evidence to support this hypothesis. Their work overturned principles of physics and philosophy that had held sway since ancient times. Later generations of scientists and philosophers, beginning with Descartes, labored to construct new principles to explain the way the physical universe behaves. The readiness of scientists, their patrons, and educated laypeople to push Copernicus's hypothesis to these conclusions came from several sources: their exposure to the intellectual innovations of Renaissance thought, the intellectual challenges and material opportunities represented by the discovery of the New World, and the challenge to authority embodied in the Reformation. Also, the new science offered

René Descartes (*second from the right*) instructs Queen Christina of Sweden and her courtiers.
(Réunion des Musées Nationaux/Art Resource, NY)

**The Revolution in Astronomy, 1543–1632**

**The Scientific Revolution Generalized, ca. 1600–1700**

**The New Science: Society, Politics, and Religion**

prestige and technological advances to the rulers, such as Christina, who sponsored it.

By the end of the seventeenth century a vision of an infinite but orderly cosmos appealing to human reason had, among educated Europeans, largely replaced the medieval vision of a closed universe centered on the earth and suffused with Christian purpose. Religion became an increasingly subordinate ally of science as confidence in an open-ended, experimental approach to knowledge came to be as strongly held as religious conviction. It is because of this larger shift in world-view, not simply because of particular scientific discoveries, that the seventeenth century may be labeled the era of the Scientific Revolution.

Because religious significance had been attached to previous explanations and religious authority defended them, the new astronomy automatically led to an enduring debate about the compatibility of science and religion. But the revolution in world-view was not confined to astronomy or even to science generally. As philosophers gained confidence in human reason and the intelligibility of the world, they turned to new speculation about human affairs. They began to challenge traditional justifica-

tions for the hierarchical nature of society and the sanctity of authority just as energetically as Copernicus and his followers had overthrown old views about the cosmos.

## QUESTIONS TO CONSIDER

- Why did new theories about astronomy lead to a broader Scientific Revolution?

- What were some of the features of the new "mechanistic" world-view?

- How did religious, political, and social conditions shape the work of scientists?

- What were the implications for political thought of the new scientific approach to the world?

## TERMS TO KNOW

| | |
|---|---|
| Nicholas Copernicus | René Descartes |
| heliocentric theory | mechanistic world-view |
| Johannes Kepler | Isaac Newton |
| Galileo Galilei | laws of motion |
| Francis Bacon | Thomas Hobbes |
| empirical method | John Locke |

## THE REVOLUTION IN ASTRONOMY, 1543–1632

THE origins of the seventeenth-century revolution in world-view lie, for the most part, in developments in astronomy. Because of astronomy's role in the explanations of the world and human life that had been devised by ancient and medieval scientists and philosophers, any advances in astronomy were bound to have widespread intellectual repercussions. By the early part of the seventeenth century fundamental astronomical beliefs had been successfully challenged. The consequence was the undermining of both the material (physics) and the philosophical (metaphysics) explanations of the world that had been standing for centuries.

### The Inherited World-View and the Sixteenth-Century Context

Ancient and medieval astronomy accepted the perspective on the universe that unaided human senses support—namely, that the earth is fixed at the center of the universe and the celestial bodies rotate around it. The regular movements of heavenly bodies and the obvious importance of the sun for life on earth made astronomy a vital undertaking for both scientific and religious purposes in many ancient societies. Astronomers in ancient Greece carefully observed the heavens and learned to calculate and to predict the seemingly circular motion of the stars and the sun about the earth. The orbits of the planets were more difficult to explain, for the planets seemed to travel both east and west across the sky at various times and with no regularity that could be mathematically understood. Indeed, the very word *planet* comes from a Greek word meaning "wanderer."

We now know that all the planets simultaneously orbit the sun at different speeds in paths that are at different distances from the sun. The relative positions of the planets constantly change; sometimes other planets are "ahead" of the earth and sometimes "behind." In the second century A.D. the Greek astronomer Ptolemy° attempted to explain the planets' occasional "backward" motion by attributing it to "epicycles"—small circular orbits within the larger orbit. Ptolemy's mathematical explanations of the imagined epicycles were extremely complex, but neither Ptolemy nor medieval mathematicians and astronomers were ever able fully to account for planetary motion.

Ancient physics, most notably the work of the Greek philosopher Aristotle° (384–322 B.C.), explained the fact that some objects (such as cannonballs) fall to earth but others (stars and planets) seem weightless relative to earth because of their composition: different kinds of matter have different inherent tendencies and properties. In this view all earthbound matter (like cannonballs) falls because it is naturally attracted to earth—heaviness being a property of earthbound things.

In the Christian era the Aristotelian explanation of the universe was infused with Christian meaning and purpose. The heavens were said to be made of different, pure matter because they were the abode of the angels. Both the earth and the humans who inhabited it were changeable and corruptible. Yet God had given human beings a unique and special place in the universe, which was thought to be a closed world with the stationary earth at the center. Revolving around the earth in circular orbits were the sun, moon, stars, and planets. The motion of all lesser bodies was caused by the rotation of all the stars together in the vast crystal-like sphere in which they were embedded.

A few ancient astronomers theorized that the earth moved about the sun. Some medieval philosophers also adopted this heliocentric thesis (*helios* is the Greek word for "sun"), but it remained a minority view because it seemed to contradict both common sense and observed data. The sun and stars *appeared* to move around the earth with great regularity. Moreover, how could objects fall to earth if the earth was moving beneath them? Also, astronomers detected no difference in angles from which observers on earth viewed the stars at different times. Such differences would exist, they thought, if the earth changed positions by moving around the sun. It was in-

Ptolemy (TOL-eh-mee)    Aristotle (AIR-is-tot-il)

## CHRONOLOGY

| | |
|---|---|
| 1543 | Copernicus, *De Revolutionibus Orbium Caelestium*; Vesalius, *On the Fabric of the Human Body* |
| 1576 | Construction of Brahe's observatory begins |
| 1603 | Accadèmia dei Lincei founded in Rome |
| 1609 | Kepler's third law of motion |
| 1610 | Galileo, *The Starry Messenger* |
| 1620 | Bacon, *Novum Organum* |
| 1628 | Harvey, *On the Motion of the Heart* |
| 1632 | Galileo, *Dialogue on the Two Chief Systems of the World* |
| 1633 | Galileo condemned and sentenced to house arrest |
| 1637 | Descartes, *Discourse on Method* |
| 1651 | Hobbes, *Leviathan* |
| 1660 | Boyle, *New Experiments Physico-Mechanical* Royal Society of London founded |
| 1666 | Académie Royale des Sciences founded in France |
| 1686 | Fontenelle, *Conversations on the Plurality of Worlds* |
| 1687 | Newton, *Principia* (*Mathematical Principles of Natural Philosophy*) |
| 1690 | Locke, *Two Treatises of Government* and *Essay on Human Understanding* |
| 1702 | Bayle, *Historical and Critical Dictionary* |

conceivable that the universe could be so large and the stars so distant that the earth's movement would produce no measurable change in the earth's position with respect to the stars.

Several conditions of intellectual life in the sixteenth century encouraged new work in astronomy and led to the revision of the earth-centered world-view. The most important was the work of Renaissance humanists in recovering and interpreting ancient texts. Now able to work with new Greek versions of Ptolemy, mathematicians and astronomers noted that his explanations for the motion

**The Traditional Universe**   In this print from around 1600 heavenly bodies are depicted orbiting the earth in perfectly circular paths. In fact, the ancient astronomer Ptolemy believed that the planets followed complex orbits within orbits, known as *epicycles,* moving around the stationary earth. *(Hulton Archive/Getty Images)*

of the planets were imperfect and not simply inadequately transmitted, as they had long believed. Also, the discovery of the New World dramatically undercut the assumption that ancient knowledge was superior. The existence of the Americas specifically undermined Ptolemy's authority once again, for it disproved many of the assertions in his *Geography,* which had just been recovered in Europe the previous century.

The desire to explain heavenly movements better was still loaded with religious significance in the sixteenth century and was heightened by the immediate need for reform of the Julian calendar (named for Julius Caesar). Ancient observations of the movement of the sun, though remarkably accurate, could not measure the precise length of the solar year. By the sixteenth century the cumulative error of this calendar had resulted in a change of ten days: the spring equinox fell on March 11

instead of March 21. An accurate and uniform system of dating was necessary for all rulers and their tax collectors and recordkeepers. And because the calculation of the date of Easter was at stake, a reliable calendar was the particular project of the church.

Impetus for new and better astronomical observations and calculations arose from other features of the intellectual and political landscape as well. Increasingly, as the century went on, princely courts became important sources of patronage for and sites of scientific activity. Rulers eager to buttress their own power by symbolically linking it to dominion over nature sponsored investigations of the world, as Ferdinand and Isabella had so successfully done, and displayed the marvels of nature at their courts. Sponsoring scientific inquiry also yielded practical benefits: better mapping of the ruler's domains and better technology for mining, gunnery, and navigation.

Finally, schools of thought fashionable at the time, encouraged by the humanists' critique of received tradition, hinted at the possibilities of alternative physical and metaphysical systems. The ancient doctrine of Hermeticism (named for the mythical originator of the ideas, Hermes Trismegistos), revived since the Renaissance, claimed that matter is universally imbued with divine (or magical) spirit. Drawing on Hermeticism was Paracelsianism, named for the Swiss physician Philippus von Hohenheim (1493–1541), who called himself Paracelsus° (literally "beyond Celsus," an acclaimed Roman physician whose works had just been recovered). Paracelsus scoffed at the notion that ancient authorities were the final word on the workings of nature. "He who is born in imagination," he wrote, "discovers the latent forces of nature."[1] Paracelsus offered an alternative to accepted medical theory, put forth by the physician Galen° (ca. 131–201), the premier medical authority of antiquity, now as revered as Aristotle. Galen believed that an imbalance of bodily "humors" caused illness. Paracelsus substituted a theory of chemical imbalance that was a forerunner of modern understandings of pathology. He was wildly popular wherever he taught because of the success of his treatments of illness and his willingness to lecture openly to laymen.

Neo-Platonism, another school of thought, had a more systematic and far-reaching impact. Neo-Platonism was a revival, primarily in Italian humanist circles, of certain aspects of Plato's thought. It contributed directly to innovation in science because it emphasized the abstract nature of true knowledge and thus encouraged mathematical investigation. This provided a spur to astronomical studies, which, since ancient times, had been concerned more with mathematical analysis of heavenly movements than with physical explanations for them. Also, like Hermeticism and Paracelsianism, Neo-Platonism had a mystical dimension that fostered creative speculation about the nature of matter and the organization of the universe. Neo-Platonists were particularly fascinated by the sun as a symbol of the one divine mind or soul at the heart of all creation.

## The Copernican Challenge

Nicholas Copernicus° (1473–1543), son of a German merchant family in Poland, pursued wide-ranging university studies in philosophy, law, astronomy, mathematics, and medicine—first in Cracow in Poland and then in Bologna and Padua in Italy. In Italy he was exposed to Neo-Platonic

Paracelsus (pair-uh-SEL-sus)    Galen (GAY-len)
Copernicus (kuh-PURR-nih-kus)

ideas. He took a degree in canon (church) law in 1503 and became a cathedral canon (a member of the cathedral staff) in the city of Frauenburg (modern Poland), where he pursued his own interests in astronomy while carrying out administrative duties. When the pope asked Copernicus to assist with the reform of the Julian calendar, he replied that reform of the calendar required reform in astronomy. His major work, *De Revolutionibus Orbium Caelestium* (*On the Revolution of Heavenly Bodies*, 1543), was dedicated to the pope in the hopes that it would help with the task of calendar reform—as indeed it did. The Gregorian calendar, issued in 1582 during the pontificate of Gregory XIII (r. 1572–1585), was based on Copernicus's calculations.

Copernicus postulated that the earth and all the other planets orbit the sun. He did not assert that the earth does in fact move around the sun but offered the heliocentric system as a mathematical construct, useful for predicting the movements of planets, stars, and the sun. However, he walked a thin line between making claims for a mathematical construct on the one hand and physical reality on the other. Scholars now believe that Copernicus was himself persuaded that the heliocentric theory was correct. He had searched in ancient sources for thinkers who believed the earth moved. Other astronomers familiar with his work and reputation urged him to publish the results of his calculations. But not until 1542, twelve years after finishing the work, did he send *De Revolutionibus* to be published. He received a copy just before his death the next year. (See the box "Reading Sources: Copernicus Justifies His Work to the Pope.")

By affirming the earth's movement around the sun while also salvaging features of the old system, Copernicus faced burdens of explanation not faced by Ptolemy. For example, Copernicus still assumed that the planets traveled in circular orbits, so he was forced to retain some epicycles in his schema to account for the circular motion. In general, however, the Copernican account of planetary motion was simpler than the Ptolemaic account. It appealed to other astronomers of the age because it was useful and because it highlighted the harmony of heavenly motion, which remained a fundamental physical and metaphysical principle. Inaccessible except to other astronomers, Copernicus's work only slowly led to conceptual revolution, as scientists worked with his calculations and assembled other evidence to support the heliocentric theory.

The most important reason that fundamental conceptual change followed Copernican theory so gradually was that Copernicus did not resolve the physical problems his ideas raised. If Copernicus were right, the earth

## READING SOURCES

# COPERNICUS JUSTIFIES HIS WORK TO THE POPE

*In this dedicatory letter to the pope that prefaced* On the Revolution of Heavenly Bodies, *Nicholas Copernicus expresses his desire to assist with calendar reform. Principally, however, he seeks to justify his novel conclusions. Note that he not only cites ancient authority for the movement of the earth but also stresses the mathematical (not metaphysical) nature of the problem and of his solution to it.*

To the Most Holy Lord, Pope Paul III

I may well presume, most Holy Father, that certain people, as soon as they hear that in this book about the Revolutions of the Spheres of the Universe I ascribe movement to the earthly globe, will cry out that, holding such views, I should at once be hissed off the stage. . . . How I came to dare to conceive such motion of the Earth, contrary to the received opinion of the Mathematicians and indeed contrary to the impression of the senses, is what your Holiness will rather expect to hear. So I should like your Holiness to know that I was induced to think of a method of computing the motions of the spheres by nothing else than the knowledge that the Mathematicians are inconsistent in these investigations. . . . Mathematicians are so unsure of the movements of the Sun and the Moon that they cannot even explain . . . the constant length of the seasonal year.

. . . I pondered long upon this uncertainty of mathematical tradition. I . . . read again the works of all the philosophers on whom I could lay a hand to seek out whether any of them had ever supposed that the motions of the spheres were other[wise]. I found first in Cicero that Hicetas [of Syracuse, fifth century B.C.] had realized that the earth moved. . . . Mathematics are for mathematicians, and they, if I be not wholly deceived, will hold that my labors contribute somewhat . . . to the Church. . . . For under Leo X, the question of correcting the ecclesiastical calendar was . . . left undecided.

Source: Thomas S. Kuhn, *The Copernican Revolution* (Cambridge, Mass.: Harvard University Press, 1985), pp. 137–143.

would have to be made of the same material as other planets. How, then, would Copernicus explain the motion of objects on earth—the fact that they fall to earth—if it was not in their nature to fall toward the heavy, stationary earth? In Copernicus's system, the movement of the earth caused the *apparent* motion of the stars. But if the stars did not rotate in their crystalline sphere, what made all other heavenly bodies move?

Copernicus was not as troubled by these questions as we might expect him to be. Since ancient times, mathematical astronomy—the science of measuring and predicting the movements of heavenly bodies—had been far more important than, and had proceeded independently of, physical explanations of observed motion. Nevertheless, as Copernicus's own efforts to support his hypothesis reveal, his theories directly contradicted many of the supposed laws of motion. The usefulness of his theories to other astronomers meant that the contradictions between mathematical and physical models for the universe would have to be resolved. Copernicus himself might be best understood as the last Ptolemaic astronomer, working within inherited questions and with known tools. His work itself did not constitute a revolution, but it did initiate one.

## The First Copernican Astronomers

In the first generation of astronomers after the publication of *De Revolutionibus* in 1543 we can see the effects of Copernicus's work. His impressive computations rapidly won converts among fellow astronomers. Several particularly gifted astronomers continued to develop the Copernican system. Thus, by the second quarter of the seventeenth century, they and many others accepted the heliocentric theory as a reality and not just as a useful mathematical fiction. The three most important astronomers to build on Copernican assumptions, and on the work of one another, were the Dane Tycho Brahe (1546–1601), the German Johannes Kepler (1571–1630), and the Italian Galileo Galilei (1564–1642).

Like generations of observers before him, Tycho Brahe° had been stirred by the majesty of the regular

Brahe (BRAH)

STELLÆBURGUM sive OBSERVATORIUM SUBTERRANEUM, A TYCHONE BRAHE Nobili Dano
IN INSULA HVÆNA, EXTRA ARCEM URANIAM, EXTRUCTUM CIRCA ANNUM M D LXXXIIII.

**Tycho Brahe's Observatory**
A gifted artist and craftsman as well as an astronomer, Brahe gathered the best talent, including German instrument makers and Italian architects, to build his state-of-the-art observatory near Copenhagen. Brahe named the complex Uraniborg, for Urania, the muse of astronomy.

*(The Fotomas Index)*

movements of heavenly bodies. After witnessing a partial eclipse of the sun, he abandoned a career in government befitting his noble status and became an astronomer. Brahe was the first truly post-Ptolemaic astronomer because he was the first to improve on the data that the ancients and all subsequent astronomers had used. Ironically, no theory of planetary motion could have reconciled the data that Copernicus had used: they were simply too inaccurate, based as they were on naked-eye observations, even when errors of translation and copying, accumulated over centuries, had been corrected.

In 1576 the king of Denmark showered Brahe with properties and pensions enabling him to build an observatory, Uraniborg, on an island near Copenhagen. At Uraniborg Brahe improved on ancient observations with large and very finely calibrated instruments that permitted precise measurements of celestial movements by the naked eye. His attention to precision and frequency of observation produced results that were twice as accurate as any previous data had been.

As a result of his observations, Brahe agreed with Copernicus that the various planets did rotate around the sun, not around the earth. He still could not be persuaded that the earth itself moved, for none of his data supported such a notion. Brahe's lasting and crucial contribution was his astronomical data. They would become obsolete as soon as data from telescopic observations were accumulated about a century later. But in the meantime they were used by Johannes Kepler to further develop Copernicus's model and arrive at a more accurate heliocentric theory.

Kepler was young enough to be exposed to Copernican ideas from the outset of his training, and he quickly recognized in Brahe's data the means of resolving the problems in Copernican analysis. Though trained in his native Germany, Kepler went to Prague, where Brahe spent the last years of his life at the court of the Holy Roman emperor after a quarrel with the Danish king. There Kepler became something of an apprentice to Brahe. After Brahe's death in 1601, Kepler kept his mentor's records of astronomical observations and continued to work at the imperial court as Rudolf II's court mathematician.

Kepler's contribution to the new astronomy, like that of Copernicus, was fundamentally mathematical. In it we can see the stamp of the Neo-Platonic conviction about the purity of mathematical explanation. Kepler spent ten years working to apply Brahe's data to the most intricate of all the celestial movements—the motion of the planet Mars—as a key to explaining all planetary motion. Mars is close to the earth, but its orbital path is farther from the sun. This combination produces very puzzling and dramatic variations in the apparent movement of Mars to an earthly observer.

The result of Kepler's work was laws of planetary motion that, in the main, are still in use. First, Kepler eliminated the need for epicycles by correctly asserting that planets follow elliptical and not circular orbits. Elliptical orbits could account, both mathematically and visually, for the motion of the planets when combined with Kepler's second law, which describes the *rate* of a planet's motion around its orbital path. Kepler noted that the speed of a planet in its orbit slows proportionally as the planet's distance from the sun increases. A third law demonstrates that the distance of each planet from the sun and the time it takes each planet to orbit the sun are in a constant ratio.

Kepler's work was a breakthrough because it mathematically confirmed the Copernican heliocentric hypothesis. In so doing, the work directly challenged the ancient world-view, in which heavenly bodies constantly moved in circular orbits around a stationary earth. Hence Kepler's laws invited speculation about the properties and movements of heavenly and terrestrial bodies alike. A new physics would be required to explain the novel motion that Kepler had posited. Kepler himself, in Neo-Platonic fashion, attributed planetary motion to the sun: "[The sun] is a fountain of light, rich in fruitful heat, most fair, limpid and pure . . . called king of the planets for his motion, heart of the world for his power. . . . Who would hesitate to confer the votes of the celestial motions on him who has been administering all other movements and changes by the benefit of the light which is entirely his possession?"[2]

## Galileo and the Triumph of Copernicanism

Galileo Galilei° holds a pre-eminent position in the development of astronomy because, first, he provided compelling new evidence to support Copernican theory and, second, he contributed to the development of a new physics—or, more precisely, mechanics—that could account for the movements of bodies in new terms. In short he began to close the gap between the new astronomy and new explanations for the behavior of matter. Just as important, his efforts to publicize his findings and his condemnation by the church spurred popular debate

---

**Galileo Galilei** (gal-ih-LAY-oh gal-ih-LAY-ee)

**Galileo Galilei** This portrait of Galileo appeared as the frontispiece in two of his publications. He is identified as "philosopher and mathematician of the grand duke of Tuscany." The cherubs above the portrait hold a military compass and a telescope—two of Galileo's inventions that he gave to his patrons. *(Image Select International)*

about Copernican ideas in literate society and helped to determine the course science would take.

Galileo's career also illustrates, in dramatic fashion, the dependence of scientists on and their vulnerability to patronage relationships. Born to a minor Florentine noble family, Galileo began studying medicine at the nearby University of Pisa at the age of 17 but became intrigued by problems of mechanics and mathematics. He began studying those disciplines at Pisa under the tutelage of a Florentine court mathematician and became a lecturer in mathematics there in 1589, at age 25, after publishing promising work in mechanics. Three years later, well-connected fellow mathematicians helped him secure a more lucrative and prestigious professorship at the University of Padua, where Copernicus had once studied. Galileo skillfully cultivated the learned Venetian aristocrats (Venice ruled Padua at this time) who controlled academic appointments and secured renewals and salary raises over the next eighteen years.

During his years at Pisa and Padua, Galileo pursued his revolutionary work in mechanics, although he did not publish the results of his experiments until much later. Galileo's principal contribution to mechanics lay in his working out of an early theory of inertia. As a result of a number of experiments with falling bodies (balls rolling on carefully constructed inclines—not free-falling objects that, according to myth, he dropped from the Leaning Tower of Pisa), Galileo ventured a new view of what is "natural" to objects. Galileo's view was that uniform motion is as natural as a state of rest. In the ancient and medieval universe, all motion needed a cause, and all motion could be explained in terms of purpose. "I hold," Galileo countered, "that there exists nothing in external bodies . . . but size, shape, quantity and motion."[3] Galileo retained the old assumption that motion was somehow naturally circular. Nevertheless, his theory was a crucial step in explaining motion according to new principles and in fashioning a world-view that accepted a mechanical universe devoid of metaphysical purpose.

The results of this work were, for the most part, not published until the end of his life. In the meantime, Galileo became famous for his astronomical observations, which he began in 1609 and which he parlayed into a position back at the Florentine court. Early that year Galileo learned of the invention of a primitive telescope (which could magnify distant objects only three times) and quickly improved on it to make the first astronomically useful instrument. In *Sidereus Nuncius* (*The Starry Messenger*, 1610) he described his scrutiny of the heavens with his telescope in lay language. He documented sighting previously undetectable stars, as well as moons orbiting the planet Jupiter. In another blow to ancient descriptions of the universe, he noted craters and other "imperfections" on the surface of the moon. Three years later he published his solar observations in *Letters on Sunspots*. Sunspots are regions of relatively cool gaseous material that appear as dark spots on the sun's surface. For Galileo sunspots and craters on the moon proved that the heavens are not perfect and changeless but rather are like the supposedly "corrupt" and changeable earth. His telescopic observations also provided further support for Copernican heliocentrism. Indeed, Galileo's own acceptance of Copernicanism can be dated to this point because magnification revealed that each heavenly body rotates on its axis: sunspots, for example, can be tracked across the visible surface of the sun as the sun rotates.

Galileo had already been approached by various Italian princes and in turn sought to woo their support with gifts of some of his earlier inventions, such as a military compass. He aimed his *Starry Messenger* at the Medici dukes of Florence, naming Jupiter's moons the "Medicean Stars" and publishing the work to coincide with the accession of the young Cosimo II, whom he had tutored as a youth. In 1610 he returned in triumph to his native Tuscany as court philosopher to the grand duke. Soon, however, his own fame and the increasing acceptance of Copernicanism, especially vindicated by his work on sunspots, aroused opposition. In 1615 Galileo was denounced to the Inquisition by a Florentine friar. (See the box "The Continuing Experiment: Galileo Asserts Science and Religion Are Compatible.") After an investigation, the geokinetic theory (that the earth moves) was declared heretical, but Galileo himself was not condemned. He could continue to use Copernican theory, but only as a theory. Indeed, a number of the most fervent practitioners of the new science continued to be clergymen who followed Galileo's work with interest. A new pope, elected in 1623, was a Tuscan aristocrat and an old friend of Galileo. Galileo dedicated his work on comets, *The Assayer* (1624), to Urban VIII in honor of his election.

Now in his 60s, Galileo began to work on a book that summarized his life's work—*Dialogue on the Two Chief Systems of the World* (1632), structured as a conversation among three characters debating the merits of Copernican theory. Given the work's sensitive subject matter, Galileo obtained explicit permission from the pope to write it and cleared some portions with censors before publication. The work was the most important single source in its day for the popularization of Copernican theory, but it led to renewed concerns in Rome. Galileo had clearly overstepped the bounds of discussing Copernicanism in theory only and appeared to advocate it. Simplicio, the character representing the old world-view, was, as his name suggests, an example of ignorance, not wisdom.

Moreover, the larger political context affecting Galileo's patrons and friends had changed. The pope was being threatened by the Spanish and Austrian Habsburgs for his tepid support in the Thirty Years' War, in which Catholic forces were now losing to Protestant armies, and he could no longer be indulgent with his friend. (The pope tended to favor French foreign policy as a counterweight to the enormous power of the Habsburgs.) Galileo was forced to stand trial for heresy in Rome in 1633. When, in a kind of plea-bargain arrangement, he pled guilty to a lesser charge of inadvertently

# Galileo Asserts Science and Religion Are Compatible

After Galileo Galilei's work on sunspots was released, many learned followers grew anxious about the implications of the new science. In the letter excerpted here, published in 1615 and widely circulated, Galileo reassures the mother of Cosimo II, the dowager grand duchess of Tuscany, that the new science does not contradict Christianity. The Catholic Church would eventually condemn Galileo for his beliefs, arguing that it was wrong to contradict established knowledge about the heavens. Although the church's actions constrained the development of science in some (predominantly Catholic) regions, throughout Europe investigators continued to find ways to make the new science fully compatible with their faiths.

Some years ago, as Your Serene Highness well knows, I discovered in the heavens many things that had not been seen there before our own age. The novelty of these things, as well as some consequences which followed from them . . . stirred up against me no small number of professors—as if I had placed these things in the sky with my own hands in order to upset nature and overturn the sciences. . . . [These professors] go about invoking the Bible, which they would have minister to their deceitful purposes. Contrary to the sense of the Bible and the intention of the holy Fathers, if I am not mistaken, they would extend such authorities until even in purely physical matters—where faith is not involved—they would have us altogether abandon reason and the evidence of our own senses in favor of some biblical passage, though under the surface meaning of its words this passage may contain a different sense. . . .

I think that in discussions of physical problems we ought to begin not from the authority of scriptural passages, but from sense experience and necessary demonstrations. . . . I should judge that the authority of the Bible was designed to persuade men of those articles and propositions which, surpassing all human reasoning, could not be made credible by science, or by any means other than through the very mouth of the Holy Spirit. . . .

But I do not feel obliged to believe that the same God who has endowed us with senses, reason and intellect has intended to forgo their use and by some other means to give us knowledge which we can attain by them. He would not re-

quire us to deny sense and reason in physical matters which are set before our eyes and minds by direct experience or necessary demonstrations. This must be especially true in those sciences of which but the faintest trace . . . is to be found in the Bible. Of astronomy, for instance, so little is found that none of the planets except Venus are so much as mentioned. . . .

Now, if the Holy Spirit has purposely neglected to teach us propositions of this sort as irrelevant to the highest goal (that is, to our salvation), how can anyone affirm that it is obligatory to take sides on them, and that one belief is required by faith, while another side is erroneous? . . . I would assert here something that was heard from [a respected cleric]: . . . "the intention of the Holy Ghost is to teach us how to go to heaven, not how heaven goes." . . . [And] in St. Augustine we read: "If anyone shall set the authority of Holy Writ against clear and manifest reason, . . . he opposes to the truth not the meaning of the Bible, which is beyond his comprehension, but rather his own interpretation. . . ."

Moreover, we are unable to affirm that all interpreters of the Bible speak with divine inspiration, for if that were so there would exist no differences between them about the sense of a given passage. Hence [it would be wise] not to permit anyone to usurp scriptural texts and force them in some way to maintain any physical conclusion to be true, when at some future time the senses . . . may show the contrary. Who indeed will set bounds to human ingenuity? Who will assert that everything in the universe capable of being perceived is already discovered and known?

## QUESTIONS

1. How does Galileo justify pursuing scientific investigation against certain claims of faith? What is the tone of his argument? Is he confident about the future progress of science?

2. Do you think that Galileo's arguments would have been reassuring to the grand duchess? Why or why not?

3. Why might the arguments have further angered those church officials already hostile toward Galileo's work?

SOURCE: *Discoveries and Opinions of Galileo*, by Galileo Galilei, translated by Stillman Drake, copyright © 1957 by Stillman Drake. Used by permission of Doubleday, a division of Random House, Inc.

advocating Copernicanism, Pope Urban intervened to insist on a weightier penalty. Galileo's book was banned, he was forced to formally renounce his "error," and he was sentenced to house arrest. Galileo lived confined and guarded, continuing his investigations of mechanics, until his death seven years later.

# THE SCIENTIFIC REVOLUTION GENERALIZED, CA. 1600–1700

GALILEO'S work found such a willing audience in part because Galileo, like Kepler and Brahe, was not working alone. Dozens of other scientists were examining old problems from the fresh perspective offered by the breakthroughs in astronomy. Some analyzed the nature of matter, now that it appeared that all matter in the universe was somehow the same despite its varying appearances. Many of these thinkers addressed the metaphysical issues that their investigations inevitably raised. They began the complex intellectual and psychological journey toward a new world-view, one that accepted the existence of an infinitely large universe of undifferentiated matter with no obvious place in it for humans.

## The Promise of the New Science

No less a man than Francis Bacon (1561–1626), lord chancellor of England during the reign of James I, wrote a utopian essay extolling the benefits of science for a peaceful society and for human happiness. In *New Atlantis,* published one year after his death, Bacon argued that science would produce "things of use and practice for man's life."[4] In *New Atlantis* and *Novum Organum* (1620) Bacon reveals his faith in science by advocating patient, systematic observation and experimentation to accumulate knowledge about the world. He argues that the proper method of investigation "derives axioms from . . . particulars, rising by gradual and unbroken ascent, so that it arrives at the most general axioms of all. This is the true way but untried."[5]

Bacon himself did not undertake experiments, although his widely read works were influential in encouraging both the empirical method (relying on observation and experimentation) and inductive reasoning (deriving general principles from particular facts). Indeed, Bacon was a visionary. Given the early date of his writings, it might seem difficult to account for his enthusiasm and confidence. In fact, Bacon's writings reflect the widespread interest and confidence in science within his elite milieu, an interest actively encouraged by the state. In another of his writings he argues that a successful state should concentrate on effective "rule in religion *and nature,* as well as civil administration."[6]

Bacon's pronouncements reflect the fact that an interest in exploring nature's secrets and exercising "dominion over nature" had become an indispensable part of princely rule. Princely courts were the main sources of financial support for science and the primary sites of scientific work during Bacon's lifetime. Part of the impetus for this development had come from the civic humanism of the Italian Renaissance, which had celebrated the state and service to it and had provided models both for educated rulers and for cultivated courtiers. Attention to science and to its benefits for the state also reflect the scope, and pragmatism, of princely resources and ambitions: the desire of rulers for technical expertise in armaments, fortification, construction, navigation, and mapmaking. (See the feature "Weighing the Evidence: Modern Maps" on pages 600–601.)

The promise of the New World and the drive for overseas trade and exploration especially encouraged princely support of scientific investigation. A renowned patron of geographic investigation, from mapmaking to navigation, was Henry, prince of Wales (d. 1612), eldest son of James I. Prince Henry patronized technical experts such as experienced gunners and seamen, as well as those with broader and more theoretical expertise. One geographer at his court worked on the vital problem of calculating longitude, sketched the moon after reading and emulating Galileo's work with the telescope, and, in the spirit of empiricism often associated with Bacon, compiled information about the new territory Virginia, including the first dictionary of any Native American language.

Science was an ideological as well as a practical tool for power. Most courts housed collections of marvels, specimens of exotic plants and animals, and mechanical contrivances. These demonstrated the ruler's interest in investigation of the world—in other words, his or her status as an educated individual. These collections and the work of court experts also enhanced the ruler's reputation as a patron and person of power. Galileo was playing off such expectations when he named his newly discovered moons of Jupiter "Medicean Stars." Like all patronage relationships, the status was shared by both partners; indeed, the attention of a patron was a guarantee of the researcher's scientific credibility.

By the beginning of the seventeenth century, private salons and academies where investigators might meet on their own were another significant milieu of scientific

**A Collection of Naturalia**    Displays of exotica, such as these specimens in Naples, symbolized the ruler's authority by suggesting his or her power over nature.    *(From Ferrante Imperato, Dell' Historia Naturale [Naples, 1599]. By permission of the Houghton Library, Harvard University)*

investigation. These, too, had their roots in the humanist culture of Italy, where circles of scholars without university affiliations had formed. Though also dependent on private resources, these associations were an important alternative to princely patronage, since a ruler's funds might wax and wane according to his or her other commitments. Private organizations could avoid the stark distinctions of rank that were inevitable at courts yet mimicked courts in the blend of scholars and educated courtiers they embraced. This more collegial but still privileged environment also fostered a sense of legitimacy for the science pursued there: legitimacy came from the recognition of fellow members and, in many cases, from publication of work by the society itself.

The earliest academy dedicated to scientific study was the *Accadèmia Segreta* (Secret Academy) founded in Naples in the 1540s. The members pursued experiments together in order, in the words of one member, "to make a true anatomy of the things and operations of nature it-

self."[7] During the remainder of the sixteenth century and on into the seventeenth, such academies sprang up in many cities. The most celebrated was the *Accadèmia dei Lincei°*, founded in Rome by an aristocrat in 1603. Its most famous member, Galileo, joined in 1611. The name "Lincei," from *lynx*, was chosen because of the legendary keen sight of that animal, an appropriate mascot for "searchers of secrets."

Galileo's notoriety and the importance of his discoveries forced all such learned societies to take a stand for or against Copernicanism. Throughout the seventeenth century, specific investigation of natural phenomena would continue in increasingly sophisticated institutional settings. The flowering of scientific thought in the seventeenth century occurred because of the specific innovations in astronomy and the general spread of

---

**Accadèmia dei Lincei** (ack-uh-DAY-mee-uh day-ee lin-CHAY-ee)

scientific investigation that had been achieved by the end of Bacon's life.

## Scientific Thought in France: Descartes and a New Cosmology

Philosophers, mathematicians, and educated elites engaged in lively debate and practical investigation throughout Europe in the first half of the seventeenth century. In France the great questions about cosmic order were being posed, ironically, at a time of political disorder. The years following the religious wars saw the murder of Henry IV, another regency, and further civil war in the 1620s (see pages 516–518). In this environment questions about order in the universe and the possibilities of human knowledge took on particular urgency. It is not surprising that a Frenchman, René Descartes° (1596–1650), created the first fully articulated alternative world-view.

Descartes's thinking was developed and refined in dialogue with a circle of other French thinkers. His work became more influential among philosophers and laypeople than the work of some of his equally talented contemporaries because of its thoroughness and rigor, grounded in Descartes's mathematical expertise, and because of his graceful, readable French. His system was fully presented in his *Discours de la méthode* (*Discourse on Method*, 1637). Descartes described some of his intellectual crises in his later work, *Meditations* (1641).

Descartes accepted Galileo's conclusion that the heavens and the earth are made of the same elements. In his theorizing about the composition of matter he drew on ancient atomic models that previously had not been generally accepted. His theory that all matter is made up of identical bits, which he named "corpuscles," is a forerunner of modern atomic and quantum theories. Descartes believed that all the different appearances and behaviors of matter (for example, why stone is always hard and water is always wet) could be explained solely by the size, shape, and motion of these "corpuscles." Descartes's was an extremely mechanistic explanation of the universe. It nevertheless permitted new, more specific observations and hypotheses and greater understanding of inertia. For example, because he re-imagined the universe as being filled with "corpuscles" free to move in any direction, "natural" motion no longer seemed either circular (Galileo's idea) or toward the center of the earth (Aristotle's idea). The new understanding of motion would be crucial to Isaac Newton's formulations later in the century.

---

**Descartes** (day-KART)

In his various works Descartes depicts and then firmly resolves the crisis of confidence that the new discoveries about the universe had produced. The collapse of the old explanations about the world made Descartes and other investigators doubt not only what they knew but also their capacity to know anything at all. Their physical senses—which denied that the earth moved, for example—had been proved untrustworthy. Descartes's solution was to re-envision the human rational capacity, the mind, as completely distinct from the world—that is, as distinct from the human body—and the unreliable perceptions it offers the senses. In a leap of faith Descartes presumed that he could count on the fact that God would not have given humans a mind if that mind consistently misled them. For Descartes, God became the guarantor of human reasoning capacity, and humans were distinguished by that capacity. This is the significance of his famous claim "I think, therefore I am." (See the box "Reading Sources: Descartes: 'I think, therefore I am.'")

Descartes thus achieved a resolution of the terrifying doubt about the world—a resolution that exalted the role of the human knower. The Cartesian universe was one of mechanical motion, not purpose or mystical meaning, and the Cartesian human being was pre-eminently a mind that could apprehend that universe. In what came to be known as "Cartesian dualism," Descartes proposed that the human mind is detached from the world and yet at the same time can objectively analyze the world.

Descartes's ambitious view of human reason emphasizes deductive reasoning (a process of reasoning in which the conclusion follows necessarily from the stated premises), a natural consequence of his philosophical rejection of sense data. The limits of deductive reasoning for scientific investigation would be realized and much of Cartesian physics supplanted by the end of the century. Nevertheless, Descartes's assumption about the objectivity of the observer would become an enduring part of scientific practice. In Descartes's day the most radical aspect of his thought was the reduction of God to the role of guarantor of knowledge. Many fellow scientists and interested laypeople were fearful of Descartes's system because it seemed to encourage "atheism." In fact, a profound faith in God was necessary for Descartes's creativity in imagining his new world system—but the system did work without God.

Although Descartes would have been surprised and offended by charges of atheism, he knew that his work would antagonize the church. He moved to the Netherlands to study in 1628, and his *Discourse* was first published there. He had lived in the Netherlands and in

## READING SOURCES

## DESCARTES: "I THINK, THEREFORE I AM"

*In the passages leading up to this one in his* Discourse on Method, *René Descartes has made it clear that he does not advocate, or anticipate, any social or political upheaval as a consequence of his search for truth. On the contrary, he acknowledges his duty to abide by the tenets of religion and the laws of his country. The only status quo he wants to challenge is the habits of his own mind, in order to build a sure foundation for reasoning. Notice that he assumes his senses may deceive him and therefore sure knowledge cannot be based on sensory data.*

For a long time I had remarked that it is sometimes requisite in common life to follow opinions which one knows to be most uncertain, as [I have stated] above. But because in this case I wished to give myself entirely to the search for Truth, I thought that it was necessary for me to take an apparently opposite course, and to reject as absolutely false everything as to which I could imagine the least ground of doubt, in order to see afterwards if there remained anything in my belief that was entirely certain. Thus, because our senses sometimes deceive us, I wished to suppose that nothing is just as they cause us to imagine . . . and judging that I was as subject to error as was any other [man], I rejected as false all the reason formerly accepted by me as demonstrations. . . . I resolved to assume that everything that ever entered into my mind was no more true than the illusions of my dreams. But immediately afterwards I noticed that whilst I thus wished to think all things false, it was absolutely essential that the "I" who thought this should be somewhat, and remarking that this truth, "I think, therefore I am" was so certain and so assured that all the most extravagant suppositions brought forward by the skeptics were incapable of shaking it, I came to the conclusion that I could receive it without scruple as the first principle of the Philosophy for which I was seeking.

Source: René Descartes, *Discourse on the Method of Rightly Conducting the Reason,* trans. Elizabeth S. Haldane and G. R. T. Ross, in *Great Books of the Western World,* vol. 28, ed. Mortimer Adler (Chicago: Encyclopaedia Britannica, 1990), p. 275.

Germany earlier in his life; fearful of the tense atmosphere during the renewed war against French Protestants, he now left France virtually for good. Unlike Galileo, Descartes enjoyed personal wealth that enabled him to travel widely, work in solitude, and sample the intellectual environment of courts and universities without depending on powerful patrons. Long residence in the Netherlands led him to advocate religious toleration late in his life. In 1649, at the urging of an influential friend with contacts at the Swedish court, Descartes accepted the invitation of Queen Christina to visit there. Christina was an eager but demanding patron, who required Descartes to lecture on scientific topics at 5:00 a.m. each day. The long hours of work and harsh winter weather took their toll on his health, and Descartes died of pneumonia after only a few months in Sweden.

A contemporary of Descartes, fellow Frenchman Blaise Pascal° (1623–1662), drew attention in his writings and in his life to the limits of scientific knowledge. The son of a royal official, Pascal was perhaps the most brilliant mind of his generation. A mathematician like Descartes, he stressed the importance of mathematical representations of phenomena, built one of the first calculating machines, and invented probability theory. He also carried out experiments to investigate air pressure, the behavior of liquids, and the existence of vacuums.

Pascal's career alternated between periods of intense scientific work and religious retreat. Today he is well known for his writings justifying the austere Catholicism known as Jansenism (see page 543) and explored the human soul and psyche. His *Pensées* (*Thoughts,* 1657) consists of the published fragments of his defense of Christian faith, which remained unfinished at the time of his death. Pascal's appeal for generations after him may lie in his attention to matters of faith and of feeling. His most famous statement, "The heart has its reasons which reason knows not," can be read as a declaration of the limits of the Cartesian world-view.

**Pascal** (pahss-KAHL)

## Science and Revolution in England

The new science had adherents and practitioners throughout Europe by 1650. Dutch scientists in the commercial milieu of the Netherlands, for example, had the freedom to pursue practical and experimental interests. The Dutch investigator Christiaan Huygens° (1629–1695) worked on a great variety of problems, including air pressure and optics. In 1657 he invented and patented the pendulum clock, the first device to measure accurately small units of time, essential for a variety of measurements.

England proved a unique environment for the development of science in the middle of the century. In a society torn by civil war, differing positions on science became part and parcel of disputes over Puritanism, church hierarchy, and royal power. Scientific investigation and speculation were spurred by the urgency of religious and political agendas. Scientific, along with political and religious, debate was generally encouraged by the collapse of censorship beginning in the 1640s.

During the 1640s natural philosophers with Puritan leanings were encouraged in their investigations by dreams that science, of the practical Baconian sort, could be the means by which the perfection of life on earth could be brought about and the end of history—the reign of the saints preceding the return of Christ—could be accelerated. Their concerns ranged from improved production of gunpowder (for the armies fighting against Charles I) to surveying and mapmaking. Perhaps the best-known member of this group was Robert Boyle (1627–1691). In his career we can trace the evolution of English science through the second half of the seventeenth century.

Boyle and his colleagues were theoretically eclectic, drawing on Cartesian mechanics and even Paracelsian chemical theories. They attacked the English university system, still under the sway of Aristotelianism, and proposed widespread reform of education. They were forced to moderate many of their positions, however, as the English civil wars proceeded. Radical groups such as the Levellers used Hermeticism and the related Paracelsianism as part of their political and religious tenets. The Levellers and other radical groups drew on the Hermetic notion that matter is imbued with divine spirit; they believed that each person was capable of divine knowledge and a godly life without the coercive hierarchy of church and state officials.

Boyle and his colleagues responded to these challenges. They gained institutional power, accepting posi-

tions at Oxford and Cambridge. They formed the core of the Royal Society of London, which they persuaded Charles II to recognize and charter on his accession to the throne in the Restoration of 1660. They worked to articulate a theoretical position that combined the orderliness of mechanism, a continued divine presence in the world, and a Baconian emphasis on scientific progress. This unwieldy set of notions was attractive to the educated elite of their day, who embraced the certainties of science but also clung to certain authoritarian aspects of the old Christian world-view.

Their most creative contribution, both to their own cause and to the advancement of science, was their emphasis on and refinement of experimental philosophy and practice. In 1660 Boyle published *New Experiments Physico-Mechanical*. The work describes the results of his experiments with an air pump he had designed, and it lays out general rules for experimental procedure. Descartes had accounted for motion by postulating that "corpuscles" of matter interact, thereby eliminating the possibility of a vacuum in nature. Recent experiments on air pressure suggested otherwise, however, and Boyle tried to confirm their findings with his air pump.

Boyle's efforts to demonstrate that a vacuum could exist—by evacuating a sealed chamber with his pump—were not successes by modern standards because they could not readily be replicated. Boyle tied the validity of experimental results to the agreement of witnesses to the experiment—a problematic solution, for only investigators sympathetic to his hypothesis and convinced of his credibility usually witnessed the results. In response to a Cambridge scholar who criticized his interpretation of one of his experiments, Boyle replied that he could not understand his critic's objections, "the experiment having been tried both before our whole society [the Royal Society of London], and very critically, by its royal founder, his majesty himself."[8] Rather than debate differing interpretations, Boyle appealed to the authority and prestige of the participants. In English science of the mid-seventeenth century, therefore, we have a further example of the fact that new truths, new procedures for determining truth, and new criteria for practitioners were all being established simultaneously.

## The Newtonian Synthesis:
## The Copernican Revolution Completed

The Copernican revolution reached its high point with the work of the Englishman Isaac Newton (1643–1727), born one year almost to the day after Galileo died. Newton completed the new explanation for motion in the

---

**Huygens** (HI-ghenz)

**Isaac Newton**    Pictured here about fifteen years after the publication of *Principia,* Newton was also one of the developers of calculus. The cumbersome mathematics he still relied on, however, has led one scholar to ponder: "What manner of man he was who could use as a weapon what we can scarcely lift as a burden."[9]    *(By courtesy of the National Portrait Gallery, London)*

heavens and on earth that Copernicus's work had initiated and that Kepler, Galileo, and others had sought.

After a difficult childhood and an indifferent education, Newton entered Cambridge University as a student in 1661. Copernicanism and Cartesianism were being hotly debated, though not yet officially studied. Newton made use of Descartes's work in mathematics to develop his skill on his own, and by 1669 he had invented calculus. (He did not publish his work at the time, and another mathematician, Gottfried von Leibniz°, later independently developed calculus and vied with Newton for credit.)

Newton was elected to a fellowship at Cambridge in 1667 and was made a professor of mathematics in 1669 at the recommendation of a retiring professor with whom he had shared his work on calculus. With less demanding teaching assignments, he was able to devote

**Leibniz** (LIBE-nits)

much of the next decade to work on optics—an important area of study for testing Descartes's corpuscular theory of matter.

In the 1680s Newton experienced a period of self-imposed isolation from other scientists after a particularly heated exchange with one colleague, provoked by Newton's difficult temperament. During this decade he returned to the study of alternative theories about matter. As a student at Cambridge he had been strongly influenced by the work of a group of Neo-Platonists who were critical of Cartesian dualism. This controversial theory posited God as a cause of all matter and motion but removed God, or any other unknown or unknowable force, as an explanation for the behavior of matter. The Neo-Platonists' concerns were both religious and scientific. As Newton says in some of his early writing while a student, "However we cast about we find almost no other reason for atheism than this [Cartesian] notion of bodies having . . . a complete, absolute and independent reality."[10]

Newton now read treatises in alchemy and Hermetic tracts and began to imagine explanations for the behavior of matter (such as for bits of cloth fluttered from a distance by static electricity) that Cartesian corpuscular theory could not readily explain. Precisely what the forces were that caused such behavior he was not sure, but his eclectic mind and his religious convictions enabled him to accept their existence.

It was this leap that allowed him to propose the existence of gravity—a mysterious force that accounts for the movements of heavenly bodies in the vacuum of space. Others had speculated about the existence of gravity; indeed, the concept of inertia as so far elaborated by Galileo, Descartes, and others suggested the need for the concept of gravity. Otherwise, if a planet were "pushed" (say, in Kepler's view, by the "motive force" of the sun), it would continue along that course forever unless "pulled back" by something else.

Newton's extraordinary contribution to a new mechanistic understanding of the universe was the mathematical computation of the laws of gravity and planetary motion, which he combined with a fully developed concept of inertia. In 1687 Newton published *Philosophia Naturalis Principia Mathematica* (*Mathematical Principles of Natural Philosophy;* usually called *Principia*). In this mathematical treatise—so intricate that it was baffling to laypeople, even those able to read Latin—Newton laid out his laws of motion and expressed them as mathematical theorems that can be used to test future observations of moving bodies. Then he demonstrated that these laws also apply to the solar system, confirming the data already gathered about the planets and even predicting the existence of an as yet unseen planet. His supreme achievement was his law of gravitation, with which he could predict the discovery of the invisible planet. This law states that every body, indeed every bit of matter, in the universe exerts over every other body an attractive force proportional to the product of their masses and inversely proportional to the square of the distance between them. Newton not only accounted for motion but definitively united heaven and earth in a single scheme and created a convincing picture of an orderly nature.

Neither Newton nor anyone else claimed that his theorems resolved all questions about motion and matter. Exactly what gravity is and how it operates were not clear, as they still are not. Newton's laws of motion are taught today because they still adequately account for most problems of motion. The fact that so fundamental a principle as gravity remains unexplained in no way diminishes Newton's achievement but is clear evidence of the nature of scientific understanding: science provides explanatory schemas that account for many—but not all—observed phenomena. No schema explains everything, and each schema contains open doorways that lead both to further discoveries and to blind alleys. Newton, for example, assumed that the forces that accounted for gravity would mysteriously work on metals so that, as alchemists predicted, they might "quickly pass into gold."[11]

After the publication of *Principia* Newton was more of a celebrated public figure than a practicing scientist. He helped lead resistance to James II's Catholicizing policies in the university, and he became the familiar of many other leading minds of his day, such as John Locke (see page 596). Newton became the president of the Royal Academy of Sciences in 1703 and was knighted in 1705, the first scientist to be so distinguished. By the end of his life universities in England were dominated by men who acclaimed and built on his work. The transformation of the institutional structure of science in England was complete.

## Other Branches of Science

The innovations in astronomy that led to the new mechanistic view of the behavior of matter did not automatically spill over to other branches of science. In astronomy innovation came after the ancient and medieval inheritance had been fully assimilated and its errors disclosed. Other branches of science followed their own paths, though all were strongly influenced by the mechanistic world-view.

In chemistry the mechanistic assumption that all matter was composed of small, equivalent parts was crucial to understanding the properties and behaviors of compounds (combinations of elements). But knowledge of these small units of matter was not yet detailed enough to be of much use in advancing chemistry conceptually. Nevertheless, the flawed conceptual schema did not hold back all chemical discovery and development. Lack of understanding of gases, and of the specific elements in their makeup, for example, did not prevent the development and improvement of gunpowder. Indeed, unlike the innovations in astronomy, eventual conceptual innovation in chemistry and biology owed a great deal to the results of plodding experiment and the slow accumulation of data.

A conceptual leap forward was made in biology in the sixteenth and seventeenth centuries. Because biological knowledge was mostly a byproduct of the practice of medicine, biological studies remained very practical and experimental. The recent discovery of *On Anatomical Procedures,* a treatise by the ancient physician Galen, encouraged dissection and other practical research. Andreas Vesalius° (1514–1564), in particular, made important advances by following Galen's exhortation to anatomical research. Born in Brussels, Vesalius studied at the nearby University of Louvain and then at Padua, where he was appointed professor of surgery. He ended his career as physician to Emperor Charles V and his son, Philip II of Spain. In his teaching at Padua Vesalius acted on the newly recovered Galenic teachings by doing dissections himself rather than giving the work to technicians. In 1543 he published versions of his lectures as an illustrated compendium of anatomy, *De Humani Corporis Fabrica* (*On the Fabric of the Human Body*).

The results of his dissections of human corpses, revealed in this work, demonstrated a number of errors in Galen's knowledge of human anatomy, much of which had been derived from dissection of animals. Neither Vesalius nor his immediate successors, however, questioned overall Galenic theory about the functioning of the human body, any more than Copernicus had utterly rejected Aristotelian physics.

The slow movement from new observation to changed explanation is clearly illustrated in the career of the Englishman William Harvey (1578–1657). Much like Vesalius, Harvey was educated first in his own land and then at Padua, where he benefited from the tradition of anatomical research. He also had a career as a practicing physician in London and at the courts of James I and Charles I.

Harvey postulated the circulation of the blood— postulated rather than discovered, because owing to the

---

**Vesalius** (vuh-SAY-lee-us)

**Vesalius on Human Anatomy**     The meticulous illustrations in Vesalius's work helped ensure its success. The medium of print was essential for accurate reproduction of scientific drawings. Note also the way the human body, in this drawing of musculature, is depicted as dominating the landscape. *(Courtesy, Dover Publications)*

technology of the day, he could not observe the tiny capillaries where the movement of arterial blood into the veins occurs. After conducting vivisectional experiments on animals that revealed the actual functioning of the heart and lungs, he reasoned that circulation must occur. He carefully described his experiments and his conclusions in *Exercitatio Anatomica de Motu Cordis et Sanguinis in Animalibus* (1628), usually shortened to *De Motu Cordis* (*On the Motion of the Heart*).

Harvey's work challenged Galenic anatomy and, like Copernicus's discoveries, created new burdens of expla-

nation. According to Galenic theory, the heart and lungs helped each other to function. The heart sent nourishment to the lungs through the pulmonary artery, and the lungs provided raw material for the "vital spirit," which the heart gave to the blood to sustain life. The lungs also helped the heart sustain its "heat." This heat was understood to be an innate property of organs, just as "heaviness," in traditional physics, had been considered an innate property of earthbound objects.

From his observations Harvey came to think of the heart in terms consonant with the new mechanistic notions about nature: as a pump to circulate the blood. But he adjusted, rather than abandoned, Galenic theories concerning "heat" and "vital spirit." The lungs had been thought to "ventilate" the heart by providing air to maintain "heat," just as a bellows aerates a fire. In light of his discovery of the pulmonary transit (that all of the blood is pumped through the lungs and back through the heart), Harvey suggested instead that the lungs carried out some of these functions for the blood, helping it to concoct the "vital spirit." Only in this sense did he think of the heart as a machine, circulating this life-giving material throughout the body.

Harvey's explanation of bodily functions in light of his new knowledge did not constitute a rupture with Galenic tradition. But by the end of his life Harvey's own adjustments of Galenic theory were suggesting new conceptual possibilities. His work inspired additional research in physiology, chemistry, and physics. Robert Boyle's efforts to understand vacuums can be traced in part to questions Harvey raised about the function of the lungs and the properties of air.

## THE NEW SCIENCE: SOCIETY, POLITICS, AND RELIGION

SCIENTISTS wrestled with questions about God and human capacity every bit as intently as they attempted to find new explanations for the behavior of matter and the motion of the heavens. Eventually the profound implications of the new scientific world-view would affect thought and behavior throughout society. Once people no longer thought of the universe in hierarchical terms, they could question the hierarchical organization of society. Once people questioned the authority of traditional knowledge about the universe, the way was clear for them to begin to question traditional views of the state, the social order, and even the divine order. Such profound changes of perspective took hold very gradually, however. The advances in science did lead to revolutionary cultural change, but until the end of the seventeenth century traditional institutions and ideologies limited its extent.

## The Beginnings of Scientific Professionalism

Institutions both old and new supported the new science developing in the sixteenth and seventeenth centuries. Some universities were the setting for scientific breakthroughs, but court patronage, a well-established institution, also sponsored scientific activity. The development of the Accadèmia dei Lincei, to which Galileo belonged, and other academies was a step toward modern professional societies of scholars, although these new organizations depended on patronage.

In England and France, royally sponsored scientific societies were founded in the third quarter of the century. The Royal Society of London, inaugurated in 1660, received royal recognition but no money and remained an informal institution sponsoring amateur scientific interests as well as specialized independent research. The Académie Royale des Sciences in France, established in 1666 by Jean-Baptiste Colbert, Louis XIV's minister of finance (see page 542), sponsored research and supported chosen scientists with pensions. These associations were extensions to science of traditional kinds of royal recognition and patronage. Thus the French Académie was well funded but tightly controlled by the government of Louis XIV, and the Royal Society of London received little of Charles II's scarce resources or precious political capital. Like the earlier academies, these royally sponsored societies published their fellows' work; in England the *Philosophical Transactions of the Royal Society* began in 1665.

The practice of seventeenth-century science took place in so many diverse institutions—academies, universities, royal courts—that neither *science* nor *scientist* was rigorously defined. Science as a discipline was not yet detached from broad metaphysical questions. Boyle, Newton, Pascal, and Descartes all concerned themselves with questions of religion, and all thought of themselves not as scientists but, like their medieval forebears, as natural philosophers. These natural philosophers were still members of an elite who met in aristocratic salons to discuss literature, politics, or science with equal ease and interest. Nevertheless, the beginnings of a narrowing of the practice of science to a tightly defined, truly professional community are evident in these institutions.

The importance of court life and patronage to the new science had at first enabled women to be actively

**Astronomers Elisabetha and Johannes Hevelius**   The Heveliuses were one of many collaborating couples among the scientists of the seventeenth century. Women were usually denied pensions and support for their research when they worked alone, however.   *(From Hevelius,* Machinae coelestis. *By permission of the Houghton Library, Harvard University)*

involved. Women ran important salons in France; aristocratic women everywhere were indispensable sources of patronage for scientists; and women themselves were scientists, combining, as did men, science with other pursuits. Noblewomen and daughters of gentry families had access to education in their homes, and a number of such women were active scientists—astronomers, mathematicians, and botanists. The astronomer Maria Cunitz° (1610–1664), from Silesia (a Habsburg-controlled province, now in modern Poland), learned six languages

---

**Cunitz** (KOO-nits)

## READING SOURCES

## MARGARET CAVENDISH CHALLENGES MALE SCIENTISTS

*In her preface to her earliest scientific work,* The Philosophical and Physical Opinions *(1655), Margaret Cavendish addresses scholars at Oxford and Cambridge Universities with deceptive humility. She implies that the seeming limitations of women's abilities are in fact the consequence of their exclusion from education and from participation in worldly affairs.*

Most Famously Learned,

I here present to you this philosophical work, not that I can hope wise school-men and industrious laborious students should value it for any worth, but to receive it without scorn, for the good encouragement of our sex, lest in time we should grow irrational as idiots, by the dejectedness of our spirits, through the careless neglects and despisements of the masculine sex to the female, thinking it impossible we should have either learning or understanding, wit or judgment, as if we had not rational souls as well as men, and we out of a custom of dejectedness think so too, which makes us quit all industry towards profitable knowledge, being imployed only in low and petty imployments which take away not only our abilities towards arts but higher capacities in speculations, so that we are become like worms, that only live in the dull earth of ignorance, winding ourselves sometimes out by the help of some refreshing rain of good education, which seldome is given us, for we are kept like birds in cages, to hop up and down in our houses . . . ; thus by an opinion, which I hope is but an erroneous one in men, we are shut out of all power and authority by reason we are never imployed either in civil or martial affairs, our counsels are despised and laughed at and the best of our actions are trodden down with scorn, by the overweening conceit men have of themselves and through a despisement of us.

Source: Moira Ferguson, ed., *First Feminists: British Women Writers, 1578–1799* (Bloomington and New York: Indiana University Press and The Feminist Press, 1985), pp. 85–86.

with the encouragement of her father, who was a medical doctor. Later she published a useful simplification of some of Kepler's mathematical calculations. Women from artisanal families might also receive useful training at home. Such was the case of the German entomologist Maria Sibylla Merian (1647–1717). Merian learned the techniques of illustration in the workshop of her father, an artist in Frankfurt. She later used her artistic training and her refined powers of observation to study and record the features and behaviors of insects and plants in the New World.

Margaret Cavendish, duchess of Newcastle (1623–1673), wrote several major philosophical works, including *Grounds of Natural Philosophy* (1668). She was a Cartesian but was influenced by Neo-Platonism. She believed matter to have "intelligence" and thus disagreed with Cartesian dualism, but she criticized fellow English philosophers on the grounds that, like Descartes, she distrusted sensory knowledge as a guide to philosophy.

Women were routinely accepted as members of Italian academies, but they were excluded from formal membership in the academies in London and Paris, although they could use the academies' facilities and received prizes from the societies for their work. One reason that women were barred was the purse: the amount of available patronage was limited, and coveted positions automatically went to men. Moreover, the hierarchical distinction signified by gender made the exclusion of women a useful way to define the academies as special and privileged.

Margaret Cavendish was aware of the degree to which her participation in scientific life depended on informal networks and on the resources available to her because of her aristocratic status. (See the box "Reading Sources: Margaret Cavendish Challenges Male Scientists.") Women scientists from more modest backgrounds, without Cavendish's resources, had to fight for the right to employment as public institutions gained importance as settings for the pursuit of science. The German astronomer Maria Winkelman° (1670–1720), for example,

---

**Winkelman** (VINK-el-mahn)

tried to succeed her late husband in an official position in the Berlin Academy of Sciences in 1710, after working as his unofficial partner during his tenure as astronomer to the academy. The academy withheld an official position from Winkelman after her husband's death, however, despite her experience and accomplishments (she had discovered a new comet, for example, in 1702). The secretary of the academy stated: "That she be kept on in an official capacity to work on the calendar or to continue with observations simply will not do. Already during her husband's lifetime the society was burdened with ridicule because its calendar was prepared by a woman. If she were now to be kept on in such a capacity, mouths would gape even wider."[12]

Winkelman worked in private observatories but was able to return to the Berlin Academy only as the unofficial assistant to her own son, whose training she herself had supervised. As the new science gained in prestige, women scientists often found themselves marginalized.

## The New Science, the State, and the Church

The new natural philosophy had implications for traditional notions about the state. The new world-view that all matter was identical and answerable to discernible natural laws gradually undermined political systems resting on a belief in the inherent inequality of persons and on royal prerogative. By the middle of the eighteenth century a fully formed alternative political philosophy would argue for more "rational" government in keeping with the rational, natural order of things. But the change came slowly, and while it was coming, traditional rulers found much to admire and utilize in the new science.

Technological possibilities of the new science were very attractive to governments. Experiments with vacuum pumps had important applications in the mining industry, for example. Governments also sponsored pure, and not only applied, scientific research. A French naval expedition to Cayenne, in French Guiana, led to refinements of the pendulum clock but had as its main purpose progressive observations of the sun to permit the calculation of the earth's distance from the sun. Members of the elite saw the opportunity not only for practical advances but also for prestige and, most important, confirmation of the orderliness of nature. It is hard to overestimate the psychological impact and intellectual power of this fundamental tenet of the new science—namely, that nature is an inanimate machine that reflects God's design not through its purposes but simply by its orderliness. Thus, in the short run, the new science

supported a vision of order that was very pleasing even to a monarch of absolutist pretensions such as Louis XIV.

As we have seen, scientists themselves flourished in close relationships with princes and actively sought their patronage for its many benefits. Christiaan Huygens left the Netherlands to accept the patronage of Louis XIV, producing in France some of his most important work in optics and mechanics. Huygens had learned from his father, secretary to the princes of Orange in the Netherlands, that a princely court not only offered steady support but also opened doors to other royal academies and salons. Huygens published some of his early research through the Royal Society in London, thanks to contacts his father had established. When Galileo left his position at Padua for the Medici court in Florence, he wrote to a friend, "It is not possible to receive a salary from a Republic [Venice] . . . without serving the public, because to get something from the public one must satisfy it and not just one particular person; . . . no one can exempt me from the burden while leaving me the income; and in sum I cannot hope for such a benefit from anyone but an absolute prince."[13]

Scientists and scientific thought also remained closely tied to religion in both practical and institutional ways during the seventeenth century. Both religion and the Catholic Church as an institution were involved with scientific advancement from the time of Copernicus. Copernicus himself was a cleric, as were many philosophers and scientists after him. This is not surprising, for most research in the sciences to this point had occurred within universities sponsored and staffed by members of religious orders, who had the education, time, and resources necessary for scientific investigation. Some of Descartes's closest collaborators were clerics, as were certain of Galileo's aristocratic patrons and his own protégés. Moreover, religious and metaphysical concerns were central to the work of virtually every scientist. The entire Cartesian edifice of reasoning about the world, for example, was grounded in Descartes's certainty about God. Copernicus, Kepler, Newton, and others perceived God's purpose in the mathematical regularity of nature.

The notion that religion was the opponent of science in this era is a result of Galileo's trial, and represents a distortion even of that event. It is true that the new astronomy and mechanics challenged traditional interpretations of Scripture, as well as the fundamentals of physics and metaphysics that were taught in universities. Thus, in its sponsorship of universities, the church was literally invested in the old view, even though individual clerics investigated and taught Copernican ideas.

**Science and Royal Power**    This painting memorializes the founding of the French Académie des Sciences and the building of the royal observatory in Paris. Louis himself is at the center of the painting, reflecting the symbolic importance of royal power in the sponsorship of science. *(Château de Versailles/Laurie Platt Winfrey, Inc.)*

The rigid response of the church hierarchy to Galileo is partially explained by the aftermath of the Protestant Reformation, which, in the minds of many churchmen—including Galileo's accusers and some of his judges—had demonstrated the need for a firm response to any challenge to the church's authority. Galileo seemed particularly threatening because he was well known, wrote for a wide audience, and, like the Protestants, presumed to interpret the Scriptures. Galileo may well have escaped punishment entirely had it not been for the political predicament faced by the pope coincident with his trial, however.

The condemnation of Galileo shocked many clerics, including the three who had voted for leniency at his trial. Clerics who were also scientists continued to study and teach the new science where and when they could. Copernicanism was taught by Catholic missionaries abroad. (See the box "Global Encounters: Jesuits and Astronomy in China.") To be sure, Galileo's trial did have a chilling effect on scientific investigation in most Catholic regions of Europe. Investigators could and did continue their research, but many could publish results only by smuggling manuscripts to Protestant lands. Many of the most important empirical and theoretical innovations in science occurred in Protestant regions after the middle of the seventeenth century.

Protestant leaders, however, were also not initially receptive to Copernican ideas because they defied scrip-

# Jesuits and Astronomy in China

The Italian Matteo Ricci (1552–1610) was one of the first Jesuit missionaries to establish himself at the imperial court in China. Ricci's willingness to learn the Chinese language and his own scientific knowledge was crucial to his acceptance at the Chinese court. Jesuit missionaries who followed Ricci in the seventeenth century found their scientific expertise equally valued, and several openly taught Copernican theory in the East. Chinese interest in European knowledge was itself new. In previous centuries Europeans had eagerly borrowed from China, including knowledge of papermaking and printing.

The Chinese have not only made considerable progress in moral philosophy but in astronomy and in many branches of mathematics as well. At one time they were quite proficient in arithmetic and geometry, but in the study and teaching of these branches of learning they labored with more or less confusion. They divide the heavens into constellations in a manner somewhat different from that which we employ. Their count of the stars outnumbers the calculations of our astronomers by fully four hundred, because they include in it many of the fainter stars which are not always visible. And yet with all this, the Chinese astronomers take no pains whatever to reduce the phenomena of celestial bodies to the discipline of mathematics. Much of their time is spent in determining the moment of eclipses and the mass of the planets and the stars, but here, too, their deductions are spoiled by innumerable errors. Finally they center their whole attention on that phase of astronomy which our scientists term astrology, which may be accounted for by the fact that they believe that everything happening on this terrestrial globe of ours depends upon the stars.

Some knowledge of the science of mathematics was given to the Chinese by the Saracens [Mongols], who penetrated into their country from the West, but very little of this knowledge was based upon definite mathematical proofs. What the Saracens left them, for the most part, consisted of certain tables of rules by which the Chinese regulated their calendar and to which they reduced their calculations of planets and the movements of the heavenly bodies in general. The founder of the family which at present regulates the study of astrology prohibited anyone from indulging in the study of this science unless he were chosen for it by hereditary right. The prohibition was founded upon fear, lest he who should acquire a knowledge of the stars might become capable of disrupting the order of the empire and seek an opportunity to do so.

## QUESTIONS

1. In what ways is Ricci both appreciative and critical of Chinese science?

2. What do Ricci's comments about Chinese science reveal about his own assumptions concerning astronomy and mathematics and how to study them appropriately?

SOURCE: Louis J. Gallagher, trans., *China in the Sixteenth Century: The Journals of Matthew Ricci: 1583–1610* (New York: Random House, 1953), pp. 30–31. Copyright 1942, 1953 and renewed 1970 by Louis J. Gallagher, S.J. Used by permission of Random House, Inc.

tural authority as well as common sense. In 1549 one of Martin Luther's associates wrote: "The eyes are witnesses that the heavens revolve in the space of twenty-four hours. But certain men, either from love of novelty or to make a display of ingenuity, have concluded that the earth moves. . . . Now it is want of honesty and decency to assert such notions publicly and the example is pernicious. It is part of a good mind to accept the truth as revealed by God and to acquiesce in it."[14]

Protestant thinkers were also as troubled as Catholics by the metaphysical dilemmas that the new theories seemed to raise. In 1611, one year after Galileo's *Starry Messenger* appeared, the English poet John Donne (1573–1631) reflected on the confusion that now reigned in human affairs, with the heavenly hierarchy dismantled:

[The] new Philosophy calls all in doubt,
The Element of fire is quite put out;
The Sun is lost, and th'earth, and no man's wit
Can well direct him where to look for it.
. . . . . . . . . . . . .
Tis all in pieces, all coherence gone;
All just supply, and all Relation:
Prince, Subject, Father, Son, are things forgot,
For every man alone thinks he hath got
To be a Phoenix, and that then can be
None of that kinde, of which he is, but he.[15]

The challenge of accounting in religious terms for the ideas of Copernicus and Descartes became more urgent for Protestants as the ideas acquired an anti-Catholic status after the trial of Galileo in 1633 and as they became common scientific currency by about 1640. A religious certainty about divine force that could account for the motion of bodies in a vacuum enabled Newton to develop his theories on motion and gravity. In short, religion did not merely remain in the scientists' panoply of explanations; it remained a fundamental building block of scientific thought and central to most scientists' lives, whether they were Catholic or Protestant.

## The New Science and Human Affairs at the End of the Seventeenth Century

Traditional institutions and ideologies checked the potential effects of the new science for a time, but by the middle of the seventeenth century political theory was beginning to reflect the impact of the mechanistic world-view. Political philosophers began to doubt that either the world or human society was an organic whole in which each part was distinguished in nature and function from the rest. Thomas Hobbes, John Locke, and others recast the bonds that link citizens to one another and to their rulers.

Because of the political turmoil in England, Thomas Hobbes (1588–1679) spent much of his productive life on the Continent. After the beginnings of the parliamentary rebellion he joined a group of royalist émigrés in France. He met Galileo and lived for extended periods in Paris, in contact with the circle of French thinkers that included Descartes. Like Descartes, he theorized about the nature and behavior of matter and published a treatise on his views in 1655.

Hobbes is best known today for *Leviathan*° (1651), his treatise on political philosophy. *Leviathan* applies to the world of human beings Hobbes's mostly Cartesian view of nature as composed of "self-motivated," atom-like structures. Hobbes viewed people as mechanistically as he viewed the rest of nature. In his view, people are made up of appetites of various sorts—the same kind of innate forces that drive all matter. The ideal state, he concluded, is one in which a strong sovereign controls the disorder that inevitably arises from the clash of desires. Unlike medieval philosophers, Hobbes did not draw analogies between the state and the human body (the king as head, judges and magistrates as arms, and so

*Leviathan* (luh-VIE-uh-thun)

forth). Instead, he compared the state to a machine that "ran" by means of laws and was kept in good working order by a skilled technician—the ruler.

Hobbes's pessimism about human behavior and his insistence on the need for restraint imposed from above reflect, as does the work of Descartes, a concern for order in the wake of political turmoil. This concern was one reason he was welcomed into the community of French philosophers, who were naturally comfortable with royalty as a powerful guarantor of order. But Hobbes's work, like theirs, was a radical departure because it envisioned citizens as potentially equal and constrained neither by morality nor by natural obedience to authority.

Another Englishman, John Locke (1632–1704), offered an entirely different vision of natural equality among people and, consequently, of social order. Locke's major works, *Essay on Human Understanding* (1690) and *Two Treatises of Government* (1690), reflect the experimentalism of Robert Boyle, the systematizing rationality of Descartes, and other strands of the new scientific thought. In his *Essay* Locke provides a view of human knowledge more pragmatic and utilitarian than the rigorous mathematical model of certainty used by many other philosophers. He argues that human knowledge is largely the product of experience. He agrees with Descartes that reason orders and explains human experience, but unlike Descartes, he doubts that human reason had unlimited potential to comprehend the universe. Locke, however, offered a more optimistic vision of the possible uses of reason. Whereas Descartes was interested in mentally ordering and understanding the world, Locke was interested in actually functioning *in* the world.

Locke's treatises on government reflect his notion of knowledge based on experience, as well as his particular experiences as a member of elite circles following the Restoration in England. Trained in medicine, he served as personal physician and general political assistant to one of the members of Parliament most opposed to Charles II's pretensions to absolutist government. When James II acceded to the throne in 1685, Locke remained in the Netherlands, where he had fled to avoid prosecution for treason. He became an adviser to William of Orange and returned to England with William and Mary in 1688. Locke's view of the principles of good government came to reflect the pro-parliamentary stance of his political milieu.

Unlike Hobbes, Locke argued that people are capable of self-restraint and mutual respect in their pursuit of self-interest. The state arises, he believed, from a contract that individuals freely enter into to protect themselves, their property, and their happiness from possible

**Gentleman Surveying a Town**   This illustration appears in a seventeenth-century book on surveying by a mathematician who helped design the gardens at Versailles. The book aimed to teach elites the math necessary for precise measurements of landscapes—for example, for the purpose of siege warfare. The presence of the gentleman in the foreground, estimating the proportions of the town by sight, reveals that the author expected his audience to be interested in the mathematical computations he sought to teach them.   *(Bibliothèque nationale de France)*

aggression by others. They can invest the executive and legislative authority to carry out this protection in monarchy or any other governing institution, though Locke believed that the English Parliament was the best available model. Because sovereignty resides with the people who enter into the contract, rebellion against the abuse of power is justified. At the core of Locke's schema is thus a revolutionary vision of political society based on human rights.

Locke's experience as an English gentleman is apparent in his emphasis on private property, which he considered a fundamental human right. Nature, he believed, cannot benefit humankind unless it is worked by human hands, as on a farm, for example. Private ownership of property guarantees its productivity and entitles the owner to participate in Locke's imagined contract. Indeed, Locke's political vision is unequivocal, and unbending, on the nature of property. Locke even found a justification for slavery. He also did not consider women to be political beings in the same way as men. The family, he felt, is a separate domain from the state, not bound by the same contractual obligations.

Locke and many other seventeenth-century thinkers were unable to imagine a new physical or political reality without invoking a notion of gender as a "natural" principle of order and hierarchy. Although Margaret Cavendish (see page 592) and other women disputed the validity of such gender distinctions, men frequently used them. Locke's use of gender as an arbitrary organizing principle gave his bold new vision of rights for certain men a claim to being "natural." The use of gender-specific vocabulary to describe nature itself had the effect of making the new objective attitude toward the world seem "natural." Works by seventeenth-century scientists are filled with references to nature as a woman who must be "conquered," "subdued," or "penetrated."

Traditional gender distinctions limited and reinforced most facets of political thought, but in other areas the fact of uncertainty and the need for tolerance were embraced. Another of Locke's influential works was the impassioned *Letter on Toleration* (1689). In it he argues that religious belief is fundamentally private and that only the most basic Christian principles need be accepted by everyone. Others went further than Locke by entirely removing traditional religion as necessary to morality and public order. Fostering this climate of religious skepticism were religious pluralism in England and the self-defeating religious intolerance of Louis XIV's persecution of Protestants.

Pierre Bayle° (1647–1706), a Frenchman of Protestant origins, argued that morality can be wholly detached from traditional religion. Indeed, Bayle concluded, one need hardly be a Christian to be a moral being. Bayle cited as an example of morality the philosopher Baruch Spinoza° (1632–1677), a Dutch Jew who had been cast out of his local synagogue for supposed atheism. Even so, Spinoza believed the state to have a moral purpose and human happiness to have spiritual roots.

**Bayle** (BAIL)   **Spinoza** (spin-OH-za)

Bayle's skepticism toward traditional knowledge was more wide-ranging than his views on religion. His best-known work, *Dictionnaire historique et critique* (*Historical and Critical Dictionary*, 1702), was a compendium of observations about and criticisms of virtually every thinker whose works were known at the time, including such recent and lionized figures as Descartes and Newton. Bayle was the first systematic skeptic, and he relentlessly exposed errors and shortcomings in all received knowledge. His works were very popular with elite lay readers.

Bayle's countryman Bernard de Fontenelle° (1657–1757), secretary to the Académie des Sciences from 1699 to 1741, was the greatest popularizer of the new science of his time. His *Entretiens sur la Pluralités des Mondes* (*Conversations on the Plurality of Worlds*, 1686) was, as the title implies, an informally presented description of the infinite universe of matter. A great success, it went through numerous editions and translations. As secretary to the Académie, Fontenelle continued his work as popularizer by publishing descriptions of the work of the Académie's scientists. At his death (at age 99) in 1757, it was said that "the Philosophic spirit, today so much in evidence, owes its beginnings to Monsieur de Fontenelle."[16]

## SUMMARY

FONTENELLE is a fitting figure with whom to end a discussion of the Scientific Revolution because he represents, and worked to accomplish, the transference of the new natural philosophy into political and social philosophy—a movement we know as the "Enlightenment." The Scientific Revolution began, as innovation in scientific thinking often does, with a specific research problem whose answer led in unexpected directions. Copernicus's response to traditional astronomical problems led to scientific and philosophical innovation because of his solution and because of the context in which it was received. Recent recoveries of new ancient texts in the Renaissance and the discovery of previously unknown lands in the New World made it possible to imagine challenging ancient scientific authority. The interest of princes in both the prestige and the practical use of science helped support the work of scientists.

Other scientists, following Copernicus, built on his theories, culminating in the work of Galileo, who supported Copernican theory with additional data and widely published his findings. The Frenchman Descartes was the first to fashion a systematic explanation for the operations of nature to replace the medieval view. The political and intellectual climate in England, meanwhile, encouraged the development of experimental science and inductive reasoning. Isaac Newton provided new theories to explain the behavior of matter and expressed them in mathematical terms that could apply to either the earth or the cosmos. With his work traditional astronomy and physics were overturned, replaced by a vision of a universe of matter that behaves not according to a higher purpose but rather as a machine. New institutions in the form of private as well as officially sponsored scientific societies rose up to support scientists' work. These societies were particularly important before the new science became accepted in universities, although they excluded some practitioners of the new science, particularly women.

Rulers made use of the new science for the practical results it offered despite the ideological challenges it presented to their power. The relationship of religion to the new science was equally complex and contrary. Some religious leaders scorned the new science; most scientists, whether Catholic or Protestant, worked to accommodate both the new science and their religious beliefs. Indeed, religious faith—in the case of Newton, for example—was a spur to innovation. By the end of the seventeenth century, the hierarchical Christian world-view grounded in the old science was being challenged on many fronts, most notably in the work of the political philosophers Hobbes and Locke. A fully articulated secular world-view would be the product of the Enlightenment in the next century.

## ■ Notes

1. Quoted in *Encyclopaedia Britannica,* 15th ed., vol. 9, p. 135.
2. Quoted in Thomas S. Kuhn, *The Copernican Revolution* (Cambridge, Mass.: Harvard University Press, 1985), p. 131.
3. Quoted in Margaret C. Jacob, *The Cultural Meaning of the Scientific Revolution* (Philadelphia: Temple University Press, 1988), p. 18.
4. Quoted ibid., p. 33.
5. Quoted in Alan G. R. Smith, *Science and Society in the Sixteenth and Seventeenth Centuries* (New York: Science History Publications, 1972), p. 72.
6. Quoted in Jacob, p. 32 (emphasis added).
7. Quoted in Bruce T. Moran, ed., *Patronage and Institutions: Science, Technology and Medicine at the European Court* (Rochester, N.Y.: Boyden Press, 1991), p. 43.
8. Quoted in Steven Shapin, *A Social History of Truth* (Chicago: University of Chicago Press, 1994), p. 298.

**Fontenelle** (fon-tuh-NEL)

9. Quoted in Smith, p. 130.

10. Quoted in Jacob, p. 89.

11. Quoted ibid., p. 25.

12. Quoted in Londa Schiebinger, *The Mind Has No Sex?* (Cambridge, Mass.: Harvard University Press, 1989), p. 92.

13. Quoted in Richard S. Westfall, "Science and Patronage," *ISIS* 76 (1985): 16.

14. Quoted in Kuhn, p. 191.

15. *Complete Poetry and Selected Prose of John Donne*, ed. John Hayward (Bloomsbury, England: Nonesuch Press, 1929), p. 365, quoted in Kuhn, p. 194.

16. Quoted in Paul Edwards, ed., *The Encyclopedia of Philosophy*, vol. 3 (New York: Macmillan, 1967), p. 209.

■ **Suggested Reading**

Biagioli, Mario. *Galileo, Courtier.* 1993. A study that stresses the power of patronage relations to shape scientific process.

Dear, Peter. *Revolutionizing the Sciences: European Knowledge and Its Ambitions, 1500–1700.* 2001. An excellent general overview of the era of the Scientific Revolution.

Kuhn, Thomas. *The Copernican Revolution.* 1985. A classic treatment of the revolution in astronomy that lucidly explains the Aristotelian world-view; to understand the Copernican revolution, start here.

Schiebinger, Londa. *The Mind Has No Sex?* 1989. An examination of the participation of women in the practice of science and an explanation of how science began to reflect the exclusion of women in its values and objects of study—above all, in its claims about scientific "facts" about women themselves.

Shapin, Steven, and Simon Schaffer. *Leviathan and the Air-Pump.* 1985. One of the most important studies of seventeenth-century science; traces the conflict between Cartesian science, as represented by Hobbes, and experimental science, in the work of Boyle; shows the relationship of Hobbes and Boyle to their respective contexts and the widespread philosophical implications of each school of thought.

Westfall, Richard S. *Never at Rest: A Biography of Isaac Newton.* 1993. A biography by one of the best-known historians of science.

www. **For a searchable list of additional readings for this chapter, go to college.hmco.com/students.**

# Modern Maps

We take for granted that contemporary maps will provide accurate representations of geography and present information in standardized ways we can easily read. But how did these standards of clarity and accuracy come about?

Modern mapping was developed during the Scientific Revolution. Like most of the changes we have labeled the "Scientific Revolution," changes in mapping were the result of several influences: innovations in Renaissance art, knowledge gleaned from voyages of exploration, the impact of new astronomical discoveries, and the interest and support of princely patrons. All of these factors enabled Europeans of this era to have a literally new view of their world.

Let us look at Christopher Saxton's map of Somerset, a county in England. This map was printed in 1579 in one of the first atlases ever published. We might be struck by how different this map appears from contemporary maps; many of its features seem decorative or even quaint. Ships, not drawn to scale, ride at anchor or sail off the coast. Towns are represented not by dots of various sizes but by miniature town buildings. Relief in the landscape is depicted with hills drawn, like the town buildings, from a side view inconsistent with the aerial perspective of the map as a whole. The large royal coat of arms that occupies the upper left quadrant of the map seems the most antiquated and irrelevant feature.

But is it irrelevant? Let us try to appreciate what a striking and powerful image this map must have been for its original viewers. Because the features are represented in ways that we consider decorative, it is easy for us to overlook the fact that this map illustrates a revolutionary method of depicting space. Saxton provides an aerial view of an entire county, with all locales arrayed in accurate spatial relationship to one another. This accurate rendering of space was, first, the result of the discovery of linear perspective by Renaissance artists. This discovery, which enabled space to be imagined from the perspective of a distanced observer, created the illusion of three-dimensional space in Renaissance paintings. Saxton's maps—and the few others published at about the same time—represented the first time Europeans could take

**The County of Somerset, England, 1579** *(British Library)*

**The French Coastline, 1693**
*(Bibliothèque nationale de France)*

"visual possession" of the land they lived in, in the way we now take for granted whenever we buy a road map.*

Precise measurement of landforms—the location of hills in this map, for example—still relied on the established craft of systematic surveying. And here is where the royal coat of arms enters the picture, literally. Saxton's surveying and the production of his atlas were sponsored by the government of Queen Elizabeth. Thus just as this map enabled contemporary observers to envision for the first time, in its entirety, the land they lived in, it simultaneously marked royal power over that land.

Now let us look at a 1693 map of the coastline of France. We immediately note that most decorative elements are gone: no ships sail the abundant seas, for example. The figure of a compass marks the Paris meridian—the site of the city, we are shown, has been precisely determined by means of its longitude and latitude. More accurate calculation of longitude had been made possible by the work of Johannes Kepler and Galileo Galilei, whose mapping of heavenly bodies provided known points in the night sky from which to calculate the longitude of the observer's position on earth. (Calculation of latitude had

always been easier, since it involved only determining the angle of the sun above the horizon, but it was also improved by better instrumentation in the seventeenth century.) After 1650 French cartographers, among others, systematically collected astronomical observations from around the world so they could map all known lands more precisely.

This map superimposes a corrected view (the darker line) of the coastline of France over an older rendering. The power of this coastline map lies in the way it dramatically advertises the progress of mapmaking itself. Royal power remains connected to scientific effort: the title reads, "Map of France, corrected by order of the King by the observations of Messieurs of the Academy of Sciences."

Thus both of these maps glorify royal power: one by linking it with a new visualization of the land it ruled, the other by presenting royalty as a patron and guarantor of knowledge. But in the second map royal identity is no longer pictured along with the land it claims. Instead, the king is mentioned discreetly, in what came to be a standardized label.

Like all innovations of the Scientific Revolution, those in mapmaking had unintended consequences. Claims to royal power articulated on maps lost their force as the information the maps conveyed was increasingly valued for itself. Royal power had many practical and ideological uses for the new science but in the end would be undermined by the world-view the new science made possible.

---

*Richard Helgerson, "The Land Speaks: Cartography, Chorography, and Subversion in Renaissance England," *Representations* 16 (Fall 1986): 51. This discussion of Saxton's map and the evolution of mapmaking is drawn from Helgerson and from Norman J. W. Thrower, *Maps and Civilization* (Chicago: University of Chicago Press, 1996), chaps. 5 and 6.

# Glossary

**This Glossary covers the complete text, Chapters 1 through 30.**

**absolutism** Extraordinary concentration of power in royal hands, achieved particularly by the kings of France, most notably **Louis XIV,** in the seventeenth century. Proponents argued that hereditary monarchy was the divinely ordained form of government. *(Ch. 16)*

**Act of Supremacy (1534)** Act of the English Parliament during the Protestant Reformation that finalized the break with the Catholic Church by declaring the king to be head of the Church of England. Henry VIII required a public oath supporting the act, which Sir **Thomas More** refused to take; More was then executed for treason. *(Ch. 14)*

**Adenauer, Konrad (1876–1967)** Leading statesman of post–World War II Germany. As chancellor (1949–1963), he oriented the country toward western Europe and the United States and proved to Germans that democracy could mean effective government, economic prosperity, and foreign policy success. *(Ch. 29)*

**agricultural revolution** Dramatic increase in food production from the sixteenth to eighteenth centuries, brought about by changes in agricultural practices, cultivation of new crops, greater availability of animal manure, and introduction of the nutrient-rich potato from the Americas. *(Ch. 18)*

**Alexander the Great (356–323 B.C.)** King of **Macedon** (r. 336–323) and conqueror of the **Persian Empire.** Son of **Philip II** of Macedon, Alexander was an ingenious warrior who, in the course of his conquests, spread Greek civilization to western Asia, Egypt, and India. His despotism and ruler-worship set a precedent for later monarchs, including many Roman emperors. *(Ch. 4)*

**Alexandria** Mediterranean seaport in northern Egypt founded by **Alexander the Great** in 332 B.C. It was a thriving Hellenistic city with great harbors, marketplaces, banks, inns, courts, shipbuilding facilities, and a renowned library. *(Ch. 4)*

**Amarna reform** Term for the ancient Egyptian king Amenhotep IV's seizure of power from temple priests by replacing the god Amun-Re with Aten and renaming himself Akhenaten. After Akhenaten's death, the Amun-Re cult regained power. *(Ch. 1)*

**Anabaptists** Radical religious reformers in Germany and Switzerland during the Reformation. They rejected the practice of infant baptism, believing that baptism should occur only after confession of sin. They also believed that Christians should live apart in communities of the truly redeemed. Mennonites and Hutterites are their modern descendants. *(Ch. 14)*

**Antigonids** Dynasty of Macedonian rulers founded in 276 B.C. by Antigonus Gonatas, grandson of Antigonus the One-Eyed, a general of **Alexander the Great.** The Antigonid dynasty lasted about 140 years, until the Roman conquest. *(Ch. 4)*

**Antioch** Greatest of the cities founded by Seleucus, a general of **Alexander the Great.** Located near the present-day Turkish-Syrian border, it became one of the wealthiest and most luxurious of all eastern Mediterranean cities. *(Ch. 4)*

**anti-Semitism** Centuries-old prejudice against and demonization of Jews. Anti-Semitism became virulent in Europe in the 1880s with the emergence of the ultranationalist and racist "New Right" ideologies and political movements. An essential part of the Nazi world-view, it led to the Holocaust. *(Ch. 24)*

**appeasement** The term for the policy employed by Britain's prime minister, Neville Chamberlain, to defuse the 1938 crisis with Germany's **Adolf Hitler.** Chamberlain acquiesced to Hitler's demands to annex the Sudetenland portion of Czechoslovakia, which proved a giant step toward the war that broke out less than a year later. *(Ch. 27)*

**Aquinas, Thomas (1225–1274)** Dominican friar and theologian. In his two most famous works, *Summa Contra Gentiles* and *Summa Theologiae,* he distinguished between natural truth, or what a person could know by reasoning, and revealed truths, which can be known only through faith in God's revelation. No one before him had so rigorously followed the dialectical method of reasoning through a whole field of knowledge. *(Ch. 10)*

**Archaic Greece** Period of ancient Greek history from around 700 to 500 B.C. Archaic Greece was characterized by artistic achievement, increased individualism amid communal solidarity, and a moving away from divine and toward abstract, mechanistic explanations. The Western philosophical tradition began during this period. *(Ch. 3)*

**Arianism** Popular heresy advocated by the priest Arius (ca. 250–336), emphasizing that Jesus was the "first born of all creation." It sought to preserve and purify Christianity's monotheism by making Jesus slightly subordinate to the Father. It was condemned by the **Council of Nicaea.** *(Ch. 7)*

**Aristotle (384–322 B.C.)** Ancient Greek philosopher, student of **Plato** and tutor of **Alexander the Great.** Aristotle emphasized the goal (*telos* in Greek) of change; in his view the entire cosmos is teleological, and every one of its parts has an essential purpose. Aristotle's scientific writings were the most influential philosophical classics of Greek and Roman civilization and remained so during the Middle Ages. *(Ch. 3)*

**Armada (1588)** Massive fleet of Spanish warships sent against England by **Philip II** but defeated by the English navy and bad weather. The tactics used by the English helped set the future course of naval warfare. *(Ch. 15)*

**Assyrians** Warlike people who ruled the ancient Near East during the first millennium B.C. Their innovations included using cavalry as their main striking force and having weapons and armor made of iron. *(Ch. 2)*

**Augsburg Confession (1532)** Document written by Philip Melanchthon (1497–1560), with the approval of **Martin Luther,** that became the most widely accepted statement of the Lutheran faith. It constitutes part of the creedal basis for today's Lutheran churches. *(Ch. 14)*

**Augustine (354–430)** North African bishop and one of the most influential Christian thinkers. Augustine wrote that all people were sinners in need of God's redemption, that history is the struggle between those who call on divine grace and those who sin, and that learning was useful only to the extent that it equipped individuals to read and understand the Bible's message of salvation. *(Ch. 7)*

**Augustus (63 B.C.–A.D. 14)** Honorific title of Gaius Julius Caesar Octavianus, grandnephew of **Julius Caesar** and first Roman emperor. After defeating Mark Antony and Cleopatra at the Battle of Actium (31 B.C.), Augustus ruled the empire for forty-five years. His rule laid the foundations of two hundred years of prosperous Roman peace. See also **Principate.** *(Ch. 6)*

**Auschwitz-Birkenau** The largest and principal extermination center of Nazi Germany's six death camps, all of which were located in what had been Poland. The Nazis shipped Jews from all over Europe to Auschwitz, which killed about twelve thousand people a day at the height of its operation in 1944. *(Ch. 28)*

**avant-garde** French for "forefront," the term refers to early-twentieth-century artists who, inspired by novel or unconventional techniques, considered themselves precursors of new styles. Avant-garde movements proclaimed idiosyncratic manifestos and constantly called for the rejection of existing forms of expression and the creation of new ones. *(Ch. 24)*

**Aztecs** Amerindian people that dominated central Mexico from the fourteenth through the sixteenth centuries from their capital Tenochtitlán (present-day Mexico City). Weakened by exposure to virulent Old World diseases, they were conquered in 1521–1523 by Spanish forces led by **Hernán Cortés.** *(Ch. 13)*

**Babylonian Captivity of the Papacy** Term used to describe the period from 1308 to 1378 when popes resided north of the Alps rather than in central Italy or Rome, where the pope was the bishop. The term refers to the period when the tribes of Israel lived in exile. *(Ch. 11)*

**Bacon, Francis (1561–1626)** England's lord chancellor during the reign of James I and author of a utopian essay extolling science's benefits for a peaceful society and human happiness. His influential works encouraged the empirical method and inductive reasoning. See also **empirical method.** *(Ch. 17)*

**barbarian kingship** Central institution in a succession of kingdoms (ca. 300–600) ruled by barbarian (non-Roman) leaders, which evolved from former Roman provinces. Most such kings had been political or military leaders under Roman authority before becoming independent rulers. *(Ch. 7)*

**baroque** Style of European art and architecture popular from the late sixteenth to early eighteenth century. Baroque artists, such as Peter Paul Rubens, modified Renaissance techniques, adding dynamism and emotional energy. Baroque painting used light to portray dramatic illusion, and baroque churches were both impressively grand and emotionally engaging. *(Ch. 15)*

**Bauhaus** An influential German art school, founded in 1919, that sought to adopt contemporary materials to develop new forms of architecture, design, and urban planning in response to the cultural uncertainty that followed World War I. Though it arguably failed in its immediate German context, the Bauhaus helped shape the whole idea of "the modern" in the West and throughout the world for decades to come. *(Ch. 26)*

**Bernard of Clairvaux (1090–1153)** Monk, church reformer, and influential adviser to kings and popes. Bernard believed

that faith and divine inspiration were more important than dialectical reasoning. He was instrumental in the success of the Cistercian religious order. *(Ch. 10)*

**Bismarck, Otto von (1815–1898)** Nineteenth-century German statesman. A Prussian aristocrat, Bismarck was the autocratic architect who, through a series of aggressive wars, united Germany and served as the nation's first chancellor. He administered an emperor-controlled country that became the dominant power in Europe. See also **Realpolitik.** *(Ch. 22)*

**Black Death (1348–1351)** First of a series of epidemics, probably bubonic plague, that raged in Europe and western Asia for three centuries. The Black Death killed about 60 percent of those infected. The huge population decline fueled the economic and social transformations of the late Middle Ages. *(Ch. 11)*

**Bolsheviks** Members of a faction of the Russian Socialist Party led by **Vladimir Ilich Lenin** (1870–1924), a zealous Marxist who insisted that a revolutionary cadre could seize power on behalf of the working class. The Bolsheviks gained control of Russia in November 1917. *(Ch. 24)*

**Bonaparte, Napoleon.** See **Napoleon Bonaparte.**

**bourgeois century** Characterization of the nineteenth century, especially the latter half. In western Europe, the bourgeois elites (middle classes), which had expanded dramatically in the wake of industrialization, helped fashion much of society. *(Ch. 23)*

**Brandenburg-Prussia** Group of German territories ruled by the Hohenzollern family that became one of Europe's most powerful states in the seventeenth century. Its military strength was supported by its hereditary landowners, who were granted autonomy in their territories. *(Ch. 16)*

**Brandt, Willy (1913–1992)** Socialist West German chancellor (r. 1969–1974). Brandt's widely popular policy of opening to the East, or *Ostpolitik,* made possible closer economic ties between West and East Germany and broader opportunities for ordinary citizens to interact across the east-west border. *(Ch. 29)*

**Brest-Litovsk, Treaty of (1918)** Treaty in which Russia accepted its defeat by Germany and its allies in World War I. The treaty forced the Russians to cede much of European Russia to Germany. After Germany's defeat by the Allies later in the year, the **Bolsheviks** recaptured Ukraine and the Caucasus region. *(Ch. 25)*

**British blockade** Britain's naval blockade of Germany during World War I. By means of this tactic, which cut off supplies to Germany but which also violated several provisions of international law, the British seriously impeded the German war effort. *(Ch. 25)*

**Caesar, Gaius Julius (100–44 B.C.)** Roman general gifted at war and politics. Named dictator in 49 B.C., he was assassinated by the members of the **senate** in 44 B.C. He introduced to Europe the calendar of 365¼ days. He was succeeded as ruler by his grandnephew Octavian (**Augustus**). Later Roman emperors were also called *caesar.* *(Ch. 5)*

**caliphate** Arab empire established by the successors of **Muhammad;** *caliph* means "successor to the prophet." The Umayyad caliphate, with its capital in Damascus, ruled from 661 to 750; the Abbasid caliphate, based in Baghdad, from 750 to 1258. *(Ch. 8)*

**Calvin, John (1509–1564)** Franco-Swiss theologian and founder of the Reformed Church in Geneva. Calvin's theological writings, most notably *Institutes of the Christian Religion* (1536), were widely disseminated and hugely influential. Calvin stressed the absolute power of God and the need for moral reform of the Christian community. *(Ch. 14)*

**canon law** Collection of orderly rules for the government of the Catholic Church, based on papal decrees and decisions of church councils. In 1140 the monk Gratian published the *Decretum,* the first systematic collection of canon law. *(Ch. 10)*

**Carlowitz, Treaty of (1699)** Treaty imposed by the European allies on a weakening Ottoman Empire. The Habsburgs, Venetians, Russians, and Poles gained territory and power at the Turks' expense. *(Ch. 16)*

**Carolingian Renaissance** Major revival of learning, combined with reform of religious and political institutions, that occurred under **Charlemagne** and his successors. The revival encompassed the founding of schools in religious institutions, production of textbooks, dissemination of early church teachings and of **canon law,** as well as secular reforms such as regularization of royal estates. *(Ch. 8)*

**Catherine the Great (r. 1762–1796)** Empress of Russia. Through an astute policy of wars and alliances, Catherine expanded her country's borders south to the Black Sea and west into Europe. An "enlightened despot," she advanced the westernizing reforms begun by **Peter the Great.** *(Ch. 18)*

**Cato the Censor (234–149 B.C.)** Marcus Portius Cato, Roman general and statesman. Known as Cato the Censor because he denounced luxury goods, he was the first Roman historian to write in Latin. *(Ch. 5)*

**Charlemagne** Frankish king (r. 768–814), crowned emperor in 800. He carried out a program of legal and ecclesiastical reform, patronized learning, and revitalized the western Roman Empire. See also **Carolingian Renaissance.** *(Ch. 8)*

**Charles V (r. 1519–1558)** Holy Roman emperor and, as Charles I, king of Spain. His empire included Spain, Italy, the Low Countries, and Germany. Though he vigorously opposed the spread of Protestantism during the Reformation, he was forced to sign the Religious Peace of Augsburg in 1555, which acknowledged the right of German princes to choose the religion to be practiced in their territories, Lutheran or Catholic. Charles abdicated his imperial and royal titles the next year, ceding the empire to his brother Ferdinand and his Spanish possessions to his son **Philip II.** *(Ch. 14)*

**Chartism** Nineteenth-century British political movement whose goal was to transform Britain from an oligarchy to a democracy. The Chartists' demands were contained in the 1838 "people's charter," which called for universal male suffrage, electoral districts with equal population, salaries and the abolition of property qualifications for Members of Parliament, the secret ballot, and annual general elections. The movement failed, but most of its measures eventually became law. See also **Second Reform Bill.** *(Ch. 21)*

**chivalry** Initially, a medieval code of conduct for mounted warriors, focusing on military prowess, open-handed generosity, and earning a glorious reputation. Later it evolved into an elaborate set of rules governing relations between men and women. *(Ch. 10)*

**Christianity** Sect originally rooted in Judaism that emerged as a fully separate religion by around A.D. 200. Emphasizing belief in one God and the mission of his son, **Jesus of Nazareth,** as savior, Christianity offered salvation in the next world and a caring community in the present one. A mes-sianic religion, Christianity emphasized Christ's return, leading to the beginning of a heavenly kingdom on earth. *(Ch. 6)*

**Churchill, Winston (1874–1965)** British prime minister (1940–1945; 1951–1955). As the leader of his country during World War II, Churchill's courage, decisiveness, memorable words, and boundless energy made him widely seen as one of Britain's greatest leaders of the twentieth century. See also **Yalta conference.** *(Ch. 28)*

**Cicero, Marcus Tullius (106–43 B.C.)** Philosopher, writer, and statesman who was Rome's greatest orator. He was crucial in making the Latin language a vessel for the heritage of Greek thought. *(Ch. 5)*

**city-state** State consisting of an independent city and the surrounding territory under its control. Early examples were the Sumerian city-states in the third millennium B.C. *(Ch. 1)*

**civic humanism** An ideology, championed by Florentine writers and public officials during the Renaissance, that emphasized their city's classical republican virtues and history. They argued that a moral and ethical value was intrinsic to public life. *(Ch. 12)*

**Civil Code** Law code established under Napoleon in 1801 that included limited acceptance of revolutionary gains, such as a guarantee of equality before the law and taxation of all social classes. Also known as the Napoleonic Code, it enshrined modern forms of property ownership and civil contracts, enhanced paternal control of families, outlawed divorce in most circumstances, and placed women under the legal domination of fathers and husbands. *(Ch. 19)*

**Classical Greece** Period of ancient Greek history from about 480 to 323 B.C. Classical Greek culture emphasized public life as the central theme of art and literature, and its sculpture was the most anatomically precise yet. Classical Greece set many standards for modern Western culture. See also **demokratia.** *(Ch. 3)*

**Cluny (Cluniacs)** A spiritual reform begun in 910 in central France. The movement emphasized strict adherence to the Benedictine Rule, as well as the ideas that the church should pray for the world without being deeply involved in it and must be free from lay control. *(Ch. 10)*

**cold war** The hostile standoff between the Soviet Union and the United States that began after World War II, when communist governments, relying on Soviet support, took control of most of east-central Europe. The Soviets' first atomic bomb explosion in 1949 intensified the conflict, which shaped world affairs for the next forty years. *(Ch. 28)*

**collectivization** The program that reshaped agriculture in the Soviet Union under **Joseph Stalin** during the early 1930s. By forcing peasants into government-controlled collective farms, the Soviet regime sought to take control of agricultural production in order better to finance rapid industrialization. *(Ch. 27)*

**Columbian Exchange** Historians' term for the blending of cultures between the Old World and the New after Christopher Columbus's arrival in the New World in 1492. The Spanish and other Europeans brought their plants, domesticated animals, and diseases to the Americas. The Americas contributed New World crops, most notably maize (corn) and potatoes, transforming the Old World diet. *(Ch. 13)*

**Comintern (Third, or Communist, International)** An association founded in March 1919 by the communists (formerly

**Bolsheviks)** to translate their success in Russia into leadership of the international socialist movement. Its program of tight organization and discipline under Russian leadership produced a schism between communists and socialists in Europe and throughout the world. *(Ch. 26)*

**Common Agricultural Policy (CAP)** A major pillar of the **European Union,** accounting for half of its budget by 2000, the Common Agricultural Policy entailed subsidies to protect farmers from outside competition. The CAP was widely criticized by advocates of freer world trade. *(Ch. 30)*

**communes** Form of government in Italian towns that rose in the eleventh century. Despite numerous local variations, communes involved common decision making by local notables, including both landed aristocrats and wealthy merchants or industrialists. *(Ch. 9)*

**Compromise of 1867** Agreement that divided the Habsburg Empire into Austria in the west and Hungary in the east, a dual monarchy under Emperor Franz Joseph called Austria-Hungary. The compromise confirmed Magyar dominance in Hungary. *(Ch. 22)*

**conciliarists** These people argued that the pope was not a universal monarch, but rather the first among equals in the Church. Thus, church councils had the right and duty to reform and correct even the pope. *(Ch. 11)*

**congress system** System of European international relations in the first half of the nineteenth century in which the major European states cooperated to preserve the balance of power. This system disappeared as political leaders increasingly used force to pursue their narrow interests. *(Ch. 22)*

**Congress of Vienna (1814–1815)** Conference called by the victorious powers—Austria, Great Britain, Prussia, and Russia—who defeated Napoleon. Guided by the Austrian foreign minister, Prince Metternich, the Great Powers drew new territorial boundaries advantageous to themselves. They also attempted to provide long-term stability on the European continent and restored some of the rulers who had been overthrown. See also **congress system.** *(Ch. 21)*

**conservatism** Ideology underlying the order established in Europe in 1815. Conservatives emphasized resistance to change and preservation of the existing order of monarchy, aristocracy, and an established church. *(Ch. 21)*

**Copernicus, Nicholas (1473–1543)** Polish astronomer who initiated the Scientific Revolution by proposing that the earth and other planets orbit the sun, a theory called the heliocentric, or sun-centered, system. See also **heliocentric theory.** *(Ch. 17)*

**corporative state, corporativism** The system established in fascist Italy beginning in 1926 that sought to involve people in public life not as citizens but as producers, through their roles in the economy. A system based on such occupational groupings eventually replaced parliament as the basis of political representation in fascist Italy. *(Ch. 26)*

**Cortés, Hernán (1485–1546)** Spanish commander who conquered the **Aztecs** and claimed the Valley of Mexico for Spain. Cortés had only five hundred men but was aided by an outbreak of smallpox and the help of Amerindian peoples eager to end Aztec control. *(Ch. 13)*

**Cossacks** Originally the term (from a Russian word meaning "free man" or "adventurer") for peoples of Tater origin who inhabited the hinterland of the Black and Caspian seas. Their numbers swelled, after 1500, by peasants who fled serfdom in Poland-Lithuania and the growing Russian state. The Cossacks helped to provide a military buffer between the Polish-Lithuanian and Russian states and the Ottomans to the south, and resisted Polish domination in the seventeenth century, but slowly lost their autonomy to the expanding Russian state in the eighteenth century. *(Ch. 16)*

**Council of Constance (1414–1418)** Assembly convened by Holy Roman Emperor Sigismund to heal deep religious and civil divisions. The council declared that its rulings were binding even on the pope. Its selection of Pope Martin V ended the **Great Schism.** *(Ch. 11)*

**Council of the Indies** Body established by the king of Spain in 1524 to oversee Spain's colonial possessions. Located at court, eventually in Madrid, it supervised all legal, administrative, and commercial activity in the colonies until the early eighteenth century. *(Ch. 13)*

**Council of Nicaea (325)** History's first ecumenical, or "all-church," council, convened by the emperor Constantine. The council condemned **Arianism** and proclaimed key elements of the Nicene Creed, especially the doctrine that Christ was "one in being with the Father," co-equal and co-eternal. *(Ch. 7)*

**Council of Trent (1545–1563)** Ecumenical council of the Roman Catholic Church during the Reformation. Though rejecting many Protestant positions, the council reformed and reorganized the church partly in response to Protestant criticisms. Its decrees reaffirmed and defined the basic tenets of Roman Catholicism for the next four hundred years. *(Ch. 14)*

**covenant** As told in the Hebrew Bible, the pact God made with Abraham, the first patriarch of **Israel.** In return for the land of Canaan and the promise of becoming a great nation, the Israelites agreed to worship no other gods. *(Ch. 2)*

**Cromwell, Oliver (1599–1658)** English Puritan general and statesman. A military genius and leader in the English Civil War, Cromwell governed as Lord Protector during the Interregnum from 1653 to 1658. *(Ch. 16)*

**Crusades (1095–1270)** A series of largely unsuccessful wars waged by western European Christians to recapture the Holy Land from the Muslims and ensure the safety of Christian pilgrims to Jerusalem. Later, the term came to designate any military effort by Europeans against non-Christians. *(Ch. 9)*

**Crystal Night (*Kristallnacht*)** Organized Nazi assault on Jewish businesses and synagogues during the night of November 9–10, 1938, following the assassination of a German diplomat in Paris. Almost all the synagogues in Germany and about seven thousand Jewish-owned stores were destroyed. The broken shop windows gave the episode its name. Although the German public generally deplored this wanton destruction of property, the Crystal Night pogrom initiated a more radical phase of Nazi anti-Jewish policy. *(Ch. 27)*

**cuneiform** First writing system in Mesopotamia, consisting of wedge-shaped impressions in soft clay. Named from the Latin word for "wedge-shaped," it was developed about 3500–3100 B.C. *(Ch. 1)*

**Darwinism** Profoundly influential theory of biological evolution, first put forth by Charles Darwin (1809–1882). He proposed that all forms of life continuously develop through natural selection, whereby those that are better adapted to the environment have the advantage and are more likely to survive and pass on their beneficial traits to their offspring. *(Ch. 23)*

**D-Day**  The complex Allied amphibious landings in Normandy, France, on June 6, 1944, that opened a second major European front in World War II. In the aftermath of this invasion, American-led forces in the west began moving toward Germany, completing the Soviet effort, which was already forcing the Germans back on the eastern front. *(Ch. 28)*

**Decembrists**  Group of Russian military officers who led the December 1825 rebellion after the death of Tsar Alexander I, seeking to install a constitutional monarchy with Alexander's eldest brother, Constantine, as tsar. They were defeated and executed by Constantine's younger brother, Nicholas. The Decembrists were seen as martyrs by later Russian revolutionaries. *(Ch. 21)*

**Declaration of the Rights of Man and the Citizen (1789)**  Document issued by the **National Assembly** of France in August 1789. Modeled on the U.S. Constitution, the declaration set forth the basis for the new French government and asserted "the natural, inalienable and sacred rights of man." *(Ch. 19)*

**De Gaulle, Charles (1890–1970)**  The youngest general in the French army, he called on French forces to follow his lead and continue the fight against Nazi Germany after the fall of France in June 1940. As the leader of the new Free French force that emerged thereafter, he won renewed respect for France as a major power and sought to exercise political leadership after France's liberation in 1944. Though he retired from public life in 1946, disillusioned with politics, he returned in 1958 to spearhead the creation of the new Fifth Republic. He served as its president from 1958 to 1969. *(Ch. 28)*

**demokratia**  Term coined in Athens in the fifth century B.C. to describe the city's system of direct government. It means "the power *(kratos)* of the people *(demos)*." Athenian society pioneered today's key democratic principles, including freedom, equality, universal citizenship, and the rule of law. *(Ch. 3)*

**Descartes, René (1596–1650)**  French philosopher, scientist, and mathematician. Descartes emphasized skepticism and deductive reasoning in his most influential treatise, *Discourse on Method.* He offered the first alternative physical explanation of matter after the Copernican revolution. *(Ch. 17)*

**digital divide**  A term for the disparity in access to the computing and Internet technologies that seemed essential to compete in the twenty-first-century global economy. It was one way that new technologies were widening the gap between the world's haves and have-nots. *(Ch. 30)*

**Directory**  French revolutionary government from 1795 to 1799, consisting of an executive council of five men chosen by the upper house of the legislature. It was overthrown in a coup led by **Napoleon Bonaparte.** *(Ch. 19)*

**Dominic**  Dominic de Guzman (1170–1221), Spanish priest and founder of the spiritually influential Dominican mendicant order. The order was known for the irreproachable life of its members, its learning, and its desire to emulate the apostolic life of the early church by poverty and preaching. *(Ch. 10)*

**Dutch East India Company**  Commercially innovative Dutch company formed in 1602 that combined government management of trade with both public and private investment. The formation of the company created a permanent pool of capital to sustain trade and resulted in a dramatic expansion of commerce with Asia. *(Ch. 16)*

**Edict of Milan (313)**  Proclamation issued primarily by Emperor Constantine that made Christianity a legal religion in the Roman Empire. Constantine promoted the Christian church, granting it tax immunities and relieving the clergy of military service. *(Ch. 7)*

**Edict of Nantes (1598)**  Edict of Henry IV granting France's Protestants (**Huguenots**) the right to practice their faith and maintain defensive garrisons. They were also guaranteed access to schools, hospitals, royal appointments, and separate judicial institutions. The edict was revoked by **Louis XIV** in 1685. *(Ch. 15)*

**Elizabeth I (r. 1558–1603)**  First woman to occupy the English throne successfully. Elizabeth's adroit rule brought stability to England after the turmoil of previous reigns. She firmly established Protestantism in England, encouraged English commerce, defended the nation against the Spanish **Armada,** and fostered the English Renaissance in poetry and drama. *(Ch. 15)*

**empirical method**  Philosophical view developed by the seventeenth-century English philosophers **Francis Bacon** and **John Locke,** asserting that all knowledge is based on observation and experimentation and that general principles should be derived from particular facts. *(Ch. 17)*

**encomienda**  A Spanish royal grant of protectorship over a group of Amerindians. The receivers of the grants (encomenderos) were obliged to Christianize the people under their charge, but instead most forced the natives to work as virtual slaves in mines and on Spanish lands. See also **Bartolomé de Las Casas.** *(Ch. 13)*

**enlightened despotism**  Term for the reform-oriented rule of eighteenth-century monarchs such as **Frederick the Great,** Joseph II of Austria, and **Catherine the Great.** Enlightened despots applied Enlightenment remedies to economic problems, encouraged education and legal reform, and improved agricultural productivity by enabling some peasants to own the land they worked. *(Ch. 18)*

**entrepreneurs**  People who assume the risks of organizing and investing in a new business venture. Entrepreneurship is closely connected with the inventions and innovations made during the industrial age. *(Ch. 20)*

**Epicureans**  Adherents of the Athenian philosopher Epicurus (341–270 B.C.), who taught that the soul is made up of atoms that do not exist after death. Epicureans emphasized the avoidance of pain and the pursuit of intellectual pleasure. *(Ch. 4)*

**Erasmus, Desiderius (1466–1536)**  Prominent Dutch humanist during the Renaissance, best known for his satire *Praise of Folly.* Erasmus's works reinterpreted Greek and Roman wisdom and emphasized tolerance, reason, and faith in the goodness and educability of the individual. *(Ch. 12)*

**ethnic cleansing**  A term describing attempts to remove an unwanted ethnic group from an area, which can include forced relocation and mass killing. Beginning in 1991, this tactic was implemented by Yugoslavian ruler Slobodan Milosevic (b. 1941) to unite all Serbs, many of whom lived in neighboring Croatia, Bosnia-Herzegovina, and **Kosovo.** *(Ch. 30)*

**Etruscans**  Inhabitants of twelve loosely confederated city-states north of Rome in Etruria that flourished in the seventh to sixth centuries B.C. They were conquered by the Romans by the early third century B.C. *(Ch. 5)*

**euro** The common currency launched by the **European Union** in 1999 to eliminate the cost of currency exchange and boost trade and economic interaction. As of January 1, 2002, it replaced the national currencies of the participating countries (the "Eurozone"). *(Ch. 30)*

**European Economic Community (EEC) (1957–1967)** Common market formed by Belgium, France, West Germany, Italy, Luxembourg, and the Netherlands to promote free trade. The EEC was replaced by the European Community (EC) in 1967. *(Ch. 29)*

**European Union (EU)** New name for the European Community after the **Maastricht agreement** of 1991. By 2001 the European Union had nine members in addition to the original six members of the **European Economic Community:** Britain, Denmark, Ireland (joined 1973); Greece (joined 1981); Portugal, Spain (joined 1985); and Austria, Finland, Sweden (joined 1995). See also **euro.** *(Ch. 30)*

**euthanasia program** The Nazi program of systematically killing people, overwhelmingly ethnic Germans, whom the Nazis deemed superfluous or threatening to the German racial health. Victims included chronic mental patients, the incurably ill, and people with severe physical handicaps. Initiated in 1939, the program had claimed 100,000 lives by the time it was discontinued in 1941. *(Ch. 27)*

**existentialism** A philosophical and cultural movement, influential from the late 1940s into the 1950s, that explored life in a world cast adrift from its cultural moorings. Highly influential were the Frenchmen Jean Paul Sartre (1905–1980) and Albert Camus (1913–1960), for whom an authentic human response to an apparently meaningless universe entailed commitment and responsibility. *(Ch. 29)*

**factories** Centralized workplaces where a number of people cooperate to mass-produce goods. The first factories of industrializing Europe were made possible by the development of the **steam engine** as a central power source. The mechanized production of factories led to huge productivity increases in the nineteenth century. See also **industrialization, mass production.** *(Ch. 20)*

**fascism** A violent, antidemocratic movement founded by **Benito Mussolini** in Italy in 1919. The term is widely used to encompass Hitler's Nazi regime in Germany and other movements stressing disciplined national solidarity and hostile to liberal individualism, the parliamentary system, and Marxist socialism. *(Ch. 26)*

**February Patent (1861)** Enactment issued in February 1861 by the Austrian emperor Franz Joseph (r. 1848–1916) that established a constitutional monarchy in the old Austrian Empire. The patent guaranteed civil liberties and provided for local self-government and an elected parliament. *(Ch. 22)*

**feudal revolution** The societal change in tenth-century France from prince-dominated territories with loyal, reliable, but few vassals to the advent of many locally powerful magnates with numerous vassals whose fidelity was uncertain and who primarily provided military service. *(Ch. 9)*

**Five Pillars of Islam** The basic teachings of Islam: (1) the profession of faith, "There is no God but Allah and **Muhammad** is His Prophet"; (2) individual prayer five times daily, plus group prayers at noon on Friday; (3) the sunup-to-sundown fast during the month of Ramadan; (4) giving generous alms to the poor; and (5) pilgrimage to Mecca at least once in a person's lifetime. *(Ch. 8)*

**Flavians** Dynasty of the Roman emperors Vespasian (r. 69–79), Titus (r. 79–81), and Domitian (r. 81–96), whose rule was a time of relative peace and good government. Unlike the Julio-Claudians, the Flavians descended from Italian landowners, not old Roman nobility. Domitian persecuted the nobility and was assassinated. *(Ch. 6)*

**Fourteen Points** Proposals by U.S. president Woodrow Wilson (1856–1924) to guide the new international order that would follow an Allied victory in World War I. Specifics included open diplomacy, free trade, reduced armaments, self-determination for nationalities, and a league of nations. *(Ch. 25)*

**Francis of Assisi (1181–1226)** Italian monk and founder of a new order of friars ("brothers," from the Latin *fratres*). Francis was born wealthy but adopted a life based on the scriptural ideals of poverty, preaching, and service. His apostolate to the urban poor was highly popular. *(Ch. 10)*

**Frankfurt Assembly (1848–1849)** Popularly elected national assembly that attempted to create a unified German state. The assembly drew up a constitution and offered the German throne to Friedrich Wilhelm IV, king of Prussia, who declined, fearing a war with Austria and not wanting an office offered by representatives of the people. *(Ch. 21)*

**Frederick the Great (r. 1740–1786)** Autocratic king of Prussia who transformed the country into a major military power, acquired Polish Prussia, and waged three wars against Austria. He participated in and encouraged the study of philosophy, history, poetry, and French literature. *(Ch. 18)*

**Freud, Sigmund (1856–1939)** Austrian founder of psychoanalysis, a method of treating psychic disorders by exploring the unconscious. Freud believed that people were motivated in part by their unconscious feelings and drives. He helped call attention to the concept that irrational forces play a significant role in human behavior. *(Ch. 24)*

**friendly societies** Nineteenth-century organizations formed by workers; members pooled their resources to provide mutual aid. Combining business activity with feasts, drinking bouts, and other social functions, friendly societies promoted group solidarity and a sense of working-class identity. *(Ch. 20)*

**G-8 (Group of 8)** Originally a Group of Seven, or G-7, this informal association of the world's seven largest economic powers (the United States, Japan, Germany, France, Britain, Italy, and Canada) began meeting during the 1970s in an effort to coordinate economic policies. After the fall of communism, the group added Russia, thereby becoming the G-8. *(Ch. 30)*

**Galileo Galilei (1564–1642)** Italian physicist and astronomer who provided evidence supporting the **heliocentric theory** of **Nicholas Copernicus** and helped develop the physics of mechanics. His publication of his astronomical observations and his subsequent condemnation by the Catholic Church spurred popular debate and greatly influenced the future of science. *(Ch. 17)*

**gentry** Class of wealthy, educated, and socially ambitious families in western Europe, especially England, whose political and economic power was greatly enhanced during the sixteenth century. They shared with traditional old-family warrior-aristocrats certain legal privileges, security of landownership, and a cooperative relationship with the monarchy. See also **price revolution.** *(Ch. 15)*

**Girondins**  Political faction during the French Revolution. Republicans and members of the Jacobin Club, the Girondins dominated the French Legislative Assembly when it began to meet in 1791. They favored an activist government but were less radical than other members of the club, called the **Jacobins.** The Girondins were purged from the National Convention in 1793, and many were executed during the **Terror.** *(Ch. 19)*

**glasnost**  Russian term meaning "greater openness." Glasnost was the leading motif in the Great Reforms begun in 1861 by Tsar Alexander II (r. 1855–1881), who sought to strengthen Russia by restructuring its institutions in the wake of defeat in the Crimean War. Glasnost was also part of the reform efforts of **Mikhail Gorbachev** in the Soviet Union during the 1980s. *(Ch. 22)*

**Glorious Revolution (1688)**  Bloodless English revolution in which Parliament replaced the Catholic King James II with William (of Orange) and his wife Mary (James's Protestant daughter). Parliament imposed on the new sovereigns a Bill of Rights that confirmed Parliament's power and protected freedom of speech. *(Ch. 16)*

**Golden Bull of 1356**  Edict of Holy Roman Emperor Charles IV establishing the method of electing a new emperor. It acknowledged the political autonomy of Germany's seven regional princes. *(Ch. 11)*

**Gorbachev, Mikhail (b. 1931)**  The Soviet Communist Party secretary who, beginning in 1985, attempted to reform the Soviet communist system through arms reduction; liberalization in the satellite states; **glasnost,** or "openness" to discussion and criticism; and *perestroika,* or economic "restructuring." Though widely admired in the West, these measures failed, and Gorbachev ended up presiding over the end of the Soviet communist regime. *(Ch. 29)*

**Gothic**  Period in European architecture, sculpture, and painting from the twelfth to early sixteenth centuries. Gothic architecture was distinguished by the pointed arch, ribbed vault, and point support, which produced a building characterized by verticality and translucency. Examples are the Cathedral of Notre-Dame of Paris and the royal portal at Chartres Cathedral. *(Ch. 10)*

**Gracchi**  Ancient Roman faction led by Tiberius Sempronius Gracchus (163–133 B.C.) and later his brother, Gaius (153–121 B.C.), both of whom were killed by their political opponents. They challenged the conservative **senate** on behalf of the poor. *(Ch. 5)*

**"the Great Patriotic War"**  Term for World War II devised by **Joseph Stalin** to rally Soviet citizens against the German invasion. Stalin appealed to Russian nationalism and recalled past heroic defenses of Russia rather than communist themes. *(Ch. 28)*

**Great Reform Bill (1832)**  British law that broadened the franchise and provided parliamentary seats for new urban areas that had not previously been represented. The bill was a major victory for the government and middle classes over the aristocracy. *(Ch. 21)*

**Great Schism (1378–1417)**  Period during which two, then three, rival popes claimed to rule the Christian Church. The schism ended when the **Council of Constance** deposed all three competing previous popes and elected Martin V as the new pope. *(Ch. 11)*

**guilds**  Merchant groups and associations of crafts and trades established in European cities and towns beginning in the thirteenth century. Guilds expanded greatly during the later Middle Ages. They provided economic benefits, fostered a sense of community, and served as mutual assistance societies. *(Ch. 9)*

**gulag**  Network of 476 forced labor camps for political prisoners in the Soviet Union. The *gulag* (an acronym for "main camp administration") was first used by Lenin in 1918 but was greatly expanded by **Joseph Stalin** in the 1930s. *(Ch. 27)*

**Gutenberg, Johann (ca. 1399–1468)**  German inventor of movable metal type. His innovations led to the publication of the first printed book in Europe, the Gutenberg Bible, in the 1450s. Printed books and broadsheets played a critical role in disseminating the ideas of the Renaissance and the Reformation. *(Ch. 12)*

**Hagia Sophia**  Largest Christian church ever built, constructed in Constantinople from 532 to 537 for the Roman emperor **Justinian.** The church consists of two intersecting rectangular basilicas that incorporate arches; the whole is surmounted by a huge dome. *(Ch. 7)*

**Hanseatic League**  Late medieval association of over a hundred trading cities, centered on the German city of Lübeck. The league dominated coastal trade in northern Europe from the fourteenth to the fifteenth centuries, until Dutch, English, and south German merchants finally gained shares of the wool, grain, and fur trades. *(Ch. 11)*

**heliocentric theory**  Theory advanced by **Nicholas Copernicus** that the earth and other planets orbit the sun. Supported by the scientific and mathematical discoveries of **Johannes Kepler** and **Galileo Galilei,** heliocentrism, which means "sun-centered," won acceptance by the end of the seventeenth century. *(Ch. 17)*

**Hellenism**  Term used to designate ancient Greece's language, culture, and civilization, especially after **Alexander the Great** spread them to other parts of the Mediterranean, western Asia, and North Africa. *(Ch. 4)*

**Helsinki Accords (1975)**  Agreements signed by thirty-five countries in Helsinki, Finland, that committed the signatories to recognize existing borders, to increase economic and environmental cooperation, and to promote freedom of expression, religion, and travel. Dissidents in Soviet bloc countries soon fastened on these provisions to highlight the lack of human rights and to discredit the ruling communist governments. *(Ch. 29)*

**Henry VIII (r. 1509–1547)**  King of England. Initially a defender of traditional Christianity, Henry broke with the papacy over the issue of his divorce. He needed a divorce, he argued, in order to marry a younger woman who might be able to produce a male heir to the kingdom. As a result of the dispute, Henry supported Reformers in the English Church. *(Ch. 14)*

**Henry "the Navigator" (1394–1460)**  Portuguese prince and director of Portugal's exploration and colonization of Africa's western coast. The Portuguese quickly established trading stations in the region, laying the foundations for their overseas empire. *(Ch. 13)*

**Herodotus (ca. 485–425 B.C.)**  Ancient Greek historian; with **Thucydides,** a founder of history-writing in the West. The word *history* comes from a word used by Herodotus, *historiai,* meaning "inquiries" or "research." In his history of the Persian Wars, Herodotus saw the fall of the Persian Empire as part of a perpetual cycle of the rise and fall of empires. *(Ch. 3)*

**Hildegard of Bingen (1098–1179)**  German abbess who was perhaps the most profound psychological thinker of her age. More than anyone before her, Hildegard opened up for discussion the feminine aspects of divinity. She was also adept in music and biblical studies. *(Ch. 10)*

**Hitler, Adolf (1889–1945)**  The German dictator who, after being legally named chancellor in 1933, militarized Germany and started World War II in 1939, leading the country to defeat in 1945. His enforcement of state-sponsored **anti-Semitism** and racial purity among German people led to the murder of millions of Jews, Gypsies, and Slavic peoples. *(Ch. 27)*

**Hobbes, Thomas (1588–1679)**  English philosopher. In his treatise *Leviathan,* Hobbes asserted that people are made up of mechanistic appetites and so need a strong ruler to hold them in check. However, he also envisioned citizens as potentially equal and constrained neither by morality nor by natural obedience to authority. *(Ch. 17)*

**Homer**  Greatest ancient Greek poet, credited as the author of the epics the *Iliad* and the *Odyssey,* both written during the eighth century B.C. His dramatic stories inspired, moved, and educated the Greeks. *(Ch. 2)*

**hominids**  The primate family *Hominidae,* which includes humans. The modern human being, *Homo sapiens sapiens,* is the only species of this family still in existence. *(Ch. 1)*

**hoplite phalanx**  Battlefield tactic of **Archaic Greece** that relied on a tightly ordered unit of heavily armed, pike-bearing infantrymen. It was the dominant military force in western Asia and the Mediterranean region until 197 B.C. *(Ch. 3)*

**Huguenots**  French Protestants, followers of the teachings of **John Calvin.** Huguenots battled Catholics throughout the sixteenth and seventeenth centuries. Many emigrated to other western European countries and England's American colonies, especially after the revocation of the **Edict of Nantes.** French Protestants gained full religious freedom in the nineteenth century. *(Ch. 15)*

**humanism**  Western European literary and cultural movement of the fourteenth and fifteenth centuries. Humanists emphasized the superiority of ancient Greek and Roman literature, history, and politics, and focused on learning and personal and public duty. See also **Desiderius Erasmus, Francesco Petrarch, Thomas More.** *(Ch. 12)*

**Hundred Years' War (1337–1453)**  Series of conflicts between the ruling families of France and England over territory in France and the succession to the French crown. Sporadic raids and battles devastated the French countryside and checked population growth. The inspirational leadership of **Joan of Arc** contributed to France's eventual success in expelling the English from nearly all of the disputed land. *(Ch. 11)*

**hunter-gatherers**  Food-collecting society in which people live by hunting, fishing, and gathering fruits and nuts, with no crops or livestock being raised for food. During the **Neolithic Revolution,** some hunter-gatherers developed agriculture. *(Ch. 1)*

**Hus, Jan (ca. 1370–1415)**  Czech religious reformer who strongly attacked clerical power and privileges and advocated reform of church practice. His execution for heresy at the **Council of Constance** provoked a civil war in Prague and Bohemia. *(Ch. 11)*

**iconoclasm**  Rejection of, or even the destruction of, religious images in worship. Iconoclasm was the official policy of the Byzantine Empire from 726 to 843 and played a role in the continuing estrangement of Byzantium from the West. *(Ch. 8)*

**impressionism**  Late-nineteenth-century style of painting pioneered by the French artists Degas, Monet, Pissarro, Renoir, Sisley, and Morisot. Influenced by new theories that images were transmitted to the brain as small light particles, which the brain then reconstituted, the impressionists sought to capture what things looked like before they were "distorted" by the brain. *(Ch. 23)*

**Inca**  A flourishing sixteenth-century empire administered from the mountains of Peru and extending from modern Ecuador to Chile. It was conquered for Spain by Francisco Pizarro (1470–1541), aided by a smallpox epidemic and native peoples seeking to end Inca domination. *(Ch. 13)*

***Index of Prohibited Books***  A list of books banned by the Roman Catholic Church because of moral or doctrinal error. First announced in 1559, it was only sporadically enforced and had little effect. The Index was suppressed in 1966. *(Ch. 14)*

**industrialization**  Beginning in Britain in the later eighteenth century, a system of **mass production** of goods in which specialization and mechanization made manufacturing efficient and profitable. Early industrialization enabled Britain to become the dominant world power in the nineteenth century. See also **factories.** *(Ch. 20)*

**information technology**  Term for the revolution in information availability and communications resulting from the late-twentieth-century development of personal computers and the Internet. See also **digital divide.** *(Ch. 30)*

**Interregnum (1649–1660)**  Literally "between reigns," the period in English history from the execution of Charles I to the restoration of Charles II. During these years England was a republic—a Commonwealth—ruled by **Oliver Cromwell,** who became Lord Protector in 1653. *(Ch. 16)*

**iron curtain**  Term used by Winston Churchill in a speech on March 5, 1946, to warn that, thanks to Soviet policy, a formidable de facto barrier was emerging in Europe, cutting the Soviet sphere off from the West and threatening the long-term division of the continent. Though the term was not coined by Churchill, his phrasing dramatically affected public opinion in the west. The "iron curtain" suggested both the division of Europe and Soviet culpability throughout the cold war period. *(Ch. 28)*

**Israel**  People who settled on the eastern shore of the Mediterranean around 1200 B.C., or perhaps earlier. Their belief in one God directly influenced the faith of Christians, Muslims, and modern Jews. See also **monotheism.** *(Ch. 2)*

**Ivan IV, "the Terrible" (r. 1533–1584)**  First Russian ruler routinely to use the title "tsar" (Russian for "Caesar"), he presided over the expansion and centralization of the Russian state. Ivan continued Moscow's expansion, begun by his grandfather Ivan III, south and east against Mongol-controlled states. Under Ivan IV, Russians moved east across Siberia for the first time. Within his expanding empire, Ivan ruled as an autocrat; he was able to bypass noble participation and intensify the centralization of government by creating ranks of officials loyal only to himself. *(Ch. 15)*

**Jacobins**  In revolutionary France, a political club named for a monastic order. One of the most radical of republican groups, the Jacobins purged the **Girondins,** originally fellow members of the club, from the National Convention in 1793.

Leaders of the **Terror,** such as **Maximilien Robespierre,** came from their ranks. *(Ch. 19)*

**Jesus of Nazareth (ca. 4 B.C.–A.D. 30)** Founder of **Christianity.** A forceful preacher and reformer who, to his followers, was Christ, "the anointed one" (from the Greek *Christos*), foretold in the Hebrew Bible as the redeemer of Israel who would initiate the kingdom of heaven. The dynamism and popularity of his teachings led to a clash with Jewish and Roman authorities in Jerusalem and to his crucifixion by the Romans. *(Ch. 6)*

**Joan of Arc (d. 1431)** Charismatic French military leader during the **Hundred Years' War.** A late medieval mystic, Joan heard "voices" telling her to assist in driving the English from France. She was captured and burned as a heretic by the English. Later she was canonized as Saint Joan, patron saint of France. *(Ch. 11)*

**Julio-Claudians** Dynasty of Roman emperors founded by **Augustus** and ruling from A.D. 14 to 68. The succession consisted of Augustus's stepson Tiberius, great-grandson Caligula, grandnephew Claudius, and great-great-grandson Nero. For elite Romans, this era was one of decadence and scandal; for ordinary people, it was a time of stability and peace. *(Ch. 6)*

**July Revolution (1830)** Uprising in Paris in July 1830 that forced King Charles X to abdicate and signaled a victory for constitutional reform over an absolute monarchy. The liberal Louis Philippe was proclaimed "King of the French," with limited powers, by the chamber of deputies. The revolution sparked democratic uprisings in Belgium, Germany, Italy, and Russian Poland and helped persuade British peers to vote for the **Great Reform Bill.** *(Ch. 21)*

**justification by faith** Doctrine professed by **Martin Luther** that Christians can be saved (justified) only by faith, a free gift of God, and not by penitential acts or good works. Luther's doctrine directly challenged the authority and fundamental practices of the Roman Catholic Church. *(Ch. 14)*

**Justinian (r. 527–565)** One of the greatest of all Rome's emperors. His comprehensive collection of Roman law is the most influential legal collection in human history. He built **Hagia Sophia,** reformed the imperial administration, and fought constant wars to expand the empire. *(Ch. 7)*

**Kepler, Johannes (1571–1630)** German astronomer. Kepler developed the three laws of planetary motion, known as Kepler's Laws, which are still accepted, and mathematically confirmed the Copernican **heliocentric theory.** *(Ch. 17)*

**Kriegsrohstoffabteilung (KRA)** The "War Raw Materials Office" that coordinated Germany's World War I economy. The KRA produced synthetic substitute products and created new mixed (private and government) companies to allocate raw materials. This body served as a model for later economic planning and coordination in Germany and elsewhere. *(Ch. 25)*

**Kristallnacht** See **Crystal Night.**

**laissez faire** French term meaning "to leave alone," it was applied to the economic doctrine put forward by **Adam Smith** in 1776. Smith advocated freeing national economies from the fetters of the state and allowing supply and demand to shape the marketplace. Laissez-faire ideas contributed to the drive to lower tariffs in the nineteenth century. See also **liberalism.** *(Ch. 21)*

**Las Casas, Bartolomé de (1474–1566)** First bishop of Chiapas, in southern Mexico. A former *encomendero,* Las Casas passionately condemned the brutality of the Spanish conquests. In 1542 King Charles accepted Las Casas's criticisms, abolishing Indian slavery and greatly restricting the transfer of **encomiendas.** *(Ch. 13)*

**Latin** Indo-European language of ancient Rome and its empire, from which today's Romance languages developed. *(Ch. 5)*

**laws of motion** The natural laws of gravity, planetary motion, and inertia first laid out in the seventeenth century by **Isaac Newton.** Newton demonstrated that these laws apply to the solar system and could be used to predict the existence of an as-yet-unseen planet. *(Ch. 17)*

**lay investiture** Control of church appointments by laymen. Emperor Henry IV (1066–1106) and Pope Gregory VII (1073–1085) disputed who should have this authority in the Christian world. The 1122 Concordat of Worms stipulated that bishops could be invested by kings only after a free church election. *(Ch. 9)*

**League of Nations (1919–1946)** An international alliance established at the end of World War I without the membership of the United States. Though its covenant called for the peaceful settlement of disputes among member states and for sanctions against a member that went to war in violation of League provisions, it failed to prevent the escalating violence that culminated in World War II. *(Ch. 25)*

**legion** Innovative and highly successful ancient Roman battle formation. The legion included many flexible, adaptable, and semi-independent groups that broke their enemies' order with javelins at long range, then charged with sword and shield. *(Ch. 5)*

**Lend-Lease Act (1941)** Act by the U.S. Congress authorizing President **Franklin Roosevelt** to lend or lease weapons or other aid to countries the president designated. A major declaration of American support for the threatened British, lend-lease was later extended to several other countries. *(Ch. 28)*

**Lenin, Vladimir Ilyich (1870–1924)** Russian revolutionary. Leader of the **Bolsheviks** since 1903, he launched the November 1917 revolution that overthrew the **provisional government.** He concluded the **Treaty of Brest-Litovsk** with Germany and began the establishment of communism in the Soviet Union. See also **New Economic Policy.** *(Ch. 25)*

**Leonardo da Vinci (1452–1519)** A painter, engineer, and scientist, da Vinci rejected arguments and ideas based on imitation of the ancients. Rather, he advocated careful study of the natural world. *(Ch. 12)*

**liberalism** Nineteenth-century economic and political theory that called for reducing government powers to a minimum. Liberals worked to impose constitutional limits on government, establish the rule of law, eliminate state regulation of the economy, and ensure a voice in government for men of property and education. *(Ch. 21)*

**linear perspective** Revolutionary technique developed by early-fifteenth-century Florentine painters for representing three-dimensional objects on a two-dimensional plane. The technique is based in part on the observation that as parallel lines recede, they appear to converge. *(Ch. 12)*

**Livia (58 B.C.–A.D. 29)** Wife of **Augustus** and mother of Tiberius, his successor. As one of Augustus's main advisers, she intrigued to secure the succession for Tiberius and was suspected of poisoning several family members, including Augustus himself. *(Ch. 6)*

**Locarno, Treaty of (1925)** Treaty that introduced a new, more conciliatory spirit in international affairs. France and Germany accepted the postwar border between them, and Germany was again accepted as a diplomatic equal and entered the League of Nations in 1926. *(Ch. 26)*

**Locke, John (1632–1704)** English philosopher. In his influential *Two Treatises of Government,* Locke asserted that the state arises from a contract that individuals freely endorse. Therefore, because sovereignty resides with the people, rebellion against abuse of power is justified—a revolutionary vision of a political society based on human rights. See also **empirical method.** *(Ch. 17)*

**Louis XIV (r. 1643–1715)** Longest-reigning ruler in European history, who imposed absolute rule on France and waged several wars attempting to dominate Europe. He was known as the Sun King, and his reign marked a great flowering of French culture. *(Ch. 16)*

**Loyola, Ignatius (1491–1556)** Spanish nobleman and founder of the Society of Jesus, or Jesuits, which has been called the vanguard of the Catholic reform movement. After papal approval of the order, the Jesuits focused primarily on educating Catholics and reconverting Protestants. *(Ch. 14)*

**Luddites** Organized groups of British workers formed in 1811–1812, who smashed machines and rioted to protest against industrialization, which they felt would threaten their livelihood. The name comes from their mythical leader, General Ned Ludd. *(Ch. 20)*

**Luther, Martin (1483–1546)** German theologian and religious reformer. Luther began the Protestant Reformation in 1517 with the publication of his *Ninety-Five Theses,* which challenged indulgences and Catholic teachings on penitential acts. His translation of the Bible into German in 1522 standardized the modern German language. See also **Augsburg Confession, justification by faith, sola scriptura.** *(Ch. 14)*

**Maastricht agreement (1991)** Agreement among twelve European Community countries at Maastricht, the Netherlands, to form the **European Union.** The member states agreed to expand cooperation on social, foreign, judicial, and security matters and adopted a timetable for a common policy on workers' rights, a common currency (the **euro**), and a common central banking structure. *(Ch. 30)*

**Maccabees** Traditionalist Jews led by the Hasmonean family, who in 168 B.C. revolted against Hellenizing laws and influences. Their success is celebrated today during the Jewish holiday of Hanukkah. *(Ch. 4)*

**Macedon** Weaker, less culturally advanced state on Greece's northern border. It was unified and led to power by **Philip II** and **Alexander the Great,** who became rulers of Greece. *(Ch. 4)*

**Machiavelli, Niccolò (1469–1527)** Florentine politician and political theorist. His most famous work, *The Prince,* describes the methods a prince can use to acquire and maintain power. Often misunderstood as a defender of despotism, Machiavelli emphasized that a successful ruler needed to anticipate and consider the consequences of his actions. *(Ch. 12)*

**Magellan, Ferdinand (1480?–1521)** Portuguese-born Spanish explorer who led the first expedition to sail around the world. After finding the South American passage to the Pacific Ocean, he sailed to the Philippines, where he was killed by natives. Survivors on one of his ships completed the circumnavigation. *(Ch. 13)*

**Maginot Line** A 200-mile system of elaborate permanent fortifications on France's eastern border, named for war minister André Maginot, and built primarily during the 1930s. It was a defense against German frontal assault; in 1940 the Germans invaded by flanking the line. *(Ch. 26)*

**Magna Carta (1215)** Momentous document that England's barons forced King John to sign. It required the king to respect the rights of feudal lords, not abuse his judicial powers, and consult the barons—in essence, it put the king under the law, not above it. *(Ch. 9)*

**manifest destiny** Term coined in 1845 for the belief that the expanding United States was destined to occupy the North American continent from coast to coast. The rhetoric of manifest destiny was invoked to justify war with Mexico in 1846 and the acquisition of California and the southwest from Mexico in 1848. *(Ch. 22)*

**manor** In western Europe, a type of estate that developed under the Carolingians. One-quarter to one-half of the land was set aside as a reserve (or demesne), to be worked on behalf of the landlord; the remainder was divided into tenancies worked by individual peasants for their own support. *(Ch. 8)*

**Maria Theresa (r. 1740–1780)** Habsburg archduchess of Austria and queen of Hungary and Bohemia. After successfully defending her right to the Austrian throne against attacks by **Frederick the Great** and others, she reformed and centralized the administration of her Austrian and Bohemian lands. *(Ch. 18)*

**Marina, Doña (Malintzin) (1501–1550)** An Aztec by birth, she was sold to the Mayas and eventually became a translator and guide for the Spanish. After her critical role in the conquest, she married a Spaniard and lived as a Spanish noblewoman. *(Ch. 13)*

**Marxism** Political and economic theories of the two German philosophers and revolutionaries, Karl Marx (1818–1883) and Friedrich Engels (1820–1895), which they called scientific **socialism** and which gave birth to modern communism. Marxism argued that the oppressed working class should and inevitably would rebel against the capitalist owners and build a communist society. *(Ch. 21)*

**mass production** System in which great numbers of people work in centralized, mechanized **factories** to produce large quantities of goods; an essential feature of **industrialization.** A series of eighteenth-century inventions, culminating in the **steam engine,** enabled Britain to mass-produce textiles and benefit from the resulting increases in productivity. *(Ch. 20)*

**Matteotti murder** The 1924 killing by fascist thugs of Italian moderate socialist Giacomo Matteotti after he denounced the fascist violence accompanying national elections. The public outcry following the murder eventually led **Mussolini** to commit to a more radical direction, which included the creation of a new fascist state. *(Ch. 26)*

**mechanistic world-view** Seventeenth-century philosophical view that saw the world as a machine that functions in strict obedience to physical laws, without purpose or will. Experience and reason were regarded as the standards of truth. *(Ch. 17)*

**Mehmed II (r. 1451–1481)** Ottoman sultan who completed the conquest of the Byzantine Empire by capturing Constantinople in 1453. Mehmed established Constantinople as the Ottoman capital and repopulated the city with a mix of Greek, Armenian, Jewish, and Muslim communities. *(Ch. 11)*

**mercantilism** Economic policy pursued by western European states in the seventeenth and eighteenth centuries, stressing self-sufficiency in manufactured goods, tight government control of trade to foster the domestic economy, protectionist policies, and the absolute value of bullion. *(Ch. 16)*

**Minoans** Society that flourished between 2000 and 1375 B.C. on the Aegean island of Crete, where Greece's first civilization appeared. Their sophisticated culture and economy were administered from their magnificent palaces. See also **Mycenaeans.** *(Ch. 2)*

**mir** Russian peasant commune. After Tsar Alexander II freed the serfs in 1861, the mir determined land use and paid the government mortgages and taxes. Peasants could leave the land only with the mir's permission. *(Ch. 22)*

**monasticism** Ascetic way of life. Christian monasticism was founded by an Egyptian layman, Anthony (d. 356), who renounced all worldliness and pursued a life of prayer in the desert. A more communal form of monasticism was created by Pachomius (290–346), who wrote the first monastic Rule—a code for daily living in a monastic community. Monasticism quickly spread throughout the Christian world. *(Ch. 7)*

**Monophysitism** Fifth-century theological doctrine emphasizing the divine nature of **Jesus of Nazareth.** The Council of Chalcedon condemned monophysitism and pronounced that Christ had two authentic natures—he was true God and true man. *(Ch. 7)*

**monotheism** Belief that there is only one God. The Hebrew Bible places this belief as originating about 2000–1500 B.C., when God commanded Abraham to give up Mesopotamian polytheism for belief in one God. *(Ch. 2)*

**More, Thomas (1478–1535)** Chancellor of England under Henry VIII. More's best-known work, *Utopia,* was highly critical of contemporary European kingdoms. It describes a fictional land of peace and harmony that has outlawed private property and all forms of wealth. More was executed when he refused to take an oath to support the **Act of Supremacy.** See also **humanism.** *(Ch. 12)*

**Muhammad (570–632)** Prophet and founder of Islam. In 610 he began to receive revelations commanding him to teach all people a new faith that called for an unquestioned belief in one god, Allah, and a deep commitment to social justice for believers. Before his death, he had converted most of Arabia. See also **Five Pillars of Islam, Quran.** *(Ch. 8)*

**Mussolini, Benito (1883–1945)** Italian fascist dictator. Mussolini founded the fascist movement in 1919 and took power in 1922. He replaced Italy's parliamentary democracy with a **corporative state** and pursued an expansionist foreign policy. He concluded the Pact of Steel with **Adolf Hitler** in 1939 and took Italy into World War II in 1940. Deposed in 1943, he was killed by partisans in 1945. *(Ch. 26)*

**Mycenaeans** Militaristic people from the Greek mainland who conquered the *Minoans* around 1550–1375 B.C. Mycenaean civilization was a center of Bronze Age culture until its destruction around 1100 B.C. *(Ch. 2)*

**mystery religions** Popular Hellenistic cults featuring the initiation of worshipers into secret doctrines. Mystery religions replaced the traditional Greek religion of the Olympian gods. Some ancient Egyptian cults were recast as mystery religions, influencing early Christianity. *(Ch. 4)*

**Napoleon Bonaparte (1769–1821)** Emperor of the French (r. 1804–1815). A French general who took part in a coup in 1799 against the **Directory,** Napoleon consolidated power as first consul and proclaimed himself emperor with the approval of a national plebiscite in 1804. His military conquests exported French revolutionary reforms to the rest of Europe. He was finally defeated and exiled in 1815. *(Ch. 19)*

**National Assembly (1789–1791)** Legislative body formed in France in 1789 after the Third Estate insisted on being certified as members of the Estates General as a whole. The National Assembly drafted the **Declaration of the Rights of Man and the Citizen** and a constitution that called for a constitutional (not absolute) monarchy. *(Ch. 19)*

**National Socialist (Nazi) Party** The political party that grew from the movement that German dictator **Adolf Hitler** made his vehicle to power. Originating from the radical right in Munich in 1919, the Nazi Party won voting support during the early 1930s, paving the way for Hitler to be named German chancellor in 1933. *(Ch. 27)*

**nationalism** Belief arising in the eighteenth century that people derive their identity from their nation and owe it their primary loyalty. The criteria for nationhood typically included a common language, religion, and political authority, as well as common traditions and shared historical experiences. Nationalism was a major force in most of the revolutions of 1848 and in the subsequent unification of Italy and of Germany. *(Ch. 21)*

**Nazi-Soviet Pact (1939)** Surprise agreement between the Soviet Union and Nazi Germany in August 1939 that each would remain neutral if either got into a war with some other nation. The pact freed Germany to attack Poland a few days later without fear of Soviet reprisal. *(Ch. 27)*

**Neo-Babylonians** Rulers of western Asia between 612 and 539 B.C. who elaborately rebuilt Babylon, creating the famous Hanging Gardens. They destroyed Jerusalem, deporting many Judeans in what is known as the Babylonian Captivity. *(Ch. 2)*

**Neolithic Revolution** Human discovery and spread of agriculture, between about 13,000 and 5000 B.C. People first domesticated dogs and other animals and then learned how to cultivate crops. *Ch. 1)*

**New Economic Policy (NEP) (1921–1928)** A Russian economic liberalization measure aimed at reviving an economy in crisis. The NEP restored considerable scope for private enterprise and allowed peasants to sell some of their harvest. After initial economic success, it was eventually considered a threat to the socialist state and was replaced by state-controlled central planning. *(Ch. 26)*

**new imperialism** Era of European overseas expansion launched in the 1880s. In the following decades, Europeans subjugated 500 million people in Africa and Asia—one half of the world's non-European population. *(Ch. 24)*

**Newton, Isaac (1643–1727)** English physicist, mathematician, and natural philosopher. Newton's mathematical computation of the laws of gravity and planetary motion, which he combined with a fully developed theory of inertia, completed the explanation for motion initiated by **Nicholas Copernicus.** See also **laws of motion.** *(Ch. 17)*

**nongovernmental organizations (NGOs)** A network of organizations unaffiliated with governments but central to the international community, such as the Red Cross, Amnesty International, and Doctors Without Borders, that had gradually emerged by the early twenty-first century to deal with humanitarian relief and human rights issues. *(Ch. 30)*

**North Atlantic Treaty Organization (NATO)** An alliance for regional defense, created in 1949 by the United States, Canada, and western European nations, whose members agree to defend one another from attack by nonmember countries. Its original aim was to contain the Soviet Union. *(Ch. 29)*

**Nuremberg trials** The war crimes trials conducted in Nuremberg, Germany. Most of the twenty-four defendants were convicted of war crimes and "crimes against humanity." *(Ch. 28)*

*On the Donation of Constantine* Work by Lorenzo Valla (1407–1457) proving that the *Donation of Constantine* was not written at the time of the emperor Constantine. The forged *Donation* purported to record Constantine's transfer to the pope of jurisdiction over Rome and the western half of the empire. Valla's work undermined the papacy's claim to political rule in central Italy. *(Ch. 12)*

**Orthodoxy** The Catholic Christian faith of Byzantium. It differed from Roman Catholicism by its use of Greek instead of Latin, the inclusion of icons in worship, an adherence to the Greek church fathers, some differences in basic theology, and many differences in customs and practices. *(Ch. 8)*

**papacy** Name for the institution ruled by the bishop of Rome who, in Roman Catholic tradition, is the successor to Peter, the most prominent apostle. Since Peter was believed to be the leader of the original followers of Christ, his successors, the popes (from *papa* by the fourth century), were believed to be the leaders of the whole church. *(Ch. 7)*

**Papal Monarchy** Period during the twelfth and thirteenth centuries when the power of the Catholic Church was increasingly expanded and centralized in the hands of the popes, as papal policy focused on recovering lost lands and rights in central Italy. *(Ch. 9)*

**Papal States** Beginning in the eighth century, territories held by the popes in central Italy under the protection of the Frankish kings. *(Ch. 8)*

**papyrus** Paperlike writing material used by the ancient Egyptians, Greeks, and Romans. Made primarily in Egypt from the papyrus plant, it was durable, flexible, and easy to write on. *(Ch. 1)*

**Paris Commune (1871)** Parisian workers' uprising intended to establish a workers' government under home rule. Stemming from labor discontent and the radicalization of workers during the siege of Paris in the Franco-Prussian War, the commune was suppressed by the army of the conservative French government. *(Ch. 22)*

**Parliament** English legislative institution, consisting of a House of Lords and a House of Commons, whose ancestors were the royal courts that met in 1265 and 1295. The king considered the courts a device to win support for royal agendas; the barons viewed them as opportunities to play a real policymaking role in government. In the late sixteenth and early seventeenth centuries, Parliament used control over monies to bargain with the crown over foreign and domestic policies, leading to resistance to and eventual deposition of Charles I. The power of parliament within the government was definitively established when it forced William and Mary

to accept its role in government in the Glorious Revolution (1688.) See also **Glorious Revolution.** *(Ch. 9, 16)*

**paterfamilias** Oldest living male in an ancient Roman family, who had supreme legal power within the household. Only the paterfamilias could own property free and clear. *(Ch. 5)*

**Paul of Tarsus (d. ca. 67)** Christian apostle and saint. A Jew from Anatolia and a Roman citizen, Paul first persecuted the Christians but became a believer around A.D. 36. Paul taught that the life and resurrection of **Jesus of Nazareth** offered all humanity the hope of salvation through faith. Under Paul, **Christianity** began its complete separation from Judaism. *(Ch. 6)*

**pax Romana** Latin for "Roman peace," the term refers to the period of peace and prosperity in the Roman Empire from A.D. 69 to 180. During this time the emperors emphasized extending citizenship and spreading prosperity throughout the provinces, and Italy was no longer the tyrant of the Mediterranean. See also **Flavians.** *(Ch. 6)*

**Peace of Westphalia (1648)** Treaty that ended the **Thirty Years' War.** The principalities within the Holy Roman Empire were recognized as virtually autonomous, severely weakening the power of the emperor. Calvinism joined Catholicism and Lutheranism as tolerated faiths within the empire, and the treaty closed the age of religious wars. *(Ch. 15)*

**Pericles** Leader of fifth-century-B.C. Athens when **demokratia** became entrenched as the government and way of life. Distinguished for his oratory and honesty, he established Athens as a great center of art and literature as well as a great empire. *(Ch. 3)*

**Persian Empire** Vast, prosperous, and law-abiding West Asian empire, from about 550 B.C. to its conquest by **Alexander the Great** around 330 B.C. The relatively tolerant rule of the Persian emperors represented the greatest success yet of a universal kingship. The Persians also built the first great navy. *(Ch. 2)*

**Peter the Great (r. 1682–1725)** Russian tsar. Brilliant, energetic, and tyrannical, Peter revolutionized Russian society by his determined efforts to westernize his nation culturally, economically, and politically. He modernized the army and navy, secured seaports, and made Russia into a great power. *(Ch. 16)*

**Petrarch, Francesco (1304–1374)** Influential Italian poet, biographer, and humanist during the Renaissance. Petrarch advocated imitating the actions, values, and culture of the ancient Romans to reform the excesses of the present world. *(Ch. 12)*

**Petrograd Soviet** The *soviet* (council) of leaders of strike committees and army regiments elected in March 1917, when Petrograd's workers protested in response to severe wartime food and coal shortages. Central to the Bolshevik Revolution of 1917, the soviet eventually became the ruling power in the Russian capital—but only temporarily. *(Ch. 25)*

**pharaoh** Ancient Egyptians' title for their king, an absolute, all-powerful, and all-providing ruler. It was believed that the ruler represented the ancestors and guaranteed the fertility of the soil. *(Ch. 1)*

**Philip II (382–336 B.C.)** King of **Macedon.** A brilliant soldier and statesman, Philip conquered the Greek world. He developed a well-trained, professional year-round army and mastered the technology of siegecraft. He was succeeded by his son, **Alexander the Great.** *(Ch. 4)*

**Philip II (r. 1556–1598)** King of Spain, son of **Charles V.** An avid Roman Catholic, he ruled Spain at the height of its influence. Philip dispatched the ill-fated **Armada** to invade England and attempted to quash the revolt of the Netherlands. *(Ch. 15)*

**philosophes** French term referring to thinkers and critics of the Enlightenment era, including **Voltaire** and Diderot. Philosophes applied to political and social thought the confidence in human reason and the intelligibility of natural law that **Isaac Newton** and other scientists had recently achieved. *(Ch. 18)*

**Phoenicians** Canaanites whose civilization flourished about 1000–750 B.C. in present-day coastal Syria, where they established major trading ports. Master sailors, they planted colonies around the Mediterranean, many of which, including Carthage, became independent states. The Phoenicians exported the civilization of western Asia—including the Phoenician alphabet, derived from **Ugarit**—to the Mediterranean world. *(Ch. 2)*

**plantation system** Agricultural practices developed by the fifteenth-century Portuguese to produce sugar on their island colonies in the Atlantic using involuntarily transported slaves from Africa. Portugal's prototype—wealthy absentee landlords and masses of forced labor producing cash crops on vast tracts of land—was the model for the New World plantation system. In seventeenth- and eighteenth-century French and English colonies in the Caribbean, large sugar plantations owned by wealthy, often absentee, landlords replaced smaller-scale independent farming. See also **slave trade.** *(Chs. 13, 16)*

**Plato (427–348 B.C.)** Ancient Greek philosopher, student of **Socrates.** One of Western philosophy's greatest exponents of idealism, Plato believed that the senses are misleading and that truth can therefore be attained only by training the mind to overcome commonsense evidence. In the *Republic*, Plato describes an ideal state in which philosophers rule as kings, benevolently and unselfishly. *(Ch. 3)*

**polis** Term for an ancient Greek city-state, a system that reached its height around 700–300 B.C. The ideological and political organization of the polis emphasized equality and a shared community life for all citizens, not just the elite. *(Ch. 3)*

**popular front** A term for antifascist electoral alliances and governing coalitions that communists promoted from 1934 until 1939 to resist the further spread of fascism. Popular front coalitions won control of government in both Spain and France during 1936. *(Ch. 27)*

**positivism** Philosophy of the French thinker Auguste Comte (1798–1857). Comte asserted that human history progressed through distinct and irreversible stages, leading inexorably upward to the final and highest stage of development, the positive—or scientific—stage. Positivism and its optimistic outlook for human progress were influential in both Europe and Latin America during the nineteenth century. *(Ch. 23)*

**Potsdam conference** A July–August 1945 meeting held at Potsdam, Germany, between the USSR, the United States, and Great Britain to implement their earlier agreements concerning the treatment of defeated Germany. Many of the agreements reached were later abandoned amid growing hostility between the USSR and the Western democracies. *(Ch. 28)*

**Prague Spring** The attempt by Czechoslovakian reformers in 1968 to gain freer cultural expression, democratization of Communist Party procedures, and broader participation in public life within the framework of a communist state. The forcible suppression of the movement by Soviet leaders seemed to signal the end of any hope for flexibility and openness within the Soviet sphere. *(Ch. 29)*

**price revolution** Steady rise in prices in the sixteenth and seventeenth centuries, resulting from population growth and the influx of precious metals from Spain's New World territories. As wages lost one-tenth to one-fourth of their value, people sought new work, protested against taxes, and attacked scapegoats. The price revolution concentrated wealth in fewer hands and contributed to the rise of a new **gentry** class. *(Ch. 15)*

**primogeniture** A legal inheritance system that provided the first born, usually the first-born son, the right to inherit all the family land and farm. *(Ch. 20)*

**Principate** The constitutional monarchy of the Early Roman Empire, from 31 B.C. to A.D. 192. The term comes from *Princeps,* or "first citizen," an old title of respect used in the **senate.** See also **Augustus, Flavians.** *(Ch. 6)*

**professionalization** Establishment in the nineteenth century of common standards and requirements, especially in medicine, law, architecture, and engineering. Professionalization brought either government or self-regulation to vocations whose prestige rested on the claim of exclusive expertise in their fields. *(Ch. 23)*

**proletariat** Term used by Karl Marx to describe the new class of industrial workers who owned none of the means of production and were totally dependent on factory owners for their livelihoods. In Marxist thought, capitalists were destined to be overthrown by the proletariat. See also **Marxism.** *(Ch. 20)*

**provisional government** The body that ruled Russia from March to November 1917, in the wake of the revolution that overthrew the tsarist regime. Originally intended to be a temporary step to an elected constituent assembly, its policies caused discontents that the **Bolsheviks** were quick to exploit. *(Ch. 25)*

**Ptolemies** Dynasty of Egyptian kings who ruled from 304 to 30 B.C., founded by Ptolemy I, a Macedonian general of **Alexander the Great.** It was the wealthiest, most sophisticated, and longest lasting of the Hellenistic kingdoms. See also **Alexandria.** *(Ch. 4)*

**Punic Wars (264–146 B.C.)** Three wars during which the Roman Empire eventually destroyed Carthage. The Romans later adopted the Carthaginians' plantation system using massive numbers of slaves. *(Ch. 5)*

**Puritans** Radical Protestants in late-sixteenth- and seventeenth-century England. Puritans emphasized Bible reading, preaching, private scrutiny of conscience, and de-emphasized institutional ritual and clerical authority. Puritans became a majority in Parliament during the reign of Charles I and led the campaign against the king during the English Civil War. *(Ch. 15)*

**Putin, Vladimir** Elected president of Russia early in 2000, he had been director of Russia's secret police before coming to political prominence as prime minister in 1999. He cracked down on the insurgency in Chechnya and, as president, proved more energetic in dealing with Russia's problems than his predecessor, Boris Yeltsin. *(Ch. 30)*

**putting-out system** The production in country homes of thread and cloth by spinners and weavers for an entrepreneur who bought raw materials and "put them out" to be finished by individual workers. This cottage industry system expanded in eighteenth-century Europe as increased numbers of agricultural laborers needed more nonfarm work in off-seasons. *(Ch. 18)*

**Quran** Islamic sacred writings, which **Muhammad** communicated in the form of "recitations," insisting that he was transmitting a direct revelation from Allah. After Muhammad's death, his followers arranged the recitations into 114 *Suras,* or chapters, containing legal and wisdom literature and moral teaching. *(Ch. 8)*

**rabbinic Judaism** Main form of Judaism, which emerged during the first century A.D. under the leadership of the rabbis, the spiritual descendants of the Pharisees. Rabbinic Judaism amplified and interpreted the Hebrew Bible to clarify Jewish practice, elevated the oral law to equal authority with the written **Torah,** and enabled Judaism to evolve flexibly. *(Ch. 6)*

**Realpolitik** Style of governing that uses all means, including war, to expand the influence and power of a state. The best-known practitioner of Realpolitik was Prussian chancellor **Otto von Bismarck.** *(Ch. 22)*

**Reconquista** Wars of reconquest in the Iberian Peninsula from the eleventh to fifteenth centuries. Spanish and Portuguese rulers seized territories from the weakening Muslim regime. By awarding reconquered lands to their nobles, Christian kings enhanced their own status and power. *(Ch. 9)*

**remilitarization of the Rhineland** The reoccupation of Germany's Rhineland territory by German troops in March 1936, in clear violation of the **Treaty of Versailles.** When the French and British did not resist the German move, **Adolf Hitler** was emboldened to additional acts of aggression elsewhere. *(Ch. 27)*

**Renaissance** Term derived from the French word for "rebirth" used to describe a period of intense creativity between 1350 and 1500 when cultural values were based on imitation of classical Greek and Roman norms. *(Ch. 12)*

**res publica** Romans' concept of their republic, which uniquely influenced Western political institutions. *Res publica* is Latin for "public thing," as opposed to *res privata*, "private thing," as the Romans characterized monarchy. *(Ch. 5)*

**revisionism** Late-nineteenth-century argument that **socialism** could and should come about by gradual, democratic means. This idea was a "revision" of Marx's contention that socialism would require a violent revolution. Most European socialists claimed to reject revisionism while at the same time pursuing revisionist policies. *(Ch. 24)*

**risorgimento** Italian term, beginning in the late eighteenth century, for the political and cultural renewal of Italy. It later came to describe the political and military events that led to the unification of Italy in 1861. *(Ch. 22)*

**Robespierre, Maximilien (1758–1794)** French lawyer and revolutionary leader. A **Jacobin** who joined the Committee of Public Safety in 1793, Robespierre called for the **Terror** to suppress internal dissent. *(Ch. 19)*

**Romanesque** Meaning "in the Roman style," this nineteenth-century term characterized the transitional architecture and painting of the period between the waning of Carolingian art and the full emergence of **Gothic** art in the twelfth century. Distinctive features of Romanesque churches are their exuberant decoration and ornament. *(Ch. 10)*

**romanticism** Artistic movement, prevalent from the 1760s to 1840s, that rebelled against rationalism. Writers, painters, and composers rejected the Enlightenment and its rationalist values, instead praising emotion and sensitivity, and worshiping nature for its inherent beauty. *(Ch. 21)*

**Rome-Berlin Axis** Alliance between Hitler's Nazi Germany and Mussolini's fascist Italy. Beginning as an informal understanding by 1936, it was cemented by an anti-Comintern agreement and eventually by an open-ended military alliance, the Pact of Steel, in 1939. *(Ch. 27)*

**Roosevelt, Franklin Delano (1882–1945)** U.S. president who served from 1933 to 1945, through the Great Depression of the 1930s and World War II. His New Deal program, including large public works projects, was an innovative response to the Depression. *(Ch. 28)*

**Rousseau, Jean-Jacques (1712–1778)** French writer and philosopher. In his 1762 work, *The Social Contract,* Rousseau depicted a hypothetical state with direct democracy in which citizens have inalienable rights to wide-ranging liberties. He was influential as a critic of an elite society still dominated by status, patronage, and privilege. *(Ch. 18)*

**Sacred Union** An agreement made between French leaders of different political groups to cooperate during World War I. The French government had initially feared that the Socialists might sabotage the war, when, in fact, they were eager to join the new government of national defense. *(Ch. 25)*

**salons** Regular gatherings in eighteenth-century Parisian private homes, where **Voltaire** and other **philosophes** read and discussed their works in progress, with the exchange of ideas facilitated by female *salonnières* (salon leaders). Anyone with appropriate manners could participate as an equal, enabling conversation to shift from maintaining the status quo to questioning it. *(Ch. 18)*

**sans-culottes** Ordinary citizens of revolutionary Paris, whose derisive nickname referred to their inability to afford fashionable knee pants ("culottes"). Because of their effective political organization, they were able to influence the direction of the French Revolution through pressure on the government as well as direct action, such as to overthrow the monarchy in August 1792. *(Ch. 19)*

**Sappho (fl. ca. 625 B.C.)** Ancient Greek poet from the island of Lesbos. Sappho wrote odes, wedding songs, and hymns expressing intimate feelings, including love for other women. She wrote of female sexuality in a male-dominated culture. *(Ch. 3)*

**second industrial revolution** Interrelated economic changes that resulted in a significant speedup in production in western Europe after 1850. Key factors were the introduction of new products, new methods of manufacture, and new materials such as mass-produced steel, synthetic dyes, and aluminum. *(Ch. 23)*

**Second International** International socialist organization founded in 1889 that met yearly to debate issues of broad concern. Beginning in 1907, it called for workers to strike and to refuse military service in case of international conflict. *(Ch. 24)*

**Second Reform Bill (1867)** British legislation that extended suffrage by lowering property qualifications and set equal population requirements for all parliamentary districts. The legislation bolstered the existing system, as the newly enfranchised clerks, artisans, and other skilled workers felt more a part of society. *(Ch. 22)*

**Seleucids** Dynasty of rulers of Asia Minor from 312 to 64 B.C. Founded by Seleucus (ca. 358–281 B.C.), a general of **Alexander the Great,** the kingdom spread **Hellenism** by establishing seventy colonies throughout the Near East. *(Ch. 4)*

**senate** In the ancient Roman Republic and Empire, the powerful council of elders that advised the monarchs (Latin: *senatus,* from *senex,* "old man"). Romans spoke of the senate's *auctoritas,* a quasi-religious prestige. *(Ch. 5)*

**separate spheres** Notion, especially prevalent in the mid-nineteenth century, of two distinct sets of roles—one male and public, the other female and private. While the man was out in the world advancing his career, the bourgeois woman was to run her home, providing her family with an orderly, comfortable shelter. *(Ch. 23)*

**Seven Years' War (1756–1763)** The first major war between European nations started and fought largely in their overseas empires, the Seven Years' War was in part a conflict between Britain and France for control of overseas possessions. Britain emerged the decisive winner in this phase of the conflict, partly because France was simultaneously involved in the conflict on the European continent, in which France and Austria tried to contain the aggressive Prussia. *(Ch. 18)*

**show trials** Trials staged for ideological and propaganda reasons in the USSR. In the most famous, orchestrated by **Joseph Stalin** from 1936 to 1938, major communist figures were made to confess to trumped-up charges and executed. These trials helped persuade Soviet citizens that a high-level conspiracy was responsible for the USSR's economic woes. *(Ch. 27)*

**Sistine Chapel** Chapel at the Vatican Palace commissioned by Pope Sixtus IV in 1475, best known for Michelangelo's magnificent paintings of the Creation and Last Judgment. The monument vividly captures the cultural, religious, and ideological program of the papacy. *(Ch. 12)*

**slave trade** Europeans' trade with Africa in which involuntary laborers were bought and shipped to the Americas to be sold primarily to owners of plantations where sugar and other commodities were produced. The trade reached its peak in the eighteenth century, when approximately 7 million Africans were shipped across the Atlantic. The slave trade was an integral part of the "triangle trade" by which Europe, Africa, and the Americas were connected. See also **plantation system.** *(Chs. 13, 16, 18)*

**Smith, Adam (1723–1790)** Scottish economist who developed the doctrine of **laissez faire.** In his treatise *The Wealth of Nations* (1776), Smith argued that an economy regulates itself better without interference by government and without monopolies and other economic privileges. Smith suggested that people's economic activities are often "led by an invisible hand" to benefit society as a whole. *(Ch. 18)*

**social Catholics** Catholics in western Europe who believed that society bore responsibility for the well-being of the poor. They were following the ideas set out in 1891 by Pope Leo XIII (r. 1878–1903) in his encyclical *Rerum novarum* ("Of New Things"). *(Ch. 23)*

**Social Darwinism** Theory of social evolution first articulated by Herbert Spencer (1820–1902). According to Social Darwinists, human societies evolve in the same way as plants and animals, and the weak, poor, and improvident are not worthy of survival. Social Darwinism was used to justify callousness toward the poor at home and imperialist conquest abroad. See also **Darwinism.** *(Ch. 23)*

**social market economy** The late-twentieth-century socially-oriented model of capitalism practiced in continental western Europe, providing a substantial safety net in health care and a commitment to public services such as transportation and day care. It competed with the U.S. model, shared by Britain, which emphasized free enterprise. *(Ch. 30)*

**socialism** Nineteenth-century economic and social doctrine and political movement that opposed private ownership and control of the means of production. Socialists believed that the "social" or state ownership of property, unlike private ownership, would benefit society as a whole, creating a more just system. *(Ch. 21)*

**Society of Jesus (Jesuits)** Founded in 1534 by **Ignatius Loyola** (1491–1556), the Jesuits soon became leaders in the Catholic Counter Reformation. The Jesuits were famed for their schools and work as spiritual advisers. *(Ch. 14)*

**Society of Revolutionary Republican Women** In revolutionary France, a powerful political club that represented the interests of female **sans-culottes.** The society was included in a general ban on political participation by women that the Committee of Public Safety instituted in October 1793. *(Ch. 19)*

**Socrates (469–399 B.C.)** Ancient Greek philosopher, a founder of the Western philosophical tradition. Socrates changed the emphasis of philosophy from the natural world to human ethics. He believed that no one who truly understood goodness would ever choose to do evil. Accused of being an atheist and corrupting the young, Socrates was executed in 399. Socrates' teachings were recorded and transmitted by his students, including **Plato.** *(Ch. 3)*

***sola scriptura*** Doctrine put forward by **Martin Luther** in *On the Babylonian Captivity of the Church* (1520) that church authority had to be based on biblical teachings. In particular he argued that the sacraments of the Catholic Church—other than baptism and communion—were not found in the Bible. *(Ch. 14)*

**solidarism** Late-nineteenth-century policy of conservative and liberal parties to blunt the appeal of socialism. Solidarism emphasized the mutual responsibility of classes and individuals for one another's well-being and led to the passage of laws and benefits to improve the lot of the working class. *(Ch. 23)*

**Solidarity** A trade union formed from a movement of shipyard workers in communist Poland in 1980. It became the nucleus of widespread demands for change—including independent labor organizations, the right to strike, and freedom of expression. Though forced underground in 1981, the movement eventually proved crucial to the downfall of the communist regime in Poland. *(Ch. 29)*

**Solon (ca. 630–560 B.C.)** Statesman of early Athens. Appointed to a one-year term as sole archon in 594 B.C., Solon transformed Greek society through mediation, moderation, respect for law, and measures that liberated the poor and downtrodden. His economic reforms sparked a commercial boom. *(Ch. 3)*

**Spanish Inquisition** Church court that began in 1478 when King Ferdinand and Queen Isabella obtained papal approval to control the grand inquisitor. The Spanish Inquisition investigated and condemned many former Jews and Muslims who were believed to have insincerely converted to Christianity. It became an important and lucrative instrument to expand state power. *(Ch. 11)*

**SS** *(Schutzstaffel)* Nazi elite troops, led by Heinrich Himmler. Linked to the Gestapo, the secret political police, the SS specialized in institutionalized terror tactics and were responsible for some of the worst atrocities of the Nazi regime. *(Ch. 27)*

**"stab in the back" myth** The notion, widely held among Germans after their unexpected loss in World War I, that political intrigue and revolution at home had sabotaged the German military effort. It helped alienate Germans from their new democratic government. *(Ch. 25)*

**Stalin, Joseph (1879–1953)** Soviet dictator. Secretary of the Communist Party since 1922, Stalin outmaneuvered his rivals after the death of Lenin to take control of the Soviet government by 1929. Stalin jettisoned the **New Economic Policy** and instituted a program of crash industrialization and agricultural **collectivization.** He concluded the **Nazi-Soviet Pact** in 1939 but joined the Allies after the German invasion of the Soviet Union in 1941. Victorious in World War II, Stalin sponsored the takeover of governments in eastern Europe by communist regimes, contributing to the development of the **cold war.** See also **"the Great Patriotic War," gulag, Potsdam conference, show trials, Yalta conference.** *(Ch. 26)*

**Stalingrad (1942–1943)** Decisive World War II battle. The Soviet Union, at immense cost in lives, launched repeated counterattacks on Germany's Sixth Army, stopping it from advancing farther and finally forcing it to surrender. The battle is often considered the turning point of World War II in Europe. *(Ch. 28)*

**steam engine** Machine invented in England in its modern form by James Watt in 1777. The steam engine provided mechanized power for manufacturing and made **factories** and **mass production** possible. *(Ch. 20)*

**Stoics** Believers in a philosophical system begun in Athens by Zeno (335–263 B.C.). Stoicism emphasized the pursuit of wisdom, the reliability of sensory experience, and freedom from all passion. Stoics focused on intentions as well as the results of actions. *(Ch. 4)*

**Streseman, Gustav (1878–1929)** German statesman of the Weimar Republic. Leader of the conservative German People's Party, Streseman served briefly as chancellor in 1923, then as foreign secretary from 1923 to 1929. He secured a reduction of Germany's reparations payments and negotiated the **Treaty of Locarno,** paving the way for Germany's entry to the League of Nations in 1926. His death in 1929 was a blow to hopes for the development of democracy in Germany and peace in Europe. *(Ch. 26)*

**Suez crisis (1956)** Crisis prompted by Egypt's nationalization of the British-owned Suez Canal. The effort of Britain, France, and Israel to seize the canal prompted a strong negative reaction in world opinion, forcing them to withdraw. The episode demonstrated the newly limited reach of the western European powers in world affairs. *(Ch. 29)*

**suffragists** Activists who, beginning in the late nineteenth century, organized to win the vote for women. Adopting increasingly violent tactics, English suffragists (often referred to by contemporaries as "suffragettes") endured attacks by male thugs, were arrested, engaged in hunger strikes, and were force-fed. *(Ch. 24)*

**Sumerians** Dominant inhabitants of Mesopotamia in the third millennium B.C. They established the world's first civilization, thirty flourishing city-states with a common culture, commerce, and tendency to make war on one another. *(Ch. 1)*

**summa** An encyclopedic compendium of carefully arrayed knowledge on a particular subject. Examples are the two most famous works of **Thomas Aquinas,** the *Summa Contra Gentiles* and the *Summa Theologiae.* *(Ch. 10)*

**surrealism** A movement in literature and the visual arts that emerged in Paris in the early 1920s. Though indebted to dada and its mocking defiance of convention, surrealism sought to find something positive by exploring the realm of the subconscious, partly by following some of **Sigmund Freud's** insights about access to the subconscious. *(Ch. 26)*

**Tacitus, Cornelius (ca. A.D. 55–120)** Roman historian of the "Silver Age." Tacitus lauded the simple virtues of the German tribes and expressed nostalgia for the Republic. His greatest works were *The Histories,* on the civil wars of A.D. 69, and *The Annals,* chronicling the emperors from Tiberius through Nero. *(Ch. 6)*

**Tanzimat** Turkish term, meaning "restructuring," for the reform movements in the Ottoman Empire beginning in 1839. Reforms included security of property, equity in taxation, and equality before the law regardless of religion. Government officials were given fixed salaries and subjected to regular inspections. *(Ch. 22)*

**Tennis Court Oath (1789)** Pledge signed by all but one Third Estate deputy of the Estates General of France on June 20, 1789. The deputies swore to continue to meet until a constitution was drafted. *(Ch. 19)*

**Terror (1793–1794)** Systematic repression of internal enemies undertaken by revolutionary tribunals across France at the urging of **Maximilien Robespierre.** Approximately fourteen thousand people were executed, including aristocrats, **Girondins,** and **sans-culottes.** The Terror ended with the arrest and execution of Robespierre in July 1794. *(Ch. 19)*

**tetrarchy** Government ruled by four leaders. Emperor Diocletian established a tetrarchy in about 293 to address the Roman Empire's political instability, huge size, and complexity, as well as to promote experienced men and provide an orderly imperial succession. *(Ch. 7)*

**Thatcher, Margaret (b. 1925)** As Conservative prime minister of Britain from 1979 to 1990, she spearheaded a number of measures to promote privatization and free enterprise at the expense of the welfare state and the British labor unions. So dramatic was the resulting change in direction that it is sometimes characterized as Thatcher's conservative revolution. *(Ch. 30)*

**third-century crisis** Period from A.D. 235 to 284, when the Roman Empire suffered barbarian invasions, domestic economic problems, plague, assassinations, and urban decline. Attempting to fend off invasions at opposite fronts, the emperors devalued the currency, leading to massive inflation. *(Ch. 6)*

**Third Estate** In France, the common people, as distinct from the nobles (First Estate) and clergy (Second Estate). In the Estates General in 1789, it was presumed that the votes of the First and Second Estates would overrule those of the Third Estate, although the commoners vastly outnumbered the nobles and clergy. *(Ch. 19)*

**Thirty Years' War (1618–1648)** Destructive war, involving most European countries but fought in Germany, resulting from sixteenth-century religious tensions, regionalism versus centralizing forces, and dynastic and strategic rivalries between rulers. See also **Peace of Westphalia.** *(Ch. 15)*

**Thucydides (ca. 455–397 B.C.)** Ancient Greek historian; with **Herodotus,** a founder of history-writing in the West. A failed Athenian general, Thucydides made a careful study of the Peloponnesian War and prided himself on the accuracy of his account of the prolonged conflict. *(Ch. 3)*

**Torah** First five books of the Bible. Accepted as sacred by the Hebrews around 425 B.C., it relates the working out of God's pact, or **covenant,** with the Hebrews, his chosen people. *(Ch. 2)*

**Tordesillas, Treaty of (1494)** Treaty by which Pope Alexander VI divided the rights of colonization of the newly identified lands between Portugal and Spain. He had intended to give Africa to the Portuguese and the New Worlds to Spain, but by a miscalculation Brazil remained in the Portuguese area. *(Ch. 13)*

**total war** The concept, first associated with World War I, that war requires the mobilization of all a nation's resources and energies. The unexpected need to wage total war during World War I accelerated social and economic processes, from technological development to women's suffrage. *(Ch. 25)*

**Toussaint-Louverture, François (1743–1803)** Former slave who governed the island of Saint Domingue (Haiti) as an independent state after the slave revolt of 1791. In 1802 French forces captured Toussaint-Louverture, who died in prison. *(Ch. 19)*

**trading-post empire** Commercial system developed by Portugal in the sixteenth century to dominate trade in the Indian Ocean through fortified, strategically placed naval bases. All merchants were expected to acquire export licenses and ship products through Portuguese ports. *(Ch. 13)*

**tragedy** Serious play with an unhappy ending. Greek tragedy emerged and reached its height in the fifth century B.C. in the works of Aeschylus, Sophocles, and Euripides. The essence of Greek tragedy is the nobility in the spectacle of a great man or woman failing because of a "fatal flaw," but learning from failure. *(Ch. 3)*

**trasformismo** System of political manipulation used by Count Camillo di Cavour (1810–1861), Piedmont's prime minister, to create majorities in parliament to support his cabinet. The practice of using cajolery and bribery to transform foes into supporters would continue to characterize Italian government in the late nineteenth century. *(Ch. 22)*

**Triple Alliance** Military alliance established in 1882 among Germany, Austria-Hungary, and Italy to counter the Franco-Russian Alliance (later the **Triple Entente**). The system of rival alliances contributed to the escalation of international tensions. *(Ch. 24)*

**Triple Entente** Military alliance between Great Britain, France, and Russia, completed in 1907, countering the **Triple Alliance.** The system of rival alliances eventually brought all of Europe into World War I. *(Ch. 24)*

**triumph** Elaborate procession through the streets of ancient Rome. Triumphs were voted by the **senate** to salute a general's victory over a foreign army. *(Ch. 5)*

**Truman Doctrine** The U.S. policy of containment, or limiting communist expansion, as outlined by President Harry Truman in 1947. Intended most immediately to deter any communist designs on Greece or Turkey, the doctrine was used thereafter to support any country that the United States considered threatened by communism during the **cold war.** *(Ch. 28)*

**Ugarit** Cosmopolitan port on northern Syria's Mediterranean coast that was a thriving trading center, especially around 1400–1200 B.C. The alphabet invented by Ugaritic scribes is the source of today's widely used Roman alphabet. *(Ch. 1)*

**unilateralism** Term describing the increasing willingness of the United States to go its own way in world affairs after the end of the cold war, and especially after the terrorist attack on the United States in September 2001. In pursuing its own course, the United States was departing from the multilateral international system that it had sought to foster since World War II. This departure alienated many Europeans. *(Ch. 30)*

**United Nations** International organization of nations founded in 1945 to encourage peace, cooperation, and recognition of human rights. The major powers—China, France, Great Britain, the Soviet Union, and the United States—were given a privileged position as permanent members of the Security Council, each with veto power. *(Ch. 28)*

**urbanization** Term related to the growth of cities, largely connected to the **industrialization** of the late eighteenth and nineteenth centuries. Cities aided industry by providing markets for goods and a concentrated source of workers. However, with urbanization came a host of new problems such as urban slums, lack of sanitation, and pollution. *(Ch. 20)*

**utilitarianism** Political theory of Jeremy Bentham (1748–1832). Bentham argued that the purpose of government is to provide "the greatest happiness of the greatest number" and that the test of government is its usefulness. Democracy was implicit in Bentham's philosophy: the greatest number could ensure its own happiness only by voting for its rulers. *(Ch. 21)*

**Vasco da Gama (1460?–1524)** Pioneering Portuguese explorer and trader whose voyage from 1497 to 1499 around the Cape of Good Hope to Mozambique and India inaugurated a four-hundred-year-long Portuguese presence in the Indian Ocean region. *(Ch. 13)*

**vassal** Drawing on both Roman and Germanic customs, vassalage linked two men—lord and vassal—in an honorable, reciprocal bond based on loyalty and service. Eventually leading nobles and their vassals formed a social and political elite. *(Ch. 8)*

**Versailles, Treaty of (1919)** Peace treaty between the victorious Allies and defeated Germany after World War I. The harsh terms of this dictated peace produced a sense of bitterness and betrayal in Germany. *(Ch. 25)*

**Vichy France** The term for the repressive French government that followed the Third Republic after France's defeat by Nazi Germany in 1940. Headquartered in the resort town of Vichy, the government collaborated with the victorious Germans, who occupied Paris. *(Ch. 28)*

**Victorian morality** Nineteenth-century ethos wherein the values of the dominant middle class, which emphasized strict moral principles, especially regarding sex and drink, became the social norms. In Queen Victoria, who reigned for two-thirds of the century, the middle classes saw a reflection of their own values. *(Ch. 23)*

**Virgil** Roman poet whose works contributed to the Augustan renewal. In the *Eclogues,* Virgil (Publius Vergilius Maro, 70–19 B.C.) describes the blessings of peace under **Augustus;** in the *Georgics,* he glorifies Italian agriculture. His *Aeneid* mythologizes Rome and describes both the burden and glory of empire. *(Ch. 6)*

**Visigoths**  Germanic people who served as allied troops for the Romans. When threatened by the Huns, the Visigoths crossed the Danube and settled in the Balkans. Eventually they sacked Rome in 410 and expanded their rule to parts of Spain and southern France. *(Ch. 7)*

**Voltaire (François-Marie Arouet, 1694–1778)**  Prolific French writer, critic, and reformer who embodied the spirit of eighteenth-century rationalism: its confidence, its increasingly practical bent, its wit and sophistication. His satires and philosophical critiques targeted Christianity, intolerance, and tyranny. See also **philosophes.** *(Ch. 18)*

**Vulgate Bible**  Latin version of new translations of the Hebrew Scriptures and Greek New Testament written by Jerome (331–420) for Pope Damasus. It was called the Vulgate because it was the Bible for the "people" (*vulgus*), whose language was Latin. *(Ch. 7)*

**Warsaw Pact (1955–1991)**  Military-diplomatic alliance of Soviet bloc countries, created to counter NATO. The pact established a joint military command and mutual military assistance, as well as a new basis for the continuing presence of Soviet troops in the satellite states. See also **cold war.** *(Ch. 29)*

**welfare state**  The concept, especially prevalent in western countries after World War II, that government should adopt large-scale social welfare measures, while maintaining a primarily capitalistic economy. Among the welfare measures usually adopted were a national health service, old-age pensions, and insurance against unemployment, sickness, and disability. *(Ch. 29)*

**Weltpolitik**  Meaning "world politics," the term describes the policy pursued by Kaiser **Wilhelm II** (r. 1888–1918) to make Germany a world power, with colonies, a navy, and major influence among the Great Powers. The kaiser implemented his ambitious agenda with nationalistic appeals and bombastic threats. *(Ch. 24)*

**Wilhelm II (r. 1888–1918)**  German kaiser (emperor) whose aggressive diplomatic, commercial, and military policies helped trigger World War I. His pursuit of *Weltpolitik* severely aggravated international tensions. See also **Weltpolitik.** *(Ch. 24)*

**World Trade Organization (WTO)**  Growing from a multilateral trade agreement in 1947, it sought, with mixed success, to promote freer trade throughout the world. By the end of the 1990s WTO meetings were drawing large demonstrations by anti-globalization activists, most notably in Seattle in 1999 and in Cancún, Mexico, in 2003. *(Ch. 30)*

**Yalta conference**  The meeting in February 1945 at Yalta, a Soviet Black Sea resort, between Stalin, Roosevelt, and Churchill. With Allied victory assured, they began outlining plans for the postwar order, including the military occupation of Germany. See also **Potsdam conference.** *(Ch. 28)*

**Young Turks**  Term describing the young intellectuals who wanted to transform the Ottoman Empire into a more modern, Westernized state. Self-exiled in the late 1860s in Paris and London, they overthrew the sultan and seized power in 1908. The expression has subsequently come to designate any group of activists pushing for political change. *(Ch. 22)*

**Zionism**  Nationalist Jewish movement. In the late nineteenth century, faced with growing **anti-Semitism,** some Jews argued that they would be safe only in their own nation. Zionism advocated establishing a Jewish state in the Jews' ancient homeland of Palestine, an idea that became reality with the creation of Israel in 1948. *(Ch. 24)*

**Zoroastrianism**  Religion founded about 1000–550 B.C. by the Persian prophet Zarathustra (*Zoroaster* in Greek). Zoroastrians believe in a supreme deity and a cosmic contest between good and evil within each individual. *(Ch. 2)*

**Zwingli, Huldrych (1484–1531)**  Town preacher of Zurich, Zwingli became a leader of the urban reformation in Switzerland and southwest Germany, emphasizing the importance of the community in the salvation of individuals. *(Ch. 14)*

# Index